University of Memphis Libraries

COMPREHENSIVE HANDBOOK
OF
PSYCHOTHERAPY

COMPREHENSIVE HANDBOOK
OF
PSYCHOTHERAPY

VOLUME 3

INTERPERSONAL/HUMANISTIC/EXISTENTIAL

Editor-In-Chief   FLORENCE W. KASLOW

Volume Editors   ROBERT F. MASSEY and
SHARON DAVIS MASSEY

JOHN WILEY & SONS, INC.

This book is printed on acid-free paper. ∞

Copyright © 2002 by John Wiley & Sons, New York. All rights reserved.

Published simultaneously in Canada.

No part of this publication may be reproduced, stored in a retrieval system or transmitted in any form or by any means, electronic, mechanical, photocopying, recording, scanning or otherwise, except as permitted under Sections 107 or 108 of the 1976 United States Copyright Act, without either the prior written permission of the Publisher, or authorization through payment of the appropriate per-copy fee to the Copyright Clearance Center, 222 Rosewood Drive, Danvers, MA 01923, (978) 750-8400, fax (978) 750-4744. Requests to the Publisher for permission should be addressed to the Permissions Department, John Wiley & Sons, Inc., 605 Third Avenue, New York, NY 10158-0012, (212) 850-6011, fax (212) 850-6008, E-Mail: PERMREQ@WILEY.COM.

This publication is designed to provide accurate and authoritative information in regard to the subject matter covered. It is sold with the understanding that the publisher is not engaged in rendering professional services. If legal, accounting, medical, psychological or any other expert assistance is required, the services of a competent professional person should be sought.

Designations used by companies to distinguish their products are often claimed as trademarks. In all instances where John Wiley & Sons, Inc. is aware of a claim, the product names appear in initial capital or all capital letters. Readers, however, should contact the appropriate companies for more complete information regarding trademarks and registration.

Library of Congress Cataloging-in-Publication Data:

Comprehensive handbook of psychotherapy / [editor-in-chief] Florence W. Kaslow.
     p.   cm.
  Includes bibliographical references and index.
  Contents: v. 1. Psychodynamic/object relations / [edited by] Jeffrey J. Magnavita — v. 2. Cognitive-behavioral approaches / [edited by] Terence Patterson — v. 3. Interpersonal/humanistic/existential / [edited by] Robert F. Massey, Sharon Davis Massey — v. 4. Integrative/eclectic / [edited by] Jay Lebow.
    ISBN 0-471-01848-1 (set) — ISBN 0-471-38263-9 (cloth : alk. paper : v. 1) — ISBN 0-471-38319-8 (cloth : alk. paper : v. 2) — ISBN 0-471-38626-X (cloth : alk. paper : v. 3) — ISBN 0-471-38627-8 (cloth : alk. paper : v. 4)
   1. Psychotherapy—Handbooks, manuals, etc. 2. Cognitive therapy—Handbooks, manuals, etc. 3. Behavior therapy—Handbooks, manuals, etc. I. Kaslow, Florence Whiteman. II. Magnavita, Jeffrey J. III. Patterson, Terence. IV. Massey, Robert F. V. Massey, Sharon Davis. VI. Lebow, Jay.

RC480 .C593 2002
616.89'14—dc21

                                                                                             2001045636

Printed in the United States of America.

10 9 8 7 6 5 4 3 2 1

Contributors

Maurizio Andolfi, MD, is director of the Accademia di Psicoterapia dela Famiglia in Rome, Italy, professor of psychology at the University of Rome. He is an approved supervisor in the American Association for Marriage and Family Therapy and editor of *Terapia Familiare.* He researches the longitudinal effects of psychotherapy.

Harry J. Aponte, MSW, is in private practice in Philadelphia, Pennsylvania, was clinical associate professor at MCP Hahnemann University, and director of the Philadelphia Child Guidance Clinic. He was honored with awards from the American Academy of Family Therapy in 1992, the Menninger Clinic in 1997, and the American Association of Marriage and Family Therapy in 2001. His interests involve spirituality in therapy, the person of the therapist, and therapy with low income and minority families.

Marilyn Peterson Armour, PhD, is assistant professor of social work at the University of Texas at Austin, Texas.

Dorothy Becvar, PhD, is a family therapist in private practice in St. Louis, Missouri. She is president and CEO of the Haelan Center, a not-for-profit holistic healing center. Her interests are focused on marriage and family therapy.

Insoo Kim Berg, MSSW, is executive director and cofounder of the Brief Therapy Center in Milwaukee, Wisconsin, along with her husband, Steve de Shazer. She provides consultation, training, and supervision in the United States, Europe, and Asia.

Paul E. Bracke, PhD, is a licensed psychologist in private practice in Oakland and Mountain View, California. He is a senior consultant and group leader for the Meyer Friedman Institute, Mount Zion Medical Center of the University of California in San Francisco. He has conducted research on the effectiveness of reducing Type-A behavior in heart-attack victims and the role of families in developing Type-A behavior. He is interested in the future of existential-humanistic psychology.

Helen H. Braun, MIATES, is a founder of the Centro Integral de la Familia in Quito, Ecuador, and an administrator and faculty member in the master's program in family therapy at the Universidad Politechnica Salesiana Sede Quito.

Andraé L. Brown, MEd, is in the marriage and family doctoral program in the Department of Professional Psychology and Family Therapy at Seton Hall University, South Orange, New Jersey.

v

He is an American Psychological Association Minority Fellow and a Minority in Academic Careers Doctoral Fellow. His research interests include church and spirituality influences, resiliency, HIV/AIDS, school systems, and alcohol and substance abuse among adolescents and families.

James F. T. Bugental, PhD, is emeritus professor of the Saybrook Institute, San Francisco, California, emeritus clinical faculty member at Stanford University Medical School, and distinguished adjunct professor at the California School of Professional Psychology. He is past president of the Association for Humanistic Psychology.

Christine M. Chao, PhD, is in private practice as a psychologist in Denver, Colorado. She was the director of the Asian Pacific Center for Human Development in Denver. She received the Asian Women of Achievement Silk Wings Award. Her chief interests include Asian mental health and the intersection of cross-cultural psychology and Jungian thought.

Linda Combs, MSSA, LCSW, is training director at Family Service Bureau, an affiliate of New Community Corporation, in Newark, New Jersey. She has supervised interns and staff at several agencies. She is interested in psychodrama and systemic approaches to psychotherapy.

William F. Cornell, MA in phenomenological psychology from Duquesne University, is in private practice in Pittsburg, Pennsylvania. He is certified in Radix and neo-Reichian methods and is a supervising transactional analyst. He specializes in supervision, the effects of abuse, and psychotherapeutic processes.

Catherine Ducommun-Nagy, MD, is the president of the Institute for Contextual Growth, Inc. and of its subsidiary, Nagy Context, Inc. She is adjunct assistant professor in the Master of Family Therapy program at MCP/Hahnemann University in Philadelphia, Pennsylvania. Born and trained in Switzerland, she specializes in contextual therapy and residential treatment programs.

Adriana Balaguer Dunn, PhD, is associate professor in the Department of Professional Psychology and Family Therapy at Seton Hall University, South Orange, New Jersey. She has been teaching in the master's, post-master's, and doctoral programs in marriage and family since 1994 and was the doctoral clinical coordinator. She is a clinical member of the American Association of Marriage and Family Therapy, an AAMFT approved supervisor, and a member of Division 43 (Family Psychology) of the American Psychological Association. She has conducted research on Latino couples.

Mony Elkaim, MD, is director of the Institute for Family and Human Studies in Brussels, Belgium, professor at the Free University of Brussels, and past president of the European Family Therapy Association.

Eugene W. Farber, PhD, is a clinical psychologist and associate professor in the Emory University School of Medicine Department of Psychiatry and Behavioral Sciences, Atlanta, Georgia. His interests focus on HIV/AIDS mental-health intervention and psychological adaptation to adverse life events, including the role of resilience factors and meaning construction in psychological adjustment.

Anne R. Farrar, MA, is in the counseling psychology doctoral program in the Department of Professional Psychology and Family Therapy at Seton Hall University, South Orange, New Jersey. Her research interests include child maltreatment, adoption and foster care, and play therapy.

Shibusawa Fazuko, PhD, MSW, LCSW, is assistant professor at the Columbia School of Social Work, New York. She was a family therapist in private practice in Tokyo, Japan. She is a Hartford Geriatric Social Work Faculty Scholar. Her clinical and research interests focus on Asian American families, ethnic elders, and HIV risk among older adults.

Nouriman Ghahary, MS, is in the counseling psychology doctoral program in the Department of Professional Psychology and Family Therapy at Seton Hall University, South Orange, New Jersey. Her research and clinical interests include the impact of trauma on individuals and larger communities, politically based trauma, and resilience.

Eliana Gil, PhD, is coordinator of the Abused Children's Treatment Services in Fairfax, Virginia. She is director of the Starbright Training Institute for Child and Family Play Therapy and an adjunct faculty member of Virginia Tech University's Family Services. She specializes in working with abused and traumatized children and their families.

Ingeborg E. Haug, DMin, is associate professor of Marriage and Family Therapy Education and Program Chair at Fairfield University, Fairfield, Connecticut. She has published on ethics and spirituality.

Pilar Hernández, PhD, is assistant professor in the marriage and family programs in the Department of Professional Psychology and Family Therapy at Seton Hall University, South Orange, New Jersey. She specializes in the use of narrative approaches to trauma and resilience, especially regarding persons subjected to political oppression, and she focuses on feminist family therapy and domestic violence.

Gordon Hewitt, PhD, is a clinical teaching and supervising transactional analyst, president of the International Transactional Analysis Association, and a supervisor with the New Zealand Association of Psychotherapists. He was academic dean of science at Victoria University. He consults with organizations and specializes in conflict resolution.

Bianca Zwang Hirsch, PhD, was president of the Viktor Frankl Institute of Logotherapy. She worked as a school psychologist and was an associate clinical professor and consultant to the Division of Behavioral and Developmental Pediatrics at the University of California at San Francisco. She specializes in logotherapy.

Arpana G. Inman, PhD, is assistant professor in the Department of Professional Psychology and Family Therapy at Seton Hall University, South Orange, New Jersey. She specializes in research on multicultural issues in counseling, training, and supervision, Asian American ethnic and racial identities, and the psychology of women.

Alan Jacobs trained in psychodrama with Zerka Moreno, J. L. Moreno, and Abel Ossario. He is a supervising transactional analyst and received the Eric Berne Memorial Award in 1996. He is editor of TAJnet and of the Internet journal IDEA. His award winning photography of Nazi concentration camps can be found at www.remember.org.

Vann S. Joines, PhD, is president of the Southeast Institute for Group and Family Therapy, Chapel Hill, North Carolina. He is a clinical teaching and supervising transactional analyst, recipient of the 1994 Eric Berne Memorial Award, and an approved supervisor in the American Association for Marriage and Family Therapy. He has done research on personality adaptations.

C. Wayne Jones, PhD, is associate director of the Philadelphia Child and Family Therapy Training Center, Inc. (formerly the Philadelphia Child Guidance Center) and Clinical Associate Professor of Psychology in the Department of Psychiatry, University of Pennsylvania School of Medicine. He maintains a private practice and consults on family-centered approaches to strengthen the socioemotional skills of inner-city, high-risk young children and their parents.

Judith V. Jordan, PhD, is codirector of the Jean Baker Miller Training Institute of the Stone Center, Wellesley College, Massachusetts. She is an attending psychologist at McLean Hospital and assistant professor of psychology at Harvard Medical School. She was the Mary Margaret Voorhees Distinguished Professor at the Menninger School of Psychiatry and Mental Health Science in 1999. She specializes in relational psychology.

Anie Kalayjian, EdD, is adjunct professor of psychology at Fordham University, New York. She is president of the New York chapter of the International Society for Traumatic Stress Studies, founder and president of the Armenian American Society for Studies on Stress and Genocide, chairperson of the DPI/NGO United Nations Annual Conference, and vice chair of the United Nations NGO Executive Committee. She specializes in research and practice regarding trauma and disasters.

Joseph Kabali, MA, is in the marriage and family doctoral program in the Department of Professional Psychology and Family Therapy at Seton Hall University, South Orange, New Jersey. He is from Uganda and is a catholic priest. His research interests include working with couples preparing for marriage or remarriage and follow-up sports.

Marion Lindblad-Goldberg, PhD, is director of the Philadelphia Child and Family Therapy Training Center, Inc. and clinical associate professor of psychology in the Department of Psychiatry, University of Pennsylvania School of Medicine. She is an approved supervisor with the American Association for Marriage and Family Therapy. She specializes in structural family therapy, supervision, single-parent families, and in-home family therapy.

Elisabeth Lukas, PhD, completed her dissertation at the University of Vienna under Dr. Giselher Buttmann and Dr. Viktor E. Frankl. She directs the South German Institute of Logotherapy in Fürstenfeldbruck near Munich, Germany. She has written more than 40 books on logotherapy, and her works have been translated into 11 languages.

Robert F. Massey, PhD, is a professor and director of the Marriage and Family MS, EdS, and PhD programs in the Department of Professional Psychology and Family Therapy at Seton Hall University, South Orange, New Jersey. He is an approved supervisor in the American Association for Marriage and Family Therapy and a certified transactional analyst. He writes on and researches integrative systems thinking, couple and family relationships, personality theories, and spirituality in contexts.

Sharon Davis Massey, PhD, is a licensed marriage and family therapist and an approved supervisor in the American Association for Marriage and Family Therapy. She supervises the clinical work of university students and is an adjunct professor in the marriage and family programs at Seton Hall University, South Orange, New Jersey. Her professional interests center around the development of humans within their evolving contexts, supervision from an interpersonal-systemic frame of reference, and human ways of knowing.

Marisol M. Meza, MEd, is in the marriage and family doctoral program in the Department of Professional Psychology and Family Therapy at Seton Hall University, South Orange, New Jersey. Her research interests include single-parent households, Latino issues, and multicultural competence in training, supervision, and psychotherapy.

Carlo Moiso, MD, practices psychotherapy in Rome, Italy. He is a clinical teaching and supervising transactional analyst and a member of the board of trustees of the International Transactional Analysis Association. He was a recipient of the Eric Berne Scientific Memorial Award. He specializes in transferential phenomena in transactional settings and the affective involvement of psychotherapists.

Anselm Nwaorgu, PhD, works as a psychologist at the Eric J. Feldman Child/Family Development Services, Mount Carmel Guild Behavioral Health Care, Newark, New Jersey. He is a priest in the archdiocese of Newark. He specializes in working with inner-city children and adolescents.

Augustine Nwoye, PhD, is head of the University Counselling Centre, Kenyatta University, Nairobi, Kenya, East Africa. He is interested in the community contexts of human development and mental-health services.

Laura Palmer, PhD, is assistant professor and codirector of training in the Counseling Psychology Program in the Department of Professional Psychology and Family Therapy at Seton Hall University, South Orange, New Jersey. She is affiliated with Newark Beth Israel Hospital in Newark, New Jersey. She has worked in the field of pediatric mental-health services. Her research focuses on emotional and neurocognitive sequelae of trauma in children suffering emotional and physical trauma and the efficacy of current evaluation procedures.

Kwamia N. Rawls, MSEd, is in the marriage and family doctoral program in the Department of Professional Psychology and Family Therapy at Seton Hall University, South Orange, New Jersey. She received the Minority Scholar Teaching Fellowship at Passaic Community College in New Jersey. Her research interests include effective multicultural teaching strategies and marital satisfaction in arranged marriages.

Janine Roberts, EdD, is a professor at the University of Massachusetts, Amherst, Massachusetts. She is president of the American Family Therapy Academy. She is on the editorial boards of *Family Process,* the *Journal of Feminist Family Therapy,* and the *Journal of Marital and Family Therapy.* She has written on rituals and healing stories.

Robert Sherman, EdD, is professor emeritus, Queens College, City University of New York. He is a faculty member of the Alfred Adler Institute in New York and Quebec and adjunct professor at Seton Hall University. He specializes in couple and family therapy and supervision.

Joel K. Simon, MSW, practices solution-focus training and therapy at Center for Solutions, Walden, New York. He was director of an adolescent day treatment program and director of an intensive outpatient treatment center for cocaine addiction. His interests lie in solution-focused brief therapy.

Volker Thomas, PhD, is associate professor and director of the doctoral program in Marriage and Family Therapy in the Department of Child Development and Family Studies at Purdue University, Indiana. His research interests include young children in family therapy, therapy with economically disadvantaged children, and creativity and family therapy.

Norbert A. Wetzel, ThD, is a licensed psychologist, cofounder and director of training at the Center for Family, Community, and Social Justice, Inc. in Princeton, New Jersey. He is interested in the philosophical foundations of family therapy and applications of ecosystemic thinking to culturally and socioeconomically diverse populations.

Hinda Winawer, MSW, LCSW, is cofounder and director of the Center for Family, Community, and Social Justice, Inc. in Princeton, New Jersey. She is a senior faculty member at the Ackerman Institute for Family Therapy in New York and a member of the Family, Alcohol, and Drug Addiction Project.

Foreword

It is my pleasure to introduce a volume in which chapters cover so many aspects of humanistic, existential, and relational forms of psychotherapy, including my own approach, Contextual Therapy. The volume editors, Sharon and Robert Massey, have done a great job in bringing together experienced therapists and writers whose work is presented in a very practical fashion. The chapters are ordered in accordance to their relevance for children, adolescents, adults or families, and group therapy. This helps readers locate materials relevant to their clinical practice in a very effective way. The volume entails not only an in-depth discussion of several models of therapy, but also contains vast clinical material. Compelling case illustrations that should be relevant to today's clinicians in their day-to-day practice enrich most chapters. The synthesizing postscript addresses issues of ethical norms and practice in psychotherapy, supervision issues, and integration of interpersonal, existential, and humanistic processes in psychotherapy. The contents of the postscript are certainly very close to some of the issues that I have reflected on over more than fifty years of interest in what constitutes effective therapy and prevention.

The four volumes of the *Comprehensive Handbook of Psychotherapy* cover all the major schools of psychotherapy that have been in existence during the second part of the twentieth century. I have no doubts that this Handbook will serve as a beacon for an assessment of the field of psychotherapy by future generations of students and scholars. Any comprehensive review of the field of psychotherapy leads to fundamental questions about the goals of psychotherapy and its mandate. In a technical way, each school defines particular therapeutic goals, based on assumptions about what constitutes health and pathology. These assumptions also define the locus of the healing process.

It has been my life-long effort to define what constitutes effective psychotherapy, and I share with the pioneers of the family-therapy movement that health and pathology needed to be defined in supra-individual terms. One of the big risks of any system-based theory of relationships is the reification of the individual as an automaton subjected to the dynamics of group behaviors without any expectations of individual choices or responsibilities. Psychodynamic theories have broadened our understanding of individual psychology to such an extent that it would be hard to imagine what the field of psychotherapy would look like without their influence. Yet, none of these theories, object-relation theories included, provide a frame to discuss some of the fundamental questions faced by each of us as humans. We have a finite existence and a freedom of choice at any moment of our existence, yet we are determined by past relationships, and we will influence future generations that we will never meet. It is, therefore, the responsibility of therapists of any school to care about the consequences of their interventions for not only individual clients and their relatives, but for the survival of posterity at large.

In times when human survival can be effectively threatened by weapons of mass destruction or by careless use of nonrenewable resources, transgenerational solidarity at a global level is no longer dispensable. It is no more a subject for a few well-meaning environmentalists or old fogies worrying that people should care about others rather than behave in the crudely self-serving way promoted by a western culture of relentless consumerism. It is a time of urgency: As therapists of any school, we need to recognize that we have to focus not only on the individual needs of our designated clients and their families but on prevention at large. Prevention entails an understanding of relational ethics, more specifically an understanding of the interlocking justifications of relating partners based on their respective earned merits and on their respective claims. The discussion of the impact of destructive entitlement for relationships is not a new subject in the contextual-therapy literature, nor is the discussion of a realistic therapeutic optimism, based on the knowledge that fair giving benefits not only the one who receives but also the one who gives, a novel idea.

The beginning of the twenty-first century is marred by an escalating polarization between self-appointed avengers of groups claiming that their interests were ignored and established governments protecting the interests of their legal citizens. The battle is already claiming more lives of innocent bystanders than have been claimed in any other times except for periods of actual wars between nations. As therapists, we should be compelled to find ways to discover residual resources that can decrease the risks of possible mass destruction that could make any effort at reaching individual clients and their families by psychotherapy a futile venture. I would like to quote a passage from *Transgenerational Solidarity: The Expanding Context of Therapy and Prevention*.* "The requirement of a genuine species solidarity would not stop at prohibiting genocide initiated by any self-appointed master race or nation on the one hand or violent protest staged by a suppressed ethnic group on the other. Instead, species solidarity will require the formulation and documentation of each human loyalty group's claim to justification. Only if humanity will be able to listen to justifiable thought [about] conflicting demands will it become fair to expect people to devote their energies to mutually sorting out their claims and alleged justifications. As long as indignant ethnic, religious, racial, etc. groups find no ears to talk to, their energies are bound to be channelled into destruction" (p. 316).

It is my hope that the readers of this volume will get one step closer to the understanding of the dynamics that form the underpinnings of our existences as fellow humans and find their own creative ways to contribute to the survival of posterity.

IVAN BOSZORMENYI-NAGY, MD

---

*Boszormenyi-Nagy, I. (1987). *Foundations of Contextual Therapy, The Collected Papers of Ivan Boszormenyi-Nagy*. New York: Brunner/Mazel.

Preface

The world of psychotherapy theory and practice has changed markedly in the past 30 years. During this time, many forces have converged, leading to major alterations in the therapeutic landscape. Therefore, it seemed essential to produce this four-volume *Comprehensive Handbook of Psychotherapy* to illuminate the state of the art of the field, and to encompass history, theory, practice, trends, and research at the beginning of the twenty-first century.

These volumes are envisioned as both comprehensive in terms of the most current extant knowledge and as thought provoking, stimulating in our readers new ways of thinking that should prove generative of further refinements, elaborations, and the next iteration of new ideas. The volumes are intended for several audiences, including graduate students and their professors, clinicians, and researchers.

In these four volumes, we have sought to bring together contributing authors who have achieved recognition and acclaim in their respective areas of theory construction, research, practice, and/or teaching. To reflect the globalization of the psychotherapy field and its similarities and differences between and among countries and cultures, authors are included from such countries as Argentina, Australia, Belgium, Canada, Italy, Japan, and the United States.

Regardless of the theoretical orientation being elucidated, almost all of the chapters are written from a biopsychosocial perspective. The vast majority present their theory's perspective on dealing with patient affects, behaviors or actions, and cognitions. I believe these volumes provide ample evidence that any reasonably complete theory must encompass these three aspects of living.

Many of the chapters also deal with assessment and diagnosis as well as treatment strategies and interventions. There are frequent discussions of disorders classified under the rubric of Axis I and Axis II in the fourth edition of the *Diagnostic and Statistical Manual of Mental Disorders,* with frequent concurrence across chapters as to how treatment of these disorders should be approached. There are other chapters, particularly those that cluster in the narrative, postmodern, and social constructivist wing of the field, that eschew diagnosis, based on the belief that the only reality of concern is the one being created in the moment-to-moment current interaction: in this instance, the therapeutic dialogue or conversation. In these therapies, goals and treatment plans are coconstructed and coevolved and generally are not predicated on any formal assessment through psychological testing. Whereas most of the other philosophical/theoretical schools have incorporated the evolving knowledge of the brain-behavior connection and the many exciting and illuminating findings emanating from the field of neuroscience, this is much less true in the postmodern wing of the field, which places little value on facts objectively verified by consensual validation and replication.

One of the most extraordinary developments in the past few decades has been that barriers between the theoretical schools have diminished, and leading theoreticians, academicians, researchers, and clinicians have listened to and learned from each other. As a result of this cross-fertilization, the *move toward integration* among and between theoretical approaches has been definitive. Many of the chapters in Volumes 1, 2, and 3 also could fit in Volume 4. Some of the distance between psychodynamic/object-relations therapies and cognitive-behavioral therapies has decreased as practitioners of each have gained more respect for the other and incorporated ideas that expand their theory base and make it more holistic. This is one of the strongest trends that emerges from reading these volumes.

A second trend that comes to the fore is the recognition that, at times, it is necessary to combine judicious psychopharmacological treatment with psychotherapy, and that not doing so makes the healing process more difficult and slower.

Other important trends evident in these volumes include greater sensitivity to issues surrounding gender, ethnicity, race, religion, and socioeconomic status; the controversy over empirically validated treatments versus viewing and treating each patient or patient unit as unique; the importance of the brain-behavior connection mentioned earlier; the critical role assigned to developmental history; the foci on outcome and efficacy; and the importance of process and outcome research and the use of research findings to enhance clinical practice. There is a great deal of exciting ferment going on as our psychotherapeutic horizons continue to expand.

These volumes would not have come to fruition without the outstanding collaboration and teamwork of the fine volume editors, Drs. Jeffrey Magnavita, Terrence Patterson, Robert and Sharon Massey, and Jay Lebow, and my gratitude to them is boundless. To each of the contributing authors, our combined thank you is expressed.

We extend huge plaudits and great appreciation to Jennifer Simon, Associate Publisher at John Wiley & Sons, for her guidance, encouragement, and wisdom. Thanks also to Isabel Pratt, Editorial Assistant, for all her efforts. It has been a multifaceted and intense enterprise.

We hope the readers, for whom the work is intended, will deem our efforts extremely worthwhile.

FLORENCE W. KASLOW, PHD, ABPP
Editor-in-Chief

Palm Beach Gardens, Florida

Contents

FOREWORD — xi
Ivan Boszormenyi-Nagy, MD

PREFACE — xiii
Florence W. Kaslow, PhD, ABPP

SECTION ONE

PSYCHOTHERAPY WITH CHILDREN

CHAPTER 1
ECOSYSTEMIC STRUCTURAL FAMILY THERAPY — 3
C. Wayne Jones and Marion Lindblad-Goldberg

CHAPTER 2
THE CENTRAL ROLE OF CULTURE: WORKING WITH ASIAN CHILDREN AND FAMILIES — 35
Christine M. Chao

CHAPTER 3
PLAY THERAPY WITH ABUSED CHILDREN — 59
Eliana Gil

CHAPTER 4
EXISTENTIAL/EXPERIENTIAL APPROACHES TO CHILD AND FAMILY PSYCHOTHERAPY — 83
Volker Thomas

CHAPTER 5
A BIOPSYCHOSOCIAL APPROACH TO PLAY THERAPY WITH MALTREATED CHILDREN — 109
Laura Palmer, Anne R. Farrar, and Nouriman Ghahary

SECTION TWO

PSYCHOTHERAPY WITH ADOLESCENTS AND YOUNG ADULTS

CHAPTER 6
SOLUTION-FOCUSED BRIEF THERAPY WITH ADOLESCENTS — 133
Joel K. Simon and Insoo Kim Berg

CHAPTER 7
AN INTEGRATIVE APPROACH TO ASSESSMENT AND INTERVENTION WITH ADOLESCENTS OF COLOR — 153
Arpana G. Inman, Kwamia N. Rawls, Marisol M. Meza, and Andraé L. Brown

CHAPTER 8
ADLERIAN THERAPY: A CENTURY OF TRADITION AND RESEARCH — 179
Robert Sherman and Anselm Nwaorgu

CHAPTER 9
SCHOOL-BASED COMMUNITY FAMILY THERAPY FOR ADOLESCENTS AT RISK — 205
Norbert A. Wetzel and Hinda Winawer

SECTION THREE

PSYCHOTHERAPY WITH ADULTS

CHAPTER 10
A RELATIONAL-CULTURAL PERSPECTIVE IN THERAPY — 233
Judith V. Jordan

CHAPTER 11
EXISTENTIAL/HUMANISTIC PSYCHOTHERAPY — 255
Paul E. Bracke and James F. T. Bugental

CHAPTER 12
SPIRITUALLY-SENSITIVE PSYCHOTHERAPY — 279
Harry J. Aponte

CHAPTER 13
EXISTENTIAL TREATMENT WITH HIV/AIDS CLIENTS — 303
Eugene W. Farber

CHAPTER 14
LOGOTHERAPY — 333
Elisabeth Lukas and Bianca Zwang Hirsch

SECTION FOUR

PSYCHOTHERAPY WITH FAMILIES AND COUPLES

CHAPTER 15
COUPLE THERAPY AS A TRANSFORMING PROCESS: REFLECTIONS ON COUPLES' STORIES — 359
Maurizio Andolfi (Joseph Kabali, Translator)

CHAPTER 16
EXISTENTIAL DILEMMAS AND SKILL BUILDING IN COUPLE THERAPY — 389
Adriana Balaguer Dunn

CHAPTER 17
RESILIENCE AND HUMAN RIGHTS ACTIVISM IN WOMEN'S LIFE STORIES   413
  Pilar Hernández and Janine Roberts

CHAPTER 18
REDECISION FAMILY THERAPY   435
  Vann S. Joines

CHAPTER 19
CONTEXTUAL THERAPY   463
  Catherine Ducommun-Nagy

CHAPTER 20
SYSTEMS AS INTERCONNECTING SOCIAL-PSYCHOLOGICAL PROCESSES:
EXISTENTIAL FOUNDATIONS OF FAMILIES   489
  Robert F. Massey

SECTION FIVE

GROUP PSYCHOTHERAPY

CHAPTER 21
PSYCHODRAMA   529
  Alan Jacobs

CHAPTER 22
TRANSACTIONAL ANALYSIS   555
  Robert F. Massey, Gordon Hewitt, and Carlo Moiso

CHAPTER 23
BODY-CENTERED PSYCHOTHERAPY   587
  William F. Cornell

CHAPTER 24
BIOPSYCHOSOCIAL AND SPIRITUAL TREATMENT OF TRAUMA   615
  Anie Kalayjian

SECTION SIX

SPECIAL TOPICS

CHAPTER 25
INTERNATIONAL PERSPECTIVES ON PROFESSIONAL ETHICS   641
  Marilyn Peterson Armour, Ingeborg E. Haug with Dorothy Becvar, Helen Braun,
  Mony Elkaim, Shibusawa Fazuko, and Augustine Nwoye

CHAPTER 26
AN INTERPERSONAL-SYSTEMIC AND DEVELOPMENTAL APPROACH TO SUPERVISION   669
   Sharon Davis Massey and Linda Combs

CHAPTER 27
HUMANISTIC, INTERPERSONAL, AND EXISTENTIAL PSYCHOTHERAPIES: REVIEW AND SYNTHESIS   699
   Sharon Davis Massey

AUTHOR INDEX   719

SUBJECT INDEX   735

SECTION ONE

PSYCHOTHERAPY WITH CHILDREN

Chapter 1   Ecosystemic Structural Family Therapy
Chapter 2   The Central Role of Culture: Working with Asian Children and Families
Chapter 3   Play Therapy with Abused Children
Chapter 4   Existential/Experiential Approaches to Child and Family Psychotherapy
Chapter 5   A Biopsychosocial Approach to Play Therapy with Maltreated Children

CHAPTER 1

Ecosystemic Structural Family Therapy

C. WAYNE JONES AND MARION LINDBLAD-GOLDBERG

HISTORY OF THE THERAPEUTIC APPROACH

EARLY FOUNDATIONS

The earliest published version of the highly pragmatic structural family therapy (SFT) model appeared on the psychotherapy landscape in 1967 (Minuchin, Montalvo, Guerney, Rosman, & Schumer). The model was further elaborated in 1974 (Minuchin), 1978 (Minuchin, Rosman, & Baker), 1981 (Minuchin & Fishman), 1989 (Elizur & Minuchin), and 1993 (Fishman; Minuchin & Nichols). While Salvador Minuchin, the primary exponent of SFT, preferred the language of organization and role theory in describing this theoretical model, his conceptual thinking was influenced by his colleague, Jay Haley, and others who were well-versed in communication and systemic theories (e.g., Bateson, 1979; Haley, 1963; Jackson, 1957; Watzlawick, Jackson, & Beavin, 1967). Minuchin, known as much for his dramatic and compelling therapeutic style as for his theory development, credited both Nathan Ackerman's passionate clinical work and Braulio Montalvo's clinical complexity and sensitivity for his inspiration as a clinician (Minuchin, 1985; Nichols & Schwartz, 1998).

Minuchin, Montalvo, and Haley collaborated in the early development of what became known as structural family therapy. Haley (1976), however, eventually developed his own therapeutic model, termed problem-solving therapy, which emphasized a narrower focus on symptoms. Both therapy models highlight the importance of reconfiguring nonadaptive family coalitions and tie theory to a family developmental framework (Haley, 1976; Minuchin, 1974). Minuchin's life experiences, his long-standing commitment to working with low-income, multiproblem families, and his collaborative relationship with E. H. Auerswald (1968) sensitized him to the importance of examining a family's ecology. An ecological approach involves giving attention to the total field of a problem, including extended family, friends, other professionals, community agencies, and institutions. (For more detailed description of the historical origins of SFT, see Colapinto, 1991; Minuchin & Nichols, 1993; Nichols & Schwartz, 1998.)

In this model, Minuchin directed clinical attention to the recurring, often enduring patterns of interaction that come to organize and structure daily family life. This meant that understanding problem formation, problem maintenance, and change in the treatment of children and adolescents could be found within an analysis or "mapping" of family structure. Because core relational patterns are revealed primarily during family interactions, the hallmark of practice in this model has been its here-and-now action orientation to helping. In the SFT model, therapists work from within a family system. They connect with and learn about the uniqueness of the family and its members, as well as facilitate and support change by creating or capitalizing on natural emotional and relational challenges in ongoing interaction. In vivo learning through the use of in-session enactments provides one of SFT's distinctive contributions to family therapy (Diamond & Liddle, 1999; Simon, 1995).

These foundational elements of the model remain solid and intact in the contemporary theory and practice of SFT. However, like the entire child and family therapy field, stimulated by advances in theory and research from many disciplines, the model has undergone considerable development and refinement over the past 30 years. One major set of influences on current SFT practice has been findings from treatment studies that have examined the major constructs of the model and the mechanisms of change as applied to specific clinical populations. These studies use integrative models derived from classic SFT and include multidimensional family therapy (MDFT; Liddle, 2000), attachment-based family therapy (ABFT; Diamond, Diamond, & Siqueland, in press), multisystemic family therapy (MST; Henggeler, Schoenwald, Borduin, Rowland, & Cunningham, 1998), and the biobehavioral family model (BBFM; Wood, Klebba, & Miller, 2000). Other influences stem from empirical and conceptual advances in developmental science and developmental psychopathology (e.g., Cicchetti, Toth, & Lynch, 1995; Greenspan, 1992; Sameroff & Emde, 1989; Siegal, 1999; Sroufe, 1997) and family psychology (e.g., Gottman, Katz, & Hooven, 1996). SFT continues to be a highly popular model among clinicians, in part because of its reputation for effectiveness, conceptual clarity, strong training programs, and a capacity for incorporating new ideas and research advances over time.

RECENT ELABORATIONS

Much of the updating of SFT theory and practice described in this chapter has evolved at the Philadelphia Child and Family Therapy Training Center, Inc., as well as from staff in its former parent organizations, the Philadelphia Child Guidance Center and the Children's Hospital of Philadelphia. The model, as currently practiced and taught by the authors, has changed in three major ways.

First, the array of information considered important for deciding on goal setting, treatment planning, and treatment implementation has significantly broadened. Data regarding individual biological, developmental, affective, and psychological processes are as likely to be included in the thinking that goes into case formulations as is information about family and larger-system processes. Originally, in a first interview, therapists were encouraged to focus narrowly on the assessment of family interactional patterns in relation to a child's symptoms, and then be prepared to implement immediate change-producing strategies in the session. This confined therapists to here-and-now interactional data, which often contributed to underdeveloped pictures of the child or the family in either historical context or a larger community context. Having been influenced by best-practice standards emerging in the public mental-health arena, SFT therapists are encouraged to obtain a comprehensive biopsychosocial assessment of a child or adolescent in relevant social contexts at both the macro- and microlevels (Engels, 1980).

Second, the posture toward the therapist-child-family relationship has shifted to one of greater collaboration and partnership, building on the model's historical strengths-based approach. As in many of the classic models of family therapy, the therapist's role in early SFT highlighted the therapist's expertise, setting up a clear hierarchical position vis-à-vis the family. Today, practitioners of SFT directly recognize and capitalize on the respective expertise and resources of a family, child, or adolescent, other involved helpers, as well as themselves. Families, and often the focus child or adolescent, are fully and actively involved in the planning of assessment and treatment as well as in the evaluation of treatment outcomes (Hodas, 1997).

Third, emotions and emotional development in the family receive increased focus. Particular attention is given to family styles of regulating or soothing the strong affective states of members (*family emotion regulation*) and to family members' subjective internal experiences of emotional connection and attachment (*affective proximity*). Building relationships in a family, as well in other social settings, that will promote and nurture the development of specific social-emotional competencies, has assumed a central role in the current theory and practice of SFT. This goal has become a critical anchor for shaping the types of assessments and interventions used.

Minuchin (1974) highlighted the importance of preparing children to navigate their worlds competently in his early articulation of principles regarding family functioning, but the individual skills necessary for this remained vague and were rarely targeted for direct change. In part, this occurred because, until recently, not much certainty existed in the developmental field as to the nature of these skills. Now a large body of work is devoted to identifying key social-emotional skills (Mayer & Salovey, 1993), understanding the internal processes and milestones in their development (Denham, 1998; Greenspan, 1992), and specifying parenting practices or family processes that promote or constrain their development (Gottman et al., 1996; Saarni, 1999).

A focus on an individual child's social-emotional development necessitates a broadening of the overarching goals of therapy. In the earliest versions of the model, therapy was considered successful when symptoms were resolved and the family was assumed to be more "functional." Functionality was broadly defined as the fit between the demands confronting the child and family and the organizational structure in place to meet these demands. Although this concept remains very useful, it has lacked a clear referent to the developmental literature and current thinking about what constitutes "healthy" social-emotional functioning and the vast array of individual differences among children and adolescents impacting both developmental outcomes and family functioning. A strict focus on organizational functionality as a treatment outcome risks placing too much value on form over meaning.

Contemporary SFT involves focusing on *growth-promoting practices* and the strength of emotional connections. This captures specific dynamic, fluid processes at work in families and other systems that are directly tied to child outcomes. Assessment and treatment are anchored firmly in developmental theory. This allows for a more evenly dispersed emphasis between the short-term clinical goals of symptom relief and family change, and the long-term preventive goals of growth and development. This signifies fostering change at multiple system levels, including the individual child, the family, and the child-family-community interface. The current overarching goals of SFT are now defined as:

- To resolve presenting problems and to eliminate negative interaction cycles.
- To shift the developmental trajectories of children, such that they are moving toward greater capacity for self-regulation and social-emotional competence.
- To enable a family to organize and emotionally connect in such a way that they become more growth-promoting in their interactions with one another.

- To enable relevant community systems to organize in such a way that a family's efforts toward creating a growth-promoting context is nurtured.

THEORETICAL CONSTRUCTS

Contemporary SFT embraces an appreciation that the structure and dynamics of family relationships are strongly shaped by forces within the broader social context, such as culture, race, gender, politics, and economics (McGoldrick, 1998). However, the specific relationship adaptations that result from these and other influences constitute both the primary target and locus of change in the SFT model. Four major theoretical constructs guide therapists in determining the focus of observations and change in particular family relationships: *family structure, family emotion regulation, individual differences,* and *family development.*

Identifying structural patterns informs therapists about what family members are expecting from and doing with one another. This provides a snapshot of interactional sequences promoting or constraining mastery of specific challenges. Family emotion regulation shows therapists the emotional meaning embedded in these interactions and how members help one another to handle emotional distress. Therapists observe the specific types of family interactions around family members' emotional experiences that need strengthening to support the development of children's social-emotional competencies. Recognition of individual differences in the family helps a therapist become attuned to unique needs (e.g., temperament, learning styles, vulnerabilities to emotional disorders) and histories (e.g., trauma) requiring adjustments of approach, timing, and pacing of change. A focus on family development enables therapists to understand the specific emotional challenges being faced by a child and family as they move through time in a particular cultural context.

A basic assumption in contemporary SFT, rooted in the developmental work of Fraiberg (1959) and R. W. White (1959), is that children enter the world wired to move forward and adapt, despite the natural challenges and conflicts that come their ways. Likewise, families are presumed to be generally oriented toward mastery and self-regulation, regardless of how poorly they may appear to be functioning at a particular point in time. The orientation toward personal and family mastery remains a powerful motivating force and a key to understanding the strengths-based approach to treatment in SFT. In practice, this implies that therapists must tap into this powerful, though often dormant, mastery orientation to help children and their families become unstuck or to overcome barriers to moving toward greater competency and adaptation.

The four major interrelated constructs—family structure, family emotion regulation, individual differences, and family development—inform therapists about the multiple interacting forces supporting or constraining children and their family's movement toward greater mastery and development of core social-emotional competencies. These contemporary SFT constructs can be found in each of the major integrative variants of the model (e.g., MDFT, ABFT, MST, and BBFM), albeit with differing levels of emphasis and elaboration. These ideas guide assessment, intervention, and evaluation of treatment outcomes.

FAMILY STRUCTURE

Families serve both as major resources for children in mastering difficult emotional challenges and as one of the major sources of those challenges. Families represent the matrix of identity development. From its earliest days, a fundamental premise guided SFT: the "inextricable association of family and individual: the family exists for the individual, the individual exists within the family" (Colapinto, 1991, p. 422). To understand children's mastery efforts, therefore, it is important to construct a map of a family regarding how challenges are most likely to be generated from within and the family's preferred pathways for helping children to negotiate challenges, whatever their sources.

Over time, families tend to develop recurring, often enduring patterns of interaction organized around the various day-to-day instrumental tasks and emotional challenges associated with living together. These patterns have been designated *family structure,* a construct used to describe the manner in which families organize themselves (Minuchin, 1974). These interactional patterns are set in motion by family-member expectations about how tasks, needs, and connections are to be managed. Over time and with repetition, these interactions often become fixed presumptions that are prescriptive for maintaining future interactions. When similar patterns of interactions and expectations repeat themselves across a variety of family tasks and situations, they take on the status of core "rules" or "norms," invisibly regulating members' behaviors and creating coherence.

Family structure comprises both universal and idiosyncratic components. Universally, all families have a hierarchical structure, and family members tend to exercise reciprocal and complementary functions (Minuchin, 1974). Role complementarity or reciprocity refers to the degree family members accommodate to one another and their levels of rigidity or role exaggeration. The idiosyncratic aspect of family structure includes the mutual expectations of particular family members governing interactions around daily routines, such as meals, sleep, work, recreation, intimacy, and homework. This component of family structure is often strongly influenced by culture, particularly with respect to gender-role prescriptions.

Families take many shapes and forms, including single-parent, remarried, multigenerational, same-sex, and traditional. Regardless of form, all families tend to be differentiated into subsystems of members who join together to perform various instrumental and emotional tasks, generally determined by generation, age, gender, nature of task, or common interests (Minuchin, 1974). These subsystems may include the individual, the couple, the parent(s), each parent-child dyad, the siblings, the grandparents, the grandchildren, the relatives, or the nonbiological kin. Each individual belongs to more than one subsystem within a family. This can be a source of stress and strain when the demands of each subsystem are at odds or there are strong loyalty conflicts between different members. In growth-promoting families, each subsystem provides a context for learning a range of important life skills through experiencing different types of challenges, patterns of closeness and distance, emotional relationships, and levels of power. The particular family form or composition of family subsystems is far less important than how members organize along the two dimensions of family structure: boundaries and affective proximity.

Boundaries
Boundaries prove most critical for understanding the unique manner in which families actually function or regulate themselves within the organization they have constructed. Boundaries refer to a family's "rules defining who participates, and how" (Minuchin, 1974, p. 53) in a given transaction, that is, who is in, who is out, and who is for or against. Boundaries help moderate both involvement and hierarchy, thereby protecting the autonomy of the family and its subsystems. They are conceptualized along a continuum of permeability whose poles are the two extremes of *diffuse* and *rigid.*

Wood (1985) distinguished between the boundaries separating physical or psychological space among family members and boundaries dividing family roles. Role boundaries or "generational hierarchy" clarify differentiation in responsibilities among generations, such as among grandparent, parent, and child roles. A reversed generational boundary occurs when children parent their parents and become responsible for controlling or taking care of them emotionally. A collapsed generational boundary refers to situations in which parents act as peers to their children or when cross-generational alliances exist between a parent and children against the other parent. The clarity and permeability of role boundaries impact how power is distributed in a family. Power describes "the relative influence of each [family] member on the outcome of an activity" (Aponte, 1976, p. 434). In growth-promoting families, the amount of status or power afforded to different family members or subsystems is based primarily on their generational membership or developmental levels.

Boundaries also refer to the amount of contact or involvement among individual family members, family subsystems, and with people or institutions outside the family, particularly with respect to carrying out specific tasks. In this sense, the concept of boundary concerns physical or psychological space, describing the amount of separation or distance between two or more personal domains of influence. Wood (1985) drew on Goffman's (1971) list of physical and psychological territorial preserves over which an individual has "entitlement to possess, control, use, or dispose of the object or state in question" (p. 28) to highlight six common areas of life around which family members tend to negotiate regularly: contact time, personal space, emotional space, information space, conversation space, and decision space.

A family system and each subsystem can be described as excessively involved or underinvolved with one another around some or all of these personal domains. Subsystems that are highly involved and have highly permeable boundaries have been termed *enmeshed*. Individuals in enmeshed subsystems function as if they are parts of each other. At the other end of the spectrum are subsystems in which individuals are minimally involved, show little interdependence, and display a *disengaged* style. At the extremes, these types of relating can generate conditions for significant child and family problems. When adaptive mechanisms are evoked, an enmeshed family reacts to the slightest variation from the accustomed routine, whereas the disengaged family does not respond sufficiently when action is necessary. Clear boundaries promote an optimal flow of contact and information between and within subsystems (Minuchin, 1974).

Affective Proximity
Another important dimension of family structure, which represents a major elaboration from earlier versions of SFT, revolves around the degree of *affective proximity* between family members. This concept describes family interactions associated with the subjective internal experiences of emotional connection and attachment (Lindblad-Goldberg, Dore, & Stern, 1998). In contrast to *involvement*, which captures the natural struggle in families between dependency and autonomy, the affective proximity dimension of family structure refers to how secure family members feel in their relationships. This expanded concept is based on Bowlby's (1969, 1988) perspective that security and emotional proximity are biologically based needs that drive relational behavior from the cradle to the grave. The attachment system is activated by conditions of stress and perceived threat. Close and securely attached relationships occur when the people in a relationship feel they can count on one another to be attuned and responsive to distress signals.

Attachment theory is increasingly recognized as critical in guiding treatment for a wide range of clinical problems in families with children and adolescents (e.g., Byng-Hall, 1991; Marvin & Stewart, 1990) as well as in adult couple relationships (Johnson, 1996). It is a core component in three of the four major variants of SFT: ABFT (Diamond, Diamond, et al., in press), MDFT (Liddle, 2000), and BBFM (Wood et al., 2000). Developmental research indicates considerable support for the central role played by security of attachment in both psychological and behavioral outcomes (e.g., Cummings & Davies, 1996; Masten, Best, & Garmezy, 1990).

Unlike involvement, which can be overwhelming and stunting when excessive, an emotional connection in a family can never be too secure. The processes of emotional involvement, as marked by boundaries, and emotional connection, as experienced in affective proximity, were often blurred together in earlier articulations of SFT, making it difficult to explain how relationships described as enmeshed could quickly transform into a system that looked disengaged. Involvement does not necessarily predict the security of an emotional connection. For example, a mother and her 14-year-old daughter appear to be highly enmeshed, with the mother involved in every aspect of her daughter's life, yet at the same time, they behave as though their emotional connection with one another is very fragile. This happens because the mother abruptly disengages and becomes critical when her daughter attempts any autonomous action. When the child is taking the emotional risk of exploring new, more independent behavior, they are both most vulnerable, yet, at this point, the mother leaves her stranded and alone. On the other hand, a husband and his wife appear to have low levels of involvement with one another, yet are close because they both have faith that, if there were a crisis, the spouse would recognize it as such and respond with support.

Affective proximity calms and soothes the nervous system (Bowlby, 1988; Siegel, 1999), allowing other necessary instrumental and emotional tasks associated with being a family to be addressed. This proves essential for the development of emotion regulation and other social-emotional competencies in children. In the face of an inadequate, inconsistent, or ruptured emotional connection between family members, perceived distance can generate considerable distress and anxiety, setting in motion a range of behaviors designed to restore the relationship.

The more family relationships are marked by highly negative, rigidly repetitive interactions, the more likely a serious chronic disturbance with affective proximity exists. When attachments are insecure, family members become focused solely on the regulation and stabilization of their emotions and experience themselves as on the verge of being overwhelmed by absorbing negative emotional states (Johnson, 1996). Wynne's (1984) epigenetic model of relationship development and Diamond and Liddle's (1999) treatment-process research imply that family members must possess a fundamental basis for trust and attachment before they can have any hope of learning communication skills, engaging in joint problem-solving, or developing intimacy.

FAMILY EMOTION REGULATION

In contemporary SFT, the processes by which emotions regulate and inform interaction among family members and in turn generate emotional experiences and meaning for members have become central in both case formulation and treatment implementation. This emphasis flows from the increasing recognition from many disparate fields, including psychobiology (e.g., Siegel, 1999), that emotion and its regulation form the core of internal and interpersonal processes shaping the organization of self. With a model of emotions and emotional regulation in the family context, therapists can understand not only here-and-now interactions and the forces that fuel the evolution of various family structures and the experiences of connection, but also fathom the forces shaping developmental trajectories of children. Empirical studies over the past 15 years from the integrative field of developmental science imply that emotional regulation plays a key role in the development of most major child clinical problems (e.g., Cole, Michel, & O'Donnell, 1994; Cole & Zahn-Waxler, 1992; Malatesta & Wilson, 1988). For many clinical syndromes, such as disruptive behavior problems, anxiety, and depression, the dysregulation of emotions in one or more emotional arenas (i.e., anger, fear, or sadness) provides the defining feature of the disorder.

Emotion regulation, mediated in part by autonomic-nervous-system arousal processes, refers to an individual's ability to manage subjective experiences of emotions, especially their intensity and duration, as well as the capability of handling strategically one's expression or modulation of emotion in communicative contexts (Faude, Jones, & Robins, 1996; Saarni, 1999). The press to maintain some subjective sense of internal organization and to avoid out-of-control, reactive behavior or a disorganized thought process initiates a need for emotion regulation strategies at both the individual and family-system levels. The impetus to retain some sense of emotional organization powerfully shapes emotional closeness and distance in family relationships over time. In SFT today, family emotional regulation connotes the overarching goal of all relationship systems to remain organized, emotionally connected, and emotionally balanced.

In earlier models of family therapy, the concept of homeostasis was used to describe how some families seem to resist change, thus emphasizing the family's need for stability and control (Hoffman, 1981). This focus was confined to form (interactional organization) rather than extended to meaning (emotional organization). Now the emphasis has shifted to consider the extent to which family members perceive their capacities to regulate intensely felt negative emotions. In less-adaptive families, fear that the family may spiral into chaos and fragmentation often accompanies poor facility in regulating negative emotions. This frequently implies disconnection and isolation among family members. Such fear becomes particularly pronounced when one or more family members have a history of trauma or when a serious rupture of an attachment relationship has occurred. This leaves families with constricted, self-reinforcing relationship cycles (Johnson & Williams-Keeler, 1998). Although emotional arousal is unavoidable and usually desirable, both families and their members must possess ways to modulate, tolerate, or endure the experience of emotions that are perceived to be excessive (Denham, 1998). To some extent, how families approach or avoid this task of emotion regulation gives each family system and each relationship in it a unique shape and texture.

Individual emotion regulation is influenced by temperament (Kagan, Reznick, & Snidman, 1988), cognitive capacities or neurobiological conditions (Bradley, 2000), patterns of caregiving in families (Calkins, 1994; Cassidy, 1994), and a child's access to coping resources, sometimes referred to as social-emotional competencies. Through a reciprocal developmental process, a child's emotional reactivity affects the ability to incorporate and construct higher-order, social-emotional competencies. In turn, a child's social-emotional competencies affect the capacity to moderate intense emotions (Greenspan, 1992). A developmental model is based on the assumptions of a relatively predictable progression in the growth of internal capacities children bring to an interaction and that these capabilities develop from the simple to the more complex. The core-component competencies associated with emotion regulation predict the long-term relational success of children and adolescents (Mayer & Salovey, 1993). Although numerous important social-emotional skills have been identified (e.g., Goleman, 1995; Mayer & Salovey, 1993; Strayhorn, 1988), five emerge as most relevant to emotional regulation at both the individual child and the family-system levels:

- The ability to monitor one's own and others' feelings and emotions.
- The ability to discriminate among various emotional states and to evaluate their intensity levels for both self and others.

- The ability to use this information to guide thinking and actions.
- The ability to soothe or calm oneself in the midst of strong affect.
- The ability to empathize, that is, to go beyond identification of what is going on with oneself or with another person emotionally, and to also care.

In practicing contemporary SFT, therapists note the degree to which individual children and adolescents demonstrate these social-emotional skills, as well as the degree to which family interactions and relationships support their development. These core competencies represent real strengths when present and significant vulnerabilities when absent. The developmental lens puts into sharper focus observations of particular family interactions as they directly relate to the mobilization of specific social-emotional capacities in children. A major component of planning treatment begins with identifying and then encouraging specific types of interactions to promote movement of the child (and, in a preventive sense, other siblings) further up the ladder of development with respect to these core competencies. By challenging family interactional patterns that serve to detour or shut down conflict, and extending the length of a transaction, a therapist is working with family emotion regulation and attempting to shift distorted or irrational beliefs about negative emotions and family members' capacities to manage it.

Families vary considerably in definitions of what constitutes an extreme in emotional intensity, in attitudes or feelings about the role of emotions, in the emotional experiences or expressions that are favored or discouraged, and in how expressions of emotional expectations are to be handled. In his empirically based work on parental metaemotion theory, Gottman (Gottman et al., 1996) identified how parental approaches to children's emotions, particularly negatively charged ones such as anger and sadness, can promote or undermine the development of emotional regulation and its constituent social-emotional competencies. Gottman defined metaemotion theory as the thoughts and feelings or philosophy parents have about their own emotions and those of their children.

The findings from this work bear important implications for the specific types of parenting responses that need to be nurtured by therapists in treatment. For example, Gottman et al. (1996) observed that an "emotion-coaching" approach to children's negative emotions resulted in more positive child outcomes. In this process, parents (1) were attuned to low-intensity emotions in themselves and in their children; (2) viewed their children's negative emotions as opportunities for teaching or intimacy; (3) validated their children's emotions; (4) assisted their children in verbally labeling their emotions; and (5) problem-solved with their children, setting behavioral limits and discussing goals and strategies for dealing with the situation. This style contrasts with more dismissive and critical approaches.

The focus on family emotion regulation places reciprocal interactional processes in key caregiving relationships at the center of all growth and development. Therapists using contemporary SFT attend to how negative emotions are managed in a family and how this links to patterns of affective proximity and involvement. Therapists note the content of the emotions expressed, how they are expressed, who expresses them, and how other family members respond to them. From this, they discern the expectations and belief systems about different emotions. They design interventions to open avenues for supporting parents to move toward an emotion-coaching style of responding to their children, as well as addressing presenting problems or concerns. Working effectively with emotion regulation means attending to important individual family member differences affecting reactivity.

Individual Differences

Since the earliest writings on SFT, helping families construct systems to better fit individual members' needs and to promote positive growth and development have continued (Minuchin, 1974). To facilitate a good fit, however, therapists must have a clearly elaborated grasp of both sides of the intrapersonal-interpersonal equation. Case formulations in the early days of the model gave primary weight to observable family transactions, with little stress on less visible, yet powerful, intrapersonal differences that influence the particular shape of family systems as well as members' responsiveness to change efforts. Although sometimes acknowledged, these factors were generally considered strictly background phenomena. In contemporary SFT, both the interpersonal and the intrapersonal receive attention, as in MDFT (Liddle, 2000), ABFT (Diamond et al., in press), MST (Henggeler et al., 1998), and BBFM (Wood et al., 2000). Therapists are encouraged to investigate as much about who the players are as how they dance together.

Intrapersonal differences could become the focus of a therapist's attention, but the differences considered most important directly impact the quality of the therapeutic alliance, the selection of specific strategies, the structure of sessions, and the pacing of change. These individual differences include constitutionally based tendencies, such as Attention-Deficit/Hyperactivity Disorder (ADHD), learning or processing differences, anxiety-proneness, temperament, and vulnerability for various emotional disorders. More psychologically based individual differences, such as emotion-regulatory styles and the developmental capacity for organizing or constructing meaning, also prove important and equally powerful. Because these psychologically based individual differences directly influence cognitive, emotional, and behavioral flexibility, they can significantly limit or constrain an individual's capacity for forming rich, deep emotional connections with family members. Although biology does not determine destiny, biologically rooted characteristics do tend to set in motion their own unique sets of organizing dynamics distinguishable from the social contexts in which they exist. These individual-level biological and psychological characteristics are as likely to mold a family system as they are to be modified and shaped by ongoing interactions within these social systems.

Therapists working with children and adolescents must know how to identify these important individual differences, to understand the often predictable, associated interpersonal processes set in motion by them, and to appreciate the meaning attributed to them by a child and family. Far from being a search for pathology inside the individual, the focus on individual differences enables a therapist to better understand how particular profiles of strengths and resources contribute to organizing interactions over time. Real strengths and resources come to light only in the context of grasping the possible trajectory of one's life given a specific personal vulnerability. As the nature of constraints and vulnerabilities come into sharper focus, the human drama of the emotional challenges faced by both child and family become more easily visible, contextualizing the coping or mastery efforts of individual family members. Unless therapists grasp the interactional dramas in which individual differences significantly modulate outcomes, talking about strengths and resources with children and their families will likely ring hollow.

Individual differences themselves do not pose direct targets for change in SFT. Instead, they are forces to accept, work with, and incorporate into a therapist-family-child relationship system and into treatment. Calling attention to and giving a name to powerful life-impacting predispositions, such as ADHD and other neurodevelopmental processes, can foster greater empathy in a family and school for a child, and begin altering the quality and types of support available to master the unique challenges presented by them. Not uncommonly, misunderstood biologically based behavior becomes mislabeled as purposeful, resulting in blame, criticism, and rejection, thereby paving the way for coalitions, boundary problems, and attachment ruptures in a family. Children can become symptomatic given their increased vulnerabilities to chronic, failed mastery efforts, negative self-assessments, and disrupted relationships. Recognizing enduring individual differences enables children and families to make a problem less central in their lives.

Empowerment of a child and family, always a major strategy in SFT, rests on knowledge and self-understanding, making psychoeducation a very important component of treatment. This allows a therapist to highlight a family's emotional experiences of their situation and to amplify strengths with respect to how they have approached normative challenges in the context of their family's development, thereby furthering a meaningful therapeutic alliance.

FAMILY DEVELOPMENT

A family-life-cycle perspective draws attention to the normative and nonnormative demands that children and families face in the present, along with those they have encountered over the course of time (Carter & McGoldrick, 1989). From this perspective, a therapist better appreciates the nature of the current emotional challenges, which may originate from outside or within a family, and discovers clues as to a child's and family's previous experiences of mastery or failure. Information related to the life cycle allows therapists to contextualize both presenting concerns as well as individual and family efforts to handle them.

The current emphasis on challenge and mastery in SFT implies that children and families are active agents in their own learning and development, continually exploring, experimenting, and practicing new ways of handling emotional demands that come their ways within the contexts of their relationships as they move through time together. All meaningful growth and development for both children and adults occur within interpersonal contexts and are interactional by nature. According to Greenspan (1992), biological or constitutionally based factors and family/community system dynamics meet in the ongoing interactions between parents and their children, thus setting in motion internal processes that will move children toward greater internal organization and social-emotional competence. On the other hand, these interactions can also prompt greater disorganization and vulnerability.

Interactions become opportunities for significant child or adolescent growth and development when (1) a critical challenge triggers the process of active emotional exploration and dialogue between the child and family members, and (2) both child and family engage emotionally in a sustained way on efforts to negotiate a resolution of a challenge. Mastery occurs when there is a shift in both a child's internal organization of experience and the structuring of a family's relationships. The map used to navigate the territory for child and family becomes more elaborated via the process of mastery. A critical emotional challenge refers to any set of affectively charged demands that become central in a child's interactions with family members, peers, teachers, or significant others and requires a change in thinking and an alteration in emotional or relational posture to the problem at hand.

Generally, critical emotional challenges contain multilevel implications for a child, family, and other systems, setting in motion recurring feedback loops that can either promote or constrain mastery efforts. Children cannot have a critical emotional challenge separate from their close relationships, nor can the challenge be mastered easily without affective proximity. Critical emotional challenges with which children struggle may originate from their interactions with their families, teachers, or peers, and they may also stem from internal developmental shifts and conflicts. Challenges are mastered through an ongoing interplay between the challenge itself and sustained engagement in the effort to negotiate a solution while being supported by family members. Each challenge that is mastered moves the child toward more complex, differentiated, and flexible emotionally based meaning structures for organizing experience and for guiding behavior.

A family faces many challenges during the course of its life cycle. Some of these challenges relate to shifts in the primary family structures, particularly those involving the addition or subtraction of family members. These challenges are often coupled with other external stressors on the family. For example, the birth of the first child poses a fundamental emotional challenge to the existing relationship between a couple (Cowan & Cowan, 1990). Both individual self-definitions and the couple relationship now have to be reconceptualized. The change from a dyadic adult couple relationship to the establishment of a triadic relationship of parents and child proves dramatic. With the birth of other children and the family's involvement with extrafamilial systems such as day care/school, neighborhoods, religious affiliations, recreation facilities, community agencies, and institutions, new, complex structures of both intra- and interfamilial interaction and communication must form.

Additionally, throughout a family's life cycle, each member experiences developmental changes that uniquely impact on family interaction. The family will have to adapt to external stressful events as well throughout its life cycle. These internal and external changes generate challenges for all members and their habitual attitudes, strategies, roles, and privileges. Families may react with rigidity and hold to old positions, or they may adapt new forms of interaction and communication. A dilemma for all families concerns how to simultaneously preserve a continuous family style for handling developmental transitions and stressors (i.e., maintain homeostasis or coherence) and demonstrate the flexibility to change family patterns when necessary for growth to occur.

For example, the Jones family has a toddler, and a 13-year-old son. Two-year-old Sally's sudden escalation of temper tantrums is likely to have been triggered by a normative developmental push to test her growing skills with mobility, words, and imagination. She displays readiness to act on her world, but is frequently thwarted when running into physical and parental limits. The critical emotional challenge for this youngster entails mastery of anger, frustration, and limits. Prior to two weeks earlier, Sally had not been faced with either the urgency of the desire to press the limits nor the intensity of anger she has experienced in bumping up against them. She consequently becomes easily disorganized because this is not what she expected to happen, and she does not have an internal map for representing and handling this set of emotional experiences.

At the same time, the parents are faced with a corresponding critical emotional challenge. Their easygoing young daughter's recent devolution into wild screaming fits runs counter to the behavioral expectations of these somewhat conflict-averse parents. For the girl to successfully master her emotional challenge, the parents will need to find strategies for supporting her growing desire for greater independence while holding firm on important limits and providing containment when her emotions appear overpowering. In this dance for mastery, the parents as individuals and as a couple, as well as their young daughter, will be simultaneously exploring, through trial and error, new change strategies for handling the emotional challenges before them.

The parents will be observing each other's ability to tolerate Sally's expression of negative emotion and perhaps expand their tolerance of expressed negative feeling in their marital relationship. They will attend to the brother's role in enhancing or opposing Sally's new behavior. Moving beyond what has generally been defined implicitly in numerous transactions as "tolerable" within parent-child, spouse-spouse, or sibling-sibling interactions will signal the family's capacity to demonstrate change. How members of the family's social network react to preserve the status quo or to foster change will also be important variables in determining whether change occurs. Many breakdowns are likely. The outcome of a specific interaction may displease all parties, yet the sum of interactions over time shapes mastery. A drama in every sense of the term unfolds.

Optimally, each parent will eventually become more comfortable with intense negative affect and learn to contain a tendency to overreact. At the family level, one positive structural outcome would be for the parents to form a close working alliance that fosters regular communication with one another, and perhaps with their son, about the emotions Sally's behaviors evoke in them, the meaning of the behaviors, and ideas about responding to her. Sally, it is hoped, will attain increased capacity to tolerate less-than-immediate gratification and develop an expanded repertoire of strategies for regulating negative affect, all while remaining securely emotionally connected with her parents and brother.

As illustrated by Sally and her family, anxiety and discomfort tend to accompany any alteration that requires a reorganization of internal experiences and/or a restructuring of family relationships. Actually, mild to moderate levels of anxiety or discomfort, if experienced in securely attached relationships, propel the mastery process and form natural and normal components for developing core social-emotional competencies. It is assumed that most of the time, children and their families spontaneously discover strategies for handling critical emotional challenges, organizing and incorporating their experiences in ways that move everyone to the next step in their social-emotional development.

When families interpret anxiety or discomfort around change in one another as harmful, however, they may prematurely shut down the interactions necessary for mastery and derail the development of social-emotional competencies. Without access to these internal resources, both children and their parents become more vulnerable to the ordinary stresses associated with navigating day-to-day challenges, or more severe external stressors, and they may more easily develop symptoms of distress. In this way, symptoms can be viewed as misguided or derailed mastery efforts on both the individual and family levels.

MAJOR SYNDROMES, SYMPTOMS, AND PROBLEMS TREATED

SFT and its integrative variants (e.g., MDFT, ABFT, MST, and BBFM) have been applied to most clinical problems of children, adolescents, and their families, either alone or in combination with other treatment modalities, and in a variety of treatment settings. A modified version of Reiss's (1996) framework for classifying treatment foci is used for organizing the broad array of developmental and relationship-based problems targeted by SFT into three categories.

The first includes problems in which disordered relationship patterns are highly prominent and serve as the primary focus of intervention. A child or his or her parents experience severe psychological distress as a direct result of negative family or larger-system interactions, but individual-level *DSM* diagnoses (*Diagnostic and Statistical Manual of Mental Disorders;* American Psychiatric Association [APA], 1994) have little influence in organizing interventions in this category of treatment foci. These include conditions associated with dissolution of the family and hostile postdivorce relationships, such as dislocation and parental abdication syndrome (Abelsohn, 1983; Isaacs, Montalvo, & Abelsohn, 1986; Montalvo, 1982). Larger-system interventions targeting problematic family relationships with schools (Aponte, 1970; Power & Bartholomew, 1987), medical institutions (Moore, Cohen, & Montalvo, 1998; Sargent, 1985), child-welfare agencies (Colapinto, 1995; Combrinck-Graham, 1995; Minuchin, Colapinto, & Minuchin, 1998), and juvenile courts (Jones, 1985) have also been a major focus in SFT.

A second category includes clinical situations in which a child or adolescent shows symptoms clearly meeting *DSM* criteria, and these symptoms are evoked, maintained, or exacerbated by relationship problems. Both family relationships and individual symptoms provide the focus of interventions and outcomes assessment. SFT has spawned many useful, richly detailed treatment applications for addressing this category of clinical problems among troubled young children (Combrinck-Graham, 1986; Jones, 1994) as well as with adolescents and their families (Fishman, 1988; Micucci, 1998). Clinical symptoms and syndromes addressed include suicidality (Landau-Stanton & Stanton, 1985), school-based problems (Eno, 1985), drug addiction (Stanton & Todd, 1982), anorexia nervosa (Dare, Eisler, Russell, & Szmukler, 1990; Minuchin et al., 1978; Sargent, 1987), juvenile sex offending (Sefarbi, 1990; Stevenson, Castillio & Sefarbi, 1989), and selective mutism (Lindblad-Goldberg, 1986).

Children and adolescents with severe psychiatric and disruptive behavioral symptoms, often resulting in lengthy out-of-home placements, have also received significant attention in SFT, with treatment programs designed for hospital or day treatment settings (Brendler, Silver, Habor, & Sargent, 1991) and intensive home-based settings (Lindblad-Goldberg et al., 1998). Major contributions have also been made with SFT variants designed to treat highly troubled adolescents. For example, MDFT (Liddle, 2000) highlights adolescent substance abuse, MST (Henggeler et al., 1998) targets delinquent youth, and ABFT (Diamond & Siqueland, 1998) spotlights adolescent depression.

A third category of clinical situations addressed with SFT involves children or adolescents with biologically based illnesses or disorders, who are severely stressed, but who may or may not show diagnosable mental-health conditions. Intervention efforts are directed at family relationships primarily to enhance adaptation and to reduce exacerbation of physical and emotional health problems for both the child and other family members. The treatment of families who have a child with ADHD or learning disabilities (Bogas, 1993) and developmental disabilities (Jones, 1987, 1991) is included here.

Supporting children with chronic illness and their families has received enormous attention among approaches influenced by SFT (Kazak, Segal-Andrews, & Johnson, 1995; Sargent, 1983), ranging from a focus on life-threatening diseases such as cancer (Kazak & Simms, 1996) to inflammatory bowel diseases (Wood et al., 1989) to asthma and diabetes (Minuchin et al., 1978; Sargent, 1982). BBFM (Wood et al., 2000) represents a major contribution to the treatment of clinical problems associated with a wide range of childhood physical illness. At the other end of the life cycle, SFT has been applied to supporting the elderly who are faced with deteriorating health within the contexts of family and medical facilities (Montalvo, 1994; Montalvo, Harmon, & Elliot, 1998).

CASE EXAMPLE

TRANSLATING THEORY INTO PRACTICE:
METHODS OF ASSESSMENT AND INTERVENTION

Methods of assessment and treatment in contemporary SFT occur in relationship to four major stages of treatment, organized around metaprocesses guiding a therapist's relationship with a family. Thinking in terms of these metaprocesses steers therapists in their efforts to read a therapist-family relationship system and directs the timing and pacing of interventions. These overlapping stages are: (1) constructing a therapeutic system, (2) establishing a meaningful therapeutic focus, (3) creating key growth-promoting interpersonal experiences that lead to incremental changes, and (4) solidifying changes and termination.

Although the processes implicated in these four stages of treatment occur sequentially, they are neither linear nor discrete in nature. Instead of one stage clearly beginning and another definitely ending, the stages operate according to developmental principles, with each new stage building on and enriching the other. In this manner, treatment becomes more textured and multidimensional over time. For example, initial efforts toward constructing a therapeutic system begin in stage 1. Subsequent stages, however, continue to deepen a therapist's relationship with family members, promoting the objectives of future stages. The processes of each stage often spiral and repeat over the course of psychotherapy.

Vignettes from a case study highlight how the theoretical principles and methods of assessment and intervention related to each of the treatment stages described previously are translated into clinical practice. The case study involves 7-year-old Eric, who was referred by his school counselor because of his frequent, intense, and volatile tantrums, which could last for hours. During these tantrums, he would yell, curse, hit, break household objects, and sometimes even urinate on the possessions of whoever was the target of his anger. These eruptions would often be accompanied by hopeless and disparaging self-statements, such as "I shouldn't be alive; I'm so stupid and bad." The behavior occurred at home, in the neighborhood, and at school.

The family is middle-class, living in an urban neighborhood. Both parents have advanced degrees. The father, Allen, age 40 years, works long hours each week in midlevel management and confines most of his family involvement to the weekends. The mother, Sue, age 39 years, works part-time as a graphic artist. She has placed her career on hold to devote time to taking care of the children. The parents have been married for 15 years. Allen's parents and Sue's father are deceased. Sue's mother lives in a nearby retirement community. Eric's 14-year-old sister, Amy, is enrolled in the ninth grade. Her parents describe her as a well-adjusted child with friends and as doing well in school. Amy spends a lot of time outside of the home with friends or in her room at home talking with friends on the telephone.

STAGE 1: CONSTRUCTING THE THERAPEUTIC SYSTEM

Two major objectives are accomplished in the beginning stage of the treatment process. One involves identifying key members of the family and/or extrafamilial system who are invited to participate in the treatment as needed. All four family members were initially considered key for involvement in the treatment. Also, after speaking with the referring school counselor, the therapist determined that Eric's teacher would be a potential supportive resource.

Persons who are critical for inclusion in the treatment process are those who may be a part of the sequence of interactions around a problem and/or those who may be impacted by it, and those who may have the potential to establish relationships to support growth and development. Primary caregivers (e.g., parents, stepparents, foster parents, grandparents) and siblings are generally considered desired participants. Treatment may also involve extended relatives and family friends. Because children spend a significant amount of time in school and/or day care, some therapeutic involvement with these systems is also generally required. A genogram and ecomap can be important assessment tools in identifying significant familial and extrafamilial resources (Lindblad-Goldberg et al., 1998).

The second major objective of this first stage of treatment entails laying the foundation for setting up a therapeutic alliance. Without a strong therapeutic alliance, no meaningful treatment occurs. This relationship allows conversations to emerge with sufficient depth and range for making sense of and addressing the presenting problems. Within SFT parlance, "joining" connotes the process of forming a therapeutic alliance (Minuchin, 1974). Joining means to actively demonstrate acceptance of the family by initially accommodating to the family's values and preferred styles of communication and problem-solving. A therapist introduces language that validates an individual's emotional experiences and perspective. Language conveys a normalizing of problems construed as developmental challenges. Effective joining helps family members feel understood, respected, and known. Joining instills a sense of hope and remoralization in families who have felt defeated and demoralized by their problems. Joining builds an emotional scaffolding to support ongoing therapy. As collaborative alliances develop, a therapist can partner with each family member to clarify concerns and treatment expectations, foster a shared understanding of assessment issues, and ultimately coevolve treatment planning.

Initial Contact with Parents
The mother, Sue, called for an appointment and sounded very anxious about therapy. Her husband, Allen, entered the phone conversation. Both parents described feeling besieged and overwhelmed by their son's behaviors. They also seemed protective of him, frequently qualifying the slightest negative comments. The therapist joined the parents around their concern for Eric's self-esteem. Suggestions were given about what they could say to Eric and his sister regarding coming to family therapy. A beginning partnership emerged when therapist and parents discussed a potential plan to ensure that no family member would feel pathologized during a family session.

First Session with All Family Members
Subsequent sessions with all family members would solidify the therapist's initial therapeutic parental alliance as well as join with Eric and Amy. The first family session began with a discussion about positive family and individual experiences, punctuating emotional connections between the children and their parents. Allen set the emotional tone in the session, displaying a highly articulate, controlled, and precise interactional style. He assumed the role of spokesperson and responded to all of the therapist's initial questions about Eric. Sue sat quietly, deferring to her husband. Although not directly critical of his wife, Allen seemed to be subtly blaming her for Eric's problems. Consequently, the therapist intervened in a respectful manner to ensure that Sue had equal time to talk. The therapist wanted the parents to come together as a team to feel confident that their concerns about Eric were developmentally valid. This was important because parental ambivalence about the validity of the problem would weaken the therapeutic system when intensity increased later in treatment.

The therapist affirmed the parents' expert knowledge of Eric's strengths and limitations. Parental theories linking the etiology of Eric's problems to self- or other-blame were redirected. Instead, the parents' attention was focused on the kinds of support children need to achieve the normal milestones of social-emotional development. The fact that some children need more support than others was emphasized. The use of a normative developmental framework based on objective milestones helped them and Eric not to feel blamed, but optimistic, in helping Eric master his developmental dilemmas. The therapist summarized, "Eric's loss of control clearly makes him suffer and also hurts his relationships with you and his sister. However, I do not believe this is simply a matter of will power. Maybe he's trying to tell you that he is in over his head right now and needs your help trying to cope with some very big feelings. We need to learn more about how he is processing things emotionally, what is getting in the way of his ability to effectively cope with his fears, disappointments, and frustrations, and how you and his sister can help him."

Eric presented initially as shy and cautious, but soon felt safe to talk about how badly he feels when "anger gets me." Because he was already showing a natural predilection toward "externalizing the problem," a technique described by M. White (1989), the therapist capitalized on it. Eric engaged in a relatively detailed conversation about the impact of his very big feelings on himself and his parents, sister, teacher, and peers. Amy described how Eric's anger annoyed her, but she was also able to empathize with him. Eric then responded to a game of guessing where and when his anger did not "win" (e.g., during rough-and-tumble sports). Now he could eagerly accept the therapist's invitation to have a "competition with anger," using his parents as "coaches." Reasons for winning or losing would be recorded in his weekly journal. The goal of this task was to empower Eric to elicit parental support in understanding how his internal reactions combine with situational family, peer, or teacher interactions to trigger temper outbursts or to master them.

The session concluded with a brief orientation about treatment. Although most mental-health professions mandate informed consent in their ethics code, this is too often treated as a pro forma activity by therapists rather than an essential element of forming a therapeutic system. A treatment system constitutes a new social system. The expectations and procedures may not be well-known. Explaining what the treatment entails, including informed-consent procedures, significantly advances establishing collaborative alliances.

Positive relationships with family members prove essential, but inadequate, to alone sustain engagement in the absence of a clear and motivating treatment focus. Stage 2 places a major emphasis on the exploration and assessment of a child within a family context.

STAGE 2: ESTABLISHING A MEANINGFUL THERAPEUTIC FOCUS

A meaningful therapeutic focus derives from a well-grounded assessment of an individual child in the family context based on multiple perspectives and developed in partnership with both child and family. A therapist elicits detailed descriptions of a child's presenting symptoms and their impact on functioning across major social contexts, such as family, school, peer group, and community. Resources are also identified. Information about individual or family strengths and vulnerabilities are incorporated into broader clinical themes that make sense to the family. This process helps to provide a vehicle for moving toward change.

Sessions 2 through 4 (All Family Members) and 5 (Parents and Eric's Teacher)
Eric's multidimensional assessment was based on standardized questionnaire data, observed family interaction, Eric's journal of "encounters with temper," observations of Eric's play in sessions, and discussions with the parents, Amy, Eric, and Eric's teacher about situations that trigger Eric's tantrums. This assessment clarified an anxiety component related to the symptoms. For example, his tantrums occurred most frequently around transitions from one activity to another and in contexts where there was high sensory stimulation, particularly of the verbal

kind. Other anxiety-related symptoms, such as compulsions, had appeared in the months prior to the parents seeking treatment, but they had not been linked to the tantrums.

Viewing Eric as anxious and easily overwhelmed provided a new perception of his presenting problems. This perception opened up constructive dialogues between the parents, between the parents and both of their children, and between the parents and Eric's teacher. All had unwittingly been placing Eric in too many situations requiring flexibility, his greatest weakness. They examined the number, type, and intensity of demands for flexibility being made on him. Accompanying his mother on her numerous errands frequently interrupted his staying home or playing in the neighborhood each afternoon. At school, numerous demands for shifting gears, such as moving from one activity to another in the classroom, and, most significantly, stresses on the playground overextended his capacity for flexibility. Because Eric already felt he had little control over events in his life, these demands proved too much. This type of problem-solving dialogue is often overlooked when gross family interactions are examined out of the context of individual-level child data.

Examination of recurring family interactions added significantly to understanding other sources of tension and anxiety for all family members and their subsequent reciprocal responses. Emotional connections between Eric and his mother, as well as within the couple, were marked by insecurity and distance. Allen became stiff and fidgety when Sue spoke, as if he half expected her to misspeak or diverge into a tangent. Sue talked hesitatingly, frequently looking at Allen, attempting to correct herself based on whatever she read in his facial expressions. When his parents were conversing, Eric would quickly disengage and retreat into playing with toys in the room; Amy would also withdraw and do her homework. In subsequent sessions, Amy negotiated a contract with the therapist that she would come to sessions on an "as-needed" basis because of her heavy homework load and extracurricular activities. Perhaps she, too, needed time away from the parental tension.

The therapist playfully highlighted this negative interactional pattern in a family session when the father reprimanded Eric for leaving the family circle. The father had also just given an irritated glance at his wife when it looked as though she might comment on the action. The therapist brought the focus back to the parents, saying, "I think Eric has the right idea; this conversation is way too heavy for someone his size to bear. Is there something that you're trying to help Sue get out that could be useful here?" Sue haltingly pointed out that Allen was more adept with words and that she often had trouble expressing her words fast enough because she viewed herself as a slow thinker. The therapist changed the perception of this self-deprecating comment by first acknowledging Sue's observation of differences between her and Allen's processing styles. The therapist then questioned whether Sue's tendency to reflect on what she is going to say might be considered by some to be a real strength. The notion of individual differences and the importance of accepting and learning to work with them within the family (as opposed to labeling them as deficits) emerged as a theme that was played out repeatedly in this family's treatment.

By making overt this one interactional pattern between the parents, critical family history emerged as well as important information about Sue's 20-year struggle with her own emotional health and self-esteem. Allen made an effort to steer the conversation back to Eric, but the therapist briefly blocked this in the interest of stretching the family's tolerance for conflict and negative emotions, as well as to promote elevating Sue's status in the parental relationship. Sue's description of her difficulties and

Allen's efforts to deflect the conversation represented a recurring parental pattern of minimizing serious issues.

Sue spoke of her mother as being critical and intrusive and described her father as distant. The similarity to her current family was noted to create an opening for Sue to acknowledge her disappointments and begin to talk with Allen about their relationship. As Sue began to talk more openly, Allen revealed how Sue's dependency burdened him. He related that Sue frequently went to bed and slept when challenges arose and how she called him to come home to care for the children. This set of interactions maintained Eric's insecurity in his relationship with his mother. Sue acknowledged this and described her frequent bouts of low energy, crying spells, and gloomy moods. The therapist wondered aloud about the presence of clinical depression. Sue seemed surprised to hear that the condition, which she had learned to live with over the years, might not result from character flaws but instead might respond to treatment. She indicated that, in previous therapy, medication had been discussed, but the therapist had never given a diagnosis or suggested that learning more effective coping skills might help her.

Both Sue and Allen seemed to relax once this "secret" emerged. Allen began advocating for Sue to obtain an evaluation for depression and to enter treatment for it. The therapist took great care to avoid implying that Sue's depression was "the" cause of Eric's difficulties. Instead, the therapist highlighted the importance of both parents being able to work together from a position of strength to help Eric learn to cope with his big feelings. In a sense, Sue needed to learn to handle her own big feelings. She followed through with a brief series of individual-therapy sessions, resulting in an increased sense of empowerment for her and a more active, positive role in the family. This intervention served three process goals. First, it began a restructuring of the family organization by promoting a stronger, more functional parental alliance. Second, this intervention challenged the family's avoidant style regarding handling conflict and negative emotions. In the interest of protecting one another from the feared harmful impact of disappointment and hurt feelings, honest appraisals and straight talk about individual experiences had become nearly impossible for all family members. Consequently, effective problem-resolution was curtailed. Third, this intervention began to call attention to the need to appreciate individual differences such as temperament, perceptions, coping styles, and emotional needs.

By the end of the fifth session, a more complete case formulation, with clear goals and objectives, was in place. In contemporary SFT, case formulations operate as enhanced problem definitions, which establish therapeutic focus. They provide a summative activity wherein information about presenting symptoms, child and family strengths, and child and family development becomes integrated into a meaningful story. An effective problem definition or therapeutic focus offers clarity and galvanizes children and their families into action. It links the symptoms and what must be done to address them to the next step in the child's and family's development.

Following the initial five sessions, the parents began to view Eric's tantrums as an expression of his being overwhelmed by sensations and feelings too big for him to handle. They learned the two reasons Eric's coping skills were underdeveloped. One stemmed from his constitutional sensitivity and proneness to anxiety. Consequently, he often began an interaction with his parents, Amy, or others already highly aroused. To learn greater self-control and self-regulation, he needed his parents and teacher to provide more early warnings and orientation for upcoming transitions, as well as help with visualizing what he could do that was fun in the next activity. When prevention fails, and Eric becomes overwhelmed, he needs containment and soothing, rather than threats and other power-based responses. The parents also realized that, when they do not work together and overwhelm him with their own tensions and anxieties, Eric's effective coping strategies decrease. The parents must, therefore, find ways to become more supportive of one another and more tolerant of their own individual differences. In particular, father needs to stop rescuing mother, and she should remain more involved in the parenting role, exercising greater assertive parenting tactics with both children.

The case formulation clarifies both what the child needs to learn and what family structures will support this learning, and then links these understandings to the presenting problems. This opens the door to the third stage of treatment in which the focus turns primarily to problem-resolution, realignment of family relationships, and increasing emotional capacities.

STAGE 3: CREATING KEY GROWTH-PROMOTING INTERPERSONAL EXPERIENCES

To foster problem-resolution and development, the therapist organizes family relationships to create or stimulate key interpersonal experiences designed to provide intensive practice of emerging, but weak, coping skills. Both therapy sessions and family life at home become emotionally based learning laboratories for child and parents. Interventions follow the assumption that emotional skills are best understood experientially or from the inside out. Thus, the SFT therapist must remain highly attuned to emotional and interactional processes. Two major elements appear crucial for making interactions become more growth-promoting: emotional challenge and emotional support. Both seem essential in proper proportions for interactional experiences to promote growth or change rather than repetition of an unsatisfying, accustomed pattern. A therapist varies or adjusts the levels of intensity associated with an emotional challenge and the accompanying support. Here, many of the techniques associated with the SFT model generally come into play, including boundary making, raising intensity, enactments, and punctuation of interactional process (Minuchin & Fishman, 1981).

Session 6 (Eric and Parents)
A spontaneous enactment of Eric's problem in handling disappointment and discomfort occurred during the sixth session. Eric loudly demanded to go home midway through the session, proclaiming that he was bored and was missing his favorite television show. Sue attempted to empathize with him when Allen motioned emphatically to her that he would handle it. Allen sternly told Eric to "cool it" and promised to stop by the ice-cream store on the way home from the session if he behaved. Eric immediately calmed and smiled. At this moment, however, the therapist blocked the full implementation of this resolution by turning to Sue and asking, "Do you think Eric could settle down without any bribes?" This brought Sue back into the interaction, increasing the tension in every dyadic and triadic relationship in the room, particularly between the therapist and Allen, Sue and Allen, and the parents and Eric. Now both Eric and the family were presented with a slightly different, but significant, emotional challenge that needed resolution. Sue responded to the therapist's challenge haltingly, "I really don't know what Eric can handle anymore." She then glanced protectively at Allen's reddened face signifying he had felt criticized. He defensively responded that at least his directive had proven effective. The therapist supported Allen, indicating that he probably would have proceeded in the same way. However, the therapist then proposed that treatment sessions offer a safe place to question old methods and to experiment with new strategies.

This one conflictual interaction between Eric and his parents supplied rich material for an intense, constructive dialogue between the parents and the therapist for another 40 minutes. The therapist focused the parents on both Eric's internal processes and family interactional dynamics, asking "What do you think triggered his reaction just now?" After entertaining the parents' guesses, ranging from "a short attention span" to "just being difficult," the therapist highlighted recent conversations that may have made Eric anxious. Specifically, Sue had initiated discussion about the impact of Allen's unavailability the day before when she called him at work to ask for help in handling one of Eric's volatile tantrums. Allen bristled, and Sue pouted; then Eric was ready to leave. Both parents agreed with the therapist's observations. This led to a reflective examination about other tantrums and potential links to daily routines or interactions in the home. For the family, this enactment engendered a deep appreciation of the power of anxiety as a force leading to Eric's demanding, explosive behavior. It also helped to provide a rationale as to why bribing Eric with an ice-cream cone might short-circuit efforts to master this anxiety, as well as block an opportunity for them to demonstrate their capabilities in handling and resolving conflict.

As often happens with child- and adolescent-focused clinical problems, Eric's family shows a parallel difficulty in handling the same class of emotions as Eric. His family as a whole or as individuals do not tolerate tension and discomfort. Interactions are shut down before a natural resolution of issues occurs. Fear and anxiety govern interactions. When disappointment and anxiety challenge Eric, he, in turn, confronts his family. Family members display an inability to support his efforts to master these powerful feelings because they themselves feel uncomfortable with them. By terminating conflict prematurely, the parents miss opportunities to probe beneath the surface of Eric's demands and suppress hypothesizing about the possible triggers of his behavior. Eric misses a chance to become more aware of his intentions, a critical process in learning to self-regulate.

In the enactment described previously, the therapist intended to extend the dynamic tension in family relationships longer than the family would naturally tolerate to kindle these opportunities to engage in critical thinking. The possibility of promoting discovery of new ways for working with these feelings could arise. Growth and development derives from struggles with mild to moderate levels of emotional tension. The family's learning this throughout therapy helps to contain some of the anxiety associated with attempting new behaviors. Interventions such as the one described with Eric and his family constitute *core* emotional challenges because they cut across multiple system levels. They possess the potential to alter both family organization and dynamics as well as the child's internal structure and processes. Therapy with Eric and his family involved numerous similar experiences, based on the assumption that a significant level of daily practice proves necessary to incorporate new structures both intrapersonally and in the family.

Work with a variety of subsystems in a family often becomes important to provide growth-promoting experiences of sufficient intensity. In the early days of SFT and other models of family therapy, a mistaken belief prevailed that children and adolescents greatly benefited primarily from the indirect effects of change at the larger family-system level. This represented a trickle-down theory of change. In contemporary SFT, it is believed that work at one subsystem level cannot be omitted or replaced by work at another level. Meaningful change expected in a child's or adolescent's coping skills requires specific interventions directed at these specific processes.

Sessions 7 and 8 (Eric and Parents)
The parents and therapist decided mutually to use family play in the seventh session to

observe how Eric was processing different emotions and coping with overwhelming negative emotions. Eric gravitated toward toy soldiers and policemen, with overarching play themes generally involving the good guys trying to restrain the bad guys. The bad guys kept escaping from their jail. Rather than interpreting the symbolism in the play, the therapist utilized it to show the parents how Eric could incorporate new ideas and emotions into his play. The therapist wondered aloud whether the bad guys' intentions had been misunderstood by the good guys. Eric guessed, "Maybe the bad guys were really trying to save the townspeople from something they couldn't see." The therapist helped Eric to further elaborate on this idea, stretching his ability to entertain a broader range of other people's (and perhaps his own) intents and motivations. Developmentally, this skill is assumed to be a prerequisite for increasing the capacity to represent emotions at an abstract level and to mentally engage in problem-solving difficult situations (Greenspan, 1992).

Sue and Allen joined Eric in play and helped him to hypothesize about the intensity and intent of his play characters' emotions. Eric was delighted to have his parents connect with him in an arena in which he felt so competent: the world of play and imagination. The parents were urged to spend some time each day engaged in fantasy play. One objective of this task was to increase the number of interactions at home in which Eric *and* his parents experienced sustained emotional connections around nonthreatening, yet emotional, themes.

During the eighth session, family play was concentrated on increasing awareness of family members' emotion-regulation styles. Together, the family drew a cardboard "emotion scale," using different colors to symbolize varying degrees of emotional intensity. When the scale registered red, indicating high emotional intensity, each individual described what he or she could do, both autonomously *and/or* with the help of another, to bring it down to an "even-keel yellow." In this and future sessions, the emotion scale was used to help family members modulate arousal, hypothesize about the intentions of self and others, and communicate about it during discussions of emotionally charged home situations. The parents used the scale at home to defuse potentially explosive situations and to become more adept at reading each other's and their children's intents or motivations.

Over the next several sessions, the therapist and parents designed and implemented behavioral interventions to assist Eric in containing explosions and to ensure that his tantrums would no longer work to avoid uncomfortable situations. The parents kept negative consequences or punishments for behavior to a minimum, and instead waited out the upsets. Eric identified "safety zones" on each floor of the house where he could go whenever he felt that he would explode. He chose tight, dark, and quiet places such as under the sofa or in closets.

Through continued subsystem work, both Eric and his family practiced the types of growth-promoting interactional experiences outlined above for approximately one month. Gradual changes occurred both in the ways the family operated and in Eric's presenting symptoms. Stage 4 began with the accomplishment of agreed-upon goals.

STAGE 4: SOLIDIFY CHANGES AND TERMINATE

Although a therapist helps family members continually to integrate different themes generated during treatment, this task becomes more central in stage 4. Families need a clear conceptual understanding of how their actions produce desired outcomes to solidify changes, especially when relapses occur. A therapist wants to know how a family will right themselves when one member slips. Here, family members take the lead roles, and the therapist serves as a partner or guide. Changes must generalize beyond the therapy context and be sustained long after treatment ends.

Subsequent Sessions (Eric and Parents)
For Eric and his family, stage 4 began with a small crisis. Symptoms, which had significantly improved, suddenly escalated. Until the relapse, Eric's volatile tantrums decreased from 15 to 16 per week to 2 or fewer, with recovery time shortened from over an hour to less than 10 minutes. A relapse presents rich opportunities for linking various strands of the therapy and for solidifying changes. In the session following the relapse, the parents and therapist reviewed possible changes either at home or school that could have played a role in Eric's relapse. Here, the parents took a leadership role. These previously conflicted parents worked more as partners, requiring only mild support, readily drawing on a more elaborated case formulation they had developed over the course of therapy.

Sue confidently suggested that interactions with a new child in Eric's class could be stressing him. The therapist asked her to pursue this hunch with Eric. Initially, Eric rebuffed her inquiries, leaving Allen poised to shut down this avenue (albeit with less impatience than previously) and to open another. The therapist quickly recommended that Sue find another way to open the dialogue with her son. In contrast to her previous style of backing away from challenge, she moved forward, knelt on the floor beside Eric, and joined him briefly in play. With this level of support and engagement, Eric talked about his difficulties with a new child in his class. He felt jealous because his friends expressed more interest in the new child than in playing with him. Allen now teamed with Sue and Eric to problem-solve the situation. All three explored the emotional signals behind the problem behavior, examined changes in the social context, and then worked together to develop solutions. The therapist reviewed his observations of the family's approach to this new challenge, highlighting how little he needed to help. The family then identified what made their problem-solving successful. In this way, the family used an opportunity to internalize a method for self-reflection—an essential process for self-correction.

Before treatment ended, the family was invited to reflect on their vulnerabilities and to think ahead about preventive strategies for the future. The family also reviewed each member's progress throughout treatment and identified coping resources for future challenges. These types of dialogue helped to solidify therapy themes related to conflict tolerance, acceptance of individual differences, and emotional expressiveness that had emerged in various forms throughout the treatment.

Posttreatment
By the follow-up visit nine months later, Eric showed further decreases in tantrums and continued growth in social-emotional competencies. He was now engaging in sports activities that he had always admired but was too anxious to try. He was better able to verbalize his worries and to request support when needed. The parents had grown closer and more secure with one another, as had Eric and his mother. A more relaxed, tolerant attitude about negative emotions and conflict pervaded the family. The treatment consisted of 18 sessions in total over the course of 10 months.

SUPPORTING RESEARCH

A strong commitment to both family-process and treatment-outcome research has continued ever since the first approximations of the model began to emerge in the early 1960s at the Wiltwyck School for Boys in New York. Over the past 35 years, empirical studies using SFT-inspired practitioners have made major contributions to the larger body of research establishing family-based treatment in general as viable and efficacious for a variety of child and adolescent disorders (Diamond, Serrano, Dickey, & Sonis, 1996). Liddle (2000) in MDFT, Diamond et al. (in press) in ABFT, and Henggeler et al. (1998) in MST are currently generating the strongest empirical support for many of the core constructs and practices of SFT in their three integrative, highly specified, research-based models.

The SFT model represents the product of a quasi-experimental process, bearing some resemblance to the inductive stepwise process Kazdin (1994) recommended for treatment-development studies. For example, Minuchin and his colleagues (1967) began their work with only a few sketchy concepts derived from sociology and anthropology. They let their systematic observations of families in therapy guide model development. Their early adoption of one-way mirrors and then of videotape recordings of clinical sessions to document family and therapeutic processes reflect the value placed on keeping theory grounded in concrete, observable phenomena. Observational methodology has always held a central position in research related to SFT, with a reliance on various family tasks or assignments to evoke interactional behaviors that could be coded for patterns.

As with the therapy, studies related to SFT since Wiltwyck have tended to be population-centered. With social context as central to this model, most of the initial studies during the first 25 years were focused more on understanding specific groups of families and charting the interactional landscape around specific problem areas than on the documentation of treatment outcomes. The population studied at Wiltwyck included behaviorally disordered children and adolescents living in families described as "the ghetto-living, urban, minority group member, who is experiencing poverty, discrimination, fear, crowdedness, and street-living" (Minuchin et al., 1967, p. 22). A total of 11 families constituted the treatment group. Early outcome studies in SFT, as was true for much of the treatment field in the 1960s and 1970s (Gurman & Kniskern, 1981), tended to have very small samples and did not involve control groups. These researchers relied primarily on pre- and postmeasures of change in child symptoms and family interactional patterns.

Despite the methodological limitations of the early studies, the results proved very encouraging regarding the model's potential for effectiveness. For example, 7 of 11 families followed at Wiltwyck showed improvement in interactional flexibility and quality of the communication process at the end of six months of family intervention (Minuchin et al., 1967). This study of underorganized, unstable families solidified the conviction "that families need some kind of structure, some form of hierarchy, and some degree of differentiation between subsystems" (Colapinto, 1991, p. 419). The thrust of the simple, early study at Wiltwyck has been validated by current, more sophisticated research with this population (see comprehensive reviews by Henggeler, Borduin, & Mann, 1992; Tolan, Cromwell, & Brasswell, 1986).

Controlled research based on the MST model developed by Henggeler and colleagues (1998) has been built on and significantly extended the early exploratory empirical work begun by Minuchin at Wiltwyck. In this SFT-informed model, closely supervised community-based practitioners, available 24 hours per day, provide treatment in the homes and communities over a period of four to six months, with interventions guided by a highly specified treatment manual. Henggeler (1999) and colleagues have published eight randomized clinical trials comparing MST with other models for intervening with seriously troubled, delinquent youth. They consistently demonstrated success in reducing delinquent behavior, drug use, and out-of-home placements (such as incarceration and hospitalization). Current MST studies spotlight treatment retention, cost-effectiveness, and quality assurance.

Ecosystemic structural home-based family therapy (ESSFT; Lindblad-Goldberg et al., 1998), also a home-based expansion of the model begun at Wiltwyck, was developed to serve a population of children and adolescents with a broad spectrum of severe mental-health disorders who are considered to be at high risk for out-of-home placement. Eight months of treatment is provided by cotherapy teams, with interventions including family therapy, community linking, 24-hour crisis availability, family support services, and respite care. Therapists receive three years of intensive training in the model and three hours of weekly supervision. A seven-year study of ESSFT treatment outcomes targeting 1,968 diverse families across more than 40 different community agencies showed significant reductions both in presenting symptoms (from both the child's and parents' perspectives) and in the use of out-of-home placement (Dore, 1996). Significant positive changes were also observed in family functioning and a child's or adolescent's psychosocial functioning. These changes were maintained up to one year posttreatment. ESSFT and MST as variants of SFT significantly expand an emphasis on treating a family within the ecology of a community.

Another early research area of Minuchin and his colleagues at the Philadelphia Child Guidance Center dealt with middle-class families with children showing psychosomatic conditions. On both physiological and interactional measures, the special vulnerabilities of some children with chronic illness correlated with certain overorganized family patterns, such as enmeshment, rigidity, overprotectiveness, and absence of conflict resolution. SFT proved effective in treating families with diabetic children who showed frequent, medically unexplained emergency hospitalizations for acidosis, and children who experienced intractable asthma and relied heavily on steroids (Minuchin et al., 1975). In summarizing the results of treating 53 cases of anorexia nervosa, Minuchin et al. (1978) reported a 90% improvement rate, with the positive effects maintained at follow-up intervals of up to two years. In more recent well-designed studies comparing individual therapy and a modified, integrative version of SFT with young anorexic girls, researchers have replicated these early findings (Dare et al., 1990; Russell, Szmukler, Dare, & Eisler, 1987).

During this same time-period, Stanton and Todd (1982) applied SFT to the treatment of heroin addicts receiving methadone and their families. In one of the earliest controlled studies of SFT, they compared this treatment model with a family placebo condition and individual therapy. Those in the SFT treatment condition showed significant symptom reduction, with the level of positive change doubling that achieved in the other two conditions; these positive effects persisted at 6- and 12-month follow-ups. Numerous subsequent studies with substance-involved adolescents using family-based treatment have replicated and expanded these findings (e.g., Freidman, 1989; Henggeler, Borduin, Melton, Mann, & Smith, 1991; Lewis, Piercy, Sprenkle, & Trepper, 1990). These studies also highlight the power of the model in fostering engagement with treatment. For example, compared to a rate of 49% to 50% for peer groups, family treatments resulted in attrition rates of 11% to 30%. Szapocznik et al. (1988) increased the attendance of substance-involved youth at first sessions by 40% using a strategy derived from SFT.

Liddle's (2000) research using MDFT included some of the most rigorous testing of core SFT constructs with a clinical population in treatment for drug and alcohol abuse. In addition to a focus on family interactions, MDFT incorporates an emphasis on individual developmental themes and family affect. Three randomized trials have established the model's efficacy with adolescent substance abusers (Liddle et al., in press). Process studies have also received a major emphasis in Liddle and colleagues' research agenda, including a focus on the relationship between in-session patterns of change and resolution of parent-child conflict (Diamond & Liddle, 1999) and strategies for improving poor therapist-adolescent alliances (Diamond, Liddle, Hogue, & Dakof, in press).

Although SFT has been applied to the treatment of a wide range of child and adolescent disorders, there are fewer family-based treatment outcome studies reported in the literature targeting childhood internalizing disorders such as anxiety and depression. In one well-designed study, Szapocznik et al. (1989) compared SFT with psychodynamic therapy and a nontreatment control condition for Hispanic school-age boys presenting with a variety of problems typically seen in an outpatient setting. About half of the boys displayed behavior problems, the rest evidenced anxiety and adjustment difficulties. Though equivalent in their effectiveness at reducing levels of behavioral and emotional symptoms and in increasing general social-emotional adaptation, the two treatment conditions differed significantly in their impact on family functioning. The families of the boys receiving psychodynamic therapy deteriorated in functioning during the treatment and at one-year follow-up. In contrast, the families of the boys receiving SFT showed improved family functioning that was maintained through the one-year follow-up.

Studies are currently underway by Diamond and colleagues (Diamond & Siqueland, 1998; Diamond, Diamond, & Siqueland, et al., in press) using an SFT-derived model, ABFT, with depressed adolescents. The model highlights reduction of blame in the family, improving communication and problem-solving skills, fostering authoritative parenting styles, and strengthening family social supports. Early results are promising. Significant reductions in depressive symptoms were reported by the treatment group, as compared to wait-listed patients, in a randomized pilot study of 32 mostly African American clinically depressed adolescents (Diamond, 1998).

SUMMARY

SFT has proven to be an influential and effective treatment model for use with children and adolescents who present with a wide variety of clinical problems. The developers of several strong research-based treatment models (e.g., MDFT, MST, ABFT, and BBFT) have incorporated core concepts and intervention strategies from SFT and rigorously tested them with specifically defined clinical populations. This complements the focus in contemporary family-therapy-treatment outcome research, which has shifted from comparative studies of different broad-based family therapy models to testing more integrated, highly specified versions of family-focused approaches. The current trend toward greater specification and operationalization of the goals and methods of treatment throughout the field of psychotherapy (see Roth & Fonagy, 1996) can only strengthen the model and make it more effective and more teachable. As is evident in the integrative effort of this chapter, SFT is unlikely to maintain the status quo, even in reference to itself. Instead, its proponents will continue to develop, reorganize, and respond to the endless challenges and circles of feedback, influencing while being influenced.

REFERENCES

Abelsohn, D. (1983). Dealing with the abdication dynamic in the post-divorce family: A context for adolescent crisis. *Family Process, 22,* 359–383.

American Psychiatric Association. (1994). *Diagnostic and statistical manual of mental disorders* (4th ed.). Washington, DC: Author.

Aponte, H. J. (1970). The family-school interview: An eco-structural approach. *Family Process, 15,* 303–311.

Aponte, H. J. (1976). Underorganization in the poor family. In P. J. Guerin (Ed.), *Family therapy: Theory and practice* (pp. 432–448). New York: Gardner Press.

Auerswald, E. H. (1968). Interdisciplinary versus ecological approach. *Family Process, 7*, 202–215.

Bateson, G. (1979). *Mind and nature.* New York: Dutton.

Bogas, S. (1993). An integrative treatment model for children's attentional and learning problems. *Family Systems Medicine, 2*, 385–396.

Bowlby, J. (1969). *Attachment and loss. Volume I: Attachment.* New York: Basic Books.

Bowlby, J. (1988). *A secure base.* New York: Basic Books.

Bradley, S. J. (2000). *Affect regulation and the development of psychopathology.* New York: Guilford Press.

Brendler, J., Silver, M., Habor, M., & Sargent, J. (1991). *Madness, chaos, and violence: Therapy with families on the brink.* New York: Basic Books.

Byng-Hall, J. (1991). The application of attachment theory to understanding and treatment in family therapy. In C. M. Parkes, J. Stevenson-Hinde, & P. Marris (Eds.), *Attachment across the life cycle* (pp. 199–215). New York: Routledge.

Calkins, S. D. (1994). Origins and outcomes of individual differences in emotion regulation. *Monographs of the Society for Research in Child Development, 59*, 53–72.

Carter, E., & McGoldrick, M. (1989). *The changing family life cycle: A framework for family therapy.* New York: Gardner Press.

Cassidy, J. (1994). Emotion regulation: Influences of attachment relationships. *Monographs of the Society for Research in Child Development, 59*, 228–249.

Cicchetti, D., Toth, S. L., & Lynch, M. (1995). Bowlby's dream comes full circle: The application of attachment theory to risk and psychopathology. *Advances in Child Clinical Psychology, 17*, 1–75.

Colapinto, J. (1991). Structural family therapy. In A. S. Gurman & D. P. Kniskern (Eds.), *Handbook of family therapy* (Vol. 2, pp. 417–443). New York: Brunner/Mazel.

Colapinto, J. (1995). Dilution of family process in social services: Implications for treatment of neglectful families. *Family Process, 34*, 59–74.

Cole, P., & Zahn-Waxler, C. (1992). Emotion dysregulation in disruptive behavior disorders. In D. Cicchetti & S. Toth (Eds.), *Rochester symposium on developmental psychopathology: Developmental perspectives on depression* (Vol. 4, pp. 173–209). Rochester, NY: University of Rochester Press.

Cole, P. M., Michel, M. K., & O'Donnell, L. (1994). The development of emotion-regulation and dysregulation: A clinical perspective. *Monographs of the Society for Research in Child Development, 59*, 73–100.

Combrinck-Graham, L. (Ed.). (1986). *Treating young children in family therapy.* Rockville, MD: Aspen Press.

Combrinck-Graham, L. (1995). *Children in families at risk: Maintaining the connections.* New York: Guilford Press.

Cowan, P. C., & Cowan, P. A. (1990). *When partners become parents: The big life change for couples.* New York: Basic Books.

Cummings, E. M., & Davies, P. (1996). Emotional security as a regulatory process in normal development and the development of psychopathology. *Development and Psychopathology, 8*, 123–139.

Dare, C., Eisler, I., Russell, G. F. M., & Szmukler, G. I. (1990). The clinical and theoretical impact of a controlled trial of family therapy in anorexia nervosa. *Journal of Marital and Family Therapy, 16*, 39–57.

Denham, S. A. (1998). *Emotional development in young children.* New York: Guilford Press.

Diamond, G. S. (1998). *Pilot work on family therapy for depressed adolescents.* Paper presentation, American Psychological Association, San Francisco.

Diamond, G. S., Diamond, G. M., & Siqueland, L. (in press). Family therapy for depressed adolescents: A program of research. *Clinical Child and Family Psychology Review.*

Diamond, G. S., & Liddle, H. A. (1999). Transforming negative parent-adolescent interactions in family therapy: From impasse to dialogue. *Family Process, 38*, 5–26.

Diamond, G. S., Liddle, H. A., Hogue, A., & Dakof, G. A. (in press). Alliance-building interventions with adolescents in family therapy: A process study. *Psychotherapy: Theory, Research, Practice, and Training.*

Diamond, G. S., Serrano, A. C., Dickey, M., & Sonis, W. A. (1996). Current status of family-based outcome and process research. *American Academy of Child and Adolescent Psychiatry, 35*, 6–16.

Diamond, G. S., & Siqueland, L. (1998). Emotions, attachment and the relational frame. *Journal of Structural and Strategic Therapy, 17,* 36–50.

Dore, M. M. (1996). *Annual research report on family-based services.* Harrisburg, PA: Bureau of Children's Services, Pennsylvania Office of Mental Health.

Elizur, J., & Minuchin, S. (1989). *Institutionalizing madness.* New York: Basic Books.

Engels, G. L. (1980). The clinical application of a biopsychosocial model. *American Journal of Psychiatry, 137,* 535–544.

Eno, M. M. (1985). Children with school problems: A family therapy perspective. In R. Ziffer (Ed.), *Adjunctive techniques in family therapy* (pp. 151–180). Orlando, FL: Grune & Stratton.

Faude, J., Jones, W., & Robins, M. (1996). The affective life of infants: Theoretical and empirical foundations. In D. Nathanson (Ed.), *Knowing feeling* (pp. 219–256). New York: Norton.

Fishman, H. C. (1988). *Treating troubled adolescents.* New York: Basic Books.

Fishman, H. C. (1993). *Intensive structural family therapy: Treating families in their social context.* New York: Basic Books.

Fraiberg, S. H. (1959). *The magic years: Understanding and handling the problems of early childhood.* New York: Scribner's Sons.

Freidman, A. S. (1989). Family therapy vs. parent groups: Effects on adolescent drug abusers. *American Journal of Family Therapy, 17,* 335–347.

Goffman, E. (1971). *Relations in public: Micro studies of the public order.* New York: Harper & Row.

Goleman, D. (1995). *Emotional intelligence.* New York: Bantam Books.

Gottman, J. M., Katz, L. F., & Hooven, C. (1996). Parental meta-emotion philosophy and the emotional life of families: Theoretical models and preliminary data. *Journal of Family Psychology, 10*(3), 243–268.

Greenspan, S. (1992). *Infancy and early childhood: The practice of clinical assessment and intervention with emotional and developmental challenges.* Madison, CT: International Universities Press.

Gurman, A., & Kniskern, D. (Eds.). (1981). *Handbook of family therapy.* New York: Brunner/Mazel.

Haley, J. (1963). *Strategies of psychotherapy.* New York: Grune & Stratton.

Haley, J. (1976). *Problem-solving therapy.* San Francisco: Jossey-Bass.

Henggeler, S. W. (1999). Multisystemic therapy: An overview of clinical procedures, outcomes, and policy implications. *Child Psychology and Psychiatry Review, 4,* 2–10.

Henggeler, S. W., Borduin, C. M., & Mann, B. J. (1992). Advances in family therapy: Empirical foundations. In T. H. Ollendick & R. J. Prinz (Eds.), *Advances in clinical child psychology* (Vol. 15, pp. 207–241). New York: Plenum Press.

Henggeler, S. W., Borduin, C. M., Melton, G. B., Mann, B. J., & Smith, L. A. (1991). Effects of multisystemic therapy on drug use and abuse in serious juvenile offenders: A progress report from two outcome studies. *Family Dynamics of Addiction Quarterly, 1,* 40–51.

Henggeler, S. W., Schoenwald, S. K., Borduin, C. M., Rowland, M. D., & Cunningham, P. B. (1998). *Multisystemic treatment of antisocial behavior in children and adolescents.* New York: Guilford Press.

Hodas, G. (1997). *Guidelines for best practice in child and adolescent mental health services.* Harrisburg, PA: CASSP Training and Technical Assistance Institute.

Hoffman, L. (1981). *Foundations of family therapy: A conceptual framework for systems change.* New York: Basic Books.

Isaacs, M. B., Montalvo, B., & Abelsohn, D. (1986). *The difficult divorce: Therapy for children and families.* New York: Basic Books.

Jackson, D. D. (1957). The question of family homeostasis. *Psychiatric Quarterly Supplement, 31,* 79–90.

Johnson, S. M. (1996). *The practice of emotionally focused marital therapy: Creating connection.* New York: Brunner/Mazel.

Johnson, S. M., & Williams-Keeler, L. (1998). Creating healing relationships for couples dealing with trauma: The use of emotionally focused marital therapy. *Journal of Marital and Family Therapy, 24,* 25–40.

Jones, W. (1985). Problem formulation in juvenile court interventions with unruly children and their families. *Juvenile and Family Court Journal, 36*(1), 37–45.

Jones, W. (1987). Coping with the young handicapped child in the single-parent family: An ecosystemic perspective. In M. Lindblad-Goldberg (Ed.), *Clinical issues in single parent households* (pp. 85–100). Rockville, MD: Aspen Press.

Jones, W. (1991). Role adjustment among low-income, single parents with a retarded child: Patterns of support. *Journal of Family Psychology, 4*(4), 497–511.

Jones, W. (1994). Cultivating the language of play: The young child in family counseling. In C. S. Huber (Ed.), *Transitioning from individual to family counseling* (pp. 33–47). Alexandria, VA: American Counseling Association.

Kagan, L. F., Reznick, J. S., & Snidman, N. (1988). Biological basis of childhood shyness. *Science, 240*, 167–171.

Kazak, A. E., Segal-Andrews, A., & Johnson, K. (1995). Pediatric psychology research and practice: A family systems approach. In M. Roberts (Ed.), *Handbook of pediatric psychology* (pp. 84–104). New York: Guilford Press.

Kazak, A. E., & Simms, S. (1996). Children with life-threatening illnesses: Psychological difficulties and interpersonal relationships. In F. W. Kaslow (Ed.), *Handbook of relational diagnosis and dysfunctional family patterns* (pp. 225–238). New York: Wiley.

Kazdin, A. E. (1994). Methodology, design, and evaluation in psychotherapy research. In L. Garfield & A. E. Bergin (Eds.), *Handbook of psychotherapy and behavioral change* (3rd ed., pp. 19–71). New York: Wiley.

Landau-Stanton, J., & Stanton, M. D. (1985). Treating suicidal adolescents and their families. In M. Pravder-Merkin & S. L. Koman (Eds.), *Handbook of adolescents and family therapy* (pp. 309–328). New York: Gardner Press.

Lewis, R. A., Piercy, F. P., Sprenkle, D. H., & Trepper, T. S. (1990). Family-based interventions for helping drug-abusing adolescents. *Journal of Adolescent Research, 50*, 82–95.

Liddle, H. A. (2000). *Multidimensional family therapy treatment manual for Cannabis Youth Treatment Multi-Site Collaborative Project.* Rockville, MD: Center for Substance Abuse Treatment.

Liddle, H. A., Dakof, G. A., Parker, K., Diamond, G., Barrett, K., & Tejeda, M. (2001). Multidimensional family therapy for adolescent drug abuse: Results of a randomized clinical trial. *American Journal of Drug and Alcohol Abuse, 27*(4), 651–688.

Lindblad-Goldberg, M. (1986). Elective mutism in families with young children. In J. Hansen (Series Ed.) & L. Combrinck-Graham (Vol. Ed.), *Treating young children in family therapy* (pp. 38–50). Rockville, MD: Aspen Press.

Lindblad-Goldberg, M., Dore, M., & Stern, L. (1998). *Creating competence from chaos: A comprehensive guide to home-based services.* New York: Norton.

Malatesta, C., & Wilson, A. (1988). Emotion cognition interaction in personality development: A discrete emotions functional analysis. *British Journal of Social Psychology, 27*, 91–112.

Masten, A. S., Best, K. M., & Garmezy, N. (1990). Resilience and development: Contributions from the study of children who overcome adversity. *Development and Psychopathology, 2*, 425–444.

Marvin, R. S., & Stewart, R. B. (1990). A family systems framework for the study of attachment. In D. Greenberg, D. V. Cicchetti, & E. M. Cummings (Eds.), *Attachment in the preschool years: Research and intervention* (pp. 51–86). Chicago: University of Chicago Press.

Mayer, J. D., & Salovey, P. (1993). The intelligence of emotional intelligence. *Intelligence, 17*, 433–442.

McGoldrick, M. (Ed.). (1998). *Re-visioning family therapy: Race, culture and gender in clinical practice.* New York: Guilford Press.

Micucci, J. A. (1998). *The adolescent in family therapy: Breaking the cycle of conflict and control.* New York: Guilford Press.

Minuchin, S. (1974). *Families and family therapy.* Cambridge, MA: Harvard University Press.

Minuchin, S. (1985, November). *My many voices.* Unpublished manuscript, Evolution of Psychotherapy conference, Milto H. Erickson Foundation, Phoenix, AZ.

Minuchin, S., Baker, L., Rosman, B., Liebman, R., Milman, L., & Todd, T. (1975). A conceptual model of psychosomatic illness in children. *Archives of General Psychiatry, 32*, 1031–1038.

Minuchin, P., Colapinto, J., & Minuchin, S. (1998). *Working with families of the poor.* New York: Guilford Press.

Minuchin, S., & Fishman, H. C. (1981). *Family therapy techniques.* Cambridge, MA: Harvard University Press.

Minuchin, S., Montalvo, B., Guerney, B., Rosman, B., & Schumer, F. (1967). *Families of the slums.* New York: Basic Books.

Minuchin, S., & Nichols, M. (1993). *Family healing.* New York: Free Press.

Minuchin, S., Rosman, B., & Baker, L. (1978). *Psychosomatic families.* Cambridge, MA: Harvard University Press.

Montalvo, B. (1982). Interpersonal arrangements in disrupted families. In F. Walsh (Ed.), *Normal family processes* (pp. 277–296). New York: Guilford Press.

Montalvo, B. (1994). Assisting terminally ill patients and their families: An orientation model. *Family Systems Medicine, 12*(3), 269–279.

Montalvo, B., Harmon, D., & Elliot, M. (1998). Family mobilization: Work with angry elderly couples in declining health. *Contemporary Family Therapy, 20*(2), 163–178.

Moore, M., Cohen, S., & Montalvo, B. (1998). Sensitizing medical residents to fantasies and alignments in the family: Mastering psychosocial skills in the medical encounter. *Contemporary Family Therapy, 20*(4), 417–432.

Nichols, M., & Schwartz, R. (1998). *Family therapy: Concepts and methods.* Needham Heights, MA: Allyn & Bacon.

Power, T. J., & Bartholomew, K. L. (1987). Family-school relationship patterns: An ecological assessment. *School Psychology Review, 16,* 498–512.

Reiss, D. (1996). Foreword. In F. W. Kaslow (Ed.), *Handbook of relational diagnosis and dysfunctional family patterns* (pp. ix–xv). New York: Wiley.

Roth, A., & Fonagy, P. (1996). *What works for whom? A critical review of psychotherapy research.* New York: Guilford Press.

Russell, G. F. M., Szmukler, G. I., Dare, C., & Eisler, I. (1987). An evaluation of family therapy in anorexia nervosa and bulimia nervosa. *Archives of General Psychiatry, 44,* 1047–1056.

Saarni, C. (1999). *The development of emotional competence.* New York: Guilford Press.

Sameroff, A., & Emde, R. (1989). *Relationship disturbances in early childhood.* New York: Basic Books.

Sargent, J. (1982). Family systems theory and chronic childhood illness: Diabetes mellitus. In K. Flomenhaft & A. E. Christ (Eds.), *Psychosocial family interventions in chronic pediatric illness* (pp. 125–138). New York: Plenum Press.

Sargent, J. (1983). The sick child: Family complications. *Developmental and Behavioral Pediatrics, 4,* 50–56.

Sargent, J. (1985). Physician-family therapist collaboration: Children with medical problems. *Family Systems Medicine, 3,* 454–465.

Sargent, J. (1987). Integrating family and individual therapy for anorexia nervosa. In J. E. Harkaway (Ed.), *Eating disorders* (pp. 105–116). Gaithersburg, MD: Aspen Press.

Sefarbi, R. (1990). Admitters and deniers among adolescent sex offenders and their families: A preliminary study. *American Journal of Orthopsychiatry, 60,* 460–465.

Siegal, C. (1999). *The developing mind: Toward a neurobiology of interpersonal experience.* New York: Guilford Press.

Simon, G. M. (1995). A revisionist rendering of structural family therapy. *Journal of Marital and Family Therapy, 21,* 17–26.

Sroufe, L. A. (1997). Psychopathology as an outcome of development. *Development and Psychopathology, 9,* 251–268.

Stanton, M. D., & Todd, T. C. (1982). *The family therapy of drug abuse and addiction.* New York: Guilford Press.

Stevenson, H. C., Castillio, E., & Sefarbi, R. (1989). Treatment of denial in adolescent sex offenders and their families. *Journal of Offender Counseling, Services, and Rehabilitation, 14,* 37–50.

Strayhorn, J. (1988). *The competent child: An approach to psychotherapy and preventive mental health.* New York: Guilford Press.

Szapocznik, J., Murray, E., Scopetta, M., Hervis, O., Rio, A., Cohen, R., et al. (1989). Structural family versus psychodynamic child therapy for problematic Hispanic boys. *Journal of Consulting and Clinical Psychology, 57,* 571–578.

Szapocznik, J., Perez-Vidal, A., Brickman, A., Foote, F., Santisteban, D., Hervis, O., et al. (1988). Engaging adolescent drug abusers and their families into treatment: A strategic structural systems approach. *Journal of Consulting and Clinical Psychology, 56,* 552–557.

Tolan, P. H., Cromwell, R. E., & Brasswell, M. (1986). Family therapy with delinquents: A critical review of the literature. *Family Process, 25,* 619–649.

Watzlawick, P., Jackson, D., & Beavin, L. (1967). *Pragmatics of human communication.* New York: Norton.

White, M. (1989). The externalizing of the problem and the re-authoring of lives and relationships.

In M. White (Ed.), *Selected papers* (pp. 5–28). Adelaide, Australia: Dulwich Centre.

White, R. W. (1959). Motivation reconsidered: The concept of competence. *Psychological Review, 66,* 297–333.

Wood, B. L. (1985). Proximity and hierarchy: Orthogonal dimensions of family interconnectedness. *Family Process, 24,* 487–507.

Wood, B. L., Klebba, K. B., & Miller, B. D. (2000). Evolving the biobehavioral family model: The fit of attachment. *Family Process, 39,* 319–344.

Wood, B. L., Watkins, J. B., Boyle, J. T., Nogueira, J., Zimand, E., & Carroll, L. (1989). The psychosomatic family model: An empirical and theoretical analysis. *Family Process, 28,* 1–21.

Wynne, L. C. (1984). The epigenesis of relational systems: A model for understanding family development. *Family Process, 23,* 297–318.

CHAPTER 2

The Central Role of Culture: Working with Asian Children and Families

CHRISTINE M. CHAO

Several children who had been at the reading asked about *Aida*.

One wondered simply why Aida was her favorite role.

"When I sang Aida," Ms. Price answered, "I used the most important plus that I have. You have it; I have it: this beautiful skin. When I sang Aida, my skin was my costume."

—Leontyne Price, age 73, talking to fourth- and fifth-graders from PS 180, Harlem, New York (Tommasini, 2000)

To see the "beautiful skin" of others as leading into the drama of their lives, and in that drama to listen for the story lines, come to know the characters, major and minor, identify the tensions, and then declare, in true humility, that we do not know how the stories will end—but they are their stories, and we will be there to nurture, safeguard, and protect their stories as they unfold—that is the aim of working with children and their families in the context of their cultures.

HISTORY OF THE THERAPEUTIC APPROACH

Until Asian American psychologists, following in the footsteps of their African American colleagues (e.g., Banks, 1975; Block, 1968; Cheek, 1976; Grier & Cobbs, 1968), began publishing articles highlighting the critical role that culture plays in working with Asian clients, little had been written on this topic. Dropping out of therapy prematurely could be traced to the fact that Asians encountered non-Asian therapists who had little understanding of the dynamics operating in Asian cultures. These encounters left non-Asian clinicians puzzled over why some Asian clients did not make eye contact, or would nod and say, "Yes, yes," but then not comply with treatment suggestions, or would miss a scheduled appointment and then show up at another time without an appointment (D. Sue & Sue, 1977; S. Sue & Zane, 1987). Issues of "loss of face" and feelings of shame (S. Sue & Morishima, 1982), when not taken into account and addressed with sensitivity, could scuttle a therapeutic relationship before it was even established, thus leading to underutilization of mental-health services.

As Asian American scholars and practitioners began addressing these issues, studies proliferated and added to the breadth, depth, and subtlety of understanding Asian American mental health in all its complexities. In recent years, strong and steady growth in such work has continued. Publication of *Asian-Americans: Psychological Perspectives* (S. Sue & Wagner, 1973) represented one of the early breakthroughs in the field. A companion text, *Asian-Americans: Social and Psychological Perspectives* (Endo, Sue, & Wagner, 1980), followed. *The Mental Health of Asian Americans* (S. Sue & Morishima, 1982) provided another landmark work. In *Asian Americans: Personality Patterns, Identity, and Mental Health*, Uba (1994) expanded both theoretical and practical frameworks for working with Asians. E. Lee (1997) fleshed out some of the complexities of applied work in *Working with Asian Americans: A Guide for Clinicians*. At this time, the *Handbook of Asian American Psychology* (L. Lee & Zane, 1998) offers the most current and comprehensive work encompassing research on Asian Americans covering all ethnic subgroups. Finally, Chin (2000) addressed Asian women's issues specifically in *Relationships among Asian American Women*. Clearly, a solid literature in this area has not emerged; however, anchored by the cited works, writers can continue to expand the field as more clinicians and researchers recognize the urgency of the issues involved.

RESEARCH

The works of Chin (2000), Endo et al. (1980), E. Lee (1997), L. Lee and Zane (1998), S. Sue and Morishima (1982), S. Sue and Wagner (1973), and Uba (1994) attest to the burgeoning understanding of Asians in the United States, whether they are fourth- or fifth-generation, newly or recently arrived immigrants, or have come to the United States because they were refugees from war-torn Southeast Asia. Some current research about Asian groups touches on areas of high clinical valence: family violence (Lum, 1998), the use of drugs and gambling (Zane & Huh-Kim, 1998), and issues that arise with Asian elderly (Kao & Lam, 1997; P. Wong & Ujimoto, 1998).

Another branch of clinical inquiry concerns specific groups of Asians: South Asian women (Kakaiya, 2000), gay and lesbian Asian Americans (Aoki, 1997), refugees suffering from PTSD (Du & Lu, 1997), and multiracial persons with Asian ancestry (Root, 1996). Current psychological research and scholarly thought encounter rich veins of study and inquiry to mine. These and other needed studies mirror the depth and complexity of Asian experiences in the United States and around the world where Asians have immigrated.

CONCEPTUAL FRAMEWORK OF THE APPROACH

RACE, ETHNICITY, AND CULTURE: DEFINITIONS AND DISTINCTIONS

To speak of doing therapy with "Asian" children and families or to write about "Asian" mental health, one must first realize the enormous differences that exist among various Asian groups even while pointing to similarities, such as the importance of family, deference to elders and experts, and a group orientation as opposed to an individualistic stance (Chung, 1997; Huang, 1997; L. Lee, 1997; Uba, 1994). These differences, traced back to the particular country of origin of either the people themselves or their ancestors, prove crucial in understanding the psychology of a family and the people who make up that family, be they the grandparents, parents, uncles, aunts, cousins, adolescents, younger children, or infants.

Race, ethnicity, and culture are often used interchangeably, reflecting at best ignorance and misunderstanding, and, at worst, biases and prejudices that, when coupled with the power a therapist possesses, can wreak havoc on any therapy relationship. A person seeks out a professional for help and is categorized by being assigned a "race," a phenotypic marker. Based on physical appearance, including aspects such as skin color, hair color and texture, and shape of nose and eyes, a person is assigned a niche. But that tells very little about a person and may leave an observer clueless in the case of someone who is racially mixed (Chao, 1995; Root, 1992, 1996). Race alone provides no guarantee of even approximating a cultural understanding of a person.

Ethnicity proves more problematic. McGoldrick (McGoldrick, Pearce, & Giordano, 1982) offered one of the best definitions, which honors the complexity of this concept. Ethnicity comprises "a sense of commonality transmitted over generations by the family and reinforced by the surrounding community. It is more than race, religion or national and geographic origin. It involves conscious and unconscious processes that fulfill a deep psychological need for identity and historical continuity" (p. 4). Whereas the term "Asian" puts a person in a broad racial category, only refinement by an ethnic classification helps one to understand what a person's story might be. A Chinese Laotian clinician implied this in commenting to a pan-Asian group of mental-health workers from over half a dozen Asian countries, "We don't even eat rice the same!" (Chao, 1992, p. 158).

Culture grows out of ethnicity. It evolves from the shared behaviors, attitudes, values, and spiritual and philosophical tenets of a group of people. Culture encompasses the foods eaten and how they are prepared, the holidays celebrated, and the history of one's immediate family, extended family, and ancestral line. For some, culture will include the experience of war, whether that war was the Second World War involving internment in camps in the United States (Nagata, 1991) or escaping the killing fields of Cambodia (Kinzie et al., 1990) and somehow getting to the United States. Culture comes from the language(s) spoken, the names given, and the names changed.

Cultures within a racial grouping can often clash. A therapist working with Asian clients needs to be aware of the history of various countries and how long-held animosities and enmities can surface. At a peer-counseling retreat attended by the teenage children of Southeast Asian refugees, the sons and daughters of Korean immigrants, and fourth- and fifth-generation Japanese American adolescents, tensions had to be acknowledged, explored, and dealt with when a Korean teen announced that her parents allowed no items made in Japan in their house and that she would give up a Japanese American boyfriend rather than risk her father "disowning" her. Stereotypes abounded about which group of Asians wore the "flashiest clothes," were the best dancers, were the toughest with the most gang involvement. Finally, the fourth- and fifth-generation Japanese American teens, who did not speak fluent Japanese, had their identities questioned by children of more recent arrivals—were they "really Asian"?

In another instance, school officials had placed a recently arrived 12-year-old Southeast Asian refugee boy in a class with a number of Vietnamese boys who had been in the United States several years. The officials were perplexed when there seemed to be almost no interaction, and they sought consultation. They discovered that, whereas the boy's origins derived from Southeast Asia, as did his classmates', this boy was Cambodian. He and his mother had escaped while Vietnamese forces were driving Pol Pot from Cambodia. While the rest of the world breathed a sigh of relief that the Cambodian genocide might come to an end, his experiences and trauma were such that he drew pictures of himself as a grown-up soldier killing Vietnamese. The caveat to the therapist necessitates asking questions and assuming nothing.

Acculturation implies many meanings. It can denote learning the language of the majority group that holds the power in the place one lives. It can connote becoming savvy in the ways of the group that holds power such that one can move between worlds effortlessly or not, as the case may be. It can be a measure of adaptation and adjustment, but whether that is "good" or "bad" is a judgment call. Children of parents just coming to the United States, for example, are said to acculturate at a faster rate than their parents (Sluzki, 1979), especially given that the children spend a large portion of their days in school while their parents may be working at jobs that give them only minimal exposure to and limited opportunities to engage and interact with English-speaking persons other than what it takes to get a job done.

A therapist born in Korea and studying in the United States for an advanced degree was called on to do family therapy for an immigrant Korean family whose children were what has been called the "1.5 generation." This means that, though both children and parents may have been born in Korea, because the children were so young when they came to the United States and because they had been in U.S. schools for a comparatively long time, they seem more acculturated, and their attitudes and behaviors appear to be those of a second-generation person. Thus, not quite like their first-generation parents and yet not truly second-generation, which their children will be called, the appellation "1.5" has emerged as a marker that, in cultural shorthand, denotes the psychological orientation of these youngsters. In this instance, the therapist actually had to help translate between the parents and their children. The parents had bought a donut shop, worked very long hours, but had mastered only "survival English" to sell coffee and pastries to their customers and to fill out order forms to buy ingredients. The children were young and quickly became more fluent in English than their parents. Because the parents spent such long hours at their job and they had no extended family in close proximity, nor were they living in an area with many other Korean families, the children lost their fluency in Korean. The therapist literally became a translator for the family.

Differences and Similarities among Asian Cultures: The Importance of Knowing the Story

It is important to understand from the beginning that it is impossible for any therapist to know every single story of every single Asian individual, couple, family, or child one encounters. This is true whether or not one is an Asian clinician, from the fourth, third, second, or even first generation. A Vietnamese clinician confessed that he had never spoken with any Chinese Vietnamese until coming to the United States, even though, when he lived in Saigon, he knew where the "Chinatown" was and had numerous opinions and stereotypes about how this group functioned.

The collective story of Vietnam and its history, language, food, philosophy, culture, and psychology differ from the history, language, food, philosophy, culture, and psychology of other Asian countries. Korea, the Philippines, Laos, China, Cambodia, India, Thailand, Indonesia, Myanmar, Japan, Tibet, Taiwan, Malaysia, Hong Kong, and Pakistan—each conveys a different story, each a different psychology. So I apologize when I do not know my client's story and do not know my client's language. I may know only sketchy details of the history of my client's group. Along with my disclosure forms, I disclose that I am ignorant. While this might fly in the face of what has been written about the need to be assertive and directive with Asian clients (Sue & Sue, 1990; Uba, 1994), what I do not know is also fact, and it generally provides a good place to start.

Along with whatever psychological expertise a therapist offers, a crucial element in successful work with clients occurs when a therapist can both value and be a witness to a client's story. This becomes an exchange of gifts, which is very consonant with Asian cultures (S. Sue & Zane, 1987): Clients give the story of themselves, their families, children, and ancestors; the therapist receives these stories, offers hope, and bears witness to their pains and struggles. Time and again, as clients from various Asian backgrounds have translated for me the word for psychologist in the language of their group, it is often a variation of, if not the same as, the literal translation in Chinese, *xinlixuejia*, which means "doctor/expert of the inner heart" (Chao, 1992). So, our task together is to understand hearts: to heal them, to fix them, to understand them, to bring them into harmony. It requires that each person better understand his or her own heart and then in turn understand the heart of partner, child, father and mother, and many other relatives. With families, this also implies helping the parents to a place where they can become the "doctors" of their own children's hearts.

THE DIFFERENT STORIES OF ASIANS IN THE UNITED STATES: THIRD, FOURTH, AND FIFTH GENERATIONS

Japanese Americans
Among Japanese Americans whose parents and grandparents were born in the United States, perhaps the most salient psychological issue of their story stems from the fact that their grandparents, and many times their parents, were among the nearly 120,000 people who were compelled to leave their homes under Executive Order Number 9066, which was signed by President Franklin D. Roosevelt on February 19, 1942, approximately two months after Japan attacked the U.S. naval base at Pearl Harbor, Hawaii. This was "the single largest forced relocation in U.S. history" (Burton, Farrell, Lord, & Lord, 1999, p. 1). After being herded into assembly centers, 11 of which were fairgrounds or racetracks where families were put in stables full of the stench from their former animal occupants, people were sent to 1 of 10 internment camps located in desert areas, swamps, and otherwise isolated, inhospitable sections of the United States. To quote from a document published by the National Park Service, U.S. Department of the Interior (Burton et al., 1999):

Even though the justification for the evacuation was to thwart espionage and sabotage, newborn babies, young children, the elderly, the infirm, children from orphanages, and . . . children adopted by Caucasian parents were not exempt from removal. Anyone with 1/16th or more Japanese blood was included. In all, over 17,000 children under 10 years old, 2,000 persons over 65 years old, and 1,000 handicapped or infirm persons were evacuated. (p. 34)

That forced relocation has had reverberations down the generations (Nagata, 1991). In an attempt to deal with the trauma themselves and, hopefully, and at least consciously, to shield their children from the pain they had endured, "Be American" was a parental command that many third-, fourth-, and fifth-generation Japanese Americans continuously heard. In part because of this, many lost their fluency in Japanese, and the rates of out-marriage were and have been high (Iwasaki-Mass, 1992). For some families, this was fine. For others, there was the caveat: "Be American—but marry a nice Japanese boy," which then laid the groundwork for conflicts between parents and children if their offspring did not comply.

Those interned in the camps tell stories of amazing resiliency, courage, strength, and coping (Nagata, 2000). They embodied the Japanese word *gaman*, which can be loosely translated to mean quiet perseverance, uncomplaining endurance. As one client commented, "*Gaman* has so much to do with Japanese culture. You accept things, but not in a downtrodden way. You're patient; you wait till it gets played out." This is the way they were raised; this was the way their parents were raised. These values are now at times questioned and seen as problematic as people struggle over whether they should, at least consciously, imbue their children with them.

The following poems were written by Japanese Americans interned in camps. Soga, Mori, Takei, and Ozaki (1983) composed poems whose form dates back to fifth-century Japan and is called *tanka* and consists of 31 syllables (5-7-5-7-7). In the introduction to a collection of poetry written by Japanese Americans interned in camps, Soga, Mori, Takel, and Ozek. The authors noted:

> In view of the scarcity of writing paper, these short poems being less cumbersome than long diaries, were ideal forms for the internees' expression of their pent-up emotions. It also perpetuates the Japanese tradition of expressing their innermost emotions through short poems instead of prose.... Tanka speaks of nature as well as human emotions and allows the reader to perceive the unsaid and the intimated. (pp. vii–viii)

Arrest

ko no negao ni	I bid farewell
wakarete samuku	To the faces of my sleeping children
kikare yuku	As I am taken prisoner
yami shojyo to	Into the cold night rain.
ame furi idenu	

—Muin Ozaki (p. 15)

At the Sand Island Camp

han-nen buri	After a long half year
tsuma to aksuhu shi	I take my wife's hand into mine
sono to o ba	And for at least half a day
han-nichi bakari	I do not wash away her touch
arawazu ni ori	

—Keiho Soga (p. 23)

Fort Sill Internment Camp

komi ageru	A wretching anguish rises
ikidori ari	As the number "111"
hyakujyuichi to	Is painted
munehada ni bango	On my naked chest
akaku kakareshi	In red.

—Muin Ozaki (p. 39)

Clinicians are trained to listen for the "unsaid and the intimated." In listening for the story, it is important to ask if one does not know, and to know that, even when working with children of parents born as infants in the camps, the historical story bears psychological implications for the entire family through the generations.

The "unsaid and the intimated" often reflect the psychological dynamics operating within an Asian American family. A clinician may not see overt and extroverted displays of affection between parents and children who are no longer toddlers, but that does not mean that strong feelings are absent. Often, Asian American therapists act as cultural go-betweens when children tell them that they wish their parents would be more demonstrative in their affection or more vocal and verbal with expressions of encouragement and approval.

Sometimes, a therapist provides "cultural education," pointing out that a universal Asian characteristic is to frown on those considered too boastful either of their own, their family's, or their children's accomplishments. It can be an enlightening exercise to have children ask their parents how they were raised: When did they know their parents were proud of them? How did they talk about their accomplishments and their failures? How did they experience a restrained style of communication? One family doing this exercise ended up laughing when one parent relayed how his father (the children's grandfather) would introduce him to the father's friends: "Oh, this is my stupid son whom I am afraid will amount to nothing because, unfortunately, he is very ignorant." Given that memory, the father never used this sort of introduction when speaking of his children. He thought he had made an enormous shift in parenting styles. His children, however, felt they could never do anything to win his approval; they experienced him as taciturn and withholding of any praise. The end of this story? The father did not really change his communication style that much; the children announced that, when they had children, they would be a lot more verbally demonstrative, but both acknowledged there had been a shift in their awareness and understanding. That brought a little more peace to the family.

Chinese Americans
The ideogram for China looks roughly like a square with a slash through the center. It translates as "Middle Kingdom," the center of the universe. Psychologically, one can see the pride of the Chinese and a sort of egocentric strength, which enabled so many to leave their homeland and come to *Gam Saan* (Gold Mountain) after gold was discovered in California in 1848. The sojourn of the Chinese in the United States was difficult. In 1870, Governor Edward M. McCook of Colorado felt it necessary to speak to his state regarding the presence of Chinese immigrants:

> They may be of inferior race, and lower in national traits than ourselves; they are undoubtedly pagan in religion, but notwithstanding all these moral disabilities, they are exceedingly muscular; and if we can first avail ourselves of their muscles, we can attend to their habits and their morals afterwards. (Rudolf, 1964, p. 23)

This quotation proves instructive on many dimensions. It shows the dehumanizing sentiment that Chinese in the United States faced, an attitude that culminated in legislative fiat when a series of restrictive laws were instituted, beginning with the Chinese Exclusion Act of 1882. These laws were not repealed until 1943. Initially, the laws suspended immigration of Chinese laborers for 10 years. The Geary Act of 1892 extended that for an additional 10 years. However, these laws also meant that no Chinese could become naturalized citizens of the United States, unlike the waves of immigrants who came from Italy, Ireland, Germany, Poland, and Russia. Under these laws, no Chinese seeking redress for a wrong committed could bring suit in a court of law. It took action by the Supreme Court in 1898 to say that children born on U.S. soil to Chinese parents could be recognized as citizens (B. Wong, 1998).

Filipino Americans
Filipinos have also been in the Americas since the eighteenth century, with many coming in the early 1900s as immigrants to work on farms in California or in the pineapple plantations of Hawaii (along with Japanese immigrants). Rightly called "the forgotten Asian Americans" (Cordova, 1983), no single culture can characterize the Philippines, which has experienced colonization by Spain, Japan, and the United States and has been influenced by the cultures of China, India, and Indonesia as well as Arabic culture (Sustento-Seneriches, 1997). Defying easy categorization, Filipinos can be Muslim, Roman Catholic, or Buddhist, with surnames that are Spanish or Chinese. Depending on how long a family has been in the United States, a Filipino American may speak only English, or may, for example, speak Tagalog, English, and Chinese. Early Filipino immigrants could not own land or intermarry. Parallel to Governor McCook's prejudice toward Chinese, Filipinos were denigrated by being called names such as "pineapples" and "little brown monkeys" (Sustento-Seneriches, 1997, p. 103).

The struggles, endurance, and survival of these early groups have led to their descendents now comprising groups of third-, fourth-, and fifth-generation Asian Americans who find themselves labeled the "model minority." This simplistic appellation arises out of loosely shared common characteristics among peoples from Asian countries. These are values such as harmony, nonconfrontational ways of solving disputes, and a hierarchical structure predicated on respect, obedience, and loyalty to those in positions of higher status. A general understanding can serve a useful heuristic purpose when clinical issues arise with an Asian child or family, yet it can be as hopelessly general as a therapist relying on "Yankee ingenuity" or "Southern hospitality" to understand the dynamics of a European American family experiencing problems with an acting-out teenager. The label "model minority" also can serve as a convenient cover-up, obscuring problems in the Asian American community such as alcoholism (Ja & Yuen, 1997) and domestic violence (Tran & Jardins, 2000).

What Are You? Issues of Identity

What are the psychological issues of this group of Asian Americans? Many times, they center on questions of identity. Growing up in the United States of Asian ancestry, this group is already bicultural. Important questions involve to what degree and whether a person experiences psychological stress regarding identity. Children can present with a myriad of issues: "I'm the only Japanese American kid in my class, and I get called 'chink'" and "My parents want me to go to Saturday Chinese school, and I hate it!" Or, conversely, "Why didn't my parents teach me to speak Japanese, and why has our family talked so little about what it was like when Grandma and Grandpa were sent to the camps?" Children of "model-minority" parents who have achieved high educational status and financial success can present with issues of anomie and acting-out behavior that can range from bleaching and "punking" their hair in spikes to body piercing. The clinician's job then becomes helping both the individual child and the family sort out the real issue: Is this an expression of individuality in a family that is bicultural but also has strong traditional Confucian underpinnings? Is this an acting out of a family issue, with the child sounding a protest alarm about family dynamics in which an underlying unhappy or destructive marital dyad is not being addressed?

Asian children, adolescents, and their families also need to explore in therapy how they deal with the theme of racism. Every person of color living in the United States has had to evolve some strategy for dealing not only with prejudice (which can range from the humorous to the annoying) but also with racism. Racism can be defined as a feeling, attitude, or behavior that combines prejudice with power, a power that can harm physically and/or psychologically. For example, the 1980s and 1990s saw many of the U.S. economic difficulties blamed on Japan. Correspondingly, Asian Americans have experienced a rise in anti-Asian violence, especially in areas with large percentages of Asian Americans in the population. (A few Asians can be considered "interesting" or "exotic." More than that evoke cries of "yellow peril.") In June 1982, Vincent Chin went with coworkers to a bar to celebrate his upcoming marriage. In the bar, two White autoworkers shouted, "It's because of you motherfuckers that we're out of work." Outside of the bar, the same two autoworkers bludgeoned Chin to death with a baseball bat (Tien, 2000). On February 26, 1992, *The New York Times* reported on a Japanese man killed in Ventura County, California: "The stabbing death this week of a Japanese businessman who had reportedly been the target of anti-Japanese remarks and a death threat heightened fears today among Japanese-Americans of a spread of racial harassment" (Mydans, 1992, *The New York Times*, p. A12). The same article also reported incidents involving Asian American children: A Girl Scout Troop made up predominately of Japanese American girls "... tried to sell cookies outside a supermarket in affluent West Los Angeles. They were out there in their uniforms," Mr. Ron Wakabayashi (executive director of the Los Angeles City Human Relations Commission) said. "The crueler people were calling them Japs. Other folks were saying, 'I only buy from Americans'" (p. A12).

An extremely useful model to remind clinicians of the interactions of a number of variables that need to be weighed and factored in when dealing with clients of color has been offered by Jones (1991). Originally designed to help clinicians understand and facilitate therapeutic work with African American clients, the structure of the model has much to offer in work with Asian Americans. Jones posited that, when a person presents with a problem, the therapist must take into account four sets of variables. He portrays these as intersecting circles that can take on various valences of import: (1) reactions to racial oppression, (2) influence of the majority culture, (3) influence of African American culture, and (4) personal experiences and endowments.

In the model, Jones (1991) pointed out that every African American must evolve some coping style in dealing with encountered racism while acknowledging that these coping styles may be in flux. Second, the influence wielded by White American culture has to be understood. Thus, a process of assimilation occurs even while White European culture is being influenced by the presence of African American culture. Third, the influence of traditional African American culture perdures; this brings richness and depth and provides an underpinning, even if, at times in a person's life, this support may appear quite vitiated. Finally, the model supports accounting for personal attributes and occurrences in a person's life and/or psychological makeup that may stand outside racial or ethnic categories, such as being born with a physical disability. Jones considers this model to be interactive, with each factor conceived as a circle that shrinks or expands, depending on its valence at a particular time and for a particular client. The therapist needs to be aware of each of these aspects in the life of a client.

This model offers a valuable conceptual framework to a clinician working with Asian children and their families. Asians in the United States face racism. They are continually undergoing a process of assimilation, for good or ill. While Asian parents pressed their children to "be good Americans" during the years of World War II, many newly arrived Asian immigrants and refugees fear the "Americanization" of their children and try to hold on to what is distinctly Cambodian, Vietnamese, Laotian, or Hmong. Finally, under the heading of "personal experiences and endowments," we must factor in the story of each Asian group as they come to the United States.

Miyamoto's (1971) poem, which follows, can serve as a summation of the psychological dynamics encountered by third-, fourth-, and fifth-generation Asian Americans. Though the poem is written by a Japanese American and specifically references Japanese American history, the psychological processes ring true for other Asian groups. From the psychological wounds it addresses, to the issues of identity that it raises, to the naming of the process of pitting one community of color against another, to the poem's conclusion, which tells us all is not easy in the psyche of the writer, this poem illustrates what a therapist can encounter when working with an Asian American client.

What Are You?

When I was young
kids used to ask me
what are you?
I'd tell them what my mom told me
I'm an American
chin chin Chinaman
you're a Jap!
flashing hot inside
I'd go home
my mom would say
don't worry
he who walks alone
walks faster

people kept asking me
what are you?
and I would always answer
I'm an American
they'd say
no, what nationality?
I'm an American!
that's where I was born
flashing hot inside
and when I'd tell them what they
wanted to know
Japanese
. . . Oh, I've been to Japan

I'd get it over with
me they could catalogue and file me
pigeon hole me
so they'd know just how
to think of me
priding themselves
they could guess the difference
between Japanese and Chinese

they had me wishing
I was American
just like them
they had me wishing I was what I'd
been seeing in movies and on TV
on billboards and magazines
and I tried

while they were making laws in California against us
    owning land
we were trying to be American
and laws against us intermarrying with white people
we were trying to be American
when they put us in concentration camps
we were trying to be American
our people volunteered to fight against their own
    country
trying to be American
when they dropped the atom bomb Hiroshima and
    Nagasaki
we were still trying

finally we made it
most of our parents
fiercely dedicated to give us
a good education
to give us everything they never had
we made it
now they use us as an example
to the blacks and browns
how we made it
how we overcame

but there was always
someone asking me
what are you?

Now I answer
I'm an Asian
and they say
why do you want to separate yourselves
now I say
I'm Japanese
and they say
don't you know this is the greatest country in the world
Now I say in America
I'm part of the third world people
and they say
    if you don't like it here
    why don't you go back
        —Joanne Nobuko Miyamoto
            (1971, pp. 50–51)

ASIAN IMMIGRANTS

Asian immigrants are the new arrivals on U.S. shores. Distinguishing Asians who came willingly from Asian refugees of war, who did not know to where they were escaping and who ended up in the United States, often by default, facilitates understanding the psychological dynamics at work. The categories employed in this chapter can be misleading. When does someone become Asian American? When one becomes a "naturalized" citizen? When one achieves citizenship based on being born in the United States? And what is the psychological difference between a Chinese American, a Japanese American, a Vietnamese American, and an "Asian American"? How are they the same and how are they different? Immigrants can come from Eastern Hemisphere countries such as Hong Kong (now returned by Britain, after a 99-year lease, to the People's Republic of China), Japan, Taiwan, India, Samoa, Guam, or Indonesia. Under the 1965 Immigration and Nationality Act Amendments (Takaki, 1998), 20,000 immigrants each, with no quota imposed on family members, may be admitted from eligible countries. In recent years, as the numbers of Asian Americans have grown from less than 0.5% of the U.S. population in the 1960s (fewer than 1 million) to 2.9% (7,272,662), most Asians in the United States will be foreign-born (Uba, 1994, pp. 2–3).

KOREAN AMERICANS AND THE CRISIS OF SA-I-GU

Although each group has a unique story, given the space limitations of a single chapter, the issues faced by Korean immigrants in the United States will be highlighted in this section and can be viewed as paradigmatic to illustrate clinical issues that may confront a therapist. According to 1990 U.S. census estimates, Koreans make up 11% of the Asian American population, with 71% of these persons being foreign-born. A defining moment for Korean immigrants occurred during the Los Angeles riots of April 29, 1992, following the all-White jury acquittal of White police officers in the beating of African American Rodney King. In the riots, "Some 2,400 Korean-owned stores in South Central and Koreatown were looted or burned during the rampage" (Lin, *Asian Week,* April 25, 1997). Thousands of calls to police for help were recorded, but the police did not respond. Many in the community feel that police deliberately allowed Korean stores to burn, keeping rioters in Koreatown, so they would not threaten more affluent, White areas of Los Angeles. Estimated losses were placed at nearly half a billion dollars. *Sa-i-gu* translated literally means "4-29," that is, the fourth month, the 29th day. On this day, one minority was pitted against another who had emigrated from a country that was incredibly homogeneous, both racially and ethnically.

Koreans commemorate and remember other dates also. *Sa-il-gu* refers to 4-19 or April 19, 1960, when student protests erupted over Korean government corruption and injustices. These student clashes lasted over a year and resulted in the deaths of many students. Another date in Korea's history is known by all as *yook-i-o* or June 25, which in 1950 was the beginning of that country's civil war. Coming to the United States, Koreans never imagined they could be the recipients of injustice such as that perpetrated in difficult times of Korea's history. What occurred in Los Angeles represented in many ways the death of immigrant dreams. The English-language newspaper *Asian Week* did an in-depth report five years after *sa-i-gu.* Angela Oh, an attorney and community activist working on behalf of many Korean riot victims, commented:

> April 29 was the day of our passage in becoming Americans. I think for most minorities to become American requires some painful experience. Koreans really could not relate to what it meant to be a minority, because there was this belief this was something other people talked about. They thought, "We work hard. We have our own culture. We're defined. We're proud. We're people who lasted for thousands of years as independent and with a distinct bloodline. We're not affected by this talk about minorities in this country." (*Asian Week,* April 25, 1997, p. 13)

In an editorial in that issue of *Asian Week,* Oh noted "The implosion of 1992 provides a proper reason to re-examine critical urban issues such as economic disenfranchisement, race relations, police-community relations and political empowerment" (p. 7). It may appear that we are venturing into the realm of the political and not the psychological, but this is not the case. Lawyer Oh reveals the deep psychological wounds suffered by members of this group:

> Most of the 2,500 Korean American families who suffered the losses in Los Angeles in the spring of 1992 are not interested in talking. These were deeply personal tragedies, never redressed; and the internal crises continue. There is no honor in revealing these deeply private matters.... For some, it was a rebellion; for Korean Americans it was *sa-i-gu*—and its real meaning can never be translated into the English language for consumption once a year. (p. 7)

Koreans coming into this country often pool family money together looking for a place to start up a business where survival English will suffice. Banks never seem to give them loans that will allow them to set up shop in affluent areas, so they drift to poorer sections of towns where other people of color are congregated, who also cannot get business loans from banks, but who do not have the long history of *kye,* "a uniquely Korean private money-lending system" (Kang, May 25, 1990, *Asian Week,* p. 1). Resentments build, and clashes appear to be inevitable.

Many Korean immigrants see themselves as leaving a country where a rigid class system helps keep intact an equally rigid education system that allows only relatively few to be admitted to the best schools. So parents come here hoping that, if they work hard, they can acquire for their children access to good schools that might have been impossible to get into at home. Koreans also come from one of the most homogeneous of Asian cultures. Throughout their history, they have fought off attempts of subjugation by both China and Japan. A Confucian ethic instills a hierarchy of obligations that children owe to parents and teachers and that adults owe to bosses and older family members. Coming to the United States brings multiple culture shocks. Children who are part of the 1.5 (in Korean, *il-jum*-o) generation assimilate mainstream United States culture along with their relative ease of English-language acquisition. Often, their parents remain at a cultural disadvantage.

Come to this country, I tell immigrant and refugee clients, and you are in danger of catching the diseases of this country. You can be the recipient of racism and/or you can become a carrier of this disease. You can inoculate yourself by learning the history of minority groups (both Asian and non-Asian) in this country and by realizing the debt Asians in America owe to African Americans in the struggle for justice. Listen to the comments written two years before *sa-i-gu*, that highlight, among other things, the consequences of cultural ignorance that can result in the pitting of one group of color against another:

> What struck me more than anything was a recent remark by a black resident: "The Koreans are a very, very rude people. They don't understand you have to smile." I wondered whether her reaction would have been the same had she known that Koreans don't smile at Koreans either without a reason. To a Korean, a smile is not a facial expression he can turn on and off mechanically. Koreans have a word for it—*mu-ttuk-ttuk-hada* (stiff). In other words, the Korean demeanor is *muy-po-jung*—lack of expression.
>
> It would be an easy thing for blacks who are naturally friendly and gregarious to misunderstand Korean ways.... In our culture, a smile is reserved for people we know and for a proper occasion; herein lies a big problem when newcomers from Korea begin doing business in America's poor inner-city neighborhoods. As a Korean American I've experienced this many times. Whenever I'm in Korea . . . I'm chided for smiling too much. "Why do you smile so easily? You act like a Westerner." (Kang, 1990, p. 1)

Another factor, with social-political roots, makes it taboo for a Korean woman to smile at male customers. There is a long memory of the prostitution encouraged, at least tacitly, by the U.S. military at bases in Korea. To smile at a male customer, to place money directly into his hand, could be misinterpreted. This attribution does not necessarily apply to all Korean women in the United States. Exploring this when relevant in therapy may help to resolve family tensions.

CASE EXAMPLES

A 1.5-Generation Adolescent and Her Family from Korea

The daughter had been in the United States with her parents since they emigrated from Korea when she was 7 years old. She was bilingual and spoke colloquial English. She helped in her parents' liquor store after school. Her parents stopped letting her help in the front of the store because they felt she was smiling and talking too much with the customers. They were also afraid their fellow Korean church members would come in and see their daughter's "trashy-bar-girl behavior." Their daughter had taken a business/marketing class in her high school and very much wanted to "chat up" her parents' customers, learn their special likes and dislikes, and help her parents build a solid customer base. In addition, she was acutely aware of tensions between African Americans and Asians, and, in an individual session, stated that her parents held racist views, but felt it was largely out of ignorance. She wanted to show everyone that "Koreans are not prejudiced!" In family sessions, we discussed how relationships between men and women have been conducted in Korea, dating back to the time of her parents' grandparents and great-grandparents.

We talked about the evolving nature of social conduct: what is "proper," what is "scandalous." The mother commented that her grandmother would have been shocked to see her working. The parents related that they had met and decided to marry without benefit of a formal arrangement between their families; this initially angered their parents.

The daughter had to do a project for her business class and decided to write a paper on how to keep the customer happy when you have Korean and non-Korean customers. She enlisted her parents' help on the Korean section. She then tried out some of their suggestions when Korean patrons came into her parents' store. After her paper received an A, her parents took some of her suggestions, and would say to their non-Korean customers such phrases as "Have a nice day" or "Come back soon." (We also discussed that smiling and saying that to the opposite sex was not considered flirting or improper.)

The therapist and the family talked together about race and the history of African Americans in this country, of which the parents knew hardly anything; the daughter understood a lot more through classes in school and contact with other students of color. Her parents referred to a relative who had been born in Japan and yet for years had not been allowed to be a citizen and had taken a Japanese name to avoid discrimination. Her parents spoke about the "comfort women" who had been forced into sexual slavery when Japan occupied Korea during World War II. As the parents and the daughter exchanged "stories," the son, two years younger (14 years old), and the youngest child, an 11-year-old daughter, began to clamor for more stories of when their parents were little. Though the family rarely had time to eat together because of the hours they spent at their store, when they had a meal together, they decided to have each parent take a turn and tell a family story, a personal story from the past, or a story about Korea.

The family still experienced tensions and there were still outbursts from the oldest daughter ("You want us to succeed in America, but, when I act American, you hate me!"), but they all agreed that family life was more satisfactory. After the youngest daughter was invited to a Kwanzaa celebration (the African American cultural holiday based on harvest festivals in Africa) by a girl in her class, she asked to invite this girl to her family's next celebration of Chusook (the Korean harvest moon festival).

An Indian Mother Experiencing the Dynamics of Acculturation

Kakaiya (2000) noted, "*Acculturation* is the process of maintaining an identity with one's culture of origin while adapting to the host culture" (p. 139, italics added). But to what extent should one adapt? What should one adopt? What should be left behind? When does acculturation slide into *assimilation* and loss of the culture by which one knows oneself? In an illustration of this, a South Asian woman spoke of how she left her husband in India and took her three daughters to the United States. She tells relatives it is to get them the best education; she tells a non-South Asian woman friend that she feels Hindu culture is too oppressive to women. She then invites this woman to a local temple to see her daughters perform classical, traditional Indian dances. So what part is true: a patriarchal culture unfriendly to women, or the need to preserve a part of that culture so she and her children will not lose something of what defines them?

Balancing Expectations

A young woman, whose parents are devout Sikhs and who emigrated from the North of India, spoke of the tension she embodies as she lives out both an ethnic and religious biculturism. Religiously observant Sikhs do not cut their hair. As an adolescent, she was content to keep her hair long, yet felt she would be completely ostracized from her Western peers if she did not shave her legs and under her arms. She spoke of "hiding a lot and covering my tracks.... Lying and deceit became a coping mechanism. I'd wear long pants, then change into miniskirts, and then change back into pants in the parking lot before going home." A deeply spiritual woman whose identity as a Sikh is paramount, hers was a juggling act: to reassure parents of her love and obedience, to be accepted by her teenage compatriots, to be one with her cohorts in her community and at the Sikh place of worship, the gurdwara. She summed up the psychological dynamic that served to undergird this: "You can't be happy unless your parents are happy. Our families have made so many sacrifices; this is the least I can do. I don't want to hurt them or lose them. They are all I have" (P. K., personal communication, July 14, 2000).

As Western-trained therapists, do we label this enmeshment, or do we understand it as an exquisitely poignant and at times painful example of cultural rapprochement? As therapists, we are often the bridge builders between parents and children. If we listen carefully, respectfully, and with the requisite humor and humility, we can be given permission by children and their families to serve as cultural go-betweens.

Cultural reentrenchment also surfaces as a dynamic that needs to be recognized when it occurs in families. In the country of origin, there will be all sorts of changes occurring within the culture, both subtle and not so subtle. For example, people from groups that historically were enemies meet, fall in love, and marry. In the United States, however, without the benefit of a country's changing cultural dynamics, the immigrant parent often feels he or she is marooned in a cultural outpost and must retrench, guarding against any processes that do not represent the traditional culture. In addition, for parents, the immigrant experience always contains a fantasy escape clause: You can go home if this country drives you crazy. If the smells are all wrong, the language gives you a headache, everyone looks and acts strangely, and the dislocation is too painful, you can call home, you can write, and finally, you can leave. The fantasy implies that the country of origin has not and will not be changed. Of course, for the children, this also is not easy. Asian American offspring have grown up only on their parents' nostalgic stories. When they visit the homeland of their parents, they may experience severe cultural anomie. The young Sikh professional woman concluded: "It's so very complex. India continues to progress, but immigrant parents clench their children even tighter. Our parents are not a part of that process that's occurring in India. It puts us kids in a tougher position. Our parents always promised themselves, 'I'm going to go back. I'm going to go back,' but it's not reversible." Finally speaking for herself, born in a small village in India and having come to the United States at the age of 4 years, she mused: "I'd love to create a country of 1.5 Indians, where we could learn Indian ways but also have all the luxuries of living in the United States. You can't go back. There's no physical home for us. It will have to be in our heart and soul" (P. K., personal communication, September 20, 2000).

Summing up many of the issues that the children of Asian immigrants deal with, University of California, Berkeley, Professor Elaine Kim (1993) spoke of issues of ethnicity, race, and identity and how gender is intertwined with them:

> In my day, a young Korean American woman who wanted to be transformed into a "real" Korean would have to learn to behave "like a Korean woman," according to twentieth century interpretations of Korean Confucian ideals of feminine modesty, frugality, chastity, fidelity, and maternal sacrifice. She would have to learn to

speak Korean, something I struggled with hopelessly for many years only to end in dismal failure.... Every time I spend more than a month in South Korea, I need a month or more to recover my self-esteem.

When I was 23 years old, I went to work in Seoul for a year, armed with an Ivy League education and buoyed by a burning desire to "become Korean." I returned feeling neither "Korean" nor "American." Moreover, my sense of gendered identity was shaken, and my encounters in Korea convinced me that I was clumsy, ugly and hopelessly inadequate as a woman, besides.

Noticing that Korean American men, far from losing confidence in themselves after a sojourn in Seoul, seemed psychologically galvanized by the experience, I finally realized ... that what I had been feeling was not a loss of a sense of self from "culture clash" but rather confusion because I had been thinking about ethnicity and not about gender, and I could not recognize the similarities between American and South Korean patriarchies due to their differences in form. (p. 20)

SOUTHEAST ASIAN REFUGEES: YOU CAN'T GO HOME AGAIN

Many Asian refugees now in the United States did not realize they would end up in this country. They knew only that they wanted to escape the horrors of war. They came from refugee camps in Thailand, Hong Kong, and the Philippines, they fled from Cambodia, Laos, and Vietnam. They are Vietnamese, Cambodian, Laotian, White Hmong, Blue H'Mong, Lao Lu, Khmer, Chinese Vietnamese, Cambodian Chinese. Often, they did not know what country would accept them. Persons illiterate in Vietnamese, who were fishermen and had descended from generations of fishermen, found themselves in the mountains of Colorado because they had been sponsored by a U.S. church or resettled by a U.S. agency. Others were doctors, lawyers, and engineers, trilingual, fluent in Vietnamese, French, and English. Some came after the fall of Saigon in April 1975. Others escaped by boat, suffering rape by Thai pirates on the open seas. Many lost children to starvation and disease. Some had children die of accidental opium overdose when they tried to quiet a crying infant as they escaped through a jungle hoping to get to the border of Thailand. Some came because they were the offspring of an Asian mother and a U.S. military father. Their backgrounds can include any race crossed by any ethnicity: a Cambodian mother and a European American father, a Vietnamese mother and a Latino (with a range of cultural roots, including Puerto Rico, Cuba, Mexico) father, a Laotian mother and an African American father.

An overarching truism for Asian culture, no matter what country a person originates from, flows from the word and meaning of family, extending far beyond the nuclear family to include grandparents on the mother's side, grandparents on the father's side, aunties and uncles all numbered and designated as to what side and which generation they are from, cousins and those married to cousins, and, finally, ancestors on both sides. Thus, it is of paramount importance to inquire not only Who is in the family? but also Who was left behind? Who did not survive? In what other states or countries do other family members live? Has the family erected an altar for their ancestors? This last question can have numerous ramifications. Some refugees were sponsored by Christian churches that were very kind and supportive in helping people resettle. To be polite, as well as show their appreciation, some families began to attend church, and some decided to formally convert to Christianity. Some continued to honor their ancestors; others opted for their Christian church's teaching that to revere one's ancestors in a special place or to pray using incense constituted ancestor "worship" and, as such, was akin to idolatry. Rifts over religion have developed within families and add to the stress and tension a family may already be experiencing (Chao, 2000).

"ALL OF US, WE ALL HAVE SOME PTSD"

This comment was made by a Vietnamese physician who had successfully rebuilt a medical practice after escaping from Vietnam by boat (Hue Vo, M.D., personal communication, 1987). The presence of symptoms of Posttraumatic Stress Disorder (PTSD) surfacing at some time, ranging from mild to moderate to severe, and lasting from a short while to a long duration should be expected of immigrants from strife-torn areas. Neither parents nor children easily shake off the scars of war, and the traumas persist (Kinzie, Sack, Angell, Clarke, & Rath, 1989). Yet, for some refugee adolescents traumatized as children, symptoms of PTSD can persist, but become less intense over time (Sack et al., 1993). In interviewing 170 Cambodian youth and 80 of their mothers, Sack, Clarke, and Seeley (1996) discovered a consistent relationship among traumatic events suffered in the past, stress in constructing new lives, and symptoms of PTSD. It did not matter that many years had passed since escaping from Cambodia. Some families talk to their children about their experiences in the war; many more, however, do not. Having to remain silent in the face of atrocity is one of the traumas that many Cambodians now living in the United States endured:

> In Khmer, explains Chan Than, the word for the Kabok tree is "koh," which also means "mute." During the Khmer Rouge era, an oft-repeated saying had it that, "If you want to live, plant a koh tree in front of your house." In other words, keep quiet if you don't want to die. "We had to remain silent about everything we saw, knew, or heard." (Stephens, 2000, p. 81)

Working with people who are Khmer (Cambodian), as with other children and families who are originally from Southeast Asia, a therapist must sometimes walk a tightrope: How much of the horrors that were endured should be talked about? What part may be retraumatizing, and what part may be active witnessing to the strength and endurance that will become part of that family's story? Should the children who were born here in the United States be told? What are the dynamics in a family when older children went through the war and the escape and younger children did not? Sometimes, to keep alive, people commit acts that they never would have done in less extreme times. Are these to be aired? When is the right time to talk of something? What should be talked about and with whom? These questions have no one right answer. Therapists must realize that these are the questions lurking in the room when they meet with a child and/or family. Sometimes timing may be most crucial: Sometimes, time has to pass and trust has to be built; sometimes, a therapist acts as the go-between, meeting first with one family subsystem and then with another, for example, father and mother; father, mother and mother's mother; father, mother, and child; child and father; child and grandparent; father and father's oldest uncle. Some therapists are concerned that clients will bring up material that is too terrifying and could precipitate a psychotic episode. Of course, solid diagnosis, caution, and respect for silence are imperative; clients should never be pushed to reveal traumatic events when they do not want to discuss them. However, many times, the therapist's discomfort becomes the issue. Listening to stories of pain, terror, cruelty, and suffering poses challenges.

A CAMBODIAN FAMILY

A Cambodian father requested that the author see his 15-year-old daughter after having brought her in to see a European American therapist from his HMO. He felt the therapist only castigated him for being too controlling. In fact, he said his wife accused him of being too lenient with their daughter, as when he had bailed her out after having a number of accidents with the family car and letting her stay out late.

The first meeting occurred with the father, then with the daughter, and then with both of the parents. At this time, the father voiced his opposition to his daughter's Cambodian boyfriend. The parents reported that the boyfriend, though Khmer, had "too dark skin," which for them meant that he and his family must have been members of Pol Pot's Khmer Rouge. Then the father said he had called friends he knew in the city to learn about the boyfriend's family. Reports came back that the boyfriend's father was in jail for incest committed against a younger sister.

In a separate session, when the boyfriend and the daughter were presented with these objections from her parents, the boyfriend said that his family were never Khmer Rouge. He related that his father had abandoned his mother in the refugee camps of Thailand where he was born, and that one day he wanted to go and search for his father. The boyfriend stated that there was another Khmer family with the same last name in the same apartment complex where his mother lived and that was the father who was in jail for incest. Which account was accurate? There was no way to tell. The therapist offered a safe place to contain both the parents' pain and the daughter's protestations that her family was in a new country. She was born on U.S. soil, and the crimes of the past, though not to be forgotten, should not be laid on her shoulders.

During a session with only the parents, the father spoke of the loss of his own father, who was killed by the Khmer Rouge by being tied to a large rock and drowned. Later, unable to deal with the atrocities he witnessed, the father's grandfather committed suicide. Two years prior to this session, the father's oldest brother, who had remained in Cambodia, died at the age of 50 of a heart attack. (Like Holocaust survivors [Etinger & Strom, 1973], Cambodians who have endured extreme deprivation, starvation, and torture experience a higher risk of death from cardiovascular disease and hypertension; The Roots of the Cambodian Health Crisis, 2000: online Web page.) Without his own father, grandfather, or elder brother, the father felt extremely pressured to achieve everything he could to honor the legacy of suffering his family had endured.

The next crisis arose when the daughter discovered she was pregnant. The daughter and the therapist had discussed in individual sessions that she was sexually active, the daughter saying that she and her boyfriend had used condoms. When the therapist asked if the daughter had thought of birth control pills, she replied that, recently, her father had said he would take her to Planned Parenthood for birth control pills. The daughter commented that she was too embarrassed to have her parents know she was sexually active.

A joint meeting was scheduled with the parents, the daughter, and her boyfriend. The therapist had no idea if anyone would come. Then the father called, saying that he and his wife would come in for 10 minutes only, to tell their daughter they would disown her if she did not terminate the pregnancy. The daughter and her boyfriend came 15 minutes before the scheduled time, saying that they wanted to bring the pregnancy to term and that her grandmother did not believe in abortion and supported her. The therapist placed extra chairs in the office and, when the parents came, had the younger people vacate the more comfortable chairs for the parents to sit in. The therapist poured cups of tea for the parents only. In part, this was to acknowledge the hierarchy in Asian culture as well as to thank them for coming. The boyfriend greeted the parents with his hands pressed together over his forehead, head bent, and eyes lowered to the ground, in a traditional Cambodian gesture of respect. The therapist asked him who had taught him the traditional greeting, and he responded that his mother had. It was a challenging session lasting an hour and a half, but the parents stayed the entire time.

The daughter spoke of her frustration that her parents never recognized any good she had done. The parents talked of how they had decided to marry, allowing their respective families to investigate: "I see your mother. I like her, but I then ask the old people, 'What do you think?' Background is important. We checked it out. Her mother investigated me!" Each member talked about his or her biggest worry. The parents worried that, in addition to bringing shame to the family, their daughter would not finish college, and thus they would have failed in giving her a secure footing in the United States. The daughter was concerned about the loss of her parents love: "I would not see them. Would they love me? They would not be proud of me." The boyfriend declared, "Her parents have to be there for her. They're the ones that raised her. She needs them to be in her life for her to be successful. You can't buy another parent."

The daughter asked her mother whether, if she and the boyfriend stayed together and had the baby, her mother would attend her high school graduation. Her mother said, "No." The daughter asked whether, if she finished college, her mother then would acknowledge the baby, the boyfriend, and come to her graduation. Her mother said, "Yes," though she doubted it would happen; if it did, she would be clear that they would be worthy of commendation.

The therapist acknowledged the painfulness of the dilemma for everyone. There were decisions that had to be made by the daughter and her boyfriend. The boyfriend would have to tell his mother and ask her advice. The two young people would have to decide if they wanted to bring the pregnancy to term. Did they want to get married? If they wanted to marry, did they want to marry soon or at some later date? Informing the daughter and the boyfriend that the ultimate decisions were theirs was also a way to tell the parents that they had to trust what they had imparted to their daughter. Though they had tried to give her all they felt she needed to succeed in the United States, so she would be a credit to them, this was her decision. The session ended with none of these questions answered, but with an appointment scheduled with the daughter for the next week.

Next, at the request of the daughter and her parents, the therapist spoke with her school counselor, who had been very supportive of her in the past. The counselor talked about a program he would enroll her in where pregnant teens could still attend school and graduate on schedule. He said that he would also apprise her teachers of her status. The parents were appreciative, seeing the school counselor as a go-between. They had assumed school officials would throw their daughter out of school in disgrace.

The daughter canceled the next appointment because her younger brother had gone driving with a friend who had taken the family car without permission and landed in a ditch. The boys called his sister in a panic to help get them out of the scrape with neither father knowing. The therapist noted to the daughter that this was the type of occurrence that parents always find out about in the end, and asked, though it was admirable to help a younger brother, was this another instance of her helping out everybody but herself? (This had been a theme we had touched on, as she had chosen boyfriends with problems and whom she had "rescued.") The daughter went to help her brother, and another appointment was scheduled.

Before that could take place, however, the daughter and her parents called separately to say that the decision the daughter made was to have an abortion. Did the parents browbeat her? Did she do it just to please her parents? At the next session, the daughter said that initially, she told her boyfriend she had had a miscarriage, but she thought he knew the truth. She talked of how hard the decision was for her. She said she could not stand losing her parents' approval and love. She felt she understood what they were feeling and what they wanted for her. She worried about whether she was acting just to please them. She related that her parents told her she could pick her own boyfriends and that, if she wanted to keep her current boyfriend, that was okay with them.

The therapist recounted to the daughter an oft-repeated verse from the Analects of Konzi (Confucius): "The Master said: 'In serving his parents a son may remonstrate with them but gently; when he sees that they do not incline to follow his advice, he shows an increased degree of reverence, *but he does not abandon his purpose*; and should they punish him, he does not allow himself to murmur.'" The tension between not abandoning one's purpose and not merely obeying parents but showing them "an increased degree of reverence" poses a dilemma with which all Asian American adolescents grapple. This will persist as an ongoing issue with this girl. (Interestingly, the author has increasingly shown and discussed the previous quotation with non-Asian clients, for whom it also resonates.)

The parents will also continue to cope with being Cambodian refugees in a country that will reward them if they adhere to its concept of a "model minority." How will they resolve the tremendous sorrow of all they have lost? How will this family deal with this spirited daughter who is the opposite of the koh tree—the mute tree—and who questions and challenges everything?

The family is invited to meet as needed. They know that any member can ask the others to come in. The boyfriend may try to get his high-school-equivalency diploma; he may move back to his mother's house, which is in another state. The daughter and he may or may not stay together. The father reported that he has had a recurring nightmare; he will come in individually for some sessions. The daughter requested that her brother be included in future sessions; the father agreed, and says that his wife also will come. An unanswered question remains: Should the grandmother and great-grandmother have been included?

THE PRINCIPLE OF YIN AND YANG

A host of unanswered questions remain. Is there a right way and a wrong way to conduct psychotherapy with Asian clients? Should a therapist self-disclose with Asian clients, and, if so, when, why, and how much? Should the therapist accept gifts of food, eat with Asian clients, or have dinner with them? Can only Asian therapists treat Asian clients? The answer to all of these questions is yes and no.

In my office lies a small, purple and beige yin/yang circle made of clay by my daughter. She constructed the wavy line separating the yin and the yang, representing the female and male principles, the passive and active, or, basically, whatever is opposite. However, the most important principle, which my daughter remembered to incorporate, was to put a dot of beige in the purple section and a dot of purple in the beige section. That is, each position contains the seeds of destruction of itself; each position must ultimately give way to the other. The process remains dynamic and always in flux.

THE RIGHT THERAPY FOR ASIAN CLIENTS

Asian culture is hierarchical. Research suggests that Asians subscribe to the premise that therapy proves most successful when a therapist is viewed as an authority figure and gives prescriptions, whether for medication or a course of action (E. Lee, 1982; Leong, 1986). And yet, insight-oriented and psychoanalytic therapy also can be successful (Tang, 2000). So the answer emerges in reading everything possible about Asian psychology and poring over the bibliographies to find articles and books that might be relevant to a particular case (Chin, 2000; E. Lee, 1997; L. Lee & Zane, 1998; Uba, 1994), and then knowing that a client who has walked into the office may fit none of the categories.

Perhaps the answer lies not in worrying so much about which is the correct approach to therapy (though that is important), but in making sure of living truly as what the Chinese word for a psychologist means: *xinlixuejia* ("doctor of the inner heart") or in Vietnamese, *tam ly gia* ("the expert who helps one understand the heart") (Chao, 1992). To deal with matters that reside in the "inner heart" means to create a place of safety, security, and respect. It connotes cultivating what in Korean is known as *jeong*, "expressing a combination of empathy, sympathy, compassion, emotional attachment, and tenderness in varying degrees according to the social context" (B. Kim, 1996, p. 288).

SELF-DISCLOSURE AND ISSUES OF TRANSFERENCE AND COUNTERTRANSFERENCE

I believe that the therapist must hold the tension between being the "expert" and admitting that he or she knows nothing at all, or, in the words of Lao Tsu, "Give up learning, and put an end to your troubles" (Feng & English, 1972, p. 20). Out of this position, mixed with the aforementioned *jeong*, I disclose, along with state-mandated disclosure forms, my own ethnic background (Chao, 1995), and, if I am to ask my Asian clients to explore "heart" issues, I also must present who I am. They are curious and interested. I tell my clients of my biracial and bicultural background. Coming in with a Chinese name and Chinese ancestors, I have a certain amount of ascribed credibility, but that may mean nothing, and I can lose whatever advantage I may have had if I do poor therapy. Similarly, a non-Asian therapist may initially start out with very little ascribed credibility, but can attain high levels of achieved credibility by being successful with clients (S. Sue & Zane, 1987). These therapists may become the recipient of invitations to dinner, gifts, and presentations of food.

For some clients, the fact that I am racially mixed stirs up issues of Asian purity, fears that their children might marry outside their racial or ethnic group, and/or fears that their children will lose the language of their particular group. On days when I am tired, perplexed, and feeling lost in my work with clients, I can fantasize: If only I were full Chinese, spoke Putonghua (Mandarin Chinese) and Cantonese, and grew up in Beijing and New York, and then lived in Vietnam and spoke Khmer (Cambodian), and went to graduate school in Korea, and did postdoctoral work in Japan. Or conversely, If only I were full European American, no one would refer this impossible family to me, and I would work only with White people who would never make me feel inadequate. Thus, countertransference issues can arise as well as transference issues (Chin, 1993).

GIFTS, FOOD, AND EATING WITH ASIAN CLIENTS

S. Sue and Zane (1987) noted that, within the context of working with a client, a therapist offers a gift of hope, and this is reflective of the gift giving that is ego-syntonic with many Asian cultures. I agree, and, concretely, I usually serve my Asian clients a cup of tea. With non-Asian clients, or with Asian American clients who are the fourth or fifth generation in this country, I will *ask* if they would like a cup of tea or coffee. With first-generation immigrants and refugees, I will just pour the tea. I pour the tea out of respect for what I know I might hear, out of respect for the story of how they came here, out of deference to how difficult it can be for Asian clients to come to someone not in their family and to talk about their lives being in turmoil or how they fear they have lost their sons or daughters to U.S. culture and no longer feel they respect them. I apologize that I have only tea bags and cannot give them a proper cup of tea, with leaves steeped in boiling water. Usually, in the beginning, a client never drinks the tea. That is all right. When the tea cup is picked up (and that may be in the second or third session), it can mean that a certain level of trust has been achieved. We have gotten through the issue of "loss of face" or the "shame" of having to consult a therapist, and now we are venturing into the heart of issues. Sometimes in family work, serving tea to the parents helps delineate boundaries between parents and children and can reassure parents that they are the ones who hold "the mandate of heaven," even in the face of rebellious children.

Many times, Asian clients will bring in small gifts of food reflective of the cuisine of their country. A general rule of thumb is to accept this graciously and not go into interpretations, which generally come out of our own unease and desire to establish a hierarchy with clients (Chao, 1994). In all of this, a psychological awareness of the issues, common sense, and an awareness of one's own issues serve as good guides. Codes of ethics enjoin therapists to protect the welfare of their clients and not exploit their professional relationships with them. Working with clients from a very traditional background means realizing that therapists at times will need to protect the emotional welfare of their clients by accepting a gift they bring. To reject a gift could cause the client to "lose face," thereby doing damage to the psychological integrity of the person. Each case, however, must be examined according to its own merits.

I supervised two Asian therapists. In one case, after the therapist had successfully helped a family deal with a daughter who was developmentally delayed, the father invited the therapist to their home for dinner. The therapist and I spoke about the significance of this because, if anything, an invitation to dinner in a restaurant is more usual, as, ordinarily, only family members are invited into a home. However, the family felt very comfortable with and grateful to the therapist. Going to dinner was not engaging in a dual relationship or exploiting their professional relationship; to refuse the invitation would cause definite loss of face for the family. The family felt empowered by the therapist and no longer were as reticent in claiming services for their daughter. They were not of the same ethnic background as their therapist, and they wanted to show off their country's cuisine. The therapist went to dinner.

In the second instance, the therapist was working with a wife and children abused by a husband. The therapist had helped the woman and her young children move to a safe house after couple therapy had broken down. The therapist came to me, her supervisor, saying that the husband had called wanting to take the therapist out to dinner to thank her for helping his wife. The therapist and the client were of the same ethnic Asian background. The therapist's intuitive hunch was that the husband wanted to harangue her about causing a potential divorce, and how this was bad for the entire community, and how could she, as a member of this Asian community, sanction that? Here, the therapist and I devised a "face-saving" way out that was a refusal to what could be a potentially threatening situation for the therapist by telling the husband that the agency as well as her supervisor, who was more advanced in the hierarchy, had a policy of no dinners with clients. The therapist did not go to dinner.

THE NEED FOR THE TRAINING OF
ASIAN THERAPISTS

Even if one is Asian, one cannot know every culture. And yet, we have to examine our own institutions that graduate professionals to provide mental-health services, that graduate scholars to study human development and social psychology. Where are the Hmong psychologists, the Laotian researchers, the Vietnamese and Cambodian developmental psychologists? Are we so afraid of differences that we feel we must wait for a few more generations to pass, and then, when the offspring of the Vietnamese, Cambodian, or Hmong are so "acculturated" and homogenized, we will let them into our graduate schools and grant them doctorates and master's degrees in counseling, or social work, or psychology? We need to study different patterns of child rearing, what is considered normal and abnormal within a particular culture, and how culture influences the ways family members interact, argue, and settle differences. Different cultures perceive problems differently, ask for help differently, seek healing differently. If we open ourselves up to it, our understanding of what it means to be human will be enlarged, and more of what we call the mystery of life can enter in. If our academic and training institutions actively recruit Asian American students and truly value the fact that they have been raised in a paradigm different from that of a European American, and if our academicians can see those differences as assets and strengths, then our psychology has a chance to truly become a science of mind and behavior joined to the study of the inner heart.

Epilogue. An awkward young girl timidly approached the microphone and asked Leontyne Price, in a soft voice, "Was it difficult for you growing up?" Ms. Price, moved, said, "Well, sweetheart, let me turn the question around. Is it difficult for you growing up?" The girl nodded her head and said, "Yes." Ms. Price inquired further. Was it problems with friends, school, homework, family, things like that? The girl nodded yes again. "Angel," Ms. Price said, "What I can tell you is that it does get better. All the things you think are negative now will change. I promise you; I promise you." (Tommasini, 2000)

REFERENCES

Aoki, B. K. (1997). Gay and lesbian Asian Americans in psychotherapy. In E. Lee (Ed.), *Working with Asian Americans: A guide for clinicians* (pp. 411–419). New York: Guilford Press.

Banks, H. C. (1975). The Black person as client and therapist. *Professional Psychology, 6,* 470–474.

Block, J. B. (1968). The White worker and the Negro client in psychotherapy. *Social Work, 13,* 36–42.

Burton, J. F., Farrell, M. M., Lord, F. B., & Lord, R. W. (1999). *Confinement and ethnicity: An overview of World War II Japanese American relocation sites.* U.S. Department of the Interior, National Park Service, Western Archeological and Conservation Center.

Chao, C. M. (1992). The inner heart: Therapy with Southeast Asian families. In L. Vargas & J. Koss-Chiono (Eds.), *Working with culture: Psychological interventions with ethnic minority children and adolescents* (pp. 157–181). San Francisco: Jossey-Bass.

Chao, C. M. (1994). Confessions of a supervisee/supervisor or an apologia for doing something different. *Child, Youth and Family Services Quarterly, 17*(2), 13–15.

Chao, C. M. (1995). A bridge over troubled waters: Being Eurasian in the U.S. of A. In J. Adleman & G. Enguidanos (Eds.), *Racism in the lives of women: Testimony, theory and guides to antiracist practice* (pp. 33–43). New York: Harrington Park Press.

Chao, C. M. (2000). Ancestors and ancestor altars: Connecting relationships. In J. L. Chin (Ed.), *Relationships among Asian American women* (pp. 101–107). Washington, DC: American Psychological Association.

Cheek, D. K. (1976). *Assertive Black . . . puzzled White.* San Luis Obispo, CA: Impact.

Chin, J. L. (1993). Transference. In J. L. Chin, J. H. Liem, M. D. Ham, & G. H. Hong (Eds.), *Transference and empathy in Asian American psychotherapy: Cultural values and treatment needs* (pp. 117–129). Westport, CT: Praeger.

Chin, J. L. (Ed.). (2000). *Relationships among Asian American women.* Washington, DC: American Psychological Association.

Chung, W. (1997). Asian American children. In E. Lee (Ed.), *Working with Asian Americans: A guide for clinicians* (pp. 165–174). New York: Guilford Press.

Cordova, F. (1983). *Filipinos: Forgotten Asian Americans.* Dubuque, IA: Kendall/Hunt.

Du, N., & Lu, F. G. (1997). Assessment and treatment of Posttraumatic Stress Disorder among Asian

Americans. In E. Lee (Ed.), *Working with Asian Americans: A guide for clinicians* (pp. 275–294). New York: Guilford Press.

Endo, R., Sue, S., & Wagner, N. W. (Eds.). (1980). *Asian-Americans: Social and psychological perspectives*. Palo Alto, CA: Science and Behavior Books.

Etinger, L., & Strom, A. (1973). *Mortality and morbidity after excessive stress: A follow-up investigation of Norwegian concentration camp survivors*. New York: Humanities Press.

Feng, G. F., & English, J. (1972). *Lao Tsu: Tao te ching*. New York: Vintage Books.

Grier, W. J., & Cobbs, P. M. (1968). *Black rage*. New York: Basic Books.

Huang, L. N. (1997). Asian American adolescents. In E. Lee (Ed.), *Working with Asian Americans: A guide for clinicians* (pp. 175–195). New York: Guilford Press.

Ja, D., & Yuen, F. K. (1997). Substance abuse treatment among Asian Americans. In E. Lee (Ed.), *Working with Asian Americans: A guide for clinicians* (pp. 295–308). New York: Guilford Press.

Jones, A. C. (1991). Psychological functioning in African Americans: A conceptual guide for use in psychotherapy. In R. L. Jones (Ed.), *Black psychology* (3rd ed., pp. 577–589). Berkeley, CA: Cobb and Henry.

Kakaiya, D. (2000). Identity development and conflicts among Indian immigrant women. In J. L. Chin (Ed.), *Relationships among Asian American women* (pp. 133–149). Washington, DC: American Psychological Association.

Kang, K. C. (1990, May 25). A battle of cultures in New York. *Asian Week*, p. 1.

Kao, R. S., & Lam, M. L. (1997). Asian American elderly. In E. Lee (Ed.), *Working with Asian Americans: A guide for clinicians* (pp. 208–226). New York: Guilford Press.

Kim, B. C. (1996). Korean families. In M. McGoldrick, J. Giordano, & J. K. Pearce (Eds.), *Ethnicity and family therapy* (2nd ed., pp. 281-294). New York: Guilford Press.

Kim, E. H. (1993, January 13). Speech delivered November 13, 1992 to Women Organized to Reach Koreans. *Asian Week, 17*, p. 20.

Kinzie, J. D., Boehnlein, J. K., Leung, P. K., Moore, L. J., Riley, C., & Smith, D. (1990). The prevalence of Posttraumatic Stress Disorder and its clinical significance among Southeast Asian refugees. *American Journal of Psychiatry, 147*, 913–917.

Kinzie, J. D. Sack, W. Angell, R. Clarke, G., & Rath, B. (1989). A three-year follow-up of Cambodian young people traumatized as children. *Journal of the American Academy of Child and Adolescent Psychiatry, 28*(4), 501–504.

Lee, E. (1982). A social systems approach to assessment and treatment of Chinese American families. In M. McGoldrick, J. Pearce, & J. Giordano (Eds.), *Ethnicity and family therapy* (pp. 527–551). New York: Guilford Press.

Lee, E. (Ed.). (1997). *Working with Asian Americans: A guide for clinicians*. New York: Guilford Press.

Lee, L. C., & Zane, N. W. S. (Eds.). (1998). *Handbook of Asian American psychology*. Thousand Oaks, CA: Sage.

Leong, F. T. (1986). Counseling and psychotherapy with Asian Americans: Review of the literature. *Journal of Counseling Psychology, 33*, 196–206.

Lin, S. C. (1997, April 25). Hope and resignation in LA: APAs give mixed review to the progress made since the Los Angeles riots. *Asian Week*, pp. 12–13.

Lum, J. L. (1998). Family violence. In L. C. Lee & Zane, N. W. S. (Eds.), *Handbook of Asian American psychology* (pp. 505–526). Thousand Oaks, CA: Sage.

McGoldrick, M., Pearce, J., & Giordano, J. (Eds.). (1982). *Ethnicity and family therapy*. New York: Guilford Press.

Miyamoto, J. (1971). "What are you?" *Asian Women's Journal: University of California, Berkeley, Asian American Studies Center*, 50–51.

Mydans, S. (1992, February 26). Killing alarms Japanese-Americans. *The New York Times*, p. A12.

Nagata, D. (1991). Transgenerational impact of the Japanese American internment: Clinical issues in working with children of former internees. *Psychotherapy, 28*, 121–128.

Nagata, D. (2000). World War II internment and the relationships of Nisei women. In J. L. Chin (Ed.), *Relationships among Asian American women* (pp. 49–70). Washington, DC: American Psychological Association.

Oh, A. (1997, April 25). Still bitter after all these years: The crisis continues for Korean Americans in Los Angeles. *Asian Week*, p. 7.

Root, M. P. P. (Ed.). (1992). *Racially mixed people in America*. Newbury Park, CA: Sage.

Root, M. P. P. (Ed.). (1996). *The multiracial experience: Racial borders as the new frontier.* Thousand Oaks, CA: Sage.

The Roots of the Cambodian Health Crisis. (2000). Available from www.hartnet.org/khmer/pagepapr.html

Rudolf, G. (1964). The Chinese in Colorado 1869–1911 (Master's thesis). *DU Library Microfilm, M., Number 4,* Item 10.

Sack, W. H., Clarke, G., Him, C., Dickson, D., Goff, B., Lanham, K., et al. (1993). A 6-year follow-up study of Cambodian refugee adolescents traumatized as children. *Journal of the American Academy of Child and Adolescent Psychiatry, 32*(2), 431–437.

Sack, W. H., Clarke, G., & Seeley, J. (1996). Multiple forms of stress in Cambodian adolescent refugees. *Child Development, 67*(1), 107–116.

Sluzki, C. (1979). Migration and family conflict. *Family Process, 18*(4), 379–390.

Soga, K., Mori, T., Takei, S., & Ozaki, M. (1983). *Poets behind barbed wire.* Honolulu, HA: Bamboo Ridge Press.

Stephens, S. (2000). The legacy of absence: Cambodian artists confront the past. *Persimmon: Asian Literature, Arts, and Culture, 1*(2), 80–83.

Sue, D. W., & Sue, D. (1977). Barriers to effective cross-cultural counseling. *Journal of Counseling Psychology, 24,* 420–429.

Sue, D. W., & Sue, D. (1990). *Counseling the culturally different.* New York: Wiley.

Sue, S., & Morishima, J. (1982). *The mental health of Asian Americans.* San Francisco: Jossey-Bass.

Sue, S., & Wagner, N. N. (Eds.). (1973). *Asian Americans: Psychological perspectives.* Palo Alto, CA: Science and Behavior Books.

Sue, S., & Zane, N. (1987). The role of culture and cultural techniques in psychotherapy: A critique and reformulation. *American Psychologist, 42,* 37–45.

Sustento-Seneriches, J. (1997). Filipino American families. In E. Lee (Ed.), *Working with Asian Americans: A guide for clinicians* (pp. 101–113). New York: Guilford Press.

Takaki, R. (1998). *Strangers from a different shore: A history of Asian Americans.* New York: Back Bay Books.

Tang, N. M. (2000). Psychoanalytic psychotherapy with Chinese Americans. In E. Lee (Ed.), *Working with Asian Americans: A guide for clinicians* (pp. 323–341). New York: Guilford Press.

Tien, L. (2000). U.S. attitudes toward women of Asian ancestry: Legislative and media perspectives. In J. L. Chin (Ed.), *Relationships among Asian American women* (pp. 29–47). Washington, DC: American Psychological Association.

Tommasini, A. (2000, May 30). A soprano takes her favorite story to class: Leontyne Price reads her book version of *Aida* and sings for school children. *The New York Times,* p. B1.

Tran, C., & Jardins, K. D. (2000). Domestic violence in Vietnamese refuge and Korean immigrant communities. In J. L. Chin (Ed.), *Relationships among Asian American women* (pp. 71–96). Washington, DC: American Psychological Association.

Uba, L. (1994). *Asian Americans: Personality patterns, identity and mental health.* New York: Guilford Press.

Wong, B. (1998, April 30). Wong Kim Art's legacy: Family history as national treasure. *Asian Week,* p. 6.

Wong, P. T. P., & Ujimoto, K. V. (1998). The elderly: Their stress, coping and mental health. In L. C. Lee & N. W. S. Zane (Eds.), *Handbook of Asian American psychology* (pp. 165–210). Thousand Oaks, CA: Sage.

Zane, N. W. S., & Huh-Kim, J. (1998). Addictive behaviors. In L. C. Lee & N. W. S. Zane (Eds.), *Handbook of Asian American psychology* (pp. 527–554). Thousand Oaks, CA: Sage.

CHAPTER 3

Play Therapy with Abused Children

ELIANA GIL

Play therapy has gained legitimacy and credibility in the past two decades as more mental health professionals study and practice this therapeutic modality and as research mounts to substantiate its effectiveness (Bratton & Ray, 2000). Differential uses of play therapy include diagnostic understanding of a child, establishing a working relationship, breaking through defenses against anxiety, helping children verbalize conscious material and associated feelings, assisting the acting out of unconscious material and relief of accompanying tension, and developing play interests to be carried over into daily life (Amster, 1982). In work with children, play therapy embodies a range of curative qualities, including the potential for expression and communication, problem-solving, affective discharge, assimilation of difficult experiences, and relationship enhancement (Schaefer, 1993). Play therapy can be utilized with a range of presenting problems (Kaduson, Cangelosi, & Schaefer, 1997; Kottman & Schaeffer, 1993).

The field of play therapy has also grown in tandem with professional interest. The Association for Play Therapy was organized in 1982. A certification process was launched in 1992 (there are currently 367 Registered Play Therapists and 474 Registered Play Therapy Supervisors across the United States and abroad). Approximately 10 university courses are offered in play therapy. Each annual conference, now in the seventh year, attracts over 900 professionals. As more and more professionals seek certification in play therapy, undergraduate and graduate schools as well as independent agencies will likely provide play therapy courses for interested students. Play therapy training is currently more accessible than ever, with several educational programs dedicated to the spread of education on this subject (e.g., the Center for Play Therapy at the University of North Texas and Starbright Training Institute in Fairfax, Virginia). This represents a revival of interest in play therapy since pertinent theory was cultivated at the beginning of the twentieth century. Although several pioneers piqued professional curiosity and originated experimentation with play therapy, a discrete *field of play therapy* has only truly flourished in the past two decades.

HISTORICAL BACKGROUND

Historical Development of Using Play in Therapy

Although Hug-Hellmuth (1921) first proposed play as an essential part of child analysis, Anna Freud (1928) initiated play in therapy as a way to strategically engage children and to enhance a sense of comfort with analytical processes. Melanie Klein (1932), in contrast, viewed play as a substitute for verbalization and, therefore, relied on interpretation of play to understand a child's experience. Basing their techniques on psychoanalytic theory, Klein and A. Freud originated play as a viable component of child therapy. Others quickly followed. Levy (1938) developed a more structured and goal-oriented approach, which he called release therapy. He postulated that repetitive, literal play had the potential to be therapeutic through facilitating repetition compulsion and subsequent discharging of affect. Levy provided play materials to help children re-create traumatic events, so they could *play out* their concerns about situations, therefore making the events more tolerable and children could achieve a sense of mastery over them. Hambridge (1955) followed Levy's use of re-creation by directly reproducing anxiety-producing events in the middle phase of treatment, after a therapeutic relationship was well-grounded. Neither Levy's or Hambridge's work gained momentum at the time, but currently serve as foundations for posttrauma play theory and technique (Gil, 1998; Marvasti, 1993; Schaefer, 1994; Terr, 1990).

Solomon (1938) used play to allow aggressive children to *play out* anger without feared negative consequences. Play therapists continue to question the benefits and dangers of facilitating or encouraging aggressive play in therapy sessions. Rank (1936) focused on the patient-therapist relationship and the patient's life in the *here and now*. He emphasized the negative role of birth trauma in children's lives. Moustakas (1959) developed *relationship* therapy based on establishing a deep and secure relationship between therapist and child to facilitate helping a child to individuate. Axline (1947) adapted the approach of Rogers (1939); she cultivated child-centered play therapy, which has been popularized by Landreth (Landreth & Sweeney, 1997) and has become one of the current prevailing play-therapy approaches.

Major Theories of Play Therapy

An array of theories serves as the foundation for and shapes the contemporary field of play therapy. The following represents a cursory overview of the leading theories from which many others are derived. (See O'Connor & Braverman, 1997, for a thorough overview of play-therapy theories.)

Psychoanalytic Play Therapy

The ultimate goal of child psychoanalysis is to "explore, understand, and resolve the etiology of the arrests, fixations, regressions, defensive operations that bind the important sources of psychic energy, in order to aid the resumption of normal development" (Lee, 1997, p. 54). Psychoanalysts employ a verbally based play therapy and rely on interpretations designed to evoke insights that children may then use to alter their behaviors. Most child psychoanalysts work with children over the age of 5 years and use a limited selection of toys to either help develop rapport or assist children to symbolize their underlying concerns. They encourage child patients to build a strong and dependent relationship with the therapist. Toys prove critical to the formation of a therapeutic relationship, according to A. Freud, and often help to prepare a child for analytic work. She did not, however, encourage transferential responses to herself by being neutral. In fact, she recommended that a therapist exhibit "greater strength and authority than the other adults in the child's life . . . [and that an analyst] should put herself in the position of the child's ego ideal" (Oliver James, 1997, p. 116).

A. Freud also contributed the earliest guided imagery techniques with her *let's-see-a-picture* technique, offering a child a vehicle for expressing feelings. This technique is an extension or a modification of S. Freud's well-known technique of *free association,* in which patients were asked to verbalize fantasies to understand their internal world. S. Freud also used dream interpretation and drawings to understand his patients' psyches more fully, and A. Freud adapted Freudian concepts in recognition of the uniqueness of a child's world.

A. Freud saw toys as useful to build a therapy relationship and to allow a child who has not developed full verbal strength to "explain a personal environment" (Oliver James, 1997, p. 117). Klein (1932) took a very different approach to toys in providing a box with personalized toys for each child. She selected toys representative of objects and persons in the child's real world. These toys were kept in boxes in a closet and were taken out only during therapy sessions. Klein prompted child patients to act out feelings during play and used play instead of adult conversation with them. She also interpreted a child's play, believing this would help the child deal with anxiety. A. Freud and Klein disagreed about the type and extent of interpretation and about a child's use of transference with a therapist.

Cognitive-Behavioral Play Therapy
Cognitive-behavioral play therapists use play to alter the ways people construe their life experiences, so that their affects and behaviors become more adaptive and functional (Knell, 1993, 1997). Behaviorists focus on problem behaviors by studying sequential behaviors and determining the type and degree of reinforcement that have maintained behaviors. By applying very specific reinforcers, they aim to alter a child's problem behaviors without the need to understand what intrapsychic issues might be fueling the behaviors.

Cognitive-behavioral play therapists base their work on six basic tenets: (1) Involve a child in treatment via play; (2) focus on a child's thoughts, feelings, fantasies, and environment; (3) provide a strategy for developing more adaptive thoughts and behaviors; (4) be structured, directive, and goal-oriented rather than open-ended; (5) incorporate empirically demonstrated techniques; and (6) allow for empirical examination of treatment. They use role playing, reinforcements such as stickers and praise, modeling, behavioral contingencies, and positive reinforcement. Toys, puppets, and board games are used to reinforce new lessons or skills (Knell, 1993).

Jungian Play Psychotherapy
Jungian therapists nurture individuation processes by helping a child to "develop his or her unique identity, to overcome or to come to terms with his or her losses or traumas, activate and adapt to the healthy demands of family, school, and society at large" (Allan, 1997, p. 105). Jung suggested that the essence of a reparative healing experience results not from "what the therapist does directly to the client, but how the therapist sets the conditions in the therapeutic setting" (Oliver James, 1997, p. 128). Jung further believed that, under these conditions of consistent safety, individuals have the power to heal themselves. In addition, Jung affirmed that the power of transference lies in its capacity to help individuals feel empowered, which then promotes healing. Almost daily during his midlife, Jung became deeply engrossed in play, using "twigs, stones, and mud along the lake shore to build towns and villages" (De Domenico, 1994, p. 254). Jung (1961) made a great contribution to the importance of play by chronicling his own personal work to address painful or blocked childhood memories using symbolic, reconstructive play. He promoted play as one of the primary means to

self-realization, and Jungian play therapists base their techniques on Jung's own healing journey into the "archetypal world of play and fantasy" (De Domenico, 1994, p. 254). They commit themselves to creating safe environments, consider inner and outer worlds as vital learning environments, and value uninterrupted play from the unconscious, restricting themselves from offering interpretations, judgments, or directives. In addition to the Freudian theory of unconscious drives, Jung offered his belief in a collective unconscious that "creates psychological images and mythological experiences that actually teach the child and adult the meaning-making matrices of their ancestors" (De Domenico, 1994, p. 259).

Developmental Play Therapy
A developmental play therapist seeks "to provide the child with the condition needed to develop his core self—the inner self that guides and controls him from the inside out" (Brody, 1997, p. 162). The guiding technique of this theory involves the appropriate use of human touch. The necessity for bonding behaviors to occur between mother and child during a child's infancy proves central in this type of therapy. These bonding behaviors lead to a child's developing appropriate and secure attachment, which in turn affects a child's ability to interact and develop relationships with others. Brody (1992) suggested that children's emotional problems can be healed only by providing human touch. She, therefore, holds, rocks, and cradles children to develop sufficient safety, so that a child can begin a process of leaving the physical safety of a therapist and exploring the environment, returning to the therapist as he or she needs emotional support or encouragement. Developmental play therapists, therefore, provide bonding opportunities to allow a child to move to the next developmental stage of separation and individuation.

Child-Centered (Nondirective) Play Therapy
Rogers (1951) proposed a theory of personality structure that Axline (1955) adapted to working with children. Child-centered play therapists focus on the person of the child rather than the child's problem. Therapy relationships are built without necessarily knowing about the causes or extent of a child's maladjustment. Maladjustments are "viewed as resulting from an incongruence between what the child actually experienced and the child's concept of self" (Landreth & Sweeney, 1997, p. 21). Child-centered play therapists specialize in reaching children thorough understanding and acceptance. They believe this encourages a child to achieve self-actualization in learning to be less defensive and more open to a wider range of experiences. Eventually, a child's feelings of liking and self-acceptance no longer depend on external figures. Rather, a child feels more confident and capable of self-direction (Landreth, 1982), therefore "discovering the self the individual is capable of becoming" (Landreth & Sweeney, 1997, p. 17).

Landreth (1991) has revised and expanded Axline's basic principles of child-centered therapy. Thus, a therapist:

1. Is genuinely interested in a child and develops a warm, caring relationship.
2. Experiences unqualified acceptance of a child and does not wish that a child were different in some way.
3. Creates a feeling of safety and permissiveness in a therapeutic relationship, so a child feels free to explore and express self completely.
4. Is always sensitive to a child's feelings and gently reflects those feelings in such a manner that a child develops self-understanding.
5. Believes deeply in a child's capacity to act responsibly and unwaveringly respects and resists any urge to direct a child's play or conversation.
6. Trusts a child's inner-direction, allows a child to lead in all areas of a therapeutic relationship, and resists any urge to direct a child's play or conversation.

7. Appreciates the gradual nature of the therapeutic process and does not attempt to hurry the process.
8. Establishes only those therapeutic limits that help a child accept personal and appropriate relationship responsibility.

Filial Therapy

Filial therapists (L. Guerney, 1997) promote psychological adjustment in children by helping parents acquire the skills of a play therapist. They can apply them in everyday life when relating to their children, thus improving parent-child relationships. L. Guerney (2000) provided five major arguments for using the filial therapy approach:

1. Child problems usually result from parental lack of knowledge and skills, not parental pathology.
2. Playing with their children allows parents to relate more positively and allows children to communicate thoughts, feelings, and needs through play that might not be expressed in real life.
3. Many parents engage in the tradition of playing with their children.
4. Given the primary role of change agents, parents may feel less resistant to their children's treatment.
5. A parent-child relationship nearly always remains the most significant in a child's life; therefore, if a child experiences expression, insight, and adult acceptance in the presence of this powerful person, the greatest effect results.

Filial therapy might be new to many child and family therapists, yet it has a long and successful track record and has attained the status of an empirically validated treatment easily duplicated. As such, it has gained much popularity in the past decade, even though it was first introduced in the literature in the early 1960s (B. Guerney, 1964).

Other play therapy approaches, such as Gestalt (Oaklander, 1978, 1994), Adlerian (Kottman & Warlick, 1990), ecosystemic (O'Connor & Ammen, 1998), and strategic play therapy (Ariel, 1994) are summarized elsewhere (O'Connor & Braverman, 1997; Oliver James, 1997). In addition, the concepts of family play therapy (Bailey, 2000; Gil, 1994; Schaefer & Carey, 1994) and dynamic play therapy that primarily use the expressive or creative arts (Harvey, 1990; Malchiodi, 1998) are gaining popularity.

THE THERAPEUTIC ASPECTS OF PLAY AND CURRENT APPLICATIONS

The differences between young child and adult clients abound, but, most obviously, adults can find greater comfort in language and verbal expression, a skill that allows them to make themselves understood by others. Adults are more or less effective in their abilities to communicate distress, concerns, fears, problems, and potential solutions. Children, on the other hand, have cognitive, emotional, and language limitations that can diminish their abilities to perceive, understand, and cope with challenging or difficult situations. They much more likely use an ample range of behaviors to communicate internal stress and distress, and professionals must be prepared to decode symptomatic behaviors. Even the brightest and most articulate child can feel stymied to explain wants or needs, so that parents or caretakers can comprehend and react appropriately. Children often come to treatment because their behaviors are a problem to concerned parents or professionals. Child clients may not experience their presenting issue as dilemmas and often find therapy structure unfamiliar and stressful.

Initial clinical challenges in child therapy include understanding youngsters' nonverbalized internal experiences and facilitating their communication. Play therapists believe that children's communication occurs not only through language but also through play, art, stories, symbols, and verbal metaphors. "Toys are a young child's words, and play is his natural language" (Schaefer, 1993, p. 6). Play embodies "a more fantastic, drive-dominated form of communication that is full of images and emotions" (p. 6). A 6-year-old who was brought to see me after witnessing a murder had been interviewed by four professionals. In his first play activity, he constructed a little scenario in a sand box using miniature cars and fences. In his scenario, every car was in its garage. The only car that ventured out arrived at a four-way intersection; here, three cars had a stop sign but the child's car had a green light and could "get away and go on vacation." This child clearly communicated his internal state, although he spoke no words. I respected his need to stop me from asking questions and his need for a fantasy escape.

Besides a vehicle for communication, play therapy fosters many other potential therapeutic benefits. Through play activities, children can experience mastery by creating stories or artistic productions or competing in a board game. The use of pretend play, role play, storytelling, and other play techniques that encourage a child to expand fantasy and invention promote creative thinking. Many traumatized children struggle with integrating aspects of their stressful and overwhelming experiences. Through play, they exercise the capacity to use objects to symbolize aspects of a trauma and to then contain, manage, and assimilate thoughts and feelings associated with trauma. In so doing, they can discharge withheld affect and can change from a passive to an active stance by having controlled recall through play (Gil, 1998).

Because play proves pleasurable to most children, therapists offer children enjoyable experiences in which they are valued and accepted as they are. A therapist can thus become a healthy attachment figure in the child's life, and a child may experience enhancement of self through the process of building a therapeutic relationship (Schaefer, 1993). Because of these advantages, play therapists have treated children experiencing a wide range of problems, including abuse and neglect, aggression and acting out, hospitalization, learning disabilities, reading difficulties, selective mutism, difficulties with self-concept and self-esteem, social adjustment problems, speech difficulties, traumatization, and withdrawal (Landreth, Homeyer, Glover, & Sweeney, 1996), depression, fears and phobias, divorce and separation, attachment disorders, and Attention-Deficit Disorder (Kaduson et al., 1997). The writings that document play therapy as a powerful, natural, and effective assessment and treatment approach with troubled children have increased (Gil, 1991; Kaduson et al., 1997; McMahon, 1992; Schaefer, Gitlin, & Sandgrund, 1991; Webb, 1991).

THE ROLE OF PLAY IN CHILDHOOD: THE INHERENT VALUE AND USE OF PLAY IN NORMATIVE DEVELOPMENT

Those interested in play and play therapy most frequently draw on the definition of play developed by Erikson (1950) who construed play as "a function of the ego, an attempt to synchronize the bodily and social processes with the self" (p. 211). Schaefer and O'Connor (1983) characterized typical elements of play as being pleasurable, intrinsically complete, not depending on external rewards or other people, tending to be person- rather than object-dominated, noninstrumental, having no intrapersonal or interpersonal goal, and not occurring in novel or frightening situations.

Play activity happens universally across cultures, classes, and socioeconomic strata: "Play is the singular central activity of childhood, occurring at all times and in all places" (Landreth, 1993, p. 41). Most children do not need lessons in playing, a "spontaneous, enjoyable, voluntary, and non-goal directed [experience]" (Landreth, 1993, p. 41). Cattanach (1993) cited Huizinga's insistence that play is a function of culture from its earliest beginnings, that play is a cultural factor in life and that the spirit of playful competition is, as a social impulse, older than culture itself and pervades all life like a veritable ferment. . . . Ritual grew up in sacred play; poetry was born in play and nourished on play; music and dancing were pure play. (p. 30)

Several theories have been advanced about why play is helpful to humans. Schaefer (1993) listed these as (1) the surplus energy theory of play (children have extra energy that can build up and exert internal pressure unless released); (2) recreation theory (play restores energy expended in work); (3) practice theory (play gives children opportunities to practice skills they will need in the future); (4) psychoanalytic theory (play allows a child to relive stresses previously experienced passively); (5) cognitive theory (play promotes a child's creativity and flexible thinking); and (6) arousal theory (persons seek optimum levels of arousal through play).

THE APPLICATION OF PLAY THERAPY WITH ABUSED CHILDREN

Martin (1976) initiated the study of the psychological impact of abuse on children. He focused on physically abused children and explored physiological, educational, and psychological problems that could emerge from children's experiences of abuse. He presented an innovative approach by discussing not only physical and medical consequences of child maltreatment but by also emphasizing the need for therapeutic interventions for abused children and their families.

In the past three decades, the literature on this subject has grown concurrently with the development of a substantial professional community specializing in identification, assessment, and treatment of abused children. Gil (1991), James (1994), Friedrich (1995), Deblinger and Heflin (1996), Ciottone and Madonna (1996), and Vaughn Heineman (1998) have proposed a variety of therapeutic issues to be addressed in treatment. A consensus regarding the treatment needs of abused children has emerged and is focused on relieving specific symptomatology (Posttraumatic Stress Disorder [PTSD] responses), encouraging ego development, promoting attachment, and addressing problems in affective and behavioral dysregulation. Treatment approaches to address these problems vary, however. Most professionals who work with children use play therapy either as a primary or adjunctive modality.

EMPIRICAL FINDINGS REGARDING ABUSED CHILDREN'S COMMON SYMPTOMATOLOGY

Kendall-Tackett, Williams, and Finkelhor (1993) reviewed 42 methodologically sound research studies conducted on sexually abused children. They did not discern a "profile" for sexually abused children, but noted several problem areas appearing consistently throughout research efforts: fear and anxiety (symptoms of PTSD), depression, aggression, and sexual acting out. Children of different ages may manifest these four processes differentially. A 3-year-old aggressive child might throw or break toys whereas a 12-year-old might pick fights with peers. In addition, gender and personality differences may predispose children to exhibit different symptomatology while experiencing the same underlying issue. A depressed 10-year-old girl may develop an eating disorder in contrast to a boy of the same age who might become provocative and oppositional. Friedrich (1995) observed that sexual abuse does not result in a consistent cluster of symptoms because "the same acts, in different children, can be manifested in seemingly disparate immediate and long-term sequelae" (p. 2). A host of variables affect outcome, including the context in which incidents of abuse occur. Sexual abuse may transpire in multiproblem families with chaotic lifestyles and unwieldy social environments of violence, housing instability, poverty, isolation, drug abuse, and mental illness. Families in which abuse arises vary in their interaction patterns (Trepper & Niedner, 1996). In the past decade, more and more emphasis has emerged regarding understanding children's resiliency as well as temperamental, personality, age, and gender factors that might make children more stress-resistant or invulnerable (Rutter, 1984; Wener & Smith, 1989; Wolin & Wolin, 1993).

Briere (1992) noted "seven major types of psychological disturbances, all of which are frequently found in adolescents and adults who were abused in childhood: post-traumatic stress, cognitive distortions, altered emotionality, dissociation, impaired self-reference, disturbed relatedness, and avoidance" (p. 19). Children also appear to be vulnerable to these problem areas, although they are discussed in alternative language: fear and anxiety, self-blame, guilt and shame, affect dysregulation, depersonalization, impaired self-image and self-esteem, and attachment problems. Moreover, Friedrich (1995) underscored that young children have developmental vulnerabilities, so attention must be focused on the development of the self and view of others. Finally, Friedrich recognized the work of Watkins and Bentovim (1992), focused on gender vulnerabilities, and concluded that "the three sexual abuse effects thought to be more or less unique to male victims are (1) confusion/anxiety over sexual identity, (2) inappropriate attempts to reassert masculinity, and (3) recapitulation of the victimizing experience" (p. 216). In addition, younger children may display more overt behavioral acting out than older children and adults because they may feel less inhibited about their behaviors and may have developed fewer self-regulation skills. Friedrich also emphasized that "children cannot be adequately understood unless they are appreciated as developing organisms who must be evaluated and treated within the context of their family" (p. 2).

TREATMENT NEEDS OF ABUSED CHILDREN

Understanding of the impact of sexual abuse on young children guides and informs treatment responses. Although effects of abuse vary from mild to extreme, for many sexually abused children it is experienced as a traumatic event in their lives. The treatment needs of sexually abused children require attention to *enhancement of ego skills in coping with trauma*. Sexually abused children can feel overwhelmed by the experiences they endure. Their feelings might overpower their abilities to defend against emotional pain. They may resort to psychological defenses such as denial, splitting, repression, suppression, or dissociation to withstand an assault. These defenses can be used rigidly or become maladaptive as children mature. For example, a sexually abused child who learns the dissociative strategy of taking emotional flight may develop psychogenic amnesia for significant events or periods in his or her life. Although dissociation helps abused children escape immediate pain, long-term use of this defense can be counterproductive. Helping children learn more adaptive coping strategies leads to their learning and identifying feelings, developing safe and appropriate outlets for feelings, finding alternative behaviors that are respectful, and learning to monitor and control impulses.

Kendall-Tackett et al. (1993) cited PTSD symptoms as one of the most common acute or chronic problems for abused children. Because of this finding, manifestations of fear and anxiety are expected to be frequent presenting problems in this population. Directive approaches such as use of cognitive-behavioral techniques have so far been shown to be most effective in decreasing these symptoms (Cohen & Mannarino, 1996;

Smith, Perrin, & Yule, 1998) and, therefore, serve as a treatment of choice when assisting children to develop adequate coping strategies to relieve symptoms.

Abuse victims need to *rework and integrate trauma.* Traumatic events can be laid down in memory in dissociated fashion. As long as aspects of the traumatic memory remain fragmented and vulnerable to reactivation by internal or external triggers, individuals will have ongoing experiences of helplessness. When traumatic events are integrated as coherent memories, individuals will feel less need to use defenses and experience a greater sense of control. Traumatic memories are processed and reworked as manageable and in the past. Schaefer (1994) noted that children will have mastery over the traumatizing event when they "(1) feel in control of the outcome of the play, (2) play out a satisfactory ending to the play, (3) feel free to express and release negative affect, and (4) exhibit a cognitive reappraisal of the event" (p. 305). *Facilitating corrective emotional experiences* aids the process of healing and constitutes another primary goal of therapy with abused children. Because they were abused in a context of interpersonal relationships, they learn that those they love, trust, and depend on also become those who hurt or exploit them. Interpersonal relationships thereby become unpredictable and risky. Therapists can offer a real opportunity for children to develop trust by providing a reliable, safe, and consistent human affiliation.

Many abused children are removed from their homes and live in foster-care placements where they are constantly negotiating issues of separation and loss. It is critical for therapists to examine the unique consequences of multiple separations, longing, and negotiating attachment to different caretakers because these complicate and expand the consequences of abuse and neglect (Bowlby, 1980; Gil & Bogart, 1982; Jewett, 1982; Osmond, Durham, Leggett, & Keating, 1998). Establishing healthy boundaries also proves crucial for children with violated physical or emotional boundaries. Children may enter therapy expecting that clinicians will invade their trust and may experience anticipatory anxiety that affects their behaviors. One 4-year-old who came into my office for the first time took off her underwear and spread her legs, so that I could see her vagina. This child had been sexually abused by her mother, and my interpretation of her behavior was that, in this new and unfamiliar context of meeting an unknown adult female, she became acutely anxious and resorted to known behavior in an effort to regain control and decrease her anxiety. She expected that I would be interested in seeing her genitals. I picked up her underwear, handed it to her, and said, "This is a place where you keep your underwear on, and I keep my underwear on." She visibly relaxed, and we were able to proceed with our first session, although she often asked for this type of limit setting or reassurance that she was safe.

Clinical work with all children involves enhancing their self-esteem (Marvasti, 1994). Sexually abused children often feel culpable, guilty, ashamed, and stigmatized. Clinical efforts to normalize and enhance children's self-image must be a consistent and persistent focus of treatment. Children under stress may constrict awareness and communication about affect and need opportunities for self-expression and mastery. Sex-abuse therapists often discuss helping child victims find their voices, so that they can experience personal power by saying what could not be articulated during abuse. Role plays, letter writing, making audiotapes, and singing songs facilitate this. Most abuse-specific therapists offer children ample opportunities to make cognitive reappraisals and to develop alternative explanations with increased input (Ciottone & Madonna, 1996; Schaefer, 1994). I have worked with many sexually abused children who feel they were responsible for the abuse because they did not stop their abusers. Once they understand that they did the best they could, given their limitations and the fact that the adults had substantial power over them, they can begin to hold themselves less culpable and view an adult's actions more realistically.

Sexual abuse does not occur in a vacuum. Everyone in the family is affected by the abuse, whether the offender is a family member or not. It is important, therefore, to assist all family members to process their thoughts, feelings, and reactions about the abuse, so that they may respond appropriately to child victims (Trepper & Barrett, 1986). Terr (1983) recommended that families be brought together for "ventilation, abreaction, and interpretation" (p. 18). When children are believed, supported, and cared for, they tend to fare better than when parents distrust or blame them or convey their wishes that disclosures had not been made. When immediate family members are not available physically or emotionally, therapists are well-advised to look for supportive relationships for a child. Often, extended family, school or day-care providers, and neighbors can become important resources for children. Crisis intervention and stress-reduction strategies prove important for sexually abused children and their families (Brenner, 1984; Johnson, 1989; Schaefer, 1994).

RATIONALE FOR THE USE OF PLAY THERAPY WITH ABUSED CHILDREN

Sexually abused children experience discrete acts or incidents of abuse within a larger context. Whether the abuser is a family member and how family members respond to a child's disclosure modify this context. When a family member commits a sexual offense, a child is compromised by loyalty conflicts that may seriously affect disclosure. Secrecy may be enforced by emotional manipulation. Children may sense the danger of disclosing sexual abuse, or they may fear consequences, such as loss of family stability. Children may be told that other family members already know and approve of what is going on. Or they may be told that others will be angry with them, not the adult. When abuse occurs outside the home, children still have serious issues to endure. They often feel worried that they will not be believed or that they will be seen as "bad." If they have maintained secrecy, they may fear parental discipline for not telling sooner. Abusers may have threatened harm to children or their families if they disclose what occurred.

Parental responses range from positively responsive to a child to less than optimal to extremely negative. Parental responses intensely influence children's recovery processes. Parents must be encouraged to provide safe, secure, and loving responses, so that abused children feel believed, supported, and protected. Children can be viewed as responsible for abuse, and may get accused of wrongdoing. Worse, others may perceive them as eliciting abusive responses from an abuser. Parents can also deny that abuse has occurred or choose to disbelieve a child and to form alliances with an abuser. Play therapy offers a nonthreatening approach to invite and permit frightened children real opportunities to access their internal resources without imposing additional pressure to communicate verbally about their experiences.

Only the cognitive-behavioral treatment approach to working with abused children has been systematically studied, so it is difficult to make conclusive statements about the treatment of choice for sexually abused children. Thus, although play therapy tends to be seen as helpful to most clinicians working with sexually abused children, current research (Berliner & Saunders, 1996; Cohen & Mannarino, 1996, 1998; Deblinger, McLeer, & Henry, 1990) primarily supports cognitive-behavioral theory and application as a tried-and-tested method of working with these children. This therapeutic approach implies an emphasis on verbal communication. Cognitive-behavioral approaches may be more amenable to research opportunities because of a clearly defined theory and technique that can be tested after application.

Empirical studies are needed to explore other play-therapy approaches, such as dynamic play therapy and family play therapy. In addition, posttraumatic play, as a distinctive and promising type of play, needs further attention and study (Gil, 1998; Marvasti, 1993; Terr, 1981). All these techniques have been documented in the literature as potentially effective, but are not currently empirically supported. The United States Office of Victims of Crime conducted a survey of treatment approaches in the field of child sexual abuse to determine a consensus of questionable as well as generally accepted and empirically supported treatments. Survey results were used to develop a document entitled *Guidelines for the Psychosocial Treatment of Intrafamilial Child Physical and Sexual Abuse.* (These guidelines are currently available on the Internet at www.adobe.com/products/acrobat/readstep2.html.)

RATIONALE FOR A PRESCRIPTIVE APPROACH OR INTEGRATED TREATMENT APPROACHES

Schaefer and Millman (1977) cautioned that "rather than attempting to force a child into one 'all purpose' therapeutic mold . . . therapists are now trying to individualize, to fit the remedies or techniques to the individual child" (pp. 1–2). This prescriptive approach seems warranted when working with abused children who have a range of responses to their experiences. Specifically, some sexually abused and traumatized children seem to have conflicting drives toward mastery and avoidance. Some, therefore, present in therapy ready, almost eager, to face, process, and overcome the impact of traumatic events whereas others avoid facing traumatic experiences because of painful emotions that overwhelm them. Clinicians need to evaluate children's individual responses and to react accordingly, either in a nondirective or a directive style.

CASE EXAMPLE

REFERRAL INFORMATION AND PSYCHOSOCIAL HISTORY

Chabita, an 8-year-old girl from a country in Central America, caught her teacher's attention when she broke into tears at school. She was referred to the school counselor, who spent two hours in an attempt to find out the source of this child's distress. Chabita, completely fluent in English and Spanish, felt comfortable speaking with the school counselor in English. But not until a Spanish-speaking counselor was asked to join this meeting did Chabita reluctantly talk about feeling afraid of her teenage brother, Miguel.

Chabita described a terrifying situation in which she was left alone with Miguel, who was often explosive and physically abusive. She showed both counselors a number of bruises on her arms and back. When Chabita referred to "other things" that her brother did to her that she didn't like, both counselors became concerned about sexual abuse. She was unwilling to elaborate what "other things" Miguel did, but finally nodded when one of the counselors asked if her brother touched private parts of her body. Chabita cried loudly that she did not want her father to know and that she was afraid that both her parents would be mad at her for letting Miguel touch her in this way. The counselor reassured Chabita that they would explain the situation to her parents and that it was not her fault that her brother was hitting her or being sexual with her. The counselors explained to Chabita that they were going to call Child Protective Services and that she would probably need to tell her story again. The emergency response team was able to come to Chabita's school promptly. She repeated her story in a more calm state. She was then taken to the local hospital to have a medical exam by the Sexual Abuse Nurse Examiners.

Positive medical findings confirmed that Chabita had been sexually abused. The exam also noted several injuries around her vaginal area and inner thighs that were consistent with Chabita's description of being physically assaulted. She was taken into custody and transferred to an emergency foster placement until her parents could be located and informed of the situation. Chabita was referred to the Abused Children's Treatment Services at this time. Our first appointment with Chabita's mother, Marta, occurred within the next two days. By the time I met with her mother to obtain a developmental history, Chabita was back at home after her brother Miguel had been arrested and placed in a juvenile facility. A hearing would be imminent, at which point, legal decisions would be made about Miguel.

Marta, 42-years-old, looked much older than her years. She walked slowly with her head down. She dressed in a simple way without vanity (no makeup, short unmanicured nails, loose clothing, hair pulled back into a braid held by a rubber band). She was visibly distraught and cried throughout most of our hour-long meeting. My goal was to learn about the family situation as well as specifics of how Chabita and her parents were functioning at this time and, in particular, how they were supporting and helping each other.

Marta was relieved that I spoke Spanish since she had not learned English; Chabita was her customary interpreter. Marta noted that Chabita had always been a shy, quiet child who stayed to herself, hardly ever communicating with the rest of the family. She explained that both she and her husband, Carlos, had become accustomed to Chabita's self-isolation and lack of conversation. She and her husband had once discussed the possibility that something was wrong with Chabita because she seemed "sad," but Chabita denied that there was anything wrong. "Why wouldn't she tell me that something so bad was going on right in our house?" she exclaimed earnestly. I explained that Chabita had been physically and sexually abused by her brother and by all accounts felt very frightened. By now, I had learned that Miguel had threatened to kill Chabita if she told. Marta sobbed, saying she could not understand how God had let this happen, and she could not believe that Miguel had done these things. She offered that he was always a good boy, that perhaps she should not have left him behind in her country, that not having her love had probably changed him. I noticed Marta's tendency to shift the conversation to Miguel, and I also understood her concern that he was locked up and surrounded by other boys who might hurt him. I reassured her that I was familiar with this particular juvenile facility and that I knew firsthand that they had good security and that the staff would take care of Miguel and make sure he was safe.

I asked Marta how she was dealing with recent events and whom she counted on for support. She related that her husband and she had a distant and conflictual relationship and that he was quite angry with her that she had not known what was going on under her nose. Carlos seemed to hold Marta responsible for wanting to bring Miguel to this country when he was doing fine in his country of origin. Carlos was angry that the family now had to deal with the "American system" and felt that his personal control was being compromised. Marta mentioned that her sister Flora had been quite helpful to her by listening and letting her "discharge" her emotions. Flora had also offered to allow Miguel to live with her (and her husband and her in-laws), so that he would not have to go to a foster home.

Marta told me repeatedly that she had made numerous attempts to get Chabita to talk about what was bothering her. She maintained vehemently that she had never observed her son's physical aggression toward Chabita. In fact, she noted that Chabita and Miguel never wanted to be together and that she often encouraged them to act more like brother and sister and to spend time or go out together. Apparently, Chabita stayed away from Miguel when her mother was present and usually spent most of her time in her room. Marta reported that Miguel was raised by his maternal grandparents in a small village in Central America and had never sought much contact with his parents. He did not like talking on the phone with his mother or father, although there were monthly phone calls to inquire about his progress.

Marta and her husband had come to this country 12 years earlier (when Miguel was 3 years old). They felt it would be better for them to come without the child and to devote themselves to working and making money. Marta became pregnant unexpectedly, and, in spite of Carlos's objections to having the child, Chabita was born in this country. Chabita was also taken back to Central America and was cared for by mother's parents for the first two years of her life. When Carlos and Marta felt they could afford to have Chabita come to the States, they sent for her, but decided that Miguel was doing fine and could be brought later. (Marta added that Miguel, as a boy, was better able to fend for himself, but Chabita, as a girl, would require more of her mother's attention when she was young.) By then, Marta's sister and brother had also migrated to this country, and her sister offered to help with child care for a small stipend. Marta and Carlos had always hoped to have Miguel join them when they were financially stable and finally brought him to this country when he was 13, two years prior to this referral.

Apparently, Miguel did not want to come, did not speak English, and was very attached to his grandparents. He was sullen and distant from the beginning and apparently had not made an easy transition at school. Marta complained that Miguel had gotten in with "the wrong crowd," older kids who influenced him to make mischief.

Miguel had been arrested once for petty theft and disorderly conduct. Marta noted that Miguel's friends were older, and both Marta and her husband had given up trying to get him to follow rules around the house or to return on time. "Not even whippings helped anything. He did what he wanted, and my husband said he would have to return to his grandparents, who could handle him." Marta refused to accept that Miguel was "a bad child," and committed herself to showing him that he was loved by buying him special presents, giving him spending money, and overlooking his resistance to doing household chores. Marta and Carlos have each worked two jobs as far back as they could remember, and they sent money home to support both sets of parents and a few siblings. Their general goal appeared to be to save enough money to buy a house, so that they could take care of their elderly parents in this country.

Until Chabita was 5, Marta's sister took care of her during the day. As soon as Chabita was about 7 years old, Marta left her at home alone, asserting that she was a "good child," "didn't mind being by herself," and was "never in trouble until now." I noted that Chabita was not "in trouble," but that she had been victimized by her brother and had gone through a painful and difficult experience. "I know," Marta responded, "but now the family is in trouble because of what's happened to her." I again responded that Chabita had not done anything wrong and that it was positive that she had been able to tell someone at school about what was going on, so that the abuse could stop. I also told her that Miguel obviously had some problems with anger and would need specialized help because what he had done to Chabita was very serious and dangerous. Marta cried inconsolably, but did mutter that "Miguel has a sickness, it's true." She did not ask any questions about Chabita and what she could do for her; however, questions about Miguel abounded. "When will they set him free? Will he go to jail? Should we send him back home?" I did not have answers for her, but told her I would try to find out what I could and would be available to her to help in any way that I could.

Marta was not a reliable source of information about Chabita's medical or developmental history, saying that she could not remember much. She stated that she had had a normal pregnancy and that Chabita was born at home with her sister's help. Chabita did not have regular medical attention, but had colds from time to time. Marta described her as "self-reliant" since she was small. Reportedly, Chabita knew how to cook and often had a warm meal ready for her parents when they arrived home late. She had done very well at school and gotten good grades. She also liked to read and constantly brought home books from the school library. When I asked Marta what Chabita liked to read, she said she did not know. When I asked what kind of contact she had with her child's teacher, she said she always went to the meeting at the start of the year and after that the school never really called her because "everything was fine with Chabita." She noted that this was not the case with Miguel and that the school was always calling with complaints about her son. The school had recommended therapy for Miguel, but Marta commented she did not know where to find a counselor and could not afford therapy. She took this as an opportunity to ask how much it would cost for Chabita for therapy. I informed her that she could fill out financial statements and that we could use a sliding-scale fee. Our program also has the good fortune to have scholarship money, so no one is turned away for financial reasons. Marta looked visibly relieved when I gave her this information.

ASSESSMENT

Marta's reading skills in English and Spanish were equally low. I read and explained several items of the Spanish version of the Child Behavior Checklist (CBCL) (Achenbach & Edelbrock, 1983), and we completed it together. The CBCL showed elevated scores in the areas of depression and anxiety. Chabita's social worker agreed to help her fill out the Trauma Symptom Checklist for Children (TSCC) (Briere, 1989), which was mailed to me prior to my first visit with Chabita. The TSCC revealed clinically significant scores in the areas of depression, anxiety, and sexual distress. I also translated and helped Marta complete the Child Sexual Behavior Inventory, which showed no clinical significance. Marta's inability to respond to many of the items of the Behavioral and Emotional Rating Scale dramatically confirmed her lack of familiarity with her daughter's personality traits, interests, or strengths.

CASE FORMULATION

Several cultural issues emerge as salient in this case. Quite often, siblings in Central-American families are raised separately from their biological parents. Frequently, parents travel to the United States to establish economic stability to either support extended family members or eventually help them come to the United States. Limited resources and opportunities spur many Central Americans to idealize the "American dream," which often provides minimum political stability and work options. This migration to the United States produces family situations in which young children are separated from their known primary caretakers and reunited with them after many years of separation, rendering them virtual strangers to each other. The "incest inhibition mechanism" that Finkelhor (1984) described does not become well-established. Siblings close in age may perceive each other as peers or friends rather than as relatives. In addition, sibling jealousy may arise among children who are selected to make the initial trip to the States with their parents and those left behind.

Parents arriving in the United States experience great pressure to establish themselves economically. To make ends meet, they often take whatever jobs they can, earning low wages and working exceptionally long hours. Children are expected to be autonomous and self-reliant and to contribute to the family goal of stabilization by cooking or caring for younger siblings. To build an economic foundation for their family, Chabita's parents had woefully neglected their children's emotional and spiritual development and created an expectable level of emotional distance, which emerged from a systemic commitment to work, survival, and providing for extended family members. Both parents had thrown themselves into a relentless schedule that allowed for little attention to emotional sustenance or growth.

Marta and Carlos were physically and emotionally unavailable to their children and did not have the insight to attend to the conflicts that arose when Miguel was integrated into the family. They simply assumed that Miguel would be happy to be home with his parents and that whatever difficulties he experienced would pass with time. They minimized the toll that Miguel would face by leaving his known caretakers, trying to learn English, meeting new family members, and shifting from a situation in which he felt competent to one in which he experienced helplessness and dependency. When Miguel asked questions about school or social difficulties, Marta and Carlos would tell him to ask Chabita for information. This created additional resentment for Miguel, and his therapist later told me that Miguel had felt that his masculinity was compromised by having to depend on Chabita.

Miguel was treated with great leniency by the justice system. He was placed on probation, ordered into juvenile-sex-offender treatment, and allowed to live with his maternal aunt. He was not permitted contact with Chabita and to date expresses little willingness to participate in an "accountability" session, in which he would assume responsibility for his behavior and ask for Chabita's forgiveness. His therapist reports that little progress has been made even one and a half years later.

EARLY INTERVENTION

The initial intervention at the Abused Children's Treatment Services (ACTS) involves conducting a developmental assessment to consider the impact of trauma on a child's functioning and to tailor a treatment plan based on an understanding of the unique coping strategies of each child. The developmental assessment includes nondirective play therapy designed to allow children to establish a sense of safety by not placing demands on them, following their interests (activities), creating opportunities for mastery, and encouraging the use of internal resources and controls. In addition, because most children who come to ACTS have been interviewed by a number of investigative personnel (child protective services and/or police), they are wary of questions and reticent to repeat their stories yet again. A nondirective approach removes the focus from verbal expression. At the same time, staff assure children that their counselors work with children who have been touched or hurt in their private parts.

Chabita appeared extremely shy and withdrawn and, over time, shifted to reserved and guarded affect-expression. She never became affectively expansive, although some progress occurred. Marta commented on her daughter's change as she became more relaxed and less isolated. During our initial sessions, Chabita's depressive symptoms were most obvious and were followed by a hypervigilant stance and heightened startle response, as evidenced by her flinching at any loud and unexpected noises. She was initially hesitant to play or explore the play therapy room, but eventually responded to a variety of play techniques, including sand therapy, art therapy, puppet play, dollhouse play, and board games. In sand therapy, children are directed to use as few or as many miniatures as they wish to build a "world"—a scenario in a sand box containing fine white sand and painted blue on the bottom (Labovitz Boik & Goodwin, 2000). Art therapy provides opportunities for creating lines, shapes, colors, or representational art using a continuum of media from fluid to rigid (Malchiodi, 1998; Rubin, 1978). Board games include the "Talking, Feeling, Doing Game" (Gardner, 1983), in which children respond to a variety of questions about their thoughts or feelings or are instructed to act out situations to earn chips and get closer to the finish line. In physical activities, children exercise opportunities to run, jump, kick balls, or play structured games such as hockey and basketball. Relaxation techniques (Allen & Klein, 1996; Williams, 1996) encourage children to use guided imagery and visualization to calm themselves as well as teach them how to constrict and release muscle groups, so that a feeling of physical relaxation follows. Generic play therapy includes puppets, a dollhouse, and a variety of other props, such as feeling cards, arts and crafts, masks, and musical instruments. The play-therapy room is stocked with those toys generally used by play therapists, but also contains a replica of a courtroom, because so many children testify in court, and a toy hospital and ambulance, because the children who come to our program have recently had a medical exam at a nearby hospital.

Chabita was initially diagnosed as manifesting the symptoms of Dysthymic Disorder (*DSM-IV*, 300.4; APA, 1994). The following play activities supported this diagnosis as well as the presence of anxious features associated with the stress of living in a violent home environment with few emotional supports. Chabita's initial sand scenarios depicted a small animal "lost" in a forest. The small animal (cat) was placed in the corner of the sand box surrounded by large trees. "He got lost," Chabita stated. Chabita then constructed a village with many structures and two rainbows. When I inquired how the animal had gotten lost, or what it was like to be lost, she simply replied, "He's little. They don't see him." She did not sustain dialogues, but often simply looked away and continued to play. I did not insist on her talking to me, but felt that her sand scenarios spoke volumes about her fear and isolation. Not until three or four months into therapy did this scenario begin to include a fence with a door so that the animal could enter and exit at will. The singular animal used during the first few sand trays later became a "duo": a cat and, as she described the dog, "his friend who keeps him company."

Chabita's initial drawings also depicted isolation. Next to a picture of a house with no windows or doors, she drew a floating body and explained, "That's me, I don't draw good." I told her that her picture was very clearly a house and a person, and I thought she had made a good effort to draw it, even though she didn't think she drew very well. "It's not so bad," she added. "I think it's very well done," I replied and took great pleasure seeing this child smile when I put her picture inside a black frame and gave it to her. Her mother told me she asked that it be hung in her room.

I asked Chabita to complete the World Test, which provides a visual representation of a child's perception of external resources (people in her world). The results of the World Test were stunning: She listed her teacher as a resource and no one else. She also did not include herself in the primary group of circles, but placed herself in a corner of the page. As Chabita became less depressed and felt more safe with me, I began more directive abuse-specific work. I used play themes and play activities to decrease her anxiety, to activate hope, and to facilitate expression of affect. I also attempted to broaden her resource base. Toward that end, we arranged conjoint parent-child sessions with her mother, so they could experience new and pleasurable interactions with each other. Carlos was unwilling to participate throughout the therapy process with Chabita, but was court-ordered to attend family sessions with Miguel. Miguel's therapist reported that Carlos found it impossible to be open in the group or to actively participate in group discussions, although his attendance was good.

Chabita made good use of art. She was able to spread bold colors across large pieces of paper following my directives to show her anger, her sadness, her happy feelings. One day, she did a spontaneous picture of Miguel (she had often refused to make a family picture), and then she covered the figure with bold black strokes. When the figure disappeared, she crumpled up the wet painting and jammed it into a full trash can. When I asked her to put words to the motion of stuffing the painting in the trash, she exclaimed, "Be gone with you. Be gone with you now!"

We used puppets to role-play what Chabita wanted to say to Miguel but had never been able to. Initially, her voice was small as she said, "You were bad to hurt me. I'm not scared of you no more." Together, we made a megaphone with construction paper, and eventually she was able to shout loudly and freely. During the first session with the megaphone, she seemed to physically relax after yelling. We audiotaped what she wanted to say to Miguel, and we would often listen to it in session. Once, she spontaneously uttered, "All right!" She responded well to relaxation techniques and guided imagery. She spent many hours "in her head." She easily imagined herself elsewhere; she created a "safe place" on the beach, and could quickly and easily fantasize herself there when she felt tense or scared.

I showed Chabita some videotapes about child abuse, emotional abuse, secrets, fear, and expression of feelings (J. Gary Mitchell Film Company, Sebastopol, California). She easily discussed the situations in the videotapes. In contrast to her generally guarded stance, she projected her thoughts and feelings onto characters in the tapes. She showed great empathy for and insight about others. I would constantly challenge her to think about situations that had been similar for herself.

We seemed to be speaking in code for most of our time together, but I noticed slight changes in Chabita's willingness to assert her own thoughts and feelings. She expressed herself by using words conservatively. She called between sessions once to report that her cousin had been killed in a car accident. Her reaching out attested to a newfound ability to identify personal needs and to mobilize resources to get help for herself. I thanked and praised her for calling me and asked her permission to speak with her mother, whom I then coached to provide Chabita with physical comfort and special attention. Marta herself was clearly overcome with grief, and we scheduled a joint emergency session to talk about grieving. Marta brought her sister to the session as well, also demonstrating an appropriate use of reaching out for help.

TREATMENT PLAN AND TIME FRAMES

A developmental assessment may take anywhere from 4 to 10 sessions. Children are allowed to express as much or as little as they want and to choose their play activities. The context of therapy is always made specific by telling child clients that we work with sexually abused children. Children are told they will not be asked questions initially, but that their counselors are available to answer any questions. Clinicians introduce children to play-therapy opportunities and remain emotionally present and willing to help and support children. Occasionally, a clinician will verbalize a child's activities, so that a youngster feels seen and heard. Rogerian principles of client-centered therapy serve as a foundation for child-centered therapy (Landreth & Sweeney, 1997), promoting communication of four basic messages: "I am here, I hear you, I understand, and I care" (p. 44).

Once assessment reveals the unique fashion in which a child has had stressful experiences such as abuse or parental neglect, a clinician tailors a treatment plan to meet his or her needs. The play therapist develops goals that are then promoted through the use of play techniques, often working in metaphor, rather than stripping the child of critical defensive mechanisms. For example, when Chabita sets up a scenario in which a cat is secluded and "lost," I trust that she is speaking about her own experiences. Rather than rushing to provide the lost cat with directions, I allow her the time to access her own internal resources and thus to become more self-reliant. Chabita eventually found a "friend" for the cat; this might have symbolized the therapeutic relationship or her newly enhanced relationship with her mother.

Because Chabita's primary symptoms indicated depression (flat affect, self-isolation, lack of appetite, and oversleeping), I attempted to address those symptoms in a variety of ways. These included more emotional and physical contact with her mother, physical activities in the play-therapy room, such as throwing a ball and playing hockey in our gym, and focusing her on activities like painting that offered her a feeling of competence and satisfaction. I also recommended that the school counselor see Chabita once a week to assure her that she had resources in both school and home environments. Chabita responded to individualized attention and gradually appeared less sad and pessimistic.

I observed that, in addition to dysthymic problems, Chabita also exhibited anxious features and frequently seemed hypervigilant and jumpy. She reacted positively both to guided imagery and to relaxation techniques. I gave her the homework task of teaching her mother one of the techniques. Together, we translated one of the written relaxation exercises that she liked, and we made an audiotape to take home and play for her mother. The concept of relaxation seemed odd for Marta, but I had called her ahead of time and asked her to set aside a half-hour for Chabita. Marta reported that she was pleasantly surprised about the exercise, but that she had not used it since the first time she heard the tape.

Chabita needed abuse-specific work as well. She benefited greatly from watching a videotape of four children who spoke about their experiences (Shapiro, 1994). She identified strongly with a sexually abused girl who happened to look very much like her. As we watched, she would comment, "I felt that way" and "I know the answer." We also reviewed several lessons from a comprehensive child sexual abuse prevention model called "Good Touch/Bad Touch." I concentrated on those lessons that reinforced her telling about abuse. This promoted an understanding that "most touch is good." We made a list of all the kinds of touch that were positive and desirable and all that were uncomfortable or hurtful. I was keenly aware that Chabita did not have "quality time" with either parent and that they were not physically affectionate people. In one of the guided-imagery exercises, I encouraged her to imagine a nurturing parent and to identify those behaviors that would make her feel cared for. She identified a very loving grandmother who used to "squeeze" her so hard she had to hold her breath. She also acknowledged that her own parents did not really like to be "huggy," and that her mother did not respond to my coaching, as she seemed to feel uncomfortable with showing physical affection. Marta did indicate that she loved to make time to cook with Chabita and that she was able to attend to her in that way.

Chabita realized very clearly that Miguel's behavior was inappropriate or "bad" and that she had not done anything wrong. I helped her understand that people are not good or bad, but that their behaviors can be labeled that way. Eventually, she came to admit that she liked Miguel when he was nice to her (apparently, very sporadically), but that she did not like his hitting her or using his penis to hurt her.

The assessment phase with Chabita lasted two months. The directive therapy occurred over a five-month period. Finally, to ensure that Chabita did not feel stigmatized because of her abuse, I referred her to a 12-week group-therapy process. Although she was very shy and withdrawn, other children were very positive toward her, and she tolerated the group process. "I didn't know this happened to other kids," she commented, "and sometimes it's the dad, not the brother . . . gross!"

I have made follow-up phone calls with Chabita and her mother, and they seem to be doing well. Marta has been able to cut back on her jobs and tells me she is feeling less stressed. The marital relationship continues to be strained, at best, and Marta speaks about it with resignation. Marta says that she now realizes that Miguel is a very complicated youth who needs more help than she can provide. She has a trusting relationship with Miguel's therapist and is still considering sending him back to live with his grandparents in Central America once his probationary period is over. Miguel has had no contact with Chabita, and she states that she has little interest in reestablishing contact.

SUMMARY

Chabita, a sexually abused Hispanic child, was terrorized by a disturbed and angry older brother, Miguel. After the abuse was disclosed, Miguel was removed to an aunt's home and has been in juvenile sex-offending therapy for the past year and a half, with guarded progress. Several cultural issues complicated the treatment for this child. The parents had been separated from their teenage son for 13 years and were unable to facilitate his successful integration into the family system. Both parents had severe demands on their time and emotional energies. They were seeking to establish and build economic stability that would allow them to help extended family members. The parents displayed a pattern of emotional distance that was normalized by their joint goal of self-sacrifice and extreme, unrealistic work demands. They felt under intense pressure to secure economic freedom and comfort.

Chabita's birth was not planned. Her father had actually suggested an abortion, for which her mother never forgave him. The parents have not been sexual with each other for years, and the mother indicated calmly that she assumed her husband engaged in extramarital affairs, for which she claims apathy and relief. When I inquired if she had ever considered separation or divorce, she replied this was out of the question: "We don't believe in divorce." I was never able to recruit the father's participation in therapy even after a hopeful phone conversation. His belief that therapy amounts to "superstition" never changed.

The mother-child relationship was initially distant and cold, mostly because of the mother's discomfort with physical affection as well as her limited time and energy. I used some of the principles of filial therapy (L. Guerney, 1997) to enhance their emotional closeness. In addition, I gave Marta and Chabita the opportunity to participate in some family-play-therapy tasks to facilitate joint pleasurable experiences (Gil & Sobol, 2000). Marta was sporadically involved with Chabita, and her progress was good, although not ideal.

Chabita made adequate strides over the course of therapy. I feel that our relationship allowed her to experience the possibilities of unconditional support, validation, encouragement, and safety. Her relationship with her school counselor became stable and rewarding. Chabita is virtually asymptomatic at this time. She views her mother as a greater resource than she did initially. She has developed the ability to self-comfort as well as to express herself through painting. As a termination gift, I presented Chabita with a set of paints and an easel.

LIMITATIONS OF NONDIRECTIVE PLAY THERAPY

Some children do not respond to play therapy, although in my experience, these are few and far between. There are several reasons this can occur. Some children are comfortable talking with adults and seem to enjoy the chance of sitting with a therapist and engaging in a therapeutic dialogue. Others, even latency-age children, may regard toys or play activities as "child play" and may feel unwilling to participate with play. Still others may use initial play activities to calm themselves when feeling anxious about meeting with a therapist; once calm, they will discard play in favor of dialogue. Some child clients seem to have limited interest or capacity to engage in symbolic play and prefer generic play such as ball throwing, Lego building, or reenactments of recreational activities (e.g., skateboarding). With some behavioral problems or symptomatic behaviors, generic play may have limited value. Especially when working with abused children, a combination of nondirective and directive techniques will likely be required to meet designated goals.

On occasion, children appear to feel overwhelmed by the number of choices available in a play-therapy room. Children with Attention-Deficit/Hyperactivity Disorder, in particular, may feel overstimulated and become agitated, going from one play activity to another with disorganized fervor. In such cases, clinicians might obtain more cooperation if they select a few toys and move to an office with fewer choices. Some children use play as a way to avoid addressing disturbing emotions or behaviors. In these cases, clinicians might negotiate a balance of a session, so that play-therapy work is done in one portion and generic play or free play in the other. For example, a child who is having problems with aggression at school and who feels unwilling to discuss this concern in therapy may opt instead to paint pictures or construct standard puppet stories. Therapists can listen to a child's unscripted puppet story and then ask a child to compose a story with the theme of aggression between friends. They may also accept free paintings some of the time and request specific drawings such as Kinetic Family Drawings and others that might elicit images of affective states or concerns (Webb, 1991).

Just as many children do not require or may not fully utilize play therapy, therapists may not feel capable of conducting play therapy. Some clinicians believe that little preparation is required to offer play therapy because many toys, such as paper and crayons, dollhouses, puppets, and board games, have been standard equipment in the offices of many therapists who work with families. At the same time, to achieve full benefits of play therapy, clinicians must obtain additional training that maximizes their understanding of this therapy as a primary or adjunctive therapy approach. Many universities are now providing graduate courses in play therapy, and workshops and conferences are offered to provide continuing education credits in this area. As more and more professionals develop a higher comfort level and feel more competent in the use of play therapy, this medium may become more integrated as a standard credible and substantive therapeutic theory and approach.

Play therapy constitutes one of the few therapeutic modalities that inherently provide pleasure and a sense of well-being even when exploring difficult, emotionally charged issues. Those who utilize play therapy routinely with children and their families are constantly impressed with the positive outcome of addressing painful material within a context of safety and enjoyment. Play therapists assist children and families by allowing and encouraging them to experience rewarding interactions with each other, deepen their communication through symbols and metaphors, and change their often limited perceptions of each other.

Sexually abused children, in particular, are often resistant to verbal communication, either because they have been told not to speak or because they sense that sexual abuse is not discussable. Frequently, as a result of an initial disclosure, children are exposed to multiple interviewers who conduct lengthy interviews, thus adding to the demands placed on a child. Play therapists are best equipped to overlook the necessity of verbal communication in favor of communication and processing that can occur via play. Play therapists may use a combination of directive and nondirective techniques to balance concerns about colluding with the child's natural tendency to deny or minimize problems. Chabita once noted, "It was fun to come and see you even when we were talking about yucky stuff."

RESEARCH

Bratton and Ray (2000) chronicled 82 studies supporting the effectiveness of play therapy techniques. They pointed out, however, that "play therapy research lacks credibility in a few areas of what is considered hard research" (p. 81). They appealed to play therapists to design and conduct research studies to "investigate both the immediate and long-term effects of play therapy. Specifically . . . there is a need to compare its effectiveness with other child psychotherapeutic techniques" (p. 81).

REFERENCES

Achenbach, T. M., & Edelbrock, C. (1983). *Manual for the Child Behavior Checklist and the revised Child Behavior Profile.* Burlington: University of Vermont, Department of Psychiatry.

Allan, J. (1997). Jungian play psychotherapy. In K. J. O'Connor & L. M. Braverman (Eds.), *Play therapy: Theory and practice* (pp. 100–131). New York: Wiley.

Allen, J., & Klein, R. (1996). *Ready, set, relax.* Watertown, WI: Innercoaching.

American Psychiatric Association. (1994). *Diagnostic and statistical manual of mental disorders* (4th ed.). Washington, DC: Author.

Amster, F. (1982). Differential uses of play in treatment of young children. In G. L. Landreth (Ed.), *Play therapy: Dynamics of the process of counseling with children* (pp. 33–42). Springfield, IL: Charles C. Thomas.

Ariel, S. (1994). *Strategic family play therapy* (2nd ed.). Chichester, England: Wiley.

Axline, V. (1947). *Play therapy.* Boston: Houghton Mifflin.

Axline, V. (1955). Play therapy procedures and results. *American Journal of Orthopsychiatry, 25,* 618–626.

Bailey, C. E. (Ed.). (2000). *Children in therapy.* New York: Norton.

Berliner, L., & Saunders, B. (1996). Treating fear and anxiety in sexually abused children: Results of a controlled 2-year follow-up study. *Child Maltreatment, 1*(4), 294–309.

Bowlby, J. (1980). *Attachment and loss. Volume III: Loss: Sadness and depression.* New York: Basic Books.

Bratton, S., & Ray, D. (2000). What the research shows about play therapy. *International Journal of Play Therapy, 9*(1), 47–88.

Brenner, A. (1984). *Helping children cope with stress.* New York: Lexington Books.

Briere, J. N. (1989). *Trauma Symptom Checklist for Children.* Los Angeles: University of Southern California School of Medicine, Department of Psychiatry.

Briere, J. N. (1992). *Child abuse trauma: Theory and treatment of the lasting effects.* Thousand Oaks, CA: Sage.

Brody, V. (1992). The dialogue of touch: Developmental play therapy. *International Journal of Play Therapy, 1*(1), 21–30.

Brody, V. (1997). Developmental play therapy. In K. J. O'Connor & L. M. Braverman (Eds.), *Play therapy: Theory and practice* (pp. 160–183). New York: Wiley.

Cattanach, A. (1993). *Play therapy with abused children.* London: Jessica Kingsley.

Ciottone, R. A., & Madonna, J. M. (1996). *Play therapy with sexually abused children: A synergistic clinical-developmental approach.* Northvale, NJ: Aronson.

Cohen, J. A., & Mannarino, A. P. (1996). Factors that mediate treatment outcome of sexually abused preschool children. *Journal of the American Academy of Child and Adolescent Psychiatry, 34*(10), 402–410.

Cohen, J. A., & Mannarino, A. P. (1998). Interventions for sexually abused children: Initial treatment outcome findings. *Child Maltreatment 3*(1), 17–26.

Deblinger, E., & Heflin, A. H. (1996). *Treating sexually abused children and their nonoffending parents: A cognitive approach.* Thousand Oaks, CA: Sage.

Deblinger, E., McLeer, M. D., & Henry, D. (1990). Cognitive behavioral treatment for sexually abused children suffering post-traumatic stress: Preliminary findings. *Journal of the American Academy of Child and Adolescent Psychiatry, 29*(5), 747–752.

De Domenico, G. (1994). Jungian play therapy techniques. In K. J. O'Connor & C. E. Schaefer (Eds.), *Handbook of play therapy: Advances and innovations* (pp. 253–282). New York: Wiley.

Erikson, E. (1950). *Childhood and society.* New York: Norton.

Finkelhor, D. (1984). *Child sexual abuse: New theory and research.* New York: Free Press.

Freud, A. (1928). *Introduction to the technique of child analysis* (L. P. Clark, Trans.). New York: Nervous and Mental Diseases.

Friedrich, W. N. (1995). *Psychotherapy with sexually abused boys: An integrated approach.* Thousand Oaks, CA: Sage.

Gardner, R. A. (1983). The Talking, Feeling, and Doing game. In C. E. Schaefer & K. J. O'Connor (Eds.), *Handbook of play therapy* (pp. 251–258), New York: Wiley.

Gil, E. (1991). *The healing power of play: Working with abused children.* New York: Guilford Press.

Gil, E. (1994). *Play in family therapy.* New York: Guilford Press.

Gil, E. (1998). Understanding and responding to post-trauma play. *Association for Play Therapy Newsletter, 17*(1), 7–10.

Gil, E., & Bogart, K. (1982, January/February). Foster children speak out: A study of children's perceptions of foster care. *Children Today,* 11–1.

Gil, E., & Sobol, B. (2000). Engaging families in therapeutic play. In C. E. Bailey (Ed.), *Children in therapy: Using the family as a resource* (pp. 341–382). New York: Norton.

Guerney, B. G., Jr. (1964). Filial therapy: Description and rationale. *Journal of Consulting Psychology, 28*(4), 303–310.

Guerney, L. (1997). Filial therapy. In K. J. O'Connor & L. M. Braverman (Eds.), *Play therapy: Theory and practice* (pp. 131–159). New York: Wiley.

Guerney, L. (2000). Filial therapy into the 21st century. *International Journal of Play Therapy, 9*(2), 1–17.

Hambridge, G. (1955). Structured play therapy. *American Journal of Orthopsychiatry, 25,* 601–617.

Harvey, S. (1990). Dynamic play therapy: An integrated expressive arts approach to the family therapy of young children. *Arts in Psychotherapy, 17*(3), 239–246.

Hug-Hellmuth, H. (1921). On the technique of child analysis. *International Journal of Psycho-Analysis, 2,* 287–305.

James, B. (1994). *Handbook for treatment of attachment-trauma problems in children.* New York: Lexington Books.

Jewett, C. L. (1982). *Helping children cope with separation and loss.* Harvard, MA: Harvard Common Press.

Johnson, K. (1989). *Trauma in the lives of children: Crisis and stress management techniques for teachers, counselors, and student service professionals.* Claremont, CA: Hunter House.

Jung, C. (1961). *Memories, dreams, and reflections.* New York: Vintage.

Kaduson, H. G., Cangelosi, D., & Schaefer, C. (Eds.). (1997). *The playing cure: Individualized play therapy for specific childhood problems.* New York: Aronson.

Kendall-Tackett, K. A., Williams, L. M., & Finkelhor, D. (1993). Impact of sexual abuse on children: A review and synthesis of recent empirical studies. *Psychological Bulletin, 113*(1), 164–180.

Klein, M. (1932). *The psychoanalysis of children.* London: Hogarth Press.

Knell, S. M. (1993). *Cognitive-behavioral play therapy.* Northvale, NJ: Aronson.

Knell, S. M. (1997). Cognitive-behavioral play therapy. In K. J. O'Connor & L. M. Braverman (Eds.), *Play therapy: Theory and practice* (pp. 79–97). New York: Wiley.

Kottman, T., & Schaefer, C. (Eds.). (1993). *Play therapy in action: A casebook for practitioners.* New York: Aronson.

Kottman, T., & Warlick, J. (1990). Adlerian play therapy. *Journal of Humanistic Education and Development, 28,* 69–83.

Labovitz Boik, B., & Goodwin, E. A. (2000). *Sandplay therapy: A step-by-step manual for psychotherapists of diverse orientations.* New York: Norton.

Landreth, G. L. (Ed.). (1982). *Play therapy: Dynamics of the process of counseling with children.* Springfield, IL: Charles C. Thomas.

Landreth, G. L. (1991). *Play therapy: The art of the relationship.* Muncie, IN: Accelerated Development.

Landreth, G. L. (1993). Self-expressive communication. In C. E. Schaefer (Ed.), *The therapeutic powers of play* (pp. 41–63). New York: Aronson.

Landreth, G. L., Homeyer, L. E., Glover, G., & Sweeney, D. S. (1996). *Play therapy interventions with children's problems: Case studies with DSM-IV diagnoses.* New York: Aronson.

Landreth, G. L., & Sweeney, D. S. (1997). Child-centered play therapy. In K. J. O'Connor & L. M. Braverman (Eds.), *Play therapy: Theory and practice* (pp. 17–45). New York: Wiley.

Lee, A. C. (1997). Psychoanalytic play therapy. In K. J. O'Connor & C. E. Schaefer (Eds.), *Handbook of play therapy: Advances and innovations* (pp. 46–78). New York: Wiley.

Levy, D. (1938). Release therapy in young children. *Psychiatry, 1,* 387–389.

Malchiodi, C. A. (1998). *Understanding children's drawings.* New York: Guilford Press.

Martin, H. P. (Ed.). (1976). *The abused child: A multidisciplinary approach to developmental issues and treatment.* Boston: Ballinger.

Marvasti, J. A. (1993). Please hurt me again: Posttraumatic play therapy with an abused child. In T. Kottman & C. Schaefer (Eds.), *Play therapy in action: A casebook for practitioners* (pp. 485–525). Northvale, NJ: Aronson.

Marvasti, J. A. (1994). Play diagnosis and play therapy with child victims of incest. In K. J. O'Connor & C. E. Schaefer (Eds.), *Handbook of play therapy: Advances and innovations* (pp. 253–282). New York: Wiley.

McMahon, L. (1992). *The handbook of play therapy.* London: Routledge.

Moustakas, C. (1959). *Psychotherapy with children.* New York: Harper & Row.

Oaklander, V. (1978). *Windows to our children: A Gestalt approach to children and adolescents.* New York: Gestalt Journal Press.

Oaklander, V. (1994). Gestalt play therapy. In K. J. O'Connor & C. E. Schaefer (Eds.), *Handbook of play therapy: Advances and innovations* (pp. 43–156). New York: Wiley.

O'Connor, K. J. (1998). Ecosystemic play therapy. In K. J. O'Connor & C. E. Schaefer (Eds.), *Handbook of play therapy: Advances and innovations* (pp. 61–84). New York: Wiley.

O'Connor, K. J., & Ammen, S. (1998). *Play therapy treatment planning and interventions: The ecosystemic model.* San Diego, CA: Academic Press.

O'Connor, K. J., & Braverman, L. M. (Eds.). (1997). *Play therapy theory and practice: A comparative presentation.* New York: Wiley.

Oliver James, O. (1997). *Play therapy: A comprehensive guide.* New York: Aronson.

Osmond, M., Durham, D., Leggett, A., & Keating, J. (1998). *Treating the aftermath of sexual abuse: A handbook for working with children in care.* Washington, DC: Child Welfare League of America.

Rank, O. (1936). *Will therapy.* New York: Knopf.

Rogers, C. R. (1939). *The clinical treatment of the problem child.* New York: Houghton Mifflin.

Rogers, C. R. (1951). *Client-centered therapy.* Boston: Houghton Mifflin.

Rubin, J. A. (1978). *Child art therapy: Understanding and helping children grow through art* (2nd ed.). New York: Van Nostrand-Reinhold.

Rutter, M. (1984, March). Resilient children. *Psychology Today,* 57–65.

Schaefer, C. E. (Ed.). (1993). *The therapeutic powers of play.* New York: Aronson.

Schaefer, C. E. (1994). Play therapy for psychic trauma in children. In K. J. O'Connor & C. E. Schaefer (Eds.), *Handbook of play therapy: Advances and innovations* (pp. 297–318). New York: Wiley.

Schaefer, C. E., & Carey, L. (Eds.). (1994). *Family play therapy.* Northvale, NJ: Aronson.

Schaefer, C. E., Gitlin, K., & Sandgrund, A. (1991). *Play diagnosis and assessment.* New York: Wiley.

Schaefer, C. E., & Millman, H. L. (1977). *Therapies for children.* San Francisco: Jossey-Bass.

Schaefer, C. E., & O'Connor, K. J. (Eds.). (1983). *Handbook of play therapy.* New York: Wiley.

Shapiro, A. (1994). *Breaking the silence: Kids against child abuse* [Videotape]. Minneapolis, MN: Community Interventions.

Smith, P., Perrin, S., & Yule, W. (1998). Post-traumatic stress disorders. In P. Graham (Ed.), *Cognitive-behaviour therapy for children and families* (pp. 127–142). Cambridge, MA: Cambridge University Press.

Solomon, J. C. (1938). Active play therapy. *American Journal of Orthopsychiatry, 8* 479–498.

Terr, L. C. (1981). Forbidden games: Post-traumatic child's play. *Journal of the American Academy of Child Psychiatry, 20,* 741–760.

Terr, L. C. (1983). *Play therapy and psychic trauma: A preliminary report.* In C. E. Schaefer & K. J. O'Connor (Eds.), *Handbook of play therapy* (pp. 308–319). New York: Wiley.

Terr, L. (1990). *Too scared to cry.* New York: Harper & Row.

Trepper, T. S., & Barrett, M. J. (1986). *Treating incest: A multiple systems perspective.* New York: Haworth Press.

Trepper, T. S., & Niedner, D. M. (1996). Intrafamilial child sexual abuse. In F. W. Kaslow (Ed.), *Handbook of relational diagnosis and dysfunctional family patterns* (pp. 394–406). New York: Wiley.

Vaughn Heineman, T. (1998). *The abused child: Psychodynamic understanding and treatment.* New York: Guilford Press.

Watkins, B., & Bentovim, A. (1992). The sexual abuse of male children and adolescents: A review of current research. *Journal of Child Psychology and Psychiatry, 33,* 197–248.

Webb, N. B. (1991). Play therapy crisis intervention with children. In N. B. Webb (Ed.), *Play therapy with children in crisis* (pp. 26–42). New York: Guilford Press.

Wener, E., & Smith, R. (1989). *Vulnerable but invincible: High risk children from birth to adulthood.* New York: Cornell University Press.

Williams, M. L. (1996). *Cool cats, calm kids.* Atascadero, CA: Impact.

Wolin, S., & Wolin, S. (1993). *The resilient self.* New York: Villard Books.

CHAPTER 4

Existential/Experiential Approaches to Child and Family Psychotherapy

VOLKER THOMAS

HISTORY

Child psychotherapy has been practiced almost as long as adult psychotherapy (A. Freud, 1928). Originally derived from psychoanalysis, child psychotherapy developed along several different branches (Adler, 1930; A. Freud, 1946; S. Freud, 1933; Klein, 1932). The use of language distinguishes child from adult psychotherapy: Adult psychotherapy involves mainly talk therapy; an adult client and therapist cognitively process internal and external experiences, thoughts, and emotions by putting them into verbal language and converse about them during the therapeutic process. Young children have limited skills for verbal articulation and for cognitively processing complex therapeutic interpretations. For them, adult therapeutic conversations do not prove very effective. Thus, therapists accepted alternative avenues through which children can express themselves and process interactions with adults and other children. Play provides the preferred medium through which children can process their experiences and communicate their thoughts, feelings, and worldview. Play constitutes the internal and external language through which children present themselves experientially.

The historical routes of existential-experiential child psychotherapy have flowed from three perspectives: psychoanalytic-psychodynamic, cognitive-behavioral, and systems-oriented. These approaches all utilize play for entering children's worlds and for providing therapeutic opportunities responsive to children's needs to express themselves and to experience the world in age-appropriate ways. Although the three approaches employ the same therapeutic medium, their underlying philosophies differ markedly. Psychoanalytic-psychodynamic child psychotherapists focus on the internal emotional and cognitive processes while encouraging a child to display them through play. Cognitive-behavioral child psychotherapists aim at changing a child's behavior and thoughts in a direction that adults prefer. Systems-oriented child psychotherapy or family play therapy centers around the interactional patterns and relationships a child has established with significant people in his or her life, usually other family members; the goal of therapy lies in changing the interactional patterns in a desired direction and improving relationships between a child and other family members.

Psychoanalytic-Psychodynamic Approaches to Child Psychotherapy

Child-focused psychotherapy links inevitably back to Sigmund Freud and his treatment of Little Hans (S. Freud, 1933). However, Freud did not work directly with Hans, but through written correspondence with Hans's father (Kratochwill & Morris, 1991). Hermine von Hug-Hellmuth introduced the idea of working directly with a child by engaging in play (O'Connor & Schaefer, 1994; Schaefer & O'Connor, 1983). In the 1930s and 1940s, Anna Freud (1928, 1946) and Melanie Klein (1932) applied their advances in child theory to clinical work with children. While A. Freud encouraged children to verbalize their inner lives (Landreth, 1991), Klein viewed play as symbolic of a child's unconscious, and helped children through interpretation of their play (Brown & Prout, 1989). Alfred Adler's work on the significance of a child's position in a family and on the influence of parents, teachers, and peers on the development of social interest, as he demonstrated through interviewing children in front of their parents and teachers in schools, also influenced the development of psychoanalytic-psychodynamic child psychotherapy at that time (Adler, 1956; Schaefer & Carey, 1994; Schaefer & O'Connor, 1983). After World War II, Virginia Axline, in her classic book, *Play Therapy* (1947), further advanced psychoanalytic thinking in clinical work with children. Her principles of play therapy have become the foundation for all recent approaches to child psychotherapy. Clark Moustakas (1959) built on Axline's theory and expanded the focus to the child-therapist relationship.

Cognitive-Behavioral Child Psychotherapy

Behavioral child psychotherapists applied the principles of classical conditioning, operant conditioning, and social learning theory (Bandura, 1977) to clinical work with children. Cognitive therapy derives from Beck (1976), who developed a structured approach with the goal of changing clients' thinking and perceptions, ultimately leading to behavioral changes. More recently, many behavioral therapists have applied cognitive-behavioral therapy to working with children. For Knell (1994), one of its leading proponents, cognitive-behavioral therapy "offers a potentially powerful method for children to learn to change their own behavior and to become active participants in treatment" (p. 112). Knell offered principles focusing more on children's affective experiences and how they perceive them in interaction with their environment. Contrary to traditional psychoanalytic child therapy, in which a child was subject to interpretations by a therapist, cognitive-behavioral therapists encourage a child's existential experiences as they are played out in concrete perceptions and behaviors.

Systems-Oriented Child and Family Psychotherapy

As a reaction to the internal focus of psychoanalysis and the individual focus of behaviorism, systems-oriented approaches to therapy for individuals and families developed in the 1950s and 1960s. Bateson's (Bateson, Haley, Jackson, & Weakland, 1956) research on schizophrenia proposed that child problems do not originate within a child's psyche, but represent an expression of certain interactional patterns commonly occurring in families. General systems theory (von Bertalanffy, 1968) provided the theoretical underpinnings for Bateson's assertions. Several approaches to family therapy that focus on existential-experiential aspects of child-adult interaction emerged based on Bateson's and von Bertalanffy's work (Bailey, 2000; Freeman, Epston, & Lobovits, 1997; Johnson & Lee, 2000; Keith & Whitaker, 1994).

This brief historical review shows a clear development of child psychotherapy as helping children use their inner resources, express and experience them in the safe environment of the therapeutic relationship, and incorporate their social environment into the therapeutic process. The following discussion of the underlying therapeutic constructs illustrates this development more clearly.

EXISTENTIAL-EXPERIENTIAL APPROACHES AND RELATED CONSTRUCTS

Carl Whitaker's symbolic-experiential family therapy, Susan Johnson's emotionally focused family therapy, and Michael White's narrative therapy are three of the major existential-experiential approaches to child and family psychotherapy.

WHITAKER'S SYMBOLIC-EXPERIENTIAL FAMILY THERAPY

Whitaker strongly agreed with Winnicott (1971) that "psychotherapy is play. Where playing . . . is not possible, then work done by the therapist is directed toward bringing the patient from a state of not being able to play into a state of being able to play" (p. 38). Thus, working therapeutically with children requires play. Keith and Whitaker (1994) proposed a series of nine constructs that they apply when working with children and their families:

1. Family therapy and play are learned mainly by experience. Children spontaneously use play to process and communicate what they experience. Therapists learn from children how to play; they provide the structure to make play therapeutic.
2. Therapy requires rules and structure, for which a therapist is responsible. However, therapists know how to use their own experience and are aware when structure interferes with the therapeutic process.
3. Magic and rituals increase the scope of therapy. The as-if world of play and therapy offers a safe space for children and their parents to explore the problem areas that brought them to therapy and creatively try new ways of overcoming those problems.
4. Therapeutic play constantly mixes the symbolic and the real. Children display their reality symbolically in play.
5. In psychotherapy, the primary reality is metaphorical. Metaphors are the entrance to a child's world. Toys in the therapy room embody such metaphors, which convey multiple meanings.
6. During the therapeutic process, therapist and clients repeatedly shift from metaphor to reality and back. Discovering the multiple meanings of reality as represented in the metaphors explains a child's view of the world. A therapist serves as an explorer of a child's reality and translates it into abstract adult language.
7. Play reflects an interpersonal experience projected onto a therapist. Thus, the metaphorical meaning of therapeutic child play is not limited to a child's expression of internal experience, but also takes place within the interpersonal space between child and therapist.
8. Body language is an implicit way in which children communicate their internal affective states to the outside world. In the therapy room, body language adds another level of meaning to the therapeutic play.
9. Symbolic cues are used in administrative reality. For example, a child comes into the

therapy room being bored with the toys that used to excite her; this may be the girl's symbolic expression that she is ready to terminate therapy.

Symbolic-experiential child and family clinicians define therapy as a process of clients' exploring their metaphorical messages, how they are stuck in an unsafe world. The therapist helps them in a constant interchange between metaphor and reality to find new and creative ways to get unstuck and "have access to their self-actualizing potential. Play is a medium for expanding their reality" (Keith & Whitaker, 1994, p. 194).

JOHNSON'S EMOTIONALLY FOCUSED FAMILY THERAPY

Johnson (Johnson & Lee, 2000) based her emotionally focused family therapy (EFFT) on Bowlby's (1969) attachment theory. Psychoanalyst Bowlby, departing from traditional Freudian psychoanalysis, proposed that an attachment bond between child and parent regulates their proximity and supports a sense of security. Johnson derived four assumptions from attachment theory:

1. Human beings experience a continuous need for seeking and maintaining contact with other human beings.
2. Attachment figures, by providing such contact, nurture comfort and security; lack of contact with an attachment figure generates distress. Positive attachments build a secure base, a safe haven that buffers against stress. Conversely, separation from attachment figures or a lack of confidence in their availability and responsiveness leads to insecure attachments.
3. Emotional accessibility and responsiveness form the building blocks of secure attachments.
4. When attachment bonds are threatened and affective reactions fail to restore a secure base, separation distress occurs. This process involves angry protest, clinging, depression and despair, and detachment.

The goal of therapy consists of modifying the distressing cycles of interaction that maintain attachment insecurity in family members while also fostering positive cycles of accessibility and responsiveness (Johnson, 1996; Johnson, Maddeaux, & Blouin, 1998). To reach this goal, the therapist encourages the child and other family members via play and conversation to identify attachment needs and to express them. Therapeutic process in EFFT proceeds in three stages that include nine steps:

Stage 1: De-Escalation

Step 1. Delineating the conflict issues and attachment struggles in a family: This step involves exploring how family members regulate closeness and distance, and how they interact around theses issues.

Step 2. Identifying and clarifying negative interactional cycles that maintain insecure attachments: When children experience neglected attachment needs, negative interactional cycles develop over time around failed attempts to deal with the associated stress. For example, a child who feels neglected may cling to a mother who is depressed. In reaction, the mother may push the child away; this increases a child's distress. The more the child clings, the more the mother rejects the youngster.

Step 3. Accessing unacknowledged emotions underlying interactional positions in a family: The therapist assists the child in identifying and experiencing unmet attachment needs and fears of rejection through a variety of play techniques. At the same time, the therapist encourages a depressed mother to become more aware of her emotions.

Step 4. Redefining the problem: Once family members have accessed the underlying problems and the therapist has identified the negative interactional cycles, the therapist helps the family to redefine the problem. For example, the child learns to approach the mother in a nonclinging way when he or she has identified an unmet attachment need; at the same time, the mother learns to deal with her depression differently and to avoid rejecting the child.

Stage 2: Interactional shifts

Step 5. Promoting identification with disowned needs and aspects of self: During this step family members are encouraged to accept their emotions that led to the negative interactional cycles. For example, via role plays, the therapist and the mother reinforce the child's need for closeness and attachment, rather than perceiving them as parental rejection. The mother learns to accept her depressive emotions and to separate them from her child's attachment needs.

Step 6. Fostering the acceptance of each family member's experience and new interactional responses: Now the mother learns to identify and accept the child's need for attachment as different from her emotional state and to embrace the child's desire as easily accomplished. The child learns to accept that the mother feels depressed at times and that this does not mean that she no longer loves the child.

Step 7. Facilitating the expression of needs and wants to restructure interactions: At this point, the therapist works with the child to express needs openly and directly to the mother without clinging. This helps the mother to respond positively without rejecting the child. The mother can identify her own needs underlying the depression and develop strategies for meeting her needs so that she can nurture her child appropriately.

Stage 3: Consolidation of change

Step 8. Establishing the emergence of new solutions to previously problematic situations: In rehearsing role plays, mother and child practice new solutions when attachment needs arise.

Step 9. Consolidating new positions: Mother and child, with the help of the therapist, experience the difference between the old and new interactional patterns. Once a new pattern has been achieved, the therapist coaches clients to reenact the old, negative pattern to experience the difference emotionally.

White's Narrative Therapy

Freeman et. al. (1997) applied White's (White & Epston, 1990) narrative therapy to working with children and families. Narrative therapy uses clients' imagination to transform problem-saturated stories into alternative stories to change clients' lives (Simons & Freedman, 2000). Language provides the vehicle of this transformation. However, in therapy with children, the metaphoric and symbolic language of children serves as the playground for transformation. Troubled children regain control over their lives by reauthoring their life stories.

Several therapeutic constructs form the foundation for narrative therapy with children. The technique of *externalization* allows for separating a person from a problem. This relieves a child and all other family members from the pressure of blame and defensiveness. When children realize that problems are put on the spot instead of them, they enthusiastically participate in playful pursuits to overcome the problem. Understanding a child apart from a problem facilitates progress. Once a therapist validates a family's worries and complaints about a child, all can view the child as a totality embracing more than the problem that brought the family to therapy.

Problem-saturated stories shape people's lives (White & Epston, 1990). They orient how family members perceive their lives. Selective memory leads family members to filter information that confirms fixed suppositions about the problems a child encounters. As therapy participants examine the constraining effects of problem-saturated stories, they discover and enact exceptions to the problems then and there. The exceptions or unique outcomes consist of thoughts, motives, intentions, feelings, or actions at odds with the problem-saturated story (Freeman et al., 1997). Ultimately, unique outcomes lead to an alternative story that transforms people's lives. The family changes the plot of the problem-saturated story into a counterplot, in which the protagonist conspires to undermine the problem or contests the matter directly with the antagonist. Just as a complex relationship transpires between a family and a problem, so a complex relationship exists between a problem and wider social forces. Because problem-saturated stories are nested in social, cultural, economic, and gender assumptions about roles and behavior, narrative therapists inquire about these factors and strive to be aware of how they are affecting different family members, particularly a child. Narrative child and family therapists want to foster an atmosphere of validation and safety that encourages a child to explore problem stories with other family members, to identify unique outcomes, and to develop alternative stories that overcome the presenting problem.

METHODS OF ASSESSMENT AND INTERVENTION

Existential-experiential approaches to child and family psychotherapy do not involve instruments to assess clients' level of functioning. The philosophical underpinnings of these approaches favor experientially based clinical or informal assessments that encourage clients to enact and experience their functional and dysfunctional patterns. These forms of assessment continue during therapeutic processes and are not limited to the initial phase of therapy.

SYMBOLIC-EXPERIENTIAL FAMILY THERAPY

Whitaker (Keith & Whitaker, 1994) was strongly opposed to formal assessment. He encouraged clients to give meaning to symbolic interactions via expressing and experiencing them, rather than by using self-report instruments that "objectify" clients' experiences. Symbolic-experiential child and family therapists assess clients by engaging with them in play situations, humor, and absurdity. They invite clients to react to a therapist in actions that give meaning to clients' presenting problems and how they perceive the world.

Keith and Whitaker (1994) described a variety of intervention methods that have the common goal of changing children's and families' life experiences in positive ways:

1. Attendance: Children attend all interviews, and toys are available. Whitaker was a strong proponent of not seeing children alone, but in the context of their family. Interventions occur contextually, with the goal of changing the experiences and behaviors of all family members who live with the child exhibiting identified problems.
2. Three-person talk: These verbal interventions are directed at one person with the intention of being heard by other family members and with the goal of indirectly addressing expressed issues with an identified child. For example, a therapist may tell the mother of a child with a school phobia to have the child sit on her lap for two hours every morning while the other children ready themselves for school. When the child hears this exaggerated suggestion,

the youngster may experience frustration about the long time and protest.

3. Using laughter: Another intervention method that exaggerates conventional interventions applies humor and laughter to disrupt negative interactional patterns. For example, a therapist observes a parent and a child engaging in one of their frequent arguments that the parent does not care about the child. She turns to her cotherapist and exclaims, "For not caring about each other, they get into it quite a bit, don't they?"

4. Teaching acting out: In this method, a therapist encourages clients to act out interactional patterns they report. The acting out intensifies the affective experience, which is intended to open up space for change and provide a different solution for problematic interactional patterns. For example, when a child and parent argue about the parent's not caring, the therapist may invite them to get up, take a ball made of soft material, and show each other how they do not care by throwing the ball back and forth.

5. Talking silly, that is, pseudo-seriously: Children especially like this intervention. For example, a 7-year-old girl giggles in response to a therapist's question to the parents. When the parents ignore the incident, the therapist says with a smile to the girl, "Did you just giggle so beautifully? That sounded great! Are you the best giggler in the family?" When the girl shrugs her shoulders, obviously embarrassed, the therapist continues, "You should have a giggle contest with your parents." The family members look at each other, confused, then burst out laughing.

6. Using absurdity: Symbolic-experiential therapists engage in growth-producing experiences with their clients. This philosophy allows them to behave on impulse, without apparent connection to the content of the session, because they trust that their spontaneous behaviors will further the therapeutic process. For example, the parents of a misbehaving 9-year-old boy engaged in a long discussion about how overwhelmed their lives felt and how little time they had for attending to their son. The parents had started the previous session with the same complaint, totally ignoring the child. Not wanting to listen to the parents again, the therapist gets up from her chair, picks up some toys, and begins to play on the floor, right in front of the parents. The boy looks at the parents, who do not respond, gets up, and joins the therapist on the floor, while the parents continue to complain about their lives. When they finally stop and ask the therapist what she and the boy are doing on the floor, the therapist smiles at the boy and says to the parents, "We've heard your complaints so many times that we had better things to do than getting bored listening to you."

7. Playing delusion or agreeing with delusion: Again in this method, a therapist reflects back to clients how they use a destructive interactional pattern to disrupt the pattern. For example, the father of a 7-year-old girl with school phobia reports his concern that the teachers at his daughter's school are "out to get quiet girls." He proceeds to draw an extremely hostile picture of the teachers, to whom he is not willing to entrust his daughter. Knowing of the integrity of the accused teachers, the therapist suggests that he feels very uncomfortable with the father, who could be out to get him. The therapist proceeds to voice his concern that the father may sue him if he does not come up with a miracle intervention that solves his daughter's problem.

8. Giving positive feedback: A number of therapists overlook this commonsense

intervention by staying focused on problems and pathology. Praising clients and giving them positive feedback at every possible occasion change the experiences of clients, especially when they tend to be rather negative and critical.

9. Switching generations: A therapist may invite parents to become children during a role play to play the children the way they experience them. Or the children are encouraged to enact the most feared behavior of their parents. Or the therapist may switch generations. For example, when a young child refuses to join the therapist on the floor playing with toys, the therapist crawls to the mother and begins crying and whining like a little child who does not get his or her way.

All these interventions share the intent to alter during therapy sessions clients' experiences, associated affects, and negative interactional patterns linked to presenting problems. Changing clients' experiences symbolically opens the door for new ways of interacting that no longer require a presenting problem.

EFFT

Johnson's (Johnson & Lee, 2000) EFFT, consistent with its underlying philosophy of altering emotional and interactional patterns, which are difficult to measure objectively, does not include the use of formal assessment instruments. However, EFFT begins with an initial assessment phase that lasts one or two sessions: "The therapist observes the organization of family interactional patterns, the strategies used to deal with conflict and frustration, and how family members support and comfort each other" (Johnson & Lee, 2000, p. 119). Many therapists invite a family to draw a picture of the family drama that symbolizes the presenting problem.

Negative interaction cycles such as pursue/distance and criticize/withdraw are important to assess.

EFFT does not include specified intervention methods. Instead, Johnson (Johnson & Lee, 2000) recommends that therapists use their creativity and imagination when moving families and children through the three phases described earlier. Techniques such as the family puppet interview (Irwin & Malloy, 1975), mutual storytelling (Brooks, 1993; Gardner, 1993), and different forms of art therapy (Gil, 1994; Oster & Gould, 1987; Winnicott, 1971) seem particularly well-suited to set up a safe environment in which to work.

Narrative Therapy

White (1995; Simons & Freedman, 2000) opposes formally assessing and evaluating children and other family members. Formal assessment runs contrary to the philosophy and assumptions underlying this approach. Instead, narrative therapists rely on the creativity and playfulness of children with words and other activities. This helps clients to reauthor their lives and does not require the maintenance of problems. Narrative therapists rely on a series of intervention methods:

1. Using the language of externalization: Because language shapes people's experience (White & Epston, 1990), a therapist uses a client's language to identify metaphors describing the relationship between a person and a problem. For example, the encopresis problem of a 4-year-old boy is relabeled the "sneaky pooh" that runs the boy's life. Metaphors are assumed not only to be internal but also interactional. They exist in the space between family members. For example, the experience of pain that family members inflict on each other becomes the

"wall of hurt" in the family that keeps members from making meaningful connections. Frequently, therapists employ a problem as a "consultant," by using a metaphor, describing an ongoing relationship with the problem instead of one describing the effort to defeat or drive it away. For example, a family described the son's acting-out behavior in school as the "family bane." The therapist let the boy select a puppet from his toy box that represented the "family bane." Then the therapist invited the boy to take the bane to school and consult it whenever he felt the urge to act out (Thomas, 1999).

2. Helping parents participate in playful approaches: Parents may get actively involved in the therapy process in many creative ways. According to Freeman et al. (1997), parents may brainstorm ideas and solutions with a child; become coconspirators, spying on or opposing a problem; add meanings that contribute to a child's narratives as they emerge in play or conversation; participate in a ritual or game or "rite of passage"; supply details and examples that develop promising narratives or exceptions to problem-saturated stories; and form an audience to a child's restorying, corroborate that a child's behavior has changed, and celebrate the change with the youngster.

3. Facilitating the coauthoring process: A therapist collaborates with a child and family in a number of ways: hearing the presenting painful relationship the child and other family members have with the problem; joining a family as an interested and curious observer of the ways a problem operates, and the methods it uses to oppress the child and family; hearing the messages the problem uses to thicken its plot, the unexamined assumptions that the problem employs to gain its authority to malign family members; and finding out what relationship child and family would prefer to have with a problem.

4. Facilitating coherent and lasting alternative stories: Next, a therapist engages in practices with a child and family that help them develop a counterplot to the problem-saturated story. The therapist can do this by being an avid reader of exceptions to a problem's influence and by identifying unique outcomes; being curious and excited about the abilities of child and family and building these into convincing alternative descriptions; taking a keen interest in new and preexisting possibilities for changing the status quo of a problem; weaving a contrast between the ways a problem goes about its business and the way a child works to become free of it, thereby developing a detailed counterplot; and ultimately becoming a coauthor of a meaningful story of change within family life.

5. Letter writing: Narrative therapists frequently write therapeutic letters to their clients. Depending on a child's age, the letter can be directed toward and written to a youngster, or it can be written to the parents but directed toward the child. A narrative letter is literary rather than diagnostic. It tells a client's story as recorded by a therapist. A letter engages a family not so much by developing an argument as by inquiring what might happen next. It provides a structure to tell an alternative story emerging with therapy; thus, it documents history, current development, and future prospects.

Narrative therapy permits existential experiences for clients through language and literary collaboration. It differs from traditional child psychotherapy approaches in that language becomes the playful medium of therapy. Yet, it resembles traditional child psychotherapy by relying mainly on language rather than play, unlike other existential-experiential approaches to child and family psychotherapy.

MAJOR SYNDROMES, SYMPTOMS, AND PROBLEMS TREATED

Existential-experiential child and family psychotherapists have applied these methods to a range of issues: sexual abuse, physical abuse, anxiety, depression, experiencing parental divorce, oppositional defiance, attention-deficit/hyperactivity.

Treating Sexually Abused Children and Their Families

Child sexual abuse poses a common and devastating problem in many parts of the world. It is estimated that one of five children under the age of 18 is sexually abused in the United States every year (Freeman-Longo & Blanchard, 1998). According to the Australian Institute of Health and Welfare, between 10 and 15% of all children in Australia may be sexually abused every year (Australian Institute of Health and Welfare [AIHW], 2000). The United Kingdom Department of Health estimates that these numbers are about 15% for the United Kingdom and comparable to the rest of Europe (2000). A UNICEF-supported study by the 1996 World Congress Against Sexual Exploitation of Children revealed in 1995 that 47% of sexually exploited girls in Costa Rica, El Salvador, Guatemala, Honduras, Nicaragua, and Paraguay were victims of abuse and rape in their homes (United Nations Children's Fund, 1997). Similar estimates are reported for many African and Asian countries.

Existential-experiential approaches to child and family psychotherapy are well-suited for treating children who suffer from sexual abuse. Maddock and Larson (1995) proposed a treatment model to integrate a therapist's personal style with client experiences. Barrett, Cortese, and Marzolf (2000) developed a similar model based on three stages: constructing a context for change, challenging patterns and expanding realities, and consolidation. This model provides a paradigm for conducting existential-experiential therapy. The goals of therapy encompass recognition of dysfunctional patterns (Johnson & Lee, 2000), acknowledgment of exceptions or unique outcomes (Freeman et al., 1997), development of safety and clear boundaries (Keith & Whitaker, 1994), and the generation and maintenance of hope.

Stage 1: Creating a Context for Change
During this stage, the therapist works with all involved agencies, such as Child Protective Services, schools, and the legal system, to develop an environment of safety for the child. When the child feels understood and safe, the therapist has set up a context for understanding that gives the child a voice. According to Barrett et al. (2000), sufficient conditions for this context include six steps:

1. Obtain and review all materials related to the sexual abuse.
2. Determine the family constellation and the roles family members played in the abuse.
3. Delineate past and present functioning and behavior patterns, such as attachment disturbances (Johnson & Lee, 2000) and post-traumatic behaviors and reactions (e.g., self-blame, powerlessness, loss and betrayal, eroticization, destructiveness, dissociative behaviors, the issue of body integrity, and difficulty in regulating affect).
4. Identify the child's stress response, such as fight/flight or numbing responses, the triggers, and the sexual contexts of the affective arousal.
5. Select a "bridge person" who can be supportive and help the child develop and maintain safety and security.

6. Determine whether the child is exhibiting and/or engaging in sexual behaviors that concern caregivers and if other children may be at risk.

The therapist works with the child and the "bridge person" mainly using play therapy techniques that help the child feel safe and express feelings and reactions to trauma experienced.

Stage 2: Challenging Patterns and Expanding Alternatives

Once the child has developed a trusting relationship with the therapist, enabling the child to give voice to his or her trauma and to feel heard, the therapist establishes a trusting work relationship with the parents. This proves essential to achieve a positive and lasting change in stage 2. Barrett et al. (2000) recommend a multisystem-level treatment approach in stage 2 to address the emotional experiences of all family members involved. This multimodal approach may include a variety of constellations. Individual child sessions help the child to separate from parents and other family members still in denial. Individual sessions with parents can advance the goal of furthering their understanding of their responsibilities in supporting repetition of abuse patterns. Sessions with siblings aid them in dealing with their roles in the family trauma. Whole-family treatment proves important in making problematic patterns in the family overt, to discover the role each member takes in maintaining the pattern, and then to find ways to meet a family's intimacy needs without victimization. Parent-child sessions facilitate better attachment (Johnson & Lee, 2000) and relationships. Group therapies by family roles provide outlets for family members outside their own family. This form of treatment includes groups for molesting fathers, mothers of victims, and siblings of victims.

Transition from stage 2 to stage 3 is indicated when the child exhibits fewer symptoms, when caregivers display improved ability to problem-solve independently, and when the child focuses less on power, control, safety, and attachment themes during play therapy sessions.

Stage 3: Consolidation

In this stage, the child learns that he or she can count on adult caregivers and can use resources in the future to prevent further abuse. The therapist works with the family to design ending rituals that consolidate the hope the child has gained during treatment. A relapse prevention plan is devised and discussed with all family members. The plan includes steps to identify future warning signals and actions to be taken to prevent further abuse.

TREATING PHYSICALLY ABUSED CHILDREN AND THEIR FAMILIES

The effects of physical abuse and violence on children are well documented and include externalizing or acting-out behaviors such as aggression, defiance, or delinquency (frequently diagnosed as Oppositional Defiant Disorder [ODD] in younger children, and/or Conduct Disorder [CD] in older children and adolescents), and internalized responses such as depression, anxiety, or withdrawal (Fatout, 1990; Hullings-Catalano, 1996).

Parents of abused children are often abuse survivors themselves. This makes the treatment quite challenging. As in the work with sexually abused children, stopping abuse and establishing a safe and secure treatment environment remains paramount. Most existential-experiential approaches to the treatment of physically abused children and their families are based on a multisystems model. A therapist works closely with all social service agencies involved in a case (e.g., Child Protective Services, schools, legal services) and provides a multimodal treatment, which includes individual play therapy sessions with the child, sessions with parents, and sessions with the entire family.

Busby and Smith (2000) proposed an excellent model for working with physically abused children and their families. Their model follows six steps:

1. Locating alternatives to violence: After establishing initial safety and trust, the therapist explores alternative ways of relating free of violence, using methods and techniques similar to those of Johnson and Lee (2000) in their EFFT approach.
2. Improving connections: After investigating alternatives to violence, the therapist encourages family members to develop violence-free connections and works with them on the improvement of their relationships. This is analogous to Johnson and Lee's steps 4, 5, and 6, which have the goal of healing damaged attachments (i.e., connections).
3. Letting go of the past: The next step in the healing process includes the parents' working through the guilt and shame associated with the abuse, and the child's dealing with the guilt and anger flowing as consequences of trauma. The therapist actively coaches children and other family members in role plays to let go of the affects linked with abuse and to gain confidence in the newly established trust and safety.
4. Making space for uniqueness: Once the connections among family members have improved, they can grant and accept more space to explore different ways of relating that move beyond attempts to control affect and behavior (to prevent angry and violent outbursts).
5. Strengthening support systems: Not only do child and family learn and experience healing within the family, the therapist also emboldens them to develop and maintain support systems external to the family. Extended family, neighbors, and school personnel can support the family in preventing any further violence in the future.

Once family members have broken the cycle of silence about the abuse and have openly dealt with guilt and shame, they can use external resources for maintaining violence-free connections.

6. More play: Finally, a therapist works with a family to apply play therapy techniques in the form of family play at home. Being playful and having fun with each other offer the best predictors for violence-free connections in a family in which a child has suffered from physical abuse.

TREATING ANXIOUS CHILDREN AND THEIR FAMILIES

According to the *Diagnostic and Statistical Manual of Mental Disorders,* fourth edition (*DSM-IV*) (American Psychiatric Association [APA], 1994), it is mostly adults who experience anxiety disorders. Separation anxiety is the only child anxiety disorder listed. However, clinicians treat many anxiety disorders that children experience, such as specific phobias (e.g., school phobia), social phobias, and general anxiety disorders. Associated symptoms include being compulsive, shy, inattentive, and distractible, restless, and/or having academic problems. Stone Fish, Jensen, Reichert, and Wainman-Sauda (2000) provided a useful summary describing how to work with anxious children and their families from an existential-experiential perspective. Additionally, Breunlin, Schwartz, and Karrer (1992) as well as White and Epston (1990) delineated experiential approaches to working with anxious children.

TREATING DEPRESSED CHILDREN AND THEIR FAMILIES

Depression and other mood disorders evolve in the context of dysfunctional interactional family patterns (Hammen, 1991; Kaslow, Deering, & Ash, 1996; Oster & Caro, 1990; Sholevar,

1994). Thus, the treatment of childhood depression, according to experiential therapists, proceeds most effectively within a family context (Kaslow, Mintzer, Meadows, & Grabill, 2000). Most depressed children come to a therapist's office with symptoms of depressed or irritable mood; anhedonia (inability to experience pleasure); decreased weight or appetite or failure to make expected weight gains; sleep disturbance; psychomotor agitation or retardation; fatigue or loss of energy; feelings of worthlessness, low self-esteem, or inappropriate guilt; concentration difficulties or indecisiveness; thoughts of death and/or suicide; somatic complaints; feelings of helplessness; and social withdrawal. These symptoms frequently can cause so much impairment in a child that a *DSM-IV;* (APA, 1994) diagnosis of Major Depressive Disorder or Dysthymic Disorder is justified.

Kaslow and her colleagues (Kaslow & Racusin, 1994) developed an experiential approach to the treatment of depressed school-age children and their families that they call interpersonal family therapy (Racusin & Kaslow, 1991). The approach combines family systems theory, cognitive-behavioral psychology, object-relations theory, and developmental psychopathology. In collaboration with other professionals (e.g., physicians who prescribe medication, school personnel who monitor achievement and grades), a systematic assessment leads to a treatment plan that includes the child and family. Sessions during the 16-week therapy program vary in focus: Sessions 1 and 2 highlight joining and assessment, session 3 feedback and disposition, session 4 psychological symptomatology, sessions 5 and 6 cognitive functioning, sessions 7 and 8 affective functioning, sessions 9 and 10 interpersonal functioning, session 11 adaptive behavior, sessions 12 and 13 family functioning, and sessions 14 to 16 review, synthesis, and postassessment. Successful treatment not only reduces symptoms in the child, but improves family interactions that may have contributed to the child's depression.

TREATING CHILDREN OF DIVORCE AND THEIR FAMILIES

Divorce, though common, affects children in major ways. Children have to make emotional and psychological adjustments and go through geographical changes, and their economic circumstances frequently worsen. The degree of impact divorce has on children depends on many factors (Wallerstein & Blakeslee, 1989). Although most children master the challenges of postdivorce adjustment without major psychological and emotional symptoms, many need therapeutic assistance to work through the trauma of loss and anxiety during an adjustment period, and residual effects can be expected as many as 10 or more years after the divorce, both in separated spouses and their offspring.

Griffith and Thiessen-Barrett (2000) proposed a three-phase family-based model for working with issues of divorce adjustment. They drew on many creative, experiential play techniques applied to children and families. In phase 1, the therapist *establishes rapport, assesses, and develops a plan.* After establishing rapport with all family members, the therapist uses projective drawings and questionnaires to assess members' level of functioning and adjustment. Instruments used may include the Kinetic Family Drawing (Burns & Kaufman, 1970) and the Kinetic House-Tree-Person Drawings (Burns, 1987). Both instruments allow family members to express their views and feelings about the changing family situation. Depending on a family's specific circumstances, a therapist develops treatment goals in collaboration with all members involved in the sessions.

In phase 2, the therapist *implements a treatment plan.* During this phase, the therapist may draw from a variety of experiential techniques to help the family make necessary adjustments. Some of these techniques include play activities (Gil, 1994), art activities such as family drawings (Riley & Malchiodi, 1994; Warren,

1996), puppet play (Gil, 1994; Mesalam & Griffith, 1993), sand play (Allan & Berry, 1993; Bradway & McCoard, 1997), sand play in combination with storytelling (Boik & Goodwin, 2000; Miller & Boe, 1990), school interventions (Aponte, 1994; Griffith & Coleman, 1988; Lusterman, 1985), filial therapy (Van Fleet, 1994), family storytelling (Gil, 1994), and reading story books (Pardeck, 1990).

In phase 3, *close and termination* occur. Therapy is commonly terminated when therapist and family agree that they can continue with improving their adjustment processes on their own and use the techniques they have learned in therapy.

Treating Children with Oppositional Defiant Disorder and Their Families

According to the *DSM-IV* (APA, 1994), ODD is characterized by a recurrent pattern of negativistic, defiant, disobedient, and hostile behavior that may include losing one's temper, arguing with adults, actively defying or refusing to comply with the requests or rules of adults, deliberately doing things that will annoy other people, blaming others for one's own mistakes or misbehavior, being angry and resentful, and being spiteful and vindictive. These behaviors occur so frequently that they lead to an impairment in social, academic, or occupational functioning. Because ODD is expressed in the interactional context of a family and other interactional systems such as schools, treatment occurs best within a family context.

Keim (2000) designed a four-stage experientially based family intervention approach. Stage 1 transits *from blame to empowering descriptions*. Treatment during this stage has the goal of helping parents shift their focus from a blaming mode to a problem-solving mode. Parents and children learn that they have different perceptions of power and control that interfere with their abilities to effectively solve problems. In stage 2 the *gentle disempowerment of a child begins*. Most parents of ODD children are consumed by disempowering fights with their children. This puts a child into a position of power that he or she cannot handle, except by fighting even more. The parents experience that their child's acting out is a cry for help with being a child and a challenge to the parents to be and act as parents. In stage 3, emphasis falls on *rules and consequences*. Once parents have begun to gently take charge and a child has accepted the shift with relief, the therapist works with all family members to develop realistic rules and consequences. The rules have to be unambiguous and clear to the child. The consequences need to be enforceable and acceptable to both parents and child. In stage 4, parents engage in *soothing an oppositional child*. Once the parents feel more confident about their parenting and have developed a more positive attitude toward their child, the therapist encourages them to help the child to change his or her mood. Assuming that oppositional behaviors are misdirected needs for connection and attachment, the parents learn about and accept their child's emotional needs and practice developing soothing strategies to meet those needs.

Throughout treatment, the therapist models for parents and children appropriate behaviors and responses to attachment needs (Johnson & Lee, 2000) not met in the family. Changing the atmosphere in the family during therapy sessions helps parents and children to modify the atmosphere at home in positive ways that do not require ODD behaviors.

Treating Children with Attention-Deficit/Hyperactivity Disorder and Their Families

Attention-Deficit/Hyperactivity Disorder (ADHD) ranks as one of the most prevalent childhood disorders in the mental-health field (Barkley, 1997). According to *DSM-IV* (APA, 1994) criteria,

ADHD is characterized by inattentiveness, impulsivity, and hyperactivity occurring so frequently that they lead to an impairment in social, academic, or occupational functioning. The most reliable and valid assessment of ADHD consists of an empirical assessment based on self-report data, behavioral observation, and a medical evaluation (DuPaul & Stoner, 1994). A differential diagnosis related to ODD is also important, because almost 50 percent of children with ADHD may also develop ODD (Barkley, 1990).

Similar to the treatment of ODD, Polson (2000) offered an ADHD family-centered model reliant on an experiential perspective. The goals of this model encompass (1) inducing parents to work together on establishing firm rules and behavior constraints, and holding the children responsible for their behavior; (2) removing children from parental roles; (3) developing parental and child support networks; (4) preventing family members from accommodating a child's misbehavior; and (5) promoting more positive, warm, nurturing patterns of interaction within a family.

The model proceeds in four phases. *Assessment procedures* fill the initial two sessions in phase 1. In addition to the therapist's clinical impression, parents and teachers fill out the Child Behavior Checklist: Parent, Teacher Report Forms (Achenbach & Edelbrock, 1983) and the Conners' Parent and Teacher Rating Scale (Conners, 1989). Based on the results and the clinical diagnosis, the therapist consults with a physician, who prescribes a medication (if applicable), and derives a treatment plan in collaboration with the family. In phase 2, *psychoeducation* serves as the intervention. During this phase, the therapist provides all necessary information about ADHD that the family needs to understand the child and the family dynamics associated with ADHD. Phase 3 involves *providing alternative ways of interacting around a child*. This constitutes the experiential phase of treatment. The interventions resemble those utilized in the four stages of the ODD approach described by Keim (2000). Phase 4 is concentrated on *maintaining changes*. Parents are encouraged to participate in a local chapter of Children and Adults with Attention-Deficit/Hyperactivity Disorder (CHAADD), which helps a family to network with other families in similar situations. This operates as reinforcement of attained affective and behavioral changes the ADHD child and parents have accomplished during treatment.

CASE EXAMPLES

THE BROWN FAMILY AND THE SYMBOLIC-EXPERIENTIAL APPROACH

A few years ago, a couple with a 9-year-old girl, Anna, entered the therapist's office with her parents, Mr. and Mrs. Brown. Anna sat down on the comfortable recliner while her parents chose the hard chairs on the other side of my chair. Jack and Jill Brown, both in their early 30s, married right after they graduated from college, when Jill became pregnant with Anna during her senior year. Jill stayed home while Jack continued on to graduate school for a master's degree in business administration. Jill had grown up as the middle child of five children. Both of her parents were professionals working full time when Jill was born. She was raised partly by her two older sisters and was used to having people around at home. Jack, on the other hand, was the only child of older parents who had struggled with infertility until they finally conceived him. When his mom was pregnant, she quit her job and put all her energy into what became her most precious accomplishment in life, raising Jack, who consequently grew up well-nurtured and protected. Coming from very different family backgrounds, the Browns had little time to adjust to each other and to learn about those differences.

Following a rather casual courtship, they became pregnant, after having lived together for only a few months. Jack's parents were very upset that he "had to get married" and implied in secret statements to Jack that they were concerned that Jill had "tricked" him into the marriage by getting pregnant. After Anna's birth, Jill wanted to pursue a graduate degree, but Jack opposed this and wanted her to stay home, just as his mom had. Jill resented Jack's lack of support and felt isolated and lonely staying at home with a small child. During Anna's early childhood, Jill would accept odd jobs, against Jack's wishes, to get out of the house and to have adult contact. The tension between the couple grew. Jack accused Jill of being a "neglectful" mother and withdrew increasingly into his studies and job. Jill resented Jack's withdrawal, accusing him of not doing his share around the house and with Anna. Both were very achievement-oriented and rather competitive. Both felt "on the short end of the stick" regarding their marriage, and both considered getting a divorce several times. Yet, Jack did not want to provide his parents with the satisfaction of knowing that the marriage would not work out, as they had predicted, and Jill's value system did not include divorce as a viable option.

Thus, Anna grew up in the midst of this tension about parental roles and accomplishments. She became quite achievement-oriented herself. She observed her parents' strong wills and the frequency with which they engaged in open arguments. Over the years, she learned to take advantage of her parents' struggles by playing them against each other. She would complain to dad that mom would leave her alone too much, which would make him angry at mom and lead him to spoil her with the intent to make up for mom's neglect. When Jill found out about her husband taking Anna places behind her back, she would get angry with him. Or Anna would complain to mom that dad had yelled at her unjustly; then Jill would get angry with Jack and withdraw into her bedroom with Anna. There, Jill would read to Anna for hours while giving Jack the "silent treatment." In turn, he would get angry and withdraw even more into his job and graduate school.

Over the years, this cycle became so powerful that eventually Anna ran the family, manipulating her parents as she pleased. Although she was very sad that her parents became angry so frequently and were unhappy as well, she thought that was how life was supposed to be and did not know what else to do. When Jill finally felt so desperate that she threatened to divorce Jack despite her values, Jack agreed to seek family therapy.

This background provides the context for understanding why and when the Brown family ended up seeking treatment for their unruly child and themselves. However, before they came to the office, they and the therapist went through what Keith and Whitaker (1994) termed the *battle for control*. Jill, who had made the initial phone call and scheduled the appointment, called back the next day, reporting that Jack was so busy with school and work that he could not make the appointment. According to Jill, Jack had suggested that she and Anna proceed with the session because it would be more important to them anyway. The therapist insisted that he would see them only if all three came in at the time of the scheduled appointment and suggested that Jill talk this over with Jack and call him back. The following day, Jack called to make his case personally with the therapist, who stayed firm and insisted on his coming in with Jill and Anna, assuring Jack that the therapist considered him a crucial part of the family. Finally, Jack gave in, and the family showed up at the scheduled time.

Jack and Jill entered the office in a depressed and discouraged mood and sat down helplessly on the hard chairs while Anna placed herself in the recliner. This image of the family in the office reflected the way they saw their family world. The therapist engaged Anna in playing with his toys on the floor (something the parents had rarely done), which she greatly enjoyed. After a while, he invited the parents to join them on the floor because Anna revealed her feelings through play. Both parents had excuses for not wanting to sit on the floor, being apparently uncomfortable; yet, the therapist did not give up and insisted. Finally, the parents awkwardly kneeled down next to Anna. The therapist had found a way to join with them and to give them positive feedback as Keith and Whitaker (1994) recommended (in intervention 8). At the end of the first session, he gave them the homework of playing with Anna once a day for 15 minutes until the next session.

Based on clinical impressions from the first session, the family members were given the following *DSM-IV* (APA, 1994) diagnoses: Anna, ODD (313.81); Jack and Jill, Adjustment Disorder with Mixed Disturbance of Emotions and Conduct (309.4), Partner Relational Problem (V61.1), and Parent-Child Relational Problem (V61.20). The family had a score of 50 on the Global Assessment of Relational Functioning Scale (GARF) (Group for the Advancement of Psychiatry Committee on Family, 1996), which ranges from 0 to 100.

When the family came back the following week, the therapist could feel the increased tension in the office. They reported that the playtime had been a disaster: Anna had argued with her parents about what to play, dictated and controlled their actions, and threw tantrums when they did not do what she had demanded. After two attempts, the parents discontinued the playtime, which also led Anna to throw temper tantrums. Apparently, the negative cycle had escalated; the family felt more scared and desperate than before. The therapist decided to listen to the family and let them take the initiative at the beginning of the second session (Keith & Whitaker, 1994, intervention 8). The longer the therapist and family sat there with the family not knowing what to do, the more the intensity in the room increased. Finally, Jill suggested trying playtime again, hoping that the therapist would help to facilitate the process and keep Anna from "running the show." Jill got down on the floor and asked Jack and Anna to join her, which Jack did after a few moments. However, Anna refused to get up from the recliner, accusing her parents of being bad playmates. In response, the parents accused each other of being insensitive to Anna's needs. The therapist witnessed the grotesque picture of two adults sitting on the floor with toys arguing about their child while Anna lay in the reclined chair berating her parents.

At this point, the therapist got so disgusted with this family that he rose from his chair and, employing the use of absurdity (Keith & Whitaker's, 1994, intervention 6), announced that he would leave the room until they were ready to do therapy. He told them that he understood how they were acting at home and that they did not have to waste their time and money doing the same in his office. He would take a book and read in the waiting room. When they were ready to do therapy, one of them could come and call him. As all three family members sat in quiet shock, their mouths and eyes wide open, the therapist left the office. After five minutes, Anna came out and politely asked him to come back. She promised that they would not fight any longer and that they wanted to try to be a happy family. When he again entered the office, Jill was in tears and Jack was furious. They were sitting on the hard chairs, full of emotions they did not know how to handle. Only Anna went quietly back to the floor and began to play with the dollhouse. The therapist ignored the parents and asked Anna what she wanted to show him (intervention 4: teaching acting out). She took a male doll and put it in a big box in the attic. Then she proceeded to place a female doll in a bed in the basement. Another female child-size doll started preparing a meal in the kitchen. "This is my family after a big fight," Anna exclaimed. I shared with Anna how impressed I was that she kept taking care of the family even after a fight and asked what would happen next. She cooked for a while, then brought a plate with food to the basement and quietly handed it to mom (the female doll). She repeated the same with another plate, brought it to the attic, and placed it quietly on top of the closed box in which dad (the male doll) lay. "How nice of you to bring Mom and Dad something to eat when they are sad," I commented and added, "What a responsibility for a 9-year-old girl to take care of her mom and dad!" (intervention 8: giving positive feedback). Anna looked at me, surprised, and teared up. She turned and looked at her mom, who was still crying quietly. Their eyes met, both expressing great sadness. Mom got up and held her little daughter, who was sobbing. While Jill was holding Anna on the floor, I went over to Jack, sat down next to him, and put my arm around his shoulder. He fought his tears as hard as he could, but they were too insistent to be held back. "You may join them if you like. There is room for everybody in this family, even in pain and sadness." Relieved by the therapist's permission, Jack got up and joined Jill and Anna in their embrace. Without any reluctance, they welcomed him. When they rose from the floor, something astonishing happened. Anna asked to sit on Jack's lap. After some awkward tiptoeing around each other, Jack ended up in the recliner with Anna on his lap while Jill moved one of the hard chairs next to the recliner.

When I asked what had happened, Anna responded first: "I want to be a little girl and not have so much responsibility. It's much more fun sitting on Dad's lap than bringing him food he does not eat anyway." Jack and Jill looked at each other and confirmed that they both had forgotten that Anna was just 9 years old, and that they wanted to learn to be better parents and to be a more compatible husband and wife.

For Jack and Jill to accomplish their goals, and for Anna to fully accept being a 9-year-old girl, rather than a parentified child who ran the house, required several months of weekly and later biweekly sessions. Anna had to learn to let go of the power that came along with the parentification and to assent to the limits her parents set. Jack and Jill had to learn to work through their family-of-origin issues, which had led them into negative cycles. That freed up energy so that Jack and Jill could attend to each other's needs and, most of all, could recognize and meet Anna's needs according to her developmental stage. The therapist learned how to deal with the intensity of three people who had greatly unmet needs and to appreciate the power of emotional connections that arise out of fear and pain.

THE SMITH FAMILY AND EMOTIONALLY FOCUSED FAMILY THERAPY

Joe and Cindy, a couple in their late 20s, sought therapy for their 7-year-old first-grader, Cody. Cody refused to go to school, frequently feeling sick to his stomach and expressing fear that terrible events would happen at home while he was in school. He had repeated nightmares and was afraid to be alone. His fears paralyzed the whole family in that Joe and Cindy would take turns staying home with Cody three to four days a week. The school personnel had become increasingly concerned and recommended that Cody repeat first grade because of his frequent absences.

Joe and Cindy lived together bound by Joe's fear of Cindy having an affair and by Cindy's fear of violence perpetrated by Joe. He grew up as the youngest of seven children. His father was an alcoholic who died of liver problems when Joe was 10 years old. His mom, although severely depressed at times, raised the children by herself and never remarried. When Joe was 14 years old, he went to live with his mother's sister's family until he graduated from high school and went away for college. Since he moved in with his aunt, Joe always worked to support himself, besides going to school. He quit college after his junior year and took a job with a landscaping company because he loved to be outdoors.

Cindy grew up as the eldest sibling of two brothers in a lower-middle-class home. Both of her parents worked to make ends meet, which left Cindy with the responsibility of taking care of the house and her younger brothers until her mom returned home from work. Cindy's parents instilled a very strong sense of the value of education in their children, so that they would have a better life than their parents, who were both high school graduates. Cindy did well in school and also succeeded in college, despite having to work to pay her own way.

Cindy and Joe met in a class at the beginning of their junior year in college. Because Joe was struggling with school at that time, Cindy helped him with assignments and studied with him. They dated for about six months and then moved in together because Joe thought that way they could save some money. Cindy felt that Joe was clingy and controlling from the first day they lived together. He always wanted to know where she was and did not show any interest in spending time with other people. Cindy hoped that Joe would change after they had lived together for some time. When Cindy realized that Joe would not change, she began to resent him and accused him of holding her hostage in her own house. At the same time, she felt guilty for wanting to be away from him because she genuinely loved Joe. Because she needed somebody to converse with about her dilemma, she increasingly went out with her girlfriends in the hope of figuring out how to improve her friendship with Joe.

At the beginning of their relationship, Joe was so in love with Cindy that he wanted to spend as much time with her as possible. He was convinced that he had finally found a person who would unconditionally nurture him for the rest of his life. He pushed Cindy to move in with him so that they could be together all the time. He quit college so that he could make more money and become a "good man" who could provide well for her. His father had never managed to do that because most of his money went for alcohol. Joe proposed to Cindy, hoping that getting married would make him feel safer in the relationship.

From the beginning of their marriage, Joe sensed Cindy's discomfort when they stayed home every night. He tried to tolerate her need to go out and socialize with her girlfriends. When Cindy became pregnant a few months later, Joe's fears temporarily decreased. Cindy went out less than before the pregnancy, and their relationship improved considerably. This changed dramatically after Cindy gave birth to Cody. Joe became increasingly jealous of and felt excluded from the close relationship Cindy had formed with Cody. Cindy felt falsely accused of not caring about her husband and was struggling herself, feeling isolated from her social support network. However, she felt so responsible for Cody that she concentrated all her energy on the infant.

The relationship between Joe and Cindy began to deteriorate even more when Cindy returned to work and Cody spent his days with a baby-sitter. Cindy increasingly sought to reconnect with her female friends while Joe felt even more neglected and rejected than when Cindy was at home with the baby. Both grew increasingly frustrated. Cindy avoided Joe more and more, and he became increasingly frustrated and controlling. Joe thought that if they engaged more in sex, Cindy would feel better about him and their marriage, and she would stay home more often. His anxious approaches turned off Cindy, who felt used as a sexual object. Consequently, she refused any sexual contact with Joe. Instead, she went out with her girlfriends, leaving Cody in Joe's care at home.

After a few months, the couple agreed on a compromise to reconcile their relationship for the sake of their young son. Cindy stayed home more often, and Joe tried to tolerate her independence. Yet, at the same time, both built up considerable resentment toward each other. In this atmosphere, Cody grew up to be a quite anxious and sensitive toddler who needed constant care and attention. Until he entered kindergarten, he insisted that one of his parents lie down with him every night to go to sleep. He developed a separation anxiety requiring considerable energy from parents and school. However, Cody made the transition, forming a close relationship with his kindergarten teacher. At that time, Cindy experienced more freedom and independence, allowing her to spend more time away from home. Joe reacted with upset, yet tried very hard to "keep it together" because he did not want his son to know about his parents' conflict.

However, when Cody entered first grade and did not like his new teacher, he began to develop a fear of going to school. Joe could empathize well with Cody, but Cindy became increasingly frustrated. Their marriage deteriorated quickly as Cody's school phobia worsened. Joe aligned himself with his son, and Cindy felt excluded and rejected. She needed time away and spent more time with her friends again.

One day, Joe found a pack of condoms in Cindy's car after one of her nights out, which convinced him that Cindy was having an affair. Her explanation that one of her girlfriends had left the pack in her car only increased Joe's resentment toward Cindy when she wanted to go out with them. He began to check up on her, and would get very angry when she came home later than they had agreed on. The resentment and tension between them increased until one day he hit her when she stayed out late and he could not find her at the place she was supposed to be. Cindy threatened to leave him if he did not agree to engage in family therapy.

Joe was so afraid of losing Cindy that he called an EFFT therapist to set up a first appointment. He felt comfortable that the therapist was a woman, hoping that she would convince Cindy to be more open and honest, to quit the affair he was convinced she was having, and help Cody overcome his fear of going to school. Cindy also was glad to have a female therapist, expecting that she would receive support in dealing with a clinging, insecure husband and her fearful son.

At the conclusion of the assessment phase, the therapist diagnosed the family members according to the *DSM-IV* (APA, 1994): Cody, Separation Anxiety Disorder (309.21), Joe and Cindy, Adjustment Disorder with Mixed Disturbance of Emotions and Conduct (309.4), Partner Relational Problem (V61.1), and Parent-Child Relational Problem (V61.20). The family had a GARF score of 45 (Group for the Advancement of Psychiatry Committee on Family, 1996) representing significantly impaired current level of functioning.

Using Johnson's (1996; Johnson & Lee, 2000) step-by-step treatment manual discussed above, the therapist met with Cindy, Joe, and Cody for 12 sessions over a three-month period and engaged in nine steps:

Step 1. Delineating the conflict issues and attachment struggles in the family: During the first session, the therapist identified Cindy's fear of violence, Joe's anger and obsession that Cindy was cheating on him, and Cody's fear of going to school. The therapist linked these fears to insecure attachment styles in all three family members. Cindy had an avoidant insecure style, Joe an ambivalent insecure style, and Cody an avoidant insecure attachment style (Bowlby, 1969).

Step 2. Identifying and clarifying negative interactional cycles that maintain insecure attachment: The couple learned that Joe pursues and intimidates Cindy, whereas she tries to distance herself out of fear of being hurt. The couple also identified the reciprocity of this negative cycle: The more Joe pursues, the more Cindy distances, and the more she distances, the more he pursues. Cody's fear became part of this negative cycle as well. His fear was an attempt to break the cycle between the parents, yet operated as fuel on the fire. Both Joe and Cindy used Cody's fear to justify their own positions and to blame the other for Cody's problems.

Step 3. Accessing unacknowledged emotions underlying interactional positions in the family: Once the couple gained some understanding of the negative cycle feeding their secondary emotions, the therapist worked with each partner on becoming aware of primary emotions (Johnson, 1996). Joe experienced his fear of abandonment when he got angry and controlling; Cindy got in touch with the loneliness she felt when her husband did not want to talk to and cuddle with her. They noticed that Cody's school phobia reflected their own fears and unmet needs.

Step 4. Redefining the problem: The therapist reframed the fear of abandonment, which actually served as a veiled expression of attachment needs and often led to blaming or withdrawing, as an attempt to protect oneself from another loss and emotional betrayal. This helped the couple to identify their negative cycles in terms of their attachment needs. The therapist reframed Cindy's fear of Joe as her strong need to feel emotionally connected with him. Joe's anger was relabeled as his need to be close to his wife, a feeling that she longed for but also feared. Finally, the therapist identified Cody's fear of going to school as his attempt to be a good son and do his part in meeting his parents' attachment needs by staying at home with them.

Step 5. Promoting identification with disowned needs and aspects of self: Once the couple had identified their disowned attachment needs, the therapist worked with them on expressing these needs to each other and on bringing them directly into the relationship. During this stage, the therapist coached Joe to share his fears and concerns when Cindy wanted to go out with her girlfriends; Cindy learned to acknowledge Joe's fear and to validate it, rather than get defensive and push it aside. Conversely, the therapist encouraged Cindy to express her need to have relaxed conversations with Joe (which she, instead, seeks with her girlfriends) and to feel close to him; the therapist coached Joe to accept Cindy's expressed needs, even if it was difficult for him to meet them. Both learned to identify Cody's emotional needs and to encourage him in communicating them. They acknowledged his needs more sensitively, which decreased his fears considerably.

Step 6. Fostering acceptance of each family member's experiences and new interactional responses: Once Joe and Cindy learned to accept each other's experiences, Joe became less anxious and angry and let go of his fear that Cindy had an affair, and Cindy felt more secure and safe with her husband and did not distance herself as much as before. At the same time, they had more energy for dealing with Cody. They devoted more time to playing with him and helping him with homework and established a bedtime routine with him that included reading and cuddling.

Step 7. Facilitating expression of needs and wants to restructure interactions: Now the couple was ready to ask for and have more closeness, to have dinner together, and to go for walks. The therapist practiced with the couple staying engaged in conversation, even when they felt anxious and uncomfortable. Cody learned to identify his needs and fears and to express them openly to his parents, who dealt with them appropriately. For example, Joe, on his return from work, made an effort to go for a walk with Cody, who would ride his bike and tell dad about his day at school.

Step 8. Establishing the emergence of new solutions to previously problematic situations: After a few more sessions, Cindy and Joe were ready to find new solutions to the daily problems they faced without falling back into the negative cycles that brought them to therapy. The safer the couple felt and the more they engaged with each other, the less Cindy wanted to go out with her girlfriends, and the less Joe felt threatened when she did go out. Both parents had gained so much emotional energy they could devote to Cody that his school phobia disappeared. They worked out a deal that they would take turns driving him to school in the morning and that he would return home on the bus, where his baby-sitter waited for him.

Step 9. Consolidating new positions: During this final phase of therapy, Cindy and Joe were able to stay emotionally connected, even when dealing with stress, openly expressed their needs, and met each other's needs. Eventually, the couple learned to have fun with each other and with Cody, who slowly grew into a more confident little boy. He felt increasingly more secure, enjoyed school, became a good student, and established friendships with boys in the neighborhood.

RESEARCH ON THE APPROACH: EFFICACY AND EFFECTIVENESS DATA

Little empirical research has been conducted to validate the efficacy and effectiveness of Whitaker's symbolic-experiential and White's narrative approaches. The only experiential approach that has generated relevant outcome research is Johnson's emotionally focused couple therapy (EFCT), the original couple version of the EFFT approach. For example, Johnson and Greenberg (1995) found that helping an angry and attacking (secondary emotions) partner reveal his or her softer feelings (primary emotions) was associated with positive therapy outcome. In another study, Greenberg, Ford, Alden, and Johnson (1993) concluded that, when couples express primary emotions in therapy, they have more productive sessions and feel more intimate with each other. In a comparison of several empirically based treatment approaches derived from rigorous methodological research studies, Alexander, Holtzworth-Munroe, and Jameson (1994) reported that EFCT was one of the most effective approaches to treating distressed couples. In a meta-analysis that included many outcome studies within and across different treatment approaches, Dunn and Schwebel (1995) confirmed the efficacy and effectiveness of EFCT.

SUMMARY

Existential-Experiential orientations have considerably advanced the approaches to child treatment. This chapter discussed three major schools of thought, Whitaker's symbolic-experiential family therapy, Johnson's emotionally focused family therapy, and White's narrative therapy. All three approaches represent system-oriented child and family psychotherapy that focus on existential-experiential aspects of child-adult interaction based on Bateson's (Bateson et al., 1956) and von Bertalanffy's (1968) work.

REFERENCES

Achenbach, T., & Edelbrock, C. (1983). *Manual for the Child Behavior Checklist and revised Child Behavior profile*. Burlington: University of Vermont.

Adler, A. (1930). *The science of living*. London: Allen & Unwin.

Adler, A. (1956). *The individual psychology of Alfred Adler: A systematic presentation in selections from his writings* (H. L. Ansbacher & R. R. Ansbacher, Eds.). New York: Harper & Row.

Alexander, J. F., Holtzworth-Munroe, A., & Jameson, P. (1994). The process and outcome of marital and family therapy: Research review and evaluation. In A. Bergin & S. Garfield (Eds.), *Handbook of psychotherapy and behavior change* (4th ed.). New York: Wiley.

Allan, J., & Berry, P. (1993). Sandplay. In C. E. Schaefer & D. M. Cangelosi (Eds.), *Play therapy techniques* (pp. 117–123). Northvale, NJ: Aronson.

American Psychiatric Association. (1994). *Diagnostic and statistical manual of mental disorders* (4th ed.). Washington, DC: Author.

Aponte, H. J. (1994). The family-school interview: An ecostructural approach. In H. J. Aponte (Ed.), *Bread and spirit: Therapy with the new poor* (pp. 83–97). New York: Norton.

Australian Institute of Health and Welfare. (2000). *Australia's children: Their health and well-being.* Canberra, Australia: Author.

Axline, V. M. (1947). *Play therapy.* New York: Ballantine Books.

Bailey, C. E. (Ed.). (2000). *Children in therapy: Using the family as a resource.* New York: Norton.

Bandura, A. (1977). *Social learning theory.* Englewood Cliffs, NJ: Prentice-Hall.

Barkley, R. A. (1990). *Attention-Deficit/Hyperactivity Disorder: A handbook for diagnosis and treatment.* New York: Guilford Press.

Barkley, R. A. (1997). *ADHD and the nature of self-control.* New York: Guilford Press.

Barrett, M. J., Cortese, J., & Marzolf, K. (2000). Treatment of the sexually abused child. In C. E. Bailey (Ed.), *Children in therapy: Using the family as a resource* (pp. 137–163). New York: Norton.

Bateson, G., Haley, J., Jackson, D., & Weakland, J. (1956). Toward a theory of schizophrenia. *Behavioral Science, 1,* 251–264.

Beck, A. T. (1976). *Cognitive therapy and the emotional disorders.* New York: International Universities Press.

Boik, B. L., & Goodwin, E. A. (2000). *Sandplay therapy: A step-by-step manual for psychotherapists of diverse orientations.* New York: Norton.

Bowlby, J. (1969). *Attachment and loss. Volume I: Attachment.* New York: Basic Books.

Bradway, K., & McCoard, B. (1997). *Sandplay: Silent workshop of the psyche.* New York: Routledge.

Breunlin, D., Schwartz, R., & Karrer, B. (1992). *Metaframeworks: Transcending the models of family therapy.* San Francisco: Jossey-Bass.

Brooks, R. (1993). Creative characters. In C. E. Schaefer & D. M. Cangelosi (Eds.), *Play therapy techniques* (pp. 211–224). New York: Aronson.

Brown, D. T., & Prout, H. T. (1989). *Counseling and psychotherapy with children and adolescents: Theory and practice for school and clinic settings.* Brandon, VT: Clinical Psychology.

Burns, R. C. (1987). *Kinetic-House-Tree-Person Drawings (K-H-T-P).* New York: Brunner/Mazel.

Burns, R. C., & Kaufman, S. H. (1970). *Kinetic Family Drawings (K-F-D): An introduction to understanding children through kinetic drawings.* New York: Brunner/Mazel.

Busby, D. M., & Smith, G. L. (2000). Family therapy with children who are victims of physical violence. In C. E. Bailey (Ed.), *Children in therapy: Using the family as a resource* (pp. 164–191). New York: Norton.

Conners, C. K. (1989). *Conners' Parent and Teacher Questionnaire.* North Tonawanda, NY: Multi-Health Systems.

Dunn, R. L., & Schwebel, A. I. (1995). Meta-analysis of marital therapy outcome research. *Journal of Family Psychology, 9,* 58–68.

DuPaul, G., & Stoner, G. (1994). *ADHD in schools: Assessment and intervention strategies.* New York: Guilford Press.

Fatout, M. F. (1990). Consequences of abuse on the relationships of children. *Families in Society, 71,* 76–81.

Freeman, J., Epston, D., & Lobovits, D. (1997). *Playful approaches to serious problems: Narrative therapy with children and their families.* New York: Norton.

Freeman-Longo, R., & Blanchard, G. (1998). *Sexual abuse in America: Epidemic of the 21st century.* Brandon, VT: Safer Society.

Freud, A. (1928). *Introduction to the technique of child analysis.* New York: Nervous and Mental Diseases.

Freud, A. (1946). *The psychoanalytic treatment of children.* London: Imago.

Freud, S. (1933). *Collected papers.* London: Hogarth Press.

Gardner, R. A. (1993). Mutual storytelling. In C. E. Schaefer & D. M. Cangelosi (Eds.), *Play therapy techniques* (pp. 199–211). New York: Aronson.

Gil, E. (1994). *Play in family therapy.* New York: Guilford Press.

Greenberg, L. S., Ford, C. L., Alden, L., & Johnson, S. M. (1993). In-session change in emotionally focused therapy. *Journal of Consulting and Clinical Psychology, 61,* 78–84.

Griffith, M., & Coleman, R. (1988). *Family therapy: An ecological perspective*. Greeley, CO: Health Psychology.

Griffith, M., & Thiessen-Barrett, J. (2000). Creative activities for children of divorce. In C. E. Bailey (Ed.), *Children in therapy: Using the family as a resource* (pp. 242–277). New York: Norton.

Group for the Advancement of Psychiatry Committee on the Family. (1996). Global Assessment of Relational Functioning Scale (GARF): I. Background and rationale. *Family Process, 35,* 155–172.

Hammen, C. (1991). *Depression runs in families: The social context of risk and resilience in children of depressed mothers.* New York: Springer-Verlag.

Hullings-Catalano, V. (1996). Physical abuse of children by parents. In D. M. Busby (Ed.), *The impact of violence on the family: Treatment approaches for therapists and other professionals* (pp. 43–74). Boston: Allyn & Bacon.

Irwin, E. C., & Malloy, E. S. (1975). Family puppet interview. *Family Process, 14,* 170–191.

Johnson, S. (1996). *The practice of emotionally focused marital therapy: Creating connection.* New York: Brunner/Mazel.

Johnson, S. M., & Greenberg, L. S. (1995). The emotionally focused approach to problems in adult attachment. In N. S. Jacobson & A. S. Gurman (Eds.), *Clinical handbook of couple therapy.* New York: Guilford Press.

Johnson, S. M., & Lee, A. C. (2000). Emotionally focused family therapy: Restructuring attachment. In C. E. Bailey (Ed.), *Children in therapy: Using the family as a resource* (pp. 112–133). New York: Norton.

Johnson, S. M., Maddeaux, C., & Blouin, J. (1998). Emotionally focused family therapy for bulimia: Changing attachment patterns. *Psychotherapy, 35,* 238–247.

Kaslow, N. J., Deering, C. G., & Ash, P. (1996). Relational diagnosis of child and adolescent depression. In F. W. Kaslow (Ed.), *Handbook of relational diagnosis and dysfunctional family patterns* (pp. 171–185). New York: Wiley.

Kaslow, N. J., Mintzer, M. B., Meadows, L. A., & Grabill, C. M. (2000). A family perspective on assessing and treating childhood depression. In C. E. Bailey (Ed.), *Children in therapy: Using the family as a resource* (pp. 215–241). New York: Norton.

Kaslow, N. J., & Racusin, G. R. (1994). Family therapy for depression in young people. In W. M. Reynolds & H. F. Johnston (Eds.), *Handbook of depression in children and adolescents* (pp. 345–363). New York: Plenum Press.

Keim, J. P. (2000). Oppositional behavior in children. In C. E. Bailey (Ed.), *Children in therapy: Using the family as a resource* (pp. 278–307). New York: Norton.

Keith, D. V., & Whitaker, C. A. (1994). Play therapy: A paradigm for work with families. In C. E. Schaefer & L. J. Carey (Eds.), *Family play therapy* (pp. 185–202). Northvale, NJ: Aronson.

Klein, M. (1932). *The psycho-analysis of children.* London: Hogarth Press.

Knell, S. M. (1994). Cognitive-behavioral play therapy. In K. J. O'Connor & C. E. Schaefer (Eds.), *Handbook of play therapy. Volume 2: Advances and innovations* (pp. 111–142). New York: Wiley.

Kratochwill, T. R., & Morris, R. J. (1991). *The practice of child therapy.* New York: Pergamon Press.

Landreth, G. L. (1991). *Play therapy: The art of the relationship.* Bristol, PA: Accelerated Development.

Lusterman, D. (1985). An ecosystemic approach to family-school problems. *American Journal of Family Therapy, 13,* 22–30.

Maddock, J., & Larson, N. (1995). *Incestuous families: An ecological approach to understanding.* New York: Norton.

Mesalam, B., & Griffith, M. (1993). Using puppets to facilitate the acceptance of a second mother by a four-year-old boy. *Association for Play Therapy, Newsletter, 12,* 2–4.

Miller, C., & Boe, J. (1990). Tears into diamonds: Transformation of child psychic trauma through sandplay and storytelling. *Arts in Psychotherapy, 17,* 247–257.

Moustakas, C. E. (1959). *Psychotherapy with children: The living relationship.* New York: Carron.

O'Connor, K. J., & Schaefer, C. E. (Eds.). (1994). *Handbook of play therapy. Volume 2: Advances and innovations.* New York: Wiley.

Oster, G. D., & Caro, J. E. (1990). *Understanding and treating depressed adolescents and their families.* New York: Wiley.

Oster, G. D., & Gould, P. (1987). *Using drawings in assessment and therapy.* New York: Brunner/Mazel.

Pardeck, J. T. (1990). Using bibliotherapy in clinical practice with children. *Psychological Reports, 67,* 1043–1049.

Polson, M. (2000). Attention-Deficit/Hyperactivity Disorder: Working with children and their families. In C. E. Bailey (Ed.), *Children in therapy: Using the family as a resource* (pp. 308–338). New York: Norton.

Racusin, G. R., & Kaslow, N. J. (1991). Assessment and treatment of childhood depression. In P. A. Keller & S. R. Heyman (Eds.), *Innovations in clinical practice: A sourcebook* (Vol. 10, pp. 223–242). Sarasota, FL: Professional Resource Exchange.

Riley, S., & Malchiodi, C. (1994). *Integrative approaches to family and art therapy.* Chicago: Magnolia Street.

Schaefer, C. E., & Carey, L. J. (1994). *Family play therapy.* Northvale, NJ: Aronson.

Schaefer, C. E., & O'Connor, K. J. (1983). *Handbook of play therapy.* New York: Wiley.

Sholevar, G. P. (1994). *The transmission of depression in families and children: Assessment and intervention.* Northvale, NJ: Aronson.

Simons, V. A., & Freedman, J. (2000). Witnessing bravery: Narrative ideas for working with children and families. In C. E. Bailey (Ed.), *Children in therapy: Using the family as a resource* (pp. 20–45). New York: Norton.

Stone Fish, L., Jensen, M., Reichert, T., & Wainman-Sauda, J. (2000). In C. E. Bailey (Ed.), *Children in therapy: Using the family as a resource* (pp. 192–214). New York: Norton.

Thomas, V. (1999). David and the family bane: Therapy with a gifted child and his family. *Journal of Family Psychotherapy, 10,* 15–24.

United Kingdom Department of Health. (2000). *Children and child protection registers 1999–00.* London: Department of Health.

United Nations Children's Fund. (1997). *State of the world's children–1996.* New York: UNICEF.

Van Fleet, R. (1994). *Filial therapy: Strengthening parent-child relationships through play.* Sarasota, FL: Professional Resource.

von Bertalanffy, L. (1968). *General systems theory.* New York: Braziller.

Wallerstein, J., & Blakeslee, S. (1989). *Second chances: Men, women and children a decade after divorce.* New York: Ticknor & Fields.

Warren, B. (Ed.). (1996). *Using creative arts in therapy.* New York: Routledge.

White, M. (1995). *Re-authoring lives: Interviews and essays.* Adelaide, Australia: Dulwich Centre.

White, M., & Epston, D. (1990). *Narrative means to therapeutic ends.* New York: Norton.

Winnicott, D. W. (1971). *Playing and reality.* New York: Basic Books.

CHAPTER 5

A Biopsychosocial Approach to Play Therapy with Maltreated Children

LAURA PALMER, ANNE R. FARRAR, AND NOURIMAN GHAHARY

The maltreatment of children results in various degrees of impact across the spectrum of development. The consequences evolve contingent on multiple factors related to the type of abuse, relationship to the perpetrator, level of violence involved, age of onset, and chronicity. Additionally, multiple mediating factors shape outcomes (Kendall-Tackett, Williams, & Finkelhor, 1993; Trickett, 1993), including responsiveness of a nonoffending parent (Everson, Hunter, Runyan, Edelsohn, & Coulter, 1989), early intervention, temperament of the child, economic variables (Trickett, Aber, Carlson, & Cicchetti, 1991), and genetic factors (Davidson, Hughes, Blazer, & George, 1991; Yehuda, Schmeidler, Giller, Binder-Brynes, & Siever, 1998). Maltreatment can potentially affect a child interpersonally (Cicchetti & Toth, 1995), academically (Eckenrode, Laird, & Doris, 1993), vocationally (Malinosky-Rummell & Hansen, 1993), and spiritually. Finally, maltreatment and abuse can potentially be transmitted intergenerationally. Given this complex web of factors, treatment and assessment cannot be linear, but require multifactorial, directive, and dynamic models. Play provides a child's primary vehicle for cognitive, social, and physical growth and development. Crucial neural development occurs in and supports the biopsychosocial process of development in childhood. Erikson's (1950/1963) developmental theory, when viewed beyond the primary tasks, offers an integrative perspective for understanding both trauma and the facilitation of normal development in interfacing solid theory and practice for effective intervention in assessment and therapy involving a known history of child maltreatment.

HISTORY OF PLAY THERAPY

Psychologists have expressed interest in children and play since the later part of the nineteenth century (Schaefer & Cangelosi, 1993). Rousseau was the first author to seek an understanding of children through their play. Later, Sigmund Freud was quoted as describing play as a "poetic creation" (p. 1). This implies that "play allows the child to transpose passive experiences into active experiences" (p. 1). Melanie Klein (1999), from the English school of psychoanalysis, and Anna Freud (1999), associated with the Vienna school of psychoanalysis, both spent their careers demonstrating that play acts as a "partial substitution for the more verbal methods of child treatment" (p. 1).

Jackson (1998) noted that play therapists focus on "helping the child heal, using the natural language of play" (p. 1). During the 1940s, Virginia Axline introduced play therapy into the "mainstream of psychotherapy" (Schaefer & Cangelosi, 1993, p. 19). In 1998, Phillips and Landreth conducted a survey of play therapists and found that 44% identified as counselors or therapists, 22% as psychologists, 18% as social workers, and 1% as psychiatrists. Today, clinicians use a variety of approaches and techniques, ranging from D. W. Winnicott's Squiggle Game to Richard Gardner's mutual storytelling to his use of the Talking, Feeling, and Doing Game. Play within a therapeutic environment ranges from symbolic, such as the use of puppets, costumes, and blocks, to techniques using natural media of sand, water, and food, to drawing and art techniques (e.g., finger painting), the use of board games such as chess and checkers, and the use of computers and video games.

Play forms a central aspect of a child's life. Gitlin-Weiner, Sandgrund, and Schaefer (2000) viewed play as a less stressful way for children to share and experience their strengths and weaknesses. Florey (1999) described play as one of the most common phenomena for children, one that "is singularly difficult to define, describe, and delimit" (p. 62). She added that "it is known that play is a biological, psychological, and sociocultural phenomenon" (p. 62) capable of facilitating development in a number of arenas and reflective of evolution in each of these areas.

Frank (1999b) discussed children's exploration through play, referring to children as innately "curious and exploratory" (p. 77) and generally capable of utilizing play as a "method of trial and error" (p. 77) to help cope with the world. Depicting an adult's world as too gigantic and chaotic for a child to comprehend, Frank noted that children need to develop and accomplish a way for them to cope and to not be as threatened—through the use of play. Through engagement in all types of play, whether free or imaginative, children can "resolve some of the perplexities and clarify their feelings" (p. 74). Play provides a process for personality development as a child explores, manipulates, uses objects, animals, people, and events to learn, and repeatedly goes over these changes until the time for "creating his own life space" arrives (Frank, 1999a, p. 51).

Terr (1990) characterized the everyday play of childhood as free, light-spirited, and easy. A few games will evolve for an ordinary child when needing to master an upcoming step in life, gratify an inner wish, deal with an uncomfortable fear, or cope with the aftereffects of an unpleasant event. A child will move away from the self in ordinary play and can pretend to be an animal, a superhero, or a professional. The further a child moves away from self, the more successfully play will help to achieve mastery. Frank (1999b) observed that maltreated children are "suppressed and robbed of their spontaneity and denied of the opportunities they need for learning and growing" (p. 77).

Children who come to therapy may present as angry, frustrated, shy, withdrawn, inhibited, and frightened, and they may further express these emotions by exhibiting temper tantrums, refusing to speak, and running around the office (Bow, 1993). The therapist's goal involves enticing and engaging a child in the therapeutic process by using several tasks. As a first task, a therapist joins, works with a resistant child, and develops an alliance. Second, a therapist needs to observe the play and assess the underlying themes and dynamics, that a child presents. Third, a therapist helps a child develop greater insight and awareness. Fourth, a therapist assists a child in interpreting behaviors and emotions and facilitates increased awareness of these "feelings, attitudes, and the relationship between events in his life that he is unaware of at the present time" (Dodds, 1987, as cited in Bow, 1993, p. 23). Bow discussed the importance of toys in play therapy, indicating that they are used to facilitate contact with children by both gaining their interest and their attention. Toys, therefore, allow a child an opportunity for emotional release along with a "medium for sublimation" (p. 23).

ASSESSMENT

Assessment forms an essential part of every therapeutic process, including play therapy. Bow (1993) indicated that children can vary widely in their social, emotional, and cognitive development. Because these developmental factors prove crucial in working effectively, therapists need to be aware of these aspects when assessing a child's level of difficulty. Therapists' awareness of the chronological and mental ages of children who present in therapy and the ability to make distinctions between the two and to plan treatment based on such information represents a crucial step in treating children. Developmental knowledge also affects a child-therapist relationship and interaction. Just as children grow and become more developmentally complex, so does their play. Hence, a therapist faces a more difficult challenge in seeking to interact with a child who, based on his or her developmental task demands, engages only in solitary or parallel play, than in interacting with a child who is developmentally prepared to engage with others in the course of the play.

The assessment of play therapy can occur in multiple ways. A child's interactions with others in the play can give the therapist useful information as to level of social development. Parten's (1932) model of social participation spans four areas: unoccupied, onlooker, solitary, and group. This model details the developmental progression of play from a social interaction perspective, marking the progression of the child from that of an onlooker, to independent and parallel play through cooperative, dynamic play involving more than the individual. Play can also indicate cognitive maturation by assessing how a child reviews a playroom and selects toys of interest from a range of items including infant and toddler toys and preschool-level toys and activities. A youngster may select toys designed for a much younger child for various reasons, including degree of comfort. The toys may represent current issues; for example, a 7-year-old may select a baby rattle and bottle after the birth of a new sibling, wanting to be the baby again; a 10-year-old may choose a puzzle designed for toddlers because of feeling more competent solving this level of puzzle. Children often pick toys that will expand their current levels of cognitive and physical competence; some stay away from such toys. The challenge lies in determining if the challenge proves too overwhelming.

Assessment can also transpire across the process of therapy and the symbolism involved in play. Additionally, how a child incorporates a therapist in play (unoccupied, onlooker, solitary, group), the choice of toys, and process of how play evolves within and across a relationship offers a very informative source of data about the child's level of ego development, expectations of or experience with relationships, moral development, cognitive ability, and worldview.

Gil (1991) noted that assessment is a continuous part of play therapy: "Children may unfold during therapy, sharing their emotions and feelings as they begin to trust" (p. 61), as they constantly experience developmental changes occurring alongside changes in their personality. Play is central to the life of preschoolers; it is a way they can demonstrate their concerns, their fears, and the cognitive style by which they understand their experiences, in addition to their abilities to imitate and interact with their environments.

Models of Play Therapy

Influenced by Seyle's (1936) work on stress and coping, Webb (1991) proposed that children, like adults, experience stress in the normal course of their lives. Children differ, however, in that their defense mechanisms are limited because of their age as well as their more restricted exposure to a variety of events. Webb suggested that, therefore, children are vulnerable to stress and may require assistance in learning new coping methods. Similarly, Mann and McDermott (1983), portrayed children who have been abused or neglected as tending to be inhibited, confused, and unimaginative. They may present at a more primitive level attributable to regression or being fixated at a particular stage. Themes of stealing, hiding, and hoarding commonly emerge.

Clinicians have proposed and used various models of play therapy for the treatment of maltreated children. Oaklander (1988) offered a model in which the "process of work with the child is a gentle, flowing one—an organic event" (p. 53), indicating that therapists will find their own styles of guiding a session and following a child's lead. The purpose of therapy always remains helping children become aware of their existence in the world. Gil (1991) stated that because children who have been abused, whether physically or sexually, have suffered an intrusive act, the therapist's interventions should be nonintrusive, allowing the child emotional and physical space.

Directive Play Therapy

Several authors have discussed directive play therapy, each employing and advocating a unique form and level of interaction between child and therapist. The best-known work was introduced and published by Ann Jernberg (1979), who credited the work of Austin Des Lauriers (1962) as the forerunner of the Theraplay method. This form of play therapy is based on children's developmental as opposed to chronological age, making it an appropriate approach "for the one who behaves in ways that keep distance between himself and the kind of relationship his therapist, as parent surrogate, knows he needs" (Jernberg, 1979, p. 26), such as the autistic child. According to Jernberg, in this method of treatment, the adult is in charge, and any and all of the following purposes may be targeted for attainment in the course of therapy: (1) structuring—guiding and defining; (2) challenging—intruding to both arouse and excite; and (3) nurturing—for caring, feeding, and cuddling.

This method of treatment is not deemed appropriate for children with a recent history of traumatic experience, such as children experiencing the recent loss of a parent, molestation, or a major surgery (Jernberg, 1979). These typically may benefit more from treatment involving crisis intervention. Instead, children, especially foster or adopted children with a distant history of abuse or other past trauma, would be suited for Theraplay. The goals encompass assisting such children in viewing themselves as more lovable, having the parents evolve a lovable infancy with them (creating a "normal infancy"), and helping the children stop "abuse-evoking mannerisms" by eliminating testing, teasing, and "provocative" behaviors.

When children begin the course of this directive approach to play therapy, they are informed by the therapist that the sessions will be fun, clearly directed by the therapist, and action-oriented, and that, in addition, the sessions will be clearly delineated as to the roles of the therapist and patient, and time and space. Jernberg (1979) presented the example of a "good nursery school day" as characterizing the course of each Theraplay session, with activities occurring in a predetermined way. She articulated 26 "do's and don'ts" for a Theraplay therapist, among which are therapist insisting on eye contact, using every opportunity for physical contact, helping the children see themselves as "unique, special, separate, and outstanding" (p. 29), and looking for opportunities to differentiate self from a child. In this approach, the therapist is considered to be the primary object in the playroom.

Nondirective Play Therapy
Virginia Axline (1969) is credited for the development of nondirected or client-centered play therapy. In this mode of treatment, the "therapist leaves the responsibility and the direction to the child" (p. 9). Axline presented the case of Dibs in her 1964 book discussing his treatment from the beginning of their relationship to the end. For Axline, an "individual becomes aware of the part he can play in directing his own life—freedom from this inner authority—that he is better able to see his course of action with more accuracy" (p. 11). She described children as resilient and typically quick to forgive and forget negative experiences. She noted that, unless experiences are "extremely bad," a child "is accepting of life as he finds it, and accepting of the people with whom he lives" (p. 12). Axline experienced children as displaying eagerness, curiosity, and a great love for the simplest pleasures in life.

Nondirective therapy allows "children to be themselves," to experience complete acceptance without the "evaluation or pressure to change" (Axline, 1969, p. 15). This form of treatment allows opportunities for children to learn about themselves and to chart a personal course openly. Play provides the natural medium for self-expression. In play therapy, "the child is given the opportunity to play out his accumulated feelings of tension, frustration, insecurity, aggression, fear, bewilderment, confusion" (p. 16). The play therapy room offers "good growing ground" (p. 16), replete with toys and potential for activities, while allowing a child freedom to choose. In this room, children exercise control, are in command of the situation, and are permitted to "spread their wings." For Axline, children must feel comfortable to express themselves completely. A child should perceive the therapist in the room as accepting, friendly, and understanding and as implementing only a few limitations, which typically convey a feeling of both reality and security. Therefore, a therapist needs to demonstrate acceptance of a child; the development of rapport proves essential to the process.

Psychodynamic Play Therapy
Melanie Klein and Anna Freud have both been named as the forerunners of psychoanalytic play therapy. For Klein (1999), play offered unique access to the unconscious of a child. She described the playroom as a very simple environment in which each child would have a personal drawer and would keep his or her own simple, small, and nonmechanical playthings locked. She indicated that this gives the child a sense of privacy with the therapist.

Klein (1999) observed that children are capable of insight and of fully understanding interpretations when both salient and stated succinctly. Interpretations need to be presented in a manner a child can comprehend. Anna Freud (1999) tended to focus more on a transference relationship occurring between therapist and child. She regarded the playroom as a manageable place for a child to carry out all of the real-world activities, but in the confinement of a fantasy experience. Freud emphasized the task of psychoanalytic play therapy as removing obstacles that block children's development. This allows them to progress, so they can be effective human beings.

Anna Freud (1999) did not consider play to be equivalent to an adult's free associations. Rather, it allows for an ego-mediated mode of behavior, which supplies an abundant amount of information. The therapist also needs to gather collateral information, such as including the parents (Esman, 1983). Gil (1991) indicated that Klein proposed play as a direct substitute for verbalizations whereas Freud endorsed play to facilitate the relationship between child and therapist.

CONCEPTUAL FRAMEWORK: ERIKSON'S MODEL AND CONSEQUENCES OF CHILD MALTREATMENT

ERIK ERIKSON: A PRESCRIPTIVE-HOLISTIC GUIDE TO INTERVENTION

Review of the sequelae of child sexual abuse makes clear that any attempt at intervention needs to be comprehensive, addressing the developmental systems as well as the larger macrosystem of a child in relationship to family, peer group, institution, and culture. Erikson (1950/1963) has provided the most inclusive theory, spanning all aspects of development. His far-reaching theory encompasses biopsychosocial, cognitive, cultural, and institutional factors that are affected by, and affect, a history of child maltreatment. Most important, he has given us a prescriptive plan for intervention for maltreated children.

Erikson organized his theory around eight primary tasks that occur across the life span. Tasks are achieved at various levels of mastery, allowing for progression onto the next stage. If there is optimal task-resolution in the current stage, the individual will have more psychological resources available to address the challenges in the subsequent stages. If there is less-than-optimal task-resolution, the individual will still advance through the next stage, but the likelihood of optimal task-resolution is lessened. Erikson's theory provides for progression through all of the stages of development in spite of less-than-optimal task-resolution. Thus, there is room for optimism, but the consequences of poor task-resolution can set up the individual for a lifetime of interpersonal challenges, negatively impacting potentially all areas of functioning. The emergence of psychological structures occurs because of a dynamic person-environment interaction across critical periods of brain development. The following brief review delineates the processes that facilitate development as well as provides a backdrop for understanding the possible impact of maltreatment across the various critical stages.

Neurological Development and the Impact of Trauma

Psychological development is contingent on the range of ego functions being expanded as the number of cognitive structures increases. The neurological underpinnings of this concept can be supported by Fischer and Rose's (1994) work on neural development. They have outlined a framework for a theory of dynamic development of the human brain in coordination with behavior. They portrayed brain development as a dynamic process involving myelination, synaptic density, dendritic branching, brain mass, pruning of neurons and synapses, and brain electrical activity that all change systematically with age, throughout childhood into young adulthood. They further delineated the process as contingent on the establishment of neural networks "that support these control systems or skills.... Each network is composed of many connected components, which are distributed across brain areas and typically operate in parallel" (p. 5). Further, Fischer and Rose explained what is known about competition and coordination of these neural networks. Competition occurs between neurons and neural connections for survival and growth; those that receive less input are pruned, and those that are active are sustained. Understanding that this process is critically related to early experience is essential in recognizing the potential lifelong effects of an abusive environment.

An equally significant and related process concerns synaptogenesis. Huttenlocher (1994) elaborated on synaptogenesis as a dynamic process spanning infancy and childhood:

Growth of connections predominates during infancy; this is followed by pruning of connections in early childhood, which may be necessary for the emergence of efficient cortical processing.... The period during which there are an excess number of synapses appears to coincide with the period during which the brain exhibits increased functional plasticity.... It suggests that the fine structure or connectivity of the cerebral cortex may undergo permanent changes in response to environmental modification during infancy and childhood. (p. 148)

Cyclical cortical reorganization constitutes a relevant and essential aspect of cortical development. Thatcher (1994) postulated iterative "growth spurts" of cortical connections based on his EEG coherence analyses from 436 children and adolescents ranging in mean age from 6 months to 16 years. Based on his findings, he suggested that the first cycle occurs from the age of 1.5 to 5 years. The second cycle occurs around age 5 to 10 years, and the third cycle typically happens from the age of 10 to 14. Thatcher proposed that the left hemisphere consists of a developmental process by which the anterior-posterior and lateral-medial gradients are lengthened sequentially between the posterior sensory areas and the frontal regions. The right hemisphere consists of a sequential growth from the long-distance frontal connections. These cycles of the left and right hemisphere cycles may repeat throughout the life span. Thatcher also believed that a specific cognitive function, mediated by either the left or right hemisphere, continues to experience or participate in cyclic reorganization and reintegration at each cycle or subcycle of development rather than expand at a specific age and then cease to grow.

In summary, the developing neurophysiological system appears to have critical or sensitive periods of growth and development. Susceptibility to injury and disruption resulting from environmental stressors may be linked to these various critical or sensitive periods. The effects of emotional distress and psychological trauma on the neurophysiological developments of humans, although well conceptualized by Luria (1973), remain in the infancy stage of research. However, the significance of maternal deprivation, a well-established source of psychological trauma on emotional and cognitive development, has been well-documented in the work of Spitz (1945) and Bowlby (1951). Additionally, the level of environmental enrichment or deprivation during critical periods has been shown to have significant effects on the level of brain density in laboratory-reared animals (Forgays & Forgays, 1952; Hebb, 1949). The specifics of the process of neurological development have yet to be thoroughly explained. Epstein (1974, 1980) has proposed critical periods of postnatal neurological development that correlate with Piaget's periods of cognitive development:

The first phase is the genetically specified plan, which allows for the ontogenesis of the complex architecture of the brain and regulates the timing of developmental processes, such as neural cell proliferation and migration (prenatally) and competitive neuronal elimination and myelination. The second phase, overlapping with the latter part of the first, pertains to the post-natal phenomenon whereby neuronal networks and connections are established via a variety of mechanisms, including environmental stimulation, hormone, stress, and so on.... This sculpting process presumably is biologically advantageous since it reduces the need for a genetic plan for programming an enormous number of synaptic connections and allows for optimal flexibility of the nervous system in response to evolving environmental demands. The loss of synapses continues into adolescence.... The third phase of neural development consists of the daily process of adaptive synaptic modification that allows for memory of ongoing experiences and continuing changes in neural maps throughout the life-span. (Epstein as cited in Dawson, Panangiotides, Grofer-Klinger, & Hill, 1992, p. 154)

Although Erikson (1950/1963) did not articulate the role of brain development as it relates to psychosocial development, his theory spans the various mediating and facilitating factors that are directly related to the aforementioned neural processes. The interface of child with environment is absolutely required for the effective cultivation of neural development. Adaptive responsiveness of the environment will facilitate optimal neural development; neglectful or abusive responsiveness will advance neural development that supports the organism's survival, but may be less adaptive interpersonally and psychosocially in alternative situations. Simply put, the organism's genetically programmed neural development remains responsive to experience. A less-than-optimal environmental response will alter development.

A final concept, relative neural plasticity, requires emphasis. This signifies the brain's capacity to "learn" or develop new neural connections in the face of altered experience. Plasticity is not absolute, nor is it fully understood. However, studies (Black & Greenough, 1998; Greenough, 1987; Klintsova & Greenough, 1999) increasingly support that the brain does respond to altered experience, and that plasticity actually extends across the life span, although this may occur to some diminished capacity. Erikson understood environmental responsiveness as essential for optimal development and provided a delineation of specific and necessary task-facilitating factors across each of the eight stages. He also recognized play as a critical vehicle in facilitating development across childhood.

Developmental Processes and Play
Erikson (1950/1963) appreciated play as the process by which a child attempts to synchronize internal and external processes for further self-definition. He realized that play permits the child to work off "pent-up emotions and to find imaginary relief for past frustrations" (p. 215). To elaborate: Play actually provides a vehicle for mastery of conflict, abandonment, and fears.

Erikson's theory is also congruent with current trauma theory in that he viewed an individual as striving toward integration, mastery, and recovery rather than remaining fixed in a stage. Revisiting Erikson's primary delineation of his stages in conjunction with an overlay of a history of child maltreatment provides a pertinent perspective. His theory encompasses task-facilitating factors that can be interpreted through play-therapy interventions that target the less-than-optimal task-resolution occurring in many children with a history of maltreatment.

Stage 1: Basic Trust versus Basic Mistrust. Stage 1 transpires during infancy, from birth to approximately 18 months of age, and parallels Freud's oral stage. This stage is organized around an infant's need to develop an adequate sense of trust in relation to mistrust. Optimal achievement emerges in this stage as infants develop a sense of basic trust in living and a basic faith in their own existences. Confidence grows that physiological needs will be met by caregivers, resulting in diminished anxiety as well as the beginning ability to tolerate a small amount of anxiety. Across the stage, the infant needs to develop a sense of the world as being safe, predictable, and sufficient. Optimal task-resolution here will result in a drive to continue growing with sufficient motivation to address the challenges of the next stage. An overarching and necessary goal for this stage entails development of attachment to another person. Related is the capacity for trust that evolves and establishes the foundation for the ability to establish loving relationships later in life. Combined, the preceding achievements form the foundation for the development of a sense of self-worth.

Specific factors necessary for facilitating optimal mastery at stage 1 are necessarily localized in environment-infant interactions. An infant requires consistency and predictability in having physical and emotional needs met. Natural biological rhythms must be respected. This necessitates that an infant be fed when hungry, be kept clean and warm, and be allowed undisturbed sleep. A child needs to be protected from harm, which includes falls, disease, and overstimulation. Another basic need involves tactile stimulation, which conveys the fundamental notion of being loved. At this stage, the consistent presence of the primary caregiver(s) proves essential for transmitting a sense of trustworthiness and security.

Undesirable task-resolution at this stage may result in a wide range of behaviors. A child may present as withdrawn or apathetic, with deep-seated rage reactions, or with feelings of dependency. The incentive for growth is stifled. A child with poor resolution of stage 1 may display persistent feelings of suspicion or insecurity. An overriding inability to trust others results in impaired intimate relationships. A correlating lack of trust of the external world may appear as generalized anxiety.

A history of any form of child maltreatment in this first and critically formative stage easily predicts many of the behavioral and emotional symptoms of Posttraumatic Stress Disorder, Reactive Attachment Disorder, generalized anxiety, and pervasive developmental disorders. It also coincides with previous research (Kendall-Tackett et al., 1993) indicating that the level of relationship between the child victim of maltreatment and the perpetrator poses a critical factor in predicting severity and chronicity of psychological harm.

The utility of Erikson's theory becomes clearer when therapists draw on it to interpret the task-facilitating factors as age-appropriate play-therapy interventions. Whether one subscribes to a purely dynamic orientation to play therapy or a more interactive or even directive approach, task-facilitating factors can guide therapeutic process toward facilitating mastery of the heretofore-incomplete task-resolution. Obviously, consistency across a therapeutic relationship is paramount, as a therapist represents the responsive environment, anticipating the need for safety, security, stimulation, and protection. A therapist needs to exercise foresight regarding a child's age-appropriate natural needs, such as hunger, fatigue, and warmth; a therapist can begin by providing necessary and appropriate labels for these feelings states. In accordance with the Eriksonian principles and traditional dynamic play therapy, this will most frequently happen symbolically. Therapists working with chronically traumatized children often have witnessed their inabilities to adequately express not only affective states, but also basic needs. This sometimes occurs because a child's ability for accurate reading of physiological cues as well as perceptions of the intensive behaviors of adults have been consistently and intentionally discredited. This inability for self-perception and assertion of basic needs also arises in neglected children.

Although physical touch as an accepted activity in therapy is debated, appropriate tactile stimulation can also serve as reparation. Again, this can occur directly or symbolically. All therapists are cautioned to be aware of the range of possible interpretations of direct physical touch as experienced by physically or sexually maltreated children. Perhaps the most conservative approach is achieved through symbolic parallel play, when the child witnesses the therapist appropriately touching, cuddling, and soothing a toy and labeling the possible emotional responses. As a child increases a sense of trust in the therapist, a representation of appropriate touch as demonstrated in his or her own play may emerge. A child may also begin to initiate or request a hug from a therapist.

The desirability of a therapist transmitting a sense of trustworthiness remains paramount in this stage of recovery. A therapist may need to review many times the purpose of therapy, clarification of roles, expectations, limits of confidentiality, schedules, and rules. The testing of limits is understood to be a direct consequence of poor task-resolution and essentially the failing of the responsible caregiver (i.e., a primary parent, the system, or society). Responsibility for earning trust through the facilitating factors lies with the therapist, not with children being expected to give what they do not yet possess. The length of time required for reasonable task-resolution resulting in an adaptive level of trust will vary across clients and is dependent on numerous factors both inside and outside the therapeutic relationship. Increasing the responsiveness of a child's current environment to replicate what is occurring in the therapeutic relationship will advance the goal of trust development.

Stage 2: Autonomy versus Shame and Doubt. Erikson's second stage revolves around the development of an adequate sense of autonomy in relation to shame and doubt. Across normal development, this stage spans from approximately 18 months to 3 years of age. After achieving desirable task-resolution, an individual is able to relate more deeply to caregivers and siblings. A toddler's awareness is extended as he or she becomes more capable of a larger awareness of the personal world. Toddlers begin to demonstrate control in response to limits imposed by caregivers. Additionally, with adequate task-resolution, tolerance increases, for frustration and anxieties are understood to be normal and transitory. Toddlers strive for independence, a beginning sense of competency, exertion of self-will, and increased self-awareness. Poor mastery at this stage results in self-doubt, fear of loss of love, withdrawal into self, unhealthy narcissism, shame, or perhaps defiant shamelessness. Personality traits or behaviors that may manifest later as results of poor task-resolution of this stage include some phobias, compulsions, eating disorders, communication disorders, enuresis, encopresis, and intimacy difficulties.

The task-facilitating factors that can be instructive to play therapy specific to this stage include providing a child freedom to explore the environment in a safe way. This involves stimulating and interesting objects in the environment. Firmness and setting limits of the therapy should not be overly restrictive. As should have occurred during normal development, a therapist will serve the function of surrogate ego. Praise and encouragement should be offered consistently and directed toward actual achievements, contributions, and age-appropriate risk-taking. Behavioral control is best gained through environmental restructuring and physical limiting.

At this stage in dynamic play therapy, the games will reveal exploration of issues of safety and risk-taking, punishment and control, the battle of good and evil, and bodily functions. The role of the therapist entails accurate reflection, acceptance, providing clear limits and boundaries, encouragement, and praise.

Stage 3: Initiative versus Guilt. The third stage spans ages 3 to 6 years and parallels Freud's Oedipal stage. During this stage, the developmental task concerns developing an adequate sense of initiative in relation to guilt. If a child achieves optimal task-resolution, he or she will demonstrate a sense of morality or conscience. A child's energies are focused on family relationships, family roles and boundaries, and gender identity. Fantasy play and imagination evolve. This represents an important cognitive ability, allowing a child to explore feelings symbolically, playing out conflicts, desires, and demands without self-loathing and guilt. A child extends perception of reality significantly during this stage. Children emerging with a healthy sense of autonomy from the previous stage appear more capable of engaging in cooperative play in stage 3, display an increased ability for sharing and extension of self in relation to others, and show increased capacity for accepting limits and for direction and purpose.

Poor task-resolution may appear as a sense of guilt over goals contemplated and acts initiated. Confusion about gender identity or family roles and boundaries may also indicate impaired task-resolution, as can disabling guilt about fantasies, especially relating to feelings about the opposite-sex parent. Anxiety, self-centeredness, overconformity, and continued symbiosis are frequent sequelae of undesirable task-resolution. This stage is facilitated by clearly delineated age boundaries and roles in a family. Unity in the primary caregivers' relationship or adequate personal adjustment of a single caregiver has to be secure enough to resist the child's demand for possessiveness. And adequate opportunities for a child to experience and establish relationships outside of the family prove important.

The therapeutic equivalents of task-facilitating factors include games involving symbolic play that can further healthy use of fantasy and exploration of family roles and gender. Puppets, mutual storytelling, and sand play provide excellent vehicles for fostering the unfolding of these issues in the protected space of the therapy. Therapists need to be careful to monitor for potentially high levels of anxiety that may emerge, even when a child is involved in well-disguised symbolic play. The use of guided imagery and relaxation training are valuable exercises to incorporate in this stage of therapy. Therapists will need to be cognizant of clearly delineating their roles, with clarification of the boundaries of a relationship. Rules and roles can be explored safely and in a meaningful way through the use of board games. Therapy also helps the child extend and confirm a sense of personal reality, offering a necessary alternative to the worldview instilled by a history of abuse and/or neglect. Small therapeutic playgroups can advance this goal as well.

Stage 4: Industry versus Inferiority. The primary goal of Erikson's fourth stage is evolving a sense of industry in relation to inferiority. This stage spans the period between 6 and 12 years of age and parallels a child's early academic experience. The positive psychological outcome of this stage includes a high level of self-efficacy as a learner and development of "know-how" across a wide variety of activities. A child develops a sense of responsibility and the capacity to live up to expectations. A sense of fair play and of justice commence. During this stage, a child enjoys cooperative play with others, generally with same-sex peers. Gender identification further increases. An adaptive child learns to achieve recognition by producing either academically or through personal interests, hobbies, or activities. Youngsters generally channel libidinal and aggressive drives into work and play. They identify with adult work roles and understand the interdependence of roles within larger society.

A child with poor task-resolution during this stage will present with a sense of inadequacy and inferiority and may demonstrate a lack of achievement or inability to learn. Overpowering anxiety may appear as well as a sense of being alone. These individuals may experience diminished enjoyment of activities, incompetence in participating in cooperative efforts, and, in all likelihood, difficulty moving outside the family and so may withdraw from outside contacts.

Task-facilitating factors implicate successful experiences in school or in other extracurricular activities such as in religious affiliations, athletics, music and art groups, and Scouts. Parents need to recognize the need for children to have positive relationships and experiences outside of the family. Additionally, positive parent role models also prove facilitative at this stage, giving children a template for developing and managing multiple roles, both inside and outside of a family. Siblings play an important part in providing interactions that promote a sense of self-confidence in competitive situations. Siblings also allow for additional opportunities for gender identification and broader experience in relationships. A stimulating environment with multiple opportunities for new experiences and growth proves crucial to a child's healthy development during this stage, as do adults who show understanding and patience in teaching new skills and knowledge.

Therapists nurturing or remediating this stage can provide various activities that foster in children new learning and self-efficacy as a learner. If the child is experiencing academic lags or failure, it is critical to initiate appropriate evaluations and interventions directed at facilitating learning. Academic failure compounds a child's sense of inferiority and can understandably lead to multiple, devastating consequences, including school dropout, unwanted pregnancy, unemployment, substance abuse, and juvenile delinquency (Hinshaw, 1992). A therapist can also act to encourage a child's connection with activities and mentors outside of therapeutic and family relationships, extending a sense of perspective and adaptive worldview. Beneficial play during this stage may include symbolic play incorporating perspective taking, role assignment, and bibliotherapy. As with the previous stages, small group therapy can also assist in advancing cooperative play, leadership skills, developing a sense of division of labor, and a notion of fair play.

The scope of this chapter is limited to childhood, precluding extending the theoretical application across adolescence. However, there continues to be utility across Erikson's remaining four stages for therapists working with clients who have experienced trauma interpreting the task-facilitating factors into supportive clinical interventions.

THE SYNDROME OF CHILD SEXUAL ABUSE: SYMPTOMS AND PROBLEMS TREATED

Sequelae of Child Maltreatment and Influences on the Development of Victims

Children view, understand, and respond to interpersonal events in unique and distinctive ways in accordance with their development level. Developmental task mastery and, therefore, the healthy growth of a child may be hindered through maltreatment, which may traumatize and nullify a victim. Child maltreatment constitutes a human-inflicted problem with potentially devastating consequences for victims, families, communities, and society at large. According to Terr (1990), psychic trauma results when there is a surprising and overwhelming emotional occurrence from the external world. Glaser (2000) proposed that the definition of child abuse and neglect encompasses both quantitative aspects of a single event or repeated events and qualitative dimensions of a pattern of interaction typical of a relationship between an abuser and a child. Glaser cited prior work (2000) that distinguished physical and sexual abuse as descriptive of the nature of events whereas neglect and emotional abuse characterize the relationship between an adult caregiver and child.

Documented research has evidenced a strong correlation between childhood maltreatment and failure in the areas of emotional, social, behavioral, and cognitive development, which can adversely influence individuals in childhood as well as in their adult lives (Cicchetti & Toth, 1995). Greenwald and Leitenberg (1990) suggested that thousands of children who are maltreated and traumatized each year exhibit a range of psychological, behavioral, cognitive, and physical symptoms, some of which are encompassed under the diagnosis of Posttraumatic Stress Disorder (PTSD).

PTSD often occurs in response to exposure to traumatic and stressful events, which loom as so extraordinary or severe that they are perceived as dangerous to one's integrity and sense of safety. The fourth edition of the *Diagnostic and Statistical Manual of Mental Disorders* (American Psychiatric Association [APA], 1994) incorporates severe psychological reactions to victimization under this diagnosis. Apart from the existence of a recognizable stressor, determining PTSD hinges on two major characteristic features that describe the experiences of victims of trauma: (1) reexperiencing a traumatic event, often through repetitive, intrusive memories or recurrent dreams, thoughts, and flashbacks of the event, and (2) numbing or reduced responsiveness demonstrated by feelings of detachment from the outside world, constricted affect, or diminished interest in specific activities.

Among others, Terr (1987) has offered more specific explanation regarding the sequelae of child abuse. Terr related four characteristics of childhood trauma: (1) memories, visualized or perceived, of the traumatic event; (2) repetitive behaviors; (3) trauma-specific fears; and (4) changes in attitudes about people, life, and the future, regardless of what diagnosis a traumatized individual ultimately receives. Repetitive dreams may not always occur as part of the symptomatology of a traumatized child. Discovering repeated dreams in most traumas that occur before a person is 5 years of age appears unlikely. Terr (1990) also observed that mutism, paralysis, and nighttime sensation of weight pressing on the chest often link back to traumatic incidents.

Documentation shows that, in the aftermath of trauma, children tend to have two behavioral options: to play or to enact. According to Terr (1990), if a child repeats behavioral reenactments frequently enough, personality changes may take place. Most personality shifts following from childhood psychic trauma prove problematic. These changes occur because children unconsciously need to repeat trauma-related thoughts, wishes, and behaviors. When the repetitive actions occur frequently enough to amount to "personality traits," a child's parents may notice a change for the worse: The child will seem quieter, bossier, meaner, more babyish, or more like a clown. Repetition of such behaviors as self-anesthesia and dissociation and of such primitive defenses as splitting and identification with the aggressor lead to large-scale personality problems.

Posttraumatic play (Terr, 1990), the repetitive reenactment of one's trauma, differs from ordinary child's play in being deliberate, unappeasable, somber, and "obsessively repeated." Play does not stop easily when traumatically inspired, and it may not change much over time. Personality reflects a more extreme deviation when a trauma is long-standing or frequently repeated.

Children instantaneously respond to maltreatment with fright; repeated and prolonged childhood trauma may result in extreme rage and its mirror image, inertia (Terr, 1990). Maltreatment, such as a history of sexual and emotional abuse, is associated with peer-relationship problems in childhood and sexual difficulties in adulthood (Cicchetti & Carlson, 1989). Furthermore, Terr has suggested that sexually misused children may become enraged and show their anger in three different ways: (1) identifying with the aggressor and becoming cruel and abusive themselves; (2) sustaining the role of the victim for life, falling into passivity and reconstituting the old victimization; or (3) becoming self-destructive when frustrated. Terr also proposed that children who experience prolonged sexual abuse may develop dissociative disorders, become numb, or use avoidance in coping with pain. If a perpetrator is a family member, if force and threats have not accompanied the abuse, and if the child has received privileges because of and has been enticed by the relationship, then the youngster faces cognitive dissonance.

In this regard, Davis and Frawley (1992) have noted that sexually abused children often assume responsibility for their own abuse because either the sexual acts frequently correspond with their age-appropriate fantasies and desires or they unconsciously identify with an abuser's desires in an attempt to heal the perpetrator.

From an object-relational perspective, early traumatic events have damaging effects on the ego and result in psychic helplessness. In this theoretical model, the central issue around the trauma concerns the extent to which abusive behavior represents a psychic abandonment and an intense betrayal of the child. Therefore, the relationship of the perpetrator to the child as well as parental action or failure to protect the child from abuse become important factors to consider.

From this theoretical perspective, in an atmosphere of respect and tolerance for their feelings, children in the phase of separation will be able to give up symbiosis with their caregivers and accomplish the steps toward individuation and autonomy. However, if the primary caregivers fail to provide safe, secure, and unconditional loving environments for them and expect them to accommodate their (parental) needs, often, but not always, the children will develop an "as-if personality," described by Winnicott as the "false self" (Miller, 1981). Such children, to prevent the loss of parental love, grow up revealing only what is expected of them and fusing completely with what they reveal. In doing so, they cannot develop and differentiate their "true" selves because they are unable to live them. According to Miller, one serious consequence of this early adaptation implies the impossibility of consciously experiencing certain feelings of their own either in childhood or later in adulthood.

Object-relations theorists also believe that, because early relationships are based on identification with the primary objects, if the parents or caregivers are abusive or neglectful, children will feel that their self is "bad." The internalization of the "bad" parental object symbolizes an effort to control those objects. Children, however, attempt to internally control objects that in the external world have control over them. Dissociation occurs when the child fails to control the objects. The child splits off, or dissociates the "bad" aspects of the object and of the self. Youngsters do this to sustain the good image of the self and that of the caretaker, whom they need and cannot abandon.

The Changed Child, the Changed World

According to Janoff-Bulman (1985), persons tend to hold three major assumptions about self and the world around them: belief in personal invulnerability; perception of the world as a meaningful, just, and orderly place; and a view of self as positive. Ordinarily, these assumptions allow for setting goals and developing expectations about self and environment. They affect how people go about their lives from day to day, assisting in planning activities and ordering one's life and self. These presuppositions can change as the result of victimization. The illusion of total control and order is shattered in the face of victimization, which occurs when individuals feel helpless in the face of a sudden, unexpected, devastatingly profound emotional blow or a succession of assaults.

Saporta and van der Kolk (1992) maintained that incomprehensibility, disrupted attachment, traumatic bonding, and inescapability contribute four primary features of traumatic events, which account for the overpowering nature of trauma. The core of trauma results from the overwhelming of a victim's psychological and biological coping mechanisms, which transpires when internal and external resources prove inadequate to manage an external threat. They termed this inability to make sense of traumatizing occurrences outside the normal range of experience and knowledge *incomprehensibility*. Assumptions about oneself and one's place in the world partly constrain the capacity to integrate such events into one's experiences. After confrontation with violence and abuse, a victim's views of self as invincible and the world as a safe and just place can never be the same again. In reconstructing one's view of self and the world, one's reactions often involve negative contemplations of oneself as worthless, helpless, and inadequate.

Regarding the role of attachment in coping with the aftermath of trauma, Saporta and van der Kolk (1992) inferred that human beings have a biological need to form attachments with others and that this need increases in times of stress and danger. Becker (as cited in Saporta & van der Kolk, 1992) asserted that pain, fatigue, fear, and loss motivate efforts to draw greater care from others. Those with less adequate internal coping resources during these times may cling to others to reconstitute a sense of stability and safety. Stable attachments may help to limit overwhelming physiological arousal, and prior experiences can help make sense of what has happened.

Several other authors have also demonstrated the relationship between the degree of posttraumatic dysfunction and loss of attachment and interpersonal supports (Pynoos & Eth, 1986). Lindy (1985) indicated that traumatized people often show lasting difficulties in developing subsequent relationships and tend to alternate between withdrawing socially and attaching impulsively and maladaptively. This undermining of interpersonal resources in turn maintains a traumatic situation. Saporta and van der Kolk (1992) also maintained that the need to stay attached contributes to the denial and dissociation of a traumatic experience. To preserve an image of safety and avoid losing the hope of the existence of a protector, victims may then begin to organize their lives around keeping a bond with and appeasing their abusers.

Although the actual victimizing events may occur only once, the experience of victimization and the emotional responses of victims are often long-lived, which gives the process of coping and recovering great importance. Ordinary children are not exempt from holding assumptions about a positive self and an orderly and controllable world; in fact, more often than not, children cannot conceive that misfortune and disorder can affect anyone by chance, thinking that they are responsible for what happens and can control what goes on around them. According to Terr (1990), when children are victimized, the two major feelings of shame and guilt may overwhelm their senses. She indicated that shame comes from the public exposure of one's vulnerabilities whereas guilt is a private sense of failing to meet one's own internal and private standards.

CASE EXAMPLE

Diagnosis and Assessment

Adam is a biracial (African American and Puerto Rican) boy. He was 8 years old when he was referred for individual therapy following an evaluation for child sexual abuse to address the emotional and behavioral sequelae of sexual abuse. He, along with his two siblings, had a history of physical and sexual abuse and subsequent adjustment and behavioral difficulties. Adam experienced multiple out-of-home placements before his eventual adoption. Biological family history was remarkable for instability. His mother suffered from depression/anxiety and was in treatment, including counseling and medication. Child Protective Services became involved with Adam and his siblings in 1990, when he was 3 years old, when allegations of neglect were made against Adam's mother. Although this was when the initial concern was documented, it is unlikely that Adam's initial experiences were sufficient with regard to adequate caregiving. In late 1991, his arm was dislocated by his purported father. After trial placements with other family members, Adam, then age 7, and his two sisters were placed in foster care. The following year, Adam was placed with a maternal aunt. He resided with his aunt for two years, and was later removed at the age of 9 because of physical and emotional abuse. He was placed in a therapeutic group home with a stated goal of preparing him for an adoptive placement. Adam joined an adoptive family at the age of 10. This placement failed within the first six months, and he returned to the group home. Multiple factors led to dissolution of the adoptive placement. Most prominently, the adoptive father placed rigid, unyielding expectations on Adam, and Adam experienced difficulty in shifting his primary attachment and sense of security from the group home staff to his adoptive family. He did not perceive this family to be warm or supportive. The placement was perhaps hastily decided on out of fear that he would have limited opportunities for adoption.

The record reflects that Adam had previously been diagnosed with Pervasive Developmental Disorder and Attention-Deficit/Hyperactivity Disorder (*DSM-IV*; APA, 1994). Adam has been involved in psychotherapy since the age of 8 with a diagnosis of Posttraumatic Stress Disorder. Academically, he is classified as perceptually impaired. Since he was placed in the therapeutic group home, Adam made considerable gains in his reading ability. Past medical history was unremarkable for head injury, loss of consciousness, extended high fevers with convulsions. His record indicates that he was the product of a full-term pregnancy. All developmental milestones were reported to be achieved within normal limits. The birthmother denied using drugs or alcohol during her pregnancy with Adam. Adam has a prior history of aggressive and sexualized acting-out behaviors. These behaviors significantly decreased following his placement at the therapeutic group home.

Adam was evaluated in 1996 to determine current neuropsychological functioning. That examination evidenced significant weaknesses in language-based academics, with a lack of phonemically based awareness, slow automatic retrieval of phonemically based information, and slow naming of information that should be overlearned by his age. He was also impulsive. However, he did show relative strengths in the area of visual-perceptual problem-solving and visual memory. His ability to communicate his wants and needs was determined to be significantly compromised. His IQ was measured at the 12th percentile (low average), with verbal indices in the 6th percentile (borderline range) and visual performance indices in the average range (25th percentile).

Adam was a well-liked youngster who generally got along well with his peers and staff. His primary difficulty while living at the group home involved accepting consequences and responsibility for infractions. Additionally, he was very fearful. There was only one serious incident of aggression toward peers during his placement. Adam was well able to utilize interpersonal relationships, coping skills, and expressive tools for problem-solving.

Case Formulation

Adam's history of multiple traumas, displacement, and losses affected his psychosocial development beginning at the first stage. He entered therapy with a high level of mistrust and an inadequate sense of autonomy, initiative, and industry. These features were manifest in his relationships with caregivers, his siblings, and his therapist. Adam demonstrated very poor academic performance, inadequate social skills, minimal self-efficacy with regard to any type of activity, and secretive, sexualized aggression toward younger children. The primary goal of therapy entailed assisting Adam in preparation for adoption by working on the ongoing goal of addressing the impact of multiple traumas on his sense of self. There also had to be a primary focus on the impact of the sexual reenactment behaviors he engaged in with his sisters. These behaviors, understandably, are generally not tolerated well by prospective adoptive parents if there are other children in the home. Additionally, if left unaddressed, these behaviors can become more driven and compulsive, as seen in adult pedophiles.

Adam was initially very resistant to addressing his history of sexual abuse and sexually aggressive behavior with younger children, which he demonstrated through anger, denial, and shame. He was increasingly able to address his memories of the events, feelings, and thoughts about how this may have impacted his sisters. His recollection is somewhat different from those of his sisters', as represented in a report furnished by their therapist. Adam vacillates in his willingness to actually address these issues, demonstrating anger at his sisters for wanting to "keep bringing this up." He has been able to address his anger toward his therapist for bringing this history into discussion, believing that he has previously discussed it sufficiently. He reports that this exploration has negatively impacted his academic work, as he is less attentive in class. He also relates that he feels pressured by his teacher to tell her why he is distracted. It is likely that this is actually affecting Adam's work, but it is also clear that he would rather not continue to explore this history.

Adam has been able to acknowledge that it is likely that his sisters participated in sexual activity with him when they did not want to. He maintained that they also initiated some of the activity. Adam recalled most of the sexual contact occurring with Caroline rather than with Jamie. He was able to recall that most of his behavior was related to his experiences with his mother and to wanting to know what it would be like to engage in some of the sexual behaviors he had witnessed occurring with his mother and her partners. Adam struggled with having complete empathy with his sisters' reactions, tending to minimize or deny their emotional reactions. This continued to be a focus in therapy.

Treatment Approach and
Rationale for Its Selection

Using Erikson's theory and task-facilitating factors, the goals and objectives of Adam's therapy were prioritized, starting with the most fundamental: establishing basic trust. It was essential that therapy be predictable, with consistent "rhythms" and sufficient caregiving. These task-facilitating factors involved establishing a safe, predictable environment. Essentially, therapy occurred in the same place, on the same day, and at the same time every week. Familiar toys were in place, and a predictable routine was set up and included a snack-and-talk time. This routine was generally invariable, unless Adam requested alteration. If any unanticipated changes arose, he would react with anxiety or irritation. The process of establishing a basic and functional level of trust spanned at least the first two years of therapy. Part of the difficulty stemmed from the "background noise" of frequent disruptions, such as the emotional and physical abuse by his aunt, his sisters' placement together and apart from him, and his stay in the group home. Each of these factors resulted in revisiting the original separation from his mother and the multiple foster placements that followed.

Across this period of early attachment in the therapy, it was not only important to anticipate and meet appropriate needs for Adam, but also to teach him to articulate his needs, learn to recognize and tolerate mild anxiety, and develop adequate self-soothing skills. The therapist understood the sexualized and aggressive behaviors that Adam demonstrated as efforts toward mastery of the trauma he had experienced as well as ineffective, modeled attempts at discharge of anxiety and frustration.

Play therapy became the primary vehicle for expression of feelings, allowing the therapist to gain a view of Adam's perceptions of provocation and others' intentions, along with his inability to articulate associated feelings and cognitions. After sufficient assessment of the themes of the play, the therapist would enter into the play, introducing alternative ways of solving problems, of relating, and of expressing feelings. The play remained symbolic until Adam moved from third-person to first-person themes. He became increasingly more comfortable doing this as basic trust developed within the therapy. This was facilitated even further when there were parallels of safe, trusting, and loving relationships occurring across his placement at the group home.

Adam demonstrated highly adaptive coping mechanisms in most of his daily functioning. When faced with this level of personal history, which is quite painful for him, he resorts to denial and cognitively distancing himself from the material. He will continue to benefit from the consistent support and encouragement he receives from his group-home staff and teachers. He benefited from the many extracurricular activities in which he engaged; these serve to develop in him the need to live a "normal" life. Permanency planning continues to be a primary need for this young man.

The subsequent tasks of autonomy and initiative were facilitated across a similar process, incorporating the task-facilitating factors into the therapy. Regarding Adam's developing autonomy, it was important to allow him both the physical and emotional freedom to explore issues in an environment of safety. Although limits and boundaries were clear, and often revisited, Adam had many opportunities to explore his feelings, thoughts, behaviors, and relationships in a safe, accepting environment. He met with consistent praise, encouragement, and appropriate redirection.

The third- and fourth-stage issues also emerged for Adam in therapy. Recalling that stage 3 involves the development of a healthy sense of initiative as opposed to guilt, it was important to work through the confusion that resulted from so many abusive relationships with caregivers. Therapy was also a place for Adam to explore his perceptions about his body. His sense of physical well-being and sexuality had been significantly compromised during his history of abuse. He would often use dolls to act out his gender-role and racial-identity confusion and sense of personal injury. The play often resulted in direct, first-person discussions about gender, sexual orientation, and appropriate physical contact between children and adults. Adam used both the play and the psychoeducational discussions to develop more adaptive cognitive schema, which facilitated improved self-concept, interpersonal relationships, and appropriate expectations about parent-child interactions. Additionally, he drew on the play to more carefully examine his own gender role and developing sexual orientation, becoming clearer that one's experience does not determine one's sexual orientation. Although Adam's sexual abuse had occurred in his relationship with his mother, he had experienced chronic emotional abuse that involved demasculinating and racially confusing remarks. It remained a possibility that he had also been sexually abused by one of his mother's male paramours, although that had never been confirmed. These combined experiences left him with questions about his own sexuality, as well as appropriate display of affection, and confusion between sexual and aggressive feelings. There were visible gains made across therapy in this area.

The final confrontation for Adam came toward the end of therapy, when he had to address his sisters' need for explanation and apology for the sexually aggressive behaviors he had displayed toward them. The goal was to work with Adam to increase his empathic understanding of how the sexualized behaviors affected his sisters, and how those experiences may have paralleled his own history of being molested by his mother. This was a painful process for Adam and was approached at a slow pace. He understood that the primary goal was to move toward some form of closure by acknowledging the experience in some manner for his sisters. Adam used role play, puppets, and letter writing to practice how he would eventually address this issue in a joint session with his sisters. The acknowledging session occurred in Adam's fourth year of therapy and just prior to his preparation for what would become his final adoption. It is likely that this issue will need to be revisited at various times between Adam and his sisters, but the process has definitely been initiated.

The final stage that Adam addressed across this course of therapy, industry versus a sense of inferiority, was facilitated more outside of therapy than in since this is best achieved through larger social interactions and experiences. The stable living environment provided at the group home gave Adam the type of milieu he needed to address academic issues. Additionally, many opportunities were put into place for him to develop "know-how" in a wide variety of activities, including softball, learning to play the piano, and developing a social network. These experiences were often presented in therapy for multiple reasons, including a need for affirmation and as opportunities to explore doubts, fears, or disappointments. Sometimes, Adam would introduce these situations during the snack-and-talk time; at other times, he would introduce them symbolically through play.

POSTTERMINATION SYNOPSIS AND REFLECTIONS

Adam was successfully placed in his adoptive family prior to the termination of therapy. This allowed for a successful termination of therapy, with a receptive and responsible family to assist him as he moved into later stages of development. He was able to effectively review the gains he had made in therapy. A termination project, a life book, was started two months before the planned ending of treatment. This provided a physical means of review and comment. The life book moved with Adam from therapy to his new family with many unfilled pages, anticipating the growth and developments to come in his life.

With traumatized children, it is often the case that therapy is sequential, with issues reemerging at later points in life triggered by age-appropriate crises, such as dating, marriage, parenting, and death of loved ones. Within this framework, this process of revisiting the issues becomes adaptive and facilitative, as an individual gains a greater capacity for understanding with an expanding perspective of earlier life traumas.

To move from the psychosocial, cognitive, and emotional framework for a moment, it is important to recognize that a deliberate and informed process in the therapy with this child likely facilitated the parallel processes in his neurocognitive structures to develop. The processes within the relationship in therapy and those that occurred in the group home and his expanding social network provided new experiences that mapped onto or literally changed existing neural networks, producing new memories, broader understanding, more options for effective and appropriate behavioral and emotional responses to situations, and improved cognitive functions. Play served as the primary vehicle, but a clear biopsychosocial template provided a road map for effective intervention.

RESEARCH REGARDING APPROACH

Heretofore, there have been no specific investigations of the model delineated in this chapter. There is modest, but growing, literature on the efficacy of play therapy specific to maltreated children. Bratton and Ray (2000) reported that play therapy is often scrutinized because of lack of outcome studies. They indicated that, despite managed-care companies demanding "evidence of effectiveness" (p. 48), research in the area of play therapy has declined over the past two decades. They reviewed the quantitative empirical studies that examined multiple areas of play-therapy research and reported that the studies contained many areas of weakness, such as not clearly defining the theory and practice of the play therapy used; therefore, the studies cannot be easily replicated. They indicated that there were three studies published regarding the use of play therapy with children who are sexually abused.

Perez (1987) conducted a study of 55 sexually abused children, ages 4 to 9 years, who participated in 12 sessions of individual-relationship play therapy, group-relationship play therapy, or a control group. Perez reported that no differences were reported on whether a child participated in either individual or group play therapy; however, children in the two treatment groups scored higher on a locus of control and a self-mastery inventory whereas the children in the control group actually had lower scores at posttest evaluation. Perez found that, for her sample, the children in the control group actually were in worse shape than observed previously, and those children receiving play therapy evidenced significant improvement. Saucier (1986) noted that her sample of 20 children between the ages of 1 and 7 years scored significantly higher on a scale of personal-social development than a control group after eight sessions of either directive or indirective play therapy. Phillips and Landreth (1998) related that it is not enough for clinicians to feel confident that their forms of play therapy are useful, but they should evaluate each case individually to determine that it is the most effective modality of treatment.

The application of Erikson's theory can be examined using scientific methods of inquiry. The model easily lends itself to both qualitative and quantitative methods, incorporating multiple measures of behaviors across time and treatment paradigms. Erikson's task-facilitating factors can be taught to clinicians in a standardized method. Maltreated children can be assessed for levels of psychosocial development using either theoretical constructs or standardized instruments. The Measures of Psychosocial Development (Hawley, 1988) could be standardized for administration to younger children; currently, Hawley's norms extend down only to age 13. The apparent merits of the theory support the rationale for future research in the efficacy of its application in interventions with maltreated children.

SUMMARY

Erik Erikson (1950/1963) has provided a comprehensive, instructive developmental theory that uniquely informs psychotherapy with abused and neglected children. In accordance with the theory, play is demonstrated in this chapter to be the primary vehicle for cognitive, social, and physical growth and development during childhood in general and in psychotherapy with abused children specifically. The theory is instructive in directing therapists in adjusting the interventions to more specifically facilitate optimal development. Finally, the theory can be evaluated for effectiveness through either qualitative or quantitative research designs.

REFERENCES

American Psychiatric Association. (1994). *Diagnostic and statistical manual of mental disorders* (4th ed.). Washington, DC: Author.

Axline, V. M. (1964). *Dibs: In search of self.* New York: Ballantine Books.

Axline, V. M. (1969). *Play therapy.* New York: Ballantine Books.

Black, J. E., & Greenough, W. T. (1998). Developmental approaches to the memory process. In J. L. Martinez & R. P. Kesner (Eds.), *Neurobiology of learning and memory* (pp. 55–88). San Diego, CA: Academic Press.

Bow, J. N. (1993). Overcoming resistance. In C. Schaefer (Ed.), *The therapeutic use of child's play* (pp. 17–40). Northvale, NJ: Aronson.

Bowlby, J. (1951). Maternal care and mental health. *World Health Organization Monograph Series, 2,* 179.

Bratton, S., & Ray, D. (2000). What the research shows about play therapy. *International Journal of Play Therapy, 9*(1), 47–88.

Cicchetti, D., & Carlson, V. (Eds.). (1989). *Child maltreatment: Theory and research on the causes and consequences of child abuse and neglect.* New York: Cambridge University Press.

Cicchetti, D., & Toth, S. L. (1995). A developmental psychopathology perspective on child abuse and neglect. *Journal of the American Academy of Child and Adolescent Psychiatry, 34,* 541–565.

Davidson, J. R. T., Hughes, D., Blazer, D. G., & George, L. K. (1991). Post-Traumatic Stress Disorder in the community: An epidemiological study. *Psychological Medicine, 21,* 713–721.

Davis, J., & Frawley, M. (1992). *Treating the adult survivor of childhood sexual abuse: A psychoanalytic perspective.* New York: Basic Books.

Dawson, G., Panangiotides, H., Grofer-Klinger, L., & Hill, D. (1992). The role of frontal lobe functioning in the development of infant self-regulatory behavior. *Brain and Cognition, 20,* 152–175.

Des Lauriers, A. (1962). *The experience of reality in childhood schizophrenia.* New York: International Universities Press.

Eckenrode, J., Laird, M., & Doris, J. (1993). School performance and disciplinary problems among abused and neglected children. *Developmental Psychology, 29,* 53–62.

Epstein, H. T. (1974). Phrenoblysis: Special brain and mind growth periods. *Developmental Psychobiology, 7,* 207–224.

Epstein, H. T. (1980). EEG developmental stages. *Developmental Psychobiology, 13,* 629–631.

Erikson, E. H. (1963). *Childhood and society* (2nd ed.). New York: Norton. (Original work published 1950)

Esman, A. H. (1983). Psychoanalytic play therapy. In C. E. Schaefer & K. J. O'Connor (Eds.), *Handbook of play therapy* (pp. 11–20). New York: Wiley.

Everson, M. D., Hunter, W. M., Runyan, D. K., Edelsohn, G. A., & Coulter, M. L. (1989). Maternal support following disclosure of incest. *American Journal of Orthopsychiatry, 59,* 197–207.

Fischer, K. W., & Rose, S. P. (1994). Dynamic development of coordination of components in brain and behavior: A framework for theory and research. In G. Dawson & K. Fischer (Eds.), *Human behavior and the developing brain* (pp. 3–66). New York: Guilford Press.

Florey, L. (1999). Development through play. In C. Schaefer (Ed.), *The therapeutic use of child's play* (pp. 61–70). Northvale, NJ: Aronson.

Forgays, D. G., & Forgays, J. W. (1952). The nature of the effect of free-environmental experience in the rat. *Journal of Comparative and Physiological Psychology, 45,* 322–328.

Frank, L. K. (1999a). Play in personality development. In C. Schaefer (Ed.), *The therapeutic use of child's play* (pp. 43–59). Northvale, NJ: Aronson.

Frank, L. K. (1999b). Validity of play. In C. Schaefer (Ed.), *The therapeutic use of child's play* (pp. 71–77). Northvale, NJ: Aronson.

Freud, A. (1999). The role of transference in the analysis of children. In C. Schaefer (Ed.), *The therapeutic use of child's play* (pp. 141–149). Northvale, NJ: Aronson.

Gil, E. (1991). *The healing power of play: Working with abused children.* New York: Guilford Press.

Gitlin-Weiner, K., Sandgrund, A., & Schaefer, C. (2000). Introduction: Emergence and evolution of children's play as a focus of study. In K. Gitlin-Weiner, A. Sandgrund, & C. Schaefer (Eds.), *Play diagnosis and assessment* (2nd ed., pp. 1–11). New York: Wiley.

Glaser, D. (2000). Child abuse and neglect and the brain: A review. *Journal of Child Psychology and Psychiatry and Allied Disciplines, 41*(1), 97–116.

Greenough, W. T. (1987). Behavioral biology. In N. A. Krasnegor & E. M. Blass (Eds.), *Perinatal development: A psychobiological perspective* (pp. 195–221). San Diego, CA: Academic Press.

Greenwald, E., & Leitenberg, H. (1990). Posttraumatic Stress Disorder in a nonclinical and nonstudent sample of adult women sexually abused as children. *Journal of Interpersonal Violence, 5*(2), 217–228.

Hawley, G. A. (1988). *Measures of psychosocial development: Professional manual.* Odessa, FL: Psychological Assessment Resources.

Hebb, D. O. (1949). *The organization of behavior: A neuropsychological theory.* New York: Wiley.

Hinshaw, S. P. (1992). Externalizing behavior problems and academic underachievement in childhood and adolescence: Causal relationships and underlying mechanisms. *Psychological Bulletin, 111*(1), 127–155.

Huttenlocher, P. R. (1994). Synaptogenesis in human cerebral cortex. In G. Dawson & K. Fischer (Eds.), *Human behavior and the developing brain* (pp. 137–152). New York: Guilford Press.

Jackson, Y. (1998). Applying APA ethical guidelines to individual play therapy with children. *International Journal of Play Therapy, 7*(2), 1–15.

Janoff-Bulman, R. (1985). The aftermath of victimization: Rebuilding shattered assumptions. In R. Figley (Ed.), *Trauma and its wake* (pp. 15–25). New York: Brunner/Mazel.

Jernberg, A. M. (1979). *Theraplay: A new treatment using structured play for problem children and their families.* San Francisco: Jossey-Bass.

Kendall-Tackett, K. A., Williams, L. M., & Finkelhor, D. (1993). Impact of sexual abuse on children: A review and synthesis of recent empirical studies. *Psychological Bulletin, 113*(1), 164–180.

Klein, M. (1999). The psychoanalytic play technique. In C. Schaefer (Ed.), *The therapeutic use of child's play* (pp. 125–140). Northvale, NJ: Aronson.

Klintsova, A. Y., & Greenough, W. T. (1999). Synaptic plasticity in cortical systems. *Current Opinion in Neurobiology, 9*(2), 203–208.

Lindy, J. D. (1985). The trauma membrane and other clinical concepts derived from psychotherapeutic work with survivors of natural disasters. *Psychiatric Annals, 15*(3), 153–160.

Luria, A. R. (1973). *The working brain: An introduction to neuropsychology.* New York: Basic Books.

Malinosky-Rummell, R., & Hansen, D. J. (1993). Long-term consequences of childhood physical abuse. *Psychological Bulletin, 114*(1), 68–79.

Mann, E., & McDermott, J. F. (1983). Play therapy for victims of child abuse and neglect. In C. E. Schaefer & K. J. O'Connor (Eds.), *Handbook of play therapy* (pp. 283–307). New York: Wiley.

Miller, A. (1981). *Prisoner of childhood: The drama of the gifted child and the search for the true self.* New York: Basic Books.

Oaklander, V. (1988). *Windows to our children: A Gestalt therapy approach to children and adolescents.* Highland, NY: Gestalt Journal Press.

Parten, M. B. (1932). Social participation among preschool children. *Journal of Abnormal Psychology, 27,* 243–269.

Perez, C. (1987). A comparison of group play therapy and individual play therapy for sexually abused children. (Doctoral dissertation, University of Northern Colorado). *Dissertation Abstracts International, 48.*

Phillips, R., & Landreth, G. L. (1998). Play therapists on play therapy. I: A report of methods, demographics, and professional practices. *International Journal of Play Therapy, 4,* 1–26.

Pynoos, R. S., & Eth, S. (1986). Witness to violence: The child interview. *American Academy of Child Psychiatry, 25*(3), 306–319.

Saporta, J. A., & van der Kolk, B. A. (1992). Psychobiological consequences of severe trauma. In M. Basoglu (Ed.), *Torture and its consequences: Current treatment approaches* (pp. 151–181). New York: Cambridge University Press.

Saucier, B. (1986). An intervention: The effects of play therapy on developmental achievement levels of abused children (Doctoral dissertation, Texas Women's University). *Dissertation Abstracts International, 48,* 1007.

Schaefer, C. E., & Cangelosi, D. M. (1993). Introduction. In C. E. Schaefer & D. M. Cangelosi (Eds.), *Play therapy techniques* (pp. 1–5). Northvale, NJ: Aronson.

Seyle, H. (1936). A syndrome produced by diverse nocuous agents. *Nature, 138,* 32–34.

Spitz, R. A. (1945). Diacritic and coenesthetic organizations: The psychiatric significance of a functional division of the nervous system into a sensory and emotive part. *Psychoanalytic Review, 32,* 146–162.

Terr, L. (1987). Childhood trauma and the creative product. *Psychoanalytic Study of Children, 42,* 45–572.

Terr, L. (1990). *Too scared to cry: Psychic trauma in childhood.* New York: Basic Books.

Thatcher, R. W. (1994). Cyclic cortical reorganization: Origins of human cognitive development. In G. Dawson & K. Fischer (Eds.), *Human behavior and the developing brain* (pp. 232–268). New York: Guilford Press.

Trickett, P. K. (1993). Maladaptive development of school-aged, physically abused children's relationships with the child-rearing context. *Journal of Family Psychology, 7*(1), 134–147.

Trickett, P. K., Aber, J. L., Carlson, V., & Cicchetti, D. (1991). Relationship of socioeconomic status to the etiology and developmental sequelae of physical child abuse. *Developmental Psychology, 27*(1), 148–158.

Webb, N. B. (1991). Assessment of the child in crisis. In N. B. Webb (Ed.), *Play therapy with children in crisis: A casebook for practitioners* (pp. 3–25). New York: Guilford Press.

Yehuda, R., Schmeidler, J., Giller, E. L., Binder-Brynes, K., & Siever, L. J. (1998). Relationship between PTSD characteristics of Holocaust survivors and their adult offspring. *American Journal of Psychiatry, 155,* 841–843.

SECTION TWO

PSYCHOTHERAPY WITH ADOLESCENTS AND YOUNG ADULTS

Chapter 6   Solution-Focused Brief Therapy with Adolescents

Chapter 7   An Integrative Approach to Assessment and Intervention with Adolescents of Color

Chapter 8   Adlerian Therapy: A Century of Tradition and Research

Chapter 9   School-Based, Community Family Therapy for Adolescents at Risk

CHAPTER 6

Solution-Focused Brief Therapy with Adolescents

JOEL K. SIMON AND INSOO KIM BERG

At least since Freud, psychotherapy practice has been guided by theory. Solution-focus brief therapists tend to view their investigations and practices as proceeding less from a theory and more from a curiosity to learn what works. From its inception, solution-focus practice developed inductively. The solution-focus brief therapist remains curious about what clients do that is helpful to them (de Shazer, 1985). With a diversity of clients, constantly learning by listening leads to developing even more useful interventions. Solution-focus brief therapy constitutes a dynamic orientation to doing psychotherapy as each client represents new possibilities for understanding and integration.

HISTORICAL CONTEXT

In 1970, Steve de Shazer moved from Milwaukee, Wisconsin, to Palo Alto, California. De Shazer states that his first contact with the term "psychotherapy" occurred in reading *Strategies of Psychotherapy* by Jay Haley. There, he discovered the ideas and work of the innovative psychiatrist, Milton H. Erickson. The book had a profound influence on de Shazer, and, coupled with the work of the Mental Research Institute (MRI) in Palo Alto, formed the foundations for what would later be called solution-focus brief therapy (de Shazer, 1985).

Erickson became best known for his study and use of hypnotherapy. Although he had practiced from the 1940s until his death in 1980, the major interest in his work began to gather momentum only in the early 1980s. Erickson's ideas reached far beyond hypnotic technique. He posed radical ideas regarding the role of the therapist, the competency of clients, and the meaning of therapy in general. Erickson's approach involved using the client's own language and worldview as the focus of his work. Hence, he designed therapy differently for each patient. Cade and O'Hanlon (1993) expanded on the significance of this principle of utilization: "Since we have no general explanatory models or normative models to guide us, clients' goals and visions of the future become our compass settings and help us map our way to their hoped-for destinations" (p. 60).

One of Erickson's primary approaches entailed first learning the problem pattern and then prescribing a small change in the pattern. Several of the researchers at MRI, among them John Weakland, Jay Haley, and Gregory Bateson were interested in Erickson's work and especially in his use of pattern disruption (de Shazer, 1991). These researchers saw problems as socially contextual and reasoned that an individual's social situation serves to maintain a problem. Accordingly, they strategized ways of disrupting problem patterns.

By 1972, de Shazer had developed a therapy practice that included the use of a one-way mirror. At this time, he collaborated on two projects with Joseph Berger, a professor of sociology at Stanford University. In the first project, Berger watched de Shazer working with clients behind the mirror and described the conversations from his sociological point of view. In the second project, de Shazer attempted to develop a theory based on the work of Erickson. In reflecting on his lack of success in attempting this application of Erickson's work, de Shazer (1999) concluded that "this latter part was never successful. There were too many cases that were unique and thus we ended up with almost as many categories as cases. Erickson, it turned out, was correct in saying that he did not have a Theory. (p. 4)

During 1972, de Shazer first came in contact with John Weakland from MRI. Along with Erickson, Weakland's ideas have had a major influence on de Shazer and the development of the solution-focus approach. In 1974, the therapist Kim Berg, then a therapist in a family clinic in Milwaukee, traveled to Palo Alto to train with John Weakland at MRI. She asked Weakland where she might observe brief therapy in action and he suggested she contact de Shazer. This was the beginning of a collaboration that currently spans 28 years and has had a profound effect on the practice of therapy.

In 1976, Weakland invited de Shazer to participate in a panel at the second Don D. Jackson Memorial Conference. The topic was entitled "Techniques of Brief Therapy" and this represented de Shazer's first presentation of his evolving ideas to an international audience. Later that year, de Shazer and Weakland presented a workshop at a second conference, entitled "Unorthodox Techniques of Brief Therapy." De Shazer (1999) reflects on this topic:

> The audience thought it rather peculiar, or unorthodox, that we would ask the client about what the problem was and further that we would take their answers seriously! This sort of dissonance between what I think of as normal and ordinary and what the audience thinks unorthodox and/or bizarre has continued but the dissonance lessened over the years as I have become used to it. (p. 5)

In 1977, de Shazer described a particular session in which a therapist working with a client and a team were experiencing a disagreement regarding approach. Out of frustration, the therapist asked the client to excuse him and he went behind the mirror to talk to the team. Both therapist and team found this was particularly helpful to the client and so began the practice of taking a break, which has been part of the solution-focus identity and procedure ever since.

De Shazer returned to live in Milwaukee in 1978, when he and Berg invested their limited financial resources in a training center they named the Brief Family Therapy Center (BFTC). They intended to create a research center patterned after MRI. In 1979, de Shazer worked with Elam Nunnally, a family sociologist, to research the effect of session lengths on outcome. They imposed a 30-minute limit on sessions—this included taking the break. De Shazer (1999) concluded:

> In none of the 40 or so cases did we have trouble designing an intervention message. We always found that we had "enough" information. Furthermore, this arbitrary time limit had no effect on outcomes, task performance, or on whether or not the client would return for the subsequent session. (p. 12)

This research served to unshackle the therapists from the traditional 50-minute session and refocused from time to content.

In response to a growing interest in their approach at the BFTC, de Shazer, Berg, and their colleagues established a training institute in the early 1980s. Around the same time, they moved BFTC to larger quarters to allow for trainees to sit behind the mirror and watch solution-focus therapists working with actual clients. In 1982, Wallace Gingerich coined the phrase solution-focus brief therapy (SFBT) to describe the perspective developing at BFTC.

Berg was working with a client behind the mirror in 1983. The client appeared hopeless and burdened with multiple problems. Although Berg searched relentlessly for a small ray of hope to expand on, she met with despair. Finally, the client said that a miracle would have to happen for her situation to improve. Berg had the client suppose that the miracle had already happened, and this significantly improved the tenor of the session. During the break, the team members expressed an excitement for the question and they suggested that the therapists experiment with what would become known as the "Miracle Question." This story exemplifies how solution-focus therapists listen intently to clients to learn how to do effective therapy.

De Shazer published the first book describing the solution-focus approach, *Keys to Solutions in Brief Therapy,* in 1985. Interest in developments at BFTC increased. The later portion of the 1980s and throughout the 1990s saw an expansion of attention to SFBT. Currently, de Shazer and Berg engage in training professionals throughout world.

THEORETICAL CONSTRUCTS

USEFUL CONVERSATIONS

Language can be conceptualized to function in two ways: (1) Language represents reality; (2) language constructs reality. The first orientation suggests that language describes reality, that two individuals conversing use words as symbols of reality (de Shazer, 1991). Thus, if two therapists talk about a client as having depression (or being depressed), they assume that they both accept a similar meaning for the word "depression." They do not need to discuss what depression means. The meaning of depression survives the therapists' conversation and transcends a particular conversational context. "Depression" carries a constant meaning independent of who participates and where and when the conversation takes place.

Making sense of a solution-focus conversation requires the second orientation, a very different way of thinking about language (de Shazer, 1994). Conversations form the contexts in which therapists and clients make useful meanings of the words they use. Each new conversation provides an opportunity for new meanings. Solution-focus conversations can be described as at least two individuals engaged in the process of meaning making (de Shazer, 1991).

Both talking and doing happen at the same time; the talking cannot be separated from the action (G. Miller, 1997). In his *Philosophical Investigations,* Ludwig Wittgenstein (1958) suggested this connection between language and action:

> We can also think of the whole process of using words as in one of those games by means of which children learn their native language. I will call these games "language-games" and will sometimes speak of a primitive language as a language-game. I shall also call the whole, consisting of language and the actions into which it is woven, the "language-game." (p. 5)

Wittgenstein expanded on this concept of language-game and its connection to action: "Here the term *language-game* is meant to bring into prominence the fact that the *speaking* of language is part of an activity, or a form of life" (p. 11).

Conventional diagnosis denotes that someone *is* or *has*; for example, "He is depressed," or "She has schizophrenia." However, observations show that when clients talk about depression, they appear depressed. From Wittgenstein's point of view, a conversation about depression results in doing depression; language cannot be separated from action. Solution-focus brief therapists simply (and minimally) coconstruct useful conversations with clients—conversations that make meaning of possibilities and capabilities.

If language (1) makes meaning and (2) inevitably results in action, the questions that solution-focus practitioners ask not only gather information, but also cannot help but give information (Tomm & Lannamann, 1988). Questions convey to clients what therapists are interested in knowing and what they think will be most helpful to focus on. While acknowledging a lack of expertise in client lives, professionals bring proficiency as to what constitutes a useful process. This process comes from working over many years with many clients and an investment in finding out what makes a difference for them.

BASIC ASSUMPTIONS

To a large degree, how therapists converse with clients flows from the assumptions they make and determines where therapists will focus. The practice of SFBT proceeds from a useful set of assumptions about clients, therapists, and the helping process (Simon & Berg, 1999):

1. *Change is constant and inevitable.* Experience suggests that change is already happening even before a client sees a therapist. The therapist does not initiate change, but focuses on changes already happening. Even in an inpatient psychiatric setting, most individuals will say that things are already getting better within 24 hours of admission (that is, if they are asked).

2. *Small change leads to bigger changes.* Once clients experience positive changes making a difference in their lives, the effects multiply. Conversations about possibilities serve to enhance further possibilities. It matters less where clients choose to begin making a difference in their lives. The very act of entertaining a future vision represents the key element in what is useful to many clients. After clients report a small positive difference, they very often relate that they have gotten what they needed from therapy—good therapy is a good-enough beginning.

3. *The past cannot be changed.* De Shazer (1985) quoted Erickson: "Emphasis should be placed more on what the patient does in the present and will do in the future than on a mere understanding of why some long-past event occurred" (p. 78). Solution-focus therapists are interested in the details of clients' past successes. De Shazer expanded on Erickson's comments: "The past, particularly the problematic areas of the past, can then be seen as potentially detrimental to solution. Of course, past successes, deliberate or accidental, can be used in constructing a solution" (p. 79).

4. *People have the resources necessary.* They are the experts on themselves: Although solution-focus brief therapists perceive themselves as having expertise on a useful process, they view client as being experts on themselves. If asked, clients will relate what is useful to them in their everyday lives. A therapist's area of expertise still depends on clients' expertise on themselves.

5. *Every human being, relationship, and situation is unique.* Erickson designed his therapy differently for each client (O'Hanlon, 1987). Solution focus begins with the uniqueness of every individual. This process of fitting the therapy to a client requires client input and feedback.

6. *What people do has an impact on other people.* The meteorologist Edward Lorenz coined the term "the butterfly effect" (Butz, Chamberlain,

& McCown, 1997), connoting that a butterfly's flapping its wings in China alters the weather system in the United States. Lorenz's tongue-in-cheek phrase implies that only a small variable can make a big difference. In complex systems, small variables generate unpredictable consequences. Human beings operate within multiple social contexts: friends, work, religious affiliation, family, local grocery store, and neighborhood fitness club. Given the complexity of human social systems, simple cause-and-effect thinking cannot accurately predict human behavior. Many parents know that adolescents can be unpredictable. Viewing this unpredictability as a possible resource may be helpful.

7. *Every problem has at least one exception.* At times, a client is either doing something other than the problem or experiences a problem as less important. De Shazer, Berg, and their colleagues imagined having conversations about exceptions as key to building solutions (Simon & Berg, 1999):

> However, as they listened to clients describing the details of a problem, they began to notice that clients also described exceptions, times when a problem was either absent or minimal. At this point, the focus of the therapy shifted from the description of the problem to details of exceptions. It was this shift that moved the therapy from problem resolution to solution development. (p. 117)

8. *Changes come from many directions.* Therapy is not the only way people change. According to S. Miller, Duncan, and Hubble (1997): "Research shows, in fact, that *improvement between treatment sessions is the rule rather than the exception* (p. 50)." Clients talk about the useful differences that happen outside of therapy offices. Solution-focus therapists take advantage of the many resources clients can utilize by highlighting what occurs between sessions to enhance their lives.

BUILDING SOLUTIONS

An SFBT conversation has two major foci, which occur simultaneously: (1) developing *with a client* a well-formed goal and (2) constructing a conversation that helps build solutions. Therapists can use the following eight guidelines to assist in indicating whether they are developing well-formed goals with their clients (Berg & Miller, 1992).

1. *A goal important to the client and meaningful to the therapist is best.* Often, what appears to be a simple and inconsequential goal, in fact, will make a big difference to a client.

2. *Select a small goal.* A solution-focus therapist looks for small differences (often already happening) and expands on them. As a client is helped to realize that a small change is possible, this often leads to success. Where a therapist and client choose to start matters less than that a client experiences success.

3. *Concrete, specific, and behavioral goals are achievable.* Solution-focus therapists find it most helpful when a client can describe what will be different and how that will make a difference. The more detail a client gives the therapist, the more possible the goal becomes. Paradoxically, solution-focus therapists expand on possibilities by focusing on details.

4. *The goal describes the presence of behavior.* Very often, clients talk about goals by describing what will not be happening. For example, "My daughter will not do drugs anymore," or "My son and I won't argue all the time." Instead, a solution-focus therapist can simply ask what it is clients want to be doing (feeling or thinking) instead. In this way, clients can expand on the details of desired differences. A client may find it much more difficult to articulate what will be happening instead of "doing drugs," "sneaking out at night," or "lying all the time." Rather than detailing what makes parents upset, describing goals by the presence

of desired behaviors will help parents look for positive changes in their children.

5. *A useful goal describes a good-enough beginning.* Life is about constant change and transformations. Solution-focus brief therapists tend to be practical about when therapy has reached a useful end. They are interested in what will tell clients that they have made a good- enough-start and can continue the process on their own.

6. *The client's own life context will determine which goals are realistic and achievable.* Asking clients what makes them think that the goal is attainable provides a clarifying intervention with them. As they detail the evidence that the goal can happen in their lives, they make the possibilities even more real for themselves.

7. *Clients should either be able to describe how they are already noticing the goal happening in their lives, or describe how the first steps toward the goal might happen within a couple of weeks.* Clients will more likely achieve their goals when they can detail how they are beginning or might begin to accomplish the goal.

8. *The goal must be seen as requiring hard work.* There is a tendency to value what requires effort to attain. Therapists can use this in two ways. They can ask those who are already accomplishing a goal how they were able to put in the hard work to make it happen, and they can inquire of clients how much hard work they are willing to exert to accomplish their goals.

QUESTIONS AS USEFUL TOOLS

Clients develop realistic and achievable goals through the use of six useful questions. These questions encompass presession change questions, future-oriented questions, the Miracle Question, scaling questions, exception questions, and coping questions. Solution-focus therapists ask *presession change questions* to identify what useful actions clients take before they see a therapist. For many clients, the very act of thinking about how therapy will make a difference for them raises possibilities (S. Miller et al., 1997). The act of picking up the telephone means a client already thinks about how therapy will help achieve a better future. In "Building on Pretreatment Change to Construct the Therapeutic Solution: An Exploratory Study," Weiner-Davis, de Shazer, and Gingerich, (1987) discovered that a high percentage of clients provide substantive answers to presession change questions.

When clients describe what is already better, they are well on the road to solution building within the first few moments of the session. Once clients begin talking about possibilities, they tend to generate even more possibility-talk. To a large extent, the solution-focus brief therapist asks questions to encourage solution-building conversations. Presession change questions invite a client into solution-building conversations right from the beginning. Such questions immediately let a client know what information interests a therapist. Very often, when solution-focus brief therapists contact clients to arrange a first session, they ask the client to notice improvements prior to a first meeting.

Solution-focus therapists ask clients *future oriented questions.* These questions move the conversation from details of a problem to possibilities of how clients' lives will be better in the near future. For example, when a client states a problem, the therapist might explore how a client's life will be better once that particular problem is solved.

The *Miracle Question* offers another way to encourage conversations about a better future. Over countless experiments with a variety of presenting complaints and in a multitude of settings, precise wording in asking the Miracle Question has been found to make a difference:

> I'm going to ask a strange question. [Pause.] Let's suppose that after our conversation, you go home tonight and go to sleep. [Pause.] While you're sleeping, a miracle happens. The miracle is that the problems that brought you here to see me are gone. [Pause.] You can't know about the miracle

since you're asleep. When you wake up in the morning, what will tell you that the problem that brought you here is gone?

Once solution-focus therapists ask the Miracle Question, they help clients describe the details of what will be different, how it will make a positive difference for them, and how a positive difference will occur within their social context.

Even when the Miracle Question is so carefully phrased, often a client immediately responds, "I don't know." Solution-focus therapists view this response as logical because most clients have been preoccupied and have never thought about a different life beyond articulated problems. Given time and patience, clients slowly begin to consider the solution picture. As solution-focus therapists ask about the details of the miracle, clients often describe the miracle in the present tense, as if elements of the miracle have already occurred. Solution-focus brief therapists listen for these exceptions. They then become very curious and ask *exception questions* about times when the problem is either not occurring or better; they ask clients how the exceptions happen, how clients help to make exceptions come about and what differences the exceptions make not only to the clients but also to significant others in their lives. Beyond the initial response of "I don't know," most teenagers will come up with an answer if a therapist gives them time to think. A therapist can then begin to ask questions that will build on the answer by filling in the details.

Scaling questions expand on both exceptions and future visions. Solution-focus therapists ask clients to rate themselves on a scale from 0 to 10, usually with 10 as the most desirable outcome. For example, after detailing the miracle picture, the therapist might ask clients to rate themselves, with 10 as the miracle already happening and 0 as the worst things have been. A therapist will choose the appropriate scale from the unlimited possibilities based on the relevancy to the client. Solution-focus therapists often use confidence scales, determination scales, and effort scales. Many times, a client will suggest which scales might be appropriate. Sometimes, a client will introduce scales spontaneously because many people commonly use scales in their everyday lives. Following a client's lead by using the same language to structure a scale proves helpful. A client might say, "The problem is 50 percent better"; a therapist would then construct the scaling questions using percentages.

The majority of clients place themselves somewhere above 0 on the scale; surprisingly, clients rarely rate themselves at 0. The numbers themselves have only the meanings that result from conversations with clients (Berg & de Shazer, 1993); the scale does not indicate an absolute or normative standard. Therefore, clients rating themselves above 0 is encouraging and suggests that they are already on the way toward a 10. Logically, 1 on the scale exceeds 0. It is usually helpful to ask clients their thoughts on the differences between 0 and 1. A 1 might mean that exceptions are in fact happening, or that pieces of the miracle are already occurring.

Once clients are asked how they have managed to be above 0, therapists can find out how that has made a difference for clients and others. Solution-focus therapists next inquire how clients will know that they have moved to just one more number above where they are currently, and how that will make differences in their lives. Clients detail the difference and are also assisted in constructing a rich conversation about how it makes a useful difference to them.

Clients often talk about their problems as being multiple, complex, and unsolvable. At these times, *coping questions* can prove advantageous. Asking clients how they are able to cope with a situation often results in conversations about their strengths and resources. A well-timed coping question will often change the conversation from problems to possibilities, even with a client who seems to be in a dire situation and feels quite hopeless. This question elicits any action clients have done (even "getting out of bed this morning") implying that they have made a positive effort toward solving a problem. The follow-up conversation might begin with "How did you do it?" This reminds clients that they have been successful in achieving small tasks.

The use of the questions is not bound by a rigid set of rules or procedures. If a particular question is not working, a therapist should move to another one that might be more productive. Solution-focus brief therapists follow a very simple but effective principle: Find out what works and do more of it.

Taking the Break

When clients first meet with a solution-focus therapist, they are informed that the therapist will take a short break and give some thought to the conversation (Campbell, Elder, Gallagher, & Simon, 1999). After the break, the therapist invites the client back into the room for feedback. Most clients relate that the break and feedback is a very positive experience for them. If the therapist is fortunate to work with an observing team behind a one-way mirror, the clinician will take a break with the team, and together they will develop the feedback. Because most practitioners work alone, however, a therapist will generally formulate the feedback on his or her own.

When a client returns, the therapist will usually normalize the reaction to the current situation as perfectly understandable. Many parents respond with relief in hearing that they are not alone in having troubles with their adolescents. The therapist will reflect on all the skills, abilities, resources, smart thinking, courage, and strengths that the clients spoke about during the conversation. The feedback is taken directly from what clients have said, and the client's key words are used as much as possible. The session usually ends with a simple suggestion of what the client might think about, notice, or try between sessions.

MAJOR SYNDROMES, SYMPTOMS, AND PROBLEMS TREATED

Insurance companies require diagnoses and licensing bodies expect professionals to provide relevant assessment information to proper requests. Accordingly, solution-focus therapists comply with such requirements. Even when engaged in solution-focus conversations, clients provide enough information regarding the problems they face for therapists to formulate a suitable diagnosis. Beyond what third-party payers require, solution-focus therapists find little relevance or usefulness in diagnosis. Solution-focus therapists have successfully applied the approach to a wide range of clients with a diversity of stated problems. SFBT enjoys wide applicability and flexibility because of emphases on individuals' goals, competencies, resources, and future possibilities.

CASE EXAMPLES

An Adolescent Male in the Criminal Justice System

As with adults, working with adolescents requires that a therapist be alert to the smallest possible exceptions, especially to a bad reputation that the adolescent may have developed over the years. Some years ago, Leroy took part in family treatment for adolescent boys being released from youth correctional institutions, the very last and most restrictive setting for teenagers. Leroy, a tall, strong-looking, 16-year-old from the toughest part of the city, had not lived with his mother and his three siblings for four years. He had exhausted various service options available for children like him: foster homes, group homes, and residential treatment homes. He finally ended up in a correctional school, a euphemism for juvenile prison.

When the therapist (Kim Berg) first saw Leroy, he was housed in the institution's most restrictive room because he had recently attacked a female staff member. When Berg came to meet with Leroy, the referring person wanted to post a guard outside the room. Leroy had garnered a reputation as an angry, violent, and hostile young man with a long history of abusing substances that contributed to his various criminal activities. He had a long string of violations of rules against drinking and using drugs at the many institutions. Frequently, police were called to control him because his drinking led to violent fights with other residents.

The therapist declined the offer of a guard and reassured her colleague that she would be fine without one. She did not want to convey a message to Leroy that she feared him nor that she anticipated that he might become aggressive. Many professionals with the best of intentions had reported numerous unsuccessful attempts at "helping" Leroy. The therapist realized that she had to take a "not-knowing stance" every step of the way if she were to connect with him. Most of the professionals had emphasized Leroy's deficits and attempted to convince him that his notion of getting what he wanted through violence was mistaken. All the professional efforts to control, manage, correct, and reeducate him were ironically generated from the idea that he did not know right from wrong, lacked the right information, or could not predict the consequences of his actions. This therapist disagreed with these views and wanted to find a way to see from Leroy's perspective. The therapist had no idea what she was looking for, but she needed the smallest possible exception to what shaped his negative view of himself. She wanted him to know that someone recognized that he had worthwhile and successful personal traits.

Driving to the institution, the therapist picked up his mother. The therapist learned about the mother's perspective on her son's difficulties and her frustrations at the lack of progress with Leroy. Leroy's mother loved him very much and wanted him home, but was doubtful it could really happen. As they entered the security area where he was confined, the therapist saw Leroy bend down and lovingly kiss his mother on her cheek. This observation gave the therapist clarity about her direction.

As mother and son busily caught up on family news, the therapist interrupted and asked, "Leroy, I'm really confused. How come nobody knows what a loving and gentle person you are?" He gruffly spat out, "I don't know!" His mother elaborated on what a loving and gentle child he was when he was younger. This exchange was repeated about three or four times during the next three visits.

One day, the therapist was interviewing another young man. She saw Leroy talking with other youths, and smoking. Delighted that Leroy was released to his usual cottage, but surprised to see him smoke, the therapist walked up to him and remarked, "I didn't know you smoked!" He replied, "I don't smoke in front of my mother because it is disrespectful." The therapist's repertoire of questions expanded and now alternated between "loving and gentle" and "respectful and thoughtful." To everyone's surprise, Leroy's behavior improved remarkably, and he was eventually released to the custody of his mother after a relatively brief stay.

Whether the presenting complaint is substance abuse, criminal behavior, anger, or aggression, solution-focus therapists build solutions in the same way: First, discover the adolescent's dreams and aspirations; next, find out what the adolescent already has done toward accomplishing his or her goals; finally, find the next small steps that need to be taken toward what the teenager wants, and continually assess the progress toward that goal. It is important to establish a respectful posture, including noticing whatever skills a teenager may have already displayed (e.g., in music, computer games, sports, artistic, or other creative activities), and use these successes as resources to achieve what the teenager wants. Recounting past mistakes, poor judgment, and immaturity serves only to turn off teenagers. No wonder that when professionals engage teenagers in such problem-laden conversations, the teenagers shut down. Conventional methods of talking to teenagers about their faults and problems has resulted in the false sense that adolescents are difficult to work with.

Usually, adolescents appear in therapists' offices because their parents or other adults in their lives are concerned about problems. Most adolescents view therapists as useless and interfering, and they see little if any possible gain from therapy. Adults' interactions with teenagers have focused on problems, usually trying to force them to do something an adolescent views as useless. Rather than educating or enlightening the youth, solution-focus therapists find that inquiring what matters to adolescents is more productive. Successful work with teenagers requires that therapists find out what is important to them, and then explore with compassion and honesty what they want from their lives.

Developing supportive relationships with parents proves essential to successful treatment outcomes with teenagers. Respectful relationships with parents entail finding out about their own hopes and wishes for their children and giving credence to their concerns and goals. This includes helping them to view themselves as caring parents and as experts on their own children, as well as working with them as consultants in the treatment. Solution-focus therapists ask such questions as, "What do you know about your son (or daughter) that tells you that he (or she) can go back to school (learn to follow the rules, be respectful, have a better attitude, or be honest with you)?"

An Adolescent Female Hospitalized Psychiatrically: "Just Let Me Do What I Want"

Fourteen-year-old Jessica and her family originally relocated to the southern United States because her father's company had transferred him. The mother recently decided to return North because, as she relayed, Jessica had lost control. The mother complained that Jessica had been staying out late, had become sexually active and did not obey her parents' rules. While in the South, Jessica had been hospitalized twice. Although she responded appropriately during the hospitalizations, she maintained the gains after her release, by her own account, for only about a week before she reverted back to the behaviors of concern to her parents.

Jessica's mother and father agreed that it would be best if mother and children returned North. They hoped this would remove Jessica from those friends whom they felt were influencing her problem behaviors the most. The move did not seem to have the desired effect, and Jessica's mother had called her managed care case manager to request another psychiatric hospitalization. The case manager suggested that Jessica and her mother see a therapist at a local community mental health clinic.

Session 1
The therapist (J. Simon) began by explaining that in each session a team would observe behind a one-way mirror and that the team would take a break to discuss how to proceed.

THERAPIST: You were willing to come? (Jessica shakes her head in disagreement.) You weren't willing to come. But you're here.
JESSICA: I'll sit here, but I won't talk!
THERAPIST: Okay, Mom, so you were willing to come here today. (Mom agrees.) So, what is it that gave you some hope that coming here will be useful for you?

MOM: I don't know how to deal with it; I really don't know how to deal with her. Her moods are so aggressive. She is nasty. She doesn't have anything nice to say about anybody. I'm at the point that I don't know. Her behavior is not normal. She's out of control. She tells us to go "f" ourselves. She calls us sluts. I can't handle it anymore. She's really nasty. She shoves.

THERAPIST: Now, she's been in therapy for six months before.

[The mother talks at length about Jessica's past behaviors and what led up to the first hospitalization.]

Usually, therapy is one of the last remedies that families turn to when trying to solve a problem. Jessica's parents first thought that the solution was to move Jessica back to the North. Unfortunately, this did not work. Other people will try different ways of addressing the problem, usually talking to friends and family. Before people even consult a therapist, usually quite a bit of problem talk and exploration has occurred. Not surprisingly, clients expect to do the same when seeing a therapist. A strong assumption exists that problem talk will eventually lead to problem solution. The therapist uses the first part of the session to define who wants change to happen, what change is desired, what were past successes, and how best to invite the family into a conversation that builds solutions.

MOTHER: They referred us to a place called Lakeside.
JESSICA: It was a psycho ward.
THERAPIST: So, how long were you there?
JESSICA: A week.
THERAPIST: Did they think she was ready to leave?
MOTHER: They did, but it has a lot to do with insurance too.
JESSICA: I bullshitted my way out.

MOTHER: She did, she has the ability to play the game.
THERAPIST: Wow, I want to hear more about that. This ability to play the game. How are you able to do that?
JESSICA: I'm very manipulative. I know how to manipulate.
THERAPIST: You must have been showing them some behavior that convinced them.
JESSICA: When I'm in a place like that, I'm on my best behaviors.
THERAPIST: You are? So, how do you do that?
JESSICA: I know not to make a scene in front of certain people. It'll get me into a worse situation.

In this section, the therapist listened for solutions and focused on Jessica's ability to know how to practice "best behaviors." He did not accept the assumption, which Jessica and her mother seemed to make, that being "manipulative" is inherently bad. He became curious about how Jessica was able to do that. This suggested that being manipulative required that she have some control over her behavior, that she knows what people expect of her, and can even demonstrate useful behaviors when the context warrants it. The therapist both used and accepted what the client brought to the session.

THERAPIST: Mom, when they told you she was ready to leave, what did they say they were noticing?
MOTHER: They told us that we should seek outside counseling and a psychiatrist for her medications.
THERAPIST: Makes sense. To keep the good stuff going. But what were they saying they were seeing that told them she was ready to go?
MOTHER: They just told us to seek outside counseling.
JESSICA: They said the maximum stay was one week.

THERAPIST: Oh, so you just kind of maxed out. (Mother agrees.)
JESSICA: I made progress in that place. For about a week. They pissed me off so I hit them.
THERAPIST: What progress did you make?
JESSICA: I learned some ways to cope with my anger. I walked away, but my freaking father won't let go.
THERAPIST: So, what is it that you learned at the hospital that you used outside?
JESSICA: Those hospitals aren't helpful. 99% of the kids that are in there bullshit their way out.
THERAPIST: Let's see if I got this right. You made progress while you were in there, but not when you were out?
JESSICA: No, I went right back.
THERAPIST: When you left, were you hoping that you would continue the progress?
JESSICA: Yeah, but oh well!
THERAPIST: What progress were you hoping to continue?
JESSICA: That I'd be better, but I'm not, so, oh well.
THERAPIST: Better in what way?
JESSICA: I don't even know what triggered me to being bad.
THERAPIST: Yeah, so what progress were you hoping would happen?
JESSICA: That I would be talking to my parents.
THERAPIST: So, you thought about that while you were there?
JESSICA: Yeah.
THERAPIST: How did you come to that conclusion that this was something you wanted?
JESSICA: I was in my room one night; I was crying and couldn't sleep. I'm still pissed off at them and will never forgive them for putting me in that damned psycho institution!
THERAPIST: Sure. So, you're in your room and you're crying. What did you think about?
JESSICA: I was thinking about my parents and what I did and stuff like that.

The therapist stayed focused on solution building. Jessica made many provocative statements to which he might have responded, but he maintained the direction of the conversation. As a result, the conversation moved toward what might motivate Jessica to change her behaviors.

THERAPIST: (To mother.) Were you aware of how she was thinking that night?
MOTHER: No, that was the hardest thing we've ever had to do.
JESSICA: You did it anyway; you put your daughter in a psycho institute.
THERAPIST: Wait, Jessica. (To mother.) You weren't aware of this and hadn't had this conversation?
MOTHER: No, every night she would call home and say she's sorry.
THERAPIST: Jessica, you weren't faking that night?
JESSICA: No, that was the night I left. I couldn't sleep that night. I was afraid they wouldn't let me go. I won't forgive them forever; they put me in a psycho institute. Why should I forgive them for that?
THERAPIST: So, Jessica came back home and went into therapy?
MOTHER: We thought that maybe this wasn't the best place for her and sent her back up North to live with her grandmother. At Christmas time, we came up, and she wanted to come back with us, so we said sure.
THERAPIST: What convinced you that you were going to give it a try with her?
MOTHER: You don't give up on your kid.
THERAPIST: So, you have hope that you can turn this around.
MOTHER: Of course, I have hope. At least, I hope I have hope. I know the real Jessica.
THERAPIST: Who is the real Jessica?
MOTHER: The real Jessica is loving. She is thoughtful.

[The discussion turns to the events leading up to the second hospitalization.]

THERAPIST: Let's say that coming here will be helpful. What will be different?

MOTHER: I'll be able to deal with her.

JESSICA: I told you what to do, and then you'll have your little girl back again.

MOTHER: What am I supposed to do?

JESSICA: Let me do what I want, and I will listen.

THERAPIST: Jessica, let me ask you the same question. Let's suppose coming here will be helpful: How will things be just a little bit better?

JESSICA: They're not going to be better. She's not giving me what I want, so why should I give her what she wants?

THERAPIST: So, what would Mom be getting?

JESSICA: I'd love her and be a family. I mean I love her now, but just a little bit.

THERAPIST: So, you're thinking that there's some hope that it could grow a little bit.

JESSICA: It would grow. I know it would!

The therapist began the session looking for presession change, knowing that this usually sets up a solid foundation for asking the Miracle Question. He has learned quickly that neither Jessica nor her mother was able to acknowledge any positive differences at that point. He had prepared for further discussion as the pair moved into a solution-building conversation. Jessica had the ability to know what she needed to do and to accomplish her goal when she was in a context where this would benefit her.

With less success in eliciting evidence of presession change, the therapist opted to continue by asking Jessica and her mother what they were hoping to get from therapy. The question itself implied that, although the therapist had a role, Jessica and her mother were responsible for defining the goal.

[The therapist asks the Miracle Question]

JESSICA: I would wake up happy and want to go to school.

MOTHER: She would want to go to school.

THERAPIST: So, both of you agree with that?

JESSICA: I'd be up and ready. It's not going to happen because I hate school. I want to blow it up.

THERAPIST: So, you'd wake up happy and want to go to school. So what would be the first sign that you wake up and things will be different?

JESSICA: If I was actually able to get up at 5:30 in the morning.

THERAPIST: 5:30 in the morning. So, just if you were able to get up at 5:30 in the morning.

JESSICA: Yeah, if I were able to get up and say: I want to go to school. But it's not going to happen.

THERAPIST: Sure, miracles don't usually happen—just getting some possibilities here. What would be the first point where Mom would say, "Wow, something's different about Jessica"?

JESSICA: That I was up.

THERAPIST: That you got up.

JESSICA: Yeah, I don't get up.

THERAPIST: (To mother.) So, what would that mean to you if you saw that?

MOTHER: I would think something's different.

THERAPIST: What would it mean to you if you saw Jessica doing that?

MOTHER: That she's trying.

THERAPIST: So for you, what would be the next sign that this miracle happened?

MOTHER: A good attitude.

THERAPIST: What do you mean?

MOTHER: Like cheerful, without her telling you to go "f" yourself.

THERAPIST: What would she be saying instead?

MOTHER: "Mom, where's my shoe?" Normal teenage stuff.

THERAPIST: So, you said "cheerful." How would you know she's cheerful?
MOTHER: She'd be smiling and warm. She doesn't look happy.
JESSICA: I'm not happy.
THERAPIST: So, when she is happy, what does she look like?
MOTHER: Different, she just looks happy.
THERAPIST: (To mother.) What would that mean to you?
MOTHER: That she's trying.
THERAPIST: What would be the next sign that the miracle happened?
MOTHER: Her attitude. She'd be cheerful. Normal teenage. She'd be smiling and warm. Her whole facial expression would be different. She doesn't look happy.
THERAPIST: How does she look when she look's happy?
MOTHER: Her face lights up.
THERAPIST: When was the last time you saw that? Even only for a moment?
[At this point, Jessica interrupted to state that the last time it happened was when she was in bed with her boyfriend just before her mother interceded. Much to her mother's credit, she avoided the obvious attempt at provocation and stated that she thought that there was in fact a more recent occasion when she saw Jessica happy. Jessica angrily disagreed and stated that she never has been happy in the North.]
THERAPIST: So, on this day after the miracle, she'd be happy. What else would you notice?
MOTHER: She would care about family. For example, she would care about her grandfather. She used to care about him.

Thus, the Miracle Question can be used to refocus the conversation on solutions. When Jessica or her mother digressed into problem description, the therapist simply asked how the problem will be different once the miracle happens.

THERAPIST: Jessica, is that what you meant when you talked about being more part of the family?
JESSICA: Yeah.
THERAPIST: (To mother.) If I asked your husband what he would notice about this miracle day, what would he say?
MOTHER: Her attitude.
THERAPIST: When would he first notice it?
MOTHER: When she got up in the morning.
THERAPIST: What would be the first sign for him?
MOTHER: She would just say "Hi" to him.
THERAPIST: What would that mean to him?
MOTHER: It would mean a lot. We love her, but she doesn't get that.
THERAPIST: So, if she knew you loved her, what difference would it make?
MOTHER: It would make a big difference. I don't think she likes being the way she is.
JESSICA: I do right now. Nothing is going to change.
THERAPIST: Jessica, let's suppose after this miracle happened, you have a relationship with your family that changes. How will things be different?
JESSICA: I'd tell them I love them. I'd hug them.

The questions put the miracle picture in Jessica's and her mother's life situations. The therapist inquired how others would know that the miracle was happening and what difference it would make to them, concentrating on their lives outside of the therapy office.

THERAPIST: If I had this scale and 10 on the scale is the miracle we just talked about, 0 is what it was like the first time you went to the hospital. Where would you put yourself right now?
MOTHER: 2.
JESSICA: 1.
THERAPIST: 2, 1—not high, something to work with. How is 2 different from 0?

MOTHER: There's still hope.
THERAPIST: After all you've been through, how do you still have hope?
MOTHER: I'm the one in the family with the hope.
THERAPIST: How do you do it?
MOTHER: She's my kid. I don't want anything to happen to her.
THERAPIST: Jessica, what's the difference between 1 and 0?
JESSICA: There's just a little love.

[The therapist asks the mother and Jessica where the father would be on the scale. They both agree at 0. The therapist comments that, given their scale responses, both concurred they had just a little more hope than the father that things could change.]

THERAPIST: Mom, if 3 were happening, what would be happening?
MOTHER: She'd be treating us like people—with a little more respect. Talking to me like normal.
THERAPIST: Jessica, how will you know that you have moved just to a 2 on the scale?
JESSICA: She's giving me what I wanted.
THERAPIST: What would be the first thing she'd be giving you?
JESSICA: I need new sneakers and a pair of jeans.
THERAPIST: One last scale. On a scale of 0 to 10, where 10 is that in reference to this problem, you'd do anything to make this relationship better, and 0 is the only thing you would do is hope and pray it will change—where are you right now?
MOTHER: 9 and a half.
JESSICA: I'll put in some as long as I don't have to go to the hospital. If I have to go to a hospital, I won't put in any.
THERAPIST: So, where are you on the scale?
JESSICA: About a 5.
THERAPIST: That's halfway there. How come so high?
JESSICA: I'm willing to meet her halfway.

While doing scales, the therapist knew that the numbers that Jessica and her mother used will begin to mean something *only* as they are discussed (Berg & de Shazer, 1993). The therapist noted that 1 or 2 on the scale is not high; he carefully paced the mother's cautiousness regarding the possibilities for her daughter. He then moved to defining 1 or 2 as being higher than 0 and therefore "something to work with." The therapist could have asked the mother and Jessica why they are so low on the scale; no doubt, this would have taken the conversation in a very different direction. The therapist consistently used scales to enhance possibilities. He asked questions about how the numbers are different from 0 and how Jessica and her mother would know that progress was being made. He assumed that progress was not only possible, but also probable, and his questions reflected that assumption.

[At this point, the therapist confers with the team. When he returns, he compliments Jessica on her willingness to come and participate, her ability to make strong connections to people, and her intelligence in knowing how to control her behavior when she felt it was necessary. The team complimented the mother for her concern, and willingness to work things out with her daughter. The team suggested that the mother's concerns made perfect sense to them.]

THERAPIST: It's clear to us that you're not crazy at all. You're trying to do what's best. We thought that both of you are not quitters. (To mother.) You could have taken her to the hospital. You chose not to. You could have said to the hospital, "We're not going to take her back." You didn't. (To Jessica.) You could have refused to come home. You didn't. Our sense is, yeah, you're not quitters. You're at least willing to give this one more chance. It's clear that respect is important to both of you. Part of the issue here is trying to figure that out. We are also impressed that both of you said that, while there's not a lot of love there, that could grow. Jessica has had a lot of therapy. Doesn't sound like a lot of it has been helpful. We don't think people should stay in therapy unless it's helpful. We find that the hard work people put in happens between sessions. We can do some cheerleading. I might ask a few useful questions. Since both of you are willing to put in the effort, Jessica you said 5, Mom you said 9 on that scale, we have a simple, I don't think it'll be easy, but simple, suggestion. Notice what happens that moves each one of you up one point. That would be helpful to us.

Session 2: Taking Control
Jessica's mother called during the next week to state that the parents had decided to hospitalize Jessica. Jessica was hospitalized for about a week before returning home. This next appointment was held three weeks after the previous one. Jessica's father came up from the South to attend the session.

THERAPIST: Okay, let's start with a scale. If 10 were being on track, whatever that means to you, and 0 is the day that you decided you needed to bring Jessica back to the hospital, where are you today?
JESSICA: About 7.
THERAPIST: 7, wow! Dad, where would you put things?
FATHER: From last time I saw her, I'd put her around 5 to 6. A lot of improvement but...
THERAPIST: Some room to grow. 5 to 6, that's high, that's good. Over halfway there. Mom, what about you?
MOTHER: 5, I think.

In general, the acronym EARS (elicit, amplify, reinforce, start again) (De Jong & Berg, 1998) had been developed to provide a useful format for subsequent solution-focus sessions.

The therapist begins by *eliciting* positive change since the client was last seen. The therapist *amplifies* the change and then *reinforces* the change and finally *starts again*, by simply asking, "What else is different?" The EARS sequence can also be initiated at the beginning of the next session by using a scale. Very often, the session is built around the scale and naturally follows the EARS format.

THERAPIST: Jessica, let me start with you. Why 7?
JESSICA: I worked this time. When I was in the hospital, I didn't bullshit my way out.
THERAPIST: What do you mean?
JESSICA: Last time, I just said things to get out. This time I didn't. I proved to them that I can do it.
THERAPIST: So, tell me about working.
JESSICA: I talked about my anger and stuff. We had good family sessions, and my parents were able to see that I was changing.
THERAPIST: What told them you were changing?
JESSICA: My attitude. I was happy, but still upset. My personality changed. It was different. I'd wake up with a smile on my face.
THERAPIST: How did you finally decide you were going to do some work?
JESSICA: I was sick of being hurt.
THERAPIST: Mom, you said 5. I remember last time—5 is pretty high.
MOTHER: She's got work to do. At least you can talk to her.
THERAPIST: What tells you that?
MOTHER: Before, she was ready to bite your head off. She was so up and down. I think now she's calmed down, and you can talk to her. She's more workable.
THERAPIST: What have you noticed that tells you that she's more workable?
MOTHER: You can talk to her. On the phone, when she was upset, she'd walk away instead of staying there and saying the things she usually said.

THERAPIST: So, Dad, you put yourself around that range, 5 to 6. What are you noticing?

FATHER: She's just got a different attitude. She's not as quick to react without thinking. She thinks about what she's going to do first before saying or doing anything. People say we're similar because I couldn't walk away from her. Now, even I control it a little better. I guess I'm a last-word person.

THERAPIST: So, I guess we have two last-word people here. Jessica, how have you been doing that?

JESSICA: I've been thinking more about what the consequences will be before I say anything.

Interestingly, although the father was new to this therapy, he was not new to scales and could very quickly participate. Because a solution-focus approach does not require learning a specialized language, it facilitates clients' involvement. The role of feelings in SFBT is exemplified here. The family focused on feeling states at the hospital; instead, the therapist chose to focus this session on what the family was noticing that was different. It has long been the assumption that the client needs to explore and express emotions as primary curative factors. G. Miller and de Shazer (2000) expressed a different point of view: "Like other social constructionists, we also reject claims that the emotions category refers to an essential or universal reality that exists independent from the practical social contexts within which people live their lives, or independent from persons' interpretations of those contexts" (p. 3).

[The therapist and family continue to discuss other changes they have noticed. A discussion regarding the usefulness of medications takes place. Jessica reasons that the positive changes have been because of the medications she is taking.]

THERAPIST: Okay, how about a scale? Where 0 is all these good changes are all because of the medication and 10 is that it's all you—nothing to do with the medication. Where are you on that scale?

JESSICA: About 5.

THERAPIST: So, it's a 50/50 thing: 50% is the medication, 50% is your effort.

Often, clients who have been in the mental health system attribute positive changes to an almost magical effect of psychiatric medications. In those cases, many solution-focus therapists have found it helpful to restructure clients' thinking around ways in which they have some authorship of change. The therapist used the opportunity to challenge Jessica's thinking that medications have been responsible for all the positive changes. Using her answer, he suggested that "50% is your effort."

[As the discussion continued, Jessica acknowledged that the parents' refusal to take her home proved beneficial to her. She affirmed that she had to act differently, and it was up to her to prove to the hospital staff and parents that she was serious. The mother responded that she began to notice the difference after about a week.]

THERAPIST: How would you know that she came up one point on that scale?

MOTHER: If she walked away and didn't say anything.

THERAPIST: Dad, what would move you up?

FATHER: I guess the same thing. She would think before acting.

THERAPIST: Jessica, what would move you up one point?

JESSICA: Control my anger. When I get angry, talk to someone about it.

THERAPIST: What tells you that's possible?

MOTHER: Well, she is reaching out to us more.

THERAPIST: In terms of your confidence that this is the last hospitalization for Jessica, 10 is that's it—the corner has been turned; 0 is we're taking her back tomorrow. Where are you right now?

JESSICA: 8
MOTHER: 5, I'm never going to be sure.
FATHER: 6.
THERAPIST: Jessica, what make you so sure?
JESSICA: Something inside of me tells me I can.
THERAPIST: What's there now that wasn't three weeks ago?
JESSICA: Confidence. Self-esteem. I was able to do it on my own. That gave me confidence that I could do it. I also realized my family was behind me and pushing for me.
THERAPIST: What told you your parents were behind you?
JESSICA: They put me in the hospital. Dad talked to me first time in a long time. Mom told me I had to get out myself; she wasn't going to get me out.
THERAPIST: Dad, why 6?
FATHER: She's handling things differently. Her attitude toward herself, me, my wife, her brothers and sisters. I mean brothers and sisters will argue. Now, she'll walk away instead of fighting. Last night she was helping put fake fingernails on her sister. That's something we hadn't seen before.
THERAPIST: Mom, given all that you've been through, I'm amazed you're at 5. How is 5 different from 0?
MOTHER: I think she's trying. It's little things. She's calmer. She walks away from arguments. She's laughing now and is more relaxed. She's having fun now.
THERAPIST: How long would she need to continue to do what she's doing before you thought that she was just one step higher?
FATHER: A month; up to a month. (Mother and Jessica agreed.)

At this point, the therapist took a break and consulted with the team. He complimented Jessica for all the progress she had made. He again reinforced that, although the medication might be helpful to her, much of the credit goes to her hard work. He complimented both parents for having the good sense to hospitalize their daughter and acknowledged how difficult that decision must have been. He also applauded them for their patience and conviction that Jessica had the ability to change.

THERAPIST: We have a suggestion for between now and the next time you come back. It may take some time for the next point on the scale to happen. It usually doesn't just happen like that. Pieces of that next step happen along the way.
FATHER: Like a jigsaw puzzle.
THERAPIST: Right, so we want you to look for the pieces of that jigsaw puzzle.

Jessica was seen with her mother for one last session about two weeks later. She had not only maintained the gains, but they acknowledged some other significant positive changes. She was being paid for helping her aunt do work around her house, and her older brother was taking her along when he went out with his friends. The mother originally thought that the brother felt sorry for what Jessica had been going through; however, as the brother continued, the mother realized that he genuinely enjoyed being with his sister now. She credited Jessica's new behaviors for this development. Jessica talked at length about the growing importance of her family to her. As a result of the continued progress Jessica was making, the mother had been giving her more privileges, for example, extending her curfew. Both Jessica and the mother were reasonably confident that they could continue the process. The family decided to make this their last session.

This case illustrates the usefulness of SFBT with adolescents. The therapist was able to concentrate on maintaining a conversation that builds solutions. The approach anchored the therapist and allowed him to direct the conversation even when Jessica and her mother digressed into problem talk. Finally, this example demonstrates the requisite elements for successful engagement with adolescents: mutual respect, active listening, pacing, and discovering who most wants change and how that change will make a difference.

RESEARCH

In a comprehensive review, Gingerich and Eisengart (2000) summarized 15 controlled studies of SFBT. To meet the definition of SFBT, the process had to include one or more of the following core components: a search for presession change, goal setting, use of the Miracle Question, use of scaling questions, a search for exceptions, a consulting break, and a message including compliments and tasks. To be considered a well-controlled study, the research not only met the above requirements, but also met three additional criteria. The study demonstrated some form of experimental control, assessed client behavior or functioning, and assessed end-of-treatment outcomes. Of the 15 studies considered, the 5 meeting all requirements involved depression in college students, parenting skills, rehabilitation of orthopedic patients, recidivism in a prison population, and antisocial adolescent offenders. The authors concluded that "The wide variety of settings and populations studied and the multiplicity of modalities used suggest that SFBT may be helpful in a broad range of applications, however, this tentative conclusion awaits more careful study" (p. 495).

De Jong and Hopwood (1996) presented a study completed at the Brief Family Therapy Center in Milwaukee. Of the 275 clients seen in treatment between November 1992 and August 1993, 57% identified themselves as African American, 5% as Latino, 3% as Native American, and 36% as White; 15% of cases were adolescents, and 33% were younger than 13. At time of treatment termination, 49% demonstrated moderate progress and 25% showed significant progress. This total of 74% compares favorably to the 66% expected outcome when conventional models are used (Garfield & Bergin, 1986). Seven to nine months after their last interview, 136 of the participants were asked whether their treatment goal was met or if significant progress had been made toward that goal; 45% stated that their goals were met and 32% stated that significant progress had been made. The authors state in their summary:

- More than three-fourths of clients receiving solution-focused therapy met their treatment goals or made progress toward them.
- This level of effectiveness occurred over an average of 3.0 sessions.
- Solution-focused therapy was equally effective with a diversity of clients.
- Effectiveness did not vary by client-therapist gender or racial mix.
- The same therapeutic procedures were effective across a range of client-identified problems. (De Jong & Hopwood, 1996, p. 294)

Specific to adolescents, there are a number of studies which suggest that SFBT proves an effective intervention with this age group in various settings (Geil, 1998; LaFountain & Garner, 1996; Littrell, Malli, & Vanderwood, 1995; Seagram, 1997; Triantafillou, 1997).

The results of research are promising and show that SFBT is time-effective. A worldwide research project is planned using the SFBT protocol designed by the European Brief Therapy Association. In addition, other planned research will focus on the adaptability and effectiveness of the solution-focus approach in a diversity of settings.

SUMMARY

As with many other populations, the SFBT approach has proven effective with adolescents. The approach inherently fosters a respect for clients and maintains a focus on their stated goals. Solution-focus therapists are guided by a client's vision of a positive outcome. This simple focus on the individual has the effect of broadening the approach to include a wide variety of individuals. No matter what the problem, every client has the ability to create a detailed vision of a more satisfying future. In addition, no matter what the diagnosis, solution-focus practitioners can be relentlessly curious about the client's abilities and resources. Ultimately, solution-focus therapists have learned from countless clients throughout nearly 30 years of working this way that a simple conversation about possibilities may have the most useful results.

REFERENCES

Berg, I., & de Shazer, S. (1993). Making numbers talk: Language in therapy. In S. Friedman (Ed.), *The new language of change: Constructive collaboration in psychotherapy* (pp. 5–24). New York: Guilford Press.

Berg, I., & Miller, S. (1992). *Working with the problem drinker: A solution-focused approach.* New York: Norton.

Butz, M., Chamberlain, L., & McCown, W. (1997). *Strange attractors: Chaos, complexity, and the art of family therapy.* New York: Wiley.

Cade, B., & O'Hanlon, W. H. (1993). *A brief guide to brief therapy.* New York: Norton.

Campbell, J., Elder, J., Gallagher, D., & Simon, J. (1999). Crafting the "tap on the shoulder:" A compliment template for solution-focused therapy. *American Journal of Family Therapy, 27*(1), 35–47.

De Jong, P., & Berg, I. (1998). *Interviewing for solutions.* Belmont, CA: Brooks/Cole.

De Jong, P., & Hopwood, L. E. (1996). Outcome research on treatment conducted at the Brief Family Therapy Center, 1992–1993. In S. Miller, B. Duncan, & M. Hubble (Eds.), *Handbook of solution-focused brief therapy* (pp. 272–298). San Francisco: Jossey-Bass.

de Shazer, S. (1985). *Keys to solution in brief therapy.* New York: Norton.

de Shazer, S. (1991). *Putting difference to work.* New York: Norton.

de Shazer, S. (1994). *Words were originally magic.* New York: Norton.

de Shazer, S. (1999, January). *Beginnings.* Available from http://www.brief-therapy.org

Garfield, S., & Bergin, A. (1986). *Handbook of psychotherapy and behavior change.* New York: Wiley.

Geil, M. (1998). *Solution focused consultation: An alternative consultation model to manage student behavior and improve classroom environment.* Unpublished doctoral dissertation, University of Northern Colorado, Greeley.

Gingerich, W., & Eisengart, S. (2000). Solution-focused brief therapy: A review. *Family Process, 39*(4), 477–498.

LaFountain, R., & Garner, N. (1996). Solution-focused counseling groups: The results are in. *Journal for Specialists in Group Work, 21*(2), 128–143.

Littrell, J., Malli, J., & Vanderwood, M. (1995). Single-session brief counseling in a high school. *Journal of Counseling and Development, 73*(4), 451–458.

Miller, G. (1997). *Becoming miracle workers: Language and meaning in brief therapy.* New York: Aldine De Gruyter.

Miller, G., & de Shazer, S. (2000). Emotions in solution-focused therapy: A re-examination. *Family Process, 39*(1), 5–23.

Miller, S., Duncan, B., & Hubble, M. (1997). *Escape from Babel: Toward a unifying language for psychotherapy practice.* New York: Norton.

O'Hanlon, W. (1987). *Taproots: Underlying principle of Milton Erickson's therapy and hypnosis.* New York: Norton.

Seagram, B. (1997). *The efficacy of solution-focused therapy with young offenders.* Unpublished doctoral dissertation, York University, York, PA.

Simon, J., & Berg, I. (1999). Solution-focused brief therapy with long-term problems. *Directions in Rehabilitation Counseling, 10*(10), 117–127.

Tomm, K., & Lannamann, J. (1988, September/October). Questions as interventions. *Family Therapy Networker,* 38–41.

Triantafillou, N. (1997). A solution-focused approach to mental health supervision. *Journal of Systemic Therapies, 16*(4), 305–308.

Weiner-Davis, M., de Shazer, S., & Gingerich, W. (1987). Building on pre-treatment change to construct the therapeutic solution: An exploratory study. *Journal of Marital and Family Therapy, 13*(4), 359–363.

Wittgenstein, L. (1958). *Philosophical investigations* (3rd ed.). New York: Macmillan.

CHAPTER 7

An Integrative Approach to Assessment and Intervention with Adolescents of Color

ARPANA G. INMAN, KWAMIA N. RAWLS, MARISOL M. MEZA, AND ANDRAÉ L. BROWN

Marcia (1980) construed identity as "a self-structure—an internal, self-constructed, dynamic organization of drives, abilities, beliefs, and individual history" (p. 159). Thus, a person's identity remains fluid, incorporating and changing based on experience and history. Although the process of identity formation begins at infancy, late adolescence poses a critical time when individuals negotiate multiple identities related to sexual, vocational, and sociocultural expectations. With consistency and continuity in experience and/or history, individuals are able to develop a stable sense of self in relation to various contexts. This provides them with stronger, well-developed identities. However, when experiences become inconsistent, individuals may experience dissonance and have to rely on external sources to validate a sense of self, thus complicating their processes of identity development. The extent to which adolescents experience congruency in different contexts will influence the synthesis of various identities, facilitating a smooth transition into adulthood.

Adolescents of color living in the United States are confronted with integrating multiple cultures: the dominant culture, the ethnic culture of origin, and the adolescent culture. They are enculturated and socialized within their own cultures of origin while also receiving messages from the dominant culture (Berry, 1993). They thus are faced with the normal developmental tasks and expectations within their own cultures while being confronted with values and expectations from what may be a relatively incompatible culture (Huang, 1994). Apart from dealing with the already complex issue of identity formation in personal, social, and sexual contexts, their development is often complicated by factors such as acculturation, experience in a racial/ethnic context that may influence the retention of racial/ethnic identities, and parental and personal migration histories. Some adolescents of color negotiate the multiple demands of the developmental tasks without much conflict; others experience several challenges in blending potentially disparate cultural values, worldviews, behaviors, attitudes, beliefs, norms, and expectations (Inman, Ladany, Constantine, & Morano, 2001). In light of this, it becomes relevant to examine their experiences from within both an emic (culture-specific) and an etic (culture-general) perspective. In understanding the sociocultural realities within which adolescents of color grow and function, exploring the dialectical interaction of all these factors becomes important.

The focus of this chapter concerns the challenges faced by three groups of adolescents—Asian Americans, African Americans, and Latino Americans—as viewed through an integrative model of assessment emphasizing developmental tasks.

THEORETICAL CONSTRUCTS

Typically, a therapist grounded in a theoretical orientation finds some flexibility in dealing with the common fluctuations of human behavior attributable to personality and circumstance. However, despite similarities in problems, stories, or backgrounds, client experiences can neither be duplicated nor examined in exactly the same light. Furthermore, with the increasing ethnic/racial diversity in the United States, therapists are challenged not only by the diverse cultural landscape of their clients but also by the additional complexity of negotiating developmental challenges within multiple contexts. This requires more than a solid footing in a particular theoretical framework: Therapists need a governing paradigm or lens for conceptualizing clients and their problems—a paradigm that examines the development of clients of color within multiple contexts while also acknowledging the delicate role that therapists play in a therapeutic context.

In light of this, we propose an integrative model based in a multicultural perspective. This model is not meant to take the place of a clinician's own theoretical orientation, but to enhance its effectiveness by allowing therapists to examine the impact of an adolescent's personal development within multiple cultures and to acknowledge the impact of therapists' own role in the therapeutic process. Such an approach allows therapists to address complex developmental systems that adolescent clients of color must negotiate in a pluralistic society such as the United States.

Specifically, two theories form the theoretical basis of our approach. Bronfenbrenner's (1989) ecological systems theory examines the interplay of different levels of contexts (e.g., family, school, migration, racial relations in society) along which an adolescent develops. The second-order cybernetic perspective of the ecosystemic model (Keeney, 1983) involves exploring the role of a therapist in facilitating the process of therapy.

In discussing ecological systems theory, Bronfenbrenner (1989) identified the interaction of time and environment as important in understanding human development. Developmental changes triggered by internal (puberty) or external (birth of a sibling) life events can alter the relational dynamic between person and environment. Bronfenbrenner observed the development of an individual as occurring within four ecological systems (micro-, meso-, exo-, and macrosystem), which are nested levels of dynamic contexts. These contexts form a complex web of interconnecting systems in which an individual negotiates interactions with others and various sociocultural systems directly or indirectly throughout life. Specifically, a microsystem constitutes the smallest element within a context (e.g., school) in which an adolescent of color engages in a set of roles (e.g., student), activities (e.g., learning), and interpersonal relations (e.g., student-teacher). The mesosystem represents a layer above the microsystem and refers to the linkage between two or more systems, for example, the relationship between African American families and the workplace. The exosystem, nested over the mesosystem, encompasses the influence of events within specific social structures that indirectly impact an adolescent of color, for example, the impact of a Latino father's experience of discrimination in the workplace and his parenting of his adolescent. Finally, the macrosystem encompassing the different levels may be thought of as a "societal blueprint for a particular culture, subculture, or other broader social context" (p. 228). This social or cultural context carries information and endows institutions and activities with motivation and meaning. Thus, for adolescents of color, the macrosystem includes negotiating the influences of societal norms, messages from the media, political policies, and judicial laws.

This model of social structure captures the complexity within which individuals develop from birth to death. Thus, it can be very valuable in assessing the relative significance of various interconnecting relationships (families, friends, clergy), systems (house of worship, school), and contexts (discrimination, racism, immigration, sexism) in the lives of Asian, African, and Latino American adolescents. Acknowledging and using the different levels and cultural contexts are important in delivering comprehensive, culturally sensitive psychological services to these families.

The second theoretical basis for our model comes from the ecosystemic perspective and implies reflecting on the role and impact of a therapist in the therapeutic process. In a therapeutic relationship, a therapist must walk a tightrope, negotiating how to be a part of the process while also being separate from a client. This skill proves even more important to negotiate when dealing with adolescents of color who are similarly balancing their development and experience on a daily basis in the larger society.

The ecosystemic perspective embraces multiple patterns of personal and contextual interaction within two differing epistemologies, referred to as first-order and second-order cybernetics (Amatea & Sherrard, 1994). First-order change signifies viewing an individual in context, as a part of a system or systems of interrelating persons and circumstances (e.g., a client and a client's family, or a client, a client's family, and their economic status). This view implies that one can observe something, such as another's behavior, without changing it or having an impact on it. Thus, a therapist becomes an observer from the outside, occupying a position of power over the client, resulting in a potentially incongruent hierarchical power structure (see Madanes, 1981). Such a relationship or environment may mimic the challenges of unequal power differentials faced by persons of color on a daily basis, thus failing to foster a culturally supportive atmosphere needed to work successfully with such populations.

On the other hand, a second-order cybernetic perspective suggests that one cannot observe an interaction without impacting it (or being impacted by the interaction). According to Becvar and Becvar (1994), Daniels and White (1994), Hoffman (1990), and other family therapists, clinicians are no longer directors of change, but agents of change. As a result, clinicians become "involved observers" by becoming a part of the system and also a part of what must change.

This second-order perspective forms the second basis of our model. In incorporating the second-order perspective, clinicians place themselves as an equal facilitator, a part of the treatment. It allows for an environment in which a client's identity is unchallenged and a process is set in motion to empower a minority client, to reduce feelings of inadequacy, stress, inferiority, unmanliness, and unmachismo. Such a setting has a greater potential for clients to complete treatment because their cultural and social ideologies are embraced and they are not forced to adapt to mainstream beliefs/attitudes/ways of behaving. This fosters an environment sensitive to the challenges and struggles of persons of color.

To effectively employ this integrative approach, examining potential issues impacting an adolescent of color becomes important. The following sections address some significant factors impacting Asian, African, and Latino American adolescents. Before we begin our discussion, it is important that the reader view this material as a "cultural guideline" that needs to be adjusted with each adolescent of color, keeping in mind that the terms Asians, Africans, and Latinos describe many nationalities with great diversity within groups.

CULTURAL-GROUP PROCESSES AND ILLUSTRATIVE CASES

Asian American Adolescents

Asian Americans currently constitute one of the fastest growing minorities in the United States. They comprise a very heterogeneous group, diverse in country of origin, socioeconomic status, language, religious practices, cultural values, beliefs, and acculturation levels. Despite this diversity, under the notion of "model minority," Asian Americans typically have been viewed as well-adjusted, highly educated, financially stable and successful, and as encountering few psychological difficulties (Sue & Sue, 1999). This myth has not only influenced the perceptions of the dominant culture, but has also proved to be problematic for Asian Americans, resulting in underutilization of mental-health resources (Durvasula & Mylvaganam, 1994).

Asian adolescents living in Asia develop identities and behaviors that are embedded within their own cultural values and socially and developmentally desirable to their own cultures (Inman et al., 2001). Conversely, Asian American adolescents living in the United States are exposed to value-laden messages from both the Asian ethnic and the dominant U.S. cultures. They are faced with attitudinal options, values, and lifestyles (Dona & Berry, 1994) that necessitate social, psychological, and cultural adjustments with reference to both cultures. Thus, their developmental task is compounded by a need to negotiate a sense of self in a context that reflects neither the experiences of their parents nor the experiences of the majority culture. Developing a congruent sense of self in a context of inconsistent messages between socialization agents (i.e., familial and nonfamilial) can pose significant challenges in the formation of strong social, psychological, ethnic identities. Thus, examining their experiences within a sociocultural context becomes relevant. Several influences shape the Asian American adolescent identity: family, immigration, acculturation, and ethnic identity. These influences are discussed in the context of the Asian conceptualization of adolescence and illustrated through the case example of Meena, an Asian American adolescent.

Conceptualization of Adolescence in the Asian Context
There appears to be no stage of adolescence in Asian cultures comparable to that in the dominant culture (Almeida, 1996; Huang, 1994). Asian American adolescents are socialized in a collective value orientation that de-emphasizes developing an identity separate from their families. The shift from childhood to adulthood does not involve a differentiation of the self (as in the dominant culture); rather, there is an emphasis on clarification of roles within a family while sharing greater responsibilities (e.g., economic, cultural) for the welfare of family members (Ahmed, 1999). Such a focus allows little room for "experimentation within couple relations in dating, or exploration of one's sexual orientation, career, and work choices" (Almeida, 1996, p. 407). In Asian American cultures, issues related to sexuality continue to be taboo and often are not discussed across generational lines. Dating is often associated with premarital sex rather than seen as a way to define oneself within the context of relationships with the opposite sex (Mehta, 1998). In a similar light, career and vocational decisions tend to be based on familial consensus, reflecting parental and cultural values, and can typically be a point of contention in families.

Asian American Families

Subsumed within a patriarchal society, Asian families tend to be hierarchical in structure, with clear role expectations based on gender, birth order, position, and status in a family and social hierarchy within a society (Huang, 1994; Jayakar, 1994; Sodowsky & Carey, 1987). Behaviors and values stress family harmony, respect toward elders, formality and social restraint in relationships, and specific obligations for males and females (Jayakar, 1994; Sodowsky & Carey, 1987). Individual actions and behaviors are perceived to affect the welfare and integrity of the immediate family, the extended family (related/nonrelated members of the community), as well as ancestors, with family needs superseding individual needs. Furthermore, prolonged dependence on family is typically encouraged (Huang, 1994); it is not uncommon to find adults (e.g., 22 to 28 years of age) continuing to live with their parents. Because of the collective nature of the Asian culture, exploring the makeup of the actual household, the influence of the extended family (whether in the United States or the country of origin), and the different alliances in the community becomes necessary.

In addition, a major force shaping the identities of Asian American adolescents arises in the context of an emigrational experience. Many families migrate to the United States for the betterment of their families and children. The kinds of sacrifices they make in leaving their countries of origin, the current sacrifices being made to take care of the family, postimmigration adjustment, changes in socioeconomic status, and potential gender-role reversals become important influential factors in the responsibilities and expectations that family members place on these youth. The fear of cultural obliteration impacting their children and the need to protect cultural legacies and family patterns may also push parents to impose significant pressures and rigid boundaries on their children to engage in or hold onto their ethnic cultures (Almeida, 1996; Dasgupta & Dasgupta, 1996). Negotiating competing familial expectations of dependence, dominant cultural expectations of autonomy, and peer pressures of dating and anticipations of developing social relationships can have great implications on the adjustment of these adolescents. In this context, Asian American adolescents have to develop a range of roles to function effectively within the multiple cultures (LaFromboise, Coleman, & Gerton, 1993). Some potential consequences resulting from this include divided loyalties between personal and family identities (Inman et al., 2001), intergenerational stress (Huang, 1994), and dissonance within one's ethnic/psychological identity (Phinney, 1990), culminating in psychological distress related to depression and low self-esteem.

Immigration

Asians have a long history of immigration to the United States, dating back to the 1800s. This immigration has occurred for economic, political, and educational reasons as well as because of a relaxation of immigration laws (Sue & Sue, 1999). With the waves of immigration, great variations have occurred in terms of country of origin, age at and reasons for immigration, level of intergenerational conflict prior to immigration, immigration status on entry to the United States (voluntary or involuntary), length of stay in the United States, exposure to Western values prior to immigration, level of community support, educational and skill levels, socioeconomic status/social class in the country of origin and current status, and religiosity. These significant factors need to be considered in understanding the adjustment and socialization of Asian American adolescents and their families (Almeida, 1996; Hines, Garcia-Preto, McGoldrick, Almeida, & Weltman, 1992).

To understand immigrant histories, learning about the socioeconomic status of an adolescent's family constitutes an important indicator of the kinds of resources currently available to a family. Given the myth of the model minority, Asian Americans are often perceived as economically and educationally successful (Sue & Sue, 1999). However, as with the diversity within the Asian American racial group, great variations occur in education levels and social class (Sandhu, 1997). Gaining an awareness of parental education, past and current occupations, and changes in social class from pre- to postimmigration become important in this context. These issues may impact on the academic expectations placed on Asian American adolescents by their parents, for example, career and vocational choices/pressures imposed and the focus placed on academics versus other activities (Eaton & Dembo, 1997).

Acculturation
Within the experiences of immigration, a significant factor that influences Asian American adolescents and their families revolves around acculturation. Acculturation involves a bidirectional change process that occurs when an individual simultaneously encounters two or more distinct cultures firsthand, thus spurring attitudinal, value, and behavioral changes (Berry, 1993; Marin, 1992). Typically, young children tend to acculturate more easily compared to their parents or recent immigrants (Sodowsky & Lai, 1997). Thus, parents may come to depend on their children to assist in certain interactions with the dominant culture, and, at the same time, they may struggle with the immersion of their children within the dominant culture, leading to the "Americanization" of their children. In such situations, acculturative influences continuing over generations can result in diluted or reorganized role structures (Huang, 1994). Such reorganization can generate conflicting messages for an adolescent functioning in this multicultural context. These conflicting messages may result in compartmentalization of roles (e.g., adhering to the dominant cultural values when outside the home and to ethnic values at home) (Inman, Constantine, & Ladany, 1999) and role confusions.

In examining the impact of acculturation, one needs to be cognizant of the fact that there are significant differences in terms of generational status and level of acculturation. Being the first to immigrate to the United States versus being born here has significant implications in terms of an adolescent's worldview and level of acculturation. A recent immigrant is likely to be immersed in Asian customs, values, and beliefs, whereas a third- or fourth-generation Asian American is likely to be quite Americanized and to identify more with the dominant U.S. value system. According to Marin (1992), the degree of contact between the dominant and the ethnic culture also influences acculturation levels. For example, Asian Americans living in a relatively homogeneous Asian community may be less acculturated than adolescents and their families who are geographically isolated from members of their culture. Research has also shown that immigrants typically engage in a process of selective acculturation (Prathikanti, 1997); that is, they may adapt easily to overt aspects of the dominant culture (e.g., language, clothing) while holding on to more central aspects of the original culture, such as family relations and sex-role expectations (Dhruvarajan, 1993; Naidoo, 1985; Sodowsky & Carey, 1988, Sue & Sue, 1987). Thus, noting the acculturation level in different areas becomes an important variable in the assessment process of Asian American adolescents and their families (Inman et al., 1999).

Ethnic Identity
Ethnic identity or identification with one's own ethnic culture (Marin, 1992) represents yet another important factor in the acculturative experiences of immigrants. Ethnic identity concerns individuals' ties to their cultural identities and takes on unique importance in a pluralistic society. Forming an ethnic identity involves an active process of self-evaluation, self-exploration,

and decision-making about the role of ethnicity in one's life. Several models of minority ethnic identity formation have been proposed (for a description of these, see Phinney, 1990; Sue & Sue, 1999). These describe individuals going through a series of experiences, such as alienation from their cultures to being able to develop integrated cultural identities.

Development of a personal sense of ethnic identity occurs primarily within one's family, whose support is a significant variable in the development of ethnic pride and self-worth (Phinney & Chavira, 1992). Research shows that levels of parental ethnic identification as well as extent of family interaction with the dominant culture influence adolescent ethnic identity development (Huang & Ying, 1989; Sodowsky & Lai, 1997). The extent to which parents are able to prepare their children for functioning in a bicultural context will impact on an adolescent's experience of connection or alienation, marginalization or integration within the identity-formation process as well as the development of a sense of self (esteem/worth).

Case Presentation
Meena, an 18-year-old, second-generation Asian Indian female, sought counseling for depression resulting from conflicts with her parents. One point of contention stemmed from her living at home with her parents. She indicated a desire to find an apartment as soon as she was able to save some money because of her parents' constant involvement in her daily activities. She further reported frustration with their wanting her to major in engineering, although she had a strong desire to specialize in history. Meena indicated that she was dating a Caucasian American man, but had not revealed this to her parents. While the parents were aware of their friendship, according to her, they suspected that she may be dating him and would make comments about the importance of staying focused on her education as well as the significance of marrying within her community. She also felt forced to attend Indian celebrations and hated wearing Indian clothes on these occasions.

Family History. Meena came from an intact family and was the older of two siblings; her younger sister, 16 years of age, was currently in high school. Meena's father was unemployed, and her mother worked as a nurse. Meena perceived her parents as very strict, holding high expectations for their children. They not only desired them to excel academically, but also were "controlling" in terms of their socialization with peers (e.g., whom Meena could go out with, how long she could be out of the house). Both parents were bilingual and had migrated to the United States 20 years earlier. They kept in regular contact with their parents, siblings, and other extended family members. They were fairly traditional and very involved in the Indian community.

Case Conceptualization. Meena's depression appeared to be a function of feeling caught between two cultures. On one hand, she had been enculturated within her own ethnic culture; on the other, she was getting potentially conflicting messages from the dominant culture. Meena's anger at her parents for their "lack of understanding" was being internalized and leading to depressive symptoms of poor sleep and appetite, decreased energy and concentration, and frequent crying spells. She and her parents were experiencing typical intergenerational cultural conflicts that are experienced between immigrant parents and second-generation children. Specifically, like most immigrant parents, Meena's parents may have been fearful of Meena's losing her sense of cultural identity, and thus imposed stronger pressures to engage in culturally specific ways. Additionally, Meena was dealing with her emerging sexual identity, an issue that her parents may have wanted to deny. Thus, acculturative, ethnic identity, and intergenerational conflicts clearly posed significant problems for Meena and her parents.

Treatment Approach. Treatment focused on examining the contextual factors impacting on Meena's depression. The notion of a multicultural identity and the implicit demands in negotiating such an identity were explored with her. Acculturative conflicts that typically arise out of these experiences for second-generation adolescents were discussed and normalized. In addition, Meena was given some literature to read on cultural value conflict. She was also encouraged to explore parental expectations in the context of their immigration history and acculturation level. Specifically, she was encouraged to talk to her parents about their reasons for immigration; their decision process involved in immigrating; the sacrifices they may have made in leaving their families, friends, and social status; and their own struggles with holding onto their sense of ethnic identification in their postmigration adaptations. She was encouraged to talk to her mother about her own gender-role socialization in her family of origin and issues related to sexuality. These issues were then discussed with her as a way to understand her parents' expectations and behaviors regarding the academic, social, and sexual aspects of her life.

Posttermination Synopsis and Reflections. Negotiating developmental tasks within multiple cultures can be quite challenging for Asian American adolescents. According to the dominant culture, Meena should have developed a sense of individuation and independence from her family (Carter, 1991). Through increased peer socialization and dating, she would have been working on developing a sense of self as a woman separate from her family with a personal sexual identity that laid the foundation for the tasks of intimacy in young adulthood. Integration into the dominant culture would be seen as important to being successful in society. But according to the Asian Indian culture, Meena should have been more focused on her education, fulfilling the dutiful role of the daughter in the family by attending to and staying connected to ethnic celebrations and functions. Disconnecting from the culture would not only have been stressful in providing an experience of cultural discontinuity for Meena's ethnic-identity development, but her need to disengage from the family would have been culturally incongruent. Furthermore, within the Asian Indian context, dating and premarital sex seem to be implicitly connected (Mehta, 1998); the fear of their daughter's becoming "Americanized" and bringing shame to the family may have been at play. Understanding her own development within the context of multiple cultures as well as listening to her parents' narratives about their immigration histories seemed relevant (Almeida, 1996). Externalizing the pressures as a function of acculturation rather than seeing these primarily as familial conflicts allowed Meena and her family to negotiate the challenges together.

AFRICAN AMERICAN ADOLESCENTS

Much has been written in an attempt to describe the plight of the African American adolescent in the United States. Although issues related to high-risk social behaviors are apparent among adolescents of all socioeconomic levels and racial/ethnic backgrounds (Hechinger, 1992; National Commission on Children, 1991; Zill & Rogers, 1988), on a daily basis we are bombarded by the media's attempt to negatively characterize and stereotype African American youth (e.g., as criminals, drug users, street thugs, uneducated, pregnant adolescents, poor, violent).

From birth, African Americans are socialized to recognize, negotiate, and navigate in the White-dominated society of the United States (hooks, 1997). In this context, African American adolescents are challenged to become and remain psychologically and socially healthy in the midst of failing school districts, discrimination in employment, economic disparities, racial profiling, increased health risks, poverty, high morbidity, below-average life span, and often-invisible and more-sophisticated forms of racism (Booker, 1998; Jones, 1997; Madhubuti, 1991; Noguera, 1996; Schoenbaum & Waidman, 1997; Woodard, 1957). Given the many contextual levels and systems that these youth must contend with, a more comprehensive perspective is needed to understand the experiences of African American adolescents.

Often, attention is given to the perceived negative behaviors of these adolescents, with little understanding of the experiences and motivations behind their actions (Dyson, 1997; Payne & Brown, in press; Utsey, Bolden, & Brown, 2001; Wyatt, 1999). It is imperative to reformulate conceptualizations of this diverse group, to demystify the stereotypes and myths associated with them, and to make a concerted effort to gain a realistic perspective of their present situations. In this section, we take a look at the significant influences on the development of African American adolescents and elucidate the issues and interventions through a case study of Edwin, a teenage African American male.

Invisibility

Franklin (1999) investigated the interaction of racism and identity development in African American adolescents and proposed the invisibility-syndrome paradigm. Invisibility implies "an inner struggle with the feelings that one's talents, abilities, personality, and worth are not valued or even recognized" (p. 761). The invisibility syndrome represents a global experience for all people of African descent and should be explored within an historical and contemporary perspective that includes gender roles, racism, prejudice, and all other oppressive manifestations under conditions of White supremacy (Jones, 1997; Parham, 1999; Wyatt, 1999).

During adolescence, many African Americans begin to find and develop their own identities and to face the world on their own with limited familial protection. Also during this time, they are bombarded by society's ills, including both overt and covert acts of discrimination, racism, sexism, prejudice, and crime. The impact and fallout of all these issues are coupled with myriad developmental challenges and interpersonal circumstances. The interpersonal conflicts that occur may take on varying expressions, including parental and sibling conflicts, exploration of sexuality, confronting death, peer pressure, experimentation with drugs and alcohol, maintaining a social network, and developing social and racial consciousness (Helms, 1995; Lefrancois, 1996).

In clinical work, the invisibility paradigm leads to assessing African American men and women for how recognition, legitimacy, validation, respect, dignity, and identity interact in an intrapsychic manner to determine their visibility or invisibility (Franklin, 1999). Many adolescents feel as if they have to make people recognize their existences and contributions to society. Some adolescents turn to education, music, and sports to assert themselves; others, who are isolated, mistrusting, confused, and without proper guidance, may choose less positive pathways to developing their identities as adults, individuals, family members, and persons of color. They begin to assert their manhood and womanhood in a society that negates their attempts and to discover where they can excel.

Sites of resilience represent the psychological and/or physical spaces that help African American adolescents cope. Several sites of resilience identified by different authors warrant our attention. Specifically, Elder (1985) noted the family (i.e., reorganization, kinship, generational patterns, individual histories, and historical events) as a source that has fostered resilience and adaptive traits for African Americans. Payne and Brown (in press) have further identified racial identity, street life, and religion/spirituality as added sources of resilience for inner-city Black males.

African American Families

The most widely misunderstood and misrepresented structures in African American life under the weight of European psychological-cultural oppression are African American families (Kambon, 1998). Despite increasing percentages of single male- and female-headed African American households, these families are embedded within extended networks of support. Children are typically reared by a large number of relatives, older siblings, godparents, and close friends because of the value attached to sense of community, group orientation, cooperation, and interdependence (Todisco & Salomone, 1991). A major strength of African American families flows from the great flexibility and adaptability of family roles, with men, women, and children adopting multiple roles in a family (e.g., men accepting of women's professional work roles, men sharing traditional female responsibilities, older children taking on parental roles), and strong kinship bonds (e.g., grandmother sharing child-rearing responsibilities). Because of the possibility of nontraditional/extended family arrangements, it is important to explore the complex structure of a family household and the significant relationships that compose a family (Boyd-Franklin, 1989; Sue & Sue, 1999).

Racial Identity Development

Psychological functioning in African Americans has been typically associated with their racial identity development (Carter, 1991), with sociopolitical influences (e.g., inequalities and prejudice based on race) serving as a major catalyst for the development, ownership, and experience of African American racial identity (Helms, 1995). Helms (1990, 1995) perceived racial identity as a dynamic construct, consisting of ego statuses defined by one's feelings, thoughts, and behaviors in relation to one's own race or other races. A major component of racial-identity development involves overcoming internalized negative stereotypes and conceptions of one's own racial group (Helms & Cook, 1999).

It is within the family that African American adolescents first develop an understanding of race and racial issues. Parents are charged with the role of helping these adolescents define themselves in their multiple identities. Billingsley (1968) observed the African American family as a social system embedded in a network of mutually interdependent relationships with the Black community and the larger society. The major institutions in this larger society set the conditions for educational, economic, political, health, welfare, and community subsystems for African American families. The type of racial socialization that occurs in a family is guided by a family's experiences as African Americans in the context of these systems in the dominant society. Their experiences of prejudice, poverty, urban living, educational and occupational opportunities (Wyatt, 1999), as well as racist policies and practices in these systems tend to complicate and add to these families' difficulties in promoting healthy racial identity for their children (Meyers, 1993). The manner by which families address issues of race with their children defines the kind of coping strategies their adolescents develop in their racial-identity development.

Wyatt (1999) contended that the ability or inability to assimilate into the dominant culture often serves as a source of tension over the life span of a family. Racial identity and pride entail developmental processes; hence, family members may never be on the same level of assimilation or acceptance of each other's perspectives. Families thus may find themselves deeply divided on issues of who is "too White" or "too Black," resulting in intergenerational divides on these issues. Unlike their counterparts, African

American adolescents experience the challenge of developing a positive identity in a context of multiple familial messages, historical influences, and societal images that are often incongruent with their own personal experiences. Thus, the ability of African American adolescents to develop positive racial identities, despite the negativity in their surroundings, is an important resilience factor.

Street Life
Although involvement in street life has been perceived as a negative coping strategy and associated with issues such as gangs and substance abuse, Payne and Brown (in press) believe that behaviors associated with street life can serve as a means of establishing resilience for some young, inner-city Black men. Street life can help organize meaning for the context within which these adolescents exist and can serve as a means to survive and endure what may be an economically depressed, racist environment. In many instances, a strong sense of camaraderie may be established through a new and/or extended family found on inner-city streets. This new family can take the place of traditional families in helping Black men feel adequate, respected, and accomplished. Although engaging in street life appears neither glamorous nor typically psychologically/physically constructive, understanding how such a lifestyle evolves to preserve and establish integrity and resilience, particularly for African American men, may be useful.

Spirituality
Religious or spiritual beliefs play a very significant role in the lives of African Americans. Spirituality has been identified as an important coping strategy to deal with stressors. African Americans may have strong ties to a certain religion or church group and may experience a strong spiritual orientation or an ingrained belief in God. This affiliation may serve as a social network, sanctuary, economic entity, political power base, employment provider, cultural vehicle, leadership reservoir, and mechanism for psychological liberation (Dyson, 1997; Payne & Brown, in press; Tinney, 1981). In addition, for many, a special significance arises from a "church family" consisting of ministers, deacons, brothers, and sisters in a church as an integral part of the extended family (Boyd-Franklin, 1989). Thus, the role of religion, the house of worship, and the clergy should be considered a potential resource in working with African American adolescents (Sue & Sue, 1999).

Case Presentation
Edwin, a 16-year-old African American male residing in a juvenile facility in a major urban city in the Northeast, was referred for counseling by the court. Edwin had been arrested for possession of stolen property (a car) and possession of an illegal substance (marijuana). This was not his first arrest, but the most recent and serious offense in a series of arrests and confrontations with law enforcement over a three-year period. The court mandated that he complete comprehensive treatment as an alternative to the state juvenile penitentiary.

Edwin reported beginning to participate in illegal drug use at age 13. He related that a loss of trust occurred with his parents when his stepfather, Charles, reported Edwin to the police for stealing a neighbor's bike. Edwin felt betrayed by his mother for supporting Charles's decision to turn him over to the police. He referred to Charles as a "sellout" and an "Oreo" and stated that he always wanted to be White, talking and acting White, living in a White neighborhood, working for the government, and maintaining friendships with the police.

While incarcerated, Edwin began to recognize that his life had gotten out of control. He accepted the fact that this not only negatively impacted his education and social life but also damaged the relationships that he cherished. Now Edwin wanted to begin to change his lifestyle and to reconcile with his family.

Family History. Edwin was the younger of two sons born to Mary, age 45, and Fred, age 46. When Edwin and his brother, Brian, age 19, were 2 and 3 years old, their parents separated because of Fred's addictions and infidelity. Mary later married Charles, age 50. As a middle-class family, they owned their own home in the suburbs surrounding the city where Edwin was arrested and detained. Mary worked as a teacher at a local public middle school, and Charles had recently retired as a social worker for the city.

Edwin reported that he had had a good childhood, and that he had always maintained a loving, but conflicted, relationship with his mother, stepfather, and brother. He respected his brother and tried to emulate him. He experienced mixed feelings about his biological father, Fred, with emotions ranging from deep adoration to an intense hatred. He blamed his mother for Fred's addiction, his abusive behavior, and the resulting disintegration of the family.

Edwin tried to reestablish a relationship with Fred, and was disappointed and mortified to witness Fred's attempt to buy crack and his arrest for stealing. Hurt, confused, and isolated, Edwin turned to his friends, drugs, and women for solace and support and to become his "own man." He began selling drugs as a means of earning money to maintain the lifestyle he wanted. Relatively successful, he started a savings account and gave his mother money to pay small bills and to buy groceries on occasion. As time progressed, Edwin's turning to other family members proved futile; they judged and labeled him as untrustworthy and a liar.

Edwin did not subscribe to any traditional Western religion, but affirmed that he was a very spiritual person. He credited his belief in and search for a spiritual connection with his God as the reason he has been able to endure his hardships and keep hope about having a productive future. Mary and Charles were reported to be Christians and Brian a member of the Nation of Islam. These spiritual/religious differences have traditionally been both a strength and a point of conflict in the family.

Case Conceptualization. Edwin had a romanticized sense of street life, coupled with normal adolescent challenges to society, tradition, and parental influence. While attempting to negotiate biological, environmental, and social changes, he became increasingly distant, rebellious, and disillusioned. He felt invisible within the family and in the larger society. He was not recognized for any positive behaviors, and his negative behaviors were either punished or overlooked by his parents. He was unable to articulate his need for support, love, and acceptance by his family, and his inability to successfully negotiate the different tasks of adolescence resulted in criminal activities, arrest, and entrance into the juvenile justice system.

He longed for a relationship with his biological father, and felt rejected and unable to connect with his stepfather. In attempting to find a role model, he perceived only two options: becoming a "crackhead" like his biological father or a "sellout" like his stepfather. The age-appropriate/expected parental conflicts between Charles and Edwin were coupled with the diverging levels and ideals of "Blackness" as related to family members' racial-identity development. In attempting to identify with his biological father, Edwin began to repeat the patterns of stealing, drug use and sales, and arrests, straining his relationship with his mother.

Not only was he able to assert himself and negotiate his identity on his own terms, he also began to accrue other secondary reinforcements (e.g., reputation, money, respect, and women). He further received mixed messages from his mother when she took the money offered to her. By overlooking the fact that Edwin neither received an allowance nor worked, she reinforced the notion that he needed material possessions instead of a strong character to gain respect and affection.

On the surface, it may seem as if Edwin consistently showed poor judgment, was impulsive, and based his decisions on emotions without any regard for consequences for himself and those around him. However, a closer analysis provided evidence to suggest that this was a manifestation of his internal struggles. In addition to the emotional and psychological conflicts, he had to negotiate being young, urban, Black, and male in a system that disproportionately arrests, detains, expels, and dehumanizes Black men. His struggle rested in developing coping skills, a more productive and healthy way of asserting himself, and refocusing his energies without losing all that he had gained from his street lifestyle.

Treatment Approach. Therapy involved addressing Edwin's issue as embedded in the contexts of familial and societal pressures. As parents, Mary and Charles were encouraged to examine Edwin's issue not as a series of isolated incidences but as existing in a larger sociocultural framework. As a young Black man, Edwin lived and functioned in a system that potentially targets young Black males. He was contending with a system based on prejudice, racism, discrimination, and inequality as evidenced by high disparities in educational achievement, economics, incarceration rates, homicides, and health issues (Noguera, 1996; Schoenbaum & Waidman, 1997). Edwin's sense of isolation and lack of skills in navigating the system was examined in the context of male role modeling and racial-identity development.

Psychoeducation was provided throughout therapy as the family began to understand, recognize, and identify the social, political, economic, legal, educational, emotional, and spiritual constraints that exist in a racist, White supremacist, patriarchical system and the effects it exerts on the daily functioning and identity of a Black male (Fanon, 1963; hooks, 1997; Utsey et al., 2001). This approach implied neither negating nor excusing his actions, but contextually providing a framework and viewing issues from a realistic, sociopolitical perspective.

Posttermination Synopsis. Although African American experiences might be similar to those of other adolescents, the uniqueness of African American adolescents lies in their attempts to remain psychologically healthy and establish strong social and cultural identities while existing in an environment that fosters a sense of invisibility. In addressing the issues of an African American adolescent, every aspect of his or her identity must be examined from a position of understanding and not judgment (Payne & Brown, in press). Thus, focus needs to be therapeutic and psychoeducational, with the intent to address issues that are not only unique to the individual but are shared by the collective (Utsey et al., 2001).

In working with Edwin, it was imperative to maintain a connection with all members in the system. Large generational gaps appeared between his parents and Edwin, making it difficult for the parties to communicate and to transmit their experiences. Edwin needed to develop a sense of connection with his family and also a sense of what it means to be Black. He seemed to be caught in a double bind in terms of his need for a male role model while maintaining a strong Black identity. It was important to assist him and his family to understand the struggles that Edwin was experiencing in this context and to help negotiate these different identities. Grasping the experiences of Edwin from his worldview and recognizing the realities in which he and his family existed proved crucial. An exploration from a multisystemic perspective enabled the therapist to gain an understanding of the family, and also provided an opportunity for Edwin and his family to explore and conduct a critical examination of all of the factors potentially impacting on their present functioning. This discussion included addressing issues of racism, discrimination, sexuality, school, drugs, educational difficulties, health disparities, financial resources, and independence.

Edwin was given the space and freedom to challenge, discuss, and clarify worldviews within and independent of the family. Discounting his truths would have been denying him and his family the coping skills, strategies, and family cohesion they needed for their development. In not addressing the issues (e.g., cyclical effects of institutional racism encroaching on the family structure and the adolescent), the therapist would have become a part of the system contributing to the negative forces impacting the family.

LATINO AMERICANS

Because of migratory patterns and high birthrates, it is expected that, by the year 2005, Hispanics will be the largest minority group in the United States, outnumbering the African American population in 18 of the 25 most populous states in the United States (West & Rodriguez, 2001). Hispanic Americans do not form a homogeneous group, but differ significantly in terms of country of origin, migration history, relationship to the dominant culture, socioeconomic status, values, family structure, language dialect, level of acculturation, and ethnic identity, as well as acceptance of the term used to identify themselves, such as Hispanic, Latino/Latina, Spanish American, and Chicano/a (McGoldrick, Giordano, & Pearce, 1996). Although we recognize the diversity within the group, we use the term Latino in this chapter.

Holding onto their cultural identities remains very important for Latinos because of a history of oppression, discrimination, and conquests within their own lands. Many Latinos coming to the United States for a better life are discouraged by the sociopolitical and socioeconomic oppression they experience. Families undergo significant distress because of a lack of secure foundation culturally, socially, and financially (Garcia-Preto, 1999). These issues can have a significant impact on Latino adolescents, who are negotiating their identities within a context that reinforces negative stereotypes, racism, classism, poverty, and limited educational and occupational opportunities (Garcia-Preto, 1996; Gonzalez, 1996; Sue & Sue, 1999). Although significant differences exist among Latino Americans, we identify some common contextual factors that need to be considered in working with Latino adolescents and illustrate these through the case example of Maribel, a Latina American.

Latino American Families
For Latino Americans, *familismo* signifies a cultural value whereby family relationships are held in highest regard, with one's individual identity considered to be a function of those family relationships (Ho, 1987). Family typically provides a strong sense of support and resources, with family unity and tradition perceived as important aspects of one's life. Loyalty to family and family relations takes precedence (Avila & Avila, 1995); this can be seen in children being kept home from school to take care of family obligations (Headden, 1997; Hildebrand, Phenice, Gray, & Hines, 1996).

Interpersonal relations are negotiated within the context of a large network of family (extended), friends, godparents (*compadres*), and informally adopted children (*hijos de crianza*) (Garcia-Preto, 1999), with family members having very distinct roles: grandparents—wisdom; godparents—resourcefulness; mother—abnegation; father—responsibility; and children—obedience (Ruiz, 1995). Thus, gender roles can become very restrictive in Latino families. For example, although Latino fathers are typically less involved than mothers with child rearing and daily chores (Roopnarine &

Ahmeduzzaman, 1993), they are seen as *the* authority figure in the household. Thus, in working with Latino adolescents, it is important to consider the structure of a family, the hierarchy within family roles, and the role of the adolescent within this context.

Immigration
Latinos have migrated to the United States for various reasons: to escape oppression, economic depression, and to obtain social and economic power in the "land of opportunity." They have come to the United States as refugees, illegal aliens, or political exiles (Gonzalez, 1996). The reasons for migration, the nature of immigration, the sociopolitical climates, the nature of oppression, civil wars, and political revolutions all become important factors in working with this population.

Unfortunately, relocation to the United States has come at a cost to Latino Americans, who find themselves victims of prejudice in a context of disrupted structures of emotional, financial, and social supports. Many families make substantial sacrifices by leaving their countries and giving up professional positions back home in search of better work opportunities and a better life for their children. However, their skin color, language, culture, the very essence of who they are become reasons for discrimination (Garcia-Preto, 1996). These discriminatory practices have been evident in frequent lack of employment and financial resources, language barriers, and confinement to substandard housing (Plante, Manuel, Menendez, & Marcotte, 1995). These depleted family, economic, and social supports and discriminatory practices have generated high levels of stress for Latino families, resulting in increased pressures placed on adolescents. Research has shown a significant relationship among family support, maintenance of cultural beliefs, and mental illness (e.g., Escobar, 1998). Latinos born in the United States tend not only to have fewer resources (family support) to cope with life stressors, but may also struggle to retain traditional values. These issues significantly impact the mental health of Latino adolescents and their families.

Perhaps the most important component associated with these struggles, within the context of immigration, revolves around acculturation. Olmedo and Padilla (1978) noted not only variations in acculturation levels but also a tendency to selectively acculturate among Latinos. Many Latinos have developed an ability to alternate between the two cultures, thus maintaining their national heritage while adopting some U.S. values (Falicov, 1998). Within such a context, typically less conflict arises for both the family and the adolescent. In contrast, Latino families forced to assimilate to the norms of the dominant culture may have acculturated to different degrees because of lack of opportunities for the parents (attributable to family and work obligations) and pressures experienced by adolescents to fit in with peers from the dominant culture. This can result in significant intergenerational conflicts; for example, differences in acculturation levels of parents and children have been found to contribute to reduced family cohesion (Gil & Vega, 1996).

Spirituality
Migrating to the United States can generate significant changes and disruptions for immigrant families, and these have impacted Latino family experiences as well. Latino families have experienced separation from family members, loss of emotional/family/social support, changes in socioeconomic status, and role reversals between parents and children as well as between spouses. This contributes to a sense of loss. In dealing with losses inherent in immigration experiences, religion provides a sense of comfort and continuity for Latinos.

Most Latinos are Roman Catholic. The Church and belief in its saints not only serve to reinforce values related to family, relationships, and sexuality, but also provide spaces for public support in the event of crisis or celebration. The belief in saints helps to reduce anxiety and to gain a sense of control; a person may go to church and light a candle to a particular saint in petitioning for assistance in solving a problem. A devout follower believes that the saint will intervene with God for this petition. Acknowledging this makes petitioning saints an integral part of the therapeutic process. Additionally, priests or spiritists can serve as important resources for families in distress (Falicov, 1996; Garcia-Preto, 1996).

Belief by Latinos that problems and events can be changed through the intervention of saints is typically perceived by the dominant culture as a lack of assertiveness. However, a strong reliance on religion may serve as a coping mechanism in dealing with life's events. By not validating and valuing the positive aspects of Latino culture and their religious beliefs and not recognizing the discrimination experienced by them, a therapist can, in fact, become a willing participant in the negative system that impacts on adolescents.

Identity Formation

Latino American adolescent identity develops in the context of a collective family orientation influenced by immigration history, socioeconomic-political forces within a dominant cultural context, and a family's own struggles with maintaining a strong cultural identity. Thus, identity-formation and ethnic identity go hand in hand. This entails finding a balance between sustaining one's cultural background and maintaining it in intergroup contacts. Within this context, adolescents must search for their own values and selfhood.

Several factors influence this negotiation. Experience in school plays a role. Latino Americans who are academically talented may feel pressure to hide their abilities to avoid being seen as too intelligent by their peers (Matute-Bianchi, 1986). Peer attitudes toward self and cultural background as well as awareness of inequalities within systems impact identity-formation.

Internalization of negative images of one's group as experienced in social prejudice and institutionalized racism may result in a diffusion or foreclosure on identity issues (Phinney, 1989; Streitmatter, 1988). Rejection of ethnic background and feeling torn between the dominant cultural values and family traditions also affect identity-development. Phinney (1989; Phinney & Alipuria, 1990) suggested that adolescents who achieve an ethnic identity specifically by incorporating values from their cultures of origin and the dominant culture experience a higher sense of self-esteem and mastery over the environment and benefit from more positive family and peer relationships. This not only reinforces a sense of continuity for the family, but also results in less conflict both for the family and the adolescent because of acceptance of the Latino culture and its inherent resources.

Developing a personal sexual value system also is tied to the task of forming one's identity. The ability of an adolescent to know what he or she believes will impact whether sex will be seen as a means of expressing intimacy and affection, as a casual act, or as an act that is reserved for a love relationship. Cultural and family values, religious values, and the values of an adolescent's closest friends offer important influences in developing this belief (Masters, Johnson, & Kolodny, 1995). Gender-role expectations of males and females within the Latino cultures are significantly linked to this sexual value system.

In Latino cultures, the traditional female role revolves around being La Santita, translated as "the little saint," often referring to the martyred position of women who aspire to perfection by completely submitting to every request or requirement of a male and serving their families and communities without complaint (Barkley & Mosher, 1995). This implies sublimation of sexual desires, so a woman engaging in sexual relations prior to marriage is considered to lose her self-respect and to bring dishonor to her family (Garcia-Preto, 1996). In light of this, unlike her male counterpart, the Latina adolescent celebrates a *quinceanera* (cotillion), at age 15, announcing her arrival into adulthood (Falicov, 1996). This "Sweet 15" ritual signifies an adolescent's introduction as a woman into the community; it symbolizes her readiness for being courted, albeit with a chaperone present. Thus, clear expectations in terms of sexuality and gender-role expectations exist for women. Young women socialized within the dominant culture and their own ethnic culture may question such role expectations, thus giving rise to intergenerational conflicts.

Latino adolescent males, on the other hand, face quite contradictory expectations and do not have an equivalent ritual to signal their entry into adulthood. Men in the Latino culture are expected to imbibe the notion of "machismo," which has two connotations. Machismo can mean a dedication and commitment to one's spouse and children, being a good provider (Falicov, 1998; Sue & Sue, 1999). Machismo can also denote male participation in the restrictive traditional gender roles in the Latino cultures. Machismo represents the social structure that, in the most exaggerated cases, elevates masculinity to levels of complete control and dominance, and to a privileged position (Barkley & Mosher, 1995). In the United States, machismo or being "macho" is primarily perceived as having a negative connotation, describing sexist behavior on the part of men (Garcia-Preto, 1996). Latino adolescents have the difficult task of struggling to develop their Latin identities in the midst of such prevailing negative stereotypes in society. Incongruity in the perception of Latino and American male behaviors, with Latino men's assertiveness seen as violent, can further foster dissonance within a Latino male's identity development (Gonzalez, 1996).

Case Presentation
Her parents brought Maribel, a 15-year-old, first-generation Peruvian female in her sophomore year at a Catholic high school, for counseling. Her parents reported that she was disrespectful and ungrateful toward them, and they threatened to send her back to Peru to an all-girl, residential Catholic school when she acted out. Maribel wanted to go away to college, but her father preferred that she learn how to be a housewife. Implicit within this was the norm that a daughter does not leave the parental home until marriage when a husband takes the daughter into his own home. Although Maribel's mother disagreed and advocated for her daughter, Maribel took her anger out on her mother. Maribel hated to cook, clean, and take care of her younger sister while both her parents worked the second shift. Another sore area for Maribel concerned the message she received about her sexuality. Although sexuality was never openly discussed, the message conveyed was that a woman who was not a virgin at marriage was unworthy of respect. Maribel hoped that her parents would give her more freedom after she turned 15, but this did not happen. She was not allowed to go out with the rest of her teenage friends. Although her parents would tell her to invite her friends to the house, she never did so because of her fear that her father would scare them with his look. In addition, she admitted feeling embarrassed about her friends finding out that she lived above a store. During heated arguments, her father would tell her about the sacrifices he made in Peru to give his daughters better opportunities in the United States. He felt his daughter disrespected and looked down on them because of the parents' inability to speak English and for working in a factory.

Family History. Maribel's parents, married for 16 years, had three daughters. Maribel was the older of the twins, and her youngest sister was 7 years old. Both parents were primarily Spanish-speaking; they attempted to take English as a Second Language at the local community college, but discontinued to focus on their daughters. At the time they entered counseling, both were working in a factory. Back in Peru, Maribel's father had earned an associate's degree in accounting, and her mother had studied culinary arts.

The family migrated twice to the United States. The first time was when the twins were 3 years old. The family decided to migrate as a result of their extended family moving to the United States. When Maribel was 10 years old, the family was deported; they had been in the country with a tourist visa, which eventually expired, and the father was caught working without legal documents. They moved back to Peru for a little over a year. Because of their abrupt departure, their living accommodations in Peru were meager. The family of four was forced to live in a two-room terrace in the home of their *padrinos*. In Peru, Maribel remembered her struggle with the language when attending school for one year. Upon receiving their visa, the family returned to the United States. The second trip took place when the twins were 12 years old. The twins were placed in a public school, where both were initially in the fourth grade; later, Maribel's twin was skipped to the sixth grade. Maribel recalled this experience with much resentment and promised to get into a field where she could make a lot of money and not have to suffer because of financial loss.

Case Conceptualization. It is apparent that Maribel and her parents had difficulty with the cultural differences they were each experiencing. Despite an elaborate "Sweet 15" birthday party that should have marked Maribel's movement toward adulthood, the twins were not allowed to have boyfriends until the age of 18. Had the family been living in Peru, this contingency may not have been placed on them because their parents would have been familiar with the families of their daughters' peers. The unfamiliarity with or disapproval of United States values led the parents to opt for increasing the age limit. Thus, the parent-child relationship was impaired at a critical time, when the parental role was to prepare the adolescent to enter the adult world. These difficulties resulted in Maribel's anger and resentment toward her parents. The parents' experiences of being deported and their experiences of discrimination in different contexts seemed to exacerbate the issues. The enduring losses and disruptions caused by the deportation as well as migration introduced further significant issues.

Treatment Intervention. The family's concerns were examined from a multicultural-integrative perspective. The marginalized experiences of Maribel's parents within the dominant cultural context implicated critical dynamics. Contextualizing the father's expectations in the realm of immigration, acculturation, and discrimination were crucial for Maribel to understand her parents' struggles. Specifically, his dark complexion, his inability to speak English well, and the barriers these erected in earning more money, along with feeling disrespected by his Caucasian supervisors at work, all contributed to his unwillingness to change the traditions in his home. This issue was further complicated by Maribel's behaviors toward her parents. The parents needed to find ways to feel more empowered not only in their workplaces and with outside agencies, but also in their relationships with their daughters. Because of relational difficulties, therapeutic focus turned toward increasing family cohesion by helping them understand the conflicts and disruptions within the context of acculturation. Both Maribel and her parents would benefit from understanding that they were dealing with negotiating two different cultures and experiencing the same resulting confusions and fears. Demonstrating that her parents (whom she perceived as her adversaries) felt as vulnerable as she did helped the family comprehend what they shared in common. This allowed Maribel to become more empathic toward her parents' fears and experiences of oppression. Reframing the father's behavior of "wanting to be controlling" to "being a protective father" enabled the family to engage in an open discussion about the issue.

One pivotal moment in therapy occurred when Maribel admitted that it was difficult to communicate with her parents about anything because her Spanish was not good. She felt like a fool talking to them and having them correct her constantly. Her parents, on the other hand, could not understand her when she spoke "Spanglish." This was explored in terms of the family's acculturation levels. Maribel felt she was a Peruvian living in a United States world. Becoming "American" meant giving up aspects of her culture (e.g., language) to be accepted by peers. This also connoted negotiating aspects of her identity to survive in what was originally an unfamiliar environment.

Another focus involved reframing Maribel's "disrespectful" behavior. Role playing to practice respectful questioning of her parents proved useful. Her behavior was reframed as a positive activity in her attempt to become an adult. Through conversations with her parents, Maribel could truly fathom the reasons behind their strictness. The family discussed and engaged in gradual reorganization and changing of the rules and limits, as the parents were reassured of the importance of providing the security of parental guidelines.

Posttermination Reflections. Specifically, language, values relating to sexuality, respect, and how adolescence is conceptualized in the Latino culture are what distinguish these adolescents from those in mainstream U.S. culture. When delineating potential issues in the negotiation of tasks for Latino American adolescents, contextualizing adolescent experience in the context of multilevel socializations is critical. Thus, exploring this family's struggles in the context of their migration history, the negotiation of ethnic identity (use of language), potential discrimination, and resulting socioeconomic status changes proved relevant. It was imperative to provide this family with culturally sensitive services (Rosado & Elias, 1993) by sorting through gender issues, beliefs, and values within the culture. The expectation that a Latina be submissive and accept her role graciously underpinned the very notion that contributed to Maribel's acting out aggressively against her mother. Her lashing out may have been a function of the mother's "perceived inability" to stand up to her husband and to advocate strongly for Maribel. A therapist must be sensitive to family structure, but it is also essential to empower the mother to enable the daughter to see that the mother has some authority and to move away from the myth of the submissive Latina. While acculturation helped Maribel survive outside pressures, it hindered her relationship with her parents. Moreover, although her parents were pleased to know about her biculturality (Maribel living a United States life with Latino morals), the family's problems were reflected in the discrepancy between the acculturation levels of the family members. The clash between the majority-culture's emphasis on freedom and self-determination and the father's need to protect his daughter from a hostile environment were at play. The father's refusal to allow his daughter to go away to college stemmed from his desire to protect her, but also from the belief and norm that, culturally, a young woman does not move away from the family and live on her own until she is married. Addressing both parents' contributions, while keeping in mind the father's male privilege, resulted in empowering the mother within her family.

In providing culturally sensitive treatment, cultural values such as *personalismo* were also used to engage the family. According to Bean, Perry, and Bedell (2001) *personalismo* connotes a relational, personal approach that a therapist assumes to connect and develop trust with Latino families. With this family, the therapist empathized with their experiences by self-disclosing her own family's migration story, thus allowing a foundation of trust to develop between therapist and client by "personally relating" to the family. *Familismo,* a cultural value emphasizing the importance of family (Marin, 1991), was incorporated as a way to pay tribute to the members of the extended family who provide support. For example, much time was spent in the discussion of the family's reasons for migration and their seeking help from the extended family to assist with potential loss of resources as a function of immigration. Keeping these cultural values in mind, the therapist was able to join with the family while acknowledging the importance of examining contextual factors that impacted them.

RESEARCH SUPPORT FOR THE INTEGRATIVE MODEL

Effective psychological assessment involves integrating information gathered through different sources, means, and settings. The integrative perspective discussed in this chapter provides a valuable tool for assessing the significance of multiple interlocking cultures and systemic perspectives for individuals at varying developmental levels. Given that we are examining adolescents of color in the United States, the model is particularly beneficial because it not only examines developmental issues but also takes into consideration a multicontextual perspective that parallels the multiple contexts and systems within which these youth live.

A good deal of research has emerged in support of examining experiences with a wider lens by specifically considering the ecological (sociocultural) context within which a person exists (Bronfenbrenner, 1989). Many assessment scholars have advocated the use of an ecological model to guide assessments for families and youth (Brim, 1975, Bronfenbrenner, 1977, 1989; Knoff, 1986; Nutall, Romero, & Kalesnik 1992; Paget & Nagel, 1986). Specifically, researchers have examined family process and the interaction of genetics and environment; the interaction of chronic illness/depression and social systems (Brown, Brody, & Stoneman, 2000; Kazak, 1989); the interaction of a parent's place/world of work and the family (Paulson, 1996); linkages and transitions between family and settings influencing family development, such as schools, hospitals, day care, peer groups, social/cultural networks, neighborhoods, communities (Morrison, 1997; Mulroy, 1997; Ogbu, 1988; Sucoff, 1998); and public policies that also affect families (Bogenschneider, 1996).

Bogenschneider (1996, 1997) used the ecological perspective in numerous studies examining youth and parental involvement in school, community-based prevention programs, and public policy. These studies reflect the value of the ecological perspective for explaining the multiple systems and processes that guide families, the complex relationship and interactions among individuals, families, groups and the societal systems that influence families, and also how it may be used for intervention, treatment, and community planning.

Others have also found the ecological perspective to be useful in researching the complex interactions among families, cultures, and other groups. Henggeler et al. (1986) supported the use of a family-ecological treatment model for delinquent adolescents and their families. They found that adolescents who received treatment guided by a multisystemic view (family-ecological treatment) encompassing Bronfenbrenner's system levels evidenced significant decreases in conduct problems, anxious withdrawal behaviors, immaturity, and association with delinquent peers. Ogbu's (1985) emphasis on a cultural ecological perspective for fostering competence with inner-city Blacks revealed that by viewing child-rearing practices of Black families through a cultural-ecological model, parenting practices, once viewed as illogical and incompetent, appeared as highly sensible and competent. Spencer (1995) broadened the model to view identity and developmental processes of African American youth. Using Bronfenbrenner's model as a basis, Spencer asserted that individuals must be studied within the contexts in which they develop because dialectical interaction transpires between individuals and environments, such that individuals can exercise power and involvement in their own development. Drawing on Bronfenbrenner's model, Spencer discussed further the ways in which different types of African American youth can find meaning in their environments and interactions.

The boundaries of the ecological model have also influenced cross-cultural work in the field of psychology. Eicher and Erekosima (1997) applied the model to the study of the Nigerian Kalabari society and its material use of madras (cloth). Through the use of the ecological model, their study showed the cultural significance the madras cloth held in Kalabari society. The cloth linked the present microsystems of the individual to settings of earlier and future generations in which an individual had no direct participation. Through handing down the madras cloth from one generation to another, the material cultural items were passed on from one generation to the next, thus providing a link of contemporary microsystems to those of the past, and extending mesosystem and exosystem linkages forward and backward through time among familial generations.

A particular strength of the ecological model arises from emphasis on developmental issues. The life-span perspective highlights the integration of biological, psychological, sociocultural, and historical factors important in understanding the experiences of adolescents and families of color. Specifically, Asian, African, and Latino American adolescents develop within contexts of migration, racism, employment opportunities, and intergenerational conflicts. The kinds of experiences that families of color have in these various contexts influence the socialization of the adolescent of color and his or her identity development. In working with adolescents of color, it becomes relevant to contextualize their issues within the constraints of these systems.

Furthermore, within these various interconnecting systems fit a therapist and his or her role in the therapeutic processes. The literature suggests that the therapeutic relationship and the therapeutic environment play an important role in the effectiveness of treatment (e.g., Teyber, 2000). Counseling does not occur in a vacuum. Therapists' as well as clients' worldviews are shaped by their personal histories and experiences in their own families and larger society and need to be acknowledged in the therapeutic process.

Over the years, the second-order cybernetic approach and its importance in setting a foundation for modern-day family therapy has generated interest (Fisch, Weakland, & Segal, 1982; Hoffman, 1990, 1993). Given the great diversity in today's client populations and the expanding field of counseling psychology, more is being written about the importance of the therapist being involved as a part of the process as opposed to being an observer and director of the process (Amatea & Sherrard, 1994; Becvar & Becvar, 1994; Sue, Arredondo, & McDavis, 1992). Many professionals in the field suggest that self-awareness and a personal involvement on the part of the therapist offer keys in maintaining client rapport and retention, understanding cultural diversity, and ensuring the ultimate success of therapy (Boyd-Franklin, 1989; Cross, Bazron, Dennis, & Isaacs, 1989; Helms, 1993; Sue et al., 1992; Sue & Sue, 1999).

SUMMARY

Adolescence represents a critical time for developing a sense of self-sufficiency and ego strength in relation to one's personal, social, sexual, and vocational identities. Although many of the emotional experiences (e.g., pain, hurt, love, belonging, independence) of adolescents are similar across culture, gender, race, and ethnicity, adolescents of color develop and function among myriad interconnecting cultural contexts that can complicate their smooth transitions into adulthood. The intent of this chapter was to provide a multicultural framework for working with Asian, African, and Latino American adolescents. Specifically, an integrative model of assessment and intervention was proposed to address the multiple levels within which these adolescents grow, thus allowing for treatment in a culturally sensitive environment.

REFERENCES

Ahmed, K. (1999). Adolescent development for South Asian American girls. In S. R. Gupta (Ed.), *Emerging voices: South Asian American women define self, family, and community* (pp. 37–49). Walnut Creek, CA: AltaMira Press.

Almeida, R. (1996). Hindu, Christian, and Muslim families. In M. McGoldrick, J. Giordano, & J. K. Pearce (Eds.), *Ethnicity and family therapy* (pp. 395–423). New York: Guilford Press.

Amatea, E. S., & Sherrard, P. A. D. (1994). The ecosystemic view: A choice of lenses. *Journal of Mental Health Counseling, 16,* 6–21.

Avila, D. L., & Avila, A. L. (1995). Mexican Americans. In N. A. Vacc, S. B. DeVaney, & J. Wittmer (Eds.), *Experiencing and counseling multicultural and diverse populations* (3rd ed., pp. 119–146). Bristol, PA: Accelerated Development.

Barkley, B. H., & Mosher, E. S. (1995). Sexuality and Hispanic culture: Counseling with children and their parents. *Journal of Sex Education and Therapy, 21,* 255–267.

Bean, R. A., Perry, B. J., & Bedell, T. M. (2001). Developing culturally competent marriage and family therapists: Guidelines for working with Hispanic families. *Journal of Marital and Family Therapy, 27,* 43–54.

Becvar, R. J., & Becvar, D. S. (1994). The ecosystemic story: A story about stories. *Journal of Mental Health Counseling, 16,* 22–32.

Berry, J. W. (1993). Ethnic identity in plural societies. In M. E. Bernal & G. P. Knight (Eds.), *Ethnic identity: Formation and transmission among Hispanics and other minorities* (pp. 271–296). Albany: State University of New York Press.

Billingsley, A. (1968). *Black families in White America.* Englewood Cliffs, NJ: Prentice Hall.

Bogenschneider, K. (1996). An ecological risk/protective theory for building prevention programs, policies, and community capacity to support youth. *Family Relations, 45,* 127–139.

Bogenschneider, K. (1997). Parental involvement in adolescent schooling: A proximal process with transcontextual validity. *Journal of Marriage and the Family, 59,* 178–194.

Booker, C. (1998). *The state of the Black male in America* [Online]. Available from www.tomco.net/~afrimale/stbm98.htm

Boyd-Franklin, N. (1989). *Black families in therapy: A multisystems approach.* New York: Guilford Press.

Brim, O. G. (1975). Macrostructural influences on child development and the need for childhood social indicators. *American Journal of Orthopsychiatry, 45,* 517–524.

Bronfenbrenner, U. (1977). Towards an experimental ecology of human development. *American Psychologist, 32,* 513–531.

Bronfenbrenner, U. (1989). Ecological systems theory. *Annals of Child Development, 6,* 187–249.

Brown, A. C., Brody, G. H., & Stoneman, Z. (2000). Rural Black women and depression: A contextual analysis. *Journal of Marriage and the Family, 62,* 187–198.

Carter, R. T. (1991). Racial identity attitudes and psychological functioning. *Journal of Multicultural Counseling and Development, 19,* 105–114.

Cross, T. L., Bazron, B. J., Dennis, K. W., & Isaacs, M. R. (1989). *Towards a culturally competent system of care* (Vol. 1). Washington, DC: Child and Adolescent Service System Program Technical Assistance Center.

Daniels, M. H., & White, L. J. (1994). Human systems as problem-determined linguistic systems: Relevance for training. *Journal of Mental Health Counseling, 16,* 104–118.

Dasgupta, S. D., & Dasgupta, S. (1996). Private face, private space: Asian Indian women and sexuality. In N. B. Maglin & D. Perry (Eds.), *Bad girls, good girls: Women, sex, and power in the nineties* (pp. 226–243). New Brunswick, NJ: Rutgers University Press.

Dhruvarajan, V. (1993). Ethnic cultural retention and transmission among first generation Hindu Asian Indians in a Canadian prairie city. *Journal of Comparative Family Studies, 24,* 63–79.

Dona, G., & Berry, J. W. (1994). Acculturation attitudes and acculturative stress of Central American refugees. *International Journal of Psychology, 29,* 57–70.

Durvasula, R. S., & Mylvaganam, G. A. (1994). Mental health issues of Asian Indians: Relevant issues and community implications. *Journal of Comparative Psychology, 22,* 97–108.

Dyson, M. E. (1997). *Race rules.* New York: Vintage Books.

Eaton, M. J., & Dembo, M. H. (1997). Differences in the motivational beliefs of Asian Americans. *Journal of Educational Psychology, 89,* 433–440.

Eicher, J. B., & Erekosima, T. V. (1997). Bronfenbrenner's ecological systems model and the use of imported madras cloth among the Kalabari. *Family and Consumer Sciences Research Journal, 25,* 412–431.

Elder, G. H. (1985). Household, kinship, and the life course: Perspectives on Black families and children. In M. B. Spencer, G. K. Brookins, & W. R. Allen (Eds.), *Beginnings: The social and affective development of Black children* (pp. 29–43). Hillsdale, NJ: Erlbaum.

Escobar, J. I. (1998). Immigration and mental health: Why are immigrants better off? *General Psychiatry, 55,* 781–782.

Falicov, C. J. (1996). Mexican families. In M. McGoldrick, J. Giordano, & J. K. Pearce (Eds.), *Ethnicity and family therapy* (pp. 169–182). New York: Guilford Press.

Falicov, C. J. (1998). *Latino families in therapy: A guide to multicultural practice.* New York: Guilford Press.

Fanon, F. (1963). *The wretched of the earth.* New York: Grove Press.

Fisch, R., Weakland, J. H., & Segal, L. (1982). *The tactics of change: Doing therapy briefly.* San Francisco: Jossey-Bass.

Franklin, A. J. (1999). Invisibility syndrome and racial identity development in psychotherapy and counseling African-American men. *Counseling Psychologist, 27,* 761–793.

Garcia-Preto, N. (1996). Latino families: An overview. In M. McGoldrick, J. Giordano, & J. K. Pearce (Eds.), *Ethnicity and family therapy* (pp. 141–154). New York: Guilford Press.

Garcia-Preto, N. (1999). Transformation of the family system in adolescence. In B. Carter & M. McGoldrick (Eds.), *The extended family life cycle: Individual, family and social perspectives* (3rd ed., pp. 274–286). Boston: Allyn & Bacon.

Gil, A. G., & Vega, W. A. (1996). Two different worlds: Acculturation stress and adaptation among Cuban and Nicaraguan families. *Journal of Social and Personal Relationships, 13,* 435–456.

Gonzalez, R. (1996). *Muy macho: Latino men confront their manhood.* New York: Doubleday.

Headden, S. (1997). The Hispanics dropout mystery. *U.S. News & World Report, 123,* 64–65.

Hechinger, F. (1992). *Fateful choices: Healthy youth for the 21st century.* New York: Hill and Wang.

Helms, J. E. (1990). *Black and White racial identity: Theory, research and practice.* New York: Greenwood Press.

Helms, J. E. (1993). *Black and White racial identity: Theory, research, and practice.* Westport, CT: Praeger.

Helms, J. E. (1995). An update of Helms's White and people of color racial identity model. In J. G. Ponterotto, J. M. Casas, L. A. Suzuki, & C. M. Alexander (Eds.), *Handbook of multicultural counseling* (pp. 181–198). Thousand Oaks, CA: Sage.

Helms, J. E., & Cook, D. A. (1999). *Using race and culture in counseling and psychotherapy: Theory and practice.* Boston: Allyn & Bacon.

Henggeler, S. W., Rodick, J. D., Borduin, C. M., Hanson, C. L., Watson, S. M., & Urey, J. R. (1986). Multisystemic treatment of juvenile offenders: Effects on adolescent behavior and family interaction. *Developmental Psychology, 22,* 132–141.

Hildebrand, V., Phenice, L. A., Gray, M. M., & Hines, R. P. (1996). *Knowing and serving diverse families.* Englewood Cliffs, NJ: Prentice-Hall.

Hines, P. M., Garcia-Preto, N., McGoldrick, M., Almedia, R., & Weltman, S. (1992). Intergenerational relationships across cultures. *Families in Society, 73,* 323–338.

Ho, M. K. (1987). *Family therapy with ethnic minorities.* Newbury Park, CA: Sage.

Hoffman, L. (1990). Constructing realities: An art of lenses. *Family Process, 29,* 1–12.

Hoffman, L. (1993). *Exchanging voices: A collaborative approach to family therapy.* London: Karnac Books.

hooks, b. (1997). *Cultural criticism and transformation* [video]. Northhampton, MA: Media Education Foundation.

Huang, L. N. (1994). An integrative approach to clinical assessment and intervention with Asian-American adolescents. *Journal of Clinical Child Psychology, 23*, 21–31.

Huang, L. N., & Ying, Y. (1989). Chinese American children and adolescents. In J. Gibbs & L. N. Huang (Eds.), *Children of color: Psychological interventions with minority youth* (pp. 30–66). San Francisco: Jossey-Bass.

Inman, A. G., Constantine, M. G., & Ladany, N. (1999). Cultural value conflict: An examination of Asian Indian women's bicultural experience. In D. S. Sandhu (Ed.), *Asian and Pacific Islander Americans: Issues and concerns for counseling and psychotherapy* (pp. 31–41). Commack, NY: Nova Science.

Inman, A. G., Ladany, N., Constantine, M. G., & Morano, C. K. (2001). Development and preliminary validation of the cultural values conflict scale for South Asian women. *Journal of Counseling Psychology, 48*, 17–27.

Jayakar, K. (1994). Women of the Indian subcontinent. In L. Comas-Diaz & B. Greene (Eds.), *Women of color: Integrating ethnic and gender identities in psychotherapy* (pp. 161–181). New York: Guilford Press.

Jones, J. (1997). *Prejudice and racism.* New York: McGraw-Hill.

Kambon, K. K. K. (1998). *African/Black psychology in the American context: An African-centered approach.* Tallahassee, FL: Nubian Nation.

Kazak, A. E. (1989). Families of chronically ill children: A systems and social-ecological model of adaptation and challenge. *Journal of Consulting and Clinical Psychology, 57*, 25–31.

Keeney, B. P. (1983). *Aesthetics of change.* New York: Guilford Press.

Knoff, H. M. (Ed.). (1986). *The assessment of child and adolescent personality.* New York: Guilford Press.

LaFromboise, T., Coleman, H. K., & Gerton, J. (1993). Psychological impact of biculturalism: Evidence and theory. *Psychological Bulletin, 114*, 395–412.

Lefrancois, G. R. (1996). *The lifespan* (5th ed.). Belmont, CA: Wadsworth.

Madanes, C. (1981). *Strategic family therapy.* San Francisco: Jossey-Bass.

Madhubuti, H. R. (1991). *Black men: Obsolete, single, dangerous?* Chicago: Third World Press.

Marcia, J. E. (1980). Identity in adolescence. In J. Adelson (Ed.), *Handbook of adolescent psychology* (pp. 159–187). New York: Wiley.

Marin, G. (1991). Defining culturally appropriate community interventions: Hispanics as a case study. *Journal of Community Psychology, 21*, 149–161.

Marin, G. (1992). Issues in the measurement of acculturation among Hispanics. In K. F. Geisinger (Ed.), *Psychological testing of Hispanics* (pp. 235–251). Washington, DC: American Psychological Association.

Masters, W. H., Johnson, V. E., & Kolodny, R. C. (1995). *Human sexuality* (5th ed.). New York: HarperCollins.

Matute-Bianchi, M. E. (1986). Ethnic identities and patterns of school success and failure among Mexican-descent and Japanese-American students in a California high school: An ethnographic analysis. *American Journal of Education, 91*, 233–255.

McGoldrick, M., Giordano, J., & Pearce, J. K. (1996). *Ethnicity and family therapy* (2nd ed.). New York: Guilford Press.

Mehta, P. (1998). The emergence, conflicts and integration of the bi-cultural self: Psychoanalysis of an adolescent daughter of South Asian immigrant parents. In S. Akhtar & S. Kramer (Eds.), *The colors of childhood: Separation-individuation across cultural, racial and ethnic differences* (pp. 129–168). Northvale, NJ: Aronson.

Meyers, L. J. (1993). *Understanding an African world view: Introduction to an optimal theory* (2nd ed.). Dubuque, IA: Kendall/Hunt.

Morrison, G. M. (1997). Sources of support for school-related issues: Choices of Hispanic adolescents varying in migrant status. *Journal of Youth and Adolescence, 26*, 233–253.

Mulroy, E. A. (1997). Building a neighborhood network: Interorganizational collaboration to prevent child abuse and neglect. *Social Work, 42*, 255–265.

Naidoo, J. C. (1985). Contemporary South Asian women in the Canadian mosaic. *International Journal of Women's Studies, 8*, 338–350.

National Commission on Children. (1991). *Beyond rhetoric: A new American agenda for children and families. A summary.* Washington, DC: U.S. Government Printing Office.

Noguera, P. A. (1996, Spring). Responding to the crisis confronting California's Black male youth: Providing support without furthering marginalization. *Journal of Negro Education* (65), 219–236.

Nutall, E. V., Romero, I., & Kalesnik, J. (1992). *Assessing and screening preschoolers: Psychological and educational dimensions.* Boston: Allyn & Bacon.

Ogbu, J. U. (1985). A cultural ecology of competence among inner-city Blacks. In M. B. Spencer, G. K. Brookins, & W. R. Allen (Eds.), *Beginnings: The social and affective development of Black children* (pp. 45–66). Hillsdale, NJ: Erlbaum.

Ogbu, J. U. (1988). Black education: A cultural-ecological perspective. In H. P. McAdoo (Ed.), *Black family* (pp. 169–184). Newbury Park, CA: Sage.

Olmedo, E. L., & Padilla, A. M. (1978). Empirical and construct validation of a measure of acculturation for Mexican Americans. *Journal of Social Psychology, 105,* 179–187.

Paget, K., & Nagel, R. (1986). A conceptual model of preschool assessment. *School Psychology Review, 15,* 154–165.

Parham, T. A. (1999). Invisibility syndrome in African descent people: Understanding the cultural manifestations of the struggle for self-affirmation. *Counseling Psychologist, 27,* 794–801.

Paulson, S. E. (1996). Maternal employment and adolescent achievement revisited: An ecological perspective. *Family Relations, 45,* 201–209.

Payne, Y., & Brown, A. L. (in press). Sites of resiliency: A reconceptualization of resiliency for young Black men living in the ghetto. In M. Pierre (Ed.), *New psychology for African American men.* Westport, CT: Greenwood Press.

Phinney, J. S. (1989). Stages of ethnic identity development in minority group adolescents. *Journal of Early Adolescence, 9,* 34–49.

Phinney, J. S. (1990). Ethnic identity in adolescents and adults: Review of research. *Psychological Bulletin, 108,* 499–514.

Phinney, J. S., & Alipuria, L. (1990). Ethnic identity in college students from four ethnic groups. *Journal of Adolescence, 13,* 171–183.

Phinney, J. S., & Chavira, V. (1992). Ethnic identity and self-esteem: An exploratory longitudinal study. *Journal of Adolescent Research, 7,* 156–176.

Plante, T. G., Manuel, G. M., Menendez, A. V., & Marcotte, D. (1995). Coping with stress among Salvadorian immigrants. *Hispanic Journal of Behavioral Sciences, 17,* 471–479.

Prathikanti, S. (1997). East Indian American families. In E. Lee (Ed.), *Working with Asian Americans: A guide for clinicians* (pp. 79–100). New York: Guilford Press.

Roopnarine, J. L., & Ahmeduzzaman, M. (1993). Puerto Rican fathers' involvement with their preschool-age children. *Hispanic Journal of Behavioral Sciences, 15,* 96–107.

Rosado, J. W., & Elias, M. (1993). Ecological psychocultural mediators in the delivery of services for urban, culturally diverse Hispanic clients. *Professional Psychology: Research and Practice, 24,* 450–459.

Ruiz, P. (1995). Assessing, diagnosing and treating culturally diverse individuals: A Hispanic perspective. *Psychiatric Quarterly, 66,* 329–341.

Sandhu, D. S. (1997). Psychocultural profiles of Asian and Pacific Islander Americans: Implications for counseling and psychotherapy. *Journal of Multicultural Counseling and Development, 25,* 7–22.

Schoenbaum, M., & Waidman, T. (1997, May). Race, socioeconomic status, and health: Accounting for race differences in health. *Journals of Gerontology: Series B, Psychological Sciences and Social Sciences, 52,* 61–73.

Sodowsky, G. R., & Carey, J. C. (1987). Asian Indian immigrants in America: Factors related to adjustment. *Journal of Multicultural Counseling and Development, 15,* 129–141.

Sodowsky, G. R., & Carey, J. C. (1988). Relationship between acculturation-related demographics and cultural attitudes of an Asian Indian immigrant group. *Journal of Multicultural Counseling and Development, 16,* 117–136.

Sodowsky, G. R., & Lai, E. W. M. (1997). Asian immigrant variables and structural models of cross-cultural distress. In A. Booth, A. C. Crouter, & N. Landale (Eds.), *Immigration and the family: Research and policy on U.S. immigrants* (pp. 211-234). Mahwah, NJ: Erlbaum.

Spencer, M. B. (1995). Old issues and new theorizing about African American youth: A phenomenological variant of ecological systems theory. In R. T. Taylor (Ed.), *African American youth: Their social and economic status in the United States* (pp. 37–69). Westport, CT: Praeger.

Streitmatter, J. L. (1988). Ethnicity as a mediating variable of early adolescent identity development. *Journal of Adolescence, 11,* 335–346.

Sucoff, C. A. (1998). Neighborhood context and the risk of childbearing among metropolitan-area Black adolescents. *American Sociological Review, 63,* 571–586.

Sue, D., & Sue, S. (1987). Cultural factors in the clinical assessment of Asian Americans. *Journal of Consulting and Clinical Psychology, 55,* 479–487.

Sue, D. W., Arredondo, P., & McDavis, R. J. (1992). Multicultural counseling competencies and standards: A call to the profession. *Journal of Counseling and Development, 70,* 477–486.

Sue, D. W., & Sue, D. (1999). *Counseling the culturally different: Theory and practice* (3rd ed.). New York: Wiley.

Teyber, E. (2000). *Interpersonal process in psychotherapy: A relational approach* (4th ed.). Belmont, CA: Wadsworth.

Tinney, J. S. (1981). The religious experience of Black men. In L. E. Gary (Ed.), *Black men* (pp. 269–276). Beverly Hills, CA: Sage.

Todisco, M., & Salomone, P. R. (1991). Facilitating effective cross-cultural relationships: The White counselor and Black client. *Journal of Multicultural Counseling and Development, 19,* 146–157.

Utsey, S. O., Bolden, M. A., & Brown, A. L. (2001). Visions of revolution from the spirit of Frantz Fanon: A psychology of liberation for counseling African Americans confronting societal racism and oppression. In J. G. Ponterotto, J. M. Casas, L. A. Suzuki, & C. M. Alexander (2001). *Handbook of multicultural counseling* (2nd ed., pp. 311–336). Thousand Oaks, CA: Sage.

West, Y. N., & Rodriguez, L. M. (2001, May 31). As Latinos increase in Philadelphia, strategies needed to aid them. *Philadelphia Inquirer,* p. A21.

Woodard, C. V. (1957). *The strange career of Jim Crow.* New York: Oxford Book Press.

Wyatt, G. E. (1999). Beyond invisibility of African American males: The effects on women and families. *Counseling Psychologists, 27,* 802–809.

Zill, N., & Rogers, C. (1988). Recent trends in the well-being of children in the United States and their implications for public policy. In A. Cherlin (Ed.), *The changing American family and public policy* (pp. 31–115). Washington, DC: Urban Institute Press.

CHAPTER 8

Adlerian Therapy: A Century of Tradition and Research

ROBERT SHERMAN AND ANSELM NWAORGU

Adlerian psychology, conceived over 100 years ago in Vienna, has continued to grow and evolve over the decades. It emerged from a social philosophy emphasizing human equality and democratic process, the necessity for strong community feeling toward fellow humans, and concern for a shared universe. Adlerians extend their interests beyond psychotherapy toward the improvement and advancement of all peoples through humanistic education, political action, and positive social and community connection. They believe that their philosophy and theory can assist in ameliorating problems such as stress, alienation, conflict, and mental and social dysfunction in individuals, couples, families, and communities.

The vocabulary, ideas, and techniques of Adlerian psychology were well-established internationally by the time of Adler's death in 1937. Some of his ideas and principles that have been absorbed into the general culture and language include inferiority and superiority complexes, compensation, the ideal self, lifestyle, and safe-guarding/defense mechanisms. Adlerian psychology embodies an inclusive, integrative theory that overlaps considerably with many other popular theories in concepts and practices (Mosak & Maniacci, 1999; Sherman & Dinkmeyer, 1987). This results from the breadth and depth of Adler's vision and the continued collaboration of his followers with colleagues of other persuasions.

Adlerians take the concept of holism seriously and acknowledge the interfaces with other theoretical perspectives. Adlerian psychology is often identified as a psychoanalytic theory because Adler was a founding member and president of the Psychoanalytic Society in Vienna until 1911. He split with Freud over fundamental differences in approach (Ellenberger, 1970). Adler never accepted drive theory, the central roles of sexuality and the unconscious, or the focus on the past as the controlling influence on behavior (Mosak & Maniacci, 1999). But, he did agree that much occurred in the inner workings of the mind, especially the so-called ego functions and reality testing.

Focus on thoughts, beliefs, goals, myths, stories, narratives, and the subjective meanings of experiences and behaviors pervades both

Adlerian psychology and cognitive/narrative/constructivist theories. Likewise, both groups agree that persons acquire cognitions primarily through some form of social interaction and that one's subjective interpretations create one's knowledge of reality (Forgus & Shulman, 1979; Jones, 1995). Shulman and Watts (1997), among other authors, discussed the similarities and differences between Adlerian psychology and cognitive, narrative, and constructivist therapies in a special issue of the *Journal of Cognitive Therapy* devoted to this topic. Similarly, commentators, including Disque and Bitter (1998), Stone (1998), and Walton (1998), considered the relationship between Adlerian psychology and narrative therapy in a special issue of the *Journal of Individual Psychology*. Behaviorists observe Adlerian psychologists' concerns with behavioral strategies, consequences, knowledge, and skills, and agree that behavior is both learned and chosen for its usefulness. Systems theorists could identify with the importance Adlerian psychologists place on holism, purpose, place, role, social embeddedness, hierarchy, and boundary—the elements of social organization. Articles by Sherman and Dinkmeyer (1987) and 10 others appeared in a special issue of the *Journal of Individual Psychology* on Adlerian psychology and other family therapy theories. In this publication, Dammann and Jurkovic (1986) addressed strategic therapy; Kaye, Dichter, and Keith (1986) symbolic-experiential therapy; and Lawe and Smith (1986) Gestalt therapy.

Adlerian psychology does not merely meld with other approaches; it possesses a clear and distinct core theoretical structure, which differentiates it from each of the other viewpoints. Like Jung, Adler had developed a unique perspective before collaborating with Freud, and their refusal to become disciples of Freud precipitated the rupturing of the relationships (Ellenberger, 1970). For example, Adlerian psychologists do not treat individual and system as separate entities. Adler (1933/1964b) believed that a person learns a way of being in the world, lifestyle, and private logic in social interaction because all individuals are firmly embedded in social systems. In effect, person and system interact so as to create each other. Ideally, a healthy person lives in a healthy society, and each contributes to the health of the other (Ferguson, 2000; Papanek, 1968, personal notes). Yet, each client remains a unique and indivisible individual to be studied and understood ideographically in one's own subjective context.

An Adlerian therapist approaches each case optimistically. People learn the beliefs and behaviors that contribute to difficulties and can, therefore, learn new, more constructive ones. Behavior results from learning. Psychotherapy represents an educative process helping people to face the difficulties in meeting the challenges of life more effectively. People want to creatively improve themselves, their situation, and the human condition. A therapist joins with that motivation and emphasizes purpose, strengths, and positives rather than failures and weaknesses. A therapist serves as a collaborative, democratic leader in a therapeutic system, aiding clients in discovering their productive and mistaken beliefs, goals, strategies, and the consequences of their actions. A therapist helps to reeducate clients to reorient these patterns toward more optimistic, successful, socially connected, and satisfying ones.

HISTORY OF THE THERAPEUTIC APPROACH

Alfred Adler, born in Vienna in 1870, developed individual psychology, also known as Adlerian psychology. The circumstances of his life and the stimulating intellectual Zeitgeist of his times and place influenced him greatly (Bottome, 1939; Hoffman, 1994; Mosak & Maniacci, 1999; Orgler, 1963; Stepansky, 1983). Appreciating Adler's background proves helpful in understanding the thrust of his theory.

The second born of six children, Adler suffered from rickets, spasms of the glottis, poor eyesight, and poor physical coordination. He almost died from a severe case of pneumonia at age 4. His younger brother died in bed with him when Adler was only 3. Other children teased or ignored him. He did not do well in school, and his math teacher advised his father to remove him from school and to apprentice him to a shoemaker. Despite this unpromising start, Adler's father did not heed the teacher's advice. Young Alfred took himself in hand, studied diligently, and subsequently performed well academically. He ultimately became an ophthalmologist (with poor eyesight) and an internist. Not surprisingly, Adler (1898) developed a deep concern about the relationships between physical and mental conditions and their relationships to work and social circumstances. He learned from both personal experience and observation that people have the possibility of improving themselves, of finding ways to cope with the challenges that life presents, and of choosing to do so. This became a major focus of his work. Adler's wife, Raissa, a strong feminist and political activist, supported her husband's social activism and his fight for equality for women. His theories were also influenced by his love of philosophy and his collaborative participation in the Psychoanalytic Society from 1902 to 1911. His service as a military physician during World War I reinforced his thinking about the relationships among mind, body, and behavior.

In the post-World War I era, Adler and his colleagues established at least 32 child guidance clinics in which his theory was widely implemented. Teachers, parents, and children were often seen together in an open-forum format with other clients, teachers, and students present in the session. He believed that everyone has problems, that problems form a normal part of living, and that people can assist and learn from each other. These open-forum sessions could be considered the beginnings of family therapy.

The rise of the Nazis ultimately convinced Adler that he must leave Europe. His followers spread out across the globe. He continued his work in New York, succumbing to a heart attack while on a lecture tour in Scotland in 1937. Two of his children became noted Adlerian psychiatrists and followed in his footsteps; Kurt died in 1999 and Alexandra in 2000, both in their 90s.

BEYOND ADLER

At the beginning of the twenty-first century, Adlerian psychology both emerges from an early history and has evolved through the contributions of others besides Adler. Now primarily third- to fifth-generation Adlerian theorists and practitioners work in many countries and have added a breadth of interests and developments. Adlerians are prominent leaders in developing both manual-based parent education programs and humanistic school education programs for children. Initiated by Adler (1930/1970) and stimulated by Dreikurs (Dreikurs & Grey, 1968; Dreikurs & Stolz, 1964), many manuals to conduct psychoeducational workshops have been composed, some of which have been translated into many languages and gained international popularity (Dinkmeyer & McKay, 1973; Dink-meyer, McKay, & Dinkmeyer, 1989; Dinkmeyer, McKay, & McKay, 1987; Popkin, 1993). Public schools have been organized to function according to Adlerian principles, continuing a long history of commitment to education (Allen, 2000; Corsini, 1977; Lew & Bettner, 1995). Some Adlerians (e.g., Harry Lerner and Ernst Papanek) worked closely with United Nations advisory committees in areas such as education and welfare.

Within the clinical realm, Mohr and Garlock (1959) organized social clubs for mentally ill patients to socialize with one another and with others in the general population to help them overcome social isolation. Adlerian clinicians have also been active in the fields of group therapy (Papanek, 1965; Sauber, 1971; Sonstegard, 1998) and couples and family therapy (e.g., Carlson & Sperry, 1998, 1999; Carlson, Sperry, & Lewis, 1997; Christensen & Schramski, 1983; Kern, Hawes, & Christensen, 1989; Sherman, 1999; Sherman, Oresky, & Rountree, 1991; Sherman, Shumsky, & Rountree, 1994).

Some of the major clinical contributions of Adlerian psychologists include (1) recognition of the complexity of a lifestyle in historical, interactive, and social contexts; (2) assertion that social interest and social feeling prove essential to the well-being of individual and society—emphasizing the *we* as well as the *I*; (3) implementation of a democratic relationship in all areas of life; (4) focus on strengths and encouragement; (5) respect for differences and problems as a normal part of the human condition and as opportunities for growth, rather than as invariably pathological; and (6) therapy as an educative growth process, rather than just remediation.

Some major refinements in Adlerian psychology derive their origins from other theories. Minuchin (1974) and Haley (1987) elucidated the details of social structures, role relationships, and sequences of behavior in social systems. The use of inventories in behavioral theories stimulated some Adlerians to develop their own inventories based on Adlerian theory. The importance of the emotional/feeling dimension elaborated by Goleman (1995), among others, encouraged Adlerians to look more closely at emotional behavior and its impact. Carter and McGoldrick (1999) and other clinicians offered insights on gender relationships and life cycle issues. In line with more recent attention to the spiritual dimension, a special issue of the *Journal of Individual Psychology* contained articles by Cheston (2000) on encouragement, Ellis (2000) on goals and values, and Gold and Mansager (2000) on the nature of spirituality as a task or process in human behavior. Watts (2000) considered religious approaches based on Christianity, and Haule (2000) and Noda (2000) in reference to Buddhism. Corveleyn (2000) argued against adopting any kind of spiritual strategy in therapy and favored maintaining a benevolent neutrality.

THEORETICAL CONSTRUCTS

Assumptions about human nature guide the development of Adlerian psychotherapists (Sherman, 1999, 2000; Sherman & Dinkmeyer, 1987):

1. Adlerians highlight the *unity* and *uniqueness* of individuals. A person emerges as an integrated, unique social being in a unified holistic universe.
2. Persons experience *social embeddedness*. Born of the union of two persons, humans live and develop almost entirely as members of social systems, formed in large measure by social experiences.
3. Individuals *learn* and can *choose*. Born neither good nor evil, but capable of whatever human beings do for good or ill, persons learn and choose to behave in characteristic ways.
4. *Life tasks* involve joining together in community and dealing effectively with self, love, friendship, work, and cosmos or spirituality. Individuals are here not to conquer the world, but to improve it and each other.
5. A sense of reality and *epistemology*, knowledge and meanings of personal actuality develop from *subjective perceptions* and *social experiences*.
6. In a typical *sequence of activity*, the modal pattern of human activity begins first with subjectively perceiving an object (an event), then thinking about it, feeling some degree of emotional arousal elicited by those perceptions and thoughts, and finally taking some action. These steps are interactive and sometimes vary in sequence of occurrence.
7. Humans function as both *problem-seekers* and problem-solvers, as *proactive* and reactive. Though valuing stability, and though

change may provoke stress, individuals soon become bored by sameness and look for new challenges. Excessive stability becomes rigidity and fosters dysfunction, and too much change may create chaos.

8. Like all living beings, persons *grow* and *develop* toward greater complexity, always seeking to enhance themselves. Persons strive creatively to move from a subjectively felt minus situation toward a perceived plus situation, from feelings of inferiority toward improvement, actualization, excellence, completion, and totality. Individuals encounter themes of development while moving through the life cycle (e.g., separation and new affiliations and the need to reinterpret a personal identity).

9. Humans live for and with a *purpose*. Based on perceived usefulness, individuals intentionally choose and develop ongoing patterns of behavior to move toward goals, progressing in particular directions.

The above assumptions fit together in a *profile of human behavior*. An individual subjectively perceives, thinks, feels, chooses, acts, and cares in relation to self and others. Based on subjective perception, a person develops ideas and conclusions about self, others, and the world. From the meanings given to these experiences, a philosophy of life forms. The ideas and philosophy derive primarily from participation in a family and the cultures in which the person functions. Involved in a social world, every person is motivated to improve and actualize his or her being and to achieve a sense of significance and belonging in that world. People desire to move from a lesser or inferior position to a more positive or effective position. To be "somebody" in a social world, one needs to find internal harmony between self as a subjective entity and the me as an object: my identity. This sense of self needs to be reconciled with the external world.

In the pattern of normal development, every child wants to "grow up," to be bigger, stronger, better. Based on one's philosophy or *private logic* and subjectively anticipating the future, one sets goals, consciously or unconsciously. *Strategies* (patterns of behavior) are selected in hopes of achieving those goals and/or to avoid experiences or objects that inspire fear and anxiety. One behaves "as if" one's beliefs and goals are true and accurate and as if the strategies selected will enable one to improve oneself and one's situation. The strategies are chosen patterns of behavior learned in a social environment or constructed from subjective perceptions of those patterns available. Behavior brings consequences. Strategies that persist tend to be reinforced by the resulting consequences, especially those that subjectively appear to support the established beliefs. New behaviors are fashioned or chosen if a person is sufficiently open and flexible to deal with unsatisfactory results by modifying the beliefs, goals, and/or strategies, or conversely, to build on satisfying results. High anxiety is usually coupled with rigidity and a person's perseverating in habitual behavior.

LIFESTYLE (CREATIVE SELF)

The dynamics described in the above profile combine to constitute the major elements of a person's unique self-created, organized, and unified *lifestyle*: the creative and created self. The concept of lifestyle bears similarities to the constructs of self, personality, or persona. These encompass (1) subjectively derived beliefs, myths, expectations, values, worldview, and attitudes about self and others; (2) goals toward which persons strive; (3) the behavioral strategies to achieve the goals that guide journeys through life; and (4) the impact or consequences of behaviors. Each journey is purposeful, goal-directed, and based on subjective perception. In psychotherapy, assessment and change particularly concern these four major aspects of the lifestyle (Eckstein & Baruth, 1996; Lombardi, 1975; Mosak & Maniacci, 1999).

Individuals obviously develop a multitude of beliefs and values. All do not seem equal. Persons assign much more weight to a few central ones perceived and experienced as more vital to surviving and thriving. These few become "priority" concerns and come to dominate lifestyle and to form character. People organize the bulk of their lives and behaviors primarily in the service of these priorities deemed essential to well-being or protection from anticipated harm (Bitter, 1987; Kefir, 1972). Adlerians do not consider these to be "traits," as in trait-and-factor psychology, but rather as intentional, freely chosen movements within a context of options and constraints (Slavik & Croake, 1997). Thus, symptomatic beliefs are organized in economical philosophies of life: "Everything I do will fail or turn out badly"; "I'm not good enough"; "To count, I must be able to conform and please people"; "I must be responsible and take charge because I can't count on others to come through for me."

INFERIORITY AND SUPERIORITY COMPLEXES

Persons are born naturally smaller and weaker or inferior to those around them. Children live in a world of giants. Through growing and developing, individuals soon discover that others have greater talents or assets than they, at least in some areas of life; one cannot always be above all. In understanding that, persons seek to improve and actualize themselves to become what they can be. This effort to become, to actualize, and to complete oneself signifies the Adlerian meaning of positive and healthy strivings for excellence. However, those who believe that they are inferior persons (less than they really are) may either denigrate the self (display inferiority complexes) or seek to compensate for their felt inferiority by dominating others. They desperately try to appear greater than they really are (manifest superiority complexes). This differs markedly from the healthy wish and effort to be competent, excellent, and successful in life. Both inferiority and superiority complexes lead to problematic behavior (Ansbacher & Ansbacher, 1956).

Many who recognize a particular inferiority in themselves may seek to *compensate* for it by achieving superiority in a related way or in a manner that represents the approximate opposite of the felt inferiority. For example, a person may choose to become a therapist partly because of personal difficulty with intimacy. This therapist encourages clients to share intimacies, thereby providing himself or herself with intimate experiences, but avoids sharing a real self in intimate relationships because of whatever anxieties about intimacy trouble this therapist. It is important professionally and ethically for a balanced and effective therapist to distinguish between personal difficulties needing compensation, which are most suitably taken care of through one's own growth or therapy, and having experienced challenges that allow a clinician to provide empathy for those in a similar predicament. One who is socially shy may choose a socially outgoing partner; and one lacking in self-confidence, expecting to be criticized or punished by others for apparent failings, may well strive for perfection and/or control to avoid the expected punishment or loss of esteem. Adler, who had many physical problems, specialized for years in working with circus performers and became an ophthalmologist to compensate for his own poor vision (Mosak & Maniacci, 1999).

COMMUNITY FEELING AND SOCIAL INTEREST

Hillel (Mangel, 1978) in the *Ethics of the Fathers*, commented, "If I am not for me, who will be for me? If I am only for me, who am I? If not now, then when?" This encapsulates the importance of *I and we*. Individuals live in families and social communities as part of worlds larger than themselves. Therefore, developing community feeling and *social interest*, concern about and caring for others, becomes imperative (Ansbacher, 1991). The *I* is very important, but the *we* must not be neglected. In practice, this means paying attention to others, their interests and needs, cooperating with others, and working for positive change. Cooperation does not necessarily mean conforming, but rather an agreement to participate respectfully with others in a process in good faith and with good intention (Adler, 1931/1964c; Manaster & Corsini, 1982). Yet, we are all different after all. Given individual uniqueness, Adler (1933/1964b) considered *differences* among people to be natural, appropriate, normal, and inevitable. He valued differences as the cutting edge of growth, especially when the people involved treat each other with respect and tolerance and search for agreement and synthesis. Still, he asserted that some behaviors such as abuse and oppression are plainly wrong and must be opposed.

A PSYCHOLOGY OF USE AND SELECTED LINE OF MOVEMENT

Not what people have—age, gender, strength, illness—but what they do with attributes or potentials characterizes personality or lifestyle (Ansbacher & Ansbacher, 1956). How do I think about having a learning disability or my competence as a writer? How do I use that information to organize my life? Any repetitive pattern of behavior may well have a useful purpose (behaviorists would call it instrumental) and be intended to move toward a goal. Therefore, both an individual and any system in action are viewed as coming from somewhere, are somewhere, and are heading somewhere in a specific line of movement deemed useful. The pattern can be observed and identified, and its usefulness surmised and assessed by a clinician. Beliefs, goals, and patterns of behavior are thus all regarded as subjectively organized and chosen for their anticipated usefulness, and together become directions pursued in life (Lombardi, 1975; Sherman, 1999; Sherman & Dinkmeyer, 1987).

Estimating the specific purpose of symptomatic behavior can become apparent by observing how others interact in response. If others submit to an individual's continuing aggression, for example, this leads to the hypothesis that the individual uses that aggression to dominate others and succeeds in getting at least some others to comply. Four goals of children's misbehavior stand out: to dominate, seek revenge, gain attention, or play helpless or incapable to put others in their service (Dreikurs & Grey, 1968). These can also apply to adults.

SAFEGUARDING TENDENCIES

The same principles explain the development and uses of defense mechanisms, or *safe-guarding tendencies*, as Adler (1912/1983) originally described them. Adler (Ansbacher & Ansbacher, 1956) enumerated the safeguarding strategies as depreciation/belittling of others, accusation/blaming, self-accusation/self-reproach, and undue guilt, distancing from challenges, anxiety, and exclusion of feared activities. Safeguarding strategies are employed to protect inferiority feelings, low self-esteem, and vulnerabilities. Clark (1999, 2000) further elaborated on these defenses, viewed as avoidance strategies to minimize harm to one's self-image and to manipulate the social environment in some way. He emphasized that everyone uses safeguarding devices. But when employed so persistently to avoid responsibility that they become integral to a lifestyle and personality functioning, then a maladaptive pattern emerges. Clark identified four typical safeguarding devices: the distancing complex (retreat from obstacles); hesitating attitude (rationalizing inaction and blaming others); detouring around (putting great energy into other activities); and narrowed path of approach (not completing tasks or concentrating on a few endeavors in which success is largely assured).

Adler formulated a *psychology of place, persons, and systems.* A person's place or situation shapes beliefs. Perspective depends on a point of view responsive to situations. How an individual gives meaning to an event, self, or world depends contingently on the belief system through which a person subjectively perceives and experiences. The places people occupy in families and other social systems, in turn, greatly influence beliefs. These places, such as parent, child, oldest, youngest, employer, employee, or therapist, are most easily identified by the roles attached to them.

Roles are important for assessment (Sherman & Dinkmeyer, 1987). Attached to each place are roles with concomitant responsibilities, expectations, privileges, reputations, values, and needs. Roles involve reciprocal, often complementary, relationships with others. Common reciprocal roles involve leader and follower, an active and passive person, helper and helpee, and, in business, an inside partner and an outside partner. Sometimes, roles are competitive. Two first-born children who marry each other may vie for who will be in charge of the relationship because each has grown up accustomed to that role in their family of origin (Toman, 1976). It is very different to be a child rather than a parent or adult, an employer rather than an employee, a member of the dominant cultural group rather than a member of a marginalized minority group, or rich rather than poor. Each place and its role provide a unique perspective for self and self group interests, and elicit different systems of beliefs consistent with them. This remains just as true even if one is disappointed with or rebels against the expectations attached to a particular role. The reaction is still in relation to the role. A teacher is supposed to fulfill certain responsibilities. Deviations elicit pressures to conform to the rules and expectations attached to places and roles. These relationships are thereby governed by the rules of any given social system. Such rules and relationships are constructed by the members of a group or system.

BIRTH ORDER

Because many of the ways we perceive ourselves and our worlds are shaped by childhood experiences, a person's ordinal and psychologically perceived position of birth in a family exerts a significant impact on the development of a lifestyle. Many Adlerians emphasize birth order as a major part of a family constellation and of each person's place in family, roles, and relationships. Toman (1976), Carter and McGoldrick (1999), Leman (1985), and Manaster (1977) have explored in detail the likely impacts of birth order on an eldest, middle, youngest, and only child. Many variations may ensue as a result of multiple marriages, long breaks between the birth of subsequent children, or the illness or death of a sibling or parent. Each of these conditions alters the meanings of place and the roles of occupants. Birth order may affect personality (Becker, Lerner, & Carroll, 1964), choices of marital partners, future success and positions in life (Birthnell & Mayhew, 1977; Eckstein, 2000; Phillips & Phillips, 2000), as well as family dynamics (Sulloway, 1996).

Individuals are not totally in charge of their own fates, even though they can make choices. Biology also shapes human lives. Adler discovered this dramatically early in his own life, given his poor eyesight, rickets, and clumsiness. Each person is endowed with a unique genetic code, which interacts with multiple environmental and social influences. Early in his career, Adler recognized that not all organs of an individual's body or body functions develop as equals. Some are weaker or at greater risk than others; some are stronger. Adler (1907/1917, 1923) referred to physiological vulnerability as "organ inferiority." He also recognized that mind and body influence each other:

Psychological difficulties might affect physical functioning and vice versa; physical ailments are related to depression and stress. Historically, these phenomena were termed psychosomatic or somatopsychic conditions. Understanding mind-body interactions has become more sophisticated in the past several decades. Mindfulness of the body and listening carefully to it, with its tissue memories, storehouses of energy, and its unique expressiveness, proves beneficial (M. Halem, personal communication, January 10 and 23, 2001). Recognizing and managing, in the most useful ways one can devise, physical illness or disability, mental disorder, being shorter or taller than most, having a particular skin color as a member of a minority or a majority population, or being of one gender or the other beckon as tasks for responsible responding. This includes dealing with any biological bases or concomitants of mental difficulties (Adler, 1929/1964a, 1933/1964b).

WELL PERSONS OR SYSTEMS

Adlerians go beyond the idea that, if no one is complaining, then all is well. Briefly, wellness and satisfaction with life revolve around the elements of attention, awareness, flexibility, optimism, and a sense of humor about self and life. Wellness requires willingness to take some risks and to seek new challenges sparked by openness to learning and the desire for self-actualization and significance. Self-respect, tolerance, and respect for others contribute to social connection and wellness in belonging. Positive community feeling, interest, and active participation in community expand the self as part of a larger world. Having a sense of personal competence and power, taking a proactive stance in life, and having the courage to be imperfect provide necessary energy and motivation to meet life's challenges. Striving toward excellence and perfection, rather than trying to be perfect, help an individual to set appropriate high goals and to work toward constant improvement (Adler, 1931/1980; Sherman & Dinkmeyer, 1987).

SYMPTOMATIC PERSONS

In an Adlerian perspective, individuals with clinical symptoms operate under mistaken or distorted beliefs about self and the world (Adler, 1929, 1931/1980; Sherman & Dinkmeyer, 1987; Sperry & Carlson, 1998). Typically discouraged about their plights, they tend to take extremist either/or positions, such as best/worst, good/evil, superpowerful/powerless, perfect/totally inept. They are likely to be rigid and self-protective, avoiding risks or taking reckless chances. They act disrespectfully toward self and others, or portray themselves as a kind of hero. They strive for total control, or imagine themselves as at the mercy of all. They want to dominate others, or to place themselves in a subservient role. Rigidly, they repeat old, familiar, ineffective patterns of behavior rather than learning or devising new ones. They frequently aim at a goal of either perfection or surrender. As a defense mechanism, self-denigrating people may believe that they are morally superior to others because of their suffering, even if self-inflicted. A dysfunctional person typically reacts to the world rather than taking a proactive stance. Usually, such clients experience some form of alienation or separation within the self and from the community. Adler (1933/1964b, 1931/1980) perceived alienation or separation within the self or between self and community as crucial factors in dysfunctional behavior. This represents the approximate opposite of social interest. A major source of dysfunctional beliefs and behaviors flowed from faulty parenting through neglect, abuse, or spoiling a child.

John, age 11, had difficulty relating to other children. He would not accept losing in any game or not being first in any activity. If he could not get his way, he would cheat, strike out at the other child, or begin wailing. He believed himself to be a victim cheated by others and by life. He was discouraged that he could not always overcome and dominate all others in his social world. This threatened his own feelings of inferiority, and, therefore, he had to compensate by always being the first and the best. If not, he became the least in his own eyes. He repeated the same rigid pattern of extreme behavior, which alienated him from his fellows, to protect his fragile self-image.

ASSESSMENT AND CHANGE

The processes of assessment and change intertwine in Adlerian theory (Sperry, 1997). Therapy proceeds through a fairly typical interactive four-part model. The first step encompasses *defining a problem, joining, goal setting, contracting,* and *structuring the therapy.* In this initial phase, a clear, positive, and concrete statement of the problem proves important. A therapist establishes a positive, collaborative, democratic relationship with a client. Therapist and client negotiate agreement on the nature, rules, and direction of therapy.

In the second phase, *understanding problem behavior and its purpose* receives attention. Therapist and client explore the biopsychosocial-spiritual dimensions of a presenting problem, with emphasis on a client's cognitive belief systems.

The third stage highlights *fostering change through reeducation and reorientation.* Focusing on cognition helps a client to correct distorted or mistaken beliefs, which undergird symptomatic behavior. Reorganizing the social system in which a client operates interrupts support for symptoms by changing some of the rules governing the system, shifting places, roles, boundaries, and hierarchies. Providing for the acquisition of relevant knowledge and skill, including communication skills, enables clients to initiate new ideas and new patterns of behavior. Encouraging positive attitudes such as optimism, flexibility, and the courage to be imperfect facilitates engaging in the risks of change. Intense emotions are either brought under control or refocused more constructively. Other clients need to be aroused to action. Fostering greater social interest, social feeling, and constructive connections in family, friendships, workplace, and other social systems advances client growth.

The fourth and ending period allows for *evaluation, reinforcement, termination,* and *follow-up.* Therapist and client together evaluating therapeutic experience in relation to defined problems reinforces newly acquired behaviors and helps to avert relapse. In implementing this growth-oriented theory, therapist and client collaboratively consider and evaluate next steps. Finally, agreement on a follow-up procedure proves important. Typically, if therapy is terminated before achieving the goals, striving to end on a positive and encouraging note is desirable.

Diagnosis and Assessment

Assessment includes history, clarification of a problem, and examination of the lifestyle patterns in relation to a symptom. This involves exploring relevant cognitive, emotional, environmental, social, and spiritual contexts. Therapist and client endeavor to uncover the rigidly held, distorted, or mistaken priority beliefs, expectations, and anticipations supporting a symptom and around which behavior is organized. Assessing the appropriateness of the goals that serve those beliefs, and identifying and examining strategies or sequential patterns of behavior used to attain the goals and how these impact on self and others become the next items of analysis. The entire process is then looked at as a unified and integrated whole. Generally, no matter how bizarre a problem behavior may appear to an external observer, once the internal private logic of the person is understood, the behavior will make logical sense.

Knowing how the above factors function in the systems of family, school, work, friendships, and the experience of being in the cosmos, and how other external factors may influence the integrated patterns that manifest as the symptom proves essential to assessment. Considering the continuity of past, present, and anticipation of the future; how person and system mutually influence each other; and the interrelating of thinking, feeling, and doing in a unified pattern better support accurate diagnoses.

Preliminary observation and data gathering permit the development of a *tentative hypothesis* about a client's problematic situation. A tentative hypothesis helps to anticipate the most fruitful directions for further data gathering and assessment. Once sufficient data are collected, a therapist forms *more detailed hypotheses.* A number of factors enter into the process. Realistically, a therapist actually perceives data from five different perspectives: (1) seeking to understand from a client's point of view and internal logic; (2) examining the findings in relation to "common sense," the general beliefs and expectations of the larger culture, and the immediate subculture; (3) analyzing the information as influenced by a therapist's own beliefs, values, life experiences, and cultural background; (4) filtering the data through a therapist's theory of human behavior and psychotherapy; and (5) utilizing a therapist's unique intuition and experience to empathize with a client and a client's situation to search out the essential meaning of a client's processes and contexts. These five factors affect the hypotheses chosen.

Given such a holistic approach, client and therapist benefit from continuously discussing the understandings acquired, clarifying the conclusions drawn, and evaluating and modifying a treatment plan accordingly. An efficient way to integrate the broad spectrum of data and to plumb the essence of the information is paramount. The intertwining of priority beliefs, goals, and lifestyle characteristics provide an organizing motif. The collaborative search for and analysis of the data gathered permit the development of a profile of the client and allow for completing a formula for assessment in an individualized way: Relative to the symptoms, the client believes X; chooses the goals of X to remedy the situation; strives to implement the goals through patterns of behavior such as X; with the results (including impact on self and others) of X; in the circumstances (context) of X. Assessment and diagnosis allow client and therapist to establish concrete, positive *goals* toward which to direct the therapy and to which the client will commit. These goals are best stated in concrete positive terms: "I want my brother and I to be more friendly with each other," rather than "I want him to stop fighting." During treatment, these goals will be further refined.

Change: Reeducation, Reorientation, and New Behaviors

The six factors most needing change are: private logic, systems, knowledge and skills, attitudes, emotions, and social feeling and connection to community. These are integrative and interactive and will alter lifestyle beliefs, goals, behavioral strategies, and consequences of behavior. Most theories of psychotherapy embody a concentration on only one among those six factors; Adlerians look at and generally work on all six. But each treatment plan involves a sequence of activity appropriate to a particular case and may be focused to a varying extent on any combination of the factors. The plan may be cooperatively redesigned as the therapy progresses. Fortunately, in thinking holistically, many of the techniques Adlerians employ to help bring about change address all or most of the six factors simultaneously and interactively. This streamlines therapeutic work.

Change constitutes a process of encouragement, education, growth, and development that not only remediates difficulty, but positions clients to better engage self, life, and the inevitable appearance of new challenges. Success, an increasing sense of empowerment, and personal significance provide the greatest encouragement (Bitter & Nicoll, 2000). A therapist works best with strengths, power, and resources. Clearly, Western-oriented democratic philosophy, which underlies this theory and its practices, does not necessarily reflect the values held by members of non-Western cultures, whether residing in or outside of Western societies. Adlerians recognize the need to be aware and respectful of other value systems in applying their methodologies and to learn from their clients.

Adlerians draw on a multitude of *therapeutic techniques* and tactics that either emerge directly from their theory or are easily adapted to the theory. Techniques represent neither gimmicks nor a list of "must do's." A technique is utilized in a specific case for a particular purpose in a given set of circumstances to achieve an intended purpose. When choosing a structured technique or formulating a task or assignment, the therapist typically elicits the client's permission. The technique is chosen with respect for the client and an assessment of its impact on others. Theory, sensitivity, and intuition influence the choices made. Obviously, a therapist must elect some techniques and tactics to operationalize theory and to conduct therapy (Sherman & Fredman, 1986).

Metaphors of speech, dress, posture, emotional punctuation, and interactive patterns provide many clues about a person's view of self and the world (Kopp, 1995). Noticing what a person actually does is more indicative of the primacy of particular values actually held than what the client may report or even be aware of. Action equals commitment. The direction of action helps to determine its purpose. A therapist may ask questions, administer inventories, and track symptomatic behavior, belief systems, and daily routines.

QUESTIONING

Although questioning serves as the primary technique in all talk therapy, the manner and purpose of its use differs across therapeutic frameworks. Adlerians particularly favor Socratic questioning. Through questioning and requestioning the answers to preceding questions, this dialectical method brings clients to insight about their beliefs, goals, and strategies and the consequences of their actions while simultaneously reeducating and reorienting them toward a more optimistic, successful, and satisfying lifestyle. The beauty of this art results from clients largely reaching their own conclusions and finding their own solutions. They then take new action more easily. Questions in the present elicit lifestyle issues in the context of recollections of the past and anticipations of the future, thus prompting change.

In emphasizing the direction of behavior, "Whither?" proves a more important question than "Why?" Adler (1929/1964a) was fond of using "The Question": "What would be different in your life if you did not have (the symptom)?" The answer helps reveal the threat the client is avoiding, the purpose of the behavior, and the goal the client would like to achieve despite the fear. Adler also posed the "impact question": "Who are those most affected by this symptom, how do they react, and then what do you do?" Interpretive questions, such as "Is it possible that what you really want to do is X?," prompt progress.

CONFRONTING IRRATIONAL
BELIEFS AND BEHAVIORS

Sometimes, confronting distorted perceptions or "basic mistakes" (Mosak, 1989) can help. In rational-emotive therapy, Ellis and Grieger (1977) referred to irrational beliefs such as overgeneralizations, for example, "People are hostile and just want to do you in. Nobody can be trusted." Such statements represent a philosophy of life, and constitute an essential core of the private logic of a client. Questioning provides a way to confront these irrational beliefs. Other techniques include dramatizing, interpreting, normalizing, reframing, storytelling and retelling, changing the ending of a story, eliciting repeated sentence completions, assigning readings or films, and using guided imagery.

A therapist confronts basic mistakes to help a client assume responsibility for the direction of his or her life. This type of confrontation always contains an invitation to move toward the *truth* as a system of ideas and beliefs that enable an individual to act and deal with things most rapidly, neatly, and safely, and with the minimum of irrational elements. Calming or arousing emotions not necessarily based on reason assists in deactivating distorted perceptions and beliefs.

LIFESTYLE ANALYSIS

Adlerians often elicit a lifestyle analysis (information on family constellation, possibly through a genogram, and early recollections) to uncover a person's basic integrated orientation toward life. The Life Style Inventory (Shulman & Mosak, 1988) contains questions about a client's history, members of the family and their relationships, work or school, friendships, and love relationships. Family constellation includes family history and organization as well as birth order patterns that influence a client's perception of place and role in the world. The Basis A Inventory (Kern, Wheeler, & Curlette, 1993) offers a similar, but more standardized and researched instrument, allowing for delineating behavioral profiles within a lifestyle. Sherman's (1994) Family Orientation Inventory provides a picture of family interactions around major issues such as anger and intimacy and distribution of social roles. Dagley and Dagley (1994) developed an instrument to measure the degree of encouragement experienced by children.

Early recollections signify earliest childhood memories, or specifically identified memories, such as meeting a future spouse for the first time. Early recollections symbolize the themes and patterns of a lifestyle (Ansbacher & Ansbacher, 1956). Current motivation prompts specific memories. Kern et al. (1993), Manaster and Corsini (1982), and Shulman and Mosak (1988) have developed ways to introduce and analyze early recollections.

Analysis of dreams in Adlerian psychology highlights the manifest content of a dream, rather than deeper symbolic meanings, to help clients discover the inner beliefs and meanings of their situations, their goals, and the problems they want to solve (Gold, 1979, 1981; Mosak, 1992; Shulman, 1969). Dream analysis resembles consideration of early recollections. Therapist and client survey the themes expressed, who does what to whom and how, what metaphors appear, and the ending. Dreams represent active attempts at problem solving. Therefore, inquiring about what happened the day or two before the dream and what the client anticipates for the following days provides clues to the meanings of dreams.

Therapists who perceive clients' needs *to alter places, roles, and relational functioning* may encourage them to engage in role reversal, use the empty-chair technique, shift boundaries, or sculpt. Or therapists may assign new roles as a task or a pretend task; relabel and reframe the meaning of roles; interpret the purpose of a role; strengthen, dramatize, or normalize a role; or shift a client out of an unhealthy or unsuitable system to another more appropriate one (e.g., a different school or class, job, friendship group, or residence; Minuchin, 1974; Sherman, 1999).

Some clients benefit from *acquiring new knowledge and skills*. At times, therapists teach or coach clients in session. They may recommend participation in psychoeducational groups or classes or self-help groups, use guided imagery, or assign homework tasks. To counter negative interactions and feelings, Adlerians frequently help clients to organize democratic meetings such as the Couple Conference, the Family Meeting, and the Encouragement Meeting (Manaster & Corsini, 1982). Each functions as a ritual conducted regularly, at a fixed time and place. Each requires constructive cooperation. In a Couple Conference, a couple learn to know each other better by taking turns speaking uninterrupted, usually for 30 minutes. Rather than providing a forum for problem solving, it offers a structure to increase intimacy through careful listening. In Family Meetings, members participate democratically to raise and solve issues and to plan together. An Encouragement Meeting fosters positive and affirming behavior among the members of the group as they acknowledge good deeds, important contributions, and how each is special or significant. All three enhance democratic process, evoke positive social connections, and help overcome alienation.

An Adlerian therapist helps clients to think and act positively through encouragement, reinforcement, and support for doing well. This augments *optimism, courage, social feeling,* and *connection.* Connecting with the deeper inner power and discovering ways of expressing this constructively spur energy for creative change. This enhances social interest (Ansbacher, 1991; Nikelly, 1991). A special issue on social interest in *Individual Psychology* contained articles on techniques for helping clients become more appropriately connected. LaFontaine (1996) stressed the role of social interest in developing therapeutic solutions. Brigman and Molina (1999) looked at social interest and school performance. Sherman (1997a, 1997b) described many culturally oriented techniques and methods for overcoming alienation. Sherman (1991) devised the Appreciation Party to thank each person in a family for his or her valued contributions. A therapist may also suggest tasks to develop interest in others, such as telling a self-absorbed child to play detective and carefully observe some person to see what the youngster can discover. Identifying past successes, bragging to others about one's accomplishments, and collecting positive testimony from others about oneself may be helpful to those who hold negative and pessimistic attitudes about themselves. These therapeutic processes permit great flexibility depending on the professional judgment of a therapist in selecting what to do and when. Rather than fitting only a single, prescribed way of acting, the theoretical concepts of Adlerian psychology and a democratic philosophy guide a therapist.

PROBLEMS AND POPULATIONS APPROPRIATE FOR THIS APPROACH

For Adler (1931/1980), psychology deals with how individuals interact with others in sharing this planet. Interpersonal transactions need to be grounded in the feeling of being part of a larger social system and in the willingness to contribute to the communal life for the common good (Adler, 1933/1964b; Mosak, 1989). Understandably, therefore, Adlerian psychologists strive to consider the full span of problems and issues impinging on social interest and community living. These range from individual mistakes that lead to negative lifestyles to a whole breadth of social problems such as racial conflict, religious and gender discrimination, war, poverty, drugs, issues of democracy, and inadequate parenting. Conceptualized in this way, everyone has a problem, and this remains part of the human condition.

Adlerians, therefore, work with a whole gamut of populations. They apply the principles of individual psychology to models of education, training, supervision, consultation, business organization, psychoeducation, individual, couple, family, and group therapy, and public policy. Adlerian psychology also finds application in societal issues such as leadership, nationalism, conflict resolution, social cooperation, wars, and drugs. Adlerians take seriously social discrimination based on ethnicity, gender, poverty, religion, and educational level as issues for consideration in the treatment of clients. Way (1962) stressed the need to have not only more cooperative individuals, "but a society better fitted to fulfill the needs of human beings" (p. 360). Some examples of contributions in those areas were briefly described early in the chapter.

Adlerian-based psychotherapy may be helpful in working with all types of mental disorders, especially those that fall particularly into its framework on beliefs, social relations, or lack of appropriate knowledge or skill. Therapy can assist in the management of the psychosocial-spiritual concomitants of biologically based mental disorders and, through that, perhaps even influence the biological component. There is a long history of working with all the major categories of psychopathology (Sperry & Carlson, 1998).

Adlerian theory reaches out to cover a wide spectrum of human experiences, yet each practitioner needs to work with specific populations and problems with which he or she has acquired knowledge, skill, and training. The art of referral is an important practice skill and an ethical imperative when presenting issues exceed the training and skills of a practitioner.

THE CASE OF AN ADOLESCENT AGAINST THE WORLD

DIAGNOSIS AND ASSESSMENT

The Data Collected: Client in Context
At the time of referral, David, a 17-year-old African American male, was held in detention in a residential program for adolescents, with a presenting problem of Conduct Disorder. He had previously been incarcerated several times for various offenses, ranging from drug charges to weapon possession. He was known and called a "bulldog" by his peers for constantly engaging in fights and beating up people. During the initial interview, he related that, as early as age 9, neighbors called him to come and take his alcoholic father home. His peers laughed at and made fun of his dad. They would sometimes make false calls for him to come and take his father home. "Some called me a nanny; others called me a nurse; they made me feel terrible." David said that he could not recall any day his father was present at any of the events at school or at sports that he participated in. "Other kids had their fathers there; I had nobody. Let me tell you, man, the world is not fair, and, if there is a God, I hate him."

David took to fighting and beating up his peers "to gain some respect and dignity." He was big and muscularly built and used his size to gain superiority over his peers. He had developed a concept of self that implied doing "whatever I wish to do, and it is either my way or the highway." When he was 15 years old, he allied with his mother and threw his father out of the house. For him, "My mother is my father and my mother. I buy her cards both on father's day and mother's day. She is the only woman that can tell me what to do." For David, "a woman who is not my mother should not have control or tell me what to do. Men take care of women, and that is it."

Until he turned 15, David stayed away from drugs and alcohol. His one-up against his peers stemmed from their using drugs. According to David, "A man shouldn't use drugs to get high and do things." Drugs, according to his philosophy, "is for weak people like my father." David believed that a man should take care of his wife and children.

David's maternal grandmother and grandfather died in the same year. Prior to his grandfather's death, David had promised him that he would take care of his mother and that he would not get involved with drugs and alcohol. However, a few months after his grandfather's death, David displayed even more anger, became more resolutely recalcitrant, and dropped out of school. He started drinking and using drugs, selling drugs more than he used them. "I had to take care of my mother and siblings, and I have to do it my own way. It is nobody's business what I do."

Asked why he viewed reality the way he did, David maintained that people cannot be trusted and that the only person worthy of being relied on is oneself. He believed, "All that people want to do is to use you for their own advantage, and, when you go down, they simply find somebody else." In line with these beliefs, David developed the goal that he must be smart "to avoid going down." For him, to be smart was "to beat people to their game, to use them before they use you, to take them out before they take you out." According to David, "The world is just not fair, and you don't have to be fair to the world."

David was the first of three children from the union of his father and mother. He was seven years older than his next sibling, a brother. By the age of 12, David functioned like a father figure in the home, exercising quasi-parental powers. He was not only parentified (Minuchin, 1974) by taking care of his siblings, but, even more harmful, he was also acting as a parent to his own parents. Not only did he serve as the source of emotional support for his mother, he was also the one who would usually bring his father back home from the streets. Sometimes, he beat up his father in the house, and eventually allied with his mother to evict him from the home. Disgusted with his father's ways and vowing to do better, David had taken on himself the task of caring for his family, even though he was himself a child.

During the first session, David was feeling depressed and was serving a two-week shutdown (an in-house punishment that restricts an offender to one room). He had told the director of the program (a woman), who had asked him to clean the light fixtures in the dining room, "That is a woman's job and you know it." David was constantly being punished for disobeying orders and for disrespecting female officials who worked at the residence. He actually was on the verge of being sent before a judge with the recommendation that he be returned to incarceration in the youth house. For David, "Being asked to do things, and especially being asked to do things by women, being locked up and therefore unable to take care of my mother, and breaking the promises I made to my grandfather" were related to his depression. He would not talk to anybody and professed no interest in anything.

Case Formulation: Assessment and Hypotheses
Adlerians predicate effective therapy on understanding the convictions that individuals develop early in life to help them organize, understand, predict, and control experiences. David's psychosocial history involved growing up as a deprived child, lacking in emotional nurturance partly as the consequence of having an alcoholic father and partly because of a peer group that showed him no mercy and had little sensitivity to his predicament. His position in the family and his family situation parentified him in ways that were emotionally destructive. As a child, he had become a parent both to his parents and to his siblings and had taken the responsibility of saving himself and his family from the world. He felt terrible that he broke the promise made to his grandfather and perceived his present predicament as a punishment from his grandfather. Regarding himself as different from other kids, and having "nobody" who cared, David developed inferiority feelings.

In David's *lifestyle*, convictions became organized around *distorted beliefs*, including overgeneralizations ("People cannot be trusted"; "People just want to use you for their advantage"); misperceptions of life and life's demands ("The world is wicked and unfair"; "Life doesn't give you a break, and so you just have to give yourself a break, no matter what"); and faulty values ("To be smart is to beat people to their game, to use them before they use you, to take them out before they take you out"). "The world is not fair, and you don't have to be fair to the world" constituted David's modus operandi. These beliefs left him emotionally upset, angry, discouraged, sad, isolated, and ready to fight.

Therefore, to protect himself from ego disintegration, David moved toward a self-selected *goal* that involved beating the world before the world could take advantage of him—a move he felt would give him a place in the world and provide him with security while preserving his self-esteem. Adler (1931/1980) characterized human strivings that are geared solely toward the greater glory of an individual as socially useless and, in extreme conditions, indicative of mental problems. David had to contend with both nonsupportive family dynamics and the deleterious effects of societal racism.

To achieve his goal in life, David apparently constructed a concept of self that hinged on an exaggeration of the significance of masculinity and equated this with doing what he pleased. He viewed himself as superior to women, who were there just to be taken care of. Behaviorally, he invoked the *strategy* of using *patterns of behavior* incorporating aggression, disobedience, and disrespect for female authority to suppress an underlying sense of inferiority and to preserve his sense of masculinity through an exaggerated uncooperative goal of personal superiority. Consequently, he divorced himself from the direct solution of his problems and strove for personal superiority through overcompensation, wearing a mask, and attempting aggressive and illegal actions that compensated for his low self-esteem. This behavior seems to be consistent with Mosak and LeFevre's (1976) observation that, while individuals experience themselves in conflict, unable to move, they do, in reality, create these antagonistic feelings, ideas, and values because of their unwillingness to move in the direction of solving their problems. Or they do not know how to solve their problems.

The meanings that David gave to his life experiences and the philosophy of life that he constructed led to patterns of behavior that kept him in constant conflict with most people and institutions in his social world. The *consequences* resulted in his growing isolated and alienated from most others, being incarcerated, and becoming more embittered and discouraged. These consequences further reinforced in his mind the correctness of his philosophy and the righteousness of his behavior against the world. Yet David displayed many *assets*, including strength and determination. He committed himself to what he believed in and invested his energies in accomplishing his goals. He showed purpose, singular focus, and a strong sense of loyalty to his family and to his grandfather.

Treatment

In working with David, it was important to establish, from the onset, the *goal of therapy*. David was primarily oriented to taking care of his mother and siblings. The task, then, was to convince David that this goal, though achievable, would require small progressive action steps, the first of which would be his successful completion of the residential program.

Trust posed a major issue with David. Therefore, the therapist faced the challenge of presenting an unmistakably evident willingness to listen to him without criticism, to use encouragement as a constant expression of faith in him, and to construct the therapy as a "we" experience to help encourage and sustain his hope. As Adler (1931/1980) advised, "We must be able to see with his eyes and listen with his ears" (p. 72). Concomitantly, David needed confrontation about some of his beliefs and his basic mistakes to give him an opportunity to change his personal lifestyle, his perceptions and goals, and the faulty motivations underlying his behavior and values. Changing these perceptions would, it was hoped, help decrease his inferiority feelings and overcome discouragement and enable him to start using his resources in ways that would make him a contributing member of society.

David used the tactics of deprecation and aggression to manage his inferiority feelings. Importantly, he needed to recognize how much these weapons eventually hurt him as much as they did others. Guiding David to this insight involved helping him understand that people play a role in creating their own problems and that these problems are sometimes based on faulty perceptions, inadequate or faulty learning, and, especially, faulty values. He needed to perceive himself as responsible for his actions, and not simply as blamed for them. Inviting David to take an active and responsible role in therapy represented the goal.

David's biggest problem at the residential home stemmed from his disrespect for female authority. Helping him understand his belief by questioning and deconstructing it and then modifying it proved crucial. The therapist suggested, "Is it possible that your goal in being defiant to the female staff is to show them who the real boss is or to hurt women as you feel hurt?"

DAVID: I am no boss to nobody.
THERAPIST: So what would your grandpa say to you if he were here now? (This was initiated to elicit and match a positive value against his negative one.)
DAVID: Why do you ask?
THERAPIST: I know you love your grandpa very much. I just wanted to know what he would say to you if he were here.
DAVID: To do good and get out of here.
THERAPIST: Do you want to do that?
DAVID: Yes.
THERAPIST: Doing good and getting out?
DAVID: (Quietly.) Yes.

After firming up the goal, the therapist assigned David to act "as if" he could take orders from women. He objected that he preferred not to be phony, and acting "as if" would make him hypocritical. To motivate him, the therapist explained that not all acting was fake and that people can always experiment with a new role, just as they try on a suit. This does not change the person wearing the suit, but sometimes a handsome suit that fits well can make someone feel differently and perhaps behave differently, thus enlarging oneself as a person.

Before giving a second assignment to David, the therapist aroused some curiosity by suggesting how difficult the task could be. David replied, "Nothing is too hard for a man to do." The task involved doing a good deed or giving pleasure to another resident. David rejected this because "Nobody does anything for me. I don't like them, and they don't like me."

THERAPIST: You worry that you have disappointed your grandfather, but you are still keeping up the same behavior. I wonder how you will take care of your family if you continue this way and fail to get out of here? (This comment confronts him with his therapeutic goal.)
DAVID: (Silent.)
THERAPIST: You can make choices, David, and you can help shape your life. You may not be the complete master of your fate and may not always choose what will happen to you, but you can always choose how you treat other people. You may not want to please anyone right now, but at least consider thinking about different ways you could do it, if you wanted to.

This assignment was designed to help David begin to develop social interest and to move from the role of a rebel to that of a helper.

The following week, the director of the program reported that David had actually said "Good morning" to her three times in the past week, with a smile on his face, and on two occasions had helped an inmate who was assigned to clean the kitchen. During the session, David, smiling, related that the week had gone "okay." Questioned as to what made it okay, he alluded to the fact that "it felt good to help the brother the other day in the kitchen." It was necessary to help David process this feeling in the light of his own life while encouraging and affirming courageous effort, good results, and the feelings of pride and satisfaction.

Over the next few weeks, therapy with David continued along these lines. Techniques of questioning, encouragement, and confrontation were used to help him gain insight. Many more tasks along the lines of community living in the residence were assigned to him. As the sessions progressed, it became apparent that the frustration and alienation that David had initially felt were greatly diminishing as he became more connected to the residential staff. For the next three weeks, David was not shut down once. At the end of the fourth week, he had become a prefect for the boys and a "big brother" to newer residents.

Attention was then directed to helping David construct a future for himself, so that he could take care of his mother and siblings. He presented as a very physically strong individual and expressed interest in wrestling and boxing. The idea of getting into the ring to train as a boxer excited him. The therapist continued to assign tasks to foster his present commitment to reach out to others and to be compliant with adult directives. In compensation, the residential staff allowed him more time to work out in the gymnasium located in the basement of the residence. Each week, David's experiences with these tasks were reviewed during therapy sessions. Praise and encouragement were used to foster hope, to help David continue his progress, and to maintain gains made in therapy.

Helping David to stay involved as a contributing member of the human society once he was released posed a challenge. To alter his social environment, the therapist made arrangements with the director of the local boxing club, who was willing to accept David. Life skills techniques in terms of how to look for a job and interviewing processes were addressed. David wound up enrolling in an evening class after his release in preparation for a General Education Diploma (GED) in lieu of a high school diploma.

After leaving the detention facility, David participated at the boxing club and continued outpatient treatment with this therapist for the next three months (residents were required to meet with their therapists twice a month for three months after release). He took evening classes to prepare for his GED. By the third month, he was getting ready for his first major in-club bout. The head coach at the club indicated during a telephone conversation with the therapist that he strongly believed David would make it as a professional boxer. David also got a job at a hotel as a janitor to take care of his financial needs. In a session, he indicated that he was having some problems with his mother. He was challenging his mother, who, he said, "sits around all day doing nothing to help bring some money into the family." David expressed frustration at his mother's lack of understanding of the person he had become. "She tells me that I used to make a lot more money before I was incarcerated [from selling drugs] and that she doesn't know what they did to me in that stupid place." Subsequent sessions were focused on helping David work through this conflict with his mother and enabling her to understand that he was indeed a more effective person.

David's place as eldest son and his parentified role in the family had to be addressed. As he became more connected to the larger world, he found the courage to reconnect with his father and, after getting his father into therapy, was able to step back and allow his father back into the house as husband. This opened the way for shifting family roles and hierarchies.

Follow-Up

A three-month follow-up after treatment showed that David had won all four of his boxing matches, was still working, had not gotten involved with the law, and was preparing to take his GED in two months. He looked healthier, happier, and, surprisingly, had not engaged in a single street fight since he was released. He reported that his father was attending Alcoholics Anonymous and was now in his second month of sobriety. David indicated that his father was back in the home and working part time with a neighbor in a junkyard. His mother was still not working, but David noted that their relationship had improved.

TREATMENT PROTOCOL

The treatment of this case followed the model described in the section on Assessment and Change. The therapist joined with the client, elicited pertinent history from him and relevant others, obtained lifestyle data, and arrived at a diagnostic formulation. The formulation included beliefs, goals, strategies, consequences, strengths, emotional flashpoints, and an evaluation of social interest and social connections. The context of David's circumstances were also considered. A goal for therapy was established to help him complete the program, to be released, and to take care of his family. The therapist worked to correct David's mistaken beliefs and to test out new behaviors that would connect him with others and to be helpful to others. This involved establishing new roles for him in the institution in which he was helpful to others and redirecting some of his aggression from virtually spontaneous street fighting into the discipline of boxing. The consequences of this new behavior enabled him to develop new, more positive perceptions of his social reality and himself as a person. These new perceptions were reinforced by the therapist and staff and by the new, more favorable responses he elicited in others. A three-month follow-up was conducted to assess the effect of the treatment.

POSTTERMINATION SYNOPSIS AND REFLECTIONS

David's progress in treatment tapped into the potentials already existing in him, while he was helped to direct those resources into positive outcomes. Confronting his beliefs and behaviors assisted in engendering new convictions that increased the degree of his social interest while redirecting the use of his courage and inner resources into more self-actualizing activities. Directing his energy and courage into boxing likely decreased his sense of inferiority, thereby allowing him to overcome discouragement. It is hoped that this will lead him into productive work, strengthen his personality, sustain him in his perception of uniqueness, and give him a feeling of belonging and a sense of unity and common destiny with the rest of humanity. Dreikurs (1957, 1971) observed that the meaning of life resides in doing for others and in contributing to social life and social change. When David learned to love, he was loved in return, and this gave him a new sense of joy and fulfillment.

RESEARCH

Because Adlerians do not follow a single protocol for assessment and therapy and engage in a democratic give-and-take with clients, controlled research designs pose challenges for this modality. Evaluation of the case of David illustrates the typical pathway for outcome research in Adlerian psychology. Theory determines the direction of research. Adlerian psychology highlights the unique nature of each individual, studied ideographically, and his or her contexts. Clinical observation of individual clients and client self-reports allow for measurement of change. Changes in descriptions or data, such as occur in obtaining early recollections or stories or other therapeutic activities at the beginning and then again later in therapy, indicate degrees of progress. Reduction of symptoms or positive changes manifested in concrete behaviors prove significant. For example, improved school behavior and attendance, going back to work, or performing in a feared concert indicate concrete progress. For example, David is no longer involved with the police or in beating up his peers; he does all his fighting in the boxing ring, went back to school for his GED, holds a job, and shows social interest by helping to recruit his father into treatment.

Because of this ideographic approach, Adlerians tend not to use objective instruments very often to differentiate among people based on statistical norms that describe averages. Besides looking for clinical information, Adlerians may employ the instruments as exercises to increase client understandings and options. This diminished use poses problems in formulating more common objective research designs.

Adler (1929, 1931/1964c) provided prototype examples of individual case studies as the research modus operandi. This leaves the primary responsibility in the hands of each practitioner to study his or her own cases and to report on some of them to advance knowledge in the field and to demonstrate efficacy. The availability of more such published case reports is certainly desirable, but Adlerian texts and journals contain many such reports, and there are enough to suggest that the therapy as practiced is effective. Of course, it is possible that other critical extraneous variables have intervened to produce the results reported in individual case studies. Additional outcome research would be helpful, especially research that moves beyond the case study methodology.

Most Adlerian psychology research reported in the literature relates more to some interesting point about human behavior, process issues, or how a case illustrates, expands, or reinforces some aspect of theory rather than to measuring efficacy of treatment. This is regarded by some as a serious shortcoming in the field (Watkins & Guarnaccia, 1999). A lack of an accepted treatment manual that would standardize training in and practice of Adlerian psychotherapy results in a major shortcoming inhibiting research in Adlerian psychology. The nature of the theory and the flexibility of the practice do make it difficult to conduct controlled studies. Manaster and Corsini (1982) commented that Adlerians are unified in theory, but eclectic in practice. This mistakes the large degree of overlap between Adlerian psychology and many other theories for eclecticism. Such flexibility makes possible adapting and incorporating many techniques developed in other theoretical schools consistent with Adlerian psychology theory and perhaps gives the impression of theoretical eclecticism.

In a major review of research studies reported in Adlerian psychology journals from 1970 to 1996, Watkins and Guarnaccia (1999) found numerous studies on various Adlerian concepts, including lifestyle, early recollections, social interest, and birth order, that support the value of these ideas in the theory. They believe, however, that improved instruments need to be developed, such as the BASIS A (Kern et al., 1993), to refine such studies in the future. Within-subject research designs may be helpful in accommodating the ideographic emphasis of Adlerian psychology while providing an evaluation of treatment efficacy (personal communication, A. Sherman, January 15 and 23, 2001). Formal research does not constitute the strongest facet of Adlerian psychology, even though the national organization, the North American Society of Adlerian Psychology, does have a special interest section on research.

SUMMARY

In this chapter we have described the history and major theoretical principles of Adlerian

Psychology. A four stage model for conducting the therapy was presented including some of the many techniques commonly used by Adlerian therapists. The case study of a violent adolescent dealing drugs illustrated dynamically how the theory and model actually work in practice.

We advanced the thesis that AP, as a democratic and holistic theory, which attends to a wide spectrum of human behavior and the human condition, and overlaps with many other popular theories, could, therefore, well serve as an integrative theory. This is reinforced by a century of evolution and interaction with other theories.

The essence of the theory is that a person is born into a social system and, based on subjective perception, gives meaning to self, world, and experience. The conclusions subjectively drawn constitute a philosophy of life that includes anticipations and expectations of the future. These lead to the construction of goals and strategies of behavior to achieve those goals in order to meet the challenges of life. Symptomatic clients typically engage in faulty perceptions that lead to mistaken or faulty beliefs, negative feelings and attitudes, inappropriate goals and roles, and alienation.

The therapist collaboratively assists the clients in a democratic, cooperative relationship to identify and understand those mistaken beliefs and the resulting symptomatic strategies. The therapist focuses on strengths and one's own optimism to help clients bring about change in their: (1) mistaken beliefs; (2) places, roles, and patterns of organization in their systems; (3) necessary knowledge and skills; (4) emotions and attitudes; and (5) improve social connectedness to overcome alienation. These are examined in the context of the person's life as expressed in a continuing line of movement over time.

Finally, Adlerians do take a moral stance through their belief in human equality and democratic process and hope to contribute to a better world for all. Our future anticipation is that the theory will continue to evolve and be refined in this twenty-first century.

REFERENCES

Adler, A. (1898). Gesundheitsbuch fur das Schneidergewerbe [Health book for the tailor trade]. In G. Golebiewski (Ed.), *Wegweister der Grwerbehygiene* (No. 5 of the series). Berlin, Germany: Carl Heymanns.

Adler, A. (1917). *Study of organ inferiority and its psychical compensation.* (S. E. Jelliffe, Trans.) New York: Nervous and Mental Diseases. (Original work published 1907)

Adler, A. (1923). Psychische kausalitat [Psychic causality]. *International Zeitschrift fur Individual Psychologie [International Journal for Individual Psychology], 2*(6), 38.

Adler, A. (1929). *The case of Miss R: The interpretation of a life story* (E. Jensen & F. Jensen, Trans.). New York: Greenberg.

Adler, A. (1964a). *Problems of neurosis: A book of case histories.* (P. Mairet, Ed.). New York: Harper & Row. (Original work published 1929)

Adler, A. (1964b). *Social interest: A challenge to mankind* (J. Linton & R. Vaughan, Trans.). New York: Capricorn. (Original work published 1933)

Adler, A. (1964c). The case of Mrs. A. In H. L. Ansbacher & R. R. Ansbacher (Eds.), *Superiority and social interest* (pp. 159–190). Evanston, Il: Northwestern University Press. (Original work published 1931)

Adler, A. (1970). *The education of children* (E. Jensen & F. Jensen, Trans.). Southbend, IN: Gateway Editions. (Original work published 1930)

Adler, A. (1980). *What life should mean to you.* London: Allen & Unwin. (Original work published 1931)

Adler, A. (1983). *The neurotic constitution.* (B. G. Glueck & E. Lind, Trans.). Salem, NH: Ayer. (Original work published 1912)

Allen, T. W. (2000). An Adlerian renaissance in education. *Journal of Individual Psychology, 56*(1), 115–119.

Ansbacher, H. L. (1991). The concept of social interest. *Individual Psychology, 47*(1), 38–46.

Ansbacher, H. L., & Ansbacher, R. R. (Eds.). (1956). *The individual psychology of Alfred Adler: A presentation in selections from his writings*. New York: Harper Torchbooks.

Becker, S. W., Lerner, M. J., & Carroll, J. (1964). Conformity as a function of birth order, pay off, and type of group pressure. *Journal of Abnormal Psychology, 69*, 318–323.

Birthnell, J., & Mayhew, J. (1977). Toman's theory tested for mate selection and friendship formation. *Journal of Individual Psychology, 33*(1), 18–36.

Bitter, J. R. (1987). Communication and meaning: Satir in Adlerian context. In R. Sherman & D. Dinkmeyer (Eds.), *Systems of family therapy: An Adlerian integration* (pp. 109–142). New York: Brunner/Mazel.

Bitter, J. R., & Nicoll, W. (2000). Adlerian brief therapy with individuals: Process and practice. *Journal of Individual Psychology, 569*(1), 31–44.

Bottome, P. (1939). *Adler: A biography*. New York: Putnam.

Brigman, G., & Molina, B. (1999). Social interest and school success. *Journal of Individual Psychology, 55*(3), 342–353.

Carlson, J., & Sperry, L. (1998). *The disordered couple*. Philadelphia: Brunner/Mazel.

Carlson, J., & Sperry, L. (1999). *The intimate couple*. Philadelphia: Brunner/Mazel.

Carlson, J., Sperry, L., & Lewis, J. A. (1997). *Family therapy: Ensuring treatment efficacy*. Pacific Grove, CA: Brooks/Cole.

Carter, B., & McGoldrick, M. (1999). *The expanded family life cycle: Individual, family and social perspectives* (2nd ed.). Boston: Allyn & Bacon.

Cheston, S. E. (2000). Spirituality of encouragement. *Journal of Individual Psychology, 56*(3), 296–304.

Christensen, O. C., & Schramski, T. G. (1983). *Adlerian family counseling*. Minneapolis, MN: Educational Media.

Clark, A. J. (1999). Safeguarding tendencies: A clarifying perspective. *Journal of Individual Psychology, 55*, 72–81.

Clark, A. J. (2000). Safeguarding tendencies: Implications for the counseling process. *Journal of Individual Psychology, 56*, 192–204.

Corsini, R. J. (1977). Individual education. *Journal of Individual Psychology, 33*, 21–29.

Corveleyn, J. (2000). In defense of benevolent neutrality: Against a "spiritual strategy." *Journal of Individual Psychology, 56*(3), 343–352.

Dagley, J. C., & Dagley, P. L. (1994). *The Encouragement Scale for Children*. Unpublished manuscript, University of Georgia, Athens.

Dammann, C., & Jurkovic, G. J. (1986). Strategic family therapy: A problem-focused, systemic approach. *Individual Psychology, 42*(4), 556–566.

Dinkmeyer, D. C., & Mc Kay, G. D. (1973). *Raising a responsible child*. New York: Simon & Schuster.

Dinkmeyer, D. C., McKay, G. D., & Dinkmeyer, J. S. (1989). *Parenting young children*. Minneapolis, MN: American Guidance Associates.

Dinkmeyer, D. C., Mc Kay, G. D., & Mc Kay, J. L. (1987). *New beginnings: Skills for single parents and stepfamily parents: Parents manual*. Champaign, Il: Research Press.

Disque, J. G., & Bitter, J. R. (1998). Integrating narrative therapy with Adlerian lifestyle assessment: A case study. *Journal of Individual Psychology, 54*(4), 431–450.

Dreikurs, R. (1957). Psychotherapy as correction of faulty social values. *American Journal of Individual Psychology, 13*, 150–158.

Dreikurs, R. (1971). *Social equality: The challenge of today*. Chicago: Henry Regnery.

Dreikurs, R., & Grey, L. (1968). *A new approach to discipline: Logical consequences*. New York: Hawthorne.

Dreikurs, R., & Stolz, V. (1964). *Children the challenge*. New York: Duell, Sloan & Pearce.

Eckstein, D. (2000). Empirical studies indicating significant birth-order related personality differences. *Journal of Individual Psychology, 56*(4), 481–494.

Eckstein, D., & Baruth, L. (1996). *The theory and practice of life-style assessment*. Dubuque, IA: Kendall/Hunt.

Ellenberger, H. (1970). *The discovery of the unconscious*. New York: Basic Books.

Ellis, A. (2000). Spiritual goals and spirited values in psychotherapy. *Journal of Individual Psychology, 56*(3), 277–284.

Ellis, A., & Grieger, R. (1977). *Handbook of rational-emotive therapy*. New York: Springer.

Ferguson, E. D. (2000). Individual psychology is ahead of its time. *Journal of Individual Psychology, 56*(1), 14–20.

Forgus, R., & Shulman, B. H. (1979). *Personality: A cognitive view.* Englewood Cliffs, NJ: Prentice-Hall.

Gold, L. (1979). Adler's theory of dreams: An holistic approach to interpretations. In B. Wolman (Ed.), *Handbook of dreams* (pp. 319–341). New York: Van Nostrand-Reinhold.

Gold, L. (1981). Life style and dreams. In L. Baruth & D. Eckstein (Eds.), *Life style theory, practice and research* (2nd ed., pp. 24–30), Dubuque, IA: Kendall-Hunt.

Gold, L., & Mansager, E. (2000). Spirituality: Life task or life process? *Journal of Individual Psychology, 56*(3), 266–276.

Goleman, D. (1995). *Emotional intelligence.* New York: Bantam Books.

Haley, J. (1987). *Problem solving therapy* (2nd ed.). San Francisco: Jossey-Bass.

Haule, J. R. (2000). Jung's practice of analysis: A Euro-American parallel to Ch'an Buddhism. *Journal of Individual Psychology, 56*(3), 353–364.

Hoffman, E. (1994). *The drive for self: Alfred Adler and the founding of individual psychology.* Reading, MA: Addison-Wesley.

Jones, J. V., Jr. (1995). Constructivism and individual psychology: Common ground for dialogue. *Individual Psychology, 51,* 231–243.

Kaye, D., Dichter, H., & Keith, D. (1986). Symbolic-experiential family therapy. *Individual Psychology, 42*(4), 521–536.

Kefir, N. (1972). *Priorities.* Unpublished manuscript.

Kern, R. M., Hawes, E. C., & Christensen, O. C. (1989). *Couples therapy: An Adlerian perspective.* Minneapolis, MN: Education Media.

Kern, R. M., Wheeler, M. S., & Curlette, W. L. (1993). *Basis A Inventory. Interpretive manual.* Highlands, NC: TRT Associates.

Kopp, R. R. (1995). *Metaphor therapy: Using client generated metaphors in psychotherapy.* New York: Brunner/Mazel.

LaFontaine, R. M. (1996). Social interest: A key to solutions. *Individual Psychology, 52*(2), 150–157.

Lawe, C. F., & Smith, E. W. L. (1986). Gestalt processes and family therapy. *Individual Psychology, 42*(4), 537–544.

Leman, K. (1985). *The birth order book.* New York: Dell.

Lew, A., & Bettner, B. L. (1995). *Responsibility in the classroom.* Newton Center, MA: Connexions Press.

Lombardi, D. N. (1975). *The search for significance.* Chicago: Nelson-Hall.

Manaster, G. J. (1977). Birth order: An overview. *Journal of Individual Psychology, 33,* 3–8.

Manaster, G. J., & Corsini, R. C. (1982). *Individual psychology: Theory and practice.* Itasca, IL: Peacock.

Mangel, N. (Ed. & Trans.). (1978). *Siddur Tehellat Hashem* (pp. 211–234). New York: Merkos L'Inyonei Chinuch.

Minuchin, S. (1974). *Families and family therapy.* Cambridge, MA: Harvard University Press.

Mohr, E., & Garlock, R. (1959). The social club as an adjunct to therapy. In K. Adler & D. Deutsch (Eds.), *Essays in individual psychology* (pp. 465–470). New York: Grove.

Mosak, H. H. (1989). Adlerian psychotherapy. In R. J. Corsini & D. Wedding, *Current psychotherapies* (4th ed., pp. 65–118). Itasca, IL: Peacock.

Mosak, H. H. (1992). The "traffic cop" function of dreams and early recollections. *Journal of Individual Psychology, 48,* 319–323.

Mosak, H. H., & LeFevre, C. (1976). The resolution of interpersonal conflict. *Journal of Individual Psychology, 32,* 19–26.

Mosak, H. H., & Maniacci, M. (1999). *A primer of Adlerian psychology.* Philadelphia: Brunner/Mazel.

Nikelly, A. (1991). Social interest: A paradigm for mental health education. *Individual Psychology, 42*(1), 79–81.

Noda, S. J. (2000). The concept of holism in individual psychology and Buddhism. *Journal of Individual Psychology, 56*(3), 285–295.

Orgler, H. (1963). *Alfred Adler: The man and his work.* New York: Mentor.

Papanek, H. (1965). Group psychotherapy with married couples. In J. H. Masserman (Ed.), *Current psychiatric therapies* (pp. 157–163). New York: Grune & Stratton.

Phillip, A. S., & Phillip, C. R. (2000). Birth order differences in self-attributions for achievement. *Journal of Individual Psychology, 56,* 474–480.

Popkin, M. (1993). *Active parenting today: The basics.* Atlanta, GA: Active Parenting.

Sauber, S. R. (1971). Multiple family group counseling. *Personnel and Guidance Journal, 49,* 459–466.

Sherman, R. (1991). The appreciation party. *Family Psychologist, 7*(1), 25–29.

Sherman, R. (1994). The Family Orientation Inventory. *The Family Journal, 2*(3), 262–265.

Sherman, R. (1997a). Culturally oriented techniques. *The Family Journal, 5*(1), 69–75.

Sherman, R. (1997b). Overcoming alienation. *The Family Journal, 5*(2), 164–171.

Sherman, R. (1999). Family therapy: The art of integration. In R. E. Watts & J. Carlson (Eds.), *Interventions and strategies in counseling and psychotherapy* (pp. 101–134). Philadelphia: Accelerated Development.

Sherman, R. (2000). *Thumbnail sketch of Adlerian systems theory.* Unpublished paper, Seton Hall University, South Orange, NJ.

Sherman, R., & Dinkmeyer, D. (1987). *Systems of family therapy: An Adlerian integration.* New York: Brunner/Mazel.

Sherman, R., & Fredman, N. (1986). *Handbook of structured techniques in marriage and family therapy.* New York: Brunner/Mazel.

Sherman, R., Oresky, P., & Rountree, Y. (1991). *Solving problems in couples therapy: Techniques and tactics.* New York: Brunner/Mazel.

Sherman, R., Shumsky, A., & Rountree, Y. B. (1994). *Enlarging the therapeutic circle: The therapist's guide to collaborative therapy with families and schools.* New York: Brunner/Mazel.

Shulman, B. H. (1969). The Adlerian theory of dreams. In M. Kramer (Ed.), *Dream psychology and the new biology of dreaming* (pp. 117–137). Springfield, IL: Charles C Thomas.

Shulman, B. H., & Mosak, H. H. (1988). *Manual for life style assessment.* Muncie, IN: Accelerated Development.

Shulman, B. H., & Watts, R. E. (1997). Adlerian and constructivist psychotherapies: An Adlerian perspective. *Journal of Cognitive Therapy, 11,* 181–193.

Slavik, S., & Croake, J. (1997). Social interest is not altruism. In P. Prina, C. Shelley, & C. Thompson (Eds.), *Adlerian yearbook, 1997* (pp. 46–56). London: Adlerian Society and the Institute for Individual Psychology.

Sonstegard, M. (1998). The theory and practice of Adlerian group counseling and psychotherapy. *Journal of Individual Psychology, 54*(2), 217–250.

Sperry, L. (1997). The "rediscovery" of interventive interviewing. In J. Carlson & S. Slavik (Eds.), *Techniques in Adlerian psychology.* Philadelphia: Accelerated Development.

Sperry, L., & Carlson, J. (1998). *Psychopathology and psychotherapy* (2nd ed.). Philadelphia: Accelerated Development.

Stepansky, P. E. (1983). *In Freud's shadow: Adler in context.* Hillsdale, NJ: Analytic Press.

Stone, M. (1998). Journaling with clients. *Journal of Individual Psychology, 54*(4), 511–534.

Sulloway, F. J. (1996). *Born to rebel: Birth order, family dynamics and creative lives.* New York: Random House.

Toman, W. (1976). *Family constellation: Its effects on personality and social behavior* (3rd ed.). New York: Springer.

Walton, F. X. (1998). Use of the most memorable observation as a technique for understanding choice of parenting style. *Journal of Individual Psychology, 54*(4), 487–494.

Watkins, C. E., & Guarnaccia, C. A. (1999). The scientific study of Adlerian theory. In R E. Watts & J. Carlson (Eds.), *Interventions and strategies in counseling and psychotherapy* (pp. 207–230). Philadelphia: Accelerated Development.

Watts, R. E. (2000). Biblically based Christian spirituality and Adlerian psychotherapy. *Journal of Individual Psychology, 56*(3), 316–328.

Way, L. (1962). *Adler's place in psychology.* New York: Collier Books.

CHAPTER 9

School-Based Community Family Therapy for Adolescents at Risk

NORBERT A. WETZEL AND HINDA WINAWER

PARADIGM SHIFT

The transition from an individual- to a relationship-oriented paradigm constitutes the decisive epistemological turning point in the evolution of psychotherapy during the twentieth century. This shift happened in all fields of human endeavor. Post-Newtonian physics, especially quantum mechanics, cybernetics with technological innovations such as the computer and the Internet, microbiology, literary criticism, sociology, anthropology, ecology, chaos theory, hermeneutics, and related developments in philosophy (phenomenology, existentialism, structuralism, postmodernism) all represent expressions and indications of the same epochal movement of the human mind (Auerswald, 1987, 1990; Bateson, 1971, 1979; Capra, 1984). A mechanistic worldview of fixed entities, objects, material things that exist as real "out there," independently from an observing mind, was balanced by an ecological view emphasizing the interdependence of all beings, particularly human beings, and including the observer in the observed field. In this ecological perspective, our relationship to other human beings as such is unique and profoundly different from the connectedness of material objects. We find ourselves in relationship to other human beings and challenged into responding to the other, that is, an individual who is "other" to us, before we can make a choice about being related. This openness toward and for the other and, in fact, all others defines our very uniqueness as individuals. Relatedness to others constitutes the self as such (Davis, 1996; Levinas, 1961/1992, 1974/1981).

Personal experiences with partners or friends, mass phenomena that led to genocide or ethnic wars, or the interdependence of nations on a global level equally have taught us to conceptualize individuals as embedded in a network of personal, socioeconomic, and global relations. The same holds true for larger units, such as a city or a nation. The individual, the self (i.e., the traditional subject of psychological inquiry and consideration), is woven into comprehensive intersecting networks to a degree that it threatens to disappear behind the various collectives and totalities (Mikesell, Lusterman, & McDaniel, 1995; Rabinow, 1984; Wetzel, 1994a, 1994b).

This movement of the collective mind during the past century is definitive. A return to a naïve realism or individualism is not possible. Rather, we are faced with living in two worldviews: the mechanistic world of things, which we can manipulate and which are in multiple ways interconnected; and the human, interpersonal, relational world of people and societies, where individuality and personhood are constituted through relatedness to others. In this worldview, as observing, thinking people, we are part of the observed. There is no objectivity; and we interact with others with whom we are already in a relationship prior to the act of reflecting and interrelating.

HISTORY OF THE THERAPEUTIC APPROACH

Family Therapists Discover the Other: The History of the Relational Paradigm

The relational orientation in psychology and psychotherapy forms part of the overall paradigm shift during the twentieth century. It is fitting that systemic couples and family therapy grew out of the experiences of psychiatrists and psychologists during World War II and the postwar years. Therapists discovered what social workers had always seen: the emotional power of families and the dynamics of dyadic units such as couples that deeply influence the experience of the individuals involved (Hartman & Laird, 1983). Out of initial intervention strategies, entire schools of thought and particular focus arose and led to the training of a new breed of therapists and initiated a new profession: systems therapy for families, couples and, in some instances, individuals.

Community Health Centers

Initially, the new movement of family-systems therapy was focused on people who often could not afford private, individual, long-term therapy or psychoanalysis. Together with other efforts to expand the social-welfare network (Head Start, President Johnson's anti-poverty programs), the community-health and mental-health centers network began to make therapy available for people in poverty areas and in ethnic neighborhoods who would otherwise never have received psychiatric or psychotherapeutic care (Schorr, 1997). Structural family therapy (Fishman, 1993; S. Minuchin, 1974; S. Minuchin & Fishman, 1981; S. Minuchin, Guerney, Montalvo, Rosman, & Schumer, 1967) and research into the communication processes of families with a schizophrenic offspring (Bateson, 1971; Scheflen, 1981; Sluzki & Ransom, 1976; Wynne, 1988) exemplify applications of systems models particularly fitting for couples and families outside the mainstream of psychotherapy. Recognition of local community initiatives and concern for people who live in poverty, under conditions of racial and social oppression and without access to affordable medical treatment, led to the establishment of community health centers and, in the mental health field, of community-oriented approaches (Auerswald, 1983; Brown & Parnell, 1990; Simon, 1986; Wistow, 1986) and to the growth of family-systems therapy in the 1960s and 1970s (S. Minuchin et al., 1967; Seaburn, Lorenz, Gunn, Gawinski, & Mauksch, 1996).

Stagnation of Initiatives

Two developments contributed to the stagnation of initiatives applying the principles and practice of systems therapy to the unfamiliar worlds of poor and ethnically diverse family groups. First, family therapy matured gradually into one of the accepted models of psychotherapy, similar to behavior therapy, rational-emotive therapy, and psychoanalysis. Family therapists, therefore, became a respected group of professionals and researchers who were less likely to branch out into the chaotic worlds of youngsters growing up in urban or rural poverty areas. Similarly, the development of the *Diagnostic and Statistical Manual of Mental Disorders (DSM;* American Psychiatric Association, 2000) by psychiatrists reflected a more medicalized view of human behavior. Family and couple therapists began to adopt a diagnosis-guided and pathology-oriented perspective on psychological disorders. Often, they ended up with uneasy compromises between the epistemological basis of family systems therapy (i.e., its focus on relationship, its inclusion of therapists as part of the systems that we observe and interact with in therapy, and therapists' orientations toward the relational contexts of an "identified patient") and the requirements of a professionally acceptable practice (i.e., focus on the individual who has insurance benefits, diagnosis of the individual instead of assessment of the dynamic family system, need or pressure to prescribe medication, and suggestions of hospitalization).

Second, the advances of pharmaceutical research have resulted in the medical treatment and, often, cure of conditions that hitherto were considered fatal (e.g., polio, tuberculosis, small pox). These advances, together with the establishment of health maintenance organizations, supposedly to better manage health and mental health care, also favored reductionistic thinking and the widespread prescription of psychotropic drugs based on poor research and little or no regard for the relational aspects of an individual's symptoms or behavior or for the societal impact of these drugs. The health and mental-health fields have become subject to narrowly defined pharmacological interventions. Psychopharmacology in many ways has supplanted psychotherapy. Individual human behavior is being regulated by the prescription and use of drugs researched and promoted by the pharmaceutical industry. This exclusive, medically guided focus on mind-altering drugs for problem behaviors viewed as brain disorders as the treatment of choice for many mental-health conditions, including those of adolescents, made it more difficult to advocate for psychotherapy in general and family therapy in particular (Breggin, 1999).

Many Family Forms

In recent years, one can observe another shift in the field. Family therapists are overcoming their exclusive focus on the mythological (Coontz, 1992, 1997, 1999) White, middle-class, nuclear family, and fewer therapists are Euro-American. Family psychologists are increasingly aware of the normative influence of the dominant discourse about family life in general. Family theoreticians, clinicians, and researchers have expanded and deepened their perspectives to recognize the enormous diversity in ethnic culture, socioeconomic class, gender, sexual orientation, and religious traditions among the families they encounter. Single parents, poor families, ethnic and religious minorities, gays and lesbians, the chronically sick, older people, criminals, drug- and alcohol-addicted people slowly became visible to the community of relationship-oriented therapists (Inclan & Ferran, 1990; Wetzel, 1998a). Therapists can now see them as representing one of many diverse family forms, each with often considerable strength and resilience as well as uniqueness and vulnerability (Coontz, 1997).

Therapy with Outsiders

People traditionally invisible to Eurocentric family therapists became a focus for research and practice (Wynne, 1988), especially for therapists who did not think in abstract-formalistic systems categories alone, but were able to perceive the unmistakable uniqueness of a specific relationship context that wove individuals and families together in powerful ways. These professionals had the capacities to be impressed by the mundane phenomena in the lives of others (Auerswald, 1968, 1983). They perceived the special vulnerabilities and strengths rooted in the embeddedness of an individual or family in context, even though these were alien to therapeutic observers leading middle-class lives.

Applying the relational paradigm to other than the middle-class family world involves therapy with people who live outside of middle-class society and the professional world of therapists. For many therapists, especially Euro-Americans, this process essentially constitutes an attempt to step out of the professional work context they are accustomed to and to bring the practice, concepts, insights, and creativity of systems thinking to bear on their work with people who live in areas defined by poverty, scarcity of jobs, substandard housing, and the ubiquity of drugs. The people living in these inner-city neighborhoods remained largely strangers to therapists, who rarely encountered them other than in the contexts of social-welfare agencies.

THE TRANSFORMATION PROCESS
INCLUDES THERAPISTS

These "strangers" live in schools and communities of the inner cities and in neglected rural areas. They teach therapists with European, middle-class backgrounds who listen carefully about their lives and their particular vulnerabilities and strengths. Everybody who becomes engaged in this work experiences a transformation process that originates in the encounters of strangers (Kristeva, 1991; Wetzel, 1994b). The school-based, community-oriented Family Intervention and Empowerment Program (FIEP) in New Jersey inner-city high schools exemplifies one project bringing together people from largely different backgrounds and experiences (Wetzel, 1998b). Therapists, clinicians, and supervisors with diverse cultural heritage had to learn how to listen to each other and to "see" from a specific perspective. The encounters between the teams (family therapists and community resource specialists) and the adolescents at risk (for drug abuse, school dropout, and criminalization) led to a profound reorientation of family therapeutic practice, on both the levels of personal experience and of conceptual reflection. In such a process, therapists reconnect with courageous approaches from the early phase of family therapy. At the same time, this practice constitutes the establishment of a renewed future for family therapy and theory beyond the middle-class and the dominant culture (Madsen, 1999; P. Minuchin, Colapinto, & Minuchin, 1998).

The comprehensive, resource-based, and community-oriented quality of FIEP is rooted in the awareness of the crucial importance of the psychological and socioeconomic factors affecting people's lives. It also originated in the conviction that people have the abilities to cope with their problems when provided with adequate support. The approach is based on the pioneering ideas and groundbreaking work of the early community health centers and of the originators of family systems therapy (Broderick & Schrader, 1991; McDaniel, Hepworth, & Doherty, 1995; Wetzel, 1998a).

Approaches and practices similar to the New Jersey FIEP model include:

- Multidimensional Family Therapy for Adolescent Drug Abuse, a clinical research program under the leadership of H. Liddle and J. Szapocznik at the Center for Treatment Research on Adolescent Drug Abuse at the University of Miami School of Medicine (G. S. Diamond & Liddle, 1996, 1999; G. M. Diamond, Liddle, Hogue, & Dakof, 1999; Liddle, 1995, 2000; Szapocznik & Kurtines, 1989, 1993).
- Functional Family Therapy, with affiliated sites around the country, centered around

- J. Alexander (University of Utah) and T. Sexton (Indiana University) (Alexander, Pugh, & Parsons, 1998).
- The structured Strengthening Families Program led by Karol Kumpfer, University of Utah (Kumpfer, 1994).
- The FAST program (Families and Schools Together), also structured, initiated by Lynn McDonald, Wisconsin Center for Education Research, University of Wisconsin-Madison, with centers in many states (McDonald & Frey, 1999).
- The therapeutic work rooted in the Philadelphia Child Guidance Clinic and in structural family therapy (Lindblad-Goldberg, Dore, & Stern, 1998; Lindblad-Goldberg & Dukes, 1985).
- The practice and research led by members of the Graduate School of Applied and Professional Psychology, Rutgers University (Boyd-Franklin & Bry, 2000).
- The work connected with the Family Institute of Cambridge, Massachusetts, described by Madsen (1999).

CONCEPTUAL FOUNDATIONS

POSTMODERN DIAGNOSIS AND ASSESSMENT

The process and experience of encountering the unfamiliar world of adolescents at risk makes it plain that the approach represented in projects such as the FIEP model rests on several assumptions. First, therapists need the ability to understand and work through their usual predispositions and preconceived notions, so that those living in inner-city or impoverished rural neighborhoods will be able to open up to them and teach them about their world. Second, what therapists see and learn about the world of the other depends on the perspective they take and their capacities to listen. Rather than assuming that they know what life is like for these youngsters and families or presupposing that their views are accurate, therapists need to take a postmodernist stance. They must let the young people and the families teach them. They need to listen and remain open for surprises and for what Gregory Bateson (1971) called "second-order learning." In practice, this means employing a set of variable lenses that allows an outsider to perceive the multiple facets of families' realities. These basic attitudes of listening, willingness to learn, and curiosity are crucial not only to Euro-American and middle-class therapists working with an inner-city population, but also, in varying degrees, for all therapists with cultural, racial, and socioeconomic backgrounds different from their clients'. We can never disregard the degrees to which racism, sexism, and class domination are institutionalized in society.

The Kaleidoscope

A kaleidoscope of seven perspectives or lenses helps in comprehending the various unique contexts that affect the experiences of the young people in inner-city ghettos. These perspectives themselves originated in the surprises contained in the encounters between project consultants with European background and middle-class lifestyle and high-school students with African or Hispanic heritage who grew up in a socioeconomic context of continuous deprivation (Wetzel, 1998b).

Looking at the reality of U.S. youth in impoverished inner-city and rural neighborhoods and endeavoring to understand their experiences, family therapists involved in various studies and projects (Alexander et al., 1998; Boyd-Franklin & Bry, 2000; Liddle, 2000; Lindblad-Goldberg et al., 1998; Wetzel, 1998b) learned to open the foci of their observing lenses wider to contain, if possible, the totality of people's relational and societal contexts. Specifically, it is helpful to conceptualize the various approaches to understanding adolescents in their relational contexts with the following seven lenses or particular perspectives in mind (Wetzel, 1998a):

1. A student's or family's *socioeconomic class* and *employment situation*.
2. Identification with a particular *ethnic heritage, culture,* and *race* and the family's *immigration experience*.
3. A teenager's *gender-role* experience and *gender identification*.
4. A youth's *sexual orientation*.
5. An adolescent's *religious experience* and *spirituality* and a family's *involvement* (or lack of) with *local places of worship* and *faith communities*.
6. A youngster's individual *biopsychosocial development* and maturational *age*.
7. Every family member's condition regarding *medical health* or *illness*, especially *alcohol and/or drug addiction* or *abuse*.

The conceptual and professional reflection regarding the interdependence and crossover effects among the various factors that become visible with these seven perspectives is only beginning (Comas-Diaz & Greene, 1994; McGoldrick, 1998). For the team members and consultants of the FIEP, it is indispensable to approach a teenager's experience of life in the inner city with these seven lenses in mind. Among the numerous influences that form a person's (or family's) experiences, the factors that become visible with the seven lenses are particularly crucial for the conceptualization of treatment planning and for the success of any intervention.

The seven lenses allow a participant-observer to engage in a number of assessments. First, it is possible to perceive and assess the degree of alienation, even suspicion, or familiarity that exists between family and therapist (Falicov, 2000). Without a clear understanding of the exact nature of the relationship between client family and therapist, therapy cannot succeed because the human relationship between them will fail. Second, these categories make it possible to conceptualize the level of similarity or difference in a specific family, the neighborhood community, and the surrounding society. Third, therapists begin to appreciate the complexity of family reality made visible through these perspectives when they notice how powerfully these factors influence each other.

With the use of these diverse lenses, family therapists show the courage of earlier days. They break out of the confines of professional family therapy as a treatment modality among others and use systems thinking as a paradigm for understanding human problems and dilemmas in a relational context. They risk being labeled again as subversive or as breaching the boundaries between professional clinical work and political activism.

Diagnosis
From this point of view, diagnosis evolves into a highly complex process (Kaslow, 1996). Relational therapists look at an individual and family in context, using the seven lenses and including their own relationships to the observed families. Any diagnosis has to include as referent, therefore, the perspective that has been used and awareness of the limitations of each particular view. Therapists also cease to search for pathology, a concept from the objectivistic worldview. They become reluctant to prescribe or suggest psychotropic medicines because the context-oriented perspective used in the FIEP model and similar programs usually highlights factors that would make it an improper reduction to see the problem behavior in question as a brain disorder. Adopting a much more comprehensive view, therapists find it easier to discover a given family's particular strengths and stresses. Most of the projects described earlier start with children and/or adolescents at risk and construct a version of an "interactional assessment" as part of the initial contacts (Madsen, 1999).

In part, because of similarities in ethnic and socioeconomic backgrounds, the FIEP's team members brought from the outset an intuitive and empathic understanding to their encounters with inner-city teenagers. With the seven lenses in focus, they could highlight aspects of the adolescents' and their families' lives that otherwise would have remained hidden from view or may have been ignored in planning a treatment strategy leading to empowerment, self-reliance, and community involvement (Ivey, Ivey, & Simek-Morgan, 1993).

Family therapists' experiences with the contexts of *poverty, joblessness,* and *mutual self-help* in inner-city and rural areas and their effects on family life (Ambert, 1998; Aponte, 1994; Inclan & Ferran, 1990; Wilson, 1997, 1999) make a compelling case that specific models of comprehensive care geared toward people, especially children and teenagers, living in poor communities need to be collaborative and need to reflect people's experiences of living in these neighborhoods.

Studies highlighting the relevance of *ethnicity, culture,* and *race* to family therapy have recently increased significantly in number and quality (Falicov, 1983, 2000; Fowers & Richardson, 1996; McGoldrick, Giordano, & Pearce, 1996; Pinderhughes, 1989, 1990; Saba, Karrer, & Hardy, 1990; Szapocznik & Kurtines, 1989, 1993). Many common assumptions and theories considered universal regarding psychosocial development, family dynamics, and therapeutic process are unmasked as Eurocentric when the experiences of people from different cultural and racial traditions are taken into account (Thomas & Sillen, 1979). In the ways they begin to overcome their initial mistrust, adolescents show clearly whether they feel their cultural heritages and racial identities are taken seriously by the professionals they meet (Liddle, 1995).

There is also a well-developed body of literature about *gender*-related aspects of treatment (Comas-Diaz & Greene, 1994; Goldner, 1985; Hare-Mustin & Marecek, 1990; Philpot & Brooks, 1995; Pravder Mirkin, 1994; Weingarten, 1994). In fact, professionals using the gender perspective deconstructed for the first time many common myths, assumptions, and unreflected practices in psychotherapy that were taken as universal and revealed them as White, male-oriented prejudices. The effects of differences in students' *sexual orientation* on context-sensitive treatment still need to be fully explored (Goodrich, Ellman, Rampage, Halstead, 1990; Laird, 1994; Savin-Williams, 1998; Scrivner & Eldridge, 1995).

The family-therapy field, for the most part, has hardly begun to include appreciation for *religion* and *spirituality* as traditions with enormous impact on the interpretation and meaning of life and death (McGoldrick, 1998; Walsh, 1999; Wright, Watson, & Bell, 1996). In rural and inner-city schools and neighborhoods, *faith communities* and *religious congregations* play crucial roles as sources of strength, comfort, and a sense of belonging.

Any program devoted to inner-city neighborhoods needs also to direct its focus to the individual student, specifically to his or her *age-appropriate maturity*, and *biological, psychological, social,* and *moral development*. A thorough and contextualized understanding of adolescence as a phase of individual and family life needs to be part of the perspective with which family therapy teams approach their work in inner-city high schools (Fishman, 1988; Liddle, 2000). The professional community is only at the beginning of the process of assessing how specific aspects of cultural background and childhood upbringing or life in a poverty-stricken and drug-contaminated neighborhood influence the experiences of teenagers.

Finally, close attention has to be paid to teenagers' and families' *medical* and *mental-health* and *health-care* conditions (Landau, Stanton, & Clements, 1993; Wright et al., 1996). *Alcoholism* and *drug abuse* or *drug addiction* pose factors that have particularly destructive consequences for high-school-students' lives (Kaufman & Kaufman, 1979; Krestan, 2000; Stanton & Todd, 1982; Steinglass, Bennett, Wolin, & Reiss, 1987).

Clinically and conceptually, beyond applying these seven perspectives to the daily experiences of teenagers and their families in urban and rural poverty areas lies the even greater challenge of using the kaleidoscope of the seven lenses as a multidimensional matrix (Kliman, 1994) to stimulate curiosity and understanding of their complex interplay. Recently, several authors (Boyd-Franklin, 1995; Carter & McGoldrick, 1999; Kleinman, 1980; Kliman, 1994; Moore Hines, 1988; Parnell & Vanderkloot, 1994) have addressed this multifaceted interaction (Wetzel, 1998a).

AN UNFAMILIAR WORLD

Living in the Inner City
Some U.S. inner-city neighborhoods at times resemble areas of poor developing countries. Surrounded by the ostentatious wealth resulting from the longest economic boom in U.S. economic history, children and teenagers in these areas do not live just in a context of poverty (Ambert, 1998). The environment outside their families is defined by deprivation and humiliation. Each glance at the TV and each foray into the well-to-do suburban neighborhoods reinforce in residents of poverty areas the notion that there is something wrong with them. They experience themselves as second-class citizens, marginalized, without the hopes of their more affluent contemporaries, invisible to the mainstream public (Ellison, 1947; A. J. Franklin, 1993), yet scrutinized by shopkeepers and "profiled" by the police. They are, from the outset, at a disadvantage in desegregated schools.

Families and teenagers from neglected inner-city neighborhoods hardly seem to count for the politicians, are of no concern to the executives of big corporations, and are hardly mentioned in the media (except when reporting crimes or fires) or in the broader public debates of the day. People from the surrounding society seem to have so much more at their disposal: material possessions, public respect, political influence, community services, and economic power. Young people from these areas learn that they have less power over their lives because of the neighborhoods they live in (with so many societal outcasts) or because of the color of their skins or their languages or all these factors together. Interactions with representatives of the dominant society (social-welfare offices, police, city and state bureaucracy, hospitals) often end in discouraging ways because even well-meaning gestures and initiatives for help carry with them the aura of condescension. Beyond the realm of their families and kinship networks, members of the local communities or teachers and other personnel from the inner-city high schools become the ones who show interest in them and convey to them a sense that they are worthy of support and assistance.

The Socioeconomic Perspective
People in many inner-city areas of the United States live in an environment of progressive poverty (Ambert, 1998; Imber-Black, 1990; Inclan & Ferran, 1990; Wilson, 1997). Once flourishing manufacturing enterprises have moved away or abroad in search of a cheaper labor force. Small businesses in the neighborhoods could not survive. Entire districts gradually ruined through neglect or destroyed by fire and looting during the ghetto revolts or urban revolutions of the 1960s are only now being rebuilt. Grocery stores, bank branch offices, neighborhood restaurants, churches, public transportation, hospitals, day-care centers, police stations, in short, the infrastructure of a traditional neighborhood ceased to exist in many small towns and inner-city areas. The drug trade, constant danger from gun violence, the AIDS epidemic, and the erosion of housing contributed further to the deterioration of the quality of life in the inner cities (Pravder Mirkin, 1990).

Many people in these areas work full-time, yet find it very difficult to rise above the poverty level despite long hours in low-paying jobs without health-insurance or other benefits (Ambert, 1998). Only recently have state governments established health-insurance programs for people with incomes below a certain level. Most people from impoverished areas do not have the necessary training for jobs in computer-related fields, even if the opportunity existed in inner-city areas. Through the initiatives of federal and state governments, new job opportunities were set up by granting economic incentives and tax relief for local businesses, yet these measures met only partly with success. Frequently, the necessary job-training and general-education programs were missing. The industries newly established in the neighborhoods did not add jobs for unskilled workers. And the tax relief for new companies, until recently, often prevented the financially strapped city governments from building the required infrastructure (i.e., connections to the public transit system, schools, local neighborhood centers, hospitals). Even the most recent initiatives to expand jobs for people on welfare often prove unworkable for single mothers who are unable to get to work without public transportation, cannot find access to daycare centers, cannot afford medical care for their children or themselves, and spend long hours each day to get to welfare offices, employment centers, or hospital emergency rooms.

Consequences for the Structure and Processes of Families
The consequences of the chronic scarcity of jobs in the inner cities prove worse than poverty itself: "The disappearance of work has adversely affected not only individuals, families, and neighborhoods, but the social life of the city at large as well. . . . The consequences of high neighborhood joblessness are more devastating than those of high neighborhood poverty" (Wilson, 1997, p. xiii). Socioeconomic data on joblessness, poverty, homelessness, and illness reflect the unraveling of the social fabric in the inner city (Wilson, 1997, 1999). These environmental factors constitute part of the daily experiences of young people in poor neighborhoods. Material deprivation, hunger, inadequate housing, and the absence of work alter the processes and structure of the families themselves and profoundly affect people's cognitive, emotional, and social functioning as well as physical health (Ambert, 1998; Aponte, 1994; Boyd-Franklin, 1995; D. L. Franklin, 1997; P. Minuchin, 1995). In this context, Madsen (1999) spoke of "multi-stressed families."

Strengths and Resources
Drug and alcohol abuse, physical and sexual violence, the high rate of teenage pregnancies, school dropout rates of up to one half of the students in the higher grades need to be understood in part as effects of the increasing marginalization, fragmentation, and demoralization of families in inner-city districts (Wilson, 1997). Families in these areas struggle to survive in a context of economic impoverishment, regularly experienced racial oppression, and often-witnessed institutional or personal violence. Without proper health care and adequate nutrition, they are more susceptible to physical illness. Parents, especially women who are single heads of households, have to overcome difficult hurdles daily to stay afloat economically.

Entering the world of poor families presents a challenge to therapists in multiple ways. In P. Minuchin's (1995) words, the "consideration of poor, multi-crisis families suggests that family therapists must move in a different direction: toward context, rather than toward the elaboration of internal family characteristics" (p. 124). Supposedly, in North American society, everybody has the chance to advance beyond poverty. Many therapists do not like to talk about poverty or admit to ignorance about the experience of a family living in poverty. Therapists are often not sure whether the perceived dynamics among family members are attributable to a misunderstanding of a family's ethnic culture (and racial oppression) and/or related to the family's socioeconomic class status (i.e., to an economically deprived, multi-stressed social context). Specific data about poverty in the United States and Canada and its impact on family life are very disturbing. Ambert (1998) and Wilson (1997) described the effects of poverty, in its various forms, on the structure and functioning of families, especially on children and adolescents.

However, with a context-oriented perspective and a lens focused on the culture of the poor, whatever their ethnic heritages may be, therapists can also discover strengths and resources in impoverished inner-city neighborhoods. Against the odds, many parents manage to effectively guide and support the emotional, intellectual, social, and cultural development of their children. An extensive network of personal relationships and local initiatives in the immediate neighborhood, often informally organized along ethnic or religious lines, support individual families (Boyd-Franklin, 1995; Falicov, 2000). Whoever is not blinded by traditional views of "typical" families (Coontz, 1992) will discover the manifold relational structures and networks that encompass even families who appear hopelessly fragmented and disoriented. With unbiased eyes and honest curiosity, therapists can detect personal contexts and relationship patterns that are vibrant. Traces of hitherto invisible renewal processes in the inner-city neighborhoods become obvious to those who have learned to see through the barriers that separate the various ethnically and socioeconomically defined groups. The recent inner-city rejuvenation initiatives by federal, state, and city authorities have been most successful where they support and continue already existing structures within the local communities (e.g., Schorr, 1997).

CULTURAL IDENTIFICATION AND
IMMIGRATION EXPERIENCE

Living in U.S. society inescapably leads to one's being identified with a particular ethnic group. Skin color, language, accent, gestures, eating habits, and many other subtle details render people easily identifiable as White (i.e., having a European heritage), African American (i.e., with ancestors from Africa, mainly brought in as slaves), Hispanic American (i.e., immigrated from a Spanish-speaking, mainly Latin American, country), Asian American (i.e., from the Far East), or Native American (i.e., descendant from original inhabitants of the North American continent).

People's experiences of their ethnic heritages and racial and cultural identities are vastly different for the various ethnic groups and subgroups. The same holds true for adolescents. Numerous authors have presented details about high-school-students' identifications with their ethnic heritages and cultures and the consequences and conflicts of their ethnic identities (see Boyd-Franklin, 1989; Falicov, 1983, 2000; Fowers & Richardson, 1996; McGoldrick et al., 1996; Pinderhughes, 1989, 1990; Pravder Mirkin, 1990). A number of particularly significant aspects of working with minority youth in the inner cities stand out.

Therapists' Culture-Determined Lenses
Psychotherapists working in the inner cities need to be aware of their own culturally determined lenses. We need to acknowledge that we view adolescents and their family members differently according to their different ethnic backgrounds and the different ways of experiencing race and culture as such, and whether they share our racial identities. The ways we understand and conceptualize the issues with which we are confronted in working with a particular teenager or interpret a particular family structure and process are deeply influenced by the values, ethos, practices, customs, and rules prevalent in the ethnic communities that formed our own identities and value systems.

Ethnic groups in our society are not created equal. Members of one subgroup of the dominant European American culture may experience culture or race as a dimension out of awareness until they encounter people of different ethnic backgrounds; that is, culture becomes an issue only through the encounter with people of different ethnic or racial heritages. Conversely, people who belong to one of the African American, Hispanic American, Asian American, or Native American minority populations know that their experiences of color and ethnicity are from the start inseparably part of the experiences of their own humanity. They are reminded daily that they live in a world and a society to which they have contributed, but that all too often has imposed on them its values, lifestyles, traditions, expectations, concept of spirituality, and order. Those who are not of the dominant culture are treated as strangers and outsiders; they carry with them a long history of oppression and racial injustice.

An encounter between therapist and adolescent is also significantly influenced by whether the counselor and the teenager share the same ethnic background. Therapists repeatedly experience mistrust, reservations, relational awkwardness, and closure when they are White and the student and family are Black. Equally, if a Latina counselor is part of the team, the likelihood of Hispanic students congregating in her office is significantly higher than if she is Black or White.

History of Immigration
In general, knowledge about the culture and ethnic background of high-school students and their families proves indispensable for therapists who work with them. Being curious and willing to learn is also crucial in regard to the history of immigration of the ethnic group to which a youngster belongs. Otherwise, easy generalizations can creep into our thinking. Therapists can understand a particular ethnic group only through learning about its history. African American, Hispanic American, and Asian American are general labels that do not describe the subcultures nor reflect the unique history and wanderings of the particular group of people who are the ancestors of our clients. Therapists need to respect and learn the collective memory of each racial group and to understand how it relates to the present-day experience of teenagers. This is particularly true regarding the history of oppression, torture, and murder the ancestors of most African Americans experienced during the slave trade, the ensuing centuries of slavery, and subsequent racial oppression in this country (D. L. Franklin, 1997; Pinderhughes, 1990). Similarly, most Hispanic American teenagers carry with them the collective memories of centuries of imperialist oppression and exploitation of their peoples and countries by the United States (Galeano, 1973). Being curious about the immigration histories and the collective memories of these teenagers frequently represents not only a way of honoring the sufferings of their ancestors and an act of commemorative justice (Wetzel, 1994b), but also an indispensable step toward a successful engagement with a teenager and his or her family.

Current Immigration Status
Part of being eager to learn about teenagers' and their families' constructions of their specific ethnic identities also entails exploring their current immigration status and recent histories. For example, the influx of computer specialists from countries in Europe and Asia represents a new kind of very mobile, well-adapted group of immigrants who are equally at home in many Western countries and symbolize the globalization of the labor market. The difference from earlier immigrant groups helps us not to overlook the recent immigration experiences of adolescents' families from other countries, especially from Latin America and Africa.

Many high school students in the inner cities come from families who have been separated and disrupted by the attempts to immigrate to the United States to find a better life. They often are here illegally. Sometimes, only the children are U.S. citizens, and the parents have to avoid contact with the authorities; consequently, they lack even the rudimentary services that would be available to them if their immigration status were legal. The parents' attitudes toward school personnel understandably may involve suspicion and reluctance to come to family meetings. Often, only a professional who shares the same ethnic background will be able to overcome these barriers.

People who have recently immigrated from an African country, for instance, experience the racism in our society differently compared to their African American counterparts. They may not have a history of slavery; instead, they may have grown up in a country with a long history of German, Portuguese, French, or Anglo-Saxon colonialism, which may constitute a significant difference from the centuries of slavery that define the history of African Americans.

Issues of Acculturation
Highlighting cultural experience is also important because many of the students' families present the additional issue of acculturation. Conflicts arise between the more traditional values, customs, lifestyles, and language of the parents' generation and the tendency of the young people to assimilate into the dominant U.S. culture and civilization. Each family has to work through this conflict in their own way. The desire of the young people to be accepted by their peer group, to be able to function in the school and work environment, and to be of help to their parents can often lead to a reduction of parental authority and ability to be appropriately in charge of their teenagers' lives. The adolescents often end up as the de facto leaders of their families, negotiating most outside contact and making decisions that generally would be considered beyond their competencies. This happens frequently in families in which the parents or grandparents (who often become the guardians when the parents are in jail or have died of AIDS or still live in the family's country of origin) have only limited command of the English language or are not able to read.

GENDER ROLES

Working with young people requires particular sensitivity to and knowledge about the gender roles transmitted to children and youth together with their cultural and ethnic heritages and their socioeconomic status. Manifold cross-fertilizations and confluences exist among socioeconomic class, cultural traditions, racial identification, and gender-role constructs, especially in the minds of young people (Comas-Diaz & Greene, 1994; McGoldrick, 1998).

For example, it is quite instructive for an outside observer to learn how often Black men are exposed to daily humiliations, mistrust, and small-scale aggression (Boyd-Franklin, Franklin, & Toussaint, 2000) by members of the White dominant culture. Fellow classmates sometimes give minority students from inner-city areas a hard time when they do outstanding work in school, as if people who belong to the impoverished class and to racial or ethnic minorities are not entitled to academic excellence, or are breaking loyalty bonds to their group if they flourish in their work. Poor young women from ethnic communities may become pregnant partly as a way to gain status in their communities, but also to give their lives a center of meaning otherwise unattainable for them. Many single mothers (and grandmothers) cooperate with others in the same position, gaining strength from supporting each other.

SCHOOLS IN THE INNER CITY

Transformation of Schools
Reconnecting with the very beginnings of family therapy, advocates of a renewed concern for discouraged and abandoned youth in the inner cities broke open the narrowly defined boundaries of systems therapy (Wetzel, 1994a, 1994b). A new paradigm evolved that proved particularly useful for families of lower socioeconomic status: *school-based community-oriented family therapy* (Boyd-Franklin & Bry, 2000; Winawer & Wetzel, 1999).

With the emphasis on an ecosystemic or context-oriented perspective in work with teenagers and their families from poor areas, the immediate neighborhoods of families unavoidably came into view. Family counselors could not disregard the larger human and physical environments in which adolescents grew up. The assumption that a family lives in a vacuum and that a therapist needs to focus only on intrafamilial dynamics manifested itself as an illusion in working with youngsters from poor urban or rural areas. How is the life of a grandmother attempting every day to raise her grandchildren because the children's parents died from AIDS or drug abuse comprehensible without consideration of the various environmental factors that bear on the daily life or tragic history of her family? How can a professional support a 17-year-old who saw her parents killed in a homicide/suicide, her brother later murdered in a drug deal gone sour, her only remaining brother imprisoned, so that she now lives with her 72-year-old grandfather who is grieving the recent loss of his wife of 50 years? How different is her "depression" from that of a 17-year-old who feels lonely, isolated, and discouraged while living in the context of a well-to-do family where the parents are too busy working and leave caring for her younger siblings up to her? Working with youth from the inner cities and their families forces the walls of the interview room to open up. Socioeconomic, cultural, and all other factors relevant to the immediate neighborhood become transparent because they deeply influence the dynamics of the families seen in these districts.

As soon as the perspective transcends the youths and their families, considering the schools becomes imperative. This is hardly surprising. Schools and small religious communities with roots in the surrounding district are often the sole institutional survivors of the gradual decline of the inner cities during the past 30 years. The mission of a high school located in a poor area, therefore, has to be much broader than its original educational goals. Psychotherapeutic work in poor areas inevitably has to proceed in tandem with a fundamental transformation and reorientation of the identity of a school in these districts.

Schools as Locales for Education and Therapy
For many young people from close-knit ethnic neighborhoods in the inner cities, schools seem to be the only geographically accessible institutions familiar to them (aside from places of worship) that they may not experience as hostile. Some teenagers view school as a place to learn and to prepare academically for college; others value that they can meet their friends in an environment not yet poisoned by the mercantile and criminal aspects of the drug culture; many attend school because there they can meet teachers, social workers, coaches, or other adults who will support them and make a commitment to them. For all of them, high school represents a context that suggests the hope of eventually escaping a context in which they feel powerless and disheartened.

New Tasks for High Schools in Poor Inner-City Districts
Given poverty, scarcity of jobs, drug trafficking, and racial discrimination in inner cities, it is easy to understand how the schools would end up with many roles and tasks not normally associated with the function of a high school in the United States. This development results not from careful planning. Quite the opposite: Initially, city and state administrative or human-service and health departments reacted pragmatically to what they perceived as specific needs not met by other institutions. Insufficient or unavailable medical care, lack of affordable health insurance, and higher susceptibility to illness among the student population prompted the establishment or expansion of health centers located in schools. Nurse practitioners and physicians keep regular practice hours, especially for high-school students, many of whom have not had a physical checkup for many years. The high number of pregnant students forced the establishment of day-care centers in some school buildings. Infant care became a required course for all young mothers; the infants were taken care of while their mothers attended regular school classes.

Pregnancy counseling, prenatal medical care, sexual and birth-control information belong to the normal duties of the medical personnel. In some settings, even dentists and ophthalmologists are regularly available.

For many older students from the inner city, contributing to their own and their family's earnings by working in the afternoons or evenings is an economic necessity. Consequently, employment offices were organized in which students not only receive help finding suitable jobs, but also learn proper behavior at job sites, appropriate attire, and the right language fit for doing business with adults. Through their job-related training and empowerment, these students received needed support to succeed in a fast-paced and technology-driven work environment.

Naturally, the schools had to find counselors (beyond the staff of the guidance departments and the child-study teams) who could assist students in personal or school-related crisis situations. Drugs are present everywhere, near school property or in the vicinity, and are readily available to everybody; accordingly, the number of violent incidents among students increased. Thus, counseling offices had to be made available to deal with drug-related or other crises. Many school administrators formed crisis teams made up of counselors, teachers, medical personnel, and other experts to have a rapid-response group available for quick intervention in cases of sudden violence from outside the school or between hostile groups in the school itself (e.g., rival drug-dealing gangs or hostilities motivated by ethnic antagonisms).

Integration of Services and Institutions
The need for integration of all these services and the various institutional responses to the needs of students in poor districts could no longer be overlooked. Without organizational and administrative integration, the danger of chaotic disarray of assistance, of unnecessary duplication of efforts, and, at times, of unwitting obstruction and confusion would only increase. To coordinate the well-intentioned, but disjointed, services, an attempt had to be made to envision a conceptual framework that would unify the approach and goals of student assistance. On the part of the school, as an educational institution faced with a steady accumulation of roles, the need for conceptual clarification and deepening of the understanding of its function in the inner city became evident, lest the integration of student assistance into the school remain superficial and tenuous.

MODEL: SCHOOL-BASED COMMUNITY-ORIENTED FAMILY THERAPY

The New Jersey FIEP represents an attempt to practice and implement the conceptual vision for youth and family services articulated previously. The theoretical and educational sides of the endeavor toward integration and the clarification of the educational vision of schools in poor districts remain to be defined.

The FIEP Teams and Their Administrative Contexts

During 1992 and 1993, a group of systemic family therapists (notably, Charles Fishman) and representatives of the New Jersey Departments of Health and Senior Services (T. O'Connor) and Human Services (R. Knowlton) developed and financed a school-based family intervention model for the treatment of youth at risk for drug abuse, school dropout, and other behavioral problems (originally called the New Jersey Family Intervention Program). Other states have adopted similar models of counseling for inner-city youth at risk. The FIEP model evolved further to include not only school and family contexts, but also the community. In addition to the original four counties, the FIEP model has recently been implemented in a fifth district thanks to financing through a grant from the federal Substance Abuse and Mental Health Services Administration. Despite local varieties in the functioning of the teams at the five schools, the FIEP model is operating from a similar conceptual and practical framework.

In each of the high schools, located in particularly difficult inner-city areas, the FIEP teams are administratively integrated into the School-Based Youth Services Program, which provides medical, social, and crisis counseling, usually sharing the same offices within the school building. The ecosystemic orientation of the teams and the practice of bringing all available family members into the counseling process stimulated a transformation process that, to varying degrees, led to the adoption of a more contextual view by other youth service personnel. In some settings, the shift from an individual to a family-systems perspective, even for the FIEP teams, necessitated adjustment, education, and a collaborative process in a host setting that is traditionally child-oriented.

The FIEP teams are composed of a family therapist, usually a master's-level social worker, and a community resource specialist, whose main qualification is intimate knowledge of the community from which the students come. The mission of each team encompasses the counseling and empowerment of the adolescents at risk who come to the FIEP offices. Part of the ongoing case management involves the strong effort to involve all available family members and everyone else who is part of the "intimate relational network" of a student (Wetzel, 1998a). The supervision of the teams, guided by an ecosystemic orientation, the conceptual model of the project, the annual collection and analysis of the data, and the overall guidance of the FIEP model, is in the hands of consultants from the Princeton Family Institute. Administratively, the teams are accountable to local site managers from the New Jersey School Based Youth Services program (i.e., the teams have to be part of the local administrative structure). FIEP teams do not automatically adopt views of the dominant-culture mental-health and human-services systems. In many service-delivery systems, "acceptable" client behaviors are often defined without regard to the dystonic relationship between the family's culture and style and that of the service-delivery system. The family's informal connection that continued after "treatment" and their positive experience potentially leaves a clear path for work in the future, and, most important, respects the clients' agency and competence, not only in the ending, but, by implication, in the entire therapeutic endeavor.

CONTEXTS FOR THERAPEUTIC WORK

The School Context
The gradual integration of the FIEP teams into the general school-based youth services and into the school as an institution implies the goal of an integrated school context in which the learning process includes students' acquisition of academic/curricular knowledge, their gradual mastery of social-relational dynamics, the gaining of work-related skills, and their emotional-cultural maturation. The initial steps toward these goals are pragmatic. All school-based youth services staff become one collaborative group, encompassing medical, crisis-counseling, recreational, youth-employment, and family-empowerment teams. The ecosystemic orientation of the FIEP teams helps the transformation of this group toward seeing adolescents in their most relevant context and tailoring the interactions accordingly.

Then it becomes important to intensify the collaboration between the school-based youth services and the school's administration and teachers. The boundaries between traditionally defined school roles (i.e., instruction, additional learning assistance, homework help and supervision, academic guidance) and the various youth services (i.e., medical care and prevention, social work, psychological counseling, after-school recreational activities) gradually became more and more permeable. Teachers and school administration collaborate with youth services to remove obstacles to learning in its many forms. At the same time, social workers, medical staff, and counselors are more available and able during regular school times to work with students individually or in groups because their responsibilities are no longer viewed as in competition with the learning that takes place in the classrooms. Unconstrained by school regulations, students are able to meet others during lunch hour and can address age-related problems within a group of peers in which a counselor is a resource person whenever the input of an adult is desired. With the use of questionnaires, team members attempt to understand the learning contexts and the emotional experiences of the students to deal with both. In crisis situations (group conflicts, suicide, panic), teachers and counselors are able to rely on already established and practiced communication channels.

Through patient practice steps, the relational and systemic orientation of the FIEP team exerts a transformative influence. School administration, teachers, and the staff of the preexisting youth services began to see the context-oriented FIEP teams as allies who assist them to join together disparate parts of the life context of the students in these districts (e.g., absent fathers, repressed memories of early injuries, lost siblings, neighbors who deal with drugs and others who can help).

The Family Context
With the employment of teams consisting of a context-oriented family therapist and a specialist rooted in the community, the FIEP model is founded on the critically important assumption that an individually centered perspective is hardly sufficient and rarely successful in counseling students who are at risk in so many ways. In a planful, step-by-step process, family members of students are actively drawn into the therapeutic dynamic after the students contact the team or are referred by school authorities, teachers, guidance counselors, or parents. Team members make phone calls, do home visits, visit family members in hospitals or prisons, and, in short, attempt everything that seems necessary to get all the relevant adults in the life of the students to participate in the counseling from the start. This is particularly important in cases of truancy, risk of drug abuse or drug addiction, and physical or sexual violence.

The central role of family members, especially the legal guardians, is immediately evident when a job has to be found for an adolescent, when other social agencies or the family court are involved, or when parents or grandparents are overwhelmed with the care of a teenager. Frequently, counseling happens at a youth's home. The fragmentation of family units in poor inner-city areas carries with it the consequence that many mothers or grandmothers raise their children or grandchildren alone and are unable to leave their homes at night (Wilson, 1997). Therapy at home enables everybody to participate in the counseling process: parents, partners of single mothers, and older relatives or neighbors who like to help out and support a youngster (Lindblad-Goldberg et al., 1998).

The Personal Relational Network: "Virtual Families"
The context-oriented perspective in the counseling process prompted team members to pay attention to the boundaries of the inner-city families (Aponte, 1994). Multistressed families (Madsen, 1999) do not show the same neat boundaries observed in families from other socioeconomic classes. In addition, the rigidity or porosity of boundaries varies according to family idiosyncrasies often linked to ethnic and cultural heritage (McGoldrick et al., 1996). The FIEP families' boundaries are frequently more permeable (i.e., vulnerable to outside destructive

factors) but also more able to incorporate and accept people who can contribute to stability and provide resources. While focusing on a student, counselors search the horizon for others who belong to the web of personal relationships of the student or his or her family and could be attracted to become a support in the process of "family" counseling.

FIEP guidelines emphasize making connections rather than isolating, including someone rather than separating people. In a typical "family" session, a rather disparate group of people, only some of whom are biologically related, may meet. One dynamic, the willingness to support an adolescent and to contribute to his or her success at school, connects everyone present. In some situations, the goal may be simply to help the youth complete school or to at least prevent entry into the juvenile-justice system, which, for most youths, presents almost unsurmountable obstacles for a respectable life.

A crucial task of the relationship-oriented family counselor revolves around building a group around a teenager, with everybody's agreement, that meets with the counselor until the group is strong enough to carry on their task without professional assistance. Part of the skills-repertoire of a family empowerment team, therefore, entails being able to deal with the complex relational problems and boundary issues resulting from an often unpredictable pattern of individual sessions, sessions with the teenager and the most important family members, and meetings with the entire larger relational network.

The Community Context
Consideration of community contexts leads to the next step beyond a traditional understanding of school and therapy. Active interest in the immediate neighborhood where students live and in the entire economically depressed inner-city area forms an integral part of the FIEP model (Winawer & Wetzel, 1999). The FIEP Community Resource Specialists, now middle-class professionals themselves, often come from economic backgrounds similar to the conditions prevalent in the neighborhoods. Their ethnic backgrounds and heritages usually match one of the major groups in the community. Thus, they are not strangers to the life circumstances of the students and, significantly, are well-respected in the neighborhoods. The teams receive weekly supervision and attend monthly family-therapy training sessions conducted by the authors.

Augmenting school-based teaching and family counseling with the school's and the team's active integration into the surrounding community constitutes a crucial innovation in the FIEP model. Community resource specialists incorporate and represent the commitment to this view. As part of the team, they may participate in a family session (especially during home visits); find afterschool jobs for students and train them for interaction with employers or customers; organize assistance for families who lack basic necessities of life, such as food, housing, electricity, heat, and health care; or use contacts with police or other public authorities to intervene before a student's anger or drug use causes irreparable harm.

School-based counseling and support, reintegration and renewed participation of the student in the process of learning, and conversations with the family or "virtual family" converge in a process of empowerment that generates innovative impulses to transform the environments from which the students come every day to school and to which they return. In one school, family members who had regained power over their own lives through the family meetings and who participated in retreats organized jointly by FIEP teams from several cities have begun to organize on their own and learned to address successfully some issues with their school board that were of concern for them. Thus, the three contexts—family, school, and community—overlap while remaining centered on the person of the adolescent at school.

CASE EXAMPLE

The first interview with the entire Dawson family felt tense. "Teresa Dawson," an African American Christian woman, and her four daughters sat silently with the FIEP team. The family and the team had greeted each other, and the team had acknowledged that the family members all managed to attend the meeting. A long silent pause ensued.

Teresa began, saying that the family had never been to any counseling before. Her 23-year-old daughter, "Stacey," addressed Teresa, charging her mother that she "never did anything about anything." There was an edge of rage in the daughter's voice, and the mother took up the challenge. The next few sharp, quick exchanges the FIEP team, the family therapist (FT), and the community resource specialist (CRS) could not remember verbatim. The words, however, were incendiary. Within moments, there was a physical fight between Stacey and her mother. The FIEP team, an African American middle-class Christian woman (the CRS) and an Irish/English American woman of working-class Catholic background (the FT), were eventually able to calm the fight. They used the moment to engage mother and daughter around the common ground of strong feelings about the family's situation.

The family had come into therapy because "LaToya," the youngest, 16-year-old daughter, had been referred to the FIEP team for poor school attendance, failing grades, signs of depression, and suspected abuse of marijuana. The oldest daughter, Stacey, was living in another household with her two young children, but kept a close connection with the rest of the family. Teresa's parents were deceased. Her only brother had died of AIDS. Only "Shiniqua" and "Latisha," the second and third daughters, had any knowledge of the whereabouts of their father, but had little contact with him. There was some kinship network, aunts that were not blood relatives with whom Teresa had lost contact in recent years. Stacey kept in touch with those women periodically.

The CRS had met with LaToya several times while she and the family therapist made numerous phone calls and home visits in an attempt to engage the entire family. Teresa said that she was concerned about her daughter, but was unable to set up a time when the team could visit with her and all family members. LaToya did not keep her assigned appointments, but appeared almost daily unannounced at the FIEP office. A bright and articulate teenager, she talked about school issues, but, when her feelings or home situation were addressed, she generally fell silent. During one of these meetings, Stacey, who had not been mentioned, emerged in the conversation as someone who had frequent contact with the family. With Teresa's permission and LaToya's knowledge, Stacey was called. That same week, the entire family met finally in the FIEP office, located in the high school of an economically depressed city in central New Jersey.

During the family interview, it was revealed that Teresa had been using crack cocaine with her boyfriend, who, unbeknownst to Teresa, had been molesting LaToya. Stacey launched a seething indictment of her mother, primarily to protect her younger sister. Under the protective rage she revealed years of hurt and vulnerability because she, too, had been abused by Shiniqua and Latisha's father. Stacey had been in and out of depression with frequent suicidal ideation. In fact, each of the girls had been either beaten or sexually abused by one of mother's partners. In fact, Teresa herself was being "shoved around" by her current partner.

Teresa at first denied her daughter's allegations, but Stacey used the therapy sessions as an opportunity to confront her mother. The FIEP team supported all family members in their first attempts to face their pain as a family. The team thought it remarkable that the family returned for subsequent visits given the difficult content of the sessions.

The FIEP team worked to keep the conversation open between the mother and her daughters, to enlist the mother's leadership in her family, and to help all work together to heal the interpersonal and individual wounds of the many years of abuse. The primary goal all agreed on was to help LaToya perform better in school. Although the family did not stay in formal therapy beyond 10 meetings, there were a number of changes. After therapy ended, LaToya dropped into the office now and then to give the FIEP team an update about her family, and there were occasional exchanges of phone calls between the FIEP team and family members.

The therapeutic objectives were supported by a number of efforts in the school and community. When it was clear that the family's spirituality was an untapped resource in their lives, the minister of their church was invited to a session and subsequently followed up with outreach efforts to reengage the family in the life of the church. Furthermore, the CRS, herself a spiritual person, would often assist at family therapy sessions and end those meetings by joining the family in a brief prayer.

The meetings continued for a while. Teresa was helped to find a detoxification program. The most striking event occurred when she was able to ask her partner to leave the home. The family reported that Teresa had never before ended a relationship; her partners generally drifted away. This time, Teresa's partner did go when she was clear about her position. This bold act seemed to set off a ripple effect. Stacey, who had been living away in rather stark circumstances, admitted that she had been staying away out of anger. She and her children moved back into Teresa's large apartment. Concurrent with family sessions, Stacey was assisted in securing individual psychotherapy to deal with her long-term depression. LaToya joined a homework help program in the school; her attendance and school performance improved. Teresa did not want to meet with LaToya's teachers, but did consent to the team's contact with the teachers to work out plans to help LaToya pass her subjects, which she did. LaToya's use of gateway drugs had been minimal and stopped during the course of the school year.

The involvement of Teresa and her children with FIEP is not atypical of many of the families who use the program. They did not resolve all of their problems, but made strides in areas of individual and family functioning that had been associated with an adolescent's difficulties. The adolescent improved significantly in the areas of behavioral difficulty for which she was initially referred.

From a supervisory perspective, it may be useful to examine some of the critical aspects of the team's work with the Dawson family (Winawer-Steiner, 1979). In ongoing supervisory conversations with the FIEP team who worked with Teresa and her daughters, it was clear that the team was somewhat shaken by the intensity of their first encounter with the entire family. However, they were not daunted or blinded to the resources within this multi-stressed family (Madsen, 1999). The team recognized a number of family strengths from the outset. Against many odds, the family had attended a session together. They had shown their conflicts to strangers and did not abort the session when tensions surfaced. The team was able to identify these behaviors as a probable indication of the family's investment in their relationships and in the unit as a whole. Their ability to face conflicts was seen as a sign of their courage and ability to endure emotionality. As part of their assessment, the team was able to discern both the family's common "cultural borderlands" (Falicov, 2000) with the team and the degree of social alienation experienced by the family. In many respects, the supervisor-team relationship was isomorphic to the team-client relationship. The team's expertise about their setting, cultural perspective, and firsthand experience with the family were privileged. Their interactions with each other, the supervisor, and multiple systems levels evolved through a synergy of multiple idiosyncratic factors, which gave the work its own unique imprimatur.

The cultural lenses came into focus at different phases of the work with the family and, at times, several overlapped. Socioeconomic factors (Teresa was on welfare), issues of gender and sexuality, religion and spirituality, ethnic culture, biopsychosocial development, and health issues (substance abuse) interfaced in the life of the family and in the efforts to establish a therapeutic alliance to develop conversations to help the Dawsons identify inner, interpersonal, and community resources that would clear pathways out of their despair and sense of victimization.

The social isolation, in large part associated with the mother's drug use and her reliance on public services, was a potential barrier to engagement. The team, however, was fully cognizant of the family's recurrent disappointments and fears in their encounters with other helping professionals, whom they had experienced as either ineffectual or disrespectful. The team realized that it was highly unlikely that the Dawson family would trust FIEP professionals (Ackerman, Colapinto, Scharf, Weinshel, & Winawer, 1991). In supervisory conversations, the family's suspicions were recognized as an adaptive mechanism designed to protect the family from the pseudo-kindness of strangers.

The shared "cultural borderlands" (Falicov, 2000) that did facilitate a therapeutic connection were a similar class background with one of the FIEP team members and similarities of ethnic culture with the other team member (the CRS). Recognition of the family's suppressed spiritual life as a resource provided a powerful factor in the ongoing development of the therapeutic relationship and the work. Moreover, all central figures in the family, and the pastor as well, were women. The subtext of the conversation from the start was that the sorting out of the dilemmas of this family was clearly women's work.

The team heard from Teresa that she had renewed contact with members of her personal network. Shiniqua and Latisha had talked about contacting their father's family, but had not made any concrete plans to do so; Shiniqua was rather reluctant to do so. At last contact, Teresa was in early recovery, attending Narcotics Anonymous meetings and focusing primarily on her recovery. LaToya was on a good track, too, moving toward graduation and, in her mother's words, "keeping out of trouble."

The Dawson family's work with the FIEP team supported the family's primary objective: to improve LaToya's school performance. From a positivist perspective, one could certainly identify numerous areas of difficulty that warranted further clinical attention. Whether the FIEP team should pursue the family beyond recommendations could be controversial. However, just as the steps to engage the family respected their careful path to admitting outsiders, so did the end of therapy reflect the family's knowledge about its own processes with regard to how much outside help they want or think they can benefit from and for how long. The FIEP team's response to the family's ending of the formal relationship with the program was viewed through the complexity of the kaleidoscope of the seven lenses and informed by a postmodern stance that privileges a family's expertise.

Three contexts emerged as most relevant for adolescents in the poor inner-city areas depicted earlier: school, family, and community. The model revolves around the adolescents in these contexts, viewing them through the kaleidoscope of the seven lenses.

OUTCOME RESEARCH

The feedback that the FIEP teams have received from students, families, school personnel, and community leaders is very encouraging. Initial outcome studies confirm that the school-based and community-oriented approach of FIEP contributes significantly to the transformation of students, families, and schools that are connected with it (H. C. Fishman, F. Andes, & R. Knowlton, 2001; Wetzel, 1998b).

The most recent evaluations, for the school year 1999–2000, are based on pre- and postintervention questionnaires of 223 students. The average age of the students was 15.45 years; the majority of the students were between 14 and 17 years old. In gender distribution, 63% of the students were female, 37% were male. In cultural distribution, 42% of students were African Americans, 33% were Hispanics, and 18% Caucasian. In economic distribution, 1% of the students' families were homeless, 12% were on public assistance, and 24% of the students belonged to a one-parent household below the official poverty level. Less than half (46%) of the students lived in households with two employed parents, and 12% came from middle-class families. In 64% of the families, the fathers were absent from the household.

The primary presenting problem for almost all students involved immediate risk for substance abuse or active use of illegal substances. Of those considered actively using drugs, 63% showed marked improvement through their involvement with the FIEP, and 34% reported no change. The secondary problems included violence or depression (28%), poor grades in school (18%), nonviolent behavioral problems at home (17%) or at school (15%), truancy (13%), and sexual acting out (4%). Taken as a separate issue, 28% of the students reported experiences of physical or sexual violence in the past or present. For 69.72% of the students involved in FIEP, these problems improved, whereas for 17.43%, there was no change, and for 12.84% the situation reportedly worsened.

Other programs that are similar in philosophy and practice to the New Jersey FIEP have done more extensive outcome research. Foremost among these groups is the Center for Treatment Research on Adolescent Drug Abuse at the University of Miami School of Medicine (www.miami.edu/ctrada). (Liddle and his colleagues [Liddle, Henderson, Rowe, & Dakof, 2001] presented an extensive report on this program with a comprehensive literature review during the American Family Therapy Academy's 23rd annual meeting on June 28, 2001.)

SUMMARY

Not all stories that we hear from the FIEP teams end well. Even the combined collaborative efforts of the FIEP teams can hardly diminish the destructive forces of the psychosocial and economic factors that bear on the lives of the adolescents and their families in impoverished areas. But the mood of many young people in the inner-city school systems improved after they became involved with FIEP. A higher percentage of students seem to graduate from high school and to disappear from the drug rosters of the police. Frequently, older students begin to get interested in the lives of their peers from lower grades and start to support younger students. Adults and young people speak differently to each other after participating in the meetings of the extended family relational network. In at least one inner-city high school, the adults decided to continue to meet in small groups with other families after the end of the active family-counseling phase and to organize and fight for practical changes within their housing area.

Hope and encouragement appear to have a lot to do with efforts to weave together the three contexts of school, family, and community. Thanks to initiatives by team members and to the creativity of the families, even small changes on the level of a school or within a family system work as catalysts in other contexts. So the process of transformation continues. Systemic changes that prove to be beneficial on one level (e.g., family or school) seem contagious; they tend to be transferred to other levels of systemic organization (e.g., from a family to school and community). Mothers and fathers realize that, in their interactions with the school or in the life of the community around them at home, they can apply what they learned during sessions with their teenagers and with an extended relational network.

FIEP implies the possibility of a transformative process with a ripple effect on many levels of systemic organization. At some FIEP program sites, the context-oriented and relational view of the teams has prompted, on occasion, other social-welfare agencies, even other institutions, such as the police, members of the justice system and the city bureaucracy, and child-protection agencies, to lean toward a similar ecological view, particularly those who previously had participated in meetings with FIEP teams and families. The FIEP model is viewed positively as adding new skills and new opportunities for success to the work these agencies and institutions are trying to do.

Above all, however, the transformation of those directly connected with the FIEP model is noteworthy. The teams, consultants, site administrators, involved administrators; all became encouraged and empowered themselves. Many team members have roots in groups that are ethnically and socioeconomically similar to the people they work with in these inner-city schools. The teams' work, therefore, gave them hope for the people they were familiar with.

The transformation process was particularly visible in the way team members treated each other and dealt with the difficult challenges that surfaced in their work. In regular monthly training workshops attended by all teams from the various program sites, the consequences of transcending the boundaries of traditional psychotherapy needed to be dealt with. In some cases the point had to be delineated where counseling had to respect its own limitations to be effective and where exactly the work of empowering and organizing, in the political sense of the word, would have to start (Wetzel, 1994b). These choices are not easy to make considering the deprivations, obstacles, and lack of opportunities characterizing the lives of high-school students in inner-city regions.

The deep cultural, ethnic, and socioeconomic differences and conflicts present in U.S. society in general surfaced also in the process of developing the model. The members of the diverse FIEP group of family therapists, community resource specialists, site managers, and consultants addressed these issues openly and did not squelch them. Open, sometimes difficult, conversations about race, gender, spirituality, and the challenges of the work have transformed the FIEP staff into a community. This necessitated looking at personal, hard-to-discern racist mind-sets after some team members raised awareness of these attitudes that permeate every discourse. Gender issues were intricately mixed with racist biases and stereotypes. Diversity in religious beliefs and practices prompted questions about how to build a therapist's faith into counseling sessions and deepened respect for the strengths in these beliefs and for the religious communities that are such important resources in the FIEP work.

The transformation triggered by the FIEP also encompasses the ways team members and administrators interact with each other. As a professional group committed to a school-family-community paradigm and to the hope for a chance in life for the youth served, conversations have focused not only on the clinical complexity of the work, but also on the U.S. society and on the relationship between each in that societal context. It is our hope that the process of transformation, as we could observe it within ourselves and on the various levels of FIEP, will extend into the future and empower the youth and their families and networks. When economic prosperity extends to the poorest sectors of our society, the efforts of FIEP will have an even greater chance of contributing to the evolution of a level playing field for underprivileged rural and urban youth.

REFERENCES

Ackerman, F., Colapinto, J., Scharf, C., Weinshel, M., & Winawer, H. (1991). The reluctant client: Avoiding pretend therapy. *Family Systems Medicine, 9,* 261–266.

Alexander, J. F., Pugh, C., & Parsons, B. V. (with Barton, C.). (1998). Functional family therapy. In D. S. Elliott (Series Ed.), *Blueprints for violence prevention* [Book 3]. Boulder: University of Colorado, Institute of Behavioral Science, Center for the Study and Prevention of Violence.

Ambert, A. M. (1998). *The web of poverty: Psychosocial perspectives.* New York: Haworth Press.

American Psychiatric Association. (2000). *Diagnostic and statistical manual of mental disorders* (4th ed., text rev.). Washington, DC: Author.

Aponte, H. J. (1994). *Bread and spirit: Therapy with the new poor. Diversity of race, culture, and values.* New York: Norton.

Auerswald, E. H. (1968). Interdisciplinary vs. ecological approach. *Family Process, 7,* 202–215.

Auerswald, E. H. (1983). The Gouverneur Health Services Program: An experiment in ecosystemic community health care delivery. *Family Systems Medicine, 1*(3), 5–24.

Auerswald, E. H. (1987). Epistemological confusion in family therapy and research. *Family Process, 26,* 1–12.

Auerswald, E. H. (1990). Toward epistemological transformation in the education and training of family therapists. In M. Pravder Mirkin (Ed.), *The social and political contexts of family therapy* (pp. 19–50). Needham Heights, MA: Allyn & Bacon.

Bateson, G. (1971). *Steps to an ecology of mind.* New York: Ballantine Books.

Bateson, G. (1979). *Mind and nature.* New York: Dutton.

Boyd-Franklin, N. (1989). *Black families in therapy: A multisystems approach.* New York: Guilford Press.

Boyd-Franklin, N. (1995). Therapy with African American inner-city families. In R. Mikesell, D. D. Lusterman, & S. H. McDaniel (Eds.), *Integrating family therapy: Handbook of family psychology and systems theory* (pp. 357–371). Washington, DC: American Psychological Association.

Boyd-Franklin, N., & Bry, B. H. (2000). *Reaching out in family therapy: Home-based, school, and community interventions.* New York: Guilford Press.

Boyd-Franklin, N., Franklin, A. J., & Toussaint, P. (2000). *Boys to men: Raising our African American teenage sons.* New York: Dutton.

Breggin, P. R. (1999). *Reclaiming our children: A healing plan for a nation in crisis.* Cambridge, MA: Perseus Books.

Broderick, C. B., & Schrader, S. (1991). The history of professional marriage and family therapy. In A. S. Gurman & D. P. Kniskern (Eds.), *Handbook of family therapy* (Vol. 2, pp. 3–40). New York: Brunner/Mazel.

Brown, D., & Parnell, M. (1990). Mental health services for the urban poor: A systems approach. In M. Pravder Mirkin (Ed.), *The social and political contexts of family therapy* (pp. 215–235). Needham Heights, MA: Allyn & Bacon.

Capra, F. (1984). *The Tao of physics: An exploration of the parallels between modern physics and Eastern mysticism* (2nd ed.). New York: Bantam Books.

Carter, B., & McGoldrick, M. (Eds.). (1999). *The expanded family life cycle: Individual, family, and social perspectives* (3rd ed.). Needham Heights, MA: Allyn & Bacon.

Comas-Diaz, L., & Greene, B. (Eds.). (1994). *Women of color: Integrating ethnic and gender identities in psychotherapy.* New York: Guilford Press.

Coontz, S. (1992). *The way we never were: American families and the nostalgia trap.* New York: Basic Books.

Coontz, S. (1997). *The way we really are: Coming to terms with America's changing families.* New York: Basic Books.

Coontz, S. (Ed.). (with Parson, M., & Raley, G.). (1999). *American families. A multicultural reader.* New York: Routledge.

Davis, C. (1996). *Levinas: An introduction.* Notre Dame, IN: University of Notre Dame Press.

Diamond, G. M., Liddle, H. A., Hogue, A., & Dakof, G. A. (1999). Alliance building interventions with adolescents in family therapy: A process study. *Psychotherapy: Theory, Research, Practice, and Training, 36*(4), 355–368.

Diamond, G. S., & Liddle, H. A. (1996). Resolving a therapeutic impasse between parents and adolescents in multidimensional family therapy. *Journal of Consulting and Clinical Psychology,* 64(3), 481–488.

Diamond, G. S., & Liddle, H. A. (1999). Transforming negative parent-adolescent interactions: From impasse to dialogue. *Family Process,* 38(1), 5–26.

Ellison, R. (1947). *Invisible man.* New York: Random House.

Falicov, C. J. (Ed.). (1983). *Cultural perspectives in family therapy.* Rockville, MD: Aspen Press.

Falicov, C. J. (2000). *Latino families in therapy: A guide to multicultural practice.* New York: Guilford Press.

Fishman, H. C. (1988). *Treating troubled adolescents.* New York: Basic Books.

Fishman, H. C. (1993). *Intensive structural family therapy: Treating families in their social context.* New York: Basic Books.

Fishman, H. C., Andes, F., & Knowlton, R. (2001). Enhancing family therapy: The addition of a community resource specialist. *Journal of Marital and Family Therapy,* 27(1), 111–116.

Fowers, B. J., & Richardson, F. C. (1996). Why is multiculturalism good? *American Psychologist,* 51, 609–621.

Franklin, A. J. (1993). The invisibility syndrome. *Family Therapy Networker* (17), 33–39.

Franklin, D. L. (1997). *Ensuring inequality: The structural transformation of the African-American family.* New York: Oxford University Press.

Galeano, E. (1973). *Open veins of Latin America: Five centuries of the pillage of a continent* (C. Belfrage, Trans.). New York: Monthly Review Press.

Goldner, V. (1985). Feminism and family therapy. *Family Process,* 24, 31–47.

Goodrich, T. J., Ellman, B., Rampage, C., & Halstead, K. (1990). The lesbian couple. In M. Pravder Mirkin (Ed.), *The social and political contexts of family therapy* (pp. 159–178). Needham Heights, MA: Allyn & Bacon.

Hare-Mustin, R. T., & Marecek, J. (Eds.). (1990). *Making a difference: Psychology and the construction of gender.* New Haven, CT: Yale University Press.

Hartman, A., & Laird, J. (1983). *Family centered social work practice.* New York: Free Press.

Imber-Black, E. (1990). Multiple embedded systems. In M. Pravder Mirkin (Ed.), *The social and political contexts of family therapy* (pp. 3–18). Needham Heights, MA: Allyn & Bacon.

Inclan, J., & Ferran, E., Jr. (1990). Poverty, politics, and family therapy: A role for systems theory. In M. Pravder Mirkin (Ed.), *The social and political contexts of family therapy* (pp. 193–213). Needham Heights, MA: Allyn & Bacon.

Ivey, A. E., Ivey, M. B., & Simek-Morgan, L. (1993). *Counseling and psychotherapy: A multicultural perspective* (3rd ed.). Boston: Allyn & Bacon.

Kaslow, F. W. (Ed.). (1996). *Handbook of relational diagnosis and dysfunctional family patterns.* New York: Wiley.

Kaufman, E., & Kaufman, P. (Eds.). (1979). *Family therapy approaches with drug and alcohol problems.* Boston: Allyn & Bacon.

Kleinman, A. (1980). *Patients and healers in the context of culture: An exploration of the borderland between anthropology, medicine, and psychiatry.* Berkeley: University of California Press.

Kliman, J. (1994). The interweaving of gender, class, and race in family therapy. In M. Pravder Mirkin (Ed.), *Women in context: Toward a feminist reconstruction of psychotherapy* (pp. 25–47). New York: Guilford Press.

Krestan, J. A. (Ed.). (2000). *Bridges to recovery: Addiction, family therapy, and multicultural treatment.* New York: Free Press.

Kristeva, J. (1991). *Strangers to ourselves.* New York: Columbia University Press.

Kumpfer, K. (1994). *Implementation manual for the Strengthening Families Program.* Unpublished manuscript, Salt Lake City, University of Utah, Department of Health Sciences.

Laird, J. (1994). Lesbian families: A cultural perspective. In M. Pravder Mirkin (Ed.), *Women in context: Toward a feminist reconstruction of psychotherapy* (pp. 118–148). New York: Guilford Press.

Landau-Stanton, J., & Clements, C. D. (1993). *AIDS, health, and mental health: A primary sourcebook.* New York: Brunner/Mazel.

Levinas, E. (1981). *Otherwise than being or beyond essence* (A. Lingis, Trans.). The Hague: Martinus Nijhoff. (Original work published 1974)

Levinas, E. (1992). *Totality and infinity: An essay on exteriority* (A. Lingis, Trans.). Pittsburgh, PA: Duquesne University Press. (Original work published 1961)

Liddle, H. A. (1995). Conceptual and clinical dimensions of a multidimensional, multisystems engagement strategy in family-based adolescent treatment. *Psychotherapy,* 32, 39–58.

Liddle, H. A. (2000). A family-based, developmental-ecological preventive intervention for high-risk adolescents. *Journal of Marital and Family Therapy, 26*(3), 265–279.

Liddle, H. A., Henderson, C. E., Rowe, C. L., & Dakof, G. A. (2001). *Multidimensional family therapy for adolescent substance abuse: Major findings from a clinical research program.* Miami, FL: Center for Treatment Research on Adolescent Drug Abuse.

Lindblad-Goldberg, M., Dore, M., & Stern, L. (1998). *Creating competence from chaos: A comprehensive guide to home-based services.* New York: Norton.

Lindblad-Goldberg, M., & Dukes, J. (1985). Social support in Black, low-income, single-parent families: Normative and dysfunctional patterns. *American Journal of Orthopsychiatry, 55,* 42–58.

Madsen, W. C. (1999). *Collaborative therapy with multistressed families: From old problems to new futures.* New York: Guilford Press.

McDaniel, S., Hepworth, J., & Doherty, W. (1995). Medical family therapy with somatizing patients: The co-creation of therapeutic stories. In R. Mikesell, D. D. Lusterman, & S. H. McDaniel (Eds.), *Integrating family therapy: Handbook of family psychology and systems theory* (pp. 377–388). Washington, DC: American Psychological Association.

McDonald, L., & Frey, H. E. (1999). Families and schools together: Building relationships. *Juvenile Justice Bulletin* (pp. 1–19). Washington, DC: U. S. Department of Justice, Office of Juvenile Justice and Delinquency Prevention.

McGoldrick, M. (Ed.). (1998). *Re-visioning family therapy: Race, culture and gender in clinical practice.* New York: Guilford Press.

McGoldrick, M., Giordano, J., & Pearce, J. (1996). *Ethnicity and family therapy* (2nd ed.). New York: Guilford Press.

Mikesell, R., Lusterman, D. D., & McDaniel, S. H. (Eds.). (1995). *Integrating family therapy: Handbook of family psychology and systems theory.* Washington, DC: American Psychological Association.

Minuchin, P. (1995). Children and family therapy: Mainstream approaches and the special case of the multicrisis poor. In R. Mikesell, D. D. Lusterman, & S. H. McDaniel (Eds.), *Integrating family therapy: Handbook of family psychology and systems theory* (pp. 113–124). Washington, DC: American Psychological Association.

Minuchin, P., Colapinto, J., & Minuchin, S. (1998). *Working with families of the poor.* New York: Guilford Press.

Minuchin, S. (1974). *Families and family therapy.* Cambridge, MA: Harvard University Press.

Minuchin, S., & Fishman, H. C. (1981). *Family therapy techniques.* Cambridge, MA: Harvard University Press.

Minuchin, S., Guerney, B. G., Montalvo, B., Rosman, B., & Schumer, F. (1967). *Families of the slums: An exploration of their structure and treatment.* New York: Basic Books.

Moore Hines, P. (1988). The family life cycle of poor Black families. In B. Carter & M. McGoldrick (Eds.), *The changing family life cycle: A framework for family therapy* (pp. 513–514). New York: Gardner Press.

Parnell, M., & Vanderkloot, J. (1994). Poor women: Making a difference. In M. Pravder Mirkin (Ed.), *Women in context: Toward a feminist reconstruction of psychotherapy* (pp. 390–407). New York: Guilford Press.

Philpot, C., & Brooks, G. (1995). Intergender communication and gender-sensitive family therapy. In R. Mikesell, D. D. Lusterman, & S. H. McDaniel (Eds.), *Integrating family therapy: Handbook of family psychology and systems theory* (pp. 303–325). Washington, DC: American Psychological Association.

Pinderhughes, E. (1989). *Understanding race, ethnicity, and power: The key to efficacy in clinical practice.* New York: Free Press.

Pinderhughes, E. (1990). Legacy of slavery: The experience of Black families in America. In M. Pravder Mirkin (Ed.), *The social and political contexts of family therapy* (pp. 289–305). Needham Heights, MA: Allyn & Bacon.

Pravder Mirkin, M. (Ed.). (1990). *The social and political contexts of family therapy.* Needham Heights, MA: Allyn & Bacon.

Pravder Mirkin, M. (Ed.). (1994). *Women in context: Toward a feminist reconstruction of psychotherapy.* New York: Guilford Press.

Rabinow, P. (Ed.). (1984). *The Foucault reader.* New York: Pantheon Books.

Saba, G. W., Karrer, B. M., & Hardy, K. V. (Eds.). (1990). *Minorities and family therapy.* New York: Haworth Press.

Savin-Williams, R. C. (1998). *". . . and then I became gay": Young men's stories.* New York: Routledge.

Scheflen, A. (1981). *Levels of schizophrenia.* New York: Brunner/Mazel.

Schorr, L. B. (1997). *Common purpose: Strengthening families and neighborhoods to rebuild America.* New York: Anchor Books.

Scrivner, R., & Eldridge, N. (1995). Lesbian and gay family psychology. In R. Mikesell, D. D. Lusterman, & S. H. McDaniel (Eds.), *Integrating family therapy: Handbook of family psychology and systems theory* (pp. 327–344). Washington, DC: American Psychological Association.

Seaburn, D. B., Lorenz, A. D., Gunn, W. B., Jr., Gawinski, B. A., & Mauksch, L. A. (1996). *Models of collaboration: A guide for mental health professionals working with health care practitioners.* New York: Basic Books.

Simon, R. (1986). Across the great divide: A mental health center opens doors in the South Bronx. *Family Therapy Networker, 10*(1), 20–30, 74.

Sluzki, C. E., & Ransom, D. C. (Eds.). (1976) *Double bind: The foundation of the communicational approach to the family.* New York: Grune & Stratton.

Stanton, M. D., & Todd, T. C. (1982). *The family therapy of drug abuse and addiction.* New York: Guilford Press.

Steinglass, P., Bennett, L., Wolin, S., & Reiss, D. (1987). *The alcoholic family.* New York: Basic Books.

Szapocznik, J., & Kurtines, W. (1989). *Breakthroughs in family therapy with drug-abusing and problem youth.* New York: Springer.

Szapocznik, J., & Kurtines, W. (1993). Family psychology and cultural diversity: Opportunities for theory, research, and application. *American Psychologist, 48,* 400–407.

Thomas, A., & Sillen, S. (1979). *Racism and psychiatry.* Secaucus, NJ: Citadel Press.

Walsh, F. (Ed.). (1999). *Spiritual resources in family therapy.* New York: Guilford Press.

Weingarten, K. (1994). *The mother's voice: Strengthening intimacy in families.* New York: Guilford Press.

Wetzel, N. A. (1994a). Beyond the therapy room: Therapy and politics in the global village. *Peace Psychology Bulletin, 5,* 23–27.

Wetzel, N. A. (1994b). Beyond the therapy room: Therapy and politics in the nuclear age. In B. Gould & D. H. DeMuth (Eds.), *The global family therapist: Integrating the personal, professional, and political* (pp. 22–40). Needham Heights, MA: Allyn & Bacon.

Wetzel, N. A. (1998a). Contextual dimensions of inner-city healthcare: Integrating family systems and community approaches: Reflections on the work of the St. Martin's Center for Health Services in Trenton, NJ. *Families, Systems and Health, 16*(1/2), 85–102.

Wetzel, N. A. (1998b). The Family Intervention Program: A context oriented intervention model for adolescents at risk. *New Jersey Psychologist, 48*(1), 24–27.

Wilson, W. J. (1997). *When work disappears: The world of the new urban poor.* New York: Vintage Books.

Wilson, W. J. (1999). *The bridge over the racial divide: Rising inequality and coalition politics.* Berkeley: University of California Press.

Winawer, H., & Wetzel, N. (1999). Youth in the inner cities: School-based and community-oriented family therapy. *Newsletter, American Family Therapy Academy, 78,* 37–38.

Winawer-Steiner, H. (1979). Getting started in family therapy: A preliminary guide for therapist, supervisor and administrator. In M. Dinoff & D. Jacobson (Eds.), *Neglected problems in community mental health* (pp. 154–174). Huntsville: University of Alabama Press.

Wistow, F. (1986). A safe harbor: A client constructs a new life on the mean streets of the Bronx. *Family Therapy Networker, 10*(1), 33–36, 75.

Wright, L. M., Watson, W. L., & Bell, J. M. (1996). *Beliefs and families: A model for healing illness.* New York: Basic Books.

Wynne, L. C. (Ed.). (1988). *The state of the art in family therapy research: Controversies and recommendations.* New York: Family Process Press.

SECTION THREE

PSYCHOTHERAPY WITH ADULTS

Chapter 10 A Relational-Cultural Perspective in Therapy

Chapter 11 Existential/Humanistic Psychotherapy

Chapter 12 Spiritually-Sensitive Psychotherapy

Chapter 13 Existential Treatment with HIV/AIDS Clients

Chapter 14 Logotherapy

CHAPTER 10

A Relational-Cultural Perspective in Therapy

JUDITH V. JORDAN

Traditional psychodynamic theories of therapy have emphasized intrapsychic structure, increasing the ability to function in an autonomous way, and the resolution of unconscious conflict (Freud, 1930/1958). From the perspective of these one-person psychologies, pathology resides in an individual, and the work of therapy is to help a patient rework internal psychic structure to facilitate functioning in a more self-sufficient, agentic way. The theory underlying these approaches elaborates the development of a separate self. Classical psychoanalytic models posit separateness as primary and relatedness as secondary; relationships derive from the satisfaction of drives. Freud (1920/1955) suggested that "protection against stimuli is almost more important than reception of stimuli" (p. 27). This implies that the surrounding context is impinging and distorting and that safety exists in developing protection against the surround. The assumption of primary separateness bears profound implications for many psychodynamic approaches to therapy.

Object-relations theory, while acknowledging the centrality of the mother-infant connection, is nevertheless also built on the primacy of drives, particularly the aggressive drive. In fact, Winnicott (1960), elaborating on the work of Melanie Klein (1953), suggested that the capacity for concern develops secondarily to guilt over aggression against loved ones. Fairbairn (1946) and Guntrip (1973) moved more clearly away from the drive model in the direction of appreciating the centrality of relationships in people's lives. Fairbairn noted that persons move not from dependence to independence in the life cycle but from infantile dependence to mature dependence. Their work acknowledges the ultimately interdependent nature of human lives. Rather than putting forth an ideal of independence and autonomy, unattainable standards for all people, Fairbairn and Guntrip delineated different kinds of interdependent and mutual relationships.

Although often described as relational, Kohut's (1984) self psychology most clearly concerns the development and maintenance of a separate, cohesive self. The experience of fragmentation of self generates the greatest source of pathology in his system. Many self psychologists have understood Kohut's notion of the ongoing need for self-objects as synonymous with the continuing need for relationship; but self-object is not another word for person. A self-object, much like Winnicott's (1971) transitional object, is under the fantasied control of the individual, not a distinct other person, with one's own subjectivity, and is clearly not involved in mutual relationship. The self uses a self-object for the maintenance of self-cohesion and self-esteem. In the best of all possible worlds, the self-object function would be internalized, and self-esteem and cohesion would be maintained by internally regulated structures. Thus, although Kohut acknowledged late in his work that self-object function would never be entirely internalized because no one ever receives the kind of empathic mirroring that is needed, in his ideal system this function would be internalized as intrapsychic structure. Furthermore, Kohut did not address the development of mutual relationships, but instead looked at empathy as unidirectional, from parent to child or therapist to patient. Relationships, in Kohut's model, serve as resources for the development of the self.

In the past decade, several models have been developed to emphasize a two-person psychology in a therapeutic setting. Mitchell (1988) and Aron (1996) have looked at psychoanalysis from a relational perspective, and Stolorow (Stolorow & Atwood, 1992) has fashioned a theory of intersubjectivity built on the work of Kohut and the self psychologists. But each of these systems is anchored in the primacy of intrapsychic structure. The analytic tradition of interpretation serves as the cornerstone of developing self-knowledge, and the therapeutic connection itself is rarely credited with healing power.

In the 1970s, a group of feminist theorists began to question traditional developmental and clinical models, particularly as they pertained to women. These theorists arose from both an academic research tradition (Belenky, Clinchy, Goldberger, & Tarule, 1986; Gilligan, 1982) and clinical backgrounds (Jordan, 1992b, 1997; Jordan, Kaplan, Miller, Stiver, & Surrey, 1991; Miller, 1976, 1988; Miller & Stiver, 1997).

Noting that most developmental and clinical models had been developed by men and used men as the benchmarks by which others were judged, these theorists affirmed the need to pay attention to women's experiences, to listen to women. When male standards of independence, autonomy, separation, and competition were applied to women, women were often pathologized and seen as "less than" (Broverman, Broverman, Clarkson, Rosenkrantz, & Vogel, 1970). Thus, women were perceived as too needy, too emotional, hysterical, not logical enough, or too irrational. Although it is appealing to think of diagnostic categories as culture-free, clearly, power dynamics and value judgments appear in many of the diagnostic categories, particularly the personality disorder diagnoses.

THEORETICAL CONSTRUCTS

THE RELATIONAL-CULTURAL MODEL

The relational-cultural model represents a departure from the separate-self view of development and posits that we grow in, through, and toward relationship. Psychological development involves movement toward relational mutuality, where all participants in a relationship practice mutual empathy, are responsive, and are concerned with the growth of the relationship as well as with the well-being of the individuals in the relationship. Originally elaborated to better understand and represent the psychology of women, the relational-cultural model increasingly underscores an understanding of both male and female developmental patterns. In this model, movement toward increasingly differentiated and articulated relationships, characterized by mutual empathy and mutual empowerment, constitutes the developmental trajectory. Growth-fostering relationships support the following five conditions for those engaged in them (Miller & Stiver, 1997): a sense of zest or vitality, an increasing clarity about self and other and the relationship, an increase in one's sense of self-worth, an increase in productivity and creativity, and a desire for more connection beyond this particular connection. Mutuality characterizes growth. People do not simply wish to receive from relationships (love, support, understanding) as in an essentially unidirectional, empty-vessel model, but look for engagement and participation, with each person contributing to the growth of the other. People generate a sense of well-being: clarity, creativity, authenticity, zest, and desire for more connection (Miller's "five good things") with one another, leading to mutual empowerment (Miller & Stiver, 1997). Empathy flows both ways, nurturing mutual empathy.

Empathy, a complex affective-cognitive skill, connotes the ability to put oneself in another person's shoes, to feel with the other, to join in the other's experience. Empathy never reaches perfect congruence of experience, but does involve a relaxation of one's sense of separateness, an openness to being affected by the other person, a willingness to join with the other in his or her experience, and a cognitive clarity about the source of the affect being aroused in both people (Jordan, Kaplan, Miller, Stiver, & Surrey, 1991). Descriptions of empathy have sometimes implied a picture of a regressive, merging, more primitive experience; in the relational-cultural model, empathy rests on a highly complex, sophisticated set of skills. The openness to being influenced, moved, or impacted by other people, along with the capacity to access one's own affects, contribute to this ability. Babies as young as two days old show rudimentary empathic responsiveness to the distress cries of other babies (Sagi & Hoffman, 1976; Simner, 1971). MacLean (1973) pointed to a neurological basis for empathy in the limbic system. Human beings may be hardwired to be empathically attuned to one another.

Culture shapes the predisposition for empathic responsiveness. In the socialization of children, support for empathic ability seems to differ systematically by gender. Boys are encouraged in general to restrict much affective responsiveness (Levant, 1995; Levant & Pollack, 1995; Pollack, 1999). Vulnerable affects become unacceptable in little boys and men as they mature. Thus, Levant (1995) observed what he called normative alexithymia in boys (the inability to recognize and articulate affect), despite evidence that baby boys are extremely affectively reactive. Boys are taught that they should not be influenced by others, that they should not be in the vulnerability of open feelings like sadness, tenderness, fear, and helplessness. Most likely, little boys close down empathic ability or convert it into what Levant calls action empathy, a tendency to translate empathic response into instrumental action. For girls, on the other hand, more latitude exists for fear, sadness, and uncertainty. Girls are taught that it is okay just to be with another person's feelings without having to fix or alter the person's affective experience. Girls furthermore are directed to pay attention to others' feelings. The sex differences in empathy (Hoffman, 1977) point to girls' abilities to experience vicariously what another person is feeling. Boys may correctly cognitively label another's emotional state when directed to do so, but they are less likely to feel with the other person. Perhaps this is part of what Pollack (1999) called defensive separateness instilled in boys.

Separate-self models, emphasizing aggression and autonomy, have neglected the importance of connection in many realms. For instance, recent research on coping has pointed to a possible gender-mediated biological impact on people's reactions to stress (Taylor et al., 2000). Although for decades psychology has featured the fight-or-flight response to stress as an invariant for all people, recent research indicates striking gender disparities in this response, consonant with relational-cultural theories about gender differences. The original studies done on males (rats, humans) were presented as gender-neutral. Recently, researchers scanned the data with a gender lens and discovered real differences in the ways males and females typically react to stress. Females respond with a "tend-and-befriend" response. When stress occurs, females tend to take care of others and move toward connection rather than into aggression or flight. The researchers believe this is linked to the oxytocin hormonal system in females. This new report reverses years of what has been bedrock psychological understanding and provides yet another example of the distortions that happen when standards developed on a population of males are viewed as universal and then applied to females. Some of the differences in empathy and other affiliative behaviors highlighted in the relational-cultural model may in part be mediated at a neurological and psychobiological level. Whatever the interaction of biological, psychological, and social factors in this effect, males and females typically experience stress, isolation, and empathy differently. Sex differences follow bell-shaped curves with widely overlapping populations. Similarities between boys and girls far outweigh their differences. Many men demonstrate highly developed empathy and many women do not. Still, important general sex differences need to be acknowledged.

In Eurocentric cultures, girls and women are generally given the task of taking care of others, of building relationships. Boys and men are accorded the more instrumental tasks of dealing with the inanimate world or functioning in the public world. The relational-cultural model honors the importance of context and sociopolitical forces in the shaping of group and individual psychology. Influences from far beyond the nuclear family impact each individual. Thus, power dynamics and the dynamics of marginalization weigh heavily on individuals and influence people's sense of isolation. This model posits that people grow through and toward relationship and that isolation causes enormous pain and suffering for people. Studying the forces of isolation and working with them in therapy constitute major undertakings of this work. Our focus includes internal psychological and biological factors, familial and developmental influences, as well as the sociopolitical and economic forces that disempower and isolate people.

Connections and Disconnections
Clearly, not all relationships foster growth. The failure of growth-promoting connections leads to what has been traditionally called pathology (Miller & Stiver, 1997). In the relational-cultural model, pathology arises from the experience of isolation and chronic disconnection. Acute disconnections remain inevitable and ubiquitous in relationships. The daily failures of empathy, interpersonal hurts, misunderstandings, and unresolved conflicts are endless. Disconnections in themselves do not cause pathology or isolation; chronic disconnections occurring with important, usually powerful significant people do generate pathology and pain. For example, a parent does something that hurts a child and the child tries to represent (tell, convey) the pain to a parent. In an acute disconnection, the parent might be responsive to the child's representation of feeling and apologize or express empathy or concern for the child; in this interaction, the child feels heard, understood, responded to, and effective in relationship. Misattunements handled in this way actually lead back to a stronger and more trustworthy connection and a kind of relational resilience (Jordan, 1992a). Thus, acute disconnections, responded to with empathic care, actually strengthen relationships and lead to growth. If, however, a parent reacts with denial, withdrawal, defensiveness, or attack or does not respond empathically, a child learns about not being effective in changing relationships, about not mattering to this person, and that this particular inner state and its expression (i.e., anger or sadness) is not acceptable. Under these conditions, a child begins to disconnect from inner experience, to twist himself or herself to fit into

the limited range of responses acceptable to a parent. A child begins to develop strategies of disconnection and learns not to expose vulnerability to this powerful and important other person or to other people beyond this relationship. These strategies of disconnection are sometimes strategies of survival, ways a child can keep aspects of personal experience alive, if out of connection. When a parent is chronically attacking, aggressive, or abusive, a child learns an even more profound message of not mattering: that connections are dangerous, and that vulnerability is not safe. In situations of abuse, a child finds very little empathic responsiveness and learns to develop a protective inauthenticity to survive. Thus, genuine connection begins to diminish at the same time that the yearning for connection increases. A child (or less powerful person) then experiences an intense desire for connection along with terror about the possible consequences of being in the vulnerability necessary to make a connection, and turns to strategies of disconnection to feel safe enough. This culminates in a profound sense of isolation, low self-worth, immobilization, and disempowerment.

Therapy from the Perspective of the Relational-Cultural Model

Relational-cultural therapy involves an attitudinal more than a technical change on the part of a therapist who profoundly respects the potential movement of a patient into growth-fostering relationships. Mutual respect, mutual empathy, and mutual empowerment are brought to a therapy relationship. The therapist practices a kind of *fluid expertise* (Fletcher, 1999), acknowledging that, in this relationship, the therapist is not the only one with knowledge and expertise. In therapy, patients move toward bringing themselves more fully and clearly into relationship with an increased sense of authenticity and wholeness. They experience an increased capacity for initiative, creativity, and responsiveness. Perception and desire become clearer and one's capacity to effect change is enhanced. Relational resilience is increased as the patient begins to move back into relationship following disconnections. The therapist works toward the development of increasing mutuality, self-empathy, relational resilience, courage, and the capacity for what Miller (1976) calls *good conflict*. Both therapist and patient are impacted and grow in this relationship, although the intention for change is clearly directed toward the patient, who comes seeking some relief and movement out of pain.

Therapy based on a relational-cultural model addresses issues of isolation, connection, and disconnection. Because isolation is thought to be the major (although not only) source of suffering in people's lives, and mutually empathic and mutually empowering connections are viewed as the pathways of growth, the work of therapy helps bring people back into the possibility and hope for empathic connection. Therapists work primarily with the movement of connection and disconnection and encourage the growth of mutual empathy. In the movement of the therapeutic relationship, patients rework relational images, become aware of personal patterns of disconnection, experience the healing connection offered by the therapist, connect more with their own split-off experiences and with the therapist, move into more full representation of experience in the therapeutic relationship, and begin to move out of shame and isolation.

Relational-cultural therapy is not based on a sophisticated set of techniques, but depends largely on an attitude of mutual respect and inquiry. A therapeutic relationship serves as a growth-fostering relationship to provide a relationally corrective experience for a patient. At the core of this relationship lies the engagement between therapist and patient, a healing connection (Miller & Stiver, 1997). Much of the work revolves around making meaning, understanding the relational expectations and relational images a patient brings to new relationships, and looking at the patterns of disconnections. The therapy relationship itself embodies healing.

Mutual empathy provides a key to change and growth. Most human suffering and isolation result from patterns of chronic disconnection, arising in important relationships with powerful others where there has been failure in a more powerful person's empathy and responsiveness. Therapy provides an experience during which a patient can begin to examine, wonder about, question, and ultimately rework relational expectations. A child might have learned the relational image or expectation that "If I am angry, people abandon me, and I am at risk." The grown child, now patient, may have the opportunity to learn in the therapy that "If I am angry and express it, my anger will be empathized with, and I will still be accepted. I may be effective in registering my protest." Slowly, patients begin to take small interpersonal risks, to bring themselves more fully into relationship, and to represent themselves more authentically. This allows a deepening of connection with their inner experience and the therapist. Empathy for self begins to grow where self-rejection and loss of emotional contact with oneself once predominated. Self-empathy provides an important part of the shift because it allows a reconnection with split-off, sometimes shamed aspects of personal experiences. In self-empathy, people begin to bring their empathic abilities to bear on their own unacceptable inner feelings and thoughts. Increased self-empathy moves in the direction of compassion and self-acceptance.

Mutual empathy connotes that, for empathy to make a difference, to contribute to growth, both people require empathic contact. In therapy, that means that not only does a therapist convey empathy, but a patient is attuned to the therapist's empathy. The patient is able to see, feel, know the therapist's empathic response, that is, be empathic, with the therapist being empathic with her or him. Chronic disconnection results from nonresponsiveness, abusiveness, or neglect on the part of early important people in a person's life. This leads to isolation, immobilization, a sense of being ineffective in relationship (relationally incompetent), shame, and self-blame. In these disconnections, persons learn that they cannot effectively impact relationships or do not matter to important other people. This leads to a sense of demoralization, ineffectiveness, loss of hope for empathic responsiveness from another. In such a state of disconnection and often withdrawal, individuals do not have the opportunity to unlearn these expectations because they stop bringing themselves fully into relationship. In isolation, individuals are doomed to repeat old maladaptive patterns. Only by bringing themselves more fully into relationship can individuals learn new responses and not generalize old patterns to all new relationships.

Traditional psychodynamic therapists emphasize the importance of neutrality and nongratification in therapy. In the classical paradigms, a therapist's blank screen seemed essential to the development of transference neurosis. Therapists' real engagement and responsiveness in therapy have been discouraged by many of these models; real responsiveness has been seen as threatening the unfolding of transference, putting the patient in the position of having to care for the therapist or engage in ordinary social exchange. The relational-cultural model implies a very different position. Whereas most literature on countertransference problems is focused on "loss of boundaries" and "overinvolvement" (and these can be real problems that need to be attended to), the relational-cultural model also suggests that injuries can occur to a patient when a therapist is too distant, too remote, or too opaque (Jordan, 1995; Miller & Stiver, 1997).

This model underscores that power is not distributed equally in a therapy relationship and that very strong role prescriptions exist for patient and therapist. The roles of the two individuals in this relationship differ and need to be respected and delineated. A patient comes to be helped, seeking change, hoping that this intervention will bring relief, an increase in happiness. A therapist brings expertise, a quality of attention, and the intention to assist the patient in his or her change or healing. A therapist is expected to safeguard the well-being of a patient and to promote a patient's health. Therapists usually set certain parameters, such as time of sessions, payment, and place of meeting (although some of these are negotiable). They are bound by certain legal and ethical constraints regarding proper therapeutic behavior. In the relational-cultural model, mutuality in the therapy relationship or real engagement on the part of the therapist does not imply an equality of power or sameness of role; nor does it suggest a completely open spontaneity on the part of the therapist or even a higher level of therapist self-disclosure.

In mutual empathy, a therapist's real responsiveness provides valuable information and the possibility of movement back into relationship for the patient (Jordan, 2000). Thus, in situations in which patients may not have had an opportunity to obtain feedback about their impact on another person, the therapist lets patients see that the therapist has been moved and affected by their story and feelings. In this joining in affect, in mutual empathy, patients actually experience a lessening of isolation, a sense of relational competence, and begin to trust that they can make a difference, can expect empathic responsiveness from another person around experiences that before left them feeling disconnected and isolated. A therapist's authenticity allows patients to see how the therapist is being affected by them, but the therapist is not simply engaging in knee-jerk reactivity. The therapist is judiciously responding, exercising clinical judgment, guided by concern about the possible impact of authentic responsiveness on a patient. This is therapeutic authenticity, not total honesty (Jordan, 2000; Miller et al., 1997). A therapist may feel genuinely moved by a patient's pain and begin to tear up, but not call attention to this at certain times during treatment. At other times, the therapist acknowledges tears, so that patients have an opportunity to really see how they have affected the therapist. The questions What is the likely impact on the patient at this point in therapy of seeing this response? and Will this response facilitate healing? remain in the mind of the therapist. This involves anticipatory empathy, the capacity to foresee the response of the other. Both therapist and patient work on developing anticipatory empathy, based on the understanding the therapist has gained in working with this individual patient as well as on the empathic sense in the moment with the patient. Therapists constantly modify anticipatory empathy in light of what they are learning about the patient in each interaction. This alive and growing process is not always totally accurate.

Errors in anticipatory empathy raise another important issue in the use of mutual empathy in therapy. Empathy is not always precise; misfirings and misattunements occur despite the best intentions and efforts. How empathic failures are handled often defines the success of therapy. Being empathic with someone describing pain caused by another person proves relatively easy. But when someone points out our failure to understand or the pain that a therapist induces, clinicians often react with self-protection, defensiveness, and armor. A relational-cultural therapist strives for a different process. When therapists hear about their own misattunement or hurting of a patient, they attempt to stay in empathic possibility, taking in that they have let the person down and being interested in how they did that and what impact that had. The effort to better understand and be there for the other opens therapeutic possibilities. Therapists need to let patients know that they are sorry for causing pain. This provides the corrective empathic response that was not available in the original situations, where injuries were brought about by parents and caregivers. After an empathic failure, the important question should be What happens next? All too often, therapists move into defensiveness, for instance, blaming misattunements on the patient's resistance or assuming their own overreactivity is produced only by projective identification. Thus, therapists subtly blame injured parties: the patients. When clinicians are the source of injury, staying empathic with someone they deeply care about constitutes a core part of creating a healing connection.

In these interactions, patients learn that the therapist cares more about their well-being than about personal narcissism; the clinician can receive and reflect on strong messages about the therapist's own limitations and misattunements. Chronic disconnection need not ensue, and patients will not be forced into protective inauthenticity or shame to preserve the appearance of connection (which would become less and less authentic and tenuous). This poses a profound responsibility for a therapist.

In working with disconnections, therapists need to avoid pushing or forcing people toward more connection than they are genuinely ready for. The relational-cultural model implies the importance of honoring the paradox of connection and disconnection. In working with disconnections, a clinician must both honor the longing to connect, which actually brings many people into therapy, and the terror of connection, the need to create strategies of disconnection. This entails respect for both the terror and the need to stay safe in the strategies of disconnection. Simultaneously knowing and acknowledging the deeper yearnings for connection remain paramount. When people come to therapy, they are often feeling the pain of disconnections; they are also frightened of relinquishing their strategies of disconnection, wary of the vulnerability that accompanies their longings to connect. The beginning of therapy is often fraught with the push-pull of these competing feelings. The vicissitudes of this ambivalence depend on the degree of earlier disconnections.

Therapy helps move patients toward a greater sense of authentic connection in which they can bring themselves more fully into relationship and participate in growth-fostering connections. But this does not always result in harmonious and easy relationships. If people bring themselves authentically into relationships, differences and conflict will arise with others. In unequal power situations, these potential conflicts often resolve in the direction of the more powerful person's dictating their resolution. As Miller (1976) noted, "Authenticity and subordination are totally incompatible" (p. 98). Authentic and fuller representation of one's experience depends on responsiveness in the other. And if the person cannot welcome difference, at least there must be readiness to tolerate uncertainty and conflict. Engaging in good conflict means encouraging both people to represent their differences, to learn with and to tolerate the tension of conflict, to accept that conflict is inevitable in any relationship, and to develop the belief that good conflict can actually enhance connection. If people can learn to represent their real experiences, with awareness and concern for the possible impact on the other person, both will be enhanced. Anger can serve as a resource for connection. Anger expresses hurt or injury; it provides necessary feedback in any relationship or system. People need to represent when they feel disappointed or violated, to strive for a shift, to seek justice, to be able to protest *if* there is a responsive listener. This leads to a strengthened relationship as well as a sense of personal and relational competence. Women have difficulty giving voice to anger because socialization is strongly in favor of suppressing it, whereas men in Western industrialized culture are typically taught to move into aggression or dominance to deal with conflict. Both men and women need help in learning to engage in good conflict. Developing respect for conflict and working with anger in a therapy relationship can be very helpful.

Shame

The relational cultural model helps particularly in working with shame, conceptualized as the loss of empathic possibility. When experiencing shame, a person does not feel that another can possibly respond empathically. One feels one's being as unworthy (Hartling, Rosen, Walker, & Jordan, 2000; Jordan 1989). With guilt, people feel that their actions have violated some standard and that they can make amends, whereas in shame, individuals often feel immobilized and unable to alter the experience of isolation and unworthiness. In shame, one's whole being feels inadequate in some profound way. Because one does not believe that another person could possibly respond empathically to the shameful part, one goes into withdrawal and hiding, and, in this movement, is actually deprived of the potentially healing response of another's empathic attunement. This is one of the most troubling aspects of shame. It locks people into isolation, and leads them to feel that they are to blame. This forms the core of "condemned isolation" (Miller & Stiver, 1997, p. 72). Shame arises when one feels inadequate and not worthy of connection while simultaneously maintaining awareness of desiring connection very much. Shame appears as a primary affect (Tompkins, 1987). Normative shame can serve as a prosocial affect, alerting persons to their impact on another and helping them to be responsive. It arises when one feels unworthy of connection and may lead to appropriate examination of how one is relating (as opposed to being shameless). But pathological shame disconnects and isolates.

People also shame others to control them. Thus, in any hierarchical system of power, more powerful, dominant groups often shame less powerful groups. This shaming both isolates and silences people and renders them less powerful or threatening. Marginalized groups typically experience shame from groups at the center (hooks, 1984). Thus, women, people of color, gays, and lesbians are induced to feel, by the dominant power group (in the Western world, generally White, more economically advantaged, heterosexual men), that their reality is not as worthy as that of the dominant group. The group at the center creates the standards for "good behavior" and then shames those who live by different guidelines or values. Shame serves as an effective force of disempowerment at both individual and collective levels. Working with shame in therapy, then, provides an important path toward empowerment and heals personal as well as cultural sources of shame. Relational therapy helps people move out of the isolation and silence of shame.

CASE EXAMPLES

CASE 1: SHAME

Donna, a 38-year-old lawyer, specializes in public service law. She is a particularly articulate and effective advocate for individuals who are disenfranchised. She has a keen sense of social justice and is very empathic with people's suffering. She has been married for 10 years and has two young children, both girls, ages 7 and 5. She came to treatment complaining of depression and anxiety related to her work and noted that she did not have a lot of close friends. At the beginning of treatment, Donna spoke about her sense of being cut off at work, that she was worthless, and that somehow she never measured up, despite abundant feedback that she was valued and liked by her coworkers and friends.

After suffering a particularly acute bout of depression three months into the treatment, Donna blurted out, "You know, I was married before...he beat me up....I can't believe I haven't told a soul about this ever!" (except, as it turned out, one former therapist). Donna then burst into tears, hid her face in her hands, and was unable to talk further. Slowly, she began to fill in the details of abuse from her former husband, a man to whom she was married for two years from the age of 21. He started abusing her shortly after they married and escalated from mild verbal demeaning to frank physical torture and sadistic infliction of injury. As Donna spoke of her outrage, her mortification, her fear, her immobilization, I felt her agony and acknowledged what courage it took to let me know about all this. She at first dismissed my empathy: "You're paid to be nice to me. Most people would think I was defective for putting up with this, and you probably do too, but you're not supposed to show it.... I thought you looked disapproving when I told you." I let her know I "got" how deep her conviction of her badness was. I added that she might have picked up some negative response from me, although I was not aware of disapproval. I surmised that she might have sensed my sadness that she had been so hurt and was alone with her hurt. She then reported that she was scared that I would think she was crazy because there were still aspects of this man that she admired and liked. I let her know that I knew there probably had been some good reasons why she had been drawn to him, that people are rarely all good or all bad, and that unfortunately, his destructive treatment of her had emerged only after their marriage. She feared I would blame her for "inviting" all this abuse. I assured her I in no way saw her as asking for pain or enjoying it. I also conveyed that I thought she was deeply sad, as was I, that this relationship had not lived up to her hopes, and that I knew she felt a lot of shame about all of it. I acknowledged that it took great courage to extricate herself from a relationship with this frightening and out-of-control man.

With each empathic and validating intervention, Donna moved into more connection with me, but would then also abruptly retreat into fear and guardedness. Sometimes she questioned my motives: Did I really care? Wasn't I secretly blaming and judging her? Wasn't it all her fault after all? When Donna again began to experience connection with me, she would often feel scared, alone, plunged into her shame. She found trusting the resilience of our connection difficult. At one point, she expressed open anger at me for keeping her waiting 10 minutes for our appointment. I sincerely apologized for my lateness and the distress it caused her. She searched closely for some retaliation on my part. I acknowledged that, although I found myself a little defensive and wanting to justify my lateness, I really understood why she would be angry and that it was important that she was able to let me know that, to take the risk that we could stay connected through the anger and immediate hurt. That seemed to make a difference.

In the next week, she found herself standing up for herself at a meeting at work. Although she had always been a sturdy advocate for her clients, she often had trouble speaking up on her own behalf. In this instance, she let a supervisor know that he had hurt her when he overlooked her for a particular assignment and that she thought she ought to be considered for it. She did this in a way that people could hear, could respect, and could see the accuracy of her perception.

Donna is a woman of many strengths. To apply diagnostic labels proves problematic in the relational-cultural approach. She does not fit any of the existing categories. Although the Axis I diagnoses give us some sense of etiology and intervention, the Axis II diagnoses often fail us on both accounts. These diagnoses themselves largely concern relational failures, but are presented as intrapsychic formulations. In Donna's case, she suffered shame, depression, and anxiety. She was terribly isolated, largely as a result of her shame about her history of having been battered. A terrible imbalance of mutuality and frank abuse of power occurred in her first marriage. At a cultural level, Donna grew up in a house in which her father behaved in arbitrary and dominant ways; although not physically abusive with her mother, he meted out frequent spankings to Donna and her two brothers and was "king of the castle." Her mother responded submissively, as a shadowy and nonsupportive figure for her children; her mother's world was limited to her nuclear family and a handful of friends, whereas Donna's father enjoyed considerable success and status in his role as a business executive. Donna's brothers were clearly more valued than she was and were sent to college with all expenses paid; she had to earn her own way through college and law school. She attended law school after her first marriage broke up. A woman fellow participant in a divorce group strongly encouraged Donna to enter law school.

When she began therapy with me, she was relatively isolated, although struggling to be a good wife, mother, and coworker. She was confused about her responsibility in the original abuse situation (overattributing blame to herself: "I was the problem") and felt she could not let anyone know about it. A former therapist had confirmed her worst fears by questioning her inability to "get out faster" and wondering what pattern she was repeating or what she was "getting" from being a victim. She felt mortified by these questions and left treatment with this woman shortly thereafter, without informing the therapist how horrible she had felt.

Donna had experienced a history of being devalued and suffered from low self-worth, but her isolation and silence most locked her into the painful and destructive patterns in her first marriage. Her battering husband actively imposed isolation, and her shame contributed. He ridiculed and mocked her for how inadequate she was, said she acted as if she deserved what she received, and further humiliated her for putting up with the abuse and told her no one else would understand or tolerate her. He strategically isolated her from other people. She had little reason not to believe him because her personal history had not led her to expect to be listened to or respected. But the cycle of isolation became more and more difficult for her to break. Slowly, with the support of two good friends whom she never told about the abuse, but who she thinks might have suspected it, Donna was able to mobilize herself, to gather her energy and move out of this destructive relationship. Later, through the relationships she developed in a group for newly divorced people, she began to actively believe in her own intelligence and abilities. These relationships helped her build the confidence to move out of an all-defining sense of herself as a failure, unworthy of love. They had not, however, been able to help her with the shame because she was unable to disclose the shameful parts of herself.

Donna attended therapy weekly for two years. Much of the work focused on her self-doubt, shame, poor self-esteem, depression, and her sense that she was incompetent and a fraud. In the early phase of treatment, she complained of feeling inadequate at work. As therapy progressed, her difficulties with intimate relationships emerged. As she began to feel closer to people, she became quite fearful, self-critical, and terrified that others would find out about her "past." Her self-judgment and self-rejection loomed large. Although Donna was deeply compassionate and understanding with others, bringing this empathy to bear on her own experience challenged her. Much of the therapeutic task really involved being responsive to her pain, validating her feelings, and letting her see very clearly the effects she exerted on the therapist. Although her primary relational images led Donna to fear any opening into relationship, she began to allow herself to show split-off parts of herself. A central relational image contained the expectation, if I am vulnerable, I will be despised, and people will beat me or reject me. Although she anticipated such a reaction in therapy and experienced great shame in trying to share her pain, the therapist's caring and concerned responses slowly registered with her. Thus, she was able to be empathic with the therapist's empathy, to see that she had moved the therapist, that the therapist could join her in her affect and maintain an attitude of empathy. She "moved" the therapist, affected the course of the relationship, and could begin to develop self-empathy arising from experiencing the therapist's empathy.

Despite her initial withdrawal and shameful silence in therapy, Donna began to move out of her isolation and to hope for an empathic response. As she started to represent herself more fully in relationship, she increasingly risked self-disclosure and felt more understood and more seen by others. The cycle of healing in connection affected her sense of isolation and her lack of self-worth. Slowly, she began to bring more of herself into other relationships. She was surprised to find people responding positively to her. Her strategies of disconnection, often in the form of mistrust and withholding of parts of her experience, seemed less vital to her well-being. She learned to perceive how these strategies of disconnection kept her alone and depressed and that perhaps they were not necessary for her survival anymore. Her sense of confidence increased remarkably. Donna reported that people at work noticed a change in her accessibility. She was, in fact, getting closer to one of the other women lawyers and was pleased that she had a friend whom she really liked and trusted. Her husband apparently felt she was much more present in their relationship, and she mentioned that she was enjoying being with her children much more than ever before.

Donna flourished in relational treatment, which was especially suited to deal with her issues of shame and isolation. Although the heightening of her strategies of disconnection, as she sought frantically to feel safe in this new relationship, characterized the early phases of treatment, she was able to slowly open more into the therapy relationship, to allow her vulnerability and her yearning for connection to be more present. When empathic failures occurred, she would often withdraw, reinvoking her strategies of disconnection, but she also was able to move back into connection, recognizing that these were acute disconnections and that there was a larger picture of trustworthiness and concern on the part of the therapist. She was touched by the therapist's responsiveness and felt very respected.

As she was ending therapy, Donna noted that several moments had proven pivotal to her. One time occurred when the therapist teared up in response to hearing the details of a particularly vicious beating by the first husband, and the therapist commented, "It makes me so sad and upset to know how you suffered there. I wish I or someone could have been there to help." Another time, the therapist had rushed in with premature understanding, and Donna knew she had not "gotten" it. Donna was able to be angry, and the therapist acknowledged that she had not "gotten" it and that Donna had a right to her disappointment. The therapist apologized. Donna was amazed and then grateful that the therapist had not just gone into a self-protective, "holier-than thou" mode. When she left therapy, she had developed a richer sense of connection with people in her world, and she felt infinitely more connected with herself, more "alive," as she exclaimed.

At the conclusion of their work together, Donna expressed a desire to stay in some contact with the therapist. The therapist reassured Donna that she would be happy to hear from her, although she could not promise an active correspondence in return. The therapist also let her know how much she would be missed and that the therapist would be there in the future should problems arise with which she wanted help. Both therapist and patient were openly sad about the ending of treatment, but clearly appreciative of each other and the work they had done. They shared the pleasure of reaching a point where the therapeutic contact was no longer necessary for the patient. To date, after one and a half years, the therapist has received two notes, both reporting a continued sense of well-being as well as a sense of missing their time together. The therapist responded to the second of these notes, indicating that she still thought about the patient and felt good about what they had accomplished together.

CASE 2: TRAUMA

I saw Susan, an 18-year-old woman, many years ago in individual treatment. She had been in many therapies before I began treating her. She had been hospitalized at the age of 12 with severe anorexia and had had several subsequent hospitalizations for suicidality and depression. She was hospitalized at the outset of our work together. Previous therapies had most often ended with Susan's firing her therapist for being too "shrinky" or cold.

The early months of treatment proved difficult for both of us. Susan had sought me out because she had heard that I was more "present" in therapy than some of the other therapists in the hospital. But she found me a bit disappointing initially. She learned that I made mistakes too, and she called other therapists in the system to let them know about my mistakes and my empathic failures. In the early phase of treatment, she made a lot of these phone calls, and she was very accurate in her reporting of my errors and shortcomings. I felt very exposed and inadequate as a therapist, with many other therapists in the system reporting to me the latest complaints about me that she had communicated to them. I was at the time a beginning therapist, and I was often embarrassed and defensive about how often people were hearing from Susan about my less-than-perfect empathy and many instances of therapeutic shortcomings. Both Susan and I struggled during this time. Somehow I knew she had to complain, and I had to respect her right to do that, although at the time I was not sure why. I had to work on my own sense of shame and inadequacy as a therapist. And sometimes I just wanted her to stop!

During this time, Susan initiated telling me about sexual abuse by her stepfather from the age of 6 to 10 years. She had never told any of her other therapists, although she had vivid and ongoing memories of the abuse throughout her previous treatments. Her self-loathing and suicidality increased as she started to talk about the abuse. Initially, as with many abuse survivors, she blamed herself, and she felt as if she should have found a way to tell someone, to get some help. She emphasized how unsafe and betrayed she felt. Although she had never forgotten the abuse, she had never felt anyone would believe her or be "with her" around it. Slowly, I began to make sense of some of her phone calls to other therapists and learned to appreciate how wise she had been in protecting the therapy relationship in the midst of all her fears and strategies of disconnection. For someone who has been abused, particularly by a parental figure, as a child, the therapy situation is often initially quite frightening and even triggering. Some components of the therapy setting can be quite reminiscent of abuse situations: a private relationship, behind closed doors, with two people of unequal power, one person presenting much more vulnerability than the other, and the promise that the more powerful person is trustworthy. All of these elements can serve as triggers for someone abused as a child. In her repeated calls to previous therapists about my empathic failures, Susan was making our relationship "safe enough" for her . She made each failure, which served as a sign to her of possible danger and future perpetration, public. She took our private relationship from behind closed doors and made it public. In particular, she let people know about my failures because to her, they were warning signs of a potentially unsafe relationship. Although as a child she had no way to ensure her own safety, she very effectively protected herself from too much vulnerability in therapy by making it a public relationship.

She also tested my narcissism. Would I sacrifice her to my image of myself as a good, empathic therapist, or would I be there for her even if that involved some discomfort on my part? This was an essential task of the therapy. To rework the destructive relational images gathered in the years of abuse by her stepfather and neglect by her mother, Susan had to find a different kind of connection: one that was safe, one that was responsive to and respectful of her needs and feelings. Although I took an interminably long time to "get" what Susan was doing to help protect our work together, I did finally understand and appreciate with her how effective and intelligent she had been in working out this strategy to maintain connection. And together, we built a solid connection around these early cycles of connection and disconnection.

Susan arrived with various diagnoses: anorexic, paranoid schizophrenic, depressed, borderline personality. The diagnoses seemed to better represent her treaters' specialties than her difficulties. As I have indicated, diagnoses, particularly Axis II diagnoses, do not seem of great use in a relational-cultural model of therapy. But clearly, it was helpful to know about her abuse history as that emerged. And many of her presenting complaints fit with a diagnosis of Posttraumatic Stress Disorder (PTSD).

A relational-cultural model of treatment has been used effectively in both individual treatment and in group treatment programs, including residential programs, for women suffering with PTSD or who are labeled borderline personality by others. The borderline diagnosis is particularly avoided in this model because it carries such judgment, often hidden anger, scorn, or frustration on the part of a clinician and because much of the early and defining work on this diagnosis completely overlooked the importance of abuse and early severe relational failures in the family of the individual so diagnosed (Stone, 1980). Abuse and early childhood interpersonal trauma represent severe relational failures: chronic disconnection typifies these early relationships. When a child who is abused, hurt, frightened, neglected, or disrespected by a caretaker attempts to represent his or her experience, and the parent denies, avoids, retaliates, or injures further, the youngster learns to keep authentic expression of pain and all other real feelings out of relationships. The child disconnects from herself or himself and from the other person. In many cases of abuse and trauma, these disconnections prove crucial for the actual survival of the child. The protective armoring is also essential to psychological survival.

PTSD connotes largely a condition of isolation, self-blame, shame, and immobilization. Healing trauma involves bringing a person back into connection (Herman, 1992). When trauma survivors enter treatment, they are initially quite isolated and fearful. Their relational images are filled with strongly etched expectations of hurt, disappointment, and terror in relationships. Thus, for a trauma survivor, moving into more vulnerability with another person touches enormous fear. A trauma survivor's strategies for disconnection are extremely heightened at the time of starting treatment. Although the longings to connect persist, they are dwarfed by the terrors of connecting. A therapist is thus carefully scrutinized, and there are many strong reactions to empathic failures. If a therapist misunderstands or does not "get" something or empathically misattunes, a patient may treat that as more than a failure: It may feel like an attack, a sign that a major violation or abuse is about to follow, as if at a neurological level, an *amygdala hijack* occurs, in Daniel Goleman's (1997) phrase. Under these circumstances, a patient moves into a traumatic disconnection. This happens swiftly, unexpectedly, dramatically, and sometimes alarmingly for both patient and therapist. For instance, a patient may abruptly become withdrawn and silent, manifest self-destructiveness, become rageful, suddenly leave the office, or quit therapy. Sometimes, a patient will accuse a therapist of being cruel, aggressive, or hurtful. Working with traumatic disconnections challenges therapists in treating trauma from a relational model. A therapist can easily feel ineffectual, helpless, anxious, or angry when a patient is disconnecting in these major and confusing ways.

Often, when a patient directs anger and disappointment at a therapist, the therapist will have a hard time not becoming reactive. Ideally, therapists remain responsive, but not reactive. Therapists will have a real response to what is going on, but will judiciously use that response and share it (e.g., "I am sad I have hurt you just now, and I hope we can come back and look at this together to better understand what just happened," or "I feel a bit uncertain right now, and I want to stay connected with you, but I may seem a little out of focus"—as opposed to "What makes you feel hurt right now?" or "Does this remind you of your mother?" or "You seem to need me to be confused"). Often, therapists withdraw into judgments and view a patient's behavior unfavorably (e.g., "She's being manipulative right now; she's a bottomless pit; she expects me to fill her up; she's a flaming borderline."). Therapists will often talk about maintaining boundaries or "setting limits" on patients. I prefer to talk about "stating my own limits," to let a patient know what my limitations are, to help the patient understand what can and cannot be expected from me. That involves authentic discussion, particularly helping a patient learn to deal with the inevitable limitations in any relationship. These limitations may have nothing to do with the patient, but are about the real qualities and limitations of the other and what they mean to the patient. For instance, Susan needed a lot of additional contact between sessions. Although initially I tried to be there for her, I realized that I simply could not respond as much as she needed me to. I accepted her need for more contact, but I also let her know that I could not be on the phone with her as much as she wanted and really needed. I did not pathologize her need for the contact, but I also let her know I could not do it. I told her that we needed to strategize together to see if we could come up with some creative solutions. She was not happy with my limitations, but she could see that they were real and that we had to build a relationship respectful of both of our limitations.

In a therapy relationship, real building and reworking of connection happens. Maladaptive and split-off relational images are processed. These relational images operate like expectations and keep people locked into old, often maladaptive patterns. Relational images that keep people out of current relationships are dealt with slowly, so that people begin to believe that they can come back into fuller and more authentic relationships. New relational images form. Where previously fear and doubt ruled, people start to hope for empathic responsiveness from others. Initially, this emerges in a therapy relationship but slowly generalizes to other relationships as well. The sense of empathic possibility, which grows in therapy, begins to spread into other relationships, and the convictions based on early relationships begin to fade. The person becomes open to growth-fostering relationships in the here and now. This allows for the development of an enhanced sense of vitality, increasing clarity about one's experience, and more accurate reading of others' experiences, so that one actually is able to make better use of information from others. It also leads to a greater sense of self-worth and productivity as well as an expanding desire for more connection. For people who have been suffering from isolation and distorted images of self and other, this leads to significant personal change and growth.

Empathic possibility and the development of mutual empathy lie at the heart of this change. For individuals locked into isolation by images of chronic disconnection and shame, opportunity for change emerges when they are able to begin to believe in the possibility of empathy and compassionate responsiveness. Susan engaged in a slow but significant shift out of isolation and suspiciousness when she figured out that I would not sacrifice her to my own needs and that I really wanted to understand her. She could see my responsiveness to her and that she was able to move and affect me. Although, at times, she perceived that she had upset me, more often she noticed that I cared about her and was affected by her pain; I was empathic with her pain, and I was sad or angry with her and for her, not at her. This made it possible for her to begin to question the pathological certainty of her earlier relational images. Perhaps not all relationships had to be predatory or abusive or unresponsive. Slowly, she could relinquish the fixed patterns of withdrawal and mistrust and begin to move into the vulnerability necessary to build close, growth-fostering relationships.

In working with trauma, it is very important to help a patient differentiate growth-fostering relationships from those that may be nonmutual or frankly predatory or abusive. People who have been abused are vulnerable to others' uses or misuses of them. Learning to judge more accurately when they are responded to in a caring and loving way and when they are subject to nonmutuality becomes essential. Often, this involves careful exploration of current relationships, helping a patient listen for patterns of neglect or uncaring on the part of the other person. The relational-cultural model in no way implies advocacy for sustaining all relationships. The well-being of all people dictates that they can, with the support of other people, move out of destructive relationships. For trauma survivors, many relationships are fraught with a sense of danger and with very little sense of the possibility of growth and caring. They need to learn what a growth-fostering relationship looks and feels like, that it involves an increase in energy, a sense of clarity, an increase in productivity, a desire for more connection, and a sense of self-worth. Recognition of these "five good things" (Miller & Stiver, 1997) can actually be taught to an abuse survivor.

Most trauma survivors are filled with self-blame and shame. They need to work on developing self-empathy. This often happens most dramatically in groups for abuse survivors. In these groups, women who are self-rejecting and self-blaming about their own experiences of abuse are quite empathic and compassionate with others who have lived very similar histories of abuse. Often, the women will suddenly turn to someone who is being very self-judgmental and point out that she has been very attuned and empathic with someone else in the group who had a very similar history. Together, the group will ponder what double standards they have regarding themselves and others, and slowly the empathy they bring so readily to the others in the group is turned toward themselves. Powerful healing occurs in these moments. Growth of self-empathy is more dramatic and rapid in groups of survivors than in individual therapy, where a trauma survivor will often be initially quite doubtful about the depth of a therapist's empathy and acceptance (e.g., "You're getting paid to be nice to me").

In working with trauma, relational therapists must address their own disconnections. When patients move into traumatic disconnections, a therapist often becomes unsettled and disconnected. Traumatic disconnections tend to occur under two circumstances. When there is an empathic failure on the part of a therapist, a patient may react with an abrupt, heightened disconnection, as if there is a major danger, and the therapist may even be feared as a potential perpetrator. The ordinary hurts and failures of therapy are often poorly tolerated by someone who has a history of abuse. Even at a neurochemical level (Banks, 2000; van der Kolk, 1988), overreactivity occurs. Therapists must understand that this results partly as a function of the psychobiology of trauma, the residue of repeated traumatic disconnections and violations on the part of caretaking individuals in a patient's life. This should be assessed for psychopharmacological intervention. At these moments, a therapist's work is to help patients stay grounded, remain in connection with their inner experience, and maintain enough connection with the therapist to stay in the therapy. But the therapist must also honor the strategies of disconnection and not push the patient for too much connection, for such pushing will flood a patient with affect experienced as intolerable. Therapists, then, must carry the history of the relationship, particularly the prior reworking of disconnections. They must hold the belief that further connection is possible, but must be respectful of the patient's need to reestablish safety by distancing and disconnecting.

A second frequent source of traumatic disconnection occurs, paradoxically, when a patient is beginning to feel safer and closer in therapy. As a patient starts to relinquish strategies of disconnection, often feelings of acute anxiety and of an intense lack of safety emerge. It is important to remember that connection does not connote safety and growth for abuse survivors. Closeness signals danger and impending violation. Often, as therapy moves forward toward more connection, a patient will suddenly move into a traumatic disconnection. These disconnections can confuse and frustrate therapists because they come at times of movement and progress. Often, in these paradoxical disconnections, a therapist will become angry or feel ineffectual and believe that the work has been for naught. Again, therapists must honor the disconnection, understand where it is coming from (i.e., the terror of relinquishing strategies of disconnection and of moving into the vulnerability of being more in touch with the yearning for connection), and invoke the overall movement toward connection as a hope and a reality. Therapists must also work on their own disconnections, so that they do not contribute to a patient's sense of isolation. Unfortunately, therapeutic impasses often develop around a therapist's disconnections.

RELATED RESEARCH

Although this model has been developed by listening to the voices of women in therapy, it joins a body of literature that includes research into the psychological experiences of both girls and women (Beleneky et al., 1986; Gilligan, 1982) and boys and men (Levant, 1995; Pollack, 1999). This research has documented that girls' experiences of themselves are developed primarily in relationship with others and that boys are taught to disconnect from their vulnerable feelings at an early age. More recently, several scales of mutuality (Genero, Miller, Surrey, & Baldwin, 1992) and relational health (Liang et al., 1998) have been developed to assess the effect of connection on people's well-being. A study of 12,000 adolescents (Reznick et al., 1997) indicated that the presence of simply one connection with an adult is the single most protective factor against high-risk behaviors (violence, suicide, substance abuse) for adolescents. A recent study on stress (Taylor et al., 2000) showed that males and females may respond quite differently to stressful life events: The age-old "fight-or-flight" response that had been presented as universal may, in fact, be gender-biased. Females respond to stress often with a "tend-and-befriend" response rather than "fight-or-flight."

Empirical, quantitative research on the relational-cultural model is still scant. This model grew from analysis of clinical data. But the bias favoring quantitative data over qualitative or clinical data may in itself be gender-biased. Evelyn Keller's classic work (1985) on gender and our models of science suggests that the Western model of science is heavily weighted toward a male model favoring objectivity, instrumentality, and mastery over nature. Our primarily

Baconian model of science and knowledge is based on a theory of knowing through distancing and objectivity rather than an empathic or contextual model based on a theory of knowing through joining. Furthermore, Western science is biased in the direction of elevating the importance of the individual and the separate self.

The relational-cultural model further highlights the importance of social-cultural factors in shaping individual lives. Just as individual causes give rise to disconnection, so societal forces also lead to disconnection and isolation. Thus, divisions across race, sex, class, and sexual orientation become sources of disempowerment and disconnection for individuals as well as groups. As Patricia Hill Collins (1990) noted, "People become objectified to certain categories such as race, gender, economic class and sexual orientation" (p. 228). Once categorized, persons are relegated to outsider or insider status, enjoying power or being at the mercy of others' power. This model highlights that power differentials exert a major impact on individual and group psychology. In a system that treats difference not just as difference, but as a source of more or less worth, and positions individuals hierarchically, diversity can rarely simply be "celebrated." Difference implies differential power and differential economic reward; positions of center and margin inevitably develop in these systems (hooks, 1984). The center abounds with power and privilege, and the margin lacks power and privilege. Those at the margin are treated as if they "belong" at the margin because of some innate deficiency or inability to "make it" in the dominant system. According to this line of thought, women are to blame for their deficiencies and people of color have earned their lesser status in the system. The myth of meritocracy falsely implies that people receive what they deserve—that if people only try and are intelligent, they can make it, that they compete on a level playing field. This position omits all the powerful constraints of marginalization and unseen privilege. It upholds the rationalization for those at the center that they belong there by merit, virtue, for good reason. Any systems analysis beyond the more limited system of the nuclear family has to take into account the powerful influence of these societal power issues. Power differentials occur both in families and in social institutions, and families are impacted by these societal dynamics.

Cultural values significantly influence models of health and strength. Existing models of strength in Eurocentric cultures, both in and out of the mental health field, are based on values of a dominant, privileged group. Men are particularly encouraged to deny feelings of vulnerability and weakness; yet feelings of weakness are ubiquitous and natural for all people. In addition to denial of weakness, dominant culture rests on the assumption that control and power over others provide the route to safety, well-being, and growth. The separation model posits that safety results from being separate, armored, and above others. In contrast, the relational-cultural model suggests that safety and well-being reside in building good connection and points to the development of strength in vulnerability. Relational-cultural therapists seek to build communities that can support people in their fundamental human feelings of weakness and fear. The model requires recognition that all people must struggle with vulnerability in a world where death and loss will forever remain mysteries and inevitabilities. Our traditional psychologies err in the direction of avoiding these realities of human existence.

Just as the relational-cultural model was first developed in an effort to correct the imbalances and errors in existing models of the psychology of "human beings" (supposedly gender-neutral), the model has also sought to move out of the Eurocentric position of assuming the primacy of White, middle-class, heterosexual experience. The importance of privilege or unearned advantage as well as the importance of unearned disadvantage in any individual's life is crucial to understanding a person's situation and important for a clinician or theoretician to pay attention to. Thus, to the extent that any of us enjoy unearned privilege, we need to be attentive to the impact of that on ourselves and on others (McIntosh, 1988). As a middle-class, White person, for instance, I need to take responsibility for and acknowledge all the privilege that has come to me in the United States simply because of these two identities. This privilege is largely invisible to those who enjoy it; its invisibility is destructive and hurtful to those who do not enjoy the same privilege. In the development of the relational-cultural model, we had to move from an early, privileged, and inaccurate assumption we made in defining "the psychology of women," finding "a woman's voice," to appreciating that there is no one psychology of women, no one voice, that there are many different experiences for women, textured and formed by race, class, sexual orientation, health, and ethnic differences, among other variables (Tatum, 1997; Walker, 1999). This contextual model delineates the power of our context to support or disempower us, to heal or hurt us, but clearly to define us and to have an enormous impact on well-being.

Collins (1990) concluded, "Each individual derives varying amounts of penalty and privilege from the multiple systems of oppression which frame everyone's life" (p. 229). Identifying these systems of oppression and privilege proves important because they significantly affect lives and, when invisible, often become the source of a sense of personal inadequacy, pathology, or arrogant superiority. To move toward empathy, true connection, and a model of deep human caring, each person must own his or her own vulnerability and find ways to support the vulnerabilities of others. This involves clear naming and owning of unearned advantage and disadvantage.

Hierarchical power systems involve taking advantage of the vulnerabilities of others rather than supporting and empowering them. Societies are composed of groups of dominants and subordinates, those with power and those without (Miller, 1976). The subordinates must always develop a sensitivity to the psychology of the dominants because they are dependent on the dominants. Thus, women attune to men, people of color attune to White people, children to parents, the disadvantaged to the advantaged. A lack of mutuality is inherent in this paradigm, however, because those in a position of power do not attune in the same way to those who do not enjoy power. The subordinates, then, tend to develop empathy with and sensitivity to the powerful; the powerful do not even see this attunement as being about power. Although there are many unintended benefits to the development of these abilities in the subordinate groups, the costs are enormous. Often, there is a sense of worthlessness, passivity, unwelcome dependency, inauthenticity, helpless rage, silence, or a lack of recognition of one's strengths and needs. These costs resemble the costs of chronic disconnection for individuals. Thus, when clinicians work with disconnections, it is important to assess not only an individual's nuclear family or intrapsychic causes of pain, but also the larger societal forces at work. Particularly if the clinician is someone who enjoys many areas of privilege, special work must be done to learn about and attune to the psychology of individuals who come from marginalized groups. An appreciation of the importance of power dynamics is essential. Often, clinicians who come from "the center" participate in a kind of arrogance of privilege in their assumptions about other people's lives and psyches.

The relational-cultural model addresses social issues and social change. The model contains the kernels of a reworking of the dominant Western psychology based on separation and elevation of individual above community. It fosters questions about many of the core assumptions of traditional psychodynamic models as well. In addition to use of the model in psychotherapy, work is proceeding to bring this model to organizations and institutions. Several theoreticians

(Ballard, 1999; Fletcher, 1999; Jordan & Dooley, 2000; MacMurray & Jordan, 2000) have pointed to ways that traditional business models and organizations "disappear" relational skills in the workplace. More accurate models of work would involve an open acknowledgment of the importance of relational skills such as team building, empowering others, fluid expertise, mutual learning, and caring about the well-being of the whole project. Again, the relational-cultural model poses a challenge to the old models of individualistic competition and the ascendancy of separation, stressing instead the importance of community building and resistance to existing workplace values. An ethos of competition and separation reigns in Western, Eurocentric cultures, but particularly in the United States. The dominant myths include: (1) competition always enhances performance, (2) attainable invulnerability, (3) certainty and the cultivation of pathological certainty, (4) self-sufficiency, (5) achievable objectivity, (6) unilateral change, (7) power over others creates safety, and (8) rational engagement is superior to and at odds with emotional responsiveness (Jordan, 1999). Relational competence depends on an appreciation of emotional intelligence (Goleman, 1997), awareness of the importance of integration of cognitive-affective processes (particularly in the practice of mutual empathy), and acknowledgment of our inevitable and unending mutual vulnerability and capacity for mutual support. This model questions many of the long-held and nearly invisible assumptions of some of our most cherished therapeutic traditions (e.g., neutrality, objectivity, and nonengagement on the part of a therapist). Inevitably, undertaking such a critique will arouse some well-intentioned and reasonable resistance from those invested in existing therapeutic and societal models.

The development of relational competence depends on living in a context responsive to one's voice and actions. Relational competence involves skills in empathy and attunement, and the development of relational intelligence and relational practice. In relational problem solving, the power of dialogue, of asking for help, and of sharing uncertainty are openly acknowledged. Cooperative efforts, rather than competitive one-upmanship, are encouraged. Value is placed on competence in service of community.

SUMMARY

Both at individual and systems levels, this model supports the expansion of growth-fostering connections and attempts to correct an imbalance in much existing theory that elevates the growth of a decontextualized, separate self. Although an individual's ability to participate fully in relationship lies at the center of therapeutic work, the ultimate goal actually moves beyond an individual toward the larger community. People are empowered to empower others, not to exercise power over others. This is an explicitly value-laden, pro-social model of development and treatment. Relational-cultural therapists do not push people toward perpetual connecting or toward being in constant physical touch with others. They do not force people to relinquish their strategies of disconnection when that does not seem safe. They bring people more fully back into an attitude of responsiveness and initiative, of relatedness and connectedness with others, with themselves, and with the world around them. Isolation represents a place of suffering. In isolation, an individual finds no way out of the hurtful patterns perpetuating pain, nor do contributions to community result. In contrast, connection nurtures healing, growth, meaning, possibility, and the development of communities.

REFERENCES

Aron, L. (1996). *A meeting of minds: Mutuality in psychoanalysis.* Hillsdale, NJ: Analytic Press.

Ballard, N. (1999). Equal engagement: Observations on career success and meaning in the lives of women lawyers. *Center for Research on Women, No. 292*. Wellesley, MA: Wellesley Center for Women.

Banks, A. (2000). *Posttraumatic Stress Disorder: Relationships and brain chemistry* (Project Report No. 8). Wellesley, MA: Stone Center Working Paper Series.

Belenky, M., Clinchy, B., Goldberger, N., & Tarule, J. (1986). *Women's ways of knowing: Self, voice and mind*. New York: Basic Books.

Broverman, I., Broverman, D., Clarkson, F., Rosenkrantz, P., & Vogel, S. (1970). Sex role stereotypes and clinical judgments of mental health. *Journal of Consulting and Counseling Psychology, 43*, 1–7.

Collins, P. H. (1990). *Black feminist thought: Knowledge, consciousness and the politics of empowerment*. Boston: Unwin Hyman.

Fairbairn, W. (1946). Object relationships and dynamic structure. In *An object relations theory of personality*. New York: Basic Books.

Fletcher, J. (1999). *Disappearing acts: Gender, power and relational practice at work*. Cambridge, MA: MIT Press.

Freud, S. (1955). Beyond the pleasure principle. In J. Strachey (Ed.), *The standard edition of the complete psychological works of Sigmund Freud* (Vol. 18, pp. 3–64). London: Hogarth Press. (Original work published 1920)

Freud, S. (1958). Civilization and its discontents. In J. Strachey (Ed.), *The standard edition of the complete psychological works of Sigmund Freud* (Vol. 21, pp. 59–145). London: Hogarth Press. (Original work published 1930)

Genero, N., Miller, J. B., Surrey, J., & Baldwin, L. (1992). Measuring perceived mutuality in close relationships: Validation of the mutual psychological development questionnaire. *Journal of Family Psychology, 6*(1), 36–48.

Gilligan, C. (1982). *In a different voice*. Cambridge, MA: Harvard University Press.

Goleman, D. (1997). *Emotional intelligence*. New York: Bantam Books.

Guntrip, H. (1973). *Psychoanalytic theory, therapy and the self*. New York: Basic Books.

Hartling, L., Rosen, W., Walker, M., & Jordan, J. V. (2000). Shame and humiliation: From isolation to relational transformation. *Work in Progress, No. 88*. Wellesley, MA: Stone Center Working Paper Series.

Herman, J. (1992). *Trauma and recovery*. New York: Basic Books.

Hoffman, M. (1977). Sex differences in empathy and related behaviors. *Psychological Bulletin, 84*(4), 712–722.

hooks, b. (1984). *Feminist theory: From margin to center*. Boston: South End Press.

Jordan, J. V. (1989). Relational development: Therapeutic implications of empathy and shame. *Work in Progress, No. 39*. Wellesley, MA: Stone Center Working Paper Series.

Jordan, J. V. (1992a). Relational resilience. *Work in Progress, No. 57*. Wellesley, MA: Stone Center Working Paper Series.

Jordan, J. V. (1992b). The relational self: A new perspective for understanding women's development. *Contemporary Psychotherapy Review, 7*, 56–71.

Jordan, J. V. (1995). Boundaries: A relational perspective. *Psychotherapy Forum, 1*(2), 1–4.

Jordan, J. V. (1997). *Women's growth in diversity*. New York: Guilford Press.

Jordan, J. V. (1999). Toward connection and competence. *Work in Progress, No. 83*. Wellesley, MA: Stone Center Working Paper Series.

Jordan, J. V. (2000). The role of mutual empathy in relational-cultural therapy. *Journal of Clinical Practice/In session: Psychotherapy in Practice, 56*(80), 1005–1016.

Jordan, J. V., & Dooley, C. (2000). *Relational practice in action: A group manual* (Project Report No. 6). Wellesley, MA: Stone Center Working Paper Series.

Jordan, J., Kaplan, A., Miller, J. B., Stiver, I., & Surrey, J. (1991). *Women's growth in connection*. New York: Guilford Press.

Keller, E. (1985). *Reflections on gender and science*. New Haven, CT: Yale University Press.

Klein, M. (with Riviere, J.). (1953). *Love, hate and reparation*. London: Hogarth Press.

Kohut, H. (1984). *How does analysis cure?* Chicago: University of Chicago Press.

Levant, R. (1995). *Masculinity reconstructed*. New York: Dutton.

Levant, R., & Pollack, W. (1995). *A new psychology of men*. New York: Basic Books.

Liang, B., Taylor, C., Williams, L., Tracy, A., Jordan, J., & Miller, J. (1998). The relational health indices: An exploratory study. *Wellesley Centers for Women, Paper No. 293*. Wellesley, MA: Wellesley Center for Women.

MacLean, P. (1973). *A triune concept of the brain and behavior.* Toronto, Canada: University of Toronto Press.

MacMurray, J., & Jordan, J. (2000). Women physicians: Relational dilemmas. *Work in Progress, No. 89.* Wellesley, MA: Stone Center Working Paper Series.

McIntosh, P. (1988). White privilege and male privilege: A personal account of coming to see correspondences through work in women's studies. *Center for Research on Women, Report No. 189.* Wellesley, MA: Wellesley Center for Women.

Miller, J. B. (1976). *Toward a new psychology of women.* Boston: Beacon Press.

Miller, J. B. (1988). Connections, disconnections and violations. *Work in Progress, No. 33.* Wellesley, MA: Stone Center Working Paper Series.

Miller, J. B., Jordan, J., Stiver, I., Walker, M., Surrey, J., & Eldridge, N. (1997). Therapists' authenticity. *Work in Progress, No. 82.* Wellesley, MA: Stone Center Working paper Series.

Miller, J. B., & Stiver, I. (1997). *The healing connection.* Boston: Beacon Press.

Mitchell, S. (1988). *Relational concepts in psychoanalysis.* Cambridge, MA: Harvard University Press.

Pollack, W. (1999). *Real boys.* New York: Random House.

Reznick, M., Bearman, S., Blum, R., Bauman, K., Harris, K., James, J., et al. (1997). Protecting adolescents from harm: Findings from the National Longitudinal Study on Adolescent Health. *Journal of the American Medical Association, 278*(10), 226–236.

Sagi, A., & Hoffman, M. (1976). Empathic distress in newborns. *Developmental Psychology, 12,* 175–176.

Simner, M. (1971). Newborn's response to the cry of another infant. *Developmental Psychology, 5,* 135–150.

Stolorow, R., & Atwood, G. (1992). *Contexts of being.* Hillsdale, NJ: Analytic Press.

Stone, M. (1980). *The borderline syndromes.* New York: McGraw-Hill.

Tatum, B. D. (1997). *Why are all the Black kids sitting together in the cafeteria?* New York: Basic Books.

Taylor, S., Klein, L., Lewis, B., Greunewald, T., Guring, R., & Updegraff, J. (2000). Biobehavioral responses to stress in females: Tend-and-befriend, not fight-or-flight. *Psychological Review, 107*(3), 411–429.

Tompkins, S. (1987). Shame. In D. Nathanson (Ed.), *The many faces of shame* (pp. 131–161). New York: Guilford Press.

van der Kolk, B. (1988). The trauma spectrum: The interaction of biological and social events in the genesis of the trauma response. *Journal of Traumatic Stress, 1*(3), 273–290.

Walker, M. (1999). Race, self and society: Relational challenges in a culture of disconnection. *Work in Progress, No. 85.* Wellesley, MA: Stone Center Working Paper Series.

Winnicott, D. (1960). The theory of the parent-infant relationship. *International Journal of Psychoanalysis, 41,* 585–595.

Winnicott, D. (1971). *Playing and reality.* New York: Basic Books.

CHAPTER 11

Existential/Humanistic Psychotherapy

PAUL E. BRACKE AND JAMES F. T. BUGENTAL

The value of any psychotherapy depends primarily on its ability to help individuals live with greater appreciation and realization of their true nature and of their possibilities—of their ultimate aliveness. What *is* is what exists. The existential-humanistic orientation is focused on the fact of Being itself as the central issue of life. Life offers an immense array of possibilities for our lives to be rich, satisfying, and emergent. Living also confronts each individual with the overwhelming question: How will I be most fully alive and truly actualize that which is latent in my nature? Thus, being alive immediately confronts an individual with formidable existential challenges. To meet these challenges, each individual develops a unique way of viewing self and the world and of acting in the world. Unknowingly, these patterns of living that humans develop to survive may also stand in the way of ultimate health, progress, and prosperity.

The existential-humanistic orientation is based on the recognition that an individual is assailed by a variety of factors, both personal and cultural, that pose overwhelming obstacles to becoming fully alive, that is, to maintaining a full awareness of one's sense of being. Forces that objectify the individual—including the many forms of reductionistic psychotherapy—serve only to further alienate an individual from self by insidiously fostering an increasing deadening of self-sensitivity (Bugental, 1965, 1976). As a consequence of losing this sense of inner awareness, an individual is thoroughly unable to vigorously direct his or her own life in the most healthy and satisfying ways.

Existential-humanistic psychotherapy seeks to help individuals recover this lost sense of being. Only the recovery of one's lost sense of being can alleviate the psychological distress that brings an individual to psychotherapy. Such a recovery depends on developing a strong and ongoing awareness of one's own unique subjective domain. Becoming attuned with one's innate subjective sense of self yields a greater integration of many aspects of being: an increased feeling of vitality, stronger mobilization for action, more committed choices, and more authentic intimacy and relationships (Bugental, 1965, 1976). The dual tasks of existential-humanistic psychotherapy involve disclosing the influences that block or limit patients' ability to "hear" their own subjectivity and encouraging patients to put forth committed effort to regain or enlarge the role of the subjective sense in living life.

Consequently, existential-humanistic psychotherapy contends that the only and ultimate site of significant life change resides in the subjectivity of the client. Further, only by helping clients to become genuinely aware of their own inner processes—attitudes, emotions, thoughts, intentions—in the *actual* encounter with a therapist can true life-changing therapy occur. That is, significant life change through psychotherapy happens only when therapy is focused on the actual living presence of a client. Thus, the existential-humanistic orientation underscores the atemporality of the subjective.

The foundation of existential-humanistic psychotherapy lies in respecting the primacy of a client's subjectivity as the only site of true change. Effectiveness is achieved only by making the working center of psychotherapy the actual presence and encounter between client and therapist. Growth and change evolve only by disclosing and confronting a client's current self-defeating perceptions, emotions, and attitudes as they are manifested in the lived presence of a therapeutic hour.

HISTORICAL PERSPECTIVES: THE CONVERGING SOURCES OF EXISTENTIAL-HUMANISTIC PSYCHOTHERAPY

The existential-humanistic approach, which is uniquely suited to address the most pervasive of today's psychological syndromes, has grown out of a complex confluence of existential philosophy and humanistic psychology. Although a comprehensive discussion of the psychological, philosophical, and political forces that promoted the emergence of the existential-humanistic movement exceeds the scope of this presentation, a summary provides a context for considering topics of relevance. Excellent and more thorough discussions of these historical influences are presented by Schneider and May (1995) and Yalom (1980).

PHILOSOPHICAL ROOTS

The philosophical antecedents of existential-humanistic psychology emerged from existential philosophy as developed in Europe in the nineteenth and twentieth centuries by Binswanger (1956), Heidegger (1962), Jaspers (1971), Kierkegaard (1949/1980), and other leading thinkers and clinicians. Although the existential tradition is essentially ageless, with literary roots reaching back to antiquity, the formal school of existential philosophy is generally thought to have begun in 1834 with the work of Søren Kierkegaard, the author of modern existentialism. More than 50 years before Freud, Kierkegaard had essentially developed what may be legitimately viewed as a fundamental theory of personality functioning. Further, Kierkegaard challenged the rationality, objectivism, and reductionism of his day. Thus, the emergence of existential philosophy in Europe coincided with a strong and growing dissatisfaction with the deterministic philosophies.

EXISTENTIAL ANALYSTS

The impact of existential philosophy was manifested by the emergence of a number of European psychologists and psychiatrists who rejected Freud's reductionistic model of psychic functioning and his attempts to understand the human being by using a schema borrowed from the physical sciences (Yalom, 1980). These early existential analysts contended that an analyst could only understand a patient phenomenologically—by understanding the patient's unique subjective experiences. This principle became a cornerstone of existential-humanistic theory and practice.

Although existential philosophy began to have a clear impact on psychotherapy in Europe shortly after World War II, existential thinking remained essentially unknown in the United States until the publication of *Existence* by Rollo May in 1958. In this widely influential work, May defined existentialism as "the endeavor to understand man by cutting below the cleavage between subject and object which has bedeviled Western thought and science since shortly after the Renaissance" (May, Angel, & Ellenberger, 1958, p. 11). Although the existential philosophical approach still exerts a significant influence on psychotherapy in the United States, the influence continues to be muted by the fundamental differences between the European existential tradition and the pragmatic tradition of psychotherapy in the United States (Yalom, 1980).

Humanistic Psychology: The "Third Force"

In the United States during the late 1950s, a synchronous movement was occurring in psychology. The growing discomfort with mechanistic approaches to psychotherapy was voiced by a number of personality theorists in the 1930s. This led to the establishment of the new ideological school of humanistic psychology. Theorists, including Allport (1955), Kelly (1955), Murphy (1958), and Murray (1938), shared with existential analysts the conviction that both the behaviorist and analytic approaches to psychotherapy severely limited understanding human beings. This limitation resulted from ignoring many of the essential qualities of being human: self-awareness, choice, love, creativity, and human potential (Yalom, 1980). In addition, humanistic psychologists insisted on moving beyond the reductionistic, overly objectified view of humans characterizing both classical psychoanalysis and behaviorism. Initially, Maslow (1962), Rogers (1951), May (May, Angel, & Ellenberger, 1958), Buhler (1962), Moustakas (1956), Jourard (1964), Bugental (1965), and Kelly (1955) propelled the humanistic psychology movement. In *Toward a Psychology of Being*, Maslow (1962) coined the term "third force" to contrast this movement with Freudian psychoanalysis and behaviorism.

Although existential psychotherapy and humanistic psychology share many fundamental tenets, they are not synonymous. The proliferation of humanistic psychology, which occurred in the 1960s in the context of the counterculture movement, generated a variety of humanistic orientations bearing significant implications for psychotherapy. However, because the academic community viewed many of the emergent humanistic therapies as anti-intellectual, a tenuous relationship has developed between humanistic and existential practitioners. More important, these two foundations of existential-humanistic psychotherapy emphasize significantly different aspects of the human condition. Whereas European existentialists have always highlighted human limitations and the tragic dimensions of existence (i.e., death and uncertainty), humanistic psychologists have focused more on human potential, the development of self-awareness, peak experiences, self-realization, and the inherent therapeutic power of the human encounter (Maslow, 1971; Yalom, 1980). Thus, the fundamental philosophical and theoretical agreement between existentialists and humanists coexists with a certain degree of intellectual tension, which has led to a varied and vigorous, if sometimes factious, family of existential-humanists.

PRIMARY THEORETICAL CONSTRUCTS

The Nature of Psychopathology

Psychopathology develops from the interaction of two interrelated factors: the individual's reaction to existential anxiety and the inevitable distortions and limitations that characterize each person's unique subjective vision of identity, the environing world, and a self-and-world construct system.

Existential Anxiety

Through awareness, one implicitly experiences the basic conditions of living, each of which confronts one with a particular challenge or dilemma, invariably giving rise to existential anxiety. When integrated into one's life, this anxiety becomes a strong and healthy motivation to live life fully and in accord with one's needs and values (i.e., to be authentic; Bugental, 1965). If, however, one finds life's basic dilemmas and issues too devastating, then a constrictive and dysfunctional pattern of living may evolve as a means of attempting to avoid existential anxiety. In essence, pathologies develop from constricted patterns of living employed as attempts to reduce or avoid the anxieties inevitable in confronting life's fundamental conditions of change, death and contingency, responsibility, relinquishment, a-partness:

Change. For physically embodied humans, continual change proves inescapable. Life itself is a dynamic process. Because of awareness of physical being, persons are subject to anxiety of pain, illness, or any destruction accompanying change.

Death and contingency. Confronted with finiteness, a human naturally experiences anxiety arising from awareness of death and fate (Bugental, 1965; Tillich, 1952; Yalom, 1980). Being limited, humans are confronted by both the infiniteness of potential and by limited capacity to control outcomes in life (i.e., powerlessness). Contingency means that the number and possibilities of all the influences that determine what will happen in the next instant, next hour, or in a lifetime lie beyond one's knowing and control. (Bugental, 1965). Contingency does not deny the individual's power to have some effect; it obliterates the illusion of certainty.

Responsibility. Because of the capacity to choose and to act on choices, humans are inevitably confronted with responsibility for what is chosen and done, and for what was not selected and not accomplished. Thus, guilt, sadness, and regret are inescapable and distressing aspects of life.

Relinquishment. Free to choose, humans necessarily face relinquishing—giving up "what might have been." Relinquishment represents an act of choosing to let go, rather than being forced to give something up. Through choice and relinquishment, the individual creates personal meaning. Surrendering choosing (e.g., through conformity) may result in an individual experiencing meaninglessness or emptiness.

A-partness. Humans always exist in relation to others and yet are always separate. This confronts a person with "a-partness," an anxiety-producing paradox (Bugental, 1965). In finding oneself separate yet related, an individual experiences existential anxiety generated by the threat of isolation and loneliness, or conversely, by the threat of engulfment and hence loss of self.

THE SELF-AND-WORLD CONSTRUCT SYSTEM

To organize living, a person requires some conception of the world lived in, its opportunities and dangers, and how to select and use the former and recognize and avoid the latter. These elements constitute an individual's self-and-world construct system, the unique set of personal constructs that compose the "vehicle" of personal living.

These construct systems remain inevitably subject to the flaws of perception, incorporation, and implementation that occur to some measure in each person's life. Some of these distortions arise because of social structures; most endure as exquisitely individualistic. The former often remain effectively invisible; while the latter, developed and refined through individual living experiences, often receive earlier recognition and greater attention in a person's perceptual and cognitive processes. Conversely, they can also become limited or distorted by those same exigencies. Thus, the individual writes a "story" of his or her life and advances it further each day and hour of living. One's self-and-world construct system cannot be totally accurate, for one cannot know with certainty what is "real" in an extrinsic sense. What a person can do—and, in fact, ends up doing—is formed from "best guesses."

Two areas emerge as pivotally important: perceptions of external "reality" and of one's own processes of reasoning. Because a person lives in (and is intrinsically part of) a perceptual world (i.e., the world as perceived or experienced), perception of one's own nature, including potentials of all varieties, consists of only imperfect and limited estimations. Thus, the distorted and restricting definitions and limitations that compose a person's self-and-world construct system represent a primary element in the development of psychopathology. When these limited and imperfect perceptions of self and world become significantly distorted and exert a severely constricting effect on choices, goals, and actions, then a psychological disorder develops.

Blocked Intentionality
Dispiritedness develops as a specific and pervasive type of disorder as a consequence of significant distortions and constrictions in an individual's vision of self and world. This gives rise to clinical syndromes characterized by depression, anxiety, and/or anger. The ability to translate healthy impulses and intentions into actions proves essential for psychological and physiological health. The capacity to effectively and dependably actualize positive intentions depends upon how a person defines self and world in a self-and-world construct system. Distorted self-perceptions that severely restrict expectations of what is possible or permitted of one's self and in one's world often lead to suppressing or eliminating healthy intentions. Blocked intentionality results in a deadening of vitality, which an individual experiences emotionally as dysphoria and manifests clinically as depression, anxiety, and anger.

CONCEPTUALIZATION OF THE NATURE AND PROCESS OF PSYCHOTHERAPY

The Primacy of Subjective Experience
Humans live in a perceptual world. The world as perceived provides a base or home. Human nature intrinsically involves perception, or best guesses, even about potentials. An individual can never know with surety that perceptions ultimately, objectively will prove "true," however one construes the meaning of truth. Clients enter therapy because their lived experiences are not sufficiently congruent with their anticipations (based on self-and-world constructs). Psychotherapy seeks to bring to consciousness the always implicitly present anticipations involved in these conflicts. To navigate in the "real" (external) world entails testing self-and-world anticipations, whether recognized or not.

Psychotherapy is intended to bring to consciousness anticipations involved in subjective conflicts. Existential-humanistic psychotherapy assumes that as a client recognizes such disjunctures between the anticipated and the actual, he or she will be able to amend the expectations so as to reduce or eliminate the stress, or, failing that, some compensating changes in life pattern may make the situation livable. Thus, psychotherapy is focused on a client's subjectivity and how to influence it. In therapy, matching subjective expectations with actual experiences proves essential.

The Actual: Focus of Therapeutic Attention and Clinical Change
Knowing what is "really so" about events or whether they agree or conflict with one's anticipations remains elusive. Nevertheless, perforce,

people arrive at understandings of what they term "the actual." This so-called actual comprises the described experiences of a majority of observers of particular events or experiences or the reports of persons of recognized trustworthiness who observed these occurrences. When expectations do not match actual experiences, disappointment and/or pain occurs. The source of this disjuncture needs to be explored. Psychotherapy helps to expose one's expectations and the impact of one's disappointments. This process may offer some relief from the pain of the failed expectancy and, more important, it may help the client to revise expectations so as to forestall further distress.

Essentials of the Psychotherapeutic Process

The "Search Process"

The core work of psychotherapy involves selective exploration of the subjectivity of a client through a more developed form of free association, using a client's distress as a directing criterion. In the search process, the therapist encourages a client simply to report whatever emerges in consciousness that carries any emotional loading. Thus, the therapist confines interventions chiefly to fostering as fully involved client presence as possible.

A therapist's focusing attention primarily on a client's full immersion in the exploration of personal, in-the-moment inner experiencing distinguishes the existential-humanistic orientation. In effect, a therapist supports a client in attending predominantly to what is immediately present affectively and intentionally in consciousness and to report without censorship or editing whatever is found there. This serves as the basis of the "search process." Extensive clinical experience demonstrates that, under these conditions, clients are impelled to explore distress more fully with a productive "working through." When sufficiently thorough, some alleviation of the presenting distress results, thus promoting more effective approaches to living.

Intentionality and Concern: Primary Forces in Therapeutic Direction

Experience has demonstrated that, when a person endeavors above all to report spontaneously appearing concerns and associations evoked by the feeling of distress, the individual discovers the deeper-lying conflicts, the source of distress. Helping clients learn to use this inborn capacity that empowers them toward greater self-governance is in itself a powerfully therapeutic process. The two life forces mobilized by the search process— *concern* and *intentionality*— are essential to a person's meaningful self-direction. Concern connotes the experience of emotional arousal felt when some matter of life significance is endangered or otherwise called into focal attention. Intentionality encompasses all the orienting influences that guide a person's observations, anticipations, and efforts. Intentionality brings dynamism into inner searching, making possible changes in perception and action.

Presence and Therapeutic Alliance

The ability to symbolize and subsequently manipulate symbols in order to plan actions gives human consciousness great power. This capacity for preaction consideration distinguishes humans from other species. Ironically, it also can pose one of the most intractable impediments to effective action. When truly *present* to a situation, a person more readily accepts into consciousness what is personally meaningful or emotionally charged. When one feels threatened or otherwise endangered, a primitive defense may reduce conscious presence by seemingly erecting a "shield of unawareness." In some instances, this takes the form of fainting, rage, or actual physical flight; in other, more usual instances, the defense may evoke confusion or even antagonism. Such defense results in a loss of immediacy and presence in the actual situation.

A client exercises only initial responsibility through physical presence in a therapist's office. When truly present, a client invests emotionally and intellectually in the work of psychotherapy and attends to subjective impact. This process fosters a healthy curiosity and readiness to follow one's sense of life concern. When clients invest themselves genuinely in relating to a psychotherapist and risk being as transparent as possible, therapy will prove most productive. A solid psychotherapeutic alliance of client with therapist forms one of the most powerful of human relationships and plays a major role in securing a successful psychotherapeutic outcome. Such an alliance occurs when a therapist becomes concurrently, but not identically, engaged.

THE NATURE OF RESISTANCE

The Self-and-World Construct System

A client becomes invested and participates in living and therapy through a self-and-world construct system. This unique perceptual system, which each person forms to orient and guide the conduct of life, literally forms the basis of a person's active participation in being. In interaction with personal life experiences, this construct system guides behavior and impels feelings, cognitions, and intentions. When the circumstances of life call the self-and-world construct system into question or threaten it, a person feels in jeopardy. Depending on the form, strength, and target of such threats, a person may react with any degree or form of countermeasure, including one that is life-endangering. The response to such threats constitutes a kind of resistance, which may be of any degree or form, from life-threatening (or -ending) to trivial and momentary. In psychotherapeutic interviews, a client's resistances play a crucial role in disclosing the threats the client is experiencing and the ways of countering them. This function proves central to the work of depth or life-changing psychotherapy.

The Nature of and Need for Space Suits

Persons live presence, purpose, and power in accordance with their self-and-world construct systems. These construct systems result from ultimate openness of possibilities into which individuals are born and within which they create an identity and a path of being. This constitutes a kind of "space suit" that permits directing one's life and exercising power in one's living. Yet, this very instrument for living and experiencing purpose also constrains living. Because of how humans define themselves and their nature, they can engage in an astonishing range of activities, but, at the same time, because of how those definitions identify limits, they may overlook and eliminate many possibilities.

Confronting Existential Anxiety

Recognizing that the definition of one's own nature is arbitrary and that one cannot defend against the many forces that could be injurious or lethal arouses existential anxiety—the anxiety inherent in being. In society, people construct, administer, and continually extend efforts in a shared concern for "safety" while knowing implicitly that absolute security remains always beyond reach. This existential anxiety has prompted great creativity, important alliances, and myriad original developments. Yet, these self-and-world constructs inevitably carry covertly destructive potentials. The pursuit of ultimate safety implies a constant reminder of finitude and, simultaneously, a perpetual prompting to creativity.

OPTIMAL LEVELS OF THERAPEUTIC ENGAGEMENT

The extent to which a client becomes fully and authentically involved in a psychotherapeutic interview proves critical in determining whether a genuinely therapeutic impact will occur. Presence signifies the quality of being in a situation or relationship in such a way that one intends to participate as fully as possible (Bugental, 1987,

1999). A client manifests a particular degree of presence through sensitivity to self and to the therapist and by bringing into action the capacity to respond. To be effective, the therapist manifests sensitivity to how genuinely a client is present and is prepared to devote strong and consistent efforts to increase the client's immersion in therapeutic work. This focus on evoking greater presence is a core feature in the process of existential-humanistic psychotherapy.

Bugental (1987) described two aspects of presence: *accessibility* and *expressiveness*. Accessibility refers to the extent to which a client intends that what happens in the therapeutic hour will matter, will have a significant effect. To be present in this way requires that a client invest in the therapeutic relationship and reduce typical defenses against being influenced by another. By comparison, expressiveness describes the extent to which the client intends to be fully known by the therapist. Expressiveness thus involves the effort of disclosing some of one's inner experiencing. These two facets of presence overlap, and often one will be exhibited more strongly than the other. Because clients vary tremendously in the degrees of presence that they bring to therapeutic work, it is essential that a therapist be able to assess a client's level of presence to help promote the deep immersion that is necessary for effective, life-changing psychotherapy.

The dialogue that occurs between client and therapist consists of different levels of presence. Bugental (1987) identified five levels of conversational presence, of which two prove most crucial to the success of therapy. Typically, when a client first enters therapy, conversation occurs at the first, *formal occasions,* level. Communication at the formal level involves relating between the client's objective (role) aspects and the similar impersonal facade of the therapist. This level of communication and presence typically happens in the initial intake interview. Understandably a client's presence at this formal communication level shows relatively little accessibility and expressiveness and may be marked by an emphasis on presenting a positive image to the therapist. Consequently, the therapist must seek a balance between allowing a client's minimal, comforting presence and the need to draw the client out of this superficial mode.

Early communication between therapist and client also occurs at the second level of *contact maintenance.* This transpires particularly when clients appear relaxed and ready to talk about their concerns, yet conveniently manifest significant restraint. Communication at this level includes the collection of factual and familiar information while the therapist watches for signs indicating that a client is ready to move to a deeper level of communication and presence.

Once the client has become comfortable with the nature of the initial therapeutic relationship, communication moves into the third level of *standard relating.* This level of communication symbolizes the level of presence most widely employed in most everyday situations. A client communicating in this mode displays a continued concern for the image being presented but, in addition, a greater involvement in disclosing inner experiencing. Communication at the standard level includes genuine, but limited, personal involvement, and consequently in itself, has comparatively little useful therapeutic impact (Bugental, 1987).

In order for therapy to be truly life-changing, communication needs to progress to the fourth level of *critical occasions.* Only when a client seeks to truly express to a therapist inner experiencing and encounters a therapist at this depth does lasting change and growth occur. Communication at the critical occasions level will result in genuine changes in a client's (as well as a therapist's), thoughts, feelings, words, or actions. Aiding a client in deepening involvement to the critical occasions level of presence in the therapeutic work requires a variety of therapeutic interventions. Many clients demonstrate a readiness to move from the level of standard communications to the level of critical occasions by returning repeatedly to a topic or feeling despite efforts to avoid it, unconsciously repeating a word or phrase or becoming physically restless or unusually still.

At the critical occasions level, communication primarily entails significantly greater emotional involvement by a client generally more concerned with expressing true inner experience than with constructing or preserving an image. The client at this level of presence focuses predominantly on exploring important inner experiences while the therapist at times recedes to become part of the background. Clients often manifest this greater presence by using more adjectives and adverbs in an effort to describe the complex fabric of their inner experiences. Although clients vary widely in how they display this more intense immersion and greater presence, many express themselves with more slang, exclamations, or profanity, and appear more relaxed and open in body language. All these signs indicate greater emotional presence and expressiveness.

In order to be truly effective, psychotherapy must include intervals of a genuine *intimacy*, the fifth level. Communication between therapist and client at the intimacy level involves maximum expressiveness and accessibility. Encounters of mutual intimacy characterize existential-humanistic psychotherapy. Intimate engagement emerges not through content but rather in the depth of a client's inner awareness and readiness to share that awareness with a therapist and by the therapist's deep openness and responsiveness to a client's immediate expressions of self.

Interactions at this level include intensity, emotionality, and intuition. In such engagements, the client demonstrates such deep immersion in the subjective realm that little or no concern remains about maintaining an image. Instead, most energy is thoroughly focused on expressing inner experience. Concomitantly, the therapist is maximally receptive and allowing a client's expression of self to fully impact his or her own human responsiveness. From encounters of intimacy arise the potentials for effectively confronting and changing lifelong patterns and true hope for developing a more vital way of being alive, of being more authentic. Although intimate encounters between therapist and client will end, if the therapeutic work goes well, others will follow as the client begins to apply newly found inner awareness to living.

METHODS OF ASSESSMENT

Traditional Psychodiagnostics vis-à-vis the Existential-Humanistic Perspective

The nature and importance of assessment in the practice of existential-humanistic psychotherapy emerges from its underlying view of the individual and distinguishes it from most other psychotherapeutic approaches. Traditional psychodiagnosticians have relied on formalized diagnostic categories. In existential-humanistic theory, individuals supersede the sum of their parts and, further, cannot be understood without considering the interpersonal context (Bugental, 1965). Consequently, the information that can be gathered from psychological tests, though objectively accurate, proves inadequate to the task of existential-humanistic psychotherapy: understanding the subjective experiences of a client.

Clearly, psychological testing can provide general objective information about a client's current symptoms, life stressors, general character structure and accompanying intrapsychic patterns of resistance, intellectual level, and indications of ego strength and impulse control. All this information is indeed interesting and suggestive when the goal is to treat a patient as one example of the general class of people or as representative of a specific psychological disorder. Such psychological testing, however, does not present these data in a fashion most useful in the actual work of existential-humanistic psychotherapy. Because the success of therapy depends on understanding the actual and immediate subjective experience of a client as presented in encounter with a therapist, an existential-humanistic therapist assumes that a client will present explicitly or implicitly the most important clinical data in a much more accurate, meaningful, and useful manner during the actual personal interactions of their interviews.

A more important concern about the negative impact of psychological testing stems from its interference with a therapist's ability to encounter a client as a unique and complete human being. A therapist as a person needs to come freshly to a person as a client, to encounter the client as an individual rather than as a representative of a class of people or problems, to experience a client with awareness uncontaminated by stereotypic information (Bugental, 1965). Although objective information and categorical diagnoses may be useful to the therapist who is uneasy with the uncertainty inherent in any psychotherapeutic relationship, they can prevent a unique client-therapist relationship from unfolding in its most useful and informative manner.

Similar difficulties can occur when the categories of current diagnostic systems are overutilized. Because a very common element in the psychopathology of many patients is the tendency to depersonalize and to objectify themselves, an overreliance on understanding a client and directing therapy by use of a diagnosis derived from the current *Diagnostic and Statistical Manual of Mental Disorders* (*DSM-IV*; American Psychiatric Association [APA], 1994) may only massively reinforce the pathology already present. Although understanding the specific behavioral and psychological symptoms that a patient presents may prove useful, collecting these extremely limited "facts" on the presumption that they will yield a sufficient portrait of a client and generate an effective "treatment protocol" amounts to the ultimate antithesis of the existential-humanistic approach.

Assessing Clients' Capacities for Depth Psychotherapy

A client's suitability for depth-oriented existential-humanistic therapy requires careful assessment. Depth psychotherapy by definition challenges clients to explore their subjective depths. Consequently, some individuals are not well-suited for existential-humanistic therapy. Clients who manifest significant personality disorganization in their general psychological structures must be carefully evaluated and monitored throughout the course of therapy. Specifically, clients who exhibit signs of active psychotic processes as well as those who manifest significantly fragile ego functioning (e.g., Borderline Personality Disorder) are often not good candidates for existential-humanistic therapy or for other depth therapies. Successfully exploring one's subjectivity may result in unusual actions, speech, and sounds. Although such reactions do not necessarily pose danger signs, an existential-humanistic therapist is responsible for monitoring such processes and for estimating the extent to which such cues are desirable and not indications of significant personality disorganization.

As interview processes evolve, a therapist gradually understands a client's symptoms from the existential-humanistic orientation. Clients will express the nature of life-constricting responses to existential anxiety (i.e., a client's particular dysfunctional syndrome) in the actual manner that clients relate to themselves, the presenting problem, and the therapist (i.e., the client's self-and-world construct system).

Phenomenological Assessment

The recent emergence of scientific and diagnostic methods congruent with the fundamental tenets of existential-humanistic theory offers an exciting alternative to traditional reductionistic approaches to assessment. In an attempt to develop a human science approach to understanding individuals, a growing number of theorists and researchers have adopted an approach generally labeled as existential-phenomenological (Fisher, 1989; Valle & Halling, 1989). This human science approach to assessment is intended to preserve the unity of the whole person while at the same time being an empirical and rigorous scientific discipline.

The personality theorists Halling and Nill (1989) have proposed that understanding an individual represents an *interpersonal* event; it is not something that can be achieved theoretically or abstractly. Comprehension of dysfunctional behavior results most effectively from grasping five interrelated dimensions: (1) context (the meaning of an individual's situation); (2) purpose (the conscious or unconscious intentions of a client's behaviors); (3) interpersonal dramas (the current interpersonal disturbances in a client's life); (4) critical incidents and phases (an understanding of critical incidents in stages of the client's past); and (5) embodiment (the specific physical manifestations of a client's being and distress). The principles and practice of human science in general and of existential-phenomenological assessment in particular provide a systematic method of assessing clients congruent with the basic themes of existential-humanism.

PRIMARY THERAPEUTIC INTERVENTIONS

DEVELOPING A THERAPEUTIC ALLIANCE

The clarity of a therapist's perspective for engagement with a client serves as a prerequisite for effective psychotherapy. Therefore, the therapist needs to establish in moderately specific terms his or her intentions, limits, and availability. Specifically, a therapist needs to define what one will or will not do, will or will not say, and what responsibilities will be accepted.

Further, a therapist must consider what expectations are appropriate and necessary for the client. While these responsibilities, limits, and expectations should be clear and solid, they must not be rigid and unresponsive to the therapist's evolving experiences of a client, self, and the emerging therapeutic relationship.

The Importance of Pou Sto

The mathematician Archimedes proposed that given a solid place to set his lever, he could move the earth. That place he called a *pou sto*. Bugental (1999) utilized this term to designate the conceptual position from which therapeutic interventions emanate as a therapist's pou sto. The existential-humanistic pou sto distinguishes it from other approaches to psychotherapy and is based on the concept that how the client uses her or his hour represents a valid sample of how that client conducts life. When entering therapy, the client's pou sto may be described as:

> The client is a person in the midst of his own life trying to make sense of what he experiences, trying to guide what he will do, trying to be more fulfilled and have less pain. He is talking to the therapist because he wants to be more able to be truly in his life and to accomplish his purposes more readily. When talking to the therapist, a client knows that at some level that the therapist is in a very similar situation. At that level, the client also knows that the therapist is neither all-knowing nor all-powerful. (p. 88)

Concomitantly, the authentic role and responsibilities of the therapist connote that:

> The therapist is here to aid this person in his efforts to find greater fulfillment in his life. She will do this best if she confines the bulk of her efforts to noting how this person pursues fulfillment, how well the person uses his resources, and how the person defeats himself. She can never know all there is to know about this person. He will always know more about himself. She does not know how he should live his life or

make his choices. She can, however, provide him with a trained awareness and a disciplined manner of intervening—both focused on how he uses his capacities for himself. (p. 89)

This therapeutic stance focuses the therapy on the client's unique manner of self-governance and self-defeating patterns, and how he or she uses personal resources to achieve life's goals.

Focus on the Actual
The crucial element in existential-humanistic therapy is the therapist's attention to the *actual.* A therapist seeks to identify in the immediate living moment the ways in which a client pursues or defeats fulfillment. The most impactful interventions address aspects of a client's *immediate* self-expression in exploring an important life problem. By comparison, psychotherapy directed by an effort to "understand" becomes an exercise in which client and therapist gather and arrange information in a detective-like effort to objectively analyze and describe "what the client's symptoms or problems mean." Such information-based therapy is likely to lose the power to produce real and enduring changes in a client's life.

Therapist Presence
Of equal importance is the therapist's presence in the therapeutic relationship. Therapists must bring their own subjectivity into the therapeutic work to be sufficiently sensitive to a client's attempts to reach the deeper levels of presence needed for genuine life changes. If the client is to work at the critical occasions level, the therapist must be able to enter into the therapeutic relationship as a fully alive human companion and not as a distant observer-technician.

Although much of the work of effective therapy is accomplished only at the levels of critical occasions and intimacy, the immersion that such work requires is not easily achieved or maintained. Even the most motivated clients benefit from preparatory talk at the standard conversation level. A variety of therapeutic steps are helpful in promoting a movement toward deeper communication. For instance, at some early point, the therapist explicitly transfers responsibility for the direction of the interview to the client. The therapist directly asks a client to explore the problem of concern (e.g., "Tell me what basically concerns you, matters to you, and everything you can think of or discover within yourself about what matters to you."). Similarly, the therapist can reflect in simple words what the client is so clearly manifesting but has not yet become aware of or verbalized. These initial interventions begin to penetrate into the subjective and help prepare the client for the deeper searching process. Therapists exercise patience with both themselves and the client, and yet begin helping to deepen the level of therapeutic work.

Alliance and Context
The specific amount of accessibility and expressiveness that a therapist contributes to the therapeutic process varies depending on the strength of the therapeutic alliance and the specific context or issue a client is exploring (Bugental, 1999). Consequently, assessing clients' readiness for interventions that promote working at a greater subjective depth proves essential for positive therapeutic movement. Any effective intervention must match both the status of the therapeutic alliance between client and therapist and the specific nature of the area a client is spotlighting. Attempts to push a client to work at a deeper level of subjectivity before the therapeutic relationship has developed the prerequisite trust and connection to support greater depth will lead only to greater resistance. A therapist must also be sensitive to the area that a client is currently examining in order to avoid topics or interventions that will seem too jarring. Consequently, therapists may decide to engage in explanation or direct teaching during the early interviews.

EVOKING GREATER CLIENT PRESENCE

To evoke and maintain deeper exploration of a client's central concern, the therapist must influence and help guide the direction and depth of interviews. Inevitably, as a client begins to explore a concern at a greater depth, characteristic resistances to being fully present will emerge as obstacles. The therapist's role then becomes that of aiding the client in becoming aware of and confronting these self-defeating patterns. Therapists aim interventions principally at promoting changes in the focus and intensity of how a client probes a concern, through interventions that utilize interpersonal "press" and subject-matter guidance.

Interpersonal Press

Interpersonal press refers to how strongly a therapist attempts to influence what a client will think, feel, say, or do in the actual course of their conversation (Bugental, 1978, 1987). Interpersonal press emerges in four distinct levels of therapist responses, with each successive level exerting more press on a client. The first level, *listening*, requires a dynamic alertness on the part of the therapist to "listen" on many levels simultaneously. Listening in this sense is active and involves not simply the typical forms of drawing the client out or understanding a problem, but also the therapist's active use of intuition, reflection, and keenly developed empathy. Content remains secondary to the primary message that listening conveys: Use this therapeutic opportunity to say what you need to say as fully as possible. Examples of the variety of therapeutic listening responses include silence, bridging (i.e., supporting to continue), restating, summarizing, encouraging, inviting expansion, and open-ended questions.

The second level of interpersonal press, *guiding*, requires therapists to take a more active role, even though the primary responsibility for directing the conversation remains with the client. The implicit message of guiding is: Talk to me about matters that are of concern to you. You take the lead, but I'll make more specific suggestions about how we should proceed. In this sense, guiding is used to support clients in moving from examinations of themselves that are comparatively detached to more personal and subjective ones. Thus, a therapist uses a variety of guiding comments to deepen and expand an area of a client's concern. Variations of guiding include identifying a specific part of what the client is presenting that needs expansion, pointing out choices available to a client without suggesting a preference, suggesting specific topics that the client may want to discuss, and using moderately focused questions (e.g., "What do you think are the sources of your frustration at work?"). Through such guiding, a skillful therapist can exert substantial influence over direction and depth without disrupting a client's immersion.

In using the third level of press, *instructing*, the therapist more directly leads a client through interventions based on objective information. The therapist's implicit message is: I want you to examine some specific *objective* points that are important to the area that we are discussing. When instructing, a therapist may be teaching, directing, or, in some other way, using the influence of authority to direct a client to explore certain objective issues in greater depth or with greater clarity. For instance, in response to a client's situational discouragement about progress, a therapist may respond by instructing the client: "Remember last month when you were able to deal quite successfully with that stressful situation at work. Right now, you're having a very difficult time, but, if you take a broader look at your successes, you'll see that you are making progress." Other types of instructing include questioning, rational advising (e.g., "I know you want to go confront your neighbor, but you know that, when you have done that in the past, you have regretted it."), supporting (i.e., therapist indicates a clearly rational judgment on an issue), teaching (i.e., "To pursue that job, you will need an updated resume and at least three personal references"), and directing (e.g., "You need to find out what each of your closest colleagues thinks of your proposal"). Although the value of instructing has long been debated in the therapeutic community, if it is used sensitively, it can greatly aid a client's progress.

A therapist exerts the strongest interpersonal press, *requiring*, when insisting, in a highly persuasive or confrontive manner, that a client change some manner of thinking or acting. For a variety of reasons, many therapists resist the dramatic use of strong press. The most common misunderstanding regarding therapists' employing high interpersonal press entails construing it as punishing or hostile. Nearly all the therapeutic interventions can be used in ways that are hostile and punishing or humane and respectful. With selective and appropriate use, many clients respond well to experiencing the strong convictions of their therapist. This is especially the case when a client receives strong and genuine press, like that of requiring, in the context of a mutually respectful relationship with a therapist who is clearly concerned for the client's growth and well-being. The message of requiring is: My intention is to persuade, insist, or, if need be, force you, using all my strength, to change in some way I believe is critical. I intend to do this because I believe that it is in your best interest. In this role, a therapist exercises authority, gives explicit directives, sets limits, and invites a client to experience strong emotions. Typical examples of requiring include using narrow questions (questions that suggest a response that is clearly appropriate), urging (e.g., "You know that you have a family history of heart disease; I hope that you will go and have a treadmill test"), approving, challenging, reinforcing, disapproving, and commanding.

Paralleling
Like interpersonal press, subject matter guidance or *paralleling* provides a method of helping a therapist to more fully understand a client and, hence, to be better able to direct a client to areas of greater importance and depth. Essentially, paralleling offers a means of considering the content dealt with in therapeutic interviews. More important, paralleling allows for dialoguing with a client as the therapist directs and monitors primary aspects of the interview: the topic being explored, emotions, breadth or narrowness of the topic, and the interpersonal impact of a topic. Paralleling assists both client and therapist to more fully understand the content of a topic. Monitoring the development of the content during an interview helps therapists to form hypotheses about a client's intentions and the nature of the relationship between client and therapist (Bugental, 1987).

The four types of paralleling enable a therapist to direct and monitor different aspects of the more *objective* content of therapist-client conversation. *Topical paralleling* helps to direct a topic a client is focusing on. Specifically, the therapist can follow a topic ("It's difficult for you to know which choice to make"), develop the topic ("What are the advantages and disadvantages of doing that?"), diverge from the topic ("It's a difficult decision that only you can make"), or change topics.

Feeling paralleling enables therapists to monitor and understand a client's emotional attitudes toward life and therapeutic process (Bugental, 1987). Specifically, therapists can simply follow the emotional state of the client, emphasize an emotion that seems important to explore, or help a client to grasp more reflectively the basis of a feeling.

The role and importance of feelings in psychotherapy distinguish the existential-humanistic view from other orientations. The purpose of existential-humanistic therapy rests in increasing the living awareness of clients, expanding consciousness about their being, how they use resources and powers, the limits they accept, and the choices they make. Therapy helps clients to become aware of how they are constricting their lives and awareness, and of the greater potentials that remain latent within them. The many strong feelings of pain, guilt, hope, and anxiety that inevitably accompany a deep exploration of self indicate clearly to a therapist which areas need greater examination, which are constricting views of self and others, and which may serve as potential motivations to promote therapeutic progress. Thus, although feelings are inevitable, directive, and highly instructive, they are not the "goal" or central focus of existential-humanistic therapy. Emotions in psychotherapy are similar to blood in surgery: Both are necessarily parts of the procedure, both serve cleansing and healing functions, both must be respected and addressed by the professional, but neither is the point of the procedure.

In *frame paralleling,* therapists request a client to focus more on the concrete, or conversely, to generalize from experience. Frame paralleling operates like a zoom lens on a camera; by adjusting the "frame" of therapeutic conversation, a therapist can effectively broaden or narrow the range of the client's discussion of a concern. Through *locus paralleling* therapists can direct therapeutic conversation to highlight the interpersonal arena of a client's concern (i.e., how the client's issue relates to significant others), the relationship between therapist and client, or therapist presence. The goal of helping a client become more aware of the unseen patterns constricting a client's capability to live most fully must ultimately guide a therapist's choice of how to focus and direct therapeutic conversation through paralleling.

Working with the Resistance

When persons are able to act in ways more fully in accord with their self-and-world construct systems, feelings of well-being, assurance, and optimism arise. When, however, the course of life makes such a harmonious lived experience more difficult, individuals experience despair, threat, failure, and (sometimes) rage. Anger, at times, plays a vital role in this system. Depth psychotherapy, when perceived as threatening being or worth, can elicit a variety of defensive emotions and actions. Therapists need to recognize that these feelings usually surface when a client somehow perceives personal identity as under assault. Attempts to call on or force a client to give up defensiveness and other resistances only make conflict more likely and bitter. A wise therapist acknowledges these resistance attempts as important signals and will learn from them and convert a client's opposition into a basis for working more deeply. A client's resistance expresses strength as well as feeling threatened.

The therapist may teach clients about resistance modes, which are inevitably triggered in their unconscious as a life concern is explored. This is accomplished by *tagging the immediate and consistent patterns of resistance.* Repeated identification of a client's actual resistances as they occur in the therapeutic conversation provides strong encouragement to explore the circumstances of their being elicited. The client is likely to find it possible to use this information about personal unconscious resistances through relinquishing the resistance or replacing it with other patterns. Or the client may make peace with the particular concern that had seemed an intolerable threat.

Clients also benefit from *education on the nature of resistance and its alternatives.* Working through a client's resistances poses an educative task, but does not necessarily entail primarily a cognitive exercise. As therapist and client identify and work through repeated instances of resistance and their associated subjective content, additional important material is likely to surface and can be integrated in a constructive manner.

A therapist can *intervene to loosen resistance* through teaching a client about unconscious patterns of resistance constricting living and through providing repeated opportunities to find other ways of dealing with life situations. Because so much of the impetus for the pathogenic subjective patterns happens automatically, not as the product of conscious choice, interrupting its activation and occurrence in therapeutic conversation strongly supports clients' having more choice and more conscious control. Resistance patterns that are sympathetically identified and stopped from blind repetition are more likely to be broken up and modified or discarded. Arguments or countercharges are likely to prove futile in any effort to persuade a resistant client to give up a motivated resistance pattern. However, repeated experiences of the intrusive and limiting effects of the patterned resistance, in combination with encouragement to discover more synergic paths, result in more effectively fostering a client's recovery from handicapping patterns.

MAJOR SYNDROMES, SYMPTOMS, AND PROBLEMS TREATED

A lack of centered awareness of being provides the common denominator in many forms of suffering for which clients seek help. This lack of centered awareness, often reflecting a condition of blocked intentionality attributable to the constricted and self-limiting ways in which a client views self and world, results in a deadening of vitality experienced as dysphoria and usually as anxiety. Concurrently, the individual is also confronted with severe cultural pressures. Recent economic, political, and social forces have assaulted the crucial experience of being oneself with durable boundaries and an internal locus of control (Cushman, 1990; Gendlin, 1987; Lasch, 1978). A pervasive sense of alienation and emptiness often ensues as the ultimate disabling consequence of such cultural factors.

The presenting complaints resulting from such intrapsychic constriction and cultural pressures take many forms: distorted self-awareness, depression, low self-esteem, a variety of anxiety-based syndromes, difficulties in relating, and many of the addictive syndromes. Very often, an individual's severely frustrated search for direction, completion, and meaning leads to futile attempts to fill the emptiness with status-laden consumer items, drug-induced experiences, sexual experiments, or pop spiritualism. These struggles produce many of the dysfunctional syndromes and problems confronting psychotherapists. Existential-humanistic psychotherapy is particularly well-suited to offer meaningful help to those suffering from these problems (Bugental & Bracke, 1992).

The many anxiety and depressive syndromes frequently resulting from blocked intentionality can often be very effectively treated using existential-humanistic psychotherapy. Research suggests that limited anxiety syndromes such as specific phobias and posttraumatic stress can be satisfactorily treated by a variety of cognitive-behavioral techniques (Barlow, 1988; Clum, 1990). Although a variety of therapeutic approaches can help reduce the symptoms of anxiety and depression, the underlying dynamics of these disorders are best treated by an existential-humanistic approach. Most short-term therapies are intended to develop better coping skills and improve adjustment to living, yet such changes are very often insufficient to help clients overcome the intrapsychic dynamics that chronically constrict the vitality needed to eliminate those life patterns generating the depressive and anxiety symptoms. The translation of healthy impulses and intentions into actuality proves essential for psychological and physiological health. The capacity to effectively and dependably actualize positive intentions depends on the definitions in a person's self-and-world construct system. The strength of existential-humanistic psychotherapy lies in permitting a process of discovering the many ways in which a person's unique self-and-world construct system constricts and prevents one from most vigorously and effectively acting on one's own behalf to design and maintain a meaningful and satisfying life.

Existential-humanistic psychotherapy also provides an antidote for treating two pervasive contemporary disorders: the Type A behavior pattern and workaholism. The Type A behavior pattern was identified in the late 1950s as a complex clinical syndrome that, through a variety of epidemiological and clinical studies, subsequently has been linked to premature coronary heart disease (Booth-Kewley & Friedman, 1987). The Type A behavior pattern involves behavioral dispositions (aggressiveness), specific behaviors (rapid speech), and emotional responses (impatience and anger; Thoresen & Bracke, 1993). Initially, Type A was conceptualized as an attempt to eliminate insecurity and to boost esteem through an excessive drivenness to accomplish a set of ambitious but often poorly defined goals, such as receiving recognition and advancement (Rosenman, Swan, & Carmelli, 1988). Like Type A, workaholism comprises a rampant and pervasive destructive syndrome characterized by many symptoms similar to those of Type A: difficulty in relaxing, excessive responsiveness to the expectations of others, a severely limited awareness of personal needs, perfectionism, and an intense desire to control time, events, and other people (Fassel, 1990; Schaef & Fassel, 1988).

However, both Type A behavior and workaholism have more recently been conceptualized as addictive syndromes arising from a desperate need to avoid existential anxiety (Bracke, 1992; Bracke & Bugental, 1995). Each of these syndromes exemplifies an *existential addiction:* an obsessive involvement in work or in nearly constant "doing" motivated by an intense need to avoid the basic anxieties of living. As with the treatment of depressive and anxiety disorders, cognitive-behavioral techniques can help reduce the compulsive behavioral symptoms of these disorders, but they cannot effectively address the underlying psychological dynamics.

Treatment of both of these is aided by including a primary existential-humanistic component (Bracke & Thoresen, 1995). Only through recovering a lost sense of self will a person be sufficiently powerful to confront and resolve the anxiety he or she is so desperately attempting to avoid through Type A behavior or workaholism. Exploring basic existential and spiritual questions advances effective treatment of Type A behavior (Thoresen & Bracke, 1993).

CASE EXAMPLES

Jennifer: Existential Addiction/ Type A Behavior

At 40, Jennifer is about to be promoted to vice president of a growing and successful pharmaceuticals firm. Although she has worked tirelessly on the company's behalf for the past five years and feels flattered and deserving of her impending promotion, recent personal events have dampened her excitement. She is keenly aware of the high pressure and stress of her work and knows that she has been "moving at the speed of a low-flying plane" for many years, yet she is shocked when she first experiences chest pains. The fact that a cardiologic examination does not indicate an imminent heart attack does surprisingly little to assuage her fears.

Jennifer also realizes that, although recently she has been working at a less frenetic pace, her energy is lower and her creative vigor has decreased precipitously. In short, she has suddenly lost much of the satisfaction that she had usually derived from her work. Her initial response has been to work harder in an attempt to "jump-start her creative juices." This has only increased her general sense of "burnout."

During her five years with the company, Jennifer rose rapidly to the position of top salesperson, largely through "working as long as necessary to ensure that a project was completed on time, to keep all customers satisfied."

She realized early on that this would require her to work many 14- to 16-hour days, especially on key projects. She had eagerly committed to meet this professional demand. However, she ends up working most evenings and weekends even when the actual demands of work do not require it. Thus, she has successfully created the image of a tireless, competent, hyperresponsible superstar who will never let customer or company down.

Not surprisingly, most of her personal relationships revolve around business. Although she felt that she did not have enough time for a traditional romantic relationship, she met and married a man with a similarly demanding profession as a stockbroker. Their married life consists primarily of shared commutes to work, small portions of evenings and weekends when they can put aside work, and occasional vacations to popular ski and beach resorts, usually as part of a group of business friends.

Jennifer enters psychotherapy with the goals of "managing her stress" more effectively and deciding how to deal with her impending promotion. Early therapy sessions are disrupted by urgent calls from customers received on her cell phone or by the nearly constant buzzing of the pager in her purse. Although she learns and applies the most effective stress-management techniques, she becomes increasingly distressed that the quality of her life does not improve appreciably. Even the most competent time- and stress-management strategies do not reduce the "stress" that chronically plagues her. She gradually realizes that, even when she copes exceptionally well with the demands of her work, she is somehow deeply dissatisfied.

The overwhelming distress causing her compliance with and sensitivity to the opinions of others is dramatically revealed during one pivotal therapy session. She enters the interview room in obvious embarrassment and distress. Focusing on this immediate and actual expression of self, the therapist comments on her distress. With painful self-consciousness, she apologizes emphatically for the fact that she has brought a cup of tea with her. As the therapist helps her focus on her embarrassment, her extreme sensitivity to the opinions of others becomes starkly clear to her. In this focusing on the actual, her oppressive self-denial and perfectionism emerge dramatically into her awareness.

Following this encounter, other subjective processes become more available for the psychotherapeutic work. The broader basis of Jennifer's dissatisfaction arise clearly in two powerful dreams. Ironically, when Jennifer's "burnout" requires her to rest more, she begins to have and recall dreams for the first time in many years. In the first provocative dream, Jennifer is in a hospital being prepared for "some operation that will help her." Her relief at the prospect of being helped turns to terror when she realizes that "they want to replace my heart with an indestructible high-tech heart, so that I can continue to work as hard as ever!" In her dream, she argues against the procedure and then flees.

The discussions about this dream serve to validate the crucial importance of Jennifer's having access to her subjective awareness. Her second dream packs even more power. In this dream, she is wandering through a beautiful house, a house "out of a decorating magazine." While impressed with the beauty of the upper floor, her anxiety begins to grow when she descends to the lower level. In this older and more authentic-looking part of her house, she eventually comes on a rough wooden table where she discovers two bodies wrapped in an opaque cloth. Her anxiety becomes terror when she realizes that, while still alive, these beings are suffocating! This intense subjective vision becomes the focus of subsequent sessions. With much less resistance, she realizes that she is like the bodies on the table. She is suffocating in her life. Her suffocating is further manifested by the powerful awareness that she is barely breathing during most therapy sessions.

Together, these dreams evoke a strong commitment in Jennifer to examine more carefully the value and personal cost of her professional obsession. She wonders if becoming a vice president will be worth further endangering her health. She is able to postpone her decision on the promotion. Gradually, she is also able to limit her working hours and dedicate greater efforts to carve out a few, but precious, hours of solitude in which to encourage the self-nurturing and reflection that she increasingly realizes she needs.

Although she has nearly dismissed the idea of having children, Jennifer's desire to become a mother erupts as another powerful realization stronger than she has known. "How," she laments, "can I possibly fit a child into my schedule?" As she examines her life more deeply, she is confronted with a critical, but more troubling, awareness: "So many people want a piece of me that soon there will be nothing left! How can I hope to take care of a child if I haven't learned who I am and how to care for myself?"

Comment
In living her life as a "low-flying plane," Jennifer developed the pervasive self-ignorance characteristic of individuals with some form of existential addiction, especially those who manifest Type A behavior or workaholism. Compulsive frenzy and excessive accommodation to the demands of others have thoroughly numbed her to her own needs and sense of identity. Her advanced existential addiction has enabled her to temporarily avoid the anxieties of responsibility, relinquishment, and mortality. Typical of clients manifesting an existential addiction, she has temporarily avoided the responsibility of personal choice. She allows her professional role and company to excessively determine who she is and what she does.

Although such conformity allows her to avoid the difficult task of becoming self-aware and the burden of making self-based choices, it has inevitably devolved into a deadening emptiness, superficial relationships, and, clearly, chronic depression. Like many individuals engaged in attempts to avoid existential anxieties through a workaholic or Type A lifestyle, Jennifer enters psychotherapy with the illusion that her "stress" can be effectively "managed" without making any significant changes in her life.

Jennifer's continuous connection to her company reveals another aspect of her existential addiction: Repeatedly demonstrating her crucial importance to the company may be her way of establishing her "specialness." A belief in personal specialness can serve to insulate an individual from many powerful existential anxieties that inevitably lurk beyond the edge of consciousness. For Jennifer, the talisman of specialness may help her believe that she is exempt from aging and death, an issue reflected both in her concerns about her health and her emerging ambivalence about having children.

During therapy, Jennifer begins to realize the futility of stress management as a long-term solution. For her, as for most individuals who manifest existential addictions through Type A behavior or work addiction, even the most effective strategies for managing time and stress usually prove impotent. As long as Jennifer copes with work demands by not considering her unique needs and values, she will continue to experience chronic stress and a confusing depression. The apparent avoidance of conflict that seems to come from allowing herself to be directed by others and her company will continue to undermine her sense of identity and potency. She will experience such a painful, but unconscious, loss of identity as profoundly "stressful." What must emerge in her therapy is the awareness that *living a superficial and inauthentic life is inevitably "stressful," regardless of one's coping repertoire.*

As she begins to value her sense of self, Jennifer's subjectivity becomes more available and eventually is expressed powerfully through her dreams. The dramatic contents of her dreams—not wanting a "high-tech heart" and emerging awareness of how little she allows herself to "breathe" in the world—connote Jennifer's growing desire to confront the existential dilemmas she has desperately sought to avoid. The stark and frightening awareness of her pervasive self-ignorance, self-denial, and how she is being suffocated by her overconcern for the opinions of others and for her work combine to evoke a potent motivation to rebuild her life in a healthier way. Anything short of such an intense personal confrontation might well be inadequate to dislodge her existential addiction.

PHIL: DISPIRITEDNESS, ANXIETY, AND ANGER

In his intake interview, Phil presents two contrasting selves. He portrays himself as earnest, troubled, and anxious for help. The other self is crouched behind his words, frightened, and anxious not to be seen as in any way as falling short of having a professional standard of candor and sophistication about his own psychodynamics. It is clearly the therapist's task to help him bring the strengths of the former to the service of the needy and frightened latter. This split is implicit in nearly everything he does and says.

In the first interview, a rather stiff and formal self-introduction, Phil expresses little beyond his age (37), academic status (doctoral candidate in psychology), and personal status (married to a fellow student who evidently is winning greater academic recognition). His own summary at the end of our second interview is astonishingly accurate and may be more revealing than he intended:

> Well, I've told you about all I think that's important. If you want to ask me anything, please do. I don't have anything to hide from you; it's just that I'm so worried about the prelims that I can't concentrate as I need to. It's so important to me to pass those exams because I can't afford to take another year before I start earning more. This internship in the student health service pays so little that if it weren't for Joyce's stipend at the county clinic, we just couldn't make it.

This summation comes at least figuratively through clenched teeth. Phil is so tense, so internally pressured (to seek a therapist to satisfy the psychology department's requirement for those intending a doctorate), that the therapist becomes concerned about Phil's ability to let himself use the rather brief (and often shallow) service that Student Health Service can offer doctoral candidates.

THERAPIST: You seem rather tense as you tell me about your situation. (Checking to note how much perspective Phil displays.)

PHIL: Oh! No, I, uh... (Pauses, takes deep breath.) Yes. (A wry smile.) Uh, yes, I guess I am. It's only that so much depends on my getting through and getting my degree and getting to earning again. It's been so tough for me to depend so much on Joyce's earnings. The damn student health service pays about as much as a slave factory.

THERAPIST: Really makes you mad. (Pausing to watch how Phil handles this mild confrontation.)

PHIL: Oh, don't get me wrong. I'm glad to have that stipend. It's just such a starvation-level thing that I... (Stops, eyeing the therapist, obviously aware of an assessing attention, but making his own assessment of the therapist, which is appropriate.)

THERAPIST: (Waits quietly and then observes.) You cut yourself off very abruptly just then. What happened?

PHIL: Oh, I... (Pauses, considering.) I just wondered whether I was sounding like a complainer and ungrateful for the help I'm getting. (Pauses, watching the therapist's face so intently that it transforms what he says into a question.)

THERAPIST: Well, that certainly was a kind of complaint, wasn't it? (Asking with a smile hopefully perceived as collegial, and wondering whether Phil has a mature balance to his perspective.)

PHIL: (Pauses, then a reluctant smile comes across his face.) Ulp! You got me. (Expresses a small, reluctant laugh.)

THERAPIST: (Thinks, "Good for him!"; waits.) So?

PHIL: So I wish I could earn more, not be so dependent on Joyce.

THERAPIST: Being so dependent bugs you?

PHIL: Yeah. You know it gets me two ways: First, because I'm the husband and should be earning more than she does, and, second, because even with her earnings added to mine, we are so close to the edge that we can't think about having any kids for some time, and we're both in our mid-30s. (Stops somewhat abruptly, still very watchful for my reactions.)

The interview proceeds in much the same way for the rest of the hour. The therapist's summary impression basically centers on three characteristics; Phil shows an important ability to be self-aware and self-disclosing; his dispiritedness is accompanied by an appropriate but unacknowledged anger; further, he manifests a pervasive anxiety generated by his intense need to present himself as "reasonable, balanced and self-aware"—even in the midst of a grinding, confusing, and unsatisfying life. The very self-and-world construct system that has enabled him to achieve success thus far is now abetting deep anger and depression. He is troubled by feelings that he is not fulfilling the male role as well as he should, but there too he shows some insight. He is under quite a bit of social pressure because of his wife's greater professional advancement (the stipend she has carries more prestige and pays better). Here, less evidence of insight peeks through, but in all, there is sufficient indication of a genuine potential to gain from further psychotherapy.

RESEARCH

Because of the historical roots and underlying philosophical principles of this approach, existential-humanistic psychotherapists maintain a strong fundamental skepticism about the ultimate accuracy and clinical usefulness of psychotherapy outcome research. That an individual cannot be accurately or sufficiently understood through conventional objectivist and reductionist research constitutes a fundamental premise of the existential-humanistic orientation. Specifically, the principle that individuals amount to much more than the sum of their parts and, therefore, must be considered as a whole represents the antithesis of the reductionistic basis for empirical research.

Further, enabling a client to become most fully alive and hence to bring maximum energy and commitment to the unique task of constructing and living an authentic life remains the fundamental goal of existential-humanistic psychotherapy. Consequently, although reducing a client's distressing symptoms is important, it is not the predominant goal of therapy. Therefore, whereas empirical research may be useful in measuring gross outcome variables and assessing the efficacy of a treatment in reducing specific and measurable psychological symptoms, it is generally insufficient to examine and measure those phenomena and dynamics that are most central to the therapeutic processes and to the goals of existential-humanistic therapy.

However, Yalom (1980) discussed research regarding the nature and incidence of the existential anxieties that play a primary role in the development of psychopathology. Bugental (1976) and Yalom (1989) expanded on the central processes and outcomes of individual psychotherapy cases in rich and complex detail.

Perhaps most important, the emerging field of phenomenological research and assessment holds great promise for the eventual development of a human science sufficient to accurately capture and examine a phenomenon as unique and complex as psychotherapy (Efran, Lukens, & Lukens, 1988; Howard, 1991; Polkinghorne, 1988; Triandis, 1972).

SUMMARY

Although all eras undoubtedly seem troubled and challenging to those living within them, modern life consistently confronts individuals with obstacles always formidable, sometimes overwhelming, and usually insidiously destructive to the vitality of the self. When lack of meaning and emptiness remain pervasive, effective psychotherapy in our times must seek to evoke greater aliveness, release suppressed inner sensitivity, and support the realization of potentials for being most fully alive.

REFERENCES

Allport, G. W. (1955). *Becoming: Basic considerations for a psychology of personality.* New Haven, CT: Yale University Press.

American Psychiatric Association. (1994). *Diagnostic and statistical manual of mental disorders* (4th ed.). Washington, DC: Author.

Barlow, D. A. (1988). *Anxiety and its disorders: The nature and treatment of anxiety and panic.* New York: Guilford Press.

Binswanger, L. (1956). Existential analysis and psychotherapy. In F. Fromm-Reichman & J. Moreno (Eds.), *Progress in psychotherapy* (pp. 138–148). New York: Grune & Stratton.

Booth-Kewley, S., & Friedman, H. (1987). Psychological predictors of heart disease: A quantitative review. *Psychological Bulletin, 101,* 343–362.

Bracke, P. E. (1992, March). *An existential-humanistic view of the Type A behavior pattern.* Paper presented at the Society of Behavioral Medicine, thirteenth annual scientific session, New York.

Bracke, P. E., & Bugental, J. F. T. (1995). Existential addiction: A model for treating Type A behavior and workaholism. In T. C. Pauchant (Ed.), *In search of meaning.* San Francisco: Jossey-Bass.

Bracke, P. E., & Thoresen, C. (1995). Reducing Type A behavior patterns: A structured group approach. In R. Allan & S. Scheidt (Eds.), *Heart and mind: The practice of cardiac psychology* (pp. 255–290). Washington, DC: American Psychological Association.

Bugental, J. F. T. (1965). *The search for authenticity: An existential-humanistic approach to psychotherapy.* New York: Holt, Rinehart and Winston.

Bugental, J. F. T. (1976). *The search for existential identity: Patient-therapist dialogs in humanistic psychotherapy.* San Francisco: Jossey-Bass.

Bugental, J. F. T. (1978). *Psychotherapy and process: The fundamentals of an existential-humanistic approach.* New York: McGraw-Hill.

Bugental, J. F. T. (1987). *The art of the psychotherapist.* New York: Norton.

Bugental, J. F. T. (1999). *Psychotherapy isn't what you think.* Phoenix, AZ: Zeig, Tucker.

Bugental, J. F. T., & Bracke, P. E. (1992). The future of existential-humanistic psychotherapy. *Psychotherapy, 29*(1), 28-33.

Bugental, J. F. T., & Kleiner, R. I. (1993). Existential psychotherapies. In G. Stricker & J. Gold (Eds.), *The comprehensive handbook of psychotherapy integration.* New York: Plenum Press.

Buhler, C. (1962). *Values in psychotherapy.* New York: Free Press of Glencoe.

Clum, G. A. (1990). *Coping with panic.* Pacific Grove, CA: Brooks/Cole.

Cushman, P. (1990). Why the self is empty. *American Psychologist, 45,* 599–611.

Efran, J. S., Lukens, R. J., & Lukens, M. D. (1988). Constructivism: What's in it for you? *Family Therapy Networker, 12,* 27-35.

Fassel, D. (1990). *Working ourselves to death.* San Francisco: Harper San Francisco.

Fisher, C. T. (1989). Personality and assessment. In R. Valle & S. Halling (Eds.), *Existential-phenomenological perspectives in psychology* (pp. 157–178). New York: Plenum Press.

Gendlin, E. T. (1987). A philosophical critique of the concept of narcissism: The significance of the awareness movement. In D. Levin (Ed.), *Pathologies of the modern self: Postmodern studies on narcissism, schizophrenia, and depression* (pp. 251–304). New York: University Press.

Halling, S., & Nill, D. (1989). Demystifying psychopathology: Understanding disturbed persons. In R. Valle & S. Halling (Eds.), *Existential-phenomenological perspectives in psychology* (pp. 179–192). New York: Plenum Press.

Heidegger, M. (1962). *Being and time.* New York: Harper & Row.

Howard, G. S. (1991). Culture tales: A narrative approach to thinking, cross-cultural psychology, and psychotherapy. *American Psychologist, 46,* 187–197.

Jaspers, K. (1971). *Philosophy of existence.* Philadelphia: University of Pennsylvania Press.

Jourard, S. M. (1964). *The transparent self: Self-disclosure and well-being.* New York: Van Norstrand.

Kelly, G. A. (1955). *The psychology of personal constructs.* New York: Norton.

Kierkegaard, S. (1980). *The sickness unto death* (V. Hong & E. Hong, Trans.). Princeton, NJ: Princeton University Press. (Original work published 1949)

Lasch, C. (1978). *The culture of narcissism: American life in an age of diminishing expectations.* New York: Norton.

Maslow, A. (1962). *Toward a psychology of being.* New York: Van Norstrand.

Maslow, A. (1971). *The farther reaches of human nature.* New York: Viking Press.

May, R., Angel, E., & Ellenberger, H. F. (1958). *Existence: A new dimension in psychiatry and psychology.* New York: Basic Books.

Moustakas, C. E. (1956). *The self.* New York: Harper & Row.

Murphy, G. (1958). *Human potentialities.* New York: Basic Books.

Murray, H. A. (1938). *Explorations in personality.* New York: Oxford University Press.

Polkinghorne, D. P. (1988). *Narrative psychology.* Albany: State University of New York Press.

Rogers, C. R. (1951). *Client-centered therapy: Its current practice, implications and theory.* Boston: Houghton Mifflin.

Rosenman, R. H., Swan, G. E., & Carmelli, D. (1988). Definition, assessment, and evolution of the Type A behavior pattern. In B. K. Houston & C. R. Snyder (Eds.), *Type A behavior pattern: Research, theory, and prevention* (pp. 8–31). New York: Wiley.

Schaef, A. W., & Fassel, D. (1988). *The addictive organization.* San Francisco: Harper San Francisco.

Schneider, K. J., & May, R. (1995). *The psychology of existence.* New York: McGraw-Hill.

Thoresen, C., & Bracke, P. E. (1993). Reducing coronary recurrences and coronary prone behavior: A structured group approach. In J. Spira (Ed.), *Group therapy for the medically ill.* New York: Guilford Press.

Tillich, P. (1952). *The courage to be.* New Haven, CT: Yale University Press.

Triandis, H. C. (1972). *The analysis of subjective culture.* New York: Wiley.

Valle, R., & Halling, S. (1989). *Existential-phenomenological perspectives in psychology.* New York: Plenum Press.

Yalom, I. D. (1980). *Existential psychotherapy.* New York: Basic Books.

Yalom, I. D. (1989). *Love's executioner.* New York: Basic Books.

CHAPTER 12

Spiritually-Sensitive Psychotherapy

HARRY J. APONTE

HISTORY OF THE THERAPEUTIC APPROACH

The relationship between psychology and spirituality involves a controversial history dating back centuries (Vande Kemp, 1996). In contemporary psychotherapy's history, psychoanalysis has given therapy a "reputation of being fundamentally hostile to religion" (Wulff, 1991, p. 299). Erich Fromm (1947), a representative of the secular tradition in psychoanalysis, observed: "The Enlightenment taught man that he could trust his own reason as a guide to establishing valid ethical norms and that he could rely on himself, needing neither revelation nor the authority of the church in order to know good and evil" (p. 5). Paradoxically, Fromm also noted that "modern man" has progressed to a "state of moral confusion," adopting a view that "value judgments and ethical norms are exclusively matters of taste or arbitrary preference" (p. 5). He proceeded to offer a solution of even more secular humanism, however, whereby "valid ethical norms [are] formed by man's reason and by it alone" (p. 6).

In spite of this negative legacy, there has been a persistent current of interest in religion and spirituality among leaders in the field. Jung (Wulff, 1991) directed important attention to the transcendent. Adler (1933/1973), in contrast to psychologists who held a "mechanistic" view of the human psyche, approached psychology with the assumption that "the soul is a part of life" (pp. 84–85). Frankl (1948/1975) recognized the importance of the spiritual dimension in human development and motivation. Allport (1950) explored the development of religion, conscience, and faith and their implications for mental health. Karl Menninger (1964), a pioneer U.S. psychoanalyst, sought a rapprochement: "The basis of all religion is the duty to love God and offer our help to His children—and psychiatry, too, is dedicated to the latter duty" (p. xiv).

Even though U.S. colonial history was rooted in the pursuit of religious freedom, and the founders crafted a Constitution meant to

---

Theresa Romeo-Aponte contributed substantially to the conceptualization and writing of this chapter.

guarantee freedom, contemporary U.S. society has leaned toward a secular bias (Bellah, Madsen, Sullivan, Swidler, & Tipton, 1991). The principle of separation of church and state has been interpreted so as to remove religion from the public forum. Woolfolk (1998) suggested that "secularization is sometimes thought to be the essential characteristic of modernity" (p. 10), adding that "the great tide of modernity ... washed away much of the cultural glue that had held societies and psyches together" (p. 11). Public policy in the United States has contributed to a secular culture that reflects a secular psychology.

The trend in today's society revolves around the loss of community. Putnam (2000) observed, "We are less connected" (p. 183), and further, "The classic institutions of American civic life, both religious and secular, have been 'hollowed out'" (p. 72). Self-preoccupied society has pulled people away from reliance on each other and on the supernatural. Today's technology has also depersonalized our connections. Koretz, writing in *Business Week,* (2000b), cited a study by Stanford University's Institute for the Quantitative Study of Society that some "25% of regular Web users indicate that they now are spending less time attending social events and talking on the phone to friends and family, and 13% report reduced face-to-face social and familial interactions" (p. 36). What we see in the United States, the world's most technically advanced and economically prosperous nation, is that people have become increasingly more absorbed with what they want for themselves. Community has suffered, and so have marriage and family (Aponte, 1994a).

The explosion of information through technology has also contributed to an illusion of great individual, personal power. The computer, through the Internet, has given each user access to the world. The more informed people are, the more independent they feel, not only from community but also from church and government interpreting society and directing their lives. When people can know for themselves, they can decide for themselves. A more educated U.S. society has also become a more secularized society (Bellah et al., 1991). The more skillful and competent have succeeded fabulously, while the less able in today's society, when also lacking the supports of family and community, are falling more often into personal failure. The gap between the haves and have-nots has increased (Koretz, 2000a). Today's exaggerated pursuit of personal independence and preoccupation with personal worth have contributed to a lonelier and more stressed society. Yet, there seems to be a backlash to today's soul-less and impersonal info-tech wired times. A resurgence of interest in the spiritual has arisen.

Robert William Fogel (2000), the secular-minded scientist and Nobel prize-winning economist, has recently written about modern materialistic society's most "urgent spiritual needs ... secular as well as sacred" (p. 1). Recognizing that the poor in a modern society like the United States "are rich by past or Third World standards" (p. 3), he argued that their greatest disadvantage today is not the deprivation of material but of spiritual assets, such as the "arts, theology, ethics, and moral philosophy," which lead to "self-realization" (p. 2). He perceived these secular "spiritual" needs as exemplified most evidently among the poor, but, for him, they are critically pertinent to all of modern materialistic society. Even within a secularized world, recognition of a need for the spiritual in human lives is growing.

As people in society find themselves more on their own, they live with the greater anxiety and stress of having to compete to survive. It seems self-evident that modern society needs to recognize the spiritual thirst of today's people. It follows that psychotherapists need to acknowledge that to succeed with today's more insecure, self-absorbed, and materialistic population, they must learn how to speak to the spiritual dimensions of people's human struggles.

CLIENTS CHANGE AND THERAPY CHANGES

Today's clients come more personally stressed and less supported. They arrive with more problems stemming from the strain of surviving in a competitive, lonely, and unsupportive social environment. Yet, these anxieties lie along the same axis of yesterday's problems about personal performance, troubled marriages, and troubled children. What now comes from a distinctly different axis are the moral dilemmas that today's clients present. On top of the classic personal worries, clients are also requesting help deciding on what is right to do. This is new to psychotherapy. Traditional therapy taught us to stay away from people's morality; they needed only to be freed from their neuroses, so they could choose what they believed to be good for them. Today, we encounter a new phenomenon: people who genuinely do not know how *morally* they should be living their lives, and who do not have the religious framework to inform and support their conscience. They are asking whether their children should be having sex outside of marriage, and at what age. Should their daughter undergo an abortion? What attitude should they have about their son's homosexuality? Should the terminally ill AIDS-afflicted son be assisted to suicide? People face new and proliferating moral conundrums.

Secular postmodern attitudes have supported therapies that have not only "assumed . . . functions" of traditional religions (Woolfolk, 1998, p. 10), but also have denied an objective, "'true' reality" (Goldenberg & Goldenberg, 2001, p. 96), the basis of traditional, personal morality. Speaking to the thinking of today's therapists, O'Hara and Anderson (1991) observed, "A society enters the postmodern age when it loses faith in absolute truth—even the attempt to discover absolute truth. The great systems of thought like religions, ideologies and philosophies, come to be regarded as 'social constructions of reality'" (p. 22). The postmodern perspective engenders the possibility of people forming their own subjective metaphysics and moralities. Not only does God become a tentative personal construct, but the beliefs that form the basis for a shared faith community and of a civic society become provisional. People are left to themselves to speculate about truth and morals.

Clients' religious faith is also extenuated as a source of support and consolation in trying times. Without the faith that gives meaning and purpose to the pain and anxiety of daily living, the motivation to endure and the drive to overcome depends on the thin reed of the immediate fix: feeling good by self talk, connecting with a transitional lover, or hitting the chemical high. Without principle, belief systems, and faith communities, people are hard put to discover the strength to face the inevitable frustrations and losses of life.

What, then, happens to the present-day therapist? Today's therapists face questions and situations that were not issues for yesterday's patients. Therapists cannot make any assumptions about a common moral framework or count on the supports of a spiritual belief system and faith community. Therapists frequently find themselves with clients who meander anxiously in morally uncharted territories with scant social supports. Clinicians will find themselves more alone when with clients who are themselves more isolated socially and spiritually.

Therapists are taking disparate routes to answer the challenge. Some take on the mantle of spiritual guides, others become more biologically deterministic. Those who don the roles of spiritual navigator and interpreter are themselves taking differing and contradictory courses. Doherty (1995), in *Soul Searching,* called for "the cultivation in therapists of the virtues and skills needed to be moral consultants to their clients in a pluralistic and morally opaque world" (p. 7). Becvar (1997) offered a postmodern answer: "Facts are replaced by frameworks and the views of all are understood as equally valid. . . . I attempt to operate according to five guiding principles. These include acknowledging connectedness, suspending judgment, trusting the universe, creating realities and walking the path with heart" (pp. 4–5).

Some, like Bardill (1997), emphasize a traditional Christian perspective: "The primary purpose of this discussion is to examine the spiritual reality from the Christian world view.... But, without God, from what source will we get the morals, ethics, rules to guide the path of conduct for humankind? The question of moral right and wrong cannot not be addressed" (pp. 89–93). Others advocate alternative religious traditions: "Therefore, teachers and potential mentors in the field need to expand their knowledge of other religious and spiritual traditions.... Social work educators need to develop more content relating to religious diversity beyond the Judeo-Christian tradition because the United States has become highly heterogeneous religiously" (Okundaye, Gray, & Gray, 1999, p. 380). Yet others debate whether science and the new discoveries about genes have eliminated moral choice: "In this deterministic view, the proteins unleashed by genes 'cause' or 'control' behavior" (Sapolsky, 2000, p. 68) versus "Thus it is probably incorrect to think of specific genes as determining, in particular and unchanging ways, specific behaviors. This misperception of genetic influence is often referred to as 'genetic hard wiring.' In all likelihood, genes do not have a fixed and irreversible influence on complex behaviors" (Reiss, 2000, p. 4).

Therapy has become diverse, conflictual, and contradictory in its philosophical and ethical bases, as is evidenced by the disparate and opposing views of the theorists. These differing worldviews affect the very foundation of any and every model of therapy. Technique is but a tool for a design that derives its form and its function from a philosophy about life. As clients grope for personal philosophies and morality in their quests for life solutions, therapists stretch to formulate worldviews that will add meaning, purpose, and value to their therapies. Wittingly or unwittingly, therapists impact their clients' spirituality. There is a need for a philosophy and method of working with spirituality in therapy that allows therapists to address consciously and effectively the spiritual dimension of their clients' issues. The name for one such perspective is spiritually sensitive therapy.

THEORETICAL CONSTRUCTS

Spiritually sensitive therapy does not constitute a therapeutic model per se. It is, rather, a way of thinking about spirituality in therapy applicable to both secular and religiously oriented therapies. This raises the existentialist concern for the "reality of the immediate experience in the present moment" (May, 1960, p. 15) to the level of spiritual significance. It shares in the spirit of Rollo May's assertion that existentialism in psychology "is not a set of new techniques in itself but a concern with the understanding of the structure of the human being and his experience that must underlie all techniques" (p. 15). Spiritually sensitive therapy allows for expanding the notion of a client's experience to include the spiritual dimension of life. It offers a perspective on therapy aimed at integrating a client's worldview, morality, spiritual practices, and spiritual community into clinical work. It relies on a working definition of spirituality as the transcendent aspect of life that gives to our lives meaning (philosophy and/or theology), morality (ethics and/or an understanding of virtue and sin), and spiritual practice and community (social network and/or faith community in conjunction with the spiritually transcendent).

This spirituality may be *secular*, without the acknowledgment of a transcendent being, or *religious*, with a belief in the spirit world of God. The assumption here is that everyone possesses a spirituality. Everyone has some view of life that determines what ideals ought to motivate human behavior, as well as some measure, expressed or tacit, by which actions are deemed to be good or bad, right or wrong. Everyone has determined the moral nature of people's relationships with each other and the moral basis for a relationship with God. People become a part of and depend on communities who will support them in personal growth and life tasks. These communities can be secular, such as family or neighborhood, or cultural and ethical societies. They can be religious in the sense of worship congregations, the community of spirits, and the Divinity. Spirituality constitutes a vital reality in everyday life, and not merely academic speculation.

Most therapists and their therapies reflect spiritualities, and spirituality influences their work and, thereby, their clients. Today's therapists no longer operate under the illusion that they are value-neutral; contemporary therapies are increasingly embedded in particular worldviews. Variations include Christian counseling (Bardill, 1997), humanistic-oriented therapy (Kramer, 1995), feminist-based counseling (Hare-Mustin, 1978), and postmodern, constructivist family therapy (Efran, Lukens, & Lukens, 1988). More than ever, therapists approach their clients from distinct moral, political, and philosophical perspectives. Their therapies and their philosophies are inextricably interwoven. Expectation is growing that therapists understand, formulate, and declare the philosophical underpinnings of their therapy and take responsibility for the influence on their work of their philosophical inclinations. They are challenged to do so while recognizing, respecting, and supporting the spiritualities that clients use to find solutions to their problems. The belief that all clients possess some manner of spirituality, formal or not, and that all therapists have their personal and professional preferences, acknowledged or not, prompts responsible therapists to work consciously and competently with spirituality as an essential aspect of any therapy. This has created a need for a consensually accepted way of thinking about and talking about spirituality in therapy.

BASIC ASSUMPTIONS

At the very core of spiritually sensitive therapy lies the idea that good spirituality is based on having a healthy philosophy and making good moral choices, which in turn lead to better mental health and more successful relationships. The idea is not that spiritual people do not experience mental health and relationship problems. Everyone knows "brokenness" (Nouwen, 1992a, p. 69): "Our sufferings and pains are not simply bothersome interruptions of our lives; rather they touch us in our uniqueness and our most intimate individuality" (p. 71). However, a coherent philosophy of life provides a personal framework for understanding and addressing life. A core moral code solidifies an elemental source of personal identity and self-affirmation and a referent for self-determination. Living by one's personal philosophy and moral code helps achieve control over one's life and a congruence with oneself, which in turn makes for personal peace and independence. Nouwen (1975) referred to the ability "to perceive and understand this world from a quiet inner center" (p. 38).

Thus, spiritually sensitive therapy is based on certain assumptions about people's relationships to their problems:

- People possess a kernel of freedom, the ability to choose for health or pathology, with regard to their life struggles.
- People's exercise of that free choice in harmony with or in opposition to their philosophical or moral bases helps determine whether they are on a path to healthy change.
- People need others to give them feedback, to challenge them, and to support their decisions, whether these sources be natural or transcendent.

To assert that people can exercise free will with respect to their personal problems assumes that they can exercise some degree of control over their actions and their personal issues. Frankl proclaimed: "There is always a certain residue of freedom left to his decisions. For within the limits—however restricted they may be—he can move freely; and only by this very stand which he takes toward whatever conditions he may face does he prove to be a truly human being" (1967, pp. 67–68). The alcoholic husband may not be able to choose not to be addicted or even to stop drinking, but may be able to choose at least to acknowledge the problem to his wife. There is a point of opportunity for free choice that will put him on the road to recovery, however long and arduous, or to self-destruction. That critical *point of decision*, with the potential to act toward health, is the starting block of therapy.

To claim the potential to freely choose positive over negative change suggests the moral ability to elect what is helpful over what is harmful, good over bad. From the perspective of a spiritually sensitive therapy (SST), a person is considered essentially a moral being whose struggles with life embody challenges to spiritual growth and development. Frankl also stated (1967): "An adequate view of man can only be properly formulated . . . [in] that sphere of human existence in which man chooses what he will do and what he will be in the midst of an objective world of meanings and values" (p. 61). The decisions people face in the psychological struggles of life always have some moral or philosophical basis. A couple in a troubled marriage may have to decide, among other issues, how seriously to take the marital commitment, determining, for example, whether their love should forgive all repented transgressions. Parents have to choose how firmly to set limits for their testing adolescents based on what they consider moral or immoral and responsible or irresponsible behavior, including sex. These judgments call for worldviews and moral standards by which to measure and weigh the right and wrong of human decisions. People's exercising of these moral choices directly affects how they contend with problems in their personal psychology and family relationships.

Finally, these life struggles are impossible to overcome in isolation. Spiritually sensitive therapy is founded on the proposition that a healthy spirituality calls for people not to contend with life alone. Living within one's spirituality is complemented by a healthy dependency within a relationship. Nouwen's (1975) "precious [inner] space" (p. 40) is the basis of our personal distinctness and is supplemented by the connection with the distinctness of others in "the intimacy of friendship, marriage and community life" (p. 43). Supportive relationships can spring from the natural social context of family and community and/or the transcendent realm of God and other spiritual beings. These connections with others mean that an individual, while personally grounded and differentiated, will also engage in sustaining relationships. A modern independent individual can permit personal vulnerability to another's compassion; that vulnerability in the security of another's understanding and caring becomes seeded ground open and ready for growth and change. The individual need not face contemporary life's stresses alone without the support of natural and/or supernatural others. Being not-alone is to face the challenges of life within a "community of love" (p. 42).

No matter how private and personal an issue, people need other people to see themselves and to overcome what they have not the strength to contend with alone. People may come to therapy to hear the expert opinion of a professional. They may need the emotional support of family members to admit a personal weakness. They may reach for the encouragement of a self-help group to commit to change. They may have to surrender themselves to the mercy of God in the face of what they perceive to be an intractable personal failing. People who shut down to outside help, whether natural or supernatural, or both, are likely to close off the possibility of change. People need to be willing to let go of control sufficiently to permit others to urge them along new paths they fear trekking by themselves. People need to be both confronted and comforted by others to engage in the good fight and to persevere in life's noble struggle toward change and growth.

Step 3 of the Alcoholics Anonymous (AA) 12-step program (1976) involves reaching out from the "bondage of self" by taking a "spiritual step with an understanding person, such as our wife, best friend or spiritual adviser" (p. 63), and ultimately with God. According to step 5, individuals have not braved their addiction until they have "told someone else *all* their story" (p. 73). Traditional religions offer people private confession, witnessing in community, church ritual, and clerical guidance. Today, secularly influenced and community-poor people have to take much more personal initiative to find and develop their spiritual supports.

METHODS OF ASSESSMENT AND INTERVENTION

Assessment of spirituality begins with determining the spiritual orientation of clients. Asking about religious heritage and whether clients engage in active religious practices, similar to inquiring about ethnicity and cultural backgrounds (McGoldrick, Giordano, & Pearce, 1996), helps place clients in religious as well as sociocultural contexts. The second query concerns the relationship of their spirituality to today's issues. The probe is focused both on whether there are moral difficulties linked to their personal problems and what aid spirituality may lend to client efforts to solve problems. This second question is best explored indirectly through an understanding of the issues, during an examination of decisions clients face about the problems that confront them. Underlying these questions is a look at how clients think about and articulate spirituality vis-à-vis their issues. The moral foundation of the therapy begins here.

Therapeutic interventions congruent with a spiritually sensitive model connect with a client's core free-will decision, the ignition key for change. For the woman who struggles with a poorly controlled impulse to strike her daughter, the core decision may not be the already expressed intention not to hit her daughter; rather, it may be whether she is prepared to work on letting go of the vindictiveness that surges within her whenever she experiences the feeling of being slighted, a remnant of the treatment she suffered at the hands of her own parents. The free-will decision has to carry with it the full significance of what it would mean to change. This woman may need to separate her experience as a daughter from her role as parent to a child who does not react from her parents' motives. For this woman, a deeper resolution may also call for her to let go and/or to forgive her parents for their failure to affirm and value her. In any case, she would be operating from the premise that it is better to forgive than to retaliate. Depending on the client, the therapist could intervene on the nonreligious premise of the psychological benefits of forgiveness (Sells & Hargrave, 1998) and/or on the religiously embedded call to "forgive [one's] neighbor's injustice" (Sirach 28:2, New American Bible).

In practice, the spiritually sensitive model here proposed is meant to be rooted in the practical, and not to float into academic or religious debate. It is meant to use spirituality as a resource to motivate, clarify, inform, relieve, encourage, and fortify, and not to preach or dispute. For the therapist, whose concern encompasses the emotional and relationship vicissitudes of life, discovers spirituality in the ordinary, everyday trials of life where people encounter their pains and difficulties: "Recognize the need for . . . concreteness, for what [Martin] Buber . . . calls 'the hallowing of the everyday.' Any situation may become the vehicle of the 'eternal Thou'" (Smith, 1958, p. x). Spirituality can emerge in personal interior conflicts and in family arguments. Spirituality lurks in the questions about what is right and whether to live by it; in the discouragement that prompts a person to ask whether life and relationships are worth the effort; in the lonely feeling that asks whether anyone out there cares about our troubles. Spirituality lives in the moral enigma, in the search for meaning and purpose, and in the need for a caring hand. Spirituality in therapy occurs in the *now,* when clients face the challenges to engage with today's ordinary human struggles. A spiritually sensitive therapy entails three basic tasks:

1. Identify the client issue of *today* and the moral dimensions of the related decisions a client must make to begin the change process.
2. Determine the *value platform* on which the therapy will proceed, that is, the morality and philosophy that will undergird the work.
3. Explore the *spiritual resources* clients can use, whether from within their personal interior spirituality or from the relationship and communal aspects of their spirituality.

Identifying the client issue and moral dimensions of the related decisions clients face means helping them see the potentials to be and act differently in the immediate, practical challenges of today's difficulties. The very process of clients characterizing their issues provides opportunities to assess not only the contents of the problems, but also how clients think about the challenges. Do they see little or no hope for change? Do they avoid facing their responsibilities for their troubles? Do they view the issues only as their worries, isolated from the world around them? The formulation of the issue in itself provides an occasion for critical intervention. Can they be helped to view a problem as an opportunity and possibility to improve their lives, rather than an occasion of failure and regret? Formulating an issue as a chance to change, identifying the choices they have that will make a difference, and viewing themselves as not alone in the struggle generate the momentum for positive change and growth. From a spiritual perspective, hope is implicit and emerges in the challenge, freedom, and power in moral choices, as well as in the communal spirit in the sharing of life's struggles. The spiritually oriented therapist is looking for the potential of renewal the human spirit can exercise in facing the troubles of the day.

From a spiritual perspective, the common, practical problems of the moment also contain deeper, life-defining issues embedded in the decisions clients face. This deeper structure bears its own implications for the values that will come into play in a solution. For example, a husband who debated whether to pursue an extramarital affair struggled all of his life with the need for female affirmation. His decision about whether to act on today's impulse was influenced not just by his emotional needs, but also by his moral awareness of the wrongness of marital infidelity. His values gave him the resolve not to act rashly, despite his neurotic needs. In another example, a woman distressed about giving birth to a severely handicapped child considered whether to have her baby, handicap and all, against her husband's wishes and the admonitions of family to be practical. She was torn between their wishes and her own conflicted feelings, along with the moral dilemma posed by her faith that did not countenance abortion. In her drug-abusing past, her poor self-esteem allowed friends and lovers to manipulate and exploit her. Her faith made possible her asserting control of her life and affirming her own and her child's life. These second-layer, deeper issues manifest themselves in how people deal with today's problems with their own moral challenges.

Determining the value platform on which the therapy will proceed denotes that client and therapist seek and articulate understanding about the moral and philosophical bases of their work together (Aponte, 1998). This value platform establishes the moral assumptions that will drive therapy. It offers the moral basis on which issues are defined and goals are determined and the nature of solutions selected.

These values establish what is healthy or pathological, what are personally and socially worthwhile goals, and what are both emotionally and morally acceptable solutions to a problem. Questions about what to treat as healthy or pathological have been debated in the area of homosexuality as a sickness, and, in terms of goals, whether there can be or should be a "cure" (Wylie, 2000, p. 36). That in the "euthanasia debate" (Peck, 1997) assisted suicide is thinkable raises painful moral dilemmas about what are morally acceptable solutions for terminal patients. By the standards of spiritually sensitive therapy, counseling is conducted in a way that does not violate, and ideally is congruent with, the moral standards, philosophical outlook, and religious beliefs and customs of both client and therapist (Aponte, 1985). This does not mean that client and therapist must be in synchrony about all their moral values, which would be difficult to accomplish in a heterocultural society. This concordance does mean that both client and therapist agree to the values by which they determine the nature of the problem and the goals and the means of their therapeutic undertaking. The value platform constitutes the moral soul of the therapy.

Helping clients determine the values on which they will base therapy may in itself serve as a powerful intervention toward change. This intervention can be implicit. If, for example, a therapist can assume that a troubled married couple believe in remaining together no matter what, the therapist has greater leverage and room to push changes. On the other hand, the articulation of a value base can serve as an explicit intervention. In one case, a therapist engaged an ambivalent couple in clarifying whether they wanted to base their counseling on their original standard of feeling "happily compatible" or on an alternative notion of a love that is "for keeps," even in the face of contretemps. The process of deciding on the value base of the therapy will not only set the moral parameters of therapy, but it can also move clients to revisit their motivations. Taking the time to identify their moral priorities may also move people to live up to them. When the couple looked at what made their love important to them, they agreed that the permanence of the marriage was worth the fight. Establishing the value platform gives an opportunity both to understand the spiritual context of clients' issues and to engage their spirituality in the efforts to solve the problems.

Exploring the spiritual resources of a client implies intentionally taking into account a client's spirituality as an important and legitimate asset in therapy. Looking into clients' spiritual resources serves to assess a dimension of client potential commonly overlooked in therapy. This part of an assessment helps to identify what internal spiritual conviction and development clients can count on to support change, as well as what guiding light and strength they can count on from their spiritually based associations. This assessment is directed at the spirituality that relates directly to the issues clients present in therapy, and is not a free-ranging exploration of all that is sacred and mysterious in people's spirituality.

Therapists can utilize spiritual resources in many forms. Tan (1996), working in a context of Christian counseling, spoke in terms of "religion," but helpfully distinguished between intervening *implicitly* and *explicitly:*

> Implicit integration of religion in clinical practice refers to a more covert approach that does not . . . openly, directly, or systematically use spiritual resources. . . . Explicit integration of religion in clinical practice or psychotherapy refers to a more overt approach that directly and systematically deals with the spiritual or religious issues in therapy. . . . It emphasizes the spirituality of both the therapist and client as foundational to effective therapy and human growth and healing. (p. 368)

A therapist's role in relation to client spirituality may also be active or reactive; in either of these modes, the work with spirituality may be implicit or explicit along Tan's lines. Therapists may actively look to draw out the spiritual dimension of life, or may relate to it only as it spontaneously appears in people's talk about their issues.

The spiritually sensitive model incorporates the general thrust of Tan's (1996) distinctions but involves approaching people's use of spiritually from a somewhat broader perspective. While accounting for both religious and secular spirituality, it includes looking specifically at the generic standards of people's moral conscience, their philosophical views, and their spiritually based associations, all in relation to the issues they present in therapy. Spirituality is treated as intrinsic to all human life. Therapists may relate to spirituality's tacit existence in everyday life without overt references to spirituality or to its expressed manifestation in clients' formally articulated language, practices, and associations. When therapists address spirituality, they may range from encouraging clients to mine for unused or undeveloped spiritual resources in their lives, to bringing into play in therapy spirituality already active in their lives, to sharing with clients from their own spiritual outlook what clients may consider applicable.

The spiritually sensitive model connotes a number of further distinctions that need to be assessed and that will help identify types of interventions needed. First, the internal and the external worlds of spirituality are distinguished. The internal world contains a person's depth of conviction, commitment, and dedication to spirituality. This interior life refers to the nature of the spiritual development of an individual, including individuals' progress in their spiritual path and the personal relationship they may have with the transcendent. This inner focus may take the form of fostering a spiritual disposition, along the lines of "taking the necessary steps to try to center them [clients] spiritually " (Wicks, 1991, p. 40).

A centering intervention with the interior spirituality of a client may be appropriate for clients who have lost direction in their lives, are overreactive to others' treatment of them, or use the frenzy of activity to suppress or escape their emotional pains. From a secular perspective, we may be speaking of helping clients become grounded in their own values and abilities to choose a direction for their lives. A client in his late 20s had moved from a fast life of drugs, alcohol, and sex to a career-obsessed existence. He complained about his preoccupation with control in his personal and professional life; he experienced no peace. The therapist guided him into developing a half-hour-a-day meditation that, briefly stated, consisted of (1) a period of resting his body and his mind—and pausing to hold the moment; (2) a period of picturing uncritically the reality of the situation that was preoccupying him *today*—and pausing; (3) a period of picturing himself with all of his feelings, fears, and wishes—and pausing; (4) a period of considering the choices he faced *today* and deciding if ready to do so—and pausing; and (5) giving thought to who or what could help him make the final decision and/or carry out *today's* plan—and pausing to hold the resolve. He would then be ready to act that day from his inner determination; the next day, he would go through the same process, focusing on acting that day, again from his inner space. He practiced confronting his daily challenges from the freedom and power he possessed within himself.

Eastern religious thought refers to centering, in which a therapist guides a patient "down deep into herself" to "the wisdom that she had within her and to trust that the response would be true for her" (Mason, 1997, p. 142). For a Western Christian psychologist, this centering may translate into "a radical openness to a prayerful relationship with the presence of God in oneself, in others, and in those quiet honest encounters with the Lord in silence and solitude" (Wicks, 1991, p. 40).

The external world of spirituality encompasses how the spiritual is manifested in lifestyle, personal practices, and associations with others in ritual and worship. People may live lives reflecting a spiritual orientation through habits of living, such as how and with whom they socialize, in their formal practices of prayer and meditation, and in their participation in public rituals and celebrations. One client's religious practices served to buttress a psychological intervention when she readily accepted a suggestion to concentrate on praying for divine help with her disturbing thoughts, rather than obsessively dissecting the intrusive memories she had about the sexual abuse of her childhood. A therapist can make use of a client's spiritual community to complement a strategy conducted within the therapy. In one instance, a therapist made use of the importance the client gave to this spiritual support. A divorced father whose ex-wife was moving some miles away with his 5-year-old son had become agitated with thoughts of physical violence toward her. The therapist learned that the father had consulted a priest, but blamed all on his wife. The therapist confronted the father about his extreme anger, stemming from his childhood of physical abuse more than from his wife's actions. The therapist redirected the client to the priest with the expectation that he acknowledge his lifelong struggle with his temper. Because the client leaned heavily on this priest's counsel, the therapist counted on the client's work with the priest to deepen his grasp of the depth of his struggle with anger. Further owning the anger would increase his control of the emotion.

Working with the exterior dimension of spirituality includes referring clients to their spiritual network for help specific to those resources. By its very nature, certain spiritual help cannot come from therapy; these resources include family or friend, house of worship or deity. One religious Catholic woman in anguish about her alienation from her church, and thus her God, because of an abortion in her youth, accepted encouragement to find reconciliation through confession. This kind of outside referral fulfilled a more traditional role for the therapist. A different sort of resource served a spiritual purpose for a secular-minded young woman. Having no religion, she sought meaning in her life; her therapist encouraged her decision to volunteer for a program assisting familyless street children in South America. Thus, a therapist can serve as a facilitator helping people decide what will meet their needs and where to obtain help.

In other instances, clients' personal morality, spiritual philosophy, and spiritual customs may not provide sources of strength readily accessible in therapy. Their reflections on morality may be so poorly formulated that they may be adding to their confusion about how to deal with their problems; their philosophy of life may present more impediments than help toward a positive challenge to grow and change; their faith community may be nonexistent or irrelevant for them. A client may lack or misuse spirituality, as in concocting a self-serving moral rationalization for some destructive behavior. In that case, a therapist may have to directly confront the morality of the behavior. One therapist learned that a college-age male client had become sexually involved with a disturbed, acting-out younger sister's female friend. The therapist's probes into the young man's views about the rightness and wrongness of his actions made it clear that behind his justifications, he knew this self-indulgence was risking serious trouble for his sister. Therapists are in a position to help clients articulate their undefined spirituality. They can help clients identify their moral positions in relation to issues, or to think through their philosophies and attitudes about their situations, or to look into their religious legacies for a belief system or faith community that can assist in their present circumstances.

Therapists may offer from their own spirituality as external resources. In a couple consumed with arguing and fighting each other, the husband criticized virtually everything his wife did, and she responded with sarcasm, forgetfulness, and procrastination. No reasoning could break through the determination of each to defeat the other. The therapist offered a motive that could transcend the need to win: He pointed to the young son in the waiting room as likely the most tragic victim of their battle. Did triumphing over the partner matter more than saving their family? There was hope if they could hold themselves accountable for restraining their respective vindictiveness and pour their efforts into working together to relieve the stress being generated by their household problems, such as paying overdue bills. They were moved, and volunteered a list of difficult situations they wanted help to solve as a couple. On the other hand, the suggestion of love-without-conditions as the frame for healing family conflicts freed a different family to move to a new level of effort (Aponte, 1998). They had been unable to find a principle they could believe in for continuing to work to heal in the face of discouragement and old disappointments. The therapist in each situation needed some indication that the clients would welcome the interventions. The therapist's spirituality needs to fit a situation and clients' spirituality. When uncertain, therapists may float suggestions, but clients must feel free to ignore or reject an idea without endangering the continuation or progress of therapy (Aponte, 1985). An alternative approach is to declare beforehand the therapy's philosophy. Some Evangelical Christian therapists, for instance, exemplify engaging in counseling espousing a distinct set of values (Wylie, 2000). By identifying publicly their orientation to therapy, they inform potential clients who can then chose to accept or refuse therapy involving an explicitly religiously based philosophy.

Therapists may also work from an approach that facilitates a spiritual ambience that affects the tone of the therapeutic process. Therapists' "spiritual dispositions" shape the milieu they personally generate and subtly provide an intervention. Therapists bring to their work and their relationships with their clients a dimension of where they are in their own personal journey, including their beliefs and ideals. As Anderson and Worthen (1997) put it, "The spirituality of the therapist beyond the therapy room inevitably influences the therapist's presentation of self in the room" (p. 10). For example, a therapist who sees oneself as a "wounded healer" (Nouwen, 1972) may relate to clients with the insight and empathy of a fellow pilgrim, rather than distance oneself through the paradigm of the professional fixer of pathology. Therapists may also offer clients a relationship imbued with a spiritual love, "a selfless outgoing love" (Nouwen, 1992b, p. 126), showing deep caring while expecting nothing in return from a client. Frankl (1963) implied as much when he wrote that through a therapist's "spiritual act of love . . . [a therapist] sees the potential in [a client], that which is not yet actualized but yet ought to be actualized" (pp. 176–177). This caring must be clearly within the boundaries of a professional role, and its impact on clients can be powerful. It can provide the spur to strive a little harder and can contribute to a therapeutic environment in which clients feel safe to be vulnerable and to risk change. Therapists can use these *spiritual dispositions* to put into practice a facilitating spiritual ambience in the therapy.

When therapists generate a particular spiritual environment for therapy or directly advise on spiritually related issues, they bring to therapy their own personal spirituality. Less obviously, their therapeutic model embodies a spirituality in the form of worldview, moral perspective, and outright bias about culture, politics, and religion: "Every system of therapy has an underlying ideology" (Woolfolk, 1998, p. 18). According to Browning (1987), "most of the more prominent modern psychologies, in addition to whatever scientific value they may have, do indeed cross over into what must be recognized as types of positive cultures—

cultures, indeed, which possess religio-ethical dimensions" (p. 5). From Jones's (1996) view of "Albert Ellis and B. F. Skinner ... [committing to] naturalism (to the exclusion of belief in God and the transcendent)" (p. 136), to today's postmodern therapies (Becvar, 1997) and the committed Christian therapies (Wylie, 2000), a range of quite explicitly philosophically and religiously colored therapies have evolved.

All therapists bring a complex of values from their personal spirituality to their work, their therapeutic models, and even their professional associations, which today are taking aggressive political and social positions on controversial moral issues ranging from sexual lifestyles to abortion and assisted suicide. Therapists are having to adopt and articulate their own personal position. This has meant the development of training programs that integrate, with technical training, therapists' personal life experiences that must now include consideration of their personal values and spirituality (Aponte, 1994b; Aponte & Winter, 2000). Therapists are learning the freedom to offer help from their personal and professional values, but in an environment where clients feel the freedom to accept or refuse in accordance with their own spiritual beliefs.

Spiritual interventions come in active and reactive as well as explicit and implicit forms. They are specifically targeted or broadly woven into the fabric of the therapy. They address poorly articulated morality and philosophies in addition to well-elaborated, formal philosophies or religious faiths. They are drawn from within clients, from their external practices and associations, or from therapists themselves and their therapeutic models. In any case, in spiritually sensitive therapy, the interventions pivot on clients' freely exercised decisions, which relate directly to what control they wield over their personal struggles, decisions that will make differences in their lives.

Knowing where and how to intervene in the spiritual dimensions of clients' issues calls for the same kind of diagnostic and instrumental skills that any other clinical intervention demands. In the end, hopefully, therapists will have recourse to spiritual interventions according to what is fitting for particular clients' issues and spirituality, as well as what is clinically and spiritually right for the therapists themselves. The spirituality of therapists will need to be fully integrated and implemented within the theoretical and technical frameworks of their therapeutic model. Some clients and therapists will happily engage in overt religious allusions; others, whether clients or therapists, will be turned off by any references to spirituality. Nevertheless, the moral standards by which people make the choices that affect their lives and the supports they need to follow through on their moral choices are universal issues that call for therapist attention whether or not therapists wish to speak of that aspect of their work as spiritual. Explicit references to spirituality may deepen and enrich a clinical discussion, or may distract from the affect, mood, or mindset of either or both client and therapist. Like any other intervention, a spiritually sensitive intervention must wear attire appropriate to the occasion, both for the client and for the therapist.

To conduct a spiritually sensitive therapy, clinicians need not fit any other mold but their own. They face the challenge of being grounded in their own spirituality while being able to recognize and respect their clients' spirituality. They will need to understand spirituality at the practical level of where it is lived in their clients' struggles with life, but also where it will be manifested in the therapeutic process with a therapist. Spirituality will serve as a canopy over the entire therapeutic process, giving meaning to it, but will also be encountered in the very down-to-earth give-and-take of the therapeutic relationship and therapist-client transactions. Most essentially in this model, therapists centralize their efforts around clients' freedom to change, establish a consensual value platform for the therapy, and reach for the spiritual resources that will enrich and further the work of growth and change.

MAJOR ISSUES TREATED

Spiritually sensitive therapy serves as a framework for addressing the spiritual dimension of therapeutic issues and for enriching the therapeutic process in general. Therapy serves essentially to help solve a human dilemma in a psychological or personal relationship. Aiding the spiritual life of a client supports this clinical objective at a specific or general level, but is not primary to the task. Nonetheless, because spirituality is intrinsic to human experience, a fully articulated therapy should always encompass speaking to the spiritual dimensions of client issues while communicating a spirituality that promotes sound growth and healing. A fine restaurant offers an enjoyable dining experience that is also healthy, and a good hospital offers a healthy meal that, hopefully, is also enjoyable. The therapist is not clergy, but should offer effective clinical help that is not spiritually noxious but beneficial.

Spiritually sensitive therapy is most relevant to personal issues of clients that depend more on a philosophical outlook and the exercise of moral judgment. Therefore, the further removed a client's issue from the biological components of psychiatric treatment, such as the prescription of medication and even the use of such techniques as operant conditioning, hypnosis, and EMDR, and the closer to *attitude* and *volition*, the more the spiritual comes into play. Some human predicaments, such as personal insecurity and conflictual personal relationships, depend more on attitude and moral choice for alleviation than on techniques meant to affect the more immutable processes of biology, trauma, and even social conditioning. Still, no therapy lacks spiritual components, the elemental predispositions to healing that include assuming responsibility for one's flaws and failures along with having an overriding purpose to change, the humility and openness to accept help, the hopefulness for bettering oneself and relationships, and a belief in the personal freedom and power to choose to live differently. The challenge to therapists who wish to affect the spiritual aspects of client issues depends on perceiving how the spiritual ingredients relate to the clinical concerns and on having the spiritual resources and know-how to address them in ways that further the specific therapeutic objectives.

Therefore, therapists who consistently speak to the spiritual dimensions of clients' problems in spiritually sensitive therapy will (1) treat the spirituality of clients as integral to good mental and relationship health, and (2) use the healing powers of spirituality by integrating spirituality into the basic structure of therapy—into assessment, goal setting, and intervention. An important distinction needs to be made between the spirituality inherent in a clinician's therapy and the spirituality actively promoted by the therapist. Because practitioners of most therapies have spiritual elements and characteristics, every therapy embodies some spiritual influence. However, therapists also are inclined to actively suggest ways of thinking or acting that derive from their spiritual basis and not necessarily from their clients' orientation. By way of analogy, every restaurant that takes itself seriously has a distinctive menu. A waiter or waitress may choose to suggest one item over another on a particular day to a particular customer; hopefully, the waiter feels free to be so bold because of a relationship with the customer and knowing the diner's tastes. Likewise, a therapist who believes in helping uncentered clients to articulate for themselves their values and ideals, suggested to a nonreligious Jewish client that she explore her own cultural heritage. Because she lacked religious training, the client demurred on consulting a rabbi, but agreed to read the Hebrew Bible, which gave new meaning to her life.

All psychologically healing therapies connote some general notions about how spirituality and morality affect people's functioning. Hayes, Strosahl, and Wilson (1999) contended, "It is not possible to have a theory without a philosophy" (p. 16). Frankl (1963) proposed "meaning" (p. 179) as necessary for a healthy personal psychology. Nicholas (1994) advocated "egalitarianism" (p. 224) as essential to good relationships. Doherty (1995) stressed moral "commitment" (p. 21), and Mason (1997) emphasized "commitment and caring" (p. 130). Today, therapists tend to trumpet the values that give form and direction to their therapy. This practice allows therapists to take responsibility for the spirituality characterizing their work, and makes it more feasible for clients to pick and choose the therapy that fits their personal spirituality.

When practitioners think about the general spiritual influences their therapy offers, they need to identify the spiritual principles underpinning their theories. Three principles represent the explicit values that shape the underlying philosophy of this chapter's application of a spiritually sensitive therapy: (1) Love is the primary driver of healthy growth and functioning; (2) adversity is the golden portal to overcoming the entrenched obstacles to a healthier and happier life; and (3) persons exist first to be better people, and only secondarily to achieve and accomplish. Each therapist will likewise need to articulate his or her personal beliefs.

A cardinal value permeating the application of this model stems from the belief that *love is the primary driver of healthy growth and functioning* (Aponte, 1998). Frankl (1963) affirmed, *"The salvation of man is through love and in love"* (p. 59). People cannot live, physically or emotionally, without caring about others and being cared about, including caring about themselves. Whatever people wrestle with emotionally or in relationships, somewhere at the heart of the issue lies a question about loving or being loved. The essence of a mature love requires freely choosing to care about another unconditionally. The twelfth-century spiritual writer Bernard of Clairvaux (1987) declared: [Love] "is an affection, not a contract. It is not given or received by agreement. It is given freely; it makes us spontaneous" (p. 187). In a reciprocal relationship, the lover's openness allows the lover also to be loved unconditionally. Nouwen (1992b) rounded out the picture of love when he addressed the difficulty of letting go of anxiety and control to receive love without fetters: "And still, I knew that I would never be able to live the great commandment of love without allowing myself to be loved without conditions or prerequisites" (p. 14). Love may be emotionally moved and inspired by the goodness or attractiveness of another, but is essentially chosen and chosen freely both to give and to receive. It is willed by the person who wants to love, permitting thereby the possibility of caring about another even when perceiving the other as difficult or unattractive. It permits accepting love even when feeling unlovable. A freely willed love makes it possible to engage and commit to love reliably under any and all circumstances.

All humanity hungers to be loved and is impelled to love. No self-esteem develops without a regard for and love of self. No affectionate relationship flourishes without a sharing of love. No personal virtue of charity evolves without a generous and selfless love of another. Love blossoms in an environment of freedom from anxiety, fear, acquisitiveness, competitiveness, control, and defensiveness. People grow emotionally healthy in an environment of committed and enduring love without strings. Individuals in therapy can risk change when feeling safe and valued in a therapeutic relationship, again a form of love. Whether in everyday relationships or in the connection between therapist and client, the caring or love that exists between people serves as a motivator and safe environment that deepens clients' readiness to stretch themselves for change. Love forms the foundational ingredient for a therapeutic environment that promotes growth and change.

A second supporting principle of spiritually sensitive therapy arises from the value premise that *adversity serves as the golden portal to overcoming the entrenched obstacles to a healthier and happier life.* Adversity can come from within oneself or from external circumstances. All people live with aspects of themselves that are their worst enemies. All have their specific psychological and moral vulnerabilities that characterize their particular risks to life's failures. Their genes, their families of origin, and/or early life experiences conspire to generate hitches in emotional development that predispose people to have certain kinds of problems in life. These personal hang-ups form lifelong paths of opportunity for growth and change, presenting people with uniquely personal opportunities to overcome whatever in themselves impedes taking the risks of fresh insights and new actions.

Everyone also experiences losses, reversals, and troubles from relationships and life circumstances. However, the urgency of these pains, anxieties, and personal crises offers the potential of disrupting old defenses and opening the gates to new and fresh solutions. Adversity and its implicit challenge likely opens a portal of possibility for therapy because it is immediate, compelling, and opportunistic. Whether people bring adversities on themselves or adversity happens to them, such experiences pose challenges and opportunities for growing and changing. Life's crises block old attitudes and behaviors and spur people to extend and reach deep within themselves for new thinking and new behaviors. Critical moments can serve as occasions for dramatic changes in lifestyle and relationships. However, even where external change proves impossible, internal psychological and spiritual change do not. Frankl (1963) observed the capacity of persons, even in concentration camps, to "achieve fulfillment" if they endured "sufferings in the right way—an honorable way" (p. 59). So long as people are conscious and can exercise some degree of control over their lives, even if only of the "inner life" (p. 62) of thoughts, intentions, and attitudes, they can meet challenges in ways that enhance the inner quality of life. Aponte (1999) observed that people who live in chronic poverty can aspire to self-respect and meaningful lives. A therapist can help a client discover and reformulate adversity into challenge. Instead of personal difficulties being treated as shameful and warranting self-hatred, denial, or escape, these personal hang-ups and life reversals become the "noble struggles" that can serve in therapy as the paths to renewal and sources of hope.

A third value premise extends the second and is predicated on the principle that *persons exist first to be better people, and only secondarily to achieve and accomplish.* This notion derives from the postulate that purpose remains inherent in all of life. From purpose flows opportunity and possibility. The corollary follows that people can always achieve positive change from life's adversities if they accept the essential challenge as becoming a better person. Being a "better person" means living by one's moral standards and ideals when carrying out personal, family, and social responsibilities. If one's aims encompass virtue over gain, one can do ever better, no matter how impossible a situation, because one can always adopt a better attitude or disposition. If the outcome of the situation does not serve as the measure of "better," one may fail to change the outcome but succeed in personal improvement. This philosophy implies conceding acceptance of the reality of how little humans control the course and outcome of life. To paraphrase Burns's famous refrain, the most carefully considered plans of mice and men often go astray and bring pain and disappointment instead of hoped-for joy (Untermeyer, 1942).

The lore exemplifying the notion of virtue over gain sprouts from many roots. In the Judeo-Christian biblical tradition, Moses, who was initially chosen to lead the Israelites out of Egypt

(Exodus, 3), was denied entry by God into the promised land (Deuteronomy 32:51). Was he a failure? Still clearly under God's favor, Moses completed his mission when, at the point of death, he blessed the promised-land-destined Israelites (Deuteronomy 33) and died with his eyes "undiminished" and his "vigor unabated" (Deuteronomy 34:7). Christ was executed among thieves (Luke 23:33): a failure? For his obedience, he was acknowledged by his Father to be his "beloved son, with whom I am well pleased" (Matthew 17:5). Contemporary times abound with examples of spiritual victories in worldly defeats. Frankl (1963) gained the triumph of spirit over the despair of the camps when he was able to "transcend that hopeless, meaningless world" (p. 63) through the discovery of the "existence of an ultimate purpose" (p. 64), namely, that "man's main concern is not to gain pleasure or to avoid pain, but rather to see a meaning in his life" (p. 179). Nouwen (1992b) represents a current figure; he voluntarily gave up prestige and position for humble service to pursue his own personal betterment, leaving his teaching position at Harvard to dedicate his life to the mentally impaired. In his words: "Moving from teaching university students to living with mentally handicapped people was ... the place of light, the place of truth, the place of love.... It is the place beyond earning, deserving, and rewarding. It is the place of surrender and complete trust" (p. 13).

For clients who come into therapy troubled, often feeling damaged or failures, does the measure of their worth emanate from freedom from pain and conflict or from life's ideal endings, such as success at work or a happy relationship, or from liberation from the pull of an addiction? A failure in career may open the door to a healthy personal reassessment and the reordering of priorities. A difficult relationship may offer the option of digging deeper, stretching further to learn a more selfless love that can give without always receiving. The crucible of an addiction may lead to a saving change of lifestyle even if not the eradication of the vulnerability. Clients who can count on therapists to value their efforts and incremental gains can experience a richer life even when therapy does not result in the disappearance of personal or relationship vicissitudes. Clients can discover new meaning in their lives, however flawed, and in their relationships, however difficult, when they can meet the journey's present-day challenge with greater clarity, courage, and integrity.

In general, the questions for a therapist are how to identify the forms their clients' personal life challenges are taking today and how their clients are to meet them so as to better themselves, even as they pursue their clinical solutions. The clients who can engage present challenges with constructive attitudes, positive decisions, and healthy supports will change in positive ways. Therapy builds on those spiritual platforms, sometimes in small ways, at times in major ways. Decisions about attitude, behavior, and social supports must be practical and meaningful in the context of what clients intend to happen in therapy. Their spirituality provides meaning, motivation, drive, and supportive resources.

Exploration of a spiritually sensitive therapy connotes proposing that therapists recognize the spirituality intrinsic to people's lives and the uniquenesses and mysteries inherent in that spirituality. Therapists may speak to but not tread on ground sacred to each individual. Therapists will encounter gaps in perspective between themselves and their clients; these differences will appear in the "operational applications" (Aponte, 1985, p. 329) of principle to people's personal circumstances. These will be the instances when people have to make their personal moral choices and the situations in which therapists need to make room for their clients to experience their personal struggles and the consequences of their decisions. If one can substitute the word "therapy" for "hospitality" and assume the notion of potentializing change, the following words of Nouwen (1975) are quite appropriate: "Hospitality is not to change people, but to offer them space where change can take place.... Hospitality is not a subtle invitation to adopt the life style of the host, but the gift of a chance for the guest to find his own" (pp. 73–74).

The tensions between therapist and client values form part of all therapy and can be health-promoting for a therapeutic process, no matter what the specific clinical issue. The therapist who can use those differences to stimulate discussion and open options in a free and accepting therapeutic relationship gives a gift to a client. However, the complexity and sensitivity of working at the interface of one's own and the client's spirituality requires that therapists will need personal training (Aponte, 1996) that will promote their being grounded in their own spirituality. They will thereby be better able, in the encounter with a client's spirituality, to remain firmly rooted in their own, and be freer to creatively use that meeting of spirituality for a client's benefit.

CASE EXAMPLES

An Example of Implicit Spirituality

Mr. and Mrs. Gulden entered therapy with Lori, their 12-year-old daughter, who was acting openly defiant toward her parents, although she was well-behaved and accomplished in school. Mrs. Gulden was deeply distressed that she had hit Lori in a fit of temper. Mr. Gulden was frustrated and angry with both his wife and daughter for the fighting. They were all caught in a cycle of control and countercontrol: Lori stubbornly resisted her parents; the parents, while trying to outcontrol Lori, also struggled with each other about whose way would prevail. Yet, in spite of the power plays, they all obviously cared about each other. (For those who would put a diagnosis on the family's situation, it would be Relationship Disorder with Verbal and/or Violent Conflict; Bodin, 1996, p. 380.)

The parents were attempting to control their daughter through arguments, threats, and punishments. They quarreled about how, how much, and when to discipline her. The parents' histories helped explain current dynamics. Mrs. Gulden described a childhood of emotional intimidation and neglect. She valued her father as the most important person in her life and a powerful person in the family; she longed for his approval, but received only criticism. Now, she quickly interprets as a personal slight any contradiction from her husband or defiance from her daughter. Mr. Gulden grew up in a home in which he perceived that no one listened to him. Bright and a high achiever, he felt overlooked because of his shy and quiet personality. Today, he remains sensitive to any response that seems like disrespect from a family member. As a result, both Mr. and Mrs. Gulden are quick to become defensive. They protect themselves by negotiating relationships on the basis of rights and obligations. They came to counseling asking the therapist to judge between their respective approaches to discipline and to help them devise more effective consequences for controlling Lori.

Every suggestion the therapist offered became a reason for more argument among parents and daughter. The therapist finally spoke to the underlying spirit of the family, in which interactions revolved around the theme of what was owed and not about caring. Their daughter, a good child, thrived in school, where she was liked and rewarded with positive attention. At home, she was dealing with her parents only in the currency of fairness; she cooperated solely when she judged they treated her just right. The therapist speculated with the parents that they were both hungry for love and affirmation, but, because of their respective family legacies, they feared and expected criticism and disappointment in relationships. Consequently, they protected themselves by calling for what they considered fair treatment, which translated for all practical purposes into whether they were getting their way. This led to constant power struggles, which took the form of resistance and demands. They were coconstructing their own misery and hardship. The therapist proposed examining their relationships under the light of the love that he believed they all held for each other and wanted from each other, but were afraid to give themselves over to.

The therapist proposed elevating giving and receiving love to the primary basis for resolving family issues and, therefore, the value platform for the therapy. The family tentatively agreed to test the notion. The therapist encouraged the parents to approach Lori's anger with the intention of understanding what her complaining communicated about what she was experiencing. This did not imply ignoring disrespect or necessarily surrendering to her demands. It did mean listening to her before countering her arguments. Lori tested their new resolve. As she learned to trust their openness to her, she softened and showed the side of her that wanted to please and to gain their approval.

Resolution between the parents proved more daunting. They had grown accustomed to a hardened pattern of defensiveness between them; virtually every interchange between them in therapy sessions turned into a hurtful duel. Instead of addressing the rightness or wrongness of the arguments, the therapist teased out their worries, needs, and hopes, in a word, their vulnerabilities. Initially, the therapist provided interest, caring, and safety for each, actively cultivating an environment of sensitivity, concern, and validation—an ambience of love. He made efforts to provide a safe place for them to expose their emotional needs and pain. At the same time, he took on the task of confronting their defensiveness, which at first they would accept only from him, but with time from each other also. From trusting the therapist, they moved toward trusting each other to give understanding and compassion. They gradually reoriented themselves to viewing each other as basically caring and loving, even if wounded and fearful. In this new light, they were able to reshape their relationship into a partnership in which they made extra efforts to understand and support each other even as they risked new sharing of feelings and thoughts. They changed. They accepted a new principle by which to guide their lives: love.

What worked for their daughter's relationship with them also succeeded for the couple's relationship. They had not overcome their insecurities, yet, they could trust each other to take their sensitivities into account. They gradually spaced their sessions over time until they terminated therapy.

AN EXAMPLE OF RELIGIOUS SPIRITUALITY

Michael, about 40, worked as a maintenance man in a large company. He was sent for help by his Employee Assistance Program because he was about to lose his job due to frequent absences and a general deterioration of his work performance. His story resembled a modern version of Job. In recent months, his dear mother had died; he did not know his father. During this same period, he discovered his wife was having an affair; she subsequently left him, but not before turning their two children against him and cutting off his connection to them. More recently, his house burned down, and he had no permanent place to stay. He responded to all these misfortunes by joining some drinking buddies and reveling in alcohol, drugs, and women. He spent his weekends in self-destructive self-indulgence. When he first came into the therapist's office he looked like a street person. (The diagnosis was 305.00 Alcohol Abuse, *DSM-IV*; American Psychiatric Association, 1994.)

Michael's work history evidenced that he had functioned as a responsible and respected employee who took pride in his job. At the moment, the therapist provided his only lifeline to health and sanity. The therapist spoke to Michael's sense of self-respect, but confronted him on what Michael knew amounted to suicidal behavior. The therapist would not accept his rationalizations and excuses; he would not treat Michael as a helpless, non-self-respecting victim. He spoke to Michael's pride. Michael responded to the therapist's personal connection and challenge. Then the therapist put to him the question of his readiness to take the first step to recovery. Michael needed to reach for someone or some group to walk with him through the course to health. The therapist discussed Alcoholics Anonymous and a rehabilitation program, as well as comfort and encouragement from his personal network.

Michael resisted AA and any institutional solution; neither did he foresee family or friends as being of any help to him. The therapist asked whether he belonged to a church. Because Michael is African American, the therapist hoped there might be a religious tradition in his background that could be both a social and spiritual resource for him. Michael did have a church, but had not attended in years. What about the pastor of the church: Was he someone he could trust and talk to? He thought he could.

The pastor received him with open arms. He was prompt to help in practical ways; he also invited Michael to attend services, which he did. Michael discovered a family in the congregation and a parental figure in the pastor. Moreover, he showed a spiritual inclination; he found making his life right and thinking of himself in a relationship with God meaningful. He no longer felt alone (Aponte, 1999).

Michael's passage did not prove easy. His life story, including contending with racism, poverty, and family losses, had all reinforced his vulnerability to losing his sense of personal worth. He tended to go where he was assured of a welcome: the street that his childhood buddies still frequented. Yet, at his core, he clung to a deeply ingrained sense of self-respect.

Because of his personal background, he was not ready to trust socially alien organizations such as AA or a rehabilitation center. This African American man felt familiar and safe in the church tradition of his background (Boyd-Franklin, 1989).

With the encouragement of the therapist, Michael made the first contacts with his church, but soon relapsed and stopped treatment. His situation subsequently became more desperate and shameful for him. He later returned to church on his own and then to therapy. Results this second time around seemed to perdure. Several months after ending the second round of therapy, he returned on his own initiative to say he was sober and doing well at work and, yes, still attending church.

RESEARCH

The spiritually sensitive model has the aspiration to be applicable universally, that is, to be usable by clinicians from most models of therapy. From a research perspective, the challenge exists to find studies that address a relatively inclusive formulation of spirituality. Growing research supports the importance of integrating a spiritual perspective with therapy. The research falls basically into that which is directed toward the relationship between good health (including mental health) and spirituality, and that which deals directly with the effectiveness of therapy that includes spirituality. The research adds validity to the basic premise of our model that spirituality forms an integral part of life and serves as a resource for therapy that bears consequences for individual mental health and good relationships.

Among the research efforts aimed at exploring the connection between spirituality and mental health, several are worth citing. Yahne and Miller (1999) reported on Snyder's (1994) work on hope, indicating that hope fosters happiness and coping skills. Coyle and Enright

(1997) observed that forgiveness is "correlated with a decrease in depression, anxiety, and Type A hostility in men and women who formally practice a forgiveness protocol" (Sanderson & Linehan, 1999, p. 211). Koenig (1999) attested to better physical and mental health in religious people, and specifically claimed that "religious people cope better with major stress events than those who lack the comfort of strong faith or the emotional support of a congregation" (p. 105). His research also pointed to "faith as a factor in recovery from depression among older people hospitalized for physical illness" (p. 150). According to Richards, Rector, and Tjeltveit (1999), "although religious and spiritual views were excluded from mainstream psychology and psychotherapy for nearly a century, this alienation is ending. . . . Many behavioral scientists are now . . . incorporating spiritual perspectives and interventions into psychological theory, research, and practice" (p. 138).

As reported by Miller (1999), Probst (1980), and Probst, Ostrom, Watkins, Dean, and Mashburn (1992), published results of investigations postulate significant results when clients' religion is made an active part of therapy. Matthews (1998) reported on a 1981 study conducted at the U.S. Public Health Service Hospital in Fort Worth, Texas, and published in the *American Journal of Drug and Alcohol Abuse* (Desmond & Maddux, 1981). The results showed that "patients attending the religious programs were *almost ten times as likely* as those attending nonreligious programs to remain abstinent from heroin use one year after the program ended" (p. 26). Benson (1996) has written extensively on his work with the relaxation response and reported that "a person's religious convictions or life philosophy enhance the average effects of the technique" (p. 155), which claims success both with physical complaints and emotional stress. Benson cited numerous studies reporting religious factors contributing to improved psychological treatment outcome (p. 174).

If spirituality forms an integral part of life, then spirituality actively, purposefully, and appropriately incorporated into therapy will add richness and depth to healing efforts. Therapists using spirituality in ways that fit the problem, the model of therapy, and the client's spirituality can incorporate spirituality as a valuable key to healing.

SUMMARY

Because traditional professional training has not incorporated spirituality as an integral process, clinicians lack both the comfort and the expertise to draw on this dimension in their work with clients. Obviously, from the perspective of spiritually sensitive therapy, therapy without the spiritual dimension does not take into account the whole human experience and does not include the full range of resources available to people. The fields of individual and family therapy will have to overcome the barrier of bias against considering spirituality as a legitimate aspect of therapy in the legacy of therapy. Moreover, therapists will have to learn not only new theory and techniques relating to spirituality, they will also require training to incorporate personal spirituality into a conscious, skillful, and responsible professional understanding of how to proceed in this realm. By integrating therapists' spirituality into personal training about their family of origin and unresolved issues, all of their personal life experience can be activated in providing therapy. Therapy's theorists, teachers, and researchers will need to identify the underlying values and spirituality of their therapeutic models. The professional schools and training institutes will face the challenge of relating with respect to *diverse* thinking among students and trainees, which often will be at odds with the values and preferences of the teaching institutions and their faculties. Students and trainees in turn will encounter the processes of learning respect and understanding for the spiritual and moral diversity among themselves as a precursor to acceptance of the diversity among their clients. Spirituality represents a new frontier for therapy, one that can expand the perspectives and resources of the field, but also one representing an enormous challenge to us all.

REFERENCES

Adler, A. (1973). The structure of neurosis. In H. L. Ansbacher & R. R. Ansbacher (Eds.), *Superiority and social interest* (3rd ed., pp. 83–94). New York: Norton. (Original work published 1933)

Alcoholics Anonymous World Services. (1976). *Alcoholics anonymous* (3rd ed.). New York: Author.

Allport, G. W. (1950). *The individual and his religion.* New York: Macmillan.

American Psychiatric Association. (1994). *Diagnostic and statistical manual of mental disorders* (4th ed.). Washington, DC: Author.

Anderson, D. A., & Worthen, D. (1997). Exploring a fourth dimension: Spirituality as a resource for the couple therapist. *Journal of Marital and Family Therapy, 23*(1), 3–12.

Aponte, H. J. (1985). The negotiation of values in therapy. *Family Process, 24*(3), 323–338.

Aponte, H. J. (1994a). *Bread and spirit: Therapy with the new poor.* New York: Norton.

Aponte, H. J. (1994b). How personal can training get? *Journal of Marital and Family Therapy, 20*(1), 3–15.

Aponte, H. J. (1996). Political bias, moral values, and spirituality in the training of psychotherapists. *Bulletin of the Menninger Clinic, 20*(4), 488–502.

Aponte, H. J. (1998). Love, the spiritual wellspring of forgiveness: An example of spirituality in our therapy. *Journal of Family Therapy, 20*(1), 37–58.

Aponte, H. J. (1999). The stresses of poverty and the comfort of spirituality. In F. Walsh (Ed.), *Spiritual resources in family therapy.* New York: Guilford Press.

Aponte, H. J., & Winter, J. E. (2000). The person and practice of the therapist: Treatment and training. In M. Baldwin (Ed.), *The use of self in therapy* (2nd ed., pp. 127–166). New York: Haworth Press.

Bardill, D. R. (1997). The spiritual reality: A Christian world view. In D. S. Becvar (Ed.), *The family, spirituality and social work* (pp. 89–100). New York: Haworth Press.

Becvar, D. S. (1997). Soul healing and the family. In D. S. Becvar (Ed.), *The family, spirituality and social work* (pp. 1–11). New York: Haworth Press.

Bellah, R. N., Madsen, R., Sullivan, W. M., Swidler, A., & Tipton, S. M. (1991). *The good society.* New York: Alfred A. Knopf.

Benson, H. (1996). *Timeless healing: The power and biology of belief.* New York: Simon & Schuster.

Bernard of Clairvaux. (1987). *Selected works.* New York: Paulist Press.

Bodin, A. M. (1996). Relationship conflict—verbal and physical: Conceptualizing an inventory for assessing process and content. In F. W. Kaslow (Ed.), *Handbook of relational diagnosis and dysfunctional family patterns* (pp. 371–394). New York: Wiley.

Boyd-Franklin, N. (1989). *Black families in therapy.* New York: Guilford Press.

Browning, D. S. (1987). *Religious thought and the modern psychologies.* Philadelphia: Fortress.

Coyle, C. T., & Enright, R. D. (1997). Forgiveness intervention with postabortion men. *Journal of Consulting and Clinical Psychology, 65,* 1042–1046.

Desmond, D. P., & Maddux, J. F. (1981). Religious programs and careers of chronic heroin users. *American Journal of Drug and Alcohol Abuse, 81,* 71–93.

Doherty, W. J. (1995). *Soul searching: Why psychotherapy must promote moral responsibility.* New York: Basic Books.

Efran, J. S., Lukens, R. J., & Lukens, M. D. (1988, September/October). Constructivism: What's in it for you? *Family Therapy Networker, 12* (pp. 27–35).

Fogel, R. W. (2000). *The fourth great awakening & the future of egalitarianism.* Chicago: University of Chicago Press.

Frankl, V. E. (1963). *Man's search for meaning.* New York: Washington Square Press.

Frankl, V. E. (1967). *Psychotherapy and existentialism.* New York: Washington Square Press.

Frankl, V. E. (1975). *The unconscious God: Psychotherapy and theology.* New York: Simon & Schuster. (Original work published 1948)

Fromm, E. (1947). *Man for himself.* New York: Henry Holt.

Goldenberg, H., & Goldenberg, I. (2001). *Counseling today's families* (4th ed.). Pacific Grove, CA: Brooks/Cole.

Hare-Mustin, R. T. (1978). A feminist approach to family therapy. *Family Process, 17*(2), 181–194.

Hayes, S. C., Strosahl, K. D., & Wilson, K. G. (1999). *Acceptance and commitment therapy.* New York: Guilford Press.

Jones, S. L. (1996). A constructive relationship for religion with the science and profession of psychology: Perhaps the boldest model yet. In E. P. Shafranske (Ed.), *Religion and the clinical practice of psychology* (pp. 113–147). Washington, DC: American Psychological Association.

Koenig, H. G. (1999). *The healing power of faith.* New York: Simon & Schuster.

Koretz, G. (2000a, January 31). Not enough is trickling down. *Business Week.*

Koretz, G. (2000b, June 5). The Web's chilling trend? *Business Week.*

Kramer, S. Z. (1995). *Transforming the inner and outer family.* New York: Haworth Press.

Mason, M. (1997). *Seven mountains: The inner climb to commitment and caring.* New York: Dutton.

Matthews, D. A. (with Clark, C.). (1998). *The faith factor.* New York: Viking.

May, R. (1960). The emergence of existential psychology. In R. May (Ed.), *Existential psychology* (pp. 1–48). New York: Random House.

McGoldrick, M., Giordano, J., & Pearce, J. K. (1996). *Ethnicity and family therapy.* New York: Guilford Press.

Menninger, K. (1964). Foreword. In R. G. Gassert & B. H. Hal (Eds.), *Psychiatry and religious faith* (pp. xxiii–xiv). New York: Viking Press.

Miller, W. R. (1999). Diversity training in spiritual and religious issues. In W. R. Miller (Ed.), *Integrating spirituality into treatment* (pp. 253–263). Washington, DC: American Psychological Association.

Nicholas, M. (1994). *The mystery of goodness.* New York: Norton.

Nouwen, H. J. M. (1972). *The wounded healer.* New York: Doubleday.

Nouwen, H. J. M. (1975). *Reaching out.* New York: Doubleday.

Nouwen, H. J. M. (1992a). *Life of the beloved.* New York: Crossroad.

Nouwen, H. J. M. (1992b). *The return of the prodigal son.* New York: Doubleday.

O'Hara, M., & Anderson, W. T. (1991). Welcome to the postmodern world. *Family Therapy Networker, 15*(5), 19–25.

Okundaye, J. N., Gray, C., & Gray, L. B. (1999). Reimaging field instruction from a spiritually sensitive perspective: An alternative approach. *Social Work, 44*(4), 371–383.

Peck, M. S. (1997). *Denial of soul.* New York: Harmony Book.

Probst, L. R. (1980). The comparative efficacy of religious and nonreligious imagery for the treatment of mild depression in religious individuals. *Cognitive Therapy and Research, 4,* 167–178.

Probst, L. R., Ostrom, R., Watkins, P., Dean, T., & Mashburn, D. (1992). Comparative efficacy of religious and nonreligious cognitive-behavioral therapy for the treatment of clinical depression in religious individuals. *Journal of Consulting and Clinical Psychology, 60,* 94–103.

Putnam, R. D. (2000). *Bowling alone: The collapse and revival of American community.* New York: Simon & Schuster.

Reiss, D. (2000). *The relationship code.* Cambridge, MA: Harvard University Press.

Richards, P. S., Rector, J. M., & Tjeltveit, A. C. (1999). Values, spirituality, and psychotherapy. In W. R. Miller (Ed.), *Integrating spirituality into treatment* (pp. 133–160). Washington, DC: American Psychological Association.

Sapolsky, R. (2000, April 10) It's not "all in the genes." *Newsweek,* p. 68.

Sells, J. N., & Hargrave, T. D. (1998). Forgiveness: A review of the theoretical and empirical literature. *Journal of Family Therapy, 20*(1), 21–36.

Sanderson, C., & Linehan, M. M. (1999). Acceptance and forgiveness. In W. R. Miller (Ed.), *Integrating spirituality into treatment* (pp. 199–216). Washington, DC: American Psychological Association.

Smith, R. G. (1958). Translator's preface to the second edition. In M. Buber (Ed.), *I and thou* (pp. v–xii). New York: Macmillan.

Snyder, C. R. (1994). *The psychology of hope.* New York: Free Press.

Tan, S. Y. (1996). Religion in clinical practice: Implicit and explicit integration. In E. Shafranske (Ed.), *Religion and the clinical practice of psychology* (pp. 365–387). Washington, DC: American Psychological Association.

Untermeyer, L. (Ed.). (1942). *A concise treasury of great poems.* New York: Pocket Books.

Vande Kemp, H. (1996). Historical perspective: Religion and clinical psychology in America. In E. P. Shafranske (Ed.), *Religion and the clinical practice of psychology* (pp. 71–112). Washington, DC: American Psychological Association.

Wicks, R. J. (1991). *Seeking perspective: Weaving spirituality & psychology in search of clarity.* New York: Paulist Press.

Woolfolk, R. L. (1998). *The cure of souls: Science, values, and psychotherapy.* San Francisco: Jossey-Bass.

Wulff, D. M. (1991). *Psychology of religion.* New York: Wiley.

Wylie, M. S. (2000). Soul therapy. *Family Therapy Networker, 24*(1), 26–37, 60–61.

Yahne, C. E., & Miller, W. R. (1999). Evoking hope. In W. R. Miller (Ed.), *Integrating spirituality into treatment* (pp. 217–233). Washington, DC: American Psychological Association.

CHAPTER 13

Existential Treatment with HIV/AIDS Clients

EUGENE W. FARBER

Existential psychology, a theoretical tradition founded on ontological description of the indispensable conditions of human existence (May, 1983; van Deurzen, 1999), provides a rich framework within which to conduct psychotherapy with persons living with the human immunodeficiency virus (HIV) and acquired immune deficiency syndrome (AIDS). The psychological literature has been peppered with direct and indirect references to "existential" concerns in persons living with HIV/AIDS since the start of the epidemic in the early 1980s (Davies, 1997; Schwartzberg, 1993; Winiarski, 1991). Illustrative of this is the apt characterization of HIV-related psychotherapeutic work as evocative of "... the big issues of life and death, hope and despair, how to live, and how to choose" (Blechner, 1997a, p. xix). Nevertheless, there has been surprisingly little systematic use of existential theory in discussions of the psychological aspects of HIV/AIDS. Further, in the two decades since the epidemic began, only a few reports have been published on specific applications of existential approaches in HIV-related psychotherapy (e.g., Giovinco & McDougald, 1994; Krycka, 1997; Milton, 1994).

HISTORY OF THE THERAPEUTIC APPROACH

The centerpiece of existential psychology hinges on ontology, the study of the nature of existence (May, 1983). Existential psychotherapy is unique among established psychotherapeutic schools in that its defining theoretical principles are based in philosophy rather than in psychology per se (van Deurzen, 1999). The relationship between existential psychotherapy and existential philosophy has been likened to that of basic science research in biochemistry and clinical pharmacotherapy, as philosophical descriptions of basic dimensions of human existence have provided the conceptual building blocks for the development of existentially informed psychotherapeutic applications to address real-life manifestations of psychological distress and problems in living (Yalom, 1980).

The beginnings of existential philosophy typically are identified with the work of Kierkegaard (1846/1945), who criticized the trends toward abstraction and reductionism among the intellectual elite in the emerging nineteenth-century scientific age in which he lived. His philosophy evolved from concerns with the inner life and commitments of human beings, as exemplified by his conceptualization of truth as subjectivity. In his critique of the concept of objectively derived universal truth, Kierkegaard insisted that the objective facts of life gain meaning only in relationship to the subjective point of view of the observer. Although he did not deny an objective, factual world, he argued that truth is relational in that objective facts cannot be detached from the personal commitments and passions of the individual (May, 1983). Thus, Kierkegaard regarded both the objective and subjective positions as necessary for a full understanding of the human condition. Later existential thinkers took up the task of articulating the structure of the existence of the individual. Phenomenology emerged as a method for the distillation of the essences of experiences. Developed by Husserl (1913/1967), the goal of phenomenology was to encounter beings and objects as they are, including the essential constitution of consciousness itself. Husserl emphasized the intentionality of human consciousness, the idea that mental contents are always inherently linked to objects and therefore always in relation to a world.

Although the Cartesian elements of Husserl's (1913/1967) philosophy highlighting a subject-object split and his notions about using phenomenology to articulate universal essences run counter to the existential frame of conceptualizing the unique existence of the individual in terms of an interplay of objectivity and subjectivity (Hoeller, 1990), the phenomenological approach has heavily influenced the existential emphasis on getting at the "what" of human existence. This is depicted in the work of Heidegger (1927/1962), a phenomenologist who was a student of Husserl, but who rejected his teacher's Cartesian mind-body assumptions in favor of a unitary view of existence (Solomon, 1988). In articulating his philosophy of *Dasein* (literally "being there"), Heidegger sought nothing less than to address the fundamental question of the meaning of being, and, in so doing, became one of the great twentieth-century philosophic influences on existential psychology and psychotherapy. Heidegger proposed that *Dasein* consisted simply of *being-in-the-world*, with no presuppositions about distinguishing self from world. As being-in-the-world, *Dasein* is always in relation to the world of nature and of other people. This is reflected in Heidegger's notion of care, referring to a basic orientation of concern about the world. Further, *Dasein* is concerned with the composition, meaning, and origins of its own existence.

A central theme in existential philosophy revolves around the place of choice in human existence, including the human necessity of choosing among conflicting alternatives regarding how to live and how to be. Kierkegaard (1844/1980) described the relationship of freedom and choice to *angst*, positing that existential anxiety as a central dimension of existence can serve as a catalyst for personal reflection and significant life change—a primary conceptual focus in existential psychology and psychotherapy (Hoeller, 1990; van Deurzen, 1999). Kierkegaard (1846/1945) conceptualized existence as a striving toward an end via one's commitment to specific life choices, and contrasted this approach to living with the proclivity to sidestep responsibility for one's choices or to avoid the important questions of one's life altogether.

These ideas foreshadowed later philosophical formulations of the distinction between authentic and inauthentic modes of existence. For Heidegger (1927/1962), human beings make decisions about existence either by asserting responsibility through choice or by neglecting choice. He developed a concept of *authenticity*, reflected in his notion of *Existenz*, a capacity to take personal responsibility for living through choice. Heidegger referred to *inauthenticity* as "fallenness," a propensity to live in a nonreflective and habitual manner, blending into the anonymous "they" of *das Man* (Solomon, 1988). According to Heidegger, we are not in a position to make choices about every aspect of existence because of our *thrownness,* defined as life circumstances that are not of our own choosing (e.g., the physical world, the sociocultural context into which we are born). We are limited by the constraints of *facticity,* the natural and social conditions in which we are embedded as well as the consequences of past actions and events that determine current circumstances (Solomon, 1988; van Deurzen, 1999). Although Heidegger viewed the individual as living primarily inauthentically in a state of fallenness, the anxiety generated by confrontation with the finiteness of being can propel one to an authentic mode of existence in which one accepts responsibility for authorship of one's life and asserts individual potentialities. Thus, acknowledgment of the true nature of human beings as finite allows life to be experienced with fullness and vitality.

In contrast, Sartre (1943/1956) maintained that realization of one's freedom to choose is a dizzying notion and a source of disorientation and existential angst (Schneider & May, 1995). According to Sartre, the individual tends to live inauthentically in *bad faith,* a state of self-deception where responsibility for self is disavowed by relating to oneself as if one were an inert object. Existence precedes essence, meaning that there are no specific defining attributes of human nature as such, and that individuals have absolute freedom to choose particular modes of living. To live authentically connotes affirming one's nothingness in the sense that, in each moment, one is free to reinvent oneself. Accordingly, freedom to choose means that one is always a work in progress and not a static thing (Schneider & May, 1995; van Deurzen, 1999). Sartre did not deny that one cannot change the facticity of one's existential situation, but insisted that one has absolute freedom to choose one's attitudes in relation to this facticity. Sartre's concepts of authenticity and inauthenticity of being share much in common with Heidegger (1927/1962) and Kierkegaard (1846/1945) in that each regarded authentic living as consisting of acceptance of both choice and limits, ultimately linking authenticity of being to acceptance of mortality. What distinguished Sartre, however, was his assertion that human freedom is absolute, that we are fully responsible for who we are, a viewpoint that has been criticized for its lack of acknowledgment of the influence of mitigating circumstances on human choice (Solomon, 1988).

Taken together, the philosophical contributions of Kierkegaard (1846/1945), Husserl (1913/1967), Heidegger (1927, 1962), and Sartre (1943/1956), among many others (e.g., Merleau-Ponty, 1945/1962; Nietzsche, 1872/2000), have provided a rich conceptual foundation for the development of existential psychology and psychotherapy. Their contributions influenced the work of several European psychiatrists in the early and middle decades of the twentieth century who were critical of the mechanistic aspects of Freudian theory and, therefore, turned to existential philosophy as the basis for development of an alternative view of human personality functioning (Hoeller, 1990). Notably, the Swiss psychiatrist Binswanger (1946/1958) emerged as an innovator in existential psychotherapy in articulating the therapeutic approach of *Daseinanalyse*. Also in Switzerland, Boss (1957/1963) developed an existential psychotherapy approach based on Heidegger's philosophical work. A landmark publication by May, Angel, and Ellenberger (1958) brought European ideas regarding existential psychology and psychotherapy to English-speaking readers for the first time, influencing the development of existential psychotherapy in the United States. Inspired by the works of the existential philosophers, these psychologists and psychiatrists crafted an approach to psychotherapy defined by phenomenology and such prominent existential themes as the intersubjective dimensions of existence, the meaning of living, the interdependence of life and death, and the freedom to choose within the limits of facticity.

THEORETICAL CONSTRUCTS

The Concept of Being in Existential Psychology

In an existential psychology framework, being constitutes the person who has experiences and has at least some capacity to become aware of these experiences (May, 1983). The existential concerns of human beings start with the fact that each individual is both the knower and the known, "... the being who can be conscious of, and therefore responsible for, his existence" (p. 96). As Husserl (1913/1967) observed, human consciousness involves intentionality in that it always has a reference point in the world. Human thoughts and feelings always refer to an object, so human existence inevitably occurs in relation to a world (van Deurzen, 1999). Being is not static but dynamic, and is always in process, pointing in some direction. Being itself is oriented toward the future, all the while influenced by the choices one makes vis-à-vis the legacy of one's past and one's present situation (May, 1983; van Deurzen, 1999). Accordingly, being is best understood in temporal terms, and is not regarded in existential psychology as a fixed category or object that can be spatially located. Self, from an existential perspective, at any given moment represents an amalgam of one's possibility and facticity (Maddi, 1998). Facticity in existential psychology, as influenced by Heidegger (1927/1962) and Sartre (1943/1956), refers not only to those unchangeable aspects of world into which persons are "thrown," but also potentialities that are excluded as a result of patterns of choosing a particular path in life to the exclusion of other possibilities. In this way, people become who they are by way of their decisions. Self emerges dynamically out of actions as individuals move through life (Maddi, 1998; May, 1983).

Eschewing the Cartesian subject-object split, existential psychologists construe human existence as a confluence of the subjective and objective. Thus, no subjectivity exists distinct from an objective world, but only being-in-the-world (Heidegger, 1927/1962; May, 1983). To approach a human being in terms of objectivity to the exclusion of subjectivity reduces the individual to a mechanistic product of biological, environmental, cognitive, and psychodynamic factors. And to disregard objective facts in pursuit of a purely subjective psychology ignores the influence of social and natural constraints and vulnerabilities on psychological life. A reality lies beneath both subjectivity and objectivity: the reality of the existing person, the individual who has experiences as a being-in-the-world (May, 1983).

Based on this theoretical framework, an existential therapist approaches the clinical enterprise with the assumption that, although it is important to gain knowledge *of* clinical phenomena such as psychological symptoms, patterns of behavior, interpersonal style, and psychodynamic processes, these facts come to life only in the immediacy of knowing through encounter with the living individual (May, 1983).

Modes of World

The concept of being-in-the-world refers to an essential interrelatedness of self and world such that person and world constitute a unitary whole (May, 1983). Self and world are inextricably intertwined in that one both exists in and participates in the design of one's world. Existential psychologists have delineated specific modes of being-in-the-world (May, 1983; van Deurzen, 1999).

Binswanger (1946/1958) proposed three modes of world, beginning with *Umwelt*, the natural world. This includes biological needs, drives, bodily functions, and states of physical health. It also consists of the physical environment and the world of natural laws and biological determinism. The elements that comprise *Umwelt* reflect our *thrownness,* aspects of our world that are there to start with and to which we must adjust. This involves certain *limit situations,* such as the facts of the cycle of birth and death. These circumstances cannot be overcome or avoided, but one can exercise choice in how one places oneself in relation to them.

The second mode of world, *Mitwelt,* involves the relational world. This encompasses the world of encounters with others, interrelationships among human beings, along with the social and cultural contexts defined by these interrelationships. *Thrownness* remains relevant in *Mitwelt* because persons are embedded in specific sociocultural milieux and periods of history that influence to some degree modes of encounter with others. *Eigenwelt,* the personal world, constitutes the third mode of world: the world of self in relation to itself, the realm of coming to know personal inner experiences and to understand the world in unique ways. *Eigenwelt* provides the basis for constructing the meaning of encounters. Van Deurzen (1999) has proposed a fourth mode of world, *Überwelt,* to connote the meaning construction and spiritual dimension of existence, including the values and ideals by which the individual lives.

Existential Anxiety and Existential Guilt

Existential theorists posit that anxiety and guilt are embedded in existence and are, therefore, part and parcel of the human experience (Boss, 1962/1990; May, 1983). Existential anxiety is presumed to be rooted in the dread of nonbeing and, therefore, is fundamentally concerned with threats to the integrity of existence. Anxiety becomes manifest not only in the face of mortality, but also in instances in which one encounters new possibilities for living that threaten one's existence as it is known to one—the secure present that would be destroyed by the fulfillment of a new potentiality of being. In this respect, anxiety is linked to the freedom to choose and the responsibility inherent in such freedom. At the same time, existential anxiety offers an essential source of vitality in that it reflects the existential situations faced in the presence of potentiality yet to be fulfilled. From this perspective, "Learning to be anxious in the right way . . . is the key to living a reflective, meaningful human life" (van Deurzen, 1999, p. 221).

Denial of potentiality precipitates the emergence of existential guilt (May, 1983). As with anxiety, existential guilt is linked to freedom of choice and the concomitant responsibility for living authentically. "Falling" into the anonymous everyday world of Heidegger's (1927/1962) *das Man,* connotes falling short of being oneself and thereby becoming indebted to oneself for not fulfilling potentialities. Because one can never fulfill all options and never live as fully as possible, one is always fundamentally guilty and called back by conscience to live an authentic mode of existence. And, as with existential anxiety, to the extent that existential guilt refocuses one to heed the call of one's conscience, it compels one to return to potentialities and to become as fully oneself as one can be (Boss, 1962/1990; van Deurzen, 1999; Yalom, 1980).

Existential Psychodynamics

Existential psychologists postulate that human existence consists of tension-generating dilemmas implying questions about how to live. How one responds to these dilemmas determines to a great extent who one becomes while moving through life. Existential psychotherapy, therefore, is psychodynamic in that it concerns itself with conflicting forces experienced at varying levels of awareness that influence thoughts, feelings, behaviors, and the overall shape of personality (May & Yalom, 2000; Yalom, 1980).

In his theoretical formulation of existential psychodynamics, Yalom (1980) proposed that awareness of the existential dilemmas posed by specific existential givens or "ultimate concerns" of existence give rise to anxiety against which psychological defenses are mobilized. Although these defenses serve self-preservative functions (i.e., protection against threats to the integrity of being), they also restrict the range of experiencing and thereby limit the expression of potentiality and fullness of living. Because the dilemmas posed by the ultimate existential concerns are embedded in the human condition, the presence of human suffering is not in itself regarded as psychopathological. Rather, psychopathology depends on the patterns of relationship between existential distress and the modes of psychological adaptation invoked to manage it.

In Yalom's (1980) formulation, the ultimate existential concerns are death, freedom, isolation, and meaninglessness. Among these, death most significantly influences psychological life. The dilemma of death results from wishing to perpetuate existence while simultaneously being a mortal individual for whom death is a certainty. People tend to shrink back from death by denying, avoiding, or sidestepping it. At the same time, although death is the ultimate limiting factor on existence, facing the reality of death potentially propels persons to authentic modes of living.

Yalom (1980) identified a second ultimate existential concern: freedom, reflecting the idea that one authors one's life and therefore exercises responsibility for one's life design. This implies that no inherent structure exists for one's life apart from one's choices—only the abyss of groundlessness, or what Sartre (1943/1956) referred to as nothingness. Realization of this nothingness and of the weight of the responsibility connoted by freedom constitutes a source of dizzying existential anxiety and a basis for existential guilt. The dilemma of freedom flows from the problem of the wish for a structured existence and the reality of existential groundlessness. Existential psychologists acknowledge limits on the freedom to choose, including dimensions of one's existential thrownness that one cannot alter. Presumably, however, persons use freedom in the stances taken in relation to a given dimension of thrownness, personal adversity, or other limiting circumstance. Frankl (1963) emphasized that, regardless of one's situation, one has the freedom to choose the attitude that one assumes toward that situation.

The third ultimate existential concern, isolation, refers to a fundamental aloneness, an unbridgeable gap between oneself and others (Yalom, 1980). Existential isolation is interwoven with death in that no one else can die with or for oneself; therefore, one is fundamentally alone in death. Freedom also is interlinked with isolation because, as one has personal authorship of life, one is invariably alone in one's choices and carries ultimate responsibility for those choices. At the same time, people seek belonging and connection. Existential isolation poses the dilemma of one's being fundamentally alone yet wishing for and seeking connection and protection via relationship with a larger collectivity of beings.

Yalom (1980) identified meaninglessness as the fourth ultimate existential concern. Human beings seek meaning, including answers to questions about the meaning of life (cosmic meaning) and the meaning of personal existence (terrestrial meaning). Likewise, Frankl (1969) posited a "will to meaning" as a primary motivating force in human life. However, the existential assertion of fundamental freedom implies that no inherent universal blueprint for living exists. Yalom (1980) observed, "... the world is contingent ... everything that is could as well have been otherwise" (p. 423). The dilemma of meaninglessness stems from searching for meaning within a world that has no inherent meaning. The process of meaning making represents, in effect, a process of decision making that brings forth a particular stand on life

(Maddi, 1998). Typically, people construct systems of meaning that contribute to a general sense of personal invulnerability. When faced with a traumatic circumstance, these systems of meaning may unravel, and the individual may be thrown into a crisis of meaninglessness (Janoff-Bulman & Berg, 1998; Janoff-Bulman & Frantz, 1997). Frankl (1963) suggested that, when confronting a fate that one cannot change, the challenge to find meaning in the suffering proves most crucial. Through meaning, the burden of suffering becomes, at least to some degree, bearable.

Taken as a whole, the theoretical constructs that constitute existential psychology provide an incisive perspective on the human condition and core experiences of living. HIV/AIDS serves as a lightning rod for activation of the core existential dilemmas of living. Thus, an existentially informed approach to psychotherapy can enrich and deepen clinical understanding of the psychological experiences of individuals living with HIV disease.

METHODS OF ASSESSMENT AND INTERVENTION

EXISTENTIAL ANXIETY AND CONTEXTUAL ASPECTS OF THE HIV/AIDS EPIDEMIC

Consistent with the existential framework of the embeddedness of experience, the psychotherapist who is working with individuals living with HIV/AIDS must be able to appreciate the biopsychosocial circumstances of the person as a being-in-the-world. Before focusing on the specifics of assessment and intervention, salient themes in the HIV/AIDS epidemic are reviewed to provide background and context for psychotherapeutic understanding of the experiences of an individual living with HIV disease.

The ultimate existential concern with life in relation to death stands as a towering thematic strand that runs through the very fabric of the HIV/AIDS epidemic. Just prior to the time when the first AIDS cases were reported in 1981, medical scientists were enjoying great success in the prevention and treatment of life-threatening infectious diseases and seemed to have within their grasp the capacity literally to inoculate people from death at the hands of infectious microbes. Against this historical backdrop, the appearance of AIDS was shocking, not only because it was striking the immune system of previously healthy young people with devastating lethality, but also because, initially, medical scientists were rendered helpless in their capacity to understand and treat this mysterious illness. As a newly emerging disease in an age of the ascendancy of medical science, the HIV/AIDS syndrome made focal both to affected individuals and the broader society the stark reality of human vulnerability to annihilation and the limits of science in providing a buffer from the existential reality of mortality. Thus, the psychological dynamics of the HIV/AIDS epidemic have from the start been influenced by the core existential concern with death and the existential anxiety to which it gives rise.

Defined by May (1983) as *"the experience of the threat of imminent nonbeing"* (p. 109), existential anxiety is assumed to be embedded in human existence because "to grasp what it means to exist, one needs to grasp the fact that he might not exist, that he treads at every moment on the sharp edge of possible annihilation and can never escape the fact that death will arrive at some unknown moment in the future" (p. 105). Contemplation of finiteness and death is terrifying. The existential anxiety that ensues is fiercely avoided and countered by the ubiquitous human quest for death transcendence that shapes much of the topography of psychological and cultural life (May & Yalom, 2000; Yalom, 1980). Two primary modes of defending against death anxiety include a belief in one's personal specialness, separateness, and inviolability in relation to mortality, and a belief in an ultimate rescuer. These modes of defense have been manifest in important ways in the HIV/AIDS epidemic.

The Specialness "Exemption" and HIV/AIDS Stigma

AIDS stigma represents one of the most unfortunate historical realities of the epidemic, painfully complicating the psychosocial circumstances of persons living with HIV/AIDS as well as compromising research and public health efforts to manage the epidemic and to prevent new infections (Herek & Glunt, 1988). Although it is well established that heterosexual contact is the most common mode of HIV transmission worldwide (Forstein & McDaniel, 2001), many people in the United States continue to believe that HIV/AIDS does not affect them, their families, or their communities (Winiarski, 1997). Through an accident of history, the first AIDS cases in the United States occurred mainly among younger gay men, prompting the initial classification of the disease as Gay-Related Immune Disorder (Herek & Glunt, 1988). Later, HIV "risk groups" were designated to include not only gay men but also injection drug users, perpetuating the erroneous impression that the disease posed no danger to those outside of these groups (Osborn, 1999). Employing Sullivan's (1953) concept of the "not me," defined as the dreaded personification of self that is disavowed because of its association with intense and disorganizing anxiety, Blechner (1997b) proposed that these false perceptions about risk groups allowed an individual to defend against the personal threat of HIV/AIDS by adopting a wishful illusion that the disease was relevant only to "them" and "not me." In the language of existential psychology, this psychological stance permitted the individual to avoid the existential anxiety associated with awareness of susceptibility to annihilation posed by HIV disease. In its most malignant manifestation, this pattern was expressed as social stigma, wherein the "not me" was defined not simply as "different than" but as "less than."

HIV/AIDS probably was prone to some degree of stigmatization from the start simply because of its life-threatening nature as well as the presence of visible markers of the disease that include physical frailty (e.g., wasting syndrome) and disfigurement. However, the fact that AIDS first appeared in the United States in already stigmatized and socially marginalized sociodemographic groups made it easier for the majority culture to perceive HIV/AIDS as a disease of those who were fundamentally flawed in character and approach to living and therefore to blame for their illness (Herek & Glunt, 1988). In existential terms, social stigmatization could be understood in part as a vehicle through which stigmatizing persons could defend against their existential anxiety by defining themselves as special relative to the "less than" individuals with HIV/AIDS and therefore exempt from the mortal threat posed by the disease.

Medical Science as an Ultimate Rescuer

The early years of the growing epidemic were highly stressful times, not only for those diagnosed with AIDS, who, in the absence of viable medical treatment, were confronted abruptly with the reality of impending mortality, but also for the medical care providers who were treating them. Given the remarkable prior medical successes in the treatment of infectious diseases, great hope arose that medical science could decipher quickly the etiology of AIDS and develop modes of treatment and cure. However, wishful thinking, fueled by profound fear, also played a part, contributing to an initial tendency to underestimate the tenacity and complexity of HIV and to overestimate the rapidity with which medical science could respond to this heretofore unknown disease (Blechner, 1997b; Rabkin, Remien, & Wilson, 1994). Owing in part to an implicit and unswerving societal faith in scientific progress as an instrument of death transcendence, this pattern of wishful thinking seemed to reflect the human propensity to believe in an ultimate rescuer as a defense against death anxiety. Additionally, as a pattern unfolded in which the promise of perceived breakthroughs was dashed by facing the reality of a complex disease defying quick solutions, increasing clarity emerged that the unfolding HIV/AIDS epidemic would be bounded by the polarities of hope and despair (Blechner, 1997b).

For example, the identification in late 1983 and early 1984 of HIV as the virus that causes AIDS provided a milestone galvanizing hope that a vaccine and cure would soon follow. As time went on, however, estimates of the time before a cure might be achieved kept growing, and the disease continued to spread, as initial hope for a rapid cure faded. Hope reemerged in 1987 with the introduction of zidovudine (AZT), the first antiretroviral treatment against HIV disease. Over time, however, this hope gave way to disappointment when results of clinical trials revealed that the early antiretroviral therapies proved not as effective as had initially been expected. Growing pessimism about the likelihood of an early major medical breakthrough was reflected in a 1994 decision by scientists at the International AIDS Conference to meet every two years rather than annually, as had been its custom until then (Blechner, 1997b). Hope again was raised in 1996, with the development of a new HIV treatment called highly active antiretroviral therapy (HAART). Although the hope activated by the advent of HAART has been tempered by the painful lessons of past experiences underscoring the insidious tenacity of HIV/AIDS, these new treatments have reduced the incidence of AIDS-related opportunistic infections, frequency of hospitalizations for AIDS-related complications, and overall AIDS incidence and mortality (Centers for Disease Control [CDC], 1998, 1999; Powderly, Landay, & Lederman, 1998; Torres & Barr, 1997). The emergence and widespread implementation of HAART, along with advances in the treatment of AIDS-related opportunistic infections, has changed the context of the epidemic such that HIV/AIDS increasingly is managed as a long-term chronic illness. Nonetheless, because of medical uncertainties about the enduring efficacy of antiretroviral treatments, the complexity of proper adherence to treatment regimens, the potential for adverse side effects, and the possibility of unfavorable treatment response, many individuals experience a sometimes confusing mixture of optimism and uneasiness about their health situations and a hesitance or ambivalence about fully embracing a sense of future (Farber & McDaniel, 1999; Sowell, Phillips, & Grier, 1998; Winiarski, 1997). Therefore, a predominant dilemma in the lives of individuals living with HIV/AIDS currently results from the unpredictability of this chronic and life-threatening illness and the heavy demands associated with the complexities of medical treatment.

Existential Anxiety as an Impetus toward Growth
Existential theorists assume that, although avoidance of existential anxiety can restrict experiencing, healthy acceptance of the finiteness of being and its attendant anxiety can also expand one's sense of possibility and spur progress toward fulfillment of new potentialities. This important idea is illustrated in the HIV/AIDS epidemic. Against the backdrop of pain and suffering, life-affirming growth and creativity have emerged. Not uncommonly, individuals with HIV/AIDS describe the disease as an impetus for personal development and expansion of being (Schwartzberg, 1993). Similarly, some HIV health care providers have commented that, through their encounters with patients, they have "... achieved a kind of accelerated wisdom and recognition of the fragility

and value of life" (Rabkin et al., 1994, p. i). Although HIV/AIDS continues to elude a cure, biomedical research on the disease has led to tremendous gains in knowledge and clinical techniques heretofore unrealized. Further, the HIV/AIDS epidemic has contributed to new definitions of the health care process. Heightened emphasis has emerged on doctor-patient teamwork and collaboration, along with patient empowerment through promotion of increased HIV knowledge and mastery skills for maintaining positive health practices. In some instances, HIV-affected groups have also, through exertion of sociopolitical pressure, helped advance a process of humanizing the biomedical research agenda. For example, research oversight committees for clinical trials of HIV/AIDS treatments now commonly include patient representatives to ensure that patient interests are served in the design and implementation of these research trials. Additionally, the HIV/AIDS epidemic has led to the rise of consumer-oriented patient advocacy efforts and the formation of psychosocial support organizations designed to create a community of support for persons with HIV disease.

Overall, the broad societal dynamics of the HIV/AIDS epidemic bring into bold relief the spectrum of human responses to confrontation with mortality as well as other existential dimensions of living. HIV/AIDS constitutes what Yalom (1980) referred to as a "boundary situation"—an experience that compels one to ponder one's core existential circumstances in life. In conveying the idea of an essential interdependence of life and death, Yalom asserted that "... though the physicality of death destroys us, the *idea* of death saves us" (p. 40). HIV/AIDS not only confronts one with harsh and painful experiences and limits, but also has the potential to propel one to look at life from a fresh perspective. Whether this potential is tapped, however, is dependent on patterns of choice as an individual confronts HIV-related life challenges. Existentially informed psychotherapy can play a key role in this process, opening a space within which the HIV patient can explore painful feelings, struggle with the limits imposed by the disease, and clarify potentials and options that remain.

OVERVIEW OF EXISTENTIALLY INFORMED HIV-RELATED PSYCHOTHERAPY

HIV disease affects individuals from diverse ethnic, sociocultural, and socioeconomic backgrounds. The clinical course of HIV/AIDS is marked by unpredictable fluctuations in relative health and illness. Accordingly, the psychological challenges of living with the disease arise from both acute disease-related events and ongoing uncertainty about how long periods of relative disease quiescence will last, with individuals commonly experiencing cycles of psychological reaction and adjustment to new disease-related realities as stressors arise (Farber & Schwartz, 1997; Kalichman, 1998). For these reasons, HIV-related psychotherapy requires flexibility on the part of a therapist in adapting clinical assessment and therapeutic intervention to the individualized needs of a given patient, taking into account such factors as disease phase, psychosocial situation, sociocultural background, and socioeconomic circumstance (Kalichman, 1998; Winiarski, 1991). Because the existential approach is based on the assumption that psychotherapy must be conducted according to the unique experiences of each individual patient without preconceived formulas for intervention, it offers a flexible and yet theoretically informed modality compatible with the clinical needs of patients in HIV-related psychotherapy.

Existential psychotherapy is best characterized as a frame of reference for understanding the individual and addressing psychological difficulties (May & Yalom, 2000). The existential approach does not consist of a monolithic set of therapeutic principles, nor does it depend on specific or systematized clinical procedures for psychotherapeutic intervention (Hoeller, 1990; May, 1983; van Deurzen, 1999; Yalom, 1980). Rather, existential therapists utilize a wide range of specific intervention strategies, including those developed by varied psychotherapeutic schools (May & Yalom, 2000; Schneider & May, 1995). Similarly, existential ideas have been acknowledged for their usefulness by adherents of a wide range of schools of psychotherapy (Ellerman, 1999; Ottens & Hanna, 1998; Portnoy, 1999; Rugala & Waldo, 1998). Therapeutic techniques are used in a theoretically informed way, and interventions are tailored to the needs of the individual patient as revealed in the clinical assessment process.

ASSESSMENT CONSIDERATIONS

In existential psychotherapy, *"technique follows understanding"* (May, 1983, p. 151). This means that therapist decisions about which specific intervention strategies to use at a given point in the therapeutic process are informed by a clear understanding of the present existential situation of the patient. The overarching objective of clinical assessment is to get at "the *what*" of the patient's experience as a starting point for clinical intervention. Guided by a phenomenological approach, the existential therapist endeavors to describe a dimension of the patient's experience in its immediacy rather than focusing exclusively on causal inquiry. From the existential viewpoint, understanding what an experience *is* precedes meaningful consideration of causal explanations for the experience because "... the question of *why* one is what one is does not have meaning until we know *what* one is" (May, 1979, p. 88). Therefore, although *Diagnostic and Statistical Manual of Mental Disorders (DSM-IV*; American Psychiatric Association [APA], 1994) clinical diagnosis remains important, the existential therapist reflects on the diagnosis and its associated symptom clusters in the context of the lived experience of the patient.

To gain a clear perspective on an individual as a being-in-the-world, a picture of the full range of experience proves paramount. In existential psychotherapy, this involves assessing a patient's existential situation in terms of the modes of world: *Umwelt, Mitwelt, Eigenwelt,* and *Überwelt* (van Deurzen, 1999). This approach parallels current models of HIV-related psychological functioning, including the biopsychosocial/spiritual model focused on a combination of biomedical, social/cultural, psychological, and spirituality factors influencing the psychological experiences of persons living with HIV/AIDS (Winiarski, 1997).

When exploring the patient's experience of *Umwelt*, a therapist necessarily considers how an individual experiences HIV/AIDS as a physical presence as well as construals and modes of adaptation to specific disease manifestations. Assessment incorporates laboratory indicators of disease status (CD4 lymphocyte cell counts, viral load assay findings), physical manifestations of the disease (opportunistic infections and neoplasms, bodily deterioration and weakness, fatigue, pain), HIV-related physical dysfunction, and side effect profiles for HIV medication regimens. The central nervous system impact of HIV as well as associated opportunistic infections and neoplasms affecting the brain have significant implications for psychological functioning because symptoms typically associated with depressive disorders may be indicative of an underlying HIV-related organic syndrome (Back, Miller, & Cummings, 1998; Hinkin, Castellon, van Gorp, & Satz, 1998). HIV-associated psychosis and mania also are possible (Back et al., 1998). Therefore, a therapist looks out for neurocognitive factors associated with HIV-related central nervous system complications in the assessment process. Overall, from an existential perspective, a therapist does not simply catalogue facts regarding disease manifestations, but assesses the subjective relationship of the patient to these disease-related givens.

In evaluating the existential dimension of *Mitwelt*, the issue of how HIV/AIDS is embedded in the patient's experience of social relationships as well as relationships with the public world at large becomes focal. Assessment is concentrated on the nature and quality of a patient's relationships to friends and loved ones, the community at large, health care providers and systems, social/financial service systems, and the overall sociocultural context in which a patient lives. A patient's relationship to some of the givens of *Mitwelt* emerge for consideration, including HIV stigma, limitations in accessibility of needed health care and social service resources, and cultural attitudes toward HIV disease, which frequently prove, at best, ambivalent.

Assessment of a patient's experience of *Eigenwelt* highlights self-conceptions as they relate to the patient's HIV diagnosis. This encompasses consideration of the patient's self- and role definitions, including the degree to which self is conceived of as healthy versus ill, living versus dying, and autonomous versus dependent. The patient's balance of hope versus fear as this relates to the inherent uncertainties associated with the unpredictability of disease progression also needs to be evaluated. Given the existential postulate that self is defined through choice and action within the limits of one's facticity, the dynamics associated with the ultimate existential concern of freedom are important here. They center on the very personal question of responsibility and choice as to how to go about living with HIV disease. The experience of time in relation to life trajectory also should be evaluated carefully, including the perceptions about availability of life choices, priorities, and aspirations.

The assessment process is not complete without consideration of *Überwelt* through evaluating the place of HIV disease in the guiding personal mythology of the patient. Assessing the relationship between the patient's experience of living with HIV/AIDS and religious/spiritual beliefs and/or secular personal beliefs concerning the purpose of life, the values by which life should be lived, the place of illness and suffering, and the nature of death provides pertinent information.

Because gaining experiential understanding of the lived world of the patient constitutes the goal of assessment, clinical material gleaned from the assessment process across the core domains of existence requires synthesizing to develop an existential formulation of the psychological stance of the patient in relation to living with HIV disease. Schneider and May (1995) provided a useful way of organizing case dynamics in their existential-integrative model. They assumed that within the basic polarities of freedom (i.e., the capacity for willful expression of potentiality) and limitation (i.e., the constraints imposed by nature and social reality) in which an individual lives, a person may psychologically *constrict* (tighten, narrow the experience of being), *expand* (open, spread, enlarge the experience of being), or *center* (balance and direct expansive and constricting experiences of being) the self. These concepts of constriction, expansion, and centering in the context of an existential polarity anchored by freedom and limitation have considerable heuristic value in the clinical assessment of patterns of psychological experiencing and modes of adaptation in an HIV patient. To depict a patient's psychological stance in relation to HIV disease, three basic assessment questions prove important: To what degree is the patient's range of experiencing restricted? Is the pattern of experiential restriction primarily of the hyperconstricted type (e.g., obsessional rumination about HIV/AIDS accompanied by behavioral withdrawal), the hyperexpansive type (e.g., grandiose denial of the physical health effects of HIV/AIDS), or a combination of the two? What are the existential dreads underpinning restrictions in the range of experiencing? To the degree an individual can experience a sense of choice, meaning, and willfulness, while remaining mindful of realistic HIV-related limits, the range of experiencing is broadened to recognize possibilities and to accept losses/restrictions defining one's facticity. To the extent that an individual denies or avoids the essential freedom to choose and/or disease-related limits, one may be prone to difficulties with psychological adaptation to HIV/AIDS. Understanding the stance of the patient toward HIV/AIDS within the existential polarities of freedom and limitation offers a guide for clinical intervention.

THERAPEUTIC INTERVENTION

Existential psychotherapists intend primarily to illuminate the existence of a patient (May, 1983). Accordingly, existentially informed HIV-related psychotherapists focus on exploration of the unique experience of an individual. Additionally, they employ techniques to heighten awareness of potentiality through clarification of choices within the limits imposed by HIV/AIDS. This approach parallels Schneider and May's (1995) existential-integrative model. They posited that growth and vitality ensue from confronting and integrating the full range of the freedom-limitation polarity, whereas extremes of hyperexpansion and/or hyperconstriction limit the potential of being by reducing the range of experiencing. Therapists concentrate on here-and-now exploration of a patient's existential orientation (including manifestations of existential dread associated with conflicts surrounding ultimate existential concerns), as well as future potentialities that a patient is moving toward. Therefore, existential psychotherapists combine present-oriented empathic listening with interpretations aimed at heightening patient awareness of choice and responsibility in living (Maddi, 1998).

Presence (May, 1983; Schneider & May, 1995)—"... an attitude of palpable ... *attention*" (Schneider & May, 1995, p. 154)—constitutes a cornerstone of existential technique. Presence requires a therapist to participate as fully as possible as a real person in a patient's existential reality. A therapist does not simply take the patient as an object of study, but rather seeks an authentic intersubjective encounter with a patient for the purpose of deepening the patient's understanding of self. This includes being present as a witness to expressions of pain and suffering, an essential element of effective therapy with individuals living with HIV/AIDS. In addressing the therapeutic task of "hearing people through their pain," Egendorf (1995) highlighted the profound importance of this aspect of therapeutic work, suggesting that "... pain and illumination are inextricably bound" (p. 25). Overall, to the extent that presence provides a safe context within which a patient can engage in self-exploration, including encounter with painful aspects of experience, it serves as the starting point from which existentially informed HIV-related psychotherapy proceeds. Further, just as a therapist seeks to be present with the patient, enhancing the patient's presence with self also is a therapeutic goal (May, 1983; Schneider & May, 1995).

HIV-related psychotherapy requires flexibility on the part of a therapist, who must be prepared to provide a combination of support, problem-solving, and exploratory functions in differing levels of concentration depending on the clinical needs and circumstances of a patient and the issues at hand. Within the framework of presence and openness to empathically hearing a patient's painful struggles with the challenges of living with HIV/AIDS, a therapist continually attends to the existential situation of a patient in the here-and-now, selecting therapeutic interventions accordingly. For example, for a patient who is in an acute crisis situation, the therapist may choose to focus on nonexperiential behavioral, ideational, and emotional containment functions (Schneider & May, 1995). Specific interventions might include problem solving, bolstering social support systems, cognitive restructuring (e.g., supportively challenging unwarranted catastrophic thinking, promoting ways of thinking about HIV-related stressors that suggest possibilities for solutions to present concerns), and relaxation exercises designed to lower emotional arousal (Farber & Schwartz, 1997; Kalichman, 1998; Viney, Allwood, Stillson, & Walmsley, 1992). Although mindful of the need to promote emotional relief and to ensure the safety of a patient (if, for example, the crisis is accompanied by suicide risk), the existentially informed therapist also seeks to help patients clarify options, maintain awareness of the empowering capacity for choice, and discover meaning in a crisis situation. Thus, even as the therapist is working to bring about crisis stabilization, the crisis is viewed as an opportunity to initiate a process of reflective experiential self-exploration of significant existential dilemmas that can be explored more fully once the crisis itself has been sufficiently addressed.

From the moment HIV disease is diagnosed, the issue of the impermanence of life leaps from a place of silence and invisibility into the foreground of existence. The individual is confronted with the implicit challenge of defining how life will be lived in the context of the reality of HIV disease as a threat to existence. Much of the work of existentially informed HIV-related psychotherapy is focused on working with this challenge and its manifestations in psychological conflicts surrounding the ultimate existential concerns of death, freedom, isolation, and meaninglessness.

Several psychological themes and conflicts associated with these respective ultimate existential concerns occur commonly in psychotherapy patients with HIV/AIDS. These concerns require specific modes of intervention.

Death

A core existential concept revolves around the finiteness of existence. Yet, human beings tend to disavow their essential finiteness and, in so doing, disown personal responsibility for living. In addressing this dynamic in psychotherapy, Frankl (1963) proposed that therapists invite their patients to act as though they are living for the second time and to evaluate life decisions in terms of whether they would make those same choices again. This exercise facilitates awareness of personal ownership of existence within the confines of one's essential finiteness. From the moment of immediate confrontation with finiteness that accompanies an HIV diagnosis, the individual is, in essence, faced with this very question of how to proceed with living, and has the opportunity to consider whether to proceed as before. In working with the ultimate existential concern of death in HIV-related psychotherapy, it is important to consider the patient's predominant modes of coping with death anxiety, including belief in one's specialness and/or in an ultimate rescuer (Yalom, 1980). Belief in one's own specialness inflates one's sense of imperviousness to the possibility of death, thereby providing a means of avoiding the existential anxiety associated with confronting mortality. Some degree of conviction regarding specialness can serve as an expansive experiential buffer for the HIV patient (e.g., "I can beat this disease if I take care of myself"), which is immensely helpful in confronting the reality of the disease and in feeling empowered to take on the daily challenges of living with HIV/AIDS. In its hyperexpansive manifestation, however, belief in one's specialness may be expressed as a rigidly held sense of inviolability that includes unrealistic perceptions about one's ability to transcend the vulnerabilities and dangers posed by HIV/AIDS. For example, an individual newly diagnosed with HIV may respond with a maniclike denial buoyed by the grandiose fantasy of exemption from the life-threatening limits of the disease. This idea may be accompanied by unhealthy neglect of HIV-related health care needs. Excessive reliance on belief in an ultimate rescuer prompts a psychological pulling in and therefore tends to be a hyperconstricted mode of dealing with death anxiety. It may be accompanied by passivity, lack of assertiveness, and reluctance to stand out (Yalom, 1980). The HIV-positive individual who relies on this hyperconstricted mode of living may tend to shrink back from life in avoidant fear, preferring to look outward for help and guidance in living with the disease.

Whether an individual in HIV-related psychotherapy manifests a hyperexpansive or hyperconstricted existential position vis-à-vis death anxiety, the therapeutic goal is to bring about movement to a more centered position in which the individual is able to accept the seriousness of the illness while also continuing to go about living as fully as possible within the constraints of the disease. To the extent that a therapist can facilitate a process in which life is lived as fully as possible, the fact of death may seem less foreboding (Yalom, 1980). Hyperexpansive avoidance of the reality of HIV-related limits may be addressed therapeutically by gently focusing the patient experientially on how the person feels about being HIV-positive. This is accomplished by actively making HIV/AIDS a central topic in therapy through such means as reflecting on a patient's tendency to sidestep discussion of the illness, inquiring about patient knowledge of the disease, and asking a patient about experiences with HIV medical treatment. Such interventions make HIV/AIDS a presence in the therapy, and then a therapist can guide a patient experientially by asking how the person feels in talking about HIV-related issues. With hyperconstricted modes of dealing with HIV-related death anxiety, interventions may productively converge on entertaining self-directed possibilities, encouraging a patient to explore the possibilities and perils of "daring to live," and working with the existential anxiety that is likely to be aroused by this process of therapeutic inquiry.

In the late phases of HIV disease, when its life-threatening nature is less an abstraction and more clearly a reality, a therapist provides a forum within which the patient can express the range and intensity of feelings that may arise as death nears. Existential angst, which may emerge as an individual is overcome by opportunistic infections that precipitate loss of control over body functions and dramatically reduce physical mobility, may be accompanied by feelings of shame, frustration, powerlessness, sadness, and anger. A therapist's presence and ability to be with the patient's experiences of pain become a crucial therapeutic container in supportive and palliative ways. A therapist encountering a dying patient may naturally experience challenging emotions of anxiety, sadness, and powerlessness. At these times, a therapist must be especially aware of the possibility of emotional numbing or detachment/avoidance that impedes therapeutic presence. In working with a dying patient, not concentrating exclusively on loss to the exclusion of reflections on instances of fullness and satisfaction along the life path of the individual proves important. To the extent that the patient feels that life has been lived fully, the reality of death may be more readily accepted (Yalom, 1980).

Freedom

Along with death as an existential theme in HIV-related psychotherapy, the ultimate existential concern of freedom also becomes a focal point of psychotherapeutic exploration in addressing the issue of how to live with HIV disease. Existential theorists have posited that human beings remain ambivalent about freedom because this implies a dizzying personal responsibility for authorship of the life design against the backdrop of groundlessness. Freedom awareness comes with awareness of the reality that one's decisions limit possibility, and forces acceptance of personal responsibility and, by implication, one's ultimate existential isolation (Yalom, 1980). In HIV-related psychotherapy, ambivalence about freedom and responsibility is manifested in how patients perceive their options for living within the real limits imposed by HIV disease. For some, a pattern of hyperconstriction, expressed as a pulling back from participation in life and disavowal of decision making and personal responsibility, predominates. For these individuals, "I can't" becomes a familiar expression of their stance on life with HIV/AIDS, serving as a representation of an artificially imposed restriction in living. Therapy can nudge these patients into increased awareness of this psychological outlook as a type of choice to increase patient ownership of decisions and their implications for lived existence. Equally problematic are instances in which patients live in denial of the realistic limits that HIV imposes on the options available to them. This hyperexpansive stance involves responsibility avoidance via abdication of choice by acting as if nothing about life has changed as a result of HIV disease. In such individuals, responsibility is externalized to the outside world. The therapist must direct attention to heightening patient awareness of the limits imposed by the disease and of a patient's refusal to assume responsibility for choosing a particular life design that takes into account these limits.

When dealing with themes of freedom and responsibility in existentially informed HIV-related psychotherapy, it is important to facilitate heightened patient awareness of the capacity for choice and decision making with regard to the distressing psychological concerns that serve as the foci of therapy (Ellerman, 1999; Maddi, 1998; Yalom, 1980). May (1983) defined decision as ". . . a decisive attitude toward existence, an attitude of commitment" (p. 166), and placed it at the heart of the process of change in psychotherapy. Decision presupposes will. No will occurs in the absence of wish. Therefore, therapeutic clarification of wishing is a prerequisite for willful action (May, 1969; Yalom, 1980). Repeatedly and systematically inquiring as to what the patient is wanting and how the patient is feeling in the immediacy of the here and now as the therapeutic process proceeds, cutting below content to underlying states of mind that point themselves to wishes, facilitates such clarification. Techniques in mind-body awareness, such as Gendlin's (1981) focusing, may be especially useful for this purpose. Once the wish is experientially clarified, the next step is commitment to a course of action that involves willful intention to behave in a manner consistent with pursuit of the wished-for life design—a decision to act willfully in the fulfillment of potentiality.

According to Yalom (1980), "... *the therapist's task is not to create will but to disencumber it*" (p. 332). He proposed a set of clinical strategies for this purpose: (1) introducing alternatives and facilitating a systematic process of considering various options; (2) promoting patient awareness of the ubiquity of decision and its relationship to self-definition; (3) reframing to gain a fresh perspective on a decision; and (4) exploration of the meaning of a decision, including the implicit and conflicting payoffs of decisions either to change or not. Patients can be invited to explore catastrophic fantasies about what might happen if they were to make changes that are simultaneously desired and feared. Interpretation promotes a sense of personal mastery by providing a framework for understanding core struggles in living. Disavowal of personal responsibility can be addressed by labeling and challenging instances in which a patient avoids responsibility (e.g., changing "I can't" statements into "I won't" statements) as well as pointing out instances in which a patient defers responsibility by looking to the therapist for definitive answers to personal struggles (Yalom, 1980). Frankl's (1969) prescriptive technique of paradoxical intention, in which the patient is instructed to heighten the intensity of the presenting symptom, also is useful in illustrating that the symptom is something the patient has at least some choice about. Ultimately, the process of working therapeutically with decision and will should lead to a patient's understanding that responsibility for one's life design remains an ongoing process: "... one does not create one's situation in life once and for all; rather, one is continuously creating oneself" (Yalom, 1980, p. 340).

The dynamics of freedom and responsibility prove central in addressing patient regrets about specific choices and/or paths not chosen and feelings of loss related to missed opportunities while contemplating the limits imposed by HIV disease. A therapist should be attuned to manifestations of existential guilt in facilitating a process of coming to terms with the legacy of choices from the past. These concerns are especially significant for individuals who have been long-term HIV/AIDS survivors, many of whom had made choices under an assumption that they were on a fast trajectory toward death until the new antiretroviral treatments dramatically revitalized their lives. Ambivalence about assuming the responsibilities and expectations inherent in reattaching to life and planning for the future needs to be explored. The task for patients mired in ambivalence is to gain access to their wishes, to tap into psychological propulsion for willful action in the direction of therapeutic change. In the late phases of HIV disease, therapy is increasingly devoted to acknowledging and accepting the loss of previous options as the physical toll of the disease narrows physical capacity for agency and initiative. A therapist facilitates a process of clarifying remaining options and choices while also making room for grieving as a patient comes to terms with the encroachment of HIV-related limits (e.g., physical pain, loss of cognitive sharpness and physical functions) that increasingly restrict the range of options for living.

Because most individuals contract HIV disease via specific risk behaviors, it is important to be attentive to patient perceptions of personal responsibility for their circumstances along a continuum anchored by the polarities of persecutory self-blame and complete externalization of responsibility. Some individuals grapple with the fantasy that "if only" they had behaved differently, been more careful, or taken more precautions, they would never have contracted the disease. This reflects a manifestation of existential guilt, a sense of having committed a transgression against self. At the opposite extreme are individuals who blame others for their illness, thereby avoiding contemplation of the extent to which their situation may at least in part be the legacy of personal choices and actions. The dynamics linking perceptions of past behavioral choices to a current existential situation of the HIV patient have a significant impact on the experience of self. The therapeutic aim is to help the patient discover a path somewhere between self-blame and externalization, a point of acceptance of past choices that releases an individual to concentrate instead on potentials yet to unfold, including the choices that remain within the limits imposed by HIV disease.

Isolation

In existentially informed HIV-related psychotherapy, the ultimate existential concern of isolation is intimately linked to the concerns of death and freedom. The dynamics of isolation become easily manifest in the lives of persons living with HIV/AIDS, for they alone must bear the burden of a debilitating, life-threatening illness that causes immense suffering. Although the research literature makes clear that social support can be of enormous psychological and emotional value for persons with HIV disease (Blaney et al., 1997; Pakenham, Dadds, & Terry, 1994), the stark fact remains that they alone must endure the subjective immediacy of its physical impact and its potential to shorten their lives. Problems of limited social and financial resources, challenges involved in negotiating complex health care systems, and AIDS stigma can reinforce feelings of separateness and existential isolation. Therefore, addressing a patient's sense of relative connection with or alienation from people in daily life and the societal systems in which the patient is embedded proves essential. Specifically, therapy must touch on such issues as feelings of safety and security, ambivalence about increased dependence on others in advanced phases of disease progression, apprehensiveness about the benevolence and trustworthiness of others associated with the stigmatization of HIV disease, and anticipatory abandonment fears as HIV disease progresses (Farber & Schwartz, 1997). Extremes of defending against existential isolation may include such hyperconstricted patterns as merging oneself with others or withdrawal from one's interpersonal world as well as such hyperexpansive patterns as seeking to absorb others into one's interpersonal fold or arrogant indifference toward others. In both of these modes, mutuality in relationship is sacrificed for the illusion of insulation from existential isolation, or need for relationship is avoided altogether. Relationships are sought primarily for survival rather than for mutuality and growth (Yalom, 1980).

Existential psychotherapists assume that authentic encounter between patient and therapist in itself is therapeutic (May, 1983; Portnoy, 1999; Schneider & May, 1995; Yalom, 1980). In HIV-related psychotherapy, a key focus is on using the therapeutic relationship both in the service of deeper relational understanding as well as acceptance of the limits of relationship in buffering against the existential isolation inherent in the journey of living with HIV/AIDS. Therapy emphasizes not only practical aspects of enhancing relationships but also opens a space for experiential encounter with the angst that accompanies the stark realization of one's ultimate aloneness in living with the disease. Therapy may address behavioral strategies for enhancing social support (e.g., asking for emotional/functional support from friends, family, associates; attending HIV support groups) while also making room for exploration of relational disappointment and acceptance of the limits of social support in assuaging angst associated with awareness of existential isolation. The patterns and rhythms of patient relationships may be explored in the context of the dynamics of existential isolation, guided by the assumption that, to the extent one is willing to encounter existential isolation, one is able to experience fulfilling relationships.

An individual who describes a hyperconstricted pattern of relating in which interpersonal connection is maintained with an unsatisfying partner because of extreme fear of living alone with HIV may be invited by the therapist to reflect systematically on what the experience of living alone with the disease might be like. This facilitates a process of encounter with isolation anxiety in the safe context of a therapeutic relationship. This may include direct encounter in the here and now with instances in which the limits of the therapeutic relationship itself are experienced by the patient.

From the existential perspective, treating such encounters exclusively in terms of transference phenomena obfuscates the authenticity of the patient-therapist relationship (Yalom, 1980). The painful realization that the therapeutic relationship ultimately cannot offer deliverance from existential anxiety is not simply a remnant of past experiences of separation and loss, but is a real experience occurring in the here and now between therapist and patient. To deal with it experientially in the therapeutic relationship and not just as an abstraction has substantial psychotherapeutic value. This way of conceptualizing does not deny the veracity of transference phenomena, but acknowledges the presence of a real relationship between therapist and patient, an experience of therapeutic importance in and of itself.

Meaninglessness

As a life-threatening illness, HIV/AIDS can precipitate a crisis of meaning for affected individuals, bringing to the foreground the dynamics associated with the ultimate existential concern of meaninglessness. The question "Why me?" may emerge as a familiar refrain, signaling a struggle to make sense of the personal meaning of HIV disease. Implicit in this question is the attempt to organize experience into a coherent explanatory framework of personal understanding. The dilemma of meaning springs from humans as meaning-seeking creatures who live in a world in which there are no absolutes, no specific blueprints for living, where they are free to choose and ultimately defined by the choices made (Yalom, 1980).

The meaning-making process proves crucial to HIV-related psychological adaptation. An individual who construes HIV disease as an impetus for fuller living more likely adapts positively than an individual who experiences the disease as a random, meaningless stroke of bad luck. A patient who adopts an active, stubbornly held, nihilistic view that HIV/AIDS is nothing more than a sentence of death by suffering exemplifies a clinically significant hyperexpansive manifestation of a struggle with existential meaning. This position reflects a kind of grandiosity in its steadfast insistence that any view to the contrary is merely a manifestation of foolish naïveté, an unwillingness to own up to a matter of "brutal" truth. A hyperconstricted manifestation of internal conflict emanating from HIV-related meaninglessness results in a kind of apathy and withdrawal from living, a sense that participation in life has lost its raison d'être. For such individuals, life has lost its point, there is nothing to strive for, and therefore there is no compelling reason to meet the challenges of living with HIV disease. This apathy and directionlessness begets a pattern of poor HIV-related self-care marked by low motivation to commit to positive HIV health behaviors.

The overarching challenge in psychotherapy with individuals living with HIV/AIDS who are experiencing shattered meaning or pervasive meaninglessness involves helping them to construct a sense of a meaningful place for HIV/AIDS in their lives. This entails therapeutic exploration of patient views on life purpose, personal priorities and aspirations, and possibilities for participation in living within the real physical limits imposed by HIV disease. Accordingly, a therapist may actively challenge patient perceptions held too rigidly or loosely or applied too narrowly or broadly (Farber & Schwartz, 1997; Viney et al., 1992). A patient who insists that HIV disease has rendered life unlivable can be challenged to examine the assumptions of this view and encouraged to participate in life to the extent possible, given the physical limitations imposed by the disease at a specific point in its progression.

According to the existential perspective, "... *it is good and right to immerse oneself in the stream of life"* (Yalom, 1980, p. 431). Therefore, the most important therapeutic strategy for addressing crises of meaning entails encouraging engagement in living. Meaning is contextual in that life feels meaningful only to the extent that we participate in life. To address the meaning of life by stepping back and inquiring about its meaning in a rational way makes the experience of meaningfulness elusive. Therefore, unlike therapeutic strategies with an emphasis on immersion in therapeutic exploration of the existential concerns of death, freedom, and isolation with the ultimate aim of accepting the conflicts inherent in these dimensions of being, the primary goal in therapeutic management of meaninglessness is to direct attention outside of oneself. Frankl (1963, 1969) contended that happiness ensues from meaning fulfillment, and that persons discover meaning via what they give to the world through creativity and accomplishment, what they derive from life encounters through engagement in the world and with others, and the stand they take toward suffering in the face of a situation that they cannot change. Dereflection, which focuses the patient away from internal preoccupations and toward the world outside, is a technique designed to help patients find meaning through self-transcendence rather than self-involvement (Frankl, 1963). A therapist might encourage a patient to identify activities to pursue and explore their availability. Thus, a patient who enjoys creative pursuits, such as art or writing, may be encouraged to look into community programs offering classes in these areas. Patients unable to work may become motivated to consider volunteer activities, which promote a sense of efficacy and purpose through the process of giving of time and effort.

Perhaps the greatest challenge of living with AIDS results from enduring the suffering that accompanies the disease. An important dimension of HIV-related psychotherapy involves addressing the issue of the meaning of suffering. Frankl (1963) suggested that, in confronting inescapably dire situations, human beings have choices regarding the attitudes they take, and that the pain of suffering can be softened to some degree if individuals can find meaning for these situations. A therapist can assist a patient in search of the meaning of suffering by exploring the paradox that the life-threatening nature of HIV/AIDS and the limits inherent therein also present opportunities for the deepening of experiencing and enhancement in living.

MAJOR SYNDROMES, SYMPTOMS, AND PROBLEMS TREATED

Consistent with reports in the theoretical and research literature on the psychological impact of life-threatening events (Collins, Taylor, & Skokan, 1990; Janoff-Bulman & Berg, 1998; Janoff-Bulman & Frantz, 1997; Taylor, 1983), it is common for HIV/AIDS to have an impact on core personal beliefs, central life goals, personal meaning systems, definitions of self and personal roles, and views of one's relationship to the world as a whole (Davies, 1997; Farber & Schwartz, 1997). Although a majority of individuals adjust reasonably well to living with HIV/AIDS (Chesney & Folkman, 1994; Leiberich et al., 1997; Perry et al., 1993), emotional reactions to disease-related stressors may be experienced. These range from mild sadness or anxiety to clinically significant levels of distress (Kalichman, 1998).

The most common *DSM-IV* diagnoses (American Psychiatric Association, 1994) in persons with HIV/AIDS include adjustment disorders, depressive disorders, and anxiety disorders (Kalichman, 1998). The issues and symptoms associated with these diagnoses, including the dysphoria, demoralization, and diminished sense of self-esteem of depression and the dread, foreboding, and vulnerability of anxiety, lend themselves to intervention using an existential psychotherapy framework. Further, the emphasis on the experiential dimensions of living in existential psychotherapy makes the approach well suited for working with themes of grief and bereavement, which are also commonly experienced in individuals with HIV/AIDS. Although existentially oriented psychotherapists acknowledge that clinical diagnosis has an important role in therapy treatment planning, they also caution that excessive reliance on clinical diagnostic categories in case formulation may obscure rather than illuminate clinical understanding beyond the macrolevel of clusters of behaviors and symptoms (Bugental & Sterling, 1995; Yalom, 1980). Hence, from an existential perspective, clinical facts used to derive a *DSM-IV* diagnosis are integrated into an overall picture of an individual as a being-in-the-world such that symptom clusters and diagnostic formulations are considered in the context of the unique existence of a person. At the same time, existentially informed psychotherapists must be careful not to miss important aspects of psychodiagnostics, namely, the domain of *Umwelt* as it relates to central nervous system effects of HIV disease on psychological functioning.

CASE EXAMPLE

Diagnosis and Assessment

Joe, a 30-year-old African American man with AIDS, sought psychotherapy after he began having repetitive nightmares about being pulled into a dark, murky whirlpool from which he could not escape. These nightmares occurred for several weeks and coincided with the onset of a deep dysphoria accompanied by feelings of impending doom, anhedonia, social withdrawal, self-deprecation, and poor appetite with weight loss. Joe was unusually emotionally distant, but his family and friends, while respecting his wishes to keep to himself, took turns making contact with him, maintaining a level of concerned involvement that Joe ultimately appreciated. His medical care provider, who saw this psychological state and isolative relational pattern as out of step with Joe's usual upbeat demeanor and sociability, referred him to therapy after ruling out the possibility of an HIV-related neuropsychiatric syndrome that could account for these mood changes. Given the absence of an HIV-related, central nervous system mood disorder, his symptom picture was consistent with a *DSM-IV* diagnosis of Major Depression, Single Episode. Joe was assigned a rating of 70 on the Global Assessment of Relational Functioning (Group for the Advancement of Psychiatry Committee on the Family, 1996), suggesting mild overall relational dysfunction associated with his social withdrawal.

Joe, who had never experienced this level of emotional distress, was bewildered by his psychological state, as just prior to its onset he had received the excellent news that for the first time, a new regimen of antiretroviral therapy had dramatically improved his CD4 lymphocyte cell count and reduced the serum viral burden of HIV in his body to undetectable levels. Previously, Joe had been quite ill, at one point having almost died as a result of a severe case of *pneumocystis carinii* pneumonia, an HIV-related opportunistic infection. At that time, he gave up his job as director of a nonprofit legal clinic that provided low-cost services for economically disadvantaged individuals, had gone on disability, and was preparing himself emotionally for what appeared to be a progression toward death. Joe related that letting go of his job had been emotionally difficult because he had always prided himself on his independence and belief in working for the well-being of others, stating, "I always took care of everyone else." In his family, he was the "Rock of Gibraltar." His friends relied on him as always responsive. Though he had struggled in the process of letting go of the life he had known and the independent roles he cherished, both in work and in his relationships, over time he came to be "at peace" with what "had to be" as a result of his deteriorating health. Given his zest for his previous life, however, Joe was especially confused as to why he would respond to the recent dramatic improvement in his health by feeling so down and insecure. He reported feeling "paralyzed" by the prospect of "starting over" with his life, worried that others would "disapprove" if he did not resume his previous life of selfless dedication, and concerned that he could never again live up to expectations for himself based on prior life accomplishments.

CASE FORMULATION

The onset of Joe's depression was precipitated by a change in the existential realm of *Umwelt*, namely, a dramatic improvement in health that marked a reprieve from the progression toward death. In the realm of *Mitwelt*, Joe described himself as one who previously had lived to take care of and attend to the needs of others, a role that he had reluctantly relinquished as his HIV illness worsened. Joe had clearly taken great pride in his independence and his previous role of taking charge in his relationships, which, in the context of *Eigenwelt*, had been a personal identity that was a source of considerable self-esteem. Further, he had always been passionate in his belief in the importance of selflessness and the value of working toward the good of others, a defining meaning-related theme of his being-in-the-world as reflected in *Überwelt*.

The quality of Joe's depressive symptoms suggested the presence of a hyperconstriction of experiencing, a closing off or pulling in as a way of dealing with his uncertainty about how to reattach to living after having previously prepared himself for a trajectory toward death.

This uncertainty was especially puzzling to him because of his previous enthusiasm for the life activities and roles he had been forced to surrender. Salient existential concerns regarding freedom (reflected in his self-described psychological paralysis), isolation (reflected in implied fear of aloneness owing to the perceived risk of others' "disapproval"), and death (reflected in identity confusion) contributed to the dynamics of Joe's depression.

TREATMENT APPROACH

Because of the existential dynamics contributing to Joe's depression, therapy highlighted disencumbering his sense of will and addressing angst associated with the existential themes of isolation and death. Because his recurrent nightmare provided the most immediate experiential metaphor for his conflict, therapy began with a phenomenological exploration of the contents of the nightmare. Joe was asked to describe the image of the whirlpool and the sensation of being pulled toward it using present-tense language as though it were occurring in the here and now. He identified the whirlpool as representative of life, and increasingly became aware of an intense dread of reattaching to living while simultaneously feeling pulled against his will back into the stream of life. Exploration of the nightmare image revealed experientially Joe's ambivalence about renewed health. Guided by the therapeutic question of what it would mean for him to reattach to living, he fully explored his newly articulated ambivalence. He recalled that, when he had thought he was dying and had let go of the life he had known, he found relief in not feeling the weight of responsibility of perpetual selflessness that served as the hallmark of his previous mode of being-in-the-world. When he thought about reattaching to life now with his renewed health, he believed he had no choice but to resume life according to his script of being the eternal helper, the "Rock of Gibraltar," for which previously he had been so highly valued by family and friends. He no longer wished to be that totally selfless person, but feared that, by living a more modest existence in which his needs could be considered as well as those of others, he would cease to be and would lose his value in the eyes of others. Joe's conflict in reattaching to life involved feeling bound by a sense that no room in the world existed for him as an ordinary person with needs of his own. His existence was contingent on being the "special one." In this way, he became afraid of living because of a fear of dying. At his core, he dreaded the consequences of being an ordinary person with ordinary needs.

Once this existential conflict was made clear, therapeutic work centered on the task of helping Joe relinquish his strangling perfectionism and explore his ordinariness with the eventual goal of embracing it. This involved both challenging his core belief that selflessness provided the only way to be a good person, as well as heightening his awareness of his own needs, including those arising in the context of the therapeutic relationship (e.g., Joe's need for emotional support and validation by the therapist). At each step in this process, Joe's existential anxiety was aroused and then explored, allowing him increasingly to tolerate its impact and to acquire greater latitude in experiencing and living. Although Joe continued to struggle with balancing others' needs with his own, the therapeutic work resulted in the dissipation of his nightmares and remission of his depression.

POSTTERMINATION SYNOPSIS AND REFLECTIONS

At termination, Joe was beginning to plan a future for himself, signaling a willingness to live out his "ordinariness." His sense of willfulness had been restored with the realization that it was okay to balance his own needs with those of others, and he had accepted the risks inherent in such a life stance for his relationships and sense of self. Mindful of pacing himself, he began doing community volunteer work part time, balancing this with pursuit of an interest in learning to play the guitar, a lifelong desire that he had put off in the past. Prior to becoming severely ill, Joe had defended against death anxiety through singular pursuit of a path of immortality through selflessness at the expense of fullness of being. The process of coming near to death and then back again activated a conflict within him between his sense of obligation to be in the world for others and his desire to attend to his own personal needs. As he became increasingly aware of an underlying fear of personal dissolution were he to dare to consider his own needs, Joe was able to entertain and then implement the risk of living a fuller life than he had previously allowed himself.

RESEARCH ON THE APPROACH

Because existential psychotherapy is not a standardized approach consisting of a specific set of therapeutic guidelines and intervention techniques, it does not easily lend itself to evaluation via traditional research methods. Further, many existential psychotherapists are cautious about traditional research designs that examine individuals in psychotherapy as objects of study without consideration of subjectivity. For these reasons, existential researchers have preferred qualitative and phenomenological approaches to psychological research (Bugental & Sterling, 1995), although recognizing the value and usefulness of quantitative research. While a comprehensive overview of research in existential psychotherapy exceeds the scope of this chapter, what follows is a sampling of both quantitative and qualitative research pertinent to existentially informed HIV-related psychotherapy.

RESEARCH ON MEANING AND HIV-RELATED PSYCHOLOGICAL ADAPTATION

The importance of finding meaning in adaptation to traumatic life events has consistently been underscored in the psychological literature (Janoff-Bulman & Berg, 1998; Taylor, 1983). HIV/AIDS research investigators have used both qualitative and quantitative approaches to study the role of meaning in HIV-related adaptation. Schwartzberg (1993), in a qualitative study, employed a phenomenological evaluation of detailed interviews with 19 gay men. Four general patterns of ascribing meaning to HIV disease emerged: (1) high meaning, consisting of a representation of HIV as a catalyst for personal growth; (2) defensive meaning, comprised of superficial portrayal of HIV as growth-promoting as compensation for underlying uncertainty; (3) shattered meaning, including confusion and bewilderment about the meaning of HIV disease and the pain of irrevocable loss left in its wake; and (4) irrelevant meaning, involving minimization of the personal impact of HIV disease on core conceptions of self and world. One of the conclusions drawn from this study was that meaning making is an important element of coping with HIV disease. This conclusion is consistent with a recent quantitative study using self-report measures to explore relationships between dispositional hardiness and psychological adaptation among 200 men and women with symptomatic HIV disease and AIDS (Farber, Schwartz, Schaper, Moonen, & McDaniel, 2000). The study findings suggested that persons with greater hardiness in general, and with a greater sense of meaningfulness and purpose in life in particular, are more likely to adjust positively than are those with less hardiness and less perceived meaningfulness and purpose in life.

Findings from Davies's (1997) qualitative study examining changes in time orientation among HIV-positive persons indicated that the sense of future can become dislocated, with implications for constructions of personal meaning and self-definition. The study participants, each of whom had been living with HIV disease for at least five years, described a sense of "provisional existence" characterized by simultaneous maintenance of an orientation toward death (i.e., closing off to the future) and life (i.e., expanding and projecting into the future) accompanied by a vague background feeling of angst. Three patterns of temporal orientation derived from interview data reflected ways of dealing with the angst and uncertainty engendered by an HIV diagnosis, including increased emphasis on the meaning and value of the present ("living with a philosophy of the present"), continued focus on future plans and aspirations ("living in the future"), and a shrinking back from consideration of possibility for fear of further loss or disappointment ("living in the empty present"). Individuals who indicated a pattern of experiencing consistent with "living in the empty present" tended to show the least positive psychological adjustment.

Before concluding this review of research on meaning in HIV-related psychological adaptation, it is interesting to note that research combining quantitative and qualitative methods has supported the presence of relationships between meaning and HIV-related immunological factors, including changes in CD4 lymphocyte cell count, a central marker of HIV disease progression. A study of HIV-seropositive men who had recently lost a close friend or partner to AIDS showed that individuals who found meaning as reflected in changing priorities, values, and perspectives in the course of the grieving process evidenced no mean CD4 lymphocyte cell decline over a two- to three-year follow-up window, whereas those who did not find meaning showed moderate to fast CD4 lymphocyte cell decline (Bower, Kemeny, Taylor, & Fahey, 1998). Finding meaning was associated with a lower rate of mortality from AIDS over a follow-up period of several years. A study of relationships between attributions about self and changes in CD4 lymphocyte cell count over an 18-month period among HIV-seropositive men suggested that negative attributions about the self in relation to HIV-related experiences (e.g., circumstances surrounding HIV diagnosis, HIV-related stressors and coping) were associated with more rapid CD4 lymphocyte cell decline (Segerstrom, Taylor, Kemeny, Reed, & Visscher, 1996). Findings such as these hint that in addition to its importance in HIV-related psychological adaptation, meaning making may also have implications for HIV-related immunological functioning.

Research on HIV-Related Psychotherapy

Although the usefulness of psychotherapy for persons encountering struggles in living as a result of HIV disease is widely acknowledged, relatively little research has been conducted on HIV-related psychotherapy. Only a few research reports examining existential approaches in HIV-related psychotherapy have been published. Krycka (1997) reported a qualitative study on the use of focusing, an experiential mind-body awareness technique, in psychotherapy with four men with AIDS. Emphasizing a phenomenological approach, Krycka sought to elucidate change processes in the course of psychotherapy, identifying three "movements" toward change. In the first movement, there is a struggle in encounter with unwelcome aspects of experience in the initial process of heightening experiential awareness, a pattern that gives way in the second movement to an internal dialogue with previously disavowed aspects of experience. In the third movement, this experiential dialogue facilitates a new integration of previously denied or unacknowledged dimensions of experience into the personal identity of an individual, thereby expanding the overall self-concept. A primary conclusion was that an important dimension of effective HIV-related psychotherapy involves facilitating an experiential process in which patients can listen to themselves in the presence of a therapist who is willing also to listen.

In a quantitative investigation of group interventions with HIV patients, the effectiveness of experiential group therapy was compared with cognitive-behavioral group therapy among 39 gay men with asymptomatic HIV disease (Mulder et al., 1994). The experiential group was based on humanistic-existential principles and emphasized personal awareness, addressing feelings about the implications of HIV disease, and sharing of fears and concerns. The cognitive group was centered around cognitive restructuring, behavior change, and assertiveness training. Participants in each group met for 17 sessions over a 15-week period. Results showed that participants in the psychotherapy groups showed significant decreases in psychological distress levels in comparison to a wait-list control group, with no significant differences observed between the two therapeutic modalities regarding psychological distress levels. Interestingly, despite the fact that no differences emerged in outcome measures, shortly after the group ended, participants in the experiential therapy group reported greater perceived benefit from their group than those in the cognitive-behavioral group. The investigators considered that this difference in perceived satisfaction might have been attributable to the greater opportunity for group interaction in the experiential group than in the cognitive-behavioral group. At six-month follow-up, however, no significant differences remained in perceived benefits of the two groups.

Because techniques from a broad range of therapeutic schools may be used in existential psychotherapy (May & Yalom, 2000), it is edifying to survey briefly research reports on cognitive-behavioral, social support, and interpersonal approaches in HIV-related psychotherapy, and consider their implications for existential therapy with HIV patients. For example, Lutgendorf et al. (1998) reported that gay men with symptomatic HIV disease who participated in a 10-week cognitive-behavioral, stress-management group focused on building coping skills and enhancing social support displayed enhanced coping and reduced psychological distress when compared to wait-list controls. Acceptance of the life implications of HIV infection was found to be a particularly important factor, as was positive reframing involving the capacity to view one's situation in a new light.

In a comparison study, 68 HIV-positive men with depression were randomly assigned to an eight-session cognitive-behavioral group, social support group, or no-treatment control group (Kelly et al., 1993). The cognitive-behavioral group was focused on developing cognitive and behavioral skills for reducing depression and anxiety while the social support group provided emphasis on sharing of feelings, hopes, fears, and modes of problem-solving related to HIV disease. The overall results showed significant treatment effects for both group therapy modalities in reduction of symptoms, although the social support group demonstrated higher levels of clinically significant change than did the cognitive-behavioral group, as well as greater maintenance of therapeutic benefit at three-month follow-up. In discussing their findings, Kelly et al. concluded that part of the value of the social support group stemmed from providing an arena for participants to discuss such "existential" HIV-related concerns as the impact of the disease on life choices, roles, and prospects for the future, including the likelihood of physical debilitation and an untimely death.

Markowitz et al. (1998) compared 16-week individual interventions with interpersonal psychotherapy, cognitive-behavioral therapy, supportive psychotherapy, and supportive psychotherapy with an antidepressant medication (imipramine) conducted with HIV-positive patients with depressive symptoms. Results indicated that, whereas all treatment conditions yielded a reduction in depressive symptoms over the treatment course, the strongest effects were observed for those individuals who completed interpersonal psychotherapy and supportive therapy with imipramine. In interpreting observed differential effectiveness of interpersonal psychotherapy and cognitive-behavioral therapy, the investigators suggested that the here-and-now focus in interpersonal psychotherapy, its linkage of depressive symptoms to relationship issues, and its emphasis on clarifying options for fulfillment of patient needs and desires within the limitations imposed by HIV disease may be especially important therapeutic ingredients in work with depressed HIV-positive patients.

Conclusions from Research Findings

Although a larger body of research is needed, results from existing studies indicate that both existential/experiential and nonexistential therapeutic approaches can provide therapeutic benefit for individuals living with HIV/AIDS. Taken together, these findings also point to several general conclusions that are relevant to an existentially informed approach in HIV-related psychotherapy. First, the research underscores the importance of meaning making in HIV-related psychological adaptation, suggesting that addressing meaning is crucial in psychotherapeutic work with persons living with HIV/AIDS. Of particular relevance here is the importance of providing therapeutic opportunities for patients to come to terms with the personal significance and impact of HIV/AIDS, to facilitate a process that allows identification and expression of feelings associated with HIV-related existential dilemmas, and to foster meaningful construals of HIV-related realities that permit pursuit of realistic options and choices within the acknowledged limits imposed by the disease. Second, available research supports the idea of the importance of the therapeutic relationship for a healing process, providing validation of the concept of therapist presence as an attentive listener and witness to the painful struggles expressed by patients. Third, the research showing the effectiveness of social support interventions points in particular to the therapeutic importance of communion in sharing painful experiences. Finally, regardless of modality, each of the therapeutic approaches described in these studies provides evidence for the benefits of a here-and-now focus of self-reflection and self-evaluation, as well as a future orientation that encourages making active choices about how to maximize personal potential within the limits posed by HIV/AIDS.

REFERENCES

American Psychiatric Association. (1994). *Diagnostic and statistical manual of mental disorders* (4th ed.). Washington, DC: Author.

Back, C., Miller, J., & Cummings, J. (1998). Neurobiological basis of behavioral changes in HIV-1 encephalopathy. In W. G. van Gorp & S. L. Buckingham (Eds.), *Practitioner's guide to the neuropsychiatry of HIV/AIDS* (pp. 42–64). New York: Guilford Press.

Binswanger, L. (1958). The existential analysis school of thought. In R. May, E. Angel, & H. Ellenberger (Eds., E. Angel, Trans.), *Existence: A new dimension in psychiatry and psychology* (pp. 191–213). New York: Basic Books. (Original work published 1946)

Blaney, N. T., Goodkin, K., Feaster, D., Morgan, R., Millon, C., Szapocznik, J., et al. (1997). A psychosocial model of distress over time in early HIV-1 infection: The role of life stressors, social support and coping. *Psychology and Health, 12,* 633–653.

Blechner, M. J. (Ed.). (1997a). *Hope and mortality: Psychodynamic approaches to AIDS and HIV.* Hillsdale, NJ: Analytic Press.

Blechner, M. J. (1997b). Psychodynamic approaches to HIV and AIDS. In M. J. Blechner (Ed.), *Hope and mortality: Psychodynamic approaches to AIDS and HIV* (pp. 3–62). Hillsdale, NJ: Analytic Press.

Boss, M. (1963). *Psychoanalysis and daseinsanalysis* (L. B. Lefebre, Trans.). New York: Basic Books. (Original work published 1957)

Boss, M. (1990). Anxiety, guilt, and psychotherapeutic liberation. In K. Hoeller (Ed.), *Readings in existential psychology and psychiatry* (pp. 71–92). Seattle, WA: Review of Existential Psychology and Psychiatry. (Original work published 1962)

Bower, J. E., Kemeny, M. E., Taylor, S. E., & Fahey, J. L. (1998). Cognitive processing, discovery of meaning, CD4 decline, and AIDS-related mortality among bereaved HIV-seropositive men. *Journal of Consulting and Clinical Psychology, 66,* 979–986.

Bugental, J. F. T., & Sterling, M. M. (1995). Existential-humanistic psychotherapy: New perspectives. In A. S. Gurman & S. B. Messer (Eds.), *Essential psychotherapies: Theory and practice* (pp. 226–260). New York: Guilford Press.

Centers for Disease Control. (1998). *HIV/AIDS surveillance report* (Vol. 10, No. 2). Atlanta, GA: U.S. Department of Health and Human Services.

Centers for Disease Control. (1999). Surveillance for AIDS-defining opportunistic illnesses, 1992–1997. *Morbidity and Mortality Weekly Report, 48*(Suppl. 2), 1–22.

Chesney, M. A., & Folkman, S. (1994). Psychological impact of HIV disease and implications for intervention. *Psychiatric Clinics of North America, 17,* 163–182.

Collins, R. L., Taylor, S. E., & Skokan, L. A. (1990). A better world or shattered vision? Changes in life perspectives following victimization. *Social Cognition, 8,* 263–285.

Davies, M. (1997). Shattered assumptions: Time and the experience of long-term HIV positivity. *Social Science Medicine, 44,* 561–571.

Egendorf, A. (1995). Hearing people through their pain. *Journal of Traumatic Stress, 8,* 5–28.

Ellerman, C. P. (1999). Pragmatic existential therapy. *Journal of Contemporary Psychotherapy, 29,* 49–64.

Farber, E. W., & McDaniel, J. S. (1999). Assessment and psychotherapy practice implications of new combination antiviral therapies for HIV disease. *Professional Psychology: Research and Practice, 30,* 173–179.

Farber, E. W., & Schwartz, J. A. J. (1997). Changing conceptions of self and world through the spectrum of HIV disease: Implications for psychotherapy. *Journal of Psychotherapy Practice and Research, 6,* 36–44.

Farber, E. W., Schwartz, J. A. J., Schaper, P. E., Moonen, D. J., & McDaniel, J. S. (2000). Resilience factors associated with adaptation to HIV disease. *Psychosomatics, 41,* 140–146.

Forstein, M., & McDaniel, J. S. (2001). Medical overview of HIV infection and AIDS. *Psychiatric Annals, 31,* 16–20.

Frankl, V. E. (1963). *Man's search for meaning.* New York: Pocket Books.

Frankl, V. E. (1969). *The will to meaning: Foundations and applications of logotherapy.* New York: Plume.

Gendlin, E. T. (1981). *Focusing* (2nd ed.). Toronto, Canada: Bantam Books.

Giovinco, G., & McDougald, J. (1994). Logotherapy: A journey into meaning for people with AIDS. *International Forum for Logotherapy, 17,* 76–81.

Group for the Advancement of Psychiatry Committee on the Family. (1996). Global Assessment of Relational Functioning Scale (GARF): I. Background and rationale. *Family Process, 35,* 155–172.

Heidegger, M. (1962). *Being and time* (J. Macquarrie & E. Robinson, Trans.). New York: Harper & Row. (Original work published 1927)

Herek, G. M., & Glunt, E. K. (1988). An epidemic of stigma: Public reactions to AIDS. *American Psychologist, 43,* 886–891.

Hinkin, C. H., Castellon, S. A., van Gorp, W. G., & Satz, P. (1998). Neuropsychological features of HIV disease. In W. G. van Gorp & S. L. Buckingham (Eds.), *Practitioner's guide to the neuropsychiatry of HIV/AIDS* (pp. 1–41). New York: Guilford Press.

Hoeller, K. (1990). An introduction to existential psychology and psychiatry. In K. Hoeller (Ed.), *Readings in existential psychology and psychiatry* (pp. 3–19). Seattle, WA: Review of Existential Psychology and Psychiatry.

Husserl, E. (1967). *Ideas: General introduction to pure phenomenology* (W. R. B. Gibson, Trans.). London: Allen & Unwin. (Original work published 1913)

Janoff-Bulman, R., & Berg, M. (1998). Disillusionment and the creation of value: From traumatic losses to existential gains. In J. H. Harvey (Ed.), *Perspectives on loss: A sourcebook* (pp. 35–47). Philadelphia: Brunner/Mazel.

Janoff-Bulman, R., & Frantz, C. M. (1997). The impact of trauma on meaning: From meaningless world to meaningful life. In M. Power & C. R. Brewin (Eds.), *The transformation of meaning in psychological therapies* (pp. 91–106). New York: Wiley.

Kalichman, S. C. (1998). *Understanding AIDS: Advances in research and treatment* (2nd ed.). Washington, DC: American Psychological Association.

Kelly, J. A., Murphy, D. A., Bahr, R., Kalichman, S. C., Morgan, M. G., Stevenson, Y., et al. (1993). Outcome of cognitive-behavioral and support group brief therapies for depressed, HIV-infected persons. *American Journal of Psychiatry, 150,* 1679–1686.

Kierkegaard, S. (1945). *Concluding unscientific postscript* (D. F. Swenson, Trans.). London: Oxford University Press. (Original work published 1846)

Kierkegaard, S. (1980). *The concept of anxiety* (R. Thomte & A. B. Anderson, Trans.). Princeton, NJ: Princeton University Press. (Original work published 1844)

Krycka, K. C. (1997). The recovery of will in persons with AIDS. *Journal of Humanistic Psychology, 37*(2), 9–30.

Leiberich, P., Engeter, M., Olbrich, E., Rubbert, A., Schumacher, K., Rieger, M., et al. (1997). Longitudinal development of distress, coping and quality of life in HIV-positive persons. *Psychotherapy and Psychosomatics, 66,* 237–247.

Lutgendorf, S. K., Antoni, M. H., Ironson, G., Starr, K., Costello, N., Zuckerman, M., et al. (1998). Changes in cognitive coping skills and social support during cognitive behavioral stress management intervention and distress outcomes in symptomatic human immunodeficiency virus (HIV)-seropositive gay men. *Psychosomatic Medicine, 60,* 204–214.

Maddi, S. R. (1998). Creating meaning through making decisions. In P. T. P. Wong & P. S. Fry (Eds.), *The human quest for meaning: A handbook of psychological research and clinical applications* (pp. 3-26). Mahwah, NJ: Erlbaum.

Markowitz, J. C., Kocsis, J. H., Fishman, B., Spielman, L. A., Jacobsberg, L. B., Frances, A. J., et al. (1998). Treatment of depressive symptoms in human immunodeficiency virus-positive patients. *Archives of General Psychiatry, 55,* 452–457.

May, R. (1969). *Love and will.* New York: Norton.

May, R. (1979). *Psychology and the human dilemma.* New York: Norton.

May, R. (1983). *The discovery of being: Writings in existential psychology.* New York: Norton.

May, R., Angel, E., & Ellenberger, H. (Eds.). (1958). *Existence: A new dimension in psychiatry and psychology.* New York: Basic Books.

May, R., & Yalom, I. (2000). Existential psychotherapy. In R. J. Corsini & D. Wedding (Eds.), *Current psychotherapies* (6th ed., pp. 273–302). Itasca, IL: Peacock.

Merleau-Ponty, M. (1962). *The phenomenology of perception* (C. Smith, Trans.). New York: Humanities Press. (Original work published 1945)

Milton, M. (1994). The case for existential therapy in HIV-related psychotherapy. *Counselling Psychology Quarterly, 7,* 367–374.

Mulder, C. L., Emmelkamp, P. M. G., Antoni, M. H., Mulder, J. W., Sandfort, T. G. M., & de Vries, M. J. (1994). Cognitive-behavioral and experiential group psychotherapy for HIV-infected homosexual men: A comparative study. *Psychosomatic Medicine, 56,* 423–431.

Nietzsche, F. (2000). *The birth of tragedy* (D. Smith, Trans.). Oxford, England: Oxford University Press. (Original work published 1872)

Osborn, J. E. (1999). Public health, HIV, and AIDS. In T. C. Merigan, Jr., J. G. Bartlett, & D. Bolognesi (Eds.), *Textbook of AIDS medicine* (2nd ed., pp. 123–136). Baltimore: Williams & Wilkins.

Ottens, A. J., & Hanna, F. J. (1998). Cognitive and existential therapies: Toward an integration. *Psychotherapy, 35,* 312–324.

Pakenham, K. I., Dadds, M. R., & Terry, D. J. (1994). Relationships between adjustment to HIV and both social support and coping. *Journal of Consulting and Clinical Psychology, 62,* 1194–1203.

Perry, S., Jacobsberg, L., Card, C. A. L., Ashman, T., Frances, A., & Fishman, B. (1993). Severity of psychiatric symptoms after HIV testing. *American Journal of Psychiatry, 150,* 775–779.

Portnoy, D. (1999). Relatedness: Where humanistic and psychoanalytic psychotherapy converge. *Journal of Humanistic Psychology, 39*(1), 19–34.

Powderly, W. G., Landay, A., & Lederman, M. M. (1998). Recovery of the immune system with antiretroviral therapy: The end of opportunism? *Journal of the American Medical Association, 280,* 72–77.

Rabkin, J. G., Remien, R. H., & Wilson, C. R. (1994). *Good doctors, good patients: Partners in HIV treatment.* New York: NCM Publishers.

Rugala, S. A., & Waldo, M. (1998). An integration of existential psychology and the multimodal model. *Journal of Humanistic Psychology, 38*(4), 65–79.

Sartre, J. (1956). *Being and nothingness* (H. Barnes, Trans.). New York: Philosophical Library. (Original work published 1943)

Schneider, K. J., & May, R. (1995). *The psychology of existence: An integrative, clinical perspective.* New York: McGraw-Hill.

Schwartzberg, S. S. (1993). Struggling for meaning: How HIV-positive gay men make sense of AIDS. *Professional Psychology: Research and Practice, 24,* 483–490.

Segerstrom, S. C., Taylor, S. E., Kemeny, M. E., Reed, G. M., & Visscher, B. R. (1996). Causal attributions predict rate of immune decline in HIV-seropositive gay men. *Health Psychology, 15,* 485–493.

Solomon, R. C. (1988). *Continental philosophy since 1750: The rise and fall of the self.* Oxford, England: Oxford University Press.

Sowell, R. L., Phillips, K. D., & Grier, J. (1998). Restructuring life to face the future: The perspective of men after a positive response to protease inhibitor therapy. *AIDS Patient Care and STDs, 12,* 33–42.

Sullivan, H. S. (1953). *The interpersonal theory of psychiatry.* New York: Norton.

Taylor, S. E. (1983). Adjustment to threatening events: A theory of cognitive adaptation. *American Psychologist, 38,* 1161–1173.

Torres, R. A., & Barr, M. (1997). Impact of combination therapy for HIV infection on inpatient census. *New England Journal of Medicine, 336,* 1531–1532.

van Deurzen, E. (1999). Existentialism and existential psychotherapy. In C. Mace (Ed.), *Heart and soul: The therapeutic face of philosophy* (pp. 216–235). London: Routledge.

Viney, L. L., Allwood, K., Stillson, L., & Walmsley, R. (1992). Personal construct therapy for HIV seropositive patients. *Psychotherapy, 29,* 430–437.

Winiarski, M. G. (1991). *AIDS-related psychotherapy.* New York: Pergamon Press.

Winiarski, M. G. (1997). Understanding HIV/AIDS using the biopsychosocial/spiritual model. In M. G. Winiarski (Ed.), *HIV mental health for the 21st century* (pp. 3–22). New York: New York University Press.

Yalom, I. D. (1980). *Existential psychotherapy.* New York: Basic Books.

CHAPTER 14

Logotherapy

ELISABETH LUKAS AND BIANCA ZWANG HIRSCH

BASIC ASSUMPTION OF LOGOTHERAPY

Logotherapy, conceived and developed by Viktor E. Frankl (1905–1997), a Viennese neurologist and psychiatrist, is a meaning-oriented psychotherapy. The Greek word *logos* translates as "meaning." Whereas values and traditions may be handed down from one generation to another, meaning cannot be given to individuals, but they can be helped in their search for meaning. Regardless of economic, social, and emotional status, people may be in despair, feel hopeless, lack fulfillment, and feel that their lives no longer have purpose. According to Frankl (1946/1967a, 1967b), such inner emptiness constitutes an existential frustration or frustration of the "will to meaning" and can be considered a *noogenic neurosis*. Noogenic neuroses originate in the spiritual (noetic) dimension as a result of clashes between values. By contrast, psychogenic neuroses arise in the psychic dimension as a result of conflict between drives and/or clashes among id, ego, and superego.

Although frequently listed under existential psychiatry, logotherapy differs from existential analysis because it does not concern itself merely with the existence of individuals but assumes that individuals are in search of meaning. Logotherapy represents a philosophical/psychological system whose proponents encourage patients not to focus on what has been lost but to seek meaning in spite of grief or despair. Because life has meaning under all circumstances, it becomes the task of the logotherapist to help patients discover such meaning, just as Frankl did.

If the inborn will to meaning is frustrated, then a feeling of meaninglessness results in noetic symptoms such as occur in depression, aggression, or addiction. Logotherapists cannot and do not demand meaning, but assist individuals in discovering meaning. According to Frankl, psychotherapy must address not only the physical and psychological dimensions, but also the specifically human—noetic—dimension. This human dimension enables individuals to reach beyond themselves (through self-transcendence) and focus on meaning and value as essential parts of existence. Even in the last moment of an apparently meaningless situation, the possibility for discovering meaning remains. Motivation for living stems not primarily from seeking pleasure, but pleasure comes as a by-product when accomplishing self-chosen tasks. Individuals have the will to choose, can take a stand, and assume responsibility for the choices they make and the positions they take.

Logotherapists do not concentrate only on those who are suffering because of an apparently meaningless life, but have developed specific methods for healing a variety of neurotic illnesses. For example, the fear-reducing method of paradoxical intention has proven effective in experimentally controlled research, and dereflection has been found useful as a method for reducing psychosomatic disturbances and emotional overreactions.

The foundations of logotherapy rest on three assumptions: (1) Life has meaning under all circumstances; (2) people are motivated by a will to meaning; and (3) humans have free will, within obvious limitations, to find meaning in their lives (Frankl, 1969). Frankl spoke of two levels of meaning—ultimate meaning and the meaning of the moment—stating that "the ultimate meaning of an individual's life is not a matter of intellectual cognition but rather the matter of existential commitment" (Frankl, 1967b, p. 34). Ultimate meaning—*the* meaning of life—is experienced in a higher dimension than the human dimension and may be discovered during prayer or an encounter with a beautiful piece of music or art. Fabry mused that "Ultimate meaning is like the horizon: It can be approached but never reached. Important is not the attainment but the search" (Fabry, 1979, p. 12).

The meaning of the moment is best understood when considering that each individual traverses the life cycle from birth to death through many unique experiences. Each unique situation is filled with meaning in accordance with that individual's conscience and values. To respond to the unique moment, which differs from person to person, contributes to leading a meaningful life.

Freud used the sickness/health model to point out that sickness can occur not only in the body but also in the psychological dimension. Frankl proposed that individuals have a uniquely human dimension, the noetic (spiritual) dimension (not in the religious sense) in addition to the physical and psychological dimensions. He added that, when the physical and psychological dimensions become ill, they might have to be cured with traditional medical means before logotherapy can be effectively used. Both these dimensions can block the noetic dimension, but the noetic dimension cannot become ill. The task of the logotherapist entails aiding clients in identifying and removing blocks to gain access to the resources of the spiritual dimension.

Because humans act and react as totalities, not merely in one dimension, all areas—the physical, psychological, and noetic dimensions—must be taken into consideration. In the somatic (physical) dimension, individuals have relatively little control over their cellular and/or bodily functions. The psychological area is associated with the emotional, cognitive, and social aspects of individuals. People often are motivated and driven by a need to seek pleasure, power, and prestige to move toward self-actualization. The noetic dimension constitutes the area of freedom. Individuals search for meaning and are free to make decisions, choices, and commitments. They can transcend personal needs for the sake of someone or something beyond themselves. Fabry (1987) calls the noetic dimension the "medicine chest of the logotherapist to counsel and educate clients that they have rich resources of health within" (p. 19).

HISTORY OF THE THERAPEUTIC APPROACH

Viktor E. Frankl, a Viennese neurologist and psychiatrist and the founder of logotherapy, believed that despair arose when people lacked meaning and purpose in their lives. Frankl viewed striving to find meaning as the primary motivational force and, therefore, developed logotherapy to empower clients to see that meaning exists and that they can be redirected to find it.

At the age of 15, in addition to his regular studies, Frankl attended evening classes in Applied and Experimental Psychology (Frankl, 1997b). He also attended a class in psychoanalysis conducted by two of Freud's disciples, Paul Schilder and Eduard Hitschmann. As a result of these classes, Frankl wrote to Freud; unfortunately, the correspondence that ensued disappeared during the Holocaust.

At the age of 17, Frankl gave a lecture entitled "The Meaning of Life" in his philosophy class. He proposed that life does not offer individuals meaning, but life puts the question to each individual to decide what is meaningful. He also proposed the idea that ultimate meaning represents an attainment that humans can live for and by, yet it remains that to which persons aspire but seldom reach. In 1924, at the age of 19, Frankl sent an article to Freud for publication in his *Internationale Zeitschrift fuer Psychoanalyse*, but, by the time the article was published, Frankl had already become interested in Alfred Adler's school of individual psychology. Frankl became a student of Adler, who had been an associate of Freud (Ellenberger, 1970); both Adler and Frankl were dismissed from Freud's organization (Vienna Psychoanalytic Society) because of their different emphases in therapy.

Within a few years, three schools of psychology emanated from Vienna, each with a separate emphasis: Freud's psychoanalysis, Adler's individual psychology, and Frankl's logotherapy. At first, Frankl was somewhat taken aback by this designation, as he had considered logotherapy a supplementary therapy to individual psychology. Frankl's second scientific manuscript appeared in 1925 in Adler's *Internationale Zeitschrift fuer Individualpsychologie*. Frankl was excluded from Adler's organization when discord between Adler and Frankl arose because Adler felt that patients' neurotic illness symptoms could function as a means to achieve personal goals, whereas Frankl thought that a noogenic disturbance could produce symptoms whose function was a need to express oneself. Today, this is an accepted position. Oswald Schwarz, the founder of psychosomatic medicine, and Rudolf Allers, director of a sensory/physiological clinic, supported Frankl. Reading Max Scheler's (1913/1973) book on formalizing ethics convinced Frankl that he was on the right track with his theoretical/existential approach. Together with Fritz Wittles and Maximilian Silbermann, Frankl established the *Akademischen Verein fuer Medizinische Psychologie,* in whose educational program the word "logotherapy" first appeared.

In 1926, Frankl began the manuscript for his first logotherapy textbook, *Aertzliche Seelsorge (Medical Ministry)*. The manuscript was confiscated and destroyed by the Nazis when Frankl was taken to a concentration camp. On the back of old forms and with a pencil stub, he reconstructed the manuscript in shorthand during his confinement and hid it until he was liberated. It was finally published in 1946 in German and in 1955 in English with the title *The Doctor and the Soul*. Through the use of many case illustrations, Frankl showed that attention must be paid to the noetic dimension of individuals. The noetic dimension can be mobilized to address physical manifestations of mental illness.

Frankl spent four extremely stressful years (1926–1930) at the Vienna Psychiatric Hospital, where he supervised the care of more than 12,000 very depressive patients. He developed his theories and techniques further while working in youth counseling centers during the Depression years of the 1930s. In spite of heavy responsibilities, he survived these difficult years by maintaining a positive outlook. At the time, he did not realize that the "test of his inner strength" was yet to come.

In the ominous year of 1940, Frankl, who was Jewish, could have found asylum in the United States. He had received the desired U.S. visa, which would have enabled him and his young wife to leave Austria, but he was faced with a dreadful dilemma. Because his parents were unable to obtain visas, he would have to leave them behind. He followed his conscience, remained with his family in Vienna, and let his visa expire. Under Nazi jurisdiction, as chief medical officer in the Jewish Rothschild Hospital, he was able to protect his parents temporarily, but eventually they were deported to concentration camps. In spite of high risk, he saved some of the retarded and disturbed patients from extermination by writing incorrect diagnoses. His choice to remain in Vienna was heroic, and he never regretted his decision. It can be assumed that any inconsistency with his convictions would have destroyed him more thoroughly than any torture.

Frankl survived four concentration camps before being liberated by U.S. soldiers in 1945. At that time, he was encouraged by friends to take the position of director of the Neurological Division in the Vienna Policlinic, a position he held for 25 years. After much urging, he finally published his moving manuscript, *A Psychologist Experiences Concentration Camps*, later known as *From Death Camp to Existentialism*, which eventually became the best-seller *Man's Search for Meaning* (Frankl, 1946/1967a). He dedicated his first four books to members of his family who had perished—his wife, his parents, and his brother.

Frankl felt strongly that responsibility lies with the individual and not the masses; therefore, he refused to generalize hate and vehemently spoke out against assigning "collective guilt" to all German people. He assumed an attitude of forgiveness toward those who had done so much harm, a position that became a model for future generations.

To counteract his painful experiences, he carefully expounded his theory of logotherapy, which had been developed before the Holocaust and had been validated in the concentration camps. With renewed energy, Frankl lectured at the University of Vienna and worked in the clinic while earning a second doctoral degree. He married again and started a new family. His books, some of which appeared on best-seller lists, were translated into nearly 40 languages. He undertook many lecture trips, primarily to North and South America. In 1970, the first endowed Chair for Logotherapy was established at the United States International University in San Diego, California. Four days before he died in 1997, Ohio State University honored Frankl with his twenty-ninth honorary doctorate.

Institutes and chapters of logotherapy have been established throughout the world. Two of the more active institutes are the Sueddeutsches Institute fuer Logotherapie, GmbH, in Germany, with Dr. Elisabeth Lukas as director, and the Viktor Frankl Institute of Logotherapy in the United States, with Dr. Robert Barnes as president. Dr. Robert Leslie archived a collection of Frankl's writings in English at the Graduate Theological Union in Berkeley, California; translations into Spanish and Portuguese are housed at the Iberoamerican University of Mexico. *The International Forum for Logotherapy, Journal of the Search for Meaning* is edited and published biannually by Dr. Robert Huxell.

EARLY MAJOR CONTRIBUTORS TO LOGOTHERAPY

Outstanding logotherapists, too numerous to list, have participated on national and international levels in the growth and development of the theoretical foundations and the clinical and practical applications of logotherapy. To mention only a few omits many other significant people who have worked so diligently and offered so much to the research and clinical practice of logotherapy for many years. The few early contributors mentioned exemplify the cadre of past and current logotherapists.

Joseph Fabry received his doctorate of jurisprudence in Vienna in 1933; having survived many Holocaust experiences, he immigrated to the United States in 1938 (Knight & Fabry, 1988). After a few years in New York, he moved to Berkeley, California, where he worked for many years as associate editor of the University of California magazine, *California Agriculture.* Upon his retirement, he studied with Viktor Frankl; a friendship developed between the families. Fabry established the Viktor Frankl Institute of Logotherapy in Berkeley and became its first director. In addition, he founded the *International Forum of Logotherapy* and served as its first editor. He initiated the biannual World Congress of Logotherapy, which has been held continuously since 1968. He wrote books and numerous articles on logotherapy, and translated many articles by European logotherapists. Fabry left a legacy that helped to disseminate and popularize logotherapy in the English-speaking world. His books include *The Pursuit of Meaning* (1987), a description and explanation of logotherapy; *Wege Zur Selbstfindung* (*Guidepost to Meaning,* 1988), a logotherapy self-help guide for the layperson; *Swing Shift* (1981), documenting his wartime experience as a shipbuilder; and *One and One Make Three* (Knight & Fabry, 1988), the story of a boyhood friendship with Max Knight; for many years, they coauthored numerous articles, short stories, and plays under the pen name Peter Fabrizius. He was a coeditor with Reuven P. Bulka and William S. Sahakian of *Logotherapy in Action* (1979), a compendium of articles by logotherapists; and with Elisabeth Lukas (Fabry & Lukas, 1995) of *Auf den Spuren des Logos,* a discussion and description of the framework of logotherapy through an exchange of letters of both authors with Viktor Frankl.

The Sueddeutsches Institut fuer Logotherapie, GmbH. provides therapy, directed by Elisabeth Lukas, in a clinical setting and extensive training for logotherapists. Lukas is one of Frankl's foremost students. She completed research and wrote her doctoral dissertation under his supervision. Lukas received her doctorate from the University of Vienna and is an internationally recognized authority on logotherapy. She is the author of *Logo-Test* (1968) and has written 25 books and numerous articles in professional journals. Some of her books have been translated into English, including *Meaningful Living* (1984), a book with many case studies and techniques illustrating the application of logotherapy, and *Meaning in Suffering* (1986), offering comfort in crisis through logotherapy. Her most recent book, *Auf den Stufen des Lebens* (2001), contains a collection of her most moving case studies based on Frankl's principles. Lukas has also written and made disks of several books of logophilosophical wisdom.

James C. Crumbaugh, a clinical psychologist who worked for many years at the Veterans Administration Hospital, Gulfport, Mississippi, is the coauthor of the Purpose in Life test (PIL) (Crumbaugh & Maholick, 1976) and Seeking Noetic Goals test (SONG) (Crumbaugh, 1977). Crumbaugh has written many articles and several books based on his experience using logotherapy, including *Everything to Gain: A Guide to Self-Fulfillment through Logoanalysis* (1973). He coauthored *Logotherapy: New Help for Problem Drinkers* (1980) with William M. Wood and W. Chadwick Wood. Crumbaugh was the coordinating editor of *A Primer of Projective Techniques of Psychological Assessment* (1990), in which he, Joseph Graca, Robert R. Hutzell, Michael F. Widdon, and Elaine Cabell Cooper contributed chapters.

Robert Hutzell, editor of the *International Forum for Logotherapy* for the past seven years, has worked diligently to spread an appreciation of logotherapy. The journal provides information on research and current thinking in the field of logotherapy and serves as a vehicle for communication about practice and advances by logotherapists throughout the world.

William Blair Gould (1993), whose teaching has touched many, wrote *Viktor Frankl: Life with Meaning,* a textbook that can be used to foster stimulating discussions in both philosophy and psychology classes.

THEORETICAL FOUNDATIONS OF LOGOTHERAPY

Lukas (1998b) pointed out that through exploration of the noetic dimension (the uniquely human dimension of the human spirit), Frankl discovered two fundamental phenomena that can enhance human life: the ability of self-distancing and the ability of self-transcending. Self-distancing connotes the human capacity to observe, accept, or reject oneself. It is often possible to discover meaning when an individual does not focus on the self, but looks at the self from the "outside." Self-distancing can occur in the form of inner dialogue (e.g., "I must be very careful in this situation because I am tempted to overreact"). For example, an alcoholic who pours a bottle of wine down the drain and says, "You would love to tempt me" is truly on the road to recovery. The ability to self-distance allows an individual to not focus exclusively on the self but to "stop taking all that nonsense from myself."

Self-transcendence represents the capacity to look beyond immediate personal needs to reach out to people we love and causes to serve. Self-transcendence occurs when an individual makes a commitment that surpasses personal interests by acting for the sake of something or someone other than the self. A young mother who does not go to the discotheque in the evening but instead remains at home with her child, or a firefighter who, on his day off, volunteers during a catastrophe in an adjacent town exemplify individuals forgoing personal pleasure for the sake of others. The ability to self-transcend allows individuals to develop interests and to become engaged, not in their own existences, but in the existences of others. Frankl (1967b) believed that individuals "manifest humanness only by emerging into the noological dimension or transcending themselves" (p. 137). "Meaning sets the pace for being" (p. 12).

Frankl (1967b) lauded the "defiant power of the human spirit" (p. 99) when it is activated within individuals. He illustrated with case histories that, when severe psychic and physical limitations occur, "the defiant power of the human spirit" can be activated to resist fear, suffering, and pain. Even in situations where there is no possibility of recovery, the individual can find meaning and accept the fate that has been dealt. By defying helplessness and heroically accepting what cannot be changed, passive helplessness is converted to active acceptance if the individual can find meaning in suffering. Frankl recognized that self-distancing and self-transcendence are not unconditionally available, but are bound up with meaning when the individual no longer asks "Why me?" but instead "Why not me?" In a deeper sense, this provides value and content to life and curtails possible meaninglessness.

Three other, interconnected assumptions make up the foundations of logotherapy (Frankl, 1969):

1. Life bears meaning under all conditions.
2. The "will to meaning" does not *demand* meaning but permits persons to search and *to discover* meaning, even in problematic situations in life. An individual seeks meaning to be fulfilled through a commitment (self-transcendence) to another person or a cause.
3. A person possesses the freedom, within obvious limitations, to fulfill the meaning of life.

Frankl emphasized that freedom exists within limits. Humans are not free from biological, psychological, or sociological conditions; however, an individual is free to take a stand toward these conditions. Individuals retain freedom to choose their attitudes toward themselves and are free to rise above the plane of somatic and psychic determinants of their existences.

View of Humankind

The uniqueness of logotherapy stems not from psychological tactics, strategies, or techniques, but from the creativity required for adapting logotherapy to the needs of each individual. This requires therapist improvisation designed specifically to address the unique "wholeness" of the individual patient. Frankl developed this in his theory of *dimensional ontology*. Human beings can be understood only if they are considered as a totality with all of their dimensions, generally described as consisting of three inseparable, predetermined dimensions: the somatic, psychological, and spiritual (Frankl, 1946, 1955, 1967b, 1969). None can be disregarded in psychotherapy.

Early psychology research was focused on the psychosomatic dimensions. Frankl, however, believed that the third dimension, the noetic dimension, had been neglected, even though this area is specifically human. No other scientifically oriented human discipline is based on the noetic potential of an individual, a uniquely human trait. Humans, animals, and plants live as organisms in physical form. Depending on the circumstances, the (bodily) biological dimension has feedback mechanisms that bring about automatic processes in the autonomic nervous system to help the body adapt to changed situations. Animal research has demonstrated that nonhuman animals also have a psychological dimension; they have feelings, they think and experience social interactions, but in simpler form than humans. Changes in the psychological dimension may lead to changes in behavior. However, the spiritual dimension is strictly human, regardless of culture, class, or caste. It is the dimension of life's plans and expectations, goal orientation, and willful execution of ideas, the acceptance of moral questions, ethos, and religious experiences. It is the dimension of artistic visions and scientific inspiration, the source of cultural development, and the assessment of accomplishments. It involves freedom, choices, and responsibilities as well as being able to respond and make a commitment to someone or something. In the strictly human dimension of the spirit, there is the possibility of free choice toward a given circumstance because feedback mechanisms bring about changes in self-understanding and lead to new interpretations of the self. Humans can go beyond the biological and psychological dimensions and pass into the realm of the noological dimension, in which they can take a stand not only toward the world but also toward themselves. Because they are capable of self-detachment and self-transcendence, they can reflect on and even reject themselves.

Frankl stressed that individuals are motivated to search for meaning. If the will to meaning is frustrated, it manifests itself in feelings of meaninglessness and in emotional disturbances, such as depression, aggression, or phobia. The will to meaning occupies the central place in the theory of motivation in logotherapy, and denotes that individuals strive to find and fulfill meaning and seek purpose in life. Crumbaugh and Maholick's (1964) studies in existentialism have corroborated this concept in research.

Worldview of Logotherapy

What is meaning? Logotherapy implies seeing life in general as embodying meaning and individuals as searching for ways to discover meaning in the concrete circumstances of their lives, whether felicitous or challenging. Finding meaning connotes awareness that there is an order in the universe despite chaos, destruction, and injustice, and each human being functions within this arena. In this worldview, all of creation is full of meaning, and life has meaning under all circumstances. Every life situation has its unique meaning, opportunities, and possibilities. Humans, as noetic beings (or beings of spirit), are motivated by the will to meaning and are furnished with mini-antennae (the feelers of the conscience) to capture and fulfill the meaning of the moment.

The credo that life remains meaningful under all circumstances must not, however, be wrongfully interpreted. It is not resignation under unfortunate, but temporary, circumstances. No logotherapist would ever suggest that a person should, for instance, watch patiently the death of a forest and try to discover meaning therein. Neither would a logotherapist suggest to patients that unemployment is a matter of fate and by putting their hands in their laps in resignation such a period of unemployment will become meaningful. Quite the contrary. Meaning emerges constantly in the concrete call to a concrete person to improve whatever can be improved.

Some illnesses end in death. Injustices cannot always be rectified, nor can terrible accidents be undone. In most instances, the average person cannot change the political structure. Logotherapy does not assert that horrors are in any way meaningful. It is possible, however, to demonstrate that life, in spite of all horror, does not forfeit its meaning. It is possible, especially when faced with unavoidable suffering, to find meaning in the way an individual carries such burdens. When negotiations stop because there are no more opportunities for action, when all interventions are exhausted and nothing can be changed, then, ultimately, dignified suffering reaches its finest meaning.

Logotherapy does not promote passivity, but instead allows calmness. If individuals actively pursue their responsibilities, there is no place for thoughts of despair and panic. Then fear bounces off any catastrophe without effect because the meaning of the moment conveys strength for the next moment of existence. Logotherapeutic wisdom would like to soften many pains in the world, but logotherapy cannot alter the unchangeable. When individuals are no longer able to change a situation, they must instead modify themselves.

TECHNIQUES AND WHEN TO APPLY THEM

Logotherapists not only concern themselves with the suffering of an apparently meaningless life, but also provide appropriate therapy for various neurotic illnesses. Because the somatic, psychological, and spiritual dimensions are present and inseparable in human beings, none of these can be disregarded in psychotherapy. Lukas (1984) cautioned therapists to not harm patients in one dimension while helping them in another.

Each human being is unique, and the effectiveness of logotherapy does not depend on special techniques that must be applied under all circumstances. Much depends on improvisation, intuition, and appropriate phrases. Some of the techniques used by logotherapists are: Socratic dialogue, modification of attitudes, paradoxical intention, dereflection, and the appealing technique.

Socratic Dialogue

Logotherapists use Socratic dialogue for probing, questioning, and challenging individuals to discover repressed feelings, unconscious decisions, and motives. It is used to educate patients to take charge of their lives by posing questions in such a way that patients gain new insights into their symptoms, modify current attitudes, and/or develop new attitudes to discover meaning in their lives. Socratic dialogue helps patients distance themselves from their symptoms. Patients discover that they do not have to give in to fate or identify themselves as victims, but instead learn that they have choices, even if choice involves only a change of attitude.

Modification of Attitudes

An individual's problems can be exacerbated by his or her attitude toward such problems. Depending on the individual's inner resources, problems can become a stimulus for taking action, or they can remain such a hurdle that the individual gives up in hopelessness and despair. One's attitude toward oneself and toward difficulties in life may constitute the difference between psychological illness and health. When patients gain new perspectives about themselves and their life situations, many will be able to modify their attitudes.

Lukas (1984) described a young man who, after having been fired from two jobs, turned to a therapist in despair:

PATIENT: I am no good. All my brothers and sisters are successful, but I am a failure.
THERAPIST: Every person has gifts in some areas and not in others. We'll find out (for instance, through a psychological test) in what direction your talents lie, where you will find your place. When we know that, we'll put all our energy to work to find a job in that field—and you'll see, then you *cannot* fail (pp. 34–35).

A logotherapist does not dwell on the patient's anxiety, which in this case, can most likely be diagnosed as an Adjustment Disorder with Anxiety (*DSM-IV*, 309.24; APA, 1994). Instead, the logotherapist focuses on what is healthy and where more information can lead to making positive changes. The patient's resignation blocked all efforts of will, yet only a great exercise of will and stamina can free him from his dilemma. Sometimes arguments are not enough, but must be supported by the positive philosophy of the therapist, and, when necessary, by positive suggestions. In this case, such an approach "will rekindle his courage and confidence" (p. 35).

Lukas (1984) reported the case of a 53-year-old woman who previously had been considered well, yet who experienced severe attacks of psychosomatic spasms and paralysis. She had fought an alimony suit against her ex-husband, who refused to pay anything toward her living expenses because he felt that she should go to work. She claimed that, at her age, untrained for any job, she could not find work. The judge asked a physician from the Health Department to give her a thorough physical examination to determine whether she was able to take a full-time job.

The therapist noted that the judge had taken only economic and physical considerations into account. The dimension of the spirit was overlooked. Thus, when the woman heard in ominous-sounding Latin that her blood pressure was high, that she had a curvature of the spine, a damaged heart muscle, and an enlarged thyroid gland, she panicked. The shock caused a spasm in her diaphragm. She suffered an attack of psychogenic choking and collapsed in the courtroom. This started a whole string of problems. Even though she won the court case, she was ill for many months.

In spite of good intentions, the physician's medical diagnosis failed to consider the patient's noetic dimension when he listed numerous medical terms that the patient internalized. Although she did not intentionally produce the symptoms, they caused clinically significant impairment in everyday functioning and contributed to a Generalized Anxiety Disorder (300.02) (*DSM-IV*; APA, 1994) which caused her clinically significant stress and impairment in social, occupational, and other important areas of functioning.

By addressing the human aspect of the situation and placing meaning at the center of the search, a logotherapist can reach beyond the biological and psychological dimensions and draw on the resources of the human spirit. In this case, the patient was free of her symptoms within a few weeks after the origin of her condition was clarified, and a combination of psychotherapeutic drugs, paradoxical intention, and autogenic training were initiated. (Autogenic training entails a process whereby patients are taught to become more aware of their own bodily and internal states, and then taught a new set of skills to enhance bodily functioning.)

To facilitate a different frame of reference can be therapeutic. Often, an unhealthy attitude, not the problem, causes distress. A therapist must help a patient to evaluate which of the patient's attitudes toward life are healthy and which have a negative impact and then assist the patient to see that choices are available. It is possible and therapeutic to find a meaningful attitude toward a situation, even when the situation itself appears to be meaningless. According to Frankl (1967b), even situations of unavoidable suffering, guilt, and death remain potentially meaningful: "Through the right attitude unchangeable suffering is transmuted into a heroic and victorious achievement" (p. 90). Individuals may not be able to alter a deed, but by repentance they can change themselves:

> Life can be made meaningful in a threefold way: first, through what we give to life (in terms of our creative works); second, by what we take from the world (in terms of our experiencing values); and third, through the stand we take toward a fate we can no longer change (in incurable disease, an inoperable cancer, or the like). . . . [Nor are persons spared] the tragic triad of human existence; namely, pain, death, and guilt. By pain I mean suffering; by the two other constituents of the tragic triad, I mean the twofold fact of . . . mortality and fallibility. (p. 15)

PARADOXICAL INTENTION

Although Frankl first used paradoxical intention in 1929, he did not publish his findings until 1939 in the *Schweizer Archiv fuer Neurologie und Psychiatrie*, and he did not officially incorporate this as a logotherapy technique until 1956. Since then, many therapists have effectively used paradoxical intention for a variety of conditions (Frankl, 1978). In this process, a patient is instructed by a logotherapist to confront an anxiety-producing situation. Sentences are developed to humorously exaggerate the consequences of the fear. Focusing on these exaggerated, often comical, situations usually dissolves anticipatory anxiety, and the fear disappears.

Paradoxical intention is used to change a patient's attitude toward a fearful situation or phobia. When a patient actively, but humorously, wishes for an anticipatory anxiety, the paradoxical wish produces a change of attitude, if only for a brief time. Patients who have a phobia fear the symptoms and try to avoid fearful situations. The more a patient fears symptoms and tries to avoid them, the more likely they are to occur. With the use of paradoxical intention, phobic patients stop fleeing from their fears, and obsessive-compulsive patients stop fighting their obsessions and compulsions. The fears are now replaced with a paradoxical wish.

Lukas (1986) demonstrated that paradoxical intention could be used in everyday occurrences. She described the situation of a woman threatening her husband that she would walk out on their marriage unless he gave in to her wishes. She had packed her bags several times until, one day, he decided not to go along with her continued threats. He helped her pack, encouraged her to take a lot of heavy things, and offered her three extra suitcases. The exaggerated situation became so comical that they burst out in wholehearted laughter.

In another case, Lukas (1984) used paradoxical intention and self-detachment with a patient who had a phobia about being in crowded situations (probable diagnosis, Panic Disorder with Agoraphobia, *DSM-IV*, 300.21; APA, 1994):

PATIENT: Today is especially bad; I hardly dared step out of the house. I couldn't get myself to take the bus, it was so crowded. I had to walk all the way to see you. I'm pooped!

THERAPIST: Did you bring your fear in here with you or did you leave it on the street?

PATIENT: I am not sure I understand, but I was simply overcome, and there was nothing I could do. Then it seemed to disappear without rhyme or reason.

THERAPIST: This is most likely just the way you describe it, but basically you are the same person who can think, act, plan, and decide to come to this office, and sometimes even take the bus despite occasional attacks of fear, which you have not yet learned to handle properly. During logotherapy, you will learn to manage this, and, even though your fear wants to frighten you, it will succeed less and less. You will be able to chase it away (p. 74).

The therapist desired to change the client's unhealthy obsessive attitude of "'I am full of fear, I tremble with fear' to the more detached attitude of 'I am a normal person, only sometimes I fight against some unfounded and unimportant feelings of anxiety'" (Lukas, 1984, p. 75):

> Once clients see the separation between their health and their exaggerated feelings of fear and obsession, they can be introduced to paradoxical intention. Instead of fighting the fears and obsessions, they learn to paradoxically wish to bring about the very experiences they feared and see what happens. (p. 75)

And nothing does happen. Paradoxical intention depends on an individual's capacity for self-distancing. Patients are helped to laugh at their fears and obsessions; with success, self-confidence and trust in their abilities return. The more distance patients can place between themselves and their symptoms, the more likely they are to become well.

Dereflection

Dereflection draws on the human capacity of self-transcendence and proves effective for problems such as sleeplessness, sexual dysfunction, addiction, and those caused by excessive self-observation. Dereflection encourages the use of the capacity to "forget oneself" and to focus on others. Even such autonomic body functions as falling asleep and sexual performance can become blocked if an individual concentrates too heavily on these processes. By counteracting excessive self-observation (hyperreflection, in Frankl's terms), therapy helps autonomic body functions to resume undisturbed. In therapy, clients cannot be asked to refrain from thinking of their sleep problems or sexual responsiveness because by telling them not to think about a subject, attention is drawn to that very subject. Instead, the client is encouraged to think of something or someone else. The logotherapeutic method of dereflection detaches clients from their symptoms and directs their attention to other, more positive, subjects.

Lukas (1984) used dereflection with a very intelligent high-school student who, when taking examinations, greatly feared that he would forget what he knew, and consequently he performed poorly. He also developed psychosomatic stomach aches. The symptoms were akin to those that occur during a Generalized Anxiety Disorder including Overanxious Disorder of Childhood (*DSM-IV*, 300.02; APA, 1994):

MOTHER: We are greatly worried about our son. He is intelligent and studies hard, but when he has to take exams, he does poorly. He seems to forget everything he knows.

THERAPIST: Perhaps, for the next three months, avoid questions about school and if you want to find out what he is doing, just inquire about his extra-curricular activities. Help him by enriching his free time. Have him do things that he will enjoy. It can be sports, the library, joining a choir, or doing things on weekends with the family.

FATHER: We will try—but how will these recommendations help his grades? They will probably drop even more with so many outside activities.

Whenever the son began talking about school, his parents asked him about outside activities. After a few weeks, the changes in the young man were apparent. He was enthusiastically interested, and the more he became involved in his extracurricular activities, the more he forgot about his anxieties. One night at dinner, he said, "Today we had a math test. I should have had a bellyache, but I didn't think of it." The parents perceived the therapist's suggestions as very successful, particularly when, six months later, his grades had improved from Cs to As.

In this situation, the family together with the therapist worked out a plan to help the student dereflect from his fears by not asking questions regarding tests and focusing instead on leisure-time activities. The family seemed to function satisfactorily according to the observations of the therapist and comments by the student and his family. Most likely, the Global Assessment of Relational Functioning (GARF; Group for the Advancement of Psychiatry Committee on the Family, 1996) score for this student would fall within the 90 to 95 range, suggesting a very high range of adjustment, representing a high level of interpersonal support.

Even though dereflection is a logotherapeutic technique, it runs contrary to a basic logotherapeutic principle, namely, that the relationship of therapist and client must be honest. Clients should not be manipulated and should be fully informed of the processes in progress, so they can become partners in the common search for meaning. The intent in dereflection is for a client to refrain from paying attention to a problem. However, if a client is fully informed about a logotherapist's intent in using dereflection, he or she will pay attention to that problem; therefore, it becomes impossible not to focus on the problem, and the opportunity for dereflection is lost.

In a case of sexual dysfunction, the therapist informed the impotent male patient that, although he could be intimate with his partner, it would be advisable to refrain from intercourse because his partner was taking medication (Lukas, 1984). At the same time, his partner was told to let nature take its course when she saw that he was ready to be sexually active. When the client is no longer stressed out by the expectation from his partner, himself, or the situation, he is dereflecting, and the normal body functions become unblocked. To establish a positive relationship with a client and to reduce "tricking" the patient as much as possible, Lukas frequently uses an "Alternative List" (p. 92). The procedure follows four steps:

1. After the connection between patient's symptoms and concerns about them are explained, an agreement is made for working together to reduce hyperreflection.
2. Clients are asked to make a list of activities that will enrich their lives and identify circumstances when concerns are acute and when alternative activities can be explored.
3. Clients are told to try one of these activities every time they are likely to hyperreflect. Clients are under the impression that, when trying the various activities, they will be able to select the one most suitable for future therapy. In reality, this "preparation" for therapy is already therapy: dereflection.
4. Time used to test these alternatives is, in actuality, valuable healing time during which attention to the symptoms and problems are replaced by concentration on testing alternatives. By the time clients finally decide which alternative activities can be used for dereflection, it has already taken place.

THE APPEALING TECHNIQUE

When patients are unable to gain distance between themselves and their symptoms because of addiction or psychological or physical impairment and when Socratic dialogue alone proves ineffective, Lukas (1984) employs the appealing technique. As in all methods used by logotherapists, the appealing technique depends on trust, and any appeal must be kept within the value system of the patient. This technique is based on the power of suggestion and is invoked primarily when the dimension of the spirit is temporarily blocked. The patient, however, must be minimally motivated to cooperate.

Although logotherapy by itself is not sufficient in drug/alcohol treatment, it can be a complementary or adjunct form of therapy. When patients begin treatment in detoxification clinics, logotherapists follow up this treatment with meditation and relaxation exercise tapes that patients can take home and play repeatedly. Lukas (1984) has delineated a sequence for effective use of the appealing technique when treating addiction preceded by biological detoxification. Introducing psychological relaxation exercises constitutes the first step in logotherapeutic treatment. As a transition, therapist and client engage in suggestive training of the will, during which the therapist speaks very calmly and softly, encouraging the client to feel fully relaxed and to experience willing (e.g., to become and stay well). Taped suggestions are aimed at training the will to defy a given situation, to achieve new attitudes, or to guide patients' thoughts toward new directions. By helping them to discover meaning, therapists enable patients to take charge of their lives. Using the appealing technique during the first phase of this treatment helps patients become calmer, gain distance from their problems, and learn to use the "defiant power of the human spirit" to master their anxieties, fears, and tensions. The second step in logotherapeutic follow-up involves Socratic dialogue to enable a client to discover meaning possibilities.

Lukas (1984) utilized these techniques with a mother of five who had begun taking more and more sleeping pills after her husband was incarcerated. One afternoon, after the children had been crying a long time, neighbors called the police, who broke open the door and found the mother unconscious on her bed. The children were placed temporarily with neighbors after the mother was hospitalized. On her release, she was told that, if a similar incident occurred, the children would be removed from the home. She threatened that she would kill herself if this happened. She was assessed for suicidality and informed of the need for protection. She promised to undergo counseling and was diagnosed with Depressive Disorder (*DSM-IV*, 311) and Sedative Disorder (*DSM-IV*, 292.9; APA, 1994).

During therapy, it was learned that she took sleeping pills when she was seized by fear about the future or was very upset with the children. She became tense, could not relax, and, to obtain some rest, took sleeping pills. Subsequent to relaxation exercises and suggestive training, which were reinforced with tapes at home, she began to relax and sleep more restfully. Together with the therapist, she considered what could be done for her family and herself to meet her tasks in a more positive mood. Soon she was able to make some plans and follow through on taking a part-time job with a construction company while the older children were in school and the younger children were in a day-care facility. After working there a while, she was able to secure a job for her husband when he was released from prison. A year later, both were still working there and making plans for the future of their family.

THE THREE PHASES OF PSYCHOTHERAPEUTIC COUNSELING

Three consecutive phases during the psychotherapeutic process have been delineated (Lukas, 1986). The *diagnostic phase* involves data collection; information is gathered from medical records, diagnostic interviews, questionnaires, and testing, when indicated. In this phase, an iatrogenic neurosis, a neurosis caused by the wrong message given by a physician, psychologist, or counselor, may occur. Usually, when gathering diagnostic information, heavy emphasis is placed on "what's wrong," and a patient does a lot of hyperreflecting. Lukas concluded that the wrong message is given to patients, potentially causing irreparable damage. Therefore, the message given to clients must be carefully thought out to include healthy aspects of their lives.

The *therapeutic phase* is the treatment phase in which clients are helped to overcome their difficulties by working with a therapist who is empathetic and concerned. Therapeutic encounters may include dialogue, medication, and direct and indirect counseling to help in exploring feelings and attitudes. A therapist can incorporate paradoxical intention, dereflection, and modulation of attitudes.

The value of the *follow-up phase* was not recognized until recently. When therapy has been terminated, there is no guarantee that life will be without problems or stress. Nor is it enough that the client has learned to live heroically with a loss. Through therapy, it is hoped that clients will have developed new coping skills for daily living and have found ways to enrich their value system and discover meaning potentials in daily life. Based on information gathered during the previous phases, periodic follow-up contacts may be needed to help clients consider both stress and leisure while striving toward new choices and goals to remain healthy and functional in daily life.

FIVE APPLICATIONS OF LOGOTHERAPY

The five sets of symptoms and issues for which Frankl recommended logotherapeutic interventions have been summarized by Lukas (1998b).

Noogenic Neuroses and Depressions

The noetic dimension cannot become ill. Because the spiritual dimension depends on meaning, individuals may find themselves in an existential crisis when they are not finding meaning. People in comfortable and financially sound situations may fall victim to such meaninglessness because their lives are so well-endowed that, ordinarily, no tension occurs between existence and need. They suffer from chronic boredom, a lack of goal orientation. Their lives have no direction; therefore, they take risks. Because material acquisitions no longer fill the emptiness in their hearts, they look for thrills and adventures. They have too much to live with and too little to live for to make life worthwhile. Some overindulge in drugs or alcohol and look for new neurotic excesses; others may be depressed and exhibit a nihilistic, cynical dullness and indifference.

Here, logotherapy is in its element. Logotherapy encourages a patient to search the past for buried traces of meaning, which can perhaps be reactivated: When and under what circumstances was the patient totally stimulated by something, excited by a task? Can thoughts and visions be evoked that would make the individual aware that it would be truly sad if they were not realized in the future? Logotherapy works by enlarging the field of awareness to motivate an individual beyond immediate personal references to focus on objective, meaningful goals. For example, a mother preoccupied with the needs of her small child and feeling limited by having to stay at home may come to the realization that many other mothers feel the same way. As a group, they might take turns baby-sitting so that all mothers gain some free time. Simply substituting a nagging dissatisfaction with constructive action can bring meaning into their lives and thus preempt a nooegenic neurosis and/or depression.

Psychogenic Neuroses and Psychosomatic Illnesses

The number of psychological disturbances is tremendous, yet they have a common basis: Almost always, fear lurks in the background. The absence of basic trust, coupled with weak self-confidence, prompts irrationally expecting negative responses from everyone and every situation. The individual feels pushed around, shamed, laughed at, embarrassed, unloved, and unworthy. Through self-fulfilling prophecy, the drama escalates. The more frequently and intensely a person anticipates negative happenings, the more these will occur. The person's fears drive these feelings.

In such situations, logotherapists can mobilize humor and the defiant power of the human spirit to help individuals make choices. People can learn to distance themselves playfully from mixed feelings and to laugh at their negative expectations by jokingly wishing for the threatened fears. Although these wishes can be produced only briefly and are irrational, they are sufficient for interrupting this phobic cycle. To wish for something frees it of the anticipated fear, and thus reduces the neurotic symptoms. Without symptoms, the fear disappears and confidence is regained.

In fear-evoking conditions, such as sleeplessness or sexual disturbances, therapy moves from focusing on to ignoring symptoms because, in the past, the patient has already paid too much attention to achieving these bodily functions in a forceful, almost compulsive, manner. In the therapeutic process, the patient learns to dereflect on personal needs and to reflect on the needs of others. When individuals learn to forget themselves, and, in the case of sexual dysfunction, learn to focus on their partners, they discover that their own well-being returns as an unexpected side effect. Thus, by forgetting themselves, individuals discover meaning and enhance their well-being.

In these instances, logotherapy functions partially as a nonspecific therapy. Frankl (1997a) adamantly insisted, "The neurotic person, because of some psychophysical reason, has become insecure. In order to compensate for such insecurity, the neurotic person, in particular, is in need of noetic (spiritual) strength" (p. 9). The psychotherapy that can best instill such noetic support is the one centered around the *noos*, the part of the person that cannot be damaged, and the *logos*, the unconditional meaningfulness.

ENDOGENOUS PSYCHOSES AND
INCURABLE ILLNESS

In logotherapeutic thinking, psychoses such as endogenous depression, mania, and the various symptoms associated with schizophrenia are seen as primarily somatic and must, therefore, be treated with medication. However, these patients may also benefit from psychotherapeutic interventions. Thus, when a paranoid patient no longer uses the spiritual freedom to withstand the demands of the debilitating illness with heroic resistance or accept the suffering in a conciliatory manner, logotherapeutic guidance can motivate the patient to forgive his or her hallucinated tormentors instead of fighting with them. It can also be successfully demonstrated to melancholic individuals that, above the clouds of depression, their moods can be brightened by the joy of life, even though this may not be obvious at the time. Given time and patience, the clouds usually disappear.

For individuals who are physically challenged, critically ill, and/or dying, logotherapy offers a philosophical perspective with regard to overcoming the past as well as transcending the transitory aspects of life. Reconciliation with the past can lead to a peaceful closure. The "tragic triad" of pain, death, and guilt are part of human existence. Throughout his writings, Frankl (1978) observed that even unavoidable suffering can be faced if an individual can perceive it with meaning: "When facing a fate that cannot be changed... what then counts and matters is to bear witness to the uniquely human potential at its best, which is to transform a tragedy into a personal triumph, to turn one's predicament into a human achievement" (p. 39). Frankl (1969) eloquently wrote:

Usually man only sees the stubble field of transitoriness and overlooks the full granaries of the past. In the past, nothing is irrecoverably lost but everything irrevocably preserved and saved, safely delivered and deposited. Nothing and nobody can deprive us of what we have rescued into the past. What we have done cannot be undone. This adds to man's responsibleness. For in the face of the transitoriness of his life, he is responsible for using the passing opportunities to actualize potentialities, to realize values, whether creative, experiential or attitudinal. In other words, man is responsible for what to do, whom to love, and how to suffer. Once he has realized a value, once he has fulfilled a meaning, he has fulfilled it once and forever. (p. 74)

Here, logotherapy, as medical ministry, is at its finest.

EXISTENTIAL FRUSTRATION AND
VALUE AMBIVALENCE

The questions What shall I do?, What is right?, What is wrong?, How shall I decide?, Toward which goal shall I strive?, and What direction shall I take? usually do not come from a disturbed mind, but from an awakened and mature spirit in an active process of searching. Unfortunately, individuals can become impatient, allow themselves to be easily influenced and listen to the advice of others, and surrender to the struggle. Others, who question or search, may find themselves in a labyrinth of hopelessness and, because they are unable to make up their minds, end up in an orientation crisis. Pluralistic societies, irrational breaks with traditions, and valueless educational experiments make young people especially vulnerable to problems such as drug addiction, despair, and what Frankl called an "existential vacuum"—a feeling of emptiness and hopelessness. In addition, traditional family (the nucleus of society) values are colliding with the emancipation and personal-development tendencies of modern times, producing ambivalence and a confusion of values.

To stabilize the development of values, Frankl placed primary emphasis on "education for responsibility." At all times, logotherapists refrain from moralizing, and, instead, strengthen the capacity of personal conscience to prioritize feelings. Logotherapy is founded on high regard and respect for all living beings and fosters appreciation for culture and nature. Through medical/clinical interventions, logotherapists can offer personal and existential education and thus contribute to family maintenance.

Children are aware of what happens in families and learn from their parents how to treat others: whether they address each other with respect or are more considerate of outsiders than of members of their family. A young dyslexic boy was attending a psychotherapy session in the Institute (Lukas, 1981). When his parents came to pick him up, they had to wait briefly in the waiting room, where they engaged in a heated argument. When the boy heard them, he ran out of therapy and started to scream at them. Lukas stopped the scene by calling all three into the office: "I don't know what the argument is all about, but I would like to make a suggestion to you. Continue your discussion, here in my office, but with certain basic rules. Let us sit around the table. I will not engage in the discussion, but will act as controller. I will hold a flashlight in my hand and will shine its light when one of you says something that attacks the dignity of another. When that happens, the last person who spoke will have to reword what was said in a more sensitive, gentler manner that will not be hurtful. Then the discussion can continue." The therapist instructed that only one person speak at a time.

Although the family saw no purpose in the exercise, they were willing to try it. Because the content of the discussion was not monitored, the flashlight lit up frequently at the beginning, for none of them was accustomed to maintaining a civil tone in conversation. In this situation, the emphasis was on the civil format. For example, the mother said, "I think it is outrageous what you expect of me. Who do you think you are?" The flashlight lit up. She had to restate what she had said: "Well, I don't think it is very nice of you to expect so much of me; no one can be correct 100% of the time." A great deal of concentration was demanded of the therapist, to be aware when to intercede with the flashlight and to react instantly, but this method has been found to be extremely helpful for developing self-control and discovering ways of compromising. Within a half-hour, the family could converse without hurting each other. Only then did the therapist discover what the discussion was all about, but now that seemed to be less important to the family; they quickly arrived at a solution. When the therapist asked whether they could continue being civil on their own, the wife laughingly commented, "A flashlight that would light up at the right moment would be useful around the house." The boy was diagnosed with a Learning Disorder, apparently with dyslexic features (*DSM-IV*, 315.9; APA, 1994). A GARF (Group for the Advancement of Psychiatry Committee on the Family, 1996) low score of 42 could be assigned to the family at the beginning of this case, and possibly an improved score of 69 at the end, which suggests the insight and change that had occurred in the family as a result of the logotherapist's intervention.

Pathology of the Spirit of the Times and Collective Neuroses

Each period has its opportunities and its needs, but the subsequent assessment of these by later generations makes these opportunities and needs appear quite different from when they occurred. At the time one participates, the needs appear to be very strong. Currently, many global dangers are threatening; the opportunity for all people to attain a dignified future appears to be remote. Amid such epic concerns, collective neuroses can thrive, as Frankl described during the middle of the twentieth century. Danger signals of such attitudes can be seen in statements such as "Now I want to enjoy life. After me, let the floods come!" or fatalistic views of life such as "No one cares about me anyway!" or collective negative thinking such as "The stupid foreigners!" or overzealous motivation to "Destroy the enemy." Wherever such attitudes lurk, they can be actively opposed with a comprehensive meaning-oriented belief. The unshaken belief in ourselves and in our fellow human beings is an efficient approach to prevention. Frankl (1969) quoted Albert Einstein, with whom he was in total agreement when the latter stated at the Princeton Theological Seminary "Mere thinking cannot reveal to us the highest purpose" (p. 145). Belief assumes something more than what the intellect can possibly know. Logotherapy moves between the boundaries of medicine and philosophy, psychology and religion. In logotherapy, people can discover more about who they truly are and what is meant or intended for their lives.

CASE EXAMPLES

Logotherapy is the only therapeutic approach integrating the psychosomatic and spiritual dimensions of a sick person. The psychosomatic predisposition, together with the social environment, contribute to the attitude of an individual. Logotherapy affirms that a personal change of attitude can give meaning to suffering. The final decision regarding a situation, however, arises primarily from the noos (spiritual) side of a person. To achieve positive results, a logotherapist must help patients modify their attitudes toward what they see as causes of their sufferings. By moving away from the traditional sickness model of most psychotherapies, the focus shifts from health to healing from within. Construction rather than reconstruction is demanded.

Winfried Boehm (1992) asserted that individuals are human only when they do not allow histories of their lives to be dictated or prescribed by others, but write them themselves. The formation of self means something different from an automatic becoming and passive existence, but instead implies a permanent and basic unending process. In the process of education, humans constantly surpass themselves. This becomes apparent in the cases explicated next.

Case 1

A teacher arrived at the Institute requesting a letter stating that she was disabled because of panic attacks (*DSM-IV*, 300.21: Panic Disorder with Agoraphobia and/or a Fear Neurosis; APA, 1994) while working in school (Lukas, 1998a). The therapist who had treated her for the past five years was on an extended trip to India and could not help her. She spoke with a second therapist:

THERAPIST: Is there an acute reason that prompted you to request the letter?
PATIENT: The school is planning that I should accompany my students on a trip to England. I am not only the English teacher, but also their homeroom teacher. However, I don't want to accompany them because I am afraid that something could happen to the children while they are under my supervision. I have been unable to sleep for months. I feel nauseated when I get up in the morning and can barely concentrate during the day.
THERAPIST: Have you always suffered so when special demands were made on you?
PATIENT: I have always suffered when demands are made on me. Giving grades to my students is torturous. If I give good grades, then I am afraid the children will no longer produce at home.
THERAPIST: Is this the way you feel now about the trip to England?
PATIENT: I have never felt as badly as I do this time. I can't sleep and worry that one of the children may fall onto the electric rails in a London subway station, or that a child will run into an oncoming automobile in a busy intersection and other such incidences. All kinds of fear-arousing pictures stand before my eyes. I want to be placed on the disability list, so that I do not have to travel to England.

The anxiety of the patient can be diagnosed also as a fear neurosis. Symptoms include a disproportionate number of fears based on the situation and her intensive effort to avoid fearful experiences at any price. After presenting evidence for this symptom, she was looking for a psychotherapeutic solution. The question WHY does the patient worry so much? is not relevant in logotherapy. Exploring the WHY question could lead to discovering the causal trauma basis for illness. It would lead to a BECAUSE. The BECAUSE is the item under which the cause is hidden. It is the code under which her life operates. It is not developed by her personally and would not reflect on her personally. There is no doubt that she could find enough BECAUSE answers. At the end, she would stand as a poor, panic-stricken product of coincidence and human failure.

According to logotherapy, even though the patient has symptoms, she is potentially a healthy person. As such, she can see beyond the nonhuman dimension into a meaning- and value-filled world. She was asked to participate actively in analyzing the values that are close to her heart: What stands in her way of being highly respected by her peers? What are her constant worries? Therapeutically, strength is given to the WHAT desires while the ABOUT WHAT are the concerns in life that provide the basis for rewriting the story of life in spite of any weakness. The patient was able to develop a clear ABOUT WHAT regarding her worries: the children! She worried about their well-being. But was this the truth? Was she really concerned about the children? The therapist began a Socratic dialogue:

THERAPIST: If I understand you correctly, you want to have a letter stating that you have a disability, so that you will not have to travel to England.

PATIENT: Yes, that is what I need.

THERAPIST: But even if you do not go, a child can get hurt. Even without your presence, a child can fall onto the track in a London underground station or get run over. Your absence does not preclude such accidents. Of what use is such a letter?

PATIENT: When I am not there, it is not my fault. No one can blame me for improperly supervising the children if I am at home because of illness.

THERAPIST: Do you mean to say that you don't care if a child has an accident as long as you cannot be blamed for it?

PATIENT: Yes . . . (She stops.) No, not that. But then it is not my problem.

THERAPIST: In other words, you are saying that as long as you are not there, no one can blame you, and your teacher image remains spotless?

(The therapist notices how this works on the patient.)

PATIENT: Mainly . . . perhaps you are right, although when I really think about it, I am almost embarrassed by that.

One of the questions—WHY does the patient worry so excessively?—fostered only conditioned habitual fearfulness. However, the question ABOUT WHAT is the patient worried? quickly uncovered the true "cause" of her suffering. The patient took a position about herself and regarding the world around her that was not agreeable to her or the world. She was not "honest" (we will return to that). Her fear regarding the children unfolded as pure deceit; in principle, she did not care. Worldly values were not relevant, but it appeared they contributed positive or negative feelings to the patient. Her personal well-being was highly stylized. Her main objective revolved around people being satisfied with her, liking her, considering her the perfect teacher. Significantly, she was not upset and had no guilt feelings about what slowed her down.

Egocentricity is a self-punishing process. Just as concern for objects of love allow people to gain movement and strength, so egocentric fixations rob people of strength and confidence. Individuals who consider themselves the primary objects are so overcome by fear for themselves that they cannot find their way. Herbert Huber (1996) of the State Institute for School Pedagogy and Educational Research in Munich concluded:

> Honesty refers to the fact that one does not view the world from a personal perspective, but is cognizant of *what* others are about. Honest individuals give credit to others and do not seek the glory for themselves. Honesty is nothing more than making the effort to be honest. (pp. 33–34).

According to Aristotle, justice encompasses all other virtues. Individuals who are just are interested not only in themselves but also in other people and other objects. Many people are interested in others only when they are personally useful to them. In that case, the individual loves and regards the other only when this benefits the self. Augustine termed this *amor concupiscentiae,* a love that is only egocentric. On the opposite end of the spectrum is the attitude that healthy parents show toward their children: They do not love them because it is advantageous for them, but they are happy when the children gain. Leibniz called this *amor benevolentiae,* the love of wishing well. Persons displaying this attitude want not their own well-being from others but the well-being of others. Goethe referred to this attitude as "altruism." When one can perceive persons and other creatures without concern for personal advantage, a human being transcends the somatic and psychic dimension and enters into the noetic realm.

PATIENT: Although when I really think about it, I am somewhat embarrassed.
THERAPIST: That is good. (The healthy, potential self within her has gently spoken.) Please tell me what, in your imagination, would be the worst outcome that could happen?
PATIENT: (Finally acknowledging.) It would be my failure. That the parents of my students point their fingers at me, that my colleagues would talk behind my back, and that I might have to quit my job in shame. That would be the worst.
THERAPIST: I understand. And now I have a complicated question. Could you think of something worse that you would have to fear that would embarrass you less?
PATIENT: (With a sudden gleam in her eye.) Of course. If what I am imagining actually had something to do with the fate of the children, then I would not be embarrassed by that.
THERAPIST: (Only had to dig further.) Then you would not have trouble sleeping, lack concentration, or want to avoid the field trip.
PATIENT: (Looks at therapist in disbelief.)
THERAPIST: I can prove it to you. Let's take your trip in the London subway station. If no child would be hurt, would you think about to whom the children would most likely listen, whose warning to be careful they would not ignore? Who would be such a connecting person? Most likely, a teacher with whom they are closely connected, that is, one who not only instructs them, but whom they also know as homeroom teacher.
PATIENT: Yes, we have good rapport.
THERAPIST: Therefore, you would, if it had to do with the children, insist on accompanying them to England, to have enough influence in case something goes wrong. You would personally plan exciting city tours and wholesome social activities. You would concentrate so hard that at night you would fall into bed exhausted, unable to have any fearful thoughts.
PATIENT: (Whispering.) I have to learn to think differently.
THERAPIST: A little. Up to now, what have been your main concerns will become minor. Then you are free to focus on the main concern, which is that your students will have a wonderful trip to a foreign country and return healthy.
PATIENT: And what if something should happen? If the trip is not successful?
(She falls back into her old mode of worrying.)
THERAPIST: Then you have made the best effort, and that is enough. That is all that can be asked of you!

The teacher left the Institute without requiring a disability leave. Instead, she had a new focus and accomplished the trip successfully. When her therapist returned from India, the patient explained to her that she no longer needed therapy because, in the meantime, she was able to distance herself from her egocentric orientation.

Case 2

A man told a clinician that his wife was constantly bossing him around (Lukas, 1998a). The patient explained, "Until recently I have always done what she wanted. Now she is having an affair with another man. When we married five years ago, I was so proud of her because she displayed so much self-confidence. She had a good job and a large circle of friends. Soon she began to criticize my appearance. My suits were out of style; my shoes were made of the wrong material. Therefore, we decided that she would select my clothes and determine how I should have my hair cut. From that, she took over more and more, determining my hobbies, who was to be invited to our house, and how we would spend our weekends. I had to do the work in the house when she did not feel like it, but I received no thanks. In time, I felt like her slave. In spite of that, I never rebelled because I wanted peace in the house. But now I can't anymore. I just can't take the humiliation of her having an extramarital affair."

The therapist was tempted to ask WHY: Why did the husband allow himself to be so humiliated? What mother or father figure contributed to the unreasonable line of thinking? In what early childhood experience did masochistic roots develop? Logotherapeutically, it was necessary to hasten to the ABOUT WHAT: What is the patient's main focus? Similar to the teacher in the previous example, he displayed his intentions with naïve dishonesty: To have peace, he never rebelled. Therefore, talking about peace was critical.

THERAPIST: Please define what you understand by the term "peace."
PATIENT: No arguments.
THERAPIST: Is there really peace between people when they just don't fight?
PATIENT: Peace is more than that. Harmony, mutual tolerance, and acceptance are also included. Individuals can be their own persons and live according to their own standards.
THERAPIST: That sounds wonderful. However, I am wondering about one issue. What you just described has never been realized in spite of your endless acquiescence. With that, the only accomplishment you achieved is that your wife accepted and tolerated you less and less, and you could not live with her demands.
PATIENT: (Moaning.) That's right. My wife...
THERAPIST: (Interrupts.) No! I am talking about you. You obviously have done nothing to bring about what your own definition of peace would have created!
PATIENT: (Reacting seemingly upset.) Are you trying to reproach me?
THERAPIST: Together with you, I want to find the reason for your problems. I want to fix the base, so that the marriage drama can grow. Let us consider that your slave-like submission did not create peace. Or do you see it differently?
PATIENT: (Shakes his head no.)
THERAPIST: In spite of that, you have not changed your attitude. Why not?
PATIENT: I am afraid that I will lose her. I am an insecure person who depends on others and don't know what I would do without her...

This was the "true cause." ABOUT WHAT the patient was worried came to light. He did not worry about mutual peace; he only worried about his own personal security. Psychology calls this "ambivalence." This meant he loved his wife because he needed her—as a stimulant, to provide direction, as decision maker in the daily routine. But, at the same time, he hated her, because, by needing her, she was more competent. The therapist thought that some processes like that had occurred; otherwise, he would have gladly given his "slaveholder" to another man. In spite of the fact that he berated her, he wanted to keep her.

PATIENT: I am afraid I will lose her.
THERAPIST: You are afraid for yourself.
(The statement brings this clearly into focus, and he does not deny it.)
THERAPIST: (Slipping into Socratic dialogue.) Let's do some brainstorming. Theoretically, consider yourself as being self-confident and able to manage your life better alone, but you want to bring peace into your home because of higher motives. For that you would have to operate in a peaceful manner and also to help your wife to seek more peaceful solutions, who, according to your report, seeks to start disputes. How would you have to proceed in this case?

The therapist gave him paper and pencil and encouraged him to make notes. For half an hour the therapist heard only his scribbling.

PATIENT: If I personally want to have peace, I must give my wife the freedom to choose between me and her friend. I also must offer her a conciliatory new start, should she elect to return to me.
(Tears roll down his cheeks as he continues to read.)
In order to educate her for peace, I must, however, value my identity, whether she likes it or not. When she criticizes, I would have to gently make her realize that each of us has individual preferences, and that our differences can complement the other as long as the dignity of the other is not damaged.
(Looks at the therapist as if he were a student presenting his lesson to the teacher. And truly, he had learned his lesson well.)
THERAPIST: Go and bring peace in your house.

Toward the end of the year, the therapist received a Christmas card from this man. Underneath was written, "Our marriage has held and added a new quality. With gratitude . . ." What surprised the therapist, in spite of many years of professional experience, was the exactness of the anticipatory knowledge in humans that gives directions, that cannot oppose the logic of reason nor the lack of logic in emotions. In the previous example, the reason the husband gives is that "the wife is at fault for all the problems." The feeling of the husband implies: "Become subservient to all the faults in order not to lose her." In the innermost center of his knowledge, he knew, however, "It depends on me. I have to change, including my humility."

(The diagnosis is assumed to be *DSM-IV*, 309.28, Adjustment Disorder with Mixed Anxiety and Depressed Mood; APA, 1994). Probably the GARF score would have been in the 25 to 30 range at the beginning of the case because the couple is seriously dysfunctional, but, toward the end, they seem to have made a good adjustment, with a score of 92 in all aspects.)

REVIEW OF RESEARCH

Hutzell (2000), editor of the *International Forum for Logotherapy*, provided an overview of research that has appeared in the *Forum* since its inception. Because the *Forum* has a wide audience, the format and information frequently are not presented in standard research style. Consequently, he reviewed only research that followed scientific methods for gathering data, that is, original research with descriptive methods or experimental design and statistical data. Approximately one-third of the authors who published research articles in the *Forum* used new information and descriptive methods, but few employed rigorous standards for data collection. Hutzell commented that the *Journal Des Viktor Frankl Institut* in Vienna, which was published between 1993 and 1998, had as one of its objectives to print and review articles using empirical data and strict, scientifically controlled studies. Only a few of these emerged during the years of that journal's existence.

Crumbaugh and Maholick (1964) described their experimental study in a chapter in Frankl (1967). Theses and dissertations on logotherapeutic themes and processes are listed in the bibliographies in Frankl (1978) and Fabry, Bulka, and Sahakian (1977). The authors and titles of 88 theses and dissertations are contained in Frankl (1997).

SUMMARY

Logotherapy is an existential psychotherapy developed by Viktor Frankl; it is considered the third Viennese school of psychotherapy after Freud's and Adler's. Frankl perceived that people were in despair because of an inner emptiness, an existential neurosis, because their lives lacked meaning and fulfillment. He espoused the theory that meaning cannot be given, but each individual is unique and, as such, has to discover personal meaning. Individuals cannot hold the past responsible for their present situations. People have choices, can make decisions, and must assume responsibility for their actions.

Life offers many meaning potentials, and an individual has to move from an egocentric viewpoint of What does life owe me? to What do I owe life? Meaning in life comes through commitments made to another person or a cause. Life has meaning under all circumstances. If life's conditions are such that they cannot be changed, then, until the last moment, individuals can change their attitudes and, with that change, can turn tragedy into triumph.

Logotherapists at times utilize methods of improvisation, often generated on the spur of the moment; dereflection, whereby a patient learns to shift the focus from self to another person or object; paradoxical intention often based on humor; list making; the appealing technique; and Socratic dialogue.

REFERENCES

American Psychiatric Association. (1994). *Diagnostic and statistical manual of mental disorders* (4th ed.). Washington, DC: Author.

Boehm, W. (1992). Ueber die unvereinbarkeit von Erziehung und therapie. (About the incompatibility between education and therapy). In *Vierteljahreschrift fuer Wissenschaftlliche Paedagogik, 68.*

Crumbaugh, J. C. (1973). *Everything to gain: A guide to self-fulfillment through logoanalysis.* Chicago: Nelson-Hall.

Crumbaugh, J. C. (1977). *The seeking of noetic goals (SONG).* Munster, IN: Psychometric Affiliates.

Crumbaugh, J. C. (Ed.), Graca, J., Hutzell, R. R., Widdon, M. F., & Cooper, E. C. (1990). *A primer of projective techniques of psychological assessment.* San Diego, CA: Libra.

Crumbaugh, J. C., & Maholick, L. T. (1964). An experimental study in existentialism: The psychometric approach to Frankl's concept of noogenic neurosis. *Journal of Clinical Psychology, 20,* 200–207.

Crumbaugh, J. C., & Maholick, L. T. (1976). *PIL (Purpose in Life test).* Munster, IN: Psychometric Affiliates. (Available from Viktor Frankl Institute of Logotherapy).

Crumbaugh, J. C., Wood, W. M., & Wood, W. C. (1980). *Logotherapy: New help for problem drinkers.* Chicago: Nelson-Hall.

Ellenberger, H. (1970). *The discovery of the unconscious: The history and evolution of dynamic psychiatry.* New York: Basic Books.

Fabry, J. B. (1979). Logotherapy in action: An overview. In J. B. Fabry, R. P. Bulka, & W. S. Sahakian (Eds.), *Logotherapy in action* (pp. 11–21). New York: Aronson.

Fabry, J. B. (1981). *Swing shift.* San Francisco: Strawberry Hill Press. (Original work published 1943)

Fabry, J. B. (1983). *Wege zur selbstfindung [Ways for finding oneself: How the individual gives each day its meaning].* Freiburg, Germany: Herder Verlag.

Fabry, J. B. (1987). *The pursuit of meaning.* Berkeley, CA: Institute of Logotherapy Press.

Fabry, J. B. (1988). *Guidepost to meaning.* Oakland, CA: New Harbinger Publications.

Fabry, J., & Lukas, E. (1995). *Auf den spuren des logos: Breifwechsel mit Viktor E. Frankl [In search of meaning: An exchange of letters with Viktor E. Frankl].* Berlin, Germany: Quintessenz Verlage.

Frankl, V. E. (1955). *The doctor and the soul.* New York: Alfred A. Knopf. (Original work published 1946)

Frankl, V. E. (1967a). *Man's search for meaning.* New York: Washington Square Press. (Original work published 1946)

Frankl, V. E. (1967b). *Psychotherapy and existentialism: Selected papers on logotherapy.* New York: Simon & Schuster.

Frankl, V. E. (1969). *The will to meaning.* New York: World Books.

Frankl, V. E. (1978). *The unheard cry for meaning.* New York: Simon & Schuster.

Frankl, V. E. (1997a). *Die psychotherapie in der Praxis: Eine kasuistische einfuehrung fuer aertze [Psychotherapy in the Praxis: A causal directory for doctors].* (4th Auflage). Munich, Germany: Piper Verlag.

Frankl, V. E. (1997b). *Viktor Frankl recollections: An autobiography* (J. Fabry & J. Fabry, Trans.). New York: Plenum Press. (Original work published 1995)

Gould, W. B. (1993). *Frankl: Life with meaning.* Pacific Grove, CA: Brooks/Cole.

Group for the Advancement of Psychiatry Committee on the Family. (1996). Global Assessment of

Relational Functioning Scale (GARF): I. Background and rationale. *Family Process, 35,* 155–172.

Huber, H. (1996). *Sittlichkeit und sinn [Social behavior and meaning].* Germany: Donauwoerth.

Hutzell, R. R. (2000). *International forum for logotherapy.*

Knight, M., & Fabry, J. (1988). *One and one make three: The story of a friendship.* Berkeley, CA: Benmir Books.

Lukas, E. (1968). *Logo-test.* Vienna: Deuticke Verlag.

Lukas, E. (1981). *Auch deine familie braucht sinn [Family also needs meaning].* Breisgau, Germany: Verlag Herder.

Lukas, E. (1984). *Meaningful living.* Berkeley, CA: Institute of Logotherapy Press.

Lukas, E. (1986). *Meaning in suffering.* Berkeley, CA: Institute of Logotherapy Press.

Lukas, E. (1993). *Lukas: Meaningful lines* (B. Hirsch & J. Fabry, Trans.). (Limited edition, privately published)

Lukas, E. (1998a). *Spirituelle psychology [Spiritual psychology].* Vienna: Koesal Verlag.

Lukas, E. (1998b). *Viktor E. Frankl und die logotherapie: Eine kurzinformation ueber sein leben und sein werk.* [Viktor E. Frankl and logotherapy: Brief information about his life and his work]. Fuerstenfeldbruck: Sueddeutsches Institut.

Lukas, E. (2001). *Auf den stufen des lebens* [Stepping stones to life: My most significant cases of noogenic healing according to Viktor Frankl]. Guetersloh, Germany: Quell.

Scheler, M. (1973). *Formalism in ethics and non-formal ethics of values: A new attempt toward the foundation of an ethical personalism* (M. S. Frings & R. L. Funk, Trans.). Evanston, IL: Northwestern University Press. (Original work published 1913)

Section Four

PSYCHOTHERAPY WITH FAMILIES AND COUPLES

Chapter 15 Couple Therapy as a Transforming Process: Reflections on Couples' Stories

Chapter 16 Existential Dilemmas and Skill Building in Couple Therapy

Chapter 17 Resilience and Human Rights Activism in Women's Life Stories

Chapter 18 Redecision Family Therapy

Chapter 19 Contextual Therapy

Chapter 20 Systems as Interconnecting Social-Psychological Processes: Existential Foundations of Families

CHAPTER 15

Couple Therapy as a Transforming Process: Reflections on Couples' Stories

MAURIZIO ANDOLFI
JOSEPH KABALI (TRANSLATOR)

HISTORY OF THE THERAPEUTIC APPROACH

Born in Rome in 1942, Maurizio Andolfi pursued medicine and child psychiatry at the University of La Sapienza in Rome. Andolfi first encountered family therapy in New York with Nathan Ackerman, whom he found provocative in connecting emotionally with children and families. He observed and learned about viewing a child, often through play, "as a bridge to connect to the parents" (Andolfi, 1994a; Barletta, 2000, p. 7). At the time, Andolfi perceived this as too unorthodox for his Italian colleagues; however, he has since built on the presentation of children's problems as a way of mobilizing couples and families.

As a Fellow in Social Community Psychiatry at the Albert Einstein College of Medicine in New York in the early 1970s, Andolfi was associated with Andy Ferber and worked with very disadvantaged families of various ethnic groups.

He studied at the Family Studies Section of Bronx State Hospital with Albert Scheflen and Israel Zwerling, who taught Andolfi to reconsider family in the context of community, and at the Nathan Ackerman Family Institute with Kitty LaPerrière. A little later, he went to the Philadelphia Child Guidance Clinic and observed Salvador Minuchin and Jay Haley. Andolfi views Minuchin's structural approach as a foundational basis for building a basic understanding of family processes. During this later period, he was a visiting professor at the Department of Mental Health Sciences at Hanheman Medical College in Philadelphia and also worked with poor families in South Philadelphia.

Carl Whitaker also exerted a great influence on Andolfi's development. Andolfi came to admire Whitaker for his capacity to connect with irrationality. Early in their relationship, Whitaker was interviewing an Italian psychotic adolescent with Andolfi as the translator. Whitaker ignored the adolescent and spoke only with Andolfi, with whose translation he became more and more irritated. In acting irrationally infuriated with Andolfi,

---

With appreciation to Sharon and Robert Massey for their thorough editing and organizing of this chapter.

Whitaker provided the family of the psychotic adolescent with an intervention experience almost crazier than what they lived with on a regular basis. For Andolfi, this approach contrasted with Minuchin's search for rational order and functionality.

Andolfi's training, experience, applications, and teamwork led to a series of publications in English. Andolfi (1979) advocated the consideration of family therapy as an interactional approach. He proposed prescribing a family's own dysfunctional rules as a therapeutic strategy (Andolfi, 1980) and focused on integrating structural and strategic interventions to engage families with rigid organizations. He initiated an emphasis on going behind the family mask and supporting each individual (Andolfi, Angelo, Menghi, & Nicolò-Corigliano, 1983). Later Andolfi, Angelo, and de Nichilo (1989) highlighted the use of metaphors in family therapy and the study of family myths. Since 1981, he has conducted practica in family therapy in Rome each year for English-speaking family therapists. As of 1991 he has included both Spanish- and French-speaking family therapists.

THEORETICAL CONSTRUCTS

Sociocultural Context: Couple Therapy in Italy

Request for psychotherapy by couples has begun relatively recently in Italy. Only during the past two decades has a growing interest in therapy for conjugal problems arisen. In recent years, the focus has occurred mainly concerning the multigenerational problems of a couple and the separated spouse who keeps the children. Sometimes there is a tendency for the couple to call out for help when the tension has reached a highly explosive level. At this point it is rather difficult to revitalize their relationship. Italian social and couple stereotypes relating to male and female genders are responsible for this delay in asking for help. Toward the end of the 1970s, and even more so during the 1980s, the recently-established family consultation offices, which serve as the potential places of consultation for couples' difficulties, became dispensaries for contraception and places to help women, and eventually children, in distress. Little attention was paid to the true engine of the family, the couple itself. Not much attention was given in an integrated way to observation and repair of relational damage.

Gender Issues

Clinicians tend to address and make decisions to provide public services for mother and child and tend to forget about paternal responsibility. For a long time, family consultants in Italy have ignored the male's contribution to a family, even in those issues related to couple therapy. For example, in the case of a man who is scarcely engaged in assuming his responsibilities toward his partner and children, the proposed solutions lie in the area of politically established services and legislation. Generally traditional views are implemented when concerning child rearing and development; however, these views do not support responsiveness to the profound changes that affect today's families. The paternal/masculine perspective remains utterly marginal and underused in relation to the maternal/feminine. If this continues as the prevailing social *mot d'ordre*, it is not difficult to foresee that the feminine side will continue taking precedence in the great majority of cases involving a search for solutions to motivational and other problematic processes. This mirrors the area of professional choice, where the affective world and developmental psychology seem to attend primarily to the feminine perspective. Thus, assessing a given family and intervening with painful issues frequently results in acting mostly in the areas of the competence and sensitivity of women. How, then, can we give more attention to the needs, responsibilities, and sensitivities of men, when the language of the woman, of the maternal, predominates?

How Couples Request Therapy

In the chapter "Masculine and Feminine in Psychotherapy with the Family," Andolfi (1996) noted how a couple in difficulty requested help. In Italy, usually the woman takes the initiative by calling to ask for an appointment for the two. Generally, the man has the woman do this and follows her "to make her happy." He declares that he himself would not begin such a process, although he will eventually participate and decide what to do during the consultation process. Rarely does the man call for a consultation. Rather, he acts "to save a marriage or a family" from the wife's desire to break it up. Sometimes, he brings the woman to the therapy session, hoping that the therapist will be able to "cure her."

Only infrequently do the two spouses arrive for consultation with a solid agreement on what must be done or having developed a joint plan. However, they come together. Often, couple therapists do not value this fact enough. They do not understand that the two coming together to present their difficulties sometimes takes the couple months or even years of internal wear and tear before they can decide to come together. Tradition, formal education, a certain form of religiosity, and relational self-restraint tend to undervalue the internal problems of a couple and discourage a decision to ask for help.

Judgment or fear of being judged by their respective families weighs heavily on both members of a couple and on the harmony they hope to live in. The couple suffers from their personal and relational difficulties and also assume the pains of their families of origin. All of this discourages a couple from making a simple and explicit request for couple therapy precisely in those important moments of conjugal crisis. Often, when a relationship suffers, the more "economical" way of individual therapy is chosen ("If he/she can't understand me, then I am going to find someone who will listen to me, someone who will help me"); or the couple may wait until the tension rises and causes an explosion of symptoms in a child. Looking for help for a child's or adolescent's difficulties is more easily accepted by their families and by those who know them.

The couple can become the real "target" when things no longer work out. Decisions must be made relative to separation, child custody, and care. Once the affective understandings, agreements, and fundamental ingredients of the couple are mitigated, then the social aspect (the action of lawyers, systems of justice, long-damaging waiting times, mediation by the families) begins weighing heavily on family life and generates further problems. Nevertheless, even if it is necessary to shift the responsibility and the fault for the failure of a long-term conjugal project outside of self (onto the other spouse, onto either or both their families of origin, onto lawyers, onto a lover, or even onto the children) to face the pain and the feeling of despair and impotence that follows the disintegration of a family, it is nonetheless the realization of having deceived oneself for a long time that makes one feel so bad.

The Discovery of Self-Deceit

One of the most meaningful results emerging from our research, as far as couples who began therapy because of marital difficulty is concerned, involved the discovery of self-deceit. Interviews with each one of the partners, years after the conclusion or interruption of therapy, centered around this awareness. For a long time they had "betrayed" themselves and, consequently, their children, as far as their own authenticity was concerned. The feeling brought about by this betrayal seems to produce in the personality of each individual a more considerable impact than the "damage" eventually suffered by the other partner on account of the lack of respect and of the lying behavior of the latter. In other words, through the therapeutic experience, the center of the person's life, which had shifted out of place for a long time onto the conjugal relationship and onto the "faults" of the other, begins once again to circle around the individual's personal world, and this often allows the individual to reach a rather high degree of self-awareness.

Nine years after beginning sessions, Mrs. Bardo commented to Andolfi at the end of her cycle of therapy, "Yes, to know is to suffer, especially for someone who must recognize having made the greatest, most unforgivable and irreparable kind of betrayal of self and children: allowing my own 'private kingdom' to be invaded, and forgetting about living life. But I could say that I didn't know. But isn't this the fault? Not to have wanted to know, not to have wanted to understand a reality that was self-explanatory? Even worse is the deceiving of self in a grotesque way in order not to know, to the point of undergoing enormous suffering of body and soul, which affected all the others too. When I think that I ran the risk of continuing on living a blind and uncontrolled life until the end, I feel terrorized and my sense of gratefulness toward the therapy grows immensely." This self-deceit seems to be based on voluntary actions that are in no way unconscious. The not wanting to know, not wanting to understand, not wanting to see lays the foundation for and solidifies self-deceit over the course of the years. Winnicott's (1971) concept of the *false self*, or Horney's (1950) *idealized/despised image of self* come close to the idea of self-deceit on which the whole life of an individual can be built, often at the cost of incredible pain and sacrifice.

The real self is often numbed in the development of *bad faith relations* (Vella & Ruberto, 1980). Cases in which mechanisms of mutual protectiveness, which intend to cover up sections missing in one's own self and serve to amplify those hypertrophic and irreducible areas of one's own identity and whose development precedes the coming together of the couple, take the place of intimate and authentic relations. The bad faith relation can then be synthesized in being what one is not; to this is often added what Vella and Ruberto called the *contextual bond,* exercised and sustained by the same system of family and social relationships in which the couple evolves. The silence and the halo of protectiveness, built by family members and friends of couples in crisis, reinforce feelings of immutability and irreversibility of a conjugal relationship. Only with a turn toward a definitive breaking off will everyone loudly declare that the relationship had for years been in crisis and that a separation was logical.

In his book *Passionate Marriage,* Schnarch (1997) affirmed that "differentiation in marriage is a process as long as life itself. Through this process we experience our own unities, while keeping ourselves in contact with those we love." Furthermore, "the more different we are, the stronger the awareness of self, the better we are able to remain upright in the inevitable conflicts with our partners, the more intimacy we are able to tolerate with someone whom we love without fear of losing the sense that we are separate individuals."

The majority of couples spend many years trying not to reveal to the other the ways they really are, with the purpose of maintaining an illusion of total unity. This suffocates any true affective relationship, with disastrous consequences for expression of sexuality. Actually, sexual dissatisfaction, which can be considered the true litmus test showing the deterioration of the relationship, rarely acquires sufficient strength to bring two adults to ask for outside help. At most, the dissatisfaction and existential solitude of many couples finds an indirect outlet through their children; onto the latter are often unloaded the couples' tensions and problems that were not faced squarely nor solved elsewhere.

We can see this process of affective triangulation in a family who begins family therapy because of a serious personality disorder in their adolescent son whose cyclical behavior and attitudes are, at times, destructive and manic, and other times depressive. These behaviors dominate conjugal distress and become more irreversible over time. These problems have never been confronted during 20 years of life together with three sons, who today are all adolescents. After one year of therapy centered on the son, in which everyone proposes himself or herself as a resource and after considerable progress in the relational life of the boy, we are able to renegotiate the therapeutic contract and propose a therapy centered on the couple. A contract was developed with great relief by the boy and his brothers. The couple explain that they had "tried" couple therapy many years before, long before their son became symptomatic. However, they had ended the therapy after one meeting because of their reciprocal and total incapacity to understand one another. Mrs. B., the mother, several years later, wrote the following about that first attempt at therapy: "I was feeling so bad before that now I can very much appreciate whatever freedom, autonomy, tranquility, respect for myself, and dignity I have been able to reacquire. If it is true that the present and the future have old roots, I now know that pain, when accepted to its depths, can revitalize a person. Anyone can, at any age, operate a saving turnaround and abandon a very long practice of compromises, adjustments, cowardice, and resignation in order to begin searching in all humility for one's best side, the original one, which had been distorted by the times and the vicissitudes of life (what I could have been if . . .). But this must be done in full awareness."

COUPLE THERAPY IN DISGUISE: CHILD-FOCUSED TREATMENT

Many families agree to visit us and to accept help in relation to a problem of one of their children. The child's problem is real, and sometimes shows itself as urgent or as persistent over time. No doubt, this problem exercises a sort of affective pressure on the parents and, generally speaking, on the whole family nucleus, to the point of often provoking a shared motivation and a group collaboration to look for outside professional help. We have often asked ourselves why this motivation does not provoke a similar attitude in critical situations of extreme suffering and lack of trust in the inner sanctum of the couple themselves, who often seem incapable of asking, in an explicit way, for help for their affective survival and for their own growth process. They appear to wait until faced with the specter of hostile separation and then seek help so as not to further damage their children.

In this area, one can think about the growing use of *family mediation* as the way to cut asunder family relationships in the least traumatic way possible. We can think about the scarce use of couple therapy in less dramatic situations, when there still would be many opportunities for pulling out of difficult jams and reciprocal self-deceit situations. Nevertheless, years after the completion of their therapy, a great majority of the spouses in the families who are the focus of our research tell us how empty and destructive their conjugal relationship was and what negative effects it exerted on their children. At the same time, they describe the liberating and curing effects resulting from therapy for their children and the amelioration of their marital relationship or the facilitation of an authentic kind of separation.

Over the 12 years of reflective clinical experience listening to so many families, we have understood that, to alter the "unwillingness" (to know, to understand, to see) and, consequently, the "self-deceit," an adult prefers to proceed by stages. Adults prefer first to come to *want* to help a child who is in a situation of difficulty or sickness. Only afterward, in the course of an intervention vividly desired for the child or adolescent, can they discover the mechanism of denial exercised on themselves, which is often masked under a strong form of altruism ("I only care about my child, for me it is too late to change. With my partner, there is only misunderstanding now"). Or, the opposite can be true, a mechanism permeated with a strong sense of guilt "I (or we) are responsible for the sickness of our child."

This phenomenon of arriving at a personal search by way of a child's problem appears encouraging to us because it becomes a privileged occasion to discuss again the whole order of relations in the family. In this sense, we feel deeply systemic because, although we enter here into a partial aspect of the reality of the family, we necessarily enter into its totality. This idea has been strongly confirmed by our research data in such a way that now we think that many therapies done on account of what would be classified in the *Diagnostic and Statistical Manual of Mental Disorders* (*DSM-IV*; APA, 1994) as a psychosomatic, behavioral, or relational problem of a child are really, albeit implicitly, camouflaged couple therapies.

PROBLEMS, SYMPTOMS, AND SYNDROMES TREATED

Andolfi (Barletta, 2000) prefers to know people's history through interacting with them as he makes a diagnosis. He does not rely on *DSM* categorization and medication; rather, he focuses more on people's development. He uses intake information and genograms more as discussion stimulators to see how family members describe and respond to what is reported. He helps family members play with information to deal with living issues rather than preconstructed solutions. He inquires about what others have said and their perceptions. Through this, he helps people construct a history through interaction. The more information generated, the more relative a problem becomes. He wants to enlarge the picture and will inquire about those not present in a genogram description and then focus on those present. When information stays between two people (e.g., a couple), difficulties may be amplified; adding a third person or another generation or some other concern induces the two to collaborate. Andolfi relies on psychiatric colleagues in collaborative ways to decide on medication issues. He infuses his practice with humor. Andolfi observes that therapy at times mirrors society; short, brief therapy reflects a fast-paced, instant-fix society, and may not prove effective with serious problems and issues. He regrets the diminution of collaboration among the professions as family therapy has become more established and lost some opportunities by ceasing to both foster relationships with psychiatrists and to open new doors to communities. He also favors an increase in social interest and a continued involvement in the neighborhood lives of families.

CASE EXAMPLES AND FOLLOW-UP REFLECTIONS AS RESEARCH

Disguised Couple Therapy

Case Example
Gianni, an 11-year-old boy who suffered for about two years from a "very fastidious encopresis" both at home and at school, was brought to therapy. This diagnosis naturally filled the child with shame and his parents with anxiety. Gianni's parents separated when he was 4 years of age. Truthfully, however, and this came out

clearly from the first session, the process of affective detachment has not yet been solidified, which does not allow either of them to feel clearly defined. The mother, Maria, speaks of her former husband as though he were still the center of her affective interests. The father, Mimi, has lived for a few years with a companion, but loves to still be considered the "ideal man" of the former wife, although he denies this. A pseudo-understanding of the two as remaining a couple, officially denied by them, is strengthened by Gianni. Through his excrement, he becomes a bridge between the two family nuclei revolving around the parents. They each unload onto the other the responsibility for Gianni's regressive problem.

Maria had a son whose problems intensified every time he visited his father, thus alluding to his new affective relationship as the active cause of the encopresis. On the other side, Mimi accuses Maria's family ambiance (strictness and authoritarianism of Maria's mother and the eclipsed attitude of her father) as the cause of Gianni's problems. And so, the boy's excrement has become a kind of glue that keeps all of them together in a rigid and confusing affective setup. Additionally, Gianni's father is a medical doctor. He often has to visit his sick in-laws, whom he detests; he keeps on visiting them for fear that, if he no longer does so, they may "take revenge" on the child.

We can easily define the territory of the couple as the most vulnerable and confusing area of the whole affective organization of the two families that revolve around the boy. Nevertheless, it is rare for a couple to present themselves openly to announce their own difficulties (in this case, to finalize a separation that was never completed) and to ask for help with overcoming them. It is more likely that the couple will seek an intervention in relation to their child. At this point, the choice of one therapy over another takes on a value that is more political than technical. Specifically, to treat Gianni's encopresis as the mere psychosomatic trouble of an adolescent by isolating him from the historical components of his family is not only a technical choice, it is a choice that tends to keep the family out of it, and to not recognize its right and duty to be involved as an integral part of the problem and of its possible solution.

Furthermore, to remove the parents from the cure of their children inevitably allows a therapist to think that she or he is more competent than the parents, and pushes the clinician to act accordingly. This sometimes causes further damage to the family's self-esteem. It would be equally damaging to include a family member to make him or her feel guilty for the developmental events of Gianni's life.

As described in earlier writings, the trouble of the child becomes an important relational indicator, capable of becoming a bridge in the evolutionary passage from an "area of pathology to a search for health" (Andolfi, 1979, 1995; Andolfi & Haber, 1994). Noting that the encopresis provides the first link between the family and the therapist leads to learning how to value its worth: It set up the premises for a therapeutic meeting. Today, Gianni is a 22-year-old university student, absolutely adequate to his age. The memory of the therapy with his family is still quite alive, precisely because it afforded the opportunity for a transforming process of a highly entangled couple.

Follow-Up Research

I met Mimi, Gianni's father, 11 years later in a follow-up session. He is now a mature man who learned from a "therapeutic experience" truly lived by him. He walked away from that active part of self that had kept him a prisoner of his own "couple self-deceits" and from the need to feel "indispensable" to his son's mother, his former wife and her family circle. This made him available for a new and devoted relationship with a companion whom he married recently. We can suppose that "the experience of the therapy" and the capacity of acquiring new relational competence led him to deeply modify his life and even his own medical identity; in fact, after proper training, he left the practice of family medicine to become a psychotherapist.

In relation to Gianni, his father can still see and describe the various steps of the boy's evolution: the conjugal separation and the discomfort of his child, who for many years felt pulled by affection for his mother, his father, and his grandparents. The father remembers the disturbances around Gianni's encopresis and how the boy felt bad going from one house to the other, his fear of betraying both Mommy and Daddy. The father also recalls his own turnaround, from being too possessive and judgmental in relation to his child to the discovery that he could finally feel free to play with his child. He now remembers that the therapist used to prescribe in writing tasks based on playing and having fun with his son as a king of "drug" that he had to consume regularly to meet his own son on a more personal level. When Gianni failed his studies at the end of his second year in high school, his father did not make a big deal of it; rather, he told the boy that "he had not wasted a year of life, but only a school year."

Gianni's mother went through many years of confusion because of her difficulty in separating herself from the boy's father and even more in differentiating herself from her own parents. She felt insecure as she played the role of mother in a family context in which she was never recognized as a competent human being, able to take an *I* position or to overcome the process of *intergenerational intimidation* (see Williamson, 1981). If she had been able to overcome this situation, she would not have felt and lived as a "daughter at the age of 42 years." Finally, she was able to shift her worries about her son to preoccupations about herself as she projected herself into a search for a new meaning for her life. She now happily shows signs of such a change in her life. She has lost quite a bit of weight (in the past, although keeping herself a pretty woman, she had put on some 70 pounds). She seems to have reached a greater level of self-esteem and self-confidence. Now that Gianni no longer experiences problems at school (he now serves in the police force), she can shed the suffocating role of mother, a role that she carried so deeply for so long at home by herself, and can now project herself to the outside with confidence. Now that Gianni has a girlfriend and studies administration with real interest, his mother can restart dialoguing with herself. She has relocated and has placed clearer boundaries between herself and her parents. She last heard from her former husband more than two years earlier. This in itself is a great accomplishment, because of her natural inclination to deny the conjugal separation. She now knows her limits as a woman and her capacity for building a new life for herself.

The request for therapy was at first disguised. But the therapy, which lasted a year, provided adequate space for reflection and development and answered a specific objective. First, two parents in difficulty gained competence when confronted with the bizarre symptoms of their son; second, therapy fostered a generational jump and a personal and relational process of growth for both parents, Mimi, and Maria.

MULTIGENERATIONAL CONTEXT FOR
DISGUISED COUPLE THERAPY

Case Example
Lucia, a 9-year-old girl, was taken to therapy by her parents because for two years she suffered from severe tummy ache at home and at school. No organic origin was found for her disturbances. However, her troubles tyrannized the whole family night and day because Lucia tended to be continuously in tearful crises, and often awakened her parents at night wanting to sleep with them. Her 4-year-old younger sister

received little attention from the parents because she was no problem to them and all of their attention had to go to Lucia.

Lucia's troubles may indicate another couple therapy in disguise. An element of considerable importance is the constitution of the family itself. Sophia, Lucia's mother, comes from a small rural village in the province of Veneto, where life is very austere and the expression of personal feelings, those of children included, is discouraged. Only physical sicknesses are recognized, and doctors provide cures. Sophia experienced this as a child, when she too suffered for a long time from intestinal troubles.

Renzo, the father, employed by a pharmaceutic firm in a small town in Alto Lazio. He is a very insecure person, and his family history is very painful. His father, a medical doctor employed by the local district, died at a young age; he had been recognized as a very competent doctor, yet he had seriously embarrassed his wife by being a woman-chaser. After his father's death, Renzo felt that he had to play the role of a reassuring male in the family and of caretaker of his mother and his sister, who had never been away from home.

Renzo and Sophia met because of their common insecurities. Lucia was the excuse that pressured them to marry when Sophia became pregnant. In the first therapy session, Sophia described the marriage ceremony, in which she walked to the altar carrying her 3-month-old daughter while Renzo sat a little distance from them. This image seems to characterize the later development of the family: The true couple are Sophia and Lucia, always together, while Renzo does not seem to find a spot in it all. Lucia rules the life of her parents, and the couple never spend a weekend away from Lucia and later, Clara, their second child.

Renzo had his way in only one area: He forced his wife to live, temporarily at least, in the house in which he grew up, the house that now is more spacious since the death of his father, in the company of his mother and sister.

Officially, the reason was to spend less money, but after nine years, they are still living there. The relationships among Sophia, his mother, and his sister are horrendous. This cements the relationship between Sophia and Lucia all the more strongly. It is not clear which of the two has to protect the other more.

What to do, then, in therapy? It is not easy to isolate Lucia's troubles from such complex and twisted family relationships. The fact is that Renzo and Sophia never had the chance to build their own relationship as a couple. Yet they seem very respectful toward one another; they appear to desire strongly to stay together. However, they have developed a system of avoiding coming to truly know one another, as if they did not believe enough in their own capabilities of building a solid rapport as a couple and did not fully believe in their competence as parents. Their marriage, in the words of Andolfi (1994b), was "adopted" by the family into which the relationship was born, while Lucia regulates all the affective exchanges at home.

Whereas the first case described the experience and the foundation of separation as missing, in the current case, it seems that a true union was never experienced by the couple. From the start, a triadic relationship was developed and the necessary process of detachment and affective separation from the original families never took place. The goal of therapy consists in changing the pain in Lucia's stomach from an element of blockage to a family transformation, so as to allow, first of all, a physical detachment of the nuclear family from the paternal home, and afterward, a rewriting of a nuptial rite for the parents, with the permission and emotional support of the little girl.

After just over a year of therapy, the parents are able to redesign their relationship to limit the intrusions of Renzo's family of origin and to fashion a more structured relationship with Lucia. Lucia abandons her role of guardian of the couple because Sophia and Renzo are able to reassure themselves as partners and, even more, as individuals.

It is amazing to see the flexibility of children's disturbances, which may vary in intensity, disappear altogether, or assume diverse forms and expressions according to the emotional needs of a family. This elasticity in children's symptoms allows for work on several generations at the same time, such as the level centered around the child and the one focused around a couple and their families of origin.

Follow-Up Session
Recently, a meeting took place with Lucia's family. Lucia, now 16 years old, a smiling adolescent who is well-integrated at school, still experiences occasional fears, but now looks for an individual space in which she can overcome these. As the one who brought her family to therapy, she now manages to keep a less central place in the family of origin. She allows the couple to keep discovering one another and to focus on the old, never-manifested misunderstandings and frustrations of their life as a couple. Lucia's adolescence and Clara's growing up force the parents to face in a more direct way the themes related to their approaching the "empty nest" stage so as to endeavor to fill in the "empty spaces of the couple."

MEMORY IN THE SERVICE OF
PERSONAL STORY/HISTORY

How can the search for one's best side precede the original side that seems to have been distorted by time and the vicissitudes of life? Is it a question of rebuilding one's parts *ex novo*, or of recapturing values and resources often buried and forgotten? Because one's personal story and history are built on memory, memory in some way remains at the service of personal history. This means that memories, and especially the affective tone of past events, change depending on the circumstances in which one recalls them. It is as if treason and the lies one has decided to live with in order not to change are, one at a time, used to complete diverse puzzles. Think, for example, about the situation that is created in the case of ambiguous relationships, around which the mind keeps searching for a logical meaning. The versions of the reconstructions of the scenes that follow one another in a relationship can change for a time in the attempt to inject into them contradictory details, in an effort to discover a logical sense in a series of data that are not that logical. How can a person describe or recall a relationship where love and hatred continually cross one another, in which a gesture of affection is, perhaps, contradicted by ironical words? This is the problem of foreground and background as an individual elaborates memories.

Case Example
Mrs. Bardo reflected on the effects of therapy, now distant in time, "I realize that I always and only talk about myself: a bit of sane selfishness after so much 'shaggy generosity.' Maybe it is enough to say that Emilio (and my other sons too) once absorbed and reflected the despair, the nonauthenticity and the nonlife of their parents. Now, however, he experiences the positive atmosphere and the different and more breathable air that circulates at home. Everything seems so logical now! And yet, how long a time it took us to understand it! Notwithstanding such great progress, I know that the therapy is not truly finished; it will never come to an end. Because I keep referring to it, whatever I do, say or think: I can no longer live outside of the path that I'm walking on, thanks to you."

Already in 1989 Andolfi, Angelo, and de Nichilo affirmed that therapy "begins when it ends." The time frame of a truly transforming process, whether individual or relational, takes much longer than what can be seen or understood within a therapeutic process. Change really flows from what happens outside of dependent relationships, even highly meaningful ones, such as therapeutic processes. Consequently, the task of therapy seems to originate from transforming processes rather than verifying changes in behavior. The sense of noncompletion of therapy and the suspension of a therapeutic relationship allow a family to reassign to themselves the management of their own history and story.

This awareness of times of change almost never occurs at the moment of the interruption of the therapy. At most, clients talk about a sensation of "having been fired," or even of no longer deriving personal gratification from a therapist. At times, assigning a termination to therapy is considered a kind of therapeutic provocation to force a family to reappropriate the management of what belongs to them. Naturally, the manner in which the ending of therapy is accepted is tied to the capacity of individuals to give themselves a reason for it, and for finding in themselves a sense of direction. Not infrequently, a spouse, like Mrs. Bardo, appreciates therapy because of its helping her to achieve a mature marriage separation and to end with a feeling of optimism and trust in her own resources. This is very different from the way the therapy ended for the husband, who now feels "damaged" by the outcome of the therapy because it "favored" his wife, who now "has all the children with her and can enjoy them" while he "feels alone and lonely as a dog." This emphasizing of reality in a reductive and antagonistic way, as on a battlefield where there are winners and losers, constitutes an obligatory passage that is sometimes very painful. In diverse moments, sooner or later, one can come to terms with oneself and with one's capacity to assume the "I, me" position.

Work with the Bardo family and others evidences an aspect often denied or kept in silence: the importance of self-talk. Consequently, Dr. Bardo's feeling "alone and lonely as a dog" has no connection with the possibility of having access to his children; rather, he refers to his worry because he does not know what to do with himself on the affective level. This brings him to look for space (sleeping quarters) where it is senseless to live, inducing him to feel his ex-wife's privileges rather than to confront his own transforming process. At the same time, this sense of loss motivates him to consider the therapist as an ally of his wife, almost as responsible for the ulterior damage of his life. Time alone and the need to experience thoroughly his own sense of uselessness and solitude will help him understand how much the couple's relationship was kept alive through its most destructive parts.

More than a year later, the therapist receives a phone call from Dr. Bardo, an unexpected and cordial call, during which a new element is mentioned: the presence of a new woman in his life. This seems to change all his preceding impressions on his rapport with his children, who now come to see him with pleasure. Emilio, especially, spends long periods of time with his father, with his new partner, and with her daughter. Before ending the conversation, Dr. Bardo expresses the desire to present his new partner to the therapist, and says that he has often and very positively talked about the therapy with her.

SUMMONING FAMILIES OF ORIGIN TO
COUPLE THERAPY

Murray Bowen (1978) has deeply influenced Andolfi's way of looking at intergenerational therapy, especially in emphasizing that solving a problem in the *here and now* implicates going to the *there and then*. His work, although proceeding from a psychodynamic matrix, was more similar to the work of the coach of a football team (the word *coach* recurs often in his works) than to the work of an analyst who follows the almost imperceptible movements of patients over the course of long therapeutic relationships. Bowen worked like a competent coach able to maximize the resources and the potential of individual players while keeping in view the whole team. He proposed a systems theory different from general systems theory (as described by von Bertalanffy, 1968) and from the perspectives of Watzlawick, Beavin, and Jackson (1967) at the Mental Research Institute and from the Milan School (Selvini Palazzoli, Boscolo, Cecchin, & Prata, 1978).

Bowen did not consider useful observation of communication patterns of a couple. Rather, he thought that, in many situations of serious stress, two spouses no longer know how to interact, and they end up reacting in automatic ways to each other. A vicious circle occurs with a great waste of emotional energy. Using this as a premise, Bowen placed himself as an element of discontinuity between the two spouses. He asked questions individually of each, carefully avoiding any direct exchange between the two. He automatically substituted the word *thinking* for *feeling* in the formulation of his questions and in the answers from his patients. He was convinced that the best way to help people enter into contact with their own emotional worlds results from preventing them from referring to any event in terms such as "to feel," "to live," or "to perceive." Forbidding any emotional exchange in therapy, Bowen favored individual cognitive research by alternating the position of each spouse from a reactive position of confrontation to a position of active listening to one another.

Bowen's function as emotional watershed developed further when he requested each spouse to think through his or her own position within his or her family of origin. After an accurate study of the family genogram (Bowen, 1978), each spouse is sent home and given the task of reconnecting to the original group to learn how to separate better from it and to decide what to do with any emotional cut offs, which often undergird relational misunderstandings at many levels. Bowen used the metaphor of a journey home, asking his patients to symbolically pack a bag of personal, social, and emotional possessions in searching for their true selves. For Bowen, a couple's problems revolve around being "congealed" while waiting for each to come back with a deeper awareness from his or her inner voyage to his or her family of origin, so as to start again their discourse as a couple based on better differentiation of self.

In our clinical experience, we have found it more useful to "have the bag arrive in therapy," that is, to summon the families of origin to the session, rather than send the patients home. We do this for several reasons. First, both spouses benefit from sharing an important experience that often was rather painful. In this regard, our therapy model differs from that of Framo (1982), who preferred to assemble the family of origin of one of the spouses and to exclude the partner from the session because his or her presence might impinge on the meeting. The physical presence of the other spouse in the session confirms, albeit indirectly, that we are working out the issues of the couple. This also allows us to evaluate the capacity of one partner to expose himself or herself in front of the other, and to openly show affective needs and old weaknesses that often were concealed, even after several years of life together.

Above all, a therapist can communicate efficiently to the spouses that their families of origin remain positive resources and not the causes of their difficulties, as the couple often affirms. If the older generation understands our invitation as an occasion to assign faults and guilt, the parents, feeling accused, will assume an extremely defensive posture. This often happens independent of our goodwill, as if the parents had adopted a stance of feeling responsible for their children's problems, although the latter have been adults for a long time. To overcome this impasse, we ask the parents, brothers, and sisters to serve as our consultants. They can give a therapist useful information to help in better understanding their family development. They are there not to talk about the problems of the couple, but only to help us better understand their son or daughter, brother or sister and look for family resources. Their goal, sustained by the therapist, favors the search for new relational pathways outside the customary and seemingly convenient recourse to the exchange of mutual accusations that prove useless.

Analogous to what Boszormenyi-Nagy and Spark (1973), Bowen (1978), Framo (1982), and Williamson (1981) observed, ending a meeting without any increase in aggressiveness or resentment of the members in the extended family remains essential. It is a mistake to give a son or daughter an opportunity to freely express resentment against the parents, a resentment that may have lain concealed for years. Such confrontations are unlikely to modify the relationship in a positive way. Therefore, what is more needed is to reconnect generations, to heal emotional cutoffs, and to reestablish relationships of acceptance with parents.

In the words of Williamson (1981)

> This rebalancing of intergenerational dynamics is the *sine qua non* of psychological adulthood and is the source of *personal authority* in living. The adult generation can offer support without assuming emotional responsibility or burden for the welfare, the happiness, or the survival of the aging parents. And this support may be offered "spontaneously" rather than "indebtedly."

The work of Whitaker (1989), including his concept of evolutionary normalcy, involves a search for the resources of a family. He engaged in normalizing stages of madness, violence, and disruption of fantasies. If a couple arrives in therapy presenting their *ménage* as abnormal, emphasizing the causes that produced the crisis, it might happen after experiencing Whitaker's normalizing approach that they go home confused regarding the parameters with which they defined their relationship as abnormal. The causes of the crisis, so well-catalogued by them, will dissolve in the wind, and each spouse will have questions that seem not to have any connection with the present problems. It could happen that the couple, who started their session with mutual accusations, without even noticing, will begin fantasizing and question themselves about the first time they met, about their engagement, about the marriage ceremony. Suddenly, somewhat further on during the session, the two spouses will find themselves in a "displaced" time and could jump even further back, associating their marriage to their parents' marriage. They will become children as they try to find meaning in their birth and in their relationship to their parents.

Whitaker proposed an associative modality based on producing a trip backward via true and real "leaps in time" that upset the concentration on the meanings established by the couple over time and reproduced with greater rigidity in situations of stress. If we unblock the present, then we can play at musing about "similar selves," traversing family history and stories, and afterward alighting on the present again, enriched by a perception of the time in movement.

Bringing a family of origin to a session allows for confrontation in a more efficient way, even if indirectly, of the self-deceits constructed over the years by adults. These attitudes embody intent to falsify, to cover up the real needs of an individual, and have evolved since adolescence or even earlier in very severe cases. They are proposed during meaningful relationships qualified by strong and durable affective ties such as are shared by a couple. For example, an emotional cutoff never completely resolved or a lack of differentiating oneself from one's family through the acquisition of a personal ("I") status could damage the foundation and the development of the process of intimacy of the couple. As confirmation of this, we have often witnessed that establishment of a vertical bond (father-son) allows us, almost automatically, to raise for discussion a nonauthentic process of couple intimacy. This also explains why profound changes in the way people perceive themselves happen on the occasion of important losses, such as deaths, separations, and permanent invalidity. These losses can unleash the power of undoing many false constructions of an individual's reality and unshackle the capacity to unveil the true self of each individual. This internal voyage does not allow the continuation of the highly conflictual game that often characterizes the relationships of distressed couples.

DIVORCE FOLLOWING THERAPY: THE HOUSE OR THE DOGHOUSE?

James, a 50-year-old medical doctor, came to therapy because of a very serious couple crisis. In conversation it appeared very clear that the pain and despair of this man was not only based on the loss of his partner, but even more was filled up with the absolute lack of personal and professional esteem. Therapists frequently witness situations of great emotional disarray attributed to the consequence of the crisis of a couple or the threat of a separation. This man could not see or experience anything other than the weight of the breaking up of the marriage bond. He seemed to live exclusively to defend his little son from the claws of an "evil and irresponsible" mother. Placing his life in order entailed substantial time and quite a bit of work.

In a meeting to which his sisters were invited, the core of his developmental history emerged; he had no memory at all of his mother, who had died when he was 10 years old. James did not recall a smile, a look, a caress from his mother. He was adamant in affirming that all that past had nothing to do with his conjugal problems or, as a matter of fact, with his mother and any memory of her. James, however, buries the emotional connection to his sisters, seldom sees them because of their two hours distance from Rome, and excuses the lack of understanding because they are females. If therapy led to restarting a relationship with them, "They would end up treating me like a baby!" This was a cue that to begin setting the basis for reconstructing the "I" of this man, the therapist must reaccess a context in which James can think of himself when he was a baby, in the presence of his sisters. He has to touch the defensive wall that he has built around himself over time to feel less pain for his loss. This will become the true, historical memory of his own development. He must exit the feeling that he lost everything in his marriage, and take the bigger risk of losing his personal identity in a process of progressive alienation from self. In this sense, the crisis of the couple that brings him to therapy poses a unique occasion to reorganize his own affective world and to shed the caricature-like image of a "chronic loser."

After two years, James's life changes direction. He accepts the separation with dignity and not as a beaten dog. He learns to play with his boy and stops acting like a "nervous babysitter." He substitutes the idea of living in a small apartment that he furnishes to his taste for the idea of a dog's house (a dormitory). He begins practicing as a doctor again, with joy, and starts visiting his sisters. True, he has not been able to visit the cemetery, where his mother is buried, with his sisters, but the emotional cutoffs in relation to his mother seem to have now become at least in part resolved.

From the following fragment of the evaluation phone call, it seems evident that James has again found the road to joy and now looks at reality with a newly found sense of humor:

JAMES: (Answering the phone.) It's nice hearing from you. I would like to tell you that I really appreciated your calm services, which left a nice memory in me. Besides what you led us to do, you did it with a sense of professionalism, I would even say, with affection.
THERAPIST: I'm happy about that.
JAMES: Would you like to know how things are going?
THERAPIST: Yes.
JAMES: Well, we have followed all that we decided in the sessions. I am now living by myself.
THERAPIST: In a house, not in a doghouse?

JAMES: Yes, a "doghouse," but nicely furnished.
THERAPIST: Meaning, a beautiful doghouse?
JAMES: A doghouse in its dimensions, but I consider it a rummy doghouse. There's a nice terrace, a human doghouse....
THERAPIST: Then, it's not a dormitory?
JAMES: (Laughing.) It's very cute.
THERAPIST: I'm happy for that.
JAMES: I began living this separation the wrong way because I kept a bitter resentment, at least until the beginning of this year. I really disliked this because I really had attained the perfect knowledge that this separation was needed. Rationally, I knew. Irrationally, I continued the resentment. The most beautiful dimension is that, for now, Matthew is completely calm. This has been the least expected and most pleasant aspect. He was extremely nervous during the last days [of our living together], but, since the separation, is very joyful. We divide the time. Well, we practically keep him three and a half days each. In this way, he enjoys both his parents.
THERAPIST: Meaning, you are really respecting the established plan!
JAMES: The most beautiful thing is to see how serene and happy the boy is, how he plays. I really try to do the activities that amuse him.
THERAPIST: The way you talk, you have come out of it quite well.
JAMES: (Laughing.) I filled myself with Prozac...
THERAPIST: Then it is true that this Prozac is a winner.
JAMES: It is a winner because, if I didn't take it, I would not have succeeded. Anyhow, I have now entered the real dimension of my life.
THERAPIST: Is it the Prozac, or is it you?
JAMES: At first, it was the Prozac. Afterward, I continued walking by myself, and I discovered that I am not that bad being alone. Before, I used to look at it as a tragedy, to have to separate from Veronica. But I have come to understand that all this tragedy does not exist from my personal angle and, even from the economic one, we manage. And so, all those problems of having to sacrifice the child, of not being able to see him, of being afraid of the loneliness, of feeling like a piece of junk... Nothing of this has happened.

At the end, James and the therapist discuss how his attitude toward his medical practice and his relationship with colleagues at the hospital has changed.

JAMES: Before saying goodbye, I would like to say something else: I thank you for helping me discover my mother.
THERAPIST: Oh, this is a last-minute tasty bit.
JAMES: I did not go to the cemetery, and I don't think that I will. But I think about her, and this makes me happy.
THERAPIST: Oh, now you remember that you had a mother. What happened? Tell me! The way it was before?
JAMES: No, before she did not exist. You once asked me suddenly: "Do you remember anything about your mother?" I did not remember anything. I was shocked by this. Not that I remember a lot of things now, but now I like to remember something, and this has given me serenity, not to see her as nonexistent.
THERAPIST: Did you ever tell your sisters what you are telling me now?
JAMES: No, that's not possible, not yet. There also is the fact that our father is now dying. This too has been a problem. I cried Christmas day as I saw him very dependent on us. I had been very dependent on my father; now I was very moved at seeing him so dependent on us. I discovered parents in their true roles, and not in the role of a child that I myself carried with me up to when I was 50. This happened because of his present sickness. The discovery of my mother is one that I owe to you, and that's really nice.

The rigidity of the couple can be used to search for those intergenerational blocks that seem to weigh down the evolution of a couple and the development of the family in question.

Many years of research and clinical work with families have shown that the psychosocial pact stipulated by the couple at the time of its formation and during its development contains a truly transforming force. It represents an enrichment for each of the partners only in as much as each adult individual has attained a stage of sufficient differentiation of self and personal autonomy regarding his or her family of origin.

Love, respect, loyalty, compassion toward one's own parents and brothers and sisters often become highly confused with prevarication, excessive dependence, prejudice, omnipotence, undervaluation, and inversion of roles. No doubt, the condition of an adult proves the most difficult one. Structurally, an adult must maintain boundaries regarding the parents' hierarchial positions, and this must occur likewise in relation to the children. During our therapeutic work, we often meet with stereotyped ideas relative to the supposed fragility or competence of this or that generation. For example, some parents think that children in general must be protected and sustained by the grown-ups because they are weaker and less equipped emotionally. They may also perceive the older generation as suffering from being exposed to strong affective traumas while the adult seems to be overwhelmed by the sense of responsibility of any tense and engaging situation.

Truly, we remark almost daily about the vulnerability and isolation of adults who seem to be trapped by what Horney (1950) calls "the pride system." They tend to be disconnected from their intergenerational bonds and unable to look for help and support from their extended families and from their children. An adult in difficulty tends to sever the most vital connections one has with children and one's own parents. The children, whom the adult loves so much, end up being used and often abused in their attempts to help and to detour conflicts, but they rarely are listened to as competent interlocutors. The elderly are considered too old or in too bad shape to be involved in an adult's difficulties, or they are perceived as so "negative" that it is thought better to keep them completely on the outside. In both instances, these basic prejudices are tied to an idealized image of marriage and family, an image that must be strenuously maintained even in the face of life events and transformations that seem to undermine its foundation. Adults know that the reality is less edifying. However, children and family must believe the appearances. Thus, each partner will progressively feel more and more lonely in the search for meaning and new direction for personal and family life. The difficulty in being authentic and coherent toward one's family of origin is often connected to a strong affective dependence that was never or incompletely resolved in relation to one's parents. Williamson (1981) described this as a process of *intergenerational intimidation*. How can we help the adult to become a real adult?

HAVING PARENTS TO COME TO THE THERAPY: A DRAMATIC MOVE?

Case Example
Anna reflected, "Well, there has been a change, something has changed inside. External reality does not change, but the interior one does. It is difficult to tell what happened in the past three years; at a certain moment one feels different. It occurred very gradually. At 15 years of age, we decided to get married, on the school benches. We had a very long affective bond before our marriage, and we were really too young. It was very difficult for each of us to find an identity in this suffocating relationship as a couple. When we came to therapy, for me it was the last effort before separation. I felt that I was just a quarry, trapped in a net. I had to find a way to free myself, and Rocco kept oppressing me with all his speeches, his requests for attention."

Rocco continued, "We came to therapy in the worst state possible, after meeting with a psychologist friend of ours, in order to mitigate the shock of our crisis. I was convinced, right from the beginning, that there was a wrong relationship between the two of us: I, Rocco, the eternal kid, and Anna, the mommy. I wanted to shed this baby out of myself, but I just couldn't. I was obsessed by this idea that I was a child, growing more desperate with time, until the moment I understood that my sense of desperation belonged to me, and not the game of the child and the mother."

Thus, Anna and Rocco described the beginning of their couple therapy three years after finishing it, during a first follow-up encounter. The reasons that led them to ask for therapy represent a paradigm of many couples in crisis who, after years of marriage, do not know where to vent their grief. Neither do they fathom how to evaluate what they have built together. A sense of loss and of suffering lead to irritation in the lines of communication that have marked the relationship of the couple for a long time. Anna feels hunted down and wants to escape. Rocco reproaches himself for acting as a child, but at the same time he confronts Anna's proposal of separation by reinforcing his role of the terrified kid.

Seven years later, some 10 years after the couple's therapy, Anna and Rocco are seen again in a research encounter. Both willingly agreed to relate the subsequent development of their story. We hear the voice and the feelings of the two, who are now some 50 years old, calm and alive in their judgments and in the descriptions of their own evolutionary stages. They appear very much changed physically, almost younger looking than 10 years before. Rocco shaved his mustache, symbolizing more than a simple physiognomic change in his personal history.

ANNA: I recall a lot of suffering...a great malaise which in part already existed previously, but that burned deeper with the therapy. I remember this as a sad period of my life, something I would like to live with in a different way. I remember it as an unpleasant period. It's not the fault of the therapist. (She laughs.) But I really felt bad...

INTERVIEWER: (Addressing Rocco.) Was she [Anna] the only one who felt bad, or...?

ROCCO: Naturally, there was suffering. We came to clarify something. There was suffering between us, the couple, but, when you get things out of yourself, you recognize yourself, you find yourself, and you come here with your parents, you have to do violence to yourself...Why the parents? It's our problem. However, it is a mechanism that touches everything and affects so many things, and now you have to recognize how much one suffered because of this, because of that... Sure, it's a moment of weariness...Afterwards, good came out because you are forced by suffering to analyze yourself. At the end, you come out good, more strengthened, for sure; at least, this is my own experience.

INTERVIEWER: (Addressing Anna.) Was the participation of the parents useful?

ANNA: It was a dramatic act to tell my parents to come to therapy! It was more dramatic than to tell the children. The relationship with the children is easier than the relationship with the parents. I do not know how much I have changed, also, because now we live lives that are totally different. But sure, it helped me. To see firsthand how difficult it was, how much I was used to playing the role of the "good girl," which actually was what weighed on me and conditioned me most. This has dug a big furrow within me, this fact of having to talk to my parents about something they don't understand, for me this was a new situation... At the unripe age of 40 I discovered that I was still playing the role of a girl, and still in a position of dependence.

Discussion of Research Findings

At many conferences and other, more restricted meetings, we have heard a disconsolate James Framo tell how much pain and suffering the proposal of calling the whole family of origin to therapy awakened in each member of a couple—the same kind of remarks Anna and Rocco made. After many years of clinical work with couples and families, we have been able to realize that, for an adult, the idea of calling on his or her family of origin to join in therapy poses by far the most painful and most difficult therapeutic intervention. And this, incredible as it may sound, emerges as a universal feeling mobilizing very strong emotions quite similar even among people of different sexes, genders, cultures, ethnic backgrounds, social classes, religions, and political convictions.

An adult's requesting help from parents and from siblings touches on wounds and feelings about exclusion and the generations. These feelings are reopened during a situation of vulnerability because the one asking is lying prostrate before a real-life difficulty. The presence of the other spouse modifies the affective context of the session, and prevents the sort of group regression in which one can easily reconstruct the "places at the table," where one can resume playing the games and roles that were abundantly tested during the time all lived together. The purpose changes to the one Anna describes. At age 40, she discovers during a session with her family of origin that she continues to play the role of daughter, that she is still a dependent person, and this is another part of her self-deceit.

Anna realizes that she has betrayed herself in her development as an adult, necessitating separating herself from her condition of daughter and uniting herself to a man in a more authentic manner. Anna feels that she is a daughter in her family of origin. We have coined the expression *chronic son or daughter* to underline this attitude of dependence. And yet, Anna constantly plays the mommy to Rocco, the Rocco who, because of his insecurity, goes along with the game by continually acting out the part of the baby that Anna must take care of. Anna has discovered that she still plays the role of daughter. This is nothing extraordinary; dependence represents a feeling experienced for a long time. In therapy, she lives this role in a ritualized form as witnessed by her partner, in the presence of her parents and of a third qualified person, who can be trusted. This allows her to make the leap.

The confirmation of this process derives from the experience of evaluating the sessions, viewed from a distance, as clients recall some important passages of therapy (its ritual aspects) as if it had happened "two weeks ago," and not as events that took place many years before. All this emerges in a context of gratitude toward a therapist, who has a genuine desire to be useful to families and to other therapists, by describing to them their own processes of progress.

From the description of many families, it seems that the awareness of what is not working springs up at a point of no return, in an instant, as a bolt from the blue. Consequently, we could think that change happens in a very short time, say, an hour, a day, a week. The gestation period of an individual transformation period requires time—as if life trained itself to suffer in order not to change anything, until the magical moment of the breakup, when one feels like facing the risk of suffering in order to change. Inviting families of origin to therapy often produces resistance and destructive fantasies. However, more comfortably, when encountered in an authentic fashion, this experience also becomes a most transforming experience on subjective and relational levels.

Time as an Indicator of Change: From the "No" of the Couple to the Intergenerational "No"

Case Example
Unfortunately, three years after Mario and Laura had made strides in therapy, Mario died suddenly, before his sixtieth birthday. Mrs. Vianini came with her son for a follow-up session. Marco is now a teenager and seems more mature than his age. His father passed away six months before this session of a stomach tumor, the same kind of tumor that six months

previously had taken away Laura's father. Laura, at the age of 45 years, became a widow, after having made a serious effort to alter a couple relationship that had become colder with the passage of time. She has changed quite a bit, and not only because of the recent mourning in her life. Calmly, she describes how her rapport with Mario had changed during his last years. Clearly, losing her husband prematurely has made her suffer greatly. In the late years of his life, he had become more affectionate and friendly, thanks also to the therapist.

"The positive aspect was to come to the therapy session, to sit down and talk. My husband didn't like to talk; it wasn't easy to dialogue with him. In the session, what I had wished to tell him in many years of monologue just came out." She describes therapy as a reassuring space in several ways: "I felt supported, freed by someone [the therapist] who had understood and had shown me the way to obtain access to my husband. It helped me to be able to talk about so many issues: we were there; we had to listen. I could not escape. As we came out of a session, Mario was more affectionate, more charming, I could say. He began listening more to me, he showed more esteem for me, and I stopped *growling*." Laura and Mario had asked to come to therapy after 14 years of marriage. Their difficulties with Marco, their 11-year-old son who had been thrown into the role of mediator between the two, provided the occasion for this. These difficulties soon developed in the two spouses a sense of coldness and distance from one another.

Laura smiles now and jokes with the therapist. She says that she no longer needs to *growl* when she talks. She refers to the shrill laughter, sometimes underlined during the session, with which she had often attacked Mario over many long years. Mario had always kept himself exasperatingly calm, and this made Laura explode. Even when he spoke of his car accident that left him with one arm, not even then did he show any trait of emotion. Had he been there in the follow-up session, perhaps he would have said that those therapeutic sessions that he had agreed to participate in "strictly to make Laura happy" had made him reflect on his own rigidity and on his own alienation from feelings—the Mario who had grown up in the cement of the construction company that his father directed so authoritatively, keeping himself aloof from his sons, who had been "prisoners" of the same logic of "all together, all apart." Maybe he would have said that was the only experience he had managed not to escape by taking refuge in his work. He had not missed one meeting during two years of therapy.

Laura witnessed the change in Mario. "It is very important to know the members of one's family in order to understand one's own personality. When after so many difficulties Mario brought his family here [to therapy] . . . I did not know how useful that was to him, but I know that it gave him courage, because, well, I didn't expect him to be able to want to know his family." The feeling of surprise at this "great courage" that reactivates the discourse so often interrupted in the couple usually enables the couple to restart the dialogue through indirect pathways, such as through the children, and even more through the slow sharing of complex processes of differentiation in their respective families of origin.

Mario's story was full of denials and suffering. His mother was incapacitated, and spent the 29 years before her death in bed. His father had consecutively involved his four sons in his business and imposed on them his philosophy of detachment from one another. Thus, the boys, out of respect for the father, ignored one another while working in the same firm. In this light, we can understand Mario's difficulty in asking for anything for himself since he lived in a place where all must work and ask for nothing. Mario's calm and self-control were shattered when he was asked to bring his father and his brothers to a therapy session. His "No!" resembled the cry of despair of someone who has to resign himself to living in deep loneliness within the walls of his father's business.

Mario considered the request impossible; giving a thousand reasons not to accept it. He began getting entangled in his own words, stuttering like a little boy caught up in emotions that were too big for him, unaware of what he was doing. During several sessions, the therapist and he played as if he were calling his father on the phone. The therapist disconnected the phone and gave the receiver to Mario, saying: "Call him now that the phone is disconnected. Show me after dialing how many numbers your hand begins shaking and when your face starts getting white." Then: "Who is going to talk first? What do you think that your daddy will say as he hears your voice? You know, there's a way of asking that is sure to get a refusal. You know a lot of tricks that you learned to receive no as an answer, after so many years of un-life together. Have you noticed how your own son Marco is learning fast from you how not to ask for anything, so that he may not get a no for an answer from Daddy? This is a family school, isn't it? Besides daddy business, there also is the school of no's, fabricated at home. And your wife still persists in desiring you to say yes! You, who are a professional of refusals."

Mario overcame his own resistance. He himself invited his father and his brothers to come to a session. The wall that separated these suffering men seemed to become vulnerable. For the first time, a family taboo was broken. Such requests may be explicitly verbalized; they do not have to be made in implicit terms, with the tacit expectation of receiving a refusal. For the first time, too, the members of the family of origin talked about the affective content of their relationships. The experience of Mario's "invalidity" was clarified, an invalidity that existed before the incident.

Even more surprising, we learned how Laura recently succeeded in reestablishing positive contact with her father after she was able to forgive him in her heart for his many actions of treason against the family. She had discovered an answer to the question that remained in suspense in Framo's (1990) article, "Daddy, What Are We to Each Other?" At the same time, her rapport with her mother was more unrestrained; it no longer was weighed down by the responsibilities and mistakes of the past.

Having Mario's parents come to a session proved quite a success. But this did not make it easier for Laura to invite her mother since doing this reactivated the remembrance of all the vicissitudes of her family. But it opened up new modalities that led each to feel the needs of the other. When Laura was a child, her family had to face serious economic difficulties because of the financial collapse of her father's business. All the members of the family had to leave their home in the city and hurriedly flee into Switzerland. Here, thanks to a family friend, Laura's father managed to rebuild a dignified life for himself. However, her mother, Rita, notwithstanding outward appearances, could not adapt to the new environment and always craved to return to her country, where she would be near her own parents. All this would have stayed a wish if a more serious problem had not arisen. Laura discovered that her father was having a sexual relationship with a friend of hers. Feeling doubly betrayed in her affective ties by her father and her friend, Laura decided to return to Italy. Her mother and her brother, Michele, followed her. Laura assumed the role of competent person in the family and became a point of reference and support for her mother and her brother, although they scarcely acknowledged this.

Finally, after many years of reciprocal suffering and many misunderstandings between each other, mother and daughter found the courage to overcome the affective emptiness and their emotional distance, looking for more reciprocal confidence. This allowed mother and daughter to find the strength to contact Laura's father once again and to forgive him before his death.

Follow-Up 13 Years Later

Marco, 26 years old, goes to the university and works in his father's paternal business. He is engaged and lives by himself in an apartment near Laura. The latter has lived with a partner for a few years now and has the aspect of a mature woman, reflective and able to think about the events of life with serenity and resignation. Laura often meets with her mother, who lives in another country, and with her brother, who now has his own family and is totally independent, physically and emotionally, from their mother. Laura's current preoccupation centers around Marco's work because he displays the same paternal problem of tense and difficult relations with his uncles in the business as his father did. Is it really pleasant to see how mother and son tell us about their development many years later: They share with the therapist the memories of difficult stages of their family life with freedom and openness as they talk to a significant member of their social network. Laura, laughing, observed, "Well, there isn't any doubt that one also grows. You get clobbered, you set the helmet on your head. What do you think, Dr. Andolfi? From the little straw hat . . ." The image of the little straw hat worn by Laura when she first came to the therapy sessions synthesizes the passage, across the years, and attaches the experience of change to the helmet (because of being clobbered on the head) with which she has defended herself against the difficulties of life.

When Marriage Is in Crisis from the Beginning

During follow-up evaluations, what we heard in the therapy sessions often reaffirmed that the marital crisis had begun right from the beginning of the marriage, sometimes during the honeymoon, or even during the time of preparation for the marriage. What is really surprising is that these incidents are spoken about 20 to 30 years after the wedding. We ask ourselves how a couple managed to stay together, to raise children, to share so many life experiences while knowing that they do not understand each other. If it is true that two people get married by promising mutual respect and unconditional fidelity to one another, it is also true that the life of a couple is unbearable if one does not feel understood by the person one chooses to live with. And yet, they live together and they do not change, marriage becomes an affective prison. As in all restrictive situations, one then looks for affective alternatives and escapes in children, work, friends, and sometimes in extramarital relations that do not have the strength to bring about clarification of the situation or the transformation of the relationship at its root through a decisive cutoff. Often, the partners opt for the choice of staying together in a bad situation rather than face the fearsome tunnel of feeling the pain alone, a *conditio sine qua non* to find again a personal direction in his/her own life.

In many cases, couple therapy becomes confused from the beginning because the two do not agree to pursue it. If there were agreement between them, some hope might materialize because they would have arrived at the decision of experiencing something together. This misunderstanding about finding a common ground and a shared motivation is mirrored by a psychotherapist, when a lack of understanding and a faulty grasp of a hierarchy of models and interventions result in colluding with the confusion of couples in difficulty. For example, we have many times witnessed how, in the course of a conjugal crisis, the choice of individual therapy, for one or for both of the spouses, paves the way for the development of a further distance and of lack of communication in a couple.

The reasons are easily understood. If dialogue is impossible, dialogue that would make one listened to and understood by the other, then it is better to go to a therapist to enlist listening, dialogue, and understanding. In the great majority of cases, this understanding third party who is so available and understanding to one of the spouses comes to represent a further barrier between the partners, sometimes producing an even greater feeling of affective exclusion than when one partner finds a lover. This occurs so frequently that, luckily, many therapists prefer not to initiate therapy with one individual when they notice that the crisis of a couple is so great that it requires, first and foremost, therapy for the two. Afterwards, if necessary, individual sessions may be decided on.

Research on Initial and Perduring Difficulties

In the first therapy session 10 years earlier, a couple explored why they felt bad and were going to therapy.

WIFE: We've been in crisis right from the start of our marriage.... He has never been able to understand me: I remember the first time we had a sexual relationship, which wasn't even complete, I felt as if I was being violated, something I was forced to do, something I wasn't into, where I suffered from Angelo's aggressiveness. I had grown up in a family in which my father adored me and where we were all very united and respectful toward one another. Angelo's family is a violent family. Angelo, who is an only son, was treated worse than what they could do to a dog. I was learning many useful things from individual therapy, and he took me away from my therapy and forced me to come to Dr. Andolfi.

HUSBAND: We have always had big problems about intimacy, although we are closely connected in other things, such as the house, the children... I saw how my wife was intelligent, good, everything was all right in her, so the error must have been mine alone. I was always working, and Marta never appreciated what I did. She was always accusing me because of the way my family treated us. I remember the first time we made love; it seemed as if I were raping her, and afterward our sexual life has always been like that. If I only touched her, she would instantly stiffen. I believe that a couple dialogue is valid, someone to listen to us and tell us whether we are doing right or wrong. Separated, meaning, for us to go to individual therapies [Marta kept insisting that Angelo should go individually to a parallel therapy], no I think that we cannot do it. And then, we have the children. For them this is the only way to solve the problem. Alone I would have solved the problem in a different way, maybe the wrong way.

From these brief statements it is evident that after 15 years of marriage, this couple did not allow solid affective ties to grow between them, ties that should be marked by trust and mutual respect. What keeps together so many couples who seem incapable of growing together? It is true that the birth and the affective needs of children during early infancy use a lot of parent energies and centralize the interests of everyone. Because of this, it is not rare that a couple's crisis becomes "put on ice" during that time; it will resurface, with greater intensity, a little later and, even more so, during the children's preadolescence, when the children are deeply engrossed in school and outside friendships. It is often said that the children can cause division between the parents, or can at least cause tensions within and bereavement about their conjugal life.

No doubt, the passage from being a couple to the formation of a family represents a dramatic shift in the intimate experiences of each spouse in relation to the other. However, based on the conclusions of our research, we affirm that children divide their parents to the extent that a division already exists. The growing up of a child only amplifies the conflicts that already are there in embryo in a couple. However, in many cases, when a child assumes parental functions from the time of being small, affective compensation takes place, as if the immaturity of a parent could be balanced by the hyperresponsibility of a child, who can truly sustain the weight of the grown-ups.

When a marriage fails, the premises with which one person ties oneself to a companion are often disturbed, as if a partner were chosen on the basis of scarce personal esteem, as if one were just looking for affective compensation and adjustments that, as time goes by, show themselves to be unreliable. At times, it appears that partners would rather settle for such compensations and adjustments than offer to exchange current difficulties for developing what is best in them. (On this theme of choice of partner, see Angelo, 1999.)

The situation of the empty nest, the condition that happens when older children leave home, produces a very dramatic crisis of development for those couples who had placed their disagreements, misunderstandings, and affective aloofness behind "the needs of the children," and who all of a sudden find themselves alone, without the "protection" of the children. It is not by chance that many requests for couple therapy eventuate from the difficult situation produced when children become more autonomous during adolescence.

The motivation for couple therapy is very rare when there is no guarantee that a minimal accord will be reached by the spouses. Asking together for help is a proof of relative understanding, and it is sufficient to advance, explore, and try to find other areas of agreement in the conjugal relation. Unfortunately, it is more common that one of the spouses pushes ahead for couple therapy while the other assumes the role of a cotraveler, or even becomes an obstacle to a project considered to be a menace to his or her own stability.

This is the case of the Di Livio couple. The wife feels that she has been plucked out of individual therapy to enter a forced context of couple therapy. Notwithstanding the great effort made by the therapist to rebalance a project that was very much unbalanced, after three years of therapy, during which the history of the families of origin were probed, after studying the migratory processes of Marta, the sexual aggressiveness of Angelo and his problems with work, and the school development of the children, the original "vice" was still a boulder weighing down the growing process of each of the spouses and their capacities to make a clear decision on their future as a couple, especially now that the children are grown and are students at the university. The Di Livio couple agree to come to an evaluation of research, on the condition that they come separately! This is already a piece of important information regarding their mutual trust. The meeting takes place some seven years after the end of the therapy. They still live together.

Follow-Up
INTERVIEWER: What was useful in the therapy?
WIFE: I do not know whether therapy with Angelo was useful or not. I have to be honest, when I was brought into therapy, I was not ready . . . It opened a road for me, because from then onwards I looked for what was more in my reach; I continued the road that had been interrupted, and I returned to individual therapy. The aspect that I find more intensively productive, something that has often come back to me during the last years, is a sentence said by Dr. Andolfi on the phone, when I was crying desperately because of my sexual difficulties with Angelo and his violent way of approaching me: "Lady, have you ever looked inside yourself to see what is crooked in you in the way you go into an intimate relation?"
HUSBAND: I believe that therapy was more efficacious for me than for us as a couple, even if, by rebound, there was some usefulness for the couple too. . . . With time, I understood how I undervalued myself, how I made fall on myself every one of my wife's problems. Therapy with Dr. Andolfi was useful to me; even the "slaps" were useful because they

made me wake up. Therapy was very useful to me in relation to the children: I first felt like a completely inadequate father, now they listen to me more.

INTERVIEWER: What changed afterward?

WIFE: I can't say that much changed.... It looked as if for an instant something had changed, but the mechanisms within our family did not change. Our children detached themselves from our problems, in the sense that they now say: "If you two have problems, well, they are your problems." When I came here to therapy, I was quite sure of myself, in the sense that [I felt] I am a first-class woman. I am the best, the most intelligent, and my husband is nothing. Coming here, I reevaluated my husband. I understood that, everything considered, I did not want the separation, and that quite a few qualities in my husband are okay with me. After the family session, my husband's family was transformed.... When I see them, well, I don't jump for joy, but it's okay now. Before, it was a real torment to see them. My relationship to my own family of origin also changed after the family session. Before, I couldn't stand my mother at all. Seeing her, I would instantly get goose flesh, but that no longer happens now. Before, I thought she was stupid; I no longer think that now.

HUSBAND: Now there are longer periods of understanding than before. We argue every six months, or every year. When it happens, it's a real crash. But I no longer feel like a failure and that she is always right. The fact that, at the end of each crash, she tells me that she wants to leave me no longer makes me feel bad as it did before. The session with my family was a little heavy, but I got rid of the hostility that I felt toward my dad.... I now see him as a poor old man, and I feel sorry for him. I no longer feel a lot of rage on account of what I had to suffer because of him.

INTERVIEWER: What was the problem for this couple?

THERAPIST: The general problem for which they came to see me was really that she wanted to free herself from him. She was kind of a frustrated housewife, but she wasn't even completely aware of her personal assets and resources. Angelo did everything to make the family business go on, and he presented himself as the true designated patient, in every way, the one who was always wrong. They came as a couple in despair.

INTERVIEWER: What were the difficulties?

THERAPIST: Their greatest difficulties were structural: how to free him from such a depreciative idea of self, from a devastating and violent image of a family of origin in which his best game was to play on the secondary advantages of being a "bastard son." My difficulty was to make him accept me as an assertive man, assertive, but not abusive as his father had most probably been. As far as the wife was concerned, it was extremely difficult to help her come out of her role of the pseudo-emancipated woman, to make her feel her deep insecurity, and how she had closed herself against the world outside, and also her experience of being a molested girl, which has accompanied her for her whole life. The difficulty was even greater because Marta had not chosen me as her therapist. This fault weighed heavily on the whole therapeutic process.

INTERVIEWER: How do you see the future of the Di Livio couple?

THERAPIST: I see it as I see the future of many other couples where separation is impossible, even if talk about it runs through the years, or if a scapegoat is made by one of the other. It is difficult to discover an intimacy that has never been fashioned over the course of many years or living together. This makes necessary constantly staying on the lookout in order not to feel overrun by the other. An evolutional step might suddenly appear with the death of the parents of one or the other, when the implicit pact between a child and his or her parent is loosened. Then it might be possible to recapture the direction of one's life and to feel less tied down by the weight of history. Certain knots might be undone, knots that one never before had dared to touch.

UNEXPECTED TURNS OF EVENTS

Sometimes, changes eventuate even when we do not expect them to, as illustrated in the following letter and discussion.

Dear Doctor,

I don't know whether you remember me. I am the oldest son of the family from Bologna who came to you in 1979, I believe. I was then 20 years old. My brother and I have opened an Italian language school for foreigners, and we live with our fiancées. My parents still live together, and they seem happy. My brother and I read many books on psychology, family therapy (Bandler and Grinder, Erickson and company) because we are excellent teachers of Italian, but we want to become better. Reading these books is useful. I have been thinking about writing to you for some time, and now I know why—because I want to tell you that you did a pretty good job for us. You were really good. In those days, I would have shattered everything, but you did not allow me. I think you had great sensitivity, patience, and humility since nobody realized that you got the mechanism started. I now think that I know how you did it, but that's another story. Thank you in the name of the other three. Maybe they haven't yet understood how good you were. You can place us among your successes.

Best wishes,

Giorgio Arancio
Bologna, May 31, 1991

By the time Andolfi received this letter, the research group had already enrolled the Arancio family in the subgroup of unfinished therapies and was about to contact the family again, after more than 10 years of silence, to invite them for a session to evaluate the results. The reason we decided to interrupt the therapy was tied up with the feelings of the therapist, who had dismissed the Arancio family in a premature way, at a time when the couple problem had not yet been resolved. In fact, the conclusion of therapy came shortly after a consultation with Whitaker in 1982, requested by Andolfi. After two years of therapy (to which, as usual, their children had always been invited and, occasionally, the members of their families of origin), Andolfi found himself in a stalemate position in relation to the Arancio couple. As often happened with other families and in other circumstances, Whitaker set himself as an element of separation between the family and the therapist to create a break in the therapeutic system, in the strenuous conviction that the family had to take the initiative to become in charge of their processes of change. This proved valid for Whitaker in the case of the Arancio family.

After more than two years of therapeutic sessions, Andolfi was convinced that the positions had become crystallized, that the couple was now strongly dependent on the therapist, and that, consequently, the therapy had to be interrupted. In those years, consultation within a therapeutic process had not yet been well-codified. Not infrequently, therapists found themselves in greater difficulty after a consultation for the simple reason of being unable to assume a position different from the one of the consultant, especially when the latter was a highly charismatic person. (For more information on the use of consultation in family therapy, see Andolfi & Haber, 1994.)

Andolfi did not always share Whitaker's absolute principle that the family is always capable of finding the resources to transform themselves. However, from the late 1970s to the middle of the 1990s, his clinical work was heavily influenced by Whitaker. Many families who then participated in this kind of research affirmed later that they felt as if they had been left alone halfway through the process. Andolfi is convinced that "therapy really begins when it ends," meaning that therapists cannot possibly be witnesses and observers of the changes that happen in so many families in therapy because the times of real and meaningful changes take much longer and prove more complex than clinicians sometimes think. To quote Giorgio, therapy is useful to "engage that kind of mechanism" that allows a family to elaborate afterward and over time some deep personal and relational changes.

Nevertheless, we were really surprised at receiving Giorgio's letter. It taught us once again that our assumptions about family, about the effects of therapy, and even about the meaning of our therapeutic role are at best partial and incomplete. Whenever possible, confronting personal presuppositions with those of clients and colleagues proves valuable.

In this case, it was easy to answer Giorgio's letter inviting the Arancio family to convene for a follow-up, in the hope of including them in our "therapeutic successes," as Giorgio had put it. But we needed to talk to the other three family members, those who maybe "had not understood." A follow-up session took place in 1993, two years after Giorgio's letter. In this case, therapy had been strongly desired by the wife, Vera, while the husband, Rodolfo, came with a feeling of skepticism to make Vera happy.

WIFE: (Recalling why therapy had begun.) It is natural that if I started this earthquake, it's because I wanted to grab Rodolfo by the ears... and carry him to a place where he had to listen to me and to spit out all that he felt about himself and about me. Only then, after vomiting all that icy silence of so many hard-swallowed years, could I face reality, whatever that reality was. At least, this is my side of it.

HUSBAND: I agreed to come because of Vera's insistence. I was a bit skeptical. I was always like that. But I think that I am no longer what I was, right? I remember that I was very depressed during those years. I felt a desire, so to speak, to die. I remember that Dr. Andolfi had suggested to me that I record my more somber thoughts in a notebook and bring them to him during the sessions.

GIORGIO: The main problem for me was that there was a great confusion at home in those times. They were often fighting, a continuous fight that reflected on me and on Giuseppe [the younger son]. I remember that in those days I had this idea: Both of them were okay to me if only they were separated. I would have pushed for a separation, and I was happy when they decided to go to therapy.

GIUSEPPE: I remember that the first time I was a little perplexed. Afterward, I came rather willingly. I, too, was rather scared with the fights at home between my parents. After the first time [in therapy], I understood better what it was about. We were given homework to do with the tape recorder, and we had short meetings to do it. From then on, I can say that it was an effort of collaboration by everybody.

INTERVIEWER: What was effective in the therapy, and what has changed since?

HUSBAND: It showed us what kind of people we really are. With time, we felt that we had changed as a couple. We love one another more now. I came out of my situation of latency, and I look at life in a more serene way.

WIFE: There has been a gradual intimate reapproaching between us because, as we were leaving here, it was as if our hair was sticking out straight. With time, I came to understand that our problem was but one: the fact that Rodolfo played a lot with the boys, and I wasn't doing anything else anymore at home. It's as if I was jealous: I had lost my husband. The most emotional sessions were the ones with the boys present. I thought that to present our problem to them... Instead, I had to change my mind, and I discovered that the boys both had a great way of expressing themselves in a surprising way. They were very sincere. They became competent people right away. They were no longer simply our children. The younger, Giuseppe, profited from all of this right away.

GIORGIO: They are still together, and, more or less, they agree with one another. Each one of us has his or her own life, independently we could say. There were no great divisions or special tragedies.

GIUSEPPE: I agree with Giorgio. Life goes much better now, and we are two boys who feel more united as brothers. We are no longer inside the life of Mom and Dad.

INTERVIEWER: Because of the interruption of the therapy?

WIFE: When I learned that for that Monday we were no longer going to Dr. Andolfi, I felt rather disillusioned.... Maybe, I thought, it was caused by some kind of rancor and annoyance that we had given him. He gave me the sensation that it was ... coldness. He sent us away without saying anything else except, "Today we stop here!" Why did we deserve such coldness and such a hurried attitude? Why did Dr. Andolfi perform such a volte-face after the consultation with Whitaker? We felt unjustly punished on account of something that we didn't know; we felt betrayed as bad children. If Dr. Andolfi believed he had erred toward us (although I don't believe it!), and thought that everything Whitaker had said was shining gold ... wasn't it better to give us the chance of talking it over, the three of us?

HUSBAND: Even if my wife was disillusioned and mad because of the way Andolfi ended therapy ... Well, she quoted him often afterward: she would quote his sentences.

On one hand, witnessing the Arancio family 15 years after the first meeting gives us comfort when we think of the pretty good results for each member of the family. On the other hand, it also causes us to reflect on our limitations and errors as therapists. However, we consider these errors precious material on which to develop professional competence. We make a treasure of them, so we can feel better and have more respect on the human level that plays such an important role in therapeutic relationships.

RESEARCH

Andolfi regards a good therapist as an anthropologist needing curiosity to search for and uncover what is unfamiliar and needing to be known (Barletta, 2000). The reflections on therapy in this chapter exemplify a phenomenological and ethnographic approach to research. The extensive follow-up evaluations Andolfi conducted on families in therapy as a type of qualitative research on cases perceived as successfully completed, as possibly unsuccessful, and as prematurely disrupted or terminated allow for examining the effects of therapy, the vicissitudes of life and their impacts on families. They also permit exploring dynamics implicit in personal and family development that emerge over time and bear consequences for progress or impediments in therapy and living. Andolfi has been developing a research program on long-term follow-up of family treatments. We recently published a book called *Family Therapy Narrated by Families*, published by Raffaello Corina from Milan.

This is a qualitative research project based on interviewing and videotaping family units and couples after a minimum of three years from the end of therapy, through 8 to 10 years later. The same interview was applied to the therapists who were involved in the family treatment. The main questions we asked to the families in this follow-up meeting were:

- What do you remember of the therapeutic process?
- What happened with the symptom-pathology conflict that brought you in therapy?
- In your understanding, which has been the most significant change as a result of the therapeutic process?

- In the years after the therapy, how did the family/couple cope with any new family/couple stress and individual difficulties?

We applied this research project not only to families and couples who ended their treatments, but we decided to study also the reasons for treatment which was interrupted before a significant result occurred or which involved early drop out. We have done all this in order to learn from families and couples what is really effective in therapy. Therapy in general, and family therapy in particular, would benefit from increased research of this kind on the part of clinicians.

SUMMARY

Many couples confront their own conflicts in immature and irresponsible ways, conflicts that show themselves in several forms of prevarication between males and females, with consequent disturbances in the spheres of sexuality and intimacy. These same couples in difficulty frequently implement the capabilities to transform certain dysfunctional modes of relating and to detriangulate children when they are supported and helped in their searching for their own individual resources and the group resources needed to effect change.

In his work on the masculine and the feminine in psychotherapy with families, Andolfi (1996) noted that therapists often undervalue the extraordinary energies required to maintain disturbed relationships and confused generational boundaries over a long period of time. Whenever possible, we must refer to the *strength* that structures situations of relational pathology to direct it along the lines of health. If lived in a strong way, experiences of failure and loss give a feeling of integrity to both spouses, enabling them to better understand what is left in their relationship. This analysis is very important to achieving better individuation, including even the course of a possible separation.

As we have seen in this chapter, rediscovering a vital marital relationship or gathering the courage to finish an impossible marriage are both possible therapeutic tools; they require a qualitative leap and the abandonment of gender stereotypes and protective mechanisms. These are often amplified by families of origin and their network of social and friendship relationships and are sometimes reinforced by a therapist's attitudes.

REFERENCES

American Psychiatric Association. (1994). *Diagnostic and statistical manual of mental disorders* (4th ed.). Washington, DC: Author.

Andolfi, M. (1979). *Family therapy: An interactional approach.* New York: Plenum Press.

Andolfi, M. (1980). Prescribing the family's own dysfunctional rules as a therapeutic strategy. *Journal of Marital and Family Therapy, 6*(1), 29–36.

Andolfi, M. (1986). How to engage families with a rigid organization in therapy: An attempt to integrate strategic and structural interventions. In *Evolving models for family change.* New York: Guilford Press.

Andolfi, M. (1994a). The child as consultant. In M. Andolfi & R. Haber (Eds.), *Please help me with this family: Using consultants as resources in family therapy* (pp. 73–89). New York: Brunner/Mazel.

Andolfi, M. (1994b). *Il colloquio relazionale* (Relational conversation). Rome: A.P.F.

Andolfi, M. (1995). Accademia di psicoterapia della famiglia [Academy of Family Psychotherapy]. In A. Gurman & D. Kniskern (Eds.), *A cura di, Manuale di terapia della famiglia [Manuals of family therapy].* Torino, Italy: Bollati-Boringhieri.

Andolfi, M. (1996). Maschile e femminile nella psicoterapia con la famiglia (Male and female in psychotherapy with the family). In M. Andolfi, C. Angelo, & M. de Nichilo (Eds.), *Sentimenti e sistemi* (Feelings and systems) (pp. 163–184). Milan: Raffaello Cortina Editore.

Andolfi, M., & Angelo, C. (1981). The therapist as director of the family drama. *Journal of Marital and Family Therapy, 7*(3), 255–264.

Andolfi, M., & Angelo, C. (1987). *Tempo e mito nella psicoterapia familiare [Time and myth in family psychotherapy]*. Torino, Italy: Bollati-Boringhieri.

Andolfi, M., & Angelo, C. (1988). Towards constructing the therapeutic system. *Journal of Marital and Family Therapy, 14,* 237–247.

Andolfi, M., Angelo, C., & de Nichilo, M. (1989). *The myth of Atlas.* New York: Brunner/Mazel.

Andolfi, M., Angelo, C., Menghi, P., & Nicolo-Corigliano, A. M. (1983a). *Behind the family mask: Therapeutic change in rigid family systems.* New York; Brunner/Mazel.

Andolfi, M., Angelo, C., Menghi, P., & Nicolo-Corigliano, A. M. (1983b, March/April). Provocation as a therapeutic intervention. *Family Therapy Networker,* 44–48.

Andolfi, M., & Haber, R. (Eds.). (1994). *Please help me with this family: Using consultants as resources in family therapy.* New York: Brunner/Mazel.

Andolfi, M., & Zwerling, I. (Eds.). (1980). *Dimensions of family therapy.* New York: Guilford Press.

Angelo, C. (1999). La scelta del partner (The selection of the partner). In M. Andolfi (Ed.), *La crisi della coppia (The crisis of the couple)* (pp. 23–40). Milan: Raffaello Cortina.

Barletta, J. (2000, November). *An interview with master family therapist Maurizio Andolfi.* Brisbane, Queensland: Australian Catholic University.

Boszormenyi-Nagy, I., & Spark, G. (1973). *Invisible loyalties.* Hagerstown: Harper & Row.

Bowen, M. (1978). *Family therapy in clinical practice.* New York: Aronson.

Framo, J. (1982). *Explorations in marital and family therapy.* New York: Springer.

Framo, J. (1990). Dad, what are we for each other? *Contemporary Family Therapy, 3.*

Horney, K. (1950). *Neurosis and human growth.* New York: Norton.

Schnarch, D. (1997). *Passionate marriage: sex, love, and intimacy in emotionally committed relationships.* New York: Norton.

Selvini Palazzoli, M., Boscolo, L., Cecchin, G., & Prata, G. (1975). *Paradox and counterparadox.* New York: Aronson.

Vella, G., & Ruberto, A. (1980). La relazione di malafede [The relation of bad faith]. *Terapia Familiare, 8,* 7–20.

von Bertalanffy, L. (1968). *General systems theory.* New York: Braziller.

Watzlawick, P., Beavin, J. H., & Jackson, D. D. (1967). *Pragmatics of human communication: A study of interactional patterns, pathologies and paradoxes.* New York: Norton.

Whitaker, C. (1989). *Midnight musings of a family therapist.* New York: Norton.

Williamson, D. S. (1981). Personal authority via termination of the intergenerational hierarchical boundary: A "new" stage in the family life cycle. *Journal of Marital and Family Therapy, 7*(4), 441–452.

Winnicott, D. W. (1971). *Playing and reality.* New York: Basic Books.

CHAPTER 16

Existential Dilemmas and Skill Building in Couple Therapy

ADRIANA BALAGUER DUNN

Of all dilemmas of the life cycle, the existential dilemma of coupling is probably the greatest. Marriage is the only family relationship that we swear is forever and the only one that we swear is exclusive; yet it is the one relationship that is least likely to be either exclusive or forever.

—McGoldrick (1999, p. 231)

The challenges facing couples today and the fragility of the marital bond have received increasing attention over the past few decades. The rising rate of divorce, the changing role of women, the evolving expectations of both men and women, the availability of contraceptives, and the recognition of alternative pathways to couple formation have forced a redefinition of marriage and coupling. Carl Rogers (1972), in his book *Becoming Partners: Marriage and Its Alternatives*, predicted such dramatic changes, stating that the permanence of a relationship would be determined less by external social constraints and more by "the degree to which it satisfies the emotional, psychological, intellectual, and physical needs of the partners" (p. 8). As a result, an explosion of writing has occurred in both the popular and psychological press focused on helping individuals achieve satisfying couple relationships, from identifying the right partner, to enhancing relationship satisfaction, to recognizing and correcting dysfunctional interaction patterns in relationships.

Such recognition of the centrality and complexity of couple relationships has been a fairly recent development in the field of psychology and psychotherapy, however. The present chapter examines briefly the historical development of the field of couple therapy as a backdrop for exploring the current trends and challenges of engaging in therapeutic work with couples. Special attention is given to the core or existential dilemmas faced in couple formation and to the skills required to maintain successful relationships. Implications for addressing these issues in therapy are discussed.

BRIEF HISTORICAL OVERVIEW OF THE DEVELOPMENT OF COUPLE THERAPY AS A FIELD

Although discussions of the dilemmas of couple formation and couple dysfunction have roots that extend back to original developments in individual psychology, it is not until recently that couple therapy has emerged as a distinct and influential entity in the field of therapy in general. This occurred partly because, historically, psychiatrists and psychologists, while acknowledging that relationship problems existed, continued to focus on individuals and their patterns of adaptation and viewed problems within a marriage as less serious and as not necessarily requiring psychotherapy. Couple therapy or "marital counseling" was practiced primarily outside of mainstream therapeutic circles by a variety of helping professionals, including ministers, lawyers, educators, and physicians, or as a sideline occupation by psychologists and social workers (Bevilacqua & Dattilio, 2000). As a result, couple therapy grew out of a variety of fields and schools of thought, more in response to the increasing needs of couples and families for professional advice than out of an organized theoretical or clinical movement.

According to Bevilacqua and Dattilio (2000), from the 1950s through the early 1980s, although many individuals were practicing couple therapy, there did not exist a central theoretical foundation for their work. Rather, therapists tended to borrow techniques and ideas widely from a variety of individual theories and approaches with little conceptual clarity or consistency to their work. Manus (1966), in his review of the marital therapy field, described the practice of couple therapy as a technique in search of a theory. The psychoanalytic perspective followed later by object-relations theory provided the only coherent theories somewhat systematically applied to couples' issues and treatment. However, even these theoretical applications did not result in cogent ways of conceptualizing couple relationships or in clear implications for therapeutic treatment (Gurman & Jacobson, 1986).

With the advent of family-therapy theories and approaches in the 1950s, the focus began to broaden in therapeutic circles to involve more members of a family, including spouses, children, and extended family. This led to the conceptualization of the family as a system and to the recognition of reciprocal influences between individuals and those with whom they maintain close relations. Consequently, an entirely new perspective on treatment developed highlighting the relational component of individual functioning and creating space for thinking of couples as logical units of intervention. This conceptualization was further reinforced in the 1960s and 1970s as behavioral therapists began to describe the ways in which each partner's behavior influenced that of the other in a reciprocal fashion (Bevilacqua & Dattilio, 2000).

However, despite the inherent compatibility of focus between marital and family therapy approaches, couple therapy struggled to distinguish itself within the family-therapy arena. Many in the family-therapy field argued and still contend that marital therapy is best conceived as a particular variant or subcategory of family therapy that does not require the development of distinct theoretical or therapeutic approaches (Haley, 1984). In fact, most comprehensive textbooks on the theories and approaches to family therapy continue to give only very limited, if any, attention to therapeutic interventions focused specifically on couples (e.g., Becvar & Becvar, 2000; Gurman & Kniskern, 1981, 1991; M. P. Nichols & Schwartz, 1998).

In the past decade, however, the marital therapy field has burgeoned. Failure to develop satisfying intimate relationships continues to be reported as one of the most frequently expressed presenting problems in therapy (Greenberg & Johnson, 1988). As a result, significant advances have taken place in conceptual understanding, clinical application, and empirical support for the treatment of couple dysfunction (Dattilio & Bevilacqua, 2000). Couple therapy no longer persists as the disjointed field it once was; in fact, as Gurman and Jacobson (1995) have indicated, it has now come of age and exhibits conceptual, clinical, and empirical underpinnings as strong as those found in other therapeutic arenas.

Yet, the vestiges of the historical development of couple therapy remain in the fact that the field emerged along somewhat independent branches, only recently reconnected by new integrative approaches being developed. One branch, reaching back to the roots in individual psychotherapy, has retained a focus on individual development and the core existential dilemmas that impact couple development and functioning. This branch includes both the psychoanalytic perspectives, underscoring the impact of early relationship experiences on current couple functioning, and the experiential approaches, emphasizing immediate experience and the expression of emotion as central to personal and family health (Dattilio & Bevilacqua, 2000). The other branch, an outgrowth of the behaviorally oriented and marriage-counseling approaches, has sustained a greater concentration on specific couple-interaction sequences and skills that contribute to relationship success or failure. However, more recently proposed theoretical and clinical approaches represent attempts to integrate and attend to both experiential and skill-based arenas. The significance of both arenas are discussed below in the context of explicating the essential dilemmas in couple formation and development. As will become evident, all of the critical dilemmas of couple formation involve intrapsychic, experiential, and interpersonal components that jointly determine couple interactions and relationship satisfaction and success. The importance of attending to the multiple dimensions of couples' experiences is demonstrated through a clinical example using emotionally focused couple therapy (Greenberg & Johnson, 1986, 1988; Johnson & Greenberg, 1995), an effective therapeutic model for integrating experiential and systemic traditions in working with couples.

THEORETICAL CONSTRUCTS

THE PRIMACY AND COMPLEXITY OF COUPLE RELATIONSHIPS

Frankl (1965) described the couple as an especially rich field of human experience. Whether the couple relationship is viewed as a reflection of individual dynamics, the receptacle of family-of-origin issues, or an elaborate negotiation of transactional patterns and roles, its primacy in the psychological life of individuals is generally accepted as being second only to the early parent-child relationship:

> The marital relationship, representing as it does the primary adult emotional bond, is an area of life in which feelings and their communication play some of their most powerful roles. Because so much is at stake, feelings are evoked in a marital relationship as in perhaps no other. The marital relationship provides the opportunity for interdependence, the chance to have one's feelings and needs respected, and the opportunity to be the most important person to a significant other. (Greenberg & Johnson, 1988, p. 3)

Furthermore, the couple relationship not only impacts significantly on the self-definition of an individual adult but exerts both immediate and long-term influence on future generations that are the products of that union (Boszormenyi-Nagy & Spark, 1973). Research has consistently documented the negative impact of marital distress and conflict on child outcomes (Cummings & Davies, 1994; Emery, 1988; Fincham, Grych, & Osborne, 1994; Grych & Fincham, 1990) and has highlighted the importance of maintaining a positive working relationship in cases of divorce involving children (Emery, 1988; Hetherington, 1993). As Satir (1983) discerned: "The marital relationship is the axis around which all other family relationships are formed. The mates are the 'architects' of the family" (p. 2).

Judith Wallerstein and Sandra Blakeslee (1995) eloquently described the multiple components of relationship success in their book *The Good Marriage:*

> Early in this century Carl Jung told us that marriage is the most complex of human relationships. Today marriage is more fragile than ever. But I am committed to the view that if a man and a woman begin their marriage with a healthy respect for its complexity, they stand a much greater chance of success. If they can grasp the richly nuanced, subtle needs that people bring from their childhood experiences and can understand how the past connects with the present, they can build mutual understanding and love based on true intimacy. If they can see how each domain of marriage connects with every other... and if they can acknowledge the central conflicts in all marriages and the importance of friendship and nurturance in muting those conflicts, they will be well on their way toward building an enduring relationship. Finally, if they can appreciate the myriad of ways that people grow and change through the years and realize that a happy, lasting marriage is challenged and rebuilt every day then they will have acquired the only map there is for a successful lifetime journey together. (p. 15)

Given the centrality and complexity of a couple relationship, particularly in cases of long-term coupling or marriage, researchers and clinicians alike have been struggling to determine why marriages have become so fragile and how to enhance the functioning and stability of couple relationships. One way to do so is by identifying the foundational elements and dilemmas of coupling.

EXISTENTIAL DILEMMAS IN COUPLE FORMATION AND DEVELOPMENT

Autonomy versus Intimacy: I versus We
The most basic dilemma faced by individuals in the process of couple formation involves balancing intimacy and autonomy. As Whitaker and Keith (1981) realized, "At the heart of a growthful marriage is the struggle between the two spouses to remain independent 'I's' and at the same time to join in a dependent 'we'" (p. 206). Individuals come together in couple relationships to fulfill needs for closeness, contact, comfort, and intimacy. However, these needs often conflict with similarly strong but contradictory needs for separateness, autonomy, and self-definition.

Erich Fromm (1947, 1955) proposed that the basic dilemma between maintaining a unique identity and remaining related to others is not primarily a phenomenon of couple relationships but an essential aspect of the human condition from which people cannot escape: "It is the paradox of human existence that man must simultaneously seek for closeness and for independence; for oneness with others and at the same time for the preservation of his uniqueness and particularity" (1947, p. 103). According to Fromm, in achieving autonomy from instinctual drives and in developing a sense of self-awareness, the human species is cognizant of and must retain its sense of unique identity as a species and as individuals within that species. However, along with such individuation comes a feeling of aloneness that necessitates unification with other living beings. This need for relatedness forms the basis of the full range of intimate human relations, including, but not limited to, couple formation.

Fromm (1955) further depicted the ways in which such union with others might be achieved. The first is through submission. Submission results in the individual relinquishing his or her identity by becoming a part of the other and thus achieving connection. The opposite may also occur, when individuals respond by making others a part of themselves through the process of domination. A common feature of both approaches is that they result in a symbiotic relationship. In both instances, the individuals become dependent on each other to maintain the sense of closeness and, in the process, lose their integrity and freedom as individuals. Such individuals remain ultimately dependent on those to whom they submit or whom they dominate. Thus, issues of power and domination evidence difficulty in negotiating the basic dilemma of autonomy versus intimacy.

Whitaker and Keith (1981) supported Fromm's (1955) distinction between authentic and symbiotic relationships:

> Real dependency is linked to real autonomy in the same way that intimacy and separateness are linked. A symbiotic relationship is one in which there is a fixed emotional distance. The relationship controls the two persons. Thus, two married persons may appear quite autonomous, but really are not because they are dependent on the relationship remaining distant and any changes in that relationship will result in high levels of stress. (Whitaker & Keith, 1981, p. 193)

According to Fromm (1955), the only way to achieve union with others while retaining a sense of integrity and individuality is through love. Fromm defined love as "union with somebody, or something outside oneself, under the condition of retaining the separateness and integrity of one's own self" (p. 37). This kind of love may exist between individuals in a couple, between parent and child, or in the love for oneself. It embodies the experience of sharing or communion that permits and promotes the full unfolding of each person's own inner activity and potential. Love as depicted by Fromm is paradoxical in that it makes the person stronger and more independent while at the same time requiring a temporary relinquishment of that individuality to be one with the loved person. In this polarity between separateness and union love emerges and is maintained. Fromm emphasized that love requires the presence of care, responsibility, respect, and knowledge. Care and responsibility imply active concern with the other person's growth and happiness. Respect involves an effort to see the other person as another person and not to distort the other based on one's own needs or desires. Finally, knowledge suggests a level of relating surpassing superficial interaction to connection at the core of one's being.

Fromm's work foreshadowed the theoretical developments of Bowen's (1978), family systems theory with its core concept of differentiation as critical to individual, couple, and family functioning. According to Bowen's theory, differentiation of self connotes the ability to balance autonomy and intimacy within interpersonal relationships and to regulate thinking and feeling intrapersonally. Poorly differentiated individuals tend to be easily overwhelmed by anxiety and become reactive to situations. Better-differentiated people respond to situations based on well-developed sets of internal beliefs and principles. They demonstrate a breadth of perspective, a flexibility of thought, and a capacity to observe their own behaviors and those of others while remaining aware of their interdependence on others (Papero, 2000).

The level of differentiation is also reflected in the nature of interpersonal relationships. Less-well-differentiated individuals tend to form intense relationships with others, and their actions become highly dependent on the others. Bowen (1978) characterized such relationships as fused. Such fusion might be evidenced in high levels of dependence on the other, an inability to tolerate differences in important others, and the likelihood of taking the behavior of important others personally. Such individuals might also use distance and avoidance as means of responding reactively to the fusion.

The concept of differentiation was not unique to Bowen's theory and, in fact, has origins in the works of Werner (1948) and Lewin (1935). Since then, the concept has also been discussed by various theorists, such as Fairbairn (1952), Ackerman (1958), Klein (1948, 1957), Satir (1967), Boszormenyi-Nagy (1966), Minuchin (1974), and Bowlby (1969), from diverse theoretical perspectives.

Bowen (1978; Kerr & Bowen, 1988) provided a unique perspective on differentiation. He described it as a developmental process that involves not only an individual but also his or her family on an ongoing basis and that continues to impact over multiple generations. According to Bowen, the tendency to seek some degree of fusion is related to one's incomplete differentiation from one's family of origin. Individuals who seek to complete themselves in a partner have failed to resolve their relationships with their families of origin. Untangling such issues would free them to build a new relationship based on each person's freedom to be himself or herself.

Resolution of Family-of-Origin Dynamics: My Family or Your Family versus Our Family
The renegotiation of bonds with the family of origin poses a task generally identified as an essential component of couple formation and relationship success. From early on, theorists have emphasized the importance of early family relationships as setting the stage for future relationship functioning. Object-relations theory in particular spotlights how individuals' experiences and expectations as formed in early primary relationships impact intimate interactions into adulthood (Dicks, 1963; Fairbairn, 1952; Klein, 1946; D. Scharff & Scharff, 1987): "The object relations theories have in common the view that a person's current relationships take shape from the structure and functioning of the unique pattern of internal relationships that were set down as the person interacted with and adapted to others early in life" (J. S. Scharff & de Varela, 2000, p. 81). This internal model determines the choice of a partner and the nature of a couple relationship. Individuals tend to select partners fitting their internal working models, and they project their needs and expectations onto a partner in an effort to work out unresolved issues from childhood.

Attachment theorists have stressed the importance of parent-child attachment experiences on the development of an individual. They proposed that children have innate emotional and behavioral systems prompting a search for security from the proximity and responsiveness of their primary caregivers (Bowlby, 1969; Sperling & Berman, 1994). Through parental responsiveness to an infant's needs, the infant develops internalized representations of self and other to form an "internalized working model." These internalized working models form the bases of the development of attachments in interpersonal relationships (Bowlby, 1969; Sperling & Berman, 1994). Ainsworth, Blehar, Waters, and Wall (1978) categorized these internalized working models into a typology of three attachment styles for children: secure, insecure/ambivalent, and insecure/avoidant.

From an attachment perspective, children's behaviors can be predicted from their attachment styles, which are consistent with the characteristics and attachment styles of their parents (Sperling & Berman, 1994). Securely attached children actively explore their environments and are able to tolerate separations from a caregiver because they are confident that the caregiver will be available when needed. Children with an anxious/avoidant attachment style do not expect a caregiver to be dependable and perceive the caregiver as rejecting; consequently, they tend to avoid reestablishing contact with the caregiver and are less distressed by separation. Children with an anxious/ambivalent attachment style have experienced inconsistent responsiveness on the part of caregivers and are therefore likely to become dependent and highly sensitive to the cues of a caregiver.

In their theoretical writings, Hazan and Shaver (e.g., Hazan & Shaver, 1987; Shaver & Hazan, 1993) have proposed that parallels exist between the dynamics, feelings, and behaviors associated with attachment styles of infants to their caregivers and those later identified in the romantic relationships of individuals in adulthood. Empirical research has also provided evidence that the infant's attachment style, whether avoidant, anxious/ambivalent, or secure, tends to correspond to the adult's romantic attachment style.

Family therapists also believe that an individual's overall psychological functioning is closely linked to experience in the family of origin. Kerr and Bowen (1988) took this a step further, affirming that personal relationship problems result exclusively from unresolved family-of-origin experiences. A family exercises strong influence over members' beliefs, values, attitudes, feelings, and behaviors and in the formation of a family member's sense of identity. Bowen (1978) theorized that the basic level of differentiation of self developed in each individual's family of origin, particularly in the context of the relationship with the parents during important developmental stages. In a poorly differentiated family, the parents transmit to the children chronic levels of tension and repetitive dysfunctional behaviors that become part of the children's repertoire for living and for responding in intimate relationships. Thus, the level of differentiation in the family appears to significantly determine a family's ability to adapt to social and environmental changes, individual members' developmental stages, and life-cycle transitions for the family as a whole.

According to Bowen (1978) differentiation happens as individuals explore their families-of-origin emotional functioning at a multigenerational level. Through a process of becoming a differentiated individual, a person is able to be intimate and also have a less enmeshed and reactive identity separate from the original family system. In this process, a person analyzes and neutralizes the influences of the original family and is able to distinguish his or her own thoughts and feelings as distinct from those of the family of origin (Kerr & Bowen, 1988). Individuals need to work through family-of-origin dynamics to be able to engage in healthy adult intimate relationships. In fact, Bowen believed that individuals would have greater success in resolving relationship issues if they concentrated on changing their levels of differentiation within a family of origin than if they focused only on the immediate problems of the relationship (Papero, 2000).

Bowen's belief in the need to deal with family-of-origin issues has been echoed by other theorists and practitioners also working from an intergenerational perspective. Boszormenyi-Nagy and Spark (1973) noted the impact of family myths and loyalties as having a profound effect on the functioning and relationships of individuals in a family across generations. Boszormenyi-Nagy (1973) believed that separateness and connectedness could be achieved through a process of family interaction grounded in fairness, trust, and ongoing relatedness. Such a process would facilitate the development of self-delineation in relation to significant others and self-validation within oneself (Boszormenyi-Nagy & Krasner, 1986). James Framo (1992), through an integration of object-relations and intergenerational perspectives, posited that individuals tended to internalize past family conflicts and continue to work out those contentions with their own spouses and children. Like Bowen, Framo and Boszormenyi-Nagy believed that engaging in genuine dialogue within the context of one's family of origin would support the achievement of greater differentiation and the minimization of past influences.

Other family theorists have also portrayed the family as providing the context within which issues of togetherness and individuation manifest themselves. Minuchin (1974), although not focused on intergenerational family dynamics, did explore the significance of separateness and connectedness in the family system and its subsystems. The boundaries in a family system occur on a continuum, with inappropriately rigid (disengaged) and diffuse (enmeshed) as the extremes. Disengaged families support individuality and independence of family members but lack family cohesion and support. Enmeshed families, on the other hand, foster connectedness at the expense of individual identity and development. The majority of families fall within the normal range, though they may possess subsystems with some disengaged or diffused boundaries. However, families who operate at the extremes of the continuum may experience some pathology leading to decreased individual as well as family functioning. By implication, individuals who come from such family systems will also have difficulty developing relationships with others outside the system.

Finally, McGoldrick and Carter (1999) urged that the development of a mature interdependent self must be viewed as occurring within a rich context that includes all of the intergenerational family relationships as well as cultural influences and the social influences of the time. The complex interaction of all of these factors determines the capacity for individuals to engage in intimate relationships.

Although renegotiation of family-of-origin dynamics remains a central task of couple formation, some theorists, particularly from the existential perspectives, rather than focus on intimate relationships as being the predetermined product of previous family dynamics, have highlighted committed relationships, marriage, and a new family as opportunities for developing new interaction patterns and redefining self in relation to intimate others. Such theorists view marriage as the testing ground for personal individuation from a family of origin and for renegotiation of intimacy and autonomy in one's first equally influential adult-adult relationship. Committed relationships and marriage provide the arena in which to rework one's self-views and one's relational options outside a family of origin. Thus, the couple or marriage becomes a naturally therapeutic venue. Young people who are involved in committed relationships are considered to be in a more complex phase of separation from their families of origin than are single young adults. They are struggling covertly and overtly to balance their desires for belonging with their first tastes of individual freedom and adulthood (Roberto, 1991, p. 469). Coupling, therefore, becomes a crucial vehicle for self-expression and differentiation from one's family.

Whitaker and Keith (1981), while describing couples as having to deal with the struggle of determining whose family of origin the new family will pattern itself after, also viewed new intimate relationships as the ideal venue for engaging in experiences in the present that counteract expectations and patterns established in the past. Whitaker and Keith viewed marriage as an adult model of intimacy and believed that an important contribution of marriage flows from increasing the stress and anxiety of a person's life so that continued change and growth may occur (Neill & Kniskern, 1982). Whitaker and Keith (1981) went so far as to declare that "an unstable marriage is a healthy marriage. The marriage in conflict is the marriage in movement" (p. 190). Diagnostically, Whitaker believed that marital dynamics that become static, irreversible, or remain at an impasse indicate a troubled marriage.

Facing Differences and Handling Disagreement
Contrary to Whitaker and Keith's (1981) view of conflict as a positive indicator in couple relations, the literature on couple therapy has generally identified the facing of differences and handling of disagreements as a major dilemma in the development of healthy relationships. Psychoanalytic perspectives underscore the process of projective identification in mate selection. Individuals choose each other not just based on conscious reasons of compatibility, but because, on unconscious levels, they are seeking to complete themselves in a partner. Although these processes fuel the initial attraction and contribute to a feeling of oneness, they tend to quickly result in disappointment and conflict as a partner proves unable to live up to the projected expectations (Dicks, 1967) or as the projected identifications become negatively

viewed because they involve unacceptable parts of the self seen in the partner (Scarf, 1987). Thus, once initial attraction fades, the aspects of a partner that were most attractive at first often generate the greatest conflict.

Satir (1967) observed a similar process attuned to the levels of self-esteem that partners possess when entering into an intimate relationship. For individuals with low self-esteem, differences become intolerable. Such individuals seek to enhance their levels of self-esteem in marriage based on denying their differentness from a spouse. This results in severe distortions in communication to maintain the myth of agreement: "Different-ness which leads to a conflict of interest (disagreement) is seen as an insult and evidence of being unloved" (Satir, 1983, p. 15).

Bowen (1978) also connected the process of individual development and differentiation to that of tolerance for differences within the relationship. In couples, preserving one's identity while having the capacity to be intimate represents the ideal. A couple is differentiated if individually they are able to maintain their own interests and activities while sharing other interests and activities with each other. Highly differentiated individuals seem to encounter fewer problems in marriage and to have better coping abilities to deal with the problems that do occur than poorly differentiated individuals. Poor differentiation is typically manifested in a marital dyad in either sustained conflict between the spouses or in overfunctioning or underfunctioning by one spouse. It also appears in the projection processes with family members, including children. The projection process occurs when a parental dyad attempts to relieve some of their tension by triangulating with their child. The tensions experienced by the couple are projected onto the child, with the child then developing symptoms, so the focus of the family is redirected from the marital dyad to the symptomatic child. This relieves the marital tension temporarily. Unfortunately, the issues are not resolved; they are only passed down another generation.

The cognitive-behavioral couples literature contains an emphasis on the importance of partners' skills in handling the conflicts that arise over the course of a relationship in influencing the success of a relationship. Negative communication and poor conflict-management strategies in a marriage have been consistently associated with marital distress and divorce (Christensen & Shenk, 1991; Gottman, 1994; Karney & Bradbury, 1995). Although marital conflict is not considered universally negative (Markman, 1991; Smith, Vivian, & O'Leary, 1990), researchers have been able to identify key indices of conflict management that predict marital distress. Specifically, distressed couples exhibit higher rates of negative verbal and nonverbal behavior, more negative escalation, and more frequent withdrawal during interactions than nondistressed couples (Gottman, 1993; Weiss & Heyman, 1997). Gottman (1994) identified what he labeled as the Four Horsemen of the Apocalypse for marriage: critical anger, contempt expressed by one spouse, fearful defensiveness, and withdrawal. Destructive patterns of communication begin early in the relationship and set the stage for future marital difficulties (Heavey, Christensen, & Malamuth, 1995; Markman & Hahlweg, 1993).

Researchers have been able to predict future marital satisfaction and distress from couples' premarital and newlywed interactions with increasing accuracy and sophistication (Gottman, Coan, Carrere, & Swanson, 1998; Gottman, Swanson, & Murray, 1999; Karney & Bradbury, 1995; Markman & Hahlweg, 1993; Markman, Renick, Floyd, Stanley, & Clements, 1993). Destructive communication patterns have been found to persist into subsequent marriages (Prado & Markman, 1999) and into parent-child interactions (Lindahl & Markman, 1990; Markman, Lindahl, Balaguer, & Clements, 1990).

Furthermore, substantial research exists documenting the impact on child adjustment of exposure to negative parental interactions (Cummings & Davies, 1994; Emery, 1988; Fincham et al., 1994; Grych & Fincham, 1990).

In fact, reviews of the literature have documented the value of research on couples' interactional processes in contributing to efforts in public education, premarital counseling, and marital therapy (Holmes & Boon, 1990; Karney & Bradbury, 1995; O'Leary & Smith, 1991). Specifically, when communication difficulties are addressed, researchers have demonstrated a reduction in marital distress, increases in satisfaction, and the attenuation of marital violence (Holmes & Boon, 1990; Markman et al., 1993; Sayers, Baucom, Sher, & Weiss, 1991; Smith, Vivian, & O'Leary, 1991).

Nevertheless, a strictly skills-based approach to addressing dysfunction in couple relationships has been found wanting. These interventions have generally focused on rational processes such as behavior exchange and the improvement of communication and problem-solving skills. In these approaches, expressions of intense affect were considered to be detrimental to the treatment. Negative emotion became viewed as particularly destructive and distancing, and the expression of such emotions was to be avoided (Waring, 1988). Marital therapists began to question whether affect could or should actually be controlled and assumed to change as a result of behavioral or skills-based interventions (Broderick & O'Leary, 1986). Researchers also began to acknowledge that, even though behavioral interventions did result in a reduction in marital distress, the power of those interventions was less than originally thought. In fact, only 50% of couples were reporting improved satisfaction in their relationships based on amelioration of their communication and conflict-management skills (Jacobson et al., 1984). Consequently, cognitive-behavioral theorists and researchers have begun to consider new elements that might be influencing the impact of conflict or disagreement on relationship satisfaction (Koerner & Jacobson, 1994). Such reconsideration has led to the reemergence of quality of the emotional connection between partners as essential to relationship success and positive therapy outcomes.

Johnson and Greenberg (1994) provided a conceptual framework for understanding the relationship between negative emotions and the quality of the emotional connection in couple relationships. They distinguished between basic feelings and the defensive elaborations or distortions of feelings often present in couple conflicts. Usually, basic feelings of fear—fear of rejection and abandonment or fear of loss of autonomy and engulfment—underlie the negative, defensive emotions characterizing the rigid positions taken by partners in distressed couples. According to Greenberg and Johnson (1988), the higher the level of fear, the more rigid and self-protective the positions taken by the partners. These protective positions can involve either intrapsychic distortion of emotion (e.g., shutting down, dismissing own feelings) or interactive patterns of distortion (e.g., clinging, expressions of jealousy, anger, attempts to control a partner). These patterns begin to predominate the relationship and preclude opportunities for emotional engagement, accessibility, and responsiveness that foster intimacy. Effective interventions, consequently, must focus not only on reducing negative interactions, but on accessing the primary emotions that underlie those interactions and foster emotional engagement, risk taking, and trust.

Wallerstein and Blakeslee (1995) indicated that an essential aspect of a good marriage stems from having set up a safe space for conflict. Successful marriages are not characterized by the absence of conflict, but by a sense of security in the relationship that provides a holding environment for the inevitable aggression and conflict that will arise as the two individuals negotiate conflicting interests. They viewed this ability to contain aggression in a relationship as reflective of a partner's level of maturity and sensitivity to the other's needs rather than a sign of good communication and negotiation abilities.

Conflict in a good marriage occurs in the context of connectedness and caring. Partners implicitly or explicitly acknowledge that the ties that unite the relationship hold higher value for both of them than the forces that divide the couple. This mutual commitment to the relationship enables the partners to interrupt the anger or conflict out of concern for the other or for the relationship and to expose their own vulnerabilities to each other. Thus, conflict resolution is implicitly tied to the level of trust that exists in the relationship.

The Ultimate Dilemma: To Trust or Not to Trust?
Over the long run, what is essential to the quality of intimate relationships resides in the trustable core. Adults in close relationships need access to the partner and express a desire for closeness with that person, especially in times of need or distress. The partner's presence is comforting and allays anxiety; inaccessibility leads to increased distress. Trust involves a complex integration of thoughts and emotions. The cognitive aspects of trust include expectations about the partner's reliability and dependability, based on family-of-origin legacies, one's own experiences as a child, and past experiences within the context of a current relationship. The affective aspects of trust are based on hope, a feeling of basic security, and the strength of the bond with the partner (Rempel, Holmes, & Zanna, 1985).

Issues of trust and mistrust often emerge as important issues in couples therapy. Factors contributing to a lack of trust require exploration, and new emotional bonding needs to be promoted (Greenberg & Johnson, 1988). Ivan Boszormenyi-Nagy (1987) postulated that issues of trust and fairness are core elements of couple and family relationships and that they tend to be transmitted across the generations:

"The lack of trustworthiness in one's relational world is the primary pathogenic condition of human life" (p. 230). Building trust enables partners to recognize and rework the long-standing legacies that they have brought into their relationship from their families of origin. Such recognition frees them from engaging in defensive and retributive behavior in their own interactions and from drawing their offspring into the battle and subjecting them to a legacy of unfairness and distrust (Friedman, 1992).

According to Friedman (1992), building trust requires equitable relations on every member's own terms, an integrity of give and take in relationship, a mutuality of consideration, a capacity for redistribution of past debts. This process is thought to take place through what Buber (1958) termed the "I-Thou" dialogue. This dialogue is characterized by a sense of presence (being truly present), inclusion (allowing another access to one's inner thoughts and feelings), and mutuality (genuine involvement by both parties). In an I-Thou dialogue, partners do not try to impose themselves on each other, nor do they attempt to have the other see the world from their perspectives. Rather, genuine dialogue involves responsible position taking by both partners and depends on "reciprocity of responsible caring" (Boszormenyi-Nagy & Krasner, 1986, p. 73). Under such conditions, the dialogue becomes both self-delineating and self-validating for both people: "Where there is genuine dialogue there is thus brought into being between partners who express themselves without reserve, free of semblance, a fruitful partnership that can be found in no other way. I-thou dialogue is thus in and of itself healing and generative" (Greenberg & Johnson, 1988, p. 21). It is this type of interhuman connection between partners that forms the core of trustworthiness in a relationship and that provides the vehicle for the reparation of broken trust.

Many couples come into therapy not only because of general issues of distress or distrust, but to deal with particular abandonments or betrayals that seem to have irreparably damaged the relationship. Identified as attachment injuries by Johnson and Whiffen (1999), they appear to have a significant impact on the core element of trust in a relationship and on the potential for reparation. An attachment injury denotes "a specific incident in which one partner is inaccessible and unresponsive in the face of another partner's urgent need for the kind of support and caring that we expect of attachment figures. The injurious incident is continually used as a touchstone for the dependability of the other partner" (Johnson, Makinen, & Millikin, 2001, p. 149). Examples of attachment injuries include infidelity or failure to be supportive following a miscarriage, but may also involve more "minor" incidents of invalidation such as not being seated at the head table at a wedding, which, while of great importance to one partner, may not even be remembered by the other.

Such betrayals are significant because they call into question basic assumptions about a relationship, the other, and the self. The most basic assumption of intimate relationships implies that the partner will be there when he or she is needed. Under normal circumstances, violation of this or other expectations would not necessarily harm the central core of trust in the relationship. However, when an individual is most vulnerable and in dire need of comfort, such betrayals can shatter the intimate bond and damage the relationship in critical ways.

Johnson et al. (2001) reported that partners refer to such events using the language of trauma. They speak of having been left alone and abandoned or of feeling that it was a life-and-death situation. The injured party communicates having experienced a rupture of trust and of becoming reluctant to trust in the relationship again. The significance rather than the content of such events predominates. The events may occur at any time, but are particularly likely to happen during times of transition, loss, physical danger, or uncertainty. Furthermore, what is interpersonally unbearable for one couple might be completely manageable to another:

> Much depends on how the injured partner interprets the event in question and how the other spouse responds to expressions of hurt by the injured party. When this spouse discounts, denies or dismisses the injury, this prevents the processing of the event in the relationship and compounds the injury. The unresolved event may be the topic of constant bickering, or it may lay dormant and unexpressed for a period of time. However, it eventually reemerges with a vengeance, especially when a small current incident evokes an emotional response related to the initial injury. (p. 149)

When couples experience further failed efforts to move beyond these attachment injuries, their despair and alienation deepen, and they tend to become engaged in absorbing states of negative affect and constricted interactions. These states have been identified as predicting marital distress and divorce (Gottman, 1994).

In addition to critically impacting a relationship, attachment injuries also characteristically threaten basic assumptions about the self and the sense of security and self-worth, thus inducing a sense of existential vulnerability: "The shattering of basic assumptions is, in and of itself, disorienting, and is part of the sense of helplessness that is perhaps the most salient feature of traumatic experience" (Johnson et al., 2001, p. 150). Johnson and colleagues proposed that thinking about the wounds to attachment in couple relationships in the context of trauma theory may be helpful in understanding the saliency of such events and their power in determining the future course of a relationship.

Following an attachment injury that is experienced as a traumatic abandonment, much of the relationship becomes organized around attempts at resolving that injury. The injured party may focus on either eliciting responsiveness from the partner or defending against a lack of responsiveness rather than reacting to the current circumstances of the relationship. Even though the offending partner may apologize for the transgression, the injured party is often unable to let go of the matter, but continues to ruminate about the event and reexperience the pain in a manner similar to that described in traumatic experiences (Herman, 1992). In addition, responses that are often evident in reaction to trauma, such as numbing, avoidance, and hyperarousal (van der Kolk & McFarlane, 1996), may impact emotional engagement with the partner and interfere with resolution of the attachment injury. In therapy, these strategies present themselves as an alternation by the injured party of accusing and clinging followed by withdrawal and alienation that becomes disorganizing and aversive to both partners and to the therapeutic process: "Normally positive interactions become tentative and colored by doubts. The couple is then caught in a drama in which the injured spouse sets tests and the offending spouse is always found wanting" (Johnson et al., 2001, p. 151).

Johnson et al. (2001) observed that such attachment injuries often form the crux of impasses in couple therapy. Furthermore, discussion of these injuries tends to occur at the point in therapy when the individuals are each becoming more in touch with their own feelings and more accessible to each other and when trust is beginning to be reestablished, in other words, as the I-Thou dialogue begins to take place. In the course of that dialogue, specific incidents of betrayal are raised. Unless the therapist is able to help a couple successfully resolve these perceived violations of trust, the despair and alienation of the partners deepen. Both the therapy and the relationship are seriously compromised. This view supports Friedman's (1992) assertion that building trust requires not only equitable relations on every member's own terms, an integrity of give and take in relationship, and a mutuality of consideration, but also a capacity for redistribution of past debts. In this context, the past cannot just be put in the past, but must be actively reviewed and renegotiated.

As Boszormenyi-Nagy (1987) highlighted in his definition of a dialogue of trustworthiness:

Families explore their capacity for reworking stagnant imbalance in how each of them uses the other and in how they are available to each other. The courage they invest in the review and repair of inadvertent relational corruption and exploitation yields returns in therapeutic resources, the chief among them being: earned trustworthiness. (p. 200)

Such reworking also needs to include the basic elements that have been identified in trauma theory as essential to the resolution of traumatic events, namely, being able to review and reconstruct the event, its meaning, and its consequences, while integrating the emotional experience in the context of secure connections with others.

SUMMARY

Despite our discussion of separate dilemmas or tasks of couple development, obviously the tasks all interconnect and recursively influence each other during the course of a relationship. All individuals bring individual and family legacies into their couple relationships. In those relationships, they work to maintain a sense of self-respect while balancing issues of intimacy and autonomy and finding ways to construct boundaries around the relationship (Pierce, 1994). The success of couples in accomplishing these tasks depends in part on the skills they possess in negotiating conflicts and on the capacity of the individuals to be truly present and committed to the endeavor.

Historically, treatment approaches to relationship issues have addressed the dilemmas of couple formation by focusing on personal development or individuation, either individually or in the context of a family of origin, or by attempting to enhance skills in communication and conflict resolution. Each has produced limited success. Consequently, this has generated a move for greater integration in the treatment of couple distress in giving multifaceted attention to the interactions occurring between partners as well as the emotions and meanings elicited by and that in turn influence those interactions. Clinicians who were strictly focused on intrapsychic processes have acknowledged the need to use behavioral and cognitive strategies to reduce conflict and defensiveness to lower anxiety and access primary processes. Likewise, behaviorally focused practitioners have recognized the limitations of simply focusing on changing behavioral exchanges in a couple. As a result, they have moved toward a focus on the emotional aspects of a relationship as a means of understanding how interaction patterns become rigid and of fostering acceptance of differences that may not be solvable.

The next section presents the general principles for therapeutic work with couples using emotionally focused couples therapy (Greenberg & Johnson, 1986, 1988; Johnson & Greenberg, 1995). This therapeutic approach is presented as one example of an integrative approach that has emerged in the couple therapy field to address the multidimensional nature of couple relationships. Although other integrative approaches have also been developed and shown demonstrated effectiveness (Jacobson & Christensen, 1996; W. C. Nichols, 1998), emotionally focused couples therapy is discussed here because of its primarily experiential focus.

MAJOR SYNDROMES, SYMPTOMS, AND PROBLEMS TREATED

Emotionally Focused Couples Therapy as a Context for Transformation

Emotionally focused couples therapy (EFCT) provides a therapeutic approach for working with couples while integrating experiential and systemic perspectives. Within this framework, individuals are considered to be constructive, self-organizing beings who are constantly evolving and who have inherent tendencies toward survival and growth. The process of self-formation, however, is contextually dependent and reciprocally influenced by both internal intrapsychic forces and external interactional influences (Greenberg & Johnson, 1988). Consequently, interventions are targeted at the interactional patterns that have developed and at each person's inner experiences of self and of the relationship as well as how each recursively influences the other.

Because the EFCT perspective on close relationships is grounded in attachment theory (Cassidy & Shaver, 1999; Hazan & Shaver, 1987), significant emphasis is placed on restructuring internal working models of self and others that were formed in early relationships as well as addressing attachment insecurity in current relationships. The goals of therapy involve expanding constricted emotional responses and relational beliefs about self and other that underlie negative interaction; restructuring interactions to increase partners' responsiveness and accessibility to each other; and fostering positive experiences of caring and support (Johnson et al., 2001). Consequently, it offers an approach well-suited to addressing the multidimensional complexity of the existential dilemmas of coupling presented earlier as well as providing partners with skills to address present relationship problems.

Targeted Populations and Assessment of Relational Problems

A predominant issue in couples therapy in the determination of target populations and assessment and diagnosis has been the question of reconciling individual and relational problems. The focus of assessment and diagnosis has historically been almost exclusively on disorders of individuals, despite the fact that family and relational distress is the most common presenting complaint of those seeking treatment (Veroff, Kulka, & Douvan, 1981). More recently, there has been increased attention to the assessment and diagnosis of relational problems and efforts to develop a nomenclature for relational diagnosis to be either integrated within the *Diagnostic and Statistical Manual of Mental Disorders* (*DSM-IV;* American Psychiatric Association [APA], 1994) or as an independent entity (Kaslow, 1996). Such efforts have resulted in relational diagnoses becoming a viable alternative to traditional Axis-I disorders and in the development of the Global Assessment of Relational Functioning scale (GARF; Group for the Advancement of Psychiatry Committee on the Family [GAP], 1996) as analogous to the Axis V Global Assessment of Functioning scale (GAF; GAP, 1996). Contextual influences continue to be represented in a secondary fashion on Axis IV and their impact on relation functioning inadequately addressed.

Ultimately, although relational disorders clearly impact on individual functioning and need to be reflected in assessment and diagnosis, the problem remains that relational and individual disorders pertain to unique and different levels of organization that, though interconnected, also function independently of each other. As Denton (1996) recommended, what is needed are more interactive models that take into account the complex patterns of interrelationship between different levels of influence. From a diagnostic perspective, EFCT, while targeting more directly the relational difficulties in a couple, allows for consideration of individual psychological problems, particularly those based on attachment difficulties. EFCT is focused on the repair of distressed relationships and involves working to enhance accessibility and intimacy. Thus, a basic presupposition of EFCT is that the partners are committed to improving their relationship and strengthening the emotional bond and have the capacity on some level to do so. EFCT is particularly geared to working with couples who present with problems of recurrent conflict, distancing, and lack of intimacy. These couples would probably receive a *DSM-IV* V Code diagnosis of Partner Relational Problem (APA, 1994) and are likely to retain some minimum level of trust in the relationship despite a history of painful interactions and decreased relationship satisfaction.

EFCT can also be used effectively to address individual symptoms that either have repercussions in intimate relationships or can be considered a function of the individual's position in the relationship and seen as maintained by relationship dynamics. This modality has been used in the treatment of various individual disorders such as depression, anxiety, psychosomatic problems, phobias, and Posttraumatic Stress Disorder (Greenberg & Johnson, 1988; Johnson & Williams-Keeler, 1998).

Because of the general foundation in attachment theory, EFCT may also be applicable to addressing issues of a characterological nature that presume disruption in primary attachment relationships, such as Borderline Personality Disorders and Dependent Personality Disorders. In fact, the process of therapy as outlined in EFCT is very consistent with the types of assessment and intervention suggested by Solomon (1996) and Young and Gluhoski (1996) as needed for treating couples with Borderline and other personality disorders. The major modification is that EFCT is intended to be a short-term therapy approach, whereas longer-term treatment is generally indicated when Axis-II disorders are implicated. In fact, Johnson and Whiffen (1999) suggested that those individuals who have had an experience of secure attachment in the past will more easily attain a sense of emotional reconnection in the therapy than those who have not.

The use of the GARF scale (GAP, 1996) is beneficial because the primary dimensions of relational context quantified by the GARF are congruent with those emphasized in the emotionally focused therapy framework: joint problem solving, organization (including areas of differentiation and power), and emotional climate (including level of attachment and empathy and sexual functioning). The GARF can be appropriately used to identify the initial level of relational functioning in a couple and to assess progress at different points in treatment.

According to Greenberg and Johnson (1988), EFCT is contraindicated for couples who are clearly engaged in the process of relationship dissolution. Additionally, it is not advisable as an initial treatment approach in cases of couple violence because the encouragement of open emotional engagement would likely be resisted by both the violent and victimized partners and would place the victim in an increasingly vulnerable position. Rather, the initial focus in such cases should be on controlling the violent behavior and protecting the victim (Walker, 1996). Finally, EFCT is contraindicated in cases of extreme individual symptoms such as suicidal behavior or psychosis.

Stages of Therapy

In EFCT, the process of therapy typically has been divided into three stages involving a total of nine steps (Greenberg & Johnson, 1986, 1988). The first stage of therapy involves assessment and redefinition of the problem. It includes four steps: (1) identification of the issues presented by the couple and how they reflect the core dilemmas of couple formation: separateness-connectedness and dependence-independence; (2) identification of the negative interaction cycles (usually, variants of pursue-distance and dominance-submission); (3) accessing unacknowledged feelings underlying the interactional positions of the partners; and (4) redefining the problem(s) in terms of underlying feelings. The goal by the end of this stage involves a couple being able to disengage from their negative cycles and to demonstrate an increased flexibility and willingness to access their own underlying feelings and to respond in a validating fashion to open communication by the partner.

The second stage of therapy includes: (5) promoting identification with disowned needs and aspects of self; (6) promoting acceptance by each partner of the other's experience; and (7) facilitating the expression of needs and wants to restructure the interaction. This stage of therapy has a strong experiential focus and sets the foundation for true dialogue. It goes beyond the mere expression of emotion or empathic listening to what McGuire (1991) called "felt experiencing" (p. 228):

> Rather, clients must experience, on an emotionally meaningful level, new aspects of themselves and new aspects of their partner, thereby creating new interactions. Partners must encounter each other in the session in a new way and participate in the corrective emotional experience of an I-Thou relationship. This re-establishes the possibility of having a positive human relationship with each other. (Greenberg & Johnson, 1988, p. 38)

In this stage, attachment injuries likely arise and need to be resolved successfully. A clinician assumes responsibility for providing a safe haven in a therapy context that allows for new and intense emotional experiences to be explored with confidence.

The final stage involves (8) establishing the emergence of new solutions and (9) consolidating new positions. Through engagement in this process, deeper connection, trust, and intimacy are achieved: "Partners need to be able to reveal their essential selves to each other and be accepted as they are. They need to be able to say what they think most profoundly without fear of rejection or fear of hurting the other" (Greenberg & Johnson, 1988, p. 20). To the extent that couples experience inability to reach this level of emotional bonding because of intrapersonal, historical, or contextual barriers, the level of trust in the relationship will remain tentative, positive bonding interaction cycles more circumscribed, and the possibility of relapse more probable (Johnson & Greenberg, 1988; Johnson et al., 2001).

CASE EXAMPLE

The following case example illustrates the therapy process of EFCT.

Fred and Janet, a couple in their early 50s, came into therapy after 28 years of marriage. They perceived the presenting problem in terms of an inability to communicate and a feeling of diminished intimacy. Fred felt that Janet had lost her joy of living, and Janet described Fred as irresponsible and inconsiderate. Fred indicated that Janet was angry and critical all the time and that he could not do anything right. Janet retorted that Fred just wanted to avoid all conflict and not have to deal with any difficult issue.

DIAGNOSIS AND ASSESSMENT: EFCT STEPS 1–4

The assessment phase involved exploring and validating each partner's perceptions of the problem while beginning to identify themes in the struggle between them centering on control and connectedness and separateness. The assessment included exploring the history of the relationship, the developmental stage of the relationship and its current task, and the level of commitment. Fred and Janet recounted a generally positive and rewarding relationship history. They described a relationship that began with a passionate courtship and was solidified by the joys and trials of raising two daughters together and a joint philosophical commitment to making the world a better place. They were currently in the launching stage of couple development and were struggling with issues of redefining their roles as individuals and as a couple. No diagnosable individual disorders were found to be present for either partner. The couple was asked to complete the Dyadic Adjustment Scale (DAS; Spanier, 1976); scores indicated significant levels of relationship distress and multiple conflict areas. However, the couple also expressed a strong commitment to making the relationship work.

Identifying the negative interaction cycle was a simple matter in that it was enacted frequently and with great intensity during the initial therapy sessions. Fred and Janet were engaged in the classic pattern of one partner (Janet) criticizing and complaining while the other (Fred) defends and distances. Typically, Janet would try to engage Fred in a discussion regarding her dissatisfaction with the relationship or her concerns about his health. Fred would view these attempts as dominating and become defensive and withdraw. He would reach out to Janet by inviting her for a ride in his sports car or by initiating sexual relations, only to be rejected by Janet, who labeled him irresponsible and insensitive. They had reached the point at which the pattern had changed into mutual withdrawal, and both partners realized that the relationship was in jeopardy.

As Fred and Janet accessed and explored the unacknowledged feelings underlying their interactional positions, linking the conflicts to core dilemmas regarding connectedness and independence and redefining problems in terms of underlying feelings became possible. Janet became aware of the need for connection and fear of loneliness and abandonment that undergirded her criticism and pursuit of Fred. In response, Fred was able to acknowledge his fear of not being able to meet all of Janet's attachment needs now that their daughters had left the home and the focus for connection rested completely on him.

Case Formulation

The case was conceptualized as a problem of unacknowledged fears and emotions fueling a pursuer-distancer cycle of interaction that then served to further intensify the feelings of anger and alienation. Additionally, the stage of development of the couple punctuated the core issue of connection versus independence. As they adjusted to the launching of their children, they were forced to redefine their relationship at a time when they were individually struggling with midlife issues of self-definition and aging.

In terms of the existential dilemmas of couple formation and development, Fred and Janet were revisiting the basic dilemma of couple formation, the struggle between maintaining a unique identity and remaining connected (Bowen, 1978; Fromm, 1947, 1955). For them, this dilemma, which represents a continual struggle throughout life, had been brought to the fore at this time by the launching of their children and the need to redefine the couple relationship. Furthermore, because they were having difficulty handling differences in their relationship and were unable to engage in true dialogue regarding the dilemma of autonomy versus intimacy, the trustable core of the relationship had been eroded. Thus, a dialogue of trustworthiness (Boszormenyi-Nagy, 1987) needed to be reestablished to promote the necessary self-delineation by both partners while strengthening the couple's emotional bond.

Treatment Interventions: EFCT Steps 5–7

Treatment interventions with Fred and Janet focused on the EFCT steps of continuing to identify with disowned needs and feelings, acceptance of the partner's experiences, and facilitating the expression of needs and wants. Exploring Fred's experience when he felt criticized by Janet and so withdrew proved particularly important. He tended to dismiss her comments and withdraw, which further exacerbated her need to be heard and responded to. When he did reply, he tended to try to fix the problem when Janet wanted validation of her feelings. As the interaction was explored in session, Fred was able to express how he felt like a failure who could never do anything right. This feeling reinforced feelings from his childhood of not being able to please his father. Fred was also able to begin asking for what he needed, namely, to be given a chance and not be expected to know what Janet needed from him. As Fred became more engaged and less defensive, Janet was able to increasingly focus on clearly and directly expressing her feelings and needs. She also had to counteract earlier gendered proscriptions about having needs and wants and expressing them.

As the couple's ability to engage in dialogue improved, each spouse was able to increasingly express individual vulnerabilities. Fred expressed his joy over the new sense of freedom that launching children had brought and his desire to share that independence with Janet. As Janet realized that Fred did not want to move away from her, but instead to be with her in a new way, reminiscent of their courtship, she became more secure in the relationship. Janet then revealed her fear of losing Fred, thus her hovering concern over his health, and her difficulty with becoming older. Her reticence to share Fred's lust for freedom was in part attributable to her fear that he would no longer find her attractive as he had once done.

Consolidation and Termination: EFCT Steps 8–9

Consistent with the emotionally focused therapy approach, the last stages of treatment with Fred and Janet focused on supporting the development of alternative solutions and consolidating the revised relationship positions. By the end of treatment, Fred and Janet demonstrated greater balance and flexibility in their relationship with each other. They were each able to express their needs and to negotiate differences both in and outside of therapy. They each initiated moves toward connectedness and established parameters of self-delineation. Most important, they recaptured the sense of caring and commitment that had existed throughout most of their relationship.

RESEARCH

There is considerable research-based evidence for the effectiveness of EFCT both at the termination of treatment and in follow-up studies of up to two years posttermination. Furthermore, increase in improvement appears to be greater than rates of improvement found in the general couples therapy literature (Johnson, Hunsley, Greenberg, & Schindler, 1999). Of the factors predicting success of EFCT, engagement in the therapy process emerges as more significant than initial level of relationship distress (Johnson, 2000). Additionally, the quality of the therapeutic alliance and the female partner's initial level of trust prove important determinants of the success of therapy (Johnson & Talitman, 1997).

These research findings support the assertion of Mace (1987) that the hope for the future of therapeutic endeavors lies not in an endless stream of technological developments, but in the struggle to understand and improve the fundamental quality of human relationships. They also validate the basic belief underlying EFCT and other existential approaches: the inherently curative properties of genuine relating between people.

In addition to research on specific therapeutic interventions with couples, further investigations continue to be needed on couple relationships and couple functioning in general. Researchers need to integrate conceptual understanding, clinical application, and empirical support. Another significant shortcoming of the couple literature stems from the paucity of information available regarding different cultural groups. Karney and Bradbury (1995), in a review of the literature on marital quality and stability over time, reported very little variability in the ethnic and demographic makeup of the samples used. In fact, of the 68 independent samples considered in their meta-analysis, 8% drew from Black and White populations, 17% were generally representative of married couples in the United States, and 75% consisted of Caucasian middle-class couples. The gap is particularly glaring, considering the increasing emphasis in psychology on research and treatment that includes cross-cultural approaches (Sue, 1992; Sue & Zane, 1987). Without cross-cultural investigations, it is not possible to determine whether the factors that are critical to the relationship success of Caucasian couples also apply to other racial and ethnic groups. In fact, the lack of cross-cultural research on marital and family issues constitutes a significant barrier to the development of theories and treatment approaches that are culturally valid.

Despite the fact that the field of couple therapy seems to have come of age, continued efforts are needed to further the dialogue regarding intimate relations and the therapeutic interventions aimed at redefining and improving such relationships. The research-based dialogue must encompass a gamut of methodologies (quantitative, qualitative, observational, interactional, and perceptual) and a range of theoretical perspectives as well as a consideration of the contexts within which couple relationships evolve. Only then will we be able to even begin to capture the immensely complex and interrelated phenomena of intimate relationships.

SUMMARY

Couple relationships have long been considered among the most complex and most central of human relationships. In the field of human relations, researchers and clinicians alike have been struggling to understand the increasing fragility of marriage and to develop ways of enhancing the functioning and stability of intimate relationships. To obtain a full picture of such intimate partnerships, one must first consider the foundational elements and dilemmas of coupling. These fundamental tasks of intimate relating including obtaining a balance between autonomy and intimacy, successfully resolving family-of-origin issues, being able to face differences and handle disagreements, and establishing and maintaining trust. The success of couples in accomplishing these tasks requires both the skill to negotiate conflicts and the capacity to be truly present and committed to the endeavor.

Historically, theoretical and clinical approaches to facilitating couple formation and success have focused on either the humanistic, experiential aspects of couple relationships or on the skills needed for relating. However, more recently proposed theoretical and clinical approaches represent attempts to integrate and attend to both experiential and skill-based arenas. Given that all of the critical dilemmas of couple formation involve intrapsychic, experiential, and interpersonal components that simultaneously influence couple interactions and relationship satisfaction and success, the importance of attending to the multiple dimensions of couples' experiences becomes evident. The emotionally focused couple therapy approach is presented as one example of an integrative approach that has emerged in the couple-therapy field to address the multidimensional nature of couple relationships (Greenberg & Johnson, 1986, 1988; Johnson & Greenberg, 1995). While other integrative approaches have also been developed and shown demonstrated effectiveness (Jacobson & Christensen, 1996; Nichols, 1988), emotionally focused couples therapy provides a particularly useful model for integrating experiential and systemic traditions in working with couples.

REFERENCES

Ackerman, N. W. (1958). *The psychodynamics of family life.* New York: Basic Books.

Ainsworth, M. S., Blehar, M. C., Waters, E., & Wall, S. (1978). *Patterns of attachment: A psychological study of the Strange Situation.* Hillsdale, NJ: Erlbaum.

American Psychiatric Association. (1994). *Diagnostic and statistical manual of mental disorders* (4th ed.). Washington, DC: American Psychiatric Association.

Becvar, D. S., & Becvar, R. J. (2000). *Family therapy: A systemic integration.* Needham Heights, MA: Allyn & Bacon.

Bevilacqua, L. J., & Dattilio, F. M. (2000). Overview of couples therapy. In F. M. Dattilio & L. J. Bevilacqua (Eds.), *Comparative treatments for relationship dysfunction* (pp. 1–12). New York: Springer.

Boszormenyi-Nagy, I. (1966). From family relationships to a psychology of relationships: Fictions of the individual and fictions of the family. *Comprehensive Psychiatry, 7*(5), 408–423.

Boszormenyi-Nagy, I. (1987). *Foundations of contextual therapy: Collected papers of Ivan Boszormenyi-Nagy, M.D.* New York: Brunner/Mazel.

Boszormenyi-Nagy, I., & Krasner, B. R. (1986). *Between give and take: A clinical guide to contextual therapy.* New York: Brunner/Mazel.

Boszormenyi-Nagy, I., & Spark, G. L. (1973). *Invisible loyalties: Reciprocity in intergenerational family therapy.* New York: Harper & Row.

Bowen, M. (1978). *Family therapy in clinical practice.* New York: Aronson.

Bowlby, J. (1969). *Attachment and loss. Volume I: Attachment.* New York: Basic Books.

Broderick, J. E., & O'Leary, K. D. (1986). Contributions of affect, attitudes and behavior to marital satisfaction. *Journal of Consulting and Clinical Psychology, 54,* 514–517.

Buber, M. (1958). *I and thou.* New York: Charles Scribner's Sons.

Cassidy, J., & Shaver, P. (1999). *Handbook of attachment.* New York: Guilford Press.

Christensen, A., & Shenk, J. L. (1991). Communication, conflict, and psychological distance in nondistressed, clinic, and divorcing couples. *Journal of Consulting and Clinical Psychology, 59,* 458–463.

Cummings, E. M., & Davies, P. (1994). *Children and marital conflict: The impact of family dispute and resolution.* New York: Guilford Press.

Dattilio, F. M., & Bevilacqua, L. J. (Eds.). (2000). *Comparative treatments for relationship dysfunction.* New York: Springer.

Denton, W. H. (1996). Problems encountered in reconciling individual and relational diagnoses. In F. W. Kaslow (Ed.), *Handbook of relational diagnosis and dysfunctional family patterns* (pp. 35–45). New York: Wiley.

Dicks, H. V. (1963). Object relations theory and marital studies. *British Journal of Medical Psychology, 4,* 56–121.

Dicks, H. V. (1967). *Marital tensions: Clinical studies towards a psychoanalytic theory of interaction.* London: Routledge & Kegan Paul.

Emery, R. E. (1988). *Marriage, divorce, and children's adjustment.* Newbury Park, CA: Sage.

Fairbairn, W. D. (1952). *An object-relations theory of the personality.* New York: Basic Books.

Fincham, F. D., Grych, J. H., & Osborne, L. N. (1994). Does marital conflict cause child maladjustment? Directions and challenges for longitudinal research. *Journal of Family Psychology, 8,* 128–140.

Framo, J. L. (1992). *Family of origin therapy: An intergenerational approach.* New York: Brunner/Mazel.

Frankl, V. E. (1965). *The doctor and the soul: From psychotherapy to logotherapy.* New York: Random House.

Friedman, M. (1992). *Dialogue and the human image: Beyond humanistic psychology.* Newbury Park, CA: Sage.

Fromm, E. (1947). *Man for himself: An inquiry into the psychology of ethics.* New York: Fawcett.

Fromm, E. (1955). *The sane society.* New York: Fawcett.

Gottman, J. M. (1993). A theory of marital dissolution and stability. *Journal of Family Psychology, 7,* 57–75.

Gottman, J. M. (1994). *What predicts divorce? The relationship between marital processes and marital outcomes.* Hillsdale, NJ: Erlbaum.

Gottman, J. M., Coan, J., Carrere, S., & Swanson, C. (1998). Predicting marital happiness and stability from newlywed interactions. *Journal of Marriage and the Family, 60,* 5–22.

Gottman, J. M., Swanson, C., & Murray, J. (1999). The mathematics of marital conflict: Dynamic mathematical nonlinear modeling of newlywed marital interaction. *Journal of Family Psychology, 13,* 3–19.

Greenberg, L. S., & Johnson, S. M. (1986). Emotionally focused couples therapy. In N. S. Jacobson & A. S. Gurman (Eds.), *Clinical handbook of marital therapy* (pp. 253–276). New York: Guilford Press.

Greenberg, L. S., & Johnson, S. M. (1988). *Emotionally focused therapy for couples.* New York: Guilford Press.

Greenberg, L. S., Rice, L. N., & Elliot, R. (1993). *Facilitating emotional change: The moment-by-moment process.* New York: Guilford Press.

Group for the Advancement of Psychiatry Committee on the Family. (1996). Global Assessment of Relational Functioning scale (GARF): I. Background and rationale. *Family Process, 35,* 155–172.

Grych, J. H., & Fincham, F. D. (1990). Marital conflict and children's adjustment: A cognitive-contextual framework. *Psychological Bulletin, 108*(2), 267–290.

Gurman, A. S., & Jacobson, N. S. (1986). Marital therapy: From technique to theory and back again, and beyond. In N. S. Jacobson & A. S. Gurman (Eds.), *Clinical handbook of marital therapy* (pp. 1–9). New York: Guilford Press.

Gurman, A. S., & Jacobson, N. S. (1995). Therapy with couples: A coming of age. In N. S. Jacobson & A. S. Gurman (Eds.), *Clinical handbook of couple therapy* (pp. 1–10). New York: Guilford Press.

Gurman, A. S., & Kniskern, D. P. (Eds.). (1981). *Handbook of family therapy.* New York: Brunner/Mazel.

Gurman, A. S., & Kniskern, D. P. (Eds.). (1991). *Handbook of family therapy* (Vol. 2). New York: Brunner/Mazel.

Haley, J. (1984). Marriage or family therapy? *American Journal of Family Therapy, 12,* 3–14.

Hazan, C., & Shaver, P. (1987). Romantic love conceptualized as an attachment process. *Journal of Personality and Social Psychology, 52,* 511–524.

Heavey, C. L., Christensen, A., & Malamuth, N. M. (1995). The longitudinal impact of demand and withdrawal during marital conflict. *Journal of Consulting and Clinical Psychology, 63,* 797–801.

Herman, J. L. (1992). *Trauma and recovery.* New York: Basic Books.

Hetherington, M. (1993). An overview of the Virginia longitudinal study of divorce and remarriage. *Journal of Family Psychology, 7,* 39–56.

Holmes, J. G., & Boon, S. D. (1990). Developments in the field of close relationships: Creating foundations for intervention strategies. *Personality and Social Psychology Bulletin, 16,* 23–41.

Jacobson, N. S., & Christensen, A. (1996). *Integrative couple therapy: Promoting acceptance and change.* New York: Norton.

Jacobson, N. S., Follet, W. C., Revenstorf, D., Baucom, D. H., Hahlweg, K., & Margolin, G. (1984). Variability in outcome and clinical significance of behavioral marital therapy: A reanalysis of outcome data. *Journal of Consulting and Clinical Psychology, 52,* 497–504.

Johnson, S. M. (2000). Emotionally focused couples therapy. In F. M. Dattilio & L. J. Bevilacqua (Eds.), *Comparative treatments for relationship dysfunction* (pp. 163–185). New York: Springer.

Johnson, S. M., & Greenberg, L. S. (1988). Relating process to outcome in marital therapy. *Journal of Marital and Family Therapy, 14,* 175–183.

Johnson, S. M., & Greenberg, L. S. (1994). *The heart of the matter: Perspective on emotion in marital therapy.* New York: Brunner/Mazel.

Johnson, S. M., & Greenberg, L. S. (1995). The emotionally focused approach to problems in adult attachment. In N. S. Jacobson & A. S. Gurman (Eds.), *Clinical handbook of couple therapy* (pp. 121–141). New York: Guilford Press.

Johnson, S. M., Hunsley, J., Greenberg, L. S., & Schindler, D. (1999). Emotionally focused couples therapy: Status and challenges. *Clinical Psychology, 6,* 67–79.

Johnson, S. M., Makinen, J. A., & Millikin, J. W. (2001). Attachment injuries in couple relationships: A new perspective on impasses in couples therapy. *Journal of Marital and Family Therapy, 27*(2), 145–157.

Johnson, S. M., & Talitman, E. (1997). Predictors of success in emotionally focused marital therapy. *Journal of Marital and Family Therapy, 23,* 135–152.

Johnson, S. M., & Whiffen, V. E. (1999). Made to measure: Adapting emotionally focused couples therapy to partners' attachment styles. *Clinical Psychology: Science and Practice, 6,* 366–381.

Johnson, S. M., & Williams-Keeler, L. (1998). Creating healing relationships for couples dealing with trauma: The use of emotionally focused couples therapy. *Journal of Marital and Family Therapy, 24,* 25–40.

Karney, B. R., & Bradbury, T. N. (1995). The longitudinal course of marital quality and stability: A review of theory, methods, and research. *Psychological Bulletin, 118,* 3–34.

Kaslow, F. W. (Ed.). (1996). *Handbook of relational diagnosis and dysfunctional family patterns.* New York: Wiley.

Kerr, M. E., & Bowen, M. (1988). *Family evaluation: An approach based on Bowen theory.* New York: Norton.

Klein, M. (1946). Notes on some schizoid mechanisms. *International Journal of Psychoanalysis, 27,* 99–110.

Klein, M. (1948). *Contribution to psychoanalysis, 1921–1945.* London: Hogarth Press.

Klein, M. (1957). *Envy and gratitude: A study of unconscious sources.* New York: Basic Books.

Koerner, K., & Jacobson, N. S. (1994). Emotion and behavioral couple therapy. In S. M. Johnson & L. S. Greenberg (Eds.), *The heart of the matter: Perspectives on emotion in marital therapy* (pp. 207–227). New York: Brunner/Mazel.

Lewin, K. (1935). *The dynamic theory of personality.* New York: McGraw-Hill.

Lindahl, K. M., & Markman, H. J. (1990). Communication and negative affect regulation in the family. In E. A. Blechman & M. J. McEnroe (Eds.), *Emotions and the family: For better or for worse* (pp. 99–115). Hillsdale NJ: Erlbaum.

Mace, D. (1987). Three ways of helping married couples. *Journal of Marital and Family Therapy, 13,* 179–185.

Manus, G. I. (1966). Marriage counseling: A technique in search of a theory. *Journal of Marriage and the Family, 28,* 449–453.

Markman, H. J. (1991). Constructive marital conflict is NOT an oxymoron. *Behavioral Assessment, 13,* 29–43.

Markman, H. J., & Hahlweg, K. (1993). The prediction and prevention of marital distress: An international perspective. *Clinical Psychology Review, 13,* 29–43.

Markman, H. J., Lindahl, K. M., Balaguer, A., & Clements, M. (1990, November). *Pre-marital and pre-birth communication: Longitudinal effects on parent-child interaction and functioning.* Paper presented at the Association for the Advancement of Behavior Therapy Conference, San Francisco.

Markman, H. J., Renick, M. J., Floyd, F. J., Stanley, S. M., & Clements, M. (1993). Preventing marital distress through communication and conflict management training: A 4- and 5-year follow-up. *Journal of Consulting and Clinical Psychology, 61,* 70–77.

McGoldrick, M. (1999). Becoming a couple. In B. Carter & M. McGoldrick (Eds.), *The expanded family life cycle: Individual, family, and social perspectives* (pp. 231–248). Needham Heights, MA: Allyn & Bacon.

McGoldrick, M., & Carter, B. (1999). Self in context: The individual life cycle in systemic perspective. In B. Carter & M. McGoldrick (Eds.), *The expanded family life cycle: Individual, family, and social perspectives* (pp. 27–46). Needham Heights, MA: Allyn & Bacon.

McGuire, K. N. (1991). Affect in focusing and experiential psychotherapy. In J. D. Safran & L. S. Greenberg (Eds.), *Emotion, psychotherapy, and change* (pp. 227–251). New York: Guilford Press.

Minuchin, S. (1974). *Families and family therapy.* Cambridge, MA: Harvard University Press.

Neill, J. R., & Kniskern, D. P. (Eds.). (1982). *From psyche to system: The evolving therapy of Carl Whitaker.* New York: Guilford Press.

Nichols, M. P., & Schwartz, R. C. (1998). *Family therapy: Concepts and methods.* Needham Heights, MA: Allyn & Bacon.

Nichols, W. C. (1998). Integrative marital therapy. In F. M. Dattilio (Ed.), *Case studies in couple and family therapy* (pp. 233–256). New York: Guilford Press.

O'Leary, K. D., & Smith, D. A. (1991). Marital interactions. *Annual Review of Psychology, 42,* 191–212.

Papero, D. V. (2000). Bowen systems theory. In F. M. Dattilio & L. J. Bevilacqua (Eds.), *Comparative treatments for relationship dysfunction* (pp. 25–44). New York: Springer.

Pierce, R. A. (1994). Helping couples make authentic emotional contact. In S. M. Johnson & L. S. Greenberg (Eds.), *The heart of the matter: Perspectives on emotion in marital therapy* (pp. 75–108). New York: Brunner/Mazel.

Prado, L., & Markman, H. J. (1999). Unearthing the seeds of marital distress: What we have learned from married and remarried couples. In M. Cox & J. Brooks-Gunn (Eds.), *Conflict and cohesion in families: Causes and consequences* (pp. 51–85). Mahwah, NJ: Erlbaum.

Rempel, J., Holmes, J., & Zanna, M. (1985). Trust in close relationships. *Journal of Personality and Social Psychology, 49,* 1–18.

Roberto, L. G. (1991). Symbolic-experiential family therapy. In A. S. Gurman & D. P. Kniskern (Eds.), *Handbook of family therapy* (Vol. 2, pp. 444–476). New York: Brunner/Mazel.

Rogers, C. R. (1972). *Becoming partners: Marriage and its alternatives.* New York: Delta.

Satir, V. (1967). *Conjoint family therapy.* Palo Alto, CA: Science and Behavior Books.

Satir, V. (1983). *Conjoint family therapy* (3rd ed.). Palo Alto, CA: Science and Behavior Books.

Sayers, S. L., Baucom, D. H., Sher, T. G., & Weiss, R. L. (1991). Constructive engagement, behavioral marital therapy, and changes in marital satisfaction. *Behavioral Assessment, 13,* 25–49.

Scarf, M. (1987). *Intimate partners: Patterns in love and marriage.* New York: Ballantine.

Scharff, D., & Scharff, J. (1987). *Object relations family therapy.* New York: Aronson.

Scharff, J. S., & de Varela, Y. (2000). Object relations therapy. In F. M. Dattilio & L. J. Bevilacqua (Eds.), *Comparative treatments for relationship dysfunction* (pp. 81–101). New York: Springer.

Shaver, P., & Hazan, C. (1993). Adult romantic attachment: Theory and evidence. In D. Perlman & W. Jones (Eds.), *Advances in personal relationships* (Vol. 4, pp. 29–70). London, PA: Jessica Kingsley.

Smith, D. A., Vivian, D., & O'Leary, D. K. (1990). Longitudinal prediction of marital discord from premarital expressions of affect. *Journal of Consulting and Clinical Psychology, 58,* 790–798.

Smith, D. A., Vivian, D., & O'Leary, D. K. (1991). The misnomer proposition: A critical reappraisal of the longitudinal status of "negativity" in marital communication. *Behavioral Assessment, 13,* 7–24.

Solomon, M. F. (1996). Understanding and treating couples with borderline disorders. In F. W. Kaslow (Ed.), *Handbook of relational diagnosis and dysfunctional family patterns* (pp. 251–269). New York: Wiley.

Spanier, G. (1976). Measuring dyadic adjustment. *Journal of Marriage and the Family, 13,* 113–126.

Sperling, M. B., & Berman, W. H. (Eds.). (1994). *Attachment in adults: Clinical and developmental perspectives.* New York: Guilford Press.

Sue, S. (1992). Ethnicity and mental health: Research and policy issues. *Journal of Social Issues, 48,* 187–205.

Sue, S., & Zane, N. (1987). The role of culture and cultural techniques in psychotherapy: A critique and reformulation. *American Psychologist, 42,* 37–45.

van der Kolk, B. A., & McFarlane, A. C. (1996). The black hole of trauma. In B. A. van der Kolk, A. C. McFarlane, & L. Weisaeth (Eds.), *Traumatic stress: The effects of overwhelming experience on mind, body, and society* (pp. 3–23). New York: Guilford Press.

Veroff, J., Kulka, R. A., & Douvan, E. (1981). *Mental health in America: Patterns of help seeking from 1957–1976.* New York: Basic Books.

Walker, L. E. A. (1996). Assessment of abusive spousal relationships. In F. W. Kaslow (Ed.), *Handbook of relational diagnosis and dysfunctional family patterns* (pp. 338–356). New York: Wiley.

Wallerstein, J. S., & Blakeslee, S. (1995). *The good marriage: How and why love lasts.* New York: Houghton Mifflin.

Waring, E. M. (1988). *Enhancing marital intimacy through facilitating cognitive self-disclosure.* New York: Brunner/Mazel.

Weiss, R. L., & Heyman, R. E. (1997). A clinical research overview of couples' interactions. In W. K. Halford & H. J. Markman (Eds.), *Clinical handbook of marriage and couples' interventions* (pp. 13–42). Chichester, England: Wiley.

Werner, H. (1948). *Comparative psychology of mental development.* Chicago: Follet.

Whitaker, C. A., & Keith, D. V. (1981). Symbolic-experiential family therapy. In A. S. Gurman & D. P. Kniskern (Eds.), *Handbook of family therapy* (pp. 187–225). New York: Brunner/Mazel.

Young, J. E., & Gluhoski, V. L. (1996). Schema-focused diagnosis for personality disorders. In F. W. Kaslow (Ed.), *Handbook of relational diagnosis and dysfunctional family patterns* (pp. 300–321). New York: Wiley.

CHAPTER 17

Resilience and Human Rights Activism in Women's Life Stories

PILAR HERNÁNDEZ AND JANINE ROBERTS

Mainstream approaches to family therapy have tended to underrepresent the role of gender, thereby often engaging in a form of silent sexism. Similarly, the unarticulated epistemological assumptions of these theories have often resulted in ignoring the important role of sociopolitical contexts in the ways people make meaning out of their situations. In this chapter, these issues are redressed by focusing attention on narrative and feminist approaches to family therapy. Through a review of the literature, an articulation of key concepts and assumptions, and a detailed empirical example, narrative and feminist approaches are examined. These two approaches are particularly suitable for exploring the complexities and nuances of women's lives. They highlight the ways women develop and maintain family ties, the connection between traumatic experiences and recovery, the contexts in which women live, and the challenges they face in their work environments. These perspectives also bring to the foreground ethical and political dimensions of family therapy and are adaptable for a variety of populations, especially activist women and their families and refugee populations.

HISTORY OF THE THERAPEUTIC APPROACH

The construct of gender emerged in the theory and practice of family therapy in the late 1970s. Various feminists, including Hare-Mustin (1978), Bograd (1984), Goldner (1985), and Avis (1985), raised awareness and critiqued the ways family-therapy models ignored the roles of gender and power in families. Their work began to offer a way of conceptualizing the category of gender in theory and practice.

In 1988, Luepnitz argued that feminism offered family therapy an historical perspective on its subject and a way to pose such questions as "Why does the family take the form it does at the present time?" and "Could families be differently constituted?" (p. 4). She supposed that, in practice, feminism provides a level of consciousness geared toward assisting in solving problems "that will leave the family less patriarchal and less father-absent" (p. 20). In the same year, Walters, Carter, Papp, and Silverstein (1988) introduced their feminist vision:

> It is a humanistic framework or worldview concerned with the roles, rules, and functions that organize male-female interactions. Feminism seeks to include the experience of women in all formulations of human experience, and to eliminate the dominance of male assumptions. Feminism does not blame individual men for the patriarchal social system that exists, but seeks to understand and change the socialization process that keeps men and women thinking and acting within a sexist, male-dominated framework. (p. 17)

Walters et al.'s (1988) work was based on the understanding that assuming neutrality implied a kind of silent sexism that reproduced the inherent inequalities of the status quo. Thus, they advocated general acknowledgment that women have a disadvantaged position in society. They specifically pointed out the different ways women and men are socialized to the advantage of men and called attention to the implications for clinical practice. They observed, "We need to recognize that each gender hears a different meaning in the same clinical intervention and accordingly feels either blamed or supported by an identical therapeutic stance" (p. 17).

In the early 1990s, two books edited by Marsha Pravder Mirkin (1990, 1994) added a new feminist dimension to family therapy: the view that families should be seen in a larger context. These edited books provided road maps for feminist scholars as well as scholars interested in issues of poverty, forced migration, and relocation. The contributors to these books concurred in indicating how the identity of a therapist influences therapy process and in noting the failures of various traditional models to account for the ways sociopolitical systems influence a therapeutic system. Walters (1990) urged that a feminist perspective in family therapy should include women's experience in theory and practice as well as provide an integration of feminist theory at the theoretical, methodological, and educational levels. In addition, it should incorporate a critique of sexism and the use of "female modes and models" in the development of theory and practice. In *Women and Therapy,* Mirkin (1994) contributed to the recognition of women's diversity and the multiple sources of oppression that they experience (i.e., class, race, culture, and sexual orientation).

In the recent past, feminist and empowerment approaches in family therapy (Almeida & Durkin, 1999; Almeida, Wood, Messineo, & Font, 1998) have moved away from traditional views that focus only on nuclear families. Traditional approaches promote caring and individual self-determination, but neglect the social, distributive justice dimension of the work with marginalized groups. Being caring and promoting individual well-being do not accomplish much good if they are framed by practices that define problems in asocial and deficit-oriented terms. Feminist and empowerment approaches balance issues of self-determination and distributive justice and involve interventions to change individuals and social systems. For example, the cultural-context model developed by Rhea Almeida and her colleagues (Almeida & Durkin, 1999; Almeida et al., 1998) addresses domestic violence with a political analysis of heterosexual dominance in several cultures. Their model is focused on group socioeducation for male batterers and their families in a mentoring system that spotlights changes at the level of understanding and values as well as behaviors.

The social-constructionist-feminist perspectives that evolved in the 1990s (Avis & Turner, 1996; Hare-Mustin, 1994; Laird, 1989; Weingarten, 1991, 1992, 1998; Weingarten & Cobb, 1995) revolve around examining the construction of gender discourses and their implications in day-to-day social practices. This viewpoint involves deconstructing, reconstructing, and transforming these dominant and oppressive discourses and practices. It underscores the need for a constant consideration of multiple perspectives and for taking a reflexive stance on the construction and effects of feminist theories.

Another key wave of thought emerged from scholars' and practitioners' interests in gender and the experiences of men in families and men of color and from working with men in situations of family violence. Bograd (1990, 1999) and Avis (1996) examined the experiences of men and working with them in a gender-conscious way. Jenkins (1990) and Carrillo and Tello (1998) developed frameworks for working on issues of responsibility and family violence. Green (1998) and Bepko, Almeida, Messineo, and Stevenson (1998) studied masculinity as a construct and its deconstruction at the intersection of sexual orientation, race, and class. This research proves fundamental in bringing into mainstream feminist literature the pervasive invisibility of people of color, lesbians, and gays. Espín (1994) observed that some of the negative attributions of people of color toward feminism have to do with the fact that the feminist movement has been defined mostly by the experiences of White women. Thus, she concluded that "because the feminist movement is indeed guilty of racism, the sexism that is prevalent in communities of color as in the dominant white society hides insidiously behind a cloak of ethnic loyalty" (p. 267).

THEORETICAL CONSTRUCTS

Narrative family therapists focus on the issue of language. Their epistemological positions are nonpositivist, in that proponents believe that theory and context can never be separated. Their work is located within a tradition of social constructionism, based in part on the assertion that reality cannot be known directly. This theory is founded on the assumption that the separation of the researcher (subject) and the phenomenon under discussion (object) is not feasible. Finally, a narrative approach to family therapy entails a special emphasis on the issues of power, history, and context.

Narrative approaches to family therapy are discussed in the works of White and Epston (1990), White (1995), Monk, Winslade, Crocket, and Epston, (1997), Freedman and Combs (1996), and in the feminist and narrative work of Weingarten (1991, 1992, 1998; Weingarten & Cobb, 1995), Avis and Turner (1996), and Hare-Mustin (1990, 1994, 1998). These writers assumed that, as meaning is constructed socially, it is contextual and historical. To understand their lives, people can construct meaning only within the world of language in which they are immersed. People make sense of their lives in the contexts of their social histories, and these contexts shape their stories about their identities as individuals and as members of groups. Social context becomes the basis for the possibility of providing coherence to people's personal lives. In fact, people's daily lives and practices prove meaningful only within contexts.

These narrative approaches to family therapy rely on the assumption that the meaning of a word can be established only by examining the context and manner in which the word is used, and not by appealing to abstract, logical, or grammatical rules (Wittgenstein, 1953). Language represents an activity that constructs meaning and requires intentionality. According to Anderson and Goolishian (1988), "Language does not mirror nature; language creates the natures we know" (p. 378). Through language, people construct meaning, and language itself is a shared performative activity. Words are meaningful in relation to their contexts, and the use of words in talking is a relational activity. Roberts (1994) asserted, "Everyone creates, tells, listens to, changes, and retells stories. As stories are told, people name and shape the meaning of the daily events of their lives and communicate that meaning to others" (p. 1). Storytelling is used to describe the ways people express themselves and make sense of their places in the social world. People organize their experiences and memories in the form of narratives.

At first glance, there exist many conceptual similarities between feminist and narrative approaches in family therapy. Approaches in both traditions draw on overlapping concepts in their theoretical frameworks and in their guidelines for clinical practice: constructed knowledge, deconstruction, power, and agency. Both highlight sociopolitical context as fundamental in shaping people's lives. Both developed a particular ethical stance consistent with their conceptual basis that addresses the power and agency dimensions (see Gosling & Zangari, 1996, for detailed discussion).

The feminist contribution to and integration with narrative approaches emerged as an understanding of gender as a category embedded in the whole of human experience. Avis (1996) argued that family therapy has to account for "an understanding of the symbolic dimensions by which patriarchy is embedded in language, culture, and experience, and is thus subtly communicated and internalized from the moment of birth" (p. 224). But, how can we reconcile a framework that emphasizes the relativity of human knowledge and experience with the political aims of feminism?

Feminist scholars (Mohanty, Russo, & Torres, 1991; Spivak, 1991) justified the reconciliation of the epistemological and political positions in two distinct ways. First, they noted that a feminist perspective seeks to identify a space for activism by women. This space is conceptualized as acknowledging the constructed nature of all social discourse. Nevertheless, this feminist perspective involves advocating a position of *strategic essentialism*, in which a subject position (say, feminism) is assumed to open up a space for activism, despite the acknowledgment of the constructed and contested nature of its concept (gender). Indeed, transcending the very subject position it has chosen for itself (the gendered subject) and rendering that position unremarkable represents the final goal of this position. However, such a position can be assumed only after the political project of feminism is achieved.

Second, Mohanty et al. (1991) and Spivak (1991) contextualized the experience of women under patriarchy as being but a *part* of their histories. Therefore, despite the loss of freedom under patriarchal society, there still exist, in however fragmented a form, elements of the female experience that need to be highlighted and affirmed. These elements are not invulnerable to critique, nor does the feminist critic seek to classify all elements of the female experience as antipatriarchal. However, to the extent that incommensurability with patriarchal narratives does not disqualify an experience, feminist views seek to make a case for the *politics of representation*. For instance, Garcia-Coll, Surrey, and Weingarten (1998) unmasked the oppressive effects of contemporary Western discourses on motherhood. In discussing women and power politics, Avis (1991) interrogated—or deconstructed—social discourses about gender relationships to expose the various forms of power and oppression that alienate women and to identify and offer alternatives for ways that affirm women in the world. In sum, feminist and narrative approaches to family therapy can be understood as epistemologically anchored in social constructionism and as politically rooted in feminism.

How can narrative and feminist approaches be used in family therapy in a practical manner? In this chapter, a case study of a Colombian woman is presented to illustrate the use of these theoretical frameworks. This particular case was selected to draw attention to the complexities of personal situations in which women experience simultaneously the effects of larger political struggles (e.g., against a state practice of disappearing citizens) and of personal agendas in which men use women for their own political advancement. This case illustrates various personal and political binds in which women of color or women from the Third World may find themselves struggling for larger causes and against peers and communities trying to tie them to oppressive practices.

MAJOR SYNDROMES, SYMPTOMS, AND PROBLEMS TREATED

The *Diagnostic and Statistical Manual of Mental Disorders IV-TR* (*DSM-IV-TR*) provides the standard compendium of diagnostic categories in the United States. The *International Classification of Diseases* of the World Health Organization constitutes a similar type of manual used in other countries. These manuals offer descriptive language for multiple levels of diagnosis and provide mental-health professionals with a common language to communicate their ideas and research. Feminist and narrative approaches emphasize the extent to which diagnoses are products of their time and place as well the relationships of psychiatric diagnosis to culture and history. Several authors (Hare-Mustin & Mareck, 1997; White, 1995) furnished a thorough and critical view of these systems of classification by analyzing the ways power is exercised to control individuals. Since it is not the purpose of this chapter to elaborate on this discussion, we offer one possible way to approach the use of standard diagnostic systems such as the *DSM-IV-TR* (APA, 2000).

Hare-Mustin and Mareck (1997) observed that the medical style and language of the *DSM-IV-TR* "implies that psychological disorders are closely akin to physical disorders, and that they exist apart from the life situations and cultural backgrounds of those who experience them" (p. 107). From a narrative and feminist perspective, this diagnostic system can be viewed as one way to story a client's issues. Thus, a clinician is able to comprehend and speak its language to communicate with other professionals in the mental-health system in which this represents the dominant way to address mental illnesses. However, with an understanding that this provides one way to story a client's issues, and that other ways are emphasized in therapy, a clinician will take into account the social and personal constraints implied in the *DSM-IV-TR* view to assist clients in deconstructing the effects of symptoms in their lives given their particular circumstances. White and Epston (1990) and Weingarten and Cobb (1995) have offered a variety of ways to address deconstruction in therapy through externalizing conversations, mapping questions, and collaboratively developing stories with clients.

Therefore, feminists and narrative therapists regard the multiaxial system offered by the *DSM-IV-TR* as a limited descriptor of a client's difficulties and use it to communicate with other professionals, to assist clients in understanding the meaning and implications of this view, and to deconstruct the effect that "symptoms" play in their lives. The Global Assessment of Relational Functioning Scale (GARF; Group for the Advancement of Psychiatry Committee on the Family, 1996) can be used to assist clients with scaling questions on how they view their changes in functioning. In addition, therapists may share with their clients and other professionals how they see changes in their clients' functioning. However, the personal and social levels of storytelling remain at the forefront. Clients are assisted in developing multiple and larger stories encompassing alternative ways to look at their issues.

Finally, issues regarding the evaluation of treatment effectiveness and empowerment of clients are open for future exploration. Therapists and theorists using these models may advance it by addressing the following issues: clients' beliefs in therapy's effective components, differences between narrative models in terms of process and outcome, and clients' experiences of empowerment.

CASE EXAMPLE: AN EXPLORATION INTO THE MEANING OF RESILIENCE AND HUMAN RIGHTS ACTIVISM IN WOMEN'S LIFE STORIES

CONTEXT: THE LOW-INTENSITY WAR IN COLOMBIA

To understand better the narrative of Gloria, a human rights activist from Colombia whose life story follows, it is important to be acquainted with the social context of her country. Salient aspects of this social context relevant to her life and alluded to in her conversations with a researcher (Hernández, 2000) have contributed to the kind of discourses at the foreground of her life.

Many Latin American countries have experienced internal wars and civil conflicts. Like many of their Latin American neighbors (in Guatemala, Chile, Argentina, Uruguay, El Salvador, Peru), Colombian people have suffered the effects of state terrorism and repression. However, Colombians continue to suffer under a slow and bloody 40-year dirty war. The histories of these countries have been varied as have been the nature of their violence and peace and reconciliation processes. However, they have all experienced repression by the state and its corollaries of persecution, torture, disappearances, and, most of all, impunity for the perpetrators. In Colombia, as well as in the rest of Latin America, people have coexisted with war, institutionalized violence, and social injustice for centuries. The legacy of wounds in people's hearts, minds, and bodies is partially reflected in the precariousness of social institutions and the progressive weakening of communities.

Colombia is the third most populated country in Latin America after Brazil and Mexico, with 38.5 million people. One in every 40 Colombians has been internally displaced (U.S. Committee for Refugees, 1998). The country's population is racially mixed and ethnically diverse (58% indigenous/European; 20% European descent; 14% African European; 4% African descent; 3% African/indigenous; 1% indigenous). A number of struggles are coevolving in Colombia. According to Sanchez et al. (1989), the various kinds of violence can be classified as violence arising from (1) organized group crime against politicians and journalists, (2) organized crime against private persons, (3) the guerrillas against the state, (4) the guerrillas against private persons, (5) the state apparatus to guard public order, (6) the state against social protest movements, (7) the state against ethnic minorities, and (8) organized private persons. The state of the war is characterized by this array of superimposed violence.

Since the country's independence (1810–1826), war has coexisted alongside institutionalized violence, particularly against women, the poor, and racially oppressed peoples. However, social movements have been born and reborn in spite of repression. These social movements, based in rural villages, urban shantytowns, universities, and workplaces have spawned a strong tradition of grassroots organizations. It is no surprise that sectors of Colombian educators, activists, and academics have contributed greatly to the emergence and evolution of participatory research action (Fals Borda, 1979, 1986).

Gloria's life narrative was obtained as part of a research project focused on developing stories within the marginalized narratives of survivors who became activists in human-rights forums (Hernández, 2000). This project involved exploring how these activists' experiences of discontinuity and dislocation were woven together to make meaning of their work with other victims. Gloria became involved in human-rights struggles as a way to respond to the needs of her loved ones, her community, and her belief in solidarity and social change. Her life narrative illustrates the process of making meaning out of survival experiences. From a feminist and narrative perspective, this context constitutes the foreground where discourses about womanhood, activism, and family life emerge for her. Her life narrative is tied to the historical circumstances surrounding adulthood, and her political choices are located within the realm of her life experiences. As Garbarino and Kostelny (1993) discerned, "Events taking place at the level of nations (the big picture) can reverberate down into the day-to-day life of the individual and the family (the little picture)" (p. 25). Looking at the life narratives of a human-rights activist like Gloria allows for the emergence of a larger picture about the social and political conditions of the country.

GLORIA'S LIFE NARRATIVE

Gloria grew up in an urban, working-class environment. The effects of poverty and social marginalization marked her life experiences. She has worked as a teacher and a community organizer since her adolescence. She finished her undergraduate and graduate studies in a university in a major city in Colombia and has long been involved in community and human-rights work. Gloria's life narrative illustrates issues of compassion fatigue, burnout, and gaining consciousness of her rights as a woman. Thus, these aspects are emphasized to illustrate process and change in her life as an adult.

Human-rights activists are constantly exposed to the pain and tragedies of the people they help. Figley and Kleber (1995) defined compassion fatigue as the "exposure to the knowledge of a traumatizing event experienced by a significant other" (p. 79). Figley (1995) suggested that it can emerge suddenly as a sense of helplessness, confusion, and isolation. Gloria's account of her experiences visiting Colombian jails, working with relatives of the disappeared, and internal displacement illustrates the multilevel effects of trauma in her life.

The presence of a woman caseworker representing a nongovernmental organization (NGO) was uncommon at the time in which Gloria used to visit women's and men's jails. She usually had to go through detailed checkups and harassment from the officers (women and men). Thus, she not only had to face personal stress, but also witness the suffering of political prisoners at the hands of officers. In the following excerpt, Gloria shares the impact of witnessing the pain and listening to the testimony of political prisoners while trying to develop strategies to support them emotionally and practically.

GLORIA: On one occasion I visited a political prisoner who had been tortured. His hands had been completely burnt... and one of his fingers had started to rot because he had no medical treatment. The perpetrator was [a well-known general]. We documented this and other cases. This is how I discovered what torture was about; it produced panic in me... but to address the topic in a rational manner, we developed a friendship with three physicians who examined and documented the cases.... It was like learning about the logic of the perpetrator and finding out resistance mechanisms.

It was shocking... because one would go to the jails and hear the testimony directly from the victim. At that time I used to listen to them and keep my tears inside.... I used to go to the jails in fear and had to face the humiliation of the check at the entrance and then I used to feel like weakened when leaving, after hearing all those stories.... In these jails I also met many people who never had done anything, who fell in there by chance and who were tortured. I remember that I used to get home and cry, and cry for hours. I used to share it with my team colleagues... and the way to confront the fear was by rescuing the political ideals. My work in the jails was extremely tense, so much that I used to wonder how I was able to cope with it.

There are two things that I learned in this work: first, that since I was visiting a population who is discriminated against and stigmatized, it implied a risk to my life and safety. It was valuable because this is an encounter with a human being who is very lonely and in a precarious condition.... Second, these Colombian jails are horrible places ... with social contradictions and the presence of human evil. You face human capacity for evil within the delinquents; they continue to hurt others.... Facing organized delinquency in the jails is very hard!

... When I found myself so ill I got very depressed and tried to think what I had done until that time.... My hypoglycemia used to go very high because I was not eating properly; I would only have a cup of soup during the day while visiting the jails. I used to get home late extremely tired to then work again the next day (Hernández, 2000).

In a longitudinal study with refugees and families of the disappeared, Allodi and Rojas (1985) discerned that families of the disappeared experience more symptoms than refugees because of the stress of uncertainty and the continued effects of a mode of terror that stifles resistance and expression of distress. The freezing quality of the fear associated with this experience is maintained by the perception that the family member's behavior may be used as a justification to kill the person. The effects of working closely with people who have suffered this kind of loss were a great source of pain for Gloria. At the time, she felt a tremendous fear of the possibility that she could lose her children in a similar manner.

GLORIA: The painful meaning of forced disappearance is too much for me; I have come to that conclusion, especially when it comes to women and mothers. I had a very maternal relationship with them and I became the secretary, the mediator of conflicts.... I also had to face their bitterness and lack of trust and jealously.... With time I realized that all these issues were part of their problems. However, the effect on me was fear. It produces fear when you know the extent of the human capacity for evil. One finds oneself thinking and talking repeatedly on the topic, becoming monothematic ... watching videos from Argentina, meeting regularly with the relatives. I had to stop. I felt overwhelmed and emotionally very committed to the extent of trying to do more than I could.

Forced disappearance remains a common state strategy to repress dissent. It looms as a poignant and important story in Gloria's life narrative regarding her work with women who suddenly lost their loved ones and never heard from them again. From a clinical perspective, therapy would involve encouraging her to weave the disappearance stories with wider stories of support and strategies of community solidarity. For instance, it would include exploring ways to relate to people and helping her connect with a local organization to support the relatives of the disappeared. She may find ways to help make a difference for these relatives at the level of developing support groups and work groups to educate through the media. A feminist and narrative stance would assist and support her in maintaining her political commitments while understanding victims from various perspectives to allow her distance from highly painful and emotionally volatile situations at work.

Gloria also experienced other stressful situations in her work in human rights. These occurred in the context of her already overwhelming jobs in human-rights NGOs. They added a good deal of pressure and pain in her life and became part of the process of overcoming trauma, asserting herself, and redefining her life. These experiences refer to a fundamental and often unspoken dimension of human-rights work.

In his discussion on compassion fatigue and burnout, Figley (1995) discussed that stressful working conditions in professions facing high risk of trauma exposure add a tremendous weight to the development of symptoms associated with emotional and physical exhaustion. Two issues become apparent in Gloria's narrative: (1) how nontraumatic stressful situations combine in the lives of women human-rights activists to take an additional toll in an already dangerous environment and (2) the salience of gender dynamics in some NGOs.

While working on organizing an international conference on internal displacement, Gloria went through a stressful situation that led to her becoming ill. This situation resembles burnout combined with the kind of compassion fatigue involved in human-rights work. As one of the main persons involved in organizing this conference, Gloria was responsible for its planning and outcomes. Although this was an international conference, the organizers were interested in approaching each country's situation according to its particular problems and dilemmas. As is usual in these conferences, participants have a wide variety of opinions, and controversial issues are discussed openly. However, uninformed critiques came from a foreign organization; its representatives wanted to restrict access to certain participants who were taking part in controversies. Political differences emerged both among the participants and with the organizers. She argued both that it did not appear as if they had thorough knowledge of the displaced people in Colombia and for the need to include a wide variety of participants in speaking for different political and social sectors. The controversy generated by these critiques left her feeling that her work and efforts were not valued because she received no support or recognition.

GLORIA: I was in the consulting committee for a conference on displacement: it was a topic that needed a lot of discussion, and it was difficult because the views were very polarized. For example, there were communities who were trying to resist expulsion from their lands, and their efforts were being interpreted as armed resistance. That was not the case. All the critics came to me, and afterwards I somatized. I was a moderator in a debate, and the representatives from this organization wanted me to censor certain people. I thought that all should have the right to express our views. But they thought that allowing the venting of opinions would harm their image as an objective institution. . . . Besides I also had to worry about safety issues with the participants. It was so tense that I ended up absolutely ill. I could not get up from the bed; I was immobilized with neuralgia for a week. This has happened to me several times in the last six years.

Gloria remembered feeling the effects of her work as illnesses and symptoms of different kinds. She related that the crisis that emerged after conflicts in the conference and the loss of persecuted friends were events that contributed to her developing intense and unexplained body pain:

GLORIA: I think that there have been very strong crises when I think that I am falling apart, and I sit and cry for days, especially when someone is killed. Someone with whom I worked . . . it is hard and I get depressed, I lose my appetite and sleep. I feel tired, and these neuralgias make me immobile for two or three days. I consulted a physician, thinking that it was a bone problem.

In regard to the language used in countries like El Salvador to express mind and body pain, Hunter (1991) concluded that the word *nervios* or "nerves" is a common descriptor that people use to depict their sufferings. This Spanish word "refers at once to matters of mind, body and spirit and does not make good cultural sense in relation to mind-body dualisms" (p. 151). This word is also commonly used in

Colombia and is reflective of the situation that Gloria was going through.

The effect of oppression against women exerted an underlying pressure on Gloria. Her experience points at an often-unspoken dimension embedded in human-rights work in a country with a strong legacy of machismo and entrenched patriarchal structures. Gloria worked in NGOs whose members claimed to be committed to a progressive agenda, openness, and support for political struggles. Nevertheless, the legacy of machismo in the activists' gender relationships remained poignant. Machismo connotes an ideology based on an assertion of males' "natural superiority" over females (Fisher, 1993, p. 3). Gloria shared several experiences of discrimination by men and their lack of acknowledgment of her work in public and international settings. These experiences later constituted the ground for questioning gender dynamics and for change in her personal life and work-related relationships.

For example, a common way women activists face gender discrimination arises from the traditional stereotypes about women as nonintellectual and emotional. Gloria, an accomplished writer, researcher, and activist, faced such violence against herself when working for a predominantly male NGO. Rosenbloom, Pratt, and Pearlman (1995) suggested that a factor influencing a helper's experience of compassion fatigue revolves around the organizational context. The ways an organization responds to the person and his or her work may reinforce the harmful effects of traumatic reactions. In Gloria's experience:

GLORIA: One of the most important cultural shocks for me was to face a class, or an intellectual elite very much into academic research, that did not accept activism and that saw us as people without the mental structure to produce political analysis.... At that time I felt that I did not have support. I tried to do the most I could! I did more studies in human rights overseas, and I tried to demonstrate to the male researchers my capacities. After five years I concluded that I did not have to compete with any of them.... They can talk about their sociological, anthropological and political theories, but that does not transform reality. I remembered that public debates made me very anxious. When we had our internal analysis meetings, I did not dare to speak because every time I intervened they would say that I was descriptive and not analytic! Emotional and not rational! Curiously I developed close relationships with the international human rights community and started working systematically with Amnesty International.... I proposed the presentation of cases of the disappeared at the United Nations, we presented the cases, and they were accepted!

When asked how she thought she was perceived by her colleagues, Gloria mentioned the pervasiveness of the traditional stereotypes that men use to identify women and her proactive stance to battle them:

GLORIA: I do not have the ability to express my points of view in a slow and persuasive manner. Many people think that I am a person for whom affections are very important and that then I am very subjective in how I appreciate reactions at work. For example, they label me as subjective, susceptible and emotional, yes?

INTERVIEWER: Who do you think considers you in that manner?

GLORIA: Usually co-workers. Men, that is why I feel more angry, right? Because they say that I think with my heart and not with my head. But now, having gone through my gender studies, I tell them that I do not understand how people can leave aside one part of themselves if people are integral human beings.

After Gloria moved to another organization where work with women was an important issue on the agenda, she started to be active in changing the gender dynamics in the field:

GLORIA: After I moved to another NGO, I had more time to dedicate to my son. That was very important. I also started to have more contact with the Latin American reality while keeping the work focused on Colombia. I was working on issues related to supporting unity among human-rights NGOs and also on developing democratic processes for the female and male co-workers in the NGOs and in international organizations. So we got to train groups nationally on human rights and on how to get access to the United Nations.... At that time there were a few organizations, usually run by men, lawyers, that were considered big enough and that had access to international organizations to present cases. And that— legal process to present cases—is not complicated. It requires a process, sure ... it is a technical process, strict in its regulations. It is not mysterious when you unveil it and put it to people's service, so that people know what it is, how to do it, and what it is for without the mediation of a lawyer.... When I started to work here, I went to a conference on women in Latin America. They evaluated how different countries' legislation had incorporated issues from the international convention against discrimination towards women. This was very important to me because I started to ask myself about my role as a woman in human rights. I had not asked myself that question before.

INTERVIEWER: How did you start to ask that question?

GLORIA: Basically because of the debates on equity. Some of the questions in the evaluation asked: How many women work in your organization? How many have high-level jobs? What were my opportunities to participate in public activities? And I started to realize that, besides being an activist, I was a woman and that we had an absolute deficit in our human-rights organizations, because we were not recognized as being as important as men were in public events. When there was a need to give a lecture, they will always look for men first, not women. So, we started to work with some women on how to help women have more important roles while acknowledging men's experience and abilities.

This experience reaffirmed her identity as a woman and as an activist. She incorporated the gender dimension into her educational activities. Her work was transformed as she discussed gender issues in organizations mainly composed of men. Another accomplishment that helped her regain confidence was finishing a master's degree. After receiving very positive feedback for her work, she proved to herself that the undermining environment of that previous organization was rooted in the men's prejudices against women. She noted that other types of situations occurred to maintain a gender imbalance in these organizations, for example, publishing writings without recognizing the women who collaborated on their production. A key experience in Gloria's development of a gender consciousness and a gender agenda arose through contact with women from other countries who had already made connections between oppression against women and human rights. Through these interactions, Gloria was able to position herself differently within the NGO environment in Colombia.

From a *clinical perspective*, a feminist and narrative-therapy framework could have been anchored in exploring her relationships with men at work and at home as well as her ways to resist interactions with them that she experienced as oppressive. Her identity as a woman could have been strengthened as she found a voice and a way to articulate her views in her feminist readings. She could have developed practical ways to resist and challenge her colleagues' sexism in the workplace at a personal level and by organizing other women around relevant issues. She could also have developed other stories about motherhood based on how she wanted to integrate her family and political commitments.

Exploratory ideas that might specifically address Gloria's issues in therapy embrace:

- What consequences do her present interpretations of the past have for her in the future (to relate stories of how she sees herself as a woman with her views of being an activist)?
- What family stories connect her and differentiate her from the social struggles of the women she worked for on the issue of forced disappearance?
- How do the ways she tells her stories about herself connect her with some social issues and not with others?
- What are the cultural discourses and selfhood stories regarding women's roles in the family?
- How were key stories about the ongoing Colombian civil war passed down through the generations? What themes were embodied in these stories? How do these stories speak to her today as a human rights activist? If therapy assists her in reexamining these stories, what different meanings could develop?

This case study illustrates how a feminist and narrative clinical framework provides a lens for understanding and integrating the social, political, and personal. The complexities brought up by this case point to how feminist and narrative approaches offer a clinical framework encompassing therapeutic conversations about a woman's identity within a larger political struggle. In the next section, we move from story to theory, that is, from the case to theoretical ideas on narrative and feminist approaches to family therapy. Useful concepts are elaborated to articulate clinical work at a theoretical level.

A FRAMEWORK FOR NARRATIVE AND FEMINIST ANALYSES

The processes of *discourse, story, deconstruction,* and *ethics* aid in developing a framework for narrative and feminist approaches. The concepts of discourse and story help us understand how persons construct realities while speaking and the dominance of certain ways of determining what is acceptable. Deconstruction connotes how feminist and narrative practitioners challenge, decenter, and subvert dominant patriarchal perspectives of family therapy. On the issue of ethics, these two approaches are based on the belief that the concept of a value-neutral therapist is spurious: All therapists operate from strategic subject positions, which they need to make apparent in their work.

Discourse

Therapeutic conversations involve examining issues that address a person's sense of the discourses shaping his or her life. A discourse is defined as a power-laden worldview that provides context for a variety of social and personal behaviors and attitudes. Some discourses or "larger social narratives" modulate individual stories and specify preferred ways of believing and behaving in particular contexts (Pierce & Cronen, 1980). This specificity regarding context implies that, to make sense of how other people understand their lives, it is necessary to understand their backgrounds and the contexts to which they relate. According to Hare-Mustin (1994), the concept of discourse can be understood as "a system of statements, practices, and institutional structures that share common values. A discourse includes both linguistic and nonlinguistic aspects; it is the medium that provides the words and ideas for thought and speech, as well as the cultural practices involving related concepts and behaviors" (p. 19). Weingarten (1991) added specificity to defining the concept of discourse:

1. A discourse consists of ideas and practices that share common values.
2. Any discourse reflects and constructs a specific worldview.
3. There are dominant and subjugated discourses. Dominant discourses contain and constrain what we can feel, think and do.
4. That which is not part of the discourse shapes our experiences as critically as the discourse itself.
5. Discourse evolves. Changes of discourse occur when the collective conversations people have about their lives transform culturally available dominant narratives about people's lives. . . . Individuals recognize the need to dispute and transform any discourse by reflecting on their conversations with others. (p. 286)

For example, discourses about mothers in the United States and other cultures are embedded in cultural messages about "good" and "bad" mothering. Women struggle to story their lives within these cultural messages because they do not fit with their lived experiences (Garcia-Coll et al., 1998). Another example, pertinent to the case example about Gloria presented earlier, is how mainstream media in and outside of Colombia avoid portraying the challenge of understanding and reporting about the superimposed violence in the country and the increasing intervention of the United States. Thus, discourses about Colombia and Colombians overemphasize a vision of drugs and delinquency while keeping silent about persistent and horrendous human-rights violations and the many layers of the ongoing civil war (Giraldo, 1996). In the same vein, Gloria's story about forced disappearance in Colombia makes salient a problem of national dimension. However, the mainstream media in and outside the country choose to emphasize *only* another national problem: kidnapping.

Using Gloria's case as an example of engaging in discourse, a therapist might explore the following questions:

- What are common practices and ideas about women, and women involved in human-rights struggles in Gloria's world?
- How do these practices and ideas shape her ways of being assertive? Silent? How do they mold her experiencing suffering and her choices to move away from painful situations?
- How are women's rights prioritized in the larger political struggle of her country?
- How does loyalty to a movement prevent/ allow her selection of certain personal choices?

Story

The term story alludes to people's interpretations of their past, present, and possibilities for the future. However, stories change as people reconstruct their past experiences with different lenses. White and Epston (1990) acknowledged that stories are not coherent and consistent all the time and that the "evolution of life is akin to the process of re-authoring, the process of persons entering into stories, taking them over and making them their own" (p. 13). In addition, physicality and embodiment receive emphasis in defining narratives in the realm of the experiences of people in a real world. Cronen (1994) explained that "the reality of embodiment in a real world does not determine how reality counts in our activities; its meaning must be worked out in social action" (p. 33). For Gloria, her story was located in the context of a low-intensity and dirty war, where thousands have died and more than a million have been displaced.

Deconstruction

It must always be kept in mind that a large body of research on family therapy exists that constitutes a kind of "mainstream tradition." If we are to articulate an alternative (narrative and feminist) approach to family therapy, one key task is to decenter this mainstream thinking. One of the ways this must be done is through the act of deconstruction, in which the dominant (and unarticulated) assumptions of canonical texts can be challenged. The technique of deconstruction was first popularized by Jacques Derrida (1974) and has been used extensively in family therapy.

According to Avis (1996), deconstruction entails the process by which "assumptions about women and their roles embedded in dominant cultural beliefs, 'knowledge,' and practices" (p. 233) are examined and challenged. "As what is accepted as the way things are is deconstructed, the external sources of personal beliefs are illuminated and personal choice, free from cultural gender prescriptions, becomes possible" (p. 233). For example, deconstructing traditional gender expectations with Gloria may involve an analysis of her developing awareness of her capabilities and current role at her workplace and in the public arena, and also the process of exploring internalized "mandates" that have become oppressive as they have saturated people's lives (White & Epston, 1990).

White (1995) defined deconstruction as a process that subverts taken-for-granted realities and practices, that is, the "truths" that are split off from the conditions and contexts of their production, and that subjugate people's lives. Several authors (Gottlieb & Gottlieb, 1996; Laird, 1989; Roberts, 1994; Roth, 1993) have worked on illustrating deconstruction processes on a variety of topics. Laird addressed the issue of silence in women's stories under a patriarchal system of knowledge production. For her, therapy with women is about rewriting and writing new stories that make it possible to overcome oppression against women.

Others (Avis, 1991; Hare-Mustin, 1990, 1998; Roth, 1993) have spoken of making oppression visible when political conditions constrain particular events from being narrated. For example, Roth commented on the process of naming and giving voice to and between groups of homosexual and heterosexual people working in the same organization. Hare-Mustin (1990) linked the personal with the political in pointing out how life stories are obscured by dominant knowledges. In her work with Cambodian refugee women, Robin (1992) described the empowering dimension of narration and oral history provided through the sharing and reconstruction of individual and community experiences of suffering. In a broad manner, these approaches share similar trends. They give primacy to the establishment of collaborative relationships, focus on the development of personal authority by finding a voice and becoming visible, and link everyday relationships to a political dimension. In her work on cultural and personal stories, Roberts (1994) illustrated how "cultural stories are narratives about events and issues that cut across the lives of individuals and affect groups of people and families" (p. 124). She pointed out that therapists need to be aware of the dominance that certain cultural stories may have and that they need to ask about "unheard cultural stories," so that silenced as well as stereotypical stories are challenged and revisited. In her work on child sexual abuse and the construction of identity from a feminist perspective, Davies (1995) explained how the process of rendering unprivileged stories visible is made possible through the power of words. Storied experiences break the silence on unspeakable issues in the hope that an audience will join and engage with the people and the issues to put forward a judgment on them. Human rights endeavors all over the world stand for struggles to break the silence on inhuman practices. Davies articulated the political dimension of this work:

> It is in this sense that such first-person accounts are explicitly committed to the political importance of writing and reading strategies for the creation of identity, community and political solidarity. Telling, writing and reading such accounts are linked to the important task of countering representations that have made women and children silent, invisible, deviant, perverse, aberrant or marginal. (pp. 3–4)

The integration of narrative and feminist approaches in clinical practice offers specific tools to guide the work. These approaches provide conceptual means to address clients' stories in terms of (1) relationships between everyday life practices and the multiple meanings they may have, (2) situated processes in time, and (3) politics of social discourses embedded in personal accounts. For example, Gloria's story about her conflicts with men at work illustrates her facing and developing an understanding of sexism in progressive organizations.

Ben-David's (1996) work with immigrant women in single-parent families provides another example of how to address stories. She recounted the stories of women from very different backgrounds (Ethiopia and the former Soviet Union), their migration to Israel, and the many transitions leading to change in their family structures and positions as women in the host society. She illustrated how they had to cope both with the migration process and with the responsibilities of single parenthood. She posited that these women "may be under extreme pressure to make rapid social changes in order to adapt to dominant social conventions" (p. 44) and that therapy needs to be empowering of their cultural backgrounds and sensitive to their strengths as single mothers. By addressing the meanings of the social contexts in which they were socialized as a way to interpret the new transitions, issues of child rearing, relations with extended family and daily survival, and their migration histories are taken into account to make coherent sense of their past, present, and future.

In therapy, feminist and narrative practitioners speak of empowerment to refer to the process "resulting from one person having the experience of another person accepting and collaboratively elaborating what she has to say" (Weingarten & Cobb, 1995, p. 1). This process is based on conversations among participants, clients and therapists, who pay attention to the ways they all make meaning. In Laird's (1989) words: "Therapy, then, may be described as an effort to help a client not only to comprehend her story, to choose among many possible interpretations, to rewrite it, but perhaps, in the cases of those denied their own stories through upheaval or disruption, also to compose new stories which can become models for future action" (p. 432). The empowering dimension of this kind of therapeutic approach stems from the mutual cocreation of meaning in which the therapist is key in the reconstruction of clients' life stories. With regard to therapists, this mutual cocreation implies that they acknowledge their location in the social world in terms of gender, race, class, ethnicity, and sexual preference and its implications. It also implies that therapists acknowledge the contributions of therapeutic interactions in their own lives.

Deconstruction and empowerment are intertwined processes aimed at developing personal agency. Avis (1996) conceptualized agency as "the ability to take action in one's own life and one's own behalf.... It is the freedom to make choices and to act on them. The ability to say 'no,' to assert, to do, by choice and without socialized guilt" (p. 232). This means facilitating that clients act on their own behalf based on their own self-determined goals.

ETHICAL STANCE

Within a feminist and narrative approach, clarity in the ethical dimension assumes paramount importance. As a general guide, therapeutic work is framed within an ethic of responsibility in which therapists develop the ability to appreciate their positions in therapeutic conversations (Hoffman, 1990). Weingarten (1992) explained this dimension of responsibility:

> The therapist may accept that he or she is constantly selecting aspects of the conversation to amplify or diminish, and believe that this process of selection is guided by a number of variables, including the therapist's experiences gained by virtue of being located in a particular racial, gendered, and class position in the wider sociopolitical context within which the therapy takes place. (p. 52)

Also, as when therapy is approached as a conversation with a person who has specific expertise, responsibility for the ways that the therapist's expertise is used may be shared with the client. In feminist and narrative approaches, the vocabulary and the understanding of therapists' sharing about themselves are seen as being "culturally visible." In the narrative tradition, a therapist's interventions are situated in the contexts of personal experiences, imagination, and intentional states (White, 1995). This practice contributes to constructing a context in which clients have more space to decide how they might interpret a therapist's responses.

A feminist stance emphasizes a certain attitude toward justice and the effects of oppressive gender relationships. If this perspective was not acknowledged, the approach would fall into the trap of considering interpretive descriptions as carrying their own meanings and therefore having equal value. According to Waldegrave (1990):

> Justice highlights equity in relationships between people: it involves naming the structures and the actions that oppress and destroy equity in relationships. This is reflected in families at the micro level, and beyond in social structures at the macro level. Just therapy must always take both into account. (p. 7)

Almeida (1998) critiqued personal narrative as a feminist form indicating that the privileging of personal stories by White women "privatizes gender and fails to build coalitions among diverse groups of women" (pp. 10–11). That is, personal narratives obscure the stories of women who think of themselves more as a collective in which race and colonial dimensions are key issues. She believed that narrative approaches obscure the collective dimension of political struggles that most women share around the world. "Collective" means the building of a new discourse, acknowledging the intersections of gender, class, sexual orientation, and race. Narrative and feminist therapies involve deconstructing oppressive notions of racism and classism and working toward the development of new identities. Advocates of this approach remain sensitive to the issue of gender, class, and colonial oppression. The difference is that, although it recognizes the categories as a basis for experiences of marginalization and oppression, it does not accord these categories an autonomous character; rather, it locates them within people's narratives. Therefore, a way to think about our clients and us is not only embedded in the worlds of race, class, and gender, for our identities are more than the sum total of the social and institutional effects of these identity-formations. From this perspective, Avis' (1989) training assumptions fit very well. She proposed that an understanding of gender poses an ethical imperative, that therapy implies a political process. Frames of reference organize what people see and what they know. The category of gender organizes worldviews. Recognition that all are racist and sexist remains a pivotal training assumption.

Another key ethical aspect revolves around reciprocity and a therapist's involvement and participation in a client's narrative. As meaning is negotiated and coconstructed, Weingarten (1992) cautioned:

> Therapists and their clients may be vulnerable to being "knitted" into each other's lives. Though therapy can be a close, intense, and intimate situation in which sharing and co-creation of meaning occurs, it is essential that the material about which meanings are shared and co-created is predominantly from the client's and not the therapist's life, and that the "knitting," if it occurs, does not involve the construction and protection of joined narratives. Therapists who routinely review their clinical work with colleagues are in part acting to minimize the possibility of joined narratives.... Though therapists use their life experience, as the foundation from which they do their work, their life experience must not become merged with their client's life experience. (p. 52)

In sum, key ethical components of feminist and narrative approaches include transparency, an understanding and a stance toward the gendered way in which persons view the world, and reciprocity. Within this approach, keeping in mind and discussing the participants' abilities to appreciate their positions in therapeutic conversations remain very important. An understanding of gender represents an ethical imperative in acknowledging that therapy constitutes a political process. Finally, clinicians have an obligation to avoid merging and emphasizing their personal stories with the clients' stories. The clinician's story must not become the script for clients' stories.

IMPLICATIONS FOR TREATMENT

Given the varied philosophical foundations of the feminist and narrative approaches, one cannot delineate a *model* that would represent the multiple approaches practitioners may develop guided by these ideas. However, some guidelines consistent with this approach's philosophy merit discussion in light of the case presented earlier. First, explaining at the outset the collaborative nature of the therapeutic relationship may begin to establish trust and the expectation of developing agency in the therapeutic process. Second, therapy with women in situations of political persecution will necessarily require an awareness of the sociopolitical context in which these women grew up and chose to work. It will also necessitate awareness of the meaning of defending the right to live in the midst of civil war and the implications of being involved in human-rights causes. Therapists must assume a position of transparency regarding their stance toward women and politics. Clients who have struggled so much in the public arena may need to know where the therapist stands to gain trust and to let themselves be vulnerable in therapy.

Third, the process of deconstructing or questioning assumptions about their womanhood may be a challenging endeavor because they are already politicized. These issues should be explored in light of helping them define themselves as women who do not fit certain social expectations. These issues may become clear when exploring the impact of persecution on children and partners as well as family relationships.

Fourth, therapy with these clients would be focused on the development of alternative stories that may embrace the challenging choices they have made in their lives. This entails a joint venture in comprehending their life stories, rewriting them, and composing new stories after suffering the damaging effects of upheaval and disruption. For example, a therapist might trace their development as women finding voices for their adolescent experiences of war and oppression. The therapist can give hope by projecting that development into the future as these women discover the value of their experiences as a legacy for their families and social networks.

RESEARCH

Ratliff and Randall (2001) indicated that there has been a growing body of qualitative research in family therapy over the past 10 years. In 1998, Chenail discussed the use of qualitative research and the legitimation of knowledge in systemic approaches to family therapy. Its use has expanded in the past decade because of its emphasis on social context, multiple perspectives, individual differences, and holism (Moon, Dillon, & Sprenkle, 1990). For example, Weingarten (1992) illustrated and analyzed intimate and nonintimate interactions in therapy through cases. Likewise, Sluzki (1992) used a family therapy case to explain the legacy of migration issues in the process of change in therapy.

Various qualitative research methodologies may be well-suited for studying this approach, for example, ethnography, phenomenological interviews, ethnographic content analysis, naturalistic inquiry, participant action research, and grounded theory. However, the methodological work of Riessman (1993, 1994) on narrative analysis is of particular relevance to narrative and feminist approaches. According to Riessman (1994), as personal stories become autobiographical narratives, they, in turn, blend with a community of stories articulating people's larger worldviews. Assuming that "culture speaks itself through an individual's story" (p. 69), autobiographical data portray the social and political contexts in which persons are embedded. Personal narratives are deeply embedded in historical and cultural contexts.

Because narrative analysis is intended to systematically interpret participants' perspectives on their experiences and "gives prominence to human agency and imagination, it is well suited to studies of subjectivity and identity" (Riessman, 1993, p. 5). "Narrativizing" as a collaborative investigative dialogue makes explicit the interventional nature of research, that is, the weaving together of stories as they are elaborated in the conversations between researcher and participants. It provides a space for discontinuities and dislocations of the "multistoried nature of life" (White, 1995, p. 15). Taking narratives in their own right assumes that through them we construct and express meaning. Therefore, they are key units of discourse that allow the study of the fundamental human activity of storytelling. These views were knitted together as they combined personal experiences in the midst of a country under social unrest in Detzner's (1992) research on conflict in Southeast Asian refugee families. He used life stories to investigate the refugees' adjustment patterns while he also attended to their cultural framework. This choice of methodology allowed him to explore "shared experiences and meanings across a number of life histories" (p. 88) to analyze the impact of war and forced relocation on individuals and families.

Finally, the notions of transparency and positioning emerge as of paramount importance to narrative and feminist approaches to family therapy (Hare-Mustin, 1994; Weingarten, 1991; White, 1995) because at the heart of these approaches lies an examination of the power-knowledge relationship. Researchers agree that knowledge is produced in specific social, historical contexts and is inscribed in the ways people conceive the world. White noted the transparency and self-positioning evident in the practice of a therapist's deconstructing of his or her own interventions in therapy. This is done by "situating them in the context of his/her personal experiences, imagination, and intentional states" (p. 144). Thus, a researcher becomes "culturally visible" to those with whom he or she is interacting in a situation of power.

SUMMARY

This chapter has examined how narrative and feminist approaches can be used in working with women in a context of social upheaval and political volatility. A review of the literature in family therapy on gender as well as an articulation of key concepts in narrative and feminist therapy were explored. Feminist and narrative approaches are suitable for attending to the ways women develop and maintain family ties, the relations they establish between traumatic experiences and recovery, the contexts in which they live, and the challenges they face in their work environment. A detailed empirical example from a Colombian human-rights activist illustrated how a feminist and narrative clinical framework provides a lens for understanding and integrating the social, political, and personal. The complexities brought up by this case pointed to how a therapist's preferred clinical framework encompasses certain therapeutic conversations about a working-class woman's identity within a larger political struggle. An inductive approach suggested a case to use clinical frameworks that interweave personal experience with context to break with traditional conceptions of womanhood that ultimately constrain women of color. Finally, the ethical dimension and the implications for practice were discussed.

REFERENCES

Allodi, F., & Rojas, A. (1985). The health and adaptation of victims of political violence in Latin America. In P. Pichot, P. Berner, & R. Wolf (Eds.), *Psychiatry: The state of the art* (Vol. 6., pp. 243–248). New York: Plenum Press.

Almeida, R., & Durkin, T. (1999). The cultural context model: Therapy for couples with domestic violence. *Journal of Marital and Family Therapy, 25*(3), 5–32.

Almeida, R., Wood, M., Messineo, T., & Font, R. (1998). The cultural context model: An overview. In M. McGoldrick (Ed.), *Revisioning family therapy* (pp. 414–432). New York: Guilford Press.

Almeida, R. V. (1998). The dislocation of women's experience in family therapy. *Journal of Feminist Family Therapy, 10*(1), 1–22.

American Psychiatric Association. (2000). *Diagnostic and statistical manual of mental disorders* (4th ed., text rev.). Washington, DC: Author.

Anderson, H., & Goolishian, H. (1988). Human systems as linguistic systems: Preliminary and evolving ideas about the implications for clinical theory. *Family Process, 27,* 371–393.

Avis, J. M. (1985). The politics of functional family therapy: A feminist critique. *Journal of Marital and Family Therapy, 11,* 127–138.

Avis, J. M. (1989). Integrating gender into the family therapy curriculum. *Journal of Feminist Family Therapy, 1,* 3–24.

Avis, J. M. (1991). Power politics in therapy with women. In T. J. Goodrich (Ed.), *Women and power* (pp. 42–80). New York: Norton.

Avis, J. M. (1996). Deconstructing gender in family therapy. In F. Piercey & D. Sprenkle (Eds.), *Family therapy source book* (pp. 220–255). New York: Guilford Press.

Avis, J. M., & Turner, J. (1996). Feminist lenses in family therapy research: Gender politics and science. In D. H. Sprenkle & S. M. Moon (Eds.), *Research methods in family therapy* (pp. 145–169). New York: Guilford Press.

Ben-David, A. (1996). The narrative of life: Immigrant women in single-parent families. *Journal of Feminist Family Therapy, 8*(1), 29–46.

Bepko, C., Almeida, R. V., Messineo, T., & Stevenson, Y. (1998). Evolving constructs of masculinity: Interviews with Andres Nazario Jr., William Doherty, and Roberto Font: Commentary. *Journal of Feminist Family Therapy, 10*(1), 49–80.

Bograd, M. (1984). Family systems approach to wife battering: A feminist critique. *American Journal of Orthopsychiatry, 54,* 558–568.

Bograd, M. (Ed.). (1990). *Feminist approaches for men in therapy.* New York: Harrington Park Press.

Bograd, M. (1999). Strengthening domestic violence theories: Intersections of race, class, sexual orientation and gender. *Journal of Marriage and Family Therapy, 25*(3), 275–290.

Carrillo, R., & Tello, J. (1998). *Family violence and men of color.* New York: Springer.

Chenail, R., & Tello, J. (1998). Qualitative research and the legitimization of knowledge. *Journal of Marital and Family Therapy, 17*(2), 175–180.

Cronen, V. (1994). Coordinated management of meaning: Practical theory for the complexities and contradictions of everyday life. In J. Siegfried (Ed.), *The status of common sense in psychology* (pp. 71–98). New York: Ablex.

Davies, M. (1995). *Healing Sylvia*. London: Taylor & Francis.

Derrida, J. (1974). *Of grammatology*. Baltimore: Johns Hopkins University Press.

Detzner, D. (1992). Life stories: Conflict in South East Asian refugee families. In J. F. Gilgun, K. Daly, & G. Handel (Eds.), *Qualitative methods in family research* (pp. 85–102). Newbury Park, CA: Sage.

Espín, O. (1994). Feminist approaches. In L. Comas-Díaz & B. Green (Eds.), *Women of color* (pp. 265–286). New York: Guilford Press.

Fals Borda, O. (1979). *Conocimiento y poder popular* [Knowledge and popular power]. Bogotá, Columbia: Siglo, XXI.

Fals Borda, O. (1986). *Conocimiento y poder popular* [Knowledge and popular power] (2nd ed.). Bogotá, Columbia: Siglo, XXI.

Figley, C. R. (1995). Compassion fatigue: Toward a new understanding of the costs of caring. In H. Stamm (Ed.), *Secondary traumatic stress* (pp. 3–28). Lutherville, MD: Sidran Press.

Figley, C. R., & Kleber, R. F. (1995). Beyond the victim: Secondary traumatic stress. In R. F. Kleber, C. R. Figley, & B. P. R. Gersons (Eds.), *Beyond trauma: Cultural and societal dynamics* (pp. 75–98). New York: Plenum Press.

Fisher, J. (1993). *Out of the shadows: Women, resistance and politics in South America*. London: Latin America Bureau.

Freedman, J., & Combs, G. (1996). *Narrative therapy*. New York: Norton.

Garbarino, J., & Kostelny, K. (1993). Neighborhood and community influences on parenting. In T. Lustar & L. Okaga (Eds.), *Parenting: An ecological perspective* (pp. 203–226). Hillsdale, NJ: Erlbaum.

Garcia-Coll, C., Surrey, J., & Weingarten, K. (Eds.). (1998). *Mothering against the odds*. New York: Guilford Press.

Giraldo, J. (1996). *Colombia: The genocidal democracy*. Maine: Common Courage Press.

Goldner, V. (1985). Feminism and family therapy. *Family Process, 24,* 31–47.

Gosling, A., & Zangari, M. E. (1996). Feminist family therapy and the narrative approach: Dovetailing two frameworks. *Journal of Feminist Family Therapy, 8*(1), 15–29.

Gottlieb, D. T., & Gottlieb, C. D. (1996). The narrative/collaborative process in couples therapy: A postmodern perspective. *Women and Therapy, 19*(3), 37–47.

Green, R. J. (1998). Traditional norms of masculinity. *Journal of Feminist Family Therapy, 10*(1), 81–84.

Group for the Advancement of Psychiatry Committee on the Family. (1996). Global Assessment of Relational Functioning Scale (GARF): I. Background and rationale. *Family Process, 35,* 155–172.

Hare-Mustin, R. (1978). A feminist approach to family therapy. *Family Process, 17,* 181–194.

Hare-Mustin, R. (1994). Discourses in the mirrored room: A postmodern analysis of therapy. *Family Process, 33,* 19–35.

Hare-Mustin, R. (1998). Challenging traditional discourses in psychotherapy: Creating space for alternatives. *Journal of Feminist Family Therapy, 10*(3), 39–56.

Hare-Mustin, R., & Mareck, J. (1997). The politics of madness. In D. Fox & I. Prilleltenski (Eds.), *Critical psychology* (pp. 104–120). London: Sage.

Hernández, M. P. (2000). *A personal dimension of human rights activism: Narratives of trauma, resilience and solidarity*. Unpublished doctoral dissertation. University of Massachusetts, Amherst.

Hoffman, L. (1990). Constructing realities: An art of lenses. *Family Process, 29,* 1–12.

Hunter, J. (1991). The state construction of affect: Political ethos and mental health among Salvadoran refugees. *Culture, Medicine and Psychiatry, 15,* 139–165.

Jenkins, A. (1990). *Invitations to responsibility*. Adelaide, Australia: Dulwich Centre.

Laird, J. (1989). Women and stories: Restoring women's self constructions. In M. McGoldrick, C. Anderson, & F. Walsh. (Eds.), *Women in families* (pp. 427–450). New York: Norton.

Luepnitz, D. A. (1988). *The family interpreted: Feminist theory in clinical practice*. New York: Basic Books.

Mirkin, M. P. (Ed.). (1990). *The social and political context of family therapy*. New York: Guilford Press.

Mirkin, M. P. (Ed.). (1994). *Women in context*. New York: Guilford Press.

Mohanty, C., Russo, A., & Torres, L. (Eds.). (1991). *Third world women and the politics of feminism.* Bloomington: Indiana University Press.

Monk, G., Winslade, J., Crocket, K., & Epston, D. (1997). *Narrative therapy in practice.* San Francisco: Jossey-Bass.

Moon, S., Dillon, D., & Sprenkle, D. (1990). Family therapy and qualitative research. *Journal of Marriage and Family Therapy, 16,* 357–373.

Pierce, W. B., & Cronen, V. E. (1980). *Communication, action and meaning.* New York: Praeger.

Ratliff, D. A., & Randall, R. R. (2001). Qualitative research in family therapy: A substantive and methodological review. *Journal of Marital and Family Therapy, 27*(2), 261–274.

Riessman, C. K. (1993). *Narrative analysis.* Newbury Park, CA: Sage.

Riessman, C. K. (1994). Making sense of marital violence: One woman's narrative. In C. K. Riessman (Ed.), *Qualitative studies in social work research.* Newbury Park, CA: Sage.

Roberts, J. (1994). *Tales and transformations.* New York: Norton.

Robin, P. K. (1992). From helpless victim to empowered survivor: Oral history as a treatment for survivors of torture. *Journal of Feminist Family Therapy. 1,* 141–155.

Rosenbloom, D. J., Pratt, A. C., & Pearlman, L. A. (1995). Helpers' responses to trauma work: Understanding and intervening in an organization. In B. H. Stamm (Ed.), *Secondary traumatic stress* (pp. 65–79). Lutherville, MD: Sidran Press.

Roth, S. (1993). Speaking the unspoken: A work group consultation. In E. Imber-Black (Ed.), *Secrets in families and family therapy* (pp. 268–291). New York: Norton.

Sanchez, G., Arocha, J., Camacho, A., Fajardo, D., Guzmán, A., Jaramillo, C. E., et al. (1989). *Colombia: Violencia y democracia: Informe presentado al ministerio de gobierno* [Colombia: Violence and democracy: Report present to the government]. Bogotá: Universidad Nacional—COLCIENCIAS.

Sluzki, C. E. (1992). Transformations: A blueprint for narrative changes in therapy. *Family Process, 31,* 217–230.

Spivak, G. C. (1991). Can the subaltern speak? In C. Nelson & L. Grossberg (Eds.), *Marxism and the interpretation of culture.* Urbana: University of Illinois Press.

U.S. Committee for Refugees. (1998). *Colombia's silent crisis: One million displaced by violence.* Washington, DC: Immigration and Refugee Services of America.

Waldegrave, C. (1990). Just therapy. *Dulwich Centre Newsletter, 1,* 5–46.

Walters, M. (1990). A feminist perspective in family therapy. In M. P. Mirkin (Ed.), *The social and political contexts of family therapy* (pp. 51–68). Boston: Allyn & Bacon.

Walters, M., Carter, B., Papp, P., & Silverstein, O. (1988). *The invisible web: Gender patterns in family relationships.* New York: Guilford Press.

Weingarten, K. (1991). The discourses of intimacy: Adding a social constructionist and feminist view. *Family Process. 30,* 285–305.

Weingarten, K. (1992). A consideration of intimate and non-intimate interactions in therapy. *Family Process, 31,* 45–59.

Weingarten, K. (1998). Radical listening: Challenging cultural beliefs for and about mothers. *Journal of Feminist Family Therapy, 7*(1/2), 7–22.

Weingarten, K., & Cobb, S. (1995). Timing disclosure sessions: Adding a narrative perspective to clinical work with adult survivors of sexual abuse. *Family Process, 34,* 257–269.

White, M. (1995). *Re-authoring lives: Interviews and essays.* Adelaide, Australia: Dulwich Centre.

White, M., & Epston, D. (1990). *Narrative means to therapeutic ends.* New York: Norton.

Wittgenstein, L. (1953). *Philosophical investigations.* Oxford, England: Blackwell.

CHAPTER 18

Redecision Family Therapy

VANN S. JOINES

Redecision family therapy, developed by Robert Goulding, a psychiatrist, and Mary McClure Goulding, a social worker (M. M. Goulding & Goulding, 1979; R. L. Goulding & Goulding, 1978), represents an integration of transactional analysis (TA), Gestalt therapy, and Satir family systems therapy. The Gouldings trained with Eric Berne (1961), the originator of TA, and Fritz Perls (Perls, Hefferline, & Goodman, 1951), the developer of Gestalt therapy. They were also associates of Virginia Satir (1964, 1972), who developed a model of family systems therapy. Robert Goulding and Satir co-led one of the first family therapy workshops offered in the United States at Esalen in August 1965 (Mary M. Goulding, personal communication, October 11, 1999). Perceiving TA as a clear conceptual framework and Gestalt therapy as a powerful set of experiential techniques, the Gouldings discussed with Berne and Perls how their approaches might be integrated. Berne and Perls were mavericks who had trained as psychoanalysts and then broke away to develop their own approaches in reaction to the shortcomings they perceived in psychoanalysis. Neither was very interested in talking about how his approach might be integrated with that of someone else. After their deaths (interestingly, both died within a month of each other in the summer of 1970), the Gouldings synthesized what they perceived to be the best of both approaches along with some of their own innovations. Thus, redecision therapy was born.

The Gouldings also integrated what they had learned from Satir in this new approach with families. Later, several of the Gouldings' early students, George McClendon and Ruth McClendon (1974), Ellen Bader, (1976), and Vann Joines (1977), further expanded the application of redecision therapy to families. A short time later, Ruth McClendon and Les Kadis (Kadis & McClendon, 1998; McClendon & Kadis, 1983) extended their ideas on the use of the redecision approach in marital and family therapy, and Bader and Pearson (1988, 2000) developed a unique approach to working with couples.

EARLY THEORETICAL ROOTS

Berne, Perls, Satir, and the Gouldings all participated in the human potential movement of the

1960s. They worked in close proximity of one another in the Monterey, Carmel, and Big Sur areas of California. They knew each other and shared ideas. Having trained in the psychoanalytic model, each was attempting to chart new territory with theoretical models offering greater possibilities for change and providing more optimistic views of human beings. Their theories reflect a belief that persons are organisms that naturally tend toward growth and wholeness. They emphasized that individuals have full resources and wellness rather than deficits and sickness. Each contributed a unique perspective on these ideas.

Eric Berne

Berne (1961), a psychiatrist, was concerned with the power differential that existed between therapist and patient in the psychoanalytic model. A psychoanalyst had knowledge that was often not shared with a patient and frequently made decisions about what was best without much input from the patient. To redress the imbalances, Berne (1947, 1957) first translated the concepts of psychoanalytic theory into everyday language in *The Mind in Action,* later changed to *A Layman's Guide to Psychiatry and Psychoanalysis.* Next, Berne (1961) set out to develop a completely new therapeutic model in language that could be easily understood by an 8-year-old child. With such a model, he reasoned that a patient could have access to the same information as the therapist, and together they could work in a collaborative manner. He also emphasized the use of therapeutic contracts (mutually negotiated agreements between patient and therapist regarding the outcome of therapy) in which a patient decides what is best for his or her life and provides a goal for working cooperatively with the therapist to achieve that. Berne emphasized the need for clearly specified outcomes. He often joked that, if he got on an airplane in San Francisco for a flight to New York and the pilot announced, "We are going *toward* New York," he would get off. He said he wanted to know exactly where he would end up before embarking on a journey, and therapy should be no different.

Several contemporaries greatly influenced Berne, notably neurosurgeon Wilder Penfield (Penfield, 1952; Penfield & Jasper, 1954), the first to map the cerebral cortex; ego psychologist Paul Federn (1952), who developed the concept of ego states; and psychologist Renee Spitz (1945), who conducted pioneering research on the effects of parental deprivation on institutionalized infants. Berne (1961) cited Penfield's work as supporting the idea of ego states:

> An ego state may be described phenomenologically as a coherent system of feelings related to a given subject, and operationally as a set of coherent behavior patterns; or pragmatically, as a system of feelings which motivates a related set of behavior patterns. Penfield has demonstrated that in epileptic subjects memories are retained in their natural form as ego states. By direct electrical stimulation of the bared temporal cortex, he was able to evoke these phenomena.
>
> "The subject feels again the emotion which the situation originally produced in him, and he is aware of the same interpretations, true or false, which he himself gave to the experience in the first place. Thus, evoked recollection is not the exact photographic or phonographic reproduction of past scenes and events. It is reproduction of what the patient saw and heard and felt and understood" [Penfield, 1952, p. 183]. He noted that such evocations were discrete, and "not fused with other, similar experiences" [p. 183]. (Berne, 1961, p. 17)

Regarding Federn's (1952) and Weiss's (1950) insights, Berne (1961) commented:

> Federn is the one who first stressed on psychiatric grounds what Penfield later demonstrated in his remarkable neurosurgical experiments, that psychological reality is based on complete

and discrete ego states.... Edwardo Weiss, Federn's chief proponent, has clarified and systematized Federn's ego psychology. Weiss (1950) describes an ego state as "the actually experienced reality of one's mental and bodily ego with the contents of the lived-through period" [p. 141]. Weiss points out exactly what Penfield proved: that ego states of former age levels are maintained in potential existence within the personality.... Early ego states remain preserved in a latent state, waiting to be recathected. (Berne, 1961, pp. 18–19)

Berne's (1961) contribution stemmed from organizing these ego states into categories, which he labeled archaeopsyche, commonly called Child; neopsyche, commonly called Adult; and exteropsyche, commonly called Parent, and showing how they interact both intrapsychically and interpersonally. Structurally (i.e., developmentally), the clusters of ego states evolve as archaeopsyche, neopsyche, and exteropsyche. Functionally, as experienced or observed, a Parent ego state can be experienced as critical or nurturing of self and of other people, and a Child ego state can be experienced as natural or adapted in response to a Parent ego state and to others. "Anyone functioning as an Adult should ideally exhibit three kinds of tendencies: personal attractiveness and responsiveness, objective data-processing, and ethical responsibility; representing respectively archaeopsychic, neopsychic, and exteropsychic elements 'integrated' into the neopsychic ego state" (p. 195). Using these categories, Berne developed a unique diagnostic and treatment approach with a method for establishing clear communication to facilitate problem solving.

Spitz's (1945) research showing the effects of sensory and emotional deprivation on infants who remained in hospitals led Berne (1961) to emphasize the importance of physical stimulation and social recognition in human interaction. Berne recognized the power of positive and negative attention in shaping human behavior. Behavior receiving the most attention is reinforced regardless of whether the attention is positive or negative. Human beings evidence psychological hunger for stimulation, recognition, and structure, and most of their behavior is guided by these hungers. Individuals seek familiar types of *strokes* (stimulation, recognition, or attention) as well as preferred ways of structuring time.

Berne (1961) also made a salient contribution to communication theory by developing a method for analyzing *transactions*, which he viewed as the basic units of social discourse, composed of both a transactional stimulus and a transactional response. In examining different types of transactions, he illustrated why communication takes place, fails to take place, or occurs on two different levels: social (observable) and psychological (ulterior). He pointed out that ulterior-level communication determines the ultimate outcomes of transactions.

Further, Berne (1972) observed how individuals form early conclusions about who they are, who other people are, what the world is all about, and what will eventually happen to persons like themselves. These conclusions or early decisions provide the basis of what he called an individual's *life script*—an unconscious life plan originally perceived as necessary for survival, which prompts a person to reenact certain patterns of behavior in attempts to obtain the love that was denied in childhood or, if that seems unattainable, to obtain revenge.

Once an individual has formed a life script, he or she strives to make the external world fit internal beliefs because the person feels that psychological survival is at stake. The individual maintains these beliefs by playing what Berne (1961) referred to as psychological *games*: precise sets of ulterior transactions occurring outside of Adult ego state awareness and leading to a well-known outcome. Games represent ways to justify what a person is already feeling and believing internally and to shift the responsibility for one's problem to someone or something else (J. L. Schiff et al, 1975). Distorted or double-level communication with family members, friends, and close associates involves playing these games. An individual will also tend to maintain a certain familiar set of feelings, which Berne (1972) called *rackets.* Rackets are used to elicit concern and support from others in ways that are familiar in one's family but not necessarily direct or gratifying. TA includes the analysis of all of these different elements with the goal of helping individuals to recover autonomy rather than live out a negative, destructive, or banal script, and to use direct rather than indirect means to satisfy their needs in the present.

Overall, Berne (1966) believed that human beings are born "okay," with natural, free, spontaneous perceptions and energy. As they interact with parents and significant others, they often have to adapt their behaviors to survive physically and/or psychologically. They have also incorporated both nurturing and critical aspects of their parents and others. Finally, they have an adult part of themselves that is in contact with here-and-now reality. Berne (1964) advocated the goal of therapy as *autonomy:*—"the release or recovery of three capacities: awareness, spontaneity, and intimacy" (p. 178). The process of therapy involves identifying and working through the early decisions people have made in the interest of survival and recovering the natural capacities they were born with to give up their old scripts and behave in ways that are fulfilling in the present.

Fritz Perls

Perls (Perls et al., 1951), a psychiatrist, became concerned about the overemphasis on cognitive processes he perceived in psychoanalysis. He was disturbed that, in the therapy process, clinicians often operate as if they had forgotten that any part of the body existed below an individual's neck. In contrast, Perls believed that "the truth is in the body" (Fagan & Sheppard, 1967): People can discover what is really going on by paying attention to what their bodies are telling them. One of his favorite aphorisms was "Lose your mind and come to your senses" (Fagan & Sheppard, 1967). Thus, a major emphasis in his work involved prodding individuals to gain awareness and discover new information by paying close attention to their own experiences as they made contact with people and objects in their environments. He believed in a natural, spontaneous *contact cycle,* which occurs if individuals do nothing to interrupt it. Awareness leads to excitement, which, in turn, motivates people to take action in making contact with their environment. Through such contact, an individual's needs are met. As soon as a need is satisfied, it recedes into ground, and another need emerges as figure in a continual contact-withdrawal cycle. By *contact,* Perls (Perls et al., 1951) meant as full a meeting between oneself and another person or object as is possible in the present moment. Experience and thus growth occur at the contact boundary between an organism and the environment. Out of such experience the self is formed. Thus, the self changes continually as a result of experiences.

Neurosis, according to Perls (1947), results from deadening awareness to such an extent that individuals no longer know their own needs. This deadening occurs because, at some point in pursuing excitement, contact proved painful. The pain stemmed from the lack of an accommodating response from the environment. As a result, ways to dull awareness and thus excitement were developed to prevent such painful contact: "Avoidance is a general factor to be found in probably every neurotic mechanism" (p. 71). Perls identified five such forms of resistance or defense:

1. *Retroflection:* An individual turns personal energy back onto the self and does to oneself what the person would like to do to the other or have the other do to oneself.

2. *Projection:* An individual sees in the other person what is true for oneself.
3. *Introjection:* An individual incorporates in its entirely a value or belief from another without examining it to see if it fits for oneself.
4. *Confluence:* An individual does not differentiate between self and another, but merges with the other without a proper boundary.
5. *Deflection:* An individual does not communicate directly or allow what the other person is saying to immediately impact oneself and responds tangentially. (Polster & Polster, 1973)

To grow, individuals need to become aware of these ways of avoiding contact and to allow themselves to experience fully what is possible in the present moment. According to Perls (1969a):

Awareness per se—by and of itself—can be curative. Because with full awareness you become aware of this organismic self-regulation, you can let the organism take over without interfering, without interrupting; we can rely on the wisdom of the organism. And the contrast to this is the whole pathology of self-manipulation, environmental control, and so on, that interferes with this subtle organismic self-control. (pp. 16–17)

Because individuals learn through experience, Perls (Perls et al., 1951) often invited clients to do an *experiment* to enhance awareness or contact. The purpose of the experiment was to explore behavior previously experienced as too arousing and beyond an individual's ability to manage. However, this time, he encouraged engaging in a particular behavior with sufficient environmental and self-support to be successful and to spur the recovery of spontaneity.

Perls was influenced by Wilhelm Reich (1949), Jacob Moreno (1945), and the philosophy of existentialism (Polster & Polster, 1973). From Reich he learned to attend to linguistic, postural, muscular, and gestural characteristics as indicators of an individual's character armor. Therapy consisted of helping an individual loosen these restrictions to release the excitement for the natural, spontaneous behavior the person had given up. Moreno's contribution was to demonstrate that individuals are more likely to make discoveries about themselves by participating in an experience than by merely talking about it. Thus, Perls derived from Moreno the idea of having individuals role-play parts of their self as well as of others to experience reality more fully. Finally, the existential ideas of experience, authenticity, confrontation, and the need for lively and present action became hallmarks of Perls's work.

Perls (1969a) best illustrated the process of therapy in his description of the *five layers of a neurosis.* The first layer he called the *cliché layer.* This refers to the kind of clichés we often exchange when first meeting someone, "the meaningless tokens of meeting" (p. 55). The second layer he referred to as the *gamey, phony, synthetic layer.* Here, he made reference to Berne's work on psychological games. Individuals attempt to convince themselves and others that they are really not who they actually are, and that they are really not doing what they are actually doing. He perceived his style of therapy as being a frustrator—to frustrate people out of their phoniness. He believed that "people change at the point at which they become fully who they are, rather than trying to be what they are not" (Fagan & Sheppard, 1967).

The third layer Perls (1969a) termed the *phobic layer* or the *layer of the impasse.* Once individuals give up the gamey behaviors previously thought necessary to survive, they move into the phobic layer, where one is afraid that all of the catastrophes one believed would happen if one stopped the old behaviors will now happen. At this point, two parts of the self pull or push against each other, each wanting to move in opposite directions: One wants to grow, the other to be safe. The old protective behavior no longer satisfies, and the new behavior feels too risky: "The impasse is the crucial point in therapy, the crucial point in growth... the impasse is the position where environmental support or obsolete inner support is not forthcoming any more and authentic self-support has not yet been achieved" (p. 28). As a result, a person feels stuck. A therapist can rest assured that, once individuals have fully experienced both sides, they will move through the impasse in their own time, not the therapist's. A therapist's attempt to push or pull them through an impasse will only mobilize resistance. If a client is not ready to move through an impasse, a therapist had best stop working and allow the client to resume when the client is ready. Ideally, a client's staying with the experience helps resolve the impasse or determine when to take the next step.

As an individual remains in touch with the experience, he or she moves into the fourth dimension, the *implosive layer*. Here, the person no longer engages in the behavior previously believed necessary to survive, yet is not ready to move spontaneously into new behavior. As a result, all the individual's energy implodes inwardly upon the self, and the person experiences the deadness of this layer. In staying with this realization and really experiencing this deadness, a very interesting process happens. One experiences that, even though one is not engaging in the old behaviors previously deemed necessary for survival, one is still right here, right now, and this is enough. This realization leads to spontaneously moving into the fifth stratum, the *explosive layer*. At this layer, an individual's energy is redirected into new spontaneous behaviors formerly blocked. The person comes to life and explodes with emotions such as joy, anger, grief, laughter, or assertiveness. Perls (1969a) described the goal of this therapy process as *maturation*, movement from environmental support to self-support after having recovered the spontaneity and aliveness of one's being.

VIRGINIA SATIR

Satir (1964, 1972), a clinical social worker and a pioneer of family therapy, also initially trained in psychoanalytic theory. At that time, the emphasis in psychoanalytic work revolved around a therapist's functioning as a blank screen and treating only individuals. Satir's own personal style led her toward much more intimate involvement with people and to learn through direct experience. Early in her career, while working with a schizophrenic daughter, she noticed that, as the daughter improved, the mother worsened. Satir included the mother in the work, and the father deteriorated. Satir had the father join in the therapy, and the importance of their relationship to the son became apparent. She began to realize the need to engage the whole family of clients to have additional resources available to both understand the difficulties facing clients and to help clients resolve them. By the late 1950s, Satir was recognized as one of the developers of a new approach called *family therapy* (Simon, 1989).

As one of the founders of the Mental Research Institute (MRI) in Palo Alto, California, in 1959, Satir collaborated with Don Jackson, Jules Riskin, Gregory Bateson, Jay Haley, John Weakland, and others. Satir (1964) refined her ideas on family therapy and incorporated them into her first book, *Conjoint Family Therapy*. In 1964, she left MRI to become the director of training at the Esalen Institute in Big Sur, California. Among the main proponents of the human potential movement, Satir further developed her humanistic beliefs and experiential action methods. In 1972, after leaving Esalen, she published her second book, *Peoplemaking*.

Satir (1972) embodied the spirit of the 1960s. She believed that positive change is possible for everyone. She perceived the difficulties individuals experience as resulting from low self-esteem, which, in turn, leads to incongruent forms of communication. She regarded these unproductive forms of communication as universal and described them as *blaming, placating, being super reasonable,* or *being irrelevant.* Each of these "survival stances" entails neglecting to take into account some aspect of self, other, or context (Satir, Banmen, Gerber, & Gomori, 1991). Blaming discounts the other; placating discounts the self; being super reasonable discounts both self and other; and being irrelevant discounts self, other, and context. Satir used *sculpting* (placing family members in various positions) to make these stances explicit in a humorous way that people could easily grasp.

Satir (1964) observed that the rules about how individuals should feel and act often bind and gag them and foster low self-esteem rather than support growth, communication, and self-confidence. Rules shape whether a system functions as open or closed to change. She referred to her style of therapy as a "human validation process" (J. McLendon, personal communication, September 20, 1999). She aimed to help individuals regain self-esteem and thus improve their relationships, health, and performance. Satir (1972) focused on the value of the self in relationships and emphasized the universal truths of being human. In a safe context, individuals can receive help to access their inner resources. As individuals are empowered, they experience increased choice and congruence in making contact and in communicating with others.

This dynamic therapist (Satir et al., 1991) believed in a universal spirit in each person, a life force tending toward health and wholeness. She strove to make contact with that unique spirit in everyone with whom she worked. She used herself as her most powerful tool by exercising the rare ability to make genuine, loving contact in a way that created safety and invited forth the spirit in each individual in therapy. She accomplished this even in large groups of people; often, members in the audience of one of her workshops felt personally touched by her in some way.

Active work characterized Satir's (1972) style. She encouraged individuals to experiment with different body positions to experience rather than to merely talk. She was one of the first to point out that the presenting problem is not the problem; rather, it is the way the family tries to cope that is the problem. She used simple language to communicate and was very creative in sculpting the implicit dynamics of the family to make them explicit. She employed touch freely and congruently and helped people experience what their bodies as well as their minds were telling them. For example, she would place her hand on an individual's stomach to give the person permission to express repressed sobs. She also utilized rope, linking family members by their waists, and other props to dramatize how individuals were entangled with one another or tied up by supposedly well-intended messages. In these ways, she enabled individuals to see and experience for themselves. She also assisted them in accessing inner resources to reclaim parts of themselves they had given up and to change their dysfunctional patterns to solve their problems. She developed specific techniques, such as the Parts Party (in which other people in the group play different parts of an individual) and Family Reconstruction (a central technique of Satir's in which other group members assume the roles of significant family members to reconstruct and resolve family-of-origin issues; Satir et al., 1991). Satir traveled extensively, spreading her message of hope and change to countless individuals around the world. In her later years, she focused increasingly on spiritual issues, with the ultimate goal of aiding human beings in evolving to a higher level of functioning (McLendon, 2000).

THEORETICAL CONSTRUCTS

The Gouldings integrated many common themes and what they considered the best in each model, alluded to previously, into the process they named redecision therapy. Perls, Berne, and Satir all affirmed *awareness* as a primary tool to assist individuals in change. They recognized that a significant amount of experience occurs outside of awareness, and all three developed ways to assist in bringing these aspects into consciousness. Perls (1969a) focused on the body in assisting individuals to experience what their body was communicating to them. He encouraged individuals to engage in dialogues between parts of their self and with significant others and designed numerous "experiments" based on Gestalt principles. Berne (1961) developed a unique conceptual framework to address the psychological level of experiencing as persons present themselves to others and as they interact with one another in groups and over their lifetime. Satir (1988) used sculpting and other experiential techniques to make explicit "the feelings and needs that lie beneath everyday family events. (What goes on under the table)" (p. 2). All three theorists concluded that the hidden level rather than what occurs on the surface determines the outcome of behavior. Berne (1964) most clearly described this "psychological level" in the processes he called *games*.

Perls, Berne, and Satir all believed that the problems people experience as adults result from the ways they adapted their behaviors in childhood to survive both physically and psychologically. Perls (1969b) stressed the mechanisms individuals develop to reduce contact that is painful or feels unmanageable and the impasses that result between parts of ourselves (e.g., "top dog, bottom dog" splits). Berne (1961) observed conflicts between exteropsychic (Parent) and archaeopsychic (Child) ego states and identified *injunctions* internalized in response to parental messages contributing to developing *scripts* in attempting to reestablish "okayness." Satir (1972) described the implicit rules existing in families, the communication processes that go awry when self-esteem is diminished, and the resulting incongruent stances people assume to escape threats of rejection.

All three clinicians recognized the importance of self- and other-support. Perls et al. (1951) pointed out that anxiety basically connotes excitement without adequate breath support.

Berne (1964) emphasized people's biological, psychological, and social needs for positive strokes: "If you are not stroked, your spinal cord will shrivel up" (p. 14). Satir (1964) postulated self-esteem as the crucial factor in determining what happens both within and between people. Each interpreted the task of a therapist as assisting individuals in reclaiming the power they had lost in childhood to determine their own destiny, instead of living according to others' expectations, in short, to reclaim their capacity for autonomy.

All three believed that the power of experiencing aliveness and spontaneity facilitates change. Perls et al. (1951) observed this occurring naturally in a person in full contact with self and environment. Berne (1961) believed spontaneity results from exercising innate intuition and creativity (functionally described as the Natural Child ego state). Satir et al. (1991) perceived aliveness as emerging from making meaningful contact with one's universal spirit or life force. They posited this energy as constituting the basic human essence. Robert and Mary Goulding (1978) expressed this idea in their belief that "the power is in the patient," the title of their first book.

REDECISION THERAPY

Building on the ideas of their teachers and colleagues, the Gouldings developed the principles of redecision therapy. In the foreword to their book, *Changing Lives through Redecision Therapy* (1979), Satir commented:

> The need for hope among people is crucial. Among therapists the need is critical.
>
> A philosophy of hope, an understanding of how growth and change process works in humans, techniques and approaches to make it happen, and an absolute "bone" conviction that people can change, can transform the threat of "burn-out" in therapists to a feeling of hope and conviction that they can really help.

I think Mary and Bob Goulding understand this thoroughly. This enables them to come to every person with compassion, hope, and certainty that each person can become fully human. They show in simple, straightforward ways how to accomplish this. (pp. viii–ix)

Redecision therapy, as developed by the Gouldings (1979), consists of three main processes: *contracting, impasse clarification,* and *redecision work*. Contracting refers to establishing mutual agreements with clients at the beginning of the therapy process concerning what the outcome of the therapy will be in specific, measurable, behavioral terms. Any implicit aspects are brought to awareness, so the contract is congruent on both the social and psychological levels. How the fulfillment of the contract will be pleasing or beneficial to the clients is also assessed. Contracts interrupt possible psychological games and establish therapy on a collaborative basis.

Impasse clarification signifies the process of bringing into full awareness the part of the person that wants to change and the part that is resisting change to protect the self from some earlier perceived threat to the individual's survival. Usually, a person has identified with one side and disowned and projected the other side onto another person, animal, or object. In fully experiencing both sides of the impasse, the individual gains appreciation for each side and can integrate the two sides in a way that offers greater possibilities than either side offered alone. For example, individuals who have viewed themselves as hard-working and others as wanting to play can gain an appreciation of the value of both activities and recognize the expression of both sides as benefiting themselves better than either in isolation.

Redecision work consists of, first, helping individuals reexperience early decisions made in childhood to survive physically and/or psychologically, and second, facilitating them in spontaneously "redeciding" by accessing the natural, creative part of self. The early decisions that were limited by a child's cognitive-affective capacities and environmental restrictions are replaced by new decisions based on an adult's reasoning, creative capacities and present environmental realities.

The Seven Major Components of Redecision Therapy

Seven major components constitute the process of redecision work (McNeel, 1977). The first component consists of *emphasizing a client's personal power and responsibility*. Clients need to understand that they are not the victims of events or circumstances, but rather active participants in life. They are ultimately responsible for their lives, and have the power to change. How they use language helps them experience power and responsibility. Therefore, they are asked to use "I" rather than "it" and active rather than passive verbs (e.g., "I did X" as opposed to "It happened to me"). A therapist also invites clients to own their powers by (1) confronting statements like "You make me feel"; (2) requesting the use of present tense to experience what they are talking about; (3) speaking up to claim their importance; (4) saying "I won't" rather than "I can't"; (5) confronting words like "try"; and (6) changing the conjunction "but" to "and." "But" has the effect of discounting the importance of what has come previously; "and" gives equal weight to both.

The second major component involves fostering a *nurturing environment*. Because a therapist is inviting clients to experiment with new behaviors about which they may feel vulnerable, clients will need to feel safe and protected to be willing to do so. Ways a therapist fosters a safe and protected environment include (1) positively stroking clients for strength and health; (2) being on the side of spontaneity and creativity (functionally Natural Child ego state) by offering nonjudgmental caring and indignation at past injustices imposed on them as children; (3) encouraging clients to internalize any positive strokes they receive; (4) using humor to make the process fun and enjoyable; and (5) not laughing at experiences that are negative or potentially destructive for clients.

The third component concerns a leader's own *modeling behavior*. An effective leader demonstrates the behaviors desirable for clients to experience. Therapists may do this by (1) presenting themselves as assertively healthy and excited about life (it is difficult for depressed therapists to cure depressed clients); (2) carefully attending to clients and being present each step of the way; and (3) not allowing themselves to be discounted (e.g., calling a client's attention to not responding to their question).

The fourth major component entails *separating myth from reality*. We learn many myths in childhood; change often requires giving them up. One myth intimates that somehow individuals are not separate from their parents and that the umbilical cord is still attached. Psychologically, clients need to experience that they are now separate and self-sufficient human beings. Another myth implies that other people or objects can make one feel. Other people and circumstances often provide stimuli for feeling, but what one actually feels depends on how one interprets the stimuli. Another myth suggests that feeling bad is natural or that, if one feels too good, unfortunate events will happen. Yet another myth claims that an individual can make people or reality change by feeling a certain way long enough. A final myth rests on the premise that clients cannot change until someone else changes or cannot be happy until another person is. The effects of these myths, until they are given up, result in rationalizing experiences of remaining ensconced in impasses.

The fifth component involves *confrontation of incongruity*. Clients often express themselves in ways that are inconsistent with other aspects of themselves. Examples include (1) the difference between verbal and nonverbal communication (e.g., saying yes while shaking one's head no); (2) using general words or phrases with several connotations (e.g., "secure"); (3) making comments without awareness of the full implications (e.g., "This job will be the death of me"); (4) not differentiating between thinking, feeling, and behavior (e.g., "I'm feeling that this will be difficult," meaning, "I think this will be difficult"; or "I'm afraid to get angry because I might hurt someone"); and (5) contracts motivated by Parent or Adapted Child functioning rather than the Adult ego states.

The sixth major component centers around the use of particular *techniques facilitating therapeutic processes*. Examples of these techniques include (1) game analysis to assist clients in understanding how they unconsciously set themselves up to feel bad; (2) two-chair work to enable a dialogue between parts of the self or with significant others who are not present; (3) saying goodbye to the past by expressing unexpressed resentments, regrets, and appreciations; (4) using fantasy to allow clients to experience what future situations may be like; (5) interviewing a client's parent in double-chair work (McNeel, 1976a); (6) using playful confrontations, such as "Wow, you're good at not answering my questions!"; (7) sharing therapeutic hunches; (8) saying "Of course!" to behavior that is natural and normal; and (9) using audio- and videotape recording to allow clients to observe and hear themselves.

The seventh component consists of using *clear procedural rules to assure safety* while practicing new behaviors and that help to prevent psychological games. Clients are asked to agree to these ahead of time. These rules encompass a no-gossip rule (to talk directly to rather than about others), observing clear time limits, and maintaining specific environmental rules. Examples of environmental rules include (1) no violence or threats of violence; (2) having sex only with one's partner (not with group or marathon members); (3) being present at all sessions; (4) contracting for confidentiality; (5) avoiding emergencies by asking for what one wants or needs ahead of time; and (6) using a cooperative contract to promote clients' seeking to meet needs in a cooperative versus a competitive fashion.

The Redecision Therapy Process

Robert Goulding (1972) listed 12 steps in the redecision therapy process:

1. Assess the *quality of the contact* between therapist and client. Frequently, people diffuse contact in some way. Working to improve the quality of contact makes it possible to proceed further in therapy. This proves especially important for individuals with personality disorders who are not in touch with their real self.
2. Find out the *presenting problem.* Sometimes, individuals do not know; they know only that something is wrong. By the time the problem is clear, a majority of the work may have been accomplished. At other times, people have framed a problem in a way that is unsolvable (e.g., trying to change someone else). An important aspect of this step involves clearly identifying the problem and aiding a client in framing it in a solvable way.
3. Negotiate a *contract for change.* What does the client want to change now that the problem is clear and framed in a way that is solvable? How will everyone know when the goal is accomplished? How will that benefit or please the client? How could the client sabotage the change? What will the client do instead, to make sure he or she gets what is wanted? Identifying any implicit elements and making them explicit proves important, so the contract becomes congruent on both the social and psychological levels.
4. Be aware of and probably confront the first *con.* A con denotes a discount concerning client, therapist, or the reality of a situation. A con also constitutes an invitation into a psychological game. For example, a client might say, "I want to be able to X," which implies that she does not have the ability and wants the therapist to make her able. To shift the responsibility for the change back to the client, a therapist clarifies by stating, "I'm aware that you already have the ability to accomplish this. Is that something you want to do?" Occasionally, appropriateness counterindicates confronting the first con. For example, a person might be grieving and in need of simply expressing emotion and being heard. At the point when the therapist begins to intervene, however, he or she brings the discount to the person's attention.
5. Identify the *racket*. A racket signifies a familiar bad feeling a client seeks out and maintains rather than taking direct action to solve a problem. Preserving this feeling usually amounts to a way to attempt to elicit support from others. The therapist will usually hear evidence of the racket in the presenting problem. If not, the client will often go into the racket when the first con is confronted. If the racket consists of confusion, the client will display confusion; if anxiety, anxiousness.
6. Identify the psychological *game*. A game is enacted when a person initiates a transaction with someone and has a different set of assumptions about the situation than the other person, is surprised when the interaction turns out differently than expected, and feels upset as a result. Games are used to support rackets to keep a person from feeling bad. A redecision therapist assumes that, when individuals feel stuck in current problem solving, they have moved back into familiar existential positions experienced in childhood; they are still perceiving situations and feeling about them the ways they did as children. Therefore, after detecting a game, a redecision therapist

proceeds to check out what clients are feeling and what they are telling themselves about other persons, themselves, and their destinies.

7. Find out the *early scene*. An early scene represents one of the original events in which a client had similar feelings and perceptions to those at the end of a game. Once clients share the feelings and messages experienced at the end of the game, the next step involves inquiring if those feelings and thoughts seem familiar. If so, a therapist can ask clients with whom they were interacting in that position as a child and at what age. Then the therapist invites them to envision the scene and to describe what is happening as though it were now occurring.

8. Specify the *psychological messages* (injunctions) that the client has internalized. The therapist listens to the implied messages the significant others in the scene are conveying to the client as a child. Clients are asked what they are feeling and how they are explaining to themselves what is transpiring.

9. Elicit the *early decision*. This emerges by asking what a client is deciding to do as a result.

10. Facilitate a *redecision*. This can result from clients relating to a significant other in the scene what they are going to do and the fantasy of what will happen as a result. Clients hearing themselves articulate what they decided to do as a child and their accompanying fantasy supports them in gaining empathy for self and why they had difficulty solving the problem as it reoccurs in the present. It also assists clients in appreciating how the early decision enabled them to survive as a child. A client regains a sense of power and okayness surrendered as a child and often shifts energy functionally from an Adapted Child to a Natural Child ego state or structurally into an integrated Adult ego state as a result. The redecision occurs spontaneously and addresses the part of the individual who made the original decision. A therapist's task entails providing sufficient safety, support, and opportunities for awareness so that spontaneity can occur.

11. *Anchor* the redecision. Anchoring means facilitating a client's grasping and nurturing a redecision. Perhaps humor characteristic of a Natural Child ego state provides the best way to remember to remind oneself of the redecision. For example, a women reclaimed her power to set limits on abusive behavior by speaking up with a clear strong voice. Her daughter, who was watching, broke into song with, "I am woman; hear me roar!" The woman laughed and celebrated her victory.

12. *Support and stroke* a new behavior. Reinforcement over time by significant others preserves old, familiar behaviors. To promote new behaviors, encouragement, support, and positive stroking of the new behaviors prove beneficial. Unless new behaviors receive more attention than previous behaviors, an individual may revert back to old behaviors. Thus, the system in which a person lives plays an important role in the change process.

REDECISION FAMILY THERAPY

Having developed redecision therapy for individuals and groups, R. L. Goulding (1972) naturally progressed to applying this approach with couples and families. This involved integrating Satir's (1972) sculpting techniques and ideas about family systems with redecision processes. Ruth McClendon (McClendon & McClendon, 1974), a social worker trained in family systems work before she studied with the Gouldings in the early 1970s, developed a more complete approach to working with families using redecision therapy. She and George McClendon (1974) and later Les Kadis (Kadis & McClendon, 1981, 1990, 1998; McClendon & Kadis, 1983) formulated a three-stage model of redecision family therapy: (1) systems work to assess a problem and to differentiate the individuals within the system from the system itself; (2) redecision work with individuals to disengage them from negative past influences; and (3) restructuring work to integrate the new decisions into a family system, so that a new structure is formed to support the behavior.

The systems work consists of making explicit what is occurring implicitly, so that a family can see what is actually happening beyond the social-level interactions and also each person's part in the process. The redecision work helps individuals see how the early decisions they made in their families of origin have prompted them to structure a family system in their own way and allows them to make new decisions that free them from a constricting past. Restructuring work permits members to implement new decisions in their current family, thereby creating a more functional system.

Bader and Pearson (1988) developed a unique model of couple therapy using redecision therapy by drawing on Mahler's (Mahler, Pine, & Bergman, 1975) stages regarding separation-individuation processes. They depicted how couples journey through the same developmental stages in their relationship as a mother and child progress through in the first three years of life. Couples tend to encounter difficulty at the same points where they originally faced problems in separating/individuating from their mothers. Helping a couple understand these stages and realize where they are struggling developmentally normalizes their trouble and points the way to the tasks necessary for them to resolve their conflicts.

Joines (1977) presented an integrated systems perspective using the theories of TA and systems theory to examine the link among the intrapsychic, interpersonal (marital), family, and larger social systems. He encouraged therapists to maintain such a perspective to enhance the greatest possibilities for change in therapy. Joines (1986, 1988) also offered a new approach to therapy using Ware's (1983) theory of personality adaptations along with redecision therapy. He built on Ware's insight that individuals can adapt in their family of origin in specified ways. The resulting adaptations consist of three "surviving" adaptations (schizoid, antisocial, and paranoid) and three "performing" adaptations (passive-aggressive, obsessive-compulsive, and hysterionic). The surviving adaptations concern how to survive when trust breaks down and one can no longer rely on one's parents for survival. The performing adaptations involve how to meet the expectations in one's family of origin. Each of these adaptations has an "open door" (where the person makes contact with the world), a "target door" (where interventions will be most effective), and a "trap door" (where the individual has the greatest defenses). Feeling, thinking, and behavior constitute the doors and vary for each adaptation. Knowing the doors for each adaptation allows a therapist to quickly establish rapport, target interventions to the area in which they will be most effective in producing change, and avoid becoming stuck in a client's defenses. When combined with redecision therapy, this model offers a potent approach to therapy and an effective framework for diagnosis and treatment planning.

The Redecision Family Therapy Perspective
Redecision family therapy involves focusing on both system and individual dynamics and on recognizing the influence of both the present and the past in current difficulties. Redecision family therapists believe that an individual makes early decisions and develops a life script from experiences in one's family of origin. A person chooses a partner whose script dynamics mesh compatibly with his or her own. The

two individuals develop a relationship based on their respective script dynamics. When children are born, they learn roles in accordance with those dynamics; this leads offspring to develop their own individual life scripts, and the drama continues over the generations. Thus, a couple's relationship, the family system, and the children's scripts, which influence the next generation, are all established on the basis of the drama created by the original scripts of the marital pair (Joines, 1977). According to Pesso (1975), a couple's relationship forms a lens through which their children view the world. This view and the early decisions concerning how they will deal with it shape the children's life scripts and ultimately their own marital and family dynamics.

METHODS OF ASSESSMENT AND INTERVENTION

Assessment in redecision family therapy involves understanding and diagnosing the foundational transactional-analytic processes of symbiosis and differentiation as implicated in the uses of ego states, drama triangles, basic existential life positions, stroking patterns, and family mood. Interventions are intended to alter these dynamics from dysfunctional to developmentally appropriate.

Symbiosis and Differentiation

Much of the focus in redecision family therapy concerns helping individuals achieve differentiation. Unfinished business from the past that couples bring with them into their current relationships largely results from unresolved symbiotic relationships (Schiff et al., 1975) with members of their family of origin (Figure 18.1). The most common type of symbiosis, viewed functionally, consists of one individual operating primarily out of his or her Parent and Adult

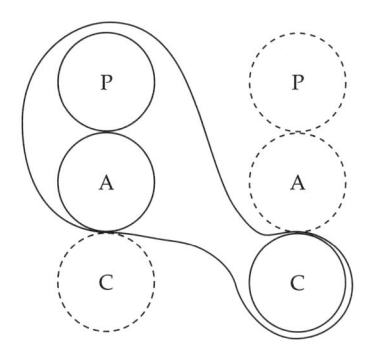

Figure 18.1 Symbiotic relationship.

ego states, while the other individual is using mainly Child ego states. In this manner, the two individuals behave as though they are one: One person takes responsibility, thinks, and directs while the other person feels and reacts (see Figure 18.1).

This type of symbiotic relationship is a normal, natural way for parents and children to relate before the child has developed Parent and Adult ego states of his or her own. During that early developmental period, it is appropriate and necessary for a parent to take responsibility for a child, to think about what the child needs, and to provide for the child. Difficulty arises if parents either do not allow and encourage the emerging Parent and Adult ego states of the child, or require the child to grow up too quickly and to assume excessive responsibility prematurely. When the former happens, the child receives a message to not grow up and tends to maintain symbiosis with others by staying primarily in the Child ego state, either complying with what others want or rebelling against them. When the latter happens, the child receives the message that he or she should not be a child and tends to maintain symbiosis by remaining primarily in the Parent and Adult ego states and taking responsibility for the feelings and behavior of others.

Viewed functionally, a person who is primarily in Parent and Adult will feel uncomfortable when the person who is primarily in Child is not doing what the former thinks he or she should, or when the person in Child is in distress of some kind. The individual who is primarily in Parent and Adult will attempt to change the other to relieve his or her own internal discomfort. The one who is operating primarily in Child will not feel that he or she is okay until the other stops trying to change him or her. Obviously, the problem for both is a lack of differentiation. The one who is in Parent and Adult needs to learn how to self-comfort and self-soothe and to remain in an okay place even when the other person is not behaving or feeling the way the first person would like. The one who is in Child needs to learn how to self-comfort and self-soothe and remain in an okay place even when the other person is uncomfortable with the first person's behavior. For example, in one couple, the man was afraid of abandonment and got upset when his partner talked to another man on an airplane. He told her that he felt as if she had betrayed him. She felt guilty that it was not okay for her to talk with other men. The differentiation issue was pointed out by saying to her, "Just because he *feels* as if you betrayed him doesn't mean that you betrayed him." Both realized that was true and felt relieved.

The symbiosis in a couple's relationship will often shift, depending on the issue or situation they are dealing with. For example, in traditional relationships, for many years women behaved as if they could not take responsibility and think outside the home, and men reciprocally acted as if they could not take responsibility and think inside the home. Women seemed to have difficulty reading the odometer on an automobile to know when the oil needed changing. Men often behaved as if they could not decipher cookbooks or find the baby's pajamas and had to ask for assistance. Fortunately, in the present, many women and men are learning that they each can be whole people both inside and outside the home. However, on a number of other issues and in other situations, couples still revert back into traditional, undifferentiated roles.

Drama Triangles

When children are born into a family with undifferentiated parents, they frequently become triangulated in a dysfunctional way into the unresolved issues of their parents (Bowen, 1978). When a couple have not resolved their conflicts, the wife may shift her need for affection from her husband to her child, and the husband may transpose his anger toward his wife to their child, who is receiving the affection he would like to have. Both are detouring conflict through their child rather than dealing with each other directly. These dynamics activate what Karpman (1968) designated the *drama triangle*. Psychological games in families can be analyzed using this triangle (Figure 18.2).

The roles in the drama triangle revolve around Persecutor, Victim, and Rescuer. Each role involves a *discount* (minimizing or ignoring some aspect of reality); in this way, they are similar to Satir's roles of Blamer, Irrelevant, and Placator. Viewed functionally, Persecutors use Critical Parent and Adult influenced by the Parent, discount their own Child ego state, and imply that they would never act as irresponsibly as the Victim. Victims discount their Parent and Adult ego states and behave as if they cannot think and manage their own behavior. Rescuers use Nurturing Parent and Adult influenced by

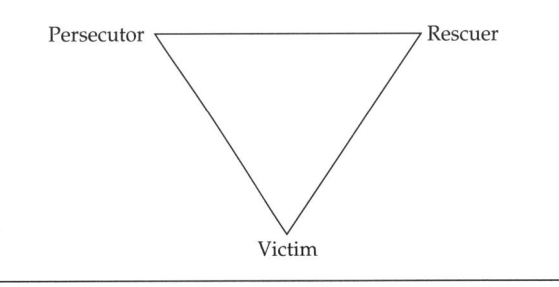

Figure 18.2 The drama triangle.

the Parent and discount their own Child ego state feelings and needs. The drama in the game is created by the switching of these roles. For example, the husband, who is angry at his child for misbehaving, may feel victimized when his wife, who is trying to rescue their child, switches to Persecutor and tells him how uncaring he is. The child, who started out as Victim, may switch to Persecutor of the father by joining with the mother. Each person seeks to justify what he or she is already feeling and believing and to shift the responsibility for the negative outcome to the other people involved. The husband may end up feeling as if he cannot win, the wife may justify her belief that all men are uncaring like her father, and the child may be reinforced in believing that it is not safe to be close to men. The primary feeling that the whole family may be maintaining is frustration.

BASIC EXISTENTIAL LIFE POSITIONS

M. M. Goulding and Goulding (1979) observed that at the end of a psychological game, individuals will justify feeling and believing what they concluded in childhood. Berne (1966) termed this the basic existential life position, consisting of a familiar way of feeling, an accustomed belief about oneself and others, and often a presupposition about one's destiny. As this basic life position emerges into an individual's awareness, the early experience in which this position was decided often spontaneously comes to mind. An individual can be guided to reflect on this early experience to rework that scene and to arrive at new decisions about self, others, and destiny, and to differentiate from parents' (or significant others') perceptions and behaviors.

STROKING PATTERNS

Berne (1964) defined a stroke as "any act implying recognition of another's presence" (p. 15). Stroking reinforces behavior; therefore, examining the stroking pattern in the family proves useful. Is it positive or negative, conditional or unconditional? Positive strokes help people feel good; negative strokes invite people to feel bad; both reinforce behavior. Parents often unwittingly reinforce in their children the opposite behavior from what they would like to reinforce by paying the most attention to that behavior, even though the attention is negative. For example, they may consciously want a child to do well, but pay the most attention when the child is making mistakes. Changing the stroking pattern in the family allows the members to reinforce a different kind of behavior. Until the stroking pattern is changed, it is difficult for individuals in the family to change because they are being reinforced for their typical behaviors.

FAMILY MOOD

Families tend to maintain a certain mood or affect. In some families, a mood of depression prevails; living in this family feels like being under a wet blanket. In other families, everyone is angry or frustrated; and in others, everyone is anxious. Berne (1972) called these feelings *rackets* and pointed out that individuals tend to seek out and maintain certain feelings to elicit attention and support from others. Rackets are the feelings that gain the attention of others in a family. In some families, expressing anger is perceived as rude or impolite, but, if the person is sad, people become concerned and try to help. In other families, sadness is seen as weakness, but people listen and respond to anger. Children learn very quickly what feelings are seen as not okay and what feelings their parents pay attention to. Parents tend to pay attention when the child experiences a parent's racket. Thus, most families teach by example. Under stress, members are expected to feel an accustomed emotion.

Implementing Assessment

Redecision family therapists employ a structured interview to observe a family's structure and dynamics. A therapist works to make the implicit explicit to help the family become aware of dysfunctional dynamics that are producing difficulties, so that together they arrive at a mutual understanding of what the problem is. Sculpting, having family members switch places, and diagramming transactions, relationships, and games are used to help a family experience as well as talk about issues. A therapist also directs a family to discuss certain issues or has them do particular tasks together, such as drawing a picture of the family to bring out the family's dynamics. Close attention is paid to the stroking patterns, coalitions, boundaries, roles, contact, family mood, implicit messages, and rules.

Interventions

The types of interventions used in redecision family therapy can help a family observe their processes, model healthy behaviors, assist the individuals in reclaiming autonomy, and aid in restructuring a family system. Examples of interventions designed to raise a family's awareness include sculpting; noticing psychological-level (implicit) messages; diagramming transactions, games, and symbiotic functioning; taking note of nonverbal communication; and helping people say what they are really feeling.

Interventions designed to model healthy behaviors encompass positively stroking family members for their strengths and health, creating safety and protection for people to feel free to be who they really are, using humor and playful interactions, transacting from an "I'm okay—You're okay" stance, teaching members how to nurture themselves and others, assigning positive stroking exercises, and creating appropriate structure and boundaries.

Interventions to help individuals reclaim autonomy involve contracting with each family member, making explicit any differentiation issues, facilitating individuating within a family system, inviting individuals to examine where they learned a certain way of thinking or a certain type of behavior, encouraging reworking earlier experiences in their family of origin or current family to make new decisions and take back the power and autonomy they may have given up earlier, and supporting each person in experiencing a personal sense of okayness as a member of the family.

Interventions that aid in restructuring a family system include having people experiment with changing their seating and positions in relation to one another, opening up new avenues for relating, providing missing boundaries and structure, assigning homework tasks, decontaminating erroneous beliefs, normalizing appropriate behavior, and helping individuals decide how they will relate to other family members in light of the new decisions they have made. All of these interventions are used to reinforce the power and autonomy of individual family members, to free their spontaneous energies, and to invite them to exercise their power and autonomy to take charge of their lives.

Redecision Family Therapy Process

Initial Session

Redecision family therapy starts in an initial session with making effective contact with each member of a family in order for the family members to experience the therapist as someone they can relate to and with whom they can feel safe. Such contact is achieved by the therapist taking time to become acquainted with each member individually and using spontaneous energy to connect in a real way with each family member. A therapist watches for the quality of contact between family members and how they stroke one another. He or she also finds qualities to stroke positively in each member and asks what each person likes about himself or herself, each other person, and being a member of the family. This process allows a therapist to assess the stroking pattern in a family, whether positive or negative, conditional or unconditional. If the stroking pattern is negative, it will need to be changed to positive to make it safe for family members to change. As in other family systems models, the therapist also observes seating arrangements, coalitions, boundaries, implicit rules, and roles throughout the therapy process.

A second step involves discovering the process the family went through in making the decision to come to therapy. This information tells the therapist a great deal about the power hierarchy in the family (i.e., who is in charge and how decisions are made in a family). It also provides an opportunity for a therapist to establish the fact that each member has in some way chosen to be there (even if it was a choice between coming or being punished in some way).

The next step involves finding out what each member of the family sees as the basic problem within the family and would like to have resolved as a result of coming to therapy. When a family discusses this with one another, the basic dynamics of the family system can be observed. During this process, a therapist helps a family become aware of behavior that is outside of the individual's awareness, identifies common themes, and works to differentiate each member within the system. Sculpting, moving the family around, exaggerating symptoms, and other similar interventions are used to highlight and make explicit the family's dynamics.

In an initial session, a therapist contracts with each family member for the changes they want to make for themselves as individuals, in relationships with the other family members, and in how the family functions as a whole. Procedural contracts are also established to create a safe environment. Administrative contracts are set up for the number and frequency of sessions and fees. A homework assignment is often given for each member to notice and positively stroke what individuals in the family do that others like and want to continue to have happen.

Subsequent Sessions

Once individuals have been differentiated from a family system and contracts for change have been established in an initial session, a therapist works with the individuals in subsequent sessions to trace their current problematic behaviors back to their origins in early decisions. These decisions represent the very best option they had available for taking care of themselves in childhood. The redecision process usually begins with the parents because they are the architects of the family system. As the parents make new decisions, this gives permission to the children to do likewise, as the children usually have modeled after the parents in some way. The new decisions change the way family members relate to one another. Time is spent restructuring a family system in light of these redecisions. The object is to construct a new system supportive of each person's autonomy and allowing for intimacy between and among the family members. This process opens healthier options for the next generation as well.

MAJOR ISSUES TREATED WITH THIS APPROACH

Stephen Schultz (1984) in *Family Systems Thinking*, described four levels of family functioning: psychotic, immature, neurotic, and mature. In families at the psychotic level, a member exhibits a psychotic disorder as defined by the *Diagnostic and Statistical Manual of Mental Disorders* (*DSM-IV-TR*, American Psychiatric Association [APA], 2000). Families at the immature level have a member with a *DSM-IV-TR* somatoform disorder, an eating disorder, or a personality disorder. Families at the neurotic level contain a member with a *DSM-IV-TR* anxiety disorder and/or depressive disorder. In families at the mature level, someone may experience a *DSM-IV-TR* adjustment disorder. Redecision family therapy is most easily applied to issues at the mature and neurotic levels, where the goal is to free individuals from their internal constraints (dysfunctional Parent or Child ego state content) in order to grow. Problems treated at this level include anxiety, depression, suicidal ideation, parent-child problems, relationship problems, grief and loss, and stepfamily issues. However, if a therapist is trained to assess and intervene in the functioning of the immature and psychotic levels, redecision family therapy can be used to treat issues at these levels as well. Problems dealt with at this level include physical and sexual abuse, drug and alcohol problems, eating disorders, somatoform disorders, personality disorders, schizophrenia, and paranoia. Berne (1961) addressed these more serious diagnoses.

At the immature level, individuals have not incorporated a Parent ego state structure adequate for setting appropriate limits on behavior both internally and externally. The individuals tend to "act in" on their bodies (psychophysiological and eating disorders) and let their bodies be the feedback mechanism limiting their behaviors, or "act out" on the environment (personality disorders) and let the environment be the controlling factor. Redecision family therapy can be used in such cases to help construct necessary structure (i.e, a new Parent ego state) to assist individuals in establishing and internalizing appropriate limits.

At the psychotic level, individuals have not learned to differentiate internal from external reality. The result is a thinking disorder manifested in tangential and irrelevant communication. Redecision family therapy can be used with families with schizophrenic members to confront the dysfunctional patterns and to establish clear communication, so that problem solving can occur. As this work is accomplished, a family may move up to the next level of functioning; work can then be done at that level and up the ladder.

CASE EXAMPLES

The Family Who Didn't Know What to Do

A family of four came for therapy because the mother was concerned that the father was physically punishing the son for acting out. She was frightened that the father might seriously injure the son and "didn't know what to do." The family consisted of the father, Jim, 38, the mother, Sally, 37, the son, Larry, 15, and the daughter, Betsy, 12. Sally had called and scheduled the appointment and was asked to bring the whole family to the initial session.

At the beginning of the first session, the Smiths, a middle-class family, all acted pleasantly and affably. Even Larry, whom the mother had characterized as acting out, seemed cooperative. Five chairs of the same type were arranged in a circle. The therapist seated himself last to see how the family would arrange themselves. Jim sat next to Larry, Sally on the other side of Larry, and Betsy next to Sally (Figure 18.3). The therapist sat between Betsy and Jim. Jim worked for a corporation, Sally was a homemaker, Larry attended tenth grade, and Betsy the seventh. All four spoke positively about themselves and each other.

When asked to describe how they decided to come for therapy, Sally indicated that it was her

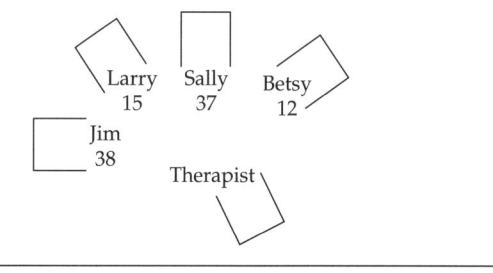

Figure 18.3 Seating arrangement.

idea. Both she and Jim had been concerned about Larry's staying out late and not obeying them. Larry was also picking on his younger sister and would not listen to his mother when she tried to discipline him. As a result, when Jim would arrive home and hear this, he would punish his son by whipping him with a belt. Sally was concerned that Jim might physically injure Larry and suggested that they come for therapy. Jim agreed. He felt at his wits' end and said he did not know what else to do. The parents had told each of the children that they had made the appointment and that the whole family was going. Larry did not want to attend, but decided to, rather than be punished. Betsy felt that they needed to enter therapy.

When Jim and Sally stated the presenting problem, both focused on Larry's being disobedient and disrespectful and picking on his sister. Betsy agreed that Larry was the reason they were there. She reported that she used to like him, but that recently he had become very mean. As they talked, the therapist noticed a high level of anxiety and pointed this out. He further remarked that Larry was sitting between his mother and father and that Jim seemed a bit remote. To move the parents together, Jim and Larry were asked to change seats; the therapist then inquired what they were feeling. The children liked seeing their parents together. Jim and Sally felt a little awkward. Sally began talking to Jim about how frightened she felt when he would physically punish Larry and how she was afraid that he might seriously injure him. The therapist advised Jim that he was obligated by law to report any behavior that might be abusive of children. Although Sally's concern was very appropriate, her anxiety seemed to be getting in the way of her owning her power and setting appropriate limits with her husband.

THERAPIST: Would you like to resolve your anxiety?
SALLY: Yes.

THERAPIST: What would you like to feel instead?
SALLY: Confident.
THERAPIST: Okay, so let yourself be in a recent situation where you are afraid of Jim hurting Larry. As you are feeling anxious, what are you saying inside your own head about Jim?
SALLY: He may seriously hurt him.
THERAPIST: And what are you saying about you?
SALLY: I wish I could do something.
THERAPIST: And what are you saying about your destiny?
SALLY: I don't know what is going to happen.
THERAPIST: Is that a familiar way of feeling?
SALLY: Yes.
THERAPIST: Who are you in that position with as a child?
SALLY: My father.
THERAPIST: How old are you?
SALLY: Twelve.
THERAPIST: Where are you and what's happening as 12-year-old Sally?
SALLY: I am in the hallway of our house. My mother is in the kitchen washing dishes. My father is in the bedroom at the end of the hallway and whipping my brother with a belt. He is angry, and my brother is yelling.
THERAPIST: What are you feeling and what are you telling yourself?
SALLY: I'm feeling scared. I'm telling myself that he is going to hurt my brother, and I can't understand why my mother isn't doing anything. I'm afraid that, if I intervene, he will hurt me too, so I'm just watching and feeling scared.
THERAPIST: What do you want to say to your father?
SALLY: Stop it!
THERAPIST: Switch and be father and respond.
SALLY: (As father.) I'm glad you said something. I don't like what I'm doing, but I love my son, and I don't want him to get into trouble. I know this is not helping, but I don't know what else to do.

THERAPIST: Be yourself again and see what else you want to say.
SALLY: I want to tell my brother that I am sorry.
THERAPIST: Tell him.
SALLY: Terry, I'm sorry that I did not say anything to stop him at the time. I was afraid that he would hurt me too. I feel very guilty for not doing something to help you.
THERAPIST: Be your brother and respond.
SALLY: (As her brother.) That's okay. I knew what I was doing. I wanted Dad to pay some attention to me, and the only time he did was when I got in trouble. Getting whipped was better than nothing. At least he was concerned for a while.
THERAPIST: Be yourself and see if there is anything else you want to say.
SALLY: I want to tell my mother something.
THERAPIST: Okay.
SALLY: Mother, why didn't you say something? Why did you just ignore the whole thing?
THERAPIST: Be mother and respond.
SALLY: (As mother.) I was scared too. My father was abusive, and I was afraid that, if I intervened, your father might hurt me also.
THERAPIST: Be yourself and see what you want to say.
SALLY: Well, you can stay scared as long as you want. I'm not doing that any longer. From now on, I'm going to speak up when I don't like what is happening.
THERAPIST: Good. Now come back to the present and see if there is anything that you want to say to Jim in light of what you have just done.
SALLY: (To Jim.) You are no longer going to physically punish him!
THERAPIST: (To Jim.) Do you want to respond?
JIM: Yes. I have been feeling just like your father. I knew that whipping Larry wasn't doing any good, but I didn't know what else to do. (Turning to Larry with tears in his eyes.) I love you, and I don't want you to get into trouble and ruin your life.

LARRY: (Tearing up.) I love you too, but, just like her brother, that's the only time you pay any real attention to me.
THERAPIST: Tell your father what you would really like for him to do with you.
LARRY: I would like for you to take me to a ballgame or fishing or go look at cars . . . things like that.
JIM: Okay. That sounds like fun.
THERAPIST: Will you do some things like that that you both will enjoy during the next week and tell us about it next time?
JIM: Yes.
LARRY: Yes.
SALLY: (Taking Jim's hand.) I feel relieved.
THERAPIST: Does anyone else want to say anything?
BETSY: (To her mother.) I have felt the same way you described feeling at 12. I felt scared and couldn't understand why you didn't tell Dad to stop. I want you to know that in the future, if you don't, I will!

The family came back for a follow-up session to solidify what they had done in the first session and reported that family life had been going well. Jim and Larry had done several activities they enjoyed together. The family seemed joyful and pleased with each other rather than feeling anxious. The father was obviously back in the family and enjoying his participation. The therapist and family worked to ensure that both children had equal access to both parents and that the parents were functioning well as marital partners and were together on their parenting. After three sessions, the family decided they had accomplished what they had come for. Larry was no longer acting out; Jim and Sally were communicating clear expectations to the children and enjoying them and each other.

Discussion
The Smiths exemplify a family who are functioning at an immature level, with the primary symptom being acting out rather than the

family talking through problem situations. Family dynamics show how life script issues are passed on and reenacted across generations. The parents' anxieties stemmed from not having effective models in their family of origin for how to handle stressful situations. They used a primarily negative conditional stroking pattern, and a mood of anxiety characterized the family. Under stress, the parents either withdrew or became punitive. The mother surrendered her power; the father abused his. The parents remained in an unresolved symbiosis, with the mother in the Child role and the father in the Parent and Adult roles. In the drama triangle, the father assumed the persecutor role, the son the victim role, and the mother the rescuer role. They maintained the existential life position of "I'm not okay—You're not okay." Using redecision work to help the mother differentiate and reclaim her power allowed her to set appropriate limits on her husband's behavior toward their son, and assisted the couple to stop the drama, change the script, feel okay, alter the stroking pattern to positive unconditional, and parent differently from their parents. As they learned how to communicate about their problems rather than to withdraw or become abusive, they stopped feeling so anxious and could be much more effective with their children and happier with each other.

Being obligated by law to report abuse of children, the therapist took a firm "Limiting Parent" stance with the father, thus modeling for the wife the possibility of setting appropriate limits when needed. This information was perhaps also helpful to the father in setting limits on his own behavior. Those types of limits are what is most needed when a family is functioning at an immature level. This family was somewhat unique in how quickly they were able to make a change once the issues were clear, and the mother was very resolved in her new decision. Possibly, the speed of change was enhanced by their dissatisfaction with the current situation and readiness to implement more effective strategies.

THE TOO-GOOD PARENTS

The Gundersons, a middle-class family of four, were concerned about their younger son, who was drinking and smoking pot. The four members included the father, Fred, 49, the mother, Lois, 48, the older son, John, 19, and the younger son, Bill, 16. Lois telephoned to make the appointment, stating that they were beginning to have problems with Bill, "who, up to this point, had always been so good."

Three of the Gundersons attended the first appointment; the older son, John, was away at college. Lois sat down with Fred to her right and Bill to his right (Figure 18.4). Bill did not look happy to be there. The therapist spent some time joining with him and he began to look more interested. After establishing rapport with the other family members, the therapist inquired how they had decided to seek therapy.

LOIS: We've never had any problems with our sons. They have always been so good. It's a little hard to understand what's going on now.
FRED: Yeah, we've always been close as a family. I've been their Scoutmaster and Little League coach. We never had any problems with them until recently, when Bill started to

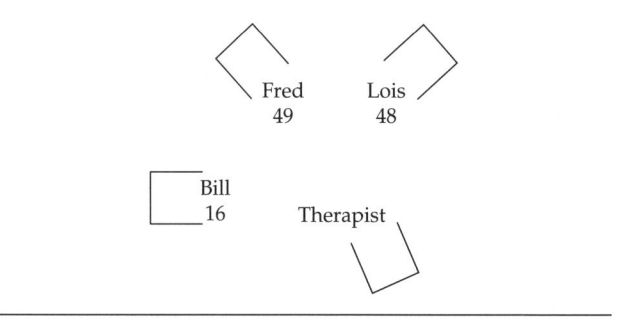

Figure 18.4 Seating arrangement.

come home a little inebriated or high on pot after being with his lacrosse team.

LOIS: He's always made good grades, but recently they have begun to slide. We wanted to do something about this before things got worse.

THERAPIST: Who initiated the idea to come for therapy?

LOIS: I did. I remembered how helpful it had been when we came for therapy earlier when we were having some marital problems, so I thought we should come back and deal with this.

THERAPIST: Did you then talk with Fred about this?

LOIS: Yes.

THERAPIST: What did you decide, Fred, when Lois talked to you about coming?

FRED: Well, I thought it was a good idea since the marital therapy had been so helpful.

THERAPIST: Did the two of you then talk to Bill about this?

BOTH: Yes.

THERAPIST: Bill, what did you decide when your parents talked with you about coming to therapy?

BILL: Well, they just told me we were coming. I didn't see the need for it, but came because they wanted to.

THERAPIST: What did you think would happen if you didn't?

BILL: I knew they would get upset.

THERAPIST: So you decided to come, so they wouldn't be upset?

BILL: Yeah.

THERAPIST: (To the whole family.) So what do you think the basic problem is that you would like to resolve as a result of being here?

LOIS: I want to find out what is going on with Bill. Why he is doing these things.

FRED: Bill, what do you think is going on?

BILL: (Stays silent and looks away.)

LOIS: (To Bill.) Are you unhappy? Is there anything you are upset about?

BILL: (Looks down and shakes his head no.)

THERAPIST: I'd like to ask you to do an experiment. Fred and Lois, will you both stand up and point your fingers at Bill like this. (He demonstrates by pointing his index finger at Bill. The parents do so and laugh and Bill perks up. The therapist then addresses Bill.) Is that what it feels like as you hear your parents talk?

BILL: (Smiling.) Yeah.

THERAPIST: (To the parents, based on a hunch that Bill is acting out the Child ego state of one of his parents.) Were either of you in that position as a child?

LOIS: No, I was always the good one who tried to do everything right.

FRED: I was.

THERAPIST: So, switch places with Bill. (He does. Bill and Lois point their fingers at him.) What does it feel like to be in that position?

FRED: Bad.

THERAPIST: How old are you, and what's going on when you are in that position as a child?

FRED: I'm a teenager. I don't have a father, and I don't get much direction from my mother either. I get in trouble at times. I sort of have to figure everything out on my own.

THERAPIST: Tell Bill what you are really wanting that you are not getting at that time.

FRED: (Begins to cry.) I want someone who will care about what is happening to me and give me some direction. I had to learn the hard way from my mistakes. (From his Parent ego state.) That's why I've done so much for you guys, so you wouldn't have to experience what I went through.

THERAPIST: (Drawing the ego states on a white board; Figure 18.5.) I think it is important to recognize that Bill now has a Parent and Adult ego state of his own. Although he will continue to want Adult information from you when he asks for it, there is very little you can say from your Parent that he cannot already tell you before you say it because he

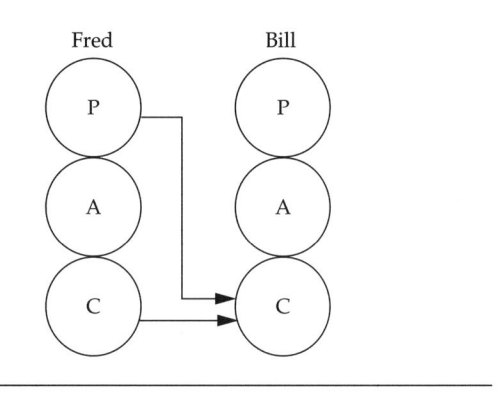

Figure 18.5 Ego state diagram.

has internalized your Parent. What he really needs to hear from you at this point is your Child ego state. Will you tell Bill from that part of you why you are concerned about what he is doing?

FRED: (Again crying.) Son, I really love you and want you to have a good life and not have to experience the problems I had growing up.

THERAPIST: (To Bill.) What do you experience as you hear what you father is saying?

BILL: (Beginning to cry also.) When he says it that way, I don't want to mess up.

LOIS: (In tears also.) I have probably been too lenient on the boys. I grew up very poor and had to do without a lot of things. I now have a career in which I make good money and don't want to deny the boys what I didn't have.

FRED: Our older son, who is in college, is not too good at managing his money. When he runs out, she just puts more in his bank account.

THERAPIST: I think the problem is that you have been "too good" as parents. In trying to prevent your sons from going through the hardships that you had to go through, you have been doing too much. The problem in doing that is that they don't learn how to take responsibility for themselves and learn to deal with problems themselves.

LOIS: I can see now that what you are saying is true.

FRED: Often, I try to set limits with the boys, and Lois thinks they are too strict and doesn't require them to stick to those limits.

THERAPIST: It sounds like you are undercutting each other's effectiveness as parents.

BILL: I think that is true.

THERAPIST: Are you wanting to work together to help your sons become more responsible and support each other rather than undercut each other?

BOTH PARENTS: Yes. (Bill seemed relieved to have the focus off him and showed interest in what his parents were doing.)

The parents were instructed to agree on age-appropriate expectations for both sons and, if these were not met, on automatic consequences on which they were willing to support each other. After a while, they had a clear list, about which they talked with Bill. Bill seemed relieved to have consistent directions. They were planning to visit the older son the next weekend and to speak with him about the list as well. They set up another appointment when the older son could join to evaluate how family life was proceeding. The mother telephoned a couple of weeks later, relating that they were progressing well and that she and Fred felt relieved.

Discussion

The Gundersons provide an example of a family who are functioning at a neurotic level. The primary issue revolved around the parents trying to give their sons what they did not have growing up. They practiced a largely negative conditional stroking pattern. The parents were locked in a symbiotic relationship with their sons by overdoing for them. The family displayed a depressed mood. The parents started out in the rescuer role in the drama triangle and switched to the persecutor role, with the sons staying in the victim role. The parents maintained the existential position of "We're okay—They're not okay." Helping the father and mother become aware of the impact of their own early experiences allowed them to recognize what they were doing and how that was detrimental to their children. As they differentiated themselves from their sons and redecided their basic orientations to living and relating, they were empowered to assist their sons in becoming responsible for themselves. This resulted in the parents experiencing happiness with their sons as they were and enjoying each other rather than worrying that their sons would feel deprived.

The approach the therapist took in the end was not very different from the one a structural (Minuchin, 1974) or a strategic (Haley, 1980) family therapist might have followed. The differences consisted of using sculpting to make the issue explicit and doing emotional work with the father and mother to assist them in experiencing new decisions regarding what would be most useful for their sons in reality rather than continuing to act out their own private rescue fantasies.

RESEARCH

Liberman, Yalom, and Miles (1973), as reported in *Encounter Groups: First Facts*, conducted the primary research on redecision therapy. This involved group rather than family therapy and included 17 different types of groups. The most productive by far was the redecision therapy group led by Robert Goulding. Twelve people began the group with him, 10 changed positively, 5 changed more than moderately, 1 remained unchanged, 1 dropped out, and there were no reported casualties. The members were enthusiastic about the group, and the group ranked first on the criterion that members reported having personally learned a great deal. The group also tied for first in the members' ratings as a constructive experience. Their ratings of the leader were equally high, with Goulding ranked highest in overall leader dimensions.

Those leader behaviors correlated with the highest outcomes in the study encompassed displaying: (1) high caring, (2) high meaning-attribution (offering explanations of what they observed and information on how to change), (3) moderate emotional stimulation (did not seduce the clients with charisma), and (4) moderate executive function (use of structured exercises and of group management). Although this study concerned group therapy, the basic redecision work remains the same in redecision family therapy.

McNeel (1976b, 1977, 1982) examined the effects of an intensive weekend group workshop conducted by the Gouldings to determine if people changed as a result of that event. He administered two measures, the Personal Orientation Inventory (POI) (Shostrom, 1966) and the Personal Growth Checklist (PGC) (McNeel, Nelson, & McNeel, 1974) just prior to the workshop and again three months after the workshop. The 15 participants changed substantially: On the POI, group members reported change at the .01 level of significance on seven scales and at the .05 level on three more; on the PGC, participants showed significant change on all five scales (two at the .01 level and three at the .05 level). Interviews with all participants before and after the workshop provided qualitative verification for the changes on the assessment instruments. Participants also indicated distinct changes they made as a result of specific segments of work done in the workshop. Overall, the experience proved very positive for the participants.

Bader (1976, 1982) studied the outcomes with five families who participated in a seven-day residential family therapy workshop using redecision therapy as compared with five similar families who did not participate and served as controls. Family members completed the Family Environment Scale (FES) (Moos, 1974), the California Psychological Inventory (CPI) (Gough, 1968), and the Personal Orientation Inventory (Shostrom, 1966) prior to the workshop, at the end of the workshop, and eight weeks later, and a Self-Report Questionnaire (SRQ) designed to identify changes that family members perceived in themselves or other family members after the workshop. Significant increases occurred at the .05 level on the Cohesiveness and the Expressiveness Scales of the FES for both posttests for the experimental group and a significant increase at the .05 level on the Independence Scale for the first posttest. Significantly greater positive changes at the .05 level emerged on the SRQ for the experimental families versus the control families. "The results obtained demonstrated that family therapy using TA with Redecision techniques is successful in effecting family systems change" (Bader, 1982, p. 37).

Sinclair-Brown (1982) evaluated a 12-week TA/redecision group psychotherapy program composed of nine physically abusive mothers and nine seriously neglectful mothers to determine the short-term effectiveness of the TA/redecision therapy model with this population. Criteria for evaluation included Minnesota Multiphasic Personality Inventory (MMPI) (Hathaway & McKinley, 1943) change scores, attendance, completion of contracts, therapists' and social workers' evaluations of behavioral change, reports about abuse and neglect, return of children, and demonstration of increased coping skills. Each of the criteria reflected significant change. The TA/redecision group psychotherapy model was found to be an effective short-term approach for treating this population.

Kadis and McClendon (1981) reported the results from using their intensive multiple-family therapy group model in which they used redecision family therapy with 59 families over a seven-year period. They employed a follow-up survey, with 37 families responding. The survey indicated that 57.7% of the parents and 74.4% of the children did not seek further therapy, that 80% of the parents and 76% of the children thought that their family had changed, and that 89% of the parents believed that they had changed in personal growth and 23.3% of the children believed that they themselves had not changed.

These studies provide evidence of the effectiveness of redecision therapy in group and family therapy. Further research to compare results with other modalities, to assess relevance in varying cultural contexts, and to evaluate the impact on both a range of diagnostic issues and of family structures in the present and multigenerationally will further clarify the processes and outcomes of redecision family therapy.

SUMMARY

Redecision family therapy, developed by Robert and Mary Goulding, provides an integration of the work of Berne, Perls, and Satir, along with general systems theory. As a growth model of therapy, redecision family therapy helps the individuals in a family experience autonomy and take charge of their lives. It combines both systems and individual work. It helps people to experience high self-esteem and be congruent in their interactions with others. The ultimate goal resides in developing awareness, spontaneity, and the capacity for intimacy in each individual within a family system along with promoting the healthy functioning of the family as a whole. The power of the redecision family therapy model arises from a basic view of people having the resources they need and the power to change.

REFERENCES

American Psychiatric Association. (2000). *Diagnostic and statistical manual of mental disorders* (4th ed., text rev.). Washington, DC: Author.

Bader, E. (1976). Redecisions in family therapy: A study of change in an intensive family therapy workshop (Doctoral dissertation, California School of Professional Psychology, 1976). *Dissertation Abstracts International, 37,* 05B, 2491.

Bader, E. (1982). Redecisions in family therapy: A study of change in an intensive family therapy workshop. *Transactional Analysis Journal, 12*(1), 27–38.

Bader, E., & Pearson, P. (1988). *In quest of the mythical mate.* New York: Brunner/Mazel.

Bader, E., & Pearson, P. (2000). *Tell me no lies: How to face the truth and build a loving marriage.* New York: St. Martin's Press.

Berne, E. (1947). *The mind in action.* New York: Simon & Schuster.

Berne, E. (1957). *A layman's guide to psychiatry and psychoanalysis.* New York: Simon & Schuster.

Berne, E. (1961). *Transactional analysis in psychotherapy: A systematic individual and social psychiatry.* New York: Grove Press.

Berne, E. (1964). *Games people play.* New York: Grove Press.

Berne, E. (1966). *Principles of group treatment.* New York: Grove Press.

Berne, E. (1972). *What do you say after you say hello?* New York: Grove Press.

Bowen, M. (1978). *Family therapy in clinical practice.* New York: Aronson.

Fagan, J., & Sheppard, I. (1967, July). *Two-hour workshop on Gestalt therapy.* Atlanta, GA: Georgia Mental Health Institute.

Federn, P. (1952). *Ego psychology and the psychoses.* New York: Basic Books.

Gough, H. (1968). *An interpreter's syllabus for the CPI.* Palo Alto, CA: Consulting Psychologists Press.

Goulding, R. L. (1972, July). *One-month workshop on redecision therapy.* Western Institute for Group and Family Therapy, Mount Madonna, Watsonville, CA.

Goulding, R. L., & Goulding, M. M. (1978). *The power is in the patient: A TA/Gestalt approach to psychotherapy.* San Francisco: TA Press.

Goulding, M. M., & Goulding, R. L. (1979). *Changing lives through redecision therapy.* New York: Brunner/Mazel.

Haley, J. (1980). *Leaving home: The therapy of disturbed young people.* New York: McGraw-Hill.

Hathaway, S. R., & McKinley, J. C. (1943). *Manual for the Minnesota Multiphasis Personality Inventory.* New York: Psychological Corporation.

Joines, V. (1977). An integrated systems perspective. In G. Barnes (Ed.), *Transactional analysis after Eric Berne: Teachings and practices of three TA schools* (pp. 257–272). New York: Brunner/Mazel.

Joines, V. (1986). Using redecision therapy with different personality adaptations. *Transactional Analysis Journal, 16*(3), 152–160.

Joines, V. (1988). Diagnosis and treatment planning using a transactional analysis framework. *Transactional Analysis Journal, 18*(3), 185–189.

Kadis, L. B., & McClendon, R. (1981). Redecision family therapy: Its use with intensive multiple family groups. *American Journal of Family Therapy, 9*(2), 75–83.

Kadis, L. B., & McClendon, R. (1990). A model of integrating individual and family therapy: The contract is the key. In J. Zeig & S. Gilligan (Eds.), *Brief therapy: Myths, methods, and metaphors* (pp. 135–150). Philadelphia: Brunner/Mazel.

Kadis, L. B., & McClendon, R. (1998). *Concise guide to marital and family therapy.* Washington, DC: American Psychiatric Press.

Karpman, S. (1968). Fairy tales and script drama analysis. *Transactional Analysis Bulletin, 7*(26), 39–43.

Liberman, M. A., Yalom, I. D., & Miles, M. B. (1973). *Encounter groups: First facts.* New York: Basic Books.

Mahler, M., Pine, F., & Bergman, A. (1975). *The psychological birth of the human infant: Symboisis and individuation.* New York: Basic Books.

McClendon, R., & McClendon, G. (1974, June). *One-week family therapy workshop.* Pajareo Dunes, CA: Author.

McClendon, R., & Kadis, L. B. (1983). *Chocolate pudding and other approaches to intensive multiple family therapy.* Palo Alto, CA: Science and Behavior Books.

McLendon, J. A. (2000). The Satir system: Brief therapy strategies. In J. Carlson & L. Sperry (Eds.), *Brief therapy with individuals and couples.* New York: Zeig, Tucker, Theisen.

McNeel, J. (1976a). The parent interview. *Transactional Analysis Journal, 6*(1), 61–68.

McNeel, J. (1976b). Redecisions in psychotherapy: A study of the effects of an intensive weekend group workshop (Doctoral dissertation, California School of Professional Psychology, 1976). *Dissertation Abstracts International, 36,* 9-B, 4700.

McNeel, J. (1977). The seven components of redecision therapy. In G. Barnes (Ed.), *Transactional analysis after Eric Berne: Teachings and practices of three TA schools* (pp. 425–441). New York: Harper & Row.

McNeel, J. (1982). Redecisions in psychotherapy: A study of the effects of an intensive weekend group workshop. *Transactional Analysis Journal, 12*(1), 10-26.

McNeel, J. K., Nelson, K., & McNeel, P. Y. (1974). *Personal Growth Checklist.* Unpublished manuscript. California School of Professional Psychology, San Francisco.

Minuchin, S. (1974). *Families and family therapy.* Cambridge, MA: Harvard University Press.

Moos, R. (1974). *Preliminary manual for the FES.* Palo Alto, CA: Consulting Psychologists Press.

Moreno, J. L. (1945). *Psychodrama.* New York: Beacon House.

Penfield, W. (1952). Memory mechanisms. *Archives of Neurology and Psychiatry, 67,* 178-198.

Penfield, W., & Jasper, H. (1954). *Epilepsy and the functional anatomy of the human brain.* Boston: Little, Brown.

Perls, F. S. (1947). *Ego, hunger, and aggression.* New York: Random House.

Perls, F. S. (1969a). *Gestalt therapy verbatim.* Moab, UT: Real People Press.

Perls, F. S. (1969b). *In and out of the garbage pail.* Moab, UT: Real People Press.

Perls, F. S., Hefferline, R. F., & Goodman, P. (1951). *Gestalt therapy.* New York: Dell.

Pesso, A. (1975, May). *Three-day workshop on psychomotor therapy.* Southeast Institute for Group and Family Therapy, Chapel Hill, NC.

Polster, E., & Polster, M. (1973). *Gestalt therapy integrated.* New York: Brunner/Mazel.

Reich, W. (1949). *Character analysis.* New York: Orgone Institute Press.

Satir, V. (1964). *Conjoint family therapy.* Palo Alto, CA: Science and Behavior Books.

Satir, V. (1972). *Peoplemaking.* Palo Alto, CA: Science and Behavior Books.

Satir, V. (1988). *The new peoplemaking.* Mountain View, CA: Science and Behavior Books.

Satir, V., Banmen, J., Gerber, J., & Gomori, M. (1991). *The Satir model: Family therapy and beyond.* Palo Alto, CA: Science and Behavior Books.

Schultz, S. (1984). *Family systems thinking.* New York: Aronson.

Schiff, J. L., Schiff, A. W., Mellor, K., Schiff, E., Schiff, S., Richman, D., Fishman, J., Wolz, L., Fishman C., & Momb, D. (1975). *The cathexis reader: Transactional analysis treatment of psychosis.* New York: Harper & Row.

Shostrom, E. (1966). *Manual for the personal orientation inventory.* San Diego, CA: Educational and Industrial Testing Service.

Simon, R. (1989). The legacy of Virginia Satir [Special feature]. *Family Therapy Networker, 13*(1) 26-56.

Sinclair-Brown, W. (1982). A TA redecision group psychotherapy treatment program for mothers who physically abuse and/or seriously neglect their children. *Transactional Analysis Journal, 12*(1), 39-45.

Spitz, R. (1945). Hospitalism: Genesis of psychiatric conditions in early childhood. *Psychoanalytic Study of the Child, 1,* 53-74.

Ware, P. (1983). Personality adaptations: Doors to therapy. *Transactional Analysis Journal, 13*(1), 11-19.

Weiss, E. (1950). *Principles of psychodynamics.* New York: Grune & Stratton.

CHAPTER 19

Contextual Therapy

CATHERINE DUCOMMUN-NAGY

Contextual therapy, founded by Ivan Boszormenyi-Nagy, MD, occupies a unique place among all the individual psychotherapy approaches on the one hand and classical family therapy on the other.* Contextual therapy is not a form of individual therapy or marital therapy, neither does it constitute a version of classical family therapy. Nonetheless, it offers in its essence a form of relational therapy. Human behaviors do not fall simply under the control of biological needs, unconscious drives, or the supraindividual forces described by classical family therapists, but are determined by what Nagy has called "relational ethics." He has discovered that, to understand the behaviors of people who are in close relationships, one needs to examine also the balance of giving and receiving that exists between them.

Contextual therapy remains unique in its focus on a central integrative principle: the unifying principle of the ethics of fairness, which is inseparable from an ethics of accountability. Nagy views fairness as a fundamental programming, regulatory, and sustaining principle of close relationships. In offering consideration to a partner, a person can experience a personal gain in the form of a personal validation that stems from willingness to care and does not depend on a partner's capacity to repay in kind. The ethics described by Nagy amount to as much an ethics of fair receiving as an ethics of fair chances to give—an ethics of receiving through giving in which both the giver and the receiver become the benefactors of the relationship. Adults in close relationships have needs that will clash at times. If they do not learn to develop a capacity for fair reciprocity, the relationship will cease to be mutually satisfying, and each can leave the relationship at any given moment. By contrast, parent-child relationships remain existentially inescapable and are asymmetric by nature, but the unfair exploitation of a

---

*The author acknowledges her indebtedness to Ivan Boszormenyi-Nagy, the founder of contextual therapy and her husband. She is grateful for his willingness to share his most recent ideas and for his editorial comments. This chapter results from a joint effort, but the author remains solely responsible for its actual contents and its possible errors or omissions. Please note that the author will refer to Ivan Boszormenyi-Nagy mostly by his abbreviated name, Nagy.

child by parents will lead to a detriment for the posterity in which they are all invested. Posterity becomes the main "client" of the contextual therapist, the vulnerable "other" toward whom each of us is accountable. As Boszormenyi-Nagy (1962/1987a) summarized: "The very ethical priority of fair availability is the foundation of transgenerational solidarity, the fiber of all higher animals' species survival" (p. xix).

For contextual therapists, the time when one partner can benefit from giving and the other from receiving constitutes a healing moment in the therapy process. To reach such moments, contextual therapists rely on a specific tool: *multidirected partiality.* They offer their partiality to anyone who can be affected by the therapist's process as someone who could benefit from giving as well as from receiving.

Whereas autonomy is the goal of many forms of therapy, contextual therapists view autonomy as a relational and dialectic phenomenon: Individual maturity results from a person's capacity for not only self-delineation and self-assertion but also for relational accountability and validation through fair consideration of others.

Between exclusion and naïve acceptance, contextual therapists can offer their consideration to exploitative family members as human beings who are hurt themselves by having lost their opportunities for self-validation because of their incapacity to care about others. Viewing people who engage in destructive actions in their families or who have turned destructive toward society as hurt givers serves as the only hope to reach them. If this is true, contextual therapy can voice a rare source of therapeutic optimism in the face of rampant intrafamilial abuse, neglect of children, and societal violence and provide a model for the prevention of interhuman exploitation on a large scale.

Over the more than 50 years of his clinical career, Nagy has consistently focused on a central question: What constitutes effective therapy? His lifelong effort at answering this question led him to the development of contextual therapy, after defining his approach as intensive family psychotherapy, intergenerational family therapy, and later, contextual family therapy.

In its newest formulation, contextual therapy offers a five-dimensional model of human relationships. The so-called four dimensions of relational reality listed as facts, psychology, transactions, and relational ethics have formed the core of the contextual therapy model since the late 1970s. The fifth dimension, characterized as the ontic dimension of relationships, was first introduced officially in 2000 at the annual conference of the Hungarian Family Therapy Association, but Nagy (Boszormenyi-Nagy, 1965) had already discussed the ontic aspects of relationships in some of his early writings. According to these writings, humans' very existence depends on the existence of others, whom we need as the ground against which to emerge as separate selves. Although Nagy insists that contextual therapy should retain any helpful aspects of other schools of psychotherapy or classical system-oriented family therapy, he is very specific in viewing the healing moment in therapy as the moment during which one gains from giving and the other from receiving. The skill of the therapist lies, therefore, in using multidirected partiality to guide one partner to the point when he or she can risk giving and the other to the point of accepting to receive.

HISTORY OF THE APPROACH

The Path of the Founder

Understanding the origins of contextual therapy would be difficult without tracing the path followed by its founder, Ivan Boszormenyi-Nagy. Some misconceptions about contextual therapy originate in considering Nagy a psychoanalyst who turned later to family therapy and to place contextual therapy within psychoanalytic family therapy (Nichols, 1998). Many generic books on family therapy have perpetuated this mistake and misled students into regarding contextual therapy as oriented toward insight and the past rather than toward action and the present.

Nagy has discussed how he became one of the founders of the family therapy movement and the developer of contextual therapy in several of his writings, but more specifically in two texts, one a short article prepared for the series entitled "Wisdom of the Elder" in the newsletter of the American Family Therapy Academy (AFTA; Boszormenyi-Nagy, 1995), and the second in *Foundations of Contextual Therapy: Collected Papers of Ivan Boszormenyi-Nagy, M.D.* (Boszormenyi-Nagy, 1962/1987b). Besides an introductory chapter in which Nagy portrayed his own path toward founding contextual therapy, the book contains a selection of articles representing varying stages of development of the approach. Short introductions to each chapter help the reader grasp the origins of the concepts.

Nagy has often repeated that the wish to help the mentally ill gave him the impetus to study medicine and to become a psychiatrist. Then, schizophrenia represented a condition without known treatment, and people suffering from this condition were often ostracized. He perceived their conditions as unfair and wanted to help them by searching for a cure to their illness. He does not believe that any specific event of his own family life accounted for his interest, nor did he personally know anyone who was suffering from a psychosis. On the other hand, he wonders if a childhood experience could have triggered his determination. As a child spending his vacations in a small village, he could see the prejudice encountered by an odd fellow who showed up every year at the local fair. In any case, he credits his father, who was a supreme court judge in a lineage of three generations of high judges, for teaching him to care about justice and to see any situation from the vantage point of each of the parties involved. Growing up in a traditional extended family, Nagy experienced the richness of life it offered. This may have contributed to his ease in inviting several generations of family members, including small children, to attend family therapy sessions.

Fathoming Nagy's path without a grasp of Hungary's history would prove difficult. As a country, Hungary lost two-thirds of its territory after World War I and fell later into the hands of two foreign destructive powers, Hitler's Germany and, later, Stalin's Soviet Union. Nagy traces his determination to fight injustices to his experience of political oppression and to his loyalty to a country not only wounded but also misjudged by history.

Nagy completed high school in Budapest. At the time, even lay schools like his insisted on an extensive teaching of classic authors and philosophers. This training helped him later to draw from philosophy to discuss relational phenomena. He graduated from medical school in Budapest in 1944 and started a residency in psychiatry just before Germany took control of the country. With his unyielding resistance to the Nazi regime came the risk of a death sentence that forced him into hiding while Budapest was under one of the longest sieges endured by a city in World War II. The "liberation" of Budapest by the Russian army allowed him to resume his training. Before World War II, the Department of Psychiatry of Budapest University, under Professor Laszlo Benedek, had gained an international reputation in functional neuroanatomy. At the time, most of the psychiatric training was geared to the diagnosis and classification of mental disorders. Nagy was determined to move beyond the field of descriptive psychiatry presented by his teachers and eager to expand his knowledge in the emerging field of biochemistry. To that effect, he studied physics and chemistry for several semesters at the University of Budapest. He would have completed a doctoral degree in sciences if he had remained in Hungary.

At the time of Nagy's studies, psychoanalysis was not taught in official psychiatry programs, and only later did he learn about the work of Freud and early analysts like Sandor Ferenczi, one of the leaders of the psychoanalytical movement and father of Hungarian psychoanalysis. Nonetheless, Nagy had grasped the value of psychotherapy and the importance of relational aspects of therapy from one of his teachers, his mentor Kalman Gyarfas, a professor of psychiatry, who left Budapest for Chicago, where he became the director of Illinois state hospitals.

Because Nagy refused to submit to the regime of Stalin, as he had refused Hitler's, he encountered new dangers that forced him to leave his country in 1948 and spend two years in Austria as a refugee. He worked there as a neurologist and psychiatrist for the International Refugee Organization. He also served regularly as a doctor on trains bringing convoys of refugees to Europe's main harbors en route for immigration to distant lands until he could himself embark for the United States, which he reached in 1950. These experiences brought him close to the issues of migration and dual loyalties to a hurt homeland and an accepting host country. As a naturalized U.S. citizen, he has not hesitated to express his respect for the democratic ideals of the United States; he believes that they parallel his family's commitment to democratic values.

Nagy is clear that his admiration for postwar U.S. psychiatry fostered his persistence in reaching that country despite many hindrances. He was impressed by the optimism displayed by many U.S. psychiatrists who were willing to search for a cure for schizophrenia rather than looking at this condition as a hopeless predicament. Some were also resolved to expand the scope of psychodynamic treatment beyond the limits set by Freud to reach clients suffering from psychosis:

> Indeed the spirit of a courageous search for new treatments, the quest for a cure for schizophrenia, and the success of psycho-dynamic treatment of American soldiers during World War II, may have determined that family therapy would start in America in the late '50s. Family therapy had fewer than a dozen early pioneers; with the exception of Ronald Laing, all were American. Most of us thought to extend the effectiveness of intensive individual therapy to the treatment of schizophrenia. (Boszormenyi-Nagy & Framo, 1965, p. 32)

At first, Nagy settled in Chicago, where he could rely on the support of his teacher and friend, Kalman Gyarfas. Instead of turning to clinical work, Nagy decided to continue his biochemical research at the University of Illinois Neuropsychiatric Institute, where he spent six years.

Nagy received the early support of the institute director, Francis J. Gerty, one of the powerful figures of U.S. psychiatry at the time. Gerty had invited to Chicago Lazlo Meduna, a Hungarian psychiatrist, who became world-famous for his idea that artificially induced seizures could cure schizophrenia. He was recognized as the father of shock treatment, and his work led to the development of the well-known electroshocks by Cerletti and the development of insulin shocks by Sakel. Today's reader may have a hard time imagining that during that time no known biological treatment for schizophrenia besides shock therapy existed, beyond the use of tranquilizers to sedate patients. The neuroleptics that appeared in Europe in the early 1950s were not yet available for use on a large scale.

Nagy had hoped to find readily accessible and measurable biological characteristics that could allow for the biological identification of patients in contrast with normal controls. In a second step, he desired to correlate such biological characteristics with a possible etiology for schizophrenia and therefore move toward an etiologically based cure for the disease. The clinical responses of some schizophrenic patients to insulin shock treatments gave Nagy the impetus to explore a correlation between an abnormal glucose metabolism at a cellular level and schizophrenia. He decided to measure the speed of a glucose-related biochemical reaction in live red blood cells collected from patients and controls to demonstrate a difference between the two rates (Boszormenyi-Nagy & Gerty, 1955). His methodology (the use of live cells) proved a technical success, earning him the respect of the scientific community, but despite promising early results, he was not able to prove a clear difference between patients and controls. This meant that he could not show that schizophrenia was connected with pervasive biological disturbances at a cellular level and that he had failed to discover a valid marker for the disease. Once he realized that, he decided to abandon his biological research and to return to clinical work. He considered the knowledge of the time too crude for yielding clues that could lead to an effective causal treatment. He was able to obtain his U.S. board certification as a psychiatrist in 1957.

From 1955 to 1958, Virginia Satir worked as a social worker at the Illinois State Hospital and taught psychiatric residents about work with families. In her introduction to *Conjoint Family Therapy* (Satir, 1964), she gives credit to Gyarfas for his help in her work. Although Nagy and Satir shared a common mentor, it would be a mistake to see Nagy as a student of Satir; in fact, he never attended her classes and met her only later, at which time both were already recognized as two of the pioneers of the family therapy movement.

Nagy moved to Syracuse in 1956, following the invitation of another Chicago teacher, Marc Hollander, who had become the chair of the Department of Psychiatry at the State University. Hollander also had brought to Syracuse Thomas Szasz, an analyst of Hungarian origin who later became a leading figure of the antipsychiatry movement. Nagy credits Szasz for introducing him to the British school of object-relations theory and, more specifically, to the work of Ronald Fairbairn (1952).

Nagy left Syracuse after only a few months, when he accepted a position in 1957 as psychiatry research director at the newly created Eastern Pennsylvania Psychiatric Institute (EPPI) in Philadelphia. Interestingly, he accepted a dual assignment as the director of a 24-bed research unit for the treatment of young adult females suffering from schizophrenia and as the director of the research unit on biochemistry of schizophrenia, a role that he later delegated to others to concentrate on clinical research. His original clinical team included James Framo, Marge Griffel, Geraldine Lincoln-Grossman, Leon Robinson, David Rubinstein, Geraldine Spark, Oscar Wiener, and Gerald Zuk. Margaret Cotroneo and Barbara Krasner, who are well-known as contextual therapists, joined the department later. Framo developed his own approach to intergenerational family therapy; others, like Spark, Krasner, and Cotroneo, contributed significantly to the literature of what evolved into contextual therapy. Nagy and his team had contacts with many early pioneers of the family therapy movement, such as Nathan Ackerman, Murray Bowen, Don Jackson, Christian Middleford, Carl Whitaker, and Lyman Wynne. Other well-known people like Gregory Bateson, Ronald Laing, and Satir visited the department.

As Nagy moved toward family therapy, his inpatient unit closed. The department was renamed the Department of Family Psychiatry and became one of the earliest and largest training centers for family therapy in the United States. Nagy's team connected with another Philadelphia group, including John Sonne and Ross Speck and headed by Alfred Friedman, who were interested in treating families in their own home. Both groups joined forces to set up the Family Institute of Philadelphia, one of the earliest freestanding family institutes in the country, even before Philadelphia became known for another family therapy training center, the Philadelphia Child Guidance Clinic, directed during a historic era by Salvador Minuchin. The

Family Institute of Philadelphia served as a model for several private family therapy training institutes around the country and continues to offer training in family therapy.

The department organized many early family therapy conferences. In 1965, Nagy and Framo edited one of the first books on family therapy (Boszormenyi-Nagy & Framo, 1965).

By the mid-1960s, the program had become a training facility reaching hundreds of professionals through its involvement with many local agencies and with the five Philadelphia medical schools. In addition, many European visitors visited the program. Amy van Heusden from The Netherlands invited Nagy and his team to visit Holland in 1967 and to teach a month-long family therapy course, the first in Europe. Helm Stierlin from Germany, who had trained as an analyst, spent several years working at Chestnut Lodge in Maryland with Lyman Wynne. Both became frequent visitors of Nagy at EPPI. Stierlin returned to Germany and in 1974 founded an institute for family therapy in Heidelberg. Mara Selvini-Palazzoli visited from Italy well before she herself became a leader in the family therapy movement. Luc Kaufman visited from Switzerland; in 1979. He opened the Centre d'Etude de la Famille in Lausanne, one of the initial family therapy centers in Europe. Nagy himself has spent a lot of time lecturing in Europe, mostly Holland, Germany, and Switzerland, and later Belgium and France. He has returned to Hungary since the late 1960s and has been invited there to teach regularly during the past decade. He has also traveled to several South American countries and to Israel.

Nagy taught at several Philadelphia-area universities, including Jefferson Medical College, University of Pennsylvania, and for more than 20 years at Hahneman University. He retired from Hahneman in 1999 with the rank of Emeritus Professor. In the late 1970s, he founded the private Institute for Contextual Growth in Ambler, Pennsylvania, which has offered contextual therapy training programs in the United States and Europe for more than two decades. He has also been one of the initiators and founding member of AFTA, recently renamed American Family Therapy Academy. He has received many honors as a founder of family therapy movements in the United States and Europe.

MAJOR CONSTRUCTS

From Biology to a Theory of Relationships: The Determinants of Relationships

One way of approaching the discussion of the main tenets of contextual therapy is to review the five dimensions of relational reality described by Nagy. Factual and psychological determinants concern individual processes. They constitute the individual characteristics of a person whether this person is interacting with others or not. Transactional, relational ethics, and ontic determinants of relationships are relational determinants that require the presence of two or more participants to manifest themselves. The determinants coexist at any given time in the relationship between relating partners. Yet, a clinician may choose to focus on one dimension more than another and to intervene accordingly. For example, a table has a certain width, length, and height that make this table unique, but one would not need to know the height of the table to buy a chair or, conversely, the surface of the table to buy a tablecloth. Contextual therapists benefit from a broad knowledge of all the dimensions of relational reality. Students need to become familiar with the therapeutic resources located in any of these dimensions. Still, the dimension of relational ethics remains the most promising for eliciting healing moments in therapy.

Nagy's major contribution to the field of therapy stems from two sources: He has been determined to build an integrative approach taking into account the complexity of human behavior and its determinants; concomitantly, he has generated a new motivational theory highlighting that entitlement, earned in relationships, serves as a comotivator for actions, besides physiological and psychological needs. His model shares common points with the biopsychosocial model of mental illness, but he adds two elements unique to contextual therapy: a dialectical view of relationships, and understanding that fairness dynamics play a crucial part in human relationships and cannot be ignored by therapists.

Factual Determinants
For Nagy, factual determinants encompass all the biological determinants of individual functioning, including a person's genetic makeup, medical conditions, physical assets or limitations, age, and sex. It also signifies the givens of a person's life: birth order, number of siblings, the age and condition of the parents, and the nature of the relationship between the parents (divorce or long-lasting union). The historical circumstances surrounding one's life (living in an affluent country with a plethora of options or in a war-stricken area where mere survival amounts to an achievement) belong to this dimension as well.

Nagy never abandoned his interest in medical or biochemical discoveries nor the hope that science will eventually discover the etiology of schizophrenia and a causal treatment for it. For that reason, he has always left a place for biology as a relational determinant in his model and is not concerned that new medical developments will affect the validity of his approach to therapy. He simply reminds us that, in the absence of a true causal treatment for mental illness, the need to look at therapeutic resources discovered outside classical psychiatry or medicine perdures. Contextual therapists do not have to ignore individual diagnosis. They can feel comfortable using the well-known *Diagnostic and Statistical Manual of Mental Disorders* (DSM-IV; American Psychiatry Association [APA], 1994) or any other prevailing classification system, such as the one developed by the World Heath Organization. Expecting that the simple restoration of a fair balance of giving and receiving among family members could eliminate disorders like schizophrenia or bipolar disorders would be naïve. Yet, helping clients suffering from chronic depression or psychosis to find avenues of giving to others rather than using them as a source of support and compensation for their hurt might increase their chances to regain self-worth based on actual merit. This would, in turn, decrease the risk that they might commit suicide.

Knowledge of the factual elements that affect the lives of clients allows for two uses. A clinician can design therapeutic interventions aimed at changing these elements or understand in what ways these elements impact on the other dimensions of relational reality, more specifically, the dimension of relational ethics. People who have been dealt a much worse lot than others (a disease or tough life circumstances) can either become giving people or turn into demanding partners who hold others accountable to compensate for the hardships they have to endure. Contextual therapists can offer their expertise to clients by helping them explore the ways the distributive injustice they experienced can turn into retributive injustice for others, if they turn toward others for compensation.

Psychological Determinants
Psychological determinants encompass all the mental characteristics of a person: thinking style and cognitive abilities, emotional reactions, unconscious motives, and defense mechanisms. A person's psychiatric symptoms as defined by a mental status examination also belong to the dimension of psychology.

Freud discovered that individual symptoms could be the result of unresolved internal conflicts among instinctual forces (the id, the ego, and the superego); he developed psychoanalysis as a method of treatment. Despite its depth, the analytical model could not offer a sufficient explanation for the complexity of the behaviors observed in family groups.

Nagy was interested in the impact of one person's needs on others and examined how family members were responding to the unconscious needs of one another. He has discussed the multipersonal implications of some phenomena described by the analysts, for instance, the loyalty implication of transference (Boszormenyi-Nagy, 1972/1987d). He has also used the notion of mourning described by Freud to explain the origin of the resistance to change in certain families.

He coined the term "collusive postponement of mourning" to account for the efforts made by family members to counteract a move toward autonomy in one of them. This construct forms the pendant in contextual therapy to Jackson's (1957) conceptualization of family homeostasis, Bowen's (1960) thoughts on undifferentiated family ego-mass, and Wynne's (Wynne, Rykoff, & Hirsch, 1958) idea of pseudo-mutuality.

Boszormenyi-Nagy (1962/1987b) coined the term "counterautonomous superego" to portray internalization by a child of a parent's disapproval of any move toward independence. This provides an explanation for children's readiness to surrender autonomy in families in which parents do not relinquish their symbiotic needs to possess the children as reliable companions. Such parents view their children as parentlike figures who protect them from facing the loss of their actual parents. Nagy was the first to name this process "parentification" (Boszormenyi-Nagy, 1965). Later, Nagy (Boszormenyi-Nagy & Spark, 1973) connected a child's sacrifice of autonomy to the notion of loyalty. Children will sometimes renounce their pursuit of autonomy as a form of repayment to their parents for the care they received.

Nagy would have already made a great contribution to the field of therapy with these discoveries only. Nonetheless, he was determined to go further and to propose a model that could bridge the gap between the theories of personality elaborated from an individual vantage point (ego psychology and object-relation theories) and systems theories that describe the functioning of family groups but tend to ignore individual determinants of observed behaviors. He used his knowledge of philosophy, most specifically of Hegel (Kaufman, 1965) and existential philosophers like Gabriel Marcel (1960), to bridge this gap. Later, he relied heavily on the work of Martin Buber (1958). In brief, he focused on the self-delineating aspect of relationships: We need one another not just for the satisfaction of our individual needs but for the satisfaction of our need for continuity as a self.

Nagy's interest in psychological determinants led him to explore the importance of trust for close relationships. This effort led to important developments in his approach. He followed the paths opened by individual therapists like Erik Erikson (1950), who connected the development of trust in children with the presence of predicable caregivers. Nagy soon realized that parents who are willing to commit to the care of their children are not just trustable but trustworthy. This notion led him to the discovery of the importance of fairness and justice for the development of individuals and for their capacity to form successful relationships. This construct also forms the link between the dimension of individual psychology and the dimension of relational ethics.

The dimension of psychology entails also the discussion of theories of moral development, such as Jean Piaget's (1965) and, later, Lawrence Kohlberg's (1981). Nonetheless, these theories serve to describe varying stages and forms of moral reasoning rather than the actual nature of the balance of giving and receiving between partners. Even Carol Gilligan (1982), who noted that girls and women present with a moral reasoning emphasizing concern for others or an ethics of care, does not focus her writings on the discussion of the balance of fairness as a determinant of relationships. Feminine ethicist, Nel Noddings (1984), also does not address the balance. Nagy makes a clear distinction between the discussion of the psychology of caring on one hand and of relational ethics on the other, but he acknowledges that working with female cotherapists broadened his understanding of what constitutes caring in close relationships.

Transactional Determinants
Transactional determinants emerge only when two or more people interact. To this dimension belong any of the supraindividual characteristics of families, the family power hierarchy or style of communication, the systemic laws that govern the observed transactions, as well as societal elements that affect relationships such as ethnicity, prevailing laws, and customs. Relevant to this dimension are communication theories and general systems theory. Nagy has shared with other family therapy theories the notions that pathology cannot be defined simply as a deviant state (or changed) state of an organism, and that there is a multipersonal texture to psychological health and illness (Boszormenyi-Nagy, 1965). Like many of his colleagues, he relied on general system theory (von Bertalanffy, 1967) to describe phenomena that they could observe in the whole family but could not identify in any of the individuals participating in interactions. Nonetheless, unlike his colleagues, he never did accept circular causality as the only explanation for observable interactions. He fashioned his own motivational theory based on his description of the dimension of relational ethics.

While Nagy was attempting to discover the nature of the supraindividual forces holding families together, he discovered in the notion of loyalty, the bridge between systemic notions like collusion, alliances, and the relational dynamics, based on an expectation of justice and fairness in relationships (Boszormenyi-Nagy & Spark, 1973). Because loyalties define a boundary between a group of persons who have a commitment vis-à-vis each other and all the others, this concept has obvious transactional implications. The concept of loyalty also implicates a triad encompassing the subject, the person toward whom the subject is loyal, and a person who could have been the recipient of the subject's commitment but is not receiving loyalty. But in essence, the concepts of loyalty as well as parentification belong to the dimension of relational ethics.

Relational Ethics
Nagy has designated the term "relational ethics" to depict an aspect of close relationships that should have been obvious to all: Close relationships are sustained by justice dynamics and specific expectations not discovered in other kinds of relationships—a capacity for fairness and commitment that in turn will be repaid by a loyalty. Nagy uses the term relational context rather than system to portray "the organic thread of giving and receiving that weaves the fabric of human reliance and interdependence.... From an ethical and existential perspective, context is a more specific concept than the texture of a given environment. It is a matrix of options and rights" (Boszormenyi-Nagy & Krasner, 1986, p. 414). Therapists know by experience that fairness issues lie at the core of many complaints by clients in all sorts of settings, but only contextual therapy gives clients a clear frame of reference to discuss these issues:

> The ledger of fairness or relational integrity between people is always partly shaped and distorted by each person's internal needs as he or she carries over displaced internalized justifications for presently inappropriate vindication even if such vindication is historically valid retrospectively. Invariably the stability of every relationship depends on its equilibrium between internal and interpersonal relational ledgers of justifiability. (p. 36)

Contextual therapy has been accorded new validation of its focus on fairness dynamics by the unlikely field of evolutionary biology and paleoanthropology. James Shreeve (1995) noted,

"At some point of our evolution our lineage must have developed the most sophisticated Machiavellian tactic of all: the ability to trust.... It was the need to balance between cooperation and competition that turned hominids' societal organization into human society" (p. 297). He added, "One other characteristic of human mate exchange sets the stage for alliances.... While it makes no adaptative sense to help complete strangers, it makes extraordinary good sense to help groups in which we have a genetic stake through marriage" (p. 328). Martin Nowak and his coworkers (Nowak, Page, & Sigmund, 2000) have developed a computer model to show the evolutionary advantages of strategies built on fairness rather than power. If this is true, a capacity for fairness and justice may be unique to the genetic makeup of our species and may have contributed to its spread as much as its capacity for speech.

In any event, no higher animal can survive without receiving some care from parents who are ready to put survival at risk to protect progeny. To that extent, parenting and the survival of the next generation cannot occur without some level of generous giving by a parent, whether consciously or not. Paradoxically, only the human species can afford irresponsible parenting without causing the rapid death of children. This exception to the rule comes with great cost for the next generations: Only humans can exploit their children. If one falls victim to an injustice, one is entitled to some form of compensation, but this entitlement can turn into an unfair liability for others. We know that the victims of injustices (distributive or retributive) tend to turn toward innocent third parties to restore the justice of their own world. The destructive entitlement of one family member can start a cascade of unfair expectations. Children who are burdened with the expectation of making up for parents' hurts will turn to others for compensations and inadvertently cripple a new generation of children. Destructive entitlement often lies at the root of the so-called patterns of multigenerational exploitation frequently discussed by family therapists.

Anyone can at times become exploitive toward others, and no one is free of some measure of destructive entitlement. Each has experienced some measure of unfairness and has turned to others to make up for it. All have the option of relying on entitlement to claim a compensation for the wrongs done to oneself. Conversely, at any moment, a person can also choose to forgo a claim. We need to remember that with our humanity comes a capacity to commit atrocities as well as acts of extraordinary generosity.

Nagy has relied heavily on Buber's (1957) insights to differentiate between guilt feelings stemming from individual psychology connected with the internalization of societal taboos and existential guilt resulting from actual harm to what Buber describes as the "justice of the human order." Existential guilt can diminish only if one is willing to repair the injustice by an act of care or giving that can be addressed directly to the person who has been hurt, if this is possible, or at least to any other person or group whose justice was hurt. If this can occur, the person who committed an injustice will experience a sense of relief and freedom, and the other will benefit from the acknowledgment that his or her justice was hurt. Experienced contextual therapists can offer a two-pronged approach to destructively entitled clients: Therapists can offer partiality to clients whose lot is unfair and, conversely, expect them to give consideration to the persons whom they have hurt by their demanding attitudes. This will help both parties.

Giving generously earns another kind of return. Nagy coined the term "constructive entitlement" to symbolize the kind of entitlement resulting from a willingness to give to others. In its psychological aspects, constructive entitlement can manifest as internal freedom and security and a feeling of satisfaction. In its ethical aspects, constructive entitlement seems similar to merit or justification. Having given to others, a person can act more freely and also can become more able to claim his or her dues. This human experience brings all to a common ground, and clinicians can view a client as not different from themselves. Any client can benefit from an offer of fair consideration and would prefer to be recognized as a potential giver than seen as a relentless taker.

Contextual therapists need to help clients who have been exploited by their parents to discover that even destructive parents share common experiences. In accepting to learn about their parents' own history, they will be able eventually to know that they are, like all others, people who have hoped to find fairness in their relationships, even if at the expense of their children. Realizing that, children may be able to exonerate their parents and overcome their need for revenge or cutoff. Conversely, by understanding the origins of their parents' demanding behaviors, children who are overgivers may be helped to set more realistic limits to their giving. In any event, by patiently exploring the circumstances that led to their parents' shortcomings, children are already giving them consideration, and this will earn them constructive entitlement.

In its essence, the concept of loyalty belongs to the realm of relational ethics. Loyalty connotes a preferential commitment of one individual to the ones from whom he or she has received care or protection. By now, the term loyalty is so frequently used in the family therapy literature that therapists have forgotten its origin. Many use the term "invisible loyalties" incorrectly to describe the unconscious attachment between an individual and a parent. In fact, invisible loyalties are indirect manifestations of loyalty. For instance, clients who are unwilling to manifest a commitment to a parent may end up sabotaging a relationship with someone else. Because they cannot commit to others, these clients remain by default available to the parent whom they were shunning, which amounts to the same result as a display of loyalty, hence the term invisible loyalty. The term "split loyalty" refers to another situation: A child is expected to display loyalty to one parent by putting down the other; if both parents present with a similar expectation, the child becomes trapped in an impossible situation and doomed to fail. For Nagy, the predicament of split loyalty is one of the most difficult and dangerous for a child because children can become hopeless and suicidal when, no matter what they try to do, any effort aimed as pleasing one parent will be seen as a betrayal by the other.

Similarly, parentification affects both dimensions (transactions and relational ethics). Parents can parentify their children by assigning them a parental role or by infantilizing them; in both cases, children become a captive of their parents' lack of capacity to mourn for the parents they missed while growing up. The structural school of family therapy later relied extensively on the notion of parentification, but examined mostly the impact of parentification on the power structure of the family. Structural family therapists tend to see parentified children as children who have grabbed the parental power and whose power needs to be curbed. Contextual therapists, on the other hand, are interested in the exploitative aspect of parentification (a reversal of giving and receiving between parent and children).

The Ontic Dimension of Relationships
The ontic dimension involves nonpsychological, relational determinants of a relationship. Understanding the ontic dimension proves impossible without grasping the dialectic nature of relationships. To understand its dimension, one needs to carefully read Nagy's early text. In Nagy's chapter "A Theory of Relationships: Experience and transaction" (Boszormenyi-Nagy, 1965), he articulated his dialectical view of relationships and then moved toward a description of the ontic versus functional nature of relatedness.

Nagy distinguishes between a mode of relating to others that is instrumental (functional dependence) and one that is independent of any individual needs or actions, which he labeled ontic. By being different from the self, the Other (antithesis) serves as a basis for the demarcation of the self (thesis), but, because the self cannot exist without an Other to define it, the self becomes the product of the synthesis of self and nonself elements (synthesis). The self becomes, therefore, dependent on the Other for its existence as a self (ontic dependence). This is true also for the Other. Nagy also defines the ontic aspect of relationship as "mutual becoming" (I. Boszormenyi-Nagy, personal communication, June 2000): "The adjective [ontic] was coined by Heidegger and is defined by Spiegelberg (1960) as 'descriptive of a structure inherent in being itself.'... The ontic element in a relationships makes the Other an essential counterpart of one's Selfhood, irrespective of any particular interactions" (Boszormenyi-Nagy, 1965, p. 37). As a result, "In a dialectic, relational sense, autonomy is a paradox; it is an innerly sensed freedom achieved through dependence on those vis-à-vis whom we realize the assertion of our needs" (Boszormenyi-Nagy, 1967/1987c, p. 88).

In his early writings, Nagy alluded to the possibility that the ontic aspect of relating could actually represent one dimension of the relational reality, but at the time, he had not yet ordered the specific elements of relationships in what became the four and later five dimensions of relational reality. In 1973, Boszormenyi-Nagy and Spark initiated a discussion of the ontic dimension:

> Phenomenological and existential studies have emphasized the ontic rather than functional dependence of man on his relationships. The writings of Martin Buber [1958], Gabriel Marcel [1960], and Jean Paul Sartre [1956] are examples of this school of thinking.... From this ontic dependence of all members on their relationship with one another arises a main component of the superordinate, multiperson level of relationship systems. The sum of all the ontologically dependent mutual dyads within the family constitutes a main source of group loyalty. (p. 43)

Nagy did not return specifically to the discussion of the ontic nature of relating until the late 1990s, when he became interested in a possible convergence between the work of the physicist I. Prigogine (1984, 1997) and his own work. Prigogine is known for his work on nonequilibrium situations in physics and chemistry and the discussion of self-organizing systems and the theories of chaos. In 1999, Boszormenyi-Nagy composed an essay on this subject that he submitted for comments to Prigogine and shortly after to two of Prigogine's close associates, Mony Elkaim and Isabelle Stengers, who both work in Brussels. The following passages of this unpublished text will give the reader an idea of this effort (Boszormenyi-Nagy, 1999):

> The original impetus for this writing is an expansion of Contextual Therapy (Boszormenyi-Nagy, 1965, 1987a; Boszormenyi-Nagy & Krasner, 1986; Boszormenyi-Nagy & Spark, 1973) which proposes the non-psychological essence of relationships. However, the emphasis has shifted from relational ethics to ontic characteristics of being and becoming. In the period between becoming and fading out, the human being, like other imaginable living entities, participates in the Earth's Biosphere. Biosphere is defined as composed of all living things we know of and their environment. This limits our knowledge of life to our planet and its geological past, present and, within limits, future.
>
> Biosphere means more than a "Zoo" of global size. It is a complex, quasi-teleologically functioning context. According to Prigogine and associates, the Universe is a self-organizing structure. If we extend this concept to the living matter in the Biosphere, we can assume that there are certain requirements of one living being's self-organization that is coordinated with the evolution of other beings. Thus, a co-existence is expected even from two beings of whom one is used by the other as food or as parasitic host. We assume that Biosphere partners as a whole are

mutually co-developing an interlocking of their individual quasi-teleological self-organization designs. Part of these designs include being homeostatically available to other Biosphere "siblings" as "object" of their needs (Boszormenyi-Nagy, 1999, pp. 49–51).

Later, Boszormenyi-Nagy (2000) listed the ontic aspects of relationships as a separate, fifth dimension of relational reality and since then has continued to expand on that theme. The full impact on this announcement on the future of contextual therapy is yet to be determined, but the basic knowledge that partners depend on each other not only for the satisfaction of their needs but for the establishment of their existence as separate selves is not a new notion. For instance, it has great clinical relevance for the understanding of couples.

The importance of relating for the continuity of the self does not represent a new topic either. One needs to remember that of all the threats to which human beings can be exposed, the threat of annihilation of the self is the most unbearable. One should not forget the threat to the continuity of the self of the solitary confinement so poignantly described by Stephan Zweig (1943) in his novel *The Chess Player*. Can unmet ontic dependency needs lead to the actual physical death of a person, such as an infant who is deprived of any relevant emotional contact in an orphanage or an elderly person cut off from any relevant relationships in a nursing home? This needs to be proven, but there are many cases of unexpected death of people who have just lost a spouse or a close relative, sometimes even a pet.

If it is true that the capacity for self-delineation and self-validation depends on opportunities to give to others, then the ability to give determines that persons can exist as autonomous selves. Thus, finding someone to give to becomes crucial to survival. Because giving appears inseparable from existing, giving becomes a right rather than an obligation. Giving connects directly with a right to existence.

Being born of parents provides a person with an immediate context for giving that does not have to depend on the quality of the parent-child relationship. Even nondeserving parents offer a context for giving by the mere fact of existing in an individual's life. If this is true, loyalty does not need to be based on the obligation to repay parents' kindnesses by commitment to them, but can be based on the mere right to give to people who are connected in a unique way by the virtue of a blood relationship. One can be criticized for giving to an undeserving parent rather than to a devoted caregiver, such as an adoptive parent, but no one can dispute that existence depends on the existence of the two people who conceived (whether or not they wanted to have children).

The ontic availability of parents for defining persons as children might be as important to survival as autonomous selves as the care that was or was not received from them. If this is true, the "custom-made" children of today (e.g., children originating from the mix of unknown sperm, an unknown ovum, later placed in the womb of a surrogate mother before being delivered as ordered to one or two persons who hope to be recognized as parents, or the cloned children of the future) could become the true abandoned children of the twenty-first century. Despite any level of commitment of the ones who want to serve as their emotional, transactional, and legal parents, they could never establish their identities on the base of an antithesis between a self and a clearly definable, "old-fashioned," biological parent.

Contextual Strategies and Therapeutic Contracts

Nagy has focused extensively on the nature of a therapeutic contract. Individual therapists tend to see the locus of pathology and change in the individual psychology of their clients. They simply need to define feasible treatment goals and to agree on a method to reach these goals. In doing so, individual therapists take the risk of overlooking the interests of family members, whom their interventions might inadvertently affect. Classical family therapists have discussed extensively the issue of change in treatment. Because frequently they use circular causality to explain the observed symptoms in a given client, they generally concentrate on interventions that affect the sequence of interactions among family members.

Contextual therapists, on the other hand, assume that family members are bound to present with conflicting interests, and none of them will benefit over time from overlooking the interest of others. Each family member needs to pursue personal goals, but no one can afford to ignore in the long run the consequences of that pursuit for others. Contextual therapists encourage family members to state their personal goals and agree to hear in what way these goals could impact on the lives of other family members. Exercising multidirected partiality, therapists give a chance to each family member to express what each expects from therapy and to help each explore the impact of personal needs for others. Individual family members can always benefit from learning to claim their dues and to fight for their rights, or to compromise with each other, but clients can also discover that they can gain from caring about the realistic needs of their family members. In experiencing satisfaction from giving rather than taking, clients may become more willing to decrease their reliance on destructive entitlement and more ready to stop using current relationships to obtain redress for past injustices. Helping clients who are parents to meet the needs of their children benefits not only these clients but also decreases the risk that their children will turn their destructive entitlements against the next generation and, therefore, perpetuate a pattern of multigenerational exploitation.

MAJOR SYNDROMES, SYMPTOMS, AND PROBLEMS TREATED

If individual autonomy and self-esteem comes from facing our responsibilities in relationships, it would be hard to see any contraindication for contextual therapy. To that extent, the principles on which contextual therapy are based should serve as a general guideline for anyone who provides therapy at any level (individual, couple, family, or group). Contextual therapy principles have been used as guidelines for the discussion of laws that affect children in the area of child custody, adoption, and child protective services, as, for instance, in Holland. Contextual therapy principles have been applied to parenting issues, divorce mediation, adoption counseling, family business matters, medically assisted reproduction issues, and other societal issues. A significant number of clergy of varying denominations has also used contextual principles to inform their work with families in their respective congregations.

Contextual therapy can be useful in situations where a client who suffers from a medical condition turns his or her destructive entitlement against others. It can also offer guidelines in the discussion of reproductive decisions. Contextual therapists can help clients come to a decision based on the balance of giving and receiving between past generations and a potential future generation rather than on general ethical considerations (the rights of the parents to have a child versus their obligation to refrain from potentially hurting someone else who could be exposed to the consequences of their decision).

Contextual therapy offers promising results in work with severely disabled clients and their relatives by enabling them to explore avenues in which a sick or disabled family member can give to others rather than remain a unilateral recipient of their care. This diminishes the risk of burnout in the caregivers and the risk of depression in the disabled person.

The case that serves as an illustration of the approach (following) demonstrates also that clients suffering from Conduct Disorder can be greatly helped by contextual therapy. Many people believe that clients with Conduct Disorder are unable to care and cannot be reached by contextual therapy because they have a superego defect and have not been able to integrate a taboo against infringing on societal rules and expectations. As the case below shows, this is far from the truth. Such clients do not have to be treated as if they were part of a separate breed of insensitive semihumans for whom there is little hope for improvement. For the contextual therapist, the challenge lies in finding a way to reach the humanity behind the crust of mistrust and delinquent behaviors.

Of all the disorders, a true Bipolar I Disorder is a good example of a disorder that needs to be treated by medications; however, one of the main issues in the treatment of this disorder is that a great number of clients who are helped by their medications stop taking them. In part, what manic individuals struggle with is the fact that, when the medication is effective at cutting down on the number of manic episodes, it also stops them from experiencing the immediate gratification they can get in engaging in buying sprees or in random sexual activities. To renounce these gratifications, they also need to come to terms with the limitations of their current life and the fact that "life" will not compensate them for past injustices. In working with a contextual therapist, they discover that they can gain from giving rather than having to take without limits and that they can renounce the kind of gratification they obtain by acting on their impulses. Only at that time will they become fully ready to comply with a cumbersome treatment. Depressed clients, on the other hand, learn to overcome the blockages that they experience in their capacity to give. When therapists address them as potential givers rather than as people who need to receive from others, they help these clients in earning entitlements that will, in turn, increase their sense of self-worth and, consequently, their self-esteem. Clients with schizophrenia can be addressed as both loyal and destructively entitled family members. Nagy does not believe in the transactional origin of schizophrenia, nor does he believe that restoring fairness between family members will cure schizophrenia. Nonetheless, contextual therapists can help parents and children delineate themselves from other family members in gaining validation from giving to others. This, in turn, will help the sick family member to reach a greater degree of personal autonomy.

CASE EXAMPLE

Tony was the second, both in age and adoption order, of three children adopted by the Joneses. His older brother had already left home for college; his younger sister was attending middle school. Tony has been enrolled as a student of special education at a good suburban high school, but, because of his truancy and multiple absences due to hospitalizations, he had to repeat a grade.

Carol and Richard Jones had known each other since childhood and came from families with strong religious backgrounds. The pair married early and were eager to start a family. When they realized that, perhaps related to an old medical condition, Mrs. Jones could not get pregnant, they quickly decided to adopt children. They contacted an agency and were willing to adopt children of any race or ethnic background who were still young. Indeed, Tony was Caucasian, one sibling was African American, and the other was of mixed origins. The Joneses were always very open about the fact of their children's adoption, and both families of origin were very supportive of their initiative and very accepting of the children, whom they treated as full-fledged family members.

There was very little information about Tony's birth mother and none about his father, but his background was Caucasian. He wanted to believe that he was of Italian descent, but had no proof of it. He was the only one of the three children who could pass easily for the Joneses' own biological child. Tony came to the family as a few-months-old baby and reached developmental milestones at an average age, possibly sooner than the other two children. He appeared as a bright and good-looking youngster who was likable, but he had difficulties staying still and following directions.

When Tony started school, his parents became more aware of his difficulties. He was disruptive and could not focus on his work. Later, he clearly became oppositional, both at home and in school, and started to react negatively to authority figures, including his father. Besides behavioral disturbances, Tony also developed severe mood swings. When he turned 9 years old, he needed to be hospitalized for a severe depression and making suicidal threats. At times, he also became hypomanic. Occasionally, he was heard talking to invisible partners, but no one could figure out for sure whether he was truly hallucinating or if he was simply trying to get people's attention by behaving strangely. Tony had bragged that he had occasionally experimented with alcohol and cannabis, but there was no evidence of a true substance abuse history. He experienced good health; the only concern for his health came from the use of potent psychotropic medications for extended periods of time and the potential risk for long-term side effects of these medications.

When Tony turned 15, his behaviors deteriorated to a new level of severity. Once, when his parents refused to give him his allowance because of his bad behavior, he held them at gunpoint until they gave him the money he wanted. Although the parents suspected that the gun was a fake, they could not take a chance of being hurt and complied with his demand, but called the police shortly after the incident. They could not resolve within themselves to press charges against him, believing that he was more sick than truly delinquent and that he could get hurt if they sent him to a facility for juvenile delinquents. Nonetheless, they felt that they could not allow him to stay at home any longer, for safety reasons, and because they had given up hope of being able to parent him effectively. They explored the possibility of giving up custody of him, so that he could be removed from their home and become a ward of the state.

When they found that child protective services could not intervene because they were adequate parents who had no history of neglect or abuse, they requested Tony's readmission to a hospital until they could find a placement for him in a residential treatment center. They planned for Tony to stay in a residential treatment program until he became stable enough to return home and to public school.

Up to that point, Tony's treatment history had included the use of psychotropic medications and other treatment modalities, including individual therapy, family therapy, intensive support services, the intervention of a behavioral specialist both at school and at home, the assistance of a mobile therapist available for home visits, and a staff person who accompanied him for many hours a day both at school and at home. In addition, as part of his program as a special education student, he was also accorded individualized services at school.

The residential treatment program that accepted Tony had a strong behavioral modification component and used a level-system to reward good behaviors. The on-grounds school offered individualized programming at the level of special education. Each client was expected to see an individual therapist weekly and to attend family therapy twice a month, generally with the same therapist, who also functioned as a case manager. The program Tony attended was typical of such residential programs, and the usual length of stay for clients like Tony ranged from four to eight months.

As the consultant psychiatrist and a trained contextual therapist, Dr. A. met Tony and his family around the time of his admission to the program and remained involved in his treatment at several levels until his discharge several months later. Dr. A. intervened on many occasions of crises and offered several family therapy consultations, which allowed her to find new directions in her own work and in the work of the individual therapist.

At the onset of his treatment, Tony made great efforts to do well and was hoping that his parents would take him home soon because of his rapid improvement. When he realized that he could not fool his parents and that a prompt discharge was not in sight, he started to show some of the behaviors that led to his admission, testing the program's capacity to contain him. This was a very difficult time, during which he placed enormous demands on all the members of his team. He was extremely provocative in school, and he constantly demanded the immediate attention of his individual therapist outside the time of scheduled appointments, but he was not making active use of the sessions. Family therapy did not go well. Tony's parents were very discouraged and felt that, after attending family therapy sessions for years without results, they too had little hope for changes to justify their participation in Tony's treatment. They were also worried about their daughter, who had started to act out and expressed anger at them for the excessive amount of time they were spending taking care of Tony.

As Tony realized that he was not succeeding in discouraging the staff from working with him and that no one was ready to send him home or to transfer him to a more restrictive program, his need to provoke the team decreased and his behaviors started to improve. Concomitantly, his parents grew confident that he could visit home without acting out and allowed him to come home for weekend visits instead of visiting him at the program's campus.

Home visits went well, but his parents started to struggle with their own ambivalence. Tony's progress pleased them, but they feared that he would revert to his bad behaviors if he were discharged from the program. In their dreams, they hoped that Tony could remain in the program until he turned 18 and would be able to graduate from the program's school. Yet they knew that children who met their treatment goals were expected to leave the program. Tony was aware of their resistance to his return, but, as he continued to improve and to spend time at home without incidents, a discharge date was set.

Very soon after that, Tony threatened to harm his parents again, and the police were called. This time, the parents were so emotionally hurt that they wanted him arrested and did not worry about his safety anymore. Tony returned to the residential program pending a court hearing. Again, soon after Tony returned to the program, his parents started to lose their resolve and began to talk about dropping the charges against him. When Tony got the message that he might escape adjudication, he threatened to assault one of his teachers and could have been arrested for making terrorist threats.

A Path toward Healing

After these two serious incidents, Dr. A. was asked to evaluate Tony. Was he hypomanic at the time of the incident? Did he need rehospitalization? At the time of the assessment, Tony was not agitated, but, on the contrary, profoundly depressed and hopeless. He yelled to the consultant, "You know that you cannot help kids like me. The only place for me is at 'Juvi,'" using the slang word for a local juvenile detention center. The consultant soon realized that his senseless act was the result of a tremendous parentification. By his recent behaviors, Tony had secured a place for himself in the juvenile delinquency system, knowing that he would burden his parents if he had to return home and that there was no other place for him to go after his discharge from the residential program. He had succeeded in finding a solution for his future, and he was effectively relieving his team and his parents from responsibility for formulating a more realistic discharge plan than a simple return home. Another statement that Tony made during the same interview also impressed Dr. A: Tony stated that he could accept his parents' decision to cut him off and that, as an adult, he would visit them to show them that he had "become somebody" despite all of his problems. He believed that he owed that to them: "They have been criticized enough because of me, but this time, they will be proud."

For the first time, the depth of Tony's depression and hopelessness concerned the consultant. Tony knew that, if his parents decided to cut him off, he would have no one to turn to for support aside from the program's staff. Furthermore, this staff would not be available to him if the police took him to a detention center. The consultant felt impelled to share her impression with Tony's parents and to review the situation with them rather than accept that Tony had taken his fate in his own hands. The parents came very reluctantly to the meeting, and, after hearing about Tony's threat toward his teacher, they became so angry that they felt fully determined to let the police arrest him. They had lost hope that the relationship with Tony could continue, but losing years of investment in their adoptive child was not easy for them. The consultant knew that the very nature of their relationship made the situation worse with Tony: They could not rely on the ultimate irreversibility of blood relationship that connects biological parents with their children. They were much less free to cut Tony loose than biological parents would have been because of the fear that nothing would remain of their relationship besides a common last name, which was difficult for them to accept. On the other hand, they could no longer tolerate Tony's behaviors and needed to put distance between him and them.

Dr. A. decided to address the parents' hurts and disappointments as a first step in a family meeting. Neither parent could probably give any credit to Tony until their own destructive entitlement was recognized, and Tony had already received the reassurance that the consultant cared about him, as she had offered to schedule the family therapy session. Giving the difficult circumstances, Dr. A. decided to start the session by turning to Mrs. Jones first. She was more open to talk about her hurt feelings than was Tony's father. Dr. A. wanted to give her credit for her generosity toward Tony, who was not even her biological child, and to recognize her hurt for not having children of her own. Tony's mother responded to the consultant's comment by saying that Tony could have been a biological child and still gotten into trouble. This comment was, again, a generous one. Dr. A. underscored that, as an adoptive mother, Mrs. Jones could not rely on the existence of blood ties to sustain her relationship with Tony, as biological parents can. As Dr. A. was talking, Tony grew more disruptive. She could see that her statements could hurt him by reminding him that he was only a "second choice" in his parents' life. On the other hand, Tony knew that the consultant's goal was to help him and his family rather than to hurt anyone. Finally, Tony interrupted Dr. A. with a stern comment: "Why do you keep reminding my mother that she could not have her own children? Don't you think that she has been hurt enough already?" Everyone stared at him, and his mother started to become teary. She had never heard Tony take her side and show his caring in such a determined way. After recovering from her surprise, Mrs. Jones thanked Tony for his caring about her feelings. Tony's father first reacted by disbelief, but was able later to recognize that Tony was, indeed, protective of his mother. Tony had just attacked Dr. A. because she was possibly hurting his mother, even if Dr. A. was one of the few remaining persons who were willing to take his side. After such a display of loyalty toward his mother, there was no place for doubt. He was committed to his adoptive mother much more than anyone knew, including her. In seeing Tony as a loyal son, his father could also develop a realistic hope that Tony could accept him as a father rather than fighting him all the time.

Following this session, the parents started to see Tony as a giving person and not just as someone who was using them. They did not want to condone his behaviors, but they were able to recognize that he had tried to take his fate into his own hands at a time when they did not know what to do for him. They decided to drop the charges against him and resolved to work more diligently toward family reunification. Tony's teacher was impressed by the changes he saw in Tony and his parents. He agreed to stop pursuing legal steps against him. Given Tony's recent deterioration, Dr. A. could ask for an extension of his stay in the program; by the same token, she encouraged the parents to set a date for Tony's return home and to commit to that plan.

Tony and his family started to attend therapy much more regularly and to regain confidence that they could be heard by each other. Tony's sister came at times, complaining that Tony received much more attention than she. Tony himself tried to be helpful by reminding her that, if she started to do the same things he had done, like cutting school, she also would be removed from her home and give up all that he himself almost lost.

Tony was able to use the sessions to ask more questions about his biological parents, knowing that the Joneses felt less threatened than before in their role as parents. He had learned that they had contacted the agency that was involved in the adoption process to track down his biological mother. She was located and contacted to determine if she was willing to provide more information about Tony or if she was willing to see him. She answered that she had a new family and did not want anything to do with him. In the past, in reaction to this story, he had pushed away Mrs. Jones because her commitment to him made his biological mother's shortcomings more obvious. Now, he was more able to talk openly about his hurt feelings and his sense of rejection. He had improvised a story to account for his biological father never being involved in his life; he had imagined him in jail, which may or may not have been true. Tony also improved in his ability to express how confused he was and how difficult it had been to not know anything about his father. Later, he became interested in learning about Mr. Jones's own growing up. Tony did not completely give up the belief that he was of Italian descent: he started to dress up and to wear trendy Italian clothes to go to school. The Joneses learned to accept his fancy attire as a mild and tolerable display of loyalty to his imagined biological parents. He did not have to reject the Joneses as the only way of displaying loyalty to his absent biological parents.

Tony's improvement was clear, but he was still vulnerable and prone to some grandiosity. Some of his behaviors, though funny, were still bordering on the bizarre. Eventually, he did well enough to go home at the scheduled time and to reenter his local high school. He was still fearful of sabotaging his return home, but was more able to request help. He was motivated to attend individual and family therapy after his discharge and to continue taking his medications. Because the agency did not provide aftercare services, he was referred to an outpatient clinic.

DIAGNOSTIC FORMULATION, GENERAL PRINCIPLES

Tony was diagnosed with Attention-Deficit/ Hyperactivity Disorder by the time he had turned 7; over the course of the years, he carried the additional diagnoses of Oppositional Defiant Disorder, Conduct Disorder, and later Bipolar II Disorder, Bipolar I Disorder, and Psychotic Disorder Not Otherwise Specified (APA; *DSM-IV*, 1994). To understand Tony, one needs to take into account the multiple factors that led to his behaviors: his mood disorder, his scholastic difficulties, his adoption, his ambivalent relationship with his parents as a young adolescent, and the rigidity of service systems like child protective agencies and the legal system. None of these factors alone could have accounted for the severity of his symptoms. For the consultant, the most significant symptoms Tony displayed were connected with his delinquent behaviors. He clearly had symptoms of Mood Disorder and Attention Deficit, but they did not affect him as directly, as they were controlled to a good extent by medication.

Tony was blocked in his capacity to give, but he was nonetheless acutely aware of issues of fairness and injustices. He was also capable of genuine caring.

The task at hand involved remobilizing Tony's willingness to risk giving and to help him move not only toward self-delineation but also toward self-validation. Tony was blocked from giving not only because of many elements in his life, but because he was also hurt as someone who could not find avenues to give to others and was deprived of opportunities to earn constructive entitlement. He was caught in a spiral of destructive entitlement. By behaving badly, he was hurting others, which, in turn, was hurting him. He had to move toward a spiral of constructive entitlement to take the risk to give so as to help not only the recipients of his caring, but himself as well.

Contextual therapy offers a multidimensional model for the understanding of pathology and for the mobilization of therapeutic resources. This approach proves quite effective for ordering therapeutic resources according to the five dimensions of relational reality. Each dimension entails specific therapeutic resources. Depending on a therapist's skills and training, a therapist may offer interventions in one or more dimensions, including the specific dimension of relational ethics, which serves as the focus of intervention for contextual therapists, or delegate some of the possible interventions to others. In Tony's case, Dr. A. was able to offer interventions in the dimension of facts because of her role as a consultant psychiatrist. Tony's individual therapist was able to coordinate the interventions of several agencies (insurance provider, school district, and others) due to her expertise in case management. She was also trained to provide more classical family therapy interventions. A turning point occurred when Dr. A. was able to extend consideration to Tony as a giving family member despite his behaviors. Whether his subsequent giving to his mother resulted from his response to Dr. A.'s caring or of a residual loyalty to Mrs. Jones remains to be seen. In any event, the challenge entailed helping other family members recognize his contribution and, in doing so, earning some measure of constructive entitlement.

Summary

Contextual therapists design interventions that benefit not only one identifiable client but also any of his or her close relatives. This design sets apart contextual therapy from most other schools of therapy, which tend to see treatment goals as either individual or familial rather than multipersonal. Tony's dynamics and his treatment implicated all five dimensions of concern to contextual therapists.

The Dimension of Facts and Interventions Connected with This Dimension

1. Tony was suffering from a mood disorder. He needed to take mood stabilizers for extended periods.

2. Tony was an adopted child who did not know his biological parents. He needed to accept this reality as part of his fate as a human being.
3. Tony shared several physical features with his adoptive parents that his adoptive siblings did not share with them, which put him under more pressure to replace a biological child. Tony's burden could be acknowledged.
4. Tony's mother was suffering from a chronic medical condition that affected her life since her teens. Her children could benefit from understanding better her vulnerability, which could in turn help them to accept her limitations.

The Dimensions of Psychology and Interventions Connected with This Dimension

1. Tony's personality development was affected by a lack of consistent care until he was adopted, even though he was very young at the time of the adoption. He needed to become more aware of the possibility that his mood swings were not simply the result of a biologically based disorder, but could also relate to early experiences of depression followed by episodes of compensatory grandiosity. As he gained a greater facility in expressing his feelings of hopelessness in individual therapy, he became less inclined to switch to grandiosity to compensate for his depression.
2. Tony had also internalized a bad mother who was abandoning and was projecting this internal image on several females who were playing a role in his life, including his adoptive mother, his therapist, and his psychiatrist, whom he all perceived as harsh and rejecting. He could discuss his feelings with his therapist, but, at times, he was so overwhelmed by negative feelings that he became almost paranoid. Individual therapy and antipsychotic medications assisted him in decreasing his reliance on his internal world to interpret external, real relationships. With time, he became more able to notice when he was projecting malevolent intentions on others and to correct his view of them.
3. Tony's Attention-Deficit Disorder had contributed to clear cognitive difficulties and to a learning impairment, which in turn affected his self-esteem. His special education teachers aided him in devising learning strategies, so that he could better focus on his schoolwork despite his attention difficulties.
4. Psychoeducation interventions belong to this dimension as well. Tony and his parents benefited from a discussion of mood disorders and their impact on family life. The psychological determinants of one person affect all the others involved in a relationship.

The Dimension of Transactions and Interventions Connected with This Dimension

1. Tony's response to his ambivalent parents illustrates the process of collusive postponement of mourning. Neither Tony nor his parents were ready to relinquish each other because of their internal needs (the mother's need for an idealized child and Tony's need for a rejecting parent). For all of his nasty behaviors, Tony had remained a more reliable member of the family than his older brother, who had managed to leave home. Tony needed to be credited for any positive actions toward his parents, and his parents would benefit from discovering his commitment to them. Perceiving him as a loyal son would reassure them that he would never cut them off completely; this, in turn, should facilitate their letting go of him.
2. Conversely, Tony's outrageous behaviors could have represented a desperate attempt

at differentiation. By his behaviors, he was forcing his parents to distance themselves from him. Contextual therapists offer their partiality to each family member, and, in doing so, they help clients to define their respective positions. This leads them to self-delineation. It liberates them to explore avenues for earning constructive entitlement or self-validation.

3. Tony's not being a natural child and the fantasy that he could be "returned" to someone else or that he himself would find his "true" parents kept weakening the Joneses' position by introducing the possibility that other people could parent Tony and that Tony did not have to listen to his adoptive parents. The therapist supported the Joneses in their parental roles and enabled them to ascertain their positions toward Tony by encouraging them to set clear limits and supporting each other in doing so.

4. Tony and his parents needed to deal with the constraints of larger systems: a mental health system that was guided by fiscal limitations, a child welfare system that could help abusive but not exhausted parents, and a judicial system that was responding only to people who had committed criminal acts. Tony's individual therapist was active in trying to coordinate the work of several persons involved outside of the residential program.

5. Parents require support to function as parents and to regain their roles in a family hierarchy, and children should not be the ones who make decisions for parents. Nonetheless, where structural therapists may perceive a manipulative child as someone who is usurping the power that should belong to the parents and may view the child as a troublemaker who needs to be contained, the contextual therapist may spot a giving aspect in a child's behavior. For that reason, contextual therapists help parents recognize the contributions of their child, as illustrated in Tony's case.

The Dimension of Relational Ethics and Interventions Related to This Dimension

Destructive Entitlement

1. In Tony's case, any of the factual elements of his life, such as his mental illness or his adoption, could have turned into a source of destructive entitlement. Contextual therapists, using the strategy of multidirected partiality, desire to assist each family member in risking new giving and in moving from a reliance on destructive entitlement to the new possibility to earn constructive entitlement and therefore to reach an autonomy that is based on earned freedom rather than on relational cutoffs. (The meeting between Dr. A. and Tony's family illustrates this effort.)

2. Staff involved with him started to express discouragement and anger toward Tony, who, more often than not, turned his destructive entitlement toward his teachers or his counselors. Sometimes, contextual therapists can be instrumental in offering partiality not only to family members but also to agency workers whom the situation affects.

3. Therapists can become the targets of their clients' destructive entitlements. Besides the well-known resistances to individual improvement described at length by psychoanalysts, another reason for the persistence of symptoms might be found in the client's destructive entitlement. To improve, clients like Tony need to relinquish expectations that someone can compensate them for past hurts and, instead, start to risk giving in offering their therapists the satisfaction of watching them heal. Letting a teacher enjoy the satisfaction of seeing a student progress involves giving as well.

Exoneration. Tony might never be able to forgive his biological mother for refusing contact with him, but he may grow to understand that she was at least human enough to care about other people when she told the agency that she could not meet him because she had a new family. Tony's willingness to think about this woman's predicament might be the best that he can realistically do for her.

Loyalties

1. Tony benefits from discovering ways to manifest his loyalty to the Joneses and to his biological parents in terms that are not mutually exclusive. He needs to know that he does not have to put down one relationship to show his commitment to the other.
2. The tragedy of adoptive children flows from learning only about the few negative behaviors of their parents that led to their adoption: a teen pregnancy, a history of drug use or criminality. they are left with two bad choices to show their commitment to their blood family: They can either push away others or imitate the behaviors of their biological parents that they have heard about, which often are destructive. If, on the other hand, children can understand that even the most disturbed parent would prefer to see a child succeed rather than fail, they may be freer to behave in a positive way and to accept the help of their adoptive parents.

In becoming a sharp dresser, Tony was able to manifest his loyalty to his biological father in a benign way, which was freeing him from expressing his criminal behaviors. Even if his biological parents are not Italian, Tony was able to show a commitment to a world that was not the Joneses'. In accepting Tony's fantasy, the Joneses themselves were giving to him, and he repaid their generosity by being more able to commit himself to the relationship with them.

The Ontic Dimension

At the current time, presenting the ontic dimension of relationships as a separate determinant of relationships still leaves open the question of interventions based strictly on that dimension. For the time being, the important factor connected with this dimension that should inform a therapist is the notion that each family member draws his or her own self-definition from an actual relationship with other family members. To ignore this aspect of close relationships could lead to the dangerous conclusion that no relationship is always better than a bad one. We know from Tony's story that at the time of risk of a permanent cutoff from his parents, he also was at risk of losing the very foundation of his existence as a son in a family. Realizing that, without a relationship with his parents, he was about to lose his very meaning as a person, he became suicidal. Helping him and his family to reconnect, therefore, proved essential to his survival.

TRAINING AND INDICATIONS FOR USAGE

Nagy never experienced the need to organize contextual therapists into a professional organization, but he has clearly defined the basic tenets of the approach. These encompass a dialectic view of autonomy, a willingness to expand the therapeutic contract to any of the persons engaged in a close relationship who could be affected by therapeutic interventions, the use of multidirected partiality as a strategy, and an understanding of a healing moment as the time of a conjunction of benefit for two partners, one gaining from giving, the other from receiving.

Therapists need to develop a good understanding of the five dimensions of relational reality, yet they are not expected to be able to intervene in all of them. When they become aware that a situation calls for interventions that they cannot provide, like any mature therapist, they need to be able to refer their clients to other professionals. Therapists should care about the impact of their interventions on anyone who could be affected by their work.

Therapists need to learn how to move from one setting to another without disruption of the treatment process (to transition, for instance, between couple sessions and sessions including children, or to alternate between individual treatment of an adult and incorporating this person's parents into therapy). Contextual therapists need also to have a good understanding of their own needs and should refrain from imposing their own relational agenda on clients. Ideally, they should be able to explore their own close relationships with the help of a senior contextual therapist. Therapists should seek supervision when their own destructive entitlements start to interfere with their capability of offering partiality to one or more family members. Usually, Nagy, like many classical family therapists, liked to rely on videotaped sessions of actual treatment cases to teach about the sequencing of interventions, as they are based on the spontaneous statements of the family members rather than on a preplanned agenda.

RESEARCH

Contextual therapy has evolved through countless hours over decades of observations of multipersonal clinical situations. To that extent, empirical research takes place each time a therapist endeavors to pinpoint what constituted the healing moment in a given session of therapy. Nagy arrived at the conclusion that the capacity of one person to exonerate a parent constitutes one of the best predictors of clinical improvement over any other element.

An undetermined but large number of students in family therapy programs in the United States, Europe, and South America have focused on contextual therapy as their field of inquiry and have published their results in the form of a significant number of masters-level theses and doctoral dissertations. A few examples of research subjects studied by students in the Master of Family Therapy Program at Hahneman University include *Contextual Family Therapy with Juvenile Delinquents: A Study of Relational Trust Resources* (Rediger, 1988); *Contextual Family Therapy and Group Psychotherapy: A Comparison of Therapeutic Approaches for Treating Parents Who Abuse Their Children* (Jamison, 1992); *Family Therapy with the Care Givers of Alzheimer's Patients: A Discussion and Review* (Bahl, 1988); and *Contextual Therapy and the Treatment of Dual Diagnosis Patients* (Schaller, 1992).

For several years in Holland, Else-Marie Van den Eerenbeemt and Dick Schluter have been gathering data about relationships from a very large sample of a population who read the popular Dutch magazine *Libelle*. They have established a series of questionnaires that address the multigenerational impact of many of the elements discussed under the dimension of relational ethics: mistrust between partners, loyalty conflicts, split loyalties, parentification, and destructive entitlement, among others. They have received answers from thousands of respondents which have confirmed the main hypothesis of contextual therapy, for example, the importance of the balance of giving and receiving for close relationships. Their results have been published in the same magazine and some of their findings have appeared as part of a book (Van den Eerenbeemt, 1997).

SUMMARY

Contextual Therapy, founded by Ivan Boszormenyi-Nagy, MD, one of the pioneers of the family therapy movement, occupies a unique place in the field of psychotherapy. While relational in its essence, the approach is not limited to family therapy and can guide the interventions of clinicians working with individual clients, couples or families, children, adolescents, or adults.

This chapter explores the origins of the core concepts of the approach. It starts with a review of the steps taken by its founder to reach a multidimensional model of relationships and to discover the importance of the dimension of relational ethics as an underlying determinant of close relationships. It contains a review of recent developments in the approach and ends with an in-depth analysis of the treatment of an adolescent male presenting with a complex picture of individually based symptoms of severe disturbances of mood, conduct, and unresolved adoption issues.

REFERENCES

American Psychiatric Association. (1994). *Diagnostic and statistical manual of mental disorders* (4th ed.). Washington, DC: Author.

Bahl, S. (1988). *Family therapy with the caregivers of Alzheimer's patients: A discussion and review.* Unpublished master's thesis, Hahneman University, Philadelphia.

Boszormenyi-Nagy, I. (1965). A theory of relationships: Experience and transaction. In I. Boszormenyi-Nagy & J. Framo (Eds.), *Intensive family therapy* (pp. 33–86). New York: Harper & Row.

Boszormenyi-Nagy, I., (1987a). *Foundations of contextual therapy.* New York: Brunner/Mazel. (Original work published 1962)

Boszormenyi-Nagy, I., (1987b). The concept of schizophrenia from the perspective of family treatment. In I. Boszormenyi-Nagy (Ed.), *Foundations of contextual therapy: Collected papers of Ivan Boszormenyi-Nagy, MD* (pp. 20–34). New York: Brunner/ Mazel. (Original work published 1962)

Boszormenyi-Nagy, I. (1987c). Relational modes and meanings. In I. Boszormenyi-Nagy (Ed.), *Foundations of contextual therapy: Collected papers of Ivan Boszormenyi-Nagy, MD* (pp. 79–97). New York: Brunner/Mazel. (Original work published 1967)

Boszormenyi-Nagy, I. (1987d). Loyalty implication of transference model in psychotherapy. In I. Boszormenyi-Nagy (Ed.), *Foundations of contextual therapy: Collected papers of Ivan Boszormenyi-Nagy, MD* (pp. 98–117). New York: Brunner/Mazel. (Original work published 1972)

Boszormenyi-Nagy, I. (1995, Summer). The field of family therapy: Review and mandate. *American Family Therapy Academy Newsletter, 60,* 32–36.

Boszormenyi-Nagy, I. (1999). *Essay on self-organization and relational ethics.* Unpublished manuscript.

Boszormenyi-Nagy, I. (2000, April 13) General address in the plenary of the annual conference of the Hungarian Family Therapy Association, Szeged, Hungary.

Boszormenyi-Nagy, I., & Framo, J. (Eds.). (1965). *Intensive family therapy.* New York: Harper & Row.

Boszormenyi-Nagy, I., & Gerty, F. (1955, July). Diagnostic aspects of a study of the intracellular phosphorylation in schizophrenia. *American Journal of Psychiatry, 112*(1), 53–58.

Boszormenyi-Nagy, I., & Krasner, B. R. (1986). *Between give and take: A clinical guide to contextual therapy.* New York: Brunner/Mazel.

Boszormenyi-Nagy, I., & Spark, G. (1973). *Invisible loyalties.* New York: Harper & Row.

Bowen, M. A. (1960). A family concept of schizophrenia. In D. D. Jackson (Ed.), *The etiology of schizophrenia* (pp. 346–372). New York: Basic Books.

Buber, M. (1957). Guilt and guilt feelings. *Psychiatry, 20,* 114–129.

Buber, M. (1958). *I and thou.* New York: Scribner.

Erikson, E. H. (1950). *Childhood and society.* New York: Norton.

Fairbairn, W. R. D. (1952). *Psychoanalytic studies of personality.* London: Tavistock.

Gilligan, C. (1982). *In a different voice: Psychological theory and women's development.* Cambridge, MA: Harvard University Press.

Jackson, D. D. (1957). The question of family homeostasis. *Psychiatric Quarterly Supplement, 31,* 79–90.

Jamison, J. (1992). *Contextual family therapy and group psychotherapy: A comparison of therapeutic approaches for treating parents who abuse their children.* Unpublished master's thesis, Hahneman University, Philadelphia.

Kaufman, W. (1965). *Hegel.* New York: Doubleday.

Kohlberg, L. (1981). *The meaning and measurement of moral development.* Worcester, MA: Clark University Press.

Marcel, G. (1960). *The mystery of being: Reflection and mystery* (Vol. 1). Chicago: Gateway.

Nichols, M. (1998). *Family therapy: Concepts and methods* (4th ed.). New York: Allyn & Bacon.

Noddings, N. (1984). *Caring: a feminine approach to ethics and moral education.* Berkeley: University of California Press.

Nowak, M., Page, K., & Sigmund, K. (2000, September 8). Fairness versus reason in the ultimate game. *Science, 289,* 1773–1775.

Piaget, J. (1965). *The moral judgment of the child* (M. Gabain, Trans.). New York: Free Press.

Prigogine, I. (1984). *Out of chaos.* New York: Free Press.

Prigogine, I. (1997). *The end of certainty.* New York: Free Press.

Rediger, S. (1988). *Contextual family therapy with juvenile delinquents: A study of relational trust resources.* Unpublished master's thesis, Hahneman University, Philadelphia.

Sartre, J. P. (1956). *Being and nothingness: Essay on phenomenological ontology* (E. Barnes, Trans.). New York: Philosophical Library.

Satir, V. (1964). *Conjoint Family Therapy.* Palo Alto, CA: Science and Behavior Books.

Schaller, J. (1992). *Contextual therapy and the treatment of dual diagnosis patients.* Unpublished master's thesis, Hahneman University, Philadelphia.

Shreeve, J. (1995). *The Neanderthal enigma.* New York: Avon Press.

Spiegelberg, H. (1960). *The phenomenological movement: A historical introduction.* The Hague: Martinus Nijhoff.

Van den Eerembeemt, E.-M. (1997). *Alle dochters: Drie generaties vrouwen en hun famiekwesties.* (All daughters: Three generations of women and their questions about family). Amsterdam: De Toort.

von Bertalanffy, L. (1967). *Robots, men and mind.* New York: Braziller.

Wynne, L. C., Rykoff, I., & Hirsch, S. (1958). Pseudo-mutuality in the family relationship of schizophrenics. *Psychiatry, 21,* 205–220.

Zweig, S. (1943). *Schachtnovelle [The chess player].* Stockholm: Berman-Fischer.

CHAPTER 20

Systems as Interconnecting Social-Psychological Processes: Existential Foundations of Families

ROBERT F. MASSEY

Social psychology revolves around the interconnecting of social and psychological processes, thus opening a path for examining the vital and inextricable intertwining of the two sets of processes (Massey, 1985/1986, 1987, 1989, 1996, 1998; Massey & Massey, 1995). The lens of social psychology allows a search for existentially justifiable ways to converse about self and system—seemingly, antinomies in terms of dimensions of being and discourse, yet equally essential for family and sociocultural living. How individual and group are fundamentally and ineluctably interconnected poses a dilemma for study and a key to unraveling the theoretical controversies that have spurred the emergence of numerous conceptual frameworks for explicating the workings of family dynamics, development, dysfunction, and therapy.

HISTORY OF THE THERAPEUTIC APPROACH

Adler (1956) focused on levels of self-esteem and cooperation in developing styles of life and relationships within families, between the genders, and among cultural/national groups. He acknowledged social context by interviewing children with problems in the presence of their parents and teachers. For Jung (1925/1971), a couple's relationship may be motivated by biological, unconscious, or parental influences or by conscious dynamics that foster individuation and unity with self and partner. Marriages frequently replicate the quality of relationships with parents. The roles between spouses (e.g., container and contained) often interlock. Though they did not work with families, the neo-Freudians/neo-Adlerians altered the tone and direction of psychotherapy by honing in on interpersonal processes. Sullivan (1953), Thompson (1950), Horney (1950/1970, 1967), Fromm (1941), and Erikson (1950/1963), though trained as Freudian psychoanalysts, elaborated on Adlerian themes regarding the impact of sociocultural dynamics (Massey, 1981, 1990, 1993; Wittels, 1939). From a psychoanalytic perspective, Bela Mittlemann (1944) observed complementary marital transactions (aggressive/submissive), indicated that these responses may be influenced by relationships with parents, and initiated concurrent marital therapy (1948). Also a psychoanalyst and a leader at Chestnut Lodge in Rockville, Maryland, Freida Fromm-Reichmann (1948) considered interpersonal and familial processes sufficiently important to write about the "schizophrenogenic mother." R. W. Lidz and Lidz (1949; T. Lidz & Fleck, 1965) observed troubled psychological, interpersonal, and child-raising processes in families with schizophrenics. Typically, parents displayed marital schism or skew (T. Lidz, Cornelison, Fleck, & Terry, 1957b). T. Lidz, Cornelison, Fleck, and Terry (1957a) and T. Lidz, Perker, and Cornelison (1956) explored the roles of fathers in these families. Wynne, Ryckoff, Day, and Hirsch (1958) noted disturbances in identity and relationships in families with schizophrenics resulting in pseudomutuality, rather than mutuality, and poor boundaries, more like rubber fences. Thinking disorders were common (Singer & Wynne, 1965a, 1965b). Bateson brought his extensive background in anthropology (1936) to bear on the study of communication, pioneered in systems thinking (1972), and with colleagues laid a foundation for innovative cognitive and interpersonal approaches to behavior sequences and therapy (Bateson & Jackson, 1968; Bateson, Jackson, Haley, & Weakland, 1956, 1963). Recognizing intrapsychic and emotional dynamics and conflicts, Ackerman (1958, 1966) viewed these in relation and as adaptations to family roles and the interpenetrating relationships within a family—a psychosocial entity and the basic unit of society (1966). As a psychiatric resident at Chestnut Lodge from 1950 to 1953, Don Jackson (1953, 1959a, 1959b, 1960) absorbed the interpersonal tradition of Sullivan.

Models

A number of models of therapy with families have emerged. A review of the main constructs of theories shows that they contain implicitly or explicitly social-psychological dynamics.

Carl Whitaker

Whitaker and Malone (1953) viewed both therapists and patients as experiencing the vestiges of infantile familial experiences as an "intrapsychic family" (p. 90). Within a marriage, as a framework or adult model of intimacy, processes remain "inevitably reciprocal or bilateral... mirror images—not one-sided" (Neill & Kniskern, 1982, p. 169). In healthy affective engagement, persons become increasingly individual while experiencing oneness with others. A three-generational perspective enhances understanding of family dynamics (Whitaker, 1976).

Jay Haley

Haley (1963, 1976; Bateson et al., 1956, 1963) specialized in communication. Meaning occurs through analogical and digital communication. Communication links family members, forms hierarchies, implies control of the type and quality of a relationship, expresses metaphors, and, when incongruent or paradoxical, gives rise to unadaptive or symptomatic behaviors.

Murray Bowen

Bowen (1985) found fuller explanations of problems by observing or interviewing more people. Couples frequently choose mates at similar levels of differentiation. Families often replicate multigenerational processes. Parents who live comfortably with each other and their families of origin allow their children to balance individuality and togetherness (Kerr & Bowen, 1988) and can express thoughts and feeling and not be overwhelmed by emotionality (Knudson-Martin, 1995). With overwhelming emotionality, unmanageable couple conflict, or serious emotional or social parental difficulty, parents often select a triangled child through a family projection process (Bowen, 1976). Societies display dynamics similar to family systems in times of anxiety.

Salvador Minuchin

S. Minuchin (1974) focused on family structures (roles, boundaries, subsystems, hierarchy) as systems in motion and as matrices of identity. To describe a person existing as both a whole and a part of a system, S. Minuchin and Fishman (1981) borrowed Koestler's (1979) term "holon" from the Greek *holos* (whole) and *on* (suggesting a particle or part). An individual holon as a self-in-context "includes the personal and historical determinants of self . . . [as well as] the current impact of the social context . . . [in] a circular, continuous process of mutual affecting and reinforcing" (p. 14). Complementarity underscores the dynamic interdependence, reciprocity, and mutuality of interacting. S. Minuchin (1984; Minuchin & Nichols, 1993) and colleagues (P. Minuchin, Colapinto, & Minuchin, 1998) called attention to the necessity of addressing larger-systems dynamics at the cultural and institutional levels.

Ivan Boszormenyi-Nagy
Boszormenyi-Nagy (Boszormenyi-Nagy & Krasner, 1986) intended to "reintroduce the truth of personal uniqueness into systemic therapy" (p. 7). Together, self and other can "create a personalized human order in the realm that exists *between an 'I' and a 'Thou'*" (Boszormenyi-Nagy & Krasner, 1986, p. 33; Buber, 1948/1957, 1923/1958). Need complementarity alludes to a pattern of interlocking motivations based on reciprocity (Boszormenyi-Nagy, 1962). The concept of need complementarity evolved into the construct of entitlement. Psychologically and ethically in a healthy, close relationship, the personal capacity for self-gratification dovetails with centrifugal, other-directed concern and offering care: "Through its relevance to trust, the concept of need-complementarity provided a cornerstone to contextual bridge-building between individual, systemic and multipersonal theories" (Boszormenyi-Nagy & Krasner, 1986, p. 36). Boszormenyi-Nagy (1965) elaborated on the intrapsychic and interpersonal dialectical relations between self and other. Other persons form constitutive elements of the symbolic structure of self and, in combination with self, constitute transactional systems. Modes of relating range from largely intrapsychic in severe pathologies to true dialogue in which both persons can serve as subject and object for self and other in a gratifying process of give and take that affirms self-delineation and demarcation from other in building a structure of shared trust.

Mara Selvini Palazzoli
Palazzoli (Palazzoli, Cirillo, Selvini, & Sorrentino, 1989) traversed three stages in her conceptualization of models to explicate clinical work: psychoanalytic, systemic, and complex multidimensional thinking. In the first transition, she moved from

> psychoanalytic reductionism, which disjoins the individual from his interactions, to holistic reductionism, which disjoins the system (family) from its individual members. Indeed, so wary had we been in the past of explicitly focusing on the individual, his intentions and aims, that for lack of "real, live people" we had found we needed to "personify" the system, endowing it with all the intentions and finalities of which we had so carefully dispossessed the individual! (p. 260)

Because individuals respond in myriad ways, she experienced the need to reclaim "the dimension of the subject" (p. 460) and concomitantly to consider the dimension of time, including process, history, and trajectory, as Prigogine advocated in understanding complex systems. In tune with Morin (1986) Palazzoli et al. (1989) sought ways to think about specific persons and instances in loops, like the rhythmic motions of a weaver, to devise a scientific theory of the subject in multidimensional thinking about complexity of an interactive system interconnected with an ecosystem. This includes accounting for how the observer participates in the endeavor.

Peggy Papp
For Papp (1983), couples bring assumptions from families of origin and negotiate these beliefs and interaction sequences, which interlock as they develop emotionally laden themes around

which they organize their system nested in extended families and larger systems. Symptoms indicate power struggles, change poses a dilemma about altering loyalty dynamics, symptoms and relationship patterns are circularly and reciprocally related. Choreography illustrates couple and family organization (Papp, 1976): "A three-generational context gives the therapist a broader gestalt from which to form a hypothesis and make interventions" (Papp, 1983, p. 23). Circular questioning and a developmental perspective facilitate understanding the Gestalt (Penn, 1982). A therapeutic debate by three therapists replicating the family's positions around homeostasis and change externalize the dynamics in which a family is knotted (Sheinberg, 1985). Projecting the current processes into a future time allows for a reflective social-psychological perspective to open alternatives and practice options (Penn, 1985). Papp (Walters, Carter, Papp, & Silverstein, 1988) provided leadership in exploring the impact of gender on interpersonal and family development and the relevance for therapy. Women and men tend to differ in the ways they handle depression (Papp, 2000).

Helm Stierlin
Stierlin, Rucker-Embden, Wetzel, and Wirsching (1977/1980) considered five perspectives essential to view human development: (1) related individuation, (2) centripetal and centrifugal forces of binding and expelling, (3) delegation, (4) multigenerational legacy and merit, and (5) state of current mutuality. Binding, expelling, and delegation interfere with individuation and engagement and indicate loyalty difficulties (Stierlin, 1974, 1983). Binding entails excessive gratification of dependency needs (id binding), interference with a child differentiating awareness and initiative by misdefining a youngster's experiences (ego binding), or concurrently fostering, thwarting, and exploiting a child's legitimate needs for dependency and cognitive guidance (superego binding). In the expelling mode, a child is seemingly encouraged to separate, but with the delegation to complete a mission (either to accomplish a parent's unfulfilled ego-ideal or to act out a parent's unowned delinquent impulses).

Cloe Madanes
Madanes (1981) focused on incongruous hierarchies, the power of caring and protection, metaphorical meanings of symptoms, and interactions. She (1984) devised a collaborative paradoxical approach, based on play rather than resistance, in using pretend techniques to alter the power arrangements involving symptoms viewed as helpful and protective, though not developmentally or hierarchically appropriate. Madanes (1990) identified the main human issue as "whether to love, protect, and help each other, or to intrude, dominate, and control, doing harm and violence to others" (p. 5). As "family members interact around the dilemmas of love and violence . . . a continuum of four dimensions of interaction which correspond to different kinds of emotional and spiritual development" (p. 6) emerges: (1) To dominate and to control, (2) the desire to be loved, (3) to love and protect, and (4) to repent and forgive. They fit together more logically when considered in a circular way rather than as a continuum (Nasca, Dunn, Massey, & Venkatachalam, 2001). Resolving these issues requires moral reference points, attention to spirituality, and reparation, and, when therapy reaches its limits, political action as another mode. Madanes (1995) rejected all forms of predetermination and emphasized

> the power to choose . . . [as] the essence of what is human. . . . The most expeditious way to change a person in therapy is to change . . . social context . . . [and the] relationships with significant others. . . . The first move in therapy of social action is to make each person responsible for . . . [his or her] existence and . . . actions. . . . A therapy of social action cannot be used to justify social injustice. (pp. 3–4)

Choices impact others in unseen ways (e.g., marrying and bearing children affect others immediately and over generations) and become a model for others. Human rights, ethical standards, and actions prove essential. In dealing with serious issues like violence as well as everyday ones, people suffer spiritual pain and can benefit from spiritual resources and inspiration.

Michael White
For White and Epston (1990), narratives, like maps, provide interpretative frameworks. Narratives allow for giving meaning to lives. People tell stories within their culturally shared cognitions and languages. Conversations, including those with self, generally involve stories. People most notice "a difference which makes a difference" (Bateson, 1972, pp. 271–272). White learned from Foucault (1965, 1980), who considered power inseparable from knowledge. Local knowledges can become isolated and obscured by globally disseminated knowledge accepted as truth. Replacing problem-saturated stories with alternatives and unique outcomes (Goffman, 1961) allows for consideration of struggle and conflict, the incorporation of unique lived experiences over time, and reflection on broader sociocultural contexts. As problems are externalized and become distinct from their previous stories, persons experience personal control and initiative.

Tom Andersen
Andersen (1991) derived inspiration from Aadel Bülow-Hansen and Gundrun Øverberg, who coordinated their physical therapy interventions with careful monitoring of clients' breathing: "A Norwegian word for inhalation is inspiration. One could literally say that the rather tense circumstances make the person reduce his/her inspiration from the surroundings" (p. 18). On the basis of Bülow-Hansen's work as well as Maturana and Varela's understanding that biological structures preserve themselves and their functions in constantly changing contexts, Andersen realized that an individual strives to maintain integrity and can respond within the limits of his or her repertoire. Gauging the sufficiently unusual requires going slowly enough to allow people to signal their responsiveness. Each participant experiences inner processes of searching for the meaning of an interpersonal conversation and reflecting on how to speak and listen, and also engages in an outer process of exchanging with another individual. These parallel inner and outer conversations revolve around preserving integrity and making connections. Building on Maturana (1978; Maturana & Varela, 1987) and Goolishian (Anderson, Goolishian, & Winderman, 1986), Andersen (1991) averred that, when people share common interests, they organize themselves as meaning systems.

DEVELOPMENT OF SOCIAL PSYCHOLOGY

Origins and History
Modern social psychology has diverged into sociological and psychological branches. The sociocentered approach as a social science with an accent on social context contrasts with the individuocentered viewpoint as a psychological science with stress on individual mind (Doise, 1997; Graumann, 2001; McGarty & Haslam, 1997). Modern social psychology's roots stem from Europe and flowered in the United States after World War II (Farr, 1996). In Europe, Volkerpsychologie and crowd psychology consisted of three viewpoints (Graumann, 2001). In Wundt's (1832–1920) version of German Volkerpsychologie, cultures and communities shape their members in myth and custom through language, to which individuals actively contribute. His attention to the importance of social processes cautions against experimentation that decontextualizes subjects. Second, crowd psychology evolved in Italy and France. Le Bon (1841–1931) and observations of suggestion (Mesmer, 1734–1815) and hypnotism and of

mental contagion in mobs or crowds contributed to this line of inquiry. After McDougall (1920) postulated a supraindividual group mind, crowd psychology as such did not continue in academic psychology. However, in the more individualized and experimental forms of research on aggression, deindividuation, and public opinion, the theme of the diminished responsibility of individuals in groups persists. Third, Durkheim (1858–1917) inaugurated the tradition of sociology in proposing that, whereas collective representations may have evolved from and been associated with interpersonal interactions, social facts exist external to and independent of individual consciousness.

As a pragmatist philosopher, Mead (1863–1931) aimed to overcome Cartesian dualisms: mind and body, knower and known, self and other (Farr, 1996). He spotlighted the "dialectical nature of the relationship between the individual and society. Individualization is the outcome of socialization and not its antithesis" (p. 54). Mead viewed language as "a form of dialogue and, hence, is intrinsically, and irreducibly, social" (p. 71). Language represents "a species-specific form of behavior and it accounts for the self-reflexive nature of human intelligence" (p. 72). Language, conversation, and thinking necessarily involve others and depend on taking the role of the other. Even a monologue implies a dialogue. In conversation, the speaker also speaks to oneself, who responds to both self and other. Mead's (1934/1964) perspective, unlike most others, encompassed all levels of theorizing: individual (mind), intermediate (self), and collective (society). Though Mead focused on self processes and language, the positivistic psychological social psychologists repudiated his influence.

In the United States, psychological social psychology became individualized (Farr, 1996; Graumann, 2001) as the core value of individualism in Western tradition gained ascendancy. The influence of the Gestalt psychologists (Kohler, Wertheimer, Heider, Lewin), who immigrated to the United States in the late 1920s and 1930s, contributed a cognitive emphasis in social psychology when this was not yet fashionable. The roots of cognitive social psychology emerged from phenomenology and involved natural rather than artificial communication in which individuals engaged in interpersonal exchanges. After World War II, interdisciplinary doctoral programs in social psychology developed in the United States; today, few links remain between the two forms of social psychology (Farr, 1996). U.S. social psychologists who took their discipline to Germany and Japan after World War II brought the psychological version. In Europe, Moscovici's (1972, 1981) contributions on social influence and minorities and representations (following in the footsteps of his French predecessor, Durkheim) offer possibly the only continuing conversation between the psychological and sociological forms of social psychology. An impressive amount of research on social representations is growing in Italian, Portuguese, and Spanish, involving a transatlantic dialogue between Europe and Latin America, with a beginning in Germany. In Canada, the influences of psychological social psychology have spread, but Canadians, more sensitized by their multilingual society and by contacts with Europe, prefer a combination of sociological and psychological formulations.

Gordon Allport (1954/1968) encapsulated the psychological orientation in defining social psychology as "an attempt to understand and explain how the thought, feeling, and behavior of individuals is influenced by the actual, imagined or implied presence of others" (p. 68). Allport acknowledged his "psychological slant" (p. 68). Most researchers focused on individual processes and did not address developmental dimensions (Graumann, 2001). With some exceptions (Lewin, 1951/1975; Newcombe, 1943; Sherif, 1936, 1958), social psychology has remained decidedly ahistorical both in not including longitudinal considerations (e.g., regarding committed relationships) and in enduring as a host of topics or subfields largely devoid of historical perspective, sociocultural context, or integration of past discoveries. Some exceptions point in different directions.

Working Definition of Social Psychology

Persons experience, are influenced by, and are interconnected by social processes. These dynamics constitute an essential dimension of human existence as individuals co-construct and are structured by interpersonal and systemic processes. The definition can be developed in several ways. Psychological social psychologists focus on persons experiencing social processes. Sociological social psychologists highlight how social influences shape the experiences of persons. The interconnections remain the least explicated. Fathoming and articulating them prove foundational to understanding persons and systems, selves and structures as mutually interdependent processes, distinguishable, but not separable.

ISOMORPHIC PROCESSES IN HISTORIES OF FAMILY TREATMENT AND SOCIAL PSYCHOLOGY

Reconciling exploration of individual experiencing and responsiveness with the impact and organizing features of groups and social influences eluded social psychologists, who largely split into psychological and sociological orientations. Psychological social psychologists established the power of *situationism* through studies on social influence, conformity, obedience, and bystander intervention. Gradually, the importance of *construal* emerged regarding impression formation and cognitive dissonance and in attribution theory. The notion of *tension systems* arose from Lewin's (1951/1975) work as the third leg of the tripod of social psychology (Ross & Nisbett, 1991). In tension systems, restraining factors may impede change, a system may precariously balance on the cusp of change, and channel factors may facilitate change and redirect a system, whereas major interventions may exert little impact and even generate resistance to change. More recently, particularly from European origins, social psychologists have noted the need to balance subjectivity and context (Fiske & Leyens, 1997), have called for more integration of research studies (Doise, 1997), have explored the importance of both personal and social identities as each person perceives from both personal and social vantage points (Turner & Oakes, 1997), have recognized the relevance of macrosocial structures and cultures as experienced in "socio-economic status, occupational role, and . . . ethno-religious identity" (Pepitone, 1997, p. 253), and have encouraged increased culture sensitivity (Triandis, 1997). Doise (1997) distinguished four levels of analyses: (1) intraindividual processes; (2) interindividual and situational processes; (3) different positions, such as status and power that actors occupy in social relations; and (4) systems of social and cultural beliefs, evaluations, norms, and representations. Moscovici (1972) and Tajfel (1981) have advocated a rapprochement and increased interchange between psychological and sociological social psychology. These concerns prompt a greater emphasis on sociocultural contexts and shared realities in European social psychology (Graumann, 2001).

MODELS AND DIMENSIONS

Family psychology and therapy arose from a background of focus on individual dynamics. Psychoanalysis, behaviorism (including the cognitive variety), and social learning involve attending primarily to individual dynamics and treatment. The humanistic and existential movements, parallel in time to the emergence of systems thinking, generated insights mostly on the potentials and human condition of individuals. Family psychologists and therapists discovered the power of family structures. Systemic thinking represented a fourth force to counteract the first three (psychoanalysis; behaviorism and social learning; phenomenology, existentialism, humanism) (Maslow, 1962). Most systemic thinking reinforced emphasis on the controlling functions of family groups, rules, and patterns. The evolving emphases of Whitaker's (Neill & Kniskern, 1982) symbolic-experiential therapy, of Nagy's (Boszormenyi-Nagy & Spark, 1973/1984) contextual therapy, and of Bowen's (1976) systems therapy on appreciation of subjective processes in relationship and systemic structures along with Palazzoli et al.'s (1989) discovery of acting subjects "with feelings and intentions" (p. 263) and Madanes's (1995) accent on personal responsibility constitute the evolution of a "fifth force" in psychology: an understanding of the inextricable and fundamental interconnecting of self and structure through "between" (Natanson, 1970, p. 47) processes in human existence (Massey, 1986, 1996). In its social-psychological form, family psychology provides a distinctively human explanation for systems thinking conceived as persons-interconnecting-in-contexts as well as a comprehensive existential and humanistic alternative explanation for systems processes as a countervalence to the use of partial and nonhuman analogies.

CONCEPTUAL FOUNDATIONS OF THE APPROACH

Social-Psychological Processes in Holistic Individual, Family, and System Development

Persons live as *embodied subjectivities* who engage in intentional-functional behavior (van Kaam, 1966/1969). Persons also live interdependently in contexts. Human existence requires biochemical, physiological, and neurological processes and structures. Only with their proper functioning can persons experience the emergence of their full capacities (Hedaya, 1996). The abstract elaboration of intentionality and subjectivity distinguishes human existence from other forms of life. Pascal encapsulated this in calling a person "a thinking reed," a being who can reflect and consequently bend or adapt to the breezes or forces of the environment. Capability of *reflective and self-transcending consciousness* empowers persons with the specifically human characteristic that allows for self-awareness, symbolic representation, language, empathy, humor, shame, guilt, love, planning and organizing altruism and aggression/violence, historical understanding, future planning, creativity, and the design of tools far exceeding human physical limitations (G. Allport, 1937/1961; Frankl, 1969; Fromm, 1941, 1947, 1955, 1964). The ability to reflect and self-transcend also permits identification with and submersion in groups as well as personal and institutional transformation.

Humans experience themselves as *multidimensional unities*. Frankl (1946/1965) specified the layers or dimensions of human existence as physical, psychic, societal field of force, and mode of existence (or noological). Nuttin (1953/1962) accented the intentionality/subjectivity processes in delineating the "three levels of psychic life" (p. 220) as psychophysiological, psychosocial, and spiritual.

The multidimensional capacities of humans both affect and make possible *interconnecting*. Persons follow the twin biospheric tendencies toward autonomy and heteronomy, toward differentiating and joining (Angyal, 1941/1969). A person is conceived through the union of two individuals and remains vitally dependent on symbiosis with a pregnant mother. An infant may receive initial nourishment from union with the mother in nursing and definitely requires attachment with a caretaking person to form a secure base (Bowlby, 1988), a necessity for both successful individuation and satisfactory social relations. Bodies, psyches, social possibilities, and specifically human capacities such as value formation and spiritual orientation *develop* and mutually influence each other (G. Allport, 1937/1961; B. Carter & McGoldrick, 1999; Erikson, 1950/1963; Gilligan, 1982; Steinglass, 1987; Sullivan, 1953).

The evolution of subjectivity necessitates and interrelates with social context while the emphasis varies in sociocentric or egocentric cultural milieux (Comas-Diaz, 1996). As cognitive and linguistic capacities mature (Piaget & Inhelder, 1969), *consciousness of other(s) and self evolve*. A youngster becomes conscious first affectively (Sullivan, 1953) and perceptually (Bower, 1974), then cognitively and linguistically (Mead, 1934/1964) of receiving feedback about self from others. A continual interchange and mutual influencing occurs between an individual's own experiences of subjectivity and others' communicated observations both about self and capabilities and appropriate ways to think of and express these (Andersen, 1991; Festinger, 1954; Laing, 1969/1971; White & Epston, 1990).

First behaviorally, and later cognitively, a youngster gains a sense of *me* from how one is treated and responded to. Self-consciousness, symbolic representation, and the use of *I* gradually emerge (Lewis & Brooks-Gunn, 1979). As perceptual, cognitive, and emotional capacities expand, an infant distinguishes self from others. With symbolic representation and language interactions, a child can solidify a self-image and self-concept with multiple capacities and valuations (G. Allport, 1955, 1937/1961). Conceptualizations of *I* and *me* continue and intertwine throughout the rest of conscious life (Mead, 1934/1964). With the growth of the capacity for active *I* experiences, a person can engage in reflective appraisals both to sort out which *mes*, offered by others, one will accept and to continually develop *mes*—awareness of and reflections on one's own self. *I* experiences involve a continuous stream of consciousness of subjectivity. *Me* experiences implicate social orientation both because individuals receive feedback from others that is assimilated as impressions regarding self and because personal reflections on self embody awareness of how others would view one's thoughts, feelings, and behaviors.

Interpersonal security (Sullivan, 1953) and *trust* (Boszormenyi-Nagy & Krasner, 1986; Erikson, 1950/1963) remain fundamental to the evolution of self. With caretakers attentive and responsive to the expression of one's needs, *real self* grows (Bowen, 1976; Horney, 1950/1970; Rogers, 1959, 1961). When others overly restrict, demand compliance, and place conditions of worth on a youngster, a person may become *alienated* both from valuing the creative potentials of self and from risking seeking attachments supportive and protective of vulnerability and genuine engagement. In the absence of nurturance or with neglect or abuse, a young person may learn to split and retain narcissistic injury (Masterson, 1988), develop neurotic self-idealization (Horney, 1950/1970), lack differentiation (Bowen, 1976), or experience self as incongruent (Rogers, 1959, 1961). This blocks constructive contact and impedes the full elaboration of self-capacities. In these cases, self may not internalize the other as facilitative of growth nor engage in mutuality with another person, but remain locked in fantasized relations about other, act simply as subject or object, or merge with another (Boszormenyi-Nagy, 1965).

The relational structures of persons involve both symbolic representations of self and other and the give and take of interpersonal contact. Whereas disturbances in interpersonal relations can be traced to earlier injury retrospectively, prior difficulties or constricting patterns do not necessarily predict later relational failures because couples may find ways to collude to balance their progressive and regressive needs through complementarity when they share the same ideal of preserving their relationship (Willi, 1984). Personality and relational structures interrelate when observing interactional rather than isolated personality dynamics. With the good fortune to engage in more satisfactory relationships later in development, individuals may experience security and trust and expand their capacities for collaboration and intimacy (Erikson, 1950/1963; Sullivan, 1953).

The capacity for perspective taking, for self-reflection and self-transcendence, which Mead (1934/1964) described as *"taking the attitude/role of the other,"* through awareness of the *mes* that others communicate to and about me, provides the pivot that expands and links consciousness of self and other. From childhood on, initially largely through play and imagination, individuals regularly take the role of the other and consider the attitude of the other when evaluating self-image and self-concept and when deciding on attitudes, feelings, and a course of action (Schachter & Singer, 1962). The capacity for taking the attitude/role of the other makes possible relationships and groupings that endure beyond momentary interactions (Massey, 1996; Mead, 1934/1964). The capacity for *social role taking* develops and makes possible empathy—a necessary ingredient for mutuality and intimacy—and higher levels of moral judgment (Hoffman, 1976; Selman, 1976). By taking the attitude/role of the other, persons can anticipate the responses of others, remember history and traditions, and imagine future alternatives. Taking the attitude/role of the other forms the cognitive basis for culture and society.

Culture and *society* involve suprapersonal dynamics and structures superseding individual cognition. Yet, these forms of organizing do not arise or continue without persons equipped to receive and give influences. A viable and relevant, valid and reliable perspective on human existence must skirt the twin fallacies of *reductionism* and *reification*. Psychodynamics do not fully explain the functioning of relationships, groups, and systems, yet suprapersonal processes do not occur without the specifically human capabilities of persons who participate in them. Nor do groups, organizations, and systems originate or perdure as entities separate from the constituent persons. A satisfactory understanding of human existence entails a *dynamic balancing of individual and structural*, personal and systemic processes. This calls for discovering the vital interconnecting of the two spheres.

Preserving the integrities of self and structure or system has proven elusive. Elucidating this relationship requires focusing on the realm of *the between*. Building on Buber (1948/1957, 1923/1958, 1947/1965), who highlighted the realm that exists *between an I and a Thou*, Natanson (1970), focused on sociality. In "the experience of self with other selves...sociality [means] what happens *between* selves" (p. 47). This responsiveness applies not only to the present because "the *between* is shared...not only by the living but by the dead and the unborn, [for]... *action in* the social world has a far wider reach than the face-to-face model intimates" (p. 54). We discover "the basis of sociality...[in] the 'subjective interpretation of meaning.'... The starting point for the entire conception of sociality...[flows from the premise] that the response of one person to another presupposes that each partner interprets the other's action as meaningful" (p. 56). A dialectical relationship between self and other continues throughout life as self and other construct "a structural relational context" (Boszormenyi-Nagy, 1965, p. 41).

Laing, Phillipson, and Lee (1966/1972) elaborated on the dimensions of *between* in human existence and relationships. Obviously, people *interact*. Second, people *interexperience*. Individuals are responsive emotionally to those with whom they form attachments. In S. Minuchin's (1974) studies on communication in families with a psychosomatic member, as long as the parents spoke in a compatible manner, all members of the family remained at base levels of free-fatty acids in the blood. When the parents expressed conflict with the children observing, the free-fatty acid level, an indicator of stress, rose only in the identified patient with a psychosomatic condition. Third, people *interperceive*

(Laing et al., 1966/1972). Each person views self from a specific *perspective*. A person surmises what another thinks of self (takes a *metaperspective*), and a person imagines what the other thinks that self is experiencing (develops a *meta-metaperspective*). A person also regards the other on the three levels (e.g., "You are X"; "You think I think you are X"; and "You think I think that you think that you are X"). Both persons in a relationship use all three levels. Congruity or disjunction among the twin sets of perceptions lead to understanding and misunderstanding, feeling (mis)understood, and being (mis)understood. Interperceptions about expectations form the rules of a relationship, and interexperiences give feedback about the degrees of felt compatibility and interpersonal fulfillment. Interperceptions and interexperiences link with taking the attitude/role of the other (Mead, 1934/1964) in providing the cognitive and affective bases for group *norms* and the development of culture and society. Those who adhere to a cultural framework in adopting the attendant beliefs and in feeling reasonably comfortable are jointly taking the role of the other (members of the culture). Those who do not follow the norms become designated as deviant for not taking the attitude of the other (members of a culture) or as outsiders. Family or group members who do not subscribe to the same set of interperceptions may feel alienated from that group and more comfortable with a different *reference group* with whom they share compatible interperceptions (Shibutani, 1955). Significant others and reference groups provide the guidelines for comparing personal qualities, abilities, and achievements to decide on the adequacy of *mes* in regard to social norms. In complex and pluralistic societies, reference groups provide perspectives, shared through communication channels, for persons who belong or aspire to groups with specific sets of interperceptions and interactions.

Elucidating *between* processes resolves the earlier social-psychological controversy over group mind that Floyd Allport (1924) rejected as the "group fallacy" (p. 9), as did others who affirmed a "strictly individual locus of mind" (G. Allport, 1968, p. 54). *Between* processes provide a way to explain "a common manner of thinking, feeling, and willing" (p. 43), so that both "the integrity of the personality system . . . [and] the existence and action of social structures which are transindividual" (p. 55) are recognized. *Between* processes also aid in answering "modern social psychology['s] . . . struggl[e] to attain ways of dealing more directly with the *interactions* of persons" (Smith, 1969, p. 34) in exploring "dual foci: *socialization* . . . and *communication*" (p. 374).

Laing et al. (1966/1972) conceptualized and provided language for the interconnecting processes between self and system. A *system* connotes *structure*. Systemic structures transcend persons, yet depend for their viability on the continual interplay of the interactions, interperceptions, and interexperiences of the constituent persons who confirm their validity as the basis for taking the attitude/role of the other (Mead, 1934/1964) in defining both personal identities and appropriate standards for social living (Tajfel & Turner, 1986; Turner & Oakes, 1997). In social change, a particular set of *between* experiences is altered (Mead, 1934/1964). There are family and cultural structures, but some from the past no longer exist. *Between* processes may not, and frequently do not, operate in awareness unless contrasted with a comparison in which experienced reality becomes a figure rather than the ground of one's being, as in multicultural encounters. Both autocentric embeddedness in context (Schachtel, 1959) and the exercise of *power* may render socialization and enculturation processes relatively involuntary. *Freedom* occurs within human limitations (G. Allport, 1937/1961; Binswanger, 1967; Frankl, 1969; Fromm, 1947, 1955, 1964) and the constraints of power relationships (Avis, 1992; Clark, 1974; Goldner, 1985; Hare-Mustin, 1978; Jacobs, 1987; Massey, 1987).

The dynamics of *between* transpire pristinely in a *dyad*. In dyads, dynamics rooted in psychological processes entwine both parties (Jackson, 1965). Defense mechanisms (A. Freud, 1936/1966) used interpersonally extend beyond intrapsychic operations to ensnare both partners in interaction, though neither might acknowledge their impact. Projective identification requires an other (Klein, 1946, 1956) and, when operationalized in an ongoing relationship, fundamentally impacts the quality of a relationship (Scarf, 1987). In behavioral and interactional complementarity, a dyad establishes a dynamic balancing of roles. In dysfunctional arrangements, the participants rigidly counterbalance each other (S. Minuchin, 1974). In the classical pursuer-distancer complementarity, a pursuer likely experienced earlier abandonment and a distancer engulfment (Gobes, 1985). Couples externalize their object-relational splittings and projective identifications in marital dances (Middleberg, 2001). They may fulfill and balance their progressive and regressive needs through collusion (Willi, 1984). Couples often circularly reinforce their interactional patterns with symmetrical or complementary arrangements (Haley, 1963; Watzlawick, Beavin, & Jackson, 1967).

Yet, a dyad lives in multiple contexts, and at least one of them (in the instance of parent and infant) emerged from other milieux. *Triadic* observations and conceptualizations prove necessary to deciphering the foundations of systems in human existence. Bowen (1976) observed triangulation as central to understanding relationships and systemic processes. S. Minuchin (1974) found conceptualization of triangulation of children between conflicting parents to be essential to assessing and treating dysfunctional families. Guerin, Fogarty, Fay, and Kautto (1996) distinguished between threesomes and triangles. In threesomes, each can engage another one-on-one while maintaining an *I* position, self-focus, and options and allow the other two to relate comfortably. In triangles, three individuals interact in rather fixed and repetitive ways, with two engaged in dependent clinging and the outsider more emotionally distant and frequently symptomatic. Triadic patterns derive meanings and implications from the cultural situations in which they occur (Falicov, 1998). Laing (1969/1971) observed that individuals internalize "not objects . . . but patterns of relationship . . . [so that] triadic relationships are collapsed into self-self relations" (p. 8). Thus, persons may treat themselves and deal with others as they experienced a relationship occurring between two significant others earlier in their lives. Persons perceive a synthesis of relationships in which they are third parties; in turn, they are seen as part of a synthesis with another by a third party (Laing et al., 1966/1972).

Multigenerational processes selectively carry on past models and legacies and shape options and opportunities for future progeny (Boszormenyi-Nagy & Spark, 1973/1984; Bowen, 1976; Whitaker, 1976). The structures of one generation impact on the organization of later ones (S. Minuchin, 1974). Internalized psychodynamics perpetuate influences from the past (Berne, 1961; Boszormenyi-Nagy, 1965), and customary social patterns reflect those of ancestors. Migration, technological innovations, expression of variability in personality and in relationship and family formation, genetic variations, handicapping conditions, intercultural marriages and exchanges, forced social change in intergroup conflict, and exercise of creativity all foster modulations of previous patterns. Resemblances and linkages across generations may occur overtly or covertly (Boszormenyi-Nagy & Spark, 1973/1984; English, 1969; Laing, 1969/1971; Palazzoli, Cecchin, Prata, & Boscolo, 1975/1978; Whitaker, 1976). Neither current nor multigenerational dynamics fully explain each other but interact, sometimes directly, sometimes subtly, in the continuous stream of persons and societies as processes with varying degrees of distinctiveness and interconnecting.

Selves, families, cultures, and *societies coevolve*. Cultural and societal forces support and constrict personal and family living. Specifically human capacities allow for social evolution transcending the limitations of space and time; they also exert immediate, everyday impacts, sometimes quite forcibly. Human existence can be deeply rooted in tradition. Technological advances interconnecting remote parts of the earth almost instantaneously and shaping production and consumption globally can blur and threaten cultural integrity and the stability of a community as a secure foundation for the development of solid selves and families. Each person experiences goals and aspirations within a *life space* (Lewin, 1951/1975), in which an individual perceives boundaries and positive and negative valences (driving and restraining forces) regarding potential opportunities. Some accomplishments seem attainable, yet may take steps to achieve. Individuals encounter barriers to inaccessible areas of endeavor. Behavior results from the combination of a situation and how a person perceives it at a particular time; both persons and situations are active in this equation.

Consideration of the institutional and societal levels underscores that individually focused social psychology does not suffice to explain the complexity of human existence. Reflective consciousness allows humans to transcend immediate spatiotemporal limitations by designing both *tools* and *cultural/social institutions*. Tools can extend human capacities (e.g., boats) and also exceed them (e.g., airplanes, computers). Tools can further constructive ends (e.g., cars for transportation) and destructive ones (e.g., weapons), and some do both (computers for knowledge versus launching missile attacks) (Fromm, 1964). Tools and cultural/social institutions can enhance quality of life or serve as instruments of oppression and exploitation. Cultural/social institutions are based on interpretations of the past and visions of the future; a systemic understanding of society conveys the truths that social institutions can facilitate, support, and reward as well as sabotage, oppress, and destroy individual, family, and group endeavors. Political and economic structures do not serve individuals and groups equally or equitably; the ranges of comfort and zones of access operate differentially. Racism, sexism, myriad forms of discrimination, and genocide set up barriers to achievement, comfort, and even survival. Resource-rich persons and groups gain advantages for social advancement.

Contexts of autocratic power and of the power to become restrain or advance the fulfillment of individual needs (Maslow, 1954/1970; Massey, 1987) and hopes for positive relational structures (Boszormenyi-Nagy, 1965). Individuals and groups modulate their expectancies in accordance with perceived situational access or barriers to their goals (Lewin, 1951/1975; Rotter, 1954). Individual/group perceptions/efforts interact with situational opportunities (Merton, 1949/1957). Some individuals/groups conform to positively and adversely valenced environments; others counter the prevailing trends (and strive to overcome obstacles or act negatively in constructive settings). Neither persons nor structures completely determine each other as they coevolve, but the strength of each may tend to sway the interactive outcome. For instance, a person with Down syndrome is unlikely to complete college. Oppressive political and economic structures can, but do not necessarily, break the wills of individuals or effectively shackle the movement of those identified as members of stigmatized and disenfranchised groups, and contain their levels of aspiration and accomplishment. Social support can operate differentially. Members of oppressed and discriminated against groups may find constructive support for self and relational development within their own communities, but experience rejection or barriers in the dominant society (Batts, 2001; Billingsley, 1968).

Individuals and groups have differential access to power and resources depending on the cooperative, competitive, or exploitive nature of social structures and the channels of opportunity. A sense of entitlement or disenfranchisement affects the emergence of *I*s and *me*s, at least regarding social identity and, often, regarding personal identity. Interactions, interperceptions, and interexperiences are altered for the participants, often subtly and unconsciously, both within and between groups, through consciousness of stigmatization and privilege. How a person or family regards and fits on the continuum of racial/ethnic/class identity modulates self- and other perceptions (within one's own group and in relation to other minority and the dominant groups) (Helms, 1990; Sue & Sue, 1999) and will impact social distance and ranges of association within and across groups.

Members of both target and nontarget groups internalize racism, sexism, and other forms of disempowerment to varying degrees. Individuals in disenfranchised and privileged groups may subscribe to pejorative stereotypes. Members of stigmatized groups may concretely be excluded from access to structural resources and sometimes accommodate psychologically to this condition. Some will chafe at the situation, and others will work actively for social change, frequently at risk to their own and their family's safety, and sometimes become prosecuted or disappeared. Concomitantly, while members of privileged groups enjoy access to resources (McGoldrick, 1998a, 1998b), in personal and social consciousness, they may engage in defensive maneuvers of group-level denial of humanity through depersonalization/deindividuation (Zimbardo, 1970) or displacement/projection of unacceptable libidinal desires, aggression, and violence onto the outgroup in fantasy or actuality. Or they may connect with the humanity of others, assume responsibility, and work cooperatively, sometimes braving risks to their own safety, for constructive superordinant goals benefiting both groups (Madanes, 1995; Sherif, 1958).

Differential access to resources and societal rewards impacts quality of social life, sense of safety, levels of physical and mental-health care, susceptibility to involvement with the criminal justice system and the likelihood of receiving punishment, educational and economic opportunities, and participation in political power. These dynamics impinge on and define parameters for self and transactional structures and set the contexts for experiencing one's life spaces within cultural and societal contexts. Both persons and social structures differ in degrees of flexibility (Triandis, 1997).

Through self-transcending consciousness, multidimensional persons ex-ist (literally, stand out of) and engage in *between* processes as beings-in-the-world (Binswanger, 1967) capable of care and violence. Humans form *coherences* (Dell, 1982) of self and family, cultural, and social structures of their own designs, so that a system is not a "what" but a "who" of persons-coconstructing-and-being-structured-by-their-contexts (Massey, 1986). The simpler structures constituting human ex-istence possess autonomy when considered at their own levels (Merleau-Ponty, 1942/1967). As they join with more complex and inclusive phenomena, they become constituents of the more intricate structures. The integration supersedes the independence of any component. The constituents still exert influences, but the overall, more complex level cannot be reduced to or explained by the functioning of a less-inclusive level.

The *levels function reflexively* (Cronen, Johnson, & Lannamann, 1982). They can be the contexts for deciding on the meaning of one for the other. Cronen et al. delineated the levels of meanings as content of communication, speech acts, episodes, relationships, life scripts, and cultural patterns. We can expand the continuum at both ends to begin with genetics, physiological processes, intrapsychic experiences of self and internalized other, and end with socioeconomic-political structures and spirituality. When persons, families, and groups interact, interperceive, and interexperience congruently and draw constructively on the resources at each level, charmed loops of reflexivity occur and support the development of selves and nurturing structures.

Contrarily, when the levels conflict, do not function properly (as in physical illness), or exert negative or oppressive forces on the other levels (e.g., either intrapsychic dynamics resulting from abuse impede appropriately trustful engagement in relationships or group life, or societal discrimination constricts equitable access to resources supportive of favorable development of selves, relationships, and cultural respect), then strange loops of disjunction, alienation, and hostility prevail. Selves and structures delicately and potently balance around their myriad interconnections.

ASSESSMENT AND INTERVENTION

From a social-psychological perspective, a clinician keeps in mind all of the points articulated in the conceptual model. Reaching this level of vision requires in-depth training in personal and multicultural flexibility, ready familiarity with theoretical frames, comprehension of the workings and appropriateness of assessment and intervention methods, and, most of all, reflective and collaborative attunement to and connectedness with self and other persons understood within multiple contexts. While open to an integrative collaboration, clinicians working from this perspective can draw on assessment techniques focused on elucidating interconnections and use some designed originally for individuals in a relational manner. The guiding principles involve using the assessment measures with systemic thinking (Nurse, 1999) and with cultural sensitivity, respect, and appropriateness (Dana, 2000). In clinical work, assessment and research overlap, each enriched by the other. Discussion of observational, projective, and standardized measures exploring processes on levels of human existence is elaborated in the research section of the chapter. These measures can be used, when respectfully contracted for and appropriately explained in clients' language competencies, as sources of understanding social-psychological processes, though some, from their therapeutic frameworks, eschew them as impersonal and objectifying.

Several techniques are geared specifically for social-psychological assessment. These include genograms, sculpting, and choreography (B. Carter & McGoldrick, 1999; Papp, 1983). S. Minuchin (1974) offered structural diagrams; Lindblad-Goldberg, Dore, and Stern (1998) updated these to include affective dynamics. Nasca et al. (2001) have developed strategic maps to depict strategic processes (Madanes, 1990). The Parent Interview (McNeel, 1976) elicits parental introjects through interviewing a client as if that person were the parent. The Fantasy Marriage Technique (Matuschka, 1972) involves asking a couple to imagine what two marriages would be like on relevant dimensions if the mother of one were married to the father of the second and the father of the first to the mother of the second. Usually, this evokes both the delightful and the distressing aspects of their partnership as situated in one or the other imagined couples. Dusay and Dusay (1989) devised an exercise in which a therapist helps each partner in a couple to trace current distressed feelings to the earliest memory of these and then encourages first self and then the partner to offer the protection or comfort that would have helped at the time of injury.

Persons live dynamics that can go awry in fairly recognizable ways and be organized within a classification system, such as the *Diagnostic and Statistical Manual of Mental Disorders (DSM-IV;* American Psychiatric Association [APA], 1994), the *International Classification of Diseases,* World Health Organization (1992), or the *Global Assessment of Relational Functioning* (GARF; Group for the Advancement of Psychiatry Committee on the Family, 1996). Placing a person in a category can rubricize rather than help an individual (Maslow, 1962) and become a self-fulfilling prophecy (Erikson, 1950/1963) as a person develops and engages in a career of deviancy or mental illness (Scheff, 1966). Yet, these categories can also give some general indication of the problem(s) needing attention. Clinicians who do not mistake accurate classification for encounters with unique persons and families and who seek understanding of the personal, transactional, systemic, and cultural/societal dynamics implicated can use the category systems as shorthand to communicate with other professionals, much as multicultural projects frequently entail mastery of several languages. A clinician who grasps the reflexive interrelationships of multiple levels of human existence can explain how an individually focused diagnosis fits dynamically with other dimensions of development.

PROBLEMS, SYMPTOMS, AND SYNDROMES TREATED

Developmental Social-Psychological Dynamics as Matrix for Preferred and Impaired Growth

The biopsychosocial-spiritual-systemic model is intended to provide a comprehensive, multidimensional model of human existence and development. Assessment of problems, deficits, disruptions of development, or abusive situations necessitates a holistic view of the resilient multidimensional unity and integrity of persons and systems reflexively influencing each other. A clinician entering from a framework of social psychology uses a diagnostic lens with a primary focus on the quality of interconnecting self and family development. Comprehensive assessment depends on broadly trained professionals and collaborative teamwork among specialists. Some difficulties involve genetics, physiology, biochemistry, and physical disabilities, but they happen to persons and occur within families who experience, respond, and adjust on social-psychological levels (McDaniel, Hepworth, & Doherty, 1992). Individuals and families may be troubled or racked by dissension over values, religious, or spiritual issues and practices. These affect their self-experiences, the quality of relationships, and, at times, the viability of continuing affiliation.

Social-psychological interventions can sometimes alter the understanding or acceptance levels of struggles on the somatic and noological levels, but never displace or substitute for them. Some dynamics stem from cultural and societal processes. These considerations may need to be addressed through political action or economic changes. This area requires great sensitivity, so that a clinician is attending to client needs and not advancing a personal agenda. However, a professional may glimpse the broader context and need to refrain from blaming persons and families when the locus of responsibility (Sue & Sue, 1999) lies outside of their efforts and gauge whether clients are ready for deconstruction of injustice structures.

Social psychologically oriented clinicians realize that mental and physical symptoms allude to "problems in living" (Szasz, 1970, p. 13) and do not subscribe to a "myth of mental illness" in regarding all psychological disturbance as illness. They realize that cultures vary in their definitions of socially proper behaviors and that, in ordinary circumstances, residual rule breaking is denied, transitory, and passes out of memory. Clinicians also realize that others may draw on stereotypes learned in childhood and assign a person the role of "mentally ill," which the person may accept with a concomitant alteration in interperceptions, interexperiences, and interactions in assuming this status as a career (Scheff, 1966). Patients and professionals can assume self-perpetuating complementary roles in institutions for the mentally ill, and these alter relationships with families and outside communities (Goffman, 1961). Understanding the social construction of deviance aids a clinician in seeking competencies, strengths, and resiliency in cultural contexts.

Social dynamics modulate the constructions of self and family. Clinicians using a social-psychological lens watch for instances of strange and charmed reflexive loops among individuals, families, and cultural/societal structures. Gender relations implicate a fertile area for discontinuity and incongruity between personal experiences and relationships vis-à-vis socially constructed definitions of self, other, and roles (Almeida, Woods, Messineo, & Font, 1998; Avis, 1988; Goldner, 1988, 1993; Hare-Mustin, 1986; McGoldrick & Carter, 2001; Walters et al., 1988). Clinicians sensitive and responsive to these dynamics assess for power imbalances and design interventions for protection and empowerment (Avis, 1992; Bogard, 1992; Dell, 1989; Goldner, Penn, Sheinberg, & Walker, 1990; Kaufman, 1992). Societal context may obscure constructive gender development (Pipher, 1994; Silverstein & Rauschenbaum, 1994) and need specific attention (Leonard, 1985). Differential opportunities and structural reinforcements can tilt, facilitate, or obstruct development and exercise of abilities and normative distributions of power between dominant and minority groups (Foucault, 1980; McGoldrick, 1998b). These inequalities invite deconstruction and consideration in assessment and effective interventions (Imber-Black, 1988; Madanes, 1990, 1995; S. Minuchin, 1984; P. Minuchin et al., 1998; White & Epston, 1990). Culture modifies the emergence and operation of these dynamics. Therapy considerations sometimes interface with legal and other institutions when therapy is mandated or when violation of a law has occurred. Both personal responsibility and safeguarding against exploitative or oppressive exercises of power need to be addressed (Madanes, 1995; McGoldrick, 1998a).

Grasp of a social-psychological perspective as a focal lens for a holistic biopsychosocial-spiritual-systemic understanding allows for entering various frameworks, including those addressed previously, and drawing on assessment and techniques in an informed and integrated manner. Different theorists have specialized and provided insights on particular symptoms, relational structures, and systemic configurations. Their conceptualizations may be specific to the syndromes studied or, when considered in a broader framework, may provide a path to fathoming other interconnections.

CASE EXAMPLE

John, born in 1902, grew up in an orphanage. Margaret's parents, George and Francine, were born in 1863 and 1868. She was the fourth of five children and born in 1905. Francine's mother died when she was 5, and she was raised by her second oldest sister, eighteen years older. John and Margaret were married in 1930. John worked long hours as manager in a service industry. He drank heavily and womanized, with his wife's knowledge. Margaret bore two children, Nelson and Nell. Nell remembers her parents always sleeping in separate bedrooms and her mother regularly wrapping her head in a warm towel and bemoaning her migraine headaches. Nell saw little of her distant father and was not close with her brother, seven years older than she. She showed artistic talents from an early age and, despite the protestations of her parents, who raised her strictly in a protective environment, insisted on attending a music institute in a neighboring metropolitan area. Nelson married a woman his parents did not approve of and moved across the country. Nell and Nelson had sporadic contact over the years. Nelson and his wife raised two sons and two daughters; when the oldest was a senior in high school and the youngest in seventh grade, Nell learned that her brother had been charged with incesting each of his children.

When Nell turned 19, she met Edward, age 23, who charmed her. Edward was the fourth of five children. Edward's parents, Giovanni and Teresa, were born soon after their parents arrived from Italy. Both fathers, Giuseppe and Marco, learned some English at work; their wives, Maria and Nicola, spoke mostly Italian. Giovanni and Teresa and their siblings spoke Italian at home as children and English with outsiders. Edward's parents favored his two older brothers, who had become an accountant and a lawyer. Two sisters, Rose and Angela, were born just before and after him. Edward struggled through high school, but was very sociable and had a good sense for business. After a short courtship, Nell and Edward married, partly so that Nell could escape from her overbearing parents.

After the wedding and reception, just before the couple left for their honeymoon, Nell's mother called her aside into a room and explained to her her wifely duties and for the first time informed her about sexual activities. Nell was shocked. She refused to consummate her marriage for a month. A month after they began having sexual intercourse, Nell discovered that she was pregnant. Two weeks after she delivered Katerina, Nell was diagnosed with postpartum depression and hospitalized for six months. Edward insisted that his mother rather than hers care for Katerina, who was taken to his family's home in another state. Three months after her release from the psychiatric hospital, Nell began to drink wine secretly. She found reasons to add wine to many of the meals she and Edward shared. Katerina remembers her mother drunk, unavailable emotionally, critical, and continually demanding of her. Nell intimated to Katerina that she dressed and undressed in the bathroom and not in the bedroom in the presence of her husband.

Eighteen months after Katerina's birth, Edward Jr. arrived. Eddy represented the desired male heir for his Italian father. Though less of a student than Katerina and more inclined to goof off, he was not reprimanded by his parents. Eddy was groomed to eventually take over his father's business. Four and six years later, Jenny and Maureen were born. Nell frequently expressed a hope that her two younger daughters would be more successful than Katerina. Nell's parents died before the birth of her two younger daughters. Edward's parents lived hundreds of miles away, so they had little contact. Katerina enjoyed the company of her single aunt, Rose, who lived close by, had helped care for her as an infant, and was warm and attentive to her. Katerina was relieved and delighted when she could spend special time with Aunt Rose and felt loved and accepted on those occasions. All of the children were sent to Catholic schools.

Katerina began college after graduating from high school. She lived on campus, failed a number of courses, and spent a lot of time socializing with friends. She felt miserable about her parents constantly checking up on her and her lack of concentration on her studies. Her parents brought Katerina to therapy and wondered how she could be so mired in a lack of discipline and a pattern of failure. The parents worked on some on their issues, mostly as parents, and experienced great difficulty in detriangulating from and not scapegoating Katerina. The more serious issues alluded to previously did not emerge until Katerina returned later for therapy and engaged in her processes of individuating/differentiating balanced with constructive rather than abusive and damaging connecting. Nell continued to drink. On occasion, Edward would become roaringly drunk; once, during Christmas holidays, when questioned about his state of intoxication, he swept a dozen crystal glasses off the kitchen counter crashing onto the floor with one swipe of his arm.

Katerina failed out of college. She moved in and out of her home twice, worked in a low-paying job, wishing that her father would hire her in his company as he had promised his son. She dated a number of men, who tended to be immature and self-interested. She began experimenting with bulimia. Two years later, she obtained decent employment and moved in with a senior executive in her company who was about her father's age. He treated her nurturingly in his opulent home. She gained some confidence from her work and his friendship and felt respected and appreciated in their sexual relationship. Katerina realized that they could not sustain a long-term relationship, however kind her friend and lover was. She moved out on her own into an apartment, which she decorated. During this period, she returned to therapy and began to work on her consternation over her parents' continuing tendencies to favor her siblings, despite her efforts to please them; her grief over her mother's alcoholism and her father's ebullient fostering of his son's career, and his low expectations for her; and her struggle with dieting and eating disorder. Katerina felt abandoned emotionally by her family and suffered low self-esteem and a lack of internal as well as external support for achievement and interpersonal comfort.

Katerina, then 22, resumed evening classes at the university and moved to a more career-oriented job in a larger company. A year later, she met Bill, the older brother of two sisters, the youngest of whom was cognitively challenged as the result of fetal alcohol syndrome and who lived in a sheltered environment. Katerina gradually explored a relationship with Bill. She viewed him as respectful, sensitive, and attractive. She was hesitant to commit herself to a relationship, though he patiently pursued her. After making progress in therapy in building her self-esteem and a positive image of herself, gaining some distance from the hurtful patterns of criticism from her parents, and advancing herself professionally, Katerina tentatively introduced thoughts and feelings about responding more fully to Bill's overtures. She decided to embark on premarital therapy. The couple worked on deepening understanding of themselves and their origins, learning communication skills, building in protection for vulnerabilities and room for growth, and developing an explicitly constructive marital contract.

Two years after marrying, Katerina, age 27, and Bill, age 29, returned for therapy. They were considering starting a family, and Katerina in particular was hesitant about becoming pregnant for fear of repeating the mistakes of her own upbringing. She explored some family-of-origin dynamics and her early years, and revived the sources of her support, particularly with her Aunt Rose. The couple decided to start a family and welcomed little Paul into their midst. Katerina dealt with the transitional issues of maternity leave and finding quality child care as she returned to her responsibilities as high-level support staff in a corporation.

Three years later, the couple inquired if they could come in with Bill's parents because Bill's father, Roger, was caring for his wife, Anna, who was suffering the advanced stages of Alzheimer's disease. The family had a number of inspirational sessions, sometimes including all four adults and at times only the elder couple. Anna came in a wheelchair; she had lost the use of her voice and could communicate only by some nodding and throat sounds. Roger retired early, devoted himself to his wife's care, and declined any nursing assistance. He considered this level of care part of his marital commitment. Bill and Katerina worried that Roger would become overwhelmed and isolated. Roger persisted until his wife's death 17 months later and gained inner peace for fulfilling his values. In his part of the therapy, Bill dealt with understanding and forgiving his mother for the effects of her drinking on the lowered levels of quality involvement with her children and husband.

Two years later, Katerina and Bill returned to therapy. Katerina continued to experience emotional rejection and social exclusion from her family. Though one of her younger sisters had already gone through an early divorce and her other sister and her brother were involved in conflictual marriages, her parents seemed unable to appreciate Katerina's personal and family growth. Occasionally, Nell would grudgingly baby-sit Paul and his new sister, Marsha, but complain persistently. Yet, Nell and Edward seemed to overlook the inconveniences of Eddy's wife, who would rather go shopping or socialize with her friends, leaving their three children with the grandparents. Edward tolerated Eddy's taking a good bit of time off from work and carrying less than his share of the responsibilities in the family business. Katerina expressed jealousy of how hard she and Bill had to work to make a living and compete in a corporate environment. Therapy involved Katerina's struggle with bulimia, her psychological concerns over her physical attractiveness, and her shyness about permitting herself to find full pleasure in affection sharing with Bill because of her preoccupation with body image. The couple ended therapy when she felt they had moved along sufficiently.

Six years later, Katerina again requested therapy. Though quite bright, well-nurtured by his parents emotionally and academically, Paul, age 13, was experiencing difficulty concentrating on home tasks and in school. The Child Study Team had classified him as Attention Deficit, Hyperactive. The parents wanted to work on maximizing his progress and minimizing family conflict around discipline. After long days of work, Bill expected more self-discipline from Paul, and Katerina expressed more sympathy for Paul's struggles. Katerina also was concerned that Paul would ignore or play roughly with his sister, five years younger. More poignantly, Katerina had suffered serious heart damage from taking diet pills that a physician prescribed but did not monitor well. She felt very vulnerable. She had to stop working and was depressed that she was not contributing financially and put an extra burden on Bill. She was fearful of dying before seeing her children grow up, and was angry at having been taken advantage of pharmaceutically. In the middle of the therapy, a natural disaster occurred that forced the family from their home. They stayed with Nell and Edward for a week in the spacious house where all four siblings had grown up. But Nell complained so much about the burden of their staying, that they had come in the middle of the night, and were using the washing machine so much, and Edward expressed so much concern for Nell's peace of mind that Katerina and Bill asked his father if it were at all possible for him to accommodate them in his one-bedroom apartment. Roger welcomed them. They remained comfortably with him for two weeks.

Shortly thereafter, Eddy, whose wife had left and with whom he was engaged in a nasty divorce, asked if his three children could stay after school with Katerina and the children. Nell was unwilling to accommodate her son's children; Katerina acquiesced. Eddy's children did not follow Aunt Katerina's instructions well, and Eddy seemed to expect that all four of them could eat regularly with his sister's family and come and go as they pleased. This stressed Katerina and Bill, who, as parents, had become more supportive of each other around guiding Paul. They set boundaries with Eddy and his children, telling him that they loved and wished his family well and that it is better if the parents in both families provide some predictable organization for their children.

Katerina's heart fortunately healed to the point where she can live a full, if somewhat physically restricted, life. She took part in an outpatient program in addition to therapy to more fully take charge of her continuing bulimic tendencies and the accumulated depression from years of parental nonsupport, the disappointment of losing her career, the trauma of a damaged heart, and the possibility of not seeing her children grow up.

In a session, Katerina reflected on her life. She recalled how her parents let her down and continued to do so. When Katerina wanted to talk as a daughter with her inebriated mother, Nell would tell her how wonderful life was for her compared to her own growing up and question why she could not be appreciative. Nell would hit Katerina and deny her feelings. Katerina grew up scared, and the heart condition rekindled that scare and anger that her parents continued to favor her siblings. Through her group and individual/family therapy, Katerina was striving to cleanse herself. She regretted that her mother never told her she was sorry for her behaviors. Katerina took comfort that she could acknowledge to her children when she was mistaken and that she can say that she is sorry. She worked on acknowledging the scare and hurt of neglect as past and on nurturing herself and gaining confidence to find peace in her efforts to value herself and her family.

DIAGNOSIS AND ASSESSMENT

From the social-psychological viewpoint, all *dimensions of human existence* become salient (Frankl, 1946/1965, 1969). Most prominently, Katerina's heart condition, the bodily implications of bulimia, and the effects of alcoholism and Alzheimer's disease implicate the *physiological* dimension. On the *psychological* level, Nell's internal model of a distant, emotionally distracted father and a debilitated, self-absorbed mother did not provide her with many resources for parenting. Katerina's internalization of rejecting, critical messages hampered her development of self-esteem, internal support for self-comfort, and motivation for self-protection and self-nurturance. She made the decision to find a supportive spouse and to provide more generous emotional care for her children. On the *social* dimension, both Katerina and Bill had to deal with pursuer-distancer complementarity while growing up and have actively communicated about and negotiated more balanced involvement with each other and their children. On the *noological* level, the values of respect for children and relationships and orientation to ultimate meaning in spirituality have inspired and sustained Katerina and Bill in everyday affairs and in crises. Ultimate meaning and evaluating the significance of living surface in the face of impending death.

On the *intrapsychic* level of analysis, through projective identification (Klein, 1946, 1956; Scarf, 1987) Nell finds in Edward a sociable persona and Edward gains acknowledged vulnerability. In their relationship, Edward did not grow more insightful and truly compassionate, though his sentimentality could be experienced as caring, but remained constricted by the not so implicit demands to follow his instructions. Nor did Nell become more comfortable with expressing feelings or being at ease without alcohol. The couple remained locked in a complementarity of socially overresponsible-underresponsible, with a somewhat ironical trading off of pursuing and distancing. Both Edward and Nell distance, he from problem solving through anger, which is actually a way of engaging intensely, and she from comfortable connection through criticism, which is also a means of involvement, though not an attractive one.

Into these vortexes of dissatisfaction unfulfilled couples draw triangulated and delegated children. Margaret inducted Nell into the wounded-and-bereft-woman syndrome (Leonard, 1985). Both Nell and Katerina experienced binding processes (Stierlin, 1974, 1983; Stierlin et al., 1977/1980). Nell received superego binding with her parents, who were very reluctant to support her growth in independence and yet threw her onto her own resources by offering her little support and guidance. This incapacitated her attachment processes with her husband and firstborn daughter. She experienced high levels of guilt and anxiety regarding sexual expression and about independent functioning as a mother. Nell imposed ego binding on Katerina by denying and mystifying her feelings and wants. Katerina has had difficulty being clear about her self, her strengths, and her goals; healing this deficiency has consumed a major portion of therapy. Edward and Nell deflected the stresses and disappointments of their incomplete and strained bonding onto their firstborn; Katerina was expected to carry the family vulnerabilities rather than the parents achieving healing and growth from their unresolved issues. Katerina and Bill's search for a secure quality of attachment for their relationship and with their children draws some nurturance from the model Roger provided for Bill and from Katerina's interludes of acceptance, understanding, and loving comfort with Aunt Rose (Bowlby, 1988). Katerina has suffered from her gendered identity. Her parents' clear favoritism and privileging of her brother's maleness, consonant with a version of traditional Italian culture (McGoldrick, Giordano, & Pearce, 1996), has frustrated, angered, and hampered Katerina in the discomforts of relating to her parents, educationally, and in support for career. She has internalized and somaticized this conflict through a hypervigilance about her weight and body image, dieting, bulimia, and ultimately taking diet pills that have permanently damaged her health and life opportunities. She has been victimized by societal pressures ambivalent about women's attractiveness and worth as reinforced by family dynamics (Pipher, 1994). She is challenged to find meaning and make the most of her opportunities within the constraints of her familial-sociocultural contexts.

Katerina has received a plethora of *me*s from significant others (Mead, 1934/1964). In internalizing reflected appraisals from others, she has accepted a debilitating number of attributions of not-as-worthy, a problem, not-worth-taking-care-of as much as more-preferred-people. In taking the roles of significant others, Katerina has perceived some affirmation of her being and indifference regarding her success from her father and hostile neglect from her mother. These leave her without solid internal models for self-care. The loving concern of her Aunt Rose and the support she did receive from her parents protected her from further damage and fostered in basic ways an adequate foundation for her existence (Difenthaller, 1997). In Katerina's family, mismatches among the interperceptions among members probably outnumber the congruences, and a high number of interactions revolve around conflictual and negative themes (Laing et al., 1966/1972). Katerina has perceived herself as wanting acceptance, approval, and love, as working to succeed and to please others and be helpful, as well as being neglected, unappreciated, and left out and being perceived as too needy, rebellious, incompetent, burdensome, and an outsider. These have led to misunderstandings, feeling misunderstood, and being misunderstood. Before her, both of her parents found themselves underappreciated by their parents and siblings. These incongruent interperceptions interlink with awkward and unsatisfying interactions and interexperiences of discomfort. As a couple, Katerina and Bill have continued to refocus on open and supportive communication to gain greater understanding in their levels of interperceptions to reach agreements on acceptable transactions and to maximize their interexperienced gratifications.

Katerina observed her father as husband treat his wife with self-distracted good humor, which lasted as long as she fulfilled his demands and then turned to anger and disgust, and her mother as wife wanting to keep up the appearances of normalcy while removing herself emotionally and from physical affection out of social shyness and personal shame. This resulted in a dance of husbandly pursuit with an overbearance without the attraction of acknowledged vulnerability and a wifely façade of okayness with emotional and affectional unavailability, resulting in a lack of connection to resolve issues and reach intimacy. Katerina incorporated this relationship triadically (Laing, 1969/1971) by becoming harsh with herself, particularly in relation to body image and weight, and wanting to cover over her shame while not asserting herself sufficiently for nurturant self-care. This results in disappointments, trying too hard to reach a fantasized perfection in body shape, and missed opportunities to live and relate fully and to experience joy in spontaneous fulfillments. Despite this, she has resisted triangulating her children into her pain and has joined more fully with Bill in establishing the rapport children need as a solid foundation for development. The reflexively related levels evidence a series of strange and charmed loops (Cronen et al., 1982). Her strivings for healthy wholeness do not match the social-psychological pains she has experienced with her family and are compatible positively with the support she shares with Bill and her children. Stressfully, her neglect and harshness with herself resonate with themes of abuse in her family.

Multilevel systemic processes have emerged and become more apparent in the case formulation. The described dynamics indicate possible *diagnoses*, but only those in therapy can be formally diagnosed. Nell suffered from Dysthymic Disorder (*DSM-IV*, 300.4, Early Onset), alcohol dependence (303.90), and Borderline Personality Disorder (301.83), and Edward from Narcissistic Personality Disorder (301.81) on Axis II with Diagnosis Deferred (799.9) on Axis I. Katerina's diagnoses have changed over the course of therapy. When Katerina and her family first entered therapy when she was 19, each of the three appeared to be suffering from an Adjustment Disorder (*DSM-IV*, 309; APA, 1994) with anxiety and depression regarding their transitions (309.28) and disappointments and with Katerina showing conduct problems (309.4). When Katerina's bulimia became apparent, she was given a diagnosis of 307.51. Now, with her heart condition, she has a diagnosis of Mood Disorder Due to Idiopathic Cardiomyopathy (293.83). Paul is diagnosed with ADHD Primarily Inattentive (314.00). During the time when Bill was going through a job transition, he was diagnosed as 309.28. At the time of their therapy, Anna was classified with Dementia of the Alzheimer's Type (290.0), and Roger with Partner Relationship Problem (v61.1). From the information given, we can assign GARF scores of 75 to Bill and Katerina, 65 to Roger and Anna before her deterioration, 45 to Nell and Edward, 30 to John and Margaret, 60 to Giovanni and Teresa. GARF scores range from 1 to 100 and indicate levels of satisfaction in a relational unit.

CASE FORMULATION

The genogram (see Figure 20.1) provides a pictorial symbolization of *multigenerational processes* over five generations, all of which represent important processes, and summarizes dynamics that the confines of the chapter do not allow for elaboration (*Bowen*, 1976, 1985). On the maternal side, differentiation has suffered as emotionality rather than rationality and feeling have impeded individuation and decreased nurturant and intimate connecting (Kerr & Bowen, 1988; Knudson-Martin, 1995). The high levels of anxiety in the nuclear family emotional system link with social impairments (John's infidelity, Nelson's perpetrating incest), physical symptoms (Margaret's migraine headaches, Katerina's bulimia), triangulation (Margaret with Nell with John in the outside position, and Nell with her other children with Katerina in the outside position), and emotional cutoff (Nelson and Nell). High anxiety and emotional discomfort have directed family projection processes. During Margaret's pregnancy with Nell, Margaret learned that John had taken a mistress, so Nell's birth coincided with her parents occupying separate bedrooms and her mother's associating her birth with severe disappointment and absorption in anger manifested in regular migraine headaches, which lessened her capacity for child care and resulted in Nell's anxious/avoidant attachment (Bowlby, 1988). Nell's position as the last born in an unsatisfying marriage, Katerina's as the first born in a fragile union with a sexually uncomfortable mother, and Paul's birth to two firstborn parents with alcoholic mothers placed them in vulnerable positions and made them recipients of excess anxiety.

In the *family structures* (S. Minuchin, 1974; S. Minuchin & Fishman, 1981) triangulation (Edward and Nell involving Katerina in ongoing triangulation) signals dysfunctional structuring (see Figure 20.2). Clear boundaries have proven the exception in this family. Rigid boundaries with a tendency toward disengagement occurred between John and Margaret; Nelson and his parents; and Nell, Anna, and her children. Diffuse boundaries with a bent toward enmeshment took place between Margaret and Nell, and Nelson and his children. The boundaries between Katerina and her parents have changed from diffuse, when she was triangulated into

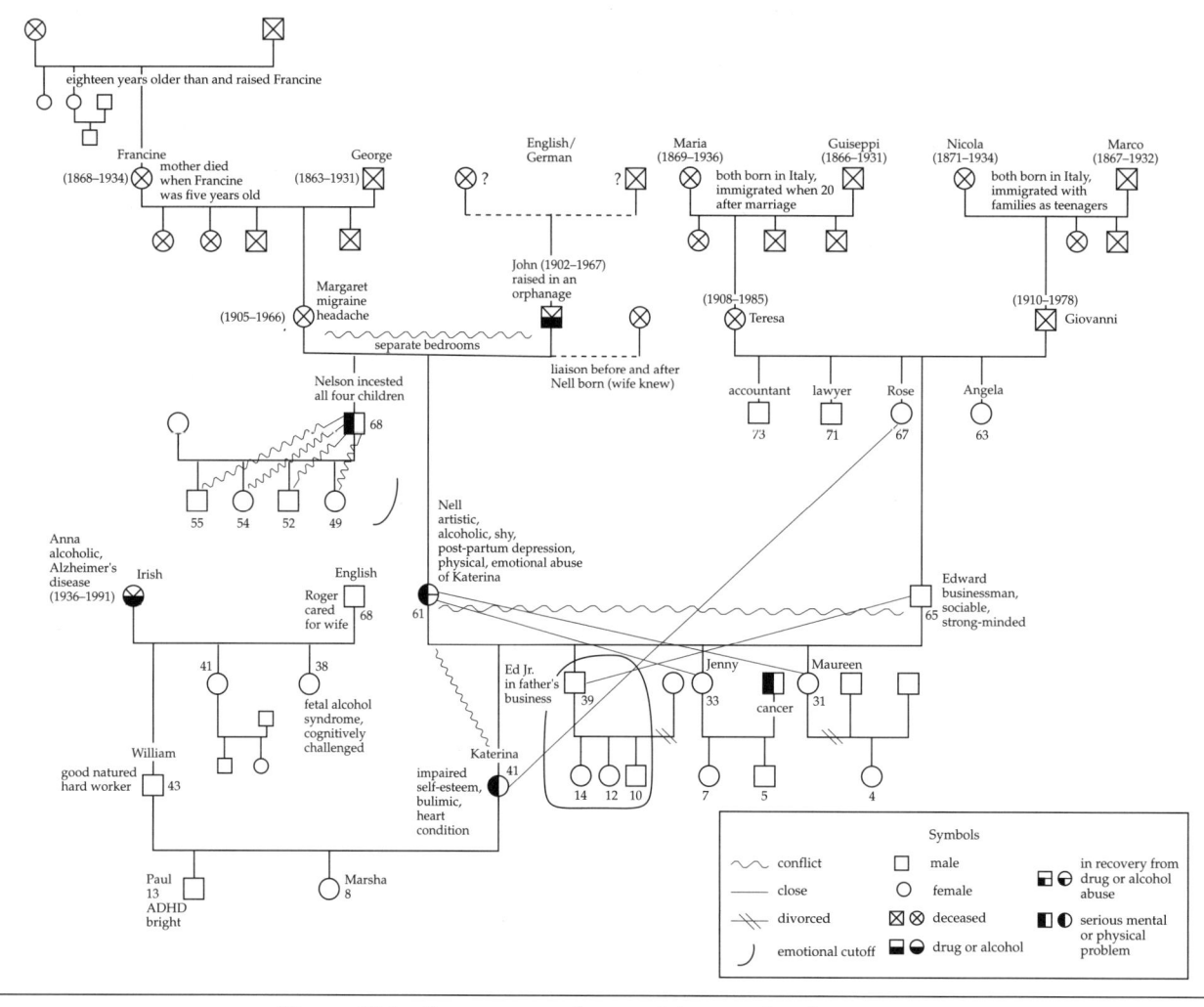

Figure 20.1 Genogram to show multigenerational processes.

their relationship (Figure 20.2b) to more rigid (Figure 20.2a), as she has become more differentiated and the recipient of rejecting anger from her mother and sisters and despairing indifference from her father (Figure 20.2c). As Eddy was divorcing, the boundaries with Katerina's family became diffuse until she and Bill insisted on clear boundaries. A lack of clear boundaries has weakened the marital subsystems (John and Margaret, Nelson and his wife, Edward and Nell) and sibling subsystems (Nell and Nelson, Katerina and her brother and sisters). Despite their age and gender differences, Katerina and Bill guide their children toward some cooperation. The upper-generation hierarchies have not been arranged for protection and support. Complementarities of pursuer-distancer and underresponsible-overresponsible have displaced comfortable accommodation encouraging competency.

Nell's alcoholism and Katerina's bulimia allude metaphorically to deprivation of nourishing nurturance in the family (Haley, 1963, 1976; Madanes, 1981, 1984). Paul's ADHD suggests that the children have had to put extra effort into eliciting attention. Symptomatic behaviors have set up incongruent hierarchies in relationships and families. Nell's alcoholism and social shyness have controlled their marital relationship as seeming helplessness has restricted the range of interaction possibilities. Katerina's

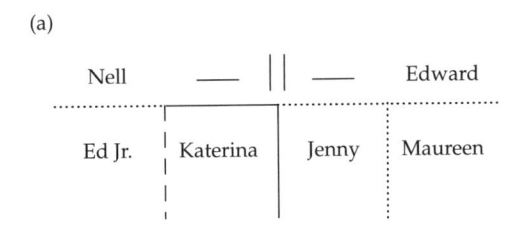

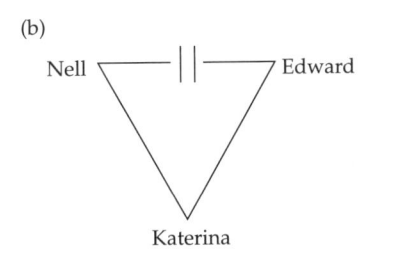

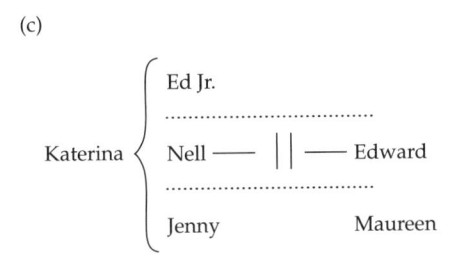

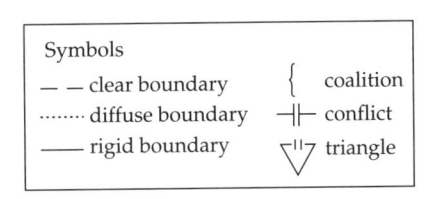

Figure 20.2 Structural diagrams (Minuchin, 1979): (a) continuing pattern, (b) Katerina triangled as teenager, and (c) current family coalition against Katerina.

academic difficulties as a college student gave her power over her parents' levels of satisfaction as they experienced frustration rather than operationalizing energy to combine support and letting go as they launched her. Simultaneously, her obstreperousness protected her parents from facing the fragility of their relationship. Katerina's preoccupation with body image has limited the couple's range of affectional experiences, hinting at sexual discomfort in earlier generations on both sides of the family because alcoholism often proves antithetical to affectional expression (Prescott, 1990, 1996). Over the generations, family members have struggled with the dilemmas of love and violence (Madanes, 1990). Difficulties on all four of the dimensions of emotional and spiritual development have affected various members, with dynamics deteriorating to the point of needing to repent and forgive in Nelson's family. Nasca et al. (2001) developed a procedure for strategic mapping to portray incongruous hierarchies, symptoms, levels of power, and disturbed dimensions of emotional and spiritual development in resolving the dilemmas of love and violence (see Figure 20.3).

On the relational ethics and ontic dimensions (C. Ducommun-Nagy, 2002), parentification has abounded (Boszormenyi-Nagy & Krasner, 1986; Boszormenyi-Nagy & Spark, 1973/1984). Children have frequently lacked provision of care. The ledgers of interpersonal justice are unbalanced. Merited trust in the give-and-take between generations has been in short supply. Katerina and Bill have worked on adequately and evenly providing for their children emotionally and spiritually. Paul's somewhat age-expected teasing and taking advantage of Marsha's younger status challenge Katerina and Bill to preserve an appropriate balance of supporting autonomy and interdependence. Katerina, as was Nell, and to some extent Bill have been used as objects by their parents (Boszormenyi-Nagy, 1965). Katerina struggles with being a subject, as does her mother. This leaves the women somewhat entrenched in fantasy or internal object relations rather than available for the mutuality of dialogue, which Katerina and Bill are aware of and achieve at times.

The therapy relationship with Katerina and Bill has allowed for reworking some of the transferences (Whitaker & Malone, 1953; Neill &

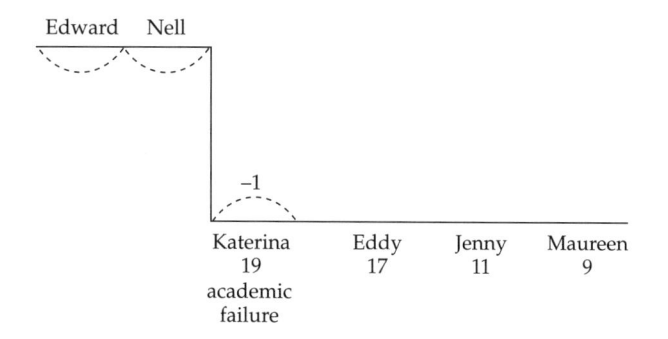

Edward   Nell

```
        −1
Katerina    Eddy    Jenny    Maureen
  19        17      11        9
academic
failure
```

Dimension II: Desire to be loved.
Therapeutic intervention:
• Foster appropriate differentiation and connection of parents and young adult.

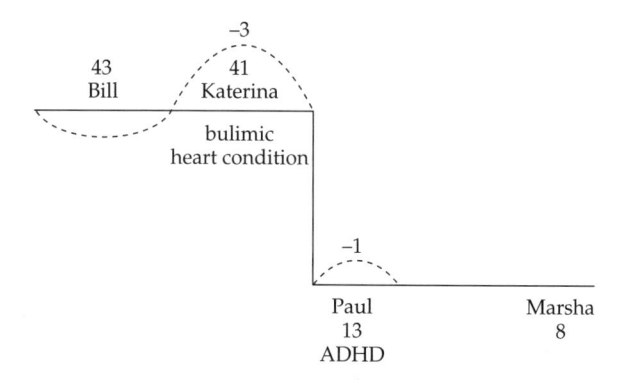

```
           −3
  43      41
  Bill    Katerina
         bulimic
       heart condition

              −1
         Paul        Marsha
          13           8
         ADHD
```

Dimension III: Desire to love and protect.
Therapeutic interventions:
• Join couple as parenting team.
• Help cope with heart condition.
• Value self so eat to nurture rather than cleanse self.

Figure 20.3 Strategic maps illustrate two-generation power arrangements and incongruent hierarchies when symptoms symbolize difficulties in the dimensions of emotional and spiritual development (Madanes, 1990). The power of symptoms can be overt or covert (indicated by dotted lines drawn above normal age- and role-developmental levels) and diminish the power of others (signified by dotted lines drawn below normal developmental levels). Positive numbers (1 to 4) point to overt power and negative numbers (−1 to −4) to covert power.

Kniskern, 1982). Katerina has used therapy to identify her actual and estranged body feelings and self-images, to deal with the discrepancies between her real-self strivings and her introjects, to experience nurturance for her gendered identity, and to receive support for her educational/social/professional development. The relationship of Bill and Katerina contrasts with many in her family and draws sustenance from his father's devotion to his wife despite her alcoholic disability (de Shazer, 1985). Both spouses have been able to identify exceptions (e.g., Aunt Rose as nurturing with Katerina, Bill's father's fidelity to an emotionally unavailable wife), which have provided them with keys for competence. As Katerina and Bill and Paul and Marsha rewrite and compose their narratives and life stories (White & Epston, 1990), they draw inspiration from their reflective conversations in therapy and with each other (Andersen, 1991).

TREATMENT APPROACH AND RATIONALE

Interventions have varied depending on assessment. Initially in family sessions with Katerina and her family, treatment focused on detriangulating and differentiation, as Edward and Nell perpetuated the fragility of their relationship and left their family-of-origin and couple grief issues unsolved. They projected vulnerabilities onto their firstborn. In sessions with Katerina as a young adult, she and the therapist engaged in coaching (E. Carter & McGoldrick Orfanidis, 1976; McGoldrick & Carter, 2001) to support both development of self-esteem and constructive attachments, as these evolved both multigenerationally and currently in cultural contexts. Multiple-chair work (James & Jongeward, 1971) allowed for examining and repairing object relations to move Katerina from symbiosis to dialogue possibilities (Boszormenyi-Nagy, 1965). The therapist continually helped Katerina and Bill to develop clear boundaries (S. Minuchin, 1974). The therapist worked with Katerina to find exceptions to the patterns of inhibition and negativity (de Shazer, 1985), to listen to herself and build constructive relationship opportunities (Andersen, 1991), to build positive self-other intrapsychic and transactional structures (Boszormenyi-Nagy, 1965; Whitaker & Malone, 1953), to detach from and heal hidden loyalties (Boszormenyi-Nagy & Spark, 1973/1984), and to learn mutual and supportive give and take in earning and relying on merited trust (Boszormenyi-Nagy & Krasner, 1986) as she and Bill (with his alcoholic mother and devoted husband/father background) rewrite and compose the narrative of the family's journey.

An explicitly social-psychological model represents a newly articulated perspective for assessment and treatment, although the dynamics have implicitly informed systemic work throughout its development. Thus, *no existing treatment protocol* has been published, and the elements appear in the texts cited and here in nascent form.

POSTTERMINATION SYNOPSIS AND REFLECTIONS

Currently, Katerina and Bill are dealing with the ramifications of her healing, but weakened, heart condition resulting from overadministration of diet pills. Metaphorically, Katerina's heart status alludes to the broken-heart sagas of elders who have suffered from parental abandonment and spousal infidelity. Over at least five generations, the family has suffered many losses through immigration and unfulfilled hopes. The case illustrates the insights and resources accruing from examining life cycles multigenerationally. This allows for exploring intrapsychic, self-other, relational, and cultural-societal structures. Over the course of two decades of intermittent involvement in therapy, Katerina has worked on differentiation, detriangulation, and extricating from embeddedness in familiar but unsupportive indifference and hostility, some of which she has internalized both from family criticism and from exploitative societal images of ideal feminine attractiveness. She is continually in the process of cleansing herself from the memories of abuse; of reaffirming her positive womanly identity; of negotiating balancing work with family life; of allowing herself connectedness, compatibility, and satisfaction in relationships of trust and nurturance with herself, Bill, and her children.

RESEARCH

Newly explicated as a model, the social-psychological perspective on assessment and treatment draws on previous research in social psychology and indicates avenues for exploration and validation.

SOCIAL PSYCHOLOGY FOUNDATIONS

Social-psychological research in general offers paradigmatic examples of addressing both social and psychological variables. Crutchfield (1955) combined personality and group leadership assessment with conformity studies and observed interactions between personality dynamics and social behavior, and between group behavior and gender as modified by age and cohort. Crutchfield's research contained a measure of the authoritarian personality (Adorno, Frenkel-Brunswick, Levinson, & Sanford, 1950), which was related to levels of conformity. As in the earlier study by Adorno et al., Crutchfield uncovered significant differences in family perceptions on objective and projective measures. Haan, Smith, and Block (1968) noted differences in participation in social protest based on levels of moral judgment as measured by Kohlberg's (1969) stages. O'Connor and Wrightsman (1972) reported greater levels of obedience in Milgram's (1963) paradigm by those scoring in the lower stages of Kohlberg's schema and also higher rates of cheating by sixth-graders with lower moral judgment scores. G. Allport and Ross (1967/1968) discovered insightful relationships between intergroup attitudes and spiritual/religious orientations. Haney, Banks, and Zimbardo (1973) uncovered that personality variables affected role behaviors in a simulated prison. Lewin's (1951/1975) field theory offers fertile ground for hypotheses regarding the interactions of personality and social-interaction variables.

With roots in academic social psychology and integrative perspectives on clinical processes, a research basis for holistic social-psychological orientation requires construct validation (Campbell, 1967; Cronbach & Meehl, 1955/1967). A multitrait-multimethod approach provides comprehensiveness (Campbell & Fiske, 1959/1967). Combining both historic and current data allows for exploring the interactions of individuals and contexts and their respective variances to more fully understand persons-in-situations (Cronbach, 1958/1967). Several examples of research paradigms with reported results set the pace for future endeavors. In the clinical field, assessment and research overlap. Accurate assessment instruments require standards of reliability and validity. Researchers, with informed consent, can utilize assessment data.

RESEARCH ON FAMILY TREATMENT
AND INTERVENTION

Some clinical paradigms suggest research possibilities for outcomes studies and for exploring the relevance and reflexivity of levels of social-psychological processing in human existence. For example, Goldner et al. (1990) proposed the relevance of dealing with several levels of description in relationship violence: ethical considerations, gendered premises, relational structures, and psychic infrastructures. Sheinberg and Fraenkel (2001) observed the importance of gathering information from several modalities (family, individual, and group) and on the self and relational levels in treating sexually abused children. In dealing with domestic violence, Almeida et al. (1998) employ sponsorship by male mentors of men, socioeducational preparation meetings, men's and women's cultural groups, and combinations of individual, couple, and family sessions. The data from all these venues can add to understanding the complexity of social-psychological dynamics.

Programmatic research on the working and relevance of a social-psychological perspective for assessment and treatment will involve a multidimensional, multilevel approach in a search for the reflexive loops between and among the factors implicated in human existence. Phenomenological listening and eliciting projective dynamics will tap into *intrapsychic* processes and *internalizations* of self-other perceptions and relationships. Reflective conversations allow for enunciation of phenomenologically experienced awarenesses of emotionally laden conceptions of self and other and of object relations (Andersen, 1991). The Millon scales (Millon, 1997) provide standardized assessment for personality trends. Loveland, Wynne, and Singer (1963) introduced the family Rorschach, building on use of the Rorschach in gaining insight into family psychological dynamics (Singer & Wynne, 1965a). The use of projective techniques could be extended to incorporate the Thematic Apperception Test (Morgan & Murray, 1935), the Children's Apperception Test (Bellak, 1993), the Tell-Me-a-Story test (TEMAS; Constantino, Malgady, & Rogler, 1988), and the Incomplete Sentences Blank Test (Rotter & Rafferty, 1950). Drawings of family compositions and activities (including family kinetic drawings) of self, others, and incidents in context (e.g., child in classroom) provide iconic information of socioemotional experiences (Nurse, 1999). The Bender-Gestalt, the Wechsler scales, the TEMAS, and the Halstead-Reitan can be used to establish accuracy and breadth of perception and information processing. The inclusion of perceptions of others in these methods crosses over into *interpersonal* considerations and shows the realistic interconnecting and reflexivity of the domains. On the enactive level, videotaped sculptings, choreographies, and communications exercises all supply data for interactional coding.

Laing et al. (1966/1972) devised the interpersonal perception method (IPM). This allows for collecting observations on the perceptions and interperceptions between a couple to evaluate their congruence and incompatibility. The Personal Authority in the Family System questionnaire (Bray, Williamson, & Malone, 1984) allows for gauging degrees of fusion/individuation, intimacy, and triangulation, largely from a Bowenian framework. The Relational Ethics Scale (Hargrave, Jennings, & Anderson, 1991) indicates vertical and horizontal loyalties from a Nagian contextual therapy viewpoint. Spanier (1976) and Waring (1984) constructed ways to assess dyadic adjustment and couple intimacy on several dimensions.

Beavers and Hampson (1990) developed both observational and inventory methods of observing family competency and style along a centripetal to centrifugal continuum. Competency ratings range from severely dysfunctional to borderline, midrange, adequate, and optimal. Studies show predictable correlations between centripetal and centrifugal styles, the continuum of competency, and symptom expression. For example, severely dysfunctional centripetal families often contain schizophrenic offspring, and their centrifugal counterparts sociopaths. In the midrange, centripetal family members frequently display neuroses, and centrifugal ones behavior disorders. Families who mix the styles as needed developmentally generally have no symptomatic members from the midrange to optimal. Beavers and Hampson's methods allow for examining and describing the relationships of family styles and levels of competency with intrapsychically and interpersonally based symptoms.

Benjamin (Humphrey, 1989; Humphrey & Benjamin, 1986) offered the Structural Analysis of Social Behavior (SASB) model and methodology as a means to measure complex relational processes encompassing both intrapsychic experiences and interpersonal transactions. Based on Sullivan's (1953) theory, the circumplex SASB model evolves from data indicating affiliation and interdependence ranging from independent or differentiated to interdependent and undifferentiated. In the pictorial model, the data are represented on three surfaces, each with two orthogonal dimensions with intermediate points— two interpersonal domains: other (endorse freedom/manage, control; tender sexuality/annihilating attack), self (freely come and go/yield, submit, give in; ecstatic response/desperate protest); and a third, self dimension (happy-go-lucky/control and manage self; love and cherish self/torture and annihilate self). The data are derived from rating scales answered in the past or present about self and relationship with others. Use of the model allowed for delineating the processes of double bind (Bateson et al., 1956), marital splits and the transmission of irrationality (T. Lidz, 1963; Lidz et al. 1957b) and pseudomutuality (Wynne, 1984) previously elusive to researchers (Humphrey & Benjamin, 1986). The SASB has proven useful with examining types of depression and in interaction with personality disorder (Benjamin & Wonderlich, 1986), schizophrenic processes (Humphrey & Benjamin, 1986), and eating disorders, exploring the triads of teenage daughters and their parents (Humphrey, 1989).

Accounting for *cultural* and *societal* factors interactive with family and self processes remains essential to comprehensive social-psychological research (Dana, 2000). Many assessment/research inventories are available. Those enumerated here provide starting points. They indicate some of the resources to draw on in designing social-psychological research to build the nomological network requisite to establishing construct validity, evaluating applicability to clients, and exploring relationship and life span developments.

By coordinating the data among members, systemic understandings of the interconnections among the persons and levels of relating can be sketched. Research can be exploratory or hypotheses-based. Given the nature of the data, both qualitative and quantitative methods are desirable. Analyses require appropriate multivariate statistics with factor analysis, regression analysis, structural-equation modeling, and PATH analyses, and meta-analysis more capable of sorting out themes and interrelationships among the variables (McGuire, 1997; Volk & Flori, 1996).

SUMMARY

The social-psychological capacities of humans make possible the development of systems. Because of self-transcending consciousness, multidimensional persons can take the attitudes and roles of others (Mead, 1934/1964) and construct between processes (Buber, 1947/1965; Natanson, 1970) while not only interacting, but also interperceiving and interexperiencing (Laing et al., 1972). Through these interconnections, symbolized in cognitions and experienced affectively and behaviorally, family, cultural, and larger groups form to give their members social identities as well as personal identities forged in the interchanges between individuals and significant others and reference groups. Access to resources and institutional controls shape family and group systemic development. An understanding involving balancing ineluctably intertwined personal and social processes, without engaging in either reductionism or reification, proves insightful and foundational in describing the existential dynamics intrinsic to persons as both contextualized and as co-constructors of the systems in which they participate. A social-psychological perspective provides a human explanation for the evolution and functioning of systems.

REFERENCES

Ackerman, N. W. (1958). *The psychodynamics of family life: Diagnosis and treatment of family relationships.* New York: Basic Books.

Ackerman, N. W. (1966). *Treating the troubled family.* New York: Basic Books.

Adler, A. (1956). *The individual psychology of Alfred Adler* (H. R. Ansbacher & R. R. Ansbacher, Eds. & Trans.). New York: Basic Books.

Adorno, T. W., Frenkel-Brunswick, E., Levinson, D. J., & Sanford, R. N. (1950). *The authoritarian personality.* New York: Harper.

Allport, F. H. (1924). *Social psychology.* Boston: Houghton Mifflin.

Allport, G. W. (1955). *Becoming.* New Haven, CT: Yale University Press.

Allport, G. W. (1961). *Pattern and growth in personality.* New York: Holt, Rinehart and Winston. (Original work published 1937)

Allport, G. W. (1968). The historical background of modern social psychology. In G. Lindzey & E. Aronson (Eds.), *The handbook of social psychology* (2nd ed., pp. 1–80). Reading, MA: Addison-Wesley. (Original work published 1954)

Allport, G. W., & Ross, M. (1968). Personal religious orientation and prejudice. In G. W. Allport (Ed.), *The person in psychology* (pp. 237–268). Boston: Beacon Press. (Original work published 1967)

Almeida, R., Woods, R., Messineo, T., & Font, R. (1998). The cultural context model: An overview. In M. McGoldrick (Ed.), *Re-visioning family therapy: Race, culture, and gender in clinical practice* (pp. 414–431). New York: Guilford Press.

American Psychiatric Association. (1994). *Diagnostic and statistical manual of mental disorders* (4th ed.). Washington, DC: Author.

Andersen, T. (Ed.). (1991). *The reflecting team: Dialogues and dialogues about dialogues.* New York: Norton.

Anderson, H., Goolishian, H., & Winderman, L. (1986). Problem determined systems: Toward transformation in family therapy. *Journal of Strategic and Systemic Therapies, 5,* 14–19.

Angyal, A. (1969). *Foundations for a science of personality.* New York: Viking. (Original work published 1941)

Avis, J. M. (1988). Deepening awareness: A private study guide to feminism and family therapy. In L. Braverman (Ed.), *Women, feminism, and family therapy* (pp. 15–46). New York: Haworth Press.

Avis, J. M. (1992). Where are all the family therapists? Abuse and violence within families and family therapy's response. *Journal of Marital and Family Therapy, 18,* 223–230.

Bateson, G. (1936). *Naven: A survey of the problems suggested by a composite picture of a culture of a New Guinea tribe from three points of view.* Cambridge, England: Cambridge University Press.

Bateson, G. (1972). *Steps to an ecology of mind.* New York: Ballantine Books.

Bateson, G., & Jackson, D. D. (1968). Some varieties of pathogenic organization. In D. D. Jackson (Ed.), *Communication, family, and marriage* (Vol. 1, pp. 200–215). Palo Alto, CA: Science and Behavior Books.

Bateson, G., Jackson, D. D., Haley, J., & Weakland, J. H. (1956). Toward a theory of schizophrenia. *Behavioral Science, 1,* 251–264.

Bateson, G., Jackson, D. D., Haley, J., & Weakland, J. H. (1963). A note on the double bind–1962. *Family Process, 2,* 154–161.

Batts, V. (2001, July). *Using transactional analysis in multicultural settings to facilitate effective healing and reconciliation.* Keynote address at the International Transactional Analysis Association/Western Pacific Transactional Analysis conference, Sydney, Australia.

Beavers, W. R., & Hampson, R. B. (1990). *Successful families: Assessment and intervention.* New York: Norton.

Bellak, L. (1993). *The TAT, CAT, SAT in clinical use* (5th ed.). New York: Grune & Stratton.

Benjamin, L. S., & Wonderlich, S. (1986). *Using social variables to differentiate among DSM-III diagnostic groups: Major Depression, Bipolar Depression, and Borderline Personality.* Unpublished manuscript, University of Wisconsin, Madison.

Berne, E. (1961). *Transactional analysis in psychotherapy.* New York: Grove.

Billingsley, A. (1968). *Black families in White America.* Englewood Cliffs, NJ: Prentice-Hall.

Binswanger, L. (1967). *Being-in-the-world* (J. Needleman, Trans.). New York: Harper.

Bogard, M. (1992). Values in conflict: Challenges to family therapists' thinking. *Journal of Marital and Family Therapy, 18,* 243–253.

Boszormenyi-Nagy, I. (1962). The concept of schizophrenia from the point of view of family treatment. *Family Process, 1,* 103–113.

Boszormenyi-Nagy, I. (1965). A theory of relationships: Experience and transaction. In I. Boszormenyi-Nagy & J. Framo (Eds.), *Intensive family therapy* (pp. 33–86). New York: Brunner/Mazel.

Boszormenyi-Nagy, I., & Krasner, B. R. (1986). *Between give and take: A clinical guide to contextual therapy.* New York: Brunner/Mazel.

Boszormenyi-Nagy, I., & Spark, G. M. (1984). *Invisible loyalties: Reciprocity in intergenerational family therapy.* New York: Brunner Mazel. (Original work published 1973)

Bowen, M. (1976). Theory in the practice of psychotherapy. In P. Guerin (Ed.), *Family therapy: Theory and practice* (pp. 42–90). New York: Gardner Press.

Bowen, M. (1985). *Family therapy in clinical practice.* New York: Aronson.

Bower, T. G. R. (1974). *Development in infancy.* San Francisco: Freeman.

Bowlby, J. (1988). *A secure base: Parent-child attachment and healthy human development.* New York: Basic Books.

Bray, J. H., Williamson, D. S., & Malone, P. E. (1984). Personal authority in the family system: Development of a questionnaire to measure personal authority in intergenerational family processes. *Journal of Marital and Family Therapy, 10,* 167–178.

Buber, M. (1957). Guilt and guilt feelings. *Psychiatry, 20,* 114–129. (Original work published 1948)

Buber, M. (1958). *I and thou* (2nd ed.). New York: Charles Scribner's Sons. (Original work published 1923)

Buber, M. (1965). *Between man and man.* New York: Collier. (Original work published 1947)

Campbell, D. T. (1967) Recommendations for APA Test standards regarding construct, trait, or discriminant validity. In D. N. Jackson & S. J. Messick (Eds.), *Problems in human assessment* (pp. 147–156). New York: McGraw-Hill.

Campbell, D. T., & Fiske, D. W. (1967). Convergent and discriminant validation by the multitrait-multimethod matrix. In D. N. Jackson & S. J. Messick (Eds.), *Problems in human assessment* (pp. 124–132). New York: McGraw-Hill. (Original work published 1959)

Carter, B., & McGoldrick, M. (Eds.). (1999). *The expanded family life cycle: Individual, family, and social perspectives* (3rd ed.). Boston: Allyn & Bacon.

Carter, E. A., & McGoldrick Orfanidis, M. (1976). Family therapy with one person and family therapist's own family. In P. Guerin (Ed.), *Family therapy* (pp. 193–219). New York: Guilford Press.

Clark, K. B. (1974). *The pathos of power*. New York: Harper & Row.

Comas-Diaz, L. (1996). Cultural considerations in diagnosis. In F. W. Kaslow (Ed.), Handbook of relational diagnosis and dysfunctional family patterns (pp. 152–168). New York: Wiley.

Constantino, G., Malgady, R. G., & Rogler, L. H. (1988). *Technical manual: TEMAS Thematic Apperception Test*. Los Angeles: Western Psychological Services.

Cronbach, L. J. (1967). The two disciplines of scientific psychology. In D. N. Jackson & S. J. Messick (Eds.), *Problems in human assessment* (pp. 22–39). New York: McGraw-Hill. (Original work published 1958)

Cronbach, L. J., & Meehl, P. E. (1967). Construct validity in psychological tests. In D. N. Jackson & S. J. Messick (Eds.), *Problems in human assessment* (pp. 57–77). New York: McGraw-Hill. (Original work published 1955)

Cronen, V. E., Johnson, K. M., & Lannamann, J. W. (1982). Paradoxes, double binds, and reflexive loops: An alternative theoretical perspective. *Family Process, 20,* 91–112.

Crutchfield, R. S. (1955). Conformity and character. *American Psychologist, 10,* 191–198.

Dana, R. H. (Ed.). (2000). An assessment-intervention model for research and practice with multicultural populations. In R. H. Dana (Ed.), *Handbook of cross-cultural and multicultural personality assessment* (pp. 5–16). Mahwah, NJ: Erlbaum.

Dell, P. F. (1982). Beyond homeostasis: Toward a concept of coherence. *Family Process, 21,* 21–41.

Dell, P. F. (1989). Violence and the systemic view: The problem of power. *Family Process, 23,* 1–14.

de Shazer, S. (1985). *Keys to solution in brief therapy*. New York: Norton.

Difenthaller, B. (1997). *Narrative therapy and the genogram: Intergenerational stories*. Unpublished manuscript, Seton Hall University, South Orange, NJ.

Doise, W. (1997). Organizing social-psychological explanations. In C. McGarty & S. A. Haslam (Eds.), *The messages of social psychology: Perspectives on mind in society* (pp. 63–76). Oxford, England: Blackwell.

Ducommun-Nagy, C. (2002). Contextual therapy. In R. F. Massey & S. D. Massey (Eds.), *Comprehensive handbook of psychotherapy. Vol. 3: Interpersonal, humanistic, existential* (pp. 463–488). New York: Wiley.

Dusay, J., & Dusay, K. (1989). *Couples therapy: A handbook of technique and theory*. San Francisco: Script Free Press.

English, F. (1969). Episcript and the hot potato game. *Transactional Analysis Bulletin, 8*(32), 77–82.

Erikson, E. (1963). *Childhood and society* (2nd ed.). New York: Norton. (Original work published 1950)

Falicov, C. J. (1998). The cultural meaning of family triangles. In M. McGoldrick (Ed.), *Re-visioning family therapy: Race, culture, and gender in clinical practice* (pp. 37–40). New York: Guilford Press.

Farr, R. M. (1996). *The roots of modern social psychology*. Oxford, England: Blackwell.

Festinger, L. (1954). A theory of social comparison processes. *Human Relations, 7,* 117–140.

Fiske, S. T., & Leyens, J.-P. (1997). Let social psychology be faddish or, at least, heterogeneous. In C. McGarty & S. A. Haslam (Eds.), *The messages of social psychology: Perspectives on mind in society* (pp. 92–112). Oxford, England: Blackwell.

Foucault, M. (1965). *Madness and civilization: A history of insanity in the age of reason*. New York: Random House.

Foucault, M. (1980). *Power/knowledge: Selected interviews and other writings*. New York: Pantheon Books.

Frankl, V. E. (1965). *The doctor and the soul: From psychotherapy to logotherapy* (2nd ed.). New York: Vintage. (Original work published 1946)

Frankl, V. E. (1969). *The will to meaning*. New York: New American Library.

Freud, A. (1966). *The ego and the mechanisms of defense*. New York: International Universities Press. (Original work published 1936)

Fromm, E. (1941). *Escape from freedom*. New York: Avon.

Fromm, E. (1947). *Man for himself.* New York: Fawcett.

Fromm, E. (1955). *The sane society.* Greenwich, CT: Fawcett.

Fromm, E. (1964). *The heart of man: Its genius for good and evil.* New York: Harper & Row.

Fromm-Reichmann, F. (1948). Notes on the development of treatment of schizophrenics by psychoanalytic psychotherapy. *Psychiatry, 11,* 263–273.

Gilligan, C. (1982). *In a different voice: Psychological theory and women's development.* Cambridge, MA: Harvard University Press.

Gobes, L. (1985). Abandonment and engulfment issues in relationship therapy. *Transactional Analysis Journal, 15,* 216–219.

Goffman, E. (1961). *Asylums: Essays in the social situation of mental patients and other inmates.* New York: Doubleday.

Goldner, V. (1985). Feminism and family therapy. *Family Process, 24,* 31–47.

Goldner, V. (1988). Generation and gender: Normative and covert hierarchies. *Family Process, 27,* 17–33.

Goldner, V. (1993). Power and hierarchy: Let's talk about it. *Family Process, 32,* 157–162.

Goldner, V., Penn, P., Sheinberg, M., & Walker, G. (1990). Love and violence: Gender paradoxes in volatile attachments. *Family Process, 29,* 343–364.

Graumann, C. F. (2001). Introducing social psychology historically. In M. Hewstone & W. Stroebe (Eds.), *Introduction of social psychology: A European perspective* (pp. 3–22). Oxford, England: Blackwell.

Group for the Advancement of Psychiatry Committee on the Family. (1996). Global Assessment of Relational Functioning Scale (GARF): I. Background and rationale. *Family Process, 35,* 155–172.

Guerin, P. J., Jr., Fogarty, T. F., Fay, L. F., & Kautto, J. G. (1996). *Working with relationship triangles: The one-two-three of psychotherapy.* New York: Guilford Press.

Haan, N., Smith, M., & Block, J. (1968). Moral reasoning of young adults: Political-social behavior, family background, and personality correlates. *Journal of Personality and Social Psychology, 10,* 183–201.

Haley, J. (1963). *Strategies of psychotherapy.* New York: Grune & Stratton.

Haley, J. (1976). *Problem-solving therapy.* San Francisco: Jossey-Bass.

Haney, C., Banks, C., & Zimbardo, P. (1973). Interpersonal dynamics in a simulated prison. *International Journal of Criminology and Penology, 1,* 69–97.

Hare-Mustin, R. T. (1978). A feminist approach to family therapy. *Family Process, 17,* 181–194.

Hare-Mustin, R. T. (1986). The problem of gender in family therapy theory. *Family Process, 26,* 15–27.

Hargrave, T. D., Jennings, G., & Anderson, W. (1991). The development of a relational ethics scale. *Journal of Marital and Family Therapy, 17,* 145–158.

Hedaya, R. J. (1996). *Understanding biological psychiatry.* New York: Norton.

Helms, J. (Ed.). (1990). *Black and White racial identity: Theory, research, and practice.* New York: Greenwood Press.

Hoffman, M. L. (1976). Empathy, role taking, guilt, and development of altruistic motives. In T. Lickona (Ed.), *Moral development and behavior: Theory, research, and social issues* (pp. 124–143). New York: Holt, Rinehart and Winston.

Horney, K. (1967). *Feminine psychology.* New York: Norton.

Horney, K. (1970). *Neurosis and human growth.* New York: Norton. (Original work published 1950)

Humphrey, L. L. (1989). Observed family interactions among subtypes of eating disorders using structural analysis of behavior. *Journal of Consulting and Clinical Psychology, 57,* 206–214.

Humphrey, L. L., & Benjamin, L. S. (1986). Using structural analysis of social behavior to assess critical but elusive family processes. *American Psychologist, 41,* 979–989.

Imber-Black, E. (1988). *Families and larger systems: A family therapist's guide through the labyrinth.* New York: Guilford Press.

Jackson, D. D. (1953). Psychotherapy for schizophrenia. *Scientific American, 188,* 58–63.

Jackson, D. D. (1959a). Family interaction, family homeostasis, and some implications for conjoint family psychotherapy. In J. Masserman (Ed.), *Individual and family dynamics.* New York: Grune & Stratton.

Jackson, D. D. (1959b). The meaning of acting out in a borderline personality. In A. Burton (Ed.), *Case studies in counseling and psychotherapy.* New York: Prentice Hall.

Jackson, D. D. (1960). *The etiology of schizophrenia.* New York: Basic Books.

Jackson, D. D. (1965). Family rules: The marital quid pro quo. *Archives of General Psychiatry, 12,* 589–594.

Jacobs, A. (1987). Autocratic power. *Transactional Analysis Journal, 17,* 59–71.

James, M., & Jongeward, D. (1971). *Born to win.* Reading, MA: Addison-Wesley.

Jung, C. G. (1971). Marriage as a psychological relationship (R. F. C. Hull Trans.). In J. Campbell (Ed.), *The portable Jung* (pp. 163–177). New York: Viking. (Original work published 1925)

Kaufman, G. (1992). The mysterious disappearance of battered women from family therapists' offices. *Journal of Marital and Family Therapy, 18,* 231–241.

Kerr, M., & Bowen, M. (1988). *Family evaluation: An approach based on Bowen theory.* New York: Norton.

Klein, M. (1946). Notes on some schizoid mechanisms. *International Journal of Psychoanalysis, 27,* 99–110.

Klein, M. (1956). On identification. In M. Klein, P. Heimann, & R. E. Money-Kyde (Eds.), *New directions in psychoanalysis* (pp. 309–345). New York: Basic Books.

Knudson-Martin, C. (1995). The female voice: Applications to Bowen's family systems theory. *Journal of Marital and Family Therapy, 20,* 35–46.

Koestler, A. (1979). *Janus: A summing up.* New York: Vintage.

Kohlberg, L. (1969). Stage and sequence: The cognitive-developmental approach to socialization. In D. Goslin (Ed.), *Handbook of socialization theory and research* (pp. 347–480). Chicago: Rand McNally.

Laing, R. D. (1971). *The politics of the family and other essays.* New York: Vintage. (Original work published 1969)

Laing, R. D., Phillipson, H., & Lee, A. (1972). *Interpersonal perception.* New York: Harper & Row. (Original work published 1966)

Leonard, L. S. (1985). *The wounded woman: Healing the father-daughter relationship.* Boston: Shambhala.

Lewin, K. (1975). *Field theory in social science.* Westport, CT: Greenwood Press. (Original work published 1951)

Lewis, M., & Brooks-Gunn, J. (1979). *Social cognition and the acquisition of self.* New York: Plenum Press.

Lidz, R. W., & Lidz, T. (1949). The family environment of schizophrenic parents. *American Journal of Psychiatry, 106,* 332–345.

Lidz, T. (1963). *The family and human adaptation.* New York: International Universities Press.

Lidz, T., Cornelison, A. R., Fleck, S., & Terry, D. (1957a). The intrafamilial environment of the schizophrenic patient. I: The father. *Psychiatry, 10,* 329–342.

Lidz, T., Cornelison, A. R., Fleck, S., & Terry, D. (1957b). The intrafamilial environment of schizophrenic patients. II: Marital schism and marital skew. *American Journal of Psychiatry, 114,* 241–248.

Lidz, T., & Fleck, S. (1965). Family studies and a theory of schizophrenia. In T. Lidz, S. Fleck, & A. R. Cornelison (Eds.), *Schizophrenia and the family* (pp. 362–376). New York: International Universities Press.

Lidz, T., Perker, B., & Cornelison, A. R. (1956). The rule of the father in the family environment of the schizophrenic patient. *American Journal of Psychiatry, 113,* 126–132.

Lindblad-Goldberg, M., Dore, M. M., & Stern, L. (1998). *Creating competence from chaos.* New York: Norton.

Loveland, N. T., Wynne, L. C., & Singer, M. T. (1963). The family Rorschach: A new method for studying family interaction. *Family Process, 2,* 187–215.

Madanes, C. (1981). *Strategic family therapy.* San Francisco: Jossey-Bass.

Madanes, C. (1984). *Behind the one-way mirror.* San Francisco: Jossey-Bass.

Madanes, C. (1990). *Love, sex, and violence.* New York: Norton.

Madanes, C. (1995). *The violence of men.* San Francisco: Jossey-Bass.

Maslow, A. H. (1962). *Toward a psychology of being.* New York: D. Van Nostrand.

Maslow, A. H. (1970). *Motivation and personality* (2nd ed.). New York: Harper & Row. (Original work published 1954)

Massey, R. F. (1981). *Personality theories: Comparisons and syntheses.* New York: D. Van Nostrand.

Massey, R. F. (1985). TA as a family systems therapy. *Transactional Analysis Journal, 15*(2), 120–141.

Massey, R. F. (1986). What/who is the family system? *American Journal of Family Therapy, 14*(1), 23–39. (Original work published in German 1985)

Massey, R. F. (1987). Transactional analysis and social psychology of power: Reflections evoked by Jacobs' "Autocratic power." *Transactional Analysis Journal, 17,* 107–120.

Massey, R. F. (1989). Script theory synthesized systemically. *Transactional Analysis Journal, 19,* 14–25.

Massey, R. F. (1990). Berne's transactional analysis as a neo-Freudian/neo-Adlerian perspective. *Transactional Analysis Journal, 20,* 173–186.

Massey, R. F. (1993). Neo-Adlerian constructs in Berne's transactional analysis. *Journal of Individual Psychology, 49,* 13–35.

Massey, R. F. (1996). Transactional analysis as a social psychology. *Transactional Analysis Journal, 26,* 91–99.

Massey, R. F. (1998). The evolution of family-systems theories. In E. P. Gielen & A. L. Comunian (Eds.), *The family and family therapy in international perspective* (pp. 27–65). Trieste, Italy: Edizioni Lint Trieste.

Massey, R. F., & Massey, S. D. (1995). Die sozial-psychologischen und systemischen Dimensionen der Transaktionsanalyse als Perspektive fur die Behandlung von Einzelnen, Paaren und Familien [The social-psychological and systemic dimensions of transactional analysis as a perspective for the treatment of individuals, couples, and families]. *Zeitschrift fur Transaktions Analyse, 12*(4), 157–197.

Masterson, J. (1988). *The search for the real self: Unmasking the personality disorders of our age.* New York: Free Press.

Maturana, H. R. (1978). The biology of language: The epistemology of reality. In G. Miller & E. H. Lennenberg (Eds.), *Psychology and biology of language and thought* (pp. 27–63). New York: Academic Press.

Maturana, H. R., & Varela, F. J. (1987). *The tree of knowledge.* Boston: New Science Library.

Matuschka, E. (1972). A fantasy marriage technique. *Transactional Analysis Journal, 2,* 81–82.

McDaniel, S., Hepworth, S., & Doherty, W. (1992). *Medical family therapy: A biopsychosocial approach to families with health problems.* New York: Basic Books.

McDougall, W. (1920). *The group mind: A sketch of the principles of collective psychology with some attempts to apply them to the interpretation of national life and character.* Cambridge, England: Cambridge University Press.

McGarty, C., & Haslam, S. A. (1997). *The messages of social psychology: Perspectives on mind in society.* Oxford, England: Blackwell.

McGoldrick, M. (1998a). Re-visioning family therapy through a cultural lens. In M. McGoldrick (Ed.), *Re-visioning family therapy: Race, culture, and gender in clinical practice* (pp. 3–10). New York: Guilford Press.

McGoldrick, M. (1998b). *Re-visioning family therapy: Race, culture, and gender in clinical practice.* New York: Guilford Press.

McGoldrick, M., & Carter, B. (2001). Advances in coaching: Family therapy with one person. *Journal of Marital and Family Therapy, 27,* 281–300.

McGoldrick, M., Giordano, J., & Pearce, J. (1996). *Ethnicity and family therapy* (2nd ed.). New York: Guilford Press.

McNeel, J. (1976). The parent interview. *Transactional Analysis Journal, 6*(1), 61–68.

Mead, G. H. (1964). *George Herbert Mead on social psychology* (A. Strauss, Ed.). Chicago: University of Chicago Press. (Original work published 1934)

Merleau-Ponty, M. (1967). *The structure of behavior* (A. L. Fisher, Trans.). Boston: Beacon Press. (Original work published 1942)

Merton, R. K. (1957). *Social theory and social structure.* New York: Free Press. (Original work published 1949)

Middleberg, C. (2001). Projective identification in common couple dances. *Journal of Marital and Family Therapy, 27,* 341–352.

Milgram, S. (1963). Behavioral study of obedience. *Journal of Abnormal and Social Psychology, 67*(4), 371–378.

Millon, T. (Ed.). (1997). *The Millon instruments.* New York: Guilford Press.

Minuchin, P., Colapinto, J., & Minuchin, S. (1998). *Working with families of the poor.* New York: Guilford Press.

Minuchin, S. (1974). *Families and family therapy.* Cambridge, MA: Harvard University Press.

Minuchin, S. (1984). *Family kaleidoscope.* Cambridge, MA: Harvard University Press.

Minuchin, S., & Fishman, H. C. (1981). *Family therapy techniques.* Cambridge, MA: Harvard University Press.

Minuchin, S., & Nichols, M. (1993). *Family healing: Tales of hope and renewal from family therapy.* New York: Free Press.

Mittlemann, B. (1944). Complementary neurotic transactions in intimate relationships. *Psychoanalytic Quarterly, 13,* 474–491.

Mittlemann, B. (1948). The concurrent analysis of married couples. *Psychoanalytic Quarterly, 17,* 182–197.

Morgan, C., & Murray, H. A. (1935). A method of investigating fantasies. *Archives of Neurology and Psychiatry, 4,* 310–329.

Morin, E. (1986). *La methode III. La connaissance de la connaissance* [The method III. The knowledge of knowledge]. Paris: Seuil.

Moscovici, S. (1972). Society and theory in social psychology. In J. Israel & H. Tajfel (Eds.), *The context of social psychology: A critical assessment* (pp. 17–68). London: Academic Press.

Moscovici, S. (1981). On social representations. In J. P. Forgas (Ed.), *Social cognition: Perspectives on everyday understanding* (pp. 181–209). London: Academic Press.

Nasca, A., Dunn, A. B., Massey, R. F., & Venkatachalam, M. (2001). *Mapping incongruous hierarchies and dimensions of love-violence: Diagrams for Madanes' perspective.* Manuscript submitted for publication.

Natanson, M. (1970). *The journeying self: A study in philosophy and social role.* Reading, MA: Addison-Wesley.

Neill, J. R., & Kniskern, D. P. (1982). *From psyche to system: The evolving therapy of Carl Whitaker.* New York: Guilford Press.

Newcombe, T. M. (1943). *Personality and social change.* New York: Dryden.

Nurse, A. R. (1999). *Family assessment: Effective uses of personality tests with couples and families.* New York: Norton.

Nuttin, J. (1962). *Psychoanalysis and personality: A dynamic theory of normal personality* (G. Lamb, Trans.). New York: Mentor Books. (Original work published 1953)

O'Connor, J., & Wrightsman, L. (1972). Moral development and the development of motives. In L. Wrightsman (Ed.), *Social psychology in the seventies* (pp. 99–129). Monterey, CA: Brooks Cole.

Palazzoli, M. S., Cecchin, G., Prata, G., & Boscolo, L. (1978). *Paradox and counterparadox: A new model in the therapy of the family in schizophrenic transaction.* New York: Aronson. (Original work published 1975)

Palazzoli, M. S., Cirillo, S., Selvini, M., & Sorrentino, A. M. (1989). *Family games: General models of psychotic processes in the family.* New York: Norton.

Papp, P. (1976). Family choreography. In P. Guerin (Ed.), *Family therapy* (pp. 465–479). New York: Gardner Press.

Papp, P. (1983). *The process of change.* New York: Guilford Press.

Papp, P. (2000). Gender differences in depression: His or her depression. In P. Papp (Ed.), *Couples on the fault line: New directions for therapists* (pp. 130–151). New York: Guilford Press.

Penn, P. (1982). Circular questioning. *Family Process, 21,* 267–280.

Penn, P. (1985). Feed-forward: Future questions, future maps. *Family Process, 24,* 299–310.

Pepitone, A. (1997). Nonmaterial beliefs: Theory and research in cultural social psychology. In C. McGarty & S. A. Haslam (Eds.), *The messages of social psychology: Perspectives on mind in society* (pp. 252–267). Oxford, England: Blackwell.

Piaget, J., & Inhelder, B. (1969). *The psychology of the child.* New York: Basic Books.

Pipher, M. (1994). *Reviving Ophelia: Saving the lives of adolescent girls.* New York: Ballantine Books.

Prescott, J. W. (1990). Affectional bonding for the prevention of violent behaviors: Neurobiological, psychological, and religious/spiritual determinants. In L. J. Hertzberg & G. F. Ostrum (Eds.), *Violent behavior. Vol. 1: Assessment and intervention* (pp. 95–124). Costa Mesa, CA: PMA.

Prescott, J. W. (1996). The origins of human love and violence. *Pre- and Peri-natal Psychology Journal, 10*(3), 143–188.

Rogers, C. R. (1959). A theory of personality and interpersonal relationships as developed in the client-centered framework. In S. Koch (Ed.), *Psychology: A study of a science* (Vol. 3, pp. 187–256). New York: McGraw-Hill.

Rogers, C. R. (1961). *On becoming a person.* Boston: Houghton Mifflin.

Rosenberg, M., & Turner, R. H. (Eds.). *Social psychology: Sociological perspectives.* New York: Basic Books.

Ross, L., & Nisbett, R. E. (1991). *The person and the situation: Perspectives of social psychology.* New York: McGraw-Hill.

Rotter, J. B. (1954). *Social learning and clinical psychology.* Englewood Cliffs, NJ: Prentice-Hall.

Rotter, J. B., & Rafferty, J. (1950). The Rotter Incomplete Sentence Blank manual: College edition. San Antonio: Psychological Corporation.

Scarf, M. (1987). *Intimate partners: Patterns in love and marriage.* New York: Random House.

Schachtel, E. (1959). *Metamorphosis.* New York: Basic Books.

Schachter, S., & Singer, J. E. (1962). Cognitive, social, and physiological determinants of emotional state. *Psychological Review, 69,* 379–399.

Scheff, T. J. (1966). *Being mentally ill: A sociological theory.* Chicago: Aldine.

Selman, R. (1976). Social-cognitive understanding: A guide to educational and clinical practice. In T. Likona (Ed.), *Moral development and behavior* (pp. 299–316). New York: Holt, Rinehart and Winston.

Sheinberg, M. (1985). The debate: A strategic technique. *Family Process, 24,* 259–271.

Sheinberg, M., & Fraenkel, P. (2001). *The relational trauma of incest: A family-based approach to treatment.* New York: Guilford Press.

Sherif, M. (1936). *The psychology of social norms.* New York: Harper.

Sherif, M. (1958). Superordinant goals in the reduction of intergroup contact. *American Journal of Sociology, 43,* 349–356.

Shibutani, T. (1955). Reference groups as perspectives. *American Journal of Sociology, 60,* 562–569.

Silverstein, O., & Rauschenbaum, B. (1994). *The courage to raise good men.* New York: Viking.

Singer, M. T., & Wynne, L. C. (1965a). Thought disorder and family relations of schizophrenics: III. Methodology using projective techniques. *Archives of General Psychiatry, 12,* 187–200.

Singer, M. T., & Wynne, L. C. (1965b). Thought disorder and family relations of schizophrenics: IV. Results and implications. *Archives of General Psychiatry, 12,* 201–212.

Smith, M. B. (1969). *Social psychology and human values.* Chicago: Aldine.

Spanier, G. B. (1976). Measuring dyadic adjustment: New scales for assessing quality of marriage and similar dyads. *Journal of Marriage and Family Therapy, 38,* 15–28.

Steinglass, P. (1987). *The alcoholic family.* New York: Basic Books.

Stierlin, H. (1974). Psychoanalytic approaches to schizophrenia in the light of a family model. *International Review of Psychoanalysis, 1,* 169–178.

Stierlin, H. (1983). Family dynamics in psychotic and severe psychosomatic disorders: A comparison. *Family Systems Medicine,* 41–50.

Stierlin, H., Rucker-Embden, I., Wetzel, N., & Wirsching, M. (1980). *The first interview with the family* (S. Tooze, Trans.). New York: Brunner/Mazel. (Original work published 1977)

Sue, D. W., & Sue, D. (1999). *Counseling the culturally different* (3rd ed.). New York: Wiley.

Sullivan, H. S. (1953). *The interpersonal theory of psychiatry.* New York: Norton.

Szasz, T. S. (1970). *Ideology and insanity.* Garden City, NY: Anchor.

Tajfel, H. (1981). *Human groups and social categories: Studies in social psychology.* Cambridge, England: Cambridge University Press.

Tajfel, H., & Turner, J. (1986). The social identity theory of intergroup behavior. In S. Worchel & W. G. Austin (Eds.), *Psychology of intergroup relation* (pp. 7–24). Chicago: Nelson.

Thompson, C. (1950). *Psychoanalysis, evolution, and development.* New York: Hermitage House.

Triandis, H. C. (1997). A cross-cultural perspective on social psychology. In C. McGarty & S. A. Haslam (Eds.), *The messages of social psychology: Perspectives on mind in society* (pp. 342–354). Oxford, England: Blackwell.

Turner, J. C., & Oakes, P. J. (1997). The socially structured mind. In C. McGarty & S. A. Haslam (Eds.), *The messages of social psychology: Perspectives on mind in society* (pp. 355–357). Oxford, England: Blackwell.

van Kaam, A. (1969). *Existential foundations of psychology.* Garden City, NY: Image Books. (Original work published 1966)

Volk, R. J., & Flori, D. E. (1996). Structural equation modeling. In D. H. Sprenkle & S. M. Moon (Eds.), *Research methods in family therapy* (pp. 336–362). New York: Guilford Press.

Walters, M., Carter, B., Papp, P., & Silverstein, O. (1988). *The invisible web: Gender patterns in family relationships.* New York: Guilford Press.

Waring, E. M. (1984). The measurement of marital intimacy. *Journal of Marital and Family Therapy, 10,* 185–192.

Watzlawick, P., Beavin, J., & Jackson, D. D. (1967). *Pragmatics of human communication.* New York. Norton.

Whitaker, C. A. (1976). The family is a four-dimensional relationship. In P. Guerin (Ed.), *Family therapy.* New York: Gardner Press.

Whitaker, C. A., & Malone, T. P. (1953). *The roots of psychotherapy.* New York: Balkiston.

White, M., & Epston, E. (1990). *Narrative means to therapeutic ends.* New York: Norton.

Willi, J. (1984). The concept of collusion: A combined systemic-psychodynamic approach to marital therapy. *Family Process, 23,* 177–185.

Wittels, F. (1939). The neo-Adlerians. *American Journal of Sociology, 45,* 433–445.

World Health Organization. (1992). *The ICD-10 classification of mental and behavioral disorders: Clinical descriptions and diagnostic guide lines.* Geneva, Switzerland: Author.

Wynne, L. C. (1984). The epigenesis of relational systems: A model for understanding family development. *Family Process, 23,* 297–318.

Wynne, L. C., Ryckoff, I. M., Day, J., & Hirsch, S. I. (1958). Pseudomutuality in the family relations of schizophrenics. *Psychiatry, 21,* 205–220.

Zimbardo, P. G. (1970). The human choice: Individuation, reason, and order versus deindividuation impulse, and chaos. In W. J. Arnold & D. Levine (Eds.), *Nebraska Symposium on Motivation, 1969* (Vol. 17, pp. 237–306). Lincoln: University of Nebraska Press.

SECTION FIVE

GROUP PSYCHOTHERAPY

Chapter 21   Psychodrama

Chapter 22   Transactional Analysis

Chapter 23   Body-Centered Psychotherapy

Chapter 24   Biopsychosocial and Spiritual Treatment of Trauma

CHAPTER 21

Psychodrama

ALAN JACOBS

Jacob L. Moreno (1946/1953), the originator of psychodrama and a lover of stories, rather typically portrayed the step that he had taken in creating the psychodrama in the statement:

> The most amusing of the early definitions of psychodrama was given to me by a Viennese poet, a chronic alcoholic, as he was walking with me one night up and down Kärtner Strasse. "Moreno," he exclaimed, "I agree with you. If I had to die I would rather die of diarrhea than of constipation. As I see it, this is the difference between you and Freud." (p. xxviii)

Psychodrama originated in Vienna, where Moreno sat on a park bench, watched, listened, told stories, and talked with children in their living theater, their natural and everyday circumstances. They would, as most children do, role-play. They would rehearse for living by becoming characters in usually mutually produced, directed, and acted minidramas typically involving characters such as the good guy, the bad guy, the baby, the mother, the scientist, the father, the teacher, the doctor.

Children learn by imitation, and one of the ways they internalize important behaviors is through psychodramatic rehearsal. This process extends into adult life, where the minidramas are often reenacted as internal dialogues with visual imagery: "What will I say to my boss?"; "How will I propose to Mary?"; "What will it be like at my driver's examination?" From this primary and essential human function Moreno developed his ideas. His theories and methods remain as fresh today as the role play of any child anywhere. As adults, we often construct these rehearsals with friends or coworkers, perhaps asking them to assist in the writing and direction of the role. One can learn the lines in the shower, in bed before falling asleep, or perhaps in the middle of the night through unconscious rehearsal, the dream.

Moreno created and developed, as Blatner says, "An existential, phenomenological, and process oriented philosophy, one that emphasizes creativity" (1988, p. 13). This extended to the nature of spontaneity and its development. His goal was, as it is with most psychotherapies, promotion of more authentic relationships and ease of functioning. His major vehicle was the improvisational theater, though his claims of revitalizing the arts as a source of mass therapy remain overly ambitious and overstated. He was variously a student of philosophy, spirituality, and medicine, a field worker in child development and creative dramatics, a practicing physician, an applied social psychologist and sociologist, an editor of a literary journal, and director of an improvisational theater (Blatner, 1988), even before Burrow (1937), Korzybski (1933), or Mead (1934/1964).

Moreno is alternatively known as a great theoretician and psychiatrist, a philosopher, and a scientist. At times, however, his reputation borders on the mythological. He is often referred to as a genius, a rather silly cultural preoccupation in the United States, as if that were enough to justify theory.

On the one hand, Blatner (1998) writes:

> Like the legendary bodhisattva of the Buddhist tradition, and with a sentiment similar to ideas of Teilhard de Chardin, Moreno wanted to help the whole world to use methods of encounter and group dynamics, to help all people develop their own creativity and thus move toward a more harmonious future. (p. 15)

On the other hand, he writes more realistically:

> Moreno's style of writing was often redundant, diffuse, rambling, turgid, and suffused with philosophical speculations and personal historical reminiscence.... [He] made no effort to compare his ideas with others in psychiatry or psychology.... The content of his talks, like his writings, could at times ramble into issues of personal history.... He could be petty, insensitive, arrogant, capricious, overly controlling, and fairly narcissistic. (pp. 39–40)

Moreno was a revolutionary and a rebel. In the early days of psychoanalysis, given Freud's influence and groundbreaking theories, it was difficult to disagree with him, let alone question the basic foundations of psychoanalytic theory. In some sense, it took a revolutionary nature to do so. Established methods do not tolerate groundbreaking innovation and change (Kuhn, 1963).

Journals Moreno published often were not particularly rigorous and rarely contained research or comparative studies. They were filled with innovative and creative ideas, but at times, their epistemology was, if not suspect, at least questionable. His decision to self-publish, thus having total control over editing, no doubt played a part in his lack of wide acceptance. These traits, sadly, contributed to reluctance in the rest of the profession to accept his ideas and methods. It seems there was often a lack of separation between Moreno's innovative and groundbreaking ideas and his personality and self-aggrandizement. His far-reaching ideas and his need to have them recognized, paradoxically, precluded them from wide acceptance because of this very same need.

Nonetheless, Moreno was a profound thinker and innovator. He deserves mention with Freud and perhaps one or two others as a great pioneer of the twentieth century in the quest to understand and aid humankind. Over the years, Moreno's wife, theoretician and therapist, Zerka T. Moreno, and other members of the second and third generations of psychodramatists, have demonstrated that it is possible to use Moreno's approaches with more understatement, less self-preoccupation, and greater attention to audience needs than Moreno at times exhibited.

HISTORY OF THE APPROACH

Between 1908 and 1911, Moreno began working in Vienna with children. In 1912, he extended Freud's individual treatment methods and started what was probably the first psychotherapy group with prostitutes, lying on couches, all in a circle (Z. Moreno, personal communication, December 1969). At the end of World War I, he worked with relocated Tyrolean refugees in a camp near Vienna. Between 1921 and 1924, he started the Theater of Spontaneity, thus starting rudimentary psychodrama.

In the United States, Moreno demonstrated role play at Mt. Sinai Hospital in New York City. A man of great ambition and sweeping action, he conducted an Impromptu Theater in 1929 and 1930, combining psychodrama and group dynamics at no less than Carnegie Hall. In 1932, he first coined the terms "group therapy" and "group psychotherapy" at the American Psychiatric Association convention. For several years beginning in 1933, he consulted at a girl's school in Hudson, New York, where he introduced role playing and developed sociometry. To that end, in 1934 he published *Who Shall Survive?*, a book of wide scope and social breadth. If somewhat peppered with self-promotion and a kind of academic salesmanship, it was nevertheless a brilliant and groundbreaking work. Renowned psychoanalyst William Allison White wrote in the foreword to the first edition (in J. L. Moreno, 1953) and republished in the later one:

Dr. Moreno's book might be described briefly as [a] study of relations between individuals. To qualify the description still further, it might be added that it is a study of the emotional relations between individuals who are functioning as a social group, or as the crosscurrents of emotion as they play back and forth between individuals. (p. cx)

In noting and lauding the scope of Moreno's imagination, he added:

And think, further, if you have no objections to the flights of the imagination, of what possibility it may offer to an understanding of the problems of democracy as they occur in a country like the United States made up of races from all the four quarters of the globe. (p. cxiv)

In 1936, Moreno started a psychiatric hospital in what was to become the Moreno Institute in Beacon, New York. He built there the first psychodrama theater in America. Many professionals trained there, some of whom were certified as directors. In 1937, Moreno first published *A Journal of Interpersonal Relations*. In 1941, at St. Elizabeth's hospital in Washington, D.C., he built a psychodrama theater. The next year, he started the first professional association for group therapists, The American Society for Group Psychotherapy and Psychodrama (ASGPP). In 1945, he published *Sociatry*, later named *Group Psychotherapy*, the official journal of the ASGPP. He died in 1974, after having his work and contributions acknowledged by such as Abraham Maslow, Eric Berne, Bill Schutz, Nathan Ackerman, William Allinson-White, and Franz Alexander.

Ackerman (in Z. T. Moreno, 1959) wrote of Moreno:

Ever since reading Moreno's *Who Shall Survive* in 1938, I have followed his original and crusading efforts in group psychotherapy with interest and admiration. . . . Moreno presents to psychotherapists of every school and vintage. He says in effect, "Let's be big about this. We've got to be. We confront nothing less than the problem of mental health for all humanity." (p. 27)

THEORETICAL CONSTRUCTS

J. L. Moreno (1946/1959) sought a deeper group method, claiming that psychodrama explored this depth to a greater extent than other therapies, that it starts where psychoanalysis and psychotherapy end. Zerka Moreno's perception was that "The psychodrama is not a single technique, it is a methodology, a synthetic method in which many dimensions of experience are mobilized in behalf of the patient" (J. L. Moreno & Moreno, 1969, p. 1). This multidimensionality in time and space, this plasticity and mobility makes the psychodramatic method adaptable to patients and other methods, theories, and cultures.

Blatner (1973) elucidated the significance of dramatic action for therapy and personal development when he said that "acting out" refers to internal impulses discharged as symbolic or actual enactment, the individual achieving little if any mastery or understanding. But if the need to act can be redirected, there can be understanding of these feelings. By acting out impulses, fantasies, memories, and projections psychodramatically, release and self-awareness are achieved. This acting out is encouraged within a structured and awareness-producing milieu. This enactment, as Blatner says, turns impulse into insight. In this sense, one might call these actions "acting in," as they apply therapeutic action methods to human understanding.

Psychodrama implies a theory of personality and provides an individual and group treatment method as well as a broader explorative tool. Its use encourages specific treatment of psychological and social problems. It has served as a teaching and training tool for a wide variety of professions and businesses, relying on action, ergo creativity/spontaneity: "flexibility of drama, and stimulation of action" (Blatner, 1988, p. vii). Although all human interaction shifts from then to now to when, from here to there, from real to pretend, from self to the universal, J. L. Moreno and Moreno (1969) were the first to articulate four universals of psychotherapy: time, space, reality, and cosmos. The objective of psychodrama was, from its inception, to construct a therapeutic setting using life as a model, to integrate it into all the modalities of living, beginning with the universals down to all the details and nuances of life and reality practice.

Even before he created psychodrama in 1921, Moreno realized the value of the group. He concluded that Freud was almost totally concerned with the individual, as opposed to Marx, for whom everything revolved around the social, or socioeconomic. He defined two antitheses to psychoanalysis: the group versus the individual and the actor versus the audience. He focused on the individual in the context of interaction with others and sought to bring the reality of the world into the group setting:

Two thousand years ago man underwent, as we do today, a crisis of the first magnitude. To the broad masses catharsis came from Christianity, due to the universality of its methods and the practicality of its instruments, love and confession, charity and hope.... In our time the social and mental sciences aim at a similar accomplishment as religion once attained. Mankind's masses suffer from social and mental unrest. Catharses will probably come, again from instruments [that] combine universality of method with great practicality. (J. L. Moreno, 1972, p. a)

As relevant as the above passage may seem, we need to remember that Moreno wrote only about the Western world. In our day, we are faced with a global crisis of population, resources, and corresponding violence. Nevertheless, psychodrama, despite Moreno's omissions and perhaps more than other psychotherapies, embodies a universal constant linking all humans: play, childlike play. On one occasion, Moreno and his wife went to see the Disney feature-length cartoon *Fantasia*. He was enraptured. As they were leaving the theater, he turned to Zerka and said in a childlike voice: "Zerka, can we come back and see it again tomorrow?" (Zerka Moreno, personal communication, January 1970). This capacity to be a child again forms the foundation for psychodrama, a capacity known to all people everywhere. It provides a locus of creativity and spontaneity.

Psychodrama summons these universal constants—creativity and spontaneity—and puts them into a very effective therapeutic form embodying the actions of life. Entering the second millennium, we find the world separated by technology, affluence, and formal education versus poverty, hunger, and ignorance. In either case, crises of great magnitude befall some and certainly threaten, like the sword of Damocles, all, whether through war, terrorism, famine, genocide, and political upheaval, cultural, racial, and sexual prejudice, or exponentially exploding populations, diminishing resources, and disease.

As mental health professionals, we cannot, even in the affluent industrialized nations, pull people out of the cascading river of social and emotional distress as fast as they are falling in. We simply cannot keep up. For the most part, our methods for healing such casualties are designed for individuals and small groups. Mass media psychology and the talk shows sensationalize and reduce most issues to their lowest common denominators, not the least of which is selling products.

Few of these large-group methods enable many people to learn from and relate to the work of a specific individual with a specific problem in a personal and meaningful way. Psychodrama, although certainly not comparable to formal or secular religion, uniquely enables large, and even mass, group catharsis via its social extension, the sociodrama.

Psychodrama uses action to solve existential dilemmas. Moreno elaborated a therapeutic modality to encourage goal-oriented action through which humans experience emotions, as Aristotle (1990) observed centuries ago:

> Tragedy is essentially an imitation, not of persons, but of action and life, of happiness and misery. All human happiness or misery takes the form of action, the end for which we live in a certain kind of activity, not a quality. Character gives us qualities, but it is in our actions—what we do—that we are happy or the reverse. In a play accordingly they do not act in order to portray the Characters; they include the Characters for the sake of the action. So that it is the action in it, i.e., its Fable or Plot, that is the end and purpose of the tragedy, and the end is everywhere the chief thing. Besides this, a tragedy is impossible without action. (p. 684)

Thus, action, whether spontaneous or scripted, makes psychodrama, and also drama, a powerful and valuable tool for human reflection and change: therapeutic, moral, philosophical. Moreno fused two apparently separate and distinct disciplines, the theater and psychotherapy, by creating distinct forms of each. He established a new form of human exploration and help for the troubled, and he generated a new dramatic form, primarily used as training for actors, known as theater games and warm-ups. Moffett, writing of the creator of improvisations for the theater, Viola Spolin (1963), wrote:

> By themselves, the [theater] games have liberating effects (accounting for their wide application in self actualization contexts); within the theater context, each clearly fosters a facet of performance technique. There are games to free the actor's tension, games to "cleanse" the actor of subjective preconceptions of the meaning of words, games of relationship and character, games of concentration—in short, games for each of the areas with which the growing actor is concerned....
>
> Key to the rubric of Spolin games are the terms physicalization ("showing and not telling"), spontaneity ("a moment of explosion"), intuition ("unhampered knowledge beyond the sensory equipment—physical and mental"), audience ("part of the game, not the lonely looker-onners"), and transformation ("actors and audience alike receive the appearance of a new reality"). (Moffett, 2000)

Although Spolin is given credit for the creation of theater warmup games, their origin is clearly in Moreno's psychodramatic warmup and spontaneity theory (see J. L. Moreno, 1972, 1947/1983; J. L. Moreno & Moreno, 1969). According to Moreno, psychodrama extends life, in contrast to Aristotle's definition of tragedy as an "imitation of action and life" (J. L. Moreno, 1972, p. 15). The actors/patients bring their own real problems to the theater rather than use those from the mind of the playwright.

The therapeutic theater, more than the traditional theater, serves as a deeper vehicle for resolving specific individual dilemmas. Psychodrama advocates claim that those in the audience with related dilemmas will gain more personally than if they see a film or a play on the same subject. Having participated in many psychodramas, in all the various functions—as patient, auxiliary ego, director, audience, and student—the author has verified this personally.

Psychodrama theory, methods, and techniques have value, even in limited application, for practitioners in various disciplines in the day-in-day-out listening to and helping of people with their pain, their existential dilemmas, their stories. The techniques and methods discovered and created by Moreno have demonstrated value in a wide range of settings and can be combined, even synthesized with many other therapeutic approaches. There is something essential to the method, something possibly universal. An established treatment method in Europe today, psychodrama suffers from a kind of second-class citizenship in the United States. This may have resulted more from Moreno's personality and his competitive stance regarding many other theories than from its essential value.

THEORETICAL CONSTRUCTS

Surplus Reality

This construct allows the protagonist to enact any scenes, real or imagined, with anyone living, dead, or imagined. They may be scenes that "have never happened, will never happen, or can never happen" (Z. T. Moreno, in Blatner, 1998, p. 178). J. L. Moreno (1972) wrote of the universes of fantasy and reality in the infant. The fantasy world is completely real for the infant; at first, no differentiation is made between the two. In this sense, fantasy, or pretend, if you will, is a reality, albeit a surplus one. Living things and objects are undifferentiated, for example, the bottle belongs to the hand that holds it, and both belong to the lips in the act of sucking. Later, as the infant learns to differentiate objects from people, there is still no differentiation between real and imagined objects or real and imagined people (1972). The psychodrama explores this surplus reality to promote the use of the protagonist's imagination (e.g., the fantasized good parent, the best job, God's approval or disapproval).

Tele

Tele (Greek for "far; influence into distance") is mutual feeling or psychic affinity between people. It is not sympathy, pity, empathy, or identification, though these may all contribute to it. It is not transference. It is

> the feeling of individuals into one another, the cement which holds groups together. It is Zweifuhlung, in contrast to Einfuhlung [dual rather than single relationship]. Like a telephone, it has two ends and facilitates two-way communication. Tele is a primary, transference a secondary structure.... The Telic relationship, between protagonist, therapist, auxiliary ego, and the significant dramatis personae of the world which they portray are crucial for the therapeutic process. (J. L. Moreno, 1972, p. xi)

In other words, it is the intuitive, spontaneous, and childlike process that occurs between people, with understanding. The understanding is unconscious as well. As the great American comedian Jonathon Winters said, it's like "putting myself in the other guy's shoes, like all day." One might say, like putting each in the other's shoes. In fact, telic capacity and ability is an important quality for any psychotherapist of any persuasion. With this conception, Moreno strove to go beyond the empathetic understanding and analysis of the transference relationship.

Encounter

In contrast to psychoanalysis, psychodrama encourages dialogue, "an encounter of two, each with opportunity for combat and repartee.... It is equally accurate to say that psychodrama is a dialogue taking place between several individuals" (J. L. Moreno, 1972, p. xiii). According to Moreno:

> Breuer and Freud were ignorant of the psychotherapeutic implication of the drama milieu to which Aristotle has referred in The Poetics.... A tragedy is filled with incidents arousing pity and fear wherewith to accomplish its catharsis of such emotions (Aristotle, 1990, p. 684). However catharsis is, for Aristotle, a secondary phenomenon, a by-product, an effect of poetry on the reader. (p. 14)

Moreno reversed Aristotle's procedure by directing attention to the beginning phase of the drama, rather than the end:

> It was from the community from which the actors spring, and the actors producing them, again it was not any community, a community in abstracto, but my village and neighborhood, the house in which I lived. The actors were not any people, people in abstracto, but my people, my father and mother, my brothers and sisters, my friends and neighbors. And the dramas in which we were interested were not the ones that mature in the minds of artists, but long before they reach them, as they sprang up in everyday life, in the minds of simple people. (pp. 14–15)

Role

"Role is the functioning form the individual assumes in the specific moment he reacts to a specific situation in which other persons or objects are involved" (J. L. Moreno, 1972, p. v). "The function of the role is to enter the unconscious from the social world and bring shape and order to it" (p. v). Before there are roles, there is the infant existing in what Moreno called an "undifferentiated universe" or "the matrix of identity": "It may be considered as the locus from which in gradual stages the self, and its branches, the roles, emerge" (p. iii). Moreno envisioned the role concept as "binding together" psychology, sociology, philosophy, and anthropology in a new way: "The theory of roles is not limited to a single dimension, the social" (p. v). Before the advent of the transactional analysis idea of "script," or plan for living (Berne, 1971), J. L. Moreno wrote that role is carried throughout life in all its dimensions and has "constructed models in which the role begins to transact from birth on" (1972, p. v).

In the social realm, role is also a pattern or stylized aggregation of behaviors designed to perform a specified task, such as being a priest or a firefighter. Role prescribes an aggregate of behaviors, attitudes, and feelings consistent with designations such as those of parent or child, which are learned either out of independent thinking or because others expect it, or both, consciously and unconsciously. It is learned within one's social position or standing. The role is a comprehensive aggregate of behaviors that is recognized by others and proves a means of placing or identifying a person in society. Borrowing the term from the formal theater, Moreno distinguished the player from the part, the actor from the script. Role is goal-directed and contains most of the instructions for living. It provides certain strategies for dealing with others in their roles, for example, wife-husband, parent-child, doctor-patient. Judge, bailiff, court stenographer, jury member, lawyer, defendant, witness, public, press, all have their assigned and acceptable systems of behavior within the context of the trial. The role remains relatively stable, even though different people may occupy a social position requiring it. People have unique styles, yet any specific style is expressed within the prescribed limits of the role. Mel Gibson and Sir Lawrence Olivier, though very different in style and approach, each must stay within Hamlet's role as written by the playwright.

Moreno was one of the very early developers of psychological role theory, and his approach revealed two levels: the role play and the ability to stand aside, or above, survey, and observe the how and why of roles: why they are assumed, acquired, rehearsed, and, above all, played. "This second level allows for greater self-reflection, and the cultivation of this 'meta-role' function is a great part of what psychotherapy is really about" (Blatner, 1998).

Role can be defined as an imaginary person created by a dramatist, for instance, a Hamlet, an Othello, or a Faust; an imaginary role may never have existed, as a Pinocchio or a Bambi. It may be a model to existence, as a Faust, or an imitation of it, as an Othello. Role can be defined also as a part of a character taken by an actor, for instance, such an imaginary person as Hamlet animated by an actor to reality. Role can also be defined as an assumed character or function within social reality, for instance, a police officer, a judge, a physician, a congressperson. Role can be defined as the actual and tangible form that the self takes. Self, ego (personality, character) are cluster effects, heuristic hypotheses, metaphysical postulations, "logoids." Role is a final crystallization of all the situations in a special area of operations through which the individual has passed (e.g., the eater, the father, the airplane pilot, the mate, the friend) (J. L. Moreno, 1972). Moreno was one of the first to see that both social and psychodynamic implications are integral parts of psychotherapy, different but inseparable. He made the connection between the two and developed his theory to reflect that observation. Role theory is a natural bridge between the two levels of human organization, addressing the group, its interactions, and the intrapsychic (Blatner, 1998).

There is a conflict between the actor on the stage and his or her private person, that is, between the given role on stage and the primary person stepping into the role. For example, each actor on stage demonstrates what Moreno called primary role-person conflict: "Behind the mask of Hamlet lurks the actor's private personality" (J. L. Moreno, 1972, p. 153). Moreover, the private person can be further distinguished as social and psychological selves; in fact, these two levels are always operating, one externally, the other internally. Roles in Moreno's sense seem to be directed toward the social or external self; that is, they are acquired. Moreno's intention was that the concept of role could be used as a tool in therapy, and indeed it forms the basis for the psychological foundation for psychodrama. He thought that roles did not emerge from the self, but were utilized by the child prior to emergence of the self:

For George Herbert Mead (1934/1964) the self—and a society of selves are language ridden, that is, dependent on language for coming to know and to understand self. Freud's exploratory outlook, too, was language ridden. Freud thought . . . that language is the main root for psychological analysis. He unconsciously assumed that it is a major container of psychological evolution, that it can catch the essence of psychic growth. Mead assigned to language a similar importance in social evolution and thought that by inference all essential information can be derived from it. Both neglect the pre-semantic and a-semantic development of the psyche and the group. (J. L. Moreno, 1972, p. 157)

Role taking, role making, role analysis, role play, and role distance have been topics for discussion by psychodrama theorists (e.g., Blatner, 1998). Role play is, of course, well-known and is used in a great variety of ways. Moreno spoke of using it, for example, to assess the capacity of hospitalized patients to deal with the world from which they had been removed. This was accomplished by getting them to talk to auxiliary egos (described next), playing the roles of significant persons: relatives, employer and employees, friends (J. L. Moreno, personal communication, October 1969). Role play is also used in different parts of the psychodrama (e.g., the warmup and the action portion). Without it, there really is no psychodrama, in the same sense that without roles, there is no social functioning.

Some of Blatner's (1998) conclusions are astute and extremely helpful. Roles are learned.

They can be lost, taken away, or relinquished. They are implicit or explicit social contracts; that is, they require an agreement by others to behave in some reciprocal fashion. Many roles are complementary (e.g., parent/child, husband/wife, supervisor/employee). Role conflict can occur when people change their role. Every relationship consists of several roles. Many roles have subroles or role components that sometimes are in conflict (e.g., a mother protects her children and at the same time encourages risk taking; a chef must pay attention to both aesthetics and cost).

Spontaneity

Imagine arriving at a theater. You show your tickets, put the stubs in your pocket or purse, check your coat, walk to your aisle, and give the usher the ticket stubs. Discreetly shining a flashlight on the floor, she makes a trail to your seat. You squiggle past the people in your aisle, taking care not to step on a foot or bang a knee, imploring "Excuse me" and "Sorry" along the path to relief and safety in your own seat. You while away the remaining minutes reading the program notes, the achievements of the actors, the history of the play. Tonight it is *Zarathustra.* After what is rarely a short enough time, the house lights dim, the footlights go up, the curtain is drawn. The audience grows silent. You sit in the dark as a masked actor steps to stage-front-center and begins a monologue announcing that he is the real Zarathustra. You are absorbed, giving yourself over to author, actor, and atmosphere.

Suddenly, someone in the audience stands and challenges the actor: "You are not the real Zarathustra," he exclaims in a loud voice. "I challenge you to take off your mask and reveal yourself as you really are." The central dramatic protagonist becomes a real-life protagonist. Just imagine, sitting in the darkened theater when this happens, out of the blue, suddenly, unexpectedly. At first, you think it is a dramatic device contrived by the director and author to instill a sense of urgency and reality. However, you soon realize that it is a genuine interruption, not part of the play in any way. Imagine your reaction, the changes in your physical state, pulse, respiration, sharpened vision. Perhaps you are annoyed or angry at the interruption, perhaps anxious, inevitably surprised.

Abruptly, the man in the audience rushes from his aisle seat and leaps onto the stage. He strides toward the actor, challenges him to take off his mask and reveal himself as he really is. There are shouts demanding the man to leave the stage and allow the play to continue. The actor, of course, solidly in role, refuses, claiming himself the real Zarathustra. The man persists, offering a persuasive argument. He is so forceful and convincing that the actor eventually relents, removes his mask, and reveals himself as he really is. Then, of course, the challenger reveals himself as the real Zarathustra. This story, retold from J. L. Moreno's original (1947/1983, pp. 24–28), illustrates the very heart of psychodrama. It reveals not only the difference between the traditional theater and the theater of spontaneity, but also the difference in audience reaction. Suddenly, they are participants in a totally unexpected, real-life drama. Nevertheless, this drama is an additional form rather than a replacement for the traditional theater.

Spontaneity is, of course, at the heart of creativity, and it was Moreno's observation that no change or problem solving of any lasting value can occur without creative imagination and thinking. If spontaneity has its origins in the unconscious miracle-working sprit, as Arnheim (1962) suggests, then it is likely that any lasting personality and behavioral changes must occur as a result of catharsis on this level. Psychodrama's connection with the creative act leads inevitably to spontaneity, the keystone of any human problem solving, be it technical, scientific, or psychological. And, though some may not see scientific discovery derived in the intuitive act, Einstein himself remarked that imagination was more important than knowledge. Relativity, after all, has its origins in a moment of intuition as, at the age of 26, Einstein swung his legs over the edge of the bed one morning, sat up, and there it was! What if the Michaelson and Morley experiments measuring the speed of light had been accurate? What if the velocity of light was a constant? At this point, he fulfilled the imaginative question he first formulated at age 14: What is it like to keep pace with a ray of light? And so began the quest to open the secrets of the atomic nucleus, what Jacobs Bronowski called the greatest collective creative act in history (Bronowski, 1973, p. 163).

Perhaps Moreno's greatest achievements were his ideas regarding spontaneity and creativity. Psychodrama, like all art, is essentially an imitative act, and dealing as it does with tragedy in the classical sense, follows the foundations set down by Aristotle (1990) in the Poetics: "Imitation is natural to man from childhood, one of his advantages over the lower animals being this, that he is the most adaptable creature in the world, and learns at first by imitation" (p. 682).

In classical times, there was no hard separation between art and science as there is today. It was only later, with the introduction of the scientific method, that they were seen as distinct. Moreno seems to have grasped the essence of the creative act in either discipline as substantially the same, and gave it to his patients and students. Without creativity there is no profound problem solving, and there is no creativity without spontaneity:

> In order to mobilize and shape ... [ad-libs], they need a transformer and catalyst, a kind of intelligence which operates here and now, *hic et nunc*, spontaneity. Mental healing processes require healing to be effective.... In psychodrama particularly, spontaneity acts not only in the direction of words but in all other dimensions of expression, such as acting, interacting, speaking, dancing, singing and drawing. It was an important advance to link spontaneity with creativity, the highest form of intelligence we know of, and to recognize them as the primary forces in human behavior. (J. L. Moreno, 1972, p. xii)

Catharsis

Psychodramatic theory develops the idea of catharsis, which becomes the major goal of psychodrama rather than the work of art as a finished product, as an alternative to Aristotle and traditional theater. J. L. Moreno (1972) wrote that ancient Greek therapeutic activity was devoted to driving out the demons from the bodies of victims. This often entailed using magical incantations and charms of one sort or another on the sick person. And the drama,

> long before it was a place for presentation of art and entertainment, was a place for therapeutics, the sick coming to it for catharsis.... Aristotle defines catharsis in the Poetics as follows: "The task of the tragedy is to produce through the exercise of fear and pity, liberation from such emotions." (p. 179)

This catharsis was to take place in the spectator. Moreno's catharsis is conjured primarily for the actor, that is, the sufferer. Regardless of his contrasting psychodrama with the traditional theater, Moreno's major focus was a correct one. It seems that no lasting alleviation of pain or changes of behavior can occur without catharsis, and he was right to design a therapy for its benefit.

Elements

According to J. L. Moreno (1972), there were five basic elements or "instruments" in classical psychodrama. *The stage*, in most cases, is simply a space in a room large enough for some physical movement. Moreno wanted a stage because it provided the patient with plastic "living space," one that affords multidimensional use of time, space, and reality, therefore enhancing maximum creativity and spontaneity. The three-tiered stage, the "therapeutic theater," was for him "where the ultimate resolution of deep group conflicts" occurs (J. L. Moreno, 1959, p. 192). Although physical spaces influence all human activity, the psychodrama stage as defined by Moreno, although preferable, is very often not a practical possibility for most therapists, even psychodramatists. It represents the ideal. Relevant, cathartic psychodrama can be achieved without this element, though it is nice to have a stage if at all possible. In Moreno's view, any place where human activity occurred was adequate.

Protagonists, or patients are encouraged to be themselves. Initially, the protagonist talks about his or her problem and then action occurs. "There are several forms of enactment, pretending to be in role, re-enactment or acting out a past scene, living out a problem presently pressing, creating life on the stage or testing oneself for the future" (J. L. Moreno, 1972, p. b).

The director, or therapist, has three functions: producer, therapist, and analyst. The producer, alert to all cues, must keep the drama attuned to the life of the protagonist. The therapist uses all kinds of techniques at his or her disposal: shocking, confronting, joking, nurturing, or empathizing. The function of the analyst is to gather as much information as possible to understand the protagonist's dilemma and to explain it.

The auxiliary ego is a member of a group of trained people, or, as J. L. Moreno (1972) called them, "therapeutic actors." They are extensions of both the therapist and the patient. They portray various others in the patient's drama as well as aspects of the patient's self: "They have three functions . . . the actor portraying roles required by the patient's world; . . . the therapeutic agent, guiding the subject; the function of the social investigator" (1972, p. c). Sometimes auxiliary egos are not available, for example, in nonpsychodrama groups. In this case, depending on their level of spontaneity, group members can, with some instruction and coaching, very often step into specific roles.

The audience usually consists of other patients or staff members not directly involved in the enactment. They can help the patient and also be helped, as in any group therapy.

Rules

Zerka T. Moreno (1965) elaborated 15 rules for psychodrama:

1. Patients, or subjects, enact and reenact their conflicts rather than only talking about them. That is, patients might set up a scene from the past based on a problem presented to the director and the group. For example, they might enact being at the dining room table of their childhood home, 30 years in the past, complete with parents and siblings, reenacting a specific incident.

2. The action is always presented as if it were actually taking place in the moment. All referencing is to what is happening now, as opposed to the past or future. The effect, somewhat hypnotic in nature, is to place patients in their own drama in action with feelings. This effect is achieved for the protagonist and other actors on stage as well as for the psychodrama audience.

3. Subjects must portray their feelings in action in the most personal and open manner possible, that is, as subjectively as possible, no matter how distorted, weird, or even "crazy" this appears to the audience. Catharsis and ultimate retraining cannot be achieved unless a full exposition of feeling occurs.

4. All expression is maximized; that is, the psychodrama is a great magnifying glass of behavior, both verbal and nonverbal. "To this end, delusions, hallucinations, soliloquies, thoughts,

fantasies, projections, [and displacements] are [encouraged] to be part of the [action]" (J. L. Moreno & Moreno, 1969, p. 3). Restraint comes after the fullest possible expression. This should always be kept in mind, because restraint is incomplete without a full expression.

5. The warmup, like any preliminary therapeutic communication, starts with the outside of the onion. This includes warming up the group, the subsequent quest for a representative protagonist, and then warming up the protagonist himself or herself.

6. Whenever possible, protagonists pick the time, the place, the scene, and the auxiliaries they require. The director acts as dramaturge in assisting the protagonist. Within this partnership, the first goal is to help the protagonist. Second, it is to give the audience-group as much of the catharsis as they can experience. If the patient/director process becomes negative, the director may ask the patient to designate another director, ask the patient to sit down and watch a mirroring of the patient performed by auxiliary egos, turn the direction over to the patient, ask the patient to choose another scene, explain the director's choice of scenes, return at a later time to scenes rejected by the patient, or insist that a scene be enacted if the benefits obviously outweigh the resistance. Care must be given to avoid dismantling defenses without a thorough understanding of why they are there in the first place.

7. The method is as much a method that encourages self-restraint, when indicated, as it is a method of self-expression. For example, "one thinks . . . of the chronic bad actor . . . , the delinquent or the psychopath, impulsive and indulgent, narcissistic personalities, the antisocial personality, whose abilities for self restraint [are limited]" (Z. T. Moreno, 1965, p. 5).

8. As in any therapy, the director and the group should accept whatever inhibitions and lack of expressiveness and spontaneity the patient has (Z. T. Moreno, 1965). In this sense, the psychodrama is always for the patient more than for the audience-group, in the same way other treatment approaches are for the individual before the group. At no time should the patient's problem and needs be secondary to a group message. The patient is first, always.

9. Interpretation takes many forms. It may be verbal, but it seems to be more effective in the construction of scenes and in the actions and words of auxiliaries.

10. Action takes precedence over interpretation. Interpretation should be given only after action. It "may be questioned, rejected, or totally ineffective" (Z. T. Moreno 1965, p. 6), as with any patient in any therapy. The theoretical discipline and personalities of the therapists and auxiliaries will influence interpretation. The psychodrama exists as a vehicle within which various approaches may be utilized.

11. As with any therapy, warming up, and the actual psychodrama itself, must be culturally, ethnically, and socially sensitive.

12. Psychodrama consists of three parts: warmup, action, and postaction sharing. In this sense, the warmup is really the group warmup. We might include a fourth part, or at least a subpart: warming up the protagonist as distinct from warming up the group.

13. "The protagonist should never be left alone with the impression that he is alone with this type of problem in this group" (Z. T. Moreno, 1965, p. 7). However, there are problems that are substantially different than others' experience (e.g., rape, torture, or unjust imprisonment). That is, there are times when the problems presented are totally out of the experience of the group. It is useful to ensure, by attitude and demeanor, that the patient is no longer alone with his or her pain, but rather has a group of supporters who, if not understanding experientially, can empathize and commiserate.

The selection of protagonists is important. Sometimes they emerge from the warmup process, sort of popping up out of the group, eager and ready to work. This is often accompanied by a spontaneous eruption of emotion. At other times, a group-appropriate protagonist is more difficult to find. Sometimes the group discusses who it thinks might be a good candidate; this process is usually accomplished during the postaction sharing phase.

14. "The protagonist must indeed learn to take the role of those to whom he is meaningfully related" (Z. T. Moreno, 1965, p. 8). In a certain sense, the protagonist must become the people with whom he or she is struggling, to understand their fears, hopes, and dreams, their problems with him or her, their existential perspective. Without this "role reversal," no lasting resolution of problems between them can be achieved.

15. "The director must trust the psychodrama method as the final arbiter and guide in the therapeutic process" (Z. T. Moreno, 1965, p. 9). This author, who has devoted a career to the exploration of power and its misuse (Jacobs, 1987, 1990, 1991, 1994), challenges this "rule" as the extension of Moreno's narcissistic grandiosity. Moreno was a great theoretician and innovator and psychodrama is a very powerful and effective method, but no therapist should ever accept any process as an act of faith, as if prostrating oneself before some religion or political ideology, an issue addressed in the classic article by Temerlin and Temerlin (1982) on "psychotherapy cults." Idealization of this sort may turn adherents into followers and true believers (Hoffer, 1951). Practitioners of psychodrama, as in most other disciplines, at times fail to take the whole spectrum of psychotherapy treatment solutions into account. This is as much a condition of psychotherapy theories and their progenitors in general as it is of psychodrama.

Parts

The parts of the psychodrama are the beginning or warmup phase, the middle or action phase, and the end or sharing phase. One might relate them to prologue, climax, and conclusion in the traditional theater. In some sense, we might also relate them to the traditional view of disease, which has onset, course, and outcome.

Warmup

This phase is as crucial to the group, director, and protagonist as any warmup is for a singer or dancer before a performance, or for any athlete before a competition. Actually, we all warm up to most everything we do. Waking in the morning, we prepare ourselves for the day's tasks, work, and enjoyments. In simply going off to the grocery store, there is a degree of warmup, in thinking about the day's meals. At the restaurant, we usually have an appetizer, followed by the main course and dessert. It is this phase, with all its various exercises, that can be useful to practitioners from other theoretical persuasions. One may never attempt a formal psychodrama, yet these psychodramatic warmup techniques can be of great help, not only in warming up a group or an individual patient, but also during therapy itself.

Action

Action is simply what it is. It is the meat of the psychodrama, where role playing and role reversal, reenactment of traumatic or problematic episodes from the past, or enactment of future scenes are performed in an operational rather than theatrical sense.

Sharing

The sharing phase is a kind of warming down, when others in the group have an opportunity to verbalize thoughts and feelings they had about themselves during the action portion. Sharing is directed toward the protagonist, but not in an interpretive way. It is designed to give the message that the protagonist is not different or alone with the problem. Interpretation is not recommended during this phase and most directors will stop any such process. In this sense, rule 15 makes sense: One must trust that the process, as executed, will have been effective enough to influence the unconscious process of the protagonist. Sometimes, interpretation deflects or may even block this process. At this final stage of the psychodrama, the director must be especially attuned to counterfeit stroking and support. Eric Berne (1964), the creator of transactional analysis, identified this as the game of "greenhouse," in which people present their feelings as though they were rare hothouse flowers on display in the "national feeling show."

SOME ESSENTIAL TECHNIQUES

Techniques are used in the service of the group; that is, they are adapted to the needs of the group and do not dictate. They are there to enhance the therapeutic environment and to help those who ask for it. Techniques that facilitate spontaneous action and a testing of alternative situations for future use are the most helpful. Although some well-known and very useful techniques are presented below, it should be kept in mind that the psychodramatist is often challenged to create new techniques as needed, even in the middle of a psychodrama (Yablonsky & Enneis, 1956). Although many techniques have been developed over the years, only basic ones are covered here, which even psychotherapists who practice other methods of treatment may find useful.

Role Reversal
Probably the single most important technique developed by Moreno, role reversal allows the patient to step into the skin, so to speak, of the other. For example, a patient may present a problem she is having with her boss. She is asked to describe the problem, then to become her boss and say the things she as patient is upset about. Then she is asked to reverse roles and respond to her boss, and so forth. An auxiliary is brought in who learns that the protagonist needs him to portray the boss. In a sense, the protagonist gives stage directions, through word and action, to the auxiliary. This helps build a replay of the original scene in a realistic manner, bringing the scene into the room and making it seem real:

> The shortest definition of role reversal is that person A becomes person B and that person B becomes person A. On the psychodramatic stage this reversal is meant as an actuality, because it is not fiction or "as if," which illustrates the revolutionary aspect of psychodramatic logic. An abbreviated form of this technique is having A take one of the "roles" of B and B take one of the "roles" of A. For certain mental patients it is an actuality. It is not a fiction or "as if." (J. L. Moreno, 1953, p. 723)

Soliloquy
As in traditional theater, the protagonist speaks to himself or herself. Therapeutic soliloquy encourages revelation of hidden or unexpressed thoughts and feelings. The difference in its use in psychodrama is that it is primarily for the benefit of the protagonist and only secondarily for the audience. This is helpful not only on the psychodrama stage, but in many forms of therapy. One need only ask patients to pause, think for a moment, look to the side, and say what they are not saying, what they are thinking or feeling.

Auxiliary ego assistant therapists can, at best, only approximate the inner life of the protagonist: "The full psychodrama of our interrelations does not emerge; it is buried in and between us. [Soliloquy] has often been used by dramatists for artistic purposes" (J. L. Moreno, 1972, p. 190) to reveal the inner life of the character and reach the inner lives of the audience in some way. In psychodrama, it is used to reveal the hidden thoughts and feelings of the protagonist in a particular enactment, that is, to duplicate earlier ones (e.g., in a scene with a parent). Moreno thought the original feelings could be exactly reproduced. Whether this is so or the original feelings are layered with years of living, decisions, and similar experiences, the point is that soliloquy does reveal what the protagonist is not saying and perhaps does not really know in full consciousness. Often, in other therapies, patients are asked "What are you feeling?" and often they reply "I don't know." Asking a person to soliloquize is often an effective way of getting by this impasse.

The Double

The protagonist is joined by a trained auxiliary or group member who functions as a support by presenting the protagonist's position and feelings. An empathetic bond with the protagonist is essential in the performance of this role (Blatner, 1988). Doubles are encouraged to assume the stance, voice tone, and physical movement of the protagonist, in much the same way that actors are required to learn and portray a role. This gives the patient additional support and, it is hoped, insight:

> Two persons, A and B are one and the same person.... B acts as the double of A and is accepted as such. The degree of non-acceptance and the conflict derived from it between the individual and his double is an important phase in double catharsis. (J. L. Moreno, 1953, p. 723)

Double catharsis means that the auxiliary ego, acting as a double, also has a catharsis.

Dream Presentation

Dreams are first described and then enacted in the now. Auxiliaries represent various parts of the dream—people, places, things, and feelings—after the protagonist has first become these various parts. Gestalt therapy techniques of asking someone to become, for example, a chair or a cloud or a cat has its origins in this technique. This is an effective way of expressing daydreams of all kinds. As in Gestalt therapy, every part of the dream—every person, object, or feeling—is considered an aspect of the dreamer.

Empty Chair

In this technique, the patient talks to an empty chair, imagining a real or fictitious person or an object or feeling. In some cases, this frees the patient from confrontation with an actual person (auxiliary) and permits greater spontaneity. Fritz Perls (1969, pp. 81–85) incorporated this technique as his most important exercise, adding a second chair, combining it with role reversal, and eliminating the auxiliary, the patient thus playing both parts. Widely known as the two-chair technique, this exercise has become synonymous with Gestalt therapy, but its origins lie with Moreno and psychodrama. After Moreno's death, his wife, who had long before taken up the torch passed by her aging husband, held a "psychodramatic, ecumenical memorial service" on the grounds of the Moreno Institute in Beacon, New York. A large tent was erected and all the people sat in chairs facing one empty chair. The audience was invited to put Moreno himself in the chair and to talk to him, to say goodbye or whatever they wished to say. The drama of the moment and, more important, the power of this exercise was demonstrated when a middle-aged woman approached the chair and implored the memory of Moreno to forgive her. She revealed that she had been hiding something for many years, something she had not even told her friends, much less Moreno. The crying woman confessed that she had hidden her Jewishness since the end of World War II. Leaving Europe for North America, she had left her religious and cultural identity as well, fearing other pogroms. The power of imagination can evoke such drama. The beauty of this technique is its simplicity, free as it is from unnecessary accoutrements.

Behind the Back

When interpretation during the action portion is considered necessary, the protagonist is asked to go to a corner, turn away from the audience or group, and listen to them discussing what they don't like or are uncomfortable with as if he or she were not there. Another name for this technique could be "fly on the wall." A variation of this exercise may be done with other kinds of psychotherapy groups, either as an individual or group exercise. This indirect interpretation tends to allay some of the defense mechanisms often seen with direct feedback. After all have participated, a group discussion may begin, often generating rich material for further exploration and possible change. After this phase, the exercise is repeated with positive feedback, though care should be taken that this phase does not cover up or reinforce denial of the first phase. Naturally, anyone may refuse, with no admonitions and with one restriction: No one may give feedback who chooses not to receive it.

Mirror

One way of helping protagonists who are stuck is to ask them to join the audience and watch an auxiliary represent them as if they were looking in a mirror. The auxiliary copies or mimics the protagonist's behavior, and may sometimes exaggerate the impression to emphasize relevant aspects for the patient: "The real purpose of the technique is to let the patient see himself as if in a mirror, provoke him and shock him into action" (J. L. Moreno, 1953, p. 723). It must be remembered that all such performances are designed for the patient and not to exhibit the talents of the auxiliaries.

Future Projection

This technique asks patients to transport themselves to a future scene. They choose the time, place, persons involved, and the scenario. This exercise is useful in a number of ways. Berne (1971) proposed the idea of "life script," in which each person creates a plan that includes many of the essential elements for living in the world as one knows it. This plan can be explored through future projection, which presupposes final outcomes of specifics such as marriage, children, job or career success, illness, death, happiness, contentment, or fulfillment. It is useful to ask persons to project themselves to a future point, perhaps near the end of life, and to describe what that is like. One can usually make some connection between present feeling, thinking, and behavior and future results, though these are not set in stone and are revised to some extent throughout life. Often, indications of paradoxical intention are revealed, where people try to avoid certain outcomes only to see them fulfilled.

Another useful application of this technique is in helping people rehearse anxiety-producing situations, for example, proposing marriage, interviewing for an important job or with a prospective business client, having children, or undergoing surgery. It also is helpful in evaluating how people will act after being released from a psychiatric facility or prison. All the relevant aspects of a person's life can be addressed: friends, children, and employers, for example. In this way, a diagnosis of their readiness may be attempted as people prepare for discharge or release.

MAJOR SYNDROMES, SYMPTOMS, AND PROBLEMS TREATED

Psychodrama has wide application because it is flexible and, therefore, adaptable to many environments and theories. Formal psychodrama need not be the only application, as psychodrama can be done literally anywhere there is a group:

> The protagonist, the problem, and the group are at the center of the session and all artifacts are on hand to help structure situations with the aid of the therapist and the auxiliary egos [assistant therapists]. This freedom for the patient to act out (present, dramatize) his problem is represented

in the freedom of space—the stage, or any open space—as a vehicle for therapeutic production. (Yablonsky & Enneis, 1956, p. 1)

A great many human problems and issues for psychotherapy can be treated with this method. For example, any number of past conflicts and origins of introjects and life decisions can be explored because time is treated as plastic and malleable; that is, we can create the illusion of going back in time so that the person and audience apparently experience it. Time may also be expanded or contracted to fit the patient's needs. For example, the director might slow the process of dialogue between, say, a parent and the protagonist, and perhaps even freeze it to explore in greater detail. This transcends traditional drama and actually was a harbinger of electronic flexibility in DVD or VHS audio and video recording, where one can pick and choose scenes at will, stop them, freeze them, rewind, or fast forward.

A distinction can be drawn between psychodramatic theory and method and its techniques. The former is a complete system with all its parts and players, requiring years of study and training. Many of its techniques and adjunctive methods, on the other hand, can be incorporated into the practice of any number of other disciplines, partly because of universal and familiar practices common to us all. According to Blatner (1988):

> Traditional training of psychodramatists is a very rigorous and time consuming discipline requiring years of training in the often frustrating and frightening caldron of spontaneous expression.... It is not for everyone and one of [its] goals is "to encourage a wider range of people to learn and utilize some of the methods while at the same time rediscovering a greater level of vitality available to us all." (p. ix)

Even with only preliminary formal psychodrama education and training, aspects of the psychodrama, such as the warmup, role play, role reversal, mirroring, and future projection, can be integrated into a wide variety of other therapies and used as techniques and adjunctive methods with relative ease. One of its greatest strengths is psychodrama's apparent universality and its availability for ready use by therapists already experienced in at least one other discipline:

> To adopt and arrange a work of art for the stage is to run counter to the classic idea of the drama. The present methods of theatrical production are destroying even the created, dogmatic type of theater. For this theater is concerned with the most faithful rendering of every word. Its value depends of faithful reproduction. It is a justification of life that is already over; it is a modern example of the cult of death, a cult of resurrection, not of creation. The present traditional theater is defended by its apologists who claim its productions are in themselves unique, and works of art. The written drama is subordinated to the machinery of the theater. (J. L. Moreno, 1972, p. 40)

Nevertheless, drama or film can be of great cathartic value for audiences as well. Why do so many flock to stages, movie theaters, and TV screens? Dramatic performances strike a chord in all of us. The reader will no doubt remember countless times sitting in a darkened theater experiencing, as much as watching, a powerful film or stage drama. Powerful catharses, the very essence of drama, are experienced in the traditional theater, where no two performances are exactly alike. Actors bring themselves to the performance with all that is happening in their own lives. Each performance is an amalgam of author, director, actors, and audience, and their individual life experiences and differences, all of which has relevance to everyday life in some way, if only by contrast. The creative acts of the writer, the director, and the actor's reactions to them cannot be cast aside, as Moreno attempts. Moreover, he failed to present enough evidence demonstrating how the traditional theater was being destroyed in the psychodrama. If we are to extend his words into other creative forms, the only essential music is jazz, in that it is, in part, improvisational. Could Moreno's criticism of the rehearsed performance mean that a chamber orchestra, faithfully playing Handel's notes, is part of the cult of resurrection? The very role play of children, spontaneous and in-the-moment as it is, becomes incorporated and stored for use in the future.

Moreno refers to traditional drama as a physician, student, and helper of human problems. This is fair enough. In this sense, the spontaneity of the present moment is essential if people are to encounter their true selves and find creative solutions to their current and old dilemmas: "Spontaneity is the variable degree of adequate response to a situation of a variable degree of novelty. Novelty of behavior, by itself, is not the measure of spontaneity. Novelty has to be qualified against its adequacy *in situ*" (J. L. Moreno, 1953, p. 722). Furthermore, this author has often found solutions to problems or learned something about life from the traditional theater and films. I am often moved deeply, to tears or anger or pity. Such feelings often cause one to ruminate about why they are elicited. If there is no thoughtful reflection, there is still unconscious processing occurring.

In response to a question from a student, Moreno pulled out a book and, before reading a passage by way of answering, said: "A definition is more substantial if it is also recorded" (J. L. Moreno, personal communication, October 1969). Is this not also true for the theater, a film, or a painting? Surely the moment of the creative act is past, the excitement and the joy of it, the manic exhilaration, yet what the creator found in that moment can be of lasting value. What matters is the content of the creation, not merely the creative act itself. In all fairness, it should be said that the creativity implicit in psychodramatic action and techniques generally exceeds that required or revealed in almost all other therapies, with the exception of art, dance, music, and children's play therapies.

CASE EXAMPLE

Case Formulation

This history was compiled during a psychodrama workshop for police, with a 36-year-old White male of stocky, athletic build and gruff demeanor, a police detective and Marine Corps Vietnam combat veteran, identified here as Jack. He had been honorably discharged after winning several decorations, which he said, like many fellow combat veterans the author has known or treated, "meant nothing."

The theme and goal of the workshop was to raise awareness of how police officers bring their entire past into every contact and encounter with the public. A second goal was, when asked for, to help participants decide to do things differently, that is, with increased social and psychological awareness of self and others, sophistication, and ease of execution.

The protagonist was referred from another jurisdiction by his superior because of repeated use of inappropriate and, in one case, excessive force. He was known by his fellow officers as very courageous, "a stand-up guy," someone they could rely on in unsafe situations. During the warmup exercises with approximately 50 participants, this man attracted the attention of everyone in the room by yelling profanities, shaking his fist, and threatening violence at the persons playing the roles of an arrogant, spoiled, young couple who had inadvertently crashed into his car during a high-speed chase of a burglar who, as a result, escaped. Jack agreed to be the protagonist in the next, or action, phase. In the psychodrama circle, a period of information gathering in a conversation between the protagonist and director produced the following history.

Jack said his father had hit him and his two brothers on many occasions throughout his youth, continuing until they were old enough to protect themselves. His mother stayed at home, cooked, cleaned, took care of the house, and tried to stay out of the way of her husband's alcoholic outbursts. She did not drink. Jack often fought in both grammar and high school. He had been a starting linebacker on the high school football team and was involved in several fights with opposing players over his three-year career. The linebacker position is at the very epicenter of the game, requiring intelligence and very focused and controlled violence. He had fought occasionally in the neighborhood, but didn't recall anyone having been seriously injured. Pressed on this point, he admitted having put a few people in the hospital who needed multiple sutures.

In "the Nam," Jack had seen over 50% of his original weapons platoon killed or severely wounded. Despite many engagements with the Viet Cong and North Vietnamese Army in jungle hamlets and fields, he emerged unscathed but for some minor lacerations and bruises. There was one particular incident, a battle in a small hamlet, that continued to bother him. After Vietnam, he was discharged, got married, was accepted into police training in another city, and had two children, a boy and a girl; after seven years, his wife divorced him. She moved to their original home with the children. Jack saw them infrequently, mostly on holidays. He remained on the city's police force, working his way up to detective. As his work on the police force was so "time-consuming," he did not have the children visit for summer vacations.

From the time he returned from the war, approximately 14 years earlier, he had slept with a loaded pistol, with the safety off, under his pillow. This, plus a lot of yelling and screaming and staying out all night "busting bad guys" contributed to his wife's deciding she wanted a divorce. Jack said he never struck anyone in his family, although one time he pushed his wife over a couch onto the floor.

Diagnosis and Assessment

Preliminary diagnosis, later confirmed, was Posttraumatic Stress Disorder, 309.81, according to the *Diagnostic and Statistical Manual of Mental Disorders* (*DSM-IV*) of the American Psychiatric Association (APA, 1994, p. 428):

1. The traumatic event was persistently re-experienced. In this case, the patient said he dreamed about it, often was awakened at night, and had thoughts of it while at work almost every day. He said there were times when he would become very angry or afraid if something reminded him of the event.
2. He said he "tried to avoid things" that reminded him of what happened, including going to veterans reunions, war movies, and contact with "slopes" (GI slang for Vietnamese people). His descriptions of his relationships with friends and family, as well as with acquaintances, also indicated detachment. He said he had a hard time loving anyone except maybe his kids. Jack thought he would die violently before 40.
3. He had difficulty falling and staying asleep, except when he drank, and had outbursts of anger. He was hypervigilant to the point of obsession and was frightened easily, though he immediately "covered it up," turning it into a stoic demeanor, anger, or, on occasion, rage.

Treatment Approach

During this interview in the warmup phase of the protagonist, Jack stopped abruptly, turned, and said he had been "carrying something" around and wanted to get rid of it. (He had witnessed another member of the group resolve a past trauma earlier in the session.) Jack shared with the director and the group that he had never told anyone about it, and said it was getting "too heavy." He was afraid he couldn't hold it much longer, that he was going to explode and "really hurt someone." On further questioning, Jack said he was afraid he was going to kill someone.

The director asked what he was carrying. Jack said he wasn't sure he could trust the director. When the director said that was okay, he didn't need to know, Jack reconsidered and, after several similar expressions of doubt and mistrust and with relaxed reassurance from the director, relented rather cautiously and began the following story.

Jack was on an extended search-and-destroy patrol with his platoon when they entered a small hamlet believed to be of Viet Cong sympathizers. At this point, the director asked him to pick several persons from the audience to act as his fellow soldiers. The director asked him to arrange them the way they looked on that day as they approached the hamlet, taking enough time to make sure this was right for him. The director asked Jack what the sky looked like, the trees, and the fields. He had some difficulty doing this, until he was asked what it smelled like. Olfactory memory often being the most lasting and powerful, this approach can be effective. It was in this instance.

Suddenly, Jack, stopped, turned, and asked, "Are you coming with me?" The director replied, "Of course." Jack's face changed, his eyes narrowed, and he said in a menacing tone, "If you don't stay with me, I'll kill you." This indicated that he was really beginning to "be" in the psychodrama; it was becoming real. In the author's experience, this does not often happen as dramatically or forcefully in talk therapy. The director put his arm through Jack's and said, "I'm here, pal. I'm not gonna leave no matter what," trying to ignore the threat. Jack reiterated his threat several times, partly to test the director's resolve to help and also because he was already in Vietnam and was making sure his lieutenant would not let him down. The director, experienced with similar threats, remained calm and supportive. Somewhat assured, they walked with the auxiliaries as a Marine weapons squad, into Vietnam, toward that hamlet, not back in time, but in the room, bringing the past into the here and now.

The hamlet was apparently deserted and quiet. Suddenly there was an eruption of gunfire from the tree line. Two or three Marines were hit and fell to the ground. Jack was looking at a buddy with whom he had been through boot camp hit in the face. He was killed instantly. He could see muzzle flashes from the trees. He hit the ground and started firing his M-79 grenade launcher, one grenade after another, into the trees, "blowing the shit out of everything and everyone I can."

As he was on the ground firing his weapon, he sensed someone behind him and turned to see a vague form. Amid the confusion, fear, and din of battle, he fired a grenade point blank, hit the person, whom he saw "sort of" explode, then quickly resumed firing into the tree line. He turned again, completely in role, and fired a grenade at another vague form. Some minutes later, when the firing stopped, he turned to see who had been behind him. Lying there were two young children with no weapons. Asked what he was feeling, he shrugged and said something like, "That's war. The little fuckin' slopes shouldn't have been there." The director asked Jack if he thought "these little slopes" were human beings. Jack started swearing again and screamed that they were stupid for sneaking up on him. This very powerful explosion of rage lasted a few minutes. Jack was given a large cushion and asked to hit and kick the children. He whacked away until he was spent. He was asked to shoot them with an imaginary pistol. He did this with great passion, then abruptly burst out in tears. He wept—deeply, almost uncontrollably, for perhaps five minutes. All this occurred with the help of auxiliaries, who crept up behind him, screamed, and fell dead as Jack relived the burden he had been carrying.

When he finished, the director asked if there was anything Jack needed from these children or anything he needed to say to them. He started crying again and said he was sorry and needed them to understand. He was instructed to reverse roles and become the children. After several reversals, and several additional techniques, while in the children's role he was able to say he forgave Jack, represented by an auxiliary. Of course, he was forgiving an externalized self-object. Reversed once more, the auxiliaries as the children forgave him. This gave Jack the direct experience of being forgiven, an externalization of the internal decision to forgive himself, thus breaking the years-long impasse. Jack was asked to explain to the children why he had done it. He found this difficult and was given a couple of doubles, who went behind him, put their hands on his shoulders, and, speaking as if they were he, gave their telic impressions. He denied some, accepted others, and suddenly turned and said, "It's my brother." Subsequently, we learned that when he was a boy of 9 or 10 years of age, while protecting himself from a blow from his father, he jerked suddenly, flailing his arms. In this act of self-protection, Jack accidentally hit his younger brother in the nose, making it bleed. There was blood everywhere. His father proceeded to give him a severe beating. Again we role-reversed and dealt with his brother forgiving him—really, his forgiving himself in the role of his brother. In both instances, in relation to his war experience in Vietnam and to his brother, it was important for Jack to be in his own role and to experience forgiveness.

The director requested that Jack return to his encounter with the civilians in the car during the group warmup, and to do it differently. After several reversals, he did make an appropriate approach and response. Jack made a promise to himself and to the group that he would continue in therapy, perhaps psychodrama, perhaps not; in any case, he would explore this scene and especially his relationship with his father. He also said he knew he would have to live with what he had done and that he would do so. Thus ended the action phase.

The sharing phase began. During this time, Jack thanked the director for staying with him and not letting him down, cried, and spontaneously apologized for threatening him. He said he would trust the director to be on the street with him anytime. Asked if this was unusual, he said he rarely, if ever, apologized. The larger group, all of them police, had a number of similar experiences they shared with Jack and the session ended.

Synopsis and Reflections

On follow-up three and then six months later, the patient reported almost complete cessation of dreams and reduced fear and resulting anger reactions in personal as well as work-related situations. He had joined a veterans group and was listening to and sharing stories with his fellow "grunts" (military slang for fellow soldiers). Jack had reestablished contact with his family, if only by telephone, started dating a woman he reported caring for, and had removed the gun from underneath his pillow, moving it to a closed case. He reported remaining in therapy for a few months and then terminating. No further follow-up was achieved. It would appear that what transpired in Jack's psychodrama directly impacted his everyday experience of self, restoring in him the self-respect he had lost in earlier incidents in which he accidentally hurt his brother and was blamed, and in which he had killed at least two children, mistaking them for soldiers.

RESEARCH REGARDING THE APPROACH

Moreno and his followers were not as focused on research as might be expected in a treatment milieu, particularly as measured against today's concern for establishing research-based treatment protocols. Nevertheless, a body of research does exist. The following is a sample across various diagnostic categories.

Randall and Stepath (1993) studied 53 inpatients (ages 62 to 87) on a geriatric psychiatric unit. The patients were exposed to two forms of reminiscence: a traditional verbal format and one using psychodramatic techniques. Participants in the psychodrama-oriented groups tended to perform on a higher level, and there was more leader activity in the psychodrama format.

Oezbay, Goeka, Oeztuerk, and Guengoer (1993) studied therapeutic factors in an adolescent psychodrama group consisting of 10 Turkish youth, ages 15 to 20. They investigated therapeutic effects (TEs), sex differences in rankings of the relative value of TEs, and changes in TEs during different periods of group development. The Therapeutic Factors List was administered after the tenth and twentieth sessions. Both at time 1 and time 2, the highest-ranked TEs for the entire group were insight, family reenactment, and existential factors. Rankings for the six females were consistent throughout, and change was seen for the four males.

Stattone (1993) studied the effects of psychodrama on prison inmates with adjustment problems in a behavior modification program. Explored were the effects of psychodrama group therapy on unacceptable behaviors of 22 prisoners. The subjects were participants in a structured residential behavior modification program and were assessed over a six-month postgroup time interval. The results suggested that psychodrama treatment techniques reduced unacceptable behavior and facilitated adjustment to life in prison.

Rezaiane, Mazumdar, and Sen (1997) studied the effects of psychodrama in changing the attitudes of depressed patients. They looked at the effectiveness of psychodrama in changing attitudes of 54 depressed male patients. Subjects were divided into three treatment groups of 18 each: a psychodrama group, a conventional psychiatric treatment group, and a combination therapy group. The Beck Depression Inventory (Beck, Ward, Mendelson, Mock, & Erbaugh, 1961) and the Sacks and Levey Sentence Completion Test (Persian adaptation) were administered before and 24 weeks after treatment to measure levels of depression and attitudes toward family, sex, interactive functions, and self before and after the clinical practice. Predictably, the psychodrama group was more effective in changing attitudes. However, the combination of psychodrama with conventional treatment produced the best results.

Mehdi, Sen, and Mazumdar (1997) also studied the usefulness of psychodrama with depressed patients. They evaluated the effectiveness of psychodrama in the treatment of 53 nonpsychotic, nonbipolar, primary depressed Iranian males ranging in age from 16 to 33. The patients were divided into three groups of equal size and received psychodrama group therapy, conventional psychiatric therapy, or a combination of both. Subjects completed the Beck Depression Inventory and the Minnesota Multiphasic Personality Inventory (short form) (Hathaway & McKinley, 1940) before treatment and six months later. Again, the combination of conventional and psychodrama treatments produced better results. Psychodrama treatment was more effective, contrasted with conventional treatment, when only one therapy was used.

Carbonelli and Partelno-Bareehmi (1999) studied psychodrama groups with middle school girls (ages 11 to 13) coping with trauma. Comparisons of treatment ($n = 12$) and control group ($n = 14$) members pre- and postintervention adjustment revealed significant decreases in participants' self-reported difficulties with withdrawn behavior and anxiety/depression. Interviews with participants reinforced the value of psychodrama group participation in the resolution of trauma and in increasing a sense of competence and self-efficacy.

Some of the various applications of psychodrama include work in prisons (Butman, 1977; Corsini, 1951; Ryan, 1976), work with schizophrenics (Bielanska, Cechniki, & Budzyna-Davidowski, 1991; Harrow, 1951, 1952; Mann, 1982), and family therapy (Baker, 1952; Barocas, 1972; Blatner, 1994). Compernolle (1981) wrote an important article recognizing Moreno's often ignored contribution to family theory and therapy. Moreno himself, along with his own family, wrote on the subject (J. L. Moreno, 1952; J. L. Moreno, Moreno, & Moreno, 1963). Zerka Moreno (1991) also has written on families. Another writer on psychodrama and family therapy is Perrott (1986).

SUMMARY

With literature and the arts at its foundations, psychodrama captures an essence Freud overlooked. Unlike many other therapies where the therapist's interpretation plays a central role, psychodrama views the patient as the truest, and even ultimate, interpretive source. This marked an important departure from the Freudian treatment approach, in which the final interpretation, especially of dreams, often rests with the therapist.

Self may be defined as the psychological and behavioral functions we control. In ancient times, creative power was seen as beyond human control and was attributed to the gods:

> Dante, while invoking the muses, was already calling on his own "high genius" (*alto ingegno*) and upon his "mind" (*mente*), which recorded what the poet saw, as though they were allies rather than his own capacities. But only the romantic movement formally introduced the decisive shift that so profoundly affected our modern thinking and according to which inspiration no longer comes from the outside but from inside, not from above, but from below. (Arnheim, 1962, p. 2)

Moreno emphasized the integral part creativity and spontaneity play in treatment. In psychodrama, this internal inspiration is revealed in the present, without editing or enhancing; although these are necessary for the film or play, they are not for the psychodrama. What is essential is spontaneity, which implies the permission to express all one cares to, and then to use this to construct alternative rehearsals for a better life.

REFERENCES

For an extensive bibliography on the Internet see www.albie.wcupa.edu/ttreadwell/tom.html

American Psychiatric Association. (1994). *Diagnostic and statistical manual of mental disorders* (4th ed.). Washington, DC: Author.

Aristotle. (1990). On poetics. In M. J. Adler (Ed.), *Great books of the Western world* (Vol. 8, p. 684). Chicago: University of Chicago Press.

Arnheim, R. (1962). *The genesis of a painting: Picasso's Guernica.* Berkeley: University of California Press.

Baker, A. A. (1952). The misfit family: A psychodramatic technique used in a therapeutic community. *British Journal of Medical Psychology, 25,* 235–243.

Barocas, H. (1972). Psychodrama techniques in training police in family crisis intervention. *Group Psychotherapy and Psychodrama, 25,* 30–31.

Beck, A. T., Ward, C. H., Mendelson, M., Mock, J., & Erbaugh, J. (1961). An inventory for measuring depression. *Archives of General Psychiatry, 4,* 561–571.

Berne, E. (1964). *Games people play.* New York: Grove Press.

Berne, E. (1971). *What do you do after you say hello? The psychology of human destiny.* New York: Grove Press.

Bielanska, A., Cechniki, A., & Budzyna-Davidowski, P. (1991). Drama therapy as a means of rehabilitation for schizophrenic patients: Our impressions. *American Journal of Psychotherapy, 45,* 566–575.

Blatner, H. A. (1973). *Acting-in: Practical applications of psychodramatic methods.* New York: Springer.

Blatner, H. A. (1988). *Foundations of psychodrama: History, theory and practice.* New York: Springer.

Blatner, H. A. (1994). Psychodramatic methods in family therapy. In C. E. Schaefer & L. J. Carey (Eds.), *Family play therapy.* Northvale, NJ: Aronson.

Blatner, H. A. (1998, August). *Theoretical foundations of psychodrama.* IAGP Conference presentation, London. Retrieved April 9, 1999, from www.blatner.com/adam/pdtheory.htm

Bronowski, J. (1973). *The ascent of man.* Boston: Little, Brown.

Burrow, T. (1937). *The neurosis of man: An introduction to a science of human behavior.* London: Routledge & Kegan Paul.

Butman, H. (1977). Role reversal in a Soviet prison camp. *Group Psychotherapy, Psychodrama and Sociometry, 30,* 155–162.

Carbonelli, D. M., & Partelno-Bareehmi, C. (1999). Psychodrama groups for girls coping with trauma. *International Journal of Group Psychotherapy, 49*(3), 285–306.

Compernolle, T. (1981). J. L. Moreno: An unrecognized pioneer of family therapy. *Family Process, 20,* 331–335.

Corsini, R. J. (1951). The method of psychodrama in prison. *Group Psychotherapy, 3,* 321–326.

Harrow, G. S. (1951). Effects of psychodrama group therapy on role behavior of schizophrenic patients. *Group Psychotherapy, 3,* 316–320.

Harrow, G. S. (1952). Psychodrama group therapy: Its effects upon the role behavior of schizophrenic patients. *Group Psychotherapy, 5,* 120–170.

Hathaway, S. R. & McKinley, J. C. (1940). A Multiphasic Personality Schedule (Minnesota): I. Construction of the schedule. *Journal of Psychology, 10,* 249–254.

Hoffer, E. (1951). *The true believer.* New York: Harper & Row.

Jacobs, A. (1987). Autocratic power. *Transactional Analysis Journal, 17,* 59–71.

Jacobs, A. (1990). *Nationalism, 20,* 221–228.

Jacobs, A. (1991). Autocracy: Groups, organizations, nations, and players. *Transactional Analysis Journal, 21,* 199–206.

Jacobs, A. (1994). Theory as ideology: Reparenting and thought reform. *Transactional Analysis Journal, 24*(1), 39–55.

Korzybski, A. (1933). *Science and sanity: An introduction to non-Aristotelian systems and general semantics.* Lakeville, CT: International Non-Aristotelian Library.

Kuhn, T. (1963). *The structure of scientific revolutions.* Chicago: University of Chicago Press.

Mann, S. J. (1982). The integration of psychodrama and family therapy in the treatment of schizophrenia. *Family Therapy, 9,* 215–225.

Mead, G. H. (1964). *On social psychology: Selected papers* (A. Straus, Ed.). Chicago: University of Chicago Press. (Original work published 1934)

Mehdi, P. R., Sen, A. K., & Mazumdar, D. P. (1997). The usefulness of psychodrama in the treatment of depressed patients. *Indian Journal of Clinical Psychology, 24*(1), 82–96.

Moffett, D. E. (2000). *Therapeutic theatre with personality-disordered substance abusers.* Retrieved March 24, 2001, from www.apa.org/journals/webref.html

Moreno, J. L. (1934). *Who shall survive? A new approach to the problem of human interrelations.* Washington, DC: Nervous and Mental Diseases.

Moreno, J. L. (1952). Sociodrama of a family conflict. *Group Psychotherapy, 5,* 20–37.

Moreno, J. L. (1953). *Who shall survive? Foundations of sociometry, group psychotherapy and sociodrama.* Beacon, NY: Beacon House.

Moreno, J. L. (1959). *Psychodrama: Foundations of psychotherapy* (Vol. 2). Beacon, NY: Beacon House. (Original work published 1946)

Moreno, J. L. (1972). *Psychodrama: First volume* (4th ed.). Beacon, NY: Beacon House.

Moreno, J. L. (1983). *The theatre of spontaneity.* Beacon, NY: Beacon House. (Original work published 1947)

Moreno, J. L., & Moreno, Z. T. (1969). *Psychodrama: Third volume: Action therapy and principles of practice.* Beacon, NY: Beacon House.

Moreno, J. L., Moreno, Z. T., & Moreno, J. (1963). The first psychodramatic family. *Group Psychotherapy, 16,* 203–249.

Moreno, Z. T. (1959). A survey of psychodramatic techniques. *Group Psychotherapy, 12,* 5–14.

Moreno, Z. T. (1965). Psychodramatic rules, techniques and adjunctive methods. *Group Psychotherapy, 18,* 73–86.

Moreno, Z. T. (1991). Time, space, reality and the family: Psychodrama with a blended (reconstituted) family. In P. Holmes & M. Karp (Eds.), *Psychodrama: Inspiration and technique*. London: Tavistock/Routledge.

Oezbay, H., Goeka, E., Oeztuerk, E., & Guengoer, S. (1993). Therapeutic factors in an adolescent psychodrama group. *Journal of Group Psychotherapy, Psychodrama and Sociometry, 46*(1), 3–11.

Perls, F. (1969). *Gestalt therapy verbatim*. New York: Bantam Books.

Perrott, L. A. (1986). Using psychodramatic techniques in structural family therapy. *Contemporary Family Therapy: An International Journal, 8*, 279–290.

Randall, M. B., & Stepath, S. A. (1993). Psychodrama and reminiscence for the psychiatric patient. *Journal of Group Psychotherapy, Psychodrama and Sociometry, 45*(4), 139–148.

Rezaiane, M. P., Mazumdar, D. P., & Sen, A. K. (1997). The effectiveness of psychodrama in changing the attitudes among depressed patients. *Journal of Personality and Clinical Studies, 13*(1/2), 19–23.

Ryan, P. R. (1976). Theater as prison therapy. *Drama Review, 20*, 31–42.

Spolin, V. (1963). *Improvisation for the theater*. Evanston, IL: Northwestern University Press.

Stattone, T. M. (1993). The effects of psychodrama on inmates within a structured residential behavior modification program. *Journal of Group Psychotherapy, Psychodrama and Sociometry, 46*(1), 24–31.

Temerlin, M., & Temerlin, J. (1982). Psychotherapy cults: An iatrogenic perversion. *Psychotherapy: Theory Research and Practice, 19*, 131–141.

Yablonsky, L., & Enneis, J. M. (1956). Psychodrama theory and practice. In F. Fromm-Reichman & J. L. Moreno (Eds.), *Progress in psychotherapy* (Vol. 1). New York: Grune & Stratton.

CHAPTER 22

Transactional Analysis

ROBERT F. MASSEY, GORDON HEWITT, AND CARLO MOISO

HISTORY OF THEORETICAL APPROACH

Relying on clinical intuition and emphasizing social processes, Eric Berne developed transactional analysis (TA) as a model of personal, interpersonal, and organizational dynamics applicable to psychotherapy, education, and group development (R. Massey, 1981). TA encompasses theories of personality, communication, social relations, and psychopathology. Berne's parents' families had immigrated to Canada from Poland and Russia (Cheney, 1971). Born in 1910 in Montreal, Eric Lennard Bernstein sometimes accompanied his father, a community physician, on house calls while riding a sleigh in the snow. He was devastated at 9 when his father, only 38, died of tuberculosis. Eric's mother supported him and his younger sister as an editor and writer and encouraged Eric to study medicine; he eventually earned his MD and Master of Surgery. He completed a two-year residency at the Psychiatric Clinic of Yale University School of Medicine. About 1938, he obtained U.S. citizenship and shortened his name to Berne. In 1941, he became an analysand of Paul Federn at the New York Psychoanalytic Institute. World War II interrupted his analysis, and from 1943 to 1946 Berne served in the U.S. Army as a psychiatrist. During the last two years of his service, he led therapy groups on the Brigham City base and for civilians in nearby Ogden, Utah. Following the war, Berne moved to Carmel, California, and resumed analysis with Erik Erikson. He held clinical and academic appointments in the San Francisco area and developed private practices both there and in Carmel. He protected his writing time by secluding himself in a cottage behind his house. He reserved Fridays and weekends for writing and Friday nights for playing poker.

Berne (1939, 1959a, 1959b, 1960a, 1960b) wrote a series of early articles on cultural issues, particularly on psychiatry in the South Sea islands. Berne (1947/1976) composed his first book, *The Mind in Action* (1947), issued in the second edition as *A Layman's Guide to Psychiatry and Psychoanalysis* (1976), with the aim of enriching popular understanding about these two areas. In 1950, Berne initiated a clinical seminar that became the San Francisco Social Psychiatry Seminar, later incorporated to fund the *Transactional Analysis Bulletin*. From the early 1950s on, he conducted an evening clinical seminar in Monterey, California. When his 1956 application for acknowledgment as a psychoanalyst was rejected with the suggestion that he engage in three or four more years of analysis and training, Berne experienced great disappointment, but determined to improve psychoanalysis. By the end of 1957, he had conceptualized the fundamental notions for his new approach: transactional analysis (Berne, 1957a, 1957b, 1958). In *Transactional Analysis in Psychotherapy*, Berne (1961) offered his most scholarly presentation of the major constructs of his theory. In *The Structure and Dynamics of Organizations and Groups*, Berne (1963) delved into the inner workings of groups and organizations through an intriguing case study about the dynamics of an esoteric group as viewed through the eyes of a social-psychiatric observer and added the only major construct (group imago) not presented in his 1961 primer.

In 1963, Berne gave a paper to the American Psychiatric Association and in subsequent years led a panel on TA. By 1970, the audience had increased to over 500 participants. *Games People Play* (Berne, 1964) was probably his most famous book. In 1964, Berne and his colleagues established the International Transactional Analysis Association (ITAA), a group that became truly international in the 1980s with increasing membership in Europe, Latin America, Asia, New Zealand, and Australia, and which publishes the *Transactional Analysis Journal*. In *Principles of Group Treatment*, Berne (1966) demonstrated his mastery of group therapy. In *Sex in Human Loving*, Berne (1970) rather humorously explored sexuality, identity, and sexual interactions. He was in a hospital correcting the galley proofs of the manuscript for this book when he died of a heart attack on July 15, 1970. In *What Do You Say after You Say Hello?*, published posthumously, Berne (1972) focused on identity (script) formation. (A legally distinct Training and Certification Council oversees training standards, written and oral examinations for transactional analysts worldwide.) Berne was also honored as a Fellow of the American Psychiatric Association and as a diplomate of the American Board of Psychiatry and Neurology.

Several participants in the San Francisco Social Psychiatry Seminar spurred the evolution of TA (Crossman, 1966; Dusay, 1977b; English, 1969, 1971, 1972, 1976; Karpman, 1968; Steiner, 1966). Steiner (1972, 1973, 1971/1974) advocated radical psychiatry: a return of psychotherapy to nonmedical origins, a realization that problems arise from interpersonal alienation, and efforts to enable people to change their contexts. Muriel James (1973, 1981b) focused on the spiritual core as a dimension of personality and social relations. She offered a TA perspective on marriage (1979) and an approach to self-reparenting (1981a). With Dorothy Jongeward she coauthored *Born to Win* (1971), which has been translated into many languages. Barnes (1977) designated this group the *classical school* (Dusay, 1977b). Robert and Mary Goulding (1978; M. Goulding & Goulding, 1979; R. Goulding, 1977) developed a second, *redecision school*.

Jacqui Schiff (1977) and her colleagues (1975) comprise a third, *cathexis school*. They viewed passivity (e.g., overadapting, violence) in thinking, feeling, and interacting as interfering with social functioning. Grandiosity or distortions of reality provide justifications for passivity. The resulting internal distress and behavior disorders stem from symbiosis or unresolved dependencies. Games represent "attempts to reenact symbiotic relationships that the children did not resolve with their parents, or . . . an angry reaction to those relationships" (p. 7). Passivity is perpetuated through discounting (e.g., the significance of problems or change options). Schiff (1970, 1977) and her colleagues (1975; Childs-Gowell, 1979) engaged in reparenting techniques with schizophrenics. They believed that they could decommission (decathect) the original internalized messages and models in the patients and provide resocialization in intensive, long-term treatment regimes in which therapists acted as surrogate parents for the patients, who were led into deep regression. These procedures led to some claims of damage and abuse and unresolved ethics charges with the ITAA. Despite the ethical controversies surrounding Schiff (Jacobs, 1994) and her colleagues in the United States, India, and Great Britain, the theory, rather than questionable practices, contains valuable insights for individual, couple, and family systems assessment (R. Massey, 1986) and for human development (Childs-Gowell, 1979; Levin, 1980).

Systemic Thinking

Berne (1961, 1963, 1966) referred to early systemic thinkers and perceived some compatibility with his ideas. He (1972) noted the impact of family drama and culture on scripting processes. Whether Berne would have followed up on the systemic implications of his theory had he lived longer remains speculation. Within a TA framework, Joines (1977) proposed working with families. Erskine (1982) focused on interlocking racket systems among family members. McClendon (1977) and Kadis and McClendon (1981, 1990) incorporated and adapted the Gouldings' (R. Goulding & Goulding, 1978; M. Goulding & Goulding, 1979) redecision therapy for individuals in their work with families. Boyd and Boyd (1981a) explored the levels of a couple relationship. Bader and Pearson (1988, 2000) drew on Mahler to delineate stages of couple formation. Dusay and Dusay (1989) developed a treatment model of couples based on ego state functioning. R. Massey (1985; R. Massey & Massey, 1995) integrated TA with multigenerational, structural, and strategic paradoxical approaches for working with families, couples (1989a, 1989e), individuals (1995), paradox (1983, 1986), and children (1989d; R. Massey & Massey, 1988; S. Massey & Massey, 1989).

Other developments in TA theory include Novellino's (1984, 1985, 1987, 1990, 1991; Novellino et al., 1998; Novellino & Moiso, 1990) and Moiso's (1985) incorporation of psychoanalytic processes, particularly transference and countertransference, while viewing Berne as more closely allied to an attachment epistemology than to the Freudian ideology of the psyche moved by the libido. Groder (1977) addressed working with inmates from a multiple-perspective approach. Erskine (1993, 1996, 1997; Erskine & Moursund, 1988) integrated concepts of self psychology with TA in emphasizing attunement and the nature of the relationship between therapist and client as central in a change process. They have concentrated on personality disorders, as have Hargaden and Sills (2001) in relation to borderline disturbances. Stern (1984) provided a collection of articles primarily by European authors.

MAJOR THEORETICAL CONSTRUCTS

Experience of Self, Ego States

Berne's theory of TA stems from and revolves around his formulations on ego states. Thirteen years of research on group therapy focusing on ego states showed it was a rapid and effective treatment with patients with rather difficult psychopathologies and a method easy to teach (Berne, 1957a). Berne (1961) acknowledged the influences of Penfield's (1952; Penfield & Jasper, 1954) experiments on memory and reactivation through electrical stimulation of the cortex, Federn's (1952) phenomenological approach to discrete ego states, and Weiss's (1950) observations on the retention of former experiences in personality. Berne (1957a) related a story by a lawyer patient. An 8-year-old boy assisting him at a dude ranch replied that he was a boy and not a cowpoke when the lawyer unsaddling a horse said, "Thanks, cowpoke!" (p. 99). The lawyer commented, "Sometimes I feel that I'm not really a lawyer, I'm just a little boy" (p. 99). Early observations like these led Berne to distinguish types of ego states.

Structural Analyses of Ego States

As patients changed postures, mannerisms, facial expressions, and tones of voice, Berne (1961) documented in detailed case illustrations that the experiences they communicated seemed to evidence different origins. Some comments reflected autistic thinking, archaic fears and anticipations, and primary process thinking as they revealed relics from the past. Some statements contained reasonable reality testing and embodied rational problem solving in the present. Other remarks resembled attitudes and actions of significant others. These observations prompted Berne to develop a tripartite classification framework. He attributed fixations or repetitions of earlier personal developmental experiences to archaeopsychic ego states; adaptations to current reality to neopsychic ego states; and imitations and internalizations of significant others to exteropsychic ego states. For Berne, these three sets of ego states constitute the structure of personality. Berne (1961, 1966) called their phenomenological and operational manifestations Child, Adult, and Parent ego states. In his definitions of the types of ego states, Berne (1961) characterized each type of ego state as a set of feelings, attitudes, and behavior patterns (pp. 75, 76, 77). He differentiated the "Parental ego state ... [as] resembl[ing] those of a parental figure" (p. 75), the "Adult ego state ... [as] an autonomous set ... which [is] adapted to the current reality" (p. 76), and the "Child ego state ... [as] relics of the individual's own childhood" (p. 77). Ego states have commonly become known by their more familiar terms, yet the more formal terms more aptly convey the theoretical and clinical richness of the constructs.

In describing ego states, Berne (1961) desired "to denote states of mind and their related patterns of behavior as they occur in nature" (p. 30) and not abstract constructs. Consequently, he differentiated ego states from Freud's psychic organs of id, ego, and superego. He regarded the "Freudian agencies ... [as] inferential concepts, while ego states are experiential and social realities" (p. 220). An individual experiences ego states; they "are not handy ideas or interesting neologisms, but refer to phenomena based on actual realities" (p. 34). Berne also distinguished ego states from roles: A person plays a role, and exists in an ego state. In elaborating on energy flow, boundaries, and sense of self, he focused on the dynamic processes of ego states. The *boundaries* between energized ego states remain relatively impermeable, yet energy can flow between them. The ego state with the current *cathexis* of unbound and free energy exercises executive power. The ego state in which a person chooses to invest free energy feels like the real self, a "completely cathected coherent state of mind" (p. 71). Executive power and feeling like real self can coincide and yield a sense of congruence.

When an archaeopsychic or exteropsychic ego state covertly or unconsciously intrudes into the neopsyche, *contamination* occurs. The intrusion of an exteropsychic rigidity appears as a prejudice and an archaeopsychic irrational belief as a delusion. Hallucinations generally represent exhibitions of exteropsychic ego states as neopsychic functioning is decommissioned and archaeopsychic ego states involving fright are activated. Psychopathology may also stem from *exclusion*, "a stereotyped, predictable attitude ... steadfastly maintained as long as possible in the face of any threatening situation" (1961, p. 44). The excluding Parent ego state may emerge in a compensated schizophrenic as a defense against archaeopsychic confusion. A person in the grips of excluding Adult relies almost solely on intellectualization and suffers from a lack of spontaneity, charm, and nurturance. Individuals with excluding Child ego states include narcissistic impulsive personalities and active schizophrenics who block off rational, judging, and nurturing ego states while persisting in seduction or confusion.

Second- and Third-Order Structural Analyses
Berne (1961) delineated developmental influences and stages by analyzing the evolution and structures of ego states in second- and third-order analyses. Through higher-order structural analyses, the complexity and nuances of earlier development become evident and available for therapeutic intervention. Second- and third-order structural analyses of the archaeopsyche uncover the nascent capacities for retaining very early images and affective experiences, for data processing at a survival level, and for internalizing primary parental influences.

In the second-order structure of the exteropsyche imitation, identification with, introjection of, or, in general, internalization of feelings, attitudes, and behaviors of parental figures are decipherable. Because parental figures internalize their exteropsychic ego states from their parental figures, the second-order exteropsyche, or Parent in the Parent, involves incorporating grandparent influences. In line with this logic, third-order structure of the exteropsyche allows for tracing the impact of great-grandparents. This exploration quickly becomes quite complex, but also more realistic in terms of actual systemic processes. Such analyses become even more complicated when we realize that each person internalizes, in reality or imagination, at least two sets of influences, maternal and paternal. The actual tracing of these multiple dynamics can occur when the information is accessed as Berne (1959a, 1959b) was able to observe among Fiji Islanders who still lived in the same location as their ancestors and maintained a continuous story tradition.

Second-order structural analysis of the neopsyche reveals the desirable qualities of an integrated Adult on three levels. When integrated neopsychic ego states embody the charm and openness reminiscent of childhood and feelings of responsibility and compassion toward other persons, they belong to the *pathos* dimension of Adult ego states. When these ego states manifest "moral qualities which are universally expected of people who undertake grown-up responsibilities, such as ... courage, sincerity, loyalty, reliability ... [they convey] a world-wide *ethos*" (Berne, 1961, p. 195; italics added) in Adult ego states. And the integrated Adult ego states exhibit sound data-processing and problem-solving functioning or *logos*.

Functional Analyses of Ego States
Berne (1961, 1972) added functional or descriptive analysis and terminology to his descriptions of ego state functioning. He distinguished between ways of exhibiting exteropsychic and archaeopsychic ego states. Prejudicial Parent ego states, or critical Parent, denote "seemingly arbitrary non-rational attitudes or parameters, usually prohibitive in nature" (1961, p. 76). Nurturing Parent ego states connote sympathy for another person. Either set can be culturally syntonic or dystonic, and pass for normal behavior or seem out of kilter with social norms. Adapted Child ego states appear as compliance or withdrawal. Natural, or free, Child ego states include autonomous behaviors showing "the ascendancy of archaic mental processes" (p. 78), as in rebellion or self-indulgence. Berne (1961) detailed the structures of ego states and initiated discussion of their functional aspects. Berne (1963, 1964, 1966) mentioned structural terms, but did not elaborate on them further. In Berne (1970, 1972), the structural nomenclature all but disappeared. John Dusay (1977a) designed the egogram to depict the distribution of energy in the functional ego states.

The conceptualization of ego states forms the foundation for TA theory. The connotations and nuances of understanding, formulating, and applying other TA constructs pivot around the particular definitions and uses of ego states.

This issue lies at the heart of theoretical controversies. Debate has ranged over the meaning and functioning of ego states (Clarkson & Gilbert, 1988; Drego, 1983a; Erskine, 1988; Erskine, Clarkson, Goulding, Groder, & Moiso, 1988; Ohlsson, 1988). This bears important implications for emphasizing research-based professional development versus popularization of TA; Berne was able to engage in both. Berne (1958) introduced structural analysis, elaborated on it in 1961, and added functional analysis, which has sometimes predominated over structural analysis in simplified presentations. Functional or descriptive analyses of ego states, when used alone, constrict the range of experiences and developmental processes available for diagnosis and treatment. Structural analyses of ego states expand the scope of assessment and clinical intervention to include epigenetic dynamics. Enlarging on Berne's heuristic inclinations and fully integrating structural analyses of ego states with relationship and script analyses enrich theory as the basis for clinical practice and research (R. Massey, 1989c, 1990b, 1991). Structural analyses of ego states better reflect the complexity and multidimensionality of actually embodied and lived human experiencing and intersubjectivity.

SOCIAL EMPHASIS

Consideration of the social dimension of human existence pervaded Berne's thinking and writing. He (1964) regarded TA as "a branch of social psychiatry" (p. 51). Social psychiatry revolves around transactions and involves studying the "inner causes and the motives that result in specific transactional stimuli and responses" (1963, p. 176) and the "events which arouse uncomfortable feelings in members of social aggregations" (p. 40). Berne viewed social psychiatry as a branch of social psychology. Later (1964), he distinguished the two, characterizing social psychiatry as more focused on personal history and as less neutral because "some implicit or explicit judgment is passed on the 'healthiness' of the games studied" (p. 51).

Berne offered an innovative appreciation of both internal experiencing and social interaction. The emergence and expressions of ego states occur in social contexts. Ego states involve responding to and internalizing social dynamics. He built his theory of communication on the experiencing of ego states in interpersonal encounters. His emphasis on the social dimension became apparent in his analysis of transactions, group imagoes, and life positions. This trend continued into his conceptualization of motivation and the development of life plans or scripts.

Transactions

Berne (1961, 1963) advanced understanding of everyday and therapeutic communication by analyzing types of transactions. In a complementary transaction, the participants exchange a stimulus and a response between the same types of ego states. For example, one person asks a factual question, and the other answers in a factual manner (both are using neopsychic ego states). If, however, the second person responds from a type of ego state different from the one that the first person directed the question at, then a crossed transaction has occurred. The first person becomes disconcerted. This pattern can either upset a previously satisfying conversation or redirect an unpleasant one.

Transactions may take place on two levels simultaneously: the social and the psychological. The social level involves what is seemingly transpiring on the surface, but, simultaneously, an ulterior, psychological communication is also transmitted. Ulterior transactions occur in both angular and duplex communications (Berne, 1963, 1972). In an angular transaction, the first person offers both a social and an ulterior stimulus. If the stimulus is successful, the second person responds from the ego state at which the psychological message was aimed. Angular transactions commonly occur in business situations to entice potential buyers to spend beyond their means. Counterparadoxical therapeutic interventions embody angular transactions (R. Massey, 1983, 1986).

Group Imago
Berne showed the relevance of cognitive dynamics in social processes through his construct of group imago. Berne (1963, 1966) used the term group imago to refer to the expectations a person brings to social and group interactions based on developmental experiences. Like a cognitive map, each individual forms a group imago through early socialization. Subsequently, one seeks others who will fulfill these transactional, functional, and need-gratifying roles. The group imago may be expanded to make room for new interaction partners and may include nonfamily members and larger systems. The roles need to fit with one's life plan. When discrepancies occur between reality and the anticipated responses based on one's group imago, one either revises the provisional group imago or attempts to change the group. In his construct of group imago, Berne offered an explanation of how cognitive structures, affective responses, and social processes intertwine in perceptual sets.

Existential Life Positions
Berne (1964, 1966, 1972) proposed that each person selects existential life positions. These contribute to psychological stability and guide interaction possibilities. This conceptualization parallels Klein's (1975) orientation regarding the cognitive-emotional residuals of the primary ego object/other object relationship, which globally permeate an individual frame of reference and form the basis of a person's life plan. These positions reflect interpretations in early developmental situations about how to value self and other(s). Fully formulated belief-generating decisions sound like "Women are (not) reliable," "Men are (not) compassionate," "I am (not) trustworthy." Each person combines the basic convictions about I/we, I am/you are okay/not-okay. These two-handed positions also can encompass three-handed positions (e.g., I am okay, you are not-okay, they are okay). The variations on this schema become apparent when substituting the array of personality attributes, social preferences, and prejudices for okay and not-okay (e.g., I a Buddhist am okay, you a Muslim are okay, they as Christians are okay). Ernst (1971, 1973) and Kertesz (1978) have expanded on use of the "OK corral."

MOTIVATION

Berne (1961, 1966) surmised that human motivation, referred to as a "hunger" (1966, p. 230), derives from multiple sources. Babies are born with *stimulus hunger*. Berne (1961) postulated that an ongoing alteration of sensory stimulation lies at the basis of the human capacity to preserve coherent ego states and cited the research of Spitz (1945) on physical and emotional deprivation. As physical contact becomes reserved for special circumstances, stimulus hunger is sublimated into *recognition hunger*. Berne (1966) termed a "unit of recognition... a stroke" (p. 230). Strokes can be positive or negative, unconditional or conditional (Steiner, 1970). People seem intolerant of extended boredom or of isolation and experience *structure hunger*.

Time Structures
Berne (1961, 1964, 1966) delineated six ways of structuring time. Boyd and Boyd (1980b, 1980c) suggested play as a seventh time structure. First, in *withdrawal*, a person may daydream, fantasize, remain inhibited, or engage in constructive and pleasurable projects alone. Second, *rituals* represent formalized recognition (e.g., "Hello"). Third, in *pastimes*, individuals discuss commonplace topics, such as favorite recreational involvements, in somewhat predictable ways. Fourth, in *activity*, interactions

center around the demands and responsibilities of work, or play for children.

Fifth, in *games*, the participants interact with concealed motivations. Whereas persons use an "operation ... for a specific, stated purpose" (Berne, 1964, p. 48), in a game each actor maneuvers the other in an ulterior way to secure an initially unstated goal and satisfaction. These sequences follow predictable rules and patterns. Berne (1961, 1964, 1966, 1972) devoted extensive attention to games. He initially analyzed games as duplex transactions involving two levels of communication. On the social dimension, two people engage in a seemingly direct exchange. However, a psychological or ulterior level is co-occurring. The true meaning of games emanates from the psychological level, which controls the process. In the relationship game of "If it weren't for you," the social dynamics revolve around control and inhibition. On the psychological level, the participants are protected from phobias and fears about closeness and intimacy because of their overt mutual antagonisms. In the game of "Alcoholic," the ulterior level hinges not on the drinking itself but on the hangover phase in which the substance abuser is mired in self-castigation and receives a scolding from a significant other. This exemplifies that "games ... are designed to defend ... [the existential life] positions" (1966, p. 270).

In his last book, Berne (1972) proposed a *game formula* consisting of (1) *con*, a maneuver to engage another in a series of transactions with a concealed motivation and thus ulterior communication; (2) *gimmick*, a second person's vulnerability; (3) *switch*, when the first individual makes a statement or behaves to convey or act on an ulterior message; (4) the second person then feels *crossed* up or confused; and (5) both *collect psychological payoffs* of successfully exploiting or of being taken advantage of. In the game of "Yes, but," the first person puts forth a query, and a second person offers help or reassurance. The switch occurs when the first person, acting on ulterior motivation, communicates that the response proved inadequate. The second person can then feel perplexed. Both then gain familiar feelings of seeking attention without gaining satisfaction and of a sense of inadequacy or frustration.

Karpman (1968) proposed the *drama triangle* as a means to conceptualize, diagram, and intervene in games. A drama triangle involves three roles: persecutor, rescuer, and victim. Drama-triangle analysis offers a graphic way to characterize the processes implicated in ulterior communications, the switches, and payoffs of games. For instance, the game of "Alcoholic" requires five roles: (1) the central role of alcoholic; (2) the persecutor; (3) the rescuer; (4) the patsy, dummy, or at times agitator, who offers the monetary means of obtaining drink; and (5) the connection who provides the supplies. The process of alcoholism involves more than imbibing fermented juices. All become accustomed to their roles. The roles can rotate. Generally feeling like a victim who can drown sorrows with drinking buddies, an alcoholic can become a belligerent persecutor, or can serve as a rescuer in recovery as a sponsor for another person. Switches in communication occur when a significant other alternates between righteously condemning the alcoholic and protecting the abusive drinker from social and legal consequences. The family suffused by alcoholism who treats community agencies in adversarial ways takes on the role of persecutor, or, concomitantly, the role of victim, when continually in need of irresponsibly used resources. Choy (1990) proposed healthy alternative roles as conducive to constructive rather than game transactions. Assertiveness replaces persecution, helpful in place of rescuing, and vulnerable instead of victim. To use Karpman's drama triangle in societal analysis, Clarkson (1987) added a fourth role, the bystander, a passive individual who does not intervene when appropriate (Jacobs, 1987). Straker (2001) disputed the validity of the designation bystander and asserted that passive acceptance more accurately results in being a beneficiary in social exploitation.

In the sixth time structure, *intimacy*, "a genuine interlocking of personalities" (Berne, 1961, p. 86) or union occurs between two people. Intimacy involves spontaneous, candid awareness, and clear perception of another person, evoking affection, spurring positive feelings and generally mutuality. Intimacy happens in unguarded moments unhindered by social programming. In intimacy, two or more individuals express meaningful emotions without reservations or ulterior motives (Berne, 1963; Boyd & Boyd, 1980a). Berne (1961, 1964, 1966) regarded pastimes and games as preliminary engagements or as substitutes for real living and as play. Only intimacy, frequently fleeting and unsustainable, fully satisfies the hunger for stimulation, recognition, and structure.

Advantages of Transactional Patterns
Building on Freud's (1905/1953) notion of gains from illness, Berne (1961, 1964) made explicit the levels of advantages that motivate individuals. The *biological advantage* stems from satisfying tactile needs or stimulus hunger. The *existential advantage* derives from confirming one's belief system. The *internal psychological advantage* concerns the use and regulation of psychological energy. A game payoff stabilizes psychic equilibrium; interruption of games, without curing the life plan that fosters them, arouses rage or existential despair. The *external psychological advantage* involves either satisfaction through relationship opportunities or protection from a feared object or situation. The *internal social advantage* arises from preferred ways of structuring time and can lead to direct satisfaction or devising reasons to avoid unappealing situations. The *external social advantage* accrues when the participants are comfortable and pleased with engaging in specific transactions. Berne explicated how these advantages may be obtained in games. In the game of "If it weren't for you," a partner's annoyance response reminds the recipient of distressing physical contact early in life (biological), reinforces the belief that all men/women are insensitive (existential), prevents the feeling of fears (internal psychological), blocks having to encounter a noxious situation (external psychological), assists in avoiding a not-desired situation (internal social), and enables one to converse with others about the negatives of one's partner (external social).

Autonomy
Berne (1964, 1972) espoused the attainment of autonomy—the "release or recovery of three capacities: awareness, spontaneity, and intimacy" (1964, p. 178)—as a primary goal motivating individuals. He exalted autonomy and subsumed intimacy as one of its characteristics. He championed liberation from "individual parental, social, and cultural background ... the demands of contemporary society at large, and finally the advantages derived from one's immediate social circle have to be partly or wholly sacrificed" (pp. 182–183). Orten (1973) questioned the sufficiency of Berne's stress on autonomy and urged consideration of the structural level and collective behavior. Baute (1979) cautioned against the adequacy of autonomy and intimacy as more than a middle-class tranquilizer and advocated a sense of community, responsiveness and accountability to others. Batts (2001) urged addressing institutional levels in practicing multiculturalism, which implies both nontarget and target persons dealing with oppression on several dimensions. Berne's position on autonomy strikes a particularly Western chord and does not accord with the twin emphases of Adler (1956, 1964) and Angyal (1965) and of contemporary research supporting the optimal development of both self and healthy attachments (Clauss, 1995; Kerr & Bowen, 1988).

Rackets, Substitute Feelings
Berne (1972) noted that families are inclined to favor certain emotions and expressions of

feelings, especially when under stress. He termed these preferred feelings "rackets" (p. 137). Reexperiencing them constitutes the payoffs in games. Racket feelings camouflage and substitute for real feelings (English, 1971, 1972). English (1977) emphasized that individuals seek familiar strokes and will cross transactions if that secures continuing the flow of these racket strokes. Ernst (1973) connected racket feelings with life positions and the quadrants (see Figure 22.1) in the "OK corral" (Ernst, 1971).

Drivers
Kahler (1977) identified five transactional processes in which a communication both sends and can be received as an invitation to reinforce customary interaction patterns. These "drivers" involve both internal discounting of positive capacities and are behaviorally manifested. The five drivers include Try Hard, Please Me (valuing the other's response more than one's own), Be Perfect, Hurry Up, and Be Strong (do not display emotions).

Patterns of Living, Scripts

Berne (1958, 1961, 1972) observed coherent life patterns, called scripts. He construed a life plan as a "transference drama...a complex set of transactions, by nature recurrent, but not necessarily recurring, since a complete performance may require a lifetime...which determines the destiny and identity of an individual" (1958, p. 156). He defined script as "an ongoing program, developed in early childhood under parental influence, which directs the individual's behavior in the most important aspects

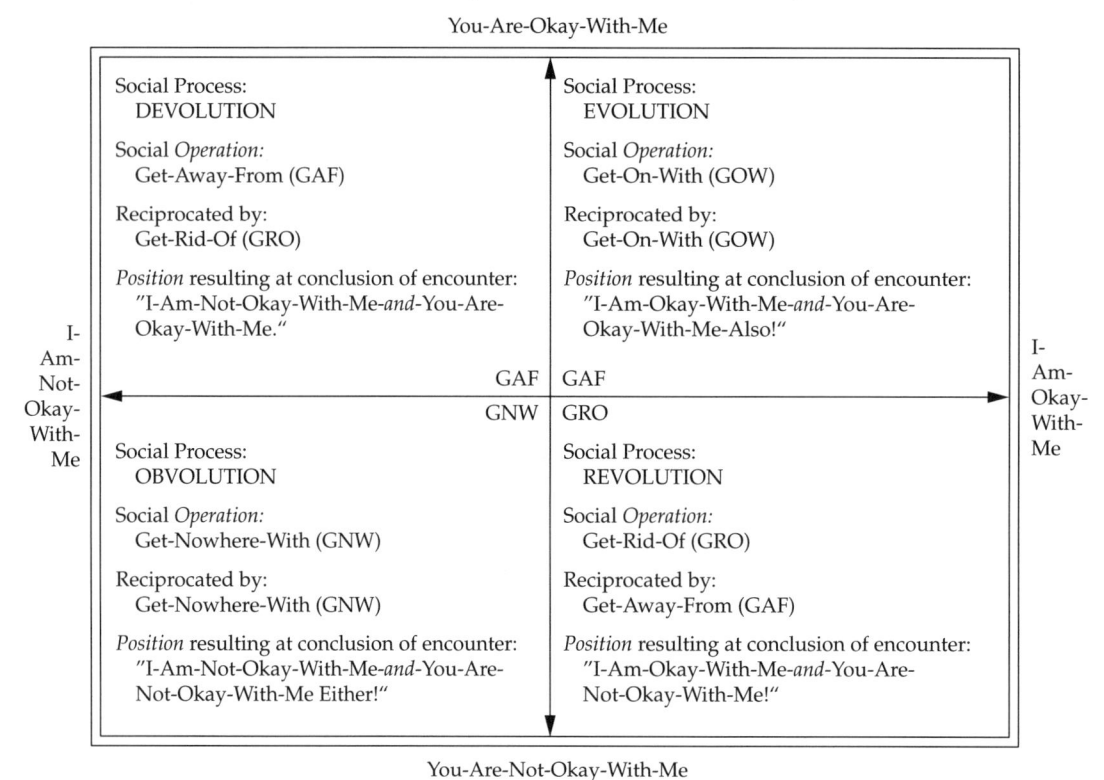

Social Process, Social Operation and Position Solution Diagram

You-Are-Okay-With-Me

I-Am-Not-Okay-With-Me	Social Process: DEVOLUTION Social *Operation:* Get-Away-From (GAF) Reciprocated by: Get-Rid-Of (GRO) *Position* resulting at conclusion of encounter: "I-Am-Not-Okay-With-Me-*and*-You-Are-Okay-With-Me."	Social Process: EVOLUTION Social *Operation:* Get-On-With (GOW) Reciprocated by: Get-On-With (GOW) *Position* resulting at conclusion of encounter: "I-Am-Okay-With-Me-*and*-You-Are-Okay-With-Me-Also!"
	GAF / GNW	GAF / GRO
	Social Process: OBVOLUTION Social *Operation:* Get-Nowhere-With (GNW) Reciprocated by: Get-Nowhere-With (GNW) *Position* resulting at conclusion of encounter: "I-Am-Not-Okay-With-Me-*and*-You-Are-Not-Okay-With-Me Either!"	Social Process: REVOLUTION Social *Operation:* Get-Rid-Of (GRO) Reciprocated by: Get-Away-From (GAF) *Position* resulting at conclusion of encounter: "I-Am-Okay-With-Me-*and*-You-Are-Not-Okay-With-Me!"

You-Are-Not-Okay-With-Me

Figure 22.1 Summary of "The OK Corral: Grid for Get-On-With." *Source:* Ernst (1971), p. 39.

of ... life" (1961, p. 418). Berne wavered between asserting that parents impose scripts and that persons exercise choices in their construction, yet he counterbalanced predetermination with personal decision making. Genetics, the conceptive scene, the quality of the couple and family dynamics, the (in)compatibility of parents' scripts, expectations for the child, the naming of the child, and developmental processes all coalesce to contribute to the growing-up environment and to the formation of identity. In this milieu, based on developmental capacities (Piaget, 1932, 1954), a child makes decisions about how to regard himself or herself and to relate to others (Berne, 1961).

From these early perceptions, experiences, and memories, a child establishes a protocol for script. The protocol or household drama first experienced with an unsatisfactory conclusion, includes a preliminary sense of which emotions and expressions are permitted and rewarded (racket processes), the existential positions regarding okayness for oneself and significant others, and preferred stroking patterns and games. "A game usually represents a segment of a script" (Berne, 1958, p. 156). Berne (1961) claimed that the protocol is repressed, but that the precipitates resurface in its preconscious derivative, the script proper. Later versions of the protocol—palimpsests—appear as a person acts out script in crucial situations. Berne observed that implementing the script proper involves compromises or adaptation in the realistic maneuverings with others. He coalesced the three terms of protocol, script proper, and adaptation into the concept of script. Steiner (1966) devised the script matrix to depict the processes involved, particularly the ego state dynamics between parents and children.

Goals, Injunctions, Decisions
Berne (1972) expanded on script development. Parental programming and script decision making involve six elements usually completed by age 6. First, a child intuits a sense of a *script payoff,* whether one will end up a winner, be cursed as a loser, or lead a nonwinning, mundane life. Second, the parents impart *injunctions,* or restrictive messages (e.g., "Don't be," "Don't think"). *Permissions* represent the opposites. R. Goulding and Goulding (1978; M. Goulding & Goulding, 1979) elaborated on the range of injunctions. They also clarified that "No one is 'scripted.' Injunctions are not placed in people's heads like electrodes. Each child makes decisions in response to real or imagined injunctions, and thereby 'scripts' him/herself" (R. Goulding & Goulding, 1978, p. 213). Third, parents entice, provoke, seduce, or reinforce offspring into a script through a *come-on,* intense messages implied in nonverbal communications, powerful whispers, or not-so-subtle pressures or setups (Berne, 1972). Fourth, parents provide *prescriptions,* counterscript messages for well-being and competence. Fifth, the same-sex parent models a *pattern.* Sixth, parents sometimes offer an *internal release* for overcoming injunctions at some later age.

In his formulation of script, Berne emphasized the negatives, the inevitable restrictive and pathological nature of scripting. He did allow that scripts can be "constructive" (1958, p. 156; 1961, p. 116) and lead to happiness if associates are chosen carefully and play their parts well, or be a "winning" (1972, p. 205) life plan. The connotation remains, however, and many transactional analysts perpetuate the notion, that scripting entails repetition of pathology. Berne contended that "a winning script payoff comes ... through the counterscript slogans" (p. 205). He contrasted script with nonscript. For Berne, nonscript emerges "with no particular time schedule, [is] developed later in life, and [is] not under parental influence" (p. 418). He equated nonscript with autonomy, reflecting his neo-Freudian and social-psychiatric proclivities. Were Berne to have activated his neo-Adlerian and social-psychological leanings more fully, he could have built on Adler's conceptualization of style of life as embodying and expressing constructive, run-of-the-mill, as well as destructive goals, plans, and patterns. Then the construct of script, like style of life, would have served as an initially value-neutral process that assumes positive or negative connotations as child and significant others coevolve in their development (R. Massey, 1989b, 1989c, 1989d, 1990a). Although Berne (1972) declared that "the crux of script theory lies in structural analysis" (p. 400), he relied almost exclusively on functional concepts and language. Utilizing higher-order structural analysis in exploring script processes would add depth and greater appreciation for realistic complexity in assessment and treatment planning (R. Massey, 1989c).

INTEGRATING BERNE'S CONSTRUCTS

Berne (1972) affirmed that "transactional analysis is...a rich mesh of intertwined concepts, all consistent with each other" (p. 49). Yet he left them unintegrated in their richness (see Figure 22.2). Berne (1961) elaborated on the structures of ego stages and their analyses, but subsequently diminished his use of structural analysis of ego states. Berne's (1961, 1964, 1970, 1972) explorations of relationship analysis and of group imagoes (1963, 1966) occurred in different books. Berne's (1961) early discussion of relationship analysis involved some structural analysis of ego states, but subsequent versions were more abbreviated and relied on functional

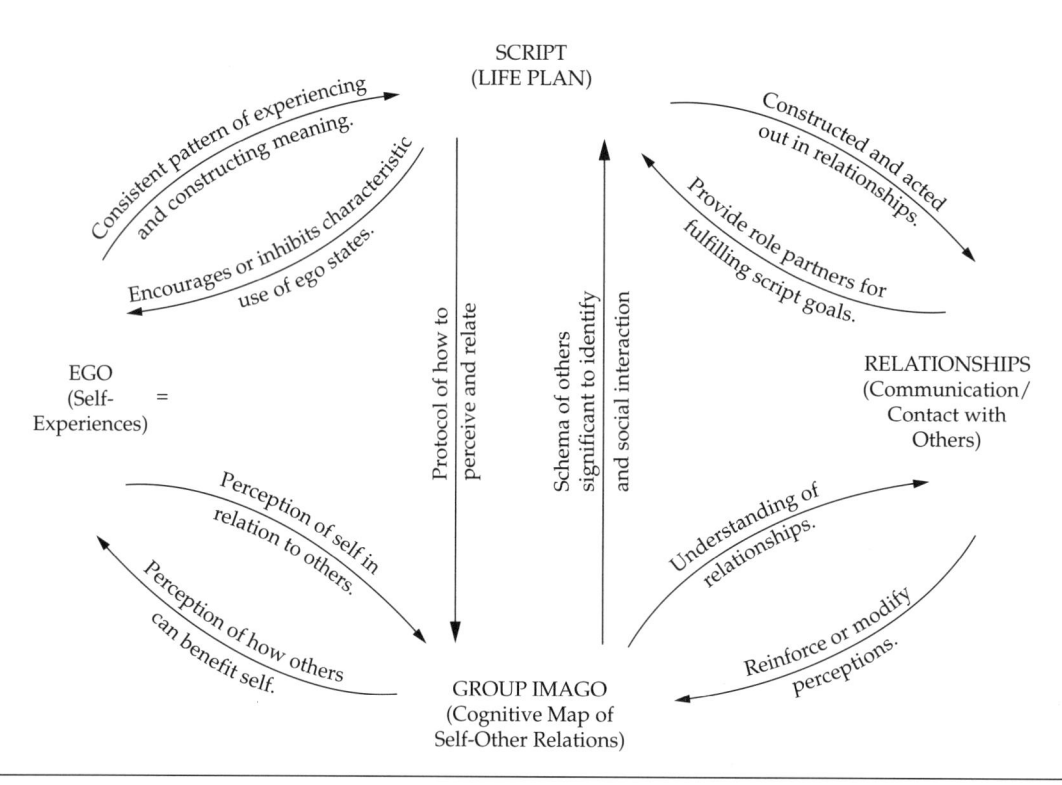

Figure 22.2 Interconnections of ego, script, group imago, and relationships. The ego, script, group imago, and relationships interconnect dynamically. Each component changes the others and is altered through mutual feedback. Through the interconnections of these processes, persons experience identities and relate to significant others with personal and socially shared meanings. *Source:* Massey (1989c), p. 14.

analysis of ego states. He never linked relationship analysis and script analysis, although in Berne (1961), the chapter on relationships follows that on scripts. Although he asserted that "the crux of script theory lies in structural analysis" (1972, p. 400), he depended almost exclusively on functional analysis in his writings on scripting.

Berne's social emphasis placed him in the *neo-Freudian/neo-Adlerian* tradition (R. Massey, 1989b, 1990a, 1993). Like Erikson, Fromm, Horney, and Sullivan, Berne trained in psychoanalysis and, hence, can be considered a neo-Freudian; he also refashioned theory in a more social/cultural direction and, thus, qualifies as a neo-Adlerian. The residues of Berne's Freudian bent toward pathology and a sometimes individual focus, particularly on autonomy as casting off social restrictions, hampered a fuller exploration of the healthy side of human development and of the implications of his theory for societal-level processes (Baute, 1979; Jacobs, 1987; R. Massey, 1987; Orten, 1973), as a more Adlerian perspective would have fostered.

Berne's (1964) distinctions between social psychiatry and social psychology depended significantly on contrasting inner and outer processes. This dynamic tension runs throughout the history of social psychology and is better handled by understanding the betweenness interconnecting person and social processes and joining persons in systems (R. Massey, 1996). Had Berne (1961) more fully appreciated the *social-psychological* implications of his theorizing, he could have discovered and more fully elaborated on the dynamic links among the concepts that he left as discrete rather than synthesized (R. Massey, 1989c, 1996). Fully utilizing his analyses of ego state structures, group imagoes, relationship dynamics, and script processes enriches the theoretical legacy of Berne in TA as a basis for more thorough assessment and treatment. This more completely actualizes his contributions as a neo-Adlerian (R. Massey, 1989b, 1990a, 1993) and solidifies his implicit systemic perspective (R. Massey, 1985; R. Massey & Massey, 1995).

METHODS OF ASSESSMENT AND INTERVENTION

In therapy, Berne (1961) recommended beginning with structural analysis, frequently in individual sessions, to master, if not resolve, internal conflicts "through diagnosis of ego states, decontamination, boundary work, and stabilization, so that the Adult can maintain control of the personality in stressful situations" (p. 90). Berne diagnosed ego states based on four criteria: (1) behavioral (demeanor, gestures, voice tone, vocabulary, and characteristics match a parental figure, integrated adult, or childlike presentation); (2) social or operational (the appropriate set of behaviors appears in the presence of someone eliciting this response, e.g., Parent ego state with another person acting like a child); (3) historical (identifying the exteropsychic figure involved or personal memories of earlier similar behaviors or feelings); and (4) phenomenological (experiencing with intensity the original occurrence).

Berne (1961) recommended analysis of transactions, generally in group therapy, as a second step after structural analyses in therapeutic processes. The analysis of transactions involves observing complementary, crossed, and duplex transactions to encourage complementary and constructively crossed interchanges and to work with duplex ones involved in games. Script analysis follows as a third step. Understanding group imagoes and observing driver behaviors add to diagnostic richness.

THE GROUP AS A THERAPEUTIC TOOL

Berne (1963, 1966) specialized in group therapy. Transactional-analytic therapists commonly work with a group of between 6 and 14 people in one of three ways: therapy of the group, therapy in the group, and therapy with the group. In the first, a therapist focuses on the functioning of a group, exploring common themes as they emerge, similar to a t-group with the addition of contracts. In the second, developed particularly by Robert and Mary Goulding in redecision therapy, a therapist works primarily one-to-one with individual clients with support, encouragement, and feedback from other members. In the third, a therapist and group deal directly with explicit transactions among group members and may analyze them in TA terms. This method is probably closest to that practiced by Berne himself. Moiso and Novellino (Moiso, 1985; Novellino, 1990; Novellino & Moiso, 1990) have developed this type in a more psychodynamic direction. They view transactions in a group as requiring an explanation of their origins and emphasize transference and countertransference processes.

Groups develop in *phases*, and individuals move through *stages* in therapy. Hewitt (1995) proposed a four-stage model of therapy based in part on the work of Steenbarger (1992). In the first stage, *contact*, a client forms connections with a therapist and group members. Clients frequently rely on their group imagoes as they begin participating in a group. They bring expectations of the roles others may play and seek ways to continue their own scripts, patterns of stroking, rackets, and structuring time, including games. Transference spurs previous defensive ways of relating. An important step occurs when a client perceives a group as safe. Then a client can make a *contract* for change. Berne (1966) advocated contractual therapy in which both therapist and client work toward a cure for a client. Contracting involves three levels: administrative (agreement on the ground rules for therapy (e.g., scheduling), therapeutic (clarity on desired change), and psychological (commitment to work through unconscious processes impeding progress). A transactional-analytic contract contains specification of outcome and actions manifesting the targeted change (Stewart, 1996). A therapy contract concerns self-development and altering one's own responses, not changing someone else; therapy does not operate by remote control. English (1975) recommended a three-cornered contract in working with mandated clients.

The second phase, *content*, revolves around discovering and changing impediments to achieving a desired goal. A therapist may help a client to externalize a felt conflict through Gestalt two-chair work, or allow a client to express conflict in actuality or symbolically with group members or the therapist and then work through the impasse in the here and now. The choice depends on the preferences of therapist and client. Frequently, both processes occur because clients experience clinicians as authority figures and, in working through transferences about negative experiences, come to find their nurturing helpful in healing. Generally, therapy occurs in the here and now between persons in the present moment. However, when clinically appropriate, with a clear contract and adequate support, a therapist can assist a client with regressive experiences. This phase ends when intrapsychic and/or interpersonal conflict is resolved in a new decision.

The third stage concerns *consolidation* and entails integrating new beliefs, attitudes, and responses. Growth necessitates behavioral change as well as insight and proceeds from dependence, possibly through counterdependence, to independence and interdependence. *Conclusion*, the fourth stage, occurs as a person finishes a segment of therapeutic work and either leaves the group or moves on to a new phase of therapy. Clients often recycle through the stages rather than proceed linearly. Moving through the stages affects the participants' group imagoes (Clarkson, 1991). Throughout the stages, clients benefit from therapists providing the "three P's of therapy" (Berne, 1972 p. 374): potency, permission, and protection (Crossman, 1966).

MAJOR SYNDROMES, SYMPTOMS, AND PROBLEMS TREATED

Berne (1961) referred to diagnosis and treatment of schizophrenia, anxiety disorders, psychosis, obsessions, compulsions, phobias, hallucinations, delusions, sexual abuse, psychopathology, neurosis, attachment disorders, alcoholism, drug abuse, suicidality, psychosomatic disorders, sexual-identity disorder, and depression. He found TA instructive and useful in assessment and providing therapy for the gamut of symptoms and clinical syndromes and attended to both intrapsychic and social dynamics. Subsequent to Berne, most transactional analysts have focused more on transactional dynamics rather than on symptom categories. Schiff et al. (1975) elaborated on the processes involved in psychoses and schizophrenia. Steiner (1971) detailed script dynamics among alcoholics and focused on their interplay with gender roles (1971/1974). Erskine (1993, 1996, 1997) and Hargaden and Sills (2001) addressed therapeutic processes in treating narcissistic and borderline conditions. TA provides a framework and terminology for diagnosing from a relational perspective (Kaslow, 1996) and offers dynamic insights to elucidate the processes implicated in the *Diagnostic and Statistical Manual of Mental Disorders* (*DSM-IV*) categorizations (American Psychiatric Association [APA], 1994).

CASE EXAMPLES

Case Study 1: Using Transference and Relationship

Alfio, age 42, enters therapy because he is divorcing for the second time. Both former wives complained bitterly about his premature ejaculation problems. Alfio appears socially likeable and treats others kindly, yet he and his spouses found sexual interaction frustrating. Alfio thus feels depressed and doubts he will ever know full love. He wants to form a new relationship with Lucia, age 36, and to not repeat past difficulties. The following dialogue took place in the fifth session of group therapy.

THERAPIST: Your colleagues in the group are saying that your behavior with women seems to follow a repetitive pattern. They believe that you are into playing a psychological game. What is your opinion?

ALFIO: Well, in fact, I am not aware of it . . . not at all . . . but I have to admit that something happens because at the end I find myself in a completely different place from where I want to be.

THERAPIST: What do you mean?

ALFIO: Well, for a long time, I've told myself not to go with women whom I see as not being affectionate or kind.

THERAPIST: Considering all that took place, you think that you deserved what happened?

ALFIO: Yes, all my life I feel inadequate and guilty for all I do . . . and I feel cheated too. . . .

THERAPIST: What comes to your mind from what you are experiencing now?

ALFIO: (Crying, after a long silence.) We already talked about it in other occasions, but I never related it to sex . . . I felt like this every time that my mother looked at me with a discounting look and ridiculed me when I was talking about some failures in school or when I spoke about admiring or missing my father, who left the family for another woman when I was 11.

THERAPIST: What do you want from me or the group?

ALFIO: Well . . . I think I want . . . support . . . from you, and the other men of the group. . . .

THERAPIST: How do you want support?

ALFIO: I want to know that you accept and trust me. I want to be accepted and trusted. When my mother caught me playing doctor with a girl when I was 6 and punished me by not letting me play with her for a week, I felt such a rush of shame and guilt and did not understand what I had done wrong.

THERAPIST: What will help you now?

ALFIO: Tell me what I have to do with women.

THERAPIST: What you need to do depends on what you really want to get. Strategies need to be based on a knowledge of one's real aim.... What do you want from women?

ALFIO: Well... to be loved by them... but... I'm not so sure... I also... I don't trust them... I am confused.... On one hand, I want to be with a woman, and, on the other hand, I am afraid of disapproval and of not finding satisfaction with a woman. And now I am very angry at the woman teacher who was harsh with my 8-year-old son after he moved to a new school a month ago. He was not familiar with those types of lessons and was picked on by some boys. That made me very angry... I mean, the teacher should have looked after him.... He is new in this school... and the teacher should have watched that he was not being bullied... and be attentive to him.

THERAPIST: What was your son's need?

ALFIO: To have special care, not be left there with the others....

Diagnosis and Assessment
Alfio presents as an anxious man. His insecurity stems from a lack of support developmentally, from his father's abandonment and his mother's negativity and ambivalence. His premature ejaculating (*DSM-IV*, 302.75; APA, 1994) expresses his anxiety in organ language (Adler, 1956). The Global Assessment of Relational Functioning (Group for the Advancement of Psychiatry Committee on the Family, 1996) (GARF) scores for his relationships with his two ex-wives would be 50. GARF scores indicate levels of relationship satisfaction in a family and range from 1 to 100.

Case Formulation
In this segment, Alfio's script and transference become apparent. He believes that he is not lovable, that other people are unreliable, and that life will be difficult for him (script beliefs). When his relationships break up, he feels confused about why this happens and depressed about repeating disappointment, as he experienced with his mother (racket behaviors). He repeats the shame around sexual issues. In situations of potential closeness with a woman, he recalls his mother's treatment of him (reinforcing memories and fantasies). Alfio decided to punish himself and the women he was involved with in response to his mother's scolding and ridiculing him and his feeling guilty. To ejaculate prematurely expressed his auto- and eterodestructive urges. (He feels guilty about not being a real man parallel to how his mother demoralized rather than nurtured and accepted her male child and to how his father had not performed in the family.)

Treatment Approach and Rationale for Selection
TA supplies the conceptual frame and the practical tools to work with object relations. Moiso (1985) regarded transference as a central aspect of transactional-analytic therapy, as Novellino (1984) has countertransference. Transference can be used therapeutically when a therapist offers a novel rather than a repetitive response, helps a client to identify an earlier unmet need and encourages finding a way to have that satisfied in the present, or provides a sufficient holding environment, so that a client can work through an externalized internal conflict or at least experience not receiving accustomed abuse.

Using the group to discover that he is lovable and can be trusted undermines Alfio's negative script and opens the possibility of finding emotional intimacy, a necessary prelude to sexual satisfaction. Alfio's remarks about his son articulate symbolic identification with and expression of his boyhood needs for caring as he seeks compensation to experience psychological safety as a foundation for a masculine identity affirmed and nurtured as a platform for receiving and giving interpersonal gratification. To cure the impasse (R. Goulding & Goulding, 1978;

Mellor, 1980; Novellino et al., 1998) of wanting to be lovable and intimate yet feeling ashamed and rejected, Alfio needs to become free of confusion and to cathect neopsychic rather than archaeopsychic and exteropsychic energies, so as to move beyond injunctions to autonomy. In a psychodynamic perspective, decontamination serves the function of supporting an observing ego, aware of the relationship between old impulses and present needs and between old controls and updated principles, values, and norms. This therapy process fulfills the three main objectives of the psychodynamic approach to TA: (1) to make the unconscious conscious, (2) to work through resistance and transference, and (3) to optimize the functioning of the ego (Novellino et al., 1998).

Because the expression of sexuality involves an interpersonal relationship, the therapist recommended couple treatment as well as group therapy. Alfio and Lucia attended four sessions together. Lucia offered her support in helping Alfio to overcome his habit of premature ejaculation. They both expressed warmth and compatibility with each other. Their script dynamics, based particularly on traditional gender roles, interlocked. As Alfio had developed a negative identity as a man and an apprehension about women's responses to him, so Lucia's mother had taught her that a woman's responsibility is to please a man and to ignore her own needs. The therapist explored with each their histories of psychosexual development and expectations and introduced psychoeducational material, which, surprisingly, despite their age and experiences, offered them unheard of knowledge (Masters & Johnson, 1970, 1975). Both were unaware of a woman's need for foreplay and of clitoral sensitivity and the range of female responsiveness to sexual attention. Lucia was encouraged to give herself permission for pleasure and Alfio to attend to her satisfaction rather than his. They were invited to play rather than pressure each other (Frankl, 1969). The therapist explained that, when their psychosexual value systems are fulfilled and they express caring with each other, their sexual responses are more likely to flow naturally and pleasurably (Boyd & Boyd, 1980a, 1981). From session to session, they reported increased satisfaction, with Alfio beginning to be less bothered with premature ejaculation. The couple sessions facilitated Alfio's moving beyond his transference toward women in vivo, and both partners incorporating new experiences of trusting and reciprocal affection as foundations for revised images of self and other.

Existing Treatment Protocol
Interpretation constitutes the core intervention of the psychodynamic approach to TA, exactly as in the classical Bernian approach, hence the appellation neo-Bernian. Interpretation addresses archaeopsychic experiences of pathology that a client presents in a coded form (transferential ulterior transactions). A therapist aims to decode these childhood experiences, cleansing them of all the original misperceptions, helping a patient to reorganize and update his or her experiences. Becoming aware of levels of experience fixated in the archaeopsyche is the goal of interpretation. The levels include (1) the unmet archeopsychic need projected on the therapist with a transferential process of concordant identification; (2) the internalized object acting as a damaging Parent (Moiso, 1985) projected on the therapist with a transferential process of complementary identification; (3) the script frame of reference (beliefs and related feelings) connected to the fixation; and (4) the ulterior level in racketeering (English, 1976) and game playing.

Dealing with unconscious material and considering the analysis of transference an essential part of the therapeutic relationship remain unavoidable. Interpretation proves effective only if preceded by decontamination because a client needs to access neopsychic functioning to ally with a therapist's neopsychic processes in dealing with material removed from consciousness for many years. To make a patient aware of the specific behavior that will be the object of therapeutic work together, the operation of *underlining* needs to precede the eight therapeutic operations described by Berne (1966). For example, if a patient nods while a therapist is saying something, a therapist may underline this by saying: "I see that you are nodding while I am talking [underlining]. What are you telling me with your nodding? [interrogation]."

Explanation and interpretation differ: *Explanation* conveys cognitive understanding of the meanings of actual behavior; with the *interpretation*, the therapist proposes a hypothesis on the unconscious origin of the same behavior. A therapist needs to elicit in a patient a strong interest in discovering in self the latent meaning of behaviors and transactions. Interpretation signifies essentially an operation of transference analysis consisting of helping patients to understand how they project on the environment personal childhood conflicts (Novellino & Moiso, 1990). Of all the possible projections, especially if made in a group setting, the ones laid on a therapist provide an especially effective channel for work. The goal of exploring through interpretation lies in viewing the protocol, seen as the narrative context constructed by a child based on the conflictual polarity of need versus injunction. Through interpretation, the psychodynamic approach to TA furthers the Bernian objective of obtaining a psychoanalytic cure by the analysis of the script, based on the analysis of actual transactions between patient and therapist and between patient and other patients.

Berne observed a protocol being reexperienced and acted out via the script—a transferential drama in action. Persons tend to unconsciously live and experience the here and now as the reenacting of situations present in their narration of a protocol. Patients will try to reinstate those symbiotic relationships through games, racketeering, and redefining process. Interpretation of a protocol's related needs requires three phases of analysis (Novellino, 1990):

(1) decontamination of the neopsyche, so as to have the Adult as an ally; (2) interpretations of the defenses (games, redefining transactions, psychodynamic defenses), to help patients understand the actual strategies with which they continue to transfer onto the here and now their childhood beliefs; and (3) interpreting the protocol's context, that is, formulating hypotheses about those specific transactions that happened in patients' childhoods that led them to fixate specific developmental needs that still influence them negatively.

Posttermination Synopsis and Reflections
Alfio brought a history of believing himself fundamentally unlovable and of relating to women in unsatisfying ways as symbolized by premature ejaculation. He tended to accentuate archaeopsychic experiences of feeling discounted and rejected as reinforced by exteropsychic models of not nurturing and being competent, messages about being unacceptable and guilty, and injunctions about "Don't be you," "Don't be a Child," "Don't be close." He transacted with intimates in duplex transactions containing an ulterior level of seeking frustration and nonsatisfaction. This reinforced his script beliefs of not being adequate and his group imago of a man leaving a woman ungratified not knowing how to really connect, and of a son remaining without a guide and the knowledge needed to function as an adult. In group therapy Alfio was able to work through his transference about men and an authority figure with the therapist and in couple therapy with Lucia about women and needing to feel demeaned. Lucia also revised her script beliefs about the value of females and entitlement to need satisfaction. Alfio is discovering his worth and acceptability as he and Lucia explore a more mutual relationship than either has experienced before, one based less on transferences and archaeopsychic processes and more on complementary transactions and intimacy on several levels.

Case Study 2: Redecision Therapy

A university counselor referred William, a second-year philosophy student, to group therapy. Though he scored straight As on his essays, he never passed a written examination. He achieved every pass in his school and university career on the basis of receiving a medical certificate from a doctor stating that he was not able to take a written examination at this time. When confronted with a written examination, he suffered such a severe anxiety attack that he did not continue. Allowing him more informal conditions and additional time made no difference in the intensity of anxiety attacks.

In the contact phase, William talked comfortably with other group members. They responded very positively to his enthusiasm for change, and he reported that he felt strongly supported. For the eight weeks of the group, William made a contract to be able to complete written examinations and to do so with a feeling of confidence rather than the anxiety he had experienced. As a new group member, he contributed during the first three sessions by providing excellent empathic feedback to other clients. He also was free and frank in speaking about his life and current experiences. The therapist and group members noted his tendency toward perfectionism. Group members gently challenged him on this inclination, which he applied mainly to himself.

In the fourth session, William chose to work one-on-one with the therapist, who asked him to describe step-by-step what happened as he went into an exam room. William replied that his anxiety built up over a day or two before the exam but was quite manageable. After sitting in the exam room, he would turn the paper over and look at the questions and think about all the reading that he had done in writing the essays associated with the topic (for which he had read prodigiously, spent many hours in very careful analysis of his reading, and then recorded his thinking very precisely and in great detail, always going to the absolute word limit allowed by his lecturer). Then he would realize that in three-quarters of an hour for each of four questions, he could not compose perfect answers. At that point, he panicked. He would shake and sweat and simply be unable to write and would end up having to leave the exam room and once more apply for pass on medical grounds.

The therapist asked William to recall when he was a child and to think for whom he would be trying to get things "right."

WILLIAM: Clearly, my mother. Nothing I ever did was good enough for her. Even if I won a race, she would tell me I could have run faster. If I were second or third in a class of 30 children, she would want to know why I wasn't first.

THERAPIST: William, will you pause and think for a moment about what it was that you most wanted from your mother when you were a little boy?

WILLIAM: What I wanted was her approval. (Pause.) No, what I really wanted was her love, and it seemed to me that I had to get her approval if I were to get her love.

THERAPIST: You seem very clear about that, William.

WILLIAM: Yes, yes, that's how it seems to be. (Pause.) I have never quite thought about it like that before, but that was how it was. I needed to get her approval before I could get her love, and it was her love that I really wanted.

The therapist (wanting to obtain permission for some work) inquired if William would be willing to do an experiment in which he would sit in one chair and talk about his own experiences, move to a different chair to speak about his perceptions of his mother's experiences, and return to the first chair and request from his mother what he wanted.

THERAPIST: Will you sit as a little boy, imagine in detail the clothes you were wearing, and how you felt?

WILLIAM: I felt quite anxious.

THERAPIST: What was happening in your life?

WILLIAM: My father had left. Mother is bringing up three children on her own and working as well as raising the children. I am scared that mother may leave as well, and then what would we do?

THERAPIST: Now look at mother and tell her what it is you want from her.

WILLIAM: (In little boy voice.) Mum, I want to know, if I get things right, will you love me?

THERAPIST: Will you change chairs and be your mother? Sit the way mother would sit, describe what clothes she was wearing, say how you were feeling.

WILLIAM: (As mother.) "I am a single mother. Working and bringing up children are quite difficult. (To William.) Well, you do all right, but you could do better, but, of course, I love you any way (said in a very unconvincing manner).

Several times, the therapist asks William to switch chairs between acting like mother and being himself as a child. The theme of the dialogue becomes apparent; each time the child asks for recognition and love, mother replies, "But you could do better; it is important that you do better; you will need to do better to do well in life."

THERAPIST: William, may I interview you as if you were your mother?

WILLIAM: Yes.

THERAPIST: (To William responding as his mother.) You hear William asking you for approval and for love. What do you feel like when William does that?

WILLIAM: (As mother.) When he asks me for that, I feel very scared. In the family in which I grew up, my father was an alcoholic, and my mother died when I was quite young. (William, as mother, looks intensely sad and starts to weep.) Nobody ever loved me. I don't know how to love anybody. I would really like to love William; he is a really nice little boy, and I just don't know how to do it.

THERAPIST: William, switch chairs and become the child again. See mother sitting over there weeping? It seems she really does not know how to love you.

WILLIAM: No, no, I can see that; she just doesn't know how.

THERAPIST: How old does mother seem when she is sitting there crying like that?

WILLIAM: She seems like just a little girl. She looks about 7 or 8; she looks younger than I am.

THERAPIST: How long are you going to go on struggling to get things perfectly right in the hope that mother will grow up and love you?

WILLIAM: (Now weeping gently in the child position.) I can see she never will. She doesn't know how. It is not that she does not want to. It is just that she does not know how. I have been trying for 20 years to get somebody to love me who is really just a little girl who does not know how. (Long pause.) I now have many people in my life who love me. I am even starting to learn how to love myself. (Laughs.) I would really like her to love me, but she is never going to, and I can get love in other places.

At this point, the rest of the group burst into applause. A group discussion followed in which William described his relationships with his friends and his partner and how much love he enjoyed in his current life.

Over the next three weeks, William reported that he had a great deal more energy because he no longer put so much energy into seeking perfection. His energy level in the group was clearly much higher, and he was even more enthusiastic about assisting his fellow group members in their work. Several group members "coat-tailed" on William's work, identifying with him and reporting that they also had been able to give away at least some of their perfectionism. By the final session of the group, William's work was clearly finished. Some group members contracted to come back for further work; for William, this was clearly unnecessary. William had completed his work by relating what he had accomplished.

Diagnosis and Assessment
William was suffering from generalized anxiety manifested particularly in written examination situations. He would probably score above average on a Wechsler Adult Intelligence Scale (WAIS-III; Wechsler, 1997) given his demonstrated capacity to compose quality essays. He would probably score high on Cattell's (1963) measure of overt or covert anxiety. However, his high anxiety levels inhibit his achieving success despite studious preparations. A *DSM-IV* diagnosis of Anxiety Disorder Not Otherwise Specified (300.00) (APA, 1994) would be appropriate. In his family of origin, a GARF score of 45 could be assigned and a GARF rating of 70 in his current relationship (Group for the Advancement of Psychiatry Committee on the Family, 1996). GARF scores range from a low of 1 to a high of 100 and indicate levels of satisfaction in family relationships.

Case Formulation
William grew up in an atmosphere of discounting his worth and abilities. He did not know if he was good enough for his father to remain in the household and to gain the acknowledgment of his mother's approval. He developed an orientation of perfectionism in the hope that, if he could follow the right procedures in a magnificent way, he could obtain the recognition he so desired. Thus, in pursuit of an actually unattainable goal, William was acting on a "be perfect" driver. He became aware of this aspect of himself (based on the script belief of not really being lovable, as derived from experiencing his father's abandonment and his mother's continual disappointment in his performances). He internalized and acted on the injunctions of "Don't be close," "Don't be you," "Don't succeed," "Don't be important." These dynamics operated largely outside of his awareness. In his own consciousness, he was a young man with enough ability to attend university classes, was comfortable with friends and a romantic partner, and felt devastated that anxiety and panic overcame him as he entered academic examination rooms after studying diligently and doing well in his preparations. He needed to highlight and build on these strengths. Gaining affectively grounded and self-affirming understanding that the dynamics motivating his mother's continual disappointment with his efforts flowed from her own developmental (script) processes rather than representing an accurate definition of himself empowered William to view his mother in her own context, to disengage himself from his earlier perception of himself as having to exert enormous efforts only to not perform well enough, and to free himself to accomplish his goals and to feel supported by others (to assume an I'm okay, You're okay position, to give and receive positive strokes for being and doing).

Treatment Approach and Rationale for Selection
William participated in group therapy based on the redecision model of transactional analysis (R. Goulding, 1972; R. Goulding & Goulding, 1978; M. Goulding & Goulding, 1979; Hoyt, 1997). Joines (2002) and McNeel (1977) have delineated the stages in this approach and Hoyt summarized eight important ingredients in redecision therapy:

1. Although not necessarily practicing a *contact* phase in session, Robert and Mary Goulding took time to become acquainted and form alliances with clients, usually in

informal settings, including over lunch and tea breaks, to build an atmosphere more supportive of intensive work.

2. *Contracts* remain foundations in TA work.
3. *Confronting*, often using humor, a *con*—any attempt by clients to discount their own abilities, the capacities of others, or possibilities for change in a situation—empowers clients. If a client states, "I want to try and get more friends," a therapist could reply, "If I offered to try and drive you home, would you come with me?" The client might respond, laughing, "No, I wouldn't!"
4. A therapist assists a client in *identifying the chief bad feelings, thinking, behaviors, and body feelings.*
5. To *uncover chronic games, belief systems and fantasies*, a therapist carefully elicits a client's thinking about the current situation and how fantasies and belief systems maintain a stuck position. Cognitive-behavioral techniques prove useful.
6. Redecision therapists help people identify *early childhood decisions* that represented their best efforts at the time but have proved limiting. Client and therapist set up a scene, as in a stage drama (M. Goulding & Goulding, 1979), in preparation for making a redecision attuned to present circumstances and potentials. The scene may be present, recent, early, imaginary, or a combination.
7. Therapists facilitate clients in working toward the *resolution of an impasse*. If this work involves regressive dimensions, returning to adult awareness and functioning need to occur in a therapy setting.
8. Anchoring a new decision proves important. In a videotaped illustration of redecision therapy (R. Goulding & Goulding, 1986), Robert Goulding noticed that a participant leaned his head to one side when focusing on his struggles. At the completion of a productive piece of work, Goulding exclaimed, "All you need to do is remember to keep your head on straight." The Gouldings encapsulated their orientation toward current transformation in a frequently used opening line: "What are you willing to change today?"

Specifically in William's therapy, he used the first three sessions to make contact and to clarify his contract. When confronted about his perfectionism, he agreed with the observations of others that this served as a primary coping mechanism in his life. He entered the group aware of his anxiety and discovered the links to the beliefs about himself as unlovable and as not living up to his mother's expectations. He engaged in a game with professors of putting out a lot of effort on the social level while preserving on the ulterior/psychological level his own racket feeling of not doing well enough through an unconscious fantasy of transferentially perceiving the professors as also expecting him to not succeed, as his mother had done. This perpetuated the original protocol or scenario and reinforced his habit of debilitated performance. To move toward an orientation of lovableness and success, William needed to make a redecision to realign his script from loyalty to the constrictions of his earlier context toward autonomy, constructive accomplishments, and positive relationship connections.

In preparation for facilitating a redecision, the therapist invited William to reexperience a significant early scene. As William was sitting in the chair speaking as his mother, the therapist watched until William fully cathected the Parent ego state containing the introjected mother. Generally, this shift is very obvious, often involving a significant change in voice, posture, and manner of speech. In addition, the person at some point will switch from saying "she" to "I." In this segment of two-chair work (James & Jongeward, 1971; Perls, 1969; Perls, Hefferline, & Goodman, 1951), the dialogue inside William's head, which took place at least largely outside his awareness on most occasions, became very clear. Robert and Mary Goulding (1978; Mellor, 1980) referred to this as "heightening the impasse."

Because this process did not prompt a spontaneous resolution, the therapist decided to interview William's Parent ego state as internalized in interaction with his mother (McNeel, 1976a) to clarify for him more fully the nature of the impasse. The therapist hypothesized that the mother's experiences as a child were interfering with her ability to parent. Reflecting on his mother's experience brought to William's awareness realization of his mother's developmental difficulties and limitations regarding providing what he so desired. This liberated him from continuing the pattern that led to further disappointment and frustration (to reinforce his racket feelings) and to highlight how he was currently enjoying being loved and beginning to value himself. When William said, "I am even starting to learn how to love myself," he laughed. This laughter followed a serious rather than a humorous statement and alluded to a gallows message (Berne, 1972). William had internalized an expectation of not having his need for love met by his mother as significant other. The gallows laughter indicated that William had learned that his need for love would not be entirely fulfilled and that he remained uncertain of this happening for sure. The gallows laughter could be confronted by asking William which parent would most likely comment on or expect him not to be lovable. This would unveil an injunction and open the possibility for a redecision or for reinforcing one. William had decided to receive the new message that he is lovable and to base his future endeavors on this realization. This produced changes in his achievement record in school and will lead to others appreciating him as he goes forward.

Posttreatment Synopsis and Reflections
At the end of the year, William finished his written examinations with a B average, which became an A in following years. He was able to benefit from short-term group therapy that targeted his difficulties through effective assessment and provided him with a safe holding environment for a reparative experience to counter the nonnurturing atmosphere in which he grew up. With an adjustment disorder, brief therapy, buttressed by the added dimension of group reinforcement for safety and change, can allow for quality contact, working on significant content, consolidation of gains, and successful conclusion through fulfilling a therapy contract.

RESEARCH

Berne (1961) drew on research in formulating TA. He cited Penfield's (1952; Penfield & Jasper, 1954; Penfield & Roberts, 1959) experiments on memory and Spitz's (1945) studies on child deprivation. Berne also derived insights from Federn's (1952) phenomenological approach to ego states and Weiss's (1950) observations of personality development. Subsequent transactional analysts have followed Berne's path of relying more on systematic observations and participant observation than on formal research.

Research on both construct validity and treatment effectiveness are desirable because TA serves as both a conceptual framework and a mode of assessment and intervention in therapy, organizational development, and education. Transactional analysts have tended to pursue applications more than formal research. With growing interest in affiliating with universities and in achieving certification and recognition in Australia, Europe, India, Japan, and New Zealand, some impetus for research has developed.

Regarding construct validity, the study of ego states has received the most attention. Ego states viewed functionally have proven the easiest to categorize and measure. Reasonably high correlations have emerged from interrater reliability studies on the meaning of behaviors as manifesting specific functional ego states (Blacklidge, 1976; Heyer, 1987; Hurley, 1973; L'Abate, 1978; Sowder & Brown, 1977; Swede, 1978; Thomson, 1972). Williams, Watson, Walters, and Williams (1983) offered a promising lead for future research in using the Adjective Check List (Gough, 1952), a validated instrument that can be scored for multiple scales, including Murray's list of needs since this allows for both a standardized measure and for comparative research with other modalities. Ego states considered structurally call for phenomenological research, as do most of the other transactional analytic constructs. There is a need for more in-depth case studies both to account for development longitudinally and to assess therapy, educational, and organizational processes multidimensionally.

The TA body of literature would benefit from initial phenomenological and qualitative research to gain leads toward potentially fruitful areas of study based on comprehensive attention to a manageable number of examples and themes through maximum variation sampling (Lincoln & Guba, 1985). Transactions could fairly easily be recorded on videotape and then coded by observers. In conjunction with interviews of the participants regarding perceptions of intention and effect, along with paper-and-pencil measures of relationship scales, multidimensional understanding of the experiences and impacts of transactions could be gleaned. As an intermediate step, Q-sorts (Stephenson, 1953) could prove useful in allowing both for expressing individual preferences and for interindividual comparisons. These combination approaches, using case studies, phenomenological analyses, and qualitative and quantitative research, can facilitate building a research understanding of scripting, group imagoes, driver behaviors, existential positions, stroking, and time structures. Some researchers have already developed instruments that can expand the research base (e.g., Drego's, 1983a, 1983b, 1996, Injunctions Scale). Researchers outside of TA circles may provide validation of constructs. Gottman and Silver's (1998) research on couples showed that destructive, argumentative interactions coalesce into two major categories, innocent victimhood and righteous indignation, parallel to Karpman's (1968) victim and persecutor. Seligman's (1975) work on learned helplessness relates to the victim role.

McClenaghan (1978) compiled an early summary of *outcome studies* on TA therapy. Thunnissen (2001) reported that, between 1963 and 1980, 124 doctoral dissertations on transactional analysis were completed. Liberman, Yalom, and Miles (1973) compared 10 group therapy approaches. One TA group yielded the most positive change scores and a second one the most negative. This may reflect the quality of the leader and the relationship between therapist and clients as the major predictor of outcome rather than differences between modalities (Miller, Hubble, & Duncan, 1995). Group cohesion, interpersonal feedback, group structure and composition, self-disclosure by leader and participants, and personal risk and responsibility may also modulate results (Bednar & Kaul, 1994). McCormick (1973) observed that juvenile delinquents treated in TA groups improved as compared to those in groups using behavior modification. McNeel (1976b, 1982), Noriega Gayol (1997), and Grünewald-Zemsch (2000) reported gains in self-esteem and quality of life following TA group treatment. No strong correlation has emerged between number of redecisions and change (Bader, 1982; McNeel, 1982), so the specific factors generating change remain undetermined. Research from the Gestalt literature (Paivo & Greenberg, 1995) indicates the usefulness of redecision techniques, but may not have sufficiently controlled for other significant factors. Most research on TA groups involves the redecision model, so other varieties need to be included in future research.

Novey (1999) examined data collected by the American Consumers Institute of Consumer Satisfaction with therapy (1995). The analysis did not differentiate between individual and group treatment, but did show higher client satisfaction with transactional analysts compared to receiving treatment from professionals identified simply as having been trained in psychiatry, psychology, social work, or marriage counseling. Satisfaction included the degree of perceiving presenting symptoms as improved, and people treated by transactional analysts achieved symptom relief significantly faster than those in therapy with clinicians with other training. Novey suggested that this satisfaction and effectiveness may result from the Transactional Analysis Certification Council's worldwide standard for training involving supervision by certified teaching members of services provided, a significant amount of theoretical instruction, and a qualifying examination generally administered by an international team. Teaching members engage in advanced training over several years and must pass a tripartite examination on theory, teaching, and supervision in an international setting.

SUMMARY

In transactional analysis Berne (1961) developed a conceptual system to describe the experiencing and observing of interacting persons. Individuals experience ego states as they are socialized and develop. They organize and interpret experiences through life plans or scripts. Analyses of ego states, transactions, and scripts provide a basis for understanding growth and dysfunction in personal and group processes, organizations, therapy, and educational settings. Several variants of TA therapy have emerged. Therapeutic approaches involving redecisions (M. Goulding & Goulding, 1979) and emphasis on transference and relationship (Novellino & Moiso, 1990) are illustrated in this chapter.

REFERENCES

Ackerman, N. W. (1958). *The psychodynamics of family life: Diagnosis and treatment of family relationships.* New York: Basic Books.

Adler, A. (1956). *The individual psychology of Alfred Adler* (H. H. Ansbacher & R. R. Ansbacher, Eds.). New York: Basic Books.

Adler, A. (1964). *Superiority and social interest* (H. H. Ansbacher & R. R. Ansbacher, Eds.). New York: Viking.

American Consumers Institute of Consumer Satisfaction. (1995, November). Mental health: Does therapy help? *Consumer Reports,* 1–6.

American Psychiatric Association. (1994). *Diagnostic and statistical manual of mental disorders* (4th ed.). Washington, DC: Author.

Angyal, A. (1965). *Neurosis and treatment: A holistic theory* (E. Hanfman & R. Jones, Eds.). New York: Viking.

Bader, E. (1976). *Redecisions in family therapy: A study of change in an intensive family therapy workshop* (Doctoral dissertation, California School of Professional Psychology, 1976). *Dissertation Abstracts International, 37,* 05B, 2491.

Bader, E. (1982). Redecisions in family therapy: A study of change in an intensive family therapy workshop. *Transactional Analysis Journal, 12*(1), 27–38.

Bader, E., & Pearson, P. (1988). *In quest of the mythical mate.* New York: Brunner/Mazel.

Bader, E., & Pearson, P. (2000). *Tell me no lies: How to face the truth and build a loving marriage.* New York: St. Martin's Press.

Barnes, G. (Ed.). (1977). *Transactional analysis after Eric Berne: Teachings and practices of three TA schools.* New York: Harper's College Press.

Batts, V. (2001, July 26). *Using transactional analysis in multicultural settings to facilitate effective healing and reconciliation.* Keynote address, International Transactional Analysis Association/Western Pacific Association of Transactional Analysis conference, Sydney, Australia.

Baute, P. (1979). Intimacy and autonomy are not enough. *Transactional Analysis Journal, 9,* 170–173.

Bednar, R. L., & Kaul, T. J. (1994). Experiential group research: Can the cannon fire? In A. E. Bergin & S. L. Garfield (Eds.), *Handbook of psychotherapy and behavior change* (4th ed., pp. xvi, 864). New York: Wiley.

Berne, E. (1939). Psychiatry in Syria. *American Journal of Psychiatry, 95,* 1415–1419.

Berne, E. (1957a). Ego states in psychotherapy *American Journal of Psychotherapy, 11,* 293–309.

Berne, E. (1957b). Intuition V: The ego image. *Psychiatric Quarterly, 31,* 611–627.

Berne, E. (1958). Transactional analysis: A new and effective method of group therapy. *American Journal of Psychotherapy, 12,* 735–743.

Berne, E. (1959a). Difficulties of comparative psychiatry: The Fiji Islands. *American Journal of Psychiatry, 116,* 104–109.

Berne, E. (1959b). Psychiatric epidemiology of the Fiji Islands. In J. H. Masserman & J. L. Moreno (Eds.), *Progress in psychotherapy* (Vol. 4, pp. 310–313). New York: Grune & Stratton.

Berne, E. (1960a). The cultural problem: Psychopathology in Tahiti. *American Journal of Psychiatry, 116,* 1076–1081.

Berne, E. (1960b). A psychiatric census of the South Pacific. *American Journal of Psychiatry, 117,* 44–47.

Berne, E. (1961). *Transactional analysis in psychotherapy: a systematic individual and social psychiatry.* New York: Grove Press.

Berne, E. (1963). *The structure and dynamics of organizations and groups.* New York: Grove Press.

Berne, E. (1964). *Games people play: The psychology of human relationships.* New York: Grove Press.

Berne, E. (1966). *Principles of group treatment.* New York: Grove Press.

Berne, E. (1970). *Sex in human loving.* New York: Simon & Schuster.

Berne, E. (1972). *What do you say after you say hello? The psychology of human destiny.* New York: Grove Press.

Berne, E. (1976). *A layman's guide to psychiatry and psychoanalysis* (3rd ed.). New York: Ballantine Books. (Original work published 1947)

Blacklidge, V. Y. (1976). The nature and nurture of the natural child. *Transactional Analysis Journal, 6*(3), 246–252.

Boyd, L., & Boyd, H. (1980a). Caring and intimacy as a time structure. *Transactional Analysis Journal, 10,* 81–83.

Boyd, L., & Boyd, H. (1980b). Play as a time structure. *Transactional Analysis Journal, 10,* 5–7.

Boyd, L., & Boyd, H. (1980c). Playing with games. *Transactional Analysis Journal, 10,* 8–11.

Boyd, L., & Boyd, H. (1981). A transactional analytic model for relationship counseling. *Transactional Analysis Journal, 11,* 142–146.

Cattell, R. B. (1963). *Self-analysis form.* Champaign, IL: Institute for Personality and Assessment Testing.

Cheney, W. (1971). Eric Berne: Biographical sketch. *Transactional Analysis Journal, 1*(1), 14–22.

Childs-Gowell, E. (1979). *Reparenting schizophrenics: The cathexis experience: Schizophrenics in treatment. An ethnographic study of ritual healing and symbolic action.* North Quincy, MA: Christopher.

Choy, A. (1990). The winner's triangle. *Transactional Analysis Journal, 20*(1), 40–46.

Clarkson, P. (1987). The bystander role. *Transactional Analysis Journal, 17,* 82–87.

Clarkson, P. (1991). Group imago and the stages of group development. *Transactional Analysis Journal, 21,* 36–50.

Clarkson, P., & Gilbert, M. (1988). Berne's original model of ego states: Theoretical considerations. *Transactional Analysis Journal, 18,* 20–29.

Clauss, K. (1995). *The relationship of family style, family competence, self-esteem, separation-individuation with social and emotional adjustment to college.* Unpublished doctoral dissertation, Seton Hall University, South Orange, NJ.

Crossman, P. (1966). Permission and protection. *Transactional Analysis Bulletin, 5*(19), 152–154.

Drego, P. (1983a). The cultural parent. *Transactional Analysis Journal, 13,* 224–227.

Drego, P. (1983b). *Injunctions Scale.* New Delhi, India: TACET.

Drego, P. (1996). Cultural parent oppression and regeneration. *Transactional Analysis Journal, 26,* 58–77.

Dusay, J. M. (1977a). *Egograms.* New York: Harper & Row.

Dusay, J. M. (1977b). The evolution of transactional analysis. In G. Barnes (Ed.), *Transactional analysis after Eric Berne: Teachings and practices of three TA schools* (pp. 32–52). New York: Harper's College Press.

Dusay, J., & Dusay, K. (1989). *Couples therapy: A handbook of technique and theory.* San Francisco: Script Free Press.

English, F. (1969). Episcript and the hot potato game. *Transactional Analysis Bulletin, 8*(32), 77–82.

English, F. (1971). The substitution factor: Rackets and real feelings. *Transactional Analysis Journal, 1*(4), 225–230.

English, F. (1972). Rackets and real feelings. *Transactional Analysis Journal, 2*(1), 23–25.

English, F. (1975). The three-cornered contract. *Transactional Analysis Journal, 5*, 383–384.

English, F. (1976). *Selected articles.* Philadelphia: Eastern Institute for Transactional Analysis and Gestalt.

English, F. (1977). Let's not claim it's script when it ain't. *Transactional Analysis Journal, 7*(2), 130–138.

Ernst, F. (1971). The OK corral: The grid for get-on-with. *Transactional Analysis Journal, 1*(4), 33–41.

Ernst, F. H., Jr. (1973). Psychological rackets in the OK corral. *Transactional Analysis Journal, 3*, 19–23.

Erskine, R. G. (1982). Transactional analysis and family therapy. In A. M. Horne & M. M. Ohlsen (Eds.), *Family counseling and therapy* (pp. 245–275). Itasca, IL: Peacock.

Erskine, R. G. (1988). Ego structure, intrapsychic function, and defense mechanisms: A commentary on Eric Berne's original theoretical concepts. *Transactional Analysis Journal, 18*, 15–19.

Erskine, R. G. (1993). Inquiry, attunement, and involvement in the psychotherapy of dissociation. *Transactional Analysis Journal, 23*(4), 184–190.

Erskine, R. G. (1996). Methods of an integrated psychotherapy. *Transactional Analysis Journal, 26*(4), 316–328.

Erskine, R. G. (1997). *Theories and methods of an integrative transactional analysis: A volume of selected articles.* San Francisco: TA Press.

Erskine, R. G., Clarkson, P., Goulding, R. L., Groder, M. G., & Moiso, C. (1988). Excerpts from the 1987 ITAA Summer Conference roundtable discussion on ego state theory: Definitions, descriptions, and points of view. *Transactional Analysis Journal, 18*, 6–14.

Erskine, R. G., & Moursund, J. P. (1988). *Integrative psychotherapy in action.* Newbury Park, CA: Sage.

Federn, P. (1952). *Ego psychology and the psychoses.* New York: Basic Books.

Frankl, V. E. (1969). *The will to meaning: Foundations and applications of logotherapy.* New York: New American Library.

Freud, S. (1953). Fragment of an analysis of a case of hysteria. In J. Strachey (Ed. & Trans.), *The standard edition of the complete psychological works of Sigmund Freud* (Vol. 7, pp. 15–122). London: Hogarth Press. (Original work published 1905)

Gottman, J., & Silver, N. (1998). *Why marriages succeed or fail: And how you can make yours last.* London: Bloomsbury.

Gough, (1952). *The Adjective Checklist.* Palo Alto, CA: Consulting Psychologists Press.

Goulding, M. M., & Goulding, R. L. (1979). *Changing lives through redecision therapy.* New York: Brunner/Mazel.

Goulding, R. L. (1972, July). *One-month workshop on redecision therapy.* Western Institute for Group and Family Therapy, Mount Madonna, Watsonville, CA.

Goulding, R. L. (1977). No magic at Mt. Madonna: Redecisions in marathon therapy. In G. Barnes (Ed.), *Transactional analysis after Eric Berne: Teachings and practices of three TA schools* (pp. 77–95). New York: Harper's College Press.

Goulding, R. L., & Goulding, M. M. (1978). *The power is in the patient: A TA/Gestalt approach to psychotherapy.* San Francisco: TA Press.

Goulding, R. L., & Goulding, M. M. (1986). *Redecision therapy* [Videotape]. San Francisco: International Transactional Analysis Association.

Groder, M. (1977). Asklepieion: An integration of psychotherapies. In G. Barnes (Ed.), *Transactional analysis after Eric Berne: Teachings and practices of three TA schools* (pp. 134–137). New York: Harper's College Press.

Group for the Advancement of Psychiatry Committee on the Family. (1996). Global Assessment of Relational Functioning Scale (GARF): I. Background and rationale. *Family Process, 35*, 155–172.

Grünewald-Zemsch, G. (2000). The "Small Project": First results, first perspectives. *Transactional Analysis Journal, 30*(1), 58–72.

Hargaden, H., & Sills, C. (2001). Deconfusion of the child ego state. *Transactional Analysis Journal, 31*, 55–70.

Hewitt, G. (1995). Cycles of psychotherapy. *Transactional Analysis Journal, 25*(3), 200–207.

Heyer, N. R. (1987). Empirical research on ego state theory. *Transactional Analysis Journal, 17*(1), 286–293.

Hoyt, M. F. (1997). Foreword. In C. E. Lennox (Ed.), *Redecision therapy* (p. xiv). Northvale, NJ: Aronson.

Hurley, J. R. (1973). Ego-state identifiability: Toward better research. *Transactional Analysis Journal, 3*(3), 32–33.

Jacobs, A. (1987). Autocratic power. *Transactional Analysis Journal, 17,* 59–71.

Jacobs, A. (1994). Theory as ideology: Reparenting and thought reform. *Transactional Analysis Journal, 24,* 39–54.

James, M. (1973). *Born to love: Transaction analysis in the church.* Reading, MA: Addison-Wesley.

James, M. (1979) *Marriage is for loving.* Reading, MA: Addison-Wesley.

James, M. (1981a). *Breaking free: Self-parenting for a new life.* Reading, MA: Addison-Wesley.

James, M. (1981b). The inner core and the human spirit. *Transactional Analysis Journal, 11,* 54–65.

James, M., & Jongeward, D. (1971). *Born to win: Transactional analysis with Gestalt experiments.* New York: Signet.

Joines, V. S. (1977). An integrated systems perspective. In G. Barnes (Ed.), *Transactional analysis after Eric Berne: Teachings and practices of three TA schools* (pp. 247–272). New York: Harper's College Press.

Joines, V. S. (2002). Roots of Satir, Perls, and Berne in redecision family therapy. In R. F. Massey & S. D. Massey (Eds.), *Comprehensive handbook of psychotherapy. Vol. III: Interpersonal, humanistic, existential.* New York: Wiley.

Kadis, L. B., & McClendon, R. (1981). Redecision family therapy: Its use with intensive mutiple family groups. *American Journal of Family Therapy, 9*(2), 75–83.

Kadis, L. B., & McClendon, R. (1990). A model of integrating individual and family therapy: The contract is the key. In J. Zeig & S. Gilligan (Eds.), *Brief therapy: Myths, methods, and metaphors* (pp. 135–150). Philadelphia: Brunner/Mazel.

Kahler, T. (1977). The miniscript. In G. Barnes (Ed.), *Transactional analysis after Eric Berne: Teachings and practices of three TA schools* (pp. 222–256). New York: Harper's College Press.

Karpman, S. (1968). Fairy tales and script drama analysis. *Transactional Analysis Bulletin, 7*(26), 39–43.

Kaslow, F. W. (Ed.). (1996). *Handbook of relational diagnosis and dysfunctional family patterns.* New York: Wiley.

Kerr, M., & Bowen, M. (1988). *Family evaluation: An approach based on Bowen theory.* New York: Norton.

Kertesz, R. (1978). *Manual de analisis transaccional de acuerdo a los program as oficiales de ALAT* [Manual of transactional analysis according to the official programs of ALAT]. Conantal, Argentina: Editorial.

Klein, M. (1975). *Envy and gratitude, and other works, 1946–1963.* London: Hogarth Press.

L'Abate, L. (1978). An experimental paper-and-pencil test for assessing ego states. *Transactional Analysis Journal, 8*(3), 262–265.

Lennox, C. (1997). *Redecision therapy: A brief, action-oriented approach.* Northvale, NJ: J. Aronson.

Levin, P. (1980). *Cycles of power.* San Francisco: Transactional Publications.

Liberman, M. A., Yalom, I. D., & Miles, M. B. (1973). *Encounter groups: First facts.* New York: Basic Books.

Lincoln, Y. S., & Guba, E. G. (1985). *Naturalistic inquiry.* Newbury Park, CA: Sage.

Massey, R. F. (1981). *Personality theories: Comparisons and syntheses.* Reading, MA: D. Van Nostrand.

Massey, R. F. (1983). Passivity, paradox, and change. *Transactional Analysis Journal, 13,* 33–41.

Massey, R. F. (1985). TA as a family systems therapy. *Transactional Analysis Journal, 15,* 120–141.

Massey, R. F. (1986). Paradox, double binding, and counterparadox: A transactional analysis perspective. *Transactional Analysis Journal, 16,* 24–46.

Massey, R. F. (1987). Transactional analysis and the social psychology of power: Reflections evoked by Jacobs' "autocratic power." *Transactional Analysis Journal, 17,* 107–120.

Massey, R. F. (1989a). Integrating systems theory and TA in couples therapy. *Transactional Analysis Journal, 19,* 128–136.

Massey, R. F. (1989b). The philosophical compatibility of Adler and Berne. *Individual Psychology, 45,* 323–334.

Massey, R. F. (1989c). Script theory synthesized systemically. *Transactional Analysis Journal, 19,* 14–25.

Massey, R. F. (1989d). Systemic contexts for children's scripting. *Transactional Analysis Journal, 19,* 186–193.

Massey, R. F. (1989e). Techniques in integrative systemic/TA couples therapy. *Transactional Analysis Journal, 19,* 148–158.

Massey, R. F. (1990a). Berne's transactional analysis as a neo-Freudian/neo-Adlerian perspective. *Transactional Analysis Journal, 20,* 173–186.

Massey, R. F. (1990b). Structural bases of games. *Transactional Analysis Journal, 20,* 20–27.

Massey, R. F. (1991). The evolution of perspectives on transference in relation to transactional analysis. *Transactional Analysis Journal, 21,* 155–169.

Massey, R. F. (1993). Neo-Adlerian constructs in Berne's transactional analysis. *Journal of Individual Psychology, 49,* 13–35.

Massey, R. F. (1995). Theoretical foundations for the treatment of individuals from an integrative systems/transactional analysis framework. *Transactional Analysis Journal, 5,* 271–284.

Massey, R. F. (1996). Transactional analysis as a social psychology. *Transactional Analysis Journal, 26,* 91–99.

Massey, R. F., & Massey, S. D. (1988). A systemic approach to treating children with their families. *Transactional Analysis Journal, 18,* 110–122.

Massey, R. F., & Massey, S. D, (1995). Die sozial-psychologischen und systemischen dimensionen der transaktionsanalyse als perspektiv fur die behandlung von einzelnen, paarenpend familien [The social-psychological and systemic dimensions of transactional analysis as a perspective for the treatment of individuals, couples, and families]. *Zeitschrift für Transaktions Analyse, 12*(4), 157–197.

Massey, S. D., & Massey, R. F. (1989). Systemic contexts for therapy with children. *Transactional Analysis Journal, 19,* 194–200.

Masters, W. H., & Johnson, V. E. (1970). *Human sexual inadequacy.* Boston: Little, Brown.

Masters, W. H., & Johnson, V. E. (1975). *The pleasure bond: A new look at sexuality and commitment.* Toronto: Bantam Books.

McClenaghan, J. C. (1978). *Transactional analysis research: A review of empirical tests and studies.* Unpublished manuscript, University of Colorado, Boulder.

McClendon, R. (1977). My mother drives a pickup truck. In G. Barnes (Ed.), *Transactional analysis after Eric Berne: Teachings and practices of three TA schools* (pp. 99–113). New York: Harper's College Press.

McCormick, P. (1973). TA and behavior modification: A comparison study. *Transactional Analysis Journal, 3,* 10–14.

McNeel, J. (1976a). The parent interview. *Transactional Analysis Journal, 6*(1), 61–68.

McNeel, J. (1976b). Redecisions in psychotherapy: A study of the effects of an intensive weekend group workshop (Doctoral dissertation, California School of Professional Psychology, 1976). *Dissertation Abstracts International, 36,* 9-B, 4700.

McNeel, J. (1977). The seven components of redecision therapy. In G. Barnes (Ed.), *Transactional analysis after Eric Berne: Teachings and practices of three TA schools* (pp. 425–441). New York: Harper & Row.

McNeel, J. (1982). Redecisions in psychotherapy: A study of the effects of an intensive weekend group workshop. *Transactional Analysis Journal, 12*(1), 10–26.

Mellor, K. (1980). Impasses: A developmental and structural understanding. *Transactional Analysis Journal, 10*(3), 213–221.

Miller, S., Hubble, M., & Duncan, B. (1995, March/April). No more bells and whistles. *Family Therapy Networker,* 53–63.

Moiso, C. M. (1985). Ego states and transference. *Transactional Analysis Journal, 15*(3), 194–201.

Noriega Gayol, G. (1997). Diagnosis and treatment of ego state boundary problems: Effects on self-esteem and quality of life. *Transactional Analysis Journal, 27*(4), 236–240.

Novellino, M. (1984). Self-analysis of countertransference in integrative transactional analysis. *Transactional Analysis Journal, 14*(1), 63–67.

Novellino, M. (1985). Redecision analysis of transference: A TA approach to transference neurosis. *Transactional Analysis Journal, 15*(3), 202–206.

Novellino, M. (1987). Redecision analysis of transference: The unconscious dimension. *Transactional Analysis Journal, 17*(1), 271–276.

Novellino, M. (1990). Unconscious communication and interpretation in transactional analysis. *Transactional Analysis Journal, 20*(3), 168–172.

Novellino, M. (1991). *Psicologia clinicva dell io* [The clinical psychology of the ego]. Rome: Astrolabio.

Novellino, M., Cavellero, G., Giovanoli Vercellino, C., Leone Guglielmotti, R., Miglionico, A., Moiso, C., et al. (1998). *L'approccio clinico dell'analisi tranzionale* [The transactional analysis clinical approach]. Milan, Italy: Franco Angeli.

Novellino, M., & Moiso, C. (1990). The psychodynamic approach to transactional analysis. *Transactional Analysis Journal, 20*(3), 187–192.

Novey, T. B. (1999). The effectiveness of transactional analysis. *Transactional Analysis Journal, 29*(1), 18–30.

Ohlsson, T. (1988). A "mandala model" of the adult ego states. *Transactional Analysis Journal, 18,* 30–38.

Orten, J. D. (1973). Societal applications of transactional theory. *Transactional Analysis Journal, 3*(3), 11–16.

Paivo, S. C., & Greenberg, L. S. (1995). Resolving "unfinished business": Efficacy of experiential therapy using empty-chair dialogue. *Journal of Consulting and Clinical Psychology, 63*(3), 419–425.

Penfield, W. (1952). Memory mechanisms. *Archives of Neurological Psychiatry, 67,* 178–198.

Penfield, W., & Jasper, H. (1954). *Epilepsy and the functional anatomy of the human brain.* Boston: Little, Brown.

Penfield, W., & Roberts, L. (1959). *Speech and brain: Mechanisms.* Princeton, NJ: Princeton University Press.

Perls, F. S. (1969). *Gestalt therapy verbatim.* Lafayette, CA: Real People Press.

Perls, F. S., Hefferline, R. F., & Goodman, P. (1951). *Gestalt therapy.* New York: Dell.

Piaget, J. (1932). *The moral judgment of the child.* New York: Harcourt, Brace.

Piaget, J. (1954). *The construction of reality in the child.* New York: Basic Books.

Schiff, J. L. (1970). *All my children.* New York: M. Evans.

Schiff, J. L. (1977). One hundred children generates a lot of TA: History, development, and activities of the Schiff family. In G. Barnes (Ed.), *Transactional analysis after Eric Berne: Teachings and practices of three TA schools* (pp. 53–76). New York: Harper's College Press.

Schiff, J. L., Mellor, K., Schiff, E., Schiff, S., Richman, D., Fishman, J., et al. (1975). *Cathexis reader: Transactional analysis treatment of psychosis.* New York: Harper & Row.

Seligman, M. E. P. (1975). *Helplessness: On depression, development, and death.* San Francisco: Freeman.

Sowder, W. F., & Brown, R. A. (1977). Experimentation in transactional analysis. *Transactional Analysis Journal, 7*(3), 279–285.

Spitz, R. (1945). Hospitalism: Genesis of psychiatric conditions in early childhood. *Psychoanalytic Study of the Child, 1,* 53–74.

Steenbarger, B. N. (1992). Toward science-practice integration in brief counseling and therapy. *Counseling Psychologist, 20,* 403–450.

Steiner, C. M. (1966). Script and counterscript. *Transactional Analysis Bulletin, 5*(18), 133–135.

Steiner, C. M. (1970). A fairy tale. *Transactional Analysis Bulletin, 9*(36), 146–149.

Steiner, C. M. (1971). *Games alcoholics play.* New York: Grove Press.

Steiner, C. M. (1972). Radical psychiatry. In H. M. Ruitenbeeck (Ed.), *Going crazy* (pp. 301–308). New York: Bantam.

Steiner, C. M. (1973). Inside TA. *Issues in Radical Psychiatry, 1*(2), 3–4.

Steiner, C. M. (1974). Principles. In J. Marcus, C. Steiner, & H. Wyckoff (Eds.), *Readings in radical psychiatry* (pp. 9–16). New York: Grove Press. (Original work published 1971)

Stephenson, W. (1953). *The study of behavior: Q-technique and its methodology.* Chicago: University of Chicago Press.

Stern, E. (Ed.). (1984). *TA: The state of the art: A European contribution.* Dordrecht, The Netherlands: Foris.

Stewart, I. (1996). *Developing transactional analysis counselling.* Thousand Oaks, CA: Sage.

Straker, G. (2001, July 27). *The dream of reconciliation: The reality of fragmentation.* Keynote speech at the International Transactional Analysis Association/Western Pacific Association of Transactional Analysis, Sydney, Australia.

Swede, S. (1978). Group Ego State Measure (GEM). *Transactional Analysis Journal, 8*(2), 163–165.

Thomson, G. (1972). The identification of ego states. *Transactional Analysis Journal, 2*(4), 196–211.

Thunnissen, M. (2001). Transactional Analysis research. *The Script, 31*(6), 1, 7.

Wechsler, D (1977). *Wechsler Adult Intelligence Scale, Third Edition.* San Antonio, TX: Psychological Corporation.

Weiss, E. (1950). *Principles of psychodynamics.* New York: Grune & Stratton.

Williams, J. E., Watson, J. R., Walters, P. A., & Williams, J. G. (1983). Construct validity of transactional analysis ego states: Free child, adult, and critical parent. *Transactional Analysis Journal, 13*(1), 43–49.

CHAPTER 23

Body-Centered Psychotherapy

WILLIAM F. CORNELL

The central organizing premises of the body-centered psychotherapies are that psyche and soma are indivisible in healthy cognitive and emotional functioning and that direct attention to cognitive, emotional, and bodily experience must be actively included in therapeutic process. The perspective underlying the body-centered therapeutic modalities goes beyond a philosophical challenge to the traditional, enculturated Cartesian split between mind and body to posit as a central therapeutic principle that somatic processes, such as sensate experience, sensorimotor development, muscular movement and structure, all constitute forms of mental organization and function, which underlie subsequent cognitive development. Any condition, concern, or symptom that brings a client into therapy will be explored simultaneously in cognitive, emotional, and bodily terms in a body-centered treatment approach. Diagnosis and treatment proceed from an understanding of the interactive influences of these different realms of mental and somatic experiencing. The integration of mental and bodily activity is promoted throughout the clinical process and is seen as an essential goal in this therapeutic perspective (M. Ludwig, personal communication, April 5, 2000).

In an overview of contemporary body-centered psychotherapies, Boadella (1997a) described the extension of the field of therapeutic attention and intervention in the body-centered modalities to include work with movement, breathing, body image, emotional expression, channels of contact, touch, and language. Perhaps more than any other characteristic, the direct work with the actual movement and activity of the body in the therapeutic session distinguishes body psychotherapy from other psychotherapeutic modalities. Boadella observed:

> Neuro-physiologically we know how dependent perception is on motility, and research into the body image shows a similar dependency. The movements of the body are a source of vitality affect, but are also intrinsic to the expression, or repression, of all other affects. The movement vocabulary of the child, during the first year and a half, is the foundation of his communicative rapport with the world: he interacts by means of motoric and vocal signs long before there is the capacity for the semantic use of language.

... All dimensions [of somatic processes] I have described are relational. Breath is relational, touch is communicative, movement is interactive, emotionality is contact-oriented, object relations become body-subject relatedness. (pp. 33, 39)

Although the body-centered modalities originally developed within the psychoanalytic tradition (Boadella, 1973; Downing, 1996; Reich, 1949; Totton, 1998), these approaches have a philosophical and attitudinal base that has much in common with the humanistic and existential traditions (Downing, 1996; D. H. Johnson & Grand, 1998; Smith, 1977b, 1985). Body-centered psychotherapies tend to be nonnormative, often challenging social and cultural norms, in support of the deepening and intensification of individual desire and interpersonal contact. The overarching therapeutic goals are not focused so much on symptom relief as on the opening up of emotional experience and motoric freedom to develop a liveliness and gracefulness of the body that "reveals an essential meaning, an embodied contact to the heart, and a motoric expression symbolizing a deep and committed life-direction" (Boadella, 1997a, p. 33).

HISTORY OF THE APPROACH

History and Evolution of Body Psychotherapy

The development of body-centered psychotherapies has paralleled and sometimes interacted with the development of psychodynamic models of psychotherapy. These therapies also have their own distinct history (Boadella, 1990). They have rarely experienced acceptance in the more traditional fields of psychotherapy and have only recently emerged to the point of forming their own professional organizations in Europe and the United States.

If the history of body psychotherapy were viewed as a family tree, virtually all of the roots would eventually wind back to Georg Groddeck, Sandor Ferenczi, and Wilhelm Reich (Boadella, 1990; Downing, 1996). During the 1920s and early 1930s, in Austria and Germany, an explosion of creativity and controversy in analytic theory and technique, led by Groddeck, Ferenczi, and Reich, formed the basis of virtually all of the body-centered psychotherapies practiced today. The work of these analysts, who endeavored to enter somatic domains to extend modes of psychological treatment, was relegated to the margins in psychoanalytic history. Their work has evolved as a separate therapeutic modality, often at the fringes of more conventional psychotherapies.

A medical pioneer who never became a member of Freud's inner circle, Groddeck (1977) practiced primarily as a physician rather than as a psychoanalyst in a residential sanitarium that offered a combination of dietary, psychoanalytic, and somatic treatments. Groddeck worked directly with the body through massage and other physical manipulations before discovering Freud's work. He continued to engage directly with the body while incorporating psychoanalytic techniques. Looking back on his career, Groddeck wrote, "The only achievement I can claim for myself with some justification is the introduction of a knowledge of the unconscious into the treatment of all patients, and particularly those who suffer from organic illnesses . . . in treatment I rely on my head and on my hands" (p. 1). He wrote frequently of the unconscious influences on both psychosomatic and organic illnesses, using a style of deep massage and other somatic treatments (baths, exercise) while drawing on dream analysis, free association, and analytic interpretations. Groddeck speculated on the importance of the pre-Oedipal, preverbal mother-infant relationship, but did not carry these ideas into therapeutic work with adults.

Groddeck served as a mentor and friend to Ferenczi, whose work, unlike that of Groddeck and Reich, is undergoing a renaissance in contemporary psychoanalysis and psychotherapy

(Aron & Harris, 1993; Haynal, 1989; Rachman, 1997). In his early analytic work, Ferenczi encouraged patients to actively suppress bodily activity, which he first viewed as an evasion of the analytic process, so as to see what analytic material would emerge if the body were stilled. In the second phase of his work, after reading and meeting Groddeck (Downing, 1996), Ferenczi began to experiment with encouraging movement. He came to see bodily activity as a form of expression rather than as an avoidance of communication and understanding. In the final stages of his work with severely disturbed clients, Ferenczi used a wide variety of physical and verbal techniques to enter as directly as possible into states of early affect and memory. Ferenczi (1955) wanted to reach "back to phases of development in which, since the organ of thought was not yet completely developed, physical memories alone were registered" (p. 122). He had come to see the necessity of working through the body and the transference-countertransference relationship to access the preverbal, infantile substratum of affective and relational experience.

Ferenczi was originally one of Freud's favorite sons and a member of the inner circle, but he became thoroughly discredited by Freud and his cohort, with his later work actively suppressed by his colleagues. Groddeck influenced Ferenczi, and Ferenczi subsequently influenced Reich (Boadella, 1990; Downing, 1996). All three seemed to make the more proper Viennese analysts, including Freud, quite nervous. Haynal (1989), in discussing the Freud/Ferenczi controversies, speculated that "probably, the most unbearable thing for Freud was the knowledge that Ferenczi had entered the 'ordeal' of severely regressed patients. This could hardly have failed to revive memories of his own early experiences of the Breuer period" (p. 31). Haynal referred to the years when Freud and Breuer collaborated to understand and treat hysterics, a period of time that gave birth to psychoanalysis but proved less than successful for their patients and rather traumatic for the two men. Emery (1995) commented on the Dionysian (i.e., uninhibited) attitude inherent in Ferenczi's life and work, in contrast to Freud's more Apollonian perspective of reserve, intellect, and discipline. Ferenczi, Groddeck, and Reich displayed a Dionysian intensity in their character and work. All three touched their patients, all three experimented with technique and wrote frankly and eloquently about their treatment failures. Ferenczi and Reich actively pressured their colleagues to speak and write more openly about technique. Ferenczi's challenges to theory and technique were mired in controversy and misrepresentation for half a century, and only now are undergoing revival and reconsideration.

Reich (1961, 1974) emerged as the ultimate theorist of the psychology of libidinous drives, writing more systematically than any other psychoanalyst about the nature of drives and about the body in conflict with itself. Groddeck and Ferenczi were primarily clinicians, each quite willing to push the boundaries of technique for the welfare of their clients, particularly those clients whom other physicians and psychoanalysts had found difficult to treat. They focused their writings more clinically than theoretically. Reich undertook the development of a comprehensive theory of direct work with the body and the drives.

Once Freud had turned away from his experiments with physical, hypnotic, and cathartic interventions, he consistently privileged cognitive processes over those of the body. Freud's writings on technique after the turn of the century came to form the canon of psychoanalytic methodology. Freud (1912) consistently warned against patients' persistent defensive and regressive movements into forms of "acting out," that is, avoiding the "psychical sphere" and yielding to instinctual impulses by entering the "motoric sphere" (p. 153). Freud (1911) argued, "Restraint upon motor discharge (upon action), which then became necessary, was provided by means of the process of *thinking*, which was developed from the presentation of ideas" (p. 221). Wittingly or unwittingly, Freud reentered the

Cartesian split of mind and body. This was a splitting that Reich opposed directly, both theoretically and technically. Reich contended that therapeutic technique needed to directly enter into vegetative and motoric realms to generate lasting change in psychic structure and that work in the psychical sphere must be grounded in work in the motoric domain. The body, in its expressions and actions, always drew Reich's therapeutic attention and intervention.

Fundamentally altering the classical psychoanalytic approach, Reich turned to face his patients as they lay on the couch. In addition to the free-associative and interpretive techniques developed by Freud, Reich's verbal interventions were descriptive and confrontive of what he first termed character resistances. These could include chronically and defensively held facial and postural expressions, attitudes, ambitions, values, self-ideals, repetitive affects, fantasies, and other habitual presentations of self and styles of relating. Reich (1949) emphasized: "What is added in character analysis is merely that we isolate the character trait and confront the patient with it repeatedly until he begins to look at it objectively and to experience it like a painful symptom; thus, the character trait begins to be experienced as a foreign body which the patient wants to get rid of" (p. 50).

But insight did not necessarily follow in the wake of Reich's (1961) characterological confrontations. He observed that his precise and rather aggressive confrontations often produced visible bodily and physiological reactions. He conceptualized these physiological reactions as a second line of defense, which he came to describe as muscular armor, in which the emotional and motoric patterns were literally turned against themselves in a "vegetative antithesis" (pp. 255–265) of the original intent of the drives. Long fascinated by the physiological relationship between pleasure and anxiety in sexual and emotional experiences, Reich believed that he had made a crucial discovery. He perceived himself leaving the psychoanalytic domain and renamed his work "vegetotherapy." In addition to the conventional work of free association and interpretation, he began to work directly with patients' bodies so as to intensify physical and emotional expression. He thereby laid the foundation for the evolution of body-centered forms of psychotherapy.

The central clinical question for Reich (1949) was not *what* or *why*, but *how*, stressing process over content: "What is specific of the character resistance is not *what* the patient says or does, but *how* he talks and acts, not *what* he gives away in a dream, but *how* he censors, distorts, etc. The character resistance remains the same in one and the same patient no matter what the material is against which it is directed" (p. 47). Reich sought to bring the patient into the subtle and immediate experience of bodily process: "We can learn much from this phenomenon [of inner emptiness and deadening] if we can make the patient relive the *transition* from the alive to the dead condition as vividly as possible, and if we pay the closest attention to the swings from one condition to the other during treatment" (pp. 325–326).

For Reich, the very essence of character analytic technique at both interpersonal and somatic levels revolved around the delicate and carefully attended experience of shifting *in the present moment* between vitality and deadness, between the motility and the constrictions of the body. The *how* of the body underlay the content of the patient's *what* and *why* of session material. Reich focused his attention on the patterns of somatic expression, including breathing, posture, eye contact, patterns of muscular movement and inhibition, changes in skin color and temperature, and the quality of the voice in speaking (in addition to the content of what was being said). Totton (1998) provided a comprehensive exploration of Reich's theories and therapeutic style during this period in the context of a discussion of the place of the body in psychoanalysis and psychotherapy.

The body emerged as central in Reich's clinical work not only through his work with resistance, but also through his attention to sexuality. From the 1920s on, sexuality represented an enduring theme in his clinical writings (Reich, 1961, 1971, 1980), his research efforts (1982, 1983), and his sociopolitical activities (1974). In many of his earliest writings as a psychoanalyst, he explored the relationship between anxiety and sexuality, postulating that the inhibition of sexuality and the capacity for intimacy undergirded many of the interpersonal and somatic character defenses. Freeing up an individual's capacity for pleasure and sexual intimacy constituted a stated goal of therapy for Reich. He also worked in the social and political realms to support sex education and counseling. In 1929, with Freud's support, Reich founded the Socialist Society for Sex Consultation and Sexological Research, which operated six free clinics for workers in Vienna, programs that were subsequently expanded in Germany before he was forced to emigrate to Scandinavia. During his years in Norway, 1934 to 1938, Reich undertook bioelectrical experiments with sexuality, foreshadowing the work of Masters and Johnson. In his radical and far-reaching efforts, fraught with clinical and social implications, Reich advocated for healthy sexuality.

As Reich left the psychoanalytic movement, he also separated from his wife, Annie, a fellow psychoanalyst. He became involved with Elsa Lindenberg, a well-known German dancer and movement specialist who had studied with Elsa Gindler and Rudolf Laban, both of whom had developed systems of body and movement training in Germany (Boadella, 1990). Their work influenced psychotherapy, physical therapy, and choreography in the 1930s, affecting the development of such diverse systems as Charlotte Selver's sensory awareness training in Europe and Kazuo Ohno's style of Buto dance in Japan. Although Reich made little direct reference in his clinical writing to these body movement specialists, clearly they exercised a strong influence on his shift to a deeply body-centered orientation. Laura Perls, too, studied with Elsa Gindler, bringing this emphasis on body movement into the therapeutic style she was developing with her husband, Fritz. Fritz Perls (Smith, 1977b) was a patient of Reich's during his characteranalytic period and, with Laura, drew heavily on this phase of Reich's work to develop what became known as Gestalt therapy.

Reich fled the Nazi movement in Germany and Austria, emigrating first to Denmark and then to Norway, where he continued to develop vegetotherapy. He emphasized that the memories and transferential experiences emerging in therapy must be accompanied by appropriate affect. He sought to elicit intense emotional expression in the therapy session. He trained many therapists and psychoanalysts in techniques that relied far less on verbal or interpersonal techniques, and instead worked directly with a client's muscular and movement patterns in a vigorous, hands-on style of therapeutic intervention. In this way, Reich desired to bring body-level patterns of defense into conscious awareness. He used a client's movements and emotional expression, combined with the therapist's direct physical intervention, to break through somatic defenses and to open up affective and cognitive awareness.

Reich emigrated to the United States in 1939. Theodore Wolfe, a physician and psychoanalyst married to Flanders Dunbar, who had written an influential textbook on psychosomatic medicine, sponsored Reich. Dunbar and Wolfe were interested in bringing Reich's psychosomatic theories to physicians and psychoanalysts in the United States. By this time, Reich was deeply involved in his orgone theories, now renaming his work "orgonomy." He came to believe that he had discovered a form of primordial energy, orgone, which was the substratum of both psychic and somatic experience. He conceptualized his therapeutic procedures as working directly with this energetic process, moving away from psychological and somatic explanations of his work.

This led to his discreditation and marginalization in mainstream psychiatry and psychoanalysis. He did, however, train and influence a number of physicians and psychologists in the United States (Baker, 1967; Lowen, 1975; Sharaf, 1983). They, in turn, have developed therapeutic models of their own and gone on to educate a generation of body-centered therapists in such modalities as orgonomy (Baker, 1967), bioenergetics (Lowen, 1958, 1975), Radix body education (Kelley, 1974), biosynthesis (Boadella, 1987), and the work of Keleman (1986, 1989). These students of Reich drew heavily on his emphasis on direct work with the body to elicit deep emotional expression and continue to have influence in North and South America and Europe. Each has viewed the body as the primary mechanism of both psychological organization and characterological defenses.

Profound changes have transpired in the conceptualization of the body in contemporary models of body-centered psychotherapy (Cornell, 1997a, 2000; Downing, 1996; D. H. Johnson & Grand, 1998). Current theoreticians are rapidly incorporating the implications of research on the mother-infant dyad, trauma, and neurological processes. Models based in dance and movement (Caldwell, 1996), sensorimotor development (Macnaughton, 1996; Marcher & Bernhardt, 1996), trauma (Bernhardt, 1996; Levine, 1997), and body work (D. H. Johnson, 1995) have moved many body-centered psychotherapies beyond the Reichian perspective. Maul (1992) edited a collection of papers that provide a comprehensive overview of body-centered psychotherapies in Europe, and Caldwell's (1997) edited volume has done the same for many of the modalities currently practiced in the United States. The relational and transferential aspects of somatic work have received increasing attention (Boadella, 1997a; Cornell, 1997a, 2000), thus emphasizing the communicative intention of bodily activity. From this perspective, all vital, intimate relationships at any age and developmental stage deeply influence the form, cohesion, and vitality of the body. A fundamental knowing of self and other forms first through the experience and use of all senses of one's body in relation to that of another's. Healthy development involves the integration of motoric and sensate processes in the context of a primary relationship, establishing subsymbolic, somatic schemas of the self in relation to one's own body, to cognitive and symbolic capacities, and to the desire for and experience of the other.

Efforts to integrate somatic experience into psychotherapeutic models are increasingly evident. Smith (1985) and Kepner (1987) significantly extended the theory and techniques of Gestalt therapy to more direct work with the body, placing bodily experience and activity at the heart of therapeutic processes. S. M. Johnson (1985), Krueger (1989), Brahler (1988), and Aron and Anderson (1998) examined the centrality of bodily experience and activity in psychoanalytic and object-relations perspectives. Experience of the body proves central in the theories of such contemporary French psychoanalytic theorists as McDougall (1989, 1995), Anzieu (1989), and Green (2000). The attitude toward the body in psychoanalytic perspectives in the United States has been far more ambivalent. From the perspective of the body-centered psychotherapies, the analytic attitude toward the body remains one step removed from the actualities of somatic processes. The body may be discussed, but is rarely worked with directly through touch and sensorimotor activity.

Related Disciplines: Phenomenology and Body Work

Phenomenological and Experiential Models
Attention to somatic and subsymbolic processes in psychological development and cognitive organization is now emerging in the theories and research of the cognitive sciences (Bermudez, Marcel, & Eilan, 1995; Bucci, 1997; Thelen & Smith, 1994; Varela, Thompson, & Rosch, 1991).

For decades, the body has been at the heart of the phenomenological perspective (Merleau-Ponty, 1964, 1967). From a phenomenological frame of reference, Gallagher drew on the work of Husserl and Merleau-Ponty to describe prenoetic consciousness. Gallagher (1995) suggested that, "Using Merleau-Ponty's model of embodied intentionality, we can develop an account of how the body, prior to or outside of cognitive experience, helps to constitute the meaning that comes to consciousness" (p. 233). He averred, "To the extent that some cognitive scientists persist in approaches that refuse to recognize the complications introduced by the various roles of the human body in cognition, they run the risk of creating abstract and disembodied paradigms" (p. 240). Bucci (1997) raised essentially the same issues with her psychoanalytic colleagues.

In the phenomenological perspective, the body forms the structure of perception and experience. The body proves fundamental, profoundly influencing consciousness while remaining largely out of conscious awareness. Phenomenologists emphasize the somatic realms of experience as *pre*conscious. This sharply contrasts to the psychoanalytic conceptualization of the *un*conscious. For phenomenologists, bodily experiences precede and shape conscious thought and expression. For example, Merleau-Ponty (1962) observed:

> In this way the body expresses total existence, not because it is an external accompaniment to that existence, but because existence comes into its own body. This incarnate significance is the central phenomenon of which body and mind, sign and significance are abstract moments. (p. 166)

The body and its senses serve as the means and fabric of all subsequent organization and knowledge. As expressed by Kwant (1963), "The body gives us a world, that the world's structure depends on the structure of our body. The reason is not that the body causally influences the world, but that the body, precisely as body, gives meaning to the world. The body is intimately permeated with meanings" (p. 41). Rooted in the phenomenological philosophies (M. Johnson, 1987; Kwant, 1963, 1969; Luijpen, 1960; Merleau-Ponty, 1962; O'Neil, 1989; Spiegelberg, 1972), a phenomenological psychology has emerged from within this philosophical tradition (Giorgi, Fischer, & von Eckartsberg, 1971; Spiegelberg, 1972; Valle & King, 1978). A phenomenological psycho*therapy*, as such, remains elusive, although phenomenology has deeply influenced psychotherapy and the existential/humanistic tradition (Binswanger, 1963; Boss, 1963; Frankl, 1967; Laing, 1960, 1961; R. May, 1966, 1969; Yalom, 1980). The mode of therapeutic inquiry in the phenomenological tradition reflects the effort to understand the world from within the lived experience of a client, in marked contrast to viewing a person from the outside in, as is more often characteristic of the classical psychoanalytic, cognitive, and behavioral traditions. The body offers the ground from which the therapy emerges, the ground of one's lived experience in the moment, but the body itself does not serve as the field of therapeutic interventions, as in the body-centered modalities (Downing, 2000).

The focus on direct, lived experience of the body provides a central organizing principle of the approaches characterized as experiential psychotherapies (Gendlin, 1962, 1981; L. S. Greenberg, Elliott, & Lietaer, 1994; L. S. Greenberg & Safran, 1987; Kepner, 1987; Sardello, 1971; Yontef, 1979). Extending the work of Gendlin (1962), Greenberg and Safran (1987) summarized the phenomenological/experiential perspective:

> Feeling in Gendlin's model is . . . a complex "bodily felt sense" that accompanies every meaningful act. It is this felt sense to which an individual attends when attempting to articulate the *meaning* of any concept or experience, whether or not it is emotionally toned. Therefore, *feeling is the bodily felt dimension of meaning*. It is the basic datum of our inwardly directed attention. It involves our preverbal, preconceptual, bodily sense of being in

interaction with the environment, an internal sense of the felt meaning of things. (p. 47; emphasis in original)

The experiential and Gestalt-oriented modalities share a great deal in common with the body-centered traditions. These approaches highlight the facilitation of felt experience in the here and now so as to deepen and broaden the range of conscious awareness. They entail processes of discovering more than of uncovering, and are thus distinguishable from psychoanalytic practices, which stress interpretation, verbalization, and uncovering. The phenomenological methods have evolved separately from the Reichian and neo-Reichian traditions, and the models have emerged with little influence on each other. The body-centered approaches bridge these two perspectives. Both the uncovering of unconscious, denied impulses and desires as well as the discovery and facilitation of novel experience and activity receive emphasis in body-centered psychotherapy.

Body Work Modalities
The broad umbrella of body work or *somato*therapies, distinct from body *psycho*therapy, refers to a second and separate tradition of work with the body. These are approaches for direct work with the body without accompanying psychological theories or systematic attention to the psychological impact of somatic intervention. Body work refers broadly to a loosely related spectrum of approaches to alleviating somatic malaise (deadness, depressiveness), chronic pain, and muscular tension. Body work practitioners seek to alter chronic postural and muscular patterns through teaching body awareness, altering movement patterns, and hands-on physical manipulation of a client's body. Many of the approaches characterized as body *work*, which include sensory awareness (Hanna, 1988, 1993), structural integration (D. H. Johnson, 1977; Rolf, 1989), the Feldenkrais method (Feldenkrais, 1950, 1981), and the Alexander technique (Alexander, 1918, 1923), typically originated with people working outside of the psychological disciplines. D. H. Johnson (1995), editor of a book of essays by and interviews with many of the originators of body work methodologies, characterized the founders of these methods in this way:

They worked quietly, wrote very little. Typically, they spent their lives outside of the vociferous worlds of university and research clinics.
 . . . These pioneers in embodiment are typically a feisty lot, unwilling to take at face value a poor medical diagnosis, a dull exercise class, ordinary states of consciousness. Rejecting the bleakness of conventional wisdom, they have chosen to survive outside the mainstream, like artists who often struggle to make a living by doing something other than their heart's work. (pp. ix, xi)

These disciplines have developed outside of academic structures and are taught and maintained by seeing, doing, practicing, and developing a kind of sensate, somatic knowledge based on accumulated and finely tuned experience rather than reading and quantitative research. Many of these originators had no academic or professional background for their contributions. Ida Rolf (1989), a biochemist at the Rockefeller Institute, developed structural integration ("Rolfing"), a method of deep tissue and fascial work to correct chronic postural distortions and inhibitions. Rolf first drew on her knowledge of yoga, osteopathy, and homeopathy to help the sister of a friend, a piano teacher who had lost the use of her hands after an accident and was unable to play the piano. She systematized her discoveries into a model of postural realignment. In a similar fashion of discovery, F. Matthais Alexander (1918, 1923), a Shakespearian actor, kept losing his voice. He watched himself speak in a mirror and gradually learned to see and feel the subtle, unconscious patterns of muscular movement, to identify chronic patterns of muscular misuse. He went on to formalize a system of deep muscular release, known as the Alexander techniques, to restore sensory perceptions and freedom of movement. This method is now used in many drama, dance, and music schools to correct subtle injuries and constrictions from the repetitive and expressive movements of the performing arts. The Alexander technique supplements conventional psychotherapies to enhance bodily awareness. Moises Feldenkrais (1950, 1981), a nuclear physicist who became fascinated with Alexander's work, fashioned his own system of body work. He focused on the body in relation to gravity, with particular emphasis on habitual, unconscious patterns of movement and sensate function. All of these and related methods involve combinations of movements and exercises to enhance sensate/bodily awareness and of direct hands-on intervention by the practitioner to facilitate somatic reorganization. Contemporary practitioners of body work are growing in awareness of the psychological and emotional implications of their work. So, too, body psychotherapists are increasingly acknowledging that many of the body work systems can enhance their skills in direct work with the body. Body workers and body psychotherapists are working more and more collaboratively. The U.S. and European Associations for Body Psychotherapy are engaged in concerted efforts to facilitate mutual dialogue and training among the diverse, though interrelated, disciplines of body work and body psychotherapy.

THEORETICAL CONSTRUCTS

Touch in Psychotherapy

The intentional and systematic utilization of direct physical contact between therapist and client remains fundamental to the body-centered psychotherapies. The use of touch in psychotherapy generates intense controversy and has contributed to the slow acceptance and, sometimes, the outright condemnation of body-centered techniques. A thorough discussion of the role of touch in psychotherapeutic change exceeds the confines of this chapter. A summary of theory, research, and clinical cautions is included here because physical contact between therapist and client occurs as standard procedure in the body-centered repertoire.

Traditionally, the taboo against touch between therapist and client is based on concerns about gratification and sexualization. Touch between therapist and client has been viewed as an intervention that places both parties at unnecessary risk of enactment of intimate, sexual, and/or aggressive impulses in the therapeutic dyad. A long-held, though now increasingly challenged, premise among psychodynamic theories implies that the gratification by the therapist of the client's needs and desires would short-circuit therapeutic motivation. Freud's (1912, 1913, 1914, 1915) insistence on the analyst as a detached, objective, anonymous, and non-gratifying presence has long held sway in the psychotherapeutic superego, even among therapists who do not practice psychoanalysis. Freud's prohibitions echo and reinforce cultural prohibitions against touch and intimacy.

Casement (1982) insisted on the maintenance of Freud's rule of abstinence and prohibitions against touch. He argued that physical contact can become a collusive action by the therapist, confusing the symbolic and the literal, thereby collapsing the "as if" exploratory space necessary for the therapeutic process. McLaughlin (1995) questioned this prohibition and offered a multilayered discussion of meaning and impact of touch, in both literal and symbolic forms, in the therapeutic process:

> I much prefer to be available to respond to what I have found to be the turmoil around early relational struggles that, more often than sexual or seductive urgencies, drive such reachings-out for hand touch or holding. I find that this responsiveness facilitates, rather than hinders, the patient's analytic seeking.... the need, now satisfied,

tends to subside as fuller verbal contact becomes possible between us. Where my responding has stirred some erotic feeling in my patient, it has remained analyzable. (p. 442)

In the psychoanalytic tradition, exceptions to the taboo on touch have been made by some clinicians who saw justification for touch during periods of intense emotional distress or regression (Balint, 1979; Fromm-Reichmann, 1950; Little, 1993; Pedder, 1976; Searles, 1965). Any systematic discussion or empirical evaluation of the therapeutic role of touch has been nearly nonexistent in the psychoanalytic literature. A few psychoanalytic authors (Burton & Heller, 1964; Forer, 1969; McLaughlin, 1995, 2000; Mintz, 1969a, 1969b) have advocated for the potential therapeutic value of occasional, nonerotic touch between therapist and patient. Mintz (1969a) outlined four meanings and potential functions of touch in psychotherapy: (1) providing direct libidinal gratification of the patient, (2) offering touch as symbolic mothering, (3) conveying a sense of being accepted, and (4) conveying a sense of reality in the here and now. While cautioning strongly against the pressures or desires to gratify and be gratified, Mintz argued that the other meanings of touch can carry therapeutic value. These challenges to the traditional cautions and taboos against touch in psychotherapy seem to disappear in the literature. Rarely are these articles referenced or considered.

In a special issue of *Psychoanalytic Inquiry,* "On Touch in the Psychoanalytic Situation" (Ruderman, Shane, & Shane, 2000), psychoanalytic clinicians were invited to discuss their views on the use of physical contact, each using Casement's 1982 paper as the starting point. The contributing authors, including Casement (2000) himself, who provided a reevaluation of his original paper and comments on each of the other authors, found reason to touch a patient under some circumstances. For example, Breckenridge (2000) concluded, "Using clinical examples I have tried to demonstrate that thoughtful, socially appropriate touching is no more inherently problematic than any other type of relational interaction in psychoanalysis" (pp. 19–20). For none of these authors, however, did touch become a standard part of the therapeutic repertoire. Holder (2000) summarized his views:

If, in conclusion, I come back to the title of my paper, "To Touch or Not to Touch: That Is the Question," I would, in general, come down on the side of "not to touch" because touching within a psychoanalytic setting involves so many imponderables and introduces so many parameters that it seems more prudent to refrain from it as much as possible and only resort to it in exceptional circumstances. To use it *actively* and *deliberately* as a technical tool seems to make the method of treatment into something that is different from psychoanalysis. (p. 63; emphasis in original)

Casement (2000, p. 166), too, while offering examples of his touching certain clients under specific circumstances, questioned the use of touch as a deliberate or frequent technique. The articles are based entirely on the authors' accumulated clinical experiences and case examples. None offer any empirical studies, but the range of perspectives provides a stimulating clinical interchange.

Numerous ethical discussions of the use of touch in contemporary psychotherapy include Cornell (1997b), Durana (1998), Epstein (1994), Fagan (1998), Goodman and Teicher (1988), Holub and Lee (1990), Kepner (1987), Kertay and Reviere (1993), Ruderman (2000), Smith (1985), and Smith, Clance, and Imes (1998). All have emphasized the importance of the clarity of therapeutic intent and the heightened responsibility of a therapist to examine the historical, interpersonal, and transferential implications of physical contact. Pope and Vasquez (1991) concluded:

If the therapist is personally comfortable engaging in physical contact with a patient, maintains a theoretical orientation for which therapist–client contact is not antithetical, and has competence (education, training, and supervised experience) in the use of touch, then the decision of whether or not to make physical contact with a particular client must be based on a careful evaluation of the clinical needs of the client at that moment. When solidly based upon clinical needs and a clinical rationale, touch can be exceptionally caring, comforting, reassuring, or healing. When not justified by clinical need and therapeutic rationale, nonsexual touch can be experienced as intrusive, frightening, or demeaning. (pp. 105–106)

In a study of physical contact between male therapists and female clients, Geib (1998) outlined several criteria that guided a positive experience of physical contact, as reported by the clients:

> The therapist provided an environment where the client felt that she, rather than the therapist, was in control; the therapist was clearly responding to the client's needs, rather than his own; the therapist encouraged open discussion of the contact, rather than avoiding the topic; and the therapist made sure that physical and emotional intimacy developed at the same pace, rather than being insensitive to the issue of timing. (p. 114)

Touch in a therapeutic relationship has also been challenged on the basis of casting such interactions as forms of countertransferential acting out and sexualization of the therapeutic relationship, resulting in the increased likelihood of boundary violations. Holroyd and Brodsky (1980) observed that therapists (heterosexual male therapists with female patients) who admitted to having intercourse with patients were more likely to use nonerotic touching with opposite-sex patients than were other therapists. In an earlier survey, Holroyd and Brodsky (1977) discovered that 80% of the therapists who acknowledged sexual involvement with a patient had become involved with more than one patient. Epstein (1994) indicated that the likelihood of touching being correlated with sexual contact is far greater when weighted with other attitudes and activities involving personalizing, exploitive, and dishonest behaviors initiated by a therapist. This suggests that touch may be one form, among others, of acting out and exploitation on the part of a therapist, but this does not necessarily mean that touch, in and of itself, causes the acting out. If a therapist is not specifically trained in the use of physical contact and is not in ongoing supervision, the use of touch remains questionable clinically and ethically.

Therapists within the humanistic tradition who advocate the use of touch in psychotherapy often frame these interventions primarily in the context of a therapist's providing a corrective emotional experience of holding, nurturance, comfort, or soothing (Durana, 1998; Williams, 1992). In the body-centered tradition, however, the use of physical contact provides a broad range of functions beyond that of comfort. These include focusing and deepening self-awareness and emotional experience, experimentation with patterns of contact and withdrawal, facilitation of sensorimotor organization and activation, sensate stimulation, provision of somatic structuring, and characterological confrontation. The case examples later in this chapter illustrate direct intervention with touch designed to move through defenses and to evoke new possibilities of bodily activity and experience, rather than to provide some form of comfort or nurturance.

MAJOR SYNDROMES, SYMPTOMS, AND PROBLEMS TREATED

Diagnosis endures as fundamental in the body-centered psychotherapies, but the diagnostic frameworks common in body psychotherapy have little in common with the symptom-cluster focus of the *Diagnostic and Statistical Manual of Mental Disorders*, fourth edition (*DSM-IV*; American Psychiatric Association [APA], 1994).

Diagnostic concerns in body psychotherapy, as in most psychotherapies, are centered, at least in part, on the alleviation of symptoms and self-generated and repetitive problems in living. A focus on the change of character structure and motoric patterns remains central to body-centered treatment. The presenting problems, identified symptoms, and initial concerns of a client represent conscious manifestations of underlying, unconscious characterological adaptations. Reich (1949) conceived of character as a narcissistic protective mechanism originally formed to manage infantile, instinctual conflict, particularly to minimize instinctual expressions that evoked disapproval or punishment by parents or other representatives of the social order.

Character constitutes a pervasive system of defenses involving habitual muscular and postural patterns, interpersonal/transferential configurations, and emotional and cognitive belief systems. The language of character types varies somewhat from one school of body psychotherapy to another, but most share a reasonably common understanding of the nature and function of character. They link character to efforts to manage severe developmental anxieties and environmental failures. Common diagnostic terms in the body-centered lexicon include schizoid, oral (depressive), psychopathic, masochistic, narcissistic, and hysteric. Schizoid defenses are organized in the face of severe and chronic environmental rejection/hatred and represent a defensive effort to avoid the intense anxieties of psychic disintegration. Oral/depressive defenses arise in encountering severe and chronic deprivation of emotional and relational needs and typify a defensive effort to manage anxieties of abandonment. The psychopathic defenses (quite distinct from the antisocial or sociopathic personality disorders in the traditional clinical literature) are constructed in reaction to an experience of being overtaken, overwhelmed by parental needs, emotions, and demands and symbolize a defensive effort to maintain rigid control to manage the anxiety of being consumed or enslaved by others. The masochistic defenses are formed in the face of highly conditional patterns of parental affection and attention, love being subtly but pervasively transformed from a means of passionate attachment into patterns of loyalty and submission. Masochism denotes a defensive effort to contain or crush one's own instinctual impulses to manage the anxieties of parental judgment and shame. Narcissistic and hysterical defenses are developed in response to parental rejection of a child's love, individuality, and autonomy, with the result that a child fears loss of self as a condition for a loving and secure relationship. Whereas the other character styles represent exaggerated, defensive efforts for self-control, the narcissistic and hysterical defenses are efforts to manage one's own anxieties of failure and loss of self/autonomy through acting out and control of others. Therapeutic efforts to treat characterological defenses then involve interventions designed to evoke and heighten awareness of characterological patterns at somatic, interpersonal, and cognitive levels to foster choice and change.

No systematic research in body psychotherapy clearly demonstrates the effectiveness of these methods with particular diagnostic categories, yet a reading of the clinical literature, particularly numerous case studies, strongly suggests that certain client populations more likely become involved in the body-centered psychotherapies. Anecdotal information and case discussions in this literature indicate that clients often seek body-centered treatments after completion of previous psychotherapy in an effort to deepen, extend, and consolidate the gains of verbally based psychotherapy. Body therapy may also be seen as a means to enter nonverbal and/or preverbal realms of experience that could not be sufficiently accessed in more traditional, language-dependent forms of psychotherapy.

The major problem areas as defined in the *DSM-IV* likely to be treated using body-centered approaches include depressive disorders, anxiety disorders, somatoform disorders, problems of sexual desire and arousal, and the personality disorders of Axis II. The adjustment disorders, the 309 codes, may be treated as well, but the symptoms of depressed mood, anxiety, and other acute disturbances of mood and well-being are more likely viewed as the tips of a characterological iceberg. To this author's knowledge, there have been no applications of the Global Assessment of Relational Functioning (GARF) scale (APA, 1994; Group for the Advancement of Psychiatry Committee on the Family, 1995; Kaslow, 1996) for assessment purposes in the body-centered literature. It would seem that this scale could be of particular value for pretreatment diagnosis and posttreatment evaluation of body-centered psychotherapies. Given the emphasis on characterological change, one would expect to see significant improvement on the GARF scale as a result of body-centered therapy, with its particular attention to altering character defenses to enhance the flexibility of relational boundaries, emotional awareness and expressiveness, and the capacity for intimacy and vulnerability.

CASE EXAMPLES

Three case illustrations describe how body-centered psychotherapy unfolds and offer examples of active intervention with the body. The first case, that of Sarah, portrays the initial stages of a body-centered psychotherapy, including diagnosis, initial contracting and negotiation, and preliminary somatic intervention and exploration. The second case, with Simon, provides an example of a body-centered intervention and its consequences in the midst of a more traditional, verbal psychotherapy. The third client, Jack, sought body-centered psychotherapy in an effort to "reclaim" his body from the sexual and emotional intrusions of his mother.

Sarah

Sarah was referred for body-centered psychotherapy by her previous psychodynamic therapist. She had entered therapy originally to address issues of chronic dysthymia and anxiety. She reported these as a part of her emotional experience since adolescence. Sarah said that it seemed appropriate that she was depressed and anxious during her adolescence, which was marked by repeated disruption and dislocation. She had managed both her depression and anxiety through the early years of her adult life by hard work, intense devotion to her career, and episodic drinking. She felt irritation with her emotions and her moods, which she described as leeching the quality out of her life. She simply forged ahead, having little patience with herself. These coping mechanisms ran out of steam, however, when she quit work to become a full-time mother of a son and daughter, ages 4 and 6, when she first entered treatment. Both her depression and her anxiety deepened significantly, interfering with her daily functioning and causing her to become unpredictably irritable and angry with her children. She sought psychotherapy and medication.

Sarah reported her psychotherapy as useful, but, after three years of productive work, she seemed to reach an impasse. She experienced a significant decrease in her depression and great improvement in self-esteem and in her relationships with her children. Her antidepressant medication contributed to significantly improving her sense of well-being, energy, and pleasure in daily life. Her anxiety, however, seemed largely unchanged. She had become dissatisfied with what now seemed like a dependency on her antidepressant and anti-anxiety medications. Her therapist suggested she try a different form of psychotherapy, one that would work more directly with her emotional patterns and her relationship to her body.

Before following the advice of her previous therapist to begin body-centered psychotherapy,

Sarah discontinued antidepressant medication on an experimental basis. She noted that her irritability returned quickly, that she had little desire to start her day, and that she experienced little pleasure. In this state of mind, she decided to contact a new therapist to do an initial (mutual) evaluation while still off her medication. She asked whether a return to her antidepressants would be wise and if it would interfere with this form of therapy. The therapist encouraged her to return to her psychiatrist and resume medication, assuring her that the medication would likely facilitate the therapy rather than interfere with it. Sarah resumed medication and entered body-centered psychotherapy.

Sarah, a bright, verbal, energetic, and tightly wound woman in her late 30s, clearly suffered from a Dysthymic Disorder (*DSM-IV*, 300.4; American Psychiatric Association [APA], 1994) and a Generalized Anxiety Disorder (*DSM-IV*, 300.02) throughout her adult life. Her anxiety could be quite severe and debilitating at times, but tended to be more episodic, whereas her dysthymia was chronic and more insidious. There was no evidence in her developmental history or current functioning of an Axis II personality disorder. Assessed on the GARF scale, Sarah rated a score of 80, reflecting functional but somewhat unsatisfactory family relationships. Sarah's ways of being and coping served the needs of her family well, so that the overall functioning of the family relational units was quite effective, though marred by a tendency to be conflict-avoidant. Her dissatisfactions were much more personal and intrapsychic. From the perspective of neo-Reichian diagnostic categories, Sarah presented as a compensated oral, that is, someone who has masked her attachment and dependency needs with a defensive self-sufficiency, so as to ward off underlying feelings of depression, loss, and anxiety.

Sarah traced the onset of symptoms to her parents' sudden divorce during her adolescence. Her parents were too self-absorbed in their own transitions and worries to notice that Sarah was suffering. She cooperated with their self-preoccupation by maintaining a high-functioning, "good soldier" attitude. She hid her sadness, loss, and worries. Looking back, she could see symptoms of depression throughout her adult life, but she had successfully "stayed on top of them" through her activity level and professional success. Then her anxiety and depression "got the best of me" until her psychotherapy helped her get back on top again. In the initial session, she reported that she had no patience with her anxiety. She hated it and wanted to be rid of it. She hoped this body therapy would help her somehow to dispose of this anxiety.

Initial treatment contracts emerged in the first session. Sarah asked that, for the time being, her previous therapist not be consulted. She felt that the new therapist's perceptions would have more impact on her if they arose anew and were not influenced by input from her previous therapist. The therapist agreed. The therapist also suggested that she needed to learn about and from her anxiety, not get rid of it, further implying that her anxiety carried meaning, which needed exploring. Reluctantly, she agreed to tentatively adopt this exploratory attitude toward her anxiety. This recommendation typifies a somatic intervention—to activate and explore, rather than control or relieve. The therapist also discussed the use of physical contact as a part of working together. The therapist assured her that the choice to use touch was entirely hers because there would be options to attend to her body and work with body processes without the use of direct physical contact. Sarah made reference to the importance of massage and chiropractic adjustments, forms of touch she found very useful and safe. She said she imagined that being touched in a psychotherapeutic process would create some anxiety and vulnerability, but felt it was necessary if she were going to gain more vitality in her life. They agreed to include touch among the means of working together, with the clear understanding that, if she needed a cessation of touching for any reason, the therapist would stop immediately. After stopping the physical contact, both would discuss what happened, what felt wrong, and whether and how to continue. They concurred that any and all experiences involving touch could be discussed, including reactions, fantasies, and dreams that might emerge between sessions.

An immediate contradiction appeared in the appearance/presentation of Sarah's body. She is slender, wears makeup in an understated fashion, and gives careful attention to her appearance with a casual style of dress. She took active care of her body, getting regular massages and chiropractic and homeopathic treatments. Yet she rarely felt at ease in her body. Her casual appearance and careful care of her body belied a more pervasive sense of tension and conflict in her body. She carried a great deal of tension in her jaw, neck, and upper body, which she experienced as normal and from which she reported no particular discomfort. Her habitual patterns of muscular tension created a subtle, but pervasive, visual impression of a person who had to simultaneously hold herself up, back, and in.

At an initial, superficial level, Sarah's body seemed quite at ease with being touched, but that changed quickly as the therapist began to use his hands to provide support to her shoulders and neck. Sarah found allowing the therapist to lift her head or support it with his hands virtually impossible. Her breathing became constricted, and her neck and shoulder muscles tensed. She tried to make herself relax. She felt embarrassed by her body's reactions, apologizing and reassuring the therapist that she trusted him. She became immediately self-critical. The therapist commented that her judgmental responses to her bodily reactions were like her judgments of her anxiety, that her judgments foreclosed the possibility of learning and exploring. Her inability to accept physical support of her neck and shoulders became the focus of attention. She reported that for days following the initial hands-on session, she felt quietly, inexplicably sad. At the same time, she felt hopeful that this style of work was "going to get through" to her. Work with her neck and shoulders continued as a part of each session, in the midst of an ongoing verbal therapy process examining her patterns of closeness and affection with her children, husband, friends, and parents.

The work with her body consistently evoked sadness, which she experienced as distinctly different from depression and anxiety. She resisted her usual temptation to take Xanax to alleviate her anxiety. There were no particular memories, associations, or dreams connected to her sadness and anxiety, only states of affect that came over her. She was pleased that she could sometimes cry and became more tolerant of her anxiety. She continued to label her body reactions as "resistant," and the therapist began to suggest other language for her body (e.g., a "protective body," a "worried body," a "cautious body"). He observed that her body seemed afraid of itself. That comment stuck with her. Sarah began to think of and experience her body as frightened rather than resistant: frightened of losing herself to her children's or husband's needs, of not taking adequate care of her kids, of becoming so depressed that she could not function and that she would suddenly fall apart. Her sadness deepened; she would often cry quietly in session and at home afterward, though she did not know what she was crying about. Gradually, her body began to accept the support of the therapist's hands: "I feel like I can rest in your hands." She realized that she was constantly attending to her body, fixing it up as though performing mechanical maintenance so that she would function properly, but that there was no real kindness, rest, or support for her body. She managed her body more than cared for it.

As she became more accepting of physical support, she reported experiencing a tenderness in the therapist's hands and way of being with her. This reminded her of her father. He encouraged her to remember her father's tenderness and to talk about it, as he held her head in his hands. She cried deeply during a pivotal dialogue:

SARAH: Oh my God, I don't think I've rested since my Dad left us. I had to stay with Mom. I had to take care of her. I don't ever even rest in my husband's arms. Even when we make love, I don't rest. I don't let go. I always hold back. I loved my Dad, but I couldn't keep him. I lost him. (Deep crying.) I'm not strong enough to feel this kind of pain.

THERAPIST: I think you're afraid you're not strong enough to feel the depth of your affections.

SARAH: What did you say? I don't understand what you mean. (Long pause.) I don't think I can tell the difference between pain and affection. They feel the same to me. I can't tell them apart.

THERAPIST: Your affections became a source of pain, not comfort. You're terrified of your affections, terrified of losing someone else you love. It's unbearable. You learned young to hold yourself back: Don't reach out, don't hold on, don't let in.

These themes formed the heart of the therapeutic work. In a fashion typical of body-centered psychotherapy, the sessions wove back and forth between verbal explorations of her affectional patterns with her husband, her children, her parents, and her therapist with the ongoing probing of her somatic patterns. Hands-on work formed a part of every session. As the shift from verbal interaction to physical interaction transpired, Sarah typically closed her eyes as the therapist asked her a series of questions to help her focus on her body and find a starting point for the body-level work. The inquiries included: "Where does your attention start to go in your body?"; "Where is your body uncomfortable?"; "What might that area of discomfort want?"; "Is there a way you want to move?"; "Is there something your body needs from me right now?"; "Where/how would you like me to touch you?" These few questions offer examples of how therapist and client begin to orient to the body and bridge to direct body intervention. Through this style of somatic exploration, Sarah began to understand the habitual reactions of her body in relation to her sadness and anxiety. Her body became more able to contain these emotions, allowing her to have deeper experiences of these feelings, gaining meaning in the context of both her history and current life choices.

Increasingly, Sarah has become aware of the somatic habits of holding her body up, back, and in, and is more able to use her body as a means of approaching and engaging others. The body-centered interventions also provided a means for her to explore her relationship with the therapist. She reflected on physical and emotional support received and her own difficulties in initiating contact, reaching out to the therapist with her own arms and hands, noticing the wishes and desires in her body for physical contact. She lessened her caretaking ways of being with her children, finding more playful means of involvement. She challenged the cooperative but passionless style of relating into which she and her husband have devolved over the years. She has spent more time outside of her home with a couple of close friends, intentionally deepening those relationships.

SIMON

Thin, almost emaciated at 31, Simon entered psychotherapy. His parents, who perceived him as purposeless and depressed, paid for his therapy. Simon suffered from a Schizoid Personality Disorder (*DSM-IV*, 301.20; APA, 1994), with some paranoid ideation and significant indications of a Depersonalization Disorder (*DSM-IV*, 300.6; APA, 1994). Within the diagnostic categorizations from a body-centered perspective, Simon would also be viewed as schizoid. On the

GARF scale in his nuclear family, Simon would rate a score of 30 reflecting a fused, symbiotic relationship with his mother and in his social life outside the home a 10 as indicated by the virtual absence of social relationships with peers.

Simon lived with his aging parents, becoming a kind of live-in, unpaid caretaker after failing at a university and in his first and only love relationship. Now and then he took an occasional college course until he got bored or the schedule became inconvenient. At times, he would worry that he was totally inept at life and then declare indifference to life and its banalities. He had no friends. He could acknowledge that he was socially awkward and probably came across as at least shy if not strange. But he tended to explain away the aloneness of his life as mostly attributable to his having to take care of his parents and the lack of privacy these living arrangements imposed on him. He occupied himself with science fiction novels and movies, computer games, and Internet fantasy chat rooms. His private reveries, as he reported them in session, were dominated by chance encounters with someone who would take an interest in him and suddenly alter the course of his life.

Simon was curious about psychotherapy, seeking an interactive, psychodynamic therapy that he thought might help him understand himself better. He looked forward to having someone to talk with regularly, as he spent much of his time alone. He knew nothing of the therapist's orientation as a body-centered psychotherapist. Simon was happy to get out of the house for his sessions, content to lie on the couch talking of internal and external events, talking mostly to himself about himself, vaguely aware of the therapist's presence. Questions, comments, and interpretations seemed to fall on deaf ears, as all possibility of change was cast into the future, only after his parents' deaths. One day, the therapist said out loud to Simon what he had often noted silently and rather sadly to himself: "Simon, you lie there like a corpse." Simon remained silent and unmoving. The therapist continued, "I used to barely notice how you lie there. It was just how you are, but now this stillness has become disturbing to me. I can't ignore it. It makes me sad. I can't stand it. I wonder how the hell you stand it? How do you stand this, Simon?" After a time, he replied, "I don't know any other way of being. How do I make you sad? What do other people do when they lie here? Is there something I'm supposed to do?"

The fact of Simon's asking questions startled the therapist. Rarely did he address the therapist directly. He seemed content to silently accept whatever the therapist might have to offer by way of linking or interpreting his dreams and fantasies. His rare questions implied a search for intellectual explanations for his feelings and fantasies. Now, in response to an observation (outburst), Simon asked three very different sorts of questions. In these questions, there were clearly two persons in the room. These questions were aimed at action, not insight, asking how rather than why. These were questions of the body, not the mind, like Reich's interest in *how* a patient did something rather than *why* it was done—questions of how to bring his body and his affect into the room. The therapist commented on how different these questions were from his usual ways of talking in sessions. Simon replied that it startled him and touched him to realize that the therapist felt something for him. He had now realized that the therapist looked at him as well as listened to him. He said he had structured his life so that he was rarely seen by anyone, that he rarely saw anyone. He wondered what else the therapist saw about him. The therapist began to make comments about noticing his way of being in the room and his way of being with the therapist. Most of the comments were purely descriptive, but at times, the observations were extended with remarks about feeling or imaginings of what he was experiencing. In contrast to Simon's usual speaking aloud to himself, periods of silence began to develop. These were not his typical silences of mental reverie of events outside the office, but quiet periods in which he attended to what was happening with him in the moment. In these silences he struggled with new ways to talk *to* another person. The therapist attended verbally to Simon's body in session and began to encourage him to pay attention to his body. The therapist inquired as to how he might begin to *show* his experience through movement, as well as speak about it. Simon remained still.

Therapy continued in this fashion for weeks. Then Simon dreamed that in a session he rolled to his side, and the therapist came over to sit at his back, with the therapist's hip and thigh against his spine. The therapist immediately saw great significance to this dream, as it brought Simon's body and the therapist's directly into the room and into relationship. The dream was the first signal that he wanted to have something to do with the therapist. The therapist knew he needed to be cautious and not impose himself on Simon's dream. He decided to wait and see if and how Simon would take up the dream. At first, Simon was embarrassed by the dream, but it struck him as very important. He could see that it was a sign of recognition of the therapist's support of him and perhaps a wish for more involvement. He reported that he was increasingly conscious of how little he noticed his body day to day, but that in his sessions, he was becoming aware of his body. The dream returned as a topic of conversation for several weeks. He sometimes feared the dream image, which he worried was a kind of regressive cry for support when he already felt so inept at life. He worried that the therapist would consider touching him to be silly or disgusting. He could make no sense of the particular body positions in the dream, that of the therapist's hip against his back.

In one session, Simon suddenly rolled to his side and asked the therapist to move over and sit with him, as in the dream. Though there had been no discussions about physical contact or direct work with the body, the therapist decided to do as Simon asked. The therapist was confident that they were now sufficiently engaged with each other that should this move prove to be a mistake, it was a mistake from which they would learn. The therapist sat with his hip against Simon's back and waited to see what would happen, encouraging Simon to allow his body to react to this new situation in any way it needed. Gradually, Simon's body began to tremble, and he began to cry softly. He said that he was stunned by the warmth of the therapist's body and touched by the strength he sensed in it. The therapist encouraged Simon to take his time and accept anything that came up inside him as they sat together. Simon found himself thinking of his father's weak and withering body, which he found disgusting. In subsequent sessions, he acknowledged that he had always seen his father as weak and disgusting. He felt as though his body had somehow absorbed the loneliness and weakness of his father's body, that he retreated to his head, where he had at least some sense of competence and even of superiority.

Every few sessions, Simon asks the therapist to sit with him, as in enacting the dream. He feels it helps him separate his experience of his own body from that of his father's. He has said that it is as though his body takes permission to become stronger directly from the contact with the therapist's body. Simon has entered into a kind of somatic partnership between his body and the therapist's. He is more able to notice his body and to talk about it. His body is becoming a source of meaning and occasionally of excitement to him. He is beginning to feel that his body, as well as his way of life, can become different from his father's. From a body-centered perspective, these changes are understood as emerging from a gradual shift from a defensive overidentification with the mind as the self, typical of the schizoid personality, to an evolving sense of the self, increasingly organized within the body. Bodily activity and meaning are beginning to coexist with mental activity and meaning.

Simon's relentless fantasies of chance meetings with strangers are being replaced by his sense of his ongoing contact with the therapist. Transferential fantasies and wishes toward the therapist are becoming more frequent and open to reflection. Attention in sessions now weaves back and forth between his experience of being with the therapist and memories of his life-long awkwardness and loneliness, his grief about his isolation, and his rage at his parents for their disinterest in him and use of him. He is beginning to consider social activities and a part-time job outside of his parents' home. He has been able to address and gradually work through his rage at his parents while continuing to live at home and provide functional caretaking as they become increasingly frail.

JACK

At 40, Jack sought body-centered psychotherapy after being in and out of psychotherapy for most of his adult life. He reported that his previous efforts at psychotherapy had always devolved into a morass of symbiotic dependency from which he could not extricate himself. He expressed the hope that a different form of therapy might help him mobilize himself and reclaim his body from his mother. Jack still lived in the same small town as his mother. He felt that she still possessed him psychologically and found her presence in the town constantly invasive in his daily life. He presented a complicated mix of somatic and interpersonal defenses, not readily representing a single diagnostic category. Assessed within the *DSM-IV* diagnostic structure, Jack was seen as fluctuating back and forth (depending on his relational circumstances of the moment) between an Avoidant Personality Disorder (*DSM-IV*, 301.82; APA, 1994) and a Dependent Personality Disorder (*DSM-IV*, 301.6;

APA, 1994), with the dependent side of his personality dominating previous therapeutic efforts. He also demonstrated significant signs of Posttraumatic Stress Disorder (*DSM-IV*, 309.81; APA, 1994). Unable to negotiate conflicts or sustain friendships through periods of stress, Jack was rated a score of 45 on the GARF scale. Within the neo-Reichian characterological diagnostic structure, Jack is predominantly a hysterical character, with underlying features of shock trauma and oral collapse.

Jack was a single child with an absent father and a severely sadistic and narcissistic mother, who may have become psychotic during periods of severe stress. His early childhood felt like a prison to him, trapped at home with a mother who loomed around him as endlessly needy, demanding, and viciously punitive when disappointed or frustrated. He experienced his mother as emotionally, physically, and sexually intrusive throughout his childhood. He took on the role of a husband substitute. Although there does not seem to have ever been actual sexual intercourse between Jack and his mother, Jack found himself the object of his mother's erotic desires. She frequently exposed her body to him. Bed times and bath times were particular points of extended, unwanted physical contact. Jack felt his mother's physical/sexual excitement. His efforts to establish private space for himself and his body evoked storms of rage. Not until adolescence was he finally able to set and enforce limits on his mother's access to his body.

As an adult, Jack was not able to sustain an intimate or sexual relationship. He was very successful at work, but able to maintain only very superficial relationships with coworkers, which did not lead to friendships outside of the office. His relationships with women typically began in bars, where he was drawn to women who appeared to him as shy and lonely. The relationships were short-lived, typically descending into patterns of mutual dependency and caretaking. There was little sexual activity.

With each breakup, Jack would feel used and devastated, dropping into a prolonged period of social withdrawal.

Jack's treatment combined participation in an ongoing transactional analysis therapy group (Berne, 1966; Grimes, 1988) and individual body-centered psychotherapy. His work in the group focused on examining his tendency to establish dependent relationships in the group and to experiment with establishing differentiated relationships among the group members. His contract in the body psychotherapy involved making use of the therapist's body (in intentional contrast to his mother's making use of his body) to experience boundaries, develop a sense of bodily coherence, and learn to titrate levels of contact and consequent affect. Work with the consequences of Jack's physical and sexual trauma is consistent with that described by Bernhardt (1996) in approaching "shock trauma" (p. 158) at a body level:

> The cardinal principle in thinking about the somatic aspects of shock work is that the initial goal is not emotional release or understanding psychodynamic meaning, per se, but to help the client find a successful resolution of the neurological and psychomotor patterns that have been overwhelmed or given up during the shock situation. (p. 158)

The direct work with the body is designed to facilitate the client's development of such psychomotor resources as "the ability to stand, walk, run, push, hit, hold off, pull toward, move sideways, move away from" (p. 158).

In the sessions, the clinician follows Jack's lead, with the therapist's body available to Jack as a resource rather than as an intrusive presence. He can sit, stand, or lie down in session as he wishes, feeling what is different from one position to another. He can be close to the therapist, move far away, or sit against the therapist as they talk. He can make use of the therapist's body literally to lean against, push against, pull to him, define and experience his body in relation to the therapist's. When Jack comes to sessions in a state of avoidant collapse, he sits with his back against the therapist's chest. The intention here is not to provide comfort but to give him the opportunity to literally feel through his body the structure, strength, and organizing activities of another body, so as to imitate and internalize in his body what he senses. Baum, Keleman, and Cornell (1999) offered a discussion of direct body work with clients with traumatized, labile body and personality structures.

RESEARCH

Empirical, systematic research into the effectiveness of body-centered psychotherapy is extremely limited. Body-centered psychotherapy has developed clinically, as in the tradition of psychoanalysis (Green, 1996), relying on the model of individual case studies as the primary means of developing and advancing clinical theory and technique. Many body-centered practitioners are highly skeptical of academic models and the objectification of the scientific model, in spite of the fact that Reich (1982) himself engaged in scientific experimentation in the 1920s and 1930s and drew on the neurological and anthropological research of his day. In a series of articles, Boadella (1991, 1992, 1997b) sought to place body psychotherapy in general and his own particular modality of biosynthesis within the scientific tradition and to gain recognition of body-centered modalities by the Swiss and European Associations for Psychotherapy. Whereas Boadella's writings did not represent empirical studies of outcome effectiveness, they did place the evolution of body psychotherapy within the evolving models of psychotherapeutic and scientific research. He underscored the consistency between body-centered theories and contemporary developmental, infant-parent, and neurophysiological research.

J. May (2000) offered the most comprehensive overview and evaluation of the status of empirical research in body-oriented psychotherapy.

May undertook a literature search for citations on body-oriented psychotherapies over the past 30 years, drawing on the American Psychological Association PsychINFO abstract service, the journals *Bioenergetic Analysis* and *Energy and Character*, and other sources of literature on body-centered methods. This yielded a bibliography of 264 sources. Of these, May found only 26 articles reporting on 23 separate studies that involved some form of empirical outcome research, most of which he found to have significant methodological limits. Eighteen of these studies provided sufficient data for more careful review of outcome effectiveness. He addressed the relevance of empirical research for body-centered treatment modalities, discussed the basic tasks of clinical research studies, and assessed the scientific characteristics of each of these studies. May opined:

> Where do we stand, then, regarding the effectiveness of body-oriented psychotherapy? Overall, 18 separate studies were reviewed. Of these, 13 could be interpreted as finding positive effects for body-oriented psychotherapy. Five showed no effects. Most studies reviewed here have significant methodological flaws that undercut to one degree or another confidence in their findings or their generalizability. It would be desirable to have additional studies with increased methodological sophistication. However, this review did not find them.
>
> At the same time, this review uncovered no reason to believe that the literature in general is contaminated by systemic flaws biased in one direction only. I am inclined to accept the overall weight of the literature, which seems to lend considerable support to the notion that body-oriented psychotherapy is effective, at least with some clients under some conditions. There is considerable support for its effectiveness as a stand-alone treatment with both clinical and non-clinical populations. (p. 364)

Difficulties for research in the body-centered traditions have been complicated by the evolution of modalities in rather competitive frames of references, overly emphasizing of the differences among varying approaches rather than the common grounds. The recent establishment of the European and U.S. associations for body-centered psychotherapy has begun to promote cooperative frames of reference and the founding of research committees. The current state of the art and science of body psychotherapy predominantly encompasses, however, many theories presently diverse and sometimes contradictory regarding explanations as to which elements of the therapy are effective and crucial to change. Clinical models are currently based on such theories as character analysis, confrontation of resistances, catharsis, reworking of intrapsychic and psychosomatic conflicts, deepening of sensory awareness, development of sensorimotor competencies, resolution of trauma, correction of developmental discontinuities or failures, and the working through of transference at a somatic level. It is imperative that these models be systematically examined through clinical observation, theoretical debate, and empirical research. The hypotheses about the causal agents in change in body-centered psychotherapy will need to be examined through systematic research for the field to advance and to gain professional credibility.

Problems of meaningful clinical research are exacerbated by the complexity and multiplicity of foci and interventions in body-centered psychotherapies. These approaches do not lend themselves as neatly to quantitative research procedures as do the more time-limited, symptom-focused, singular-technique treatment strategies of the cognitive-behavioral models, which are well-suited to research protocols. Questions, challenges, and alternatives to traditional, quantitative research models are not unique to body-centered psychotherapists (Beutler, 1998; Borkovec & Castonguay, 1998; Edelson, 1994; Goldfried & Wolfe, 1998; J. Greenberg, 1994; Horowitz, 1994; J. Sandler, Sandler, & Davies, 2000; Spence, 1994). Safran and Muran (1994) outlined elements of research endeavors better suited to in-depth, long-term dynamic psychotherapies, which body psychotherapy certainly exemplifies. Safran and Muran recommended intensive analysis of change factors by multiple judges in individual cases (in contrast to the conventional case study), sensitivity to context in which interventions are administered, use of discovery-oriented and qualitative research, a focus on underlying mechanisms of therapeutic process, identification of key change events (as now routinely done in video research of infant-parent interactions), and development of models to identify regularities in the sequencing of recurrent patient states, patient activity patterns, and the patient-therapist interaction patterns that seem related to change.

In a discussion of problems of research in the effectiveness of the experiential therapies, L. S. Greenberg et al. (1994) proposed:

> Emerging new genres of phenomenological and interpretive psychotherapy research are more consistent with basic assumptions of experiential therapists than are the traditional positivistic research methods (see Toukmanian & Rennie, 1992). These studies have begun to reveal a deeper set of processes and dimensions underlying the more observable client actions, contents, and impacts reviewed here. Rennie (1990, 1992), Angus and Rennie (1988, 1989), and Clark (1990) have provided glimpses into the operation of some of these deep structures of experiential-humanistic therapy (and perhaps of other therapies as well).
>
> Building on his elaborate analysis of clients' moment-by-moment experiences in therapy sessions, Rennie (1990, 1992) found that the center of client experience is *reflexivity,* or the turning of the client's awareness back on itself. According to Rennie (1992), the central process of therapy consists in the client's alternation between immersion in action or experience and reflexive self-awareness. (p. 524)

These models of empirical, *qualitative* research offer more hope and relevance to the assessment and understanding of effective interventions in both experiential and body-centered modalities.

SUMMARY

Grand (1998) characterized the core of the somatic psychotherapy perspective as honoring the premise that "the basis of our psychic life is the construction of bodily states, gestures, and ways of moving which have social and emotional meaning" (p. 172). Grand emphasized that "the shaping of bodily experience and the bodily structuring of emotion, feeling, and efficacy continue throughout the life span" (p. 172). With an 80-year-long history rooted in the often radical clinical explorations of Reich (1974), Ferenczi (1955), and Groddeck (1977), the body-centered psychotherapies have developed outside of the mainstream of psychoanalytic, cognitive, and behavioral modalities. Nevertheless, body-centered viewpoints provide systematic approaches to the alleviation of chronic emotional, somatic, and characterological constrictions. These methods are focused not only on the alleviation of psychological and relational distress but also on the enhancement of vitality and intimacy.

Systematic, empirical research is severely limited in the field of body-centered psychotherapy. The research studies reported by J. May (2000) indicate the utility and effectiveness of body-centered therapies within the limited scope of these research efforts. No studies to date indicate harmful outcomes, though five demonstrated no measurable improvement. No systematic studies to test the various theoretical hypotheses regarding the causal factors promoting change in body-centered work have emerged. From a research point of view, there are far more questions than answers available in the body-centered literature to date.

Therapists need to be sensitive to the elements of risk in using modalities that draw on techniques that often fall outside of cultural and professional norms, as in the use of touch, reliance on active and sometimes directive techniques, and training programs that may be strongly leader-identified and may operate outside of institutional settings and organizational controls. Therapists need to be aware of both the potential for idealization of and deference to a therapist and to the potential for undue anxiety that may be evoked by these methods. Clients may become concerned over the perceived lack of safety, lack of direction, disorientation and disruption, overstimulation, or the intrusiveness or pressure of these techniques. Active, experiential techniques may increase the possibility of transferential and/or countertransferential acting out. Ongoing supervision and consultation is recommended in the practice of body-centered psychotherapy.

Body-centered psychotherapy extends the reach of traditional psychotherapies. Body psychotherapies seem uniquely attuned and equipped to help clients address and correct preverbal developmental disruptions and traumatic intrusions on the body's cohesion and well-being. Body psychotherapists facilitate clients' explorations of interiority, with and without words, often not so much to alleviate symptoms or promote adaptation as to deepen and enrich the experience of one's self and life potentials. Body psychotherapies may promote not only self-knowing but also a sense of agency in one's bodily presence in the world and in relation to others.

REFERENCES

Alexander, F. M. (1918). *Man's supreme inheritance.* New York: Dutton.

Alexander, F. M. (1923). *Constructive conscious control of the individual.* New York: Dutton.

American Psychiatric Association. (1994). *Diagnostic and statistical manual of mental disorders* (4th ed.). Washington, DC: American Psychiatric Association.

Angus, L. E., & Rennie, D. L. (1988). Therapist participation in metaphor generation: Collaboration and noncollaborative styles. *Psychotherapy, 26,* 552–560.

Angus, L. E., & Rennie, D. L. (1989). Envisioning the representational world: The client's experience of metaphoric expression in psychotherapy. *Psychotherapy, 27,* 372–379.

Anzieu, D. (1989). *The skin ego.* New Haven, CT: Yale University Press.

Aron, L., & Anderson, F. S. (Eds.). (1998). *Relational perspectives on the body.* Hillsdale, NJ: Analytic Press.

Aron, L., & Harris, A. (1993). *The legacy of Sandor Ferenczi.* Hillsdale, NJ: Analytic Press.

Baker, E. (1967). *Man in the trap.* New York: Collier Books.

Balint, M. (1979). *The basic fault: Therapeutic aspects of regression.* New York: Brunner/Mazel.

Baum, S., Keleman, S., & Cornell, W. (1999). Clinical forum: The borderline personality and body psychotherapy. *United States Association for Body Psychotherapy Newsletter, 4,* 8–22.

Bermudez, J. L., Marcel, A., & Eilan, N. (1995). *The body and the self.* Cambridge, MA: MIT Press.

Berne, E. (1966). *Principles of group treatment.* New York: Oxford University Press.

Bernhardt, P. (1996). Somatic approaches to traumatic shock (or post-traumatic stress). In I. Macnaughton (Ed.), *Embodying the mind and minding the body* (pp. 150–171). North Vancouver, BC, Canada: Integral Press.

Beutler, L. E. (1998). Identifying empirically supported treatments: What if we didn't? *Journal of Consulting and Clinical Psychology, 66*(1), 113–120.

Binswanger, L. (1963). *Being-in-the-world.* New York: Basic Books.

Boadella, D. (1973). *Wilhelm Reich: The evolution of his work.* Plymouth, England: Vision Press.

Boadella, D. (1987). *Lifestreams.* London: Routledge & Kegan Paul.

Boadella, D. (1990). Somatic psychotherapy: Its roots and traditions. *Energy and Character, 21*(1), 2–26.

Boadella, D. (1991). Organism and organization: The place of somatic psychotherapy in society. *Energy and Character, 22,* 1–58.

Boadella, D. (1992). Science, nature and biosynthesis. *Energy and Character, 23,* 1–73.

Boadella, D. (1997a). Embodiment in the therapeutic relationship. *International Journal of Psychotherapy, 2*(1), 31–44.

Boadella, D. (1997b). Psychotherapy, science, and levels of discourse. *Energy and Character, 28*(1), 13–20.

Borkovec, T. D., & Castonguay, L. G. (1998). What is the meaning of empirically supported therapy? *Journal of Consulting and Clinical Psychology, 66*(1), 136–142.

Boss, M. (1963). *Psychoanalysis and daseinanalysis.* New York: Basic Books.

Brahler, E. (Ed.). (1988). *Body experience.* Berlin, Germany: Springer-Verlag.

Breckenridge, K. (2000). Physical touch in psychoanalysis: A closet phenomenon? *Psychoanalytic Inquiry, 20*(1), 2–20.

Bucci, W. (1997). *Psychoanalysis and cognitive science: A multiple code theory.* New York: Guilford Press.

Burton, A., & Heller, L. G. (1964). The touching of the body. *Psychoanalytic Review, 51*, 122–134.

Caldwell, C. (1996). *Getting our bodies back.* Boston: Shambhala.

Caldwell, C. (1997). *Getting in touch: The guide to new body-centered therapies.* Wheaton, IL: Quest Books.

Casement, P. J. (1982). Some pressures on the analyst for physical contact during the reliving of an early psychic trauma. *International Review of Psycho-Analysis, 9*, 279–286.

Casement, P. J. (2000). The issue of touch: A retrospective overview. *Psychoanalytic Inquiry, 20*(1), 160–184.

Clark, C. A. (1990). *A comprehensive process analysis of focusing events in experiential therapy.* Unpublished doctoral dissertation, University of Toledo, OH.

Cornell, W. F. (1997a). If Reich had met Winnicott: Body and gesture. *Energy and Character, 28*(1), 50–60.

Cornell, W. F. (1997b). Touch and boundaries in transactional analysis: Ethical and transferential considerations. *Transactional Analysis Journal, 27*(1), 30–37.

Cornell, W. F. (2000). Transference, desire and vulnerability in body-centered psychotherapy. *Energy and Character, 30*(2), 29–37.

Downing, G. (1996). *Korper und wort in der psychotherapie [The body and the word in psychotherapy].* Munich, Germany: Kosel.

Downing, G. (2000). Emotion theory reconsidered. In M. Wrathall & J. Malpas (Eds.), *Heidigger, coping and cognitive science* (pp. 245–270). Cambridge, MA: MIT Press.

Durana, C. (1998). The use of touch in psychotherapy: Ethical and clinical guidelines. *Psychotherapy, 35*(2), 269–280.

Edelson, M. (1994). Can psychotherapy research answer this psychotherapist's questions? In P. F. Talley, H. H. Strupp, & S. F. Butler (Eds.), *Psychotherapy research and practice: Bridging the gap* (pp. 60–87). New York: Basic Books.

Emery, E. (1995). A note on Sandor Ferenczi and the Dionysian itinerary in psychoanalysis. *Psychoanalytic Review, 82*(2), 267–271.

Epstein, R. S. (1994). *Keeping boundaries.* Washington, DC: American Psychiatric Press.

Fagan, J. (1998). Thoughts on using touch in psychotherapy. In E. W. L. Smith, P. R. Clance, & S. Imes (Eds.), *Touch in psychotherapy: Theory, research, and practice* (pp. 145–152). New York: Guilford Press.

Feldenkrais, M. (1950). *The body and mature behavior.* New York: International Universities Press.

Feldenkrais, M. (1981). *The elusive obvious.* Cupertino, CA: Meta.

Ferenczi, S. (1955). The principles of relaxation and neocatharsis. In S. Ferenczi (Ed.), *Final contributions to the problems and methods of psychoanalysis* (pp. 108–125). New York: Basic Books.

Forer, B. R. (1969). The taboo against touching in psychotherapy. *Psychotherapy: Theory, Research and Practice, 6*(4), 229–240.

Frankl, V. E. (1967). *Psychotherapy and existentialism.* New York: Washington Square Press.

Freud, S. (1911). Formulations on the two principles of mental functioning. In *The standard edition of the complete psychological works of Sigmund Freud* (Vol. 12, pp. 218–226). London: Hogarth Press.

Freud, S. (1912). Recommendations to physicians practicing psycho-analysis. In *The standard edition of the complete psychological works of Sigmund Freud* (Vol. 12, pp. 109–120). London: Hogarth Press.

Freud, S. (1913). On beginning treatment (further recommendations on the technique of psycho-analysis-I). In *The standard edition of the complete psychological works of Sigmund Freud* (Vol. 12, pp. 121–144). London: Hogarth Press.

Freud, S. (1914). Remembering, repeating and working through (further recommendations on the technique of psycho-analysis-II). In *The standard edition of the complete psychological works of Sigmund Freud* (Vol. 12, pp. 145–156). London: Hogarth Press.

Freud, S. (1915). Observations on transference-love (further recommendations on the technique of psycho-analysis-III). In *The standard edition of the complete psychological works of Sigmund Freud* (Vol. 12, pp. 157–171). London: Hogarth Press.

Fromm-Reichmann, F. (1950). *Principles of intensive psychotherapy*. Chicago: University of Chicago Press.

Gallagher, S. (1995). Body schema and intentionality. In J. L. Bermudez, A. Marcel, & N. Eilan (Eds.), *The body and the self* (pp. 225–244). Cambridge, MA: MIT Press.

Geib, P. (1998). The experience of nonerotic physical contact in traditional psychotherapy. In E. W. L. Smith, P. R. Clance, & S. Imes (Eds.), *Touch in psychotherapy: Theory, research, and practice* (pp. 109–126). New York: Guilford Press.

Gendlin, E. T. (1962). *Experiencing and the creation of meaning*. New York: Free Press.

Gendlin, E. T. (1981). *Focusing*. New York: Bantam Books.

Giorgi, A., Fischer, W. F., & von Eckartsberg, R. (1971). *Phenomenological psychology* (Vol. 1). Pittsburgh, PA: Duquesne University Press.

Goldfried, M. R., & Wolfe, B. E. (1998). Toward a more clinically valid approach to therapy research. *Journal of Consulting and Clinical Psychology, 66*(1), 143–150.

Goodman, M., & Teicher, A. (1988). To touch or not to touch. *Psychotherapy, 25*(4), 492–500.

Grand, I. J. (1998). Psyche's body: Towards a somatic psychodynamics. In D. H. Johnson & I. J. Grand (Eds.), *The body in psychotherapy: Inquiries in somatic psychology* (pp. 171–193). Berkeley, CA: North Atlantic Books.

Green, A. (1996). What kind of research for psychoanalysis? *International Psychoanalysis: The Newsletter of the International Psychoanalytic Association, 5,* 10–14.

Green, A. (2000). *Chains of eros: The sexual in psychoanalysis*. London: Rebus Press.

Greenberg, J. (1994). Psychotherapy research: A clinician's view. In P. F. Talley, H. H. Strupp, & S. F. Butler (Eds.), *Psychotherapy research and practice: Bridging the gap* (pp. 1–18). New York: Basic Books.

Greenberg, L. S., Elliott, R., & Lietaer, G. (1994). Research on experiential psychotherapies. In A. E. Bergin & S. L. Garfield (Eds.), *Handbook of psychotherapy and behavior change* (4th ed., pp. 509–539). New York: Wiley.

Greenberg, L. S., & Safran, J. D. (1987). *Emotion in psychotherapy*. New York: Guilford Press.

Grimes, J. (1988). Transactional analysis in group work. In S. Long (Ed.), *Six group therapies* (pp. 49–113). New York: Plenum Press.

Groddeck, G. (1977). *The meaning of illness: Selected psychoanalytic writings*. New York: International Universities Press.

Group for the Advancement of Psychiatry Committee on the Family. (1995). Beyond *DSM-IV*: A model for the classification and diagnosis of relational disorders. *Psychiatric Services, 46,* 926–931.

Hanna, T. (1988). *Somatics*. Reading, MA: Perseus Books.

Hanna, T. (1993). *The body of life*. Rochester, VT: Healing Arts Press.

Haynal, A. (1989). *Controversies in psychoanalytic method: From Freud and Ferenczi to Michael Balint*. New York: New York University Press.

Holder, A. (2000). To touch or not to touch: That is the question. *Psychoanalytic Inquiry, 20*(1), 44–64.

Holroyd, C. J., & Brodsky, A. (1977). Psychologists' attitudes and practices regarding erotic and nonerotic physical contact with patients. *American Psychologist, 32,* 843–849.

Holroyd, C. J., & Brodsky, A. (1980). Does touching patients lead to sexual intercourse? *Professional Psychology, 11,* 807–811.

Holub, E. A., & Lee, S. S. (1990). Therapist's use of nonerotic physical contact: Ethical concerns. *Psychotherapy, 21*(2), 115–117.

Horowitz, M. (1994). Psychotherapy research and the views of clinicians. In P. E. Talley, H. H. Strupp, & S. F. Butler (Eds.), *Psychotherapy research and practice: Bridging the gap* (pp. 196–205). New York: Basic Books.

Johnson, D. H. (1977). *The protean body*. New York: Harper Colophon Books.

Johnson, D. H. (Ed.). (1995). *Bone, breath, and gesture: Practices of embodiment*. Berkeley, CA: North Atlantic Books.

Johnson, D. H., & Grand, I. J. (1998). *The body in psychotherapy: Inquiries in somatic psychology.* Berkeley, CA: North Atlantic Books.

Johnson, M. (1987). *The body in the mind: The bodily basis of meaning, imagination, and reason.* Chicago: University of Chicago Press.

Johnson, S. M. (1985). *Characterological transformation: The hard work miracle.* New York: Norton.

Kaslow, F. W. (Ed.). (1996). *Handbook of relational diagnosis and dysfunctional family patterns.* New York: Wiley.

Keleman, S. (1986). *Bonding: A somatic-emotional approach to transference.* Berkeley, CA: Center Press.

Keleman, S. (1989). *Patterns of distress: Emotional insults and human form.* Berkeley, CA: Center Press.

Kelley, C. R. (1974). *Education in feeling and purpose.* Santa Monica, CA: Radix Institute.

Kepner, J. I. (1987). *Body process.* New York: Gestalt Institute of Cleveland Press.

Kertay, L., & Reviere, S. L. (1993). The use of touch in psychotherapy: Theoretical and ethical concerns. *Psychotherapy, 30,* 33–40.

Krueger, D. W. (1989). *Body self and psychological self.* New York: Brunner/Mazel.

Kwant, R. C. (1963). *The phenomenological philosophy of Merleau-Ponty.* Pittsburgh, PA: Duquesne University Press.

Kwant, R. C. (1969). *Phenomenology of expression.* Pittsburgh, PA: Duquesne University Press.

Laing, R. D. (1960). *The divided self.* London: Tavistock.

Laing, R. D. (1961). *The self and others.* London: Tavistock.

Levine, P. A. (1997). *Waking the tiger: Healing trauma.* Berkeley, CA: North Atlantic Books.

Little, M. (1993). *Transference neurosis and transference psychosis.* Northvale, NJ: Aronson.

Lowen, A. (1958), *Physical dynamics of character structure.* New York: Grune & Stratton.

Lowen, A. (1975). *Bioenergetics.* New York: Coward, McCann and Geoghegan.

Luijpen, W. A. (1960). *Existential phenomenology.* Pittsburgh, PA: Duquesne University Press.

Macnaughton, I. (Ed.). (1996). *Embodying the mind and minding the body.* North Vancouver, BC, Canada: Integral Press.

Marcher, L., & Bernhardt, P. (1996). The art of following structure. In I. Macnaughton (Ed.), *Embodying the mind and minding the body* (pp. 80–93). North Vancouver, BC, Canada: Integral Press.

Maul, B. (Ed.). (1992). *Body psychotherapy or the art of contact.* Berlin, Germany: Verlag Bernhard Maul.

May, J. (2000). A review of the empirical status of body-oriented psychotherapy. *Proceedings of the Second National Conference of the United States Body Psychotherapy Association,* 348–388. Berkeley, CA: United States Body Psychotherapy Association.

May, R. (1966). *Psychology and the human dilemma.* Princeton, NJ: Van Nostrand.

May, R. (1969). *Love and will.* New York: Norton.

McDougall, J. (1989). *Theaters of the body.* New York: Norton.

McDougall, J. (1995). *The many faces of eros.* New York: Norton.

McLaughlin, J. T. (1995). Touching limits in the analytic dyad. *Psychoanalytic Quarterly, 64,* 433–465.

McLaughlin, J. T. (2000). The problem and place of physical contact in analytic work: Some reflections on handholding in the analytic situation. *Psychoanalytic Inquiry, 20*(1), 65–81.

Merleau-Ponty, M. (1962). *Phenomenology of perception.* London: Routledge & Kegan Paul.

Merleau-Ponty, M. (1964). *The primacy of perception.* Evanston, IL: Northwestern University Press.

Merleau-Ponty, M. (1967). *The structure of behavior.* Boston: Beacon Press.

Mintz, E. E. (1969a). On the rationale of touch in psychotherapy. *Psychotherapy, Research and Practice, 6*(4), 232–234.

Mintz, E. E. (1969b). Touch and the psychoanalytic tradition. *Psychoanalytic Review, 56,* 365–376.

O'Neil, J. (1989). *The communicative body.* Evanston, IL: Northwestern University Press.

Pedder, J. R. (1976). Attachment and new beginning: Some links between the work of Michael Balint and John Bowlby. *International Review of Psycho-Analysis, 3,* 491–497.

Pope, K., & Vasquez, M. (1991). *Ethics in psychotherapy and counseling.* San Francisco: Jossey-Bass.

Rachman, A. W. (1997). *Sandor Ferenczi: The psychotherapist of tenderness and passion.* Northvale, NJ: Aronson.

Reich, W. (1949). *Character analysis.* New York: Orgone Institute Press.

Reich, W. (1961). *The function of the orgasm.* New York: Farrar, Straus and Giroux.

Reich, W. (1971). *The invasion of compulsory sex-morality*. New York: Farrar, Straus and Giroux.

Reich, W. (1974). *The sexual revolution*. New York: Farrar, Straus and Giroux.

Reich, W. (1980). *Genitality in the theory and therapy of neurosis*. New York: Farrar, Straus and Giroux.

Reich, W. (1982). *The bioelectrical investigation of sexuality and anxiety*. New York: Farrar, Straus and Giroux.

Reich, W. (1983). *Children of the future: On the prevention of sexual pathology*. New York: Farrar, Straus and Giroux.

Rennie, D. L. (1990). Toward a representation of the client's experience of the psychotherapy hour. In G. Lietaer, J. Rombauts, & R. Van Balen (Eds.), *Client-centered and experiential psychotherapy in the nineties* (pp. 155–172). Leuven, Belgium: Leuven University Press.

Rennie, D. L. (1992). Qualitative analysis of the client's experience of psychotherapy: The unfolding of reflexivity. In S. Toukmanian & D. L. Rennie (Eds.), *Psychotherapy process research: Paradigmatic and narrative approaches*. Newbury Park, CA: Sage.

Rolf, I. P. (1989). *Rolfing*. Rochester, VT: Healing Arts Press.

Ruderman, E. G. (2000). Intimate communications: The values and boundaries of touch in the psychoanalytic setting. *Psychoanalytic Inquiry, 20*(1), 108–123.

Ruderman, E. G., Shane, E., & Shane, M. (Eds.). (2000). On touch in the psychoanalytic situation. *Psychoanalytic Inquiry, 20*(1), 1.

Safran, J. D., & Muran, J. C. (1994). Toward a working alliance between research and practice. In P. F. Talley, H. H. Strupp, & S. F. Butler (Eds.), *Psychotherapy research and practice: Bridging the gap* (pp. 206–226). New York: Basic Books.

Sandler, J., Sandler, A. M., & Davies, R. (2000). *Clinical and observational psychoanalytic research: Roots of a controversy*. Madison, CT: International Universities Press.

Sardello, R. (1971). The role of direct experience in contemporary psychology: A critical review. In A. Giorgi, W. Fischer, & R. von Eckartsberg (Eds.), *Phenomenological psychology* (Vol. 1, pp. 30–49). Pittsburgh, PA: Duquesne University Press.

Searles, H. (1965). *Collected papers on schizophrenia*. New York: International Universities Press.

Sharaf, M. (1983). *Fury on earth: A biography of Wilhelm Reich*. New York: St. Martin's Press.

Smith, E. W. L. (Ed.). (1977a). *The growing edge of Gestalt therapy*. Secaucus, NJ: Citadel Press.

Smith, E. W. L. (1977b). The roots of Gestalt therapy. In E. W. L. Smith (Ed.), *The growing edge of Gestalt therapy* (pp. 3–36). Secaucus, NJ: Citadel Press.

Smith, E. W. L. (1985). *The body in psychotherapy*. Jefferson, NC: McFarland.

Smith, E. W. L., Clance, P. R., & Imes, S. (1998). *Touch in psychotherapy: Theory, research, and practice*. New York: Guilford Press.

Spence, D. P. (1994). The failure to ask hard questions. In P. F. Talley, H. H. Strupp, & S. F. Butler (Eds.), *Psychotherapy research and practice: Bridging the gap* (pp. 19–38). New York: Basic Books.

Spiegelberg, H. (1972). *Phenomenology in psychology and psychiatry*. Evanston, IL: Northwestern University Press.

Thelen, E., & Smith, L. (1994). *A dynamic systems approach to the development of cognition and action*. Cambridge, MA: MIT Press.

Totton, N. (1998). *The water in the glass: Body and mind in psychoanalysis*. London: Rebus Press.

Toukmanian, S. G., & Rennie, D. L. (Eds.). (1992). *Psychotherapy process research: Paradigmatic and narrative approaches*. Newbury Park, CA: Sage.

Valle, R. S., & King, M. (Eds.). (1978). *Existential-phenomenological alternatives for psychology*. New York: Oxford University Press.

Varela, F., Thompson, E., & Rosch, E. (1991). *The embodied mind: Cognitive science and human experience*. Cambridge, MA: MIT Press.

Williams, S. (1992). Withholding therapeutic touch. *Voices: The Art and Science of Psychotherapy, 28*(3), 58–61.

Yalom, I. D. (1980). *Existential psychotherapy*. New York: Basic Books.

Yontef, G. (1979). Gestalt therapy: Clinical phenomenology. *Gestalt Journal, 2*(1), 27–45.

CHAPTER 24

Biopsychosocial and Spiritual Treatment of Trauma

ANIE KALAYJIAN

Mass trauma has mental health repercussions on all who are touched by it, on communities and families as well as individuals. Both natural disasters and human-inflicted trauma are as old as recorded history, and no doubt predate written records. However, Posttraumatic Stress Disorder (PTSD), which is often the result, was identified as a diagnostic category only in 1980, in the third edition of the *Diagnostic and Statistical Manual of Mental Disorders* (*DSM-III;* American Psychiatric Association [APA], 1980). The discernment of PTSD as a recognizable cluster of symptoms related to overwhelming stress has facilitated theoretical development regarding etiology, encouraged research, and, perhaps most important, is leading to the development of models for treatment and prevention.

This chapter is focused on the biological, psychosocial, and spiritual impact of trauma on communities, families, and individuals and contains a six-step model for treatment that can be applied immediately. The model is also useful with individuals, families, and groups when the aftereffects of severe trauma have entered their hearts, minds, and souls, following them over a lifetime, sometimes affecting families over several generations (Kupelian, Kalayjian, & Kassabian, 1998).

A BRIEF HISTORY OF TRAUMATOLOGY

Traumatology, or the study of trauma and its effects and how to treat these, has greatly accelerated since the inclusion of PTSD in the *DSM-III* (APA, 1980). Although interest in trauma and stress reactions was building in the twentieth century, there was little agreement as to what precisely defined trauma or caused adverse reactions in some. Scholarly research and writing in the field has greatly increased in the past two decades, with numerous books published on the subject, the *Journal of Traumatic Stress* launched, and a host of articles written. The 1990s saw the advent of more than one international volume bringing together the research of traumatologists

With appreciation for the generous editorial assistance of Sharon Davis Massey.

from around the globe (Danieli, 1998). Figley (1993) recounted Veith's (1965) observation that the earliest known written records of trauma are the ancient Egyptian physicians' reports in the *Kunya Papyrus,* dating from 1900 B.C. These were of hysterical reactions to highly stressful situations, and this may have served as the world's first medical text.

Emotional reactions to highly stressful events have been documented in every century for which records of human behavior exist. Theories, explanations, analysis, and clinical interventions have varied, and symptoms of flashbacks, dissociation, and startle response have variously been interpreted as works of God, evil, the devil, and spirits (Ellenberger, 1970).

Important early contributions were made to traumatology at La Salpetrière Hospital in Paris (Briquet, 1959; Hurst, 1940; Trimble, 1985) by Jean Martin Charcot and others. Charcot was the first well-respected physician to demonstrate the psychic origins of hysteria. His work influenced Pierre Janet, Sigmund Freud, John Eric Erichsen, and Helmut Oppenheim (Figley, 1993). Janet, who was hired to work at La Salpetrière by Charcot immediately preceding the latter's death (Valsiner & Van der Veer, 2000), is considered by many in the field to be the first traumatologist. He kept and published extensive records of his more than 50 years of work with patients with hysterical and disassociative symptoms (van der Hart, Brown, & van der Kolk, 1989). In his numerous publications, which can be seen as foundational to the field, are found his observations of (1) "the inability to integrate traumatic memories as the core issues," (2) "the importance of the fundamental biphasic nature of traumatic stress," and (3) identification of symptoms of PTSD as cited in the *DSM-III* (van der Kolk, Brown, & van der Hart, 1989) and "other vital research" (Figley, 1993, p. xviii). Today's traumatologists are examining many facets of trauma, particularly its etiology, related symptoms, multigenerational transmission, and treatment.

A BIOPSYCHOSOCIAL AND SPIRITUAL APPROACH

DEFINITIONS: DISASTERS AND TRAUMA

Although knowledge about human response to mass trauma has increased significantly in the past 30 years, there are still critical theoretical and methodological problems in research on this subject, beginning with the issue of definitions.

Tierney (1989) defined *disaster* as a collective stress in a particular geographic area interfering with the ongoing social life of the community, with a sudden onset, some degree of loss, and subject to human management. Other experts (Quarantelli, 1970; Stallings, 1973; G. Warheit, 1976) distinguished between natural disasters, in which there is a community consensus, and civil disturbances, in which there is dissensus. Quarantelli (1985) further distinguished a disaster (earthquake, famine, bombing of a village) from a conflict (e.g., riots, hostages, incidents), and a community disaster (a town is flooded, there is an outbreak of cholera) from a group disaster (train derailment, sinking ship, or aircraft crash).

The Pan American Health Organization Regional Office of the World Health Organization (1993), offers a definition of *disasters* as events that occur suddenly (in most cases) and cause severe disturbances in the community. Those disturbances may be in the form of loss of life, health, or resources; of disruption of life or of environmental quality; and/or socioeconomic disruptions requiring immediate and comprehensive assistance and a variety of interventions. According to the former secretary-general of the United Nations, Boutros Boutros-Ghali (personal communication, January, 1993), "There is no hard and fast division—in terms of their effects on civilian population—between conflicts and wars, and natural disasters." According to Herman (1992), to study psychological trauma is to come face to face both with human vulnerability in the natural world and with the capacity for evil in human nature. To study psychological trauma means to bear witness to horrible events that expose the frailties and vulnerability of our humanity.

For the purposes of this chapter, *mass trauma* is defined as a mass biopsychosocial and spiritual wound that needs attention and that in many cases may benefit profoundly from a variety of professional interventions.

EFFECTS OF TRAUMA

There are many psychiatric disturbances associated with exposure to traumatic events. Although PTSD has been the most studied traumatic disorder in recent years, it is helpful to remember that it is not the only psychiatric disorder to occur following traumatic events. Major Depression, Generalized Anxiety Disorder, and substance abuse are other well-documented syndromes that may eventuate (Karem, 1991; Kulka, Schlenger, Fairbank, et al., 1990; Rundell, Ursano, Holloway, & Silberman, 1989).

It is useful to review what causes and constitutes PTSD. According to Schiraldi (2000), PTSD results from exposure to an overwhelmingly stressful event or series of events, such as war, rape, abuse, or natural disaster. It is a normal response by normal people to abnormal situations. The symptoms, if viewed apart from the traumatizing context (which may no longer be present), may appear strange and inexplicable at best, or pathological at worst, to the naïve observer. However, they make perfect sense when placed in the context of trauma. Because what has happened is out of the ordinary, it has overwhelmed the traumatized person's customary coping responses.

Trimble (1985) uses anecdotal accounts from the diary of the nineteenth-century British novelist Charles Dickens to illustrate the psychological impact of an event he experienced. Dickens was involved in a railway accident in June 1865, and was quoted as saying that at the time of the event, "the scenes amongst the dead and dying rendered his hand unsteady," and "I am not quite right within, but believe it to be an effect of the railway shaking. . . . I am weak-weak as if I were recovering from a long illness" (in Trimble, 1985, p. 7).

B. Warheit (1985) offered a more dynamic model of posttraumatic outcomes, encompassing the systematic relationships among life events, coping resources, stress, and stress outcomes. Warheit emphasized five sources that cause stressful events: (1) an individual's biological constitution, (2) an individual's psychological characteristics, (3) the social structure, (4) the culture, and (5) the geophysical environment. Slovic, Lichtenstein, and Fischoff (1979) focused on the perception of risk in mass-trauma situations, hypothesizing that persons who perceive the risk as great are more likely to heed warnings and take some individual actions to avoid or ameliorate consequences than are those who do not.

According to Laufer (1988), civilian post-trauma experiences share commonalities with those of soldiers and former members of World-War-II resistance movements. Both groups undergo a period of personal and communal readjustment that involves public recognition of survivors, communicating the experience, delayed public communication of trauma, silence and delayed response to stress and consequences of stress. Such severe stress affects the course of development and impacts the aging process. Laufer concluded by reiterating that those who survive war must cope with that trauma in its variegated forms throughout their life course, including during the readjustment period and in early, middle, and late adulthood.

A review of the literature on the Holocaust (Bergman & Jucovy, 1982; Brenner, 1980; Harel, Kahana, & Kahana, 1988; Krystal, 1968) indicates that symptoms associated with PTSD are present in this population. Research findings from World War II provide persuasive evidence that symptom patterns associated with PTSD are disproportionately high among mass-trauma survivors.

Research on the impact of the Ottoman Turkish genocide of the Armenians reveals feelings of anger and rage relating to the perpetrators' denial of the genocide (Kalayjian, Shahinian, Gergerian, & Saraydarian 1996). Salerian (1982) further noted the presence of phobias, psychosomatic disorders, and severe personality changes in populations affected by the genocide. Rates of PTSD in veterans of the Persian Gulf War appeared to be low immediately on their return (Ursano & Rosenheck, 1991). Initial systematic studies have generally supported these observations, with rates of PTSD of approximately 9%, although these rates have varied greatly (Rosenheck, Becnel, Blank, et al., 1992). Breslau, Davis, Andreski, and Peterson (1991) found that 23.6% of those exposed to a traumatic event developed PTSD. In Breslau's population, risk factors for PTSD following trauma were early separation from parents, neuroticism, preexisting anxiety or depression, and family history of anxiety.

Comorbidity is common with PTSD. Major Depression, Anxiety Disorders, and alcoholism often coexist with PTSD in the general population (Breslau et al., 1991; J.R.T. Davidson & Fairbank, 1992) and among veterans (Kulka et al., 1990; Shalev, Bleich, & Ursano, 1990). Of those with PTSD, from 62% to 92% have a previous or concurrent psychiatric disorder, compared to only 15% to 33% of non-PTSD comparison groups (J.R.T. Davidson & Fairbank, 1992; Helzer, Robins, & McEvoy, 1987).

Bowen (1976, 1978) and Boszormenyi-Nagy (Boszormenyi-Nagy & Grunebaum, 1991; Boszormenyi-Nagy & Krasner, 1986) have each, in his own distinctive systemic approach to psychotherapy, traced the multigenerational transmission of unresolved family problems. Bowen introduced the genogram as a diagnostic tool for tracing family issues. Harkness (1993) has specifically noted the transgenerational transmission of war-related trauma, and Danieli (1998) made use of information relating to the family tree in assessing and treating Holocaust survivors. Boyajian and Grigorian's study (1988) of Armenian survivors, their second-generation children, and third-generation grandchildren concluded that most first-generation participants experiencing the trauma firsthand responded with anxiety, anger, frustration, and guilt. Second-generation survivors reported manifestations of anxiety in association with parental overprotectiveness. Anger and frustration for all generations were associated with the modern Turkish government's denial of the genocide and reinforcement of the denial by other governments (Boyajian & Grigorian, 1988; Kalayjian et al., 1996). Still, against a background of losses and atrocities beyond the realm of usual life experiences, the aged survivors reflected a sense of accomplishment, tempered with anger about the perpetrators' denial of how they were victimized (Kalayjian et al., 1996).

Validation of a client's experienced trauma is essential to the undertaking of restorative psychotherapeutic work. In her work with sexual-abuse trauma, Madanes (1990, 1991) found that an explicit expression of remorse by a perpetrator to a victim had enormous healing value, and that perpetrators further needed to forgive themselves before they could fully reconnect with the community. She also noted the value of moving a victim's experience from the realm of the unique and personal (the specific trauma that happened to me) to the universal (this is a terrible thing that sometimes happens to people, others have been able to overcome it by . . .). Boszormenyi-Nagy and his associates (Boszormenyi-Nagy & Krasner, 1986; Boszormenyi-Nagy et al., 1991) examined, within the multigenerational family context, ways in which persons who have been abusive can earn existential merit and exoneration in a family, a process that might be examined for its application to larger systems. Casarjian (1992), Frankl (1955), and Kalayjian (1990) wrote of the healing that can occur through forgiveness on the part of a victim, even in the absence of remorse on the part of perpetrators, and of the meaning that can be found even in the worst of experiences.

DIFFERENCES AMONG SURVIVOR GROUPS

Some authors assume that the symptoms of PTSD are universal (Kinzie, Sack, Angell, Manson, & Roth, 1986; Kinzie et al., 1990); others object to jumping to such conclusions. Cultural differences may give rise to varied responses to trauma. For example, survivor guilt has been described as a major manifestation of the survivor syndrome among Jewish Holocaust survivors (Krystal & Niederland, 1968; Niederland, 1981). Although some, but not all, children of severely traumatized Holocaust survivors suffer pathological consequences (e.g., S. Davidson, 1980; Kestenberg, 1972; Klein, 1971; Krell, 1982; Steinberg, 1989), according to Albeck (1994), a variety of intergenerational consequences do occur. However, this guilt experience did not have a parallel among the Armenian survivors of Turkish attacks (Kalayjian et al., 1996). In Boyajian and Grigorian's (1988) sample, respondents' guilt was associated only with duties to the living (i.e., not having done enough for the Armenian community) and, among the second generation, not having done enough for their survivor parents. Kalayjian et al. (1996) found two variables unique to the Armenian survivor community: the meaning construed by the individual of the profoundly invalidating experience of the denial of the genocide by the perpetrators, and the degree of the family's involvement in the Armenian community. According to Kalayjian (1995), nightmares of second-generation genocide survivors who had experienced the devastating 1988 earthquake in Armenia were not of the earthquake, but of the Turkish gendarmes beating them on the death march, although they were not eyewitnesses to the atrocities.

Puget (as cited in Edelman, Kordan, & Lagos, 1991), who studied the trauma of dictatorship in Argentina, found that the nature of the traumatic situation affects family structure and individuals at the multigenerational and transgenerational levels. In this case, the traumatic situation comprised events of political repression (disappearance, torture, official silence) and other social repression produced by the state and implemented through the mass media.

It is well-known that anxiety and depressive disorders take different forms in different cultures, whether in terms of the dominant clinical symptoms (somatization, depressive affect, dissociative reaction) or of the importance attributed to the symptoms. Obeyesekere (1985) pointed out that among Buddhists, for example, anhedonia and low self-esteem are not considered symptoms, but rather the end results of an internal progression. This can be a positive progression, leading to a higher level of consciousness. According to Eisenbruch (1991), in Cambodian refugees, nightmares and reliving experiences, for example, cannot be interpreted outside the framework of their traditional cultural significance, that is, as a normal part of grieving for their Cambodian homeland. Rechtman (1992) pointed out that among survivors of the Pol Pot regime, the return of "ghosts" is not regarded as pathological, the way nightmares are in the West, but as a normal occurrence when the dead have not been laid to rest with proper funeral rites.

Japanese Americans underwent numerous traumata during their internment. Under the conditions of forced relocation, they feared for their safety and suffered severe economic losses and sudden unemployment, in addition to destruction of social and family networks (Loo, 1993). Internment was a culturally based trauma. Such traumas potentially serve as the "axial point for group and generational self-understanding... they define the parameters of communal conversations, thus providing the components from which collective identity is built" (Miller & Miller, 1991, p. 36). Internment was deliberate and intentional. Such traumas (internment, genocide, disappearances) of human design can lead to more severe and prolonged PTSD than trauma resulting from natural or accidental design (APA, 1994). The forced nature of the uprooting, in combination with their minority status, placed Japanese Americans at risk (Nagata, 1998). O'Sullivan and Handal (1988) noted that, whereas studies have shown either form of relocation, voluntary or compulsory, to be a significant stressor, the effects of compulsory relocation are significantly more detrimental to psychological functioning and social support. They also emphasized that minority groups are at particularly high risk for such negative effects under forced relocation, and that relocations that affect entire communities have more "profound and enduring effects" (p. 4). The work of Nobu Miyoshi (1980) provided an essential basis for documenting how the camp experiences of the Nisei (second-generation) were transmitted to their Sansei (third-generation) offspring. He postulated that family relationships are accountable to the standards of loyalty and justice from previous generations, an observation that is consistent with those of Boszormenyi-Nagy and his colleagues (Boszormenyi-Nagy & Krasner, 1986; Boszormenyi-Nagy, & Grunebaum, 1991). Within families, the "ledger" of accountability between the generations must be balanced for families and individuals to remain healthy, and ethical stagnation and poor mental health results from relating out of a sense of "destructive entitlement" (believing one is owed because of past injury), a form of ethical credit based on actually suffered past injustice. According to Stewart and Healy (1989), "The experience of psychologically significant social events at different stages of adulthood will have different consequences not only for the individual personally, but also for his or her children" (p. 33).

MAJOR SYNDROMES, SYMPTOMS, AND PROBLEMS TREATED

ASSESSING THE IMPACT OF MASS TRAUMA ON THE PSYCHOLOGICAL DIMENSION

The experience of trauma may be manifest in a variety of psychological symptoms, such as major depression, general anxiety, and substance abuse, and is exhibited in physiological and spiritual symptomatology as well. In the *DSM-IV* (APA, 1994), Posttraumatic Stress Disorder (309.81) is categorized among anxiety disorders. Those who are diagnosed with PTSD meet the following six criteria:

1. The person must experience or witness a traumatic event that is marked by a threat to well-being and strong feelings of intense fear or helplessness.
2. The person must constantly reexperience or relive the traumatic event. Reexperiencing the event can happen via hallucinations, flashbacks or dreams, and these reactions may occur if the individual is exposed to symbols of the traumatic event. Distressing physiological and psychological reactions are common responses to such symbols. Dreams of traumatized children are often frightening and their content unrecognizable. Also, children may reenact the traumatic event when exposed to related cues.
3. There is an intense desire to avoid all stimuli that seem even slightly related to the event. In addition, there is a lack of general responsiveness (such behavior was not present before the trauma), as marked by three or more of the following: avoidance of thoughts or conversations

associated with the event, repression of important memories related to the trauma, decreased interest in routine activities, withdrawal from social relationships, limitation of certain emotions, and inability to see a normal life span in the future.

4. The person must feel a persistent increased arousal in at least two of the following ways: insomnia, irritability, or unnecessary and disproportionate startle responses.
5. The symptoms mentioned in the second, third, and fourth categories must last longer than a month.
6. The symptoms must negatively affect the individual's social and occupational functioning.

Acute PTSD is specified as having a duration of symptoms for less than three months, as opposed to chronic PTSD, with duration of symptoms lasting three months or more.

Posttraumatic stress is often the result of unfortunate and overwhelming interpersonal experiences at the hands of others, or in relation to environmental disasters; these contextual circumstances do not come into focus in the definition or diagnosis in *DSM-IV*. Clearly, there are harmful psychological and societal circumstances that are deserving of attention, diagnosis, and intervention, or, better yet, prevention. At a minimum, it is helpful if these circumstances are recognized as linked to onset and etiology. The recent *Handbook of Relational Diagnosis* (Kaslow, 1996) was undertaken "from a biopsychosocial perspective, in which interpersonal and contextual factors are considered central and significant" (p. 523). The Global Assessment of Relational Functioning (GARF) scale, which is analogous to Axis V of the *DSM* Global Assessment of Functioning (GAF) scale, also "describes and quantifies the relational context within which patients live and problems occur" (Group for the Advancement of Psychiatry Committee on the Family, 1996, p. 155). These are promising as diagnostic tools that may be usefully applied in the many contexts in which PTSD arises.

Depression, anxiety, phobic symptoms, substance abuse, as well as divorce, intergenerational conflict, antisocial behavior, and career deficits have all been shown to be related to mass trauma. Both Frankl's work (1969) and the six-step model outlined here, which is in part inspired by Frankl, involve recognizing the biological, psychosocial, and noological (spiritual) dimensions of human experience, and the interrelationship of health or illness among the three dimensions. According to Frankl, symptoms that arise in any of these dimensions may be projected into others. Thus, problems in the psychosocial dimension of one's life, for example, may give rise to biological and/or spiritual as well as psychological problems.

Assessing the Impact of Mass Trauma on the Spiritual Dimension

In addition to emotional and psychological disturbances, individuals and families who have experienced mass trauma may also experience disturbances on the spiritual level. According to existential psychologist Frankl (1946/1955), one may suffer from what he terms "the existential vacuum," an inner sense of emptiness or meaninglessness. Camus (1988) once asserted, "There is but one truly serious problem, and that is . . . judging whether life is or is not worth living."

Frankl (1946/1962) was the first to note that positive use can be made even of mass trauma. The role of the therapist in logotherapy is to help a trauma survivor discover a unique personal meaning in relation to an experience of the trauma, therefore transforming the pain of the trauma into meaningful awareness and perhaps encouraging the person toward positive and active contribution to family and community.

Although Frankl (1969) asserted that meaning is available under any condition, even the worst conceivable one, it was very difficult for this author to believe that finding meaning was possible immediately after a devastating earthquake in 1988 in Armenia, which produced casualties of up to 75,000 people. It was enlightening to see how 20% of those interviewed perceived helping one another and receiving help as being very meaningful only six weeks after the earthquake. Three months after the earthquake, that percentage was doubled in Armenia. Likewise, 30% of the survivors of Hurricane Andrew in Florida in 1992 found positive meaning in their experiences three months after the hurricane (Kalayjian, 1995).

Survivors in Armenia had to endure both the sudden, natural disaster of the earthquake and the ongoing, human-made mass trauma of the civil war with the neighboring Republic of Azerbaijan. In spite of multilevel traumas, the Armenian earthquake victims talked about modification of attitude, and they found meaning through an acceptance of blind fate. They were even convinced that they were stronger, wiser, more resourceful, and more experienced for having survived the earthquake.

Alfred Adler (1924, 1956) wrote about the "psychology of use," in which he said that it was not the event itself, but how one used it that determined the goodness or badness of an experience. He also wrote of individuals organizing their personalities or "styles of life" around "fictional final goals" that represented their ways of overcoming the natural, organic "inferiority" that all humans have, being born into the world as infants, unable to take care of their basic needs. Persons who then experience other limits (abusive, neglectful, or pampering parenting, an illness, trauma) may either struggle to overcome these (e.g., Wilma Rudolph, who suffered from polio yet became an Olympic runner) or, alternatively, may see their misfortunes as determining the shape of their lives. Thus, Adler introduced the idea of personal choice in relation to the overcoming of limitations, together with the idea that it is how one chooses to view and use life's events that contributes to good or poor mental health. He felt that if one's fictional final goal of life (general outlook on life) was in line with "social interest" (the good of others as well as of oneself), the lifestyle was healthy (Adler, 1933, 1964).

Logotherapeutic Principles

Viktor Frankl, a psychiatrist and survivor of the Nazi concentration camps, who lost most of his family members there, was the originator of logotherapy, a psychotherapy that addresses what he termed the human "search for meaning." According to Frankl (1946/1962), meaning can be found in every significant life experience, including trauma: "In spite of all the enforced physical and mental primitiveness of life in a concentration camp, it was possible for spiritual life to deepen" (p. 54). One can retreat from the trauma surrounding oneself to a life of inner riches and spiritual freedom. Frankl pioneered recognizing positive outcomes resulting from traumatic situations. In logotherapy, a form of existential analysis, the human will to meaning is seen as the core for most human behavior. Frankl consistently pointed out that human beings readily sacrifice safety, security, and sexual needs for goals that are meaningful for them. In this regard, Frankl, at first glance, appears to introduce a human motivation overlooked by fellow existentialist Abraham Maslow (1943). Or perhaps he signals that self-actualization, which in Maslow's hierarchy of needs emerges after the "more basic" physiological needs and those for psychological safety, love and belonging, and esteem have been met, is the underlying spiritual drive force that leads us to attend to other needs. The spiritual motivation to seek meaning appears, in this regard, to be more basic even than physical survival. If life has no meaning, and if I as an individual am insignificant, then why live? Conversely, if I am significant but others are not, then what incentive is there to form families and communities? Clearly, both individual and community are best served by social interest, and meaning is found in positive personal engagement in communal life.

Being human, according to Frankl, is being always directed toward and pointing to something or someone other than oneself: to a meaning to fulfill or another human being to encounter, a cause to serve or a person to love. Only to the extent that one is living out this self-transcendence of human existence is one truly human or does one become one's true self (Frankl, 1978.)

Assessing the Impact of Mass Trauma on the Biological Dimension

The biological and physical aspects of human experience must also be considered when assessing the impact of mass trauma. The immune system forms the surveillance system of the body. Its primary function is to distinguish what is self and what is foreign, and to then attack and rid the body of the foreign invaders. Trauma excites the hypothalamus, which serves as a bridge between the brain and the endocrine system and ultimately triggers the "fight-or-flight" response necessary to meet the demands of the trauma. At this point, high levels of various hormones result in hypervigilance and neural hyperactivity and, therefore, lack of homeostasis. Other hormonal changes lead to accelerated heart rate and increase in the basal metabolic rate.

The thyroid gland is also involved in the trauma reaction, secreting thyroxin, which results in diarrhea, acidity, and indigestion. At the point of being threatened, one may experience all of these. This is in spite of drinking bottled water, refraining from vegetables and fruits, and eating only cooked food. At every threat, diarrhea may become more violent and uncontrollable. Trauma increases the amount of hydrochloric acid in the stomach, constricts blood vessels in the digestive tract, and reduces gastric mucus that protects the lining of the stomach. Ulcers may develop. Trauma and stress alert the rhythmic movements (peristalsis) of the small and large intestines necessary for the transport of food substances. Diarrhea results if peristalsis is too fast.

Trauma also affects the skeletal muscles by contracting them, potentially leading to tension headaches, backaches, and severe muscle tension. Trauma experience contracts the smooth muscles in the stomach walls, causing severe stomachaches, in addition to the contraction of the smooth muscles in the intestines, causing diarrhea.

THE SIX-STEP BIOPSYCHOSOCIAL AND SPIRITUAL MODEL

In the past decade, the author, in her efforts in disaster management and outreach and in relation to clinical logotherapeutic psychotherapy work with survivors, has developed a six-step model to address the biopsychosocial and spiritual needs of individual survivors, families, and the surviving community. Below are the steps of the model and explanations of its rationale, effects, and outcomes.

Step 1. Assessing Levels of Posttraumatic Stress

In this first step, participants are given a written questionnaire, the Reaction Index Scale (Frederick, 1996), to determine the level of PTSD symptomatology. The clarity and brevity of the Reaction Index Scale makes it the instrument of choice, given a chaotic postdisaster milieu in which expeditious assessment is requisite for the effective implementation of the model. The adult version includes 28 items for adults; 20 items for children have a scoring range of 0 to 4 for each item, with a total of 80 possible points. Scoring is bidirectional.

Step 2. Encourage Expression of Feelings

One at a time, each member in the group expresses what he or she is feeling in the here and now in relation to the trauma. From the author's research findings in the case of a natural disaster (e.g., earthquake), the predominant feelings expressed were that of fear—of more earthquakes as well as uncertainty of the future. Flashbacks, hearing the sounds of the earth rip apart and buildings topple, avoidance behaviors, anger, and sleep disturbances were also expressed. Among survivors of human-made disasters, those still traumatized experience predominantly the feelings of anger over the cause of the event and anger that it happened "to me" or "to us" and not "to others," fear of recurrence, and mixed feelings over survival (happiness and guilt). Flashbacks, reexperiencing of the trauma, avoidance, and numbing were also present. The facilitator (a mental-health practitioner), with a positive attitude, encourages the survivor to open the trauma membrane, dosing or titrating traumatic memory and its processing (Lindy, 1986).

Step 3. Provide Empathy and Validation

Survivors' feelings need to be validated by the group leaders' uses of statements such as "I can understand" and "It makes sense to me" and sharing information about how other survivors from around the world have coped. Intentional therapeutic touch is also used, such as holding a survivor's hand. Here, it is reinforced that the survivor's feelings of grief, fear, anger, as well as joy of surviving are all natural responses to the trauma, and need to be expressed. When trauma ruptures the individual's links with the group, an intolerable sense of isolation, disarray, and helplessness may occur. Providing validation and empathy in such a group will correct these effects by reestablishing the mutual exchange between the individual and the group.

In relation to an intergenerational support group organized to address the needs of second- and third-generation survivors of the Ottoman Turkish genocide of the Armenians, it was found that validation, even though offered by the facilitator (a psychotherapist) and not the perpetrator, had a tremendous healing effect, as reported by the participants.

Step 4. Encourage Discovery and Expression of Meaning

Survivors are asked: "What lessons, meaning, or positive associations did you discover as a result of the traumatic event?" This question is based on Frankl's psychotherapeutic principle that there can be a positive meaning discovered in the worst catastrophe. Again, each survivor is invited to focus on the strengths and meanings that naturally arise out of any disaster situation. Some of the positive lessons learned by the earthquake survivors from Armenia, California, and Turkey were: (1) Interpersonal relationships are more important than material goods; (2) it is important to release resentment and show forgiveness; and (3) it is empowering to rely not on the government, but on oneself and the community, to take charge of one's own life. The coming together of nations, communities, families, and individuals to assist restores some measure of trust or faith in self, others, and the potential for good in humankind.

Step 5. Provide Didactic Information

Practical tools and information are given on how to gradually desensitize. For survivors of natural disasters, the importance of preparation is reinforced and how to prepare is elaborated. Survivors are instructed to continue use of the biopsychosocial and spiritual model on a weekly basis. Handouts are given to teachers and prospective group leaders on how to conduct emergency drills and how to create safe and accessible exits. Booklets are given to parents and teachers on how to respond to their children's nightmares, fears, and disruptive behaviors. Assessment tools are given to psychologists and psychiatrists. Handouts on grief are provided, as well as how to take care of oneself as a caregiver.

STEP 6. PROVIDE BREATHING EXERCISES

Relaxation breathing can be used as a natural medicine and as a healing tool. Because no one can control nature, other people, or what happens outside of oneself, survivors are assisted in controlling how they respond to the trauma. This is an experiential section of the six-step model. It provides survivors with instruction on how to use breath to empower as well as to engender gratitude, compassion, faith, strength, and forgiveness in response to stress and mass trauma.

The aforementioned model has been used in Armenia, California, Florida, and Turkey following natural disasters, and in Kuwait, Yugoslavia, and Armenia after human-made disasters. Survivors stated that they benefited tremendously from this program. They reiterated statements such as: "This group has helped me a lot. Now I have some tools, I have some information, I know what to do"; "Your presence has helped us by giving us courage and encouragement. We are changed positively forever"; and "Your group has been so warm, caring and compassionate. We will remember you always."

The need for mental-health intervention after a war, for example, is self-evident. In contrast, the need for mental-health interventions in response to natural disasters is not widely accommodated. Yet, as the world becomes more heavily populated around major fault lines and along hurricane coastlines, massive human trauma pursuant to natural disasters will become more frequent. The author strongly recommends the establishment of permanent natural-disaster response teams in countries and cities affected by natural as well as human-made disasters.

CASE EXAMPLES

Ms. A.

The Family Trauma
Ms. A., age 40, the child of survivors of genocide, was seeking professional help for her sadness and continued night terrors. After a comprehensive assessment, a diagnosis of PTSD was made. Ms. A. had learned from her family and the community of the atrocities perpetrated against her people, which she described with great sadness: "During the war, the authorities declared our people enemies of the state. Adult males, particularly those identified as potential leaders, were taken from their families, escorted to a desolate area, and shot. This process was designed to deprive us of leadership and representation, so that deportations might proceed without resistance." Ultimately, forced deportations, famine, thirst, torture, epidemics, pillage, and plunder resulted in the death of two-thirds of the population in the area. Both her father's and mother's families had survived the long, forced deportation march and related hardships through desolate terrain to a neighboring country, where they were allowed to reside. There, her parents met and married. Ms. A. and her family emigrated to the United States when she was an adolescent.

The pain and suffering collectively contained in Ms. A.'s community and continued official denial of the genocide on the part of the perpetrating government have caused her tremendous psychic pain and feelings of helplessness. She said that the way she had found to best deal with those negative feelings was to sublimate them via taking positive actions. She became instrumental in groups dedicated to the scientific study of the stresses of genocide and other traumas and to advancing national and international understanding of the generational and intergenerational effects of traumatic experiences. She began to undertake systematic research on the psychosocial impact of the long-term effects of genocide on individuals and families.

When a devastating earthquake struck her family's native land, Ms. A was motivated to establish a mental-health outreach program to assist in meeting the psychosocial needs of the surviving community. Both the clinical outreach program and subsequent research with earthquake survivors revealed yet further traumatization. This generated tremendous pain and reawakened and highlighted feelings of helplessness in Ms. A. She reported having dreams and nightmares related to the traumatic stories reported to her by the survivors who participated in her research study. Ms. A. expressed a desire to help the surviving community heal from the long-term effects of the genocide. How, she wondered, could one help elderly survivors of the genocide integrate the trauma, find meaning in their experiences, and move on to the next stage of their lives? Ms. A. found ideas based on Frankl's logotherapeutic principles helpful.

Her therapist is fortunate to have met Frankl and asked his help in counseling Ms. A. with regard to her concern for helping her people heal from the injury of the genocide and enormous pain caused by its denial by successive governments. Frankl, with great understanding and empathy, responded: "Tell Ms. A. to ask your people to be the first to forgive. Your people have waited many years. Some survivors are dying as we speak. They can't wait any longer. Help her to help them forgive" (Kalayjian, 1991a). What Frankl spoke of was an individual and spiritual forgiveness, not a political one. Mrs. A. attempted to insert this concept of forgiveness in her lectures, but in vein, because people have attached forgiveness to forgetting, as in the common saying that one should "forgive and forget." This concept of forgiveness aroused yet more anger in Ms. A., as she was rejected by her colleagues and her community.

Ms. A. persevered and eventually published the first scientific research article on the psychosocial impact of the genocide after four years of revisions. She reported with anger: "One cannot help but wonder whether the demands for revisions were motivated by political concerns. The introduction of the paper, where the historical perspectives were mentioned, was changed and revised about a dozen times by the editorial board of the journal. A second study was published with the great encouragement and support of a survivor of the Nazi Holocaust."

The Personal Trauma

As Ms. A. continued her journey toward forgiveness and integration of trauma of the genocide. She submitted a paper to a conference on psychotraumatology and human rights that took place in the country of the perpetrators. Being fully cognizant of their denial of the genocide, Ms. A. reported that she revised her research paper and entitled it "Mass Human Rights Violations: Resilience vs. Resignation." A colleague submitted another paper on the genocide that was rejected. Ms. A.'s paper was accepted with some revisions. Worried about her safety, her friends and colleagues were against her going to a country that would not own its role as perpetrator. Their concern notwithstanding, Ms. A. went to the conference.

Upon her arrival at the conference, she noticed that the keynote speakers talked freely regarding the host country's more recent human rights violations against another ethnic group. Ms. A., feeling encouraged by these candid reports, decided to distribute her original abstract on the genocide against her people. At that point, the threats began. First, her life was threatened by two men claiming to represent the Secret Service of the host country, to whom she responded with skepticism, stating that she did not believe that anyone would dare kill her in front of several hundred scholars from the many countries represented at the conference. The following day, she was threatened with torture if she talked about the genocide. On the third day, the abstracts of her presentation were snatched from her hands, and on the last day of the conference, when Ms. A.'s lecture was scheduled, she was called by organizers from the host country and the head of the society (from another country), regarding presenting at the conference, for a private meeting in the basement. At this meeting, Ms. A. was presented with an ultimatum: Either she must sign a letter that was presented to her, or leave the conference without addressing the gathering. The letter indicated that Ms. A. would agree to refrain from talking about the genocide that her community had suffered. The letter was given to her only 20 minutes prior to her lecture, which was scheduled to take place during the last hour of the conference. Although Ms. A. reminded her interlocutors that they were attending a human-rights conference and were in fact violating her human rights as a presenter, it was to no avail. They reiterated that because of the political situation, they had to oblige and "protect the organizers."

Ms. A. chose to sign the letter in order to not lose the opportunity to address the conference. Colleagues helped her revise her transparencies by covering identifying words with a special transparency marker provided by the audiovisual department. When she began delivering her lecture and the first transparency was projected, Ms. A. apologized for the black lines without looking at the screen, then noticed that many of her colleagues had smirks on their faces. When she turned around to look at the screen, she saw that the censored words were showing through the black marks. Ms. A. then spontaneously said: "Whoops, it is coming through. I guess we could not hide it any longer."

Ms. A. reported noting a growing tension in the audience. Attendees from the host country were extremely tense; others were laughing, seeing the irony in her statement. Ms. A. then focused on forgiveness as a therapeutic intervention, which was the crux of her presentation. She reported feeling extremely tense while presenting, trying to decipher what to say and what not to say. Eventually, she reported communicating the importance of spiritual forgiveness as a means of getting over resentment and moving toward healthy dialogue. She focused on empowerment and moving on to the next phase of dialogue, education, and collaboration. As long as there is anger and rage, one cannot collaborate, she averred. She asserted that admission of genocide is a very difficult task to take on, especially when survivors of the perpetrators have been misinformed. She then asked the scientific community to assist the people from the country of the perpetrators in developing an emotional maturity by accepting responsibility and apologizing for the wrongs of their ancestors. They, too, she affirmed, need to forgive their ancestors to be able to overcome denial and to accept responsibility. After the lecture, numerous of Ms. A.'s international colleagues came forward and hugged and congratulated her for her courage. She reported crying in their arms, out of relief, happiness for being alive, and for having delivered that important message.

Ms. A. returned safely home, planning to write about her experience. She reported that, although she was spiritually enriched, emotionally and physically she was drained. She kept on postponing her writing out of fear of reprisal. Then an earthquake hit the country in which her former community lived, and more recently, her own life had been threatened. Ms. A., who had worked with natural disasters for over a decade, began to wonder whether she ought to go to this country to help. She decided to go and assist.

According to Ms. A., humanitarian outreach eschews geographic and political boundaries. She developed a mental-health outreach program and spearheaded a team that worked for several weeks under tents with over 500 survivors via group therapy, debriefing, and exercises to reduce the impact of the trauma. And she initiated research related to the trauma.

Ms. A.'s colleagues could not believe that, after threats to her life and the atrocities her community had suffered, she would still be willing and able to assist this country's earthquake survivors. Ms. A., having fully incorporated Frankl's message, viewed this as yet another challenge, and a step forward in her journey of forgiveness, empowerment, and transcendence.

Assessment and Diagnosis in Relation to Trauma
Ms. A. reported having severe diarrhea for weeks after her life was threatened. At every threat, her diarrhea became more violent and uncontrollable, although she reported taking Imodium, a medication intended to control it, regularly. She complained of pain in her neck and shoulders. Even after her return home, she reported experiencing an increased rate and depth of respiration, accelerated heart rate, and an increase in blood pressure and in anxiety. She was also experiencing hypervigilence, sleeplessness, and difficulty concentrating. She was diagnosed as suffering from PTSD.

Interventions for Overcoming the Impact of Trauma

The Physiological Dimension. Before Ms. A. could address her spiritual and emotional reactions to the trauma, she had to deal with her immediate physiological symptoms. On Maslow's (1943) hierarchy of prepotent needs, physiological issues are even more basic than psychological safety. The therapist asked her to see a holistic physician to control her diarrhea, fever, and dehydration. She was placed on antibiotics and Primadophilus Bifidus to compensate for the damage the antibiotics cause. This took care of her gastrointestinal disturbance. She was encouraged to seek the assistance of a doctor of chiropractic medicine to address her muscle tension and related neck and shoulder pain. Unfortunately, as she was still overwhelmed and filled with anxiety, Ms. A. fell in her backyard and severely dislocated her elbow, which called for emergency hospital intervention, a cast, and months of physical therapy after the cast was removed. Ms. A. sought the help of a nutritionist in obtaining immune-building natural supplements, such as grape seed, red wine, pine bark, and billberry extracts, as well as garlic pills.

The Spiritual Dimension. After her diarrhea had subsided, Ms. A. consulted an energy therapist who adjusted her energy field. The energy therapies are based on Eastern healing traditions that work with Chi (life energy). The energy therapist found a cold spot on her solar plexus, which in Ms. A.'s case may have had to do with fear. Because the physical body is construed as arising out of the energy field, it is thought that an imbalance or distortion in this field will lead to distress and eventually cause disease. Healing, in the energy therapies, is a matter of learning how to heal the field by restructuring, balancing, and changing it (Brennan, 1990). The energy therapist's task was to remove the trauma by removing the cold spot, releasing the negative energy, cleansing and repairing the Chi, and filling it up with warm energy.

Also in the spiritual vein, Ms. A. meditated regularly and engaged in yoga and relaxation breathing exercises, focusing on her inner strength and calling on her inner healers to take care of her wounds. Her therapist helped Ms. A. focus on what Frankl (1969) called "the last of human freedoms": the ability to choose one's own attitude in a given set of circumstances. This ultimate freedom is what we can exercise in any situation, even in the worst conceivable ones. For Ms. A., her experience of the threats on her life gave a new meaning to her struggle for truth, justice, and human rights. She now states that governments have agendas different from these, and that she will not let that alter her trust and belief in humanity. Her ability to connect with scholars and human-rights activists from the country responsible for the oppression of her people and later responsible for threats to her own person has, she reports, far superseded the negative experience of the threats she endured.

The Psychosocial and Emotional Dimensions. The therapist utilized Eye Movement Desensitization and Reprocessing (EMDR) sessions to deal with the intrusive thoughts and reexperiencing of the trauma. The trauma that Ms. A. experienced will always remain a part of her experience, but through the therapist's intervention and her own considerable efforts, using the biopsychosocial and spiritual approaches, she is well on the road to recovery. With the physiological symptoms under control, and through addressing the related psychological issues, she has taken charge of the meanings that her experiences will hold for her, and now sees how these can serve a positive function, not only for herself, but also in relation to her work with others.

Ms. D.

A Second-Generation Survivor
The following case study demonstrates that in a family where there is unresolved mass trauma with very little apparent integration, the separation-individuation process can be experienced as a crisis and another overwhelming loss, resulting in an enmeshment in the family. The case exemplifies a child's reaction to parents' trauma-related pathogenic behavior (Danieli, 1988).

Case Formulation
Ms. D., a 44-year-old, only child born in the United States, had a master's degree and a responsible position. She came for treatment after suffering intolerable rejection subsequent to her boyfriend's excluding her from a professional activity. She suffered from depression. She had moved out of her parents' home when in her late 30s to live with her boyfriend, and although deeply wounded by his behavior, had not broken off the relationship. The treatment was quickly refocused on her difficulty in separating from her parents.

It took several sessions to elicit the fact that her father was an Ottoman Turkish genocide death-march survivor. Ms. D. viewed events directed against her grandparents' generation when her parents were children as irrelevant to her life. This suggests a difficulty in her family's recognizing, articulating, and tolerating affects.

Ms. D. described her elderly father, a shoemaker, as a workaholic who refused to retire and who never stopped. Her father was a young adolescent when the genocide began. Gendarmes arrested his father in the middle of the night. He never returned. Ms. D.'s father and the eight remaining members of his family were forced onto a death march, from which only he and his mother survived. Ms. D. knew very little about his genocide experience, because he rarely talked about it without becoming tearful and overwhelmed by sadness and anger, which neither of them could tolerate.

Ms. D.'s mother, a decade younger than her husband, was born in a refugee camp to parents who had survived months of forced marches through harsh environmental and psychological conditions. She had told her daughter a few details of her parents' and their community's genocide story. When Ms. D. entered puberty, her mother began to suffer asthma attacks when distressed. Both of Ms. D.'s parents were extremely involved in the social network of the local community with other survivors.

Ms. D.'s mother was the eldest child in her family. Clinical reports indicated that the eldest child born to Holocaust-survivor parents shortly after the trauma in displaced persons camps was often severely affected (Danieli, 1982; Freyberg, 1980; Grubrich-Simitis, 1981; Russell, 1974). In this case, the mother's somaticized style suggests that she had difficulty perceiving her own affect consciously; in the verbal realm, her feelings did not become symbolically articulated (Krystal, 1988; Stolorow & Atwood, 1992). She may have lacked early validating responsiveness, which is very possible with two recently and highly traumatized parents. If she never learned to translate affect experienced first as physical sensation into the cognitive and verbal realms, she could not be expected to have helped her daughter make this translation successfully.

Her father's obsessive defense warded off intolerable affect. His manifest reaction to his own genocide story, avoiding it or being overwhelmed by it, suggests that he communicated an inability to tolerate the range of affect he needed to confront to integrate his trauma. A child who perceives that a parent cannot tolerate certain affects will stop experiencing and expressing those affects to protect the bond with that parent. In a family with a tenuous translation of affect from the physical to the verbal realm, the alienating effects of this translation will further attenuate it for the child (Stolorow & Atwood, 1992). Ms. D. would thus be unable to know or regulate her feelings when faced with a difficulty.

Based on Ms. D.'s description, her family resembled the closed system that has few internal boundaries characteristic of many Holocaust victim families (Danieli, 1985). For example, her mother freely went through Ms. D.'s personal mail and belongings. Whenever Ms. D. objected, her mother acted surprised and hurt because this signified a breach of her needed closeness. She then would have an asthma attack. This resulted both in anger and feelings of guilt in Ms. D. and a stable pattern of intrusion and ineffectual resentment. Her mother's constant worry, depression, and clinging exemplified the family atmosphere.

Ms. D.'s parents had ingrained in her a distrust of *odars* ("strangers"), a word her family used for anyone outside of the family. This maintained a strong familial overinvolvement and impeded her from establishing meaningful outside relationships. Ms. D. herself had been overinvolved with her parents, acting as their mediator, confidant, and advisor. Like her father, she worked obsessively to "get ahead"; like her mother, she somatized. Emotional distress triggered severe menstrual cramps and migraines with no apparent medical cause. At the same time, she did not have the insight to recognize the parallels with her parents' defensive styles of coping.

When Ms. D. tried to separate from her parents, her mother reacted with an asthma attack and guilt-inducing remarks. Her father attempted to use shame to force her into compliance, asking, "What would the Armenian community, our relatives, and friends say?" Ms. D. responded with immobilizing guilt, and the family's enmeshment was effectively maintained. This is the same dynamic she brought unconsciously to her relationship with her boyfriend.

Interventions

The six-step biopsychosocial and spiritual model was used with positive outcomes. At first, Ms. D. was encouraged and coached to express her feelings in the here and now. This is when feelings of anger (transmitted from her parents' anger regarding the genocide) were revealed. These feelings were superficial; beneath them lay overwhelming feelings of helplessness. Seligman and Beagley (1975) termed this "learned helplessness." Ms. D. was provided ample validation and empathy throughout the sessions. This helped to reestablish the mutual natural exchange between the individual and the larger group. Then, Ms. D. was encouraged to discover a positive meaning and lesson that she had learned in this process. This process began with forgiveness: forgiving herself, her parents, and the world for being silent about their trauma and the related overwhelming feelings. Didactic information and references to books related to her issues were shared throughout the therapy. Ms D. was then coached to learn and practice breathing exercises to assist in overcoming some of her fears and anxieties when faced with difficult situations.

Through coming to see her parents' behavior in the light of their own traumatic experiences, Ms. D. was able to understand them not as simply unjust or incomprehensible in relation to her own experienced needs as a child, adolescent, and young adult. The meanings of their behaviors were now about their own experiences and their needs, resulting from the trauma they had experienced in their own early families. Having differentiated her own experiences from theirs, she could now see her parents and the community to which she and they belonged in the context of painful experiences that many were still struggling with assimilating. She could now begin to accept and decide how to address that reality from and through her own experiences. She was now in charge of her own meanings, no longer feeling helpless, and was actively taking charge of her life.

RESEARCH

Survivors of mass trauma, like all other human beings, are unique in their responses to experience. Despite overwhelming commonalities, no two individuals or traumatic events are identical. To understand responses to traumatic events, it is important to consider the particular survivor and the unique context. Several studies have shown that the severity of the stressor is correlated with symptom severity (Helzer et al., 1987; Shore, Tatum, & Collmer, 1986; Yager, Loafer, & Gallops, 1984).

Social support contributes both directly and indirectly to the behavioral and mental-health outcomes of individuals exposed to mass trauma. Social support connotes the comfort, assistance, and information an individual or group receives from others (Kessler & McLeod, 1984; Ursano, McCaughhey, & Fullerton, 1994). Information and education were found to be empowering after natural disasters in Armenia (post-1988 earthquake) and Florida (post-1992 Hurricane Andrew) (Kalayjian, 1995). According to Hardin, Weinrich, Weinrich, Hardin, and Garrison (1994), who studied 1,482 South Carolina high-school students a year after Hurricane Hugo, social support and self-efficacy are inversely related to psychological distress. This reinforced findings from prior studies by Baum, Fleming, and Davidson (1983), Fleming, Baum, Gisriel, and Gatchel (1982), and Kalayjian (1995). Social support was an even better protector against psychological distress than self-efficacy, reinforcing the results of studies by Fleming et al. and Berndt and Ladd (1989), who found peer support to be essential for teens in distress.

Providing support during times of stress can be rewarding to the support provider, but it may also be stressful (Fullerton, McCarroll, Ursano, & Wright, 1992; S. D. Solomon, Smith, Robins, & Fischbach, 1987). Although women may be more likely than men to respond in a supportive manner (Kessler & McLeod, 1984), some women experience strong social support as burdensome during these stressful times (S. D. Solomon et al., 1987). Z. Solomon (1992) found increased somatic and psychiatric distress among wives of veterans of the Lebanon conflict who were suffering from combat stress reactions and PTSD. Solomon observed evidence of stress associated with increased responsibility thrust on the wife and possible identification with her husband's symptoms (called secondary trauma).

The appraisal of the trauma or its meaning to an individual can be construed as the evaluation of its meaning or significance in relationship to one's well-being, that is, the perceived threat to well-being and safety as well as the perceived challenge and potential for gain and growth (Lazarus & Folkman, 1984). This appraisal and ascription of meaning generally include an individual's perception of how to reconstitute life and community and how to understand, on a deeper level, what happened. Understanding what has happened after a disaster often includes attribution of responsibility (i.e., the assigning of a cause to the events). This appraisal can provide one the opportunity to grow or, in extreme cases, to submit and to be revictimized. This is where Frankl cautions people not to ask questions beginning with Why? but, rather, to ask questions beginning with What?: "What can I do about this trauma now that it has happened?" (Kalayjian, 1994).

SUMMARY

In the author's research (Kalayjian, 1995), conducted six weeks after the earthquake in Armenia, survivors were asked an open-ended question eliciting the meaning they had attributed to the earthquake. Twenty percent attributed a positive value and meaning to the disaster. This is congruent with Quarantelli's (1985) notion that disaster survivors are primarily attempting to cope with the meaning of the trauma, and with Frankl's (1962) assertion that meaning is available under any condition, even the worst conceivable one. This is somewhat contrary to Figley's (1985) belief that one of the fundamental questions a victim needs to answer to become a survivor is "Why did it happen?" The author's research findings in several countries after a variety of traumas indicate that questions related to why forced the survivor to remain in the past, in the role of victim, without a rational or satisfactory answer, and, therefore, more helpless and angry. It also left the survivor filled with feelings of self-induced guilt, and, therefore, trapped in a cycle of destructive behavior. Any question beginning with why has a built-in presumption that there is someone responsible for the trauma, or that there is always a clear cause. Trauma survivors from Armenia, California, and Turkey, who were preoccupied with the whys, were dissatisfied with the scientific answer "The plates moved, pressure was built up, and finally the tension was released." Survivors, especially in California, Florida, and Turkey, were informed regarding the why's of the earthquake and the hurricane, yet some of them still chose to remain in the why mode of thinking. Interestingly, these were the survivors who remained helpless, more depressed, and showed higher scores on the PTSD Reaction Index Scale (Kalayjian, 1995).

Although there has been increased interest in examining and researching the emotional, behavioral, and physiological consequences of mass trauma, many aspects of the health effects of trauma are not-well-understood. Further research is warranted regarding the physiological, psychosocial, and spiritual impact of mass trauma on individuals and communities and on the means of ameliorating these.

Scientists, clinicians, and health-care practitioners generally focus on the negative aspects of natural and human-made disasters. Notwithstanding the distinction, mass trauma presents opportunities for growth, development, and improvement. According to Caplan (1964), proper and prompt intervention may lead an individual and a community not only to a precrisis state but to a higher level of mental, physical, and spiritual health. If the crisis resolution is successful, the individual may learn new problem-solving behaviors and can return to a state of equilibrium, a steady state, at a higher level of functioning than that experienced before the crisis occurred.

Numerous crisis theorists (Caplan, 1964; Frankl, 1977, 1978; Gist & Stolz, 1982; Sime, 1980) have asserted that it is possible to increase resistance to mental disorders by helping individuals to extend their repertoires of effective problem-solving and life-enhancing skills.

Multiple losses, mass trauma affecting individuals, family, and community constitute real dangers that must be acknowledged, yet processing and learning to cope with these losses and finding positive meaning in them can be a challenge and an opportunity for personal and communal growth. According to Caplan's (1964) theory, a crisis becomes an opportunity when interventions occur properly, effectively, and promptly. Therefore, the primary goal of a caregiver after a mass trauma is to provide avenues to high-level, comprehensive wellness through addressing the biopsychosocial and spiritual levels, not only to restore individuals to pre-trauma health status, but to empower them to strive to surpass it.

REFERENCES

Adler, A. (1924). *The practice and theory of individual psychology.* Paterson, NJ: Littlefield, Adams.

Adler, A. (1933). *Social interest: A challenge to mankind.* New York: Capricorn Books.

Adler, A. (1956). *The individual psychology of Alfred Adler.* H. L. Ansbacher & R. R. Ansbacher (Eds.). New York: Basic Books.

Adler, A. (1964). *Superiority and social interest.* H. L. Ansbacher & R. R. Ansbacher (Eds.). New York: Viking.

Albeck, J. H. (1994). Intergenerational consequences of trauma: Refraining traps in treatment theory: A second-generation perspective. In M. B. Williams & J. F. Sommer (Eds.), *Handbook of post-traumatic therapy* (pp. 106–125). Westport, CT: Greenwood Press.

American Psychiatric Association. (1980). *Diagnostic and statistical manual of mental disorders* (3rd ed.). Washington, DC: Author.

American Psychiatric Association. (1994). *Diagnostic and statistical manual of mental disorders* (4th ed.). Washington, DC: Author.

Baum, A., Fleming, R., & Davidson, L. M. (1983). Emotional, behavioral, and physiological effects of chronic stress at Three Mile Island. *Journal of Consulting and Clinical Psychology, 51,* 565–572.

Bergman, M. S., & Jucovy, M. E. (Eds.). (1982). *Generations of the Holocaust.* New York: Basic Books.

Berndt, T. J., & Ladd, G. W. (1989). *Peer relationships in child development.* New York: Wiley.

Boszormenyi-Nagy, I., & Grunebaum, J. (1991). Contextual therapy. In A. S. Gurman & D. P. Kniskern (Eds.), *Handbook of family therapy* (Vol. 2, pp. 159–186). New York: Brunner/Mazel.

Boszormenyi-Nagy, I., & Krasner, B. (1986). *Between give and take: A clinical guide to contextual therapy.* New York: Brunner/Mazel.

Bowen, M. (1976). Theory in the practice of psychotherapy. In P. Guerin (Ed.), *Family therapy: Theory and practice* (pp. 42–90). New York: Gardner Press.

Bowen, M. (1978). *Family therapy in clinical practice.* New York: Aronson.

Boyajian, K., & Grigorian, H. (1988). Psychological sequelae of the Armenian genocide. In R. G. Hovannisian (Ed.), *The Armenian genocide in perspective* (pp. 177–185). New Brunswick, NJ: Transaction.

Brennan, B. (1990). *Light emerging: The journey of personal healing.* New York: Bantam Books.

Brenner, R. B. (1980). *The faith and doubt of Holocaust survivors.* New York: Free Press.

Breslau, N., Davis, G. C., Andreski, P., & Peterson, E. (1991). Traumatic events and Posttraumatic Stress Disorder in an urban population of young adults. *Archives of General Psychiatry, 48,* 216–222.

Briquet, P. (1959). *Traité clinique et théorique de l'hystérie* [Theoretical and clinical treatment of hysteria]. Paris: Ballière.

Brown, B. B. (1977). *Stress and the art of biofeedback.* New York: Harper & Row.

Camus, A. (1988). *The stranger.* New York: Knopf.

Caplan, A. (1964). *Principles of preventive psychiatry.* New York: Basic Books.

Casarjian, R. (1992). *Forgiveness: A bold choice for a peaceful heart.* New York: Bantam Books.

Danieli, Y. (1982). Therapists' difficulties in treating survivors of the Nazi Holocaust and their children (Doctoral dissertation, New York University, 1981). *University Microfilms International,* 949–954.

Danieli, Y. (1988). Confronting the unimaginable: Psychotherapists' reactions to victims of the Nazi Holocaust. In J. P. Wilson, Z. Harel, & B. Kahana (Eds.), *Human adaptation to extreme stress* (pp. 219–238). New York: Plenum Press.

Danieli, Y. (Ed.). (1998). *International handbook of multigenerational legacies of trauma.* New York: Plenum Press.

Davidson, J. R. T., & Fairbank, J. A. (1992). The epidemiology of Posttraumatic Stress Disorder. In J. R. T. Davidson & E. B. Foa (Eds.), *Posttraumatic*

Stress Disorder: DSM-IV and beyond (pp. 147–172). Washington, DC: American Psychiatric Press.

Davidson, S. (1980). Transgenerational transmission in the families of Holocaust survivors. *International Journal of Family Psychiatry, 1*(1), 95–112.

Edelman, L., Kordan, D., & Lagos, D. (1991). Transmission of trauma: The Argentine case. In Y. Danieli (Ed.), *International handbook of Multigenerational legacies of trauma* (pp. 447–463). New York: Plenum Press.

Eisenbruch, M. (1991). From Post-traumatic Stress Disorder to cultural bereavement: Diagnosis of Southeast Asian refugees. *Social Science and Medicine, 33*, 673–680.

Ellenberger, H. F. (1970). *The discovery of the unconscious: The history and evolution of dynamic psychiatry.* New York: Basic Books.

Figley, C. R. (1985). *Trauma and its wake.* New York: Brunner/Mazel.

Figley, C. R. (1989). *Helping traumatized families.* San Francisco: Jossey-Bass.

Figley, C. R. (1993). Foreword. In J. P. Wilson & B. Raphael (Eds.), *International handbook of traumatic stress syndromes* (pp. xvii–xix). New York: Plenum Press.

Fleming, R., Baum, A., Gisriel, M., & Gatchel, R. (1982). Mediating influences of social support on stress at Three Mile Island. *Journal of Human Stress, 8*, 14–22.

Frankl, V. E. (1955). *The doctor and the soul.* New York: Alfred A. Knopf. (Original work published 1946)

Frankl, V. E. (1962). *Man's search for meaning.* Boston: Beacon Press. (Original work published 1946)

Frankl, V. E. (1969). *The will to meaning.* New York: New American Library.

Frankl, V. E. (1973). Meaninglessness: A challenge to psychologists. In T. Millon (Ed.), *Theories of psychopathology and personality.* Philadelphia: Saunders.

Frankl, V. E. (1977). *The unconscious god.* New York: Simon & Schuster.

Frankl, V. E. (1978). *The unheard cry for meaning.* New York: Simon & Schuster.

Frederick, C. J. (1996). Children traumatized by catastrophic situation. In S. Eth & R. Pynoos (Eds.), *Posttraumatic Stress Disorder in children* (pp. 168–186). Washington, DC: American Psychiatric Press.

Freyberg, J. T. (1980). Difficulties in separation-individuation as experienced by offspring of Nazi Holocaust survivors. *American Journal of Orthopsychiatry 50*(1), 87–95.

Fullerton, C. S., McCarroll, J. E., Ursano, R. J., & Wright, K. M. (1992). Psychological responses of rescue workers: Fire fighters and trauma. *American Journal of Orthopsychiatry, 62*(3), 371–378.

Gist, R., & Stolz, S. B. (1982). Mental health promotion and the media: Community response to the Kansas City hotel disaster. *American Psychologist, 37*, 1136–1139.

Group for the Advancement of Psychiatry Committee on the Family. (1996). Global Assessment of Relational Functioning scale (GARF): I. Background and rationale. *Family Process, 35*, 155–172.

Grubrich-Simitis, I. (1981). Extreme traumatization as cumulative trauma: Psychoanalytic investigation of the effects of concentration camp experiences on survivors and their children. *Psychoanalytic Study of the Child, 36*, 415–450.

Hardin, S. B., Weinrich, M., Weinrich, S. Hardin, T. L., & Garrison, C. (1994). Psychological distress of adolescents exposed to Hurricane Hugo. *Journal of Traumatic Stress, 7*(3), 427–440.

Harel, Z., Kahana, B., & Kahana, E. (1988). Psychosocial well-being among Holocaust survivors and immigrants in Israel. *Journal of Traumatic Stress, 1*, 413–429.

Harkness, L. L. (1993). Transgenerational transmission of war-related trauma. In J. P. Wilson & B. Raphael (Eds.), *International handbook of traumatic stress syndromes* (pp. 635–644). New York: Plenum Press.

Helzer, J. E., Robins, L. N., & McEvoy, L. (1987). Post-traumatic Stress Disorder in the general population. *New England Journal of Medicine, 317*(26), 1630–1634.

Herman, J. L. (1992). *Trauma and recovery.* New York: Basic Books.

Hurst, J. (1940). *Medical diseases of war.* London: Edward Arnold.

Kalayjian, A. S. (1991, June). *Meaning in trauma: Impact of the earthquake in Soviet Armenia.* Paper presented at the VIII World Congress of Logotherapy, San Jose, CA.

Kalayjian, A. S. (1994). Emotional and environmental connections: Impact of the Armenian earthquake. In E. A. Schuster & C. L. Brown (Eds.), *Exploring our environmental connections* (pp. 155–174). New York: National League for Nursing Press.

Kalayjian, A. S. (1995). *Disaster and mass trauma: Global perspectives on post disaster mental health management.* Long Branch, NJ: Vista.

Kalayjian, A. S. (1999, December). Forgiveness and transcendence. *Clio's Psyche, 6*(3) 116–119.

Kalayjian, A. S., Shahinian, S. P., Gergerian, E., & Saraydarian, L. (1996). Coping with Ottoman-Turkish genocide: The experience of Armenian survivors. *Journal of Traumatic Stress, 9*(1), 87–97.

Karem, E. G. (1991, October). *The Lebanon wars: More data.* Presented at the annual meeting of the International Traumatic Stress Society, Washington, D. C.

Kaslow, F. W. (Ed.). (1996). *Handbook of relational diagnosis and dysfunctional family patterns.* New York: Wiley.

Kessler, R. C., & McLeod, J. D. (1984). Social support and mental health in community samples. In S. Cohen & S. L. Syme (Eds.), *Social support and health* (pp. 219–240). New York: Academic Press.

Kestenberg, J. S. (1972). Psychoanalytic contributions to the problem of children of survivors from Nazi persecution. *Israel Annals of Psychiatry and Related Disciplines, 10,* 311–325.

Kinzie, D., Boehnlein, J. K., Leung, P. K., Moore, L. J., Riley, C., & Smith, D. (1990). The prevalence of Posttraumatic Stress Disorder and its clinical significance among Southeast Asian refugees. *American Journal of Psychiatry, 147*(7), 913–917.

Kinzie, D., Sack, H. W., Angell, H. R., Manson, S., & Roth, B. (1986). The psychiatric effects of massive trauma on Cambodian children: I. The children. *Journal of the American Academy of Child and Adolescent Psychiatry, 25*(3), 370–376.

Klein, H. (1971). Families of Holocaust survivors in the kibbutz: Psychological studies. In H. Krystal & W. G. Niederland (Eds.), *Psychic traumatization: Aftereffects in individuals and communities* (pp. 67–92). Boston: Little, Brown.

Krell, R. (1982). Family therapy with children of concentration camp survivors. *American Journal of Psychotherapy, 36*(4), 513–522.

Krystal, H. (1968). *Massive psychic trauma.* New York: International Universities Press.

Krystal, H. (1988). *Integration and self-healing: Affect, trauma, alexithymia.* Hillsdale, NJ: Analytic Press.

Krystal, H., & Niederland, W. (1968). Clinical observations on the survivors syndrome. In H. Krystal (Ed.), *Massive psychic trauma* (pp. 327–348). New York: International Universities Press.

Kulka, R. A., Schlenger, W. E., Fairbank, J. A., Hough, R. L., Jordan, B. K., Marmar, C. R., et al. (1990). *Trauma and the Vietnam War generation.* New York: Brunner/Mazel.

Kupelian, D., Kalayjian, A. S., & Kassabian, A. (1998). The Turkish genocide of the Armenians: Continuing effects on survivors and their families eight decades after massive trauma. In Y. Danieli (Ed.), *International handbook of multigenerational legacies of trauma* (pp. 191–210). New York: Plenum Press.

Laufer, R. S. (1988). The serial self: War trauma, identity and adult development. In J. P. Wilson, Z. Harel, & B. Kahana (Eds.), *Human adaptation to extreme stress: From the Holocaust to Vietnam* (pp. 33–53). New York: Plenum Press.

Lazarus, R. S., & Folkman, S. (1984). *Stress, appraisal and coping.* New York: Springer.

Lindy, J. D. (1986). An outline for psychoanalytic psychotherapy of Post-traumatic Stress Disorder. In C. R. Figley (Ed.), *Trauma and its wake* (Vol. 2, pp. 195–212). New York: Brunner/Mazel.

Loo, C. M. (1993). An integrative-sequential treatment model for Posttraumatic Stress Disorder: A case study of the Japanese American internment and redress. *Clinical Psychology Review, 13,* 89–117.

Madanes, C. (1990). *Sex, love, and violence: Strategies for transformation.* New York: Norton.

Madanes, C. (1991). *Strategic family therapy.* In A. S. Gurman & D. P. Kniskern (Eds.), *Handbook of family therapy* (Vol. 2, pp. 396–416). New York: Brunner/Mazel.

Maslow, A. H. (1943). A theory of human motivation. *Psychological Review, 50,* 370–396.

Miller, D. E., & Miller, L. T. (1991). Memory and identity across generations: A case study of Armenian survivors and their progeny. *Qualitative Sociology, 14,* 13–38.

Miyoshi, N. (1980, December 19–26). Identity crisis of the Sensei and the American concentration camp. *Pacific Citizen, 91,* 41–42, 50, 55.

Nagata, D. (1998). Intergenerational effects of the Japanese American internment. In Y. Danieli (Ed.), *International handbook of multigenerational legacies of trauma* (pp. 125–140). New York: Plenum Press.

Niederland, W. (1981). The survivor syndrome: Further observations and dimensions. *Journal of the American Psychoanalytic Association, 29*(2), 413–425.

Obeyesekere, G. (1985). Depression, Buddhism, and the work of culture in Sri Lanka. In A. Kleinman & B. Good (Eds.), *Culture and depression: Studies in the anthropology and cross-cultural psychiatry of affect and disorder* (pp. 134–152). Berkeley: University of California Press.

O'Sullivan, M. J., & Handal, P. J. (1988). Medical and psychological effects of the threat of compulsory relocations for an American Indian tribe. *American Indian and Alaska Native Mental Health Research, 2*, 3–19.

Quarantelli, E. L. (1970). Emergency accommodation groups: Beyond current collective behavior typologies. In T. Sebutai (Ed.), *Human nature and collective behavior: Papers in honor of Herbert Blume* (pp. 111–113). Englewood Cliffs, NJ: Prentice-Hall.

Quarantelli, E. L. (1985). An assessment of conflicting views on mental health: The consequences of traumatic events. In C. R. Figley (Ed.), *Trauma and its wake* (pp. 173–215). New York: Brunner/Mazel.

Rechtman, N. (1992). L'apparition des ancêtres et des défunts dans les experiences traumatiques: Introduction à une ethnographie clinique chez les refugies coambodgiens de Paris [The apparition of ancestors and the dead in traumatic experiences: Introduction to a clinical ethnography in Cambodian refugees in Paris]. *Cahiers d'Anthropologie et Biometrie Humaine, 10*(1/2), 1–19.

Rosenheck, R., Becnel, H., Blank, A. S., et al. (1992). Returning Persian Gulf troops: First year findings. *Report of the Department of Veteran's Affairs to the United States Congress on the psychological effects of the Persian Gulf War*. Washington, DC: U.S. Government Printing Office.

Rundell, J. R., Ursano, R. J., Holloway, H. C., & Silberman, E. K. (1989). Psychiatric responses to trauma. *Hospital and Community Psychiatry, 40*(1), 68–74.

Russell, A. (1974). Late psychosocial consequences in concentration camp survivor families. *American Journal of Orthopsychiatry, 44*, 611–619.

Salerian, A. (1982, June 20–24). *A psychological report: Armenian genocide survivors 67 years later*. Paper presented at the International Conference on the Holocaust and Genocide, Tel Aviv, Israel.

Schiraldi, G. R. (2000). *The Post-traumatic Stress Disorder sourcebook*. Los Angeles: Lowell House.

Seligman, M. E. P., & Beagley, G. (1975). Learned helplessness in the rat. *Journal of Comparative and Physiological Association, 88*(2), 534–541.

Shalev, A., Bleich, A., & Ursano, R. J. (1990). Posttraumatic Stress Disorder: Somatic comorbidity and effort tolerance. *Psychosomatics, 31*(2), 197–203.

Shore, J. H., Tatum, E. L., & Collmer, W. M. (1986). Psychiatric reactions to disaster: The Mount St. Helens experience. *American Journal of Psychiatry, 143*, 590–595.

Sime, J. D. (1980). The concept of panic. In D. Canter (Ed.), *Free and human behavior* (pp. 63–81). London: Wiley.

Slovic, P., Lichtenstein, S., & Fischoff, B. (1979). Images of disaster: Perception and acceptance of risks from nuclear power. In G. Goodman & W. Rowe (Eds.), *Energy risk management* (pp. 223–245). London: Academic Press.

Solomon, S. D., Smith, E. M., Robins, L. N., & Fischbach, R. L. (1987). Social involvement as a mediator of disaster-induced stress. *Journal of Applied Social Psychology, 17*(12), 92–112.

Solomon, Z. (1992). *Psychological effects of the Gulf War on high-risk sectors of the Israeli population*. International Symposium on Stress, Psychiatry and War, World Psychiatric Association, Paris.

Stallings, R. (1973). The community context of crisis management. *American Behavioral Scientist, 16*, 313–325.

Steinberg, A. (1989). Holocaust survivors and their children: A review of the clinical literature. In P. Marcus & A. Rosenberg (Eds.), *Healing their wounds: Psychotherapy with Holocaust survivors and their families* (pp. 23–48). New York: Praeger.

Stewart, A. J., & Healy, J. M. (1989). Linking individual development and social changes. *American Psychologist, 44*, 30–42.

Stolorow, R. D., & Atwood, G. E. (1992). *Contexts of being: The intersubjective foundations of psychological life*. Hillsdale, NJ: Analytic Press.

Tierney, K. J. (1989). The social and community contexts of disaster. In R. Gist & B. Lubin (Eds.), *Psychosocial aspects of disaster* (pp. 11–39). New York: Wiley.

Trimble, M. R. (1985). Post-traumatic Stress Disorder: History of a concept. In C. R. Figley (Ed.), *Trauma and its wake: The study and treatment of Post-traumatic Stress Disorder* (pp. 5–14). New York: Brunner/Mazel.

Ursano, R. J., McCaughhey, B. G., & Fullerton, C. S. (1994). *Individual and community responses to trauma and disaster.* Cambridge, England: Cambridge University Press.

Ursano, R. J., & Rosenheck, R. (1991). Post-traumatic Stress Disorder in Operation Desert Storm returnees. *Report of Joint Department of Veterans Affairs and Department of Defense Working Group* (Public Law 102–25). Washington, DC: U.S. Government Printing Office.

Valsiner, J., & Van der Veer, R. (2000). *The social mind: Construction of an idea.* Cambridge, MA: Cambridge University Press.

van der Kolk, B. A., Brown, P., & Van der Hart, O. (1989). Pierre Janet's post-traumatic stress. *Journal of Traumatic Stress, 2*(4), 365–378.

van der Kolk, B. A., & Saporta, J. (1993). Biological response to Psychic trauma. In J. P. Wilson & B. Raphael (Eds.), *International handbook of traumatic stress syndromes* (pp. 25–33). New York: Plenum Press.

Veith, I. (1965). *Hysteria: The history of a disease.* Chicago: University of Chicago Press.

Warheit, B. J. (1985). A propositional paradigm for estimating the impact of disasters on mental health. In B. J. Sowder (Ed.), *Disasters and mental health: Selected contemporary perspectives* (pp. 196–214, DHHS Publication No. ADM 85–1421). Washington, DC: U.S. Government Printing Office.

Warheit, G. J. (1976). Similarities and differences in mass emergencies. *Mass Emergencies, 1,* 131–137.

World Health Organization. (1993). *Mitigation of disasters in health facilities: General issues* (Vol. 1). Washington, DC: Author.

Yager, T., Loafer, R., & Gallops, M. (1984). Some problems associated with war experience in men of the Vietnam generation. *Archives of General Psychiatry, 41,* 327–333.

Section Six

SPECIAL TOPICS

Chapter 25 International Perspectives on Professional Ethics

Chapter 26 An Interpersonal-Systemic and Developmental Approach to Supervision

Chapter 27 Humanistic, Interpersonal, and Existential Psychotherapies: Review and Synthesis

CHAPTER 25

International Perspectives on Professional Ethics

MARILYN PETERSON ARMOUR, INGEBORG E. HAUG WITH DOROTHY BECVAR,
HELEN BRAUN, MONY ELKAIM, SHIBUSAWA FAZUKO, AND AUGUSTINE NWOYE

During a 1987 visit to psychologists and psychiatrists in Moscow, Haug (1998) was asked to initiate a conversation about ethics. About 20 minutes into an ad hoc speech that addressed the development of professional ethics codes for mental-health providers in the United States and highlighted issues such as therapists' responsibility to clients, the Russian hosts interrupted. No, they objected, this is not what we think of as ethical concerns. We are struggling with the ethics of family members confiding personal information to a therapist, an outsider. Is this not disloyal? Does this not come close to betraying the family? Besides, in Soviet Russia, this action has the potential of endangering the very persons we care about.

Psychotherapy in the Western hemisphere has developed over the past 100 years into a treatment modality encompassing many different approaches to the "healing of souls." One of the founding principles of a systemic family therapy approach, a relative newcomer on the therapy scene, highlights its emphasis on understanding thoughts, feelings, and behaviors in their relational contexts, thereby locating problems and their alleviation within systems, not individuals. This contextual focus on understanding phenomena currently permeates most therapy models and, in fact, sciences in general.

The experience in Moscow was a humbling reminder that theories and practices, including reflections and understandings of ethics, remain context-dependent. They are inescapably entwined with the societies and cultures that give rise to them. Professional ethics entails translating an "ethos of care" (Peterson, 1992) into behaviors that benefit clients and their environments. They reflect the philosophical stances and virtues embraced by a professional group within a certain sociopolitical and cultural context at a particular point in time, and in the developmental history of that profession. They may be formalized in a written ethics

---

Marilyn P. Aremour and Ingeborg E. Haug are the first authors of this chapter and contributed equally. Thy recognize Dorothy Becvar, Helen Braun, Mony Elkaim, Shibusawa Fazuko, and Augustine Nwoye for their contributions and participation in the chapter.

code and/or derived from internalized and broadly accepted cultural values and personal beliefs. Professional ethics thus are not necessarily global, but local. As the international contributions in the following section demonstrate, what constitutes professional ethical behavior and is experienced as an ethical dilemma in one cultural context may differ from what is viewed as ethical or unethical in another. The international dialogue that follows can therefore challenge us to reexamine our ethical values, beliefs, and ethnocentric biases. It is hoped that it will also serve to enlarge our awareness of the ethical dimensions of our work.

Our understandings of professional ethics also are not static. As products of their times, they are always in flux and need to be revised as sociocultural and professional values and understandings shift. Ethics dialogue in the United States in the 1990s and in the new millennium, for instance, is unthinkable without including considerations of the impact of ethnic, racial, gender, sexual-orientation, socioeconomic, and religious diversity in the treatment of clients, students, and supervisees, ethical dimensions in the provision of psychotherapy that have entered professional awareness during the past two decades.

Sociopolitical factors as well greatly affect the direction our ethics dialogue takes. U.S. society may be characterized as litigious, and malpractice suits against mental-health practitioners loom as a frightening possibility. In our 1987 Moscow meeting, the U.S. focus on professional ethics as a means of preventing malpractice suits was completely foreign to Russian colleagues, who lived in an oppressive, authoritarian Soviet system that made dissent and complaints against authorities unthinkable. Ethics discussions, therefore, could not yet focus on therapists' responsibilities and accountability because a focus on consumer rights was not supported by the larger system and no functional avenues for redress were in place.

Cultural values deeply permeate our ideas of ethics, often outside awareness. In the United States, for example, individual rights are greatly prized. Professional ethical codes consequently emphasize individual clients', students', and supervisees' rights to confidentiality, self-determination, and full disclosure of the pertinent policies and procedures governing a professional's practice. The right to self-determination extends to each member of a family. In cases of releasing information, ethics codes stipulate that each family member has to give his or her consent in writing (American Association for Marriage and Family Therapy, 2001). As Tazuko Shibusawa's contribution in the following section highlights, Asian cultures, in contrast, traditionally give priority to a family unit, not an individual, assuming that an individual's good is implicitly fostered by such a collective focus. The family, not the individual, is therefore empowered to decide on such issues as an individual's access to information, even when these decisions are contrary to the individual's explicit wishes. To be even more specific, the culture accords senior males in a family the authority to decide for a family. This can create profound ethical dilemmas for family members and professionals, as in the case of cancer patients' desire to be informed of their diagnosis and a family's refusal to permit such disclosure.

The focus on the ethics of family members participating in psychotherapy, which dominated the discussions among Russian mental-health professionals in 1987, was also indicative of the developmental history of psychotherapy as a profession in their country. A 1935 decree forbade any form of psychotherapy in the Soviet Union on ideological grounds. In 1987, psychotherapy practices in general and conversations about ethics in particular were just beginning to get underway as these restrictions were lifted in the Gorbachev era. In the ensuing years, as mental-health professions gained in membership and public acceptance, professional organizations were developed, and the discussions regarding ethics shifted from a focus on clients' responsibilities to the responsibilities and appropriate behaviors expected from therapists (Misha Yerish, personal conversation, December 20, 2000). As we look at the emergence of mental-health professions around the globe, it appears that, in each country, their evolution over time includes a move from an informal code of ethics based on shared sociocultural values to more explicit, written codes that incorporate philosophical and practical professional values, formalize expectations and accountability, and help solidify professional identity.

In the following section, five international mental-health practitioners reflect on professional ethics. Although they have been trained in a variety of disciplines, such as psychology, psychiatry, pastoral counseling, and social work, they all share specialized training in marriage and family therapy and identify as family therapists. Each international colleague relates his or her personal perceptions and understandings. Each is a seasoned clinician, respected innovator, and recognized leader of high repute; none of them purports to speak for the profession at large in their countries of origin. They all, however, locate their reflections within the unique historical contexts of their societies and cultures as well as the development of the profession of marriage and family therapy within their national borders. These contributions from colleagues from Asia (Japan), Africa (Kenya), Europe (Belgium), South America (Ecuador), and North America (United States) are, as may be expected, diverse in style, organization, and content. The uniqueness of each essay and each perspective bears testimony to the contextual nature of our understanding of psychotherapy and ethics.

In the first part, the contributions of each colleague appear in alphabetical order. Following that are analyses and integration of these writings and their differing emphases from the perspectives of the five ethical principles of autonomy, beneficence, nonmalfeasance, justice, and fidelity that mental-health professions have widely adopted from medical ethics (Kitchener, 1984). Our international colleagues were not asked to specifically address these principles. Their introduction, however, provides us with a lens through which to review the richness of each of their contributions and understand them as "variations on a theme," namely, the topic of professional ethics in the theory and practice of psychotherapy, with special attention to marriage and family therapy. The chapter concludes with suggestions for further areas of study and international collaboration in regard to the evolution of professional ethics.

REFLECTIONS FROM AROUND THE GLOBE

Ethics and Family Therapy in the United States (Dorothy Becvar)

By the beginning of the new millennium, marriage and family therapy in the United States had become a recognized and distinct discipline within the mental-health professions. This was no small achievement given a history of less than 60 years. The 1940s may be understood as the period in which the seeds of the paradigm shift represented by systems theory and cybernetics were planted (Becvar & Becvar, 2000). The 1950s constituted the era in which the family therapy plant took root, evidenced by the emergence and implementation of new ways of theorizing and practicing. In the1960s, the budding of the family therapy plant splayed into a variety of distinct models and approaches. The 1970s provided the context for the blossoming of organized schools of family therapy. The 1980s evolved into a period of mature growth characterized by the connection and integration of the various models and approaches previously developed. The 1990s involved both the dying of what was old and wilted and the rebirth of new vegetation. Beginning as a time of controversy and internal conflict catalyzed by the feminist critique, it ended with a focus on transcending models and developing collaborative and respectful therapeutic dialogues. Also introduced during this period was a postmodern perspective. What is more, toward the end of both the decade of the 1990s and the old millennium, we note:

> As we approach the year 2000, we now find ourselves at a point at which including ethics, morality and spirituality in our therapeutic conversations has become an area of great interest. Apparently we see ourselves developmentally ready to address in greater depth what may be not only some of the most significant dimensions of our holistic perspective but also some of the most crucial aspects of our work. (Becvar, 1997, p. 211)

Professional associations, including the American Association of Marriage and Family Therapy (AAMFT) and the American Family Therapy Academy (AFTA), were organized and began to evolve early on as many practitioners began to identify themselves as marriage and family therapists and to look for a professional home. The AAMFT was particularly important in the quest for recognition through licensure in both the United States and Canada and also was responsible for promulgating and enforcing a code of ethics beginning as early as 1962 (Brock, 1994). Since then, there have been 10 revisions of the AAMFT Code of Ethics.

An important part of the development of family therapy in the United States emerged as many colleges and universities initiated training programs at both the master's and doctoral levels. The Commission on Accreditation of Marriage and Family Therapy Education (COAMFTE), an affiliate of AAMFT recognized by the U.S. Department of Education, has a well-established accreditation process for programs wishing to be so recognized. Both clinical membership in AAMFT and accreditation by the COAMFTE require completion of a course in ethics and professional issues in marriage and family therapy.

Despite the growth of accredited programs in marriage and family therapy, however, their number is still relatively small, and the profession remains largely multidisciplinary in nature. Just as in the early days before specialized training was available, many professionals who provide marriage and family therapy are licensed in other disciplines, such as counseling, psychology, psychiatry, and social work. Indeed, a great source of conflict over the years and continuing into the present has been disagreement over whether marriage and family therapy constitutes a separate discipline or a subspecialty within these other disciplines (Becvar, 1999).

In addition, although licensure has been attained in a majority of the states, the struggle for reimbursement with other mental-health professions has not yet been successfully resolved. What is more, private practice is fast becoming a phenomenon of the past in the context of an environment dominated by large managed-care companies. Thus, today, the majority of marriage and family therapists are employed in agency or group settings, for marriage and family therapists have not yet won the battle for reimbursement from third-party payers across the board. Given the continuing influence of the mainstream medical model, marriage and family therapists often are required to abandon, or at least compromise, their systemic, relational ways of thinking to be able to survive economically. That is, they must focus on pathology and make individual diagnoses if they are to be paid for the services they provide. This development has led to an issue of ethics at a metalevel, one that is particularly challenging for those who seek to remain consistent with a second-order cybernetics/systemic perspective. We have thus posed the following questions related to this issue:

- Is it ethical for family therapists to assign a diagnostic label to an individual, thereby defining him or her as dysfunctional, while operating out of a perspective that, even at

the level of simple cybernetics, sees family rather than individual dysfunction?
- At the level of cybernetics, what are the consequences of the previous action for our clients? What are the consequences for the larger society of our creating and maintaining a belief in pathology defined as individual rather than contextual?
- What is our ethical responsibility when we realize that we participate in a pathologizing discourse while at the same time recognizing that we devise diagnostic categories and illness labels and that they do not exist outside of our constructions (Becvar & Becvar, 2000, p. 126)?

Indeed, the introduction of a postmodern perspective, including constructivism, social constructionism, and second-order cybernetics, has introduced a whole new level of ethical awareness into the practice of marriage and family therapy. A code of ethics has been promulgated by the AAMFT since the early days of its history and has been subject to several revisions. Codes of ethics are also routinely built into state licensure laws, as are course requirements in the area of legal and ethical issues. These codes and courses generally tend to focus on such concerns as responsibility to clients; issues of confidentiality; professional competence and integrity; responsibility to students, employees, and supervisees; responsibility to research participants; responsibility to the profession; appropriate financial arrangements; and advertising.

Thus, for example, according to the AAMFT Code of Ethics, marriage and family therapists must practice within their scope of competence and must not use their influential positions to exploit their relationships with clients, students, supervisees, or research participants. Sexual intimacy between therapist and client is explicitly prohibited and may not occur between therapist and former client until two years after the termination of therapy. Less clear and often a source of ethical dilemmas for therapists is the realm of dual relationships. This refers to instances in which therapist and client may find themselves together in situations outside the therapy setting (e.g., in social gatherings or business dealings). Another illustration is a situation in which there is role confusion:

> Are you my therapist, my friend, or my lover? If you had lunch with me after the last session, why won't you today? Or consider the therapist who, in session, asks a physician client to prescribe medication for the therapist's stomach distress. The physician complies. Who is whose patient? Role confusion is a by-product of blurred boundaries and dual relationships. (Humphrey, 1994, p. 119)

A therapist faces the challenge of maintaining professional boundaries while at the same time avoiding exploitation of a client or violation of a client's confidentiality.

As difficult as ethical dilemmas such as these are, they may be relatively minor next to the challenges presented by postmodernism. Both the idea of doing therapy and the ways in which therapy has been practiced until now are called into question when one assumes a constructivist, social-constructionist, and/or second-order cybernetics perspective. From these perspectives, all of reality, including problems and pathology, are understood to be constructions generated within the minds of individuals and larger groups that are validated and supported within the language system of a given social context. Theories become stories, and truth is understood to be inaccessible in any absolute or ultimate sense (Becvar & Becvar, 2000).

Accordingly, with postmodernism comes a heightened awareness of the so-called totalizing discourses according to which societies organize themselves (Gergen, 1991). Knowledge is now understood to be framework-relative, and the idea of therapists as experts with privileged information, and thus power, is severely questioned (Anderson, 1997). Hence, for example, the ethical dilemmas around diagnosis noted previously arise. What postmodernists advocate is greater sensitivity to the expertise of clients as well as therapists, with an awareness of the influence of both as coconstructors of reality in the context of therapy. Much emphasis is given to the need for respectful, ethical behavior on the part of professionals, with a recognition that "the entire therapeutic venture is fundamentally an exercise in ethics; it involves the inventing, shaping, and reformulating of codes for living together" (Efran, Lukens, & Lukens, 1988, p. 27).

With the rise of postmodernism has come greater permission for the inclusion of both spirituality and moral/ethical issues in the therapy process (Becvar, in press). A spiritual orientation generates awareness of interdependence as the rule and of separateness as illusion; that each person represents an expression of a divine force and has an inherent urge toward growth and wholeness; that consciousness is the ground of all that is and that mind and nature form a necessary unity; that we construct realities as a function of our beliefs and perceptions; and that each person has a desire for meaning and purpose in life (Becvar, 1997). Many books and articles are appearing regarding ways to incorporate a spiritual dimension in therapy (Patterson, Hayworth, Turner, & Raskin, 2000).

From a moral/ethical perspective, a therapist is admonished to be caring and compassionate and to demonstrate courage, prudence, a willingness to use moral language, as well as the ability to respect both the interpersonal and community commitments and responsibilities of clients (Doherty, 1995). In addition, the importance of justice and truthfulness are emphasized, thereby bringing values consistent with spirituality as well as ethics to the forefront of the therapeutic process.

Family therapy in the United States not only has provided leadership in the development of viable and enforceable codes of ethics and related course work but also, as a field, has evolved to the point where many of its practitioners understand psychotherapy to be an inherently ethical endeavor. Although therapists may continue to be challenged by ethical dilemmas at a variety of levels, consciousness has been raised, and there is widespread recognition of the need to keep ethics as a primary concern, whether formulating theory or engaging in practice. Family therapy, for many, is about ethics.

PROFESSIONAL ETHICS IN FAMILY THERAPY IN ECUADOR (HELEN H. BRAUN)

Baby Family Therapy is just being carried out of the Ecuadorian delivery room for presentation to its family and the wider world. No permanent name has been given yet, and there is a long way to go before a real identity is established. Most of society is still unaware of its presence. But parents, teachers, and other family members nearby are concerned for Baby to have a good, solid, ethical, productive, helpful, successful life of service to others. And they are working on plans for a public naming party.

The definition of family therapy in Ecuador in the counseling culture of traditional helping professions generally means the inclusion of one or more family members in a counseling session in which one person is faced with the needs and opinions of the rest of the family concerning his or her behavior as well as the requirements of society. The family is there to see that the identified patient behaves according to the advice of the professional.

A systemic and relational orientation has entered the thought and world vision of Ecuadorian society at large, mainly through nongovernmental organizations (NGOs) and businesses, applying its wider and broader tenets to their own disciplines. Among these NGOs are those related to church or faith-based organizations. One of these, the family-centered service organization EIRENE, began in the late 1980s to organize courses in systemic family counseling for pastors. Although working with a very limited audience among a Protestant minority, the new approach generated interest, and the word started to spread.

Several graduates of EIRENE's family-therapy training program in 1990 formed the Center for Integrated Family Services (CIF). Over the ensuing years, requests for training and services in systemic family therapy grew. CIF staff became convinced that there was a critical need in Ecuador to establish an academically recognized program in systems-oriented family therapy for people trained in the human sciences, particularly those professionals who work full-time with families. Because of the perceived incompatability of the systemic paradigm with Freudian and Lacanian theories which dominated Ecuadorian training in the social sciences, none of the major universities was open to pioneering a family-therapy program.

In 1995, the Salesian Community, a Catholic order known for its work in educational programs for street children, especially at a technical level, established the Universidad Politecnica Salesiana in Quito, which was sympathetic to nontraditional careers and professional training opportunities. University administrators showed particular responsiveness to programs that would support families. The proposal by clinicians from the CIF to establish the first university-based master's degree program in family therapy was accepted in 1996. The program began in 1997 with psychologists, teachers, physicians, psychiatrists, lawyers, journalists, and social workers enrolled in 12-hour, biweekly weekend courses.

After two and a half years of didactic course work and clinical supervised practice, the first group of 33 persons graduated in mid-2000 with master's degrees in Intervencion, Assesoria y Terapia Familiar Sistemica (Systemic Family Intervention, Counseling, and Therapy). The director of this program until recently has been John Grimes. The program is welcomed and enthusiastically endorsed by the students, and graduates continually find their services sought after.

Additionally, a Program for Formation in Systemic Family Therapy and Intervention was started in Ecuador in 1998 as a satellite program of the Catholic University of Lovaine, Belgium. Because it follows the Belgian requirements, it is limited to psychologists and psychiatrists; social workers may attend, but will not receive a diploma. It offers a three-year curriculum with two monthly sessions over 10 months of each year.

As the new paradigm for working with families takes hold, more university-based training is becoming available. In 2000, the Central University in Quito opened a "specialty" graduate program in psychology to teach behavioral, cognitive, family, and group models of treatment within a span of 18 months. In addition, the Universidad Christiana Latinoamericana currently is also offering a one-year graduate course in family treatment for social workers.

These few incipient programs are giving shape to and influencing the growth of Baby Family Therapy in Ecuador. But there are problems. The program at the Salesian University is being viewed with caution and skepticism by the three professional organizations of clinical, industrial, and educational psychologists. Ecuadorian law is interpreted as restricting the practice of a specialty career to those prepared for a specific field at the undergraduate level. A graduate degree is expected to reinforce the skills and knowledge of an undergraduate field. Therefore, a teacher, social worker, or other person with a master's degree in family therapy would be restricted to teaching, social work, or other profession, and not expected to practice family intervention apart from the person's specific undergraduate career, regardless of the graduate degree. As the Baby grows up and gains its own voice, it will also search for its place among professional disciplines in Ecuador.

At present, one family-therapy organization has been established as a corporation and includes institutions as well as individuals as members. No associations exist as yet for the advancement, defense, promotion, or monitoring of the profession. Although most professionals, such as doctors, lawyers, and teachers, have established associations for the defense of the profession, they do not generally provide for support, the establishment of standards, or legal or ethical monitoring, including sanctions for infractions among their members. Their purpose is clearly the maintenance of professional status and influence. Graduates in family therapy are becoming aware of the need to establish a professional organization with a broader mission, though most of them plan to continue working in their original professional settings.

Ecuador's population is 25% Indian, 10% Black, 10% White, and 55% mixed or mestizo. According to the Confederation of Indigenous Nationalities in Ecuador, there are 18 ethnic groups with almost as many languages or dialects in the country (Proyecto de Desarrolla de los pueblos indogenas y negros del Ecuador, 1998).

The history of the country is one of conquest and conquerors. The Incas moved north from Peru and were conquering everything in their wake when the Spaniards arrived with their religion, horses, gunpowder, and treachery. This history of conquest leads the students in the graduate program at the Salesian University, where I am on the faculty, to describe themselves as a people who have been invaded, conquered, and dominated, whose boundaries have been violated, and for whom everything intimate has become public knowledge. They also describe themselves as multicultural, taking into account all the distinctive ethnic groups within a population of 12.5 million people. Thus, they state, "We have no identity of our own." They perceive this history of colonization as ongoing in the interventions by more industrialized countries in Ecuador's affairs. "Aid" funds for projects and programs which may or may not be appropriate to the culture, such as banking systems, management practices, and gender issues, are often felt as impositions.

Because of this history of domination and invasion of privacy, the concept of and ability to maintain confidentiality is seen as one of the major ethical problems in training and clinical practice. Everything is everyone's business, and those in authority assume the right to exercise their power above anyone else's rights. In the case of a person trained as a school psychologist and family therapist, it is difficult to protect the confidentiality of students and their families from the "need to know" of teachers and school authorities. Professionals providing requested information might find their jobs at stake. This lack of privacy and confidentiality is widespread even in places like the confessional or pastoral counseling. During the teaching of courses to priests and pastors, laments have been heard about the inability of peers and even superiors to maintain confidentiality. If this is the case, how can ordinary laypeople be expected to do so? And if the culture at large does not value confidentiality, why should an individual or professional insist on it?

For clinicians, this issue is particularly difficult in cases of sexual abuse. What information should go to legal authorities to satisfy reporting laws and also maximize the family's chances of being helped? How should the abuser be treated? When making a referral, how much information should be included?

The multicultural nature of Ecuador presents trainees and practitioners of family therapy with challenging ethical dilemmas. How will they refrain from imposing their own values and criteria for well-being on those whose culture involves viewing problems as having very diverse and different premises and solutions? Will they be able to identify and use their own countertransferences effectively to avoid harm?

A multitude of social problems in Ecuador are attributable to Indians migrating to the cities in search of work and better opportunities. Parents are at a loss to handle their children's adoption of blue jeans, weird haircuts, and makeup, their involvement in gangs and drugs, and their refusal to wear distinctive traditional clothing and follow the customary patterns of respect for elders and family traditions. At the same time, parents themselves feel displaced and hopeless. Therapists from other cultural groups recognize their own difficulties in relating to the Indians' community values and views of healthy relationships. They perceive the need for helping migrants establish networks to replace the tight community support and controls of old, and for finding replacements for the *padrinos* (godparents) left behind, who, as substitute parents, counselors, and helpers, are relied on for advice and the solution of family problems. But what cultural practices and taboos are challenged in making the changes? And are therapists' assumptions about these needs valid, or do they violate cultural values?

For therapists-in-training, there is great ambivalence about cheating, which is both a way of life and a way to show solidarity with others who may not be one's intellectual equal or may not have had time to study. One teacher at a respected university described cheating as a "national sport" and stated that it was the teacher's responsibility to prevent it by good monitoring, multiple exams, or large spaces between desks. Cheating is generally decried as a practice, yet experience has shown that no one is actually expelled for it, even though it may be so stated in the university's handbook. Should copying someone else's work be considered a cultural value, and not an ethical problem? Solidarity generally wins out, being accorded higher value than individuality.

Students of family therapy in Ecuador are learning about and studying models developed in Europe and the United States. The goodness-of-fit for material generated in the context of a different culture must be overseen. Ecuadorians in general accept goods, advertising, and ideas from more industrialized nations somewhat uncritically, as can be seen in the celebration of Halloween during the past decade, with witches and black cats almost eclipsing the traditional day of the dead with its customary bread doll figures and reverent visits to the cemetery, or the recent and already widespread sale of Christmas trees, where before there were crèches. While Ecuadorian students accept these "imported" theories and practices as applicable and useful, they also need to critically evaluate and modify them to fit the Ecuadorian context. In the process of training, students' lives and approaches to families have been deeply affected and irrevocably changed.

Graduates in family therapy begin to apply their newly acquired knowledge and skills to the specific Ecuadorian context of multiple ethnicities and languages dominated by a small ruling class. More complex and difficult ethical issues are emerging: How can socially sanctioned *machismo* (male supremacy) and its impact on family life be best dealt with? How can professional colleagues be challenged to be more respectful of families' own resources? How can professionals be held accountable for their actions in a climate of widespread indifference to corruption? How can persons be expected or taught to follow a sophisticated ethical code built on the practices of more industrialized nations if the socioeconomic-cultural reality blinds them to everything but survival? And how can the growing numbers of economically marginalized families receive effective and helpful services? With these and many other challenges ahead, we wish the Baby well, and a long and happy life.

THERAPISTS, ETHICS, AND SYSTEMS: A EUROPEAN PERSPECTIVE (MONY ELKAIM, BELGIUM)

A therapist's responsibility stands out as a primary aspect of the relationship between ethics and the systemic approach. Therapists occupy a unique position in a therapeutic system: On the one hand, they are members of this system and are therefore governed by its rules; at the same time, however, they need to feel sufficiently detached from the system to offer a possibility for change. The question facing therapists is how one can be a member of a system while simultaneously feeling free enough to act in a responsible and, therefore, ethical manner.

The Structuralist Movement in France and Latin Countries

Many family therapists from France and other Latin countries were schooled (Turkle, 1978) in the structuralist tradition before turning to family therapy and the systemic approach (Elkaim, 1993). The structuralist approach poses some problems from an ethical perspective.

Structuralism as a movement grew out of the work of Ferdinand de Saussure, whose *Course in General Linguistics* was published in 1916, three years after his death. According to this approach, elements of a language can be studied only in relation to other elements in a language. Terms in a language are interdependent and derive value from the presence of other terms. Language, therefore, is described as a structure, a system of relationships. There is no reference to the history of the system; rather, the focus remains on the circular relationships that hold among the different elements. This work was taken up in 1947 by Claude Levi-Strauss (1969), who, in *The Elementary Structures of Kinship* (published in English in 1949), applied this method to ethnology.

According to the structuralist approach, elements have no meaning in and of themselves. Rather, their meaning is derived from their relationship to the other elements composing the same system. In an article devoted to structuralism, the French philosopher Gilles Deleuze (1981) explained that the structure is all-important with respect to the actual elements that come to occupy the places in the structure; as a result, the places take precedence over the entities that fill them. The Marxist philosopher Louis Althusser (1970) might say that the real subjects in an economic structure are the spaces that are defined by relations of productions. For structuralists, "father" and "mother" are slots in a structure: The subject becomes simply an object defined by its place in the structure, and the structure itself becomes the true subject. This led Deleuze (1981) to say that structuralism is not separable from a new antihumanism.

In the same way that, for Levi-Strauss, myths operate in individuals without their being aware of it, for the French psychoanalyst Jacques Lacan (1988), there are no speakers or interlocutors; rather, language speaks through us. Lacan affirmed that everything Freud wrote was aimed at reestablishing the exact perspective of the eccentricity of the subject in relation to the ego. In Book 2 of the *Seminar,* which took place in the 1950s but was not published until 1978 (1988 in English), Lacan (1988) stressed that "with Freud a new perspective suddenly appears, revolutionizing the study of subjectivity and showing precisely that the subject cannot be confused with the individual" (p. 8). This decentration of the subject with respect to the individual led him to quote the famous phrase of Rimbaud, "I is an other" ("Je est un autre"; Lacan, 1978, p. 16).

The Systemic Approach and Individual Responsibility

The systemic approach in Europe, particularly in French-speaking countries, developed in the sphere of influence of the antipsychiatry movement and the work of David Cooper (1967) and Ronald Laing (1960). A number of psychotherapists, critical of psychiatry for humanistic reasons, turned to family therapy because it offered an alternative to considering individuals as the unique source of their problems and allowed therapists to restore dignity to individuals above and beyond their symptoms.

Imagine their surprise when they discovered that the theory underlying family therapy, which they had resorted to at least in part for political and ethical reasons, was a systemic theory governed by rules remarkably similar to the structuralist approach, an approach many of them had criticized (Guattiari, 1980). For example, history is of only limited importance; the behavior of one element cannot be separated from its relationship to the other elements; and the relationship itself can be studied only in terms of its circular link to other relationships (Watzlawick, Beavin, & Jackson, 1967).

The focus on a system rather than an individual was such that structuralist psychoanalyst Lacan (1988) and the systemic psychiatrist and researcher Albert Scheflen (1978) came to almost identical formulations. In an article published in *Family Process,* Scheflen (1978) posed a question that he had already asked me when we were working together at the Albert Einstein School of Medicine in the early 1970s: "Why did Hamlet stab Polonius in Shakespeare's play?" I gave him a number of replies, none of which seemed to satisfy him. Finally, in desperation, I asked him, "Why?" and he replied, "Because it was written in the script!" In his article, "Susan Smiled: On Explanation in Family Therapy" (1978), Scheflen described how a working group, studying a video recording of a family therapy session, attempted to interpret the behavior of a young schizophrenic girl. He gave a number of hypotheses to explain why Susan, the patient, may have smiled at various points during the session. One of his hypotheses was that, just as Hamlet's action is dictated by Shakespeare's text, the interactions of Susan and her family members are scripted by a pre-existing scenario. The family members are unaware that they are playing their roles in an unwritten scenario of the family drama.

This interpretation of an event is very similar to the one Lacan (1988) gives of Edgar Allen Poe's famous story, "The Purloined Letter," published in 1844 (1966). In this story, which starts with the narrator daydreaming about two very similar situations, Poe told the following tale: A prefect of police comes to ask Dupin, a person known for his insight, to help him find a compromising letter addressed to the queen. It appears that a minister spirited the letter away in front of the queen and in the presence of the king, without the latter realizing it. The queen, caught off guard by the king while she was reading the letter, quickly set it down, folded, on her table, without her husband's noticing. The letter, however, did not escape the attention of the minister, who walked in on the scene. The minister produced a letter from his pocket, which he pretended to read before setting it down next to the other letter. On departing, he took the letter meant for the queen, leaving his own in its place. Despite the best efforts of the prefect of police and his men, the stolen letter seemed impossible to find even though it was known that the letter was somewhere inside the minister's house. Dupin went to his house and discovered the apparently unrecognizable letter, left in an obvious place so as to better conceal it. He then seized the letter, leaving one of his own inventions in its place.

The structure of this story highlights two identical series of events, but in which the places are occupied by different objects. In the first series, the king does not see the letter, the queen leaves it out in the open so as to better conceal it, and the minister replaces this letter by another. In the second series, the police do not see anything at the minister's home; the minister leaves the letter in a prominent place so as to better hide it, and Dupin replaces the letter with another.

Lacan (1988) commented that the minister had no choice but to have this letter stolen from him because the outcome of the story "is not due to the ingenuity of Dupin but to the structure of things" (p. 201). Lacan's statement, uttered during his seminar in the 1950s, is very similar to the thoughts expressed by Scheflen (1978) some 20 years later.

European psychotherapists who had turned to family therapy for humanistic and ethical reasons were confronted with a dilemma. This new approach seemed to dismiss the notion of individual freedom and, hence, individual responsibility in favor of a "scenario" that influences the members of the human system above and beyond their own consciousness. The question facing these therapists was how to retain the advantages of the systemic approach, which locates problems at a systemic rather than an individual level, while still maintaining the idea of individual freedom and, therefore, responsibility.

Systems Far from Equilibrium and Ethics
This questioning leads to the work of Ilya Prigogine (1997; Prigogine & Stengers, 1984), a Nobel prize winner in chemistry. Unlike general systems theory, which focused on systems in equilibrium, Prigogine (Prigogine & Stengers, 1984) studied systems that change, which he called *systems far from equilibrium.* In this type of system, irreversible processes play a pivotal role, thus reintroducing the notion of time. However, time is not simply a case of linear causality. The role played by chance produces an evolution over time in these systems and cannot be reduced to causal terms. We live in a universe where general laws no longer predict the future. According to Prigogine (1997), "The new laws of nature deal with the possibility of events, but do not reduce these events to deductible, predictable consequences" (p. 189). This research allowed systemic thinkers to reintroduce the notions of time and chance into psychotherapy. In so doing, they endowed therapeutic systems with the freedom inherent in all nonpredictable systems.

Second-Order Cybernetics and the Responsibility of an Observer
The work of Heinz von Foerster (1973) on second-order cybernetics also plays a crucial role for systemic therapists concerned with ethics. Von Foerster emphasized that the observer cannot be separated from the system being observed. What the observer describes is not objective, but is coconstructed. This means that an observer can no longer hide behind the pretext of scientific classifications. Observers coconstruct what they describe, committing themselves to this description, and therefore cannot avoid taking responsibility for being part of the process.

Resonance: Freedom and Responsibility
Elkaim's (1990) creation of resonances can be situated within the mainstream of this research on ethics. Resonance occurs in situations where a feeling that emerges in a person is linked not only to that person's own past, but also has a function with respect to the person or persons with whom he or she is interacting. For example, a therapist consults with a family and finds the mother intrusive. The therapist's inclination is to establish boundaries for the mother. During a supervision with the therapist, awareness emerges that the patient reminds the therapist of her own mother, who was extremely intrusive. This discovery highlights the countertransferential aspect of the situation, yet another dimension requires consideration. This other aspect concerns the function for the patient of the amplification of this specific emotion in the therapist. In addition to asking What is the function for the therapist of the particular emotions she is experiencing?, we also need to inquire What is the function of the therapist's experience *for the patient?*

Delving deeper, we find that the mother's own mother was also intrusive, and that the mother has always tried, unsuccessfully, to be accepted and respected. The worldview that has developed from these situations leads her to believe that her childhood experiences will always be repeated. So, although she expects those around her to respect her personal space, she does not actually manage to believe that they will. When the therapist reacts the way she does, she is sculpted or molded in part by the patient. Her reaction "protects" the mother from having to call into question her worldview.

Thus, something as personal as the emotions of the therapist are in fact shaped by the deep beliefs of her interlocutor.

Resonance can be viewed as an iceberg, where the third part that is above the water line is linked to our own history; the other two thirds underwater are sculpted without our knowledge by the human system to which we belong. Resonance frequently involves rules that are shared by different systems in interrelation, for example, an institutional rule, a rule linked to the therapist's family of origin, another linked to the family in consultation, and yet another to the supervision group or the cultural context.

Resonance is a tool that allows the therapist to ask the following questions: What is the function of my experiences for the context in which I find myself? To what extent do these feelings allow the other system members to maintain their deep beliefs and remain in a repetitive cycle? The process of asking these questions allows therapists to uncover the ways in which they are influenced by a human system they have helped to develop and maintain through their own constructions and actions. The fact that we are acted upon by these systems and sculpted by the deep beliefs of the other system members does not prevent us, thanks to the tool of resonance, from becoming aware of the ways in which we are acted upon.

CONCLUSION

This text retraces the path taken by European family therapists who searched for ways of combining the advantages of the systemic approach with the idea that the subject is not only the system, but the conscious individual who coconstructs this system while at the same time being influenced by it. Through the works of Prigogine, von Foerster, and Elkaïm, concepts have been offered to these therapists so that systemics can coexist with ethics.

FAMILY THERAPY AND ETHICS: AN AFRICAN PERSPECTIVE (AUGUSTINE NWOYE, KENYA)

Background

A genuine account of the evolution of systemic/family therapy practice in postindependent Africa must be preceded by some background information on the social-psychological influences under which we live and work. Family therapy in modern Africa cannot be separated from problems in the environment. A lot of the work involves attempts to help people overcome the challenges of difficult, contradictory environments. These efforts supply a corrective to the negative impact of colonial experiences. This history is alive in the legacy of cultural traumatization, denigration, and misrepresentation. It culminates in the symbolic violence of the inferiority complex imposed on psyches through centuries of one-sided accounts and negative impressions about African values and promise as a people, perpetrated by the prejudiced writings and ethnographic reports of colonial historians and anthropologists.

Family therapy in modern Africa derives from two interrelated ancestries: first, psychotherapy as rehabilitation of culture, a movement that gained prominence in Africa from the 1940s to the early part of the 1970s; second, psychotherapy as liberation and hope for revitalization, which emerged in the 1980s and remains prominent to the present. Prior to the current emphasis on the family-therapy paradigm, the pioneers of psychotherapy initially focused on psychotherapy as rehabilitation of culture, or on psychotherapy as an agent of cultural integration of a people. At that time, the entire African society was understood as constituting one great family, suffering from the aftermath of psychological traumatization arising from the negative aspect of colonial contact with the West. The principal goal during those early years consisted of ensuring that fellow Africans, particularly the younger generation, were empowered through psychological and other related (bibliotherapy) means to gain a new affirmation of themselves as centers of initiative, and to develop some kind of solid internal structure to enable them to withstand the challenges of the new cultural dilemmas in our challenging environment. This implies that right from its inception, psychotherapy was always closely linked to the needs of community. From the 1960s, however, our focus started to shift toward educating our people on the new life of synthesized culture that formed the context of our lives postindependence.

The majority of individuals who took part in practice in this early period were not fully trained psychotherapists or family therapists. The majority were writers (e.g., Achebe, 1958; Cesaire, 1957; Senghor, 1964; Soyinka, 1976), social/political leaders of thought (e.g., Azikiwe, 1937/1969; Mandela, 1994; Nkrumah, 1970; Nyerere, 1966), artists, educators, and pastors and psychiatrists, like Lambo (1976).

The second foundation of current practice came in the wake of the 1980s and the 1990s. These were the decades of new challenges and contradictions in the African continent, most arising from the impact of the displacement of traditional values and ways of life by the modern forces of globalization, urbanization, modernization, growth in information technology, gender studies, and feminism. Some of the social stresses of these decades that directed emphasis and dictated major themes of practice were linked to the social-ecological crises in the environment. These include (1) problems of urban unemployment arising from the mass exodus of youth to the cities, (2) problems of military and ethnic conflicts in most parts of Africa, (3) growth in the number of refugee communities arising from these wars, (4) the deadly problem of uncontrollable economic recessions throughout the new nations of Africa, and (5) the general social anxiety and despair arising from the bandwagon effect of premature retirement, graduate unemployment, and the derailing of youths' aspirations.

Now, because the greatest problems of people in the face of these challenges and difficulties consist of hopelessness and disillusionment, therapeutic emphasis in Africa in the past two decades has been centered on the theme of revitalization and the mobilization of hope. The leading practitioners to address this came from the ranks of pastoral counselors and psychotherapists. These professionals organized various kinds of healing communities designed to serve as psychological/transitional centers for instilling hope and confidence and strengthening values and convictions in people demoralized by the contradictory circumstances under which we live and work. Psychotherapy as liberation provides another name for the key theme of psychotherapy practice in Africa, starting in the 1980s. This connotes psychotherapy as a process of liberating people from the crises of ennui, apathy, and general disillusionment or loss of faith in their futures.

The initial orientation of practice in Africa was grounded in psychotherapy serving as a social response for promoting mental health and preventing mental illness in communities. Thus, the two initial foundations of family therapy practice in the African context reflected images of psychological healing as applicable to the needs of the entire society and of therapists as constituting a new priesthood. As a result, family therapy in the African context, to date, has never been restricted to helping schizophrenic families or people manifesting psychiatric chronicity. Of course, in addition to the two ancestries of family therapy mentioned previously, specific agonizing circumstances generated the need for professional family therapy in modern Africa. These include societal recognition of new models of marriage (such as cohabitation and the single-parent experience); growth in street children in major cities; increasing cases of teenage pregnancies; the AIDS epidemic and growth in widow/children-headed households; growth in slum families, with their attendant dangers of child abuse, incest, and family violence; and the continuing cultural impasse experienced by youth attributable to new and contradictory definitions of how life can be best lived, filtering into print and nonprint media by modern means of communication. These new dilemmas evolved in their most relentless severity since the late 1980s and continue to generate ever greater pressures and dilemmas for families and youth.

With this very social origin of current African practice, the major goal of family therapy in context therefore becomes how to help people to develop the capacities for discernment, prudence, and psychological independence that will enable them to assimilate the principle of Goethean autonomy (Elsner, 1992) in responding to these challenges. Investing them with the principle of Goethean autonomy in this case means helping them to be able to enjoy and process the attractions and options of modern Western cultural values without being their slaves and assisting them to be able to employ these values creatively instead of either being dominated by them or trying to resist them outright. This means that over and above other activities therapists engage in to heal families, emphasis is concentrated on helping clients to evolve a balanced and synthesized adult identity, the type that does not indiscriminately succumb to foreign family values that threaten their futures or delimit their opportunities for flourishing.

Training Mode Available
Presently, few countries in Africa offer exclusive specialty training in family therapy. Training that is available is incorporated into university programs (in Nigeria, South Africa, Kenya, Ghana, Namibia, Uganda, Ethiopia, and Zimbabwe) designed for people training to become professional counselors/psychotherapists, pastoral psychologists, clinical psychologists, and psychiatrists. This inclusive model in training is intended to produce well-rounded practitioners strong in both individual-counseling and family-therapy theories, principles, and methods. Some of our existing professional associations, like the South African Association of Marital and Family Therapy and the Counselling Association of Nigeria, also organize regular conferences and workshops intended to enable members and other practitioners with previous training in other related fields to improve their skills.

Practitioners and Settings for Practice
Currently, practitioners include counselors/psychotherapists, clinical psychologists, psychiatrists, professional social workers, some educators (e.g., novelists), and pastoral psychologists. Most are employed in the universities, schools, and colleges and psychological health clinics. Some work in educational, youth, and marriage or family institutes or agencies, such as the Institutes for Justice and Peace. These are often set up and financially supported by nongovernmental organizations or the Protestant (as in Ethiopia) or Catholic churches in places like Nigeria, Kenya, Cameroon, South Africa, Ghana, and Uganda. A few clinicians are engaged in private practice in the major cities.

The Evolution of Professional Ethics
Because of the initial emphases in practice, Africans are influenced by two visions of ethics: ethics of authenticity and operational or professional ethics. The first evolved from continuing the foci of pioneers in helping to blunt the crises of current cultural and identity confusions in the face of being on the receiving end of very insistent and assertive modern Western influences. The bulk of professional-ethics evolved from what professionals learned under the professional ethics section of the initial preparation for individual counseling and

psychotherapy. Most of the reference points derive from the standard professional ethics for mental-health practitioners as approved by the American Psychological Association and the British Psychological Society. In essence, therefore, professional ethics are not unique to African situations. They are evolved with an eye on what happens elsewhere in the field as long as they are not antagonistic to African cultural standards of practice in serving the community. Consequently, we are not advocating cultural insularism in this regard.

Professional Ethics in the African Context
Professional rules of conduct, regulations, and principles are intended to set professional standards of practice and to introduce order and predictability into what clinicians do with clients. In general, such professional rules and regulations are designed to protect the autonomy and dignity of clients and to make sure they are not misused or taken advantage of in their times of need. They are also geared to help practitioners resist the temptation to resort to use of personal values, beliefs, or religious convictions in responding to clients' confrontations with the moral dilemmas of their lives.

Situations That Present Ethical Dilemmas
Situations entailing ethical dilemmas in the African context arise in those circumstances where clients confront a therapist with some vital life decisions they must make in which the issues at stake pull their loyalties to both sides of the conflicts. Such situations also challenge therapists on how to proceed: to resort to the use of personal values/beliefs in responding to client needs or to stand by what ethical guidelines dictate. Ethical violations will occur if we become coercive or fail to remain nonjudgmental in the responses given. Typical cases of ethical dilemmas include adolescents with problem pregnancies, or a mother of eight, with the last-born already in high school, who becomes pregnant and presents with the dilemma of whether to accept the unwanted pregnancy or to terminate it.

Case Vignette. Miss T., age 15, is a high school student and dormitory prefect in her school. She comes from a family with a strong Catholic background and has a mother who is known throughout the community as a shining example of how a Christian mother should behave. Miss T. sought help to deal with the torment she experienced concerning her pregnancy of two months. Because of shame and fear of what people, particularly her parents and close friends, would say, she had kept the problem to herself until she realized that she could not resolve it on her own. She presented her story and her dilemma to Ms. X., an experienced family therapist with born-again values.

Miss T.'s dilemma was such that she felt pulled in two contradictory directions, each option carrying its own share of problems and disadvantages. The critical issue at hand was whether to accept the pregnancy, carry it to term, and face the wrath of her parents as well as the social disgrace involved, or to terminate it and face a crisis of conscience. Instead of helping Miss T. to explore and weigh the options available to assist her to come to an informed decision on the matter, and to make a firm commitment to whichever option was chosen, Ms. X. violated ethical principles of the helping professions by succumbing to the temptation to respond to her client from her own personal beliefs and religious principles. Like every adult and good mother, she said she does not support the idea of children bearing children. But neither does she support abortion, as the Bible condemns it unequivocally. She cited passages from the Bible to convince Miss T. that abortion is a damnable sin and insisted that Miss T. accept the pregnancy.

After the session, Miss T. reviewed Ms. X.'s advice and biblical intimidation and felt quite unpersuaded by her view. She considered that Ms. X.'s option contained more cross than she could carry: unbearable social disgrace to herself and her parents, siblings, friends, school authorities, and admirers. Therefore, she decided to accept the abortion option. She came to this decision, however, at considerable emotional cost. It took Miss T. such a long time before Ms. X.'s internalized vehement dissenting voice subsided to enable her to come to a free decision on the matter, that she was almost at a stage when the abortion option would be very expensive and dangerous. Miss T. was nevertheless able to go through the abortion experience successfully.

Comment
The previous vignette demonstrates the kind of dangers that ethical violations in the context of our work can pose to our clients. By succumbing to the error of being judgmental and of imposing personal views on clients in distress, clinicians stand the risk of being ignored or being brushed aside by them in the "directives" issued. In doing so, therapists may lose the confidence of clients and may cause more harm than good in the psychological world of clients already encumbered.

ETHICS AND PSYCHOTHERAPY IN JAPAN
(TAZUKO SHIBUSAWA)

Case Example
A. is a clinical psychologist. She was recently asked by a psychiatrist to work with the wife of a patient treated for many years for depression. He characterizes the wife as displaying borderline personality traits because she has been having angry outbursts at home, often going on shopping binges when she is upset at her husband, and threatening to leave her husband and children whenever she cannot get her way. When the clinical psychologist begins to work with the wife, she discovers that the husband's depression does not seem to be getting any better despite many years of therapy with this psychiatrist, and that he is abusing the medication that the psychiatrist has been prescribing. The husband has also been having numerous affairs and becomes verbally abusive toward his wife when she complains of his infidelity. The clinical psychologist feels that couple therapy would be more effective than separate individual therapy. However, it is difficult for her to suggest this to the psychiatrist because he is a senior person, and she thinks that he will take her suggestion as a sign that she is casting doubt on his effectiveness. Also, the psychiatrist does not see the husband's affairs or verbal abuse as a problem. He thinks that it is the wife who provokes the husband's behaviors. This is why he referred her to A. The clinical psychologist is left with an ethical dilemma. She believes that couple therapy would be much more effective. Not only that, she believes that it would be unethical to continue seeing the wife separately when it is clear that the marital conflict is affecting both partners. She also assesses that, unless she sees the couple together, she is colluding with the psychiatrist in not addressing the husband's abusive behavior toward his wife.

Professional Context
Although therapists in Japan have worked with families in a variety of settings for many years, family therapy was first introduced in Japan as a distinct therapeutic discipline only in the 1980s. Japan's two leading professional family associations, the Japanese Association of Family Therapy and the Japanese Family Psychology Association, were both established in 1984. Presently, professionals who work with families include clinical psychologists, social workers, psychiatrists, probation officers, and family-court mediators. Their work settings include schools, medical and psychiatric hospitals, child guidance clinics, family court, residential facilities for children and adolescents, and college counseling centers. In the past 15 years, a growing number of therapists have engaged in private practice.

In recent years, the importance of psychotherapy and counseling has become increasingly acknowledged in Japan. For example, the importance of crisis intervention in preventing Posttraumatic Stress Disorder (PTSD) was recognized following the aftermath of the 1995 Hanshin Kobe earthquake, which killed 6,000 people. Counselors are now deployed by local governments whenever there is a large-scale natural disaster. In addition, all public junior and high schools are now mandated by the government to hire school counselors.

At present, however, there is no government licensing system for family therapists or psychotherapists in Japan. Currently, there are 6,000 clinical psychologists in Japan. They are certified by a private certification board, which was established in 1988. This board, which comprises leading clinicians in Japan, has been lobbying with the Japanese government for the past two decades to implement a national license, but so far has been unsuccessful. To be certified as a clinical psychologist by the board, a person must have a master's degree from a board-accredited clinical psychology program and pass written and oral examinations administered by the board.

The certification board has also stipulated a code of ethics for clinical psychologists. Clinical psychologists must (1) respect the basic human rights of their clients; (2) develop appropriate knowledge and skills for practice, and be aware of their own limitations; (3) protect client confidentiality; (4) not force psychological testing on clients; (5) choose interventions that are in the best interest of their clients; (6) respect members of related professions; and (7) not harm clients (Foundation of the Japanese Certification Board for Clinical Psychologists, 1996). An ethics committee that is part of the board evaluates cases involving ethical conduct. It has the authority to censure or cancel certification (Foundation of the Japanese Certification Board for Clinical Psychologists, 1997).

The ethical dilemmas mentioned in the previous example can be understood within the social and cultural context in which psychotherapy is practiced by clinical psychologists in Japan. First, because there is no national license, clinical psychologists have yet to be officially recognized within the medical profession as a distinct professional group. For example, physicians are the only professionals who can be reimbursed by the national health insurance system for psychotherapy sessions. It is difficult for clinical psychologists to question and challenge the authority of psychiatrists, especially when they are senior males, a traditionally privileged group in Japan. Exposing wrongdoing of someone in a senior position is very difficult among Japanese therapists. In addition, even more so than in the United States, psychiatrists often do not see the value of therapy and favor psychopharmacological treatment. Second, nonmedical professionals do not feel that they can openly question psychiatrists' conduct. Multidisciplinary team approaches are still rare in Japan, and this reinforces the power of physicians in treatment settings. As a result, clinicians can end up being caught in the middle between clients and their physicians, and are unable to take a stand even though they may not agree with a physician's treatment. Third, despite changes in societal attitudes toward the status of women in Japanese society, some professionals hold on to rigid traditional views of a woman's role in marriage, in which wives are expected to accommodate their husband's needs.

Although the ethical code requires respect for basic human rights, the notion of self-determination is rather new among Japanese. This is because Japanese culture has traditionally placed emphasis on interdependence over independence and group harmony over individual freedoms. Whereas individuation and autonomy are viewed as the main goals of human development in Western cultures, Japanese are expected to acquire skills that will enable them to understand what is expected by their social environment and to accommodate to these expectations. Quite often, families' needs and wishes are given priority over individuals' wishes, and "familial consent" is viewed as more important than "individual consent." This evokes ethical dilemmas for therapists when working with people who have life-threatening illnesses. Numerous public opinion surveys in Japan indicate that many individuals wish to know their diagnosis, yet the family's desire to "protect" a patient takes precedence, and patients often are not told of their illness. A 1994 survey of bereaved family members in Japan indicates that only one in five cancer patients was informed of the diagnosis (Benowitz, 1999).

Physicians also tend to believe that families rather than patients serve as the best judge of patients' abilities to handle information about debilitating illnesses such as cancer (Akibayashi, Fetters, & Elwyn, 1999). When no family consent for disclosure emerges, many physicians feel that they should not reveal a diagnosis to a patient. As a result, therapists can end up deceiving a patient when asked directly about prognosis (Hashimoto, 1995). Hiding diagnoses also occurs with severe chronic mental illnesses, and it is only recently that the psychoeducational approach, which teaches patients and families to cope with mental illness in an open manner, has become widespread.

The hierarchical nature of interpersonal relationships also affects therapeutic relationships. Clients expect not only physicians but also clinicians to be expert authority figures. They do not want clinicians to establish egalitarian relationships with them. Clients often look to clinicians for direct advice rather than exploring their own wishes about how to rectify a situation. Emphasis on politeness and observance of social protocol in Japanese culture also inhibit clients from questioning those in positions of authority (Shibusawa, 2001). This can produce fertile ground for therapists to abuse power. Therapists can end up disregarding the importance of informed consent or, in the worst cases, engage in dual relationships (Murayama, 1998).

Japanese families often do not seek help from outsiders unless problems become severe. As a result, they tend to seek symptom-relieving approaches that are concrete, pragmatic, and task-centered. Because of clients' tendencies to view therapists as authorities, therapists may not feel that they are able to fully engage in the process of developing and establishing solid therapeutic relationships, which would encourage clients to determine goals and styles for themselves. At the same time, Japanese therapists have actively incorporated recent trends in family therapy that emphasize empowering clients (e.g., psychoeducational approaches, narrative approaches, solution-focused approaches). Because many ethical dilemmas that therapists face in Japan stem from a patriarchal tradition, it is hoped that the empowerment perspectives will help therapists counteract the cultural pull toward paternalism and enable them to engage in interventions that are more ethical and appropriate for their clients.

DISCUSSION

Kitchener (1984) delineated five basic moral principles that form the foundation of functioning at the highest ethical level for professionals. The principles include autonomy, beneficence, nonmalfeasance, justice, and fidelity. We recognize that these principles reflect a Western bias and are being superimposed, in this analysis, on the descriptions from each of the contributors. The analysis, however, is not evaluative; rather, its focus is descriptive and additive. To that end, each principle takes on novel dimensions as viewed from different angles. For example, the principle of autonomy can be applied at the individual client level: Nwoye describes how client self-determination is violated when a family therapist imposes her own values on a young pregnant woman. The principle of autonomy can also be interpreted at a metalevel: Nwoye describes a family therapist as helping to heal communities by inoculating families and individuals against coercive Western influences. Although he uses the term "psychological independence" to describe this therapeutic goal, in effect, he is protecting the autonomy of families relative to their freedom to choose their own directions. By interpreting the principle broadly, the concept of autonomy takes on a different meaning relative to each cultural lens. The infusion of different cultural contexts, therefore, enriches and expands Kitchener's theory.

Autonomy: The Promotion of Self-Determination or the Freedom of Clients to Choose Their Own Directions

Shibusawa observes that, in Japan, the notion of self-determination as a recently introduced concept conflicts with the traditional emphasis on interdependence and group harmony. Physicians, for example, bypass an individual's right to a medical diagnosis in favor of a family's right to determine whether or not to share the information with the individual. Within the context of Japanese culture, autonomy, therefore, may not be an individual privilege. Rather, the principle of autonomy may more accurately pertain to and reflect the sanctity accorded the family unit. Indeed, Shibusawa also suggests that the culture privileges the autonomy of males and the older generation, as shown by the status of women in Japanese society.

Braun relayed that family therapy has been recently introduced at the Universidad Politecnica Salesian in Quito, Ecuador. She notes that the history of conquest leaves the students feeling invaded, conquered, and dominated, with "no identity of our own." The lack of autonomy or self-determination makes it difficult, therefore, for students of family therapy to understand the concept of client confidentiality relative to those in authority positions. While Braun observes that confidentiality is an ethical mandate that protects client autonomy, she helps us understand that the sociopolitical context for these students can alter perceptions, so that the concept of confidentiality appears insignificant: "If the culture at large does not value confidentiality, why should an individual or professional insist on it?"

Nwoye comments on the principle of autonomy in his delineation of therapeutic goals. He suggests that family therapy was viewed earlier as liberating families from the psychological traumatization of colonial contact with the West. To achieve this freedom, families were helped to develop the capacity for discernment, prudence, and psychological independence. The need to preserve the autonomy or individuality of African culture is demonstrated by Nwoye's comments on codes of ethics. He indicates support for the standard professional ethics as approved by the American Psychological Association and the British Psychological Society "as long as they are not antagonistic to African cultural standards of practice in serving the community."

Becvar comments that the principle of autonomy is a misnomer because the separateness of the client-self inherent in the principle represents an illusion. Rather, interdependence represents a more accurate description of a reality that is coconstructed between family therapists and clients. From a postmodern perspective, "all of reality, including problems and pathology, are understood to be constructions generated within the kinds of individuals and larger groups that are validated and supported within the language system of a given social context." Hence, no separateness or independence exists. Rather, Becvar challenges us to broaden our vision so as not to exclude other realities in our totalizing discourses.

Elkaim addresses the principle of autonomy by asking how any family therapist can be held responsible for decisions if he or she is a member of a system and governed by its rules. After showing how the development of family therapy and the systemic approach in Europe discounted the notion of individual freedom, he posits a both-and approach. He uses the notion of resonance to suggest that, although therapists are influenced by feelings that emerge from being with a client family, they must also become aware of the ways they are acted upon and are therefore responsible for what is being experienced. Elkaim does not address autonomy relative to client self-determination; he does address it in relation to the behavior of a family therapist.

All five contributors address the principle of autonomy, but from different lenses. In some instances, cultural context shapes the conceptualization of the principle. In other instances, philosophical arguments influence the conceptualization as well as consideration of whose autonomy is being examined.

BENEFICENCE: THE PROMOTION OF GOOD FOR OTHERS RELATIVE TO RESPECTING THE DIGNITY AND PROMOTING THE WELFARE OF CLIENTS

Shibusawa argues that Japanese social norms obscure the ability to apply the principle of beneficence. Politeness and social protocol may inhibit client families from asking those in authority the kinds of questions that keep family therapists cognizant of their influences. When this check and balance on the therapist's power is reduced, client families are more vulnerable to being harmed. Also, the social prescription of showing respect may prevent psychologists from questioning and challenging the authority of psychiatrists. The principle of beneficence can be violated when "clinicians end up caught in the middle between clients and their physicians, and are unable to take a stand even though they may not agree with a physician's treatment." Shibusawa's story about the clinical psychologist who is asked by the husband's psychiatrist to see the wife illustrates this dilemma. When the psychologist discovers that the husband is abusive, has been having numerous affairs, and misuses the medication prescribed by the psychiatrist, she is left with the dilemma that, although couple therapy is the treatment of choice, contradicting the authority of someone who is senior by virtue of training, gender, or age could have serious professional consequences. Consequently, it is difficult to defy social convention and to actively strive to promote measures that will benefit this couple.

Braun underscores the principle of beneficence in her statements about the relationship between clients and the state: "Everything is everyone's business, and those in authority assume the right to exercise their power above anyone else's rights." The need to protect clients from the state's influence comes through in her concern for confidentiality and the reporting of sexual abuse. Braun again raises the principle of beneficence in her current concern for economically marginalized families. She questions, "How can the growing numbers of these economically marginalized families receive effective and helpful services?"

Nwoye addresses the principle of beneficence in his description of the purpose of family therapy. Specifically, he portrays Africa as beset with social problems that have robbed the population of hope. "Good" is achieved by hope-healing communities dealing with the demoralization of communities: "Psychotherapy [is] the process of liberating our people from the crises of ennui, apathy, and general disillusionment or loss of faith in their future."

Becvar raises this principle of beneficence by suggesting that codes of ethics need to expand the range of issues to include spirituality and moral/ethical issues in therapy process. She invites us to articulate explicitly the beliefs that ground practice. These spiritual beliefs include recognizing that (1) each person is an expression of a divine force and has an inherent urge toward growth and wholeness; (2) consciousness is the ground of all that is, as mind and nature form a necessary unity; (3) we fashion our realities as a function of our beliefs and perceptions; and (4) each person has a desire for meaning and purpose in life.

Elkaim comments on the principle of beneficence by noting that the reaction against structuralism restored dignity to the individual above and beyond one's symptoms. He maintains that the advent of the systemic approach relieved the individual of the blame that diminished personal worth.

The principle of beneficence is demonstrated by the contributors in several ways. Shibusawa and Braun delineate the social and political mores that threaten to interfere with the welfare of clients, and Nwoye and Becvar suggest definitions of psychotherapy that highlight and expand the concept of beneficence. Elkaim comments on the historical significance of the principle in helping to redirect the focus of psychotherapy away from the practice of pathologizing individuals.

Nonmaleasance: The Promotion of Noli non Nocere: First Do No Harm

Shibusawa addresses the principle of nonmaleasance when she voices her concern about seeing a husband and wife separately, which offers protection, in this case, to an abusive husband: "Unless she [the therapist] sees the couple together, she is colluding with the psychiatrist [who is seeing the husband] in not addressing the husband's abusive behavior toward his wife." She also alludes to this principle when she describes the practice of not disclosing diagnoses to patients: "Therapists can end up deceiving the patient when asked directly of his or her prognosis."

Braun remarks on the potential for client harm by describing how therapists struggle with split loyalties. This occurs, for example, in having to choose between protecting the confidentiality of students versus protecting the livelihood of therapists who withhold information from school authorities. Braun also comments on the bind for therapists of upholding ethical principles in a culture condoning practices such as cheating. She further addresses this principle by sharing her concern about the increasing possibilities that therapists may impose their own criteria on a multicultural nation that "sees problems as having very diverse and different origins." After citing statistics to demonstrate the diversity in Ecuador's population, Braun asks questions with far-reaching implication for all family therapists: "How will [therapists] handle mysterious and little-understood family rules and premises? Will they be able to identify and use their own countertransferences effectively and in time to avoid harm?"

Nwoye comments on the potential for ethical violations if therapists are confronted by client issues challenging to their personal values. He cites the case of a pregnant teen and the damage done by a therapist who advised against abortion and used biblical references to support her view that abortion is a sin.

Becvar reminds us of the principle of nonmalfeasance by arguing against the use of the *DSM-IV* by family therapists. She indicates her concern for client harm and for therapeutic integrity when she inquires, "Is it ethical for family therapists to assign a diagnostic label to an individual, thereby defining him or her as dysfunctional, while operating out of a perspective that . . . sees family rather than individual dysfunction?" Noting that incompetence, exploitation, sexual intimacy, and some dual relationships hurt clients, she challenges us to recognize that the therapeutic realities we operate from are social constructions. When they are given the status of truth, they can block our abilities to question our practices and exclude dimensions that might allow us to be more helpful to clients. She cites the inclusion of a spiritual orientation as one example.

Elkaim addresses the principle of nonmalfeasance by focusing specifically on the responsibility of a therapist to be aware of the deep ways he or she is acted upon by a client system. Therapists are helped to be more cognizant of their powers to help or harm by asking questions such as "What is the function of my experiences for the context in which I find myself? To what extent do these feelings allow the other system members to maintain their deep beliefs and remain in a repetitive cycle?"

Each contributor comments on a different aspect of the principle of nonmalfeasance. Elkaim finds a way to address the interface between systemic influence and therapist responsibility relative to helping clients. Becvar suggests that family therapists harm clients by participating in a system of diagnosis that pathologizes individuals. Nwoye and Braun note the propensities of therapists to impose their own values when they are personally threatened by the implications of clients' struggles or are culturally biased or ignorant of cultural differences. Shibusawa and Braun describe how a therapist's loyalty to external authorities can cloud the primacy of attention to client needs.

Justice: The Promotion of Equal and Nondiscriminatory Treatment for All People

In Japan, according to Shibusawa, only psychiatrists are reimbursed by the national health system. This practice accords power primarily to senior males and lessens the status of others, such as psychologists, in the culture. It also makes it difficult to question the authority of psychiatrists and privileges psychopharmacology as the principle therapeutic intervention.

Braun also addresses the principle of justice or equal treatment by commenting on the difficulties encountered by family therapists relative to other professions. She points out that specialty practices are developed at the undergraduate level. Because a graduate degree is expected to reinforce the skills and knowledge of the undergraduate field, there is little place institutionally for family therapy. Moreover, she recounts, "because of the perceived incompatability of the systemic paradigm with Freudian and Lacanian theories that dominated Ecuadorean training in the social sciences, none of the major universities was open to pioneering a family therapy program." She indicates that there has been some headway made by the Center for Integrated Family Studies and the Universidad Politecnica Salesiana, as well as some incipient programs in family therapy started at the Catholic University of Lovaine, Belgium, and the Central University in Quito. These programs, however, are restricted to certain disciplines and/or are viewed with caution and skepticism by the professional psychology organizations.

Nwoye addresses the principle of justice in his comments about the mission of psychotherapy and family therapy in particular. Specifically, he declares that this principle forms the backbone of the therapeutic endeavor in Africa. Psychotherapy expanded in the 1980s to encompass a process of liberating people from the social ills of ennui, apathy, and disillusionment. Instead of being limited to specific diagnostic categories, psychological healing was regarded as "applicable to the needs of the entire society." Indeed, in the early years, practitioners were writers, social/political leaders, artists, educators, pastors, and psychiatrists. Nwoye's description, therefore, embodies the ethos of social justice as integral to the therapeutic endeavor and the focus on community.

Becvar highlights the principle of justice by reminding us that the struggle of family therapists in the United States for parity with other mental-health professionals has not yet been successfully resolved. She notes that marriage and family therapists "have not yet won the battle for reimbursement from third-party payors" because these payors do not recognize the effectiveness of the systemic model. Consequently, therapists are forced to compromise their systemic thinking and make individual diagnoses to receive reimbursement. In addition to noting these discriminatory practices, Becvar also focuses on the principle of justice in advocating for a model founded in recognizing the interdependence of the therapeutic endeavor and the expertise of clients as well as therapists as they coconstruct realities in the context of therapy.

The principle of justice within the field of virtue ethics is usually applied to the behavior of a professional relative to clients. The contributors to this article took metapositions by including descriptions of family therapy by the established mental-health professions. For Shibusawa, the lack of recognition from the state made it difficult to question the authority of psychiatrists; for Braun, the lack of recognition within academia obstructed establishing viable training programs in family therapy. For Becvar, the lack of recognition within the payor system complicates family therapists receiving reimbursement without having to compromise their values. Nwoye addressed the principle of justice by describing the philosophical commitment on the part of psychotherapists to combat the psychological consequences of oppression among the population as a whole.

FIDELITY: THE PROMOTION OF HONORING COMMITMENTS AND FULFILLING ONE'S RESPONSIBILITY OF TRUST IN A RELATIONSHIP

Shibusawa addresses the principle of fidelity in discussing that the needs and wishes of a family may supersede an individual's wishes. Consequently, people with life-threatening illness may not be told of their diagnosis because a family wants to "protect" a patient. This stirs up a conflict for therapists between fidelity to honor deep cultural norms and their commitments to uphold the ethical mandates of their professions. Shibusawa comments that Japanese cultural practices stem from a patriarchal tradition and that an empowerment perspective can encourage therapists to counteract the cultural pull toward paternalism.

Braun also describes conflicting pulls relative to the principle of fidelity. She describes the split loyalties for Indian parents whose children adopt behaviors betraying traditional patterns of respect for family traditions and suggests that therapists feel caught as well in terms of honoring the Indians' community values versus implementing their understanding of what makes for "healthy" relationships. Braun also addresses the principle of fidelity when she reminds us that Ecuadorians uncritically accept models of family therapy developed in Europe and the United States, but these models may have limited application to a society with multiple ethnicities and languages and a small, dominant ruling class. She cogently asks the following question relative to the relationship between fidelity, ethical principles, and contextual realities: "How can persons be expected or taught to follow an ethical code built on the practices of more industrialized nations if the socioeconomic-cultural reality blinds them to everything but survival?"

Nwoye addresses the principle of fidelity by describing the covenantal commitment made by therapists to change the legacy imposed on the population by colonialism and the modern forces of globalization and urbanization. Specifically, centuries of traumatization, denigration, and misrepresentation have given rise to a deep-seated sense of inferiority. The mission of therapists is to erase the disillusionment by establishing "centers for instilling hope and confidence, and strengthening values and convictions in people demoralized by the contradictory circumstances under which we live and work."

Becvar highlights the principle of fidelity by recommending that family therapists remain loyal to the family or systemic focus of the profession. She contends that diagnostic categories and codes of ethics are not reified truths, but the products of our own making. She admonishes family therapists for straying from their convictions and encourages them to recognize that the moral imperative for justice and truthfulness brings "values consistent with spirituality as well as ethics to the forefront of the therapeutic process."

Elkaim speaks to the principle of fidelity by asking, "How can one be a member of a system while simultaneously feeling free enough to act in a responsible and, therefore, ethical, manner?" He argues through the use of parables for a logic that allows us to remain faithful to the principles of systemic thinking while giving therapists responsibility for being aware of how they are being influenced by their pasts and the family systems they are treating. That is, he introduces the concept of resonance as a means to resolve the dichotomy between individual responsibility and systemic functioning.

The principle of fidelity is richly represented by the five contributors. The comments from Shibusawa, Braun, and Nwoye demonstrate the significance of the sociopolitical-economic context for issues of loyalty and commitment. Shibusawa observes the impact of the patriarchal tradition on the loyalty of therapists to clients. Braun points to the potential for a cultural disjuncture between the realities of a culture and the ideals of a professional code. Nyowe describes how the recognition of historical impact and foreign domination can compel therapists to develop an intense commitment to empowering a population. Becvar challenges therapists to wrestle with a paradox; specifically, she encourages therapists not to compromise their principles relative to a family focus while she reminds them to remain open to the idea that all perceived reality is constructed and therefore changeable. Elkaim recognizes the traditional dichotomy between individual responsibility and systemic functioning, but finds a way to bring together competing interests, so that therapists can remain loyal to both.

SUMMARY

As the previous discussions illustrate, international dialogue about professional ethics is unthinkable without situating it within each speaker's unique sociopolitical, cultural, and historical contexts. As these contexts change and professions evolve, so do perceptions, ideas, and written guidelines concerning ethics. Professional ethics place great responsibility on therapists to prevent abuses of power and authority and to serve the common good. Whereas cultural and professional values and philosophies frame and largely determine what we consider ethical or unethical, these values are, in the end, concretized or ignored in the actions of individual professionals. Therapists' integrations of cultural values and personal convictions, their character, maturity, education, and awareness of personal "handicaps" and vulnerabilities crucially influence the ethics of their actions. Professional ethics are shaped, therefore, by cultural contexts and their individual translations.

In our time, cultures do not exist in isolation. Our unfortunate global history of Western colonization of "other" developed countries forms the background of current international professional dialogue. As our international colleagues stated, Western ideas and practices need to be approached with discernment concerning their applicability in other contexts. At the same time, Western professionals stand to gain from opening their minds and considering expanding their understandings through international perspectives. For example, in Europe and the United States, where mental-health professions have the longest developmental history, a strong focus on client rights supported the evolution of ethics boards and laws through which harmed parties could seek retribution and justice. Over the past decade, this has led to apprehension on the part of therapists lest they be found unethical and liable for harm. In the United States, this development is also part of a larger social change in which therapy has become a commodity and consumers are aggressively pursuing their perceived rights. Overemphasis on regulatory controls and constraints may have begun to obscure the "ethos of care" (Peterson, 1992) on which mental-health professions were built. Voices such as Becvar's are suggesting a return to more communal understanding of ethics. This communal focus already persists as a strong cultural value in Japan, Ecuador, and Kenya, and is fundamental to the perception and interpretation of professional ethics in these countries, which, with respect for cultural variations, serve as representatives for Asian, Latin American, and African trends. These understandings, through international conversation and collaboration and in circular fashion, can open perspectives that may inform and shape Western practices.

In conclusion, international professional dialogue not only increases our understanding and respect for diverse viewpoints, but also may contribute to cross-fertilization of ideas and practices that enriches our global professional family.

REFERENCES

Achebe, C. (1958). *Things fall apart*. London: Heinemann.

Akibayashi, A., Fetters, M. D., & Elwyn, T. S. (1999). Family consent, communication, and advance directives for cancer disclosures: A Japanese case and discussion. *Journal of Medical Ethics, 25*, 296–301.

Althusser, L. (1970). *For Marx*. New York: Vintage Books.

American Association for Marriage and Family Therapy. (2001). *AAMFT Code of Ethics*. Washington, DC: Author.

Anderson, H. (1997). *Conversation, language and possibilities*. New York: Basic Books.

Azikiwe, N. (1969). *Renascent Africa*. London: Frank Cass. (Original work published 1937)

Becvar, D. S. (1997). *Soul healing: A spiritual orientation in counseling and therapy*. New York: Basic Books.

Becvar, D. S. (1999). Mainstream profession, countercultural paradigm. *Family Therapy News, 30*(1), 6–8.

Becvar, D. S. (in press). Spirituality and family therapy. In C. Cole, A. Cole, & V. Frusha (Eds.), *Marriage and family therapy in the new millennium*. Galena, IL: Geist & Russell.

Becvar, D. S., & Becvar, R. J. (2000). *Family therapy: A systemic integration*. Boston: Allyn & Bacon.

Benowitz, S. (1999). To tell the truth: A cancer diagnosis in other cultures is often a family affair. *Journal of the National Cancer Institute, 91*(22), 1918–1919.

Brock, G. W. (Ed.). (1994). *Ethics casebook*. Washington, DC: American Association for Marriage and Family Therapy.

Cesaire, A. (1957). *Letter to Maurice Thorez*. Paris: Presence Africaine.

Cooper, D. (1967). *Psychiatry and anti-psychiatry*. London: Tavistock.

Deleuze, G. (1981). A quoi reconnait-on le structuralisme? [The Hallmarks of structuralism?]. In F. Chatelet (Ed.), *La philosophie au eme siecle* (pp. 293–329). Paris: Marabout Universite.

Doherty, W. J. (1995). *Soul searching: Why family therapy must promote responsibility*. New York: Basic Books.

Efran, J. A., Lukens, R. J., & Lukens, M. D. (1988). Constructivism: What's in it for you? *Family Therapy Networker, 12*(5), 27–35.

Elkaim, M. (1990). *If you love me don't love me*. New York: Basic Books.

Elkaim, M. (1993). Les therapies familiales [Family therapies]. *Neuro-Psychology, 8*(7), 323–327.

Elsner, G. (1992). *Nietzsche: A philosophical biography*. Lanham, MD: University Press of America.

Foundation of the Japanese Certification Board for Clinical Psychologists. (1996). *Revised code of ethics* (Japanese). Tokyo: Author.

Foundation of the Japanese Certification Board for Clinical Psychologists. (1997). *Addendum to code of ethics* (Japanese). Tokyo: Author.

Gergen, K. J. (1991). *The saturated self*. New York: Basic Books.

Guattiari, F. (1980). Batons rompus sur de vieilles structures et de nourveaux systèmes [An informal discussion of old structures and new systems]. *Cahiers critiques de therapie familiale et de pratiques de researux 3*, 65–69.

Hashimoto, N. T. (1995). Disclosure of the cancer diagnosis. *Journal of Japan Medical Association, 113*, 937–942.

Haug, I. E. (1998). Gedanken zur Ethik in Theorie und Praxis der Familientherapie [Ethical considerations in the theory and practice of family therapy]. *Zeitschrift fuer systemische Therapie, 16*, 235–245.

Humphrey, F. (1994). Dual relations. In G. W. Brock (Ed.), *Ethics casebook* (pp. 145–155). Washington, DC: American Association for Marriage and Family Therapy.

Kitchener, K. S. (1984). Ethics in counseling psychology: Distinctions and directions. *Counseling Psychologist, 12*, 15–18.

Lacan, J. (1978). *Le seminaire: Livre II* [The seminar of Jacques Lacan]. Paris: Le Seuil.

Lacan, J. (1988). *The seminar of Jacques Lacan, Book I and Book II*. Cambridge, MA: Cambridge University Press.

Laing, R. (1960). *The divided self*. London: Tavistock.

Lambo, T. A. (1976, November). A form of social psychiatry in Africa. *World Mental-Health, 13*(4).

Levi-Strauss, C. (1969). *The elementary structures of kinship*. Boston: Beacon Press.

Mandela, N. (1994). *Long walk to freedom*. London: Little, Brown.

Murayama, S. (1998). *Clinical psychology and ethics* (Japanese). Osaka, Japan: Toki Shobo.

Nkrumah, K. (1970). *Consciencism: Philosophy and ideology for de-colonization*. New York: Monthly Review Press.

Nyerere, J. (1966). *Freedom and unity*. Dar es Salam: Oxford University Press.

Patterson, J., Hayworth, M., Turner, C., & Raskin, M. (2000). Spiritual issues in family therapy: A graduate-level course. *Journal of Marital and Family Therapy, 26*(2), 199–210.

Peterson, M. (1992). *At personal risk: Boundary violations in professional-client relationships*. New York: Norton.

Poe, E. A. (1966). *Complete stories and poems of Edgar Allan Poe*. New York: Doubleday.

Prigogine, I. (1997). *The end of certainty: Time, chaos, and the new laws of nature*. New York: Free Press.

Prigogine, I., & Stengers, I. (1984). *Order and of chaos*. New York: Bantam Books.

Proyecto de Desarrolla de los pueblos indogencas y negros del Ecuador [Development project for the indigenous and Black people of Ecuador]. (1998). Unpublished document.

Saussure, F, de. (1974). *Course in general linguistics*. London: Fontana/Collins. (Original work published 1916)

Scheflen, A. (1978). Susan smiled. On explanation in family therapy. *Family Process, 17*(1), 59–68.

Senghor, L. S. (1964). *On African socialism*. New York: Praeger.

Shibusawa, T. (2001). Japanese American parenting. In N. B. Webb (Ed.), *Culturally diverse parent-child relationships: A guide for social workers and other practitioners* (pp. 283–303). New York: Columbia University Press.

Soyinka, W. (1976). *Myth, literature and the African world*. Cambridge, England: Cambridge University Press.

Turkle, S. (1978). *Psychoanalytic politics: Freud's French revolution*. New York: Basic Books.

von Foerster, H. (1973). On constructing a reality. In W. F. D. Preiser (Ed.), *Environmental design research* (Vol. 2, pp. 35–46). Stroudsberg, PA: Dowden, Hutchison & Ross.

Watzlawick, P., Beavin, J., & Jackson, D. D. (1967). *Pragmatics of human communication*. New York: Norton.

CHAPTER 26

An Interpersonal-Systemic and Developmental Approach to Supervision

SHARON DAVIS MASSEY AND LINDA COMBS

OVERVIEW

Supervision of psychotherapy is an interpersonal and developmental human process, approached here from a moderately broad systemic level of focus. Humanistic, existential, and interpersonal themes emerge in the literature on supervision of psychotherapy from more than one theoretical approach. These allow the elaboration of an interpersonal-systemic and developmental frame of reference that affords supervisors and supervisees working from diverse theoretical frames a broad window on their work together, helpful in locating and addressing issues significant to supervisor effectiveness and supervisee development.

Supervision, as we use the term here, refers to the working relationship of an experienced, certified, or licensed therapist and someone with less experience or therapeutic skill who is in training. We focus here on the ongoing, dynamic relationship and related didactic aspects of the work. We do not address consultation, which often consists of only one or two sessions, or training programs.

THE EFFECT OF THEORETICAL FRAMES

Einstein said that whether we can observe a thing or not depends on the theory that we are using: It is the theory that allows us to see (Martínez, 1997, p. 43). What a theoretical frame focuses on is visible; what it does not highlight, although present, may go unnoticed. Here we note humanistic, existential, and interpersonal themes in the literature on supervision of psychotherapy in what may seem some unlikely places, that is, in work done in other therapeutic frames.

HISTORIC LEVELS OF ENTRY AND FOCUS

Early emphasis in psychotherapy supervision, in the psychoanalytic (Caligor, 1984), behavioral (Wolpe, 1972), cognitive (Liese & Beck, 1997; Wessler & Ellis, 1983), and client-centered humanistic (Patterson, 1997) traditions, was on individual instruction or facilitation by the supervisor of individual or intrapersonal work on the part of the supervisee, who, as therapist, then worked in the same format with clients. As the art and science of psychotherapy developed, and with greater reflection on the processes of psychotherapy and supervision, recognition and use of the inherent remediative and growth-enhancing capacities of the interpersonal experience of the dyads (client and therapist, supervisee and supervisor) has come to be perhaps the predominant mode in supervision in the psychoanalytic (Bordin, 1983; Ekstein & Wallerstein, 1972; Mueller & Kell, 1972; Reiner, 1997), Gestalt (Yontef, 1997), and interpersonal therapies (Hess, 1997). The cognitive supervisor still serves primarily as instructor (Liese & Beck, 1997), yet must model paying attention to interpersonal process, particularly when the therapist works with more difficult cases, for example, involving personality disorders (Safran & Segal, 1990). Patterson (1997), representing the client-centered approach, declines to attribute more than a modeling function to the supervisor.

With the advent of family and systems therapies in the second half of the twentieth century came new conceptualizations of training and supervision (Kaslow, 1977; Liddle, 1991; Todd & Storm, 1997), viewing the development of client, supervisee, and supervision as systemically interdependent. Psychotherapists who work from various theoretical persuasions with couples and families (Broderick & Schrader, 1991; Guerin, 1976; Gurman & Kniskern, 1981, 1991) and larger systems (Imber-Black, 1988, 1991) have come to recognize the recursive effects on one another of individuals and the multiple interpersonal systems in which they are members. Approaches to supervision from various theoretical frames on work with couples and families now incorporate systems principles (Holloway, 1995; Liddle, 1991; Liddle, Becker, & Diamond, 1997; McDaniel, Weber, & McKeever, 1983; Todd & Storm, 1997). Supervision originally focused on facilitating the *intrapersonal* development of the supervisee when psychotherapy was largely targeted toward intrapersonal healing in individual clients. Present emphasis appears to have shifted toward use of the *interpersonal* relationship, in line with a general shift in psychotherapy to use of the therapeutic alliance to facilitate client growth. There is an emerging awareness of the impact of *systemic* factors on supervisory as well as psychotherapeutic processes. Psychotherapy and supervision may be initiated at the intrapersonal, interpersonal, or systemic levels of entry, and may subsequently make use of more than one level of focus over the course of the therapeutic or supervisory experience (S. D. Massey, 1994).

HISTORIC ROOTS OF AN INTERPERSONAL-SYSTEMIC AND DEVELOPMENTAL FRAME OF REFERENCE

The interpersonal-systemic and developmental approach to supervision elaborated here is based on historic humanistic, existential, interpersonal, and developmental themes generic to psychotherapy and supervision across theoretical frames.

Humanistic Psychology

Formulated by Gordon Allport (1937/1961), Abraham Maslow (1954), Carl Rogers (1961), and others between 1941 and 1969, humanistic psychology emerged as a "third force" in academic psychology in the United States, in reaction to psychoanalysis and behaviorism. The former portrayed human behavior as determined by internal or external forces beyond the individual's awareness and control. In response, humanistic psychology addressed "specifically human" attributes of consciousness, choice, and capacity for self-development.

Humanistic psychology is social, person-centered, developmental, and growth-oriented and emphasizes self-actualization and health (Taylor, 1999). Consciousness, creativity, and teleological intent (self-actualization) are seen as essential to the therapeutic process. Individuals are understood as unique persons who come to better know and to develop themselves through personally motivated self-exploration linked to feedback from significant others. Person-centered does not mean self-absorbed or self-satisfied, as significant others contribute to one's developing sense of self and self-actualization requires continually striving to overcome limitations.

Humanistic Themes: Empathy, Positive Regard, Genuineness, Clear Communication, Self-Actualization

Empathy and unconditional positive regard for the client, genuineness, and clear communication were seen as essential in the client-centered approach to psychotherapy, whereas attention to the therapist's self was minimized (Rogers, 1951). This preserved the traditional psychoanalytic concern for not burdening or prejudicing a client with the therapist's values, beliefs, or manner of being, corrected for perceived therapist aloofness, and provided a robust caring environment. Today, Patterson (1997) continues to emphasize the therapeutic conditions and minimization of the therapist's self, and feels these should characterize the supervisor-supervisee relationship as well. The dominant level of focus in this approach has been on clients' and supervisees' intrapersonal growth and development.

Humanistic Themes across Theoretical Frames

Rogers (1951) and Carkhuff and Berenson (1967), who operationalized and researched Rogers's concepts, identified empathic understanding, positive regard, genuineness, and concreteness or specificity of expression as essential core dimensions in the "more knowing" person in any dyadic helping relationship (parent, teacher, psychotherapist, supervisor); willing self-exploration is required on the part of the "less knowing" person (child, student, client, supervisee). The need for these factors was thought to be "shared by all interactive human processes *independent of theoretical orientation*" and as accounting for facilitative or retarding effects across a variety of helping relationships (Carkhuff & Berenson, 1967, p. 4; italics added).

A review of current literature on supervision from various theoretical frames yielded the following: Liese and Beck (1997), discussing supervision of cognitive therapy, advised that therapists "should be warm, genuine, accurately empathetic, and focused" (p. 127). Fruzzetti, Waltz, and Linehan (1997), addressing supervision of behavior therapy, expected both supervisor and therapist to exhibit "therapeutic genuineness" and "interpersonal sensitivity" and asked them to make a "phenomenological empathy agreement" (pp. 88–90). Falloon (1991), writing about behavioral family therapy, stated that a goal of therapy is for each family member "to provide noncontingent (or unconditional) positive rewarding behavior to other family members" (p. 67). Regarding psychoanalytic supervision, Dewald (1997) noted the need for "intuitive and empathic" qualities in the supervisor, as well as "for clarity of conceptualization of constructs and ideas" (p. 41) in the didactic aspects of supervision. In Gestalt therapy, "empathic understanding is communicated through the therapist's genuine, congruent, authentic, and caring presence . . . genuine and unreserved communication [and] warm acceptance" (Yontef, 1997, p. 50). The therapist must also have and be able to communicate clearly specialized knowledge (of Gestalt philosophy and therapy theory). The therapeutic conditions of empathic understanding, positive regard, genuineness, and concreteness or specificity of expression appear to be accepted as generic to the role of the helping person in facilitative interpersonal relationships across therapeutic schools of thought.

Concern for initiative and personal responsibility on the part of the person being helped is universal. Presence or absence of willing client initiative in contracting for psychotherapy and then availing oneself of the therapist's skills must clearly differentiate and demarcate psychotherapy from other, quite unpleasant alternative interpersonal formats, such as interrogation or indoctrination. Current dialogue regarding the issue of therapist and supervisor power related to ability, age, caste, class, culture, education, ethnicity, gender, minority status, race, religion, and sexual orientation attests to the need for constant awareness of and vigilant attention to these issues. Supervisors are responsible for maintenance of unencumbered self-initiative supported through empathy, genuineness, positive regard, and clear communication in supervision and in therapy. Self initiative and therapist support facilitate self actualization.

Existential Psychology

The nature of existence, or *being*, and personal responsibility for *becoming* are dual concerns of existential psychology as formulated by Gordon Allport (1960), Ludwig Binswanger (1956), Medard Boss (1957), Viktor Frankl (1959), Abraham Maslow (1943, 1962), and Rollo May (1953). Existentialists emphasize the anxiety or angst felt upon recognition of the uniqueness of one's personal and contextual givenness and on confronting the paradoxical question of how best to approach life in the face of inevitable death. Each individual is held ultimately accountable for choosing to act in ways that create and give meaning and value to one's own life and that of others. Existential angst is not a symptom in need of eradication or a pain requiring sedation, but rather a lever for extricating oneself from the inertia of disengagement, or a springboard toward meaningful engagement in a world that is only partly of our choosing.

Existential Themes: Responsibility and Choice, Freedom within Limits, Transcendence

Existential psychotherapy emerged as an attempt to address the depersonalization and isolation felt by many in the aftermath of two World Wars and in response to mass trauma inflicted directly on millions, both military personnel and ordinary citizens, on the battlefield, in Nazi death camps, and in the bombings of entire cities, as in Hiroshima and Nagasaki, and vicariously on multitudes of others. In this context, the questions of individual choice and responsibility for societal wrongdoing were cast in bold relief.

For the existentialist, one's potential is achieved through engagement with the world into which one is thrown and with others, guided by an idea of transcendence. Self-actualization motivates the overcoming or transcendence of personal and social illnesses or other adversity, which in turn is indicative of mental and spiritual health. The therapist's task is to enable the client to choose, to act intentionally, based on self-selected values, to creatively embrace personal freedom within the limits set by one's unique circumstances, and to accept responsibility for the choices made. Existential psychotherapy involves a highly engaged, "interreactive" (emphasizing the need to act) interpersonal process on the part of client and therapist, in which the values and stances of each is enacted, at least verbally, vis-à-vis significant life issues confronting the client. The hierarchy between therapist and client is reduced and their roles less defined than in client-centered work. These two factors theoretically contribute to the greater freedom of choice afforded to humans who are confronting themselves and acting in relation to self-chosen values and personally selected stances regarding issues of significance (Carkhuff & Berenson, 1967; Frankl, 1959).

Existential Concern in Other Therapies

In an attempt to fill what Frankl (1959) termed the "existential vacuum," existential psychotherapy embraces the spiritual or value-related dimension of human existence, a dimension not addressed in psychoanalysis or behaviorism. Existentialism is unique among the Western psychotherapies in that it unabashedly focuses on values, the intent behind choice and action, taking responsibility for one's actions and for creating meaning in one's life. Apart from a rather radical behaviorism, however, the Western therapies are predominantly predicated on the idea of choice in relation to change. The decision to change is typically seen as emanating from understanding the intent of one's maladaptive behavior or as based on intentionally constructed therapist-client interaction, with consequent cognitive and/or affective modification, and a decision to maintain the experienced change. Change, choice, responsibility for choices, desire to better oneself, and the capacity to do so are Western psychotherapy's dominant existential stance. The therapist's making this explicit, however, in a passionate, albeit noncoercive, way, and exposing the therapist's values in the privacy of the psychotherapeutic setting (particularly in the United States, where individualism is highly valued; thus others' values possibly seen as intrusive), is for some not appealing.

Among the early Western psychotherapists, only Carl Jung (1938), envisioning unifying archetypes shared by all humans, fully embraced a spiritual dimension to human development and further explored the relationship between psychology and religion, themes later picked up by Allport (1950), Frankl (1977), and Maslow (1964). Existentialism, in its focus on the spiritual, can be seen as bridging the gap between a dominant Western tradition of healing and growth that focuses on the self-development of the individual, and contrasting Eastern traditions that focus on relationship of self with others and on the transcendent, seeing minimization of the self as the path to betterment. There is resurgent interest in the West in understanding and bridging this gap (Steinberg & Whiteside, 1999; Wilber, 1981; Zukav, 1990).

Although a client's or supervisee's existential challenges must be worked out at the intrapersonal level, this is approached in highly engaging interpersonal confrontation. This spiritual struggle operates as figure against the significant background of ethical concern for individuals and groups of others at the interpersonal and larger systemic levels of social concern. In contextual therapy with individuals, couples, and extended families, Boszormenyi-Nagy (Boszormenyi-Nagy & Grunebaum, 1991; Boszormenyi-Nagy & Krasner, 1986) acknowledges the existential responsibilities of therapists and clients (and, by extension, supervisors) to all parties affected by his multigenerational therapy. He thus addresses the intrapersonal, interpersonal, and systemic levels of focus and spiritual as well as psychological well-being. Intent, choice, freedom, and responsibility must be factored into a theoretical model of psychotherapy and supervision that purports to embody the elements generic to the human condition.

THE INTERPERSONAL THERAPIES

The term "interpersonal" has been used to refer to a broad range of theorists, from Alfred Adler (1924/1963) and Anna Freud (1965) to neo-Freudians such as John Bowlby (1988), Erik Erikson (1950, 1968), Erich Fromm (1964), and Harry Stack Sullivan (1953), and growth therapists such as Eric Berne (1961, 1963), Robert and Mary Goulding (1979), Jacob Moreno (1945, 1946), Fritz Perls (1969), and Virginia Satir (1972). All of these theorists shifted the emphasis from analysis of intrapersonal contents introjected earlier in life to modification in present interpersonal relationships of repetitious patterns that originated in past interactions with significant others. The interpersonal therapies are designed to bring to awareness and modify dysfunctional relational patterns.

The distinction between intrapersonal and interpersonal is at best subtle. Psychoanalysis emphasized uncovering and understanding the origins of early patterns and interpreting their intrapersonal motivation, whereas the interpersonal theorists, assuming a psychoanalytic or social learning explanation of origins, shifted their emphasis to noting, interrupting, altering, and healing in present therapeutic relationships old patterns that are no longer useful. The distinction may be best understood as a difference in therapeutic level of entry and of focus. Traditional psychoanalysts kept the focus on the intrapersonal and attempted to avoid the perceived "contaminating" effect of an interpersonal relationship between therapist and client. An interpersonal therapist notes origins of dysfunctional patterns in past relationships and intervenes via client-therapist transactions in the present (Teyber, 2000). The past and future are significant only in relation to their bearing on present decisions.

Interpersonal Themes: Interpersonal Reality, Nonlinear Causality, Pragmatic Solutions, Multilevel Analysis, Eudaimonia

Many therapists and supervisors identify with an interpersonal theoretical approach; however, Hess (1997), writing about supervision, only recently formulated the first statement of interpersonal precepts. Perhaps, he suggests, this is because they express a broadly held worldview regarding human experience, thus appearing to express common sense. We step back and view them only with difficulty.

Interpersonal reality is life as we experience it, based more on a "psychologic" than on rational logic, involving both cognitive and emotional processes. Communication is both analogical and digital. All behavior is communication, including remaining silent. Interpersonal interaction is the source of human experience, thus of psychopathology and corrective psychotherapeutic experience. Causality, from this perspective, often cannot be linearly traced, is affected by context, and is ultimately not so important. Metaphorically, getting the spilled milk up off of the floor is more important than finding out who spilled it or dwelling on whether the spill was accidental or not.

The interpersonal therapies help clients modify dysfunctional patterns through experiencing and choosing healthier alternatives, while reflecting on the past utility and present uselessness of now dysfunctional ones, which can be discarded. Solutions are often pragmatic, rather than right or wrong (i.e., there is more than one way to clean up spilled milk and there are various safe places to set it in the future). The specifics can be negotiated and agreed upon. Cure occurs through interpersonal experiences within a genuine, respectful, empathic therapeutic relationship involving authentic communication and a decision to change old patterns. The interpersonal paradigm thus extends these humanistic themes, the idea of self-actualization, and the existential elements of personal responsibility, choice, and transcendence to the interpersonal level of analysis. Hess (1997, p. 80) refers to Waterman's (1993) eudaimonia—"feeling challenged, competent, and assertive, having a high level of concentration and high goals, investing a great degree of effort, and knowing how well one is doing," which "leads to more actualizing needs and satisfactions"—as indicative of personal well-being within the interpersonal theoretical frame.

A particularly appealing aspect of the interpersonal perspective is its use of units of analysis that function on multiple levels. A given verbal and accompanying nonverbal communication, for example, may represent an aspect of basic personality, constitute a defensive or goal-oriented intent, and exemplify overall lifestyle (Hess, 1997). This multilayered approach to analysis moves the interpersonal theorist significantly in the direction of a systemic understanding of interpersonal reality.

In this discourse, we have used the term interpersonal to refer to the theoretical frame just elaborated, as representative of the ideas put forth by the several theorists grouped under that label. We also construe it as a systemic level of entry or focus through which therapeutic and supervisory encounters can be approached.

The Interpersonal across Therapeutic Frames

The therapeutic approach of the interpersonal therapies echoes work from other theoretical frames. Liese and Beck (1997) specifically address the misconception that cognitive therapy neglects interpersonal factors, acknowledging that "most psychological problems have interpersonal components" and that "the therapeutic relationship is *highly* important in cognitive therapy" (pp. 117, 119). In describing psychoanalytic approaches to supervision of couple and family therapy, Reiner (1997, p. 138) writes about the *"interpersonal system"* of supervisor and supervisee, after describing that relationship in psychoanalytic, object-relations, and developmental terms. In what may be a behavioral restatement of the cultural wisdom that doing unto others what one would wish done to oneself is the most likely route to attaining just that, in a chapter on behavioral marital therapy, Holtzworth-Munroe and Jacobson state, "A learning model posits that the rate of reinforcers received from the partner determines not only the degree of subjective satisfaction, but also the rate of rewards directed in return toward the partner" (1991, p. 99). Although we may speak different theoretical languages, when they are translated, there is remarkable agreement about what is essential in pragmatically maintaining positive human relationships or in remedying ones that have become problematic. The humanistic, existential, and interpersonal therapies provide a relatively nontechnical language useful in constructing a generic interpersonal-systemic theoretical frame through which to view everyday human interactions as they occur in ordinary life, in psychotherapy, and in supervision.

If it is our theoretical frame that allows us to see, that frame and a selected level of focus may mark boundaries beyond which we do not see what is there before our eyes, beyond the present range of attention. In the ensuing discussion, we look at an interpersonal-systemic level of analysis through a Western humanistic, existential, and interpersonal lens at the practice and supervision of psychotherapy. It is our belief that most, if not all, theoretical frames may be used in work at the intrapersonal, interpersonal, or systemic level of intervention in psychotherapy and in supervision, and that all theoretical frames must contend with humanistic themes and confront existential issues.

CONCEPTS THAT CONTRIBUTE TO THE APPROACH

THE DEVELOPMENTAL FACTOR

Psychotherapy and supervision are interpersonal processes designed to facilitate change. In the Wernerian sense (Glick, 1994), any process may be conceptualized developmentally. Whether developmental change is viewed as consisting of stages or as continuous may be more a matter of interval of observation or measurement than of substantial difference. Photographs do not portray motion; a series of photos taken at close intervals over a short period does not evidence development. Still, discrete photos taken of a flower, for example, at greater intervals may show in one the flower bud, in another the opening bloom, in others the full blossom, then wilting petals, depicting quite different "stages." The typical movie portrays flowers as unchanging objects. When Walt Disney placed cameras by budding flowers and took many still photos at longer intervals over an extended period of time, then placed them as separate but consecutive frames of a movie film, the world saw its first movie of the continuous process of flowers blooming. Disney discovered a time frame and intervals at which "samples" taken of the ongoing phenomenon could literally picture the longer-term, more difficult to see, continuous aspect of development.

Like theory, the observational mechanisms built into research designs frame and facilitate or hinder what we are able to see. Some supervisors may prefer to approach each discrete supervisory session similarly and feel uncomfortable viewing any cluster of those as significantly different from others. Others will find it useful to frame the course of supervision into segments or stages. Whether we see stages or continuous threads literally may depend on what we expect to find and how we look for it. Both developmental views are valid, just as more than one theoretical approach can be used to do effective therapy.

From a pragmatic viewpoint, the foregoing resolves the dispute between those who, like Patterson (1997), claim there is no drawn-out process of "so-called stages" (p. 137) in supervision and others (Bernard, 1997; Carroll, 1996; Hawkins & Shobet, 1989; Hess, 1986, 1987; Rigazio-Digilio, Daniels, & Ivey, 1997; Ronnestad & Skovholt, 1993; Stoltenberg & McNeill, 1997; Williams, 1995; Worthington, 1987) who find such constructs useful. Few supervisors are comfortable immediately placing the inexperienced therapist with the most challenging clinical case, preferring to allow time for instruction, rehearsal, experience, feedback, and assimilation, while gradually increasing the responsibilities of the supervisee and the difficulty of the work.

Supervision should facilitate supervisee development, increasing skill in building a therapeutic alliance, in assessment and conceptualizing of cases, in effective use of a broadening range of interventions, and in developing a sense of self as therapist. We find it helpful to conceptualize the beginning, middle, and later periods in the supervisor-supervisee relationship as qualitatively different, with supervisory interventions needing to be modulated to accommodate the supervisee's skill level. We recognize individual and idiosyncratic pathways through developmental sequences and expect reversals or falling back to earlier skill levels or less productive patterns under conditions of greater anxiety (e.g., a more complex case, a case that uncomfortably engages one's defenses) or under pressure in the supervisory or other personal systems that support or undermine the sense of self.

The developmental status of clients also shapes therapy (Kegan, 1982) and supervision. Supervisees need a working knowledge of how people of different ages and developmental abilities may reasonably be expected to think, feel, and behave in a normative array of contexts. When a client is out of synchrony with what might be expected, the supervisee must be able to fit this information in a meaningful way into a hypothesis that may facilitate treatment. An adult who lapses into a childlike voice around a sensitive topic, or a young child whose nonverbal and verbal communication become far too adultlike is providing information that needs to be noted. In the first instance, we may have an indication that trauma occurred when the adult was small; in the latter, we may be observing parentification in a child. Supervisors help their trainees note and use developmentally relevant information.

It is the developmental piece that allows the merging of psychoanalytic theory, which sees dysfunctional but repetitive behavioral patterns in adults as related to their function in interpersonal experiences from childhood, with systems theory. Psychoanalysts (Caligor, 1984) first recognized parallel process between interpersonal sequences that sometimes occur in therapy between therapist and client and are repeated between therapist and supervisor in the related supervision. From an interpersonal-systemic perspective, an anomalous pattern of interacting in the therapy or supervision is also considered a possible echo of something from a different systemic level, which without intervention has the potential to travel across still other levels.

Isomorphism: A Systems Principle

Supervision involves a supervisor's taking multiple roles, such as mentor, professional role model, instructor, collaborator, evaluator, and coworker in relation to the supervisee (Storm, Peterson, & Tomm, 1997). Supervision is, however, not therapy. Burns and Holloway (1989) help to clarify this significant ethical issue.

Thus, supervision is not fully isomorphic to the work of the therapist. However, at times, they do have "the same form." White and Russell (1997) mention four ways in which isomorphism has been noted in the literature on supervision from a systemic perspective:

1. The identification of repetitive or similar patterns in the therapy and the supervision. In relation to a very disorganized couple or family case, the usually focused, quite competent supervisee presents as "scattered."
2. The tendency to use the same therapeutic model and principles (Liddle & Saba, 1983). The supervisor may use a cognitive approach in working with a cognitive therapist.
3. Implementation of identical structure and process. The supervisor develops a working alliance with the supervisee, who in turn develops a therapeutic alliance with clients.
4. Use of isomorphism in intervention. A supervisor who notes that the supervisee seems atypically "scattered" in her presentation of a case intervenes to structure the supervisory session productively, providing an experience which the supervisee may then utilize in her next session with the clients.

We have noted a historical tendency toward use of the same models and principles in supervision and the related therapy, and implementation of identical structure and process, though not of content, in therapy and supervision.

CONCEPTUALIZING HUMAN SYSTEMS

Effective work with human systems is conceptualized here as focusing alternatively and productively at the intrapersonal, interpersonal, and larger (e.g., family, workplace, community, cultural) systemic levels and acknowledges the spiritual. The interpersonal-systemic frame has its deeper roots in humanistic, interpersonal, and existential themes and concepts from Gestalt psychology. According to the principle of holism, the whole of a system is greater than the sum of its parts, having qualities that cannot be found in the separate pieces. Thus, a family is more than the sum of its members, and the couple is more than the sum of the two personalities. Perception plays a role in what is seen, and therefore known. What we focus on as "figure" becomes the information available for processing; what is not in focus, although present, becomes "ground" and functionally invisible or unavailable as information, although a shift of focus can bring what was ground into focus as figure. The perceived differences among intrapersonal, interpersonal, and systems work is largely a matter of level of focus. Gestalt therapists (Perls, 1969; Yontef, 1997) tend to focus at the interpersonal level and to work dialogically.

Ludwig Wittgenstein (1922/1999, 1945/1958), who first formalized the radical positivism on which the Western idea of scientific knowledge has been based, later (partly influenced by Gestalt ideas) refuted it, adopting a postpositivist stance (Martinez, 1997). The interpersonal-systemic model adopts Wittgenstein's later philosophy (1945/1958), which speaks of the relationship of language and thus of knowledge to its use within contexts. This complements the study of persons in contexts (Dewey, 1891; James, 1890/1983; Kegan, 1982) and the idea of the social self (Mead, 1934/1964; Valsiner & van der Veer, 2000). This perspective acknowledges the personal (Polanyi, 1945, 1962) and social (Gergen, 1982) construction of knowledge. Its matrix idea is that of the simultaneous and continual development of self, other, and community within historical, current, and developing contexts.

Although open to ideas from various systems theories (e.g., biological systems, general systems, and open systems), the present approach emphasizes human systems and is not closely linked to cybernetics or communication theory or to the idea of homeostasis, as were earlier systemic models in marital and family therapy. The interpersonal-systemic perspective originates in the humanistic, interpersonal, and existential idea of continuing intrapersonal, interpersonal, and transpersonal (social and spiritual) development in response to genuine, clear, and empathic interpersonal exchange in present relationships with others and acceptance of individual and collaborative responsibility for positive personal and communal development within current contextual limits.

Several systemic models of supervision have been elaborated specific to various theoretical approaches (Kaslow, 1986; Liddle, 1991; Liddle, Breunlin, & Schwartz, 1988; McDaniel et al., 1983; Rigazio-Digilio et al., 1997; Storm & Heath, 1985; Todd & Storm, 1997). What is developed here is a broad frame providing an ample window into therapy and supervision, useful in locating areas of strength as well as aspects that, with occasional shift in focus and guided experience, can be further developed in supervisees working from a wide array of theoretical approaches.

Systemic Reality

From a systems perspective, nature is inherently whole, a seamless fabric of interlocking networks (Martinez, 1997), from the dancing molecules noted by physicists (Capra, 1975; Heisenberg, 1958) to the dissipative or open systems of chemistry (Prigogine, 1976) through those of biology (von Bertalanffy, 1968) and beyond, to the many interlocking interpersonal systems in which humans are located (S. D. Massey, 1994) and the related systems they create. Boundaries are human creations, useful in navigation of highways, seas, and conceptual or theoretical territory, harmful if used to start or maintain "border wars" between nations or conflicting theoretical camps (Wilber, 1981). These interlocking systems are constantly developing (Glick, 1994).

Psychotherapy and supervision are open, interpersonal systems, interconnected and interwoven with other interpersonal systems in which each of the parties holds membership and with other contexts, some of which they share. For the purpose of communicating meaningfully, it is important that the boundaries around these systems be recognized and empathically held in positive regard and not be viewed as rigid or impermeable in a way that overemphasizes differences among human groups. Recognition, acknowledgment of and respect for perspectives related to one's own and others' memberships in various groups helps establish clarity in communication; facilitates genuine, contactful interpersonal relating; opens discussion of differential value systems that motivate choices; validates what is common and what is unique to the persons interacting; and facilitates supervision and therapy.

Emergent Personal and Interpersonal Knowledge

In psychology, human affects, behaviors, and cognitions are the objects of study. A psychologist studying them also experiences them personally. This dual relationship of already knowing (experientially) yet seeking to know (intellectually) is further compounded by the issue that the very constructs in which the knower approaches the putative unknown and his or her objects of intellectual interest are cast in language dependent for its existence on the previous knowing by others in the linguistic group of the phenomena labeled and described by the language. If we add to this the observation that knowledge, experience, and language are shaped by cultural, historic, and other contexts (Gergen, 1982; Polanyi, 1962) and that all of these continually interact and develop over time, we begin to glimpse the complexity of truly understanding how individuals and their interlocking support systems impinge on one another. In deeply significant ways, humans and the systems they create and live within mutually shape one another.

From this perspective, knowledge is constructed in the recursive interaction of self with others, materials, and contexts. Perhaps what we term knowledge from an epistemological approach that conceives of reality or truth as objective and unchanging might more aptly be labeled, from an interpersonal-systemic and developmental frame, evolving metasubjective consensus (R. F. Massey, 1972). This does not imply that there can be no ultimate reality beyond our current capacity to know it. Rather, it pragmatically affirms that our human way of knowing is both expanded and limited by our interdependent relationships with others and that we rely on language to simultaneously contain and preserve the wisdom of the past and to conceptualize, explore, and express the new. What comes to be known both in psychotherapy and in supervision is the joint creation of all participants, using a common language to create, conceptualize, contain, store, retrieve, review, and restore or restory. The meanings are communally determined.

EMERGENCE OF SELF, OTHER, AND SYSTEMS

In seeing and selectively responding to others' varied reactions to self over time and in contexts, the individual simultaneously constructs a sense of self and other, that is, of self-in-relation to the various groups in which he or she does and does not hold membership. This experience of self and other is internalized such that any of us can recall and recreate significant interpersonal transactions that have occurred between ourselves and others in the family and other settings. The capacities for recall, replay, reflection, and choice make psychotherapy and supervision possible and useful. The interactions of supervisor and supervisee or of therapist and client are inherently intrapersonal, interpersonal, and systemic in nature. And intrapersonal work inevitably involves the interpersonal and systemic (S. D. Massey, 1994). Coming to be and to know oneself, others, and reality is a developmental and recursive process in which knower and known are at all times both present and emergent. Supervisor and supervisee, client and therapist, each become who they are, develop, and achieve their goals in a recursive, developmental, interpersonal, and systemic process.

REFLECTIVE, INTENTIONAL, SELF-ACTUALIZING, AND SELF-TRANSCENDENT HUMANS

Humans have the unique capacity among living beings to reflect intrapersonally and interpersonally on their individual and collective current, past, and anticipated thoughts, feelings, and behaviors. We decide what we will deem significant and to what we will assign value. We can choose to personally or conjointly intervene in interaction patterns in any of the many recursively interactive human systems in which we simultaneously live.

Our specifically human capacities allow the transcending of past limitations, provide the means for self-actualization in the present and ignite hope for continued improvement. Humanistic and existential themes are applicable at all levels of focus—intrapersonal, interpersonal, and systemic—and provide a framework compatible for use by supervisors examining and facilitating the work of therapists from various therapeutic frames.

SOCIAL INTEREST

Self-transcendence requires social interest (Adler, 1964). To know oneself requires feedback from others. To receive positive, encouraging feedback requires behaving beneficently toward others, setting in motion a pattern of simultaneous enhancement of self and other within the framework of attentiveness to communal standards. Individual and communal self-interest arise conjointly, not in opposition. Empathy, or the capacity to stand in the shoes of another and to see the world through others' eyes, is the social glue that binds together the social structures we create for ourselves. Communal dialogue among reflective individuals sets current standards for moral and ethical behavior and provides the means for their gradual improvement. Social interest is incompatible with abuse. The degree to which behavior evidences social interest is the common standard by which it is judged to be functional or dysfunctional by communal and professional standards. Client, supervisee, and supervisor behavior are best evaluated from the multiple perspectives of the self, one another, and others affected by the therapy and supervision (other clients, clinic director, clinic staff interacting with the case, one's professional organizations).

When larger systems are dysfunctional, as in a dysfunctional clinic or in societies where racial or gender bias and other social injustices are systemically perpetrated, intervention to correct this needs to occur at the interpersonal, organizational, and societal levels. Until such a point, some communities, families, couples, and individuals will suffer from the dysfunction or injustice, and others will internalize them as "normative" and continue to perpetrate them. Affirmation of positive and intervention in negative interpersonal transactions in therapy and in supervision both model and set the boundaries of appropriate interpersonal behavior. Advocacy for professional responsibility and social justice are the natural outgrowth of humanistic and existential ideals. Training clinics and supervisory personnel must embody the standards expected of trainees. Psychotherapy and supervision have been effectively accomplished when other persons to and for whom staff and clients are responsible are also positively benefited (Boszormenyi-Nagy & Krasner, 1986).

SIMULTANEITY

We are born into, live, develop, and interact within simultaneously coexisting levels of developing systemic reality. One is, for example, a unique individual, a family member, a friend, a coworker, and a member of a gender, racial, ethnic, national, and cultural group. All levels of systemic membership are present in ourselves at all times and potentially salient in each interaction. Exclusive focus on one or another of these levels, while blocking attention to others, can lead to numerous epistemological, sociopolitical, and treatment problems in psychotherapy and to misunderstanding or impasses in supervision as well. Particular attention needs to be paid to this concept in supervision.

Acknowledgment of and positive regard in supervision for the multiple systemic realities in which each participates helps supervisor and supervisee communicate clearly, contactfully, and with mutual respect.

PERCEPTUAL MYOPIA

At times, we interact across the boundaries of differential interpersonal systems in a way that exhibits suppressed awareness or recognition of what the other habitually or at present experiences as real. We suggest a concept of perceptual blocking of significant systemic realities affecting a current interpersonal transaction. Lack of the conscious, thoughtful reflection and open communication needed for contactful engagement in the multiple lived realities that we do and at times do not share leads to exclusion from awareness or misperception of various levels of systemic influence and related contexts over varying time frames. This perceptual myopia, an emotionally driven or experientially truncated narrowing of focus, may be out of awareness due to lack of knowledge or experience, or it may be intentional, under the mistaken belief that "it makes no difference."

Involuntary myopic responses to present experience may relate to an individual's experiences or decisions in the past (Berne, 1961; Goulding & Goulding, 1979) or they may have been intentionally shaped, historically, by a larger group (Allport, 1954) in which the individual holds membership. Such may happen when a religious, ethnic, or racial group has been maligned by members of another. Emotional cutoffs may be formed (Bowen, 1976) and accompanying myopic response patterns transmitted—intentionally at first, and reflexively, out of awareness, over time, and across generational boundaries. It is the supervisors' responsibility to monitor one's own and supervisees' breadth and depth of perceptual awareness, and to exhibit genuine positive regard for the supervisee and for all persons affected by the therapy, for which the supervisor is ultimately accountable. The holding of all persons, regardless of ability, age, caste, culture, economic status, ethnicity, gender, race, sexual orientation, social position, or religious affiliation, in positive regard is an existential value required for the successful going-on-being of all parties in a world community characterized by diversity. Therapy and supervision are practiced in this world of diversity. Values, concepts, and behaviors are subject to debate; the intrinsic worth of humans is not.

TIME AND NUMBER

The systemic level of entry or focus in psychotherapy or supervision is in no direct relationship to time or number. Intrapersonal work may be done around experiences and perceptions of the past or present and expectations of the future. The same holds true for the interpersonal and systemic levels. Nor does the number of persons seen in therapy affect the combination of time frames with levels of entry. An individual can report on unique experiences of self, of relationship with a significant other, or of the various members of family of origin in the past or present, or as anticipated or planned for in the future. A couple, family, or larger group may reflect on an individual, dyad, or other unit (couple, sibling subgroup, a triangulated child and parents, family) of their membership in relation to any time frame.

No theoretical approach is inevitably wed to a particular time frame or number of clients. While psychoanalysts have tended to work intrapersonally with a single client and to focus on the past, psychoanalytic concepts have also been applied with couples groups (Framo, 1976) and families (Bentovim & Kinston, 1991; Falloon, 1991). Framo had couples in groups first work in the present on their own current issues, then each person individually research and reflect on unresolved issues from the past with the family of origin. Later the family of origin was invited to a session (to which the spouse and other couples were not invited, only the family member) to reflect on the past, mend fences in the present, and make projections for the future. Finally, in this example of multisystemic levels of work, the couples group met again to help members whose families had met with them reflect, in the group setting, on the individual's intrapersonal experience of the emotional reconnections, new information, old patterns observed, new ones established, plans jointly made with the family for the future, and the relationship of all of this to previous or current impasses in the marital pair.

Behavioral desensitization can be undertaken in relation to experienced past trauma, present fears, or an anticipated event. The reduction of traumatic fear may be facilitated in the context of new interpersonal experience, and may conceivable be speeded or better anchored in systemic (i.e., familial) work. Similar statements can be made about cognitive therapy. Solution-focused work, which tends to focus on the present and future may be facilitated by a *brief* exploration of how the problem(s) at hand have been addressed by members of the extended family or friendship group in the past. Solutions validated by the experience of known persons may hold particular appeal. Such "family choices" are easily derived from a quickly constructed theme-oriented genogram done with an individual, or from the collective memories of family members present in a session. At all levels of systemic focus and from most theoretical frames, it can be fruitful to look at the present, past, and future, which co-exist as regards their bearing on what is happening at the moment in therapy or in supervision, with the same kind of simultaneity we attributed previously to levels of membership in various interlocking systems.

When client and therapist or supervisee and supervisor are stuck in relation to therapeutic effectiveness, a review of therapeutic frames and related interventions and an openness to exploring time frames may productively refocus attention and energy on areas previously overlooked. The supervisor's and supervisee's reflections on their perceptions of one another, their relationship, and the clinical setting when they began their work together, at present, and as anticipated in the future and of their relationship to professional support systems provide an experiential understanding of how addressing the various levels of systemic analysis and varying time frames can facilitate and anchor interpersonal-systemic work.

Mistaken Level of Focus or Time Frame

The experienced simultaneity of both time frames and levels of systemic focus can result in the misattribution of realities in one time frame or at one systemic level to another. This accounts for situations like the man who constantly fears he may behave like his father who was abusive of his mother, although he has not been abusive of his wife over their 30-year marriage; or the woman who misattributes rejection to persons at work, friends, and intimate partner, while remaining staunchly loyal to a parent whose rejection is obvious to everyone but herself; or the person who having previously experienced mistreatment by one member of a particular group now anticipates harm from or maligns all others. Differentiation work is helpful in these instances, not only between persons, but also among time frames, contexts, and systemic levels of reality. The multigenerational systems theories (Boszormenyi-Nagy & Grunebaum, 1991; Bowen, 1976; Framo, 1976) and techniques (e.g., genograms, circular questioning, multiple-chair work, or interviewing a client as though he or she were the person from whom differentiation is needed) have facilitated our work in this area. Tentative questions, framed from the position of "not-knowing" (Anderson & Goolishian, 1992), are also helpful. These can be modeled and the concept taught in supervision.

Dialectic Aspects of Assessment

Creativity, conformity, and destruction are socially defined terms differentiated by the measure to which a human activity is judged to be similar to (conformity) or different from (creativity or destruction) currently accepted and expected standards, and to which it challenges yet supports (creativity) or challenges and attacks (destruction) the same. Human activity is assessed in relationship to standards that are both present and emergent. What is termed creative and enhancing, conforming and normative, or dysfunctional and destructive is designated as such based on personal and communal values determined in relation to social interest. These standards are set within the recursive intrapersonal and interpersonal dialogues that reflective humans engage in, in the interest of simultaneous preservation and growth of the self and its supportive social systems. An individual assessing another's behavior as creative, conforming, or destructive is at the same time applying individual, value-related choice and invoking a perceived general stance of collective others who have defined the term. In this sense, not only is all behavior communication, as characterized by the interpersonal theorists; the behavior of the individual is also inevitably one pole of the eternal dialogue or dialectic between self and other or self and community. Others are inevitably affected by individual intent and choice, whether or not the individual chooses to focus on this aspect of lived reality.

Among the behaviors that affect the trajectory of other lives is the professional assessment of their behavior. A systemic approach to assessment is sensitive to the evaluative perspectives of all who are affected by it, and assessment procedures need to be evaluated against the standards of individual and social interest, which are ultimately harmonious. The same techniques that facilitate differentiation may be useful in assessing the assessment procedures used by supervisors and clinics. It is helpful if these are isomorphic in form to the therapy and the ends therapy is designed to achieve (i.e., the capacity for making personally and socially productive decisions based on an accurate assessment of one's own and others' viewpoints). An awareness and owning of the values, intents, and stances of each person/group involved in assessment helps, together with empathy and positive regard for the persons evaluated. With these, plus genuineness and clear communication, impasses can be avoided and difficulties can be transcended.

Isomorphic Patterns

Isomorphic (having the same form) patterns appear to travel with persons from one interpersonal setting to another and, often, to cross systemic levels. Familiar interpersonal patterns, even uncomfortable and dysfunctional ones, are internalized by individuals and groups and replayed. *Isomorphism* (Liddle & Saba, 1983) is the term used by systems theorists for this process.

Dysfunctional patterns and their origins that have been out of awareness can be brought into focus and, with new interpersonal experience, modified. Supervisor and therapist, working from a systemic frame, can monitor and intervene in dysfunctional patterns to redirect the energy they contain in ways that are personally and socially positive.

Shifting Focus

A shift in level of focus need not imply a shift in theory or method. The shift from intrapersonal to interpersonal or systemic level is merely that, a shift of focus, not of theory or of method. Each level of entry or focus represents a kind of lens, with differential depths and breadths, as if the clinician were adjusting the focus on the lens of a camera to accommodate both the distance at which the subjects are standing from the photographer, as well as sufficient breadth to include the number of persons or amount of surrounding context selected for inclusion in the snapshot. At different times, one may wish to zoom in for a snapshot of a selected individual, to include that individual with one or more others in their relevant contexts, or to frame the individual within the entire group.

If all levels of systemic reality were fully isomorphic to each other, there would be no need to concern oneself with the varying levels. The fact that humans vary from one another both across and within the systems they help to create and that in turn partly determine them is related to two uniquely human qualities long celebrated by the humanistic and existential psychologists: freedom and choice.

Freedom, Choice, and Change

The capacity to communicate, both in external (spoken and written language and gestures) and internal (reflective thought) forms, has arisen in historic contexts, finds new avenues of expression, develops and changes in new situations over time as unique persons shape the language they are using. In turn, the language chosen shapes and influences their communication. Choice can be made only within the limits of freedom. Culture, language, personal experience, and ability simultaneously mediate the limits of the possible and challenge or draw the self toward unique expression within the understandable limits of communicable knowledge. Thus, new avenues of expression and new choices become available. Supervisors, supervisees, and clients receive new information through the filter of established concepts. What is new must be made sense of in relation to ideas that are already established. Change is often gradual, as new ways of thinking develop incrementally. Supervisors can help trainees, eager to lead their clients promptly to change, to understand that the very human resistance to rapid change is protective of persons and cultures. To change immediately or radically is to lose one's self and is more characteristic of psychotic states than of therapeutic change, which occurs, like other positive developmental changes, incrementally and over time.

Self-Actualization and Self-Transcendence

The intent of self-actualization is to transcend former limitations. The humanistic and existential psychologies identify a drive toward self-actualization that begins with concern for physical survival, moves through psychological safety concerns to focus on love and belonging, crystallizes in relation to esteem needs, and finally centers on self-actualization (Maslow, 1962). Once physical safety is assured, the traditionally intrapsychic-focused therapies may help clients increase their sense of psychological safety through expansion of what is in self-awareness, and thus more under one's control and minimizing the need for defenses. If one then seeks love and a sense of belonging, the interpersonal therapies may provide the experiential base for facilitating those objectives. The goal of accomplishing something deemed worthy by self and others so that esteem is achieved then may arise. The humanistic and existential psychotherapies are helpful in addressing such issues.

Beyond these therapies lie the various Eastern and Western psychospiritual traditions, which Wilber (1981) included in his developmental continuum of Eastern and Western therapies. This continuum roughly parallels the trajectory from intrapersonal through interpersonal to transpersonal focus that we have just described. An interpersonal-systemic and developmental frame is open to and inclusive of all of these. What Maslow and Wilber have delineated is the human capacity for transcendence, from lesser to greater states of intrapersonal, interpersonal, and transpersonal awareness and of connection with self, others, and the universe.

The capacity to communicate, both nonverbally and verbally, to tell our experience to even one other moves the experience beyond ourselves, simultaneously substantiating it and giving us the opportunity to see our own experience through the eyes and the related but different experience of another. Just as two eyes are required for three-dimensional vision, multiple points of view are better when it comes to interpreting experience and placing it in context. What we are describing is both the essence of transcendence and of psychotherapy and supervision. Such transcendence significantly increases the freedom of choice among cognitive, affective, and behavioral options and the assignment of meanings to experiences for individuals, who have now seen their experience through more than one perspective. The more systemic levels of experience, time frames, and personal points of view explored in psychotherapy and the related supervision, the greater the degree of freedom regarding personal choice and positive self-expression, the more anchored the choices are in contextual supports and constraints, and the more likely that what is in the best social interest of self in relation to others will be determined and acted on.

The interpersonal-systemic frame of reference embraces the humanistic, existential, and interpersonal psychological traditions and the perennial philosophical and religious frames that have brought coherent meaning to humans over the millennia. Transcendence is viewed herein as a developmental human phenomenon, motivated by intrinsic human needs, incrementally achieved by persons facilitated or impeded on their journey by interpersonal relationships with others and interaction with the specific contexts of their personal universe. Success on the journey requires the development of social interest and choices based on personal and communal values, which decrease socially negative choices and increase the breadth and depth of socially positive choices available to oneself in relationship to others and the universe. In this sense, each person's evolution facilitates that of others. Psychotherapy, in this vein, facilitates development, transcendence, and choice.

METHODS OF ASSESSMENT AND INTERVENTION

Assessment

Assessment of therapeutic effectiveness, "stuckness," or oversight in the interpersonal process between therapist and client is achieved in supervision through examining the multiple perspectives of all persons in or closely affected by the therapy. The supervisor is responsible for "seeing" or "hearing" all points of view and helping the therapist (supervisee) achieve empathic understanding and establish positive regard for each client. Initially, the supervisor guides the supervisee to an accurate assessment of the clients' needs and the extent to which these are being met in the therapy. The greater the extent to which the supervisee can do this, with little prompting, the greater the skill level he or she has achieved. In earlier stages of supervisee development, the supervisor will need to highlight and label the work that supervisor and supervisee do in this area, thus providing clear, concrete information regarding their process. As the therapist develops skill in client assessment, the capacity to assess one's own work will, isomorphically, increase, because assessment in both arenas is achieved through the capacity to empathically and accurately take multiple points of view. Clarifying one's own thoughts, feelings, and values and taking responsibility for one's own behaviors enables supervisor and supervisee to more accurately see and accept those of clients. The supervisor structures and guides but refuses to take over supervisory sessions, provided client safety is not an overlooked issue, and encourages the supervisee to decide what problems need to be focused on. This is isomorphic to what the supervisee as therapist must allow clients to do, which is to identify what it is that troubles them that they wish to bring to the therapist for attention.

Techniques that bring forth related experiences and viewpoints of all persons affected by a therapeutic problem or supervisory issue facilitate accurate assessment, while also functioning as an intervention. At the systemic level, the interconnected nature of systems, such as those of assessment and intervention procedures, become apparent. Useful assessment/intervention techniques range from straightforwardly asking about viewpoints to imagining or role-playing these when one or more parties is not available to be asked. Helpful approaches to questions are those from a stance of (1) curiosity, as in solution-focused work; (2) "not-knowing," as in the collaborative language systems approach; (3) circular questioning, as in the Milan school; (4) interviewing supervisees as though they were the client; and (5) multiple-chair work, in which persons not present in the interview are "seated" in chairs and asked to "voice" their opinions (as expressed by the supervisee). Traditional forms of assessment, including client self-report and questionnaires, are also valid. Here, we focus on interpersonal and systemic techniques.

INTERVENTION

The supervisor's intervention in the therapist's work with clients is undertaken after assessment reveals specific needs in the interpersonal process between therapist and client. Interventions that are common to and useful in any of the theoretical approaches may be used, as appropriate. Interventions are generally selected in relation to the supervisee's preferred theoretical frame. At times, straightforward, didactic information is needed and is sufficient. Frequently, the supervisor's task is to create in the supervisory session interpersonal experiences that are isomorphic to those the supervisee needs to create with the client. Intervention may include any of the techniques mentioned in the discussion of assessment. Positive supervisory intervention involves modeling awareness and effective use of multiple viewpoints and varying levels of systemic focus and alternative time frames. The supervisor will exemplify empathic understanding of and positive regard for the supervisee and his or her clients, be genuine in the relationship, and provide clear, concrete communication regarding areas of strength and those that need development. Supervisors must be aware of their own values and may challenge supervisees to articulate their own. Supervisors require themselves, as well as supervisees, to adhere to the ethical and moral standards of the profession. Both assessment and intervention take place within the acknowledged multilevel and developmental, interpersonal, and systemic relationships engaged in by supervisor and supervisee.

SYNDROMES, SYMPTOMS, AND PROBLEMS TREATED

Although supervisees may evidence a variety of difficulties (e.g., less than perfect knowledge of theory or technique, oversight in relation to record keeping, a beginner's lack of experience or confidence), some issues particularly addressed from an interpersonal-systemic perspective are the following.

DYSFUNCTIONAL ISOMORPHIC PATTERNS

At times, an interaction pattern learned in the client's family is brought into therapy and reenacted with the therapist, who, out of awareness, brings the same cluster of affects, behaviors, and cognitions into the supervisory session. A supervisor who is not aware of or skilled in management of such a potentially useful assessment and training opportunity may inadvertently transmit dysfunctional patterns that have been brought into the therapy to agency, community, and/or professional organizational attention. Inadequate record keeping, for example, seen as less important by a supervisee than the interpersonal work being accomplished, if not corrected by directives and monitoring from the supervisor, can lead to vulnerability of the client, supervisor, and/or agency in later court procedures or in relation to accrediting agencies. At times, a pattern rightly needs to move across all systems; for example, when a client is actively suicidal, the alarm is spread from the supervisee to the supervisor, clinic administrator, psychiatrist, and hospital emergency personnel. Intentional use can be made of isomorphic process to correct and redirect dysfunctional patterns. When a usually competent and focused supervisee presents as disorganized and hopeless regarding a particular client family, a systemically trained supervisor's first move may be to focus clearly and methodically on the family's structure, mood during the session, what they have already tried in addressing their problem, and their receptivity to organizing around the solution, to assess whether this behavior, which is uncharacteristic of the supervisee, is isomorphic to the family's current state. If this is the case, methodical, supportive, and assured intervention with the supervisee is likely to have a productive echo when the supervisee next works with the family. Noting what may be isomorphic patterns allows the supervisor both a window for assessing what may be transpiring in therapy and an opportunity for modeling and discussing interventions or containment with the supervisee.

PERCEPTUAL MYOPIA

Perceptual blocking by supervisor and/or supervisee of simultaneous existing realities at differential levels of systemic focus truncates assessment, circumvents contactful avenues of treatment, leads to awkward and at times harmful intervention, and creates a need for corrective intervention at the overlooked or suppressed levels. The effect of membership in groups with differential levels of ascribed social power on the functioning of self in interpersonal relationships is a dimension of supervisory and clinical interaction currently being brought into sharper focus by discussion regarding privilege and power in relation to class, gender, sexual preference, and race (Burke, 1989; Dienhart & Avis, 1994; Kliman, 1994; Lappin & Hardy, 1997; Long, 1997; McGoldrick, 1998; Mirkim, 1994).

A client or supervisee may interact in ways that seem to the therapist or supervisor to be less than fully responsive to present circumstances. There may be a perceptual and emotional disconnect in one or both of two interacting persons whose life experiences are grounded in differing social systems related to ability, age, culture, economic status, ethnicity, gender, race, religion, sexual preference, social position, or other differential experience. Creating adequate awareness of and positively addressing the simultaneity of membership of clients, supervisees, and supervisors in various systems is essential to the creation of adequate empathic understanding and of genuine positive regard for whole persons within their respective contexts. Creating such awareness in supervision requires empathy for the supervisee and clients on the part of the supervisor, positive regard, genuine face-to-face interpersonal experience, and open, concrete, and specific communication of what has not been known or has been held out of awareness. The supervisee/therapist thus gains an experiential model of how to approach similar issues in clients.

Questions asked of supervisees, which are framed to ask for a client's (overlooked) perspective, can be useful. Asking first for their point of view, then their idea of each client's point of view can be followed with the suggestion that they ask about each client's viewpoint in the next interview. It is easy to fall into the habit of working from unchecked assumptions. Modeling and recommending direct communication avoids the temptation on the part of supervisor and supervisee to become "experts" at guessing what others are thinking or feeling.

MISTAKEN LEVEL OF FOCUS OR TIME FRAME

At times, a client, supervisee, or supervisor may behave as though something or someone other than oneself were effectively shaping current options. This causality may be attributed to an irrevocable past, present pressures, or future deadlines. Looking at the presenting problem empathically from the various perspectives and points of view of persons in time frames and contexts can facilitate the differentiation of persons across time frames and at different levels of systemic focus. A teenager can come to see how she may be different from her friends; a man how he differs from his abusive father; a supervisor how her supervisee's effectiveness comes from a theoretical frame other than the one preferred by the supervisor.

INFLEXIBLE USE OF LEVELS OF FOCUS AND TIME FRAMES

Flexible use of time frames and levels of focus is supportive of well-being. Reification of or overly focusing on a given time frame and systemic level can be harmful. For example, dwelling at length on the devastating experiences and affects of past sexual abuse before establishing a strong and protective present interpersonal working alliance and helping the client to internalize positive regard, protection, and self-efficacy may serve to prolong and magnify the disempowering aspects of the abuse. In the same case, exclusive focus on the present would allow no protective time or space in which the past could be reexperienced, reviewed, and assimilated.

When the supervisee feels the therapeutic process is "stuck," sessions may have become dysfunctionally focused on a nonproductive level of focus. A couple who keep coming for therapy but are stuck may benefit from individual work or from bringing in more family members. Supervisees can be coached to work with any of these modalities.

A primary benefit of an interpersonal-systemic perspective is the richly interconnected diversity of viewpoints and options it offers and the support this affords the work of clients, supervisee, and supervisor.

CASE EXAMPLE

The following is an example of a supervisory session conducted from an interpersonal-systemic and developmental frame. The therapist is a student intern in the beginning of her second year of field placement. In her early 20s, she is from an upper-middle-class family and has little exposure to some issues faced by the lower-income client population the clinic serves. This young woman has been quite successful with some difficult cases. She usually presents as calm, composed, and capable, accessing and using her considerable skills, even in the midst of apparent chaos. She has come to the supervision session presenting as quite disorganized, and professes to feel stuck in her work with a family in which the teenagers, Shauna and Shane, 15 and 16 years old, are having a lot of conflict with their parents. Their dad, Mr. Joseph, had been doing drugs, became HIV positive, passed it to his wife, then left the family. Recently, he "found God" (turned to religion for support), came back to his family, and expects to be the head of the house again. Shauna and Shane are furious with him because of his previous lifestyle, passing on the disease to their mom, and abandoning them. At present, they exhibit no respect for him and refuse to follow his rules.

SUPERVISORY APPROACH AND RATIONALE

The supervisor noted that, although professing to be stuck and presenting as disorganized, the supervisee nevertheless has quite cogently conceptualized the issues that need to be addressed. In fact, in her brief description of the family, she gave what seemed a likely statement of the father's and children's feelings and expectations, and outlined how the mother was affected by the presenting problem. The supervisor wondered what might be causing the upset, apparent confusion, and therapeutic impasse in this competent young intern. She decided, with the therapist's permission, to use an experiential approach for exploring with her the family's dynamics and the intern's reactions to and processing of them, in the hope that this might add clarity and break the impasse.

This supervisor often adds elements from psychodrama to her work, and thus is comfortable with multiple-chair work using stuffed toys to represent persons. She finds that having a client or supervisee make the toy "speak" for someone adds to the "as if" quality of exploring another's point of view, and in fact can help to differentiate between self and self-taking-the-role of someone else.

The supervisee has just completed her description of the family:

SUPERVISOR: (Negotiating structure.) There are a multitude of issues here. What would you find most useful to address now?

THERAPIST: The children are not dumb, but they're making dumb decisions just to get back at their father, and I don't blame them! But, somehow, I need to get them to all work together peacefully and for the teens to take better care of themselves. I'm *really* stuck!

SUPERVISOR: (Opening a space for and checking the supervisee's point of view.) Are you angry with the father?

THERAPIST: I know I'm not supposed to feel this way, but what a jerk! What really gets me is he just expects everyone to act like nothing bad has happened and to jump because he says so. He hasn't apologized for anything and refuses to let anybody talk about his drug use, the parents' illness, his abandoning the family, or anything related . . .

SUPERVISOR: (Bringing in another viewpoint.) What is his wife's position?

THERAPIST: She seems to be relieved that he's back and taking over parenting. It's hard to tell, because he does all the talking. She just sits and nods her head most of the time. There's something about this family that triggers unprofessional thoughts and feelings in me. I think I behave professionally with them, but I'm angry with the mother for taking her husband back and acting like a puppet! (She pauses.) I'm embarrassed. I shouldn't feel this way, but I do. And I'm afraid my feelings are getting in the way of my work with them. (The supervisor notes a tacit acknowledgment here of the likely issue.) I don't feel like I can help them very much. (This plea for help does not go unnoticed. The supervisor decides to suggest an experiential approach to the issue.)

SUPERVISOR: (Moving to introduce a multilevel focus.) Let's do something different. Shall we "bring the family into this session" with some chair work? (Her supervisees are familiar with the use of chairs to represent persons who are not present.)

THERAPIST: Sure, I need some help.

SUPERVISOR: Why don't you select a stuffed toy (from a box of these kept for this purpose) to represent each family member and put them in chairs to indicate where they would sit if they were in this office.

THERAPIST: (Puts toys in chairs, which are set up in a loose circle. "Mother" and "father" sit close to one another and opposite "the children," with the children closer to the mother. The therapist is positioned between the father and children.)

SUPERVISOR: Now, I would like for you to choose one of the chairs and take that person's position. Demonstrate one thing that person would say. I want to see and hear what happens in a session.

The therapist does that, first holding the toy representing the father and expressing what he would say, then expressing the point of view of each of the children, then of the mother. The supervisor encourages her to pay attention to the feelings she picks up in each chair.

When she has gone around once, she is asked to go around again, and to say what she thinks each family member would *really* say if he or she were brutally honest. Starting with the children this time, she states how much each hates the father for choosing drugs over them, stealing from them, and leaving them homeless a couple of times. They say how relieved they were that he left and how they did not want him back, how furious they were to find he had infected both himself and their mother with a disease that would leave them without parents in a relatively short time. Next, they vented their anger at their mother for allowing their father to return and take over as head of the household. They would never forgive their father and would not accept his telling them what to do.

As the therapist was going through this exercise, her feelings seemed to fill the room. When she took the position of the father, she began to tear up. She reported that she picked up so much shame and fear in this position that she believed he could not begin to own it, because he might be consumed by it. In the mother's position, there also was a lot of shame for not protecting her children from their father when he was doing drugs. She now seemed resigned that an early death was her punishment. Also, she wanted to support her husband in making up for being a bad parent by being the best parent he could be while he was still able.

SUPERVISOR: Now, take your own seat. (The supervisor then steps behind each "client" chair and repeats briefly what the therapist had said from each chair.) Now what are you experiencing? (She is shifting the focus again, to the supervisee's point of view.)

THERAPIST: It's awesome! I think I was holding the family's emotions and now I am not.

SUPERVISOR: Are you now?

THERAPIST: I feel so sad for them! I think the parents really love their children and are so overwhelmed by their own feelings of fear and sadness and guilt that they're not parenting the way they want to.

SUPERVISOR: (Identifying the isomorphic pattern that has come with the therapist into the supervision.) As you were so overwhelmed with feelings that you were not being the therapist you wanted to and can be?

THERAPIST: O my gosh! It's true!

SUPERVISOR: Can you now be the professional you want to be with this family?

THERAPIST: Yes.

SUPERVISOR: What has changed?

THERAPIST: I was able to step out of my position into theirs and see things from their perspective. The parents don't seem like monsters now.

SUPERVISOR: How are you going to be a competent therapist with them?

THERAPIST: The father is so defended, I want to meet with the parents and develop more support between them. (The supervisor notes that this competent young therapist has now found an empathic connection to each of the individuals in the family, and is shifting her focus to find interpersonal supports for the father, whom she had seen as most powerful and now sees as also quite weak.) Maybe if the father can talk about his feelings with his wife and find she doesn't hate him, or deal with it if she does, he may be able to be more open and honest with his children. I think they will keep on misbehaving, trying to get revenge on him, until he owns up to having been a crummy father.

SUPERVISOR: Any other ideas?

THERAPIST: Ummmm, no.

SUPERVISOR: (Exploring other systemic levels of support.) Where else can the father and ultimately the whole family get more support? (The supervisor knows that the therapist draws a lot of strength from her religion, so is confident she will appreciate the value to the family of the idea she hopes to elicit from her.)

THERAPIST: (Joining in the exploration.) They don't have many extended family members and his are into drugs and alcohol. She has one sister who lives 3,000 miles away and neither family has money for long distance calls. The only other support might be the minister the father talks with a lot. Yes. Maybe the church... except the minister tells the children to forgive their father and they think he is a jerk!

SUPERVISOR: (Assessing whether the supervisee conceptualizes a rationale for bringing in external support for the family.) Can you think of benefits to the father and mother? And if they benefit, how might it impact the children?

THERAPIST: The father really likes talking to this minister and he goes to church at least twice a week. The teens refuse to go. (The supervisee is reflective.) But if the father could forgive himself, which the minister can help with ... and he and his wife could have a more loving and supportive relationship ... he could be more *real* with his children. They may not forgive him soon, but they might accept his present love and his commitment to them now ... and quit hanging with the wrong people. (The supervisor notes that the supervisee's earlier agitation has disappeared, along with the impasse in knowing how to approach this family. She presents now as her usual confident self, eagerly approaching her work with a new and challenging family.)

SUPERVISOR: What is your next step?

THERAPIST: I will ask the parents if they will meet without the children next time and invite the minister, so we can maximize their support. I think they will go for that.

SUPERVISOR: (Noting that the supervisory hour is near the end, again negotiates for structure and moves toward closure.) I see that we are running out of time. Is there anything we did not cover or that feels unfinished?

THERAPIST: No.

SUPERVISOR: Then, tell me one or more things you got out of supervision, and also, if you would have liked something done differently, what would that have been?

THERAPIST: What I liked. I liked that I had the courage to say how I felt about these people, even though I felt ashamed of it.

SUPERVISOR: That was certainly courageous! (Again highlighting the theme of isomorphism, and reminding of its utility in redirecting a negative pattern.) Just as their feelings of anger, shame, hurt, and such infected you, you may find that your courage to face your feelings will infect them.

THERAPIST: Oh, I hope so! I also liked being able to pretend I was the father, even though I started out really disliking him. It will be easier for me to step into somebody else's shoes and not be so judgmental from now on. I like the idea of including the minister more actively in their healing. That's been so important in my life and can be a permanent part of theirs, while therapy will be brief. It seems right. The other question is if I could have done something different?

SUPERVISOR: Or I could have.

THERAPIST: I would have figured it out myself sooner and been a better therapist to them.

SUPERVISOR: Just as the parents would have figured out their stuff and been better parents sooner. (Again, the supervisor refers to the theme of isomorphism.)

THERAPIST: Oh, yeah. Thanks for not judging me but leading me to discover how I really felt and how I think they feel.

SUPERVISOR: I expect you will do the same for the clients. Remember our discussions of the isomorphic process? This has been a good example of it.

POSTSESSION SYNOPSIS AND REFLECTIONS

The supervisor here quickly noted a pattern of distress not typical of her supervisee. She assessed the supervisee's capacity to conceptualize possible interpersonal-systemic dynamics in the case, and found this strong. The difficulty seemed to lie in the affect related to "getting on" with this case. Based on an initial hypothesis that this might also be what the family was struggling with, in consultation with the supervisee, she decided to approach the sorting out of how each person involved in the therapy was feeling and thinking, using an experiential technique both were comfortable with. Another supervisor and supervisee might prefer to address what the supervisee wanted or needed more directly, with questions, exploring time frames, levels of focus, individual and family developmental issues, supports for the family, the structure and format of the supervision, or other issues raised by the supervisee.

RESEARCH REGARDING THE APPROACH

Our thesis has been that humanistic, existential, interpersonal, and developmental elements are present or evoked in supervision of psychotherapy, regardless of the theoretical preference. Investigation of the humanistic core facilitative conditions and development in the supervisory relationship offers some assurance in the former, and divided opinion in the latter. Rogers's hypothesized core dimensions of empathy, positive regard, genuineness, and concreteness emerged as valid in early research (Carkhuff, 1967; Carkhuff & Truax, 1966; Truax & Carkhuff, 1964, 1966). In their 1997 report on supervisor variables in relation to psychotherapy supervision, Neufeldt, Beutler, and Banchero (1997) reviewed recent related research. Beutler, Machado, and Neufeldt (1994) reaffirmed the importance of the facilitative conditions in therapy. Pierce and Schauble (1970, 1971), extending the line of research to supervision, found that trainees whose supervisors provided high levels of empathy, positive regard, genuineness, and concreteness developed these attributes themselves, thus indirectly supporting the hypothesis of development. Karr and Geist (1977) found supervisor genuineness, respect, and concreteness significantly related to the competence of trainees. Graduates ranked supervisors they felt contributed to their therapeutic effectiveness high on the facilitative conditions in the research of Schacht,

Howe, and Berman (1989). Bordin (1979, 1983) extended his concept of the therapeutic alliance in psychoanalytic work to that of a working alliance between supervisor and supervisee. Efstation, Patton, and Kaardash (1990) developed the Supervision Working Alliance Inventory, from which they extracted three supervisor factors (client focus, rapport, and identification) and two trainee factors (rapport and client focus) using factor analysis. That therapists and supervisors should exhibit empathy, positive regard, genuineness, and clarity of expression regardless of theoretical approach appears to be validated by a long research tradition. The variables measured are found in the perceptions of the participants in relation to an interpersonal relationship. Factors such as empathy and positive regard are not found outside of interpersonal contexts.

Holloway (1987, 1988) and Stoltenberg and Delworth (1988) have debated the relative amount of development that occurs in supervision. Worthington (1987), in a review of empirical studies, found support for changes in supervisor behavior and the supervision relationship and that supervisees and supervisors both perceived development to take place. Stoltenberg, McNeill, and Crethar (1994) also found evidence of supervisee development with training. In their reviews of the related literature, neither Ellis and Ladany (1997) nor Neufeldt et al. (1997) found clear support for supervisee development provoked by supervisor input or supervisory model. Liddle et al. (1997), who work from a family systems perspective, broaden the concept of development to include concern for the life cycle development of the individual, the family, therapy, and supervision as generic to their model, as well as, in the Wernerian sense, increasing organization and complexity in cognitive, affective, and behavioral aspects of persons interacting over time within and between various levels of systemic complexity. At the dyadic level of analysis, it can be seductively easy to fall into the assumption that one person's intent and behavior may in some linear fashion produce regular and measurable outcomes in those of another. Perhaps a more powerful correlate of developing supervisee effectiveness would result from a measure of genuine positive regard and ongoing commitment to the supervisee and clear communication on the part of the several supportive systems in which he or she is ensconsed during the period of supervision. It is not just a good pitcher who creates a good batter; the coach, team, administrator, fans, and one's family life and personal health and practice also have something to do with performance over time. We sometimes hold the individual (teacher, supervisor, trainee) responsible for what is, in effect, a "team performance." As with assessment, research related to systemic supervision needs to be isomorphic to the therapeutic model (i.e., incorporating multiple current and developing viewpoints and the recursive interaction effects among them). Lack of clarity and conflicting outcomes in research regarding supervision, which is systemic in nature and function, result from lack of addressing the multiple, developing, and simultaneous realities at play in conceptualizing the research, gathering data, and interpretation. As Ellis and Ladany (1997) suggest, "Clinical supervision appears to be a more complex phenomenon than represented in current theories about supervision and supervisees" (p. 493).

SUMMARY

The concept of human systems presented here assumes (1) multidirectional, recursive interactions among the various parts of any given interpersonal system; (2) a Gestaltic quality in which the whole of any intentional group is greater than the sum of the parts, such that dysfunction in any individual impairs the whole; (3) the capacities for self-reflection and self-regulation within contextual constraints; (4) the making and sharing of meaning; (5) intentional behavior; and (6) continuing development. Self and other are each envisioned as unique yet inseparably bound in a mutual process of coexistence and cocreation. Humans are inextricably interlinked by language, custom, culture, and biological need, initially for physical succor and safety, then for companionship, guidance, and mutual support in the physical, intellectual, and spiritual tasks required for human survival and competence within a given context. Language, custom, and culture permit the internalization of external systems; thus, systemic psychological intervention can be accomplished with individuals as well as with dyads, families, and larger groups. Intervention at the large-group level (e.g., at the cultural level, holding military personnel accountable for rape used as a tactic of war) may have a powerful, isomorphic beneficial effect at all lower levels of social organization (national, ethnic, familial, couple, individual). Conversely, the activity of an individual (e.g., the refusal of Rosa Parks, a Black woman, to sit at the back of the bus in the formerly racially segregated South) can therapeutically affect all higher levels of social organization. Therapeutic intervention undertaken at any systemic level may have positive repercussions at all others.

The supervision of psychotherapy from a variety of theoretical frames has been presented as facilitated through this interpersonal, systemic, and developmental frame of reference. It is hoped this will allow supervisor and supervisee to move comfortably across the gaps between various theoretical and experiential points of view. This broad frame should be helpful in identifying both what is enhanced and what may be obscured in a given therapy session or supervisory interview conducted from a narrower frame. We have argued that any theoretical frame from which psychotherapy and supervision are approached may be applied at all levels of therapeutic entry and focus, and that all theoretical frames involve the interpersonal and evoke the humanistic and existential.

REFERENCES

Adler, A. (1963). *The practice and theory of individual psychology.* Paterson, NJ: Littlefield, Adams. (Original work published 1924)

Adler, A. (1964). *Superiority and social interest* (3rd ed., H. L. Ansbacher & R. R. Ansbacher, Eds.). New York: Viking Press.

Allport, G. W. (1950). *The individual and his religion.* New York: Macmillian.

Allport, G. W. (1954). *The nature of prejudice.* Garden City, NY: Doubleday.

Allport, G. W. (1960). *Becoming.* New Haven, CT: Yale University Press.

Allport, G. W. (1961). *Pattern and growth in personality* (revision of personality). New York: Holt, Rinehart and Winston. (Original work published 1937)

Anderson, H., & Goolishian, H. A. (1992). The client is the expert: A not-knowing approach to therapy. In S. McNamee & K. J. Gergen (Eds.), *Therapy as social construction* (pp. 25–39). Newbury Park, CA: Sage.

Bentovim, A., & Kinston, W. (1991). Focal family therapy: Joining systems theory with psychodynamic understanding. In A. S. Gurman & D. P. Kniskern (Eds.), *Handbook of family therapy* (Vol. 2, pp. 284–324). New York: Brunner/Mazel.

Bernard, J. M. (1997). The discrimination model. In C. E. Watkins (Ed.), *Handbook of psychotherapy supervision* (pp. 310–327). New York: Wiley.

Berne, E. (1961). *Transactional analysis in psychotherapy.* New York: Grove.

Berne, E. (1963). *The structure and dynamics of groups and organizations.* New York: Ballantine.

Beutler, L. E., Machado, P. P., & Neufeldt, S. A. (1994). Therapist variables. In A. E. Bergin & S. L. Garfield (Eds.), *Handbook of psychotherapy and behavior change* (3rd ed., pp. 229–269). New York: Wiley.

Binswanger, L. (1956). Existential analysis and psychotherapy. In F. Fromm-Reichmann & J. L. Moreno (Eds.), *Progress in psychotherapy.* New York: Grune & Stratton.

Bordin, E. S. (1979). The generalizability of the psychodynamic concept of the working alliance. *Psychotherapy: Theory, Research, and Practice, 16,* 252–260.

Bordin, E. S. (1983). A working alliance model of supervision. *Counseling Psychologist, 11,* 35–42.

Boss, M. (1957). *Psychoanalysis and daseinanalysis.* New York: Basic Books.

Boszormenyi-Nagy, I., & Grunebaum, J. (1991). Contextual therapy. In A. S. Gurman & D. P. Kniskern (Eds.), *Handbook of family therapy* (Vol. 2, pp. 200–238). New York: Brunner/Mazel.

Boszormenyi-Nagy, I., & Krasner, B. R. (1986). *Between give and take: A clinical guide to contextual therapy.* New York: Brunner/Mazel.

Bowen, M. (1976). Theory in the practice of psychotherapy. In P. Guerin (Ed.), *Family therapy: Theory and practice* (pp. 42–90). New York: Gardner Press.

Bowlby, J. (1988). *A secure base: Parent-child attachment and healthy human development.* New York: Basic Books.

Broderick, C. B., & Schrader, S. S. (1991). The history of professional marriage and family therapy. In A. S. Gurman & D. P. Kniskern (Eds.), *Handbook of family therapy* (Vol. 2, pp. 3–40). New York: Brunner/Mazel.

Burke, R. A. (1989). Incorporating lesbian and gay issues into counselor training: A resource guide. *Journal of Counseling and Development, 68,* 77–80.

Burns, C. I., & Holloway, E. L. (1989). Therapy in supervision: An unresolved issue. *Clinical Supervisor, 7,* 47–60.

Caligor, L. (1984). Parallel and reciprocal processes in psychoanalytic supervision. In L. Caligor, P. M. Bromberg, & J. D. Meltzer (Eds.), *Clinical perspectives on the supervision of psychoanalysis and psychotherapy.* New York: Plenum Press.

Capra, F. (1975). *The tao of physics.* Boston: Shambhala.

Carkhuff, R. R. (1967). *The counselor's contribution to facilitative processes.* Urbana, IL: Parkinson.

Carkhuff, R. R., & Berenson, B. G. (1967). *Beyond counseling and therapy.* New York: Holt, Rinehart and Winston.

Carkhuff, R. R., & Truax, C. B. (1966). Toward explaining success and failure in interpersonal learning experiences. *Personnel Guidance Journal, 46,* 723–728.

Carroll, M. (1996). *Counseling supervision: Theory, skills, and practice.* London: Cassell.

Dewald, P. A. (1997). The process of supervision in psychoanalysis. In C. E. Watkins (Ed.), *Handbook of psychotherapy supervision.* New York: Wiley.

Dewey, J. (1891). *Psychology.* New York: American Book.

Dienhart, A., & Avis, J. M. (1994). Working with men in family therapy: An exploratory study. *Journal of Marital and Family Therapy, 20,* 397–417.

Efstation, J.F., Patton, M. J., & Kaardash, C. M. (1990). Measuring the working alliance in counseling supervision. *Journal of Counseling Psychology, 37,* 322–329.

Ekstein, R., & Wallerstein, R. S. (1972). *The teaching and learning of psychotherapy* (2nd ed.). New York: International Universities Press.

Ellis, M. V., & Ladany, N. (1997). Inferences concerning supervisees and clients in clinical supervision: An integrative review. In C. E. Watkins (Ed.), *Handbook of psychotherapy supervision* (pp. 447–507). New York: Wiley.

Erikson, E. H. (1950). *Childhood and society.* New York: Norton.

Erikson, E. H. (1968). *Identity: Youth and crisis.* New York: Norton.

Falloon, I. R. H. (1991). Behavioral family therapy. In A. S. Gurman & D. P. Kniskern (Eds.), *Handbook of family therapy* (Vol. 2, pp. 65–95). New York: Brunner/Mazel.

Framo, J. L. (1976). Family of origin as a therapeutic resource for adults in marital and family therapy: You can and should go home again. *Family Process, 15,* 193–210.

Frankl, V. E. (1959). *Man's search for meaning: An introduction to logotherapy.* Boston: Beacon Press.

Frankl, V. E. (1977). *The unconscious god: Psychotherapy and theology.* New York: Simon & Schuster.

Freud, A. (1965). *Normality and pathology in childhood: Assessments of development.* New York: International Universities Press.

Fromm, E. (1964). *The heart of man.* New York: Harper & Row.

Fruzzetti, A. E., Waltz, J. A., & Linehan, M. M. (1997). Supervision in dialectical behavior therapy. In C. E. Watkins Jr. (Ed.), *Handbook of psychotherapy supervision* (pp. 84–100). New York: Wiley.

Gergen, K. J. (1982). *Toward transformation in social knowledge.* New York: Springer-Verlag.

Glick, J. A. (1994). Heinz Werner's relevance for contemporary developmental psychology. In R. D. Parke, P. A. Ornstein, J. J. Rieser, & C. Zahn-Waxler (Eds.), *A century of developmental psychology* (pp. 291–309). Washington, DC: American Psychological Association.

Goulding, R., & Goulding, M. (1979). *Changing lives through redecision therapy.* New York: Brunner/Mazel.

Guerin, P. (Ed.). (1976). *Family therapy: Theory and practice.* New York: Gardner Press.

Gurman, A. S., & Kniskern, D. P. (1981). *Handbook of family therapy.* New York: Brunner/Mazel.

Gurman, A. S., & Kniskern, D. P. (1991). *Handbook of family therapy* (Vol. 2). New York: Brunner/Mazel.

Hawkins, P., & Shobet, R. (1989). *Supervision in the helping professions.* Milton Keynes, England: Open University Press.

Heisenberg, W. (1958). *Physics and philosophy: The revolution of modern science.* New York: Harper & Row.

Hess, A. K. (1986). Growth in supervision: Stages of supervisee and supervisor development. *Clinical Supervisor, 4*(1/2), 51–67.

Hess, A. K. (1987). Psychotherapy supervision: Stages, Buber, and a theory of relationship. *Professional Psychology: Research and Practice, 18,* 252–259.

Hess, A. K. (1997). The interpersonal approach to the supervision of psychotherapy. In C. E. Watkins Jr. (Ed.), *Handbook of psychotherapy supervision* (pp. 63–83). New York: Wiley.

Holloway, E. L. (1987). Developmental models of supervision: Is it supervision? *Professional Psychology: Research and Practice, 18,* 209–216.

Holloway, E. L. (1988). Models of counselor development or training models for supervision? Rejoinder to Stoltenberg & Delworth. *Professional Psychology: Research and Practice, 19,* 138–140.

Holloway, E. L. (1995). *Clinical supervision: A systems approach.* Thousand Oaks, CA: Sage.

Holtzworth-Munroe, A., & Jacobson, N. S. (1991). Behavioral marital therapy. In A. S. Gurman & D. P. Kniskern (Eds.), *Handbook of family therapy* (Vol. 2, pp. 96–133). New York: Brunner/Mazel.

Imber-Black, E. (1988). *Families and larger systems: A therapists' guide through the labyrinth.* New York: Guilford Press.

Imber-Black, E. (1991). A family-larger system perspective. In A. S. Gurman & D. P. Kniskern (Eds.), *Handbook of family therapy* (Vol. 2, pp. 583–605). New York: Brunner/Mazel.

James, W. (1983). *The principles of psychology.* Cambridge, MA: Harvard University Press. (Original work published 1890)

Jung, C. G. (1938). *Psychology and religion.* New Haven, CT: Yale University Press.

Karr, J. T., & Geist, G. O. (1977). Facilitation in supervision as related to facilitation in therapy. *Counselor Education and Supervision, 16,* 263–268.

Kaslow, F. (1977). Training marriage and family therapists. In F. Kaslow (Ed.), *Supervision, consultation, and staff training in the helping professions* (pp. 199–234). San Francisco: Jossey-Bass.

Kaslow, F. (Ed.). (1986). *Supervision and training; Models, dilemmas and challenges.* New York: Haworth Press.

Kegan, R. (1982). *The evolving self: Problem and process in human development.* Cambridge, MA: Harvard University Press.

Kliman, J. (1994). The interweaving of gender, class, and race in family therapy. In M. P. Mirkin (Ed.), *Women in context: Toward a feminist reconstruction of psychotherapy* (pp. 25–47). New York: Guilford Press.

Lappin, J., & Hardy, K. (1997). Keeping context in view. In T. C. Todd & C. L. Storm (Eds.), *The complete systemic supervisor: Context, philosophy, and pragmatics* (pp. 44–58). Boston: Allyn & Bacon.

Liddle, H. A. (1991). Family therapy training and supervision: A comparative review and critique. In A. S. Gurman & D. P. Kniskern (Eds.), *Handbook of family therapy* (Vol. 2, pp. 638–697). New York: Brunner/Mazel.

Liddle, H. A., Becker, D., & Diamond, G. M. (1997). Family therapy supervision. In C. E. Watkins Jr. (Ed.), *Handbook of psychotherapy supervision* (pp. 400–420). New York: Wiley.

Liddle, H. A., Breunlin, D. C., & Schwartz, R. C. (Eds.). (1988). *Handbook of family therapy training and supervision.* New York: Guilford Press.

Liddle, H. A., & Saba, G. W. (1983). On context replication: The isomorphic relationship of family therapy and family therapy training. *Journal of Strategic and Systemic Therapies, 2*(2), 3–11.

Liese, B. S., & Beck, B. S. (1997). Cognitive therapy supervision. In C. E. Watkins Jr. (Ed.), *Handbook of psychotherapy supervision* (pp. 114–133). New York: Wiley.

Long, J. K. (1997). Sexual orientation: Implications for the supervisory process. In T. C. Todd & C. L. Storm (Eds.), *The complete systemic supervisor: Context, philosophy, and pragmatics* (pp. 59–71). Boston: Allyn & Bacon.

Martínez, M. (1997). *El paradigma emergente: Hacia una nueva teoría de la racionalidad científica* [The emergent paradigm: Toward a new theory of scientific rationality]. Mexico City: Trillas.

Maslow, A. H. (1943). A theory of human motivation. *Psychological Review, 50,* 370–396.

Maslow, A. H. (1954). *Motivation and personality* (2nd ed.). New York: Harper & Row.

Maslow, A. H. (1962). *Toward a psychology of being.* New York: Van Nostrand.

Maslow, A. H. (1964). *Religions, values and peak experiences.* New York: Viking.

Massey, R. F. (1972). Metasubjectivity: A model for interracial understanding. *International Journal of Group Tensions, 2*(4), 71–85.

Massey, S. D. (1994). Unlocking interlocking systems: Creative uses of TA in individual, couples, and family-systems theory. In P. Lapworth (Ed.), *Social systems & TA: The Maastricht papers* (pp. 57–61). [Selections from the 20th European Association of Transactional Analysis, conference office, P. O. Box 1197, 3800 BD Amersfoort, The Netherlands]

May, R. (1953). *Man's search for himself.* New York: Signet.

McDaniel, S., Weber, T., & McKeever, J. (1983). Multiple theoretical approaches to supervision: Choices in family therapy training. *Family Process, 22,* 491–500.

McGoldrick, M. (1998). *Re-visioning family therapy: Race culture, and gender in clinical practice.* New York: Guilford Press.

Mead, G. W. (1964). *George Herbert Mead on social psychology* (A. Strauss, Ed.). Chicago: University of Chicago Press. (Original work published 1934)

Mirkim, M. P. (Ed.). (1994). *Women in context: Toward a feminist reconstruction of psychotherapy*. New York: Guilford Press.

Moreno, J. L. (1945). *Psychodrama: Foundations of psychotherapy* (Vol. 1). Beacon, NY: Beacon House.

Moreno, J. L. (1946). *Psychodrama: Foundations of psychotherapy* (Vol. 2). Beacon, NY: Beacon House.

Mueller, W. J., & Kell, B. L. (1972). *Coping with conflict: Supervising counselors and therapists*. New York: Appleton-Century-Crofts.

Neufeldt, S. A., Beutler, L. E., & Banchero, L. E. (1997). Research on supervisor variables in psychotherapy supervision. In C. E. Watkins Jr. (Ed.), *Handbook of psychotherapy supervision* (pp. 508–726). New York: Wiley.

Patterson, C. H. (1997). Client-centered supervision. In C. E. Watkins Jr. (Ed.), *Handbook of psychotherapy supervision* (pp. 134–146). New York: Wiley.

Perls, F. S. (1969). *Gestalt therapy verbatim*. New York: Bantam Books.

Pierce, R. M., & Schauble, P. G. (1970). Graduate training of facilitative counselors: The effects of individual supervision. *Journal of Counseling Psychology, 17,* 210–215.

Pierce, R. M., & Schauble, P. G. (1971). Follow-up study on the effects of individual supervision in graduate school training. *Journal of Counseling Psychology, 18,* 186–187.

Polanyi, M. (1945). *Science, faith and society*. Chicago: University of Chicago Press.

Polanyi, M. (1962). *Personal knowledge*. Chicago: University of Chicago Press.

Prigogine, I. (1976). Order through fluctuation: Self-organization and social systems. In E. Jantsch & C. H. Waddington (Eds.), *Evolution and consciousness: Human systems in transition*. Reading, MA: Addison-Wesley.

Reiner, P. A. (1997). Psychoanalytic approaches to supervising couple and family therapy. In T. C. Todd & C. L. Storm (Eds.), *The complete systemic supervisor: Context, philosophy, and pragmatics*. (pp. 135–155). Boston: Allyn & Bacon.

Rigazio-DiGilio, S., Daniels, T. G., & Ivey, A. E. (1997). Systemic cognitive-developmental supervision: A developmental-integrative approach to psychotherapy supervision. In C. E. Watkins (Ed.), *Handbook of psychotherapy supervision* (pp. 223–248). New York: Wiley.

Rogers, C. R. (1951). *Client-centered therapy*. Boston: Houghton Mifflin.

Rogers, C. R. (1961). *On becoming a person*. Boston: Houghton Mifflin.

Ronnestad, M. H., & Skovholt, T. M. (1993). Supervision of beginning and advanced graduate students of counseling and psychotherapy. *Journal of Counseling and Development, 71,* 396–405.

Safran, J. D., & Segal, Z. V. (1990). *Interpersonal process in cognitive therapy*. New York: Basic Books.

Satir, V. (1972). *Peoplemaking*. Palo Alto, CA: Science and Behavior Books.

Schacht, A. J., Howe, J. E., Jr., & Berman, J. J. (1989). Supervisor facilitative conditions and effectiveness as perceived by thinking- and feeling-type supervisees. *Psychotherapy, 26,* 475–483.

Steinberg, F. E., & Whiteside, R. G. (1999). *Whispers from the East: Applying the principles of Eastern healing to psychotherapy*. Phoenix, AZ: Zeig, Tucker & Co.

Stoltenberg, C. D., & Delworth, U. (1987). *Supervising counselors and therapists: A developmental approach*. San Francisco: Jossey-Bass.

Stoltenberg, C. D., & Delworth, U. (1988). Developmental models of supervision: It is development—Response to Holloway. *Professional Psychology: Research and Practice, 19,* 134–137.

Stoltenberg, C. D., & McNeill, B. W. (1997). Clinical supervision from a developmental perspective: Research and practice. In C. E. Watkins (Ed.), *Handbook of psychotherapy supervision* (pp. 184–202). New York: Wiley.

Stoltenberg, C. D., McNeill, B. W., & Crethar, H. C. (1994). Changes in supervision as counselors and therapists gain experience: A review. *Professional Psychology: Research and Practice, 25,* 416–449.

Storm, C., & Heath, A. (1985). Models of supervision: Using therapy theory as a guide. *Clinical Supervisor, 3,* 87–96.

Storm, C. L., Peterson, M., & Tomm, K. (1997). Multiple relationships in supervision: Step up to complexity. In T. C. Todd & C. L. Storm (Eds.), *The complete systemic supervisor: Context, philosophy and pragmatics* (pp. 253–271). Boston: Allyn & Bacon.

Sullivan, H. S. (1953). *The interpersonal theory of psychiatry*. New York: Norton.

Taylor, E. (1999). An intellectual renaissance of humanistic psychology? *Journal of Humanistic Psychology, 39*(2), 7–25.

Teyber, E. (2000). *Interpersonal process in psychotherapy* (4th ed.). Belmont, CA: Wadsworth.

Todd, T. C., & Storm, C. L. (1997). *The complete systemic supervisor: Context, philosophy, and pragmatics.* Boston: Allyn & Bacon.

Truax, C. B., & Carkhuff, R. R. (1964). Significant developments in psychotherapy research. In L. E. Abt & B. F. Reiss (Eds.), *Progress in clinical psychology.* New York: Grune & Stratton.

Truax, C. B., & Carkhuff, R. R. (1966). *An introduction to counseling and psychotherapy training and practice.* Chicago: Aldine.

Valsiner, J., & van der Veer, R. (2000). *The social mind: Construction of the idea.* New York: Cambridge University Press.

von Bertalanffy, L. (1968). *General systems theory.* New York: Braziller.

Waterman, A. S. (1993). Two conceptions of happiness: Contrasts of personal expressiveness (eudaimonia) and hedonic enjoyment. *Journal of Personality and Social Psychology, 64,* 678–691.

Wessler, R. L., & Ellis, A. (1983). Supervision in counseling: Rational-emotive therapy. *Counseling Psychologist, 11*(1), 43–49.

White, M. B., & Russell, C. S. (1997). Examining the multifaceted notion of isomorphism in marriage and family therapy supervision: A quest for conceptual clarity. *Journal of Marital and Family Therapy, 23*(3), 315–333.

Wilber, K. (1981). *No boundary: Eastern and Western approaches to personal growth.* Boston: Shambhala.

Williams, A. (1995). *Visual and active supervision: Roles, focus, technique.* New York: Norton.

Wittgenstein, L. (1958). *Philosophical investigations* (3rd ed., G. E. M. Anscomb, Trans.). Englewood Cliffs, NJ: Prentice Hall. (Original work published 1945)

Wittgenstein, L. (1999). *Tractatus logico-philosophicus* (C. K. Ogden, Trans.). London: Routledge. (Original work published 1922)

Wolpe, J. (1972). Supervision transcripts: II—Problems of a novice. *Journal of Behavior Therapy and Experimental Psychiatry, 3,* 199–203.

Worthington, E. L., Jr. (1987). Changes in supervision as counselors and supervisors gain experience: A review. *Professional Psychology: Research and Practice, 18,* 189–208.

Yontef, G. (1997). Supervision from a Gestalt therapy perspective. In C. E. Watkins Jr. (Ed.), *Handbook of psychotherapy supervision* (pp. 147–163). New York: Wiley.

Zukav, G. (1990). *The seat of the soul.* New York: Simon & Schuster.

CHAPTER 27

Humanistic, Interpersonal, and Existential Psychotherapies: Review and Synthesis

SHARON DAVIS MASSEY

In a volume entitled *Interpersonal/Humanistic/Existential* in this *Comprehensive Handbook of Psychotherapy*, it is helpful to outline what constitutes interpersonal, humanistic, and existential work, to indicate what is unique in these theoretical approaches, and to note what they have in common that leads to their being grouped together in a single volume. Here we describe the contexts within which each emerged and developed, trace their relationships to present concerns in the field and make brief mention of forces, time frames, and dimensions that pertain to each, referring the reader to related chapters in this volume. We broach an analysis of what is presented in the volume and suggest that synthesis (the collaborative creation of a useful narrative honoring the variant frames of reference presented) should normatively follow analysis, whether this is undertaken in the therapy room or in explication of theories. Synthesis not only facilitates therapy, but also constitutes a more comprehensive and more satisfying approach to empirical work in the human sciences.

NATURAL AND UNNATURAL PSYCHOTHERAPIES

Robert Kegan (1982) intriguingly referred to all of the psychotherapies humans have invented as "unnatural" or "self-conscious" therapies; he perceived our everyday relationships with partners, friends, family, and coworkers, when these are going well, as constituting "natural" therapy. These relationships nurture and sustain our psychological well-being; it is when they break down that we contract with a psychotherapist for time-limited nurturance and assistance in reestablishing them.

Perhaps inadvertently, Kegan helped to differentiate the humanistic, existential, and interpersonal therapies from others. The traditional psychoanalytic and behavioral approaches embraced a deterministic view of human behavior. Psychoanalysts construed human activity as determined by inescapable internal drives, by conflicting aspects of the personality, and by overbearing parental behavior in one's childhood. Behaviorists eschewed such mentalistic explanations, substituting environmental responses to human behaviors as shaping human destiny. The humanistic psychologists perceived humans as instrumental in choosing, thus determining their own unique courses of development. Existentialists added to affirmation of the freedom of choice the responsibility to choose how one will engage life in the face of inevitable death, reminded us of the limiting nature of the contexts into which we are thrown, and viewed love as facilitating transcendence. The interpersonal therapists elaborated on how the human relationships in which we participate both create opportunities for and at times limit the unique choices we make. Each of the three theoretical frames accentuates the unique, human, self-regulated, other-influenced lives that we experience.

Humanistic Psychotherapy

The roots of humanistic psychotherapy are deep, and can be traced back in the psychotherapies as far as the work of Alfred Adler (1956, 1924/1963, 1964), who envisioned each person as creating his or her own personal style of life within the physiological and contextual constraints he or she uniquely encountered. Adler observed that each person develops a unique "fictional final goal" of overcoming a sense of inferiority imposed by nature on all humans, who are born initially with insufficient resources to meet their own needs. Being dependent on others for physical and psychological safety and nurturance, each person develops particular interpersonal and social strategies for relating to these needed others. The nature and choice of strategies are influenced by interaction with others, for example, by the style of parenting. Adler thus articulated themes of human creativity, choice, desire, and capacity to transcend former limits, and the relationship of feedback from others to one's unique sense of self. Rogers wrote (1939, pp. 184–220) about "relationship therapy," foreshadowing the client-centered therapy he subsequently developed. What is generally known as humanistic psychology emerged in the 1940s and flourished through the 1960s as a "third force," recognizing and addressing the "specifically human" capacities of freedom, choice, and creativity.

Barrett-Lennard (1998) described the context in which humanistic psychology, and particularly the work of Rogers, developed. The 1920s in the United States was a period of great social change, both challenging to the collective ethos and liberating from older mores. Women were now able to vote. Greater education was within reach of both men and women. The family was less the center of life and less determining of the outlook of young people. Revolutionary jazz music, made easily available through the gramophone and radio, modern dancing and alcoholic libations, available at "speakeasies" and movies, offered glamorous alternatives to everyday experience. Freudian psychology introduced new interpretations of personal behavior and family life. Einstein's theory of relativity seemed to inject a note of uncertainty in the sciences. Modern writers such as Faulkner and Hemingway challenged the reader to greater social consciousness.

The crash of the New York stock market in 1929 and the subsequent Great Depression of the 1930s left many without work and without alternative social supports. This challenged the ethos of hard work and "rugged individualism" that had been believed to be sufficient to meet one's needs. The belief that one should be able to take care of oneself, regardless of external circumstances, left many without both external and internal resources for coping with the effects of the Depression: "Brought up to believe that success and failure in life, sound and faulty judgment, moral virtue or vice, were matters of personal character and responsibility, the predominant response was to internalize what is seen in retrospect as systemic societal failure" (Barrett-Lennard, 1998, p. 22). Public assistance programs were virtually nonexistent. Public charity was insufficient.

Barrett-Lennard pointed to the inauguration and then repeal of Prohibition (federal laws against the production and sale of alcoholic beverages, widely flouted at all social levels) and rise in the membership of the White racial hate group, the Ku Klux Klan, as evidence of social neurosis during this period.

The shift from the very socially conservative policies of Presidents Coolidge (1923–1929) and Hoover (1929–1933) to the socially progressive era of Franklin Roosevelt's presidency (1933–1945) provided a unique opportunity for professionals in the social services. Roosevelt surrounded himself by experts in these and other fields and set about constructing a more socially compassionate government and society, more supportive of its more vulnerable and needy members, and more democratically involving and empowering of the ordinary citizen. The period of Roosevelt's New Deal and of U.S. involvement, under Roosevelt, in the Second World War (1941–1945) were guided by his pragmatic, humanistic, and democratic guiding principles of social concern, empowerment, respect for diverse individuals, and engagement both in domestic social policy and in foreign affairs. Not surprisingly, these principles appeared in the humanistic psychotherapies that evolved in the United States in the first half of the twentieth century.

Humanistic psychologists assumed an intrinsic desire to better oneself, the capacity to choose and to follow through on one's intent, and the benefit of interpersonal exchange in creating unique paths for developing individuals to move toward self-actualization (Goldstein, 1934; Maslow, 1943; Rogers, 1961a). Pioneers among humanistic theoreticians were James Bugental (1965), Charlotte Buhler (1962), Sydney Jourard (1964), Abraham Maslow (1962), Rollo May (1953/1967), Hobart Mowrer (1953), and Carl Rogers (1961a). Anthony Sutich and Maslow were instrumental in the creation of both the *Journal of Humanistic Psychology*, and the American Association for Humanistic Psychology in 1961. These and a historic conference at Old Saybrook, Connecticut, in November 1964 "officially enshrined [humanistic psychology] as an intellectual movement within academic psychology" (Taylor, 1999, p. 8). Influential social and personality psychologists such as Gordon Allport (1937, 1961, 1968), Gardner Murphy (1958), and Henry A. Murray (1938) aligned themselves with the humanistic movement. Division 32, the Division of Humanistic Psychology, was created in the American Psychological Association and its journal, *The Humanistic Psychologist*, was established.

Humanistic psychotherapists directed attention away from concern for understanding historic causes of discomfort, as in psychoanalysis, and from behavioral modification of dysfunctional response patterns. They emphasized instead the uniqueness of individuals who present themselves for therapy, their capacities to choose and direct the course of therapy and of their own development, and the use of therapy to facilitate a natural human motivation toward self-actualization. Although in current texts for training counselors the humanistic therapies may be represented only by Rogers's client-centered approach, others also developed humanistic approaches. (The significant work of James Bugental is represented in this volume: Bracke & Bugental, Chap. 11.)

Although academic humanistic psychology was vigorous through the 1960s, it is judged to have lost its influence since the 1970s, when, according to Taylor (1999), it "became engulfed in the human potential movement around 1969" (p. 9) and fragmented. Adherents to the humanistic movement became "identified with Gestalt therapy, encounter group techniques, and the various body-work regimes" (p. 9). The theorists associated with the human potential movement were generally pragmatic and highly interested in helping individuals pursue self-actualization in humanistically based therapies involving near-natural, though contractual, interpersonal relationships. They were, however, more interested in the successful application of their theories than in rigorous research. Thus, they lost, or did not establish, the support of university-based programs.

Rogers, whose client-centered work is viewed as foundational to the field of counseling psychology, did pursue with his colleagues a rigorous program of research (Barrett-Lennard, 1998). Rogers (1942) was the first to publish an empirical study of psychotherapy; he continued a program of research over the course of his career, and inspired colleagues to do the same. Kurt Lewin's early work in human relations training, which led to the development of t-groups and sensitivity training, was also research-based (Bradford, Gibb, & Benne, 1964).

A U.S. populace, quite divided about issues broached in the 1960s and ambivalent about continuing to address them directly, retreated in the 1970s into a more introverted stance, withdrawing attention from the political arena. There was a collective turn toward the meditative and the spiritual, at best, or alternatively, toward self-interest. Some turned to religious cults. In the humanistic camp in psychology, some turned to the study of transpersonal and paranormal events, broadening interest in human consciousness, a theme introduced to psychology in the United States by its founder, William James (Taylor, 1999). The sense of a need to rely on oneself and distrust of others (quite unlike the sense of shared mission and felt need to change social structures prevalent among activists in the 1960s) seemed to pervade the 1980s. This was paired with the resurgence of a particularly U.S. brand of "rugged individualism" combined with renewed emphasis on the ethic of competition. The attempt to be "number one" in personal affairs, at the workplace, and equally in academia no doubt has also influenced the fate of the humanistic and interpersonal-experiential psychotherapies. A shift of dominance from humanistic to cognitive therapies (which examine and influence internal perceptions) and behavioral therapies (which promise to most quickly get to the "bottom line" of behavioral results) emerged and has endured into the present. There has also been continuing interest in those of the neo-Freudian and neo-Adlerian therapies that have come to be known as "interpersonal" therapies. And interpersonal themes are currently being introduced as "new" in some of the oldest psychotherapies (i.e., psychoanalytic). The behavioral and cognitive therapies, not coincidentally, are the two most closely attuned to the positivistic paradigm from which research-based results are sought. Although research-based evidence has been established for the efficacy of the humanistic approach, humanistic psychologists are also in the forefront (W. James, 1897; Martinez, 1997; Polanyi, 1945, 1962; Rogers, 1955, 1961a, 1961b, 1964; Taylor, 1999; Wilber,1981) of efforts to broaden and enhance the paradigms of humanistic psychology and empirical science.

The humanistic therapist, particularly as defined by Rogers (1961a) and researched by Carkhuff and Berenson (1967) and others (Barrett-Lennard, 1998), is expected to exhibit empathy for the client, to hold all persons (if not their behaviors) in positive regard, to be genuine in the therapeutic relationship, and to communicate clearly, reflecting back what is heard in the client's self-initiated explorations. These conditions are thought to facilitate all helping relationships, and thus are seen as generic to natural, supportive relationships. In this sense, the humanists were first to apply what is most natural to the practice of "unnatural therapy." Today, these natural elements, established through research and practice in the humanistic therapies, have been incorporated into the positive practice of most of the "unnatural" psychotherapies (Massey & Combs, Chap. 26).

THE HUMAN POTENTIAL MOVEMENT AND THE GROWTH THERAPIES

Working in the heady, if somewhat turbulent, 1960s and in a U.S. society struggling with issues of racial and gender inequity and embroiled in a war oversees that many perceived to be imperialistic and culturally intrusive, few in the humanistic movement applied their work directly to the amelioration of human problems at the societal level. Allport (1954), whose career in personality and social psychology was established well before the advent of the humanistic movement and who later became identified with it, wrote a volume exploring the effects of prejudice in a racially divided society. Many, however, sympathetic with the plight of minorities (Blacks, women, young men who opposed being required to participate in a war they found offensive to their moral sensibilities, and other culturally oppressed groups), aligned themselves ideologically with the countercultural movement toward expanding individual consciousness and increasing freedom from cultural oppression. During the 1960s, a young U.S. president, John F. Kennedy (1961–1963), inspired many to active expression of social interest, such as participation in the Peace Corps, in which volunteers assisted in public projects oversees. Dr. Martin Luther King Jr. led a powerful and partially transforming civil rights movement. Dr. King, President Kennedy, and his brother, Robert Kennedy, all of whom were progressive human rights leaders, were assassinated: John Kennedy in 1963, Dr. King and Robert Kennedy in 1968. During the administration of President Lyndon B. Johnson (1963–1969), increasing unrest about U.S. participation in military action in Vietnam led to civilian protests and the refusal of significant numbers of young men to submit to military service in what had come to be known as the Vietnam War. The protest was sufficiently strong that Johnson, who had contributed significantly to the improvement of civil rights related to racial issues and declared a "war on poverty," declined to run in 1968 for a second term. His successor, President Richard Nixon (1969–1974), promised in the campaign that he had a secret plan to end the war, which had never been formally declared as such by the U.S. Congress. Instead, his policies actually escalated it. The eventual end of the war in Nixon's second term was followed by the return home of soldiers who had fought in the unpopular military action and their ambivalent acceptance by a populace divided over U.S. participation in it. The broken promise to end the war earlier, an increase in bombing of Cambodia, a presidential pullback on commitment to civil rights, and the Watergate debacle, motivated by self-interest and the absence of a clear vision of the common good, generated disillusionment. Thus ended a period of social ferment. A contrasting era of societal and personal introversion and self-focus followed, isomorphic to the conservative stance and self-absorption of the president. Yet human nature yields mixed results: Nixon also opened diplomatic relations with China.

A trend toward focus on the self continued into the 1980s with what has been called the "me" generation. The tendency toward rugged individualism hampers social support for broader financing of medical and mental health care; thus, this country has the lowest levels of federal support for health care among the industrialized nations.

Some theorists, such as Eric Berne (1961, 1963/1979), Mary and Robert Goulding (R. Goulding & Goulding, 1978; M. Goulding & Goulding, 1979), Fritz Perls (1969, Perls, Hefferline, & Goodman, 1951), and Virginia Satir (1972), loosely identified with the humanistic psychotherapies, "rolled up their sleeves" during the earlier period of social activism and set to work developing therapies designed to increase individuals' consciousness of ineffective or harmful interpersonal patterns of relating. They sought to provide an experiential base of present ("here and now") interpersonal experience in the therapeutic setting on which to choose to change. J. L. Moreno's (1945, 1946) therapeutic approach, psychodrama, developed in the 1940s, enjoyed renewed popularity during this period, and

Rogers developed a large-group sensitivity training program in La Jolla, California.

Berne's (1961, 1963/1979) transactional analysis (TA) is exemplary of the therapies associated with the human-potential movement. Berne was trained in classical psychoanalysis, one of his analysts being Erik Erikson. His observations of the various shifts of state of his own analysands during a therapy hour, and finding support for this in the work of Federn, and perhaps his impatience with the lengthy process of traditional psychotherapy led Berne to the formulation of his own, highly pragmatic approach. Like Adler, Berne wanted to create a psychotherapy that the common person could understand and apply, for which academicians punished them both, finding them too "popular." Eschewing Freud's use of Latinized terms (other than "ego," used in naming "ego states," which he might, alternatively, have called states of the self), Berne sought to describe how humans in the course of development internalize aspects of parents and other significant persons.

Like the Russian developmentalist Lev Vygotsky (1962), Berne noted that a significant amount of what comes to reside in the mental process of individuals was first present in others around them (e.g., in the grown-ups who cared for them). In describing the process of development, Berne noted that the child first takes in the affective overtones of the caring relationship and internalizes the negative and positive assessments of self as influenced by others. Later, as a youngster, one learns how to function effectively in the society, learning the needed skills. Certainly, Vygotsky would agree with Berne and his early mentor, Erikson, in this regard. From adolescence on, one begins to internalize the values of one's parents and other authorities within one's culture. Berne noted that a person's nonreflective behaviors and explanations of them to self and others tended to follow scripts and at times related to injunctions learned early in life. He was a keen observer of how each of us uses the intuitive, practical/cognitive, and evaluational skills first exercised and internalized in the family of origin and was able to diagram interpersonal transactions in a manner that clarified their useful and dysfunctional interpersonal patterns. Transactional analysis provides a means of tracing and making visible for client and therapist how patterns of behavior have been passed down over several generations of family life. While undergoing a period of relative quiescence in the Unites States, where it originated, transactional analysis has a strong, internationally created and maintained training program recognized for certification at present by the national boards of several nations. There are an increasing number of practitioners in Europe, Asia, Australia/New Zealand, and Latin America. Whereas early advocates paid little attention to empirical research, some training programs outside the United States are now linking with universities.

The various growth therapies made use of therapeutic interpersonal experience to facilitate the personal growth of individuals in a society experienced as in need of and undergoing rapid change. The 1960s in the United States were a period of high drama, positive social ferment, and, at times, personal excess. Some positive results were achieved in the area of civil rights for African Americans and equal rights for women. U.S. participation in the Vietnam conflict was eventually ended, and "draft dodgers," who fled to Canada to avoid military conscription, were given amnesty. Yet, an era also marked by increased experimentation with drugs, greater expression of sexual freedom, and the flight of numerous young people from home to experience the "hippie" lifestyle left many in the mainstream culture with a sense of disquiet and, at times, of antipathy with regard to the period. Perhaps a sense of embarrassment regarding the excesses of the era or self-reproach for failure to achieve the high goals of social change, together with a bit of envy in appraisals of the times, has also been applied to the less-than-enthusiastic current appraisals of the humanistic psychotherapies that segued into a number of experiential interpersonal approaches uniquely suited to the time and still viable today. Or perhaps their strong emphasis on practice and lesser initial interest in establishing a research base was too alienating to academicians working in a period when rigorous positivistic empirical work was mandatory.

Among the therapies identified with the human potential movement and represented in this volume are psychodrama (Jacobs, Chap. 21), transactional analysis (R. F. Massey, Hewitt, & Moiso, Chap. 22), redecision therapy, Gestalt therapy, and Satir's work, later known as family reconstruction therapy (Joines, Chap. 18), and the various bodywork therapies (Cornell, Chap. 23).

THE INTERPERSONAL PSYCHOTHERAPIES

Some who dismiss the interpersonal-experiential therapies associated with the human potential movement identify with an interpersonal approach they see as new. The interpersonal approach is increasingly used in psychotherapies ranging from the traditional psychoanalytic through object-relational and self psychologies. It holds firm in the neo-Freudian and neo-Adlerian psychotherapies elaborated by Anna Freud (1965, 1936/1966), Erik Erikson (1950/1963, 1968), Erich Fromm (1941, 1964), Karen Horney (1939/1966), R. D. Laing (1969, 1960/1978), and H. S. Sullivan (1940/1953a, 1953b) where interpersonal focus in psychotherapy originated.

Once again we can refer to the work of Adler (1924/1963) as seminal. In interviewing children in front of their teachers and parents, Adler pointed to the effects of interactions with siblings, teachers, and parents on the behavior of children. He was thus capturing in vivo the effects of interpersonal experience and modifying these in the present, a hallmark of the later therapies that, in retrospect, have been labeled "interpersonal." The work of Sullivan (1940/1953a, 1953b), however, is often taken as foundational and most exemplary of this group. Sullivan's unit of focus was the person in relationship. Even the satisfaction of basic needs requires an interpersonal situation in which the other may function as provider. Sullivan was also aware of the indissoluble unity of the person and his or her environmental context. In a passage that seems to anticipate Prigogine's (1973) later formulation of open systems, Sullivan (1940/1953a) noted, "The environment flows through the living cell, becoming its very life in the process, and the cell flows and grows through the environment, establishing in the process its particular career-line as an organism" (p. 31). Sullivan was also interested in human development and noted, in particular, the importance of same-sex chums in childhood in forging a mature sense of self. The development of an interpersonal relationship in which the other becomes as important to self as oneself, or interpersonal intimacy, he felt, was foundational to full maturation. Persons exhibiting psychopathology were not, he believed, different in kind from persons who are considered emotionally healthy; the difference was in degree, not kind.

Parataxic communication, or communication that holds primarily private meanings for the person communicating, is an issue that can be addressed in therapy. If the client's anxiety can be sufficiently lowered, parataxic communication can be pointed out and addressed. Sullivan was particularly known for his ability to establish a positive working alliance, even with difficult clients. He was successful in working with schizophrenic patients, whom he treated with respect, granting them privacy in the clinic where he worked and helping them to communicate more clearly. Establishment and use of a positive therapeutic alliance is a hallmark of the interpersonal therapies.

The interpersonal therapists developed within the mainstream of psychoanalytic psychotherapy. Taking the work of Sigmund Freud as having established the field, they saw themselves as expanding his work. The interpersonal therapies represent a shift of focus from the intrapersonal (how past experience shapes present individual behavior) to the interpersonal (how interpersonal experience in the present both shapes one's options and invites creative, present-oriented response).

All psychotherapies are interpersonal, with the possible exception of bibliotherapy or a computer-assisted format, in the sense that they take place through the interaction of therapist and client. The humanistic and existential therapies, however, have historically focused on revising what transpired *within* the individual (i.e., modifying self-concept, one's idea of the other, the personal meaning of certain transactions, or examining an individual's values and life plans). The interpersonal therapies shifted the therapeutic focus to what transpires *between* individuals. Thus, the *process* of therapy, rather than its *content,* came to be seen as most relevant to creating and assessing change. Interpersonal psychotherapy is seen as having been effective, and thus no longer needed, when client-therapist and client-other transactions achieve the status of natural, authentic, functional, everyday discourse.

THE EXISTENTIAL PSYCHOTHERAPIES

Mass traumas such as the Holocaust and the bombing of civilians in the cities of Nagasaki and Hiroshima during World War II, which followed closely on the heels of another brutalizing World War, highlighted questions of personal responsibility for one's behavior and of the meaning of life in the face of ultimate death. Reaction to the horrors of the two world wars spurred interest among the general populace in the United States, Europe, and elsewhere in existential ideas that had been germinating in several places in Europe for quite some time. Gordon Allport (1955) and Rollo May, Ernest Angel, and Henri Ellenberger (1958) were the first to introduce existential and phenomenological psychology to professionals in the United States. May et al. cited "Eugene Minkowsky in Paris, Erwin Strauss in Germany and now in this country, V. E. von Gebsattel in Germany ... Ludwig Binswanger, A. Storch, M. Boss, G. Bally, Roland Kuhn in Switzerland, J. H. Van Den Berg and F. J. Buytendijk in Holland" (p. 4) as psychiatrists and psychologists having independently developed phenomenological and existential approaches to psychotherapy, largely without knowledge of each others' work. This reflected, May believed, a general response to a deep and common need.

If the events of the wars led to interest of the general populace in existential ideas, May and his coauthors made clear that the fragmentation of European culture and the internalization of that in individuals prior to either of the wars stirred the early existential writers. Martin Heidigger (1927/1962) is generally credited with inspiring the work of the existential psychologists, particularly Binswanger (1967) and Boss (1957). May et al. (1958), however, cited Kierkegaard, who wrote of existential angst, "the sickness unto death," the need for self-consciousness, the presence of inner conflict, loss of self, and psychosomatic issues 50 years before Freud developed psychoanalysis; Nietzsche, who wrote descriptively of anxiety and its repression and consequent symptom-formation 10 years ahead of Sigmund Freud; and Freud himself. They believed each identified well ahead of the two wars the "anxiety, despair, fragmentalized personality, and the symptoms of these" (p. 33) that individuals in Europe were experiencing then. This was attributable to the fragmentation of the culture that, in turn, resulted in internalized fragmentation of personalities. A hyper-rationalism, driven by the attempt, in the era of industrialization, to make oneself machine-like, and the consequent suppression of emotion seems to have been the cause of this cultural and personal fragmentation. May et al.

(1958) pointed to psychoanalysis and existential analysis as arising from the same need to address these conditions.

The existential psychotherapies developed in the European tradition of grounding psychological practice in carefully reasoned theory based on a particular philosophy. May et al. (1958) referenced Jean-Paul Sartre's "phenomenological descriptions of psychological processes" (1936) and the work of "Karl Jaspers of Germany, Gabriel Marcel in France, Nicolas Berdyaev, originally Russian but until his recent death a resident of Paris, and Ortega Gassett and Unamuno in Spain" (p. 16) as describing the existential viewpoint. They also mentioned the existential theologian Paul Tillich and referenced examples in modern literature—*The Stranger* and *The Plague* by Albert Camus; the novels of Kafka—and the art of Van Gogh, Cezanne, and Picasso as portraying the existential anguish the various psychotherapies were developed to address.

Influenced by the philosophies of Heidigger (1927/1962) and Buber (1927/1970), Binswanger (1967) and Boss (1957) of Switzerland developed existential psychotherapies that are among those known in the United States because of their translation and introduction by May et al. (1958). Laing (1969, 1960/1978) of Scotland, Viktor Frankl (1946/1965, 1946/1967) of Austria, and Maslow (1962) and May (1953/1967), both from the United States, also figured among the existential theorists.

The existentialists moved beyond noting the freedom to choose one's own way, and highlighted the necessity of doing so. Life, they asserted, has no meaning other than that which we give it. Within the very real limits of the specific (physiological, psychological, and sociological) contexts into which we are thrown at birth, each of us must decide how to responsibly engage life in the ultimate face of death to escape a paralyzing sense of meaninglessness. Thus, in existential therapy, values, personal stance, and manner of engagement with the world are challenged. In accord with Adler's (1924/1963) suggestion that context (birth order, the family constellation, gender, one's biological capacity, one's specific ecological niche, and the historic period) partly determines life choices, the existentialists used this concept as the ground against which they highlighted freedom and responsibility within one's context, thus pinpointing and strongly underscoring these humanistic concerns.

In his existential logotherapy, Frankl (1969) highlighted what he termed "the will to meaning," that is, the freedom to choose the meaning one will assign to even the most unpleasant and least controllable of situations. He developed logotherapy in relation to his own experience in Nazi concentration camps. Binswanger (1967) added to Heidigger's (1927/1962) theme of the extreme loneliness of needing to define for oneself the human capacity, in fact necessity, for love in interpersonal relationship with another for whom one cares as deeply as one does for self. Relating intimately to another is, according to Binswanger, a means of defining both self and other in a relational unity of commitment. This concept was partly inspired by reading Buber (1927/1970). Frankl has noted that human transcendence is facilitated by having a meaningful task to accomplish or someone to love; both lead us beyond self-concern. Because of his emphasis on interpersonal relationship and intimacy, Binswanger's writings have been compared with those of Sullivan (Frie, 2000).

In the present volume, Farber (Chap. 13) applies existential psychotherapy to work with persons affected by HIV/AIDS, Kalayjian (Chap. 24) applies existential concepts to working with individuals, families, and groups who are victims of mass trauma, and Lukas and Hirsch (Chap. 14) apply the same to work with a broad array of adults.

Perhaps it is fair to say, using Kegan's (1982) terms, that the humanistic, interpersonal, and existential approaches are the most natural of the unnatural therapies, for they seem most determined to replicate in the therapy, as a part of the healing process, the supportive aspects of normative caring relationships that constitute the "glue" that holds together friendship, love, the workplace—in short, civil society.

ANALYSIS, COMPARISON OF THEORIES, AND SYNTHESIS

Let us now turn to an exploration of forces time frames, descriptive dimensions, and alternative empirical and cultural frames that may be helpful in comparing and contrasting the psychotherapies just explored and others. These constructs may facilitate analysis, which is helpful in sorting and grouping things conceptually. As we find various therapies alternatively falling into one and then another group, we may begin to see various possibilities for synthesis.

FIVE FORCES IN PSYCHOLOGY

Maslow (1962) referred to the humanistic, existential, and phenomenological approaches as the "third force" in psychology. He was contrasting this group of theoreticians and practitioners to the first force of psychoanalysis and the second force of behaviorism and social learning. At that time, there was an emphasis on individuals who could self-actualize with satisfying human relations resulting as a by-product of encounter between the proactive, choosing persons. Subsequently, the family therapies emerged. Many of the leaders of systems therapy emphasized the structures of families and of societies. This more sociological orientation led to a fourth force stressing context. Recently, awareness of the need to recognize, assess, and treat both the self and structural dimensions of interconnected persons has increased. This has given rise to a fifth force: clinicians with an integrative perspective who perceive both personal experiences and contextual dynamics as highly relevant and necessary to human development, as implicated in impediments to personal and interpersonal growth, and as potential resources for healing (R. F. Massey, 1988). The psychotherapies in this volume generally fall in the third, fourth, and fifth forces.

TIME FRAMES: PAST, PRESENT, AND FUTURE FOCUS

The psychoanalytic theories emphasized understanding how the past has shaped the present, with the assumption that understanding can lead to change. The humanistic, existential, and interpersonal therapies placed more emphasis on one's ability to create and foster satisfying relationships in the present, so that present and future interactions can be more satisfying, while acknowledging, but not highlighting, that dysfunctional interpersonal patterns may have been learned or shaped in the past.

THE DIMENSIONS OF PSYCHOTHERAPY: BREADTH, HEIGHT, AND DEPTH

Interpersonal therapists somewhat broaden the frame of focus from what transpires within the individual (in the traditional psychoanalytic, cognitive, humanistic, and existential approaches) to what transpires regularly between persons. Assessment, therapeutic focus, and intervention are framed with the dyad in view, rather than the individual. A difference between the interpersonal and the other psychotherapies (humanistic and existential) in this volume is a difference in their traditional breadth of therapeutic lens, with the interpersonal therapies focusing on the relationship between dyads. Writers who have used an interpersonal focus in this volume are Gil (Chap. 3), Thomas (Chap. 4), Palmer et al. (Chap. 5), Simmon and Berg (Chap. 6), Sherman and Nwaorgu (Chap. 8), Jordan (Chap. 10), Bracke and Bugental (Chap. 11), Aponte (Chap. 12), Jacobs (Chap. 21), Massey,

Hewitt, and Moiso (Chap. 22), and Cornell (Chap. 23).

The systemic psychotherapies use an array of focal lens, focusing alternatively on individuals, couples, sibling subgroups, and entire families. Some may also include external support persons (a social worker, parole officer, priest, minister, rabbi, or other religious representative). Several systemic psychotherapies are represented in this volume: Jones and Lindblad-Goldberg (Chap. 1), Inman, Rawls, Meza, and Brown (Chap. 7), Wetzel and Winawer (Chap. 9), Andolfi (Chap. 15), Hernández and Roberts (Chap. 17), Ducommun-Nagy (Chap. 19), R. F. Massey (Chap. 20), and S. D. Massey and Combs (Chap. 26). Dunn (Chap. 16) and Joines (Chap. 18) utilize both an interpersonal and a systemic lens. Several of these authors, as well as Chao (Chap. 2) and Kalayjian (Chap. 24), also utilize a broader, cultural lens.

A unique aspect of the existential approach is the emphasis on the therapist's challenging of clients to define and embrace a unique value system and to apply it. This represents variance in a hierarchy of differential emphasis on the physiological, psychological, sociocultural, and spiritual dimensions of human existence, with existentialism ranking most high in the last. One might construe this as a difference in "height" on such a hierarchy. Authors who have written from an existential frame of reference in this volume are Farber (Chap. 13), Lukas and Hirsch (Chap. 14), Ducommun-Nagy (Chap. 19), and Kalayjian (Chap. 24). Although not formulated from a specifically existential perspective, the chapter on ethics (Peterson & Haug, Chap. 25) also targets the spiritual (value-oriented) dimension of human existence. Wetzel and Winawer (Chap. 9), Kalayjian (Chap. 24), Ducommun-Nagy (Chap. 19), R. F. Massey (Chap. 20), and S. D. Massey and L. Combs (Chap. 26) use models that are inclusive of each of these four dimensions.

Psychoanalytic therapies seek to plumb the depths of the individual psyche by examining the effects of past relationships on present functioning. This term is usually reserved for the psychotherapies of Freud, Adler, and Jung and those most closely related to them. Adlerian work, which may also be classified fairly as interpersonal, is represented by Sherman and Nwaorgu (Chap. 8). One also can count the intergenerational systems therapies that look at intergenerational transmission of family problems as depth work; these are represented by Ducommun-Nagy (Chap. 19).

Persons who identify as psychoanalytic, cognitive-behavioral, and self psychologists may elect to do interpersonal or systemic work (S. D. Massey & Combs, Chap. 26). The more persons present and interacting in the therapy, the more "natural" or humanistic and interpersonal the therapy must be; that is, the more attention must be paid to interpersonal process and to working in relation to the natural support systems. Also, the more persons in the therapy, the more sensitive the therapist must be to differential values and contexts. In family, group, and systems therapy, we must challenge ourselves and others to define and work from our own committed existential stances, from our own acknowledged, unique, as well as shared, contexts.

OLD AND NEW EMPIRICAL FRAMES:
APPRECIATING ANALYSIS, LEARNING SYNTHESIS

Today, we must adapt to the realities of daily confrontation—via television, the Internet, and other media—with large and diverse chunks of information, of constant exposure to one another's cultures and customs, of rapid social change related to technological development and the accelerating pace at which knowledge is being transmitted. Such realities create the need for greater cognitive flexibility and the capacity to readily synthesize varying sources of information into a coherent and useful whole. The capacity to synthesize information from divergent sources and viewpoints enhances communication between and among persons. Comfortably interfacing with a diversity of persons, information, and viewpoints is rapidly becoming a basic and essential skill for sustaining a positive sense of self, other, and one's everyday world.

Miguel Martinez (1997) critiqued the Western, Lockean metaphor of the human mind as a *camera oscura*, passively recording what it is focused on. In this metaphor, separate status is presumed for objects in the material world, the mind that is recording them, and transactions between the two. Constancy is a further presumption in the normative nature of each of these. The mind is initially uninformed but inquisitive, unformed but receptive to sensory data, capable of receiving, storing, and processing information that enters through the sensory receptors of the observer as "objective" data regarding a physical or intellectual "object." This has been the dominant metaphor for scientific knowledge in the Western world. Knowledge comes directly from the object to the human mind, unaltered by intervening factors (such as sensory receptor, chemical and neurological transmission of data, past experience, or learning in the person who receives this knowledge). Such a cosmological and epistemological stance, paired with a Newtonian causal approach to the material world, leads to confidence in theoretical development, research design, and measurement.

To call attention to limitations of an epistemology constrained by these assumptions, Martínez (1997) proposed a new metaphor, that of a set of television cameras. Located at several vantage points offstage, the cameras are controlled by humans who collaboratively select and alternately focus on an ongoing drama from a variety of angles, thus constructing the presentation made to the larger audience, away from the theater, of what is being played out onstage.

The experience of the television audience (seeing the presentation from many coordinated, complementary angles) contrasts with that of an individual in the theater audience, who must view the unfolding drama from only one position. These two images aptly depict contrasting paradigms of scientific rationality: the traditional approach, based on logical positivism, and an emergent paradigm consistent with aspects of postpositivism, constructivism, and our increasing experience of diversity in the way we see, interpret, and value shared information and experiences. In the latter image, the persons minding the cameras are credited for selecting the images and angles, depths, and breadths of view. Their selections, of course, are for the most part conventional and within the audience's expectations. Each new performance is portrayed within the linguistic and artistic conventions of the larger culture in which it is presented, with sufficient novelty to hold interest, make this production unique, and occasionally to convey a new idea.

What is needed and may be emerging is a more elaborated paradigm for scientific knowledge (Martínez, 1997). We need to more adequately capture the multifaceted, contextual, and developmental aspects of reality as humans individually and collectively experience it. In the present world, terms like "multinational," "multicultural," "multidimensional," and "multilateral" apply to the daily lived reality of many of us. "Change," "advancement," "growth," and "progress" are happening so quickly that at times, they overwhelm the pleasure that comes with novelty or the thrill of achievement and become associated, instead, with a sense of loss. We need a rationality, a science, and related therapies that address the multidetermination of human behavior and of events within their multiple contexts. And we need to be aware of the time-sensitive, developmental nature of behaviors and contexts and of anything we may designate as an observable, researchable variable. Neither humans nor our world is standing still. For most of us, the separation of persons from contexts is no longer a workable frame of reference in our everyday interchanges with one another.

Just as the natural sciences have discovered the inseparable nature of particles, which seem always to "dance" together (Capra, 1975; Heisenberg, 1958), and the constant exchange of open systems with their surroundings (Prigogine, 1973), so, too, in the psychotherapies we find increasing need to focus on the multiplicity of interactive points of view regarding most human events and the multidetermination of human behavior. When Wittgenstein deconstructed his own positivistic first philosophy, which informs our dominant idea of what is "scientific" knowledge (Martínez, 1997), and formulated a post-positive philosophy with which he was more comfortable, the shift was basically away from analysis to synthesis. From construing our environmental surround as composed of separate entities, which can be collected into aggregates that equaled the sum of the separate parts, he moved to recognition that, as humans, we live within interlocking systems. We have created these systems to sustain ourselves, and we, in turn, must maintain them so that they will do so. No such system can be reduced to its parts. To separate the pieces is to destroy the capacity of the system to sustain the individual members.

The studio audience in Martínez's metaphor, though "privileged" to see the drama live, must view its unfolding from one vantage point. Their counterparts in the television audience are exposed through alternative frames to multiple viewpoints. The same event viewed through the lens of opposing cameras is easily understood to be two facets of the same developing phenomenon. The viewer is aware that there are others simultaneously developing, and that all provide complementary, interrelated information. The very movement from one vantage point to another reminds that what one sees depends on the vantage point of the viewer and the instrumentation used. If we vary Martínez's metaphor slightly, and make the television production a DVD movie, we add to multiplicity of points of view the further dimension of metasubjectivity (R. F. Massey, 1972); of looking at how the movie was crafted, decisions made, what might have been or yet could be. And we can move easily from one frame of reference to another. The application of this level of analysis, this awareness and honesty in looking at how theoretical frames, personal experience and choice, the popularity of certain ideas in the current intellectual discourse (Valsiner & van der Veer, 2000), other contextual factors, and the instrumentation through which we observe the "results" of our psychotherapeutic "experiments" would greatly improve our conversations about theory and therapy. When in our scientific discourse we look for multiple complementary viewpoints and seek to find what is connected or interrelated, even in points of view that appear at first opposing, we will find that our individual and collective cognitive capacity, and likely the emotional flexibility that enhances it, will be considerably improved. What we consider as full "discovery" of approaches to an issue and adequate interpretation clearly will be more adequate, more useful. We must be more aware of contextual issues, the interrelationships among variables and viewpoints and of what might be enhanced and what thrown out of focus in a particular frame of reference. And the recognition of development—that persons, variables, and contexts change over time—will of necessity be included. From subatomic particles or waves to interpersonal systems, languages and cultures, ecosystems, weather patterns, and the multitudinous interrelationships among these, nothing in nature stands still. As scientists and as practitioners, we are in need of theories built to account for development and that themselves develop over time, and of measures that "walk along" beside the developing persons and variables they are intended to capture. Operational definitions of variables need to reflect the reality that no humanly significant variable is devoid of significant interrelationships with many others.

The experiences of our studio and television audiences/DVD viewers are not unlike the contrast between the traditional Western theoretician and the postmodern theorist in scientific work. The task of the traditional scientist has been to develop and defend a theoretical frame, linked to previous work by others, yet that appears in some significant way superior to and competitive with alternative explanations. This is based on a view of the material world as more trustworthy than that of ideas, of entities in the world as each clearly separable from the other and that counts humans among those entities and their behaviors as capable of being described within such a framework. Experiments designed to hold other variables constant and to manipulate one or two can thus "prove" whether the ones manipulated are or are not causal. Traditional, positivistic science is basically analytical work.

The subject-verb-object structure of the Indo-European languages has contributed to a linear idea of causality. In the United States, a society based on "rugged individualism," an individual is radically held responsible for his or her "successes" or "failures," and the culture prizes competition and winning. In this setting, the idea of the scientist as an individual in competition with others who are "racing" to be the first to discover what "really" is true about a particular aspect of reality becomes understandable. Thus, the unit of analysis in psychology, the study of human behavior, has been taken to be the behaviors of individuals.

In a postmodern cosmology, the universe may be seen as comprised of myriad interlocking, open, developing systems, each composed of inseparable parts in constant interaction with one another and with the surrounding context, which itself is in constant flux. Ken Wilber (1981) reminded us that the universe is whole: Any perceived dividing lines or boundaries are mental creations, elaborated (as are the lines of longitude and latitude on a globe) to assist in navigation. State or national boundaries and highways on a map facilitate travel. Theoretical constructs enable theory development and differentiation among theories. Names distinguish groups of persons who find they share beliefs and values, customs and traditions. Boundaries are human creations; no bird stops to get a passport when flying from Cairo to Istanbul, nor does the vegetation change radically along the political boundary between two states or nations. Boundaries, created for socially constructive purposes, conversely are where "border wars" break out, whether sociopolitical wars or theoretical disputes. The traditional Western scientist, ensconced in a preferred theoretical frame, and encouraged by the very nature of scientific discipline at the time to seek the material truth in a narrow discipline, often saw a theory as *truth*. We may now concede it was exactly that, but *as defined within the researcher's or theoretician's frame of reference*. At the same time, scientists felt compelled to oppose those who, coming from other, perhaps equally valid frames, claimed an alternative truth.

In a postmodern world, only the naïve can maintain that any one perspective on reality contains the whole of truth. In the previous century, the juxtaposition of what seemed opposing and irreconcilable theoretical scientific frames, (i.e., psychoanalytic psychotherapy versus a behavioral approach, behavioral versus cognitive psychotherapy, or all of these versus the humanistic) constantly seemed to raise the issue of which *one* was right. The thought that several or all could be correct, or that the various viewpoints might be interrelated was still, for most persons, quite literally unthinkable.

The author's grandfather, born in the United States in the late 1800s, probably never played a game of baseball. He may have, on occasion, hit a ball with a stick in the poor, rural county in which he was raised. Children having sufficient size and energy for such foolishness were old enough to be employed, perhaps by a neighbor who needed help with the harvest. The author's father played a few "pickup" games with boys in his neighborhood when his parents moved into town so he could attend school. There was usually at least one boy whose family owned a bat; mitts were not necessary. Her brother's generation played on Little League and Pony League teams organized by local merchants and civic organizations. Her son sat for hours with his videogame that allowed him to "buy and sell" baseball players, create teams and leagues, and play these against each other. This was on afternoons when he was not pitting armies from different historical periods against one another in another videogame or, in still another, acting as mayor of a hypothetical city, allocating assets for its many needs, and checking the positive (more public services) and negative (more smog or pollution) effects of each move. His great-grandfather not only did not, but *could not* do this.

We not only think differently about a number of experiences because the times and our world have changed: We are, in fact, *able* to think differently. Our sons and daughters may not have the cognitive difficulties we experience in understanding that multiple viewpoints, each legitimate, can be simultaneously valid, and that rather than being inevitably opposing, they are likely complementary. Where they are not, the understanding of their difference may lie in the varying personal experiences of those holding the views. Each point of view is focused on a piece of the complete picture of human experience, and each is differentially framed by the standpoint (life experience to date) of the viewer. And the tableau itself, like the drama in Martínez's metaphor and the beholder's life, is unfolding.

BRIDGING CULTURES: EASTERN AND
WESTERN FRAMES OF REFERENCE

The intrapersonal, interpersonal, systemic (sociocultural), and spiritual levels of focus may be framed as a developmental continuum of awareness, in the Western psychological tradition, moving from initial focus on what is internal to oneself, to a greater interest in what makes for positive interpersonal relating, to interest in how persons and human systems can successfully nurture and sustain one another. There is growing curiosity and increasing research about the effects of still larger, external systems: cultural (Chao, Chap. 2; Inman, Rawls, Meza, & Brown, Chap. 7; Wetzel & Winawer, Chap. 9; Hernández & Roberts, Chap. 17; Ducommun-Nagy, Chap. 19; R. F. Massey, Chap. 20; S. D. Massey & Combs, Chap. 26), and the interface of these with biological and spiritual factors, particularly as witnessed in natural and human-made disasters (Kalayjian, Chap. 24).

There is perennial interest in spirituality and religion, even in periods when psychoanalysis and behaviorism, which attempted to define psychology as separate from spiritual concerns, were dominant (Allport, 1950; Frankl, 1977; Fromm, 1950/1972; W. James 1902/1985; Jung, 1933; Maslow, 1970; Wilber, 1981). In this volume, Wetzel and Winawer (Chap. 9), Aponte (Chap. 12), Farber (Chap. 13), Lukas and Hirsch (Chap. 14), Ducommun-Nagy (Chap. 19), and Kalayjian (Chap. 24) emphasize the spiritual dimension of human experience in their therapies. Although there are greater differences within than between cultures, usually interest in the West has tended to focus at the intrapersonal and interpersonal levels, with the systemic and spiritual dimensions of human well-being left somewhat beyond the focus of the Western psychotherapies. In Eastern cultures, the spiritual and collective-systemic aspects of human well-being have traditionally been in clear focus, with the individual and dyadic aspects at times more blurred. In each case, the focus seems isomorphic to cultural norms. There are, of course, countervailing trends. Strong spiritual traditions exist in Western culture, and individuals are recognized as having shaped history and spirituality in the East, within and outside of specifically religious traditions.

Wilber (1981) elaborated a developmental taxonomy uniting the traditionally Western self-actualizing psychotherapies and the more self-effacing Eastern meditative and spiritual routes to enlightenment. This taxonomy begins with the intrapersonal (psychoanalysis), runs through the interpersonal and transpersonal therapies, and ends in the spiritual and meditative traditions of some of the world's major religions. Human growth on this continuum occurs through a developmental expansion of consciousness and of what is experienced as self. From a restricted, intrapersonal awareness of self as only the pleasing and owned aspects of one's mental contents, one can, according to Wilber, overcome the division between persona (owned contents) and shadow (disowned or unconscious contents) through psychoanalysis. With the body-related psychotherapies, one can then proceed to unite within the self one's mental and bodily awareness, overcoming the Cartesian mind-body split. With the intermediary interpersonal therapies, one can then transcend the (primarily Western) boundary that we use to artificially separate self from others; with transpersonal and meditative work, we can move even beyond this to experience self at times as merged with the ultimate transcendental Gestalt of "unity consciousness," or identification with all that is. Wilber portrayed an overall developmental perspective with broad brushstrokes, drawing into a single continuum of developing awareness all levels of systemic focus on the phenomena of human being and becoming. In his schema, the person is continually challenged to transcend older, more limiting definitions of self, constantly reaching for greater ones, until finally the boundaries of what has been experienced as self are burst, overcome, or transcended, and the occasional experience of unity with all that is results. Maslow (1962) first introduced the related ideas of existential "self-transcendence" and "peak experience" in Western psychology.

We see no inherent reason why the psychotherapies should not broaden their focus, as Wilber suggests, to include all levels of systemic concern, including the transpersonal and spiritual. Philosophy and religion, the theoretical "parents" of psychology and from whom Western psychologists wished earlier to establish a separate identity, may at this stage of the discipline's development be found to again have something both uniquely human and transcendent to offer.

The idea of being able to "see" from multiple points of view may seem quite extraordinary and new. Other concepts—of not judging the other until one has walked a mile in the other's moccasins (of Native American origin) and of doing unto others only what one would wish done to oneself (a karmic idea expressed in more than one religious tradition) are not new. Both contain the seminal idea that, to relate fully to the other, one must be able to take the other's position and to see the world from another's vantage point. Each expression is as old as the cultures from which these ideas emanate.

The ideas that others' desires and habits must be manipulated to enhance one's own material status, that status is important and hierarchy inevitable as regards power, prestige, wealth, and significance, have perhaps reached their zenith in the current entrepreneurial approach to everyday reality in the West, and in the United States in particular. Fortunately, in the "marketplace of ideas," a term coined by the pragmatic American philosopher Oliver Wendell Holmes, if the opportunity is given to freely express complementary and opposing ideas, those that best meet the needs of the persons who frequent the market will prevail. And because the market, too, changes and is shaped by the customs and cultures of those who frequent it, the excesses of one idea and the inadequacies of another may be trimmed off or fleshed out by their merchants, as need be, so that sale and purchase can continue. This will require listening carefully, respectfully hearing and comprehending the various voices in the marketplace, and collaboratively creating a market that is responsive to all. In a volume such as this, oriented toward an international market, the editors hope to facilitate discussion in the marketplace of ideas regarding what constitutes mental health and human well-being, and how one may best facilitate these where they are lacking, through the mediation of the interpersonal, humanistic, and existential psychotherapies. Whatever the answers come to be, they will likely represent a synthesis of current perspectives.

The paradigm of scientific rationality Martínez (1997) has perceived to be emerging seems well-suited to achieving multiple syntheses in an age in which many viewpoints abound, in a world in which much is constantly changing, and in which we are increasingly thrown together, exposed to one another's customs and cultures, fears, and hopes. The positivistic paradigm has proven quite useful for analytic work within specified frames and will remain useful for that purpose. We must simply be more aware of the frames of reference within which we are working and careful to record observations, measurements, and experimental results as being related to and limited by the specific frame of reference used. And it is well to challenge ourselves to be aware of and to include in any discussion of outcomes what lies outside of or is distorted by the selected frame. We will also need to find effective ways to respond to the change that is all about us. Our skills or lack of adeptness in modulating and adapting to change, in taking one another's points of view, and in cooperatively synthesizing divergent information may be the most significant determinants of the quality of human life in the twenty-first century. These three sets of skills can clearly facilitate the therapy that we give and receive, the theoretical and empirical work that we engage in, and the personal and interpersonal lives that we live.

REFERENCES

Adler, A. (1956). *The individual psychology of Alfred Adler.* (H. L. Ansbacher & R. R. Ansbacher, Eds.). New York: Basic Books.

Adler, A. (1963). *The practice and theory of individual psychology.* Paterson, NJ: Littlefield, Adams. (Original work published 1924)

Adler, A. (1964). *Superiority and social interest* (3rd ed.). (H. L. Ansbacher & R. R. Ansbacher, Eds.). New York: Viking Press.

Allport, G. W. (1937). *Personality: A psychological interpretation.* New York: Holt, Rinehart and Winston.

Allport, G. W. (1950). *The individual and his religion.* New York: Macmillan.

Allport, G. W. (1954). *The nature of prejudice.* Garden City, NY: Doubleday.

Allport, G. W. (1955). *Becoming.* New Haven, CT: Yale University Press.

Allport, G. W. (1961). *Pattern and growth in personality* (revision of personality). New York: Holt, Rinehart and Winston.

Allport, G. W. (1968). *The person in psychology.* Boston: Beacon Press.

Barrett-Lennard, G. T. (1998). *Carl Rogers' helping system: Journey and substance.* London: Sage.

Berne, E. (1961). *Transactional analysis in psychotherapy.* New York: Grove Press.

Berne, E. (1979). *The structure and dynamics of groups and organizations.* New York: Ballantine Books. (Original work published 1963)

Binswanger, L. (1967). *Being-in-the-world.* (J. Needleman, Trans.) New York: Harper.

Boss, M. (1957). *Psychoanalysis and daseinanalysis.* New York: Basic Books.

Bradford, I., Gibb, J., & Benne, L. (1964). *T-group theory and laboratory method.* New York: Wiley.

Buber, M. (1970). *I and thou.* New York: Scribner. (Original work published in 1927)

Bugental, J. F. T. (1965). *The search for authenticity.* New York: Holt, Rinehart and Winston.

Buhler, C. (1962). *Values in psychotherapy.* New York: Free Press.

Capra, F., (1975). *The tao of physics.* Boston: Shambhala.

Carkhuff, R. R., & Berenson, B. G. (1967). *Beyond counseling and therapy.* New York: Holt, Rinehart and Winston.

Erikson, E. H. (1963). *Childhood and society* (2nd ed.) New York: Norton. (Original work published 1950)

Erikson, E. H. (1968). *Identity: Youth and crisis.* New York: Norton.

Frankl, V. E. (1965). *The doctor and the soul: From psychotherapy to logotherapy* (2nd ed.). New York: Vintage. (Original work published 1946)

Frankl, V. E. (1967). *Man's search for meaning.* New York: Washington Square Press. (Original work published 1946)

Frankl, V. E. (1969). *The will to meaning: Foundations and applications of logotherapy.* New York: New American Library.

Frankl, V. E. (1977). *The unconscious god: Psychotherapy and theology.* New York: Simon & Schuster.

Freud, A. (1965). *Normality and pathology in childhood: Assessments of development.* New York: International Universities Press.

Freud, A. (1966). *The ego and the mechanisms of defense.* New York: International Universities Press. (Original work published 1936)

Frie, R. (2000). The existential and the interpersonal: Ludwig Binswanger and Harry Stack Sullivan. *Journal of Humanistic Psychology, 40*(3), 108–129.

Fromm, E. (1941). *Escape from freedom.* New York: Holt, Rinehart and Winston.

Fromm, E. (1964). *The heart of man.* New York: Harper & Row.

Fromm, E. (1972). *Psychoanalysis and religion.* New York: Bantam. (Original work published 1950)

Goldstein, K. (1934). *The organism.* Boston: Beacon Press.

Goulding, M. M., & Goulding, R. L. (1979). *Changing lives through redecision therapy.* New York: Brunner/Mazel.

Goulding, R. L., & Goulding, M. M. (1978). *The power is in the patient: A TA/Gestalt approach to psychotherapy.* San Francisco: TA Press.

Heidigger, M. (1962). *Being and time.* New York: Harper & Row. (Original work published 1927)

Heisenberg, W. (1958). *Physics and philosophy: The revolution of modern science.* New York: Harper & Row.

Horney, K. (1966). *New ways in psychoanalysis.* New York: Norton. (Original work published 1939)

James, W. (1985). *The varieties of religious experience.* Hammondsworth, England: Penguin Classics. (Original work published 1902)

James, W. (1897). *The will to believe and other essays in philosophy.* New York: Henry.

Jourard, S. M. (1964). *The transparent self: Self-disclosure and well-being.* Princeton, NJ: Van Nostrand.

Jung, C. G. (1933). *Modern man in search of a soul.* New York: Harcourt, Brace, & World.

Kegan, R. (1982). *The evolving self: Problem and process in human development.* Cambridge, MA: Harvard University Press.

Laing, R. D. (1969). *The politics of the family and other essays.* New York: Vintage.

Laing, R. D. (1978). *The divided self.* Baltimore: Penguin. (Original work published 1960)

Martínez, M. (1997). *The emergent paradigm: Toward a new theory of scientific rationality* [El paradigma emergente: Hacia una nueva teoría de la racionalidad científica]. Mexico City:Trillas.

Maslow, A. H. (1943). A theory of human motivation. *Psychological Review, 50,* 370–396.

Maslow, A. H. (1962). *Toward a psychology of being.* New York: Van Nostrand.

Maslow, A. H. (1970). *Religions, values and peak experiences.* New York: Viking.

Massey, R. F. (1972). Meta-subjectivity: A model for interracial understanding. *International Journal of Group Tensions, 2*(4), 71–85.

Massey, R. F. (1988). A critique of logotherapy as a personology. *The International Forum for Logotherapy: Journal of Search for Meaning, 11*(1), 42–52.

May, R. (1967). *Man's search for himself.* New York: Signet. (Original work published 1953)

May, R., Angel, E., & Ellenberger, H. F. (1958). *Existence.* New York: Simon & Schuster.

Moreno, J. L. (1945). *Psychodrama: Foundations of psychotherapy* (Vol. 1). Beacon, NY: Beacon Press.

Moreno, J. L. (1946). *Psychodrama: Foundations of psychotherapy* (Vol. 2). Beacon, NY: Beacon Press.

Mowrer, O. H. (1953). *Psychotherapy theory and research.* New York: Ronald Press.

Murphy, G. (1958). *Human potentialities.* New York: Basic Books.

Murray, H. A. (1938). *Explorations in personality: A clinical and experimental study of fifty college age men.* New York: Oxford University Press.

Perls, F. S. (1969). *Gestalt therapy verbatim.* New York: Bantam Books.

Perls, F. S., Hefferline, R. F., & Goodman, P. (1951). *Gestalt therapy.* New York: Julian Press.

Polanyi, M. (1945). *Science, faith and society* Chicago: University of Chicago Press.

Polanyi, M. (1962). *Personal knowledge.* Chicago: University of Chicago Press.

Prigogine, I. (1973). Irreversibility as a symmetry-breaking process. *Nature, 246,* 67–71.

Rogers, C. R. (1939). *The clinical treatment of the problem child.* Boston: Houghton Mifflin.

Rogers, C. R. (1942). The use of electronically recorded interviews in improving psychotherapeutic techniques. *American Journal of Orthopsychiatry, 12,* 429–434.

Rogers, C. R. (1955). Persons or science: A philosophical question. *American Psychologist, 10,* 267–278.

Rogers, C. R. (1961a). *On becoming a person.* Boston: Houghton Mifflin.

Rogers, C. R. (1961b). The place of the person in the new world of the behavioral sciences. *Personnel and Guidance Journal, 40,* 442–451.

Rogers, C. R. (1964). Toward a science of the person. In T. W. Wann (Ed.), *Behaviorism and phenomenology* (pp. 109–140). Chicago: University of Chicago Press.

Sartre, J. P. (1936). *The transcendence of the ego.* New York: Noonday Press.

Satir, V. (1972). *Peoplemaking.* Palo Alto, CA: Science and Behavior Books.

Sullivan, H. S. (1953a). *Conceptions of modern psychiatry.* New York: Norton. (Original work published in 1940)

Sullivan, H. S. (1953b). *The interpersonal theory of psychiatry.* New York: Norton.

Taylor, E. (1999). An intellectual renaissance of humanistic psychology? *Journal of Humanistic Psychology, 39*(2), 7–25.

Valsiner, J., & van der Veer, R. (2000). *The social mind: Construction of the idea.* New York: Cambridge University Press.

Vygotsky, L. S. (1962). *Thought and language* (E. Haufmann & G. Vakar, Eds. & Trans.). Cambridge, MA: MIT Press.

Wilber, K. (1981). *No boundary: Eastern and Western approaches to personal growth.* Boston: Shambhala.

Author Index

Abelsohn, D., 16
Aber, J. L., 109
Achebe, C., 654
Achenbach, T., 72, 97
Ackerman, F., 224
Ackerman, N. W., 393, 490
Adler, A., 83, 84, 180, 181, 185, 186, 187, 190, 192, 195, 199, 279, 489, 563, 570, 622, 673, 679, 700, 705, 707
Adorno, T. W., 515
Ahmed, K., 156
Ahmeduzzaman, M., 167
Ainsworth, M. S., 394
Akibayashi, A., 659
Albeck, J. H., 619
Alden, L., 104
Alexander, F. M., 594
Alexander, J. F., 104, 209
Alipuria, L., 168
Allan, J., 61, 96
Allen, J., 74
Allen, T. W., 181
Allodi, F., 420
Allport, F. H., 494, 499
Allport, G. W., 257, 279, 496, 497, 499, 516, 670, 672, 673, 681, 701, 703, 706, 713
Allwood, K., 321
Almedia, R., 157
Almeida, R., 156, 157, 160, 414, 415, 428, 505, 516
Althusser, L., 650
Amatea, E. S., 155, 173
Ambert, A. M., 211, 212, 213

Ammen, S., 63
Amster, F., 59
Andersen, T., 493, 497, 514, 515, 516
Anderson, D. A., 281
Anderson, F. S., 592
Anderson, H., 415, 493, 517, 645, 682
Anderson, W., 281, 517
Andes, F., 225
Andolfi, M., 359, 360, 361, 365, 367, 383, 386
Andreski, P., 618
Angel, E., 257, 305, 706
Angell, H. R., 619
Angell, R., 50
Angelo, C., 360
Angus, L. E., 608
Angyal, A., 496, 563
Ansbacher, H. L., 184, 185, 191, 192
Ansbacher, R. R., 184, 185, 191
Antoni, M. H., 327
Anzieu, D., 592
Aoki, B. K., 36
Aponte, H. J., 8, 96, 211, 213, 220, 280, 286, 290, 291, 293, 294, 295, 298
Ariel, S., 63
Aristotle, 533, 535, 538
Arnheim, R., 537
Arocha, J., 418
Aron, L., 234, 589, 592
Arredondo, P., 173
Ash, P., 94

Ashman, T., 322
Atwood, G., 234, 630
Auerswald, E. H., 3, 205, 206, 208
Avila, A. L., 166
Avila, D. L., 166
Avis, J. M., 413, 414, 415, 416, 426, 427, 428, 499, 505, 687
Axline, V., 60, 62, 84, 110, 113
Azikiwe, N., 654

Back, C., 313
Bader, E., 435, 447, 459, 460, 557, 578
Bahl, S., 486
Bahr, R., 327
Bailey, C. E., 63, 85
Baker, A. A., 551
Baker, E., 592
Baker, L., 3, 27
Balaguer, A., 389, 397
Baldwin, L., 249
Balint, M., 596
Ballard, N., 252
Banchero, L. E., 692
Bandura, A., 84
Banks, A., 248
Banks, C., 516
Banks, H. C., 35
Banmen, J., 441, 442
Bardill, D. R., 282, 283
Barkley, B. H., 168, 169
Barkley, R. A., 96, 97
Barletta, J., 359, 364, 385
Barlow, D. A., 270
Barnes, G., 556

Barocas, H., 551
Barr, M., 311
Barrett, K., 27
Barrett, M. J., 68, 92, 93
Barrett-Lennard, G. T., 700, 702
Bartholomew, K. L., 16
Barton, C., 209
Baruth, L., 183
Bateson, G., 3, 84, 104, 205, 206, 490, 493, 517
Batts, V., 501, 563
Baucom, D. H., 398
Baum, A., 631
Baum, S., 606
Bauman, K., 249
Baute, P., 563, 567
Bazron, B. J., 173
Beagley, G., 630
Bean, R. A., 171
Bearman, S., 249
Beavers, W. R., 517
Beavin, J., 500, 651
Beavin, L., 3
Beck, A. T., 84, 550
Beck, B. S., 669, 670, 671, 674
Becker, D., 670, 692
Becker, S. W., 186
Becnel, H., 618
Becvar, D. S., 155, 173, 281, 291, 390, 643, 644, 645, 646
Becvar, R. J., 155, 173, 390, 643, 645
Bedell, T. M., 171
Bednar, R. L., 578
Belenky, M., 234, 249
Bell, J. M., 211
Bellah, R. N., 280
Bellak, L., 516
Ben-David, A., 427
Benjamin, L. S., 517
Benne, L., 702
Bennett, L., 211
Benowitz, S., 659
Benson, H., 299
Bentovim, A., 66, 681
Bepko, C., 415
Berenson, B. G., 671, 672, 702

Berg, I., 136, 137, 139, 147, 148
Berg, M., 309, 322, 325
Bergin, A., 151
Bergman, A., 447
Bergman, M. S., 617
Berliner, L., 68
Berman, J. J., 692
Berman, W. H., 394
Bermudez, J. L., 592
Bernard, J. M., 676
Bernard of Clairvaux, 293
Berndt, T. J., 631
Berne, E., 435, 436, 437, 438, 442, 450, 453, 500, 535, 542, 544, 555, 556, 557, 558, 559, 560, 561, 562, 563, 564, 565, 566, 567, 568, 569, 572, 577, 579, 606, 673, 681, 703, 704
Bernhardt, P., 592, 606
Berry, J. W., 153, 156, 158
Berry, P., 96
Best, K. M., 9
Bettner, B. L., 181
Beutler, L. E., 607, 692
Bevilacqua, L. J., 390, 391
Bielanska, A., 551
Billingsley, A., 162, 501
Binder-Brynes, K., 109
Binswanger, L., 256, 305, 306, 499, 502, 593, 672, 706, 707
Birthnell, J., 186
Bitter, J. R., 180, 184, 190
Black, J. E., 116
Blacklidge, V. Y., 578
Blakeslee, S., 95, 391, 398
Blakeslee, Sandra, 391
Blanchard, G., 92
Blaney, N. T., 319
Blank, A. S., 618
Blatner, H. A., 529, 530, 531, 532, 534, 536, 543, 545, 551
Blazer, D. G., 109
Blechner, M. J., 303, 310, 311
Blehar, M. C., 394
Bleich, A., 618
Block, J., 35, 515
Blouin, J., 86
Blum, R., 249

Boadella, D., 587, 588, 589, 591, 592, 606
Bodin, A. M., 296
Boe, J., 96
Boehm, W., 350
Boehnlein, J. K., 37, 619
Bogard, M., 505
Bogart, K., 67
Bogas, S., 16
Bogenschneider, K., 172
Bograd, M., 413, 415
Boik, B. L., 96
Bolden, M. A., 161, 165
Booker, C., 161
Boon, S. D., 398
Booth-Kewley, S., 271
Bordin, E. S., 670, 692
Borduin, C. M., 4, 172
Borkovec, T. D., 607
Boscolo, L., 370, 500
Boss, M., 305, 307, 593, 672, 706, 707
Boszormenyi-Nagy, I., 371, 391, 393, 395, 399, 401, 406, 464, 465, 466, 467, 468, 470, 471, 473, 474, 475, 491, 496, 497, 498, 500, 501, 513, 514, 515, 618, 620, 673, 680, 682
Bottome, P., 180
Bow, J. N., 110, 111
Bowen, M., 369, 370, 371, 393, 394, 395, 397, 406, 449, 470, 490, 496, 497, 500, 511, 563, 618, 681, 682
Bower, J. E., 326
Bower, T. G. R., 497
Bowlby, J., 8, 9, 67, 86, 102, 115, 393, 394, 496, 510, 511, 673
Boyajian, K., 618, 619
Boyd, H., 557, 561, 563, 571
Boyd, L., 557, 561, 563, 571
Boyd-Franklin, N., 162, 163, 173, 209, 212, 213, 214, 216, 298
Boyle, J. T., 8, 12, 16
Bracke, P. E., 270, 271
Bradbury, 397, 398, 407
Bradford, I., 702
Bradley, S. J., 10

Bradway, K., 96
Brahler, E., 592
Brasswell, M., 26
Bratton, S., 59, 79, 127
Braverman, L. M., 60
Bray, J. H., 517
Breckenridge, K., 596
Breggin, P. R., 207
Brendler, J., 16
Brennan, B., 628
Brenner, A., 68
Brenner, R. B., 617
Breslau, N., 618
Breunlin, D., 94, 678
Brickman, A., 27
Briere, J. N., 66, 72
Brigman, G., 192
Brim, O. G., 172
Briquet, P., 616
Brock, G. W., 644
Broderick, C. B., 208, 670
Broderick, J. E., 398
Brodsky, A., 597
Brody, G. H., 172
Brody, V., 62
Bronfenbrenner, U., 154, 172
Bronowski, J., 538
Brooks, G., 211
Brooks, R., 90
Brooks-Gunn, J., 497
Broverman, D., 234
Broverman, I., 234
Brown, A. C., 161, 163, 165, 172
Brown, A. L., 165
Brown, B. B., 616
Brown, D., 84, 206
Brown, P., 616
Brown, R. A., 578
Browning, D. S., 290
Bry, B. H., 209, 216
Buber, M., 399, 470, 472, 474, 491, 518, 707
Bucci, W., 592, 593
Budzyna-Davidowski, P., 551
Bugental, J. F. T., 255, 257, 258, 261, 262, 263, 264, 265, 266, 267, 268, 270, 271, 275, 322, 325, 701, 708

Buhler, C., 257, 701
Bulka, R. P., 337, 354
Burke, R. A., 687
Burns, C. I., 676
Burns, R. C., 95
Burrow, T., 530
Burton, A., 596
Burton, J. F., 39
Busby, D. M., 94
Butman, H., 551
Butz, M., 136
Byng-Hall, J., 8

Cade, B., 133
Caldwell, C., 592
Caligor, L., 669, 676
Calkins, S. D., 10
Camacho, A., 418
Campbell, D. T., 516
Campbell, J., 140
Camus, A., 621
Cangelosi, D., 59, 109, 110
Caplan, A., 632
Capra, F., 205, 678, 711
Carbonelli, D. M., 550
Card, C. A. L., 322
Carey, J. C., 157, 158
Carey, L., 63, 84
Carkhuff, R. R., 671, 672, 692, 702
Carlson, J., 182, 187, 193
Carlson, V., 109, 121
Carmelli, D., 271
Caro, J. E., 94
Carrere, S., 397
Carrillo, R., 415
Carroll, J., 186
Carroll, L., 8, 12, 16
Carroll, M., 676
Carter, B., 182, 186, 212, 396, 414, 492, 497, 503, 505, 514
Carter, E., 13, 514
Carter, R. T., 160, 162
Casarjian, R., 619
Casement, P. J., 595, 596
Cassidy, J., 10, 402
Castellon, S. A., 313
Castillio, E., 16
Castonguay, L. G., 607

Cattanach, A., 64
Cattell, R. B., 575
Cavellero, G., 557, 571
Cecchin, G., 370, 500
Cechniki, A., 551
Cesaire, A., 654
Chamberlain, L., 136
Chao, C. M., 37, 39, 50, 54, 55
Chavira, V., 159
Cheek, D. K., 35
Chenail, R., 430
Cheney, W., 555
Chesney, M. A., 322
Cheston, S. E., 182
Childs-Gowell, E., 556, 557
Chin, J. L., 36, 54
Choy, A., 562
Christensen, A., 397, 402, 408
Christensen, O. C., 182, 191, 199
Chung, W., 36
Cicchetti, D., 4, 109, 120, 121
Ciottone, R. A., 65, 67
Cirillo, S., 491, 496
Clance, P. R., 596
Clark, A. J., 185
Clark, C. A., 608
Clark, K. B., 499
Clarke, G., 50
Clarkson, F., 234
Clarkson, P., 560, 562, 568
Clauss, K., 563
Clements, C. D., 211
Clements, M., 397
Clinchy, B., 234, 249
Clum, G. A., 270
Coan, J., 397
Cobb, S., 414, 415, 417, 427
Cobbs, P. M., 35
Cohen, J. A., 66, 68
Cohen, R., 16, 28
Cohen, S., 16
Colapinto, J., 3, 6, 208, 224, 491, 505
Cole, P. M., 9
Coleman, H. K., 157
Coleman, R., 96
Collins, P. H., 250, 251
Collins, R. L., 322

Collmer, W. M., 631
Comas-Diaz, L., 210, 211, 216
Combrinck-Graham, L., 16
Combs, G., 415
Combs, L., 709, 713
Compernolle, T., 551
Conners, C. K., 97
Constantine, M. G., 154, 156, 157, 158
Constantino, G., 516
Cook, D. A., 162
Coontz, S., 207, 214
Cooper, D., 650
Cooper, E. C., 337
Cordova, F., 41
Cornelison, A. R., 490, 517
Cornell, W. F., 592, 596, 606
Corsini, R. C., 185, 191, 192, 199
Corsini, R. J., 181, 551
Cortese, J., 92, 93
Corveleyn, J., 182
Costello, N., 327
Coulter, M. L., 109
Cowan, P. A., 14
Cowan, P. C., 14
Coyle, C. T., 298
Crethar, H. C., 692
Croake, J., 184
Crocket, K., 415
Cromwell, R. E., 26
Cronbach, L. J., 516
Cronen, V. E., 424, 425, 502, 510
Cross, T. L., 173
Crossman, P., 556, 568
Crumbaugh, J. C., 337, 339, 354
Crutchfield, R. S., 515
Cummings, E. M., 9, 391, 398
Cummings, J., 313
Cunningham, P. B., 4
Curlette, W. L., 191
Cushman, P., 270

Dadds, M. R., 319
Dagley, J. C., 191
Dagley, P. L., 191
Dakof, G. A., 27, 28, 208, 225
Dammann, C., 180
Dana, R. H., 503, 517

Danieli, Y., 616, 618, 629, 630
Daniels, M. H., 155
Daniels, T. G., 676, 678
Dare, C., 16
Dasgupta, S., 157
Dattilio, F. M., 390, 391
Davidson, J. R. T., 109, 618, 631
Davidson, L. M., 631
Davidson, S., 619
Davies, M., 303, 322, 325, 426
Davies, P., 9, 391, 398
Davies, R., 607
Davis, C., 205
Davis, G. C., 618
Davis, J., 121
Dawson, G., 115
Day, J., 490
Dean, T., 299
Deblinger, E., 65, 68
De Domenico, G., 61, 62
Deering, C. G., 94
De Jong, P., 148, 151
Deleuze, G., 650
Dell, P. F., 502, 505
Delworth, U., 692
Dembo, M. H., 158
Denham, S. A., 5
de Nichilo, M., 360
Dennis, K. W., 173
Denton, W. H., 403
Derrida, J., 426
de Shazer, S., 133, 134, 135, 136, 138, 139, 147, 149, 514, 515
Des Lauriers, A., 112
Desmond, D. P., 299
Detzner, D., 430
de Vries, M. J., 327
Dewald, P. A., 671
Dewey, J., 677
Dhruvarajan, V., 158
Diamond, G., 27
Diamond, G. M., 4, 12, 28, 208, 670, 692
Diamond, G. S., 4, 12, 28, 208
Dichter, H., 180
Dickey, M., 26
Dicks, H. V., 394, 396

Dickson, D., 50
Dienhart, A., 687
Difenthaller, B., 510
Dillon, D., 430
Dinkmeyer, D., 179, 180, 181, 182, 185, 186, 187
Dinkmeyer, J. S., 181
Disque, J. G., 180
Doherty, W., 208, 281, 293, 504, 646
Doise, W., 493, 495
Dona, G., 156
Dooley, C., 252
Dore, M., 8, 209, 220, 503
Doris, J., 109
Douvan, E., 403
Downing, G., 588, 589, 592, 593
Drego, P., 560, 578
Dreikurs, R., 181, 185, 198
Du, N., 36
Ducommun-Nagy, C., 513
Dukes, J., 209
Duncan, B., 137, 138, 578
Dunn, A. B., 492, 503
Dunn, R. L., 104
DuPaul, G., 97
Durana, C., 596, 597
Durham, D., 67
Durkin, T., 414
Durvasula, R. S., 156
Dusay, J., 503, 556, 557, 559
Dusay, K., 503, 557
Dyson, M. E., 161, 163

Eaton, M. J., 158
Eckenrode, J., 109
Eckstein, D., 183, 186
Edelbrock, C., 72, 97
Edelman, L., 619
Edelsohn, G. A., 109
Edelson, M., 607
Efran, J. A., 646
Efran, J. S., 276, 283
Egendorf, A., 315
Eicher, J. B., 173
Eilan, N., 592
Eisenbruch, M., 619

Eisengart, S., 151
Eisler, I., 16, 27
Ekstein, R., 670
Elder, G. H., 161
Elder, J., 140
Eldridge, N., 211, 239
Elias, M., 171
Elizur, J., 3
Elkaim, M., 650, 652
Ellenberger, H., 179, 180, 257, 305, 335, 616, 706
Ellerman, C. P., 313, 318
Elliot, M., 16
Elliott, R., 593, 608
Ellis, A., 182, 190, 669
Ellis, M. V., 692, 693
Ellison, R., 212
Ellman, B., 211
Elsner, G., 655
Elwyn, T. S., 659
Emde, R., 4
Emery, E., 589
Emery, R. E., 391, 398
Emmelkamp, P. M. G., 327
Endo, R., 36
Engels, G. L., 4
Engeter, M., 322
English, F., 500, 556, 564, 568, 571
English, J., 54
Enneis, J. M., 542, 545
Eno, M. M., 16
Enright, R. D., 298
Epstein, H. T., 115
Epstein, R. S., 596, 597
Epston, D., 85, 87, 88, 90, 91, 92, 94, 415, 417, 425, 426
Epston, E., 493, 497, 505, 514
Erbaugh, J., 550
Erekosima, T. V., 173
Erikson, E., 64, 109, 114, 116, 128, 470, 489, 497, 498, 503, 673, 705
Ernst, F., 561, 564
Ernst, F. H., Jr., 561, 564
Erskine, R. G., 557, 560, 569
Escobar, J. I., 167
Esman, A. H., 113
Espín, O., 415

Eth, S., 123
Etinger, L., 51
Everson, M. D., 109

Fabry, J., 334, 337, 354
Fagan, J., 438, 439, 596
Fahey, J. L., 326
Fairbairn, W., 233
Fairbairn, W. D., 393, 394
Fairbairn, W. R. D., 467
Fairbank, J. A., 617, 618
Fajardo, D., 418
Falicov, C. J., 167, 168, 169, 210, 211, 214, 223, 224, 500
Falloon, I. R. H., 671, 681
Fals Borda, O., 418
Fanon, F., 165
Farber, E. W., 311, 312, 316, 320, 321, 322, 325
Farr, R. M., 493, 494
Farrell, M. M., 39
Fassel, D., 271
Fatout, M. F., 93
Faude, J., 10
Fay, L. F., 500
Feaster, D., 319
Federn, P., 436, 557, 577
Feldenkrais, M., 594, 595
Feng, G. F., 54
Ferenczi, S., 589, 608
Ferguson, E. D., 180
Ferran, E., Jr., 207, 211, 212
Fetters, M. D., 659
Figley, C. R., 419, 421, 616, 632
Fincham, F. D., 391, 398
Finkelhor, D., 65, 66, 72, 109, 117
Fisch, R., 173
Fischbach, R. L., 631
Fischer, K. W., 114
Fischer, W. F., 593
Fischoff, B., 617
Fisher, C. T., 265
Fisher, J., 422
Fishman, B., 322, 327
Fishman, C., 448
Fishman, H. C., 3, 206, 211, 225, 491, 511
Fishman, J., 438, 448, 556, 569

Fiske, D. W., 495, 516
Fiske, S. T., 495
Fleck, S., 490, 517
Fleming, R., 631
Fletcher, J., 237, 252
Florey, L., 110
Flori, D. E., 518
Floyd, F. J., 397
Fogarty, T. F., 500
Fogel, R. W., 280
Folkman, S., 322, 631
Follet, W. C., 398
Fonagy, P., 28
Font, R., 414, 505, 516
Foote, F., 27
Ford, C. L., 104
Forer, B. R., 596
Forgays, D. G., 115
Forgays, J. W., 115
Forgus, R., 180
Forstein, M., 310
Foucault, M., 493, 505
Fowers, B. J., 211, 214
Fraenkel, P., 516
Fraiberg, S. H., 6
Framo, J., 370, 371, 378, 395, 466, 468, 681, 682
Framo, James, 395
Frances, A., 322, 327
Frank, L. K., 110
Frankl, V. E., 284, 290, 293, 294, 295, 308, 309, 316, 318, 321, 322, 333, 334, 335, 336, 338, 339, 342, 347, 349, 354, 391, 496, 499, 509, 571, 593, 619, 621, 622, 623, 628, 632, 672, 673, 707, 713
Franklin, A. J., 161, 212, 216
Franklin, D. L., 213, 215
Frantz, C. M., 309, 322
Frawley, M., 121
Frederick, C. J., 623
Fredman, N., 190
Freedman, J., 87, 90, 415
Freeman, J., 85, 87, 88, 91, 92
Freeman-Longo, R., 92
Freidman, A. S., 27
Frenkel-Brunswick, E., 515

Freud, A., 60, 83, 84, 110, 113, 500, 673, 705
Freud, S., 83, 84, 233, 563, 589, 595
Frey, H. E., 209
Freyberg, J. T., 629
Frie, R., 707
Friedman, H., 271
Friedman, M., 399, 401
Friedrich, W. N., 65, 66
Fromm, E., 279, 392, 393, 406, 489, 496, 499, 501, 673, 705, 713
Fromm-Reichmann, F., 490, 596
Fruzzetti, A. E., 671
Fullerton, C. S., 631

Galeano, E., 215
Gallagher, D., 140
Gallagher, S., 593
Gallops, M., 631
Garbarino, J., 419
Garcia-Coll, C., 416, 425
Garcia-Preto, N., 157, 166, 168, 169
Gardner, R. A., 74, 90
Garfield, S., 151
Garlock, R., 181
Garmezy, N., 9
Garner, N., 151
Garrison, C., 631
Gatchel, R., 631
Gawinski, B. A., 206
Geib, P., 597
Geil, M., 151
Geist, G. O., 692
Gendlin, E. T., 270, 318, 593
Genero, N., 249
George, L. K., 109
Gerber, J., 441, 442
Gergen, K. J., 645, 677, 678
Gergerian, E., 618, 619
Gerton, J., 157
Gerty, F., 467
Gibb, J., 702
Gil, A. G., 167
Gil, E., 60, 63, 64, 65, 67, 69, 77, 90, 95, 96, 111, 112, 113

Gilbert, M., 560
Giller, E. L., 109
Gilligan, C., 234, 249, 470, 497
Gingerich, W., 138, 151
Giordano, J., 37, 166, 211, 214, 285, 510
Giorgi, A., 593
Giovanoli Vercellino, C., 557, 571
Giovinco, G., 303
Giraldo, J., 425
Gisriel, M., 631
Gist, R., 632
Gitlin, K., 64
Gitlin-Weiner, K., 110
Glaser, D., 120
Glick, J. A., 675, 678
Glover, G., 64
Gluhoski, V. L., 403
Glunt, E. K., 310
Gobes, L., 500
Goeka, E., 550
Goff, B., 50
Goffman, E., 8, 493, 504
Gold, L., 182, 191
Goldberger, N., 234, 249
Goldenberg, H., 281
Goldenberg, I., 281
Goldfried, M. R., 607
Goldner, V., 211, 413, 499, 505, 516
Goldstein, K., 701
Goleman, D., 10, 182, 246, 252
Gomori, M., 441, 442
Gonzalez, R., 166, 167, 169
Goodkin, K., 319
Goodman, M., 596
Goodman, P., 435, 438, 439, 442, 576, 703
Goodrich, T. J., 211
Goodwin, E. A., 74, 96
Goolishian, H., 415, 493, 682
Gosling, A., 416
Gottlieb, C. D., 426
Gottlieb, D. T., 426
Gottman, J., 4, 5, 397, 400, 578
Gough, A., 578
Gough, H., 459
Gould, P., 90

Gould, W. B., 337
Goulding, M., 435, 442, 443, 450, 556, 557, 560, 565, 570, 575, 576, 577, 579, 673, 681, 703
Goulding, R., 673
Goulding, R. L., 435, 442, 443, 445, 446, 556, 557, 565, 570, 575, 576, 577, 703
Grabill, C. M., 95
Graca, J., 337
Grand, I. J., 588, 592, 608
Graumann, C. F., 493, 494, 495
Gray, C., 282
Gray, L. B., 282
Gray, M. M., 166
Green, A., 592, 606
Green, R. J., 415
Greenberg, J., 607
Greenberg, L. S., 104, 390, 391, 398, 399, 402, 403, 404, 405, 407, 408, 578, 593, 608
Greene, B., 210, 211, 216
Greenough, W. T., 116
Greenspan, S., 4, 5
Greenwald, E., 120
Greunewald, T., 235, 249
Grey, L., 181, 185
Grieger, R., 190
Grier, J., 311
Grier, W. J., 35
Griffith, M., 95, 96
Grigorian, H., 618, 619
Grimes, J., 606
Groddeck, G., 588, 608
Groder, M. G., 557, 560
Grofer-Klinger, L., 115
Grubrich-Simitis, I., 629
Grunebaum, J., 618, 620, 673, 682
Grünewald-Zemsch, G., 578
Grych, J. H., 391, 398
Guarnaccia, C. A., 199
Guattiari, F., 651
Guba, E. G., 578
Guengoer, S., 550
Guerin, P., 670
Guerin, P. J., Jr., 500
Guerney, B., 3, 26
Guerney, B. G., 206

Guerney, B. G., Jr., 63
Guerney, L., 63, 77
Gunn, W. B., Jr., 206
Guntrip, H., 233
Guring, R., 235, 249
Gurman, A., 26, 390, 391, 670
Guzmán, A., 418

Haan, N., 515
Haber, R., 365, 383
Habor, M., 16
Hahlweg, K., 397, 398
Haley, J., 3, 84, 104, 182, 390, 459, 490, 500, 512, 517
Halling, S., 265
Halstead, K., 211
Hambridge, G., 60
Hammen, C., 94
Hampson, R. B., 517
Handal, P. J., 620
Haney, C., 516
Hanna, F. J., 313
Hanna, T., 594
Hansen, D. J., 109
Hanson, C. L., 172
Hardin, S. B., 631
Hardin, T. L., 631
Hardy, K., 211, 687
Harel, A., 617
Hare-Mustin, R., 211, 283, 413, 414, 415, 417, 424, 426, 430, 499, 505
Hargaden, H., 557, 569
Hargrave, T. D., 285, 517
Harkness, L. L., 618
Harmon, D., 16
Harris, A., 589
Harris, K., 249
Harrow, G. S., 551
Hartling, L., 241
Hartman, A., 206
Harvey, S., 63
Hashimoto, N. T., 659
Haslam, S. A., 493
Haug, I. E., 641
Haule, J. R., 182
Hawes, E. C., 182, 191, 199
Hawkins, P., 676

Hawley, G. A., 128
Hayes, S. C., 293
Haynal, A., 589
Hayworth, M., 646
Hazan, C., 394, 402
Headden, S., 166
Healy, J. M., 620
Heath, A., 678
Heavey, C. L., 397
Hebb, D. O., 115
Hechinger, F., 160
Hedaya, R. J., 496
Hefferline, R. F., 435, 438, 439, 442, 576, 703
Heflin, A. H., 65
Heidegger, M., 256, 304, 305, 306, 307
Heidigger, M., 706, 707
Heisenberg, W., 678, 711
Heller, L. G., 596
Helms, J., 161, 162, 173, 502
Helzer, J. E., 618, 631
Henderson, C. E., 225
Henggeler, S. W., 4, 172
Henry, D., 68
Hepworth, J., 208
Hepworth, S., 504
Herek, G. M., 310
Herman, J., 246, 401, 616
Hernández, M. P., 418, 420
Hervis, O., 27, 28
Hess, A. K., 670, 674, 676
Hetherington, M., 391
Hewitt, G., 568
Heyer, N. R., 578
Heyman, R. E., 397
Hildebrand, V., 166
Hill, D., 115
Him, C., 50
Hines, P. M., 157
Hines, R. P., 166
Hinkin, C. H., 313
Hinshaw, S. P., 120
Hirsch, S., 470, 490
Ho, M. K., 166
Hodas, G., 5
Hoeller, K., 304, 305, 313
Hoffer, E., 541

Hoffman, E., 180
Hoffman, L., 10, 155, 173, 428
Hoffman, M., 235, 498
Hogue, A., 28, 208
Holder, A., 596
Holloway, E. L., 670, 676, 692
Holloway, H. C., 617
Holmes, J. G., 398, 399
Holroyd, C. J., 597
Holtzworth-Munroe, A., 104, 695
Holub, E. A., 596
Homeyer, L. E., 64
Hooks, 165, 241, 250
Hooven, C., 4, 5
Hopwood, L. E., 151
Horney, K., 362, 374, 489, 497, 705
Horowitz, M., 607
Hough, R. L., 617
Howard, G. S., 276
Howe, J. E., Jr., 692
Hoyt, M. F., 575
Huang, L. N., 36, 156, 157, 158, 159
Hubble, M., 137, 138, 578
Huber, H., 351
Hug-Hellmuth, H., 60
Hughes, D., 109
Huh-Kim, J., 36
Hullings-Catalano, V., 93
Humphrey, F., 645
Humphrey, L. L., 517
Hunsley, J., 407
Hunter, J., 421
Hunter, W. M., 109
Hurley, J. R., 578
Hurst, J., 616
Husserl, E., 304, 305, 306
Huttenlocher, P. R., 114
Hutzell, R. R., 337, 354

Imber-Black, E., 212, 505, 670
Imes, S., 596
Inclan, J., 207, 211, 212
Inhelder, B., 497
Inman, A. G., 154, 156, 157, 158
Ironson, G., 327

Irwin, E. C., 90
Isaacs, M. B., 16
Isaacs, M. R., 173
Ivey, A. E., 211, 676, 678
Ivey, M. B., 211

Ja, D., 42
Jackson, D., 3, 84, 470, 490, 500, 517, 651
Jackson, Y., 110
Jacobs, A., 499, 541, 557, 562, 567
Jacobsberg, L., 322, 327
Jacobson, N. S., 390, 391, 398, 402, 408, 695
James, B., 65
James, E., 713
James, J., 249
James, M., 514, 556, 576
James, O., 61, 63
James, W., 677, 702
Jameson, P., 104
Jamison, J., 486
Janoff-Bulman, R., 122, 309, 322, 325
Jaramillo, C. E., 418
Jardins, K. D., 42
Jasper, H., 436, 557, 577
Jaspers, K., 256
Jayakar, K., 157
Jenkins, A., 415
Jennings, G., 517
Jensen, M., 94
Jernberg, A. M., 112
Jewett, C. L., 67
Johnson, D. H., 588, 592, 594
Johnson, K., 16, 68, 502, 510
Johnson, M., 593
Johnson, S. M., 7, 8, 85, 86, 90, 92, 93, 94, 96, 102, 103, 104, 390, 391, 398, 399, 400, 401, 402, 403, 404, 405, 407, 408, 592
Johnson, V. E., 168, 571
Joines, V., 435, 447, 448
Joines, V. S., 557, 575
Jones, A. C., 42, 43
Jones, J., 161
Jones, J. V., Jr., 180

Jones, S. L., 291
Jones, W., 10
Jongeward, D., 514, 556, 576
Jordan, B. K., 617
Jordan, J., 234, 235, 236, 237, 239, 241, 249, 252
Jourard, S. M., 257, 701
Jucovy, M. E., 617
Jung, C., 61, 489, 673, 713
Jurkovic, G. J., 180

Kaardash, C. M., 692
Kadis, L. B., 435, 447, 460, 557
Kaduson, H. G., 59, 64
Kagan, L. F., 10
Kahana, B., 617
Kahana, E., 617
Kahler, T., 564
Kakaiya, D., 36, 47
Kalayjian, A. S., 615, 618, 619, 622, 626, 631, 632
Kalesnik, J., 172
Kalichman, S. C., 312, 322, 327
Kambon, K. K. K., 162
Kang, K. C., 45, 46
Kao, R. S., 36
Kaplan, A., 234, 235
Karem, E. G., 617
Karney, B. R., 397, 398, 407
Karpman, S., 449, 556, 562, 578
Karr, J. T., 692
Karrer, B., 94, 211
Kaslow, F., 210, 403, 569, 599, 621, 670, 678
Kaslow, N. J., 94, 95
Kassabian, A., 615
Katz, L. F., 4, 5
Kaufman, E., 211
Kaufman, G., 505
Kaufman, P., 211
Kaufman, S. H., 95
Kaufman, W., 470
Kaul, T. J., 578
Kautto, J. G., 500
Kaye, D., 180
Kazak, A. E., 16, 172
Kazdin, A. E., 26
Keating, J., 67

Keeney, B. P., 154
Kefir, N., 184
Kegan, R., 676, 677, 699, 707
Keim, J. P., 97
Keith, D., 85, 86, 88, 92, 98, 99, 180, 392, 393, 396
Keleman, S., 592, 606
Kell, B. L., 670
Keller, E., 249
Kelley, C. R., 592
Kelly, G. A., 257
Kelly, J. A., 327
Kemeny, M. E., 326
Kendall-Tackett, K. A., 65, 109, 117
Kepner, J. I., 592, 593, 596
Kern, R. M., 182, 191, 199
Kerr, M., 394, 395, 490, 511, 563
Kertay, L., 596
Kertesz, R., 561
Kessler, R. C., 631
Kestenberg, J. S., 619
Kierkegaard, S., 256, 304, 305
Kim, B. C., 54, 96
Kim, E. H., 48
King, M., 593
Kinston, W., 681
Kinzie, D., 619
Kinzie, J. D., 50
Kitchener, K. S., 643, 659
Klebba, K. B., 4
Kleber, R. F., 419
Klein, H., 619
Klein, L., 235, 249
Klein, M., 60, 61, 74, 83, 84, 110, 113, 233, 393, 394, 500, 509, 561
Klein, R., 74
Kleinman, A., 212
Kliman, J., 212, 687
Klintsova, A. Y., 116
Knell, S. M., 61, 84
Knight, M., 337
Kniskern, D., 26, 390, 396, 490, 496, 670
Knoff, H. M., 172
Knowlton, R., 225

Author Index

Knudson-Martin, C., 490, 511
Kocsis, J. H., 327
Koenig, H. G., 299
Koerner, K., 398
Koestler, A., 491
Kohlberg, L., 470, 515
Kohut, H., 233
Kolodny, R. C., 168
Kopp, R. R., 190
Kordan, D., 619
Koretz, G., 280
Korzybski, A., 530
Kostelny, K., 419
Kottman, T., 59, 63
Kramer, S. Z., 283
Krasner, B., 395, 399, 471, 491, 497, 513, 515, 618, 620, 673, 680
Kratochwill, T. R., 84
Krell, R., 619
Krestan, J. A., 211
Kristeva, J., 208
Krueger, D. W., 592
Krycka, K. C., 303, 326
Krystal, H., 617, 619, 630
Kuhn, T., 530
Kulka, R. A., 403, 617, 618
Kumpfer, K., 209
Kupelian, D., 615
Kurtines, W., 208, 211
Kwant, R. C., 593

L'Abate, L., 578
Labovitz Boik, B., 74
Lacan, J., 650, 651
Ladany, N., 154, 156, 157, 158, 692, 693
Ladd, G. W., 631
LaFontaine, R. M., 192
LaFountain, R., 151
LaFromboise, T., 157
Lagos, D., 619
Lai, E. W. M., 158, 159
Laing, R., 497, 498, 499, 500, 510, 517, 518, 593, 650, 705, 707
Laird, J., 206, 211, 414, 426, 427
Laird, M., 109
Lam, M. L., 36

Lambo, T. A., 654
Landau-Stanton, J., 16, 211
Landay, A., 311
Landreth, G. L., 60, 62, 64, 75, 84, 128
Lanham, K., 50
Lannamann, J., 136, 502, 510
Lappin, J., 687
Larson, N., 92
Lasch, C., 270
Laufer, R. S., 617
Lawe, C. F., 180
Lazarus, R. S., 631
Lederman, M. M., 311
Lee, A., 60, 85, 86, 90, 92, 93, 94, 96, 102, 498, 499, 500, 510, 517, 518
Lee, E., 36, 53, 54
Lee, L. C., 36, 54
Lee, S. S., 596
LeFevre, C., 195
Lefrancois, G. R., 161
Leggett, A., 67
Leiberich, P., 322
Leitenberg, H., 120
Leman, K., 186
Leonard, L. S., 505, 509
Leone Guglielmotti, R., 557, 571
Leong, F. T., 53
Lerner, M. J., 186
Leung, P. K., 37, 619
Levant, R., 235, 249
Levin, P., 557
Levinas, E., 205
Levine, P. A., 592
Levinson, D. J., 515
Levi-Strauss, C., 650
Levy, D., 60
Lew, A., 181
Lewin, K., 393, 494, 495, 501, 516
Lewis, B., 235, 249
Lewis, J. A., 182
Lewis, M., 497
Lewis, R. A., 27
Leyens, J.-P., 495
Liang, B., 249
Liberman, M. A., 459, 578
Lichtenstein, S., 617

Liddle, H. A., 4, 27, 208, 209, 211, 225, 670, 677, 678, 683, 692
Lidz, R. W., 490
Lidz, T., 490, 517
Liebman, R., 27
Liese, B. S., 669, 670, 671, 674
Lietaer, G., 593, 608
Lin, S. C., 45
Lincoln, Y. S., 578
Lindahl, K. M., 397
Lindblad-Goldberg, M., 8, 209, 220, 503
Lindy, J. D., 123, 624
Linehan, M. M., 299, 671
Little, M., 596
Littrell, J., 151
Loafer, R., 631
Lobovits, D., 85, 87, 88, 91, 92
Lombardi, D. N., 183, 185
Long, J. K., 687
Loo, C. M., 619
Lord, F. B., 39
Lord, R. W., 39
Lorenz, A. D., 206
Loveland, N. T., 516
Lowen, A., 592
Lu, F. G., 36
Ludwig, M., 587
Luepnitz, D. A., 413
Luijpen, W. A., 593
Lukas, E., 337, 338, 340, 341, 342, 343, 344, 345, 346, 348, 350, 352
Lukens, M. D., 276, 283, 646
Lukens, R. J., 276, 283, 646
Lum, J. L., 36
Luria, A. R., 115
Lusterman, D., 96, 206
Lutgendorf, S. K., 327
Lynch, M., 4

Mace, D., 407
Machado, P. P., 692
MacLean, P., 235
MacMurray, J., 252
Macnaughton, I., 592
Madanes, C., 155, 492, 496, 502, 503, 505, 512, 513, 618

Maddeaux, C., 86
Maddi, S. R., 306, 309, 315, 318
Maddock, J., 92
Maddux, J. F., 299
Madhubuti, H. R., 161
Madonna, J. M., 65, 67
Madsen, R., 280
Madsen, W. C., 208, 209, 210, 213, 220, 223
Mahler, M., 447
Maholick, L. T., 337, 339, 354
Makinen, J. A., 400
Malamuth, N. M., 397
Malatesta, C., 9
Malchiodi, C., 63, 74, 95
Malgady, R. G., 516
Malinosky-Rummell, R., 109
Malli, J., 151
Malloy, E. S., 90
Malone, P. E., 517
Malone, T. P., 490, 513, 515
Manaster, G. J., 185, 186, 191, 192, 199
Mandela, N., 654
Mangel, N., 184
Maniacci, M., 179, 180, 183, 184
Mann, B. J., 26
Mann, E., 112
Mann, S. J., 551
Mannarino, A. P., 66, 68
Mansager, E., 182
Manson, S., 619
Manuel, G. M., 167
Manus, G. I., 390
Marcel, A., 592
Marcel, G., 470, 474
Marcher, L., 592
Marcia, J. E., 153
Marcotte, D., 167
Marecek, J., 211
Mareck, J., 417
Margolin, G., 398
Marin, G., 158, 172
Markman, H. J., 397, 398
Markowitz, J. C., 327
Marmar, C. R., 617
Martin, H. P., 65

Martinez, M., 669, 677, 678, 702, 710, 711, 715
Marvasti, J. A., 60, 67, 69
Marvin, R. S., 8
Marzolf, K., 92, 93
Mashburn, D., 299
Maslow, A., 257, 501, 503, 622, 628, 670, 672, 673, 684, 701, 707, 708, 713, 714
Mason, M., 288, 293
Massey, R. F., 489, 492, 496, 498, 499, 501, 502, 503, 555, 557, 560, 561, 566, 567, 679, 711
Massey, S., 489, 557, 670, 678, 679, 709
Masten, A. S., 9
Masters, W. H., 168, 571
Masterson, J., 497
Matthews, D. A., 299
Maturana, H. R., 493
Matuschka, E., 503
Matute-Bianchi, M. E., 168
Mauksch, L. A., 206
Maul, B., 592
May, J., 606, 608
May, R., 256, 257, 282, 305, 306, 307, 309, 312, 313, 314, 315, 318, 320, 327, 593, 672, 701, 706, 707
Mayer, J. D., 5
Mayhew, J., 186
Mazumdar, D. P., 550
McCarroll, J. E., 631
McCaughhey, B. G., 631
McClenaghan, J. C., 578
McClendon, G., 435, 446, 447, 460
McClendon, R., 435, 446, 557
McCoard, B., 96
McCormick, P., 578
McCown, W., 137
McDaniel, J. S., 310, 311, 325
McDaniel, S., 206, 208, 504, 670, 678
McDavis, R. J., 173
McDermott, J. F., 112
McDonald, L., 209
McDougald, J., 303
McDougall, J., 592

McDougall, W., 494
McEvoy, L., 618, 631
McFarlane, A. C., 401
McGarty, C., 493
McGoldrick, M., 6, 37, 157, 166, 182, 186, 210, 211, 212, 214, 216, 220, 285, 389, 396, 497, 502, 503, 505, 510, 514
McGuire, K. N., 404
McIntosh, P., 251
Mc Kay, G. D., 181
Mc Kay, J. L., 181
McKeever, J., 670, 678
McLaughlin, J. T., 595, 596
McLeer, M. D., 68
McLendon, J. A., 441
McLeod, J. D., 631
McMahon, L., 64
McNeel, J., 443, 444, 459, 503, 575, 577, 578
McNeill, B. W., 676, 692
Mead, G. H., 494, 497, 498, 499, 518, 530, 536
Mead, G. W., 677
Meadows, L. A., 95
Meehl, P. E., 516
Mehdi, P. R., 550
Mehta, P., 156, 160
Mellor, K., 438, 448, 556, 569, 577
Melton, G. B., 27
Mendelson, M., 550
Menendez, A. V., 167
Menghi, P., 360
Menninger, K., 279
Merleau-Ponty, M., 305, 502, 593
Merton, R. K., 501
Mesalam, B., 96
Messineo, T., 414, 415, 505, 516
Meyers, L. J., 162
Michel, M. K., 9
Micucci, J. A., 16
Middleberg, C., 500
Miglionico, A., 557, 571
Mikesell, R., 206
Miles, M. B., 459, 578
Milgram, S., 515
Miller, A., 122
Miller, B. D., 4

Miller, C., 96
Miller, D. E., 620
Miller, G., 135, 137, 149
Miller, J., 234, 235, 236, 237, 238, 239, 240, 241, 248, 249, 251, 313
Miller, L. T., 620
Miller, S., 137, 138, 578
Miller, W. R., 298, 299
Millikin, J. W., 400
Millman, H. L., 69
Millon, C., 319
Millon, T., 516
Milman, L., 27
Milton, M., 303
Mintz, E. E., 596
Mintzer, M. B., 95
Minuchin, P., 3, 208, 213, 491, 505
Minuchin, S., 3, 26, 27, 182, 191, 194, 206, 393, 395, 459, 490, 491, 498, 500, 503, 505, 511, 514
Mirkim, M. P., 687
Mirkin, M. P., 414
Mitchell, S., 234
Mittlemann, B., 489
Miyamoto, J., 43
Miyoshi, N., 620
Mock, J., 550
Moffett, D. E., 533
Mohanty, C., 416
Mohr, E., 181
Moiso, C. M., 557, 560, 568, 570, 571, 572, 579
Molina, B., 192
Momb, D., 448
Monk, G., 415
Montalvo, B., 3, 16, 206
Moon, S., 430
Moonen, D. J., 325
Moore, L. J., 37, 619
Moore, M., 16
Moore Hines, P., 212
Moos, R., 459
Morano, C. K., 154
Moreno, J., 439, 529, 530, 531, 532, 533, 534, 535, 536, 537, 538, 539, 540, 542, 543, 544, 545, 546, 551, 673, 703
Moreno, Z. T., 531, 532, 534, 539, 540, 541, 551
Morgan, C., 516
Morgan, M. G., 327
Morgan, R., 319
Mori, T., 40
Morin, E., 491
Morishima, J., 35, 36
Morris, R. J., 84
Morrison, G. M., 172
Mosak, H. H., 179, 180, 183, 184, 190, 191, 192
Moscovici, S., 494, 495
Mosher, E. S., 168, 169
Moursund, J. P., 557
Moustakas, C., 60, 84, 257
Mowrer, O. H., 701
Mueller, W. J., 670
Mulder, C. L., 327
Mulder, J. W., 327
Mulroy, E. A., 172
Muran, J. C., 607
Murayama, S., 659
Murphy, D. A., 327
Murphy, G., 257, 701
Murray, E., 28
Murray, H. A., 257, 516, 701
Murray, J., 397
Mydans, S., 42
Mylvaganam, G. A., 156

Nagata, D., 37, 39, 620
Nagel, R., 172
Naidoo, J. C., 158
Nasca, A., 492, 503
Natanson, M., 496, 498, 518
Neill, J. R., 396, 490, 496
Neufeldt, S. A., 692
Newcombe, T. M., 494
Nicholas, M., 293
Nichols, M., 3, 390, 402, 408, 464, 491
Nichols, W. C., 402
Nicoll, W., 190
Nicolo-Corigliano, A. M., 360
Niederland, W., 619

Niedner, D. M., 66
Nietzsche, F., 305
Nikelly, A., 192
Nill, D., 265
Nisbett, R. E., 495
Nkrumah, K., 654
Noda, S. J., 182
Noddings, N., 470
Nogueira, J., 8, 12, 16
Noguera, P. A., 161, 165
Noriega Gayol, G., 578
Nouwen, H. J. M., 283, 284, 290, 293, 295, 296
Novellino, M., 557, 568, 570, 571, 572, 579
Novey, T. B., 579
Nowak, M., 472
Nurse, A. R., 503, 516
Nutall, E. V., 172
Nuttin, J., 496
Nyerere, J., 654

Oakes, P. J., 495, 499
Oaklander, V., 63, 112
Obeyesekere, G., 619
O'Connor, J., 515
O'Connor, K. J., 60, 63, 64, 84
O'Donnell, L., 9
Oezbay, H., 550
Oeztuerk, E., 550
Ogbu, J. U., 172
Oh, A., 45
O'Hanlon, W. H., 133, 136
O'Hara, M., 281
Ohlsson, T., 560
Okundaye, J. N., 282
Olbrich, E., 322
O'Leary, D. K., 397, 398
O'Leary, K. D., 398
Olmedo, E. L., 167
O'Neil, J., 593
Oresky, P., 182
Orfanidis, M., 514
Orgler, H., 180
Orten, J. D., 563, 567
Osborn, J. E., 310
Osborne, L. N., 391
Osmond, M., 67

Oster, G. D., 90, 94
Ostrom, R., 299
O'Sullivan, M. J., 620
Ottens, A. J., 313
Ozaki, M., 40

Padilla, A. M., 167
Page, K., 472
Paget, K., 172
Paivo, S. C., 578
Pakenham, K. I., 319
Palazzoli, M. S., 491, 496, 500
Panangiotides, H., 115
Papanek, H., 180, 182
Papero, D. V., 393, 395
Papp, P., 414, 491, 492, 503, 505
Pardeck, J. T., 96
Parham, T. A., 161
Parker, K., 27
Parnell, M., 206, 212
Parsons, B. V., 209
Partelno-Bareehmi, C., 550
Parten, M. B., 111
Patterson, C. H., 669, 670, 671, 676
Patterson, J., 646
Patton, M. J., 692
Paulson, S. E., 172
Payne, Y., 161, 163, 165
Pearce, J., 37, 166, 211, 214, 285, 510
Pearlman, L. A., 422
Pearson, P., 435, 447, 557
Peck, M. S., 287
Pedder, J. R., 596
Penfield, W., 436, 557, 577
Penn, P., 492, 505, 516
Pepitone, A., 495
Perez, C., 127
Perez-Vidal, A., 27
Perker, B., 490
Perls, F., 435, 438, 439, 440, 442, 543, 576, 673, 677, 703
Perrin, S., 67
Perrott, L. A., 551
Perry, B. J., 171
Perry, S., 322
Pesso, A., 448

Peterson, E., 618
Peterson, M., 641, 665, 676
Phenice, L. A., 166
Phillip, A. S., 186
Phillip, C. R., 186
Phillips, K. D., 311
Phillips, R., 128
Phillipson, H., 498, 499, 500, 510, 517, 518
Philpot, C., 211
Phinney, J. S., 157, 159, 168
Piaget, J., 470, 497, 565
Pierce, R. A., 401
Pierce, R. M., 692
Pierce, W. B., 424
Piercy, F. P., 27
Pinderhughes, E., 211, 214, 215
Pine, F., 447
Pipher, M., 505, 510
Plante, T. G., 167
Poe, E. A., 651
Polanyi, M., 677, 678, 702
Polkinghorne, D. P., 276
Pollack, W., 235, 249
Polson, M., 97
Polster, E., 439
Polster, M., 439
Pope, K., 596
Popkin, M., 181
Portnoy, D., 313, 320
Powderly, W. G., 311
Power, T. J., 16
Prado, L., 397
Prata, G., 370, 500
Prathikanti, S., 158
Pratt, A. C., 422
Pravder Mirkin, M., 211, 212, 214
Prescott, J. W., 513
Prigogine, I., 474, 652, 678, 705, 711
Probst, L. R., 299
Prout, H. T., 84
Puget, J., 619
Pugh, C., 209
Putnam, R. D., 280
Pynoos, R. S., 123

Quarantelli, E. L., 616, 632

Rabinow, P., 206
Rabkin, J. G., 310, 312
Rachman, A. W., 589
Racusin, G. R., 95
Rafferty, J., 516
Rampage, C., 211
Randall, M. B., 550
Randall, R. R., 430
Rank, O., 60
Ransom, D. C., 206
Raskin, M., 646
Rath, B., 50
Ratliff, D. A., 430
Rauschenbaum, B., 505
Ray, D., 59, 79, 127
Rechtman, N., 619
Rector, J. M., 299
Rediger, S., 486
Reed, G. M., 326
Reich, W., 439, 588, 589, 590, 591, 598, 606, 608
Reichert, T., 94
Reiner, P. A., 670, 675
Reiss, D., 15, 211, 282
Remien, R. H., 310, 312
Rempel, J., 399
Renick, M. J., 397
Rennie, D. L., 608
Revenstorf, D., 398
Reviere, S. L., 596
Rezaiane, M. P., 550
Reznick, J. S., 10
Reznick, M., 249
Richards, P. S., 299
Richardson, F. C., 211, 214
Richman, D., 448, 556, 569
Rieger, M., 322
Riessman, C. K., 430
Rigazio-Digilio, S., 676, 678
Riley, C., 37, 619
Riley, S., 95
Rio, A., 28
Roberto, L. G., 396
Roberts, J., 415, 426
Roberts, L., 577
Robin, P. K., 426
Robins, L. N., 618, 631
Robins, M., 10

Rodick, J. D., 172
Rodriguez, L. M., 166
Rogers, C., 60, 62, 160, 257, 389, 497, 670, 671, 700, 701, 702
Rogler, L. H., 516
Rojas, A., 420
Rolf, I., 594
Romero, I., 172
Ronnestad, M. H., 676
Roopnarine, J. L., 166
Root, M. P. P., 36, 37
Rosado, J. W., 171
Rosch, E., 592
Rose, S. P., 114
Rosen, W., 241
Rosenbloom, D. J., 422
Rosenheck, R., 618
Rosenkrantz, P., 234
Rosenman, R. H., 271
Rosman, B., 3, 26, 27, 206
Ross, L., 495, 516
Roth, A., 28
Roth, B., 619
Roth, S., 426
Rotter, J. B., 501, 516
Rountree, Y. B., 182
Rowe, C. L., 225
Rowland, M. D., 4
Rubbert, A., 322
Ruberto, A., 362
Rubin, J. A., 74
Rucker-Embden, I., 492, 509
Ruderman, E. G., 596
Rudolf, G., 41
Rugala, S. A., 313
Ruiz, P., 166
Rundell, J. R., 617
Runyan, D. K., 109
Russell, A., 629
Russell, C. S., 677
Russell, G. F. M., 16, 27
Russo, A., 416
Rutter, M., 66
Ryan, P. R., 551
Ryckoff, I. M., 490
Rykoff, I., 470

Saarni, C., 10
Saba, G. W., 211, 677, 683
Sack, H. W., 619
Sack, W. H., 50
Safran, J. D., 593, 607, 670
Sagi, A., 235
Sahakian, W. S., 337, 354
Salerian, A., 618
Salomone, P. R., 162
Salovey, P., 5
Sameroff, A., 4
Sanchez, G., 418
Sanderson, C., 299
Sandfort, T. G. M., 327
Sandgrund, A., 64, 110
Sandhu, D. S., 158
Sandler, A.-M., 607
Sandler, J., 607
Sanford, R. N., 515
Santisteban, D., 27
Sapolsky, R., 282
Saporta, J., 122, 123, 616
Saraydarian, L., 618, 619
Sardello, R., 593
Sargent, J., 16
Sartre, J., 305, 306, 308, 474, 707
Satir, V., 391, 393, 397, 435, 440, 441, 442, 446, 467, 673, 703
Satz, P., 313
Sauber, S. R., 182
Saucier, B., 128
Saunders, B., 68
Savin-Williams, R. C., 211
Sayers, S. L., 398
Scarf, M., 397, 500
Schacht, A. J., 692
Schachtel, E., 499
Schachter, S., 498
Schaef, A. W., 271
Schaefer, C. E., 59, 60, 63, 64, 65, 67, 68, 69, 84, 109, 110
Schaller, J., 486
Schaper, P. E., 325
Scharf, C., 224
Scharff, D., 394
Scharff, J. S., 394
Schauble, P. G., 692
Scheff, T. J., 504

Scheflen, A., 206, 651
Scheler, M., 335
Schiff, A. W., 438, 448
Schiff, E., 448, 556, 569
Schiff, J. L., 448, 556, 569
Schiff, S., 448, 556, 569
Schindler, D., 407
Schiraldi, G. R., 617
Schlenger, W. E., 617
Schmeidler, J., 109
Schnarch, D., 362
Schneider, K. J., 256, 305, 313, 314, 315, 320
Schoenbaum, M., 161, 165
Schoenwald, S. K., 4
Schorr, L. B., 206, 214
Schrader, S., 208, 670
Schramski, T. G., 182
Schultz, S., 452
Schumacher, K., 322
Schumer, F., 3, 206
Schwartz, J. A. J., 312, 316, 320, 321, 322, 325
Schwartz, R., 3, 94, 390, 678
Schwartzberg, S. S., 303, 311, 325
Schwebel, A. I., 104
Scopetta, M., 8
Scrivner, R., 211
Seaburn, D. B., 206
Seagram, B., 151
Searles, H., 596
Seeley, J., 50
Sefarbi, R., 16
Segal, L., 173
Segal, Z. V., 670
Segal-Andrews, A., 16
Segerstrom, S. C., 326
Seligman, M. E. P., 578, 630
Sells, J. N., 285
Selman, R., 498
Selvini, M., 491, 496
Selvini Palazzoli, M., 370
Sen, A. K., 550
Senghor, L. S., 654
Serrano, A. C., 26
Seyle, H., 112
Shahinian, S. P., 618, 619
Shalev, A., 618

Shane, E., 596
Shane, M., 596
Shapiro, A., 76
Sharaf, M., 592
Shaver, P., 394, 402
Sheinberg, M., 492, 505, 516
Shenk, J. L., 397
Sheppard, I., 438, 439
Sher, T. G., 398
Sherif, M., 494, 502
Sherman, R., 179, 180, 182, 185, 186, 187, 190, 191, 192
Sherrard, P. A. D., 155, 173
Shibusawa, T., 659
Shibutani, T., 499
Shobet, R., 676
Sholevar, G. P., 94
Shore, J. H., 631
Shostrom, E., 459
Shreeve, J., 471
Shulman, B. H., 180, 191
Shumsky, A., 182
Siegal, C., 4
Siegel, 9
Siever, L. J., 109
Sigmund, K., 472
Silberman, E. K., 617
Sillen, S., 211
Sills, C., 557, 569
Silver, M., 16
Silver, N., 578
Silverstein, O., 414, 492, 505
Sime, J. D., 632
Simek-Morgan, L., 211
Simms, S., 16
Simner, M., 235
Simon, G. M., 4
Simon, J., 136, 137, 140
Simon, R., 206, 440
Simons, V. A., 87, 90
Sinclair-Brown, W., 460
Singer, J. E., 490, 498, 516
Singer, M. T., 490
Siqueland, L., 4, 28
Skokan, L. A., 322
Skovholt, T. M., 676
Slavik, S., 184
Slovic, P., 617

Sluzki, C., 38, 206, 430
Smith, D., 37, 397, 398, 619, 631
Smith, E. M., 631
Smith, E. W. L., 180, 588, 591, 596
Smith, G. L., 94
Smith, L., 27, 592
Smith, M. B., 499, 515
Smith, P., 66, 67
Smith, R., 66, 285
Snidman, N., 10
Snyder, C. R., 298
Sobol, B., 77
Sodowsky, G. R., 157, 158, 159
Soga, K., 40
Solomon, J. C., 60
Solomon, M. F., 403
Solomon, R. C., 304, 305
Solomon, S. D., 631
Solomon, Z., 631
Sonis, W. A., 26
Sonstegard, M., 182
Sorrentino, A. M., 491, 496
Sowder, W. F., 578
Sowell, R. L., 311
Soyinka, W., 654
Spanier, G., 405, 517
Spark, G., 371, 471
Spark, G. L., 391, 395
Spark, G. M., 496, 500, 513, 515
Spence, D. P., 607
Spencer, M. B., 172
Sperling, M. B., 394
Sperry, L., 182, 187, 188, 193
Spiegelberg, H., 474, 593
Spielman, L. A., 327
Spitz, R., 115, 436, 437, 561, 577
Spivak, G. C., 416
Spolin, V., 533
Sprenkle, D., 27, 430
Sroufe, L. A., 4
Stallings, R., 616
Stanley, S. M., 397
Stanton, M. D., 16, 25, 211
Starr, K., 327
Stattone, T. M., 550
Steenbarger, B. N., 568
Steinberg, A., 619
Steinberg, F. E., 673

Steiner, C. M., 556, 561, 565, 569
Steinglass, P., 211, 497
Stengers, I., 652
Stepansky, P. E., 180
Stepath, S. A., 550
Stephens, S., 50
Stephenson, W., 578
Sterling, M. M., 322, 325
Stern, E., 557
Stern, L., 8, 209, 220, 503
Stevenson, H. C., 16
Stevenson, Y., 327, 415
Stewart, A. J., 620
Stewart, I., 568
Stewart, R. B., 8
Stierlin, H., 492, 509
Stillson, L., 321
Stiver, I., 234, 235, 236, 237, 238, 239, 241, 248
Stolorow, R., 234, 630
Stoltenberg, C. D., 676, 692
Stolz, S. B., 632
Stolz, V., 181
Stone, M., 180, 246
Stone Fish, L., 94
Stoneman, Z., 172
Stoner, G., 97
Storm, C., 670, 676, 678
Straker, G., 562
Strayhorn, J., 10
Streitmatter, J. L., 168
Strom, A., 51
Strosahl, K. D., 293
Sucoff, C. A., 172
Sue, D., 35, 36, 38, 156, 157, 158, 159, 162, 163, 166, 169, 173, 502, 504
Sue, S., 35, 36, 39, 54, 158, 407
Sullivan, H. S., 310, 489, 497, 498, 517, 673, 705
Sullivan, W. M., 280
Sulloway, F. J., 186
Surrey, J., 234, 235, 239, 249, 416, 425
Sustento-Seneriches, J., 41
Swan, G. E., 271
Swanson, C., 397
Swede, S., 578

Sweeney, D. S., 60, 62, 64, 75
Swidler, A., 280
Szapocznik, J., 27, 28, 208, 211, 319
Szasz, T. S., 504
Szmukler, G. I., 16, 27

Tajfel, H., 495, 499
Takaki, R., 44
Takei, S., 40
Talitman, E., 407
Tan, S. Y., 287, 288
Tang, N. M., 53
Tarule, J., 234, 249
Tatum, B. D., 251
Tatum, E. L., 631
Taylor, C., 235, 249
Taylor, E., 670, 701, 702
Taylor, S., 235, 249, 322, 325, 326
Teicher, A., 596
Tejeda, M., 27
Tello, J., 415
Temerlin, J., 541
Temerlin, M., 541
Terr, L., 60, 68, 69, 110, 120, 121, 123
Terry, D., 319, 490, 517
Teyber, E., 173, 674
Thatcher, R. W., 115
Thelen, E., 592
Thiessen-Barrett, J., 95
Thomas, A., 211
Thomas, V., 83, 91
Thompson, C., 489
Thompson, E., 592
Thomson, G., 578
Thoresen, C., 271
Tien, L., 42
Tierney, K. J., 616
Tillich, P., 258
Tinney, J. S., 163
Tipton, S. M., 280
Tjeltveit, A. C., 299
Todd, T. C., 16, 25, 27, 211, 670, 678
Todisco, M., 162
Tolan, P. H., 26
Toman, W., 186

Tomm, K., 136, 676
Tommasini, A., 35, 56
Tompkins, S., 241
Torres, L., 416
Torres, R. A., 311
Toth, S. L., 4, 109, 120
Totton, N., 588, 590
Toukmanian, S. G., 608
Toussaint, P., 216
Tracy, A., 249
Tran, C., 42
Trepper, T. S., 27, 66, 68
Triandis, H. C., 276, 495, 502
Triantafillou, N., 151
Trickett, P. K., 109
Trimble, M. R., 616, 617
Truax, C. B., 692
Turkle, S., 650
Turner, C., 646
Turner, J., 414, 415, 495, 499

Uba, L., 36, 38, 44, 54
Ujimoto, K. V., 36
Untermeyer, L., 294
Updegraff, J., 235, 249
Urey, J. R., 172
Ursano, R. J., 617, 618, 631
Utsey, S. O., 161, 165

Valle, R., 265, 593
Valsiner, J., 616, 677, 711
Vande Kemp, H., 279
Van den Eerembeemt, E.-M., 486
Van der Hart, O., 616
Vanderkloot, J., 212
van der Kolk, B. A., 122, 123, 248, 401
Van der Kolk, B. A., 616
Van der Veer, R., 616
van der Veer, R., 677, 711
Vanderwood, M., 151
van Deurzen, E., 303, 304, 305, 306, 307, 313
Van Fleet, R., 96
van Gorp, W. G., 313
van Kaam, A., 496
Varela, de, 394
Varela, F., 493, 592

Vasquez, M., 596
Vaughn Heineman, T., 65
Vega, W. A., 167
Veith, I., 616
Vella, G., 362
Venkatachalam, M., 492, 503
Veroff, J., 403
Viney, L. L., 321
Visscher, B. R., 326
Vivian, D., 397, 398
Vo, H., 50
Vogel, S., 234
Volk, R. J., 518
von Bertalanffy, L., 84, 104, 370, 471, 678
von Eckartsberg, R., 593
von Foerster, H., 652
Vygotsky, L. S., 704

Wagner, N. N., 36
Wagner, N. W., 36
Waidman, T., 161, 165
Wainman-Sauda, J., 94
Waldegrave, C., 428
Waldo, M., 313
Walker, G., 505, 516
Walker, L. E. A., 404
Walker, M., 239, 241, 251
Wall, S., 394
Wallerstein, J., 95, 391, 398
Wallerstein, R. S., 670
Walmsley, R., 321
Walsh, F., 211
Walters, M., 414, 492, 505
Walters, P. A., 578
Walton, F. X., 180
Waltz, J. A., 671
Ward, C. H., 550
Ware, P., 447
Warheit, B., 617
Warheit, G., 616
Waring, E. M., 398, 517
Warlick, J., 63
Warren, B., 95
Waterman, A. S., 674
Waters, E., 394
Watkins, B., 66
Watkins, C. E., 199

Author Index

Watkins, J. B., 8, 12, 16
Watkins, P., 299
Watson, J. R., 578
Watson, S. M., 172
Watson, W. L., 211
Watts, R. E., 180, 182
Watzlavick, P., 370
Watzlawick, P., 3, 500, 651
Way, L., 193
Weakland, J., 84, 104, 173, 490, 517
Webb, N. B., 64, 78, 112
Weber, T., 670, 678
Wechsler, D., 575
Weiner-Davis, M., 138
Weingarten, K., 211, 414, 415, 416, 417, 425, 427, 428, 429, 430
Weinrich, M., 631
Weinrich, S., 631
Weinshel, M., 224
Weiss, E., 436, 437, 557, 577
Weiss, R. L., 397, 398
Weltman, S., 157
Wener, E., 66
Werner, H., 393
Wessler, R. L., 669
West, Y. N., 166
Wetzel, N., 206, 207, 208, 209, 212, 215, 216, 219, 221, 225, 226, 492, 509
Wheeler, M. S., 191
Whiffen, V. E., 400, 403
Whitaker, C., 85, 86, 88, 92, 98, 99, 371, 392, 393, 396, 490, 500, 513, 515
White, L. J., 155
White, M., 19, 87, 88, 90, 94, 415, 417, 425, 426, 428, 430, 493, 497, 505, 514, 677
White, R. W., 6

Whiteside, R. G., 673
Wicks, R. J., 288
Widdon, M. F., 337
Wilber, K., 673, 678, 684, 702, 712, 713
Willi, J., 497, 500
Williams, A., 676
Williams, J. E., 578
Williams, J. G., 578
Williams, L., 65, 66, 109, 117, 249
Williams, M. L., 74
Williams, S., 597
Williams-Keeler, L., 10, 403
Williamson, D. S., 371, 374, 517
Wilson, A., 9
Wilson, C. R., 310, 312
Wilson, K. G., 293
Wilson, W. J., 211, 212, 213, 220
Winawer, H., 216, 221, 224
Winawer-Steiner, H., 223
Winderman, L., 493
Winiarski, M. G., 303, 310, 311, 312, 313
Winnicott, D., 85, 90, 233, 234, 362
Winslade, J., 415
Winter, J. E., 291
Wirsching, M., 492, 509
Wistow, F., 206
Wittels, F., 489
Wittgenstein, L., 135, 415, 677
Wolfe, B. E., 607
Wolin, S., 66, 211
Wolpe, J., 669
Wolz, L., 448
Wonderlich, S., 517
Wong, B., 41
Wong, P. T. P., 36
Wood, B. L., 4, 7, 8, 12, 16
Wood, M., 414
Wood, W. C., 337

Wood, W. M., 337
Woodard, C. V., 161
Woods, R., 505, 516
Woolfolk, R. L., 280, 281, 290
Worthen, D., 290
Worthington, E. L., Jr., 676, 692
Wright, K. M., 631
Wright, L. M., 211
Wrightsman, L., 515
Wulff, D. M., 279
Wyatt, G. E., 161, 162
Wylie, M. S., 287, 290, 291
Wynne, L. C., 9, 206, 207, 470, 490, 516, 517

Yablonsky, L., 542, 545
Yager, T., 631
Yahne, C. E., 298
Yalom, I. D., 256, 257, 258, 275, 303, 307, 308, 309, 312, 313, 316, 317, 318, 320, 321, 322, 327, 459, 578, 593
Yehuda, R., 109
Ying, Y., 159
Yontef, G., 593, 670, 671, 677
Young, J. E., 396, 403
Yuen, F. K., 42
Yule, W., 67

Zahn-Waxler, C., 9
Zane, N., 407
Zane, N. W., 35, 36, 39, 54
Zangari, M. E., 416
Zanna, M., 399
Zill, M., 160
Zimand, E., 8, 12, 16
Zimbardo, P. G., 502, 516
Zuckerman, M., 327
Zukav, G., 673
Zweig, S., 475
Zwerling, I., 359

Subject Index

Abused/maltreated children, 65–77. *See also* Sexual abuse
 biopsychosocial approach to play therapy with, 109–130
 case example, play therapy, 69–77
 empirical findings regarding common symptomatology, 65–66
 existential/experiential approaches to therapy, 93–94
 rationale for prescriptive approach or integrated treatment approaches, 69
 rationale for use of play therapy with, 68–69
 treatment needs of, 66–68
Accessibility, 262, 266
Acculturation, 47, 158, 216
"Actual," the, 259–260, 263–265, 266
Adaptations, performing/surviving, 447
Adjective Check List, 578
Adjustment disorder (logotherapy), 352–354
Adlerian therapy, 179–203
 assessment, 188–189
 assumptions about human nature, 182–183
 birth order, 186–187
 case example, 193–198
 change: reeducation/reorientation/new behaviors, 189–190
 community feeling and social interest, 184–185
 confronting irrational beliefs/behaviors, 190–191
 history, 180–182
 inferiority/superiority complexes, 184
 lifestyle, 183–184, 191–192
 major clinical contributions, 182
 problems/populations treated, 192–193
 psychology of place/persons/systems, 186
 psychology of use and selected line of movement, 185
 questioning in, 190
 research, 198–199
 roles, 186
 safeguarding tendencies, 185–186
 symptomatic persons, 187–188
 theoretical constructs, 182–188
 well persons/systems, 187
Adolescents/young adults:
 Adlerian therapy, 179–203
 of color (integrative approach to assessment/intervention), 153–178
 school-based, community family therapy for at-risk, 205–230
 solution-focused brief therapy with, 133–152
Adoption counseling, and contextual therapy, 476, 477–485
Adults:
 existential/humanistic psychotherapy, 255–277
 existential treatment with HIV/AIDS clients, 303–331
 logotherapy, 333–356
 relational-cultural perspective in therapy, 233–254
 spiritually-sensitive psychotherapy, 279–302
Affective proximity, 5, 8–9
Africa (therapy and professional ethics), 653–657, 659–665
African American(s):
 Adlerian psychology (case example), 193–198
 adolescents, 160–166
  case presentation, 163–166
  families, 162
  invisibility, 161–162
  racial identity development, 162–163
  spirituality, 163
  street life, 163

African American(s) *(Continued)*
  existential therapy, HIV victim (case example), 322–325
  school-based family therapy (case example), 205–230
Alcohol abuse (in case example, religious spirituality), 297–298
Amygdala hijack, 246
Anxiety:
  in case examples:
    existential/humanistic approach, 274–275
    logotherapy, 352–354
    transactional analysis/redecision therapy, 573–577
  in children, 94
  existential, 258, 261, 307, 309–312
  HIV/AIDS epidemic, contextual aspects of, 309–312
  trauma, and generalized anxiety disorder, 617
Appealing technique (logotherapy technique), 344–345
Asian American(s), 35–58, 156–160
  acculturation, 158
  adolescents, 156–160
  Cambodian family, 50–53
  case examples, 46–53, 159–160
  central role of culture in working with, 35–58
  Chinese Americans in United States, 41
  conceptual framework, 36–44
  differences/similarities among Asian cultures, 38–39
  ethnic identity, 158–159
  families, 157
  Filipino Americans in United States, 41–42
  gifts/food, and eating with Asian clients, 54–55
  history of therapeutic approach, 35–36
  identity issues, 42–44
  immigrants/immigration, 44–46, 157–158
  Indian mother experiencing dynamics of acculturation, 47
  integrative approach, 159–160
  Japanese Americans in United States, 39–41
  Korean Americans:
    case example: adolescent and family from Korea, 46–47
    and crisis of *sa-il-gu*, 44–46
  need for training of Asian therapists, 55–56
  PTSD, 50
  race/ethnicity/culture (definitions/distinctions), 36–38
  research, 36
  southeast Asian refugees, 49–50
  therapy for Asian clients, 53–56
  transference/countertransference, and self-disclosure, 54
  yin/yang, 53
Attachment-based family therapy (ABFT), 4, 8, 12, 15, 16, 26, 28
Attachment injuries, 400–401
Attachment theory/perspective, 8–9, 394–399, 402
Attention-Deficit/Hyperactivity Disorder (ADHD), 12, 16, 96–97, 481, 511
Attitudes, modification of (logotherapy technique), 340–342
Authenticity, 304–305
Autonomy, 118, 392–394, 438, 563, 660–661
Auxiliary ego (psychodrama element), 539
Avoidant personality disorder (in case example, body-centered psychotherapy), 605–606

Behavioral family model/therapy (BBFM/BBFT), 4, 8, 15, 16, 28
Being/being-in-the-world, 304, 306
Beneficence (international reflections on), 661–662
Biopsychosocial approach to play therapy with maltreated children, 109–130. *See also* Play therapy
  case example, 123–127
  conceptual framework, 114–120
  prescriptive-holistic guide to intervention, 114–120
    autonomy *vs.* shame and doubt (stage 2), 118
    basic trust *vs.* basic mistrust (stage 1), 116–118
    developmental processes and play, 116–120
    industry *vs.* inferiority (stage 4), 119–120
    initiative *vs.* guilt (stage 3), 118–119
    neurological development and impact of trauma, 114–116
  research, 127–128
  sequelae of child maltreatment and influences on development of victims, 120–122
  syndromes/symptoms/problems treated, 120–123
Biopsychosocial development, maturational age, 210, 211
Bipolar disorder, 482

Birth order, 186–187, 707
Body-centered psychotherapy, 587–613, 705
   case examples, 599–606
   experiential and Gestalt-oriented modalities and, 594
   history/evolution of, 588–592
   meanings/functions of touch in psychotherapy, 595–597
   modalities, 594–595
   phenomenological and experiential models, 592–595
   research, 606–608
   syndromes/symptoms/problems treated, 597–599
   theoretical constructs, 595–597
Borderline personality disorder, 403, 511
Boundaries, 7–8, 645
Breathing exercises, 625
Brief therapy. *See* Solution-focused brief therapy (SFBT)

Catharsis (psychodrama construct), 538
Cathexis, 556, 558
Causality, nonlinear, 674
Centering intervention, 288
Change:
   assumptions about (in solution-focused brief therapy), 136–137
   "changed child, changed world," 122–123
   contract for, 568
   existential anxiety and, 258
   existential/humanistic perspective on, 258
   freedom/choice and, 683–684
   pre-session questions, 138
   reeducation/reorientation/new behaviors (Adlerian therapy), 189–190
   time as indicator of, 376–379
Child-centered (nondirective) play therapy, 62–63, 77–79
"Child" ego state, 442
Children. *See also* Abused/maltreated children:
   Asian (central role of culture), 35–58
   biopsychosocial approach to play therapy, 109–130 (*see also* Play therapy)
   ecosystemic structural family therapy, 3–33
   existential/experiential approaches, 83–107
Children's Apperception Test, 516
Chinese Americans in United States, 41

Client-centered work, 702
Cognitive-behavioral approach, 61, 83, 84, 397
Collective neuroses, and logotherapy, 349
Communication:
   clear, 671
   parataxic, 705
Community:
   context for therapeutic work, 221–222
   feeling and social interest, 184–185
   health centers, 206
   school-based family therapy, 205–230
Conduct disorder, 93, 193–198, 477, 482
Confidentiality, 648
Conflict:
   couple, 396–399
   "good," 237
   safe space for, 398
Confluence, 439
Connections/disconnections, 236–237
Constructivism, 644
Contact cycle, 438
Contextual bond, 362
Contextual therapy, 463–488
   case example (adoption), 477–485
   factual determinants, 469, 482–483
   history: path of founder, 464–468
   indications for usage, 485–486
   ontic dimension of relationships, 473–475, 485
   psychological determinants, 469–471, 483
   relational ethics, 471–473, 484–485
   relationship theory, 468–469
   research, 486
   strategies and therapeutic contracts, 475–476
   syndromes/symptoms/problems treated, 476–477
   theoretical constructs, 468–475
   training, 485–486
   transactional determinants, 471, 483–484
Contingency, 258
Contract for change, 568
Conversation(s):
   levels (five) of presence in, 262, 266
   useful (in solution-focused brief therapy), 135–136
Countertransference. *See* Transference/countertransference
Couple therapy:
   case examples and follow-up reflections, 364–385
   child-focused treatment, 363–364

Couple therapy *(Continued)*
    contextual therapy, 463–488
    discovery of self-deceit, 361–363
    disguised, 363–368
    divorce following therapy, 372–374
    existential dilemmas and skill building in, 389–412
    families of origin and, 369–372, 374–376
    gender issues, 360–361
    history, 359–360, 390–391
    intergenerational dynamics, 369–372
    in Italy (sociocultural context), 360
    marriage in crisis from beginning, 379–383
    memory in service of personal story/history, 368–369
    multigenerational context, 366–376
    research, 385–386
    syndromes/symptoms/problems treated, 364
    theoretical constructs, 360–364
    time as indicator of change, 376–379
    as transforming process, 359–387
Crisis theorists, 632
Culture(s):
    bridging (Eastern and Western frames of reference), 713–715
    central role of, in working with Asian children/families, 35–58
    coevolving, 500–501
    ethics and, 641–643, 665–667
    relational-cultural perspective in therapy, 233–254
    social institutions, 501
    therapists' culture-determined lenses, 214–215

Death, 258, 308, 309, 316–317, 707
Deconstruction (process in narrative approach), 426–427
Deflection, 439
Delusion, playing/agreeing with, 89
Dependent personality disorder, 605–606
Depression:
    body-centered psychotherapy, 599
    dysthymia, 511, 599–602
    existential/experiential approaches (children), 94–95
    logotherapy, 346
    relational-cultural perspective in therapy, 241–245
    trauma and, 617
Depth psychotherapy, 264
Dereflection (logotherapy technique), 343–344

Desensitization, behavioral, 681
Developmental factor, 675–676
Developmental model (Erikson), and consequences of child maltreatment, 114–120
Developmental play therapy, 62
Dialectic aspects of assessment, 682–683
Differentiation, 393–394, 395, 397, 448–449
Dimensional ontology, theory of, 339
Disasters and trauma (definitions), 616–617
Discourse (process in narrative approach), 424–425
Dispositions, spiritual, 290
Divorce:
    children of (and their families), 95–96
    following therapy, 372–374
    mediation, and contextual therapy, 476
Drama. *See* Psychodrama
Drama triangles (Persecutor, Victim, Rescuer), 449–450, 562
Dream presentation (psychodrama technique), 543
Drug/alcohol abuse (logotherapy as adjunct form of therapy), 345
Dyadic Adjustment Scale (DAS), 405
Dyads, 500

EARS acronym (elicit/amplify/reinforce/start again), 148
Ecological perspective, 172–173
Ecological systems theory (Bronfenbrenner), 154–155
Ecosystemic structural home-based family therapy (ESSFT), 27
Ecuador (therapy and professional ethics), 646–649, 659–665
Ego states (Child/Adult/Parent), 436–437, 442, 557–561, 567
    defined, 436
    diagnosing, 567
    functional analysis of, 559–560
    social emphasis, 560
    structural analysis of, 558–559
Eigenwelt (personal world), 307, 313, 314
Emotionally focused couples therapy (EFCT), 104, 402–405
    case example, 405–407
    research, 407
    stages of therapy, 404–405
    targeted populations and assessment of relational problems, 402–404

Emotionally focused family therapy (EFFT), 86–87, 90, 94, 100–104
Emotion-coaching, 11
Empathy, 235, 238, 239, 624, 671
Encounter (psychodrama construct), 534–535
Epistemology, 182
Ethics/moral principles, 428–429, 641–667, 709
　autonomy, 660–661
　beneficence, 661–662
　cultural values and, 641–643, 665–667
　dilemmas, 656–657, 658
　fidelity, 664–665
　international perspectives on, 641–659, 660–665
　　from Africa, 653–657, 660–665
　　from Ecuador, 646–649, 660–665
　　from Europe, 649–653, 660–665
　　from Japan, 657–659, 660–665
　　from United States, 643–646, 660–665
　justice, 663–664
　nonmalfeasance, 662–663
　relational, 471–473, 484–485, 517
　stance (process in narrative approach), 428–429
Ethnicity, 210, 211. *See also* Culture(s)
　ethnic identity, 158–159
　vs. race/culture, 36–38
Eudaimonia, 674
Europe (therapy and professional ethics), 649–653, 659–665
Existential addiction/type A behavior, 271–274
Existential advantage, 563
Existential dilemmas, 389–412, 533
　autonomy *vs.* intimacy, 392–394
　in couple formation/development, 392–402
　facing differences and handling disagreement, 396–399
　resolution of family-of-origin dynamics, 394–399
　and skill building in couple therapy, 389–412
　solving with action in psychodrama, 533
　trust *vs.* mistrust, 399–401
Existential/experiential approaches to child/family psychotherapy, 83–107
　assessment/intervention methods, 88–92
　case examples, 97–104
　efficacy/effectiveness data, 104
　emotionally focused family therapy (EFFT), 86–87, 90, 94, 100–104
　history, 83–85
　narrative therapy, 87–88, 90–92
　perspectives (three), 83
　　cognitive-behavioral, 83, 84
　　psychoanalytic-psychodynamic, 83, 84
　　systems-oriented, 83, 84–85
　related constructs, 85–88
　symbolic-experiential approach, 85–86, 88–90, 97–100
　syndromes/symptoms/problems treated (children/families), 92–97
　　ADHD, 96–97
　　anxiety, 94
　　depression, 94–95
　　divorce, 95–96
　　oppositional defiant disorder, 96
　　physical abuse, 93–94722
　　sexual abuse, 92–93
Existential/humanistic psychotherapy with adults, 255–277
　accessibility, 262, 266
　a-partness, 258
　assessment methods, 263–265
　case examples, 271–275
　change, 258
　context, 266
　conversational presence (five levels), 262, 266
　death and contingency, 258
　depth psychotherapy, 264
　essentials of psychotherapeutic process, 260–261
　evoking greater client presence, 267–269
　existential anxiety, 258
　expressiveness, 262, 266
　focus on "the actual," 259–260, 266
　historical perspectives (converging sources of), 256–257
　intentionality and concern, 259, 260
　interpersonal press, 267–268
　optimal levels of therapeutic engagement, 261–263
　parallelling, 268–269
　phenomenological assessment, 264–265
　pou sto, 265–266
　presence, 260–261, 262, 266, 267–269
　primary therapeutic interventions, 265–270
　relinquishment, 258
　research, 275–276
　resistance, 261–263, 269–270
　responsibility, 258
　search process, 260

Existential/humanistic psychotherapy with
    adults *(Continued)*
  self-and-world construct system, 258–259, 261
  subjective experience, 259
  syndromes/symptoms/problems treated, 270–271
  theoretical constructs, 257–263
  therapeutic alliance, 260–269
  traditional psychodiagnostics, 263–264
Existential life positions, 450, 561
Existential psychology/psychotherapies, 672–673, 706–708
  analysis/comparison of theories (humanistic/interpersonal), and synthesis, 708–715
  existential concern in other therapies, 672–673
  HIV/AIDS clients, 303–331
  vs. logotherapy, 333
  responsibility and choice, 672
  themes, 672
  transcendence, 672
Experiential:
  existential/experiential approaches, 83–107
  models, and body work, 592–594
  symbolic-experiential family therapy, 85–86, 88–90, 97–100
Explanation *vs.* interpretation, 572
Expressiveness, 266
Externalization, technique of, 87
Eye Movement Desensitization and Reprocessing (EMDR), 629

Facticity, 305
False self, 362
Family(ies):
  context for therapeutic work, 220
  emotion regulation, 5, 9–11
  existential foundations of (systems as interconnecting social-psychological processes), 489–526
    assessment/intervention, 503–504, 509–511
    case example, 505–515
    coevolution of selves/families/cultures/societies, 500–501
    conceptual foundations, 496–503
    developmental social-psychological dynamics as matrix for preferred and impaired growth, 504–506
    development of social psychology, 493–495
    dyads, 500
    genogram, 512
    history, 489–493
    interconnecting, 496
    interpersonal security, 497
    isomorphic processes, 495
    models/dimensions, 489–493, 495–496
    multidimensional unities, 496
    multigenerational processes, 500
    research, 515–518
    social-psychological processes in holistic individual/family/system development, 496–503
    strategic maps, 514
    structural diagrams, 513
    subjectivity, evolution of, 497
    syndromes/symptoms/problems treated, 504–505
    triadic observations, 500
  forms, 207
  levels (four) of functioning (psychotic/immature/neurotic/mature), 452
  mediation, 363
  mood, 450
  structures, 6–9, 511
Family Environment Scale (FES), 459, 460
Family Intervention and Empowerment Program (FIEP), 209–222
  community context for therapeutic work, 221–222
  conceptual foundations, 209–218
  context (family/school), 219–220
  diagnosis, 210–212
  kaleidoscope of seven perspectives/lenses, 209–210
  model, 218–221
  personal relationship network ("virtual families"), 220–221
  postmodern diagnosis/assessment, 209–212
  socioeconomic perspective, 212–213
  strengths/resources, 213–214
  teams and administrative contexts, 218–219
  "unfamiliar world," 212–214
Family-of-origin dynamics, resolution of (my family or your family *vs.* our family), 394–399
Family therapy. *See also* Couple therapy:
  contextual, 463–488
  existential/experiential approaches, 83–107
  reconstruction, 705

redecision, 435–462
school-based, community; for adolescents at risk, 205–230
systems, 435, 440
Fantasy Marriage Technique, 503
FAST program (Families and Schools Together), 209
Feeling paralleling, 268–269
Feminist/narrative approach, 413–433. *See also* Narrative therapy
case example (exploration into meaning of resilience and human rights activism in women's life stories), 418–424
context: low-intensity war in Colombia, 418–419
life narrative, 419–424
deconstruction, 426–427
discourse, 424–425
ethical stance, 428–429
framework for analyses, 424–429
history, 413–415
narrative approaches to family therapy, 415–417
research, 430
story, 425
syndromes/symptoms/problems treated, 417–418
theoretical constructs, 415–417
treatment implications, 429
Feminist theorists, and relational-cultural perspective, 234
Fidelity (international reflections on), 664–665
Fight-or-flight, and gender bias, 249
Filial therapy, 63
Filipino Americans in United States, 41–42
Fluid expertise, 237
Frame paralleling, 269
Free association, 61
Freedom, 499, 672, 707
choice, and change, 683–684
existential concern, 308, 317–319
responsibility (ethical perspective, Europe), 652–653
Functional Family Therapy, 208–209

Game(s), 442, 445, 533, 562
Gender. *See also* Feminist/narrative approach:
bias (fight-or-flight), 249
issues, couple therapy, 360–361

role experience/gender identification, 210, 211, 216
underrepresenting role of, in therapy (silent sexism), 413
Generations, switching, 90
Genogram, 511, 512
Genuineness, 671
Gestalt therapy, 435, 594, 705
Global Assessment of Functioning (GAF) scale, 403
Global Assessment of Relational Functioning (GARF) scale, 403–404, 417, 570, 575, 599, 600, 621
Good conflict, 237
Group(s):
biopsychosocial/spiritual treatment of trauma, 615–637
body-centered psychotherapy, 587–613
imago, 561, 566
phases (*vs.* stages), 568
psychodrama, 529–553
as therapeutic tool, 567–568
transactional analysis, 555–585
Growth therapies, 702–705
Guilt, 118–119, 307

Halstead-Reitan, 516
HIV/AIDS clients, existential treatment with, 303–331, 707
assessment/intervention methods/considerations, 309–322
case example, 322–325
concept of "being" in existential psychology, 306
death, 308, 309, 316–317
freedom, 308, 317–319
history, 303–306
isolation, 308, 319–320
meaning, 325–326
meaninglessness, 308, 320–322
medical science as ultimate rescuer, 310–311
modes of world, 306–307, 313
overview of existentially informed HIV-related psychotherapy, 312–313
presence, 315–316
research, 325–328
specialness "exemption" and stigma, 310
syndromes/symptoms/problems treated, 322

HIV/AIDS clients, existential treatment with (*Continued*)
    theoretical constructs, 306–309
    therapeutic intervention, 315–322
    thrownness, 305, 307
Holism, 179, 677
Humanistic psychology, 257, 670–672, 700–702
    analysis/comparison of theories (existential/interpersonal), and synthesis, 708–715
    clear communication, 671
    empathy, 671
    genuineness, 671
    positive regard, 671
    psychotherapy, 700–702
    self-actualization, 671
    themes, 671–673
    theoretical frames and, 671–672
Human potential movement and growth therapies, 702–705
Human systems, conceptualizing, 677–678

Identity, 153
    cultural, 42–44
    ethnic, 158–159
    formation, 168–169
    racial, 162–163
Illness, incurable (logotherapy), 347–348
Immature level of family functioning (in case example, redecision family therapy), 453–456
Immigration experience, and cultural identification, 214–216
Incongruity, confrontation of, 444
Inferiority:
    complexes, 184
    vs. industry, 119–120
Integrative approach to assessment/intervention with adolescents of color, 153–178
    African American adolescents, 160–166
    Asian American adolescents, 156–160
    cultural-group processes and illustrative cases, 156–172
    ecological perspective, 172–173
    ecological systems theory (Bronfenbrenner), 154–155
    Latino American adolescents, 166–172
    research support for integrative model, 172–173
    second-order cybernetic approach, 154–155, 173
    theoretical constructs, 154–156

Intention/intentionality:
    blocked, 259
    concern and, 260
    paradoxical, 342
Interconnecting, 496
International perspectives on professional ethics, 641–667
Interpersonal perception method (IPM), 517
Interpersonal press, levels of, 267–268
Interpersonal security, 497
Interpersonal therapies, 673–675, 705–706, 708–715
    Adlerian, 179–203, 673
    analysis/comparison of theories (existential/humanistic), and synthesis, 708–715
    eudaimonia, 674
    interpersonal reality, 674
    multilevel analysis, 674
    nonlinear causality, 674
    pragmatic solutions, 674
    themes, 674–675
    therapeutic frames and, 674–675
Interpretation, *vs.* explanation, 572
Intimacy, 263, 392–394, 563
Introjection, 439
Irrational beliefs, confronting, 190–191
Isolation (existential concern), 308, 319–320
Isomorphism, 676–677, 683, 686–687
Italy, couple therapy in (sociocultural context), 360

Japan (therapy and professional ethics), 657–665
Japanese Americans in United States, 39–41, 619–620
Jungian play psychotherapy, 61–62
Justice (international reflections on), 663–664

Korean Americans:
    case example: adolescent and family from Korea, 46–47
    and crisis of *sa-il-gu*, 44–46

Language, 135, 494
Latin America:
    adolescents, 166–172
        case presentation, 169
        families, 166–167
        identity formation, 168–169

immigration, 167
spirituality, 167–168
Ecuador (therapy and professional ethics), 646–649, 659–665
Laughter, 89
Life cycle, family, 13–15
Life positions, existential, 450
Life script, 437
Life space, 501
Lifestyle, 183–184, 191–192
Life tasks, and Adlerian psychology, 182
Listening (level of interpersonal press), 267
Locus parallelling, 269
Logotherapy, 333–356, 622–623, 707
   appealing technique, 344–345
   applications, 346–349
   assumptions, 333–334, 338
   case examples, 349–354
   dereflection, 343–344
   vs. existential psychiatry, 333
   history, 334–337
   meaning and, 333
   modification of attitudes, 340–342
   noetic dimension, 339
   paradoxical intention, 342–343
   research, 354
   Socratic dialogue, 340
   techniques, 340–345
   theoretical foundations of, 338–340
   trauma, 622–623
   view of humankind, 338–339
   worldview, 339–340
Love, 293, 393

Meaning, 325–326, 333, 624
Meaninglessness (existential concern), 308, 320–322, 707
Millon scales, 516
Minnesota Multiphasic Personality Inventory, 550
Miracle Question, 138–139, 146
Mirror (psychodrama technique), 544
Mitwelt (relational world), 307, 313, 314
Modeling behavior, 444
Modes of world (natural/personal/relational), 306–307, 313, 314
Mood, family, 450
Mood disorder (in case example, contextual therapy), 482

Moral/ethical issues, 645. *See also* Ethics/moral principles
Motivation, 561–564
Multidimensional family therapy (MDFT), 4, 8, 12, 15, 16, 26, 27, 28
Multidimensional Family Therapy for Adolescent Drug Abuse, 208
Multidirected partiality, 464
Multilevel analysis, 674
Multisystemic family therapy (MST), 4, 15, 16, 26, 27, 28
Myopia, perceptual, 680–681, 687
Myth:
   of mental illness, 504
   separating reality from, 444

Narcissistic personality disorders, in case, 511
Narrative therapy, 87–88, 90–92. *See also* Feminist/narrative approach
Neurosis, layers of, 438, 439–440
Neurotic level of family functioning ("too-good parents" in case example, redecision family therapy), 456–459
Noetic dimension, 339
Nondirective (child-centered) play therapy, 62–63, 77–79, 113–114
Nonmalfeasance (international reflections on), 662–663
Noogenic neuroses and depressions (logotherapy), 346

Object-relations theory, 233
Ontic dimension, 485
Oppositional defiant disorder (ODD), 93, 96, 482

Panic disorder/fear neurosis (logotherapy), 350–352
Paradoxical intention (logotherapy technique), 342–343
Parallelling, 268–269
Parental metaemotion theory, 11
Parent Interview, 503
Peak experience, 714
Perceptual myopia, 680–681, 687
Personality disorders, 403, 511, 599, 602–606
Personal Orientation Inventory (POI), 459
Personal relationship network ("virtual families"), 220–221

Phenomenology, 264–265, 592–594, 707
Phobic patients, and paradoxical intention, 342
Physically abused children and their families, 93–94
Play:
   developmental processes and, 116–120
   role of in childhood: inherent value of use of play in normative development, 64–65
   therapeutic aspects of, and current applications, 63–64
Play therapy, 59–82
   with abused children, 59–82, 109–130
   biopsychosocial approach (with maltreated children), 109–130
   child-centered (nondirective), 62–63, 77–79
   cognitive-behavioral, 61
   developmental, 62
   directive, 112–113
   filial therapy, 63
   history, 55–65, 109–114
   Jungian, 61–62
   major theories of, 60–63
   models of, 112–113
   nondirective (child-centered), 62–63, 77–79, 113–114
   psychoanalytic/psychodynamic, 60–61, 113–114
Positive regard, 671
Posttraumatic stress disorder (PTSD). *See also* Trauma:
   abused children, 65, 66, 120
   biosocial and spiritual treatment, 615–637
   body-centered psychotherapy (in case example), 605–606
   comorbidity with, 618
   importance of crisis intervention (Japan Kobe earthquake), 658
   psychodrama (in case example), 546–549
   Reaction Index Scale, 632
   relational-cultural perspective in therapy (in case example), 245–249
   six criteria, 620–621
Pou sto, 265–266
Prescriptive-holistic guide to intervention (Erik Erikson), 114–120
   autonomy *vs.* shame and doubt (stage 2), 118
   basic trust *vs.* basic mistrust (stage 1), 116–118
   developmental processes and play, 116–120
   industry *vs.* inferiority (stage 4), 119–120
   initiative *vs.* guilt (stage 3), 118–119
   neurological development and impact of trauma, 114–116
Presence, 260–261, 262, 267–269, 315–316
Problem-solving therapy, 3. *See also* Solution-focused brief therapy (SFBT)
Projection, 439
Psychiatric hospitalization (case example, SFBT), 142–151
Psychoanalytic play therapy, 60–61
Psychodrama, 529–553, 705
   action, 533, 541
   audience, 539
   auxiliary ego, 539
   behind-the-back technique, 543–544
   case example, 546–549
   catharsis, 538
   director/therapist, 539
   double technique, 543
   dream presentation technique, 543
   elements, 538–539
   empty chair technique, 543
   encounter, 534–535
   future projection technique, 544
   history, 530–531
   mirror technique, 544
   parts, 541–542
   protagonists or patients, 539
   research, 550–551
   role concept, 535
   role reversal technique, 542
   rules, 539–541
   sharing, 541–542
   soliloquy technique, 542–543
   spontaneity, 537–538
   stage, 538–539
   surplus reality, 534
   syndromes/symptoms/problems treated, 544–546
   tele, 534
   theoretical constructs, 534–538
   warmup, 541
Psychodynamics:
   existential, 307–309
   psychoanalytic-psychodynamic child/family therapy, 83, 84
Psychogenic neuroses (logotherapy and), 346–347

Psychology:
  five forces in, 708
  unit of analysis, 712
  of use, 622
Psychopathology, nature of (existential/ humanistic perspective), 257–258
Psychosomatic illnesses (logotherapy), 346–347
Psychotherapies:
  analysis/comparison of theories, and synthesis, 708–715
  bridging cultures: Eastern and Western frames of reference, 713–715
  dimensions of psychotherapy (breadth/height/ depth), 708–709
  existential, 706–708
  existential/humanistic perspective on, 259–260
  humanistic, 700–702
  human potential movement and growth therapies, 702–705
  interpersonal, 705–706
  natural/unnatural, 699–708
  old/new empirical frames (appreciating analysis, learning synthesis), 709–713
  time frames: past/present./future focus, 708
Psychotic disorder (DSM), 452

Questioning technique, 138–140, 190
  Adlerian psychology, 190
  coping questions, 139–140
  exception questions, 139
  future oriented questions, 138
  impact question, 190
  interpretive questions, 190
  Miracle Question, 138–139
  presession change questions, 138
  scaling questions, 139
  solution-focused brief therapy, 138–140
  whither *vs.* why, 190

Race:
  vs. ethnicity/culture (definitions/distinctions), 36–38
  integrative approach to assessment/intervention with adolescents of color, 153–178
Racial identity, 162–163
Rackets, 445, 563–564
Radical positivism, 677
Reaction Index Scale, 623

Reality:
  interpersonal, 674
  separating myth from, 444
  surplus, 534
Recognition hunger, 561
Redecision family therapy, 435–462, 573–577, 705
  assessment/intervention methods, 448–452
  awareness, 441–442
  basic existential life positions, 450
  case examples, 453–459, 573–577
  components (seven major), 443–445
  confrontation of incongruity, 444
  drama triangles (Persecutor, Victim, Rescuer), 449–450, 562
  early theoretical roots (Berne/Perls/Satir), 435–441
  emphasizing client's personal power/responsibility, 443
  family mood, 450
  family therapy, 446–448
  games, 442, 445
  intervention types, 451
  issues treated, 452–453
  modeling behavior, 444
  nurturing environment, 443–444
  performing adaptations (passive-aggressive/ obsessive-compulsive/hysterionic), 447
  principles, 442–446
  procedural rules assuring safety, 444–445
  process, 443, 445–446, 451–452
  racket, 445
  research, 459–460
  separating myth from reality, 444
  stroking patterns, 450
  surviving adaptations (schizoid/antisocial/ paranoid), 447
  symbiosis and differentiation, 448–449
  techniques, 444
  theoretical constructs, 441–448
Reference group, 499
Reframing, 191
Reimbursement, and ethics, 644
Relational-cultural model, 233–254
  case examples, 241–249
  connections/disconnections, 236–237
  empathy, 235, 238, 239
  model, 234–237
  research, 249–251

shame, 241–245
theoretical constructs, 234–241
therapy from perspective of, 237–341
trauma, 245–249
Relational ethics, 471–473, 484–485, 517
Relationships, determinants of, 468–469
Religious experience/spirituality, 210, 211, 282. *See also* Spirituality
Resistance, 261–263, 269–270
Resonance: freedom and responsibility, 652–653
Responsibility and choice, 672
Retroflection, 438
Rituals, 561
Role(s), 186
    psychodrama construct, 535
    reversal (psychodrama technique), 542

Safeguarding tendencies, 185–186
Schizoid defenses, and body-centered lexicon, 598
Schizoid personality disorder, 602–605
School-based, community family therapy for adolescents at risk, 205–230
    acculturation issues, 216
    biopsychosocial development, maturational age, 210, 211
    case example, 222–224
    conceptual foundations, 209–218
    cultural identification and immigration experience, 214–216
    diagnosis/assessment, 209–212
    ethnic heritage/culture/race, immigration experience, 210, 211
    Family Intervention and Empowerment Program (FIEP), 208–209, 218–221
    gender-role experience/gender identification, 210, 211, 216
    history, 206–209
    immigration history/current status, 215–216
    inner city schools, 216–218
    kaleidoscope of seven perspectives/lenses, 209–210
    medical health/illness, alcohol and/or drug addiction/abuse, 210, 211
    outcome research, 224–225
    paradigm shift (from individual to relationship-oriented paradigm), 205
    religious experience/spirituality, 210, 211
    sexual orientation, 210, 211
    socioeconomic class/employment situation, 210, 211, 212–213
    strengths/resources, 213–214
    therapists' culture-determined lenses, 214–215
    "unfamiliar world," 212–214
Scientific knowledge/rationality, paradigms, 710, 715
Scripts, 437, 564–565
Search process (existential/humanistic perspective), 260
Second-order cybernetic approach, 154–155, 173, 644, 645, 652
Secular spirituality, 282
Self:
    emergence of self/other/systems, 679
    idealized/despised image of, 362
Self-actualization, 671, 679, 684–685, 713–714
Self-and-world construct system, 258–259, 261
Self-deceit, 361–363
Self-distancing, 338
Self psychology, 233–234
Self-realization, 280
Self-Report Questionnaire (SRQ), 460
Self-transcendence, 338, 679, 684–685, 714
Self-transcending consciousness, 496, 501
Sexism, silent, 413–414
Sexual abuse, 92–93, 648
Sexual desire/arousal disorders, 599
Sexual intimacy between therapist and client, 645
Sexual orientation, 210, 211
Shame, 118, 241–245
Simultaneity, 680
Situationism, 495
Social advantage, internal/external (transactional patterns), 563
Social-constructionist-feminist perspectives, 414–415, 644
Social embeddedness, 182
Social interest, 679–680
Social psychology:
    coevolution of selves/families/cultures/societies, 500–501
    dyads, 500
    foundations, 496–503, 515–516
    interconnections, 496
    interpersonal security, 497
    isomorphic processes in histories of family treatment and social psychology, 495

models and dimensions, 495–496
multidimensional unities, 496
multigenerational processes, 500
origins and history, 493–494
processes in holistic individual, family, and system development, 496–503
research on family treatment and intervention, 516–518
subjectivity, evolution of, 497
triadic observations, 500
working definition, 495
Socioeconomic class/employment situation, 210, 211, 212–213
Socratic dialogue (logotherapy technique), 340
Solution-focused brief therapy (SFBT), 133–152
    basic assumptions, 136–137
    building solutions, 137–138
    case examples, 140–151
    EARS acronym (elicit/amplify/reinforce/start again), 148
    future oriented questions, 138
    historical context, 133–135
    questions as useful tools, 138–140
    research, 151
    session break, 140
    syndromes/symptoms/problems treated, 140
    theoretical constructs, 135–140
    useful conversations, 135–136
Solution-focused work, 681–682
Somatoform disorders, 599
Somatotherapies, 594. *See also* Body-centered psychotherapy
Soul, 279
Space suits, 261
Spirituality:
    biopsychosocial/spiritual treatment of trauma, 615–637
    culture and, 713
    dimension of human existence, 709
    ethics and, 645
Spiritually-sensitive psychotherapy, 279–302
    active *vs.* reactive interventions, 291
    adversity, 294
    assessment/intervention methods, 285–292
    assumptions, 283–285
    case examples, 296–298
    centering intervention, 288
    client's spiritual resources, 286, 287–288
    critical point of decision, 283
    history, 279–282
    implicit *vs.* explicit intervention, 287
    implicit spirituality, 296–297
    internal *vs.* external worlds of spirituality, 288–289
    love as primary driver of healthy growth and functioning, 293
    major issues treated, 292–296
    purpose of existence, 294
    religious spirituality, 282, 297–298
    research, 298–299
    secular spirituality, 282
    spiritual dispositions, 290
    tasks (three basic), 286
    theoretical constructs, 282–285
    today's *vs.* yesterday's clients, 281–282
    value platform/premises, 286–287, 293–294
    worldview variations, 283
Spontaneity (psychodrama construct), 537–538
Spontaneity theory, 533
Story (process in narrative approach), 425
Strategic essentialism, 416
Strengthening Families Program, 209
Stroking patterns, 450
Structural Analysis of Social Behavior (SASB) model, 517
Structural family therapy (SST), 3–33
    affective proximity, 5, 8–9
    assessment/intervention methods, 16–17
    boundaries, 7–8
    case example, 16–25
    constructing therapeutic system, 17–19
    creating key growth-promoting interpersonal experiences, 22–24
    ecosystemic structural home-based family therapy (ESSFT), 27
    establishing meaningful therapeutic focus, 19–22
    family development (family life cycle), 13–15
    family emotion regulation, 5, 9–11
    family structure, 6–9
    goals, 5–6
    growth promoting practices, 5
    history, 3–6
    individual differences, 12–13
    integrative models/variants, 4, 15
        attachment-based family therapy (ABFT), 4, 8, 12, 15, 16, 26, 28

behavioral family model (BBFM), 4, 8, 15, 16, 28
multidimensional family therapy (MDFT), 4, 8, 12, 15, 16, 26, 27, 28
multisystemic family therapy (MST), 4, 15, 16, 26, 27, 28
solidifying changes and terminating, 24–25
supporting research, 25–28
syndromes/symptoms/problems treated, 15–16
theoretical constructs, 6–15
Structuralist movement in France and Latin countries, 650
Subjective experience (existential/humanistic perspective), primacy of, 259
Subjectivity, 256, 497
Superiority complexes, 184
Supervision, interpersonal-systemic/developmental approach to, 669–698
assessment/intervention methods, 685–686
case example, 688–692
conceptualizing human systems, 677–678
contributing concepts, 675–685
developmental factor, 675–676
dialectic aspects of assessment, 682–683
dysfunctional isomorphic patterns, 686–687
effect of theoretical frames, 669
emergence of self/other/systems, 679
emergent personal and interpersonal knowledge, 678–679
freedom, choice, and change, 683–684
historic levels of entry and focus, 669–670
historic roots, 670–675
inflexible use of levels of focus and time frames, 688
isomorphism: a systems principle, 676–677, 683
mistaken level of focus or time frame, 682, 687–688
overview, 669–670
perceptual myopia, 680–681, 687
reflective, intentional, self-actualizing, and self-transcendent humans, 679
research, 692–693
self-actualization and self-transcendence, 684–685
shifting focus, 683
simultaneity, 680
social interest, 679–680

syndromes/symptoms/problems treated, 686–688
systemic reality, 678
time frame and number of clients, 681–682
Surplus reality (psychodrama construct), 534
Survival stances, 441
Survivor groups, differences among, 619–620
Symbiosis and differentiation, 448–449
Symbolic-experiential family therapy, 85–86, 88–90, 97–100
Systemic approach and individual responsibility, European perspective on ethics, 650–651
Systemic reality, 678
Systemic thinking (transactional analysis), 557
"Systems far from equilibrium" and ethics, 650, 652
Systems-oriented child psychotherapy or family play therapy, 83, 84–85

Tele (psychodrama construct), 534
Tell-Me-a-Story test (TEMAS), 516
Tension systems, 495
Theater games, 533
Thematic Apperception Test, 516
Therapeutic alliance, 214–215, 238–239, 265–266, 705
Third force, 257. *See also* Humanistic psychology
Thrownness, 305, 307
Time frames, 681–682, 687–688, 708
Time structures, 561–563
Topical paralleling, 268
Touch in psychotherapy, 595–597
Training, 644, 647, 649, 655, 658. *See also* Supervision, interpersonal-systemic/developmental approach to
Transaction (dimension in contextual therapy), 483–484
Transactional analysis (TA), 460, 535, 555–585, 705
advantages (biological/existential/psychological/social) of transactional patterns, 563
assessment/intervention methods, 567–568
case examples, 569–572, 573–577
ego states (Child/Adult/Parent), 436–437, 442, 557–561, 567
existential life positions, 561
group imago, 561, 566
history, 555–557

integrating Berne's constructs, 566–567
motivation, 561–564
redecision family therapy and, 435, 437
research, 577–579
scripts (patterns of living), 535, 564–565
social emphasis, 560
syndromes/symptoms/problems treated, 569
theoretical constructs, 557–567
time structures, 561–563
transactions, 560–561
Transference/countertransference, 54, 238, 569–572
Trauma. *See also* Posttraumatic stress disorder (PTSD):
biopsychosocial and spiritual treatment of, 615–637
assessment, 621–624
biological dimension (impact of mass trauma on), 623
biopsychosocial/spiritual approach, 616–617
breathing exercises, 625
case examples, 625–631
didactic information, 624–625
empathy/validation, 624
expression of feelings, 624
logotherapeutic principles, 622–623
meaning (encouraging discovery/expression of), 624
research, 631–632
six-step model, 623–625
spiritual dimension (impact of mass trauma on), 621–622
syndromes/symptoms/problems treated, 620–623
brief history of traumatology, 615–616
definitions: disasters and trauma, 616–617
differences among survivor groups, 619–620
effects of, 617–619
language of (attachment injuries), 400–401
mass, 615, 621–622, 623, 706
relational-cultural perspective in therapy (case example), 245–249
Triadic observations/triangulation, 500, 511
Triangles, drama, 449–450
Trust, 116–118, 399–401
Type A behavior, 271–274

Überwelt, 314
Umwelt (natural world), 306–307, 313
United States (therapy and professional ethics), 643–646, 659–665
Unity consciousness, 714
Use, psychology of, 185

Value ambivalence (logotherapy), 348–349
Value platform, 286–287
Value premises (three), spiritually-sensitive psychotherapy, 293–294
Value system, existential approach, 707, 709

Warmups, 533
Wechsler scales, 516
Withdrawal, 561
Workaholism, 271

Yin/yang, 53

WITHDRAWN